ELEVENTH EDITION

FINANCIAL ACCOUNTING

Robert Libby
Cornell University

Patricia A. Libby
Ithaca College

Frank Hodge
University of Washington

FINANCIAL ACCOUNTING

This book is printed on acid-free paper.

1 2 3 4 5 6 7 8 9 LWI 27 26 25 24 23 22

ISBN 978-1-265-08392-2
MHID 1-265-08392-4

Cover Image: *Ferbies/Shutterstock*

mheducation.com/highered

To: Herman and Doris Hargenrater

Oscar and Selma Libby

Laura Libby, Brian Plummer, and Bennett Plummer

Abby, Grace, Claire, Joanne, and Richard Hodge

Dan Short

We truly appreciate the continued support of all our *Financial Accounting* team members, including our special helpers.

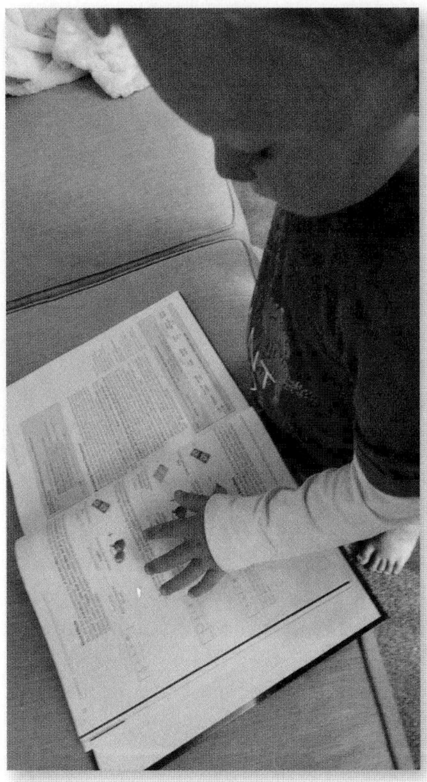

Courtesy of Patricia Libby

Courtesy of Frank Hodge

Courtesy of Patricia Libby

Courtesy of Noelle Bathurst

Courtesy of Rebecca Olson

Courtesy of Jeni McAtee

Courtesy of Kelly Delso

Courtesy of Angela Norris

Courtesy of Lauren Schur

ABOUT THE AUTHORS

ROBERT LIBBY

Courtesy of Robert Libby

Robert Libby is the David A. Thomas Professor of Accounting and Accounting Area Coordinator at Cornell University, where he teaches the introductory financial accounting course. He previously taught at the University of Illinois, Pennsylvania State University, the University of Texas at Austin, the University of Chicago, and the University of Michigan. He received his BS from Pennsylvania State University, where he was selected as the 2018 Outstanding Accounting Alumnus, and his MAS and PhD from the University of Illinois; he also completed the CPA exam (Illinois).

Bob was selected as the AAA Outstanding Educator in 2000 and received the AAA Outstanding Service Award in 2006 and the AAA Notable Contributions to the Literature Award in 1985 and 1996. He has received the Core Faculty Teaching Award multiple times at Cornell. Bob is a widely published author and researcher specializing in behavioral accounting. He has published numerous articles in *The Accounting Review; Journal of Accounting Research; Accounting, Organizations, and Society;* and other accounting journals. He has held a variety of offices, including vice president, in the American Accounting Association, and he is a member of the American Institute of CPAs.

PATRICIA A. LIBBY

Courtesy of Patricia Libby

Patricia Libby is Professor Emeritus of accounting at Ithaca College, where she taught the undergraduate and graduate financial accounting courses. She previously taught graduate and undergraduate financial accounting at Eastern Michigan University and the University of Texas at Austin. Before entering academia, she was an auditor with Price Waterhouse (now PricewaterhouseCoopers) and a financial administrator at the University of Chicago. She was also faculty advisor to Beta Alpha Psi (Mu Alpha chapter), the National Association of Black Accountants (Ithaca College chapter), and Ithaca College Accounting Association.

Patricia received her BS from Pennsylvania State University, her MBA from DePaul University, and her PhD from the University of Michigan; she also successfully completed the CPA exam (Illinois). She has published articles in *The Accounting Review, Issues in Accounting Education,* and *The Michigan CPA.*

FRANK HODGE

Christine Moody

Frank Hodge is the Orin & Janet Smith Dean at the University of Washington's Foster School of Business.

Frank joined the faculty at the University of Washington in 2000. He earned his MBA and PhD degrees from Indiana University. He has won over 30 teaching awards at the University of Washington teaching financial accounting and financial statement analysis to undergraduate students, full-time MBA students, executive MBA students, and intercollegiate athletic administrators. Frank's research focuses on how individuals use accounting information to make investment decisions and how technology influences their information choices. Frank was one of six members of the Financial Accounting Standards Research Initiative team and has presented his research at the Securities and Exchange Commission. He has published articles in *The Accounting Review; Journal of Accounting Research; Contemporary Accounting Research; Accounting, Organizations, and Society;* and several other journals. Frank lives in Seattle with his wife and two daughters.

A TRUSTED LEADER FOR STUDENTS AND INSTRUCTORS

The award-winning author team of Bob Libby, Pat Libby, and Frank Hodge continue *Financial Accounting*'s best-selling tradition of helping the instructor and student become partners in learning. Libby/Libby/Hodge uses a remarkable learning approach that keeps students engaged and involved in the material from the first day of class.

Libby/Libby/Hodge's *Financial Accounting* maintains its leadership by focusing on four key attributes:

THE PIONEERING REAL-WORLD COMPANIES APPROACH

The Libby/Libby/Hodge authors' trademark focus company approach is the best method for helping students understand financial statements and the real-world implications of financial accounting for future managers. **This approach shows that accounting is relevant and motivates students by explaining accounting in a real-world context.** Throughout each chapter, the material is integrated around a familiar focus company, its decisions, and its financial statements. This provides the perfect setting for discussing the importance of accounting and how businesses use accounting information. No other book matches this seamless integration of the real world.

A BUILDING-BLOCK APPROACH TO TEACHING TRANSACTION ANALYSIS

Faculty agree the accounting cycle is the most critical concept to learn and master for students studying financial accounting, regardless of their career aspirations. Libby/Libby/Hodge believes students struggle with the accounting cycle when transaction analysis is covered in one chapter. If students are exposed to the accounting equation, journal entries, and T-accounts for both balance sheet and income statement accounts in a single chapter, many are left behind and are unable to grasp material in the remaining chapters.

The market-leading Libby/Libby/Hodge approach spreads transaction analysis coverage over two chapters so that students have the time to master the material. In Chapter 2 of *Financial Accounting,* students are exposed to the accounting equation and transaction analysis for investing and financing transactions that affect only balance sheet accounts. This provides students with the opportunity to learn the basic structure and tools used in accounting in a simpler setting. In Chapter 3, students are exposed to more complex operating transactions that also affect income statement accounts. **By slowing down the introduction** of transactions and giving students time to practice and gain mastery, this building-block approach leads to greater student success in their study of later topics in financial accounting such as adjusting entries.** Research has shown that the accounting cycle approach used in this textbook yields learning gains that outpace approaches used in other textbooks by a significant margin.

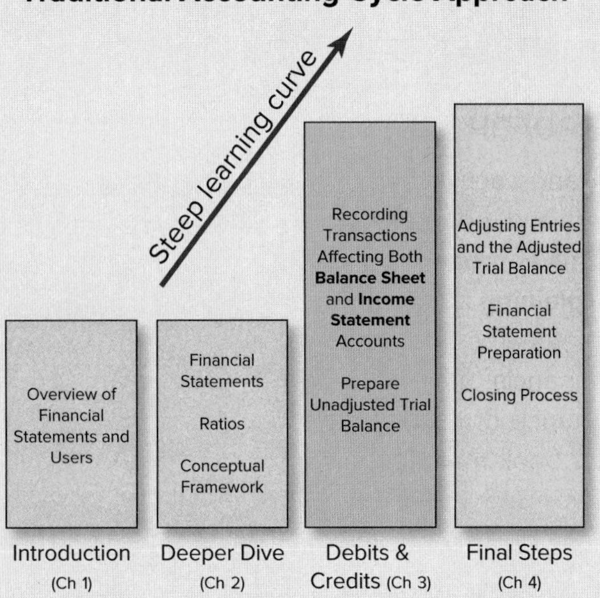

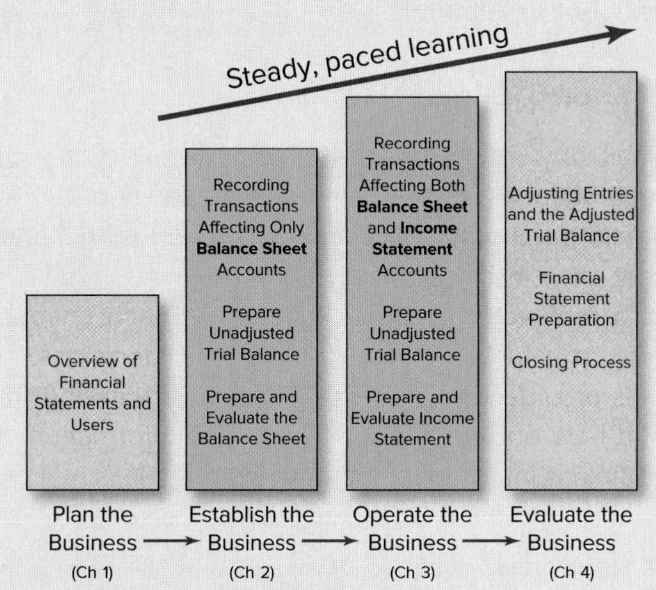

THE RIGHT BALANCE OF TRANSACTION ANALYSIS AND FINANCIAL STATEMENT ANALYSIS

A clear understanding of how transactions affect financial statements is key for sound decision-making utilizing these statements. Accountants, auditors, analysts, managers, creditors, and investors must all be aware of the effect of measuring and reporting financial activities and the power of financial statement analysis. Our balanced focus on transaction analysis and financial statement analysis based on real companies optimally prepares students regardless of their career aspirations.

POWERFUL TECHNOLOGY FOR TEACHING AND STUDY

Students have different learning styles and conflicting time commitments, so they want technology tools that will help them study more efficiently and effectively. The eleventh edition includes the best technology available with Connect's latest features—Concept Overview Videos, Integrated Excel, General Ledger problems, and other new study, practice, and assessment materials.

MARKET-LEADING PEDAGOGY AND CONTENT

Financial Accounting, 11e, offers a host of pedagogical tools that complement the different ways you like to teach and the ways your students like to learn. Some offer information and tips that help you present a complex subject; others highlight issues relevant to what your students read online and see in their other coursework. Either way, *Financial Accounting*'s pedagogical support will make a real difference in your course and in your students' learning.

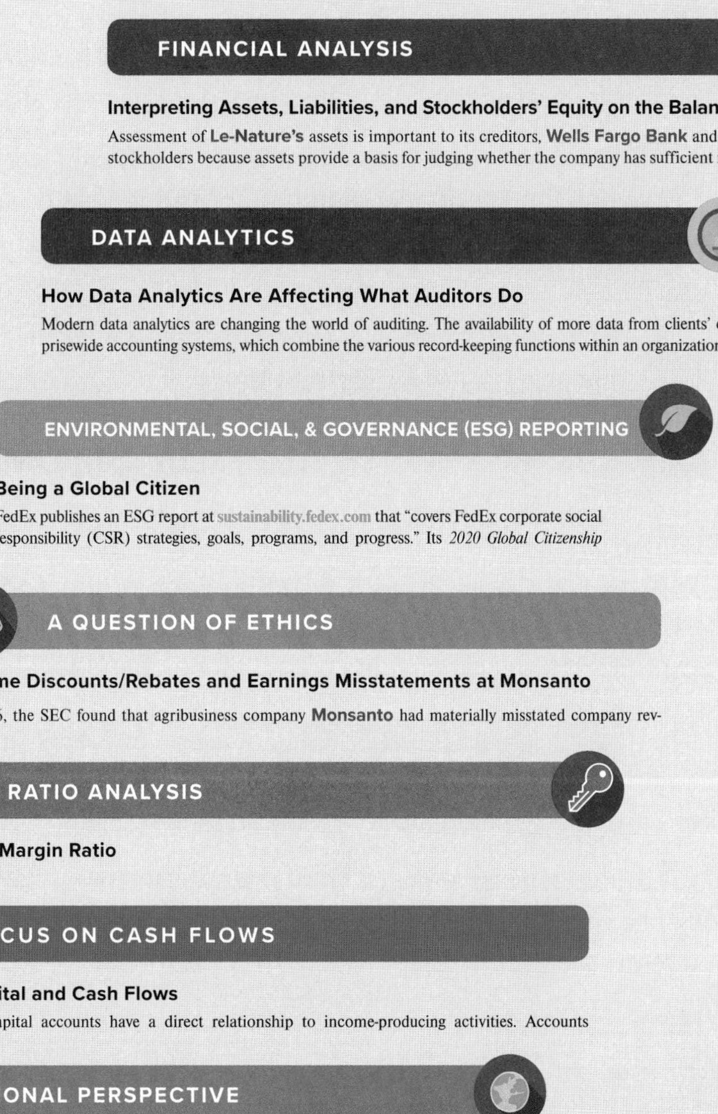

FINANCIAL ANALYSIS BOXES—These features tie important chapter concepts to real-world decision-making examples. They also highlight alternative viewpoints and add to the critical-thinking and decision-making focus of the text.

DATA ANALYTICS BOXES—This feature introduces students to how companies analyze and use data for both business decisions and accounting applications.

ENVIRONMENTAL, SOCIAL, AND GOVERNANCE (ESG) REPORTING BOXES—Most large public companies have started to publish an ESG report. These boxes illustrate how ESG reports help investors assess the long-term consequences of the company's broader business strategy.

A QUESTION OF ETHICS BOXES—These boxes appear throughout the text, conveying the importance and the consequences of acting responsibly in business practice.

> "Ethics and financial analysis boxes are excellent. Examples with real companies that students have heard of or even been to are key to their learning and understanding."
>
> —Laurie Dahlin, Worcester State University

FOCUS ON CASH FLOWS BOXES—Each of the first 11 chapters includes a discussion and analysis of changes in the cash flows of the focus company and explores the decisions that caused those changes.

KEY RATIO ANALYSIS BOXES—Each box presents ratio analysis for the focus company in the chapter as well as for comparative companies. Cautions also are provided to help students understand the limitations of certain ratios.

INTERNATIONAL PERSPECTIVE BOXES—These boxes highlight the emergence of global accounting standards (IFRS) at a level appropriate for the introductory student.

> "An excellent introduction to financial accounting that flows in a more logical manner than most texts. The extensive variety and amount of supporting materials allows for customization of the course, and the integration of key concepts such as ethics and cash flows enhance student understanding of the topics."
>
> —Joy Gray, Bentley University

PRACTICE IS KEY TO SUCCESS IN FINANCIAL ACCOUNTING

PAUSE FOR FEEDBACK AND SELF-STUDY QUIZ

Research shows that students learn best when they are actively engaged in the learning process. This active learning feature engages the student, provides interactivity, and promotes efficient learning. These quizzes ask students to pause at strategic points throughout each chapter to ensure they understand key points before moving ahead.

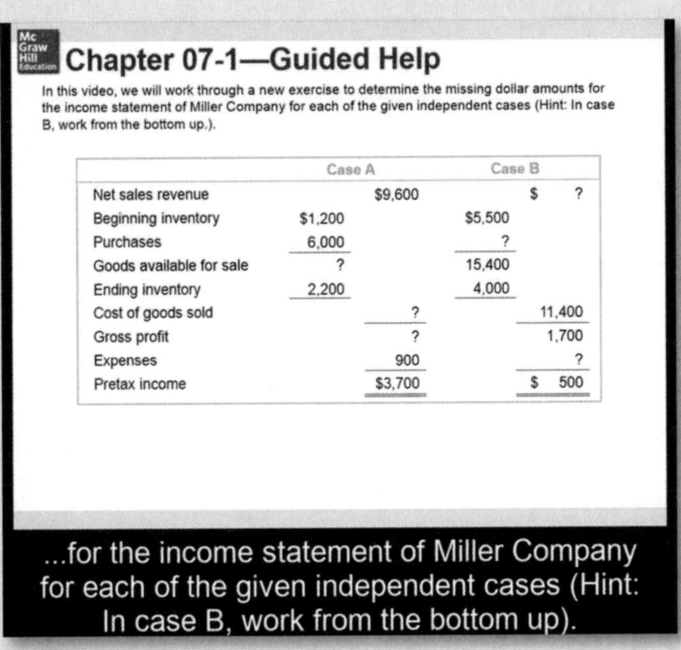

	Case A		Case B	
Net sales revenue		$9,600		$?
Beginning inventory	$1,200		$5,500	
Purchases	6,000		?	
Goods available for sale	?		15,400	
Ending inventory	2,200		4,000	
Cost of goods sold		?		11,400
Gross profit		?		1,700
Expenses		900		?
Pretax income		$3,700		$ 500

SMARTBOOK

Within Connect, SmartBook brings these features to life by interleaving reading with active practice. As students read, SmartBook encourages them to answer questions to demonstrate their knowledge—then, based on their answers, highlights those areas where students need more practice.

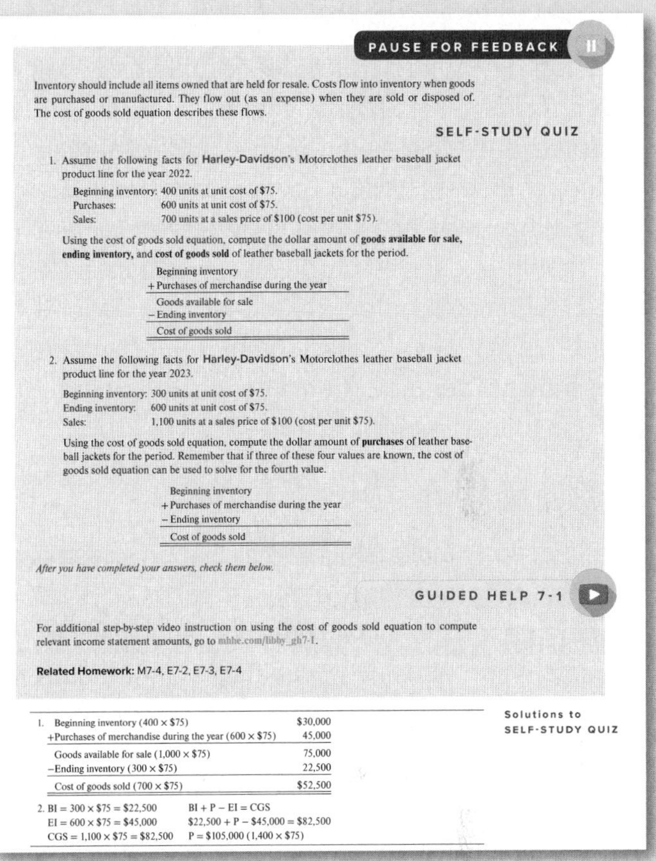

PAUSE FOR FEEDBACK

Inventory should include all items owned that are held for resale. Costs flow into inventory when goods are purchased or manufactured. They flow out (as an expense) when they are sold or disposed of. The cost of goods sold equation describes these flows.

SELF-STUDY QUIZ

1. Assume the following facts for **Harley-Davidson**'s Motorclothes leather baseball jacket product line for the year 2022.

   Beginning inventory: 400 units at unit cost of $75.
   Purchases: 600 units at unit cost of $75.
   Sales: 700 units at a sales price of $100 (cost per unit $75).

   Using the cost of goods sold equation, compute the dollar amount of **goods available for sale, ending inventory,** and **cost of goods sold** of leather baseball jackets for the period.

   Beginning inventory
   + Purchases of merchandise during the year
   Goods available for sale
   − Ending inventory
   Cost of goods sold

2. Assume the following facts for **Harley-Davidson**'s Motorclothes leather baseball jacket product line for the year 2023.

   Beginning inventory: 300 units at unit cost of $75.
   Ending inventory: 600 units at unit cost of $75.
   Sales: 1,100 units at a sales price of $100 (cost per unit $75).

   Using the cost of goods sold equation, compute the dollar amount of **purchases** of leather baseball jackets for the period. Remember that if three of these four values are known, the cost of goods sold equation can be used to solve for the fourth value.

   Beginning inventory
   + Purchases of merchandise during the year
   − Ending inventory
   Cost of goods sold

After you have completed your answers, check them below.

GUIDED HELP 7-1

For additional step-by-step video instruction on using the cost of goods sold equation to compute relevant income statement amounts, go to mhhe.com/libby_gh7-1.

Related Homework: M7-4, E7-2, E7-3, E7-4

Solutions to SELF-STUDY QUIZ

1.	
Beginning inventory (400 × $75)	$30,000
+Purchases of merchandise during the year (600 × $75)	45,000
Goods available for sale (1,000 × $75)	75,000
−Ending inventory (300 × $75)	22,500
Cost of goods sold (700 × $75)	$52,500

2. BI = 300 × $75 = $22,500   BI + P − EI = CGS
   EI = 600 × $75 = $45,000 $22,500 + P − $45,000 = $82,500
   CGS = 1,100 × $75 = $82,500   P = $105,000 (1,400 × $75)

GUIDED HELP VIDEOS

To provide students with immediate help understanding key concepts, our unique Guided Help videos provide narrated, animated, step-by-step walk-throughs for each numerical Self-Study Quiz that students can view at any time through their mobile device or online. These videos also save office hour time! We also include a Related Homework list for each Self-Study Quiz to help the students move on to their homework assignments.

COMPREHENSIVE PROBLEMS

Selected chapters include problems that cover topics from earlier chapters to refresh, reinforce, and build an integrative understanding of the course material. For practice with the completing the accounting cycle, there are two comprehensive problems in Chapter 4 that are complemented in Connect by General Ledger questions. These help students see how transactions flow from the general journal through to the financial statements.

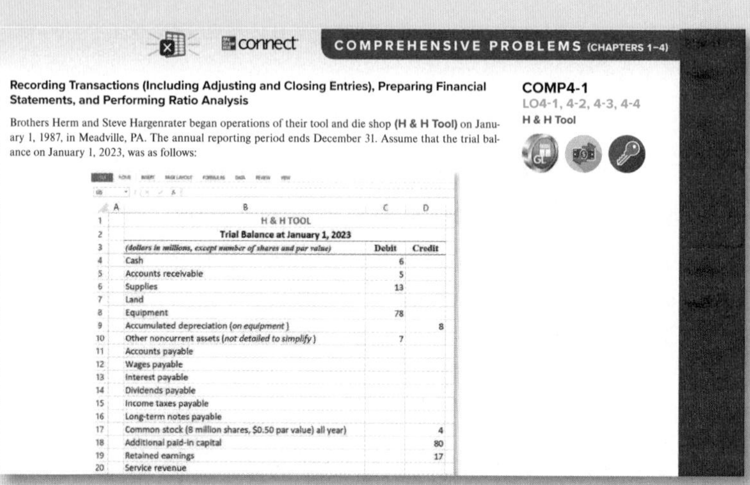

connect COMPREHENSIVE PROBLEMS (CHAPTERS 1–4)

Recording Transactions (Including Adjusting and Closing Entries), Preparing Financial Statements, and Performing Ratio Analysis

COMP4-1
LO4-1, 4-2, 4-3, 4-4
H & H Tool

Brothers Herm and Steve Hargenrater began operations of their tool and die shop **(H & H Tool)** on January 1, 1987, in Meadville, PA. The annual reporting period ends December 31. Assume that the trial balance on January 1, 2023, was as follows:

H & H TOOL
Trial Balance at January 1, 2023

(dollars in millions, except number of shares and par value)	Debit	Credit
Cash	6	
Accounts receivable	5	
Supplies	13	
Land		
Equipment	78	
Accumulated depreciation (*on equipment*)		8
Other noncurrent assets (*not detailed to simplify*)	7	
Accounts payable		
Wages payable		
Interest payable		
Dividends payable		
Income taxes payable		
Long-term notes payable		
Common stock (8 million shares, $0.50 par value) all year)		4
Additional paid-in capital		80
Retained earnings		17
Service revenue		

CASES AND PROJECTS

This section includes annual report cases, financial reporting and analysis cases, critical thinking cases, financial reporting and analysis projects, and business analytics and data visualization exercises. The real-world company analysis theme is continued in this section, giving students practice comparing Target and Walmart among other relevant companies. In each chapter, CP1 presents **auto-gradable** questions based on Target's annual report, CP2 includes **auto-gradable** questions based on Walmart's report, and CP3 provides **auto-gradable** questions comparing key ratio(s) discussed in the chapter for Target and Walmart.

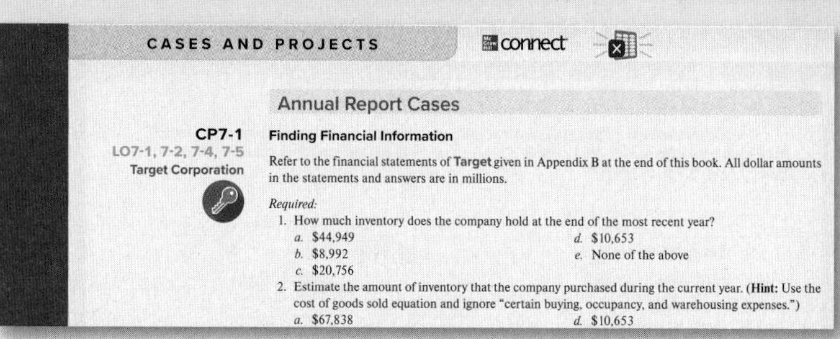

CASES AND PROJECTS connect

Annual Report Cases

CP7-1
LO7-1, 7-2, 7-4, 7-5
Target Corporation

Finding Financial Information

Refer to the financial statements of **Target** given in Appendix B at the end of this book. All dollar amounts in the statements and answers are in millions.

Required:

1. How much inventory does the company hold at the end of the most recent year?
   a. $44,949
   b. $8,992
   c. $20,756
   d. $10,653
   e. None of the above
2. Estimate the amount of inventory that the company purchased during the current year. (**Hint:** Use the cost of goods sold equation and ignore "certain buying, occupancy, and warehousing expenses.")
   a. $67,838
   d. $10,653

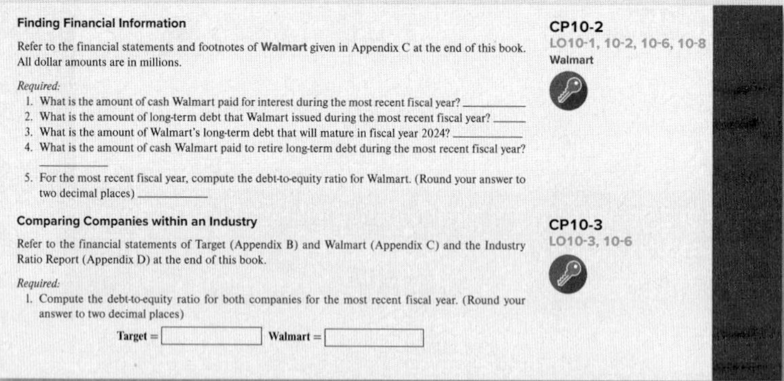

Finding Financial Information

CP10-2
LO10-1, 10-2, 10-6, 10-8
Walmart

Refer to the financial statements and footnotes of **Walmart** given in Appendix C at the end of this book. All dollar amounts are in millions.

Required:

1. What is the amount of cash Walmart paid for interest during the most recent fiscal year? ________
2. What is the amount of long-term debt that Walmart issued during the most recent fiscal year? ____
3. What is the amount of Walmart's long-term debt that will mature in fiscal year 2024? ________
4. What is the amount of cash Walmart paid to retire long-term debt during the most recent fiscal year? ________
5. For the most recent fiscal year, compute the debt-to-equity ratio for Walmart. (Round your answer to two decimal places) ________

Comparing Companies within an Industry

CP10-3
LO10-3, 10-6

Refer to the financial statements of Target (Appendix B) and Walmart (Appendix C) and the Industry Ratio Report (Appendix D) at the end of this book.

Required:

1. Compute the debt-to-equity ratio for both companies for the most recent fiscal year. (Round your answer to two decimal places)
   Target = [ ] **Walmart** = [ ]

CONTINUING PROBLEM

The continuing case revolves around Penny's Pool Service & Supply, Inc., and its largest supplier, Pool Corporation, Inc. In the first five chapters, the continuing case follows the establishment, operations, and financial reporting for Penny's. In Chapter 5, Pool Corporation, a real publicly traded corporation, is introduced in more detail. The Pool Corporation example is then extended to encompass each new topic in the remaining chapters.

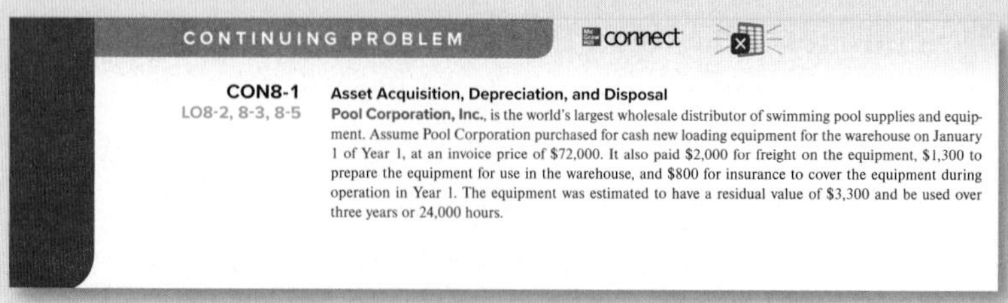

CONTINUING PROBLEM connect

CON8-1
LO8-2, 8-3, 8-5

Asset Acquisition, Depreciation, and Disposal

Pool Corporation, Inc., is the world's largest wholesale distributor of swimming pool supplies and equipment. Assume Pool Corporation purchased for cash new loading equipment for the warehouse on January 1 of Year 1, at an invoice price of $72,000. It also paid $2,000 for freight on the equipment, $1,300 to prepare the equipment for use in the warehouse, and $800 for insurance to cover the equipment during operation in Year 1. The equipment was estimated to have a residual value of $3,300 and be used over three years or 24,000 hours.

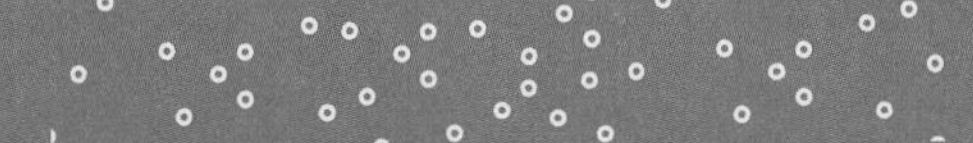

WHAT'S NEW IN THE 11th EDITION?

This edition is new in look, content, features, and resources to enhance learning by students and use by instructors.

Overall in Each Chapter:

- Greater focus on reporting by students' favorite tech companies including **Google**, **Facebook**, **Apple**, **Tesla**, **Amazon**, **Zoom**, **Microsoft** and others.
- Updated real company information throughout the edition to reflect the most recent annual report data.
- ***New*** marginal TIP feature to add clarity and remind students of important information, mostly in the text, but also in end-of-chapter assignments in early chapters to guide students in problem-solving.
- Moved marginal definitions of key terms to end-of-chapter Key Terms section with "rollover" feature in the ebook.
- ***New*** Related Homework after each Pause for Feedback Self-Study Quiz.
- ***New* Guided Help video** for each Self-Study Quiz involving numbers or calculations that are similar to popular assignments.
- ***New*** graphic highlighting key formulae.
- ***New*** Excel screen shots for trial balances, amortization schedules, and elsewhere.
- Increased use of company and individual names in end-of-chapter content to reflect more diversity.
- ***New*** parallel Alternate Problems to Problems that are also now available as algorithmic auto-graded *Connect* assignments.
- ***New*** end-of-book Annual Report Cases companies: **Target** and **Walmart.**
- ***New*** questions for Cases and Projects 1 through 3 in each chapter to allow for auto-grading, primarily using multiple-choice and fill-in-the-blank questions, often requiring an explanation for the choice.
- ***New*** structured project questions in ***You as Analyst: Online Company Research***. Flexibility is created to allow instructors to assign it as an individual or a team project.
- ***New*** auto-graded **data analytics** exercises on *Connect* titled ***Business Analytics and Data Visualization*** for most chapters.

Chapter 1

- ***New*** exhibit illustrating relationship between the income statement, statement of stockholders' equity, and balance sheet.
- ***New*** Self-Study Quiz and **Guided Help video** on the structure of the income statement, statement of stockholders' equity, and balance sheet.
- Added initial discussion of **internal controls** to Chapter 1.
- ***New*** concise discussion of the conceptual framework (moved from Chapter 2).
- ***New*** end-of-chapter Demonstration Case based on the financial statements of **Best Buy**.

Chapter 2

- ***New* Chipotle Mexican Grill** transactions for illustration that closely match with the actual first quarter 2020 results.
- ***New*** introductory discussion of operating lease right-of-use assets and related liabilities.
- ***New*** exhibit on the steps for transaction analysis for investing and financing activities that includes an example in the exhibit.
- Modified the accounting cycle graphic to add clarity.
- ***New* Guided Help video** on current ratio computation and analysis.
- ***New*** comparison company: **Shake Shack**.
- Added an exercise using real company information for **Alphabet, Inc.**, parent company of **Google**.

Chapter 3

- ***New* Chipotle Mexican Grill** transactions for illustration that closely match with the actual first quarter 2020 results.
- Briefly discussed the impact of the pandemic on Chipotle (in opening discussion and Understanding the Business).
- Renewed focus on accrual basis accounting with clarity on businesses that use cash basis accounting.
- Modified the simplified EPS formula to add clarity and consistency throughout the text.
- Integrated five-step revenue recognition principle with examples using real companies **Chipotle Mexican Grill** and **Apple**.
- ***New* Guided Help video** on identifying the accounts and amounts when recognizing revenues in the proper period.
- ***New*** exhibit on the transaction analysis steps for any transaction, with an example added to the exhibit.
- Modified several assignments: Added new transactions and updated real company information.
- Separated the analysis of cash flow requirements from recording of transactions in several assignments.

Chapter 4

- All **Chipotle Mexican Grill** illustrations updated to reflect most recent annual report data.

- Modified the Accounting Cycle graphic to add clarity.
- ***New*** Exhibit 4.2 on the types of adjustments, which also lists typical accrual and deferral accounts.
- ***New*** Exhibit 4.3 on the adjustment process, specifying the accounts to be adjusted and illustrating journal entries.
- ***New*** exhibit on the interrelationships of the financial statements, combining two graphics from the prior edition.
- ***New*** graphic illustrating the closing process.
- Changed E4-2 to the trial balance of **Facebook, Inc**. and AP4-1 to the trial balance of **Tesla, Inc**.
- Revised the continuing problem (CON4-1) for Penny's Pool Service & Supply to start with an unadjusted trial balance for completing the accounting cycle, making the assignment capable of being auto-graded using Excel and *Connect.*

Chapter 5

- Updated all internet-based sources of financial information.
- ***New*** **Environmental, Social, and Governance (ESG) Reporting** feature added with discussion of **Apple**'s ESG report.
- ***New*** **Yahoo! Finance** illustration of information available about Apple.
- ***New*** **Guided Help video** providing step-by-step instruction on how to determine the effects of transactions on key balance sheet and income statement subtotals.
- ***New*** **Guided Help video** providing step-by-step instruction on how to determine the effects of transactions of key performance ratios.
- ***New*** end-of-chapter Demonstration Case based on the financial statements of **Microsoft**.
- ***New*** end-of-chapter exercises and problems based on the financial statements of **Salesforce.com**, **Sonos, Inc.**, **Consolidated Edison**, **Nordstrom, Inc.**, and other companies.

Chapter 6

- Updated the Focus Company **Skechers**' illustrations.
- ***New*** **Guided Help video** providing step-by-step instruction on accounting for credit card discounts and sales discounts.
- Revised discussions of errors in bad debt estimates to include the effects of the pandemic on **Skechers**' bad debts.
- ***New*** end-of-chapter exercises and problems based on the financial statements of **SAP**, **Adobe**, **General Mills**, **VF Corporation**, and other companies.
- Revised discussion of **internal control** of cash.

Chapter 7

- Updated the Focus Company **Harley-Davidson**'s real company illustrations.
- ***New*** simplified discussion of how companies with perpetual inventory systems report using the LIFO cost flow assumption.
- ***New*** **Guided Help video** providing step-by-step instruction on converting ending inventory, cost of goods sold, and pretax income from LIFO to FIFO.
- ***New*** **Guided Help video** providing step-by-step instruction on correcting the income statement for errors in ending inventory.

Chapter 8

- ***New*** Focus Company: **FedEx Corporation** integrated in the chapter.
- ***New*** Understanding the Business section on package and cargo delivery industry.
- Briefly mentioned impact of pandemic in Key Ratio analysis.
- ***New*** discussion of operating lease right-of-use assets by airline and other industries as a method of acquisition.
- ***New*** comparison company **UPS** in fixed asset turnover ratio analysis.
- Revised Pause for Feedback on acquiring operational assets that more closely matches end-of-chapter assignments.
- ***New*** **Guided Help video** on recording the purchase of long-lived assets.
- ***New*** block on **Environmental, Social, and Governance (ESG) Reporting** with an excerpt from FedEx's *2020 Global Citizenship Report.*
- ***New*** discussion of **internal controls** for fixed assets.
- Illustrated depreciation schedules using Excel spreadsheets.
- Revised asset impairment test steps and illustrated applying the steps to Delta Air Lines' impairment measurement due to the pandemic.
- ***New*** illustration of determining goodwill using the purchase of **Tableau Software, Inc**. by **Salesforce.com, Inc**.
- Revised section on licenses and operating rights related to landing and take-off slots as intangible operating rights of airlines.

Chapter 9

- ***New*** and more vibrant real company pictures and illustrations of Focus Company **Starbucks**.
- Updated company names used in examples and end-of-chapter material to reflect more diversity.
- ***New*** comparison company **Monster Beverages**.
- Updated discussion of deferred revenue using Starbucks's "stored value cards" account and associated mobile app as an example.
- ***New*** real-world excerpt focused on a California lawsuit claiming that Starbucks's coffee has chemicals in it that requires a warning, and whether this lawsuit is a contingent liability.
- Added **Peloton** and **Beyond Meats** in end-of-chapter material.

Chapter 10

- ***New*** and more vibrant real company bond illustrations of Focus Company **Amazon**.
- Updated company names used in examples and end-of-chapter material to reflect more diversity.
- ***New*** **data analytics** box that highlights the role artificial intelligence plays in bond investing.
- Added **Apple** in end-of-chapter material.

Chapter 11

- ***New*** Focus Company: **Microsoft** integrated throughout the chapter with new pictures and updated illustrations.
- Updated company names used in examples and end-of-chapter material to reflect more diversity.
- ***New*** **Environmental, Social, and Governance (ESG) Reporting** feature added with discussion of **Microsoft**'s ESG report.
- ***New*** discussion of how some states (e.g., the state of Washington) do not allow treasury stock and the effects this has on financial statements.

- ***New*** comparison company **IBM**.
- ***New*** real-world excerpt focused on **Microsoft**'s equity compensation.
- Streamlined the chapter supplement that covers accounting for the equity of sole proprietorships and partnerships.
- Added **Zoom Video Communications** and **Facebook** in end-of-chapter material.

Chapter 12

- Updated the Focus Company **National Beverage** and all real company illustrations.

Chapter 13

- ***New*** and more vibrant real company pictures and illustrations of Focus Company **The Home Depot**.
- Updated company names used in examples and end-of-chapter material to reflect more diversity.
- Revised ratio titles to succinctly link to titles used in all previous chapters.
- Changed end-of-chapter material to include **Apple**, **Peabody Energy**, **Tesla**, **Boeing**, **Zoom Video Communications**, and **A-Mark Precious Metals**.
- ***New*** **Environmental, Social, and Governance (ESG) Reporting** feature added with discussion of **The Home Depot**'s ESG report.

Appendix A

- Updated the Focus Company **The Walt Disney Company**'s illustrations.
- Added marginal illustrations of the timing of transactions regarding held-to-maturity, trading securities, and available-for-sale debt and equity investments.
- ***New*** **Guided Help video** on recording transactions related to debt investments as trading securities and available-for-sale securities.
- ***New*** Pause for Feedback with a Self-Study Quiz on applying the fair value method to passive investments in equity securities.
- ***New*** **Guided Help video** on recording transactions related to applying the equity method for investments when there is significant influence.
- Added real world excerpt from **The Walt Disney Company**'s annual report regarding the impact of the pandemic and the impairment of goodwill.

Connect

- New Integrated Excel Activities - pair the power of Microsoft Excel® with the power of Connect® in a seamless live integration.
- New Tableau Dashboard Activities - easily introduce students to Tableau®. Students learn to gather the information they need from a live embedded Tableau dashboard. No prior knowledge of Tableau® is needed.
- New Alternative Problems - all the alternative problems in the text can now be found and auto-graded in Connect®.

Instructors: Student Success Starts with You

Tools to enhance your unique voice

Want to build your own course? No problem. Prefer to use an OLC-aligned, prebuilt course? Easy. Want to make changes throughout the semester? Sure. And you'll save time with Connect's auto-grading too.

65%
Less Time Grading

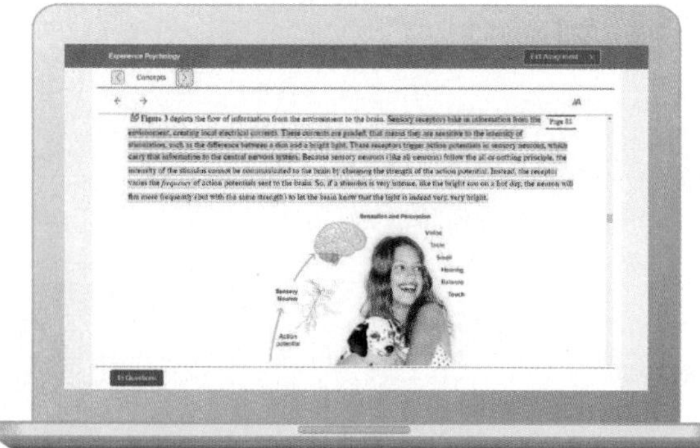

Laptop: McGraw Hill; Woman/dog: George Doyle/Getty Images

Study made personal

Incorporate adaptive study resources like SmartBook® 2.0 into your course and help your students be better prepared in less time. Learn more about the powerful personalized learning experience available in SmartBook 2.0 at **www.mheducation.com/highered/connect/smartbook**

Affordable solutions, added value

Make technology work for you with LMS integration for single sign-on access, mobile access to the digital textbook, and reports to quickly show you how each of your students is doing. And with our Inclusive Access program, you can provide all these tools at a discount to your students. Ask your McGraw Hill representative for more information.

Padlock: Jobalou/Getty Images

Solutions for your challenges

A product isn't a solution. Real solutions are affordable, reliable, and come with training and ongoing support when you need it and how you want it. Visit **www.supportateverystep.com** for videos and resources both you and your students can use throughout the semester.

Checkmark: Jobalou/Getty Images

Students: Get Learning that Fits You

Effective tools for efficient studying

Connect is designed to help you be more productive with simple, flexible, intuitive tools that maximize your study time and meet your individual learning needs. Get learning that works for you with Connect.

Study anytime, anywhere

Download the free ReadAnywhere app and access your online eBook, SmartBook 2.0, or Adaptive Learning Assignments when it's convenient, even if you're offline. And since the app automatically syncs with your Connect account, all of your work is available every time you open it. Find out more at **www.mheducation.com/readanywhere**

"I really liked this app—it made it easy to study when you don't have your text-book in front of you."

- Jordan Cunningham, Eastern Washington University

Calendar: owattaphotos/Getty Images

Everything you need in one place

Your Connect course has everything you need—whether reading on your digital eBook or completing assignments for class, Connect makes it easy to get your work done.

Learning for everyone

McGraw Hill works directly with Accessibility Services Departments and faculty to meet the learning needs of all students. Please contact your Accessibility Services Office and ask them to email accessibility@mheducation.com, or visit **www.mheducation.com/about/accessibility** for more information.

Top: Jenner Images/Getty Images, Left: Hero Images/Getty Images, Right: Hero Images/Getty Images

Online Assignments

Connect helps students learn more efficiently by providing feedback and practice material when they need it, where they need it. Connect grades homework automatically and gives immediate feedback on any questions students may have missed. The extensive assignable, gradable end-of-chapter content includes a general journal application that looks and feels more like what you would find in a general ledger software package.

End-of-chapter **auto-gradable** questions in Connect include

- Mini-Exercises
- Exercises
- Problems
- Alternate Problems
- Comprehensive Problems
- Continuing Problems
- Cases and Projects
- General Ledger Problems
- Excel Application Exercises
- Tableau Dashboard Activities

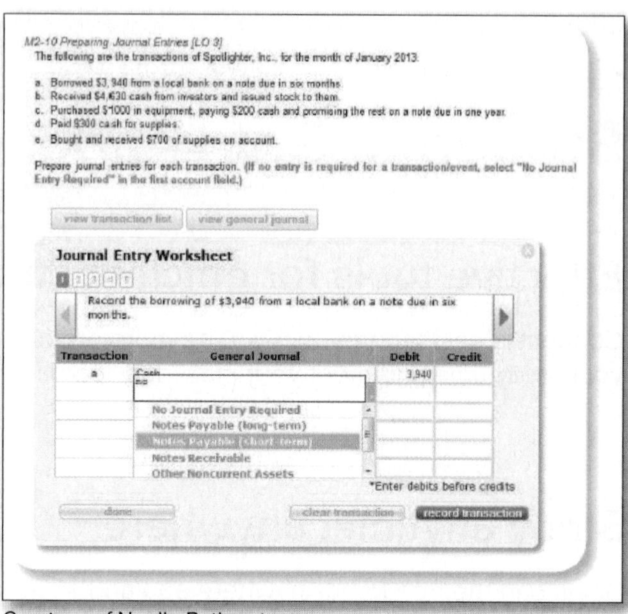

Courtesy of Noelle Bathurst

General Ledger Problems

General Ledger Problems provide a much-improved student experience when working with accounting cycle questions, offering improved navigation and less scrolling. Students can audit their mistakes by easily linking back to their original entries and can see how the numbers flow through the various financial statements. Many General Ledger Problems include an analysis tab that allows students to demonstrate their critical thinking skills and a deeper understanding of accounting concepts.

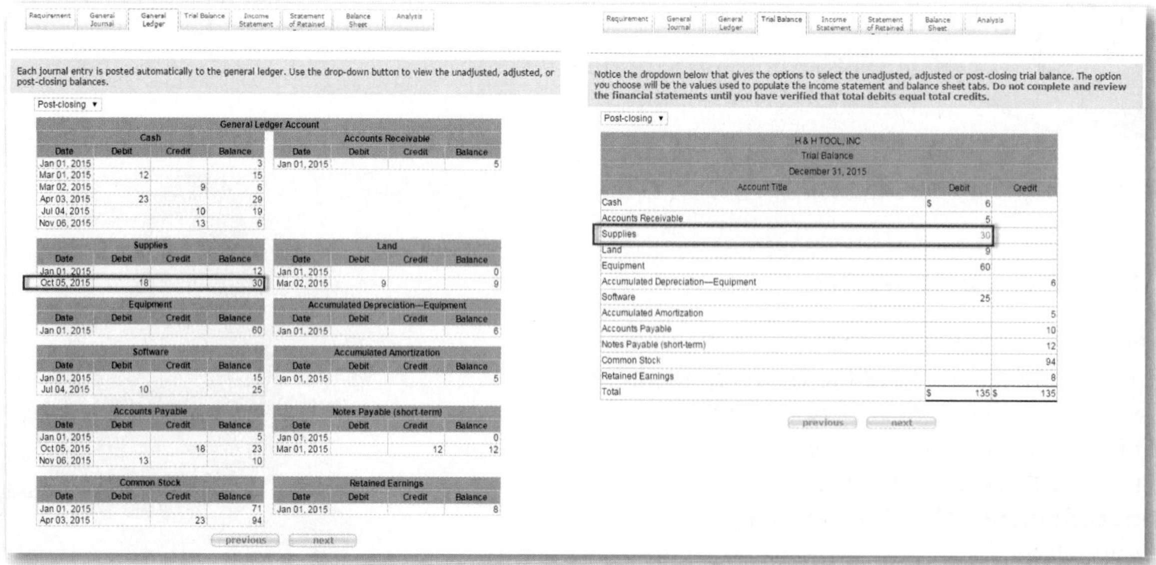

NEW!

Concept Overview Videos

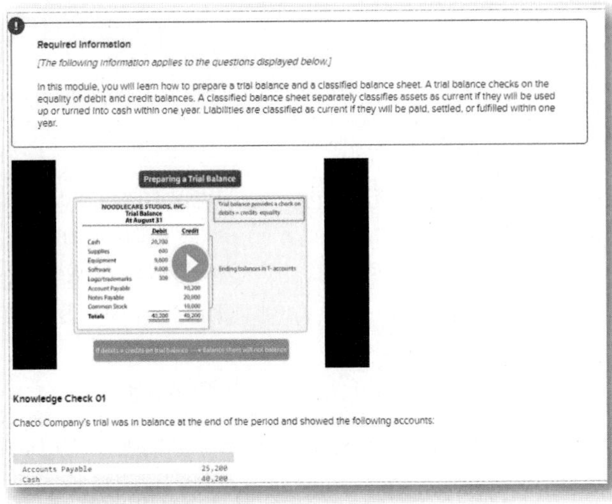

The **Concept Overview Videos** provide engaging narratives of all chapter learning objectives in an assignable and interactive online format. They follow the structure of the text and are organized to match the specific learning objectives within each chapter of *Financial Accounting.* These short presentations provide additional explanation and enhancement of material from the text chapter, allowing students to learn, study, and practice with instant feedback, at their own pace.

Tableau Dashboard Activities

Tableau Dashboard Activities easily introduce students to Tableau, allowing them to explore live dashboards directly integrated into Connect. These activities include auto-graded questions focused on both calculations and analysis. No prior knowledge of Tableau is needed.

NEW!

Integrated Excel

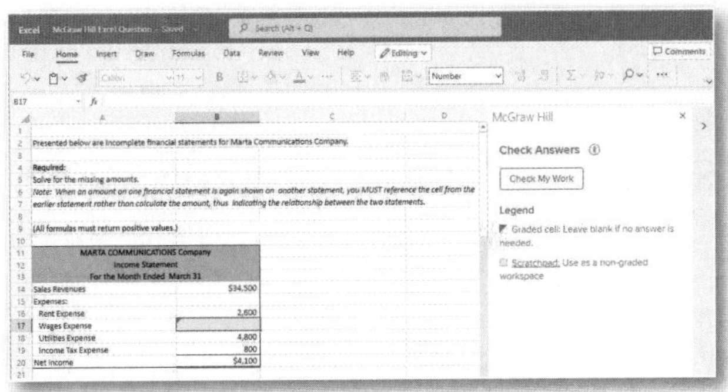

New! Integrated Excel assignments pair the power of Microsoft Excel with the power of Connect. A seamless integration of Excel within Connect, Integrated Excel questions allow students to work in live, auto-graded Excel spreadsheets—no additional logins, no need to upload or download files. Instructors can choose to grade by formula or solution value, and students receive instant cell-level feedback via integrated Check My Work functionality.

Guided Examples

The **Guided Examples, also known as Hints,** in Connect provide a narrated, animated, step-by-step walk-through of select exercises similar to those assigned. These short presentations can be turned on or off by instructors and provide reinforcement when students need it most.

> "It is a great textbook that comes with a great online work system to enhance students' learning effectiveness. Connect is user-friendly, provides many good practice opportunities, and links well with e-book."
>
> —Wan-Ting Wu, University of Massachusetts Boston

ACKNOWLEDGMENTS

Many dedicated instructors have devoted their time and effort to help us make each edition better. We would like to acknowledge and thank all of our colleagues who have helped guide our development decisions for this and previous editions. This text would not be the success it is without the help of all of you.

Reviewers

Ryan John Anthony, University of Washington
Margaret A. Atkinson, Stark State College
Progyan Basu, University of Maryland—College Park
Sheila Bradford, American University
Dale P. Burgess, William and Mary
Gretchen Charrier, University of Texas at Austin
Linda G. Chase, Baldwin Wallace University
Bingyi Chen, Suffolk University
Laurie Dahlin, Worcester State University
David L. Dassler, The University of Denver
Cathy DeHart, Gonzaga University
Peggy DeJong, Kirkwood Community College
Carleton Donchess, Bridgewater State University
Patricia Dorris-Crenny, Villanova University
Robert Duquette, Lehigh University
Donna Free, Bentley University
Joy Gray, Bentley University
Michael P. Griffin, University of Massachusetts Dartmouth
Heidi Hansel, Kirkwood Community College
David J. Harr, American University
Julie Head, Indiana University
Julie Head, Indiana University—Bloomington
Melanie Hicks, Liberty University
Barry Hollingsworth, DePaul University
Mary Jepperson, College of Saint Benedict/Saint John's University
Kevin K. Jones, University of California, Santa Cruz
Brad Kamrath, University of Washington
Christy M Lefevers, Catawba Valley Community College
Annette Leps, Johns Hopkins University
May H. Lo, Western New England University
Gina Lord, Santa Rosa Junior College
Mostafa M. Maksy, Kutztown University Pennsylvania
Oltiana Muharremi, Stonehill College
Baseemah Nance, Central Piedmont Community College
Tammy Naples, University of Minnesota
Nancy Osborne, University of Massachusetts Dartmouth
Glenn Pate, Palm Beach State College
Michael T. Paz, Cornell University
Tammy Perri, University of Nevada, Las Vegas
Kathy Petroni, Michigan State University
Usha Rackliffe, Emory University
Kelly Root, University of New Hampshire
Jamie Seitz, University of Southern Indiana
Sherrie Slom, Hillsborough Community College
Kevin R. Smith, Utah Valley University
Nancy Snow, University of Toledo
MaryBeth Tobin, Bridgewater State University
Ben Trnka, St. John's University
Suneel Udpa, University of California, Berkeley
Terri Walsh, Seminole State College of Florida
Rick Warne, University of Cincinnati
Wan Ting (Alexandra) Wu, University of Massachusetts Boston
Wan-Ting Wu, University of Massachusetts Boston

We are grateful to the following individuals who helped develop, critique, and shape the extensive ancillary package: LuAnn Bean, Florida Institute of Technology; Jeannie Folk; Beth Kobylarz, Mark McCarthy, East Carolina University; Barbara Muller, Arizona State University; Kim Temme; and Teri Zuccaro, Clarke University.

We also have received invaluable input and support through the years from present and former colleagues and students. We also appreciate the additional comments, suggestions, and support of our students and our colleagues at Cornell University, Ithaca College, and University of Washington.

Last, we applaud the extraordinary efforts of a talented group of individuals at McGraw Hill who made all of this come together. We would especially like to thank the following: our Portfolio Vice President, Tim Vertovec; our Senior Director, Rebecca Olson; our Portfolio Manager, Noelle Bathurst; our Lead Product Developer, Kelly Delso, our Marketing Manager, Lauren Shur, our Executive Program Manager, Mark Christianson; our Lead Content Project Manager, Fran Simon; our Content Project Managers, Jeni McAtee and Angela Norris; our Designers, Laurie Entringer and Matt Diamond; our Buyer, Susan Culbertson; and our Senior Content Licensing Specialist, Gina Oberbroeckling.

Robert Libby
Patricia A. Libby
Frank Hodge

CONTENTS IN BRIEF

CONTENTS

CHAPTER TEN

Reporting and Interpreting Bond Securities 522

CHAPTER ELEVEN

Reporting and Interpreting Stockholders' Equity 574

Images used throughout front matter: Question of ethics: mushmello/Shutterstock; Pause for feedback: McGraw Hill; Guided help: McGraw Hill; Financial analysis: McGraw Hill; Focus on cash flows: Hilch/Shutterstock; Key ratio analysis: guillermain/123RF; Data analytics: Hilch/Shutterstock; Tip: McGraw Hill; ESG reporting: McGraw Hill; International perspective: Hilch/Shutterstock

1 chapter

Financial Statements and Business Decisions

Le-Nature's Inc. designed its business strategy to ride the growing wave of interest in noncarbonated beverages. And apparently its strategy was a huge success. Its financial statements reported growth in sales from $156 to $275 million in just three years. How did this small family-run business compete with the likes of Coke and Pepsi in this growing market? The business press suggested the first key to its success was manufacturing a broad range of products that fit into the fastest growing "healthy" segments: flavored waters, teas, and fruit drinks. Founder and CEO Gregory Podlucky said that an obsessive drive for quality and efficiency was just as critical. Matching customers' concerns for the environment and healthy living, Le-Nature's was praised as one of the first companies to switch to environmentally friendlier PET plastic bottles and to employ safe in-bottle pasteurization. Its 21st-century manufacturing operation in Latrobe, Pennsylvania, produced everything that goes into its products, from the injection-molded PET bottles to the final packaging. Complete control over the whole process assures quality and provides the flexibility to respond quickly to changes in customers' demands. When convenience stores moved to larger-sized drinks or school cafeterias switched from carbonated beverages to healthier drinks, Le-Nature's could change its production to meet the customers' needs. The company even opened a second new state-of-the-art manufacturing facility in Arizona to meet the apparent growing demand.

But here is the twist: Just three short months later, investigators discovered that Le-Nature's phenomenal sales growth was more fiction than fact. How could this apparent success story portrayed in the financial statements really be one of the most remarkable frauds in history?

Chapter 1 concentrates on the key financial statements that businesspeople rely upon when they evaluate a company's performance as well as the importance of accurate financial statements in making our economic system work. We discuss these issues in the context of Le-Nature's rise and fall.

LEARNING OBJECTIVES

After studying this chapter, you should be able to:

1-1 Recognize the information conveyed in each of the four basic financial statements and the way that it is used by different decision makers (investors, creditors, and managers). p. 6

1-2 Identify the role of generally accepted accounting principles (GAAP) in determining financial statement content and managers', directors', and auditors' responsibilities for ensuring the accuracy of the financial statements. p.17

James F. Quinn/KRT/Newscom

FOCUS COMPANY

Le-Nature's Inc.

USING FINANCIAL STATEMENT INFORMATION TO MANAGE GROWTH

Accounting knowledge will be valuable to you only if you can apply it in the real world. Learning is also easier when it takes place in real contexts. So at the beginning of each chapter, we always provide some background about the business that will provide the context for the chapter discussion.

UNDERSTANDING THE BUSINESS

Le-Nature's Inc., our focus company for this chapter, was founded by Gregory Podlucky and his brother Jonathan, who initially were the sole owners or **stockholders** of the company. They were also the managers of the company. Using expertise gained working at their parents' brewery (**Stoney's Beer**), the brothers were early believers in the trend toward healthier, noncarbonated beverages. Like most entrepreneurs, their growth ambitions quickly outpaced their own financial resources. So they turned to banks, including **Wells Fargo Bank** and other lenders, to finance additional manufacturing facilities and equipment. Different units of Wells Fargo continued to arrange lending to Le-Nature's as the need arose, becoming its largest lender or **creditor.** Creditors make money on the loans by charging **interest.** The Podluckys also convinced others to buy stock in Le-Nature's. These individuals became part owners or stockholders along with the Podluckys. The stockholders hoped to receive a portion of what the company earned in the form of cash payments called **dividends** and to eventually sell their share of the company at a higher price than they paid. Creditors are more willing to lend and stock prices usually rise when creditors and investors expect the company to do well in the future. Both groups estimate future performance, in part, based on information in the company's financial statements.

EXHIBIT 1.1

The Accounting System and Decision Makers

Micolas/Shutterstock; nirat/iStock/Getty Images Plus; Anton Violin/Shutterstock; Pressmaster/Shutterstock; kzenon/123RF

The Accounting System

Managers (often called **internal decision makers**) need information about the company's business activities to manage the operating, investing, and financing activities of the firm. Stockholders and creditors (often called **external decision makers**) need information about these same business activities to assess whether the company will be able to pay back its debts with interest and pay dividends. All businesses must have an accounting system that collects and processes financial information about an organization's business activities and reports that information to decision makers. Le-Nature's **business activities** included:

- **Financing Activities:** borrowing or paying back money to lenders and receiving additional funds from stockholders or paying them dividends.
- **Investing Activities:** buying or selling items such as plant and equipment used in the production of beverages.
- **Operating Activities:** the day-to-day process of purchasing raw tea and other ingredients from suppliers, manufacturing beverages, delivering them to customers, collecting cash from customers, and paying suppliers.

Exhibit 1.1 outlines the two parts of the accounting system. Internal managers typically require continuous, detailed information because they must plan and manage the day-to-day operations of the organization. Developing accounting information for internal decision makers, called **managerial** or **management accounting,** is the subject of a separate accounting course. The focus of this text is accounting for external decision makers, called **financial accounting,** and the four basic financial statements and related disclosures that are periodically produced by that system.

Why Study Financial Accounting?

No matter what your business career goals, you can't get away from financial accounting. You may want to work for an investment firm, a bank, or an accounting firm that would be involved in the financing of companies like **Le-Nature's**. We will focus much of our discussion on the perspectives of **investors, creditors,** and **preparers** of financial statements. However, you might not be aware that managers within the firm also make direct use of financial statements. For example, **marketing managers** and **credit managers** use customers' financial statements to decide whether to extend credit to their customers. **Supply chain managers** analyze suppliers' financial statements to see whether the suppliers have the resources to meet demand and invest in future development. Both the employees' unions and company **human resource managers** use financial statements as a basis for contract negotiations over pay rates. Financial statement figures even serve as a basis for calculating employee bonuses. Regardless of the functional area of management in which you are employed, you will use financial statement data.

We begin with a brief but comprehensive overview of the information reported in the four basic financial statements and the people and organizations involved in their preparation and use. This overview provides a context in which you can learn the more detailed material presented in the chapters that follow. Then we will discuss the parties that are responsible for the accuracy of financial statements as well as the consequences of misstated financial statements. Le-Nature's stockholders and creditors used its financial statements to learn more about the company before making their investment and lending decisions. In doing so, they assumed that the statements accurately represented Le-Nature's financial condition.

Your Goals for Chapter 1

To understand the way in which creditors and stockholders used Le-Nature's financial statements, we must first understand what specific information is presented in the four basic financial statements for a company such as Le-Nature's. **PLEASE NOTE: Rather than trying to memorize the definitions of every term used in this chapter, try to focus your attention on learning the general content, structure, and use of the statements. Specifically:**

Content: the categories of items (often called **elements**) reported on each of the four statements.

Structure: the **equation** that shows how the elements within the statement are organized and related.

Use: how the information is **used** by stockholders and creditors to make investment and lending decisions.

The Pause for Feedback–Self-Study Quizzes at key points in the chapter will help you assess whether you have reached these goals. If you have difficulty with the Self-Study Quizzes, Guided Help videos provide narrated, animated, step-by-step walk-throughs at key points to help you with the material. Remember that because this chapter is an overview, each concept discussed here will be discussed again in Chapters 2 through 5.

ORGANIZATION OF THE CHAPTER

The Four Basic Financial Statements: An Overview

- Balance Sheet
- Income Statement
- Statement of Stockholders' Equity
- Statement of Cash Flows
- Relationships among the Statements
- Notes and Financial Statement Formats

Responsibilities for the Accounting Communication Process

- Generally Accepted Accounting Principles
- Ensuring the Accuracy of Financial Statements

LEARNING OBJECTIVE 1-1

Recognize the information conveyed in each of the four basic financial statements and the way that it is used by different decision makers (investors, creditors, and managers).

THE FOUR BASIC FINANCIAL STATEMENTS: AN OVERVIEW

Four financial statements are normally prepared by profit-making organizations for use by investors, creditors, and other external decision makers.

1. On its **balance sheet,** Le-Nature's reports the economic resources it owns and the sources of financing for those resources.
2. On its **income statement,** Le-Nature's reports its ability to sell goods for more than their cost to produce and sell.
3. On its **statement of stockholders' equity,** Le-Nature's reports additional contributions from or payments to investors and the amount of income the company reinvested for future growth.
4. On its **statement of cash flows,** Le-Nature's reports its ability to generate cash and how it was used.

The four basic statements can be prepared at any point in time (such as the end of the year, quarter, or month) and can apply to any time span (such as one year, one quarter, or one month). Like most companies, Le-Nature's prepared financial statements for external users (investors and creditors) at the end of each quarter (known as **quarterly reports**) and at the end of the year (known as **annual reports**).

The Balance Sheet

The purpose of the **balance sheet (statement of financial position)** is to report the financial position (amount of assets, liabilities, and stockholders' equity) of an accounting entity at a particular point in time. We can learn a great deal about what the balance sheet reports just by reading the statement from the top. The balance sheet Le-Nature's Inc. presented to creditors and stockholders is shown in Exhibit 1.2.

EXHIBIT 1.2

Balance Sheet

LE-NATURE'S INC. **Balance Sheet** **At December 31, 2020**[1] **(in millions of dollars)**		**EXPLANATION** *Name of the entity* *Title of the statement* *Specific date of the statement* *Unit of measure*
Assets:		***Resources controlled by the company***
Cash	$ 10.6	*Amount of cash in the company's bank accounts*
Accounts receivable	6.6	*Amounts owed by customers from prior sales*
Inventories	51.2	*Ingredients and beverages ready for sale*
Property, plant, and equipment	459.0	*Factories, production equipment, and land*
Total assets	**$527.4**	***Total amount of company's resources***
Liabilities and stockholders' equity:		***Sources of financing for company's resources***
Liabilities		*Financing supplied by creditors*
Accounts payable	$ 26.0	*Amounts owed to suppliers for prior purchases*
Notes payable to banks	381.7	*Amounts owed to banks on written debt contracts*
Total liabilities	407.7	
Stockholders' equity		*Financing provided by stockholders*
Common stock	55.7	*Amounts invested in the business by stockholders*
Retained earnings	64.0	*Past earnings not distributed to stockholders*
Total stockholders' equity	119.7	
Total liabilities and stockholders' equity	**$527.4**	***Total sources of financing for company's resources***
The notes are an integral part of these financial statements.		

Structure

Notice that the **heading** specifically identifies four significant items related to the statement:

1. **Name of the entity,** Le-Nature's Inc.
2. **Title of the statement,** Balance Sheet.
3. **Specific date of the statement,** At December 31, 2020.
4. **Unit of measure** (in millions of dollars).

Balance Sheet
Assets
=
Liabilities
+
Stockholders' Equity

The organization for which financial data are to be collected, called an **accounting entity**, must be precisely defined. On the balance sheet, the business entity itself, not the business owners, is viewed as owning the resources it uses and being responsible for its debts. The heading of each statement indicates the time dimension of the report. The balance sheet is like a financial snapshot indicating the entity's financial position at a specific point in time–in this case, December 31, 2020–which is stated clearly on the balance sheet. Financial reports are normally denominated in the currency of the country in which they are located. U.S. companies report in U.S. dollars, Canadian companies in Canadian dollars, and Mexican companies in Mexican pesos. Le-Nature's statements report in millions of dollars. That is, they round the last six digits to the nearest **million** dollars. The listing of Cash $10.6 on Le-Nature's balance sheet actually means $10,600,000.

[1]The Le-Nature's statements presented are constructed based on a simplified version of its audited 2005 statements. As we discuss in the section titled "Ensuring the Accuracy of Financial Statements," Le-Nature's statements were later found to be fraudulent. (Thus, 2020 is used in the header for illustration purposes.) The Le-Nature's fraud provides an important warning about the importance of accuracy in financial reporting.

Notice that Le-Nature's balance sheet has three major captions: assets, liabilities, and stockholders' equity. The **basic accounting equation,** often called the balance sheet equation, explains their relationship:

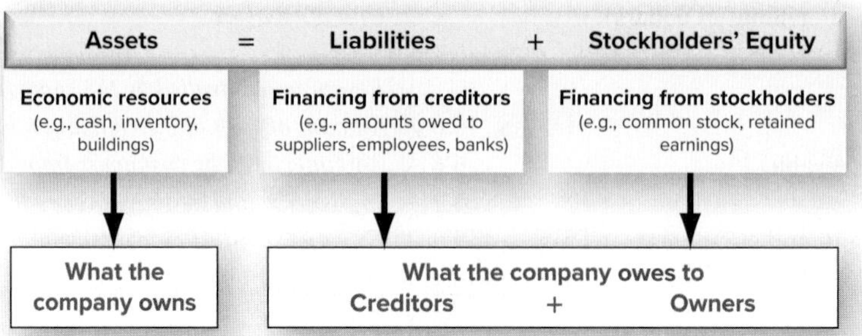

The basic accounting equation shows what we mean when we refer to a company's **financial position:** the **economic resources** that the company owns and the **sources of financing** for those resources.

Adrian Bradshaw/EPA/Newscom

Elements

Assets are the economic resources owned by the entity. Le-Nature's lists four items under the category Assets. The exact items listed as assets on a company's balance sheet depend on the nature of its operations. But these are common names used by many companies. The four items listed by Le-Nature's are the economic resources needed to manufacture and sell beverages to retailers and vending companies. Each of these economic resources is expected to provide future benefits to the firm. To prepare to manufacture the beverages, Le-Nature's first needed **cash** to purchase land on which to build factories and install production machinery (**property, plant, and equipment**). Le-Nature's then began purchasing ingredients and producing beverages, which led to the balance assigned to **inventories**. When Le-Nature's sells its beverages to grocery stores and others, it sells them on credit and receives promises to pay called **accounts receivable**, which are collected in cash later.

Every asset on the balance sheet is initially measured at the total cost incurred to acquire it. Balance sheets do not generally show the amounts for which the assets could currently be sold.

Liabilities and stockholders' equity are the sources of financing for the company's economic resources. **Liabilities** indicate the amount of financing provided by creditors. They are the company's debts or obligations. Under the category Liabilities, Le-Nature's lists two items. The **accounts payable** arise from the purchase of goods or services from suppliers on credit without a formal written contract (or a note). The **notes payable** to banks result from cash borrowings based on a formal written debt contract with banks.

Stockholders' equity indicates the amount of financing provided by owners of the business and reinvested earnings.[2] The investment of cash and other assets in the business by the stockholders is called **common stock**. The amount of earnings (profits) reinvested in the business (and thus not distributed to stockholders in the form of dividends) is called **retained earnings**.

In Exhibit 1.2, the Stockholders' Equity section reports two items. The founders and other stockholders' investment of $55.7 million is reported as common stock. Le-Nature's total earnings (or losses incurred) less all dividends paid to the stockholders since formation of the corporation equals $64 million and is reported as retained earnings. Total stockholders' equity is the sum of the common stock plus the retained earnings.

[2]A corporation is a business that is incorporated under the laws of a particular state. The owners are called **stockholders** or **shareholders.** Ownership is represented by shares of capital stock that usually can be bought and sold freely. The corporation operates as a separate legal entity, separate and apart from its owners. The stockholders enjoy limited liability; they are liable for the debts of the corporation only to the extent of their investments. Chapter Supplement A discusses forms of ownership in more detail.

FINANCIAL ANALYSIS

Interpreting Assets, Liabilities, and Stockholders' Equity on the Balance Sheet

Assessment of **Le-Nature's** assets is important to its creditors, **Wells Fargo Bank** and others, and its stockholders because assets provide a basis for judging whether the company has sufficient resources available to operate. Assets are also important because they could be sold for cash in the event that Le-Nature's goes out of business.

Le-Nature's debts are important because creditors and stockholders are concerned about whether the company has sufficient sources of cash to pay its debts. Le-Nature's debts are also relevant to Wells Fargo Bank's decision to lend money to the company because existing creditors share its claim against Le-Nature's assets. If a business does not pay its creditors, the creditors may force the sale of assets sufficient to meet their claims.

Le-Nature's stockholders' equity is important to Wells Fargo Bank because creditors' claims legally come before those of owners. If Le-Nature's goes out of business and its assets are sold, the proceeds of that sale must be used to pay back creditors before the stockholders receive any money. Thus, creditors consider stockholders' equity a protective "cushion."

PAUSE FOR FEEDBACK

We just learned the **balance sheet** is a statement of financial position that reports dollar amounts for a company's assets, liabilities, and stockholders' equity at a specific point in time. These elements are related in the basic accounting equation: **Assets = Liabilities + Stockholders' Equity.** Before you move on, complete the following questions to test your understanding of these concepts.

SELF-STUDY QUIZ

1. **Le-Nature's assets** are listed in one section and **liabilities** and **stockholders' equity** in another. Notice that the two sections balance in conformity with the basic accounting equation. In the following chapters, you will learn that the basic accounting equation is the basic building block for the entire accounting process. Your task here is to verify that total assets ($527.4 million) is correct using the numbers for liabilities and stockholders' equity presented in Exhibit 1.2.

   Assets _____ = Liabilities _____ + Stockholders' Equity _____

2. Learning which items belong in each of the balance sheet categories is an important first step in understanding their meaning. Without referring to Exhibit 1.2, mark each balance sheet item in the following list as an asset (A), a liability (L), or a stockholders' equity (SE) item.

   _____ Accounts payable
   _____ Accounts receivable
   _____ Cash
   _____ Common stock
   _____ Property, plant, and equipment
   _____ Inventories
   _____ Notes payable
   _____ Retained earnings

Tip **Don't skip the SELF-STUDY QUIZZES!** They are designed to help ensure you understand the material before moving on.

After you have completed your answers, check them below.

Related Homework: M1-1, M1-2, E1-2, E1-3

Solution to SELF-STUDY QUIZ

1. Assets ($527.4) = Liabilities ($407.7) + Stockholders' Equity ($119.7) (in millions).
2. L, A, A, SE, A, A, L, SE (reading down the columns).

The Income Statement

Structure

The **income statement (statement of income, statement of earnings, statement of operations)**[3] reports the accountant's primary measure of performance of a business, revenues less expenses during the accounting period. While the term *profit* is used widely for this measure of performance, accountants prefer to use the technical terms **net income** or *net earnings.* **Le-Nature's** net income measures its success in selling beverages for more than the cost to generate those sales.

A quick reading of Le-Nature's income statement (Exhibit 1.3) indicates a great deal about its purpose and content. The heading identifies the name of the entity, the title of the report, and the unit of measure used in the statement. Unlike the balance sheet, however, which reports as of a certain date, the income statement reports for a specified period of time (in this case for the year ended December 31, 2020). The time period covered by the financial statements (one year in this case) is called an **accounting period**. Notice that Le-Nature's income statement has three major captions: revenues, expenses, and net income. The income statement equation that describes their relationship is:

Income Statement
Revenues
+Increases
−Expenses
Net Income

Revenues	−	Expenses	=	Net Income
Resources earned from delivery of goods and services		Resources used (incurred) to earn period's revenue		Revenues earned minus expenses incurred

Elements

Companies earn **revenues** from the sale of goods or services to customers (in Le-Nature's case, from the sale of beverages). Revenues normally are amounts expected to be received for goods or services that have been delivered to a customer, **whether or not the customer has paid for the goods or services**. Retail stores such as **Walmart** and **McDonald's** often receive cash from consumers at the time of sale. However, when Le-Nature's delivers its beverages to retail stores, it receives a promise of future payment called an account receivable, which later is collected in cash. In either case, the business recognizes total sales (cash and credit) as revenue for the

EXHIBIT 1.3

Income Statement

LE-NATURE'S INC. **Income Statement** **For the Year Ended December 31, 2020** **(in millions of dollars)**		**EXPLANATION** *Name of the entity* *Title of the statement* *Accounting period* *Unit of measure*
Revenues		
Sales revenue	$ 275.1	*Cash and promises received from sale of beverages*
Expenses		
Cost of goods sold	140.8	*Cost to produce beverages sold*
Selling, general, and administrative expenses	77.1	*Other operating expenses (utilities, delivery costs, etc.)*
Interest expense	17.2	*Cost of using borrowed funds*
Income before income taxes	40.0	
Income tax expense	17.1	*Income taxes on period's income before income taxes*
Net income	$ 22.9	***Revenues earned minus expenses incurred***

The notes are an integral part of these financial statements.

[3]Comprehensive income is sometimes presented in a separate statement titled Statement of Comprehensive Income, but may be part of the Income Statement. This advanced topic is discussed in Chapter 5.

period. Various terms are used in income statements to describe different sources of revenue (e.g., provision of services, sale of goods, rental of property). Le-Nature's lists only one, **sales revenue**, in its income statement.

Expenses represent the dollar amount of resources the entity used to earn revenues during the period. Expenses reported in one accounting period actually may be paid for in another accounting period. Some expenses require the payment of cash immediately, while others require payment at a later date. Some also may require the use of another resource, such as an inventory item, which may have been paid for in a prior period. Le-Nature's lists four types of expenses on its income statement, which are described in Exhibit 1.3. These expenses include income tax expense, which, as a corporation, Le-Nature's must pay on the subtotal income before income taxes.

Net income or net earnings (often called "the bottom line") is the excess of total revenues over total expenses. If total expenses exceed total revenues, a net loss is reported.[4] We noted earlier that revenues are not necessarily the same as collections from customers and expenses are not necessarily the same as payments to suppliers. As a result, net income normally **does not equal** the net cash generated by operations. This latter amount is reported on the cash flow statement discussed later in this chapter.

FINANCIAL ANALYSIS

Analyzing the Income Statement: Beyond the Bottom Line

Investors and creditors such as **Wells Fargo Bank** closely monitor a firm's net income because it indicates the firm's ability to sell goods and services for more than they cost to produce and deliver. Investors buy stock when they believe that future earnings will improve and lead to dividends and the ability to sell their stock for more than they paid. Lenders also rely on future earnings to provide the resources to repay loans. The details of the statement also are important. For example, **Le-Nature's** had to sell more than $275 million worth of beverages to make just under $23 million. If a competitor were to lower prices just 10 percent, forcing Le-Nature's to do the same, its net income could easily turn into a net loss. These factors and others help investors and creditors estimate the company's future earnings.

PAUSE FOR FEEDBACK

As noted above, the **income statement** is a statement of operations that reports revenues, expenses, and net income for a stated period of time. To practice your understanding of these concepts, complete the following questions.

SELF-STUDY QUIZ

1. Learning which items belong in each of the income statement categories is an important first step in understanding their meaning. Without referring to Exhibit 1.3, mark each income statement item in the following list as a revenue (R) or an expense (E).

_____ Cost of goods sold	_____ Sales revenue
_____ Income tax	_____ Selling, general, and administrative

2. Assume that during the period 2020, **Le-Nature's** delivered beverages for which customers paid or promised to pay amounts totaling $275.1 million. During the same period, it collected $250.0 million in cash from its customers. Without referring to Exhibit 1.3, indicate which of these two amounts will be shown on Le-Nature's income statement as **sales revenue** for 2020. Why did you select your answer?

Keith Srakocic/AP Images

[4]Net losses are normally noted by parentheses around the income figure.

3. Assume that during the period 2020, Le-Nature's **produced** beverages with a total cost of production of $142.1 million. During the same period, it **delivered** to customers beverages that cost a total of $140.8 million to produce. Without referring to Exhibit 1.3, indicate which of the two numbers will be shown on Le-Nature's income statement as **cost of goods sold expense** for 2020. Why did you select your answer?

After you have completed your answers, check them below.

Related Homework: M1-1, M1-2, E1-6

Statement of Stockholders' Equity

Structure

Le-Nature's prepares a separate statement of stockholders' equity, shown in Exhibit 1.4. The heading identifies the name of the entity, the title of the report, and the unit of measure used in the statement. Like the income statement, the statement of stockholders' equity covers a specified period of time (the accounting period), which in this case is one year. The statement reports the changes in each of the company's stockholders' equity accounts during that period.

Le-Nature's had no changes in common stock during the period. Had it issued or repurchased common stock during the year, the transactions would be reported on separate lines. The retained earnings column reports the way that net income and the distribution of dividends affected the company's financial position during the accounting period. Net income earned during the year increases the balance of retained earnings, showing the relationship of the income statement to the balance sheet.[5] Declaring dividends to the stockholders decreases retained earnings.

The retained earnings equation that describes these relationships is:

Beginning Retained Earnings + Net Income − Dividends = Ending Retained Earnings

EXHIBIT 1.4

Statement of Stockholders' Equity

LE-NATURE'S INC. **Statement of Stockholders' Equity** **For the Year Ended December 31, 2020** **(in millions of dollars)**			**EXPLANATION** *Name of the entity* *Title of the statement* *Accounting period* *Unit of measure*
	Common Stock	**Retained Earnings**	
Balance December 31, 2019	$55.7	$43.1	*Last period's ending balances*
Net income for 2020		22.9	*Net income reported on the income statement*
Dividends for 2020		(2.0)	*Dividends declared during the period*
Balance December 31, 2020	$55.7	$64.0	*Ending balances on the balance sheet*

The notes are an integral part of these financial statements.

Solution to SELF-STUDY QUIZ

1. E, E, R, E (reading down the columns).
2. Sales revenue in the amount of $275.1 million is recognized. Sales revenue is normally reported on the income statement when goods or services have been delivered to customers who have either paid or promised to pay for them in the future.
3. Cost of goods sold expense is $140.8 million. Expenses are the dollar amount of resources used up to earn revenues during the period. Only those beverages that have been delivered to customers have been used up.

[5]Net losses are subtracted.

Elements

The statement starts with the beginning balances in the stockholders' equity accounts, lists the increases and decreases, and reports the resulting ending balances. The retained earnings portion of the statement in Exhibit 1.4 begins with Le-Nature's **beginning-of-the-year retained earnings.** The current year's **net income** reported on the income statement is added and the current year's **dividends** are subtracted from this amount. During 2020, Le-Nature's earned $22.9 million, as shown on the income statement (Exhibit 1.3). This amount was added to the beginning-of-the-year retained earnings. Also, during 2020, Le-Nature's declared and paid a total of $2.0 million in dividends to its stockholders. This amount was subtracted in computing **end-of-the-year retained earnings** on the balance sheet. Note that retained earnings increased by the portion of income reinvested in the business ($22.9 million − $2.0 million = $20.9 million). The ending retained earnings amount of $64.0 million is the same as that reported in Exhibit 1.2 on Le-Nature's balance sheet. Thus, the retained earnings portion of the statement indicates the relationship of the income statement to the balance sheet.

Statement of Stockholders' Equity

Beginning balance
+Increases
−Decreases
Ending balances

FINANCIAL ANALYSIS

Interpreting Retained Earnings

Reinvestment of earnings, or retained earnings, is an important source of financing for **Le-Nature's**, representing more than 12 percent of its financing. Creditors such as **Wells Fargo Bank** closely monitor a firm's statement of stockholders' equity because the firm's policy on dividend payments to the stockholders affects its ability to repay its debts. Every dollar Le-Nature's pays to stockholders as a dividend is not available for use in paying back its debt to Wells Fargo. Investors examine retained earnings to determine whether the company is reinvesting a sufficient portion of earnings to support future growth.

PAUSE FOR FEEDBACK

The **statement of stockholders' equity** explains changes in stockholders' equity accounts, including the change in the retained earnings balance caused by net income and dividends during the reporting period. Check your understanding of these relationships by completing the following question.

SELF-STUDY QUIZ

Assume that a company's financial statements reported the following amounts: beginning retained earnings, $5,510; total assets, $20,450; dividends, $900; cost of goods sold expense, $19,475; and net income, $1,780. Without referring to Exhibit 1.4, compute ending retained earnings.

After you have completed your answer, check it below.

Related Homework: E1-13

Solution to SELF-STUDY QUIZ

Beginning Retained Earnings ($5,510) + Net Income ($1,780) − Dividends ($900) = Ending Retained Earnings ($6,390).

Relationships Among the Income Statement, Statement of Stockholders' Equity, and Balance Sheet

Our discussion of the basic financial statements has focused on what elements are reported in each statement, how the elements are related by the equation for each statement, and how the information is important to the decisions of investors, creditors, and others. We also have discovered how the statements, all of which are outputs from the same system, are related to one another. In particular, we learned:

1. Net income from the income statement results in an increase in ending retained earnings on the statement of stockholders' equity.
2. Ending retained earnings from the statement of stockholders' equity is one of the two components of stockholders' equity on the balance sheet.

Thus, we can think of the income statement as explaining, through the statement of stockholders' equity, how the operations of the company improved or harmed the financial position of the company during the year. These relationships are illustrated in Exhibit 1.5 for **Le-Nature's** financial statements.

EXHIBIT 1.5 Relationships Among LeNature's Statements

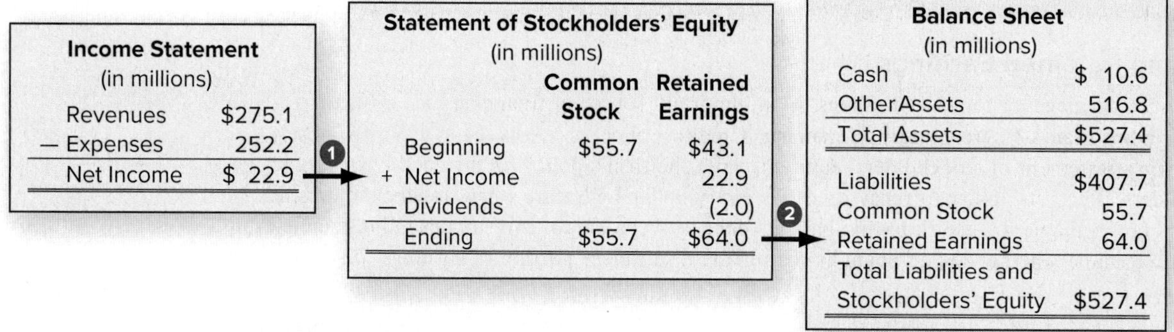

PAUSE FOR FEEDBACK

Thus far, we have covered the content (elements), structure (equation), and relationships among the income statement, statement of stockholders' equity, and balance sheet that is illustrated in Exhibit 1.5. Check your understanding of these key points by completing the following questions.

SELF-STUDY QUIZ

Assume that you are the president of Brightlight Mobile Games Company. At the end of the first year of operations (December 31), the following financial data for the company are available:

Accounts payable owed to suppliers	$ 8,000	Common stock (December 31)	$ 43,600
Cash	26,300	Dividends declared and paid during the current year	11,600
Equipment owned, at cost less used portion	41,900	Expenses (excluding income taxes)	82,000
Receivables from customers (all considered collectible)	11,800	Income tax expense at 20 percent × pretax income; all paid this year	?
Salary payable (on December 31, will be paid on January 10)	12,000	Sales revenue	117,000

(Note: The beginning balances in Common stock and Retained earnings are zero because it is the first year of operations.)

Required:

1. Prepare a summarized income statement for the year.
2. Prepare a statement of stockholders' equity for the year.
3. Prepare a balance sheet at December 31.

GUIDED HELP 1-1

For additional step-by-step video instruction on preparing the balance sheet, income statement, and statement of stockholders' equity, go to mhhe.com/libby_gh1-1.

Related Homework: E1-14, P1-1

Tip This **Guided Help video** reviews the key topics in the chapter covered to this point (balance sheet, income statement, and statement of stockholders' equity). **Watch it before moving on!**

Statement of Cash Flows

Structure

Le-Nature's statement of cash flows is presented in Exhibit 1.6. The **statement of cash flows (cash flow statement)** divides Le-Nature's cash inflows and outflows (receipts and payments) into the three primary categories of cash flows in a typical business: cash flows from operating, investing, and financing activities. The heading identifies the name of the entity, the title of the report, and the unit of measure used in the statement. Like the income statement, the cash flow statement covers a specified period of time (the accounting period), which in this case is one year.

As discussed earlier in this chapter, reported revenues do not always equal cash collected from customers because some sales may be on credit. Also, expenses reported on the income statement may not be equal to the cash paid out during the period because expenses may be incurred in one period and paid for in another. Because the income statement does not provide information concerning cash flows, accountants prepare the statement of cash flows to report inflows and outflows of cash. The cash flow statement equation describes the causes of the change in cash reported on the balance sheet from the end of the last period to the end of the current period:

+/− Cash Flows from Operating Activities
+/− Cash Flows from Investing Activities
+/− Cash Flows from Financing Activities
Change in Cash
+ Beginning Cash Balance
Ending Cash Balance

Statement of Cash Flows

+/−CFO
+/−CFI
+/−CFF
Change in Cash

Note that each of the three cash flow sources can be positive or negative.

Solution to SELF-STUDY QUIZ

1.

BRIGHTLIGHT MOBILE GAMES COMPANY
Income Statement For the Year Ended December 31, Current Year

Sales revenue	$117,000
Expenses	82,000
Pretax income	35,000
Income tax expense	7,000
Net income	$ 28,000

2.

BRIGHTLIGHT MOBILE GAMES COMPANY
Statement of Stockholders' Equity
For the Year Ended December 31, Current Year

	Common Stock	Retained Earnings
Balance January 1, Current year	-	-
Stock issuance	$43,600	
Net income		$28,000
Dividends		(11,600)
Balance December 31, Current Year	$43,600	$16,400

3.

BRIGHTLIGHT MOBILE GAMES COMPANY
Balance Sheet
December 31, Current Year

Assets	
Cash	$26,300
Receivables from customers	11,800
Equipment	41,900
Total assets	$80,000
Liabilities	
Accounts payable	$ 8,000
Salary payable	12,000
Total liabilities	20,000
Stockholders' equity	
Common stock	43,600
Retained earnings	16,400
Total stockholders' equity	60,000
Total liabilities and stockholders' equity	$80,000

EXHIBIT 1.6

Statement of Cash Flows

LE-NATURE'S INC. **Statement of Cash Flows (Summary)** **For the Year Ended December 31, 2020** **(in millions of dollars)**		EXPLANATION *Name of the entity* *Title of the statement* *Accounting period* *Unit of measure*
Cash flows from operating activities	$ 87.5	*Cash flows directly related to earning income*
Cash flows from investing activities	(125.5)	*Cash flows from purchase/sale of plant, equipment, & investments*
Cash flows from financing activities	47.0	*Cash flows from investors and creditors*
Net increase (decrease) in cash	9.0	***Change in cash during the period***
Cash balance December 31, 2019	1.6	*Last period's cash on the balance sheet*
Cash balance December 31, 2020	$ 10.6	***Ending cash on the balance sheet***

The notes are an integral part of these financial statements.

Elements

Cash flows from operating activities are cash flows that are directly related to earning income. For example, when customers pay Le-Nature's for the beverages it has delivered to them, it lists the amounts collected as cash collected from customers. When Le-Nature's pays salaries to its production employees or pays bills received from its tea suppliers, it includes the amounts in cash paid to suppliers and employees.

Cash flows from investing activities include cash flows related to the acquisition or sale of the company's plant and equipment and investments. This year, Le-Nature's had only one cash outflow from investing activities, the purchase of additional manufacturing equipment to meet growing demand for its products.

Cash flows from financing activities are cash flows directly related to the financing of the enterprise itself. They involve the receipt or payment of money to investors and creditors (except for suppliers). This year, Le-Nature's borrowed additional money from the bank to purchase most of the new manufacturing equipment. It also paid out dividends to the stockholders.[6]

The positive and negative subtotals for cash flows from operating, investing, and financing activities are added to determine the change in cash during the period. Then, the change in cash during the period is added to the beginning cash balance, resulting in the ending cash balance. This balance should be the same as the amount reported on the balance sheet at the end of the period. Thus, the cash flow statement explains how the operating, investing, and financing activities of the company affected the cash balance on the balance sheet during the year.

FINANCIAL ANALYSIS

Interpreting the Cash Flow Statement

Bankers often consider the Operating Activities section to be most important because it indicates the company's ability to generate cash from sales to meet its current cash needs. Any amount left over can be used to pay back the bank debt or expand the company. Stockholders will invest in a company only if they believe that it will eventually generate more cash from operations than it uses so that cash will become available to pay dividends and expand.

PAUSE FOR FEEDBACK

The **statement of cash flows** reports inflows and outflows of cash for a stated period of time classified into three categories: operating, investing, and financing activities. Answer the following questions to test your understanding of the concepts involved.

[6]The complete statement of cash flows is discussed in Chapter 12.

SELF-STUDY QUIZ

1. Assume that during the period 2020, **Le-Nature's** delivered beverages to customers who paid or promised to pay a total of $275.1 million. During the same period, it collected $250.0 million in cash from customers. Which of the two amounts will be shown on Le-Nature's cash flow statement for 2020?
2. Your task here is to verify that Le-Nature's cash balance increased by $9.0 million during the year using the totals for cash flows from operating, investing, and financing activities presented in Exhibit 1.5. Recall the cash flow statement equation:

+/− Cash Flows from Operating Activities (CFO)
+/− Cash Flows from Investing Activities (CFI)
+/− Cash Flows from Financing Activities (CFF)
Change in Cash

After you have completed your answers, check them below.

Related Homework: E1-15

Notes and Financial Statement Formats

At the bottom of each of **Le-Nature's** four basic financial statements is this statement: **"The notes are an integral part of these financial statements."** This is the accounting equivalent of the Surgeon General's warning on a package of cigarettes. It warns users that failure to read the notes (footnotes) to the financial statements will result in an incomplete picture of the company's financial health. Throughout this book, we will discuss many note disclosures because understanding their content is critical to understanding the company.

A few additional formatting conventions are worth noting here. Assets are listed on the balance sheet by ease of conversion to cash. Liabilities are listed by their maturity (due date). Most financial statements include the monetary unit sign (in the United States, the $) beside the first dollar amount in a group of items (e.g., the cash amount in the assets). Also, it is common to place a single underline below the last item in a group before a total or subtotal (e.g., property, plant, and equipment). For group totals (e.g., total assets), a dollar sign is placed beside each amount and a double underline is set below. The same conventions are followed in all four basic financial statements.

Summary of the Four Basic Financial Statements

We have learned a great deal about the content of the four basic financial statements. Exhibit 1.7 summarizes this information. Take a few minutes to review the information in the exhibit before you move on to the next section of the chapter.

LEARNING OBJECTIVE 1-2

Identify the role of generally accepted accounting principles (GAAP) in determining financial statement content and managers', directors', and auditors' responsibilities for ensuring the accuracy of the financial statements.

RESPONSIBILITIES FOR THE ACCOUNTING COMMUNICATION PROCESS

For decision makers to use the information in **Le-Nature's** financial statements effectively, they have to know (1) the information conveyed by the statements and the measurement rules applied in computing the numbers on the statements and (2) that the numbers on the statements are correct. The rules that determine the content and measurement rules of the statements are called generally accepted accounting principles, or GAAP.

Solutions to SELF-STUDY QUIZ

1. The firm recognizes $250.0 million on the cash flow statement because this number represents the actual cash collected from customers related to current and prior years' sales.
2.

	In millions
+/− Cash Flows from Operating Activities (CFO)	$ 87.5
+/− Cash Flows from Investing Activities (CFI)	(125.5)
+/− Cash Flows from Financing Activities (CFF)	47.0
Change in Cash	$ 9.0

EXHIBIT 1.7

Summary of the Four Basic Financial Statements

Financial Statement	Purpose	Structure	Examples of Content
Balance Sheet (Statement of Financial Position)	Reports the financial position (economic resources and sources of financing) of an accounting entity *at a point in time.*	**Balance Sheet** Assets = Liabilities + Stockholders' Equity	Cash, accounts receivable, plant and equipment, long-term debt, common stock
Income Statement (Statement of Income, Statement of Earnings, Statement of Operations)	Reports the accountant's primary measure of economic performance *during the accounting period.*	**Income Statement** Revenues +Increases −Expenses Net Income	Sales revenue, cost of goods sold, selling expense, interest expense
Statement of Stockholders' Equity	Reports changes in the company's common stock and retained earnings *during the accounting period.*	**Statement of Stockholders' Equity** Beginning balance +Increases −Decreases Ending balances	Beginning and ending stockholders' equity balances, stock issuances, net income, dividends
Statement of Cash Flows (Cash Flow Statement)	Reports inflows (receipts) and outflows (payments) of cash *during the accounting period* in the categories operating, investing, and financing.	**Statement of Cash Flows** +/−CFO +/−CFI +/−CFF Change in Cash	Cash collected from customers, cash paid to suppliers, cash paid to purchase equipment, cash borrowed from banks

Generally Accepted Accounting Principles

How Are Generally Accepted Accounting Principles Determined?

In the United States, Congress created the **Securities and Exchange Commission (SEC)** and gave it broad powers to determine the measurement rules for financial statements that companies issuing stock to the public (publicly traded companies) must provide to stockholders.[7] The SEC has worked with organizations of professional accountants and other interested parties to establish groups that are given the primary responsibilities to work out the detailed rules that become generally accepted accounting principles. Today, the **Financial Accounting Standards Board** (FASB) has this responsibility. The official pronouncements of the FASB are called the FASB **Accounting Standards Codification.**

What Concepts Guide the Setting of Accounting Standards?

The FASB relies on a **conceptual framework** outlined in Exhibit 1.8 to provide a structure for developing specific accounting standards. It states that the **primary objective of financial reporting to external users** is to provide financial information about the reporting entity that

[7]Contrary to popular belief, these rules are different from those that companies follow when filing their income tax returns. We discuss these differences further in later chapters.

Objective of Financial Reporting	Fundamental Characteristics of Useful Information	
To provide financial information that is useful to existing and potential investors, lenders, and other creditors	Relevant to users' decisions	Faithful representation of company activities
	Timely, Verifiable, Comparable, Understandable	
	Enhancing Characteristics of Useful Information	

EXHIBIT 1.8

Conceptual Framework for Financial Reporting

is useful to existing and potential investors, lenders, and other creditors in making decisions about providing resources to the company. Most users are interested in information to help them assess the amounts, timing, and uncertainty of a business's future cash inflows and outflows. To be useful, the information must be **relevant** to the decisions of these external users and be a **faithful representation** of the economic substance of the company's activities. Information is relevant if it helps evaluate the company's past behavior and predict its future activities. Faithful representation requires that the information be complete and free from bias and other forms of error.

Comparability, verifiability, timeliness, and understandability are qualitative characteristics that enhance the usefulness of information that is relevant and faithfully represented. For example, our discussions of financial analysis will emphasize the importance of comparing information for the same company over time, as well as against those of competitors. Such comparisons are valid only if the information is prepared on a consistent and comparable basis. These characteristics of useful information guide the FASB in deciding what financial information should be reported.

Why Is GAAP Important to Managers and External Users?

Generally accepted accounting principles (GAAP) are of great interest to the companies that must prepare financial statements, their auditors, and the readers of the statements. Companies incur the cost of preparing the statements and bear the major economic consequences of their publication, which include, among others:

1. Effects on the selling price of a company's stock.
2. Effects on the amount of bonuses received by management and employees.
3. Loss of competitive information to other companies.

As a consequence of these and other concerns, changes in GAAP are actively debated, political lobbying often takes place, and final rules are a compromise among the wishes of interested parties. Most managers do not need to learn all the details included in these standards. Our approach is to focus on those details that have the greatest impact on the numbers presented in financial statements and are appropriate for an introductory course.

INTERNATIONAL PERSPECTIVE

The International Accounting Standards Board and Global Accounting Standards

Financial accounting standards and disclosure requirements are adopted by national regulatory agencies. Since 2002, 144 jurisdictions have adopted **International Financial Reporting Standards (IFRS)** issued by the **International Accounting Standards Board (IASB).** Examples of jurisdictions requiring the use of IFRS currently include:

- **European Union (Germany, France, the Netherlands, Belgium, Bulgaria, Poland, etc.) and United Kingdom**
- **Australia and New Zealand**
- **Hong Kong (S.A.R. of China), Malaysia, and Republic of Korea**

- **Israel and Turkey**
- **Brazil and Chile**
- **Canada and Mexico**

In the United States, the Securities and Exchange Commission now allows foreign companies whose stock is traded in the United States to use IFRS. To prepare you to deal with statements prepared under U.S. GAAP and IFRS, we will point out key differences between IFRS and U.S. GAAP. The basic principles and practices we discuss in Chapters 1 through 4 apply equally to both sets of standards.

Source: IFRS Foundation, 2020

Ensuring the Accuracy of Financial Statements

What if the Numbers Are Wrong?

Shortly after the issuance of the statements presented in this chapter in 2005 (yes, it happened in 2005, not 2020), **Le-Nature's** worked with the Wachovia Capital Markets group from **Wells Fargo Bank** to borrow an additional $285 million from various lenders. Why would lenders agree to risk such a large amount? Le-Nature's financial statements presented a picture of a growth company with amazing future prospects. Reported revenues grew from $40 to $275 million (or nearly 600 percent) in just six years! Reported net income rose by 2,400 percent in the same period! Clearly, Le-Nature's looked like a good bet. But if the numbers are wrong, all bets are off.

The truth about Le-Nature's was revealed when several non-family-member stockholders suspected that all was not right and filed a lawsuit. Court records reveal an amazing story. Reported annual sales of $275 million were really about $32 million. Gregory Podlucky and his co-conspirators forged checks, invoices, and revenue and expense records to massively overstate revenues and profits. The $10.6 million its balance sheet claimed for cash turned out to be $1.8 million. The balance sheet also understated liabilities by $200 million. The company was never a real success–**it was all fake.**

Podlucky was borrowing more and more money and using it to pay off his earlier creditors (this is called a **Ponzi scheme**). At the same time, he was stealing cash to support a lavish lifestyle. A sample of the resulting newspaper headlines follows:

Market Predicts Le-Nature's Is All Washed Up

Le-Nature's Fraud: 2 More Sentenced in $800M Fraud

Ex-Pa. soft-drink CEO gets 20 years in prison

Accountant Guilty of Helping CEO Commit Fraud

While this crime may read like a fantastic novel, the consequences for many were severe. This was the largest fraud ever heard in the Federal District Court of Western Pennsylvania. The final prison tally is listed below.

The Prison Tally

Defendant	Sentence
Gregory Podlucky, CEO	20 years in federal prison
Robert Lynn, President	15 years in federal prison
Andrew Murin, Consultant	10 years in federal prison
Jonathan Podlucky, COO	5 years in federal prison
Karla Podlucky (CEO's wife)	4¼ years in federal prison
G. Jesse Podlucky (CEO's son)	9 years in federal prison
Donald Pollinger, Businessman	5 years in federal prison
Tammy Jo Andreycak, Bookkeeper	5 years in federal prison

Crime clearly did not pay for Podlucky and his co-conspirators. The auditors who missed the fraud agreed to pay $50 million to the creditors, and Wachovia Capital Markets, which marketed the loans, agreed to pay $80 million.

Ethical Conduct

Ethics are standards of conduct for judging right from wrong, honest from dishonest, and fair from unfair. Intentional misreporting of financial statements in the Le-Nature's case was clearly unethical and illegal. However, many situations are less clear-cut and require that individuals weigh one moral principle (e.g., honesty) against another (e.g., loyalty to a friend). When money is involved, people can easily fool themselves into believing that bad acts are justified. To avoid falling prey to this tendency, when faced with an ethical dilemma, it is often recommended that you follow a three-step process:

1. Identify the benefits of a decision (often to the manager or employee involved) and who will be harmed (other employees, owners, creditors, the environment).
2. Identify alternative courses of action.
3. Choose the one you would like your family and friends to see reported on your local news. That is usually the ethical choice.

In the Le-Nature's case, Podlucky and his co-conspirators clearly did not follow this process. Little besides the jewelry and the Latrobe plant were left to satisfy Le-Nature's over $800 million in debts. The nonfamily stockholders lost all of their money. Over 240 plant workers lost their jobs. And the town of Latrobe, Pennsylvania, suffered a severe economic blow.

Responsibility and the Need for Internal Controls

As a manager in a business, you are responsible for setting up systems to prevent and detect unethical behavior. Primary responsibility for the information in the financial statements lies with management, represented by the highest officer of the company and the highest financial officer. Companies should take three important steps to assure investors that the company's records are accurate:

1. They should maintain a system of **internal controls** over both the records and the assets of the company.
2. They should hire outside independent auditors to **audit** the fairness of the financial statements.
3. They should form a committee of the board of directors to oversee the integrity of these other safeguards.

Internal Control Alert

Three steps to ensure the accuracy of records and safeguarding of assets:

System of Internal Controls | External Auditors | Board of Directors

PhotoDisc/Getty Images; LifetimeStock/Shutterstock.com; anekoho/Shutterstock; Purestock/Getty Images

The term internal controls refers to the process by which a company safeguards its assets and provides reasonable assurance regarding the reliability of the company's financial reporting, the effectiveness and efficiency of its operations, and its compliance with applicable laws and regulations. Internal control procedures should extend to all assets: cash, receivables, investments, plant and equipment, and so on. Controls that ensure the accuracy of the financial records are designed to prevent inadvertent errors and outright fraud. External independent auditors audit the financial reports to ensure that they represent what they claim and conform with generally accepted accounting principles. Because strong internal controls increase the reliability of the financial statements, internal control procedures are also reviewed by the outside independent auditor.

These safeguards failed in Le-Nature's case. The company had no controls, the independent auditors were duped by management, and the board included only Podlucky's cronies. Although financial statement fraud is a fairly rare event, the misrepresentations in Le-Nature's statements aptly illustrate the importance of fairly presented financial statements to investors and creditors.

DEMONSTRATION CASE

At the end of each chapter, one or more demonstration cases are presented. These cases provide an overview of the primary issues discussed in the chapter. Each demonstration case is followed by a recommended solution. **You should read the case carefully and then prepare your own solution before you study the recommended solution.** This self-evaluation is highly recommended. The introductory case presented here reviews the elements reported on the income statement, statement of stockholders' equity, and balance sheet and how the elements within the statements are related.

Best Buy Co., Inc., sells a wide range of consumer electronics and home appliances from its over 1,000 stores and online. Following is a list of the financial statement items and amounts adapted from a recent Best Buy income statement and balance sheet. The numbers are presented in millions of dollars for the year ended February 1, 2020. Assume that the company did not issue or retire stock during the year. Retained earnings at the beginning of the year was $2,448 and dividends were $536.

Accounts payable	$ 8,060	Long-term debt	$ 4,052
Accounts receivable	1,149	Net income	1,541
Cash	2,229	Sales revenue	43,638
Common stock	26	Net property and equipment	6,734
Cost of sales	33,590	Retained earnings	3,453
Income before income taxes	1,993	Selling, general, and administrative expenses	7,991
Income tax expense	452	Total assets	15,591
Interest expense	64	Total liabilities	12,112
Merchandise inventories	5,479	Total liabilities and shareholders' equity	15,591
		Total shareholders' equity	3,479

Required:

1. Prepare a balance sheet, an income statement, and a statement of stockholders' equity for the year following the formats in Exhibits 1.2, 1.3, and 1.4, respectively.
2. Specify what information these three statements provide.
3. Indicate the other statement that would be included in Best Buy annual report.
4. Securities regulations require that Best Buy statements be subject to an independent audit. Suggest why Best Buy might voluntarily subject its statements to an independent audit if there were no such requirement.

Tip For more help on preparing the balance sheet, income, statement, and statement of stockholders'equity, watch the Guided Help video that can be found at mhhe.com/libby11e_gh1

SUGGESTED SOLUTION

1.

BEST BUY CO., INC
Balance Sheet
At February 1, 2020
(in millions of dollars)

Assets	
Cash	$ 2,229
Accounts receivable	1,149
Merchandise inventories	5,479
Net property and equipment	6,734
Total assets	$15,591
Liabilities and shareholders' equity	
Liabilities:	
Accounts payable	$ 8,060
Long-term debt	4,052
Total liabilities	12,112
Shareholders' equity:	
Common stock	26
Retained earnings	3,453
Total shareholders' equity	3,479
Total liabilities and shareholders' equity	$15,591

BEST BUY CO., INC
Income Statement
For the Year Ended February 1, 2020
(in millions of dollars)

Revenues	
Sales revenue	$43,638
Expenses	
Cost of sales	33,590
Selling, general, and administrative expenses	7,991
Interest expense	64
Income before income taxes	1,993
Income tax expense	452
Net income	$ 1,541

BEST BUY CO., INC
Statement of Stockholders' Equity
For the Year Ended February 1, 2020
(in millions of dollars)

	Common Stock	Retained Earnings
Balance February 2, 2019	$26	$2,448
+ Net income	–	1,541
– Dividends	–	(536)
Balance February 1, 2020	$26	$3,453

2. The balance sheet reports the amount of assets, liabilities, and stockholders' equity of an accounting entity at a point in time. The income statement reports the accountant's primary measure of performance of a business, revenues less expenses, during the accounting period. The statement of stockholders' equity reports on changes in the stockholders' equity accounts during the accounting period.

3. Best Buy also would present a statement of cash flows.

4. Users will have greater confidence in the accuracy of financial statement information if they know that the people who audited the statements were required to meet professional standards of ethics and competence.

Chapter Supplement A

Types of Business Entities

This textbook emphasizes **accounting for profit-making business entities.** The three main types of business entities are sole proprietorship, partnership, and corporation. A **sole proprietorship** is an unincorporated business owned by one person; it usually is small in size and is common in the service, retailing, and farming industries. Often the owner is the manager. Legally, the business and the owner are not separate entities. Accounting views the business as a separate entity, however, that must be accounted for separately from its owner.

A **partnership** is an unincorporated business owned by two or more persons known as **partners.** The agreements between the owners are specified in a partnership contract. This contract deals with matters such as division of income each reporting period and distribution of resources of the business on termination of its operations. A partnership is not legally separate from its owners. Legally, each partner in a general partnership is responsible for the debts of the business (each general partner has **unlimited liability**). The partnership, however, is a separate business entity to be accounted for separately from its several owners.

A **corporation** is a business incorporated under the laws of a particular state. The owners are called **stockholders** or **shareholders.** Ownership is represented by shares of capital stock that usually can be bought and sold freely. When the organizers file an approved application for incorporation, the state issues a charter. This charter gives the corporation the right to operate as a separate legal entity, separate and apart from its owners. The stockholders enjoy **limited liability.** Stockholders are liable for the corporation's debts only to the extent of their investments. The corporate charter specifies the types and amounts of stock that can be issued. Most states require a minimum of two or three stockholders and a minimum amount of resources to be contributed at the time of organization. The stockholders elect a governing board of directors, which in turn employs managers and exercises general supervision of the corporation. Accounting also views the corporation as a separate business entity that must be accounted for separately from its owners. Limited liability companies **(LLCs)** and limited liability partnerships **(LLPs)** have many characteristics similar to corporations.

In terms of economic importance, the corporation is the dominant form of business organization in the United States. This dominance is caused by the many advantages of the corporate form: (1) limited liability for the stockholders, (2) continuity of life, (3) ease in transferring ownership (stock), and (4) opportunities to raise large amounts of money by selling shares to a large number of people. The primary disadvantage of a corporation is that its income may be subject to double taxation (income is taxed when it is earned and again when it is distributed to stockholders as dividends). In this textbook, we emphasize the corporate form of business. Nevertheless, the accounting concepts and procedures that we discuss also apply to other types of businesses.

Chapter Supplement B

Employment in the Accounting Profession Today

Since 1900, accounting has attained the stature of professions such as law, medicine, engineering, and architecture. As with all recognized professions, accounting is subject to professional competence requirements, is dedicated to service to the public, requires a high level of academic study, and rests on a common body of knowledge. An accountant may be licensed as a certified public accountant, or CPA. This designation is granted only on completion of requirements specified by the state that issues the license. Although CPA requirements vary among states, they include a college degree with a specified number of accounting courses and a total of 150 credit hours, good character, professional experience, and successful completion of a professional examination. The CPA examination is prepared by the American Institute of Certified Public Accountants.

Accountants (including CPAs) commonly are engaged in professional practice or are employed by businesses, government entities, nonprofit organizations, and so on. Accountants employed in these activities may take and pass a professional examination to become a certified management accountant, or CMA (the CMA examination is administered by the Institute of Management Accountants), or a certified internal auditor, or CIA (the CIA examination is administered by the Institute of Internal Auditors). Specialists in areas such as fraud examination may also apply for certification in those specialty areas (e.g., CFE).

Practice of Public Accounting

Although an individual may practice public accounting, usually two or more individuals organize an accounting firm in the form of a partnership (in many cases, a limited liability partnership, or LLP). Accounting firms vary in size from a one-person office, to regional firms, to the Big Four firms (**Deloitte**, **Ernst & Young (EY)**, **KPMG**, and **Pricewaterhouse Coopers (PwC)**), which have hundreds of offices located worldwide. Accounting firms usually render three types of services: audit or assurance services, management consulting or advisory services, and tax services.

Audit or Assurance Services

Audit or assurance services are independent professional services that improve the quality of information for decision makers. The most important assurance service performed by the CPA in public practice is financial statement auditing. The purpose of an audit is to lend credibility to the financial reports, that is, to ensure that they fairly represent what they claim. An audit involves an examination of the financial reports (prepared by the management of the entity) to ensure that they conform with GAAP. Other areas of assurance services include electronic commerce integrity and security and information systems reliability.

Management Consulting or Advisory Services

Many independent CPA firms offer management consulting services. These services usually are accounting based and encompass such activities as the design and installation of accounting and profit-planning and control (budget) systems; financial advice; forecasting; inventory controls; cost-effectiveness studies;

and operational analysis. To maintain their independence, CPAs are prohibited from performing certain consulting services for the public companies that they audit.

Tax Services

CPAs in public practice usually provide income tax services to their clients. These services include both tax planning as a part of the decision-making process and the determination of the income tax liability (reported on the annual income tax return). Because of the increasing complexity of state and federal tax laws, a high level of competence is required, which CPAs specializing in taxation can provide. The CPA's involvement in tax planning often is quite significant. Most major business decisions have significant tax impacts; in fact, tax-planning considerations often govern certain business decisions.

Employment by Organizations

Many accountants, including CPAs, CMAs, and CIAs, are employed by profit-making and nonprofit organizations. An organization, depending on its size and complexity, may employ from a few to hundreds of accountants. In a business enterprise, the chief financial officer is a key member of the management team. This responsibility usually entails a wide range of management, financial, and accounting duties.

In a business entity, accountants typically are engaged in a wide variety of activities, such as general management, general accounting, cost accounting, profit planning and control (budgeting), internal auditing, and information systems management. A primary function of the accountants in organizations is to provide data that are useful for internal managerial decision making and for controlling operations. The functions of external reporting, tax planning, control of assets, and a host of related responsibilities normally also are performed by accountants in industry.

Employment in the Public and Not-for-Profit Sector

The vast and complex operations of governmental units, from the local to the international level, create a need for accountants. The same holds true for other not-for-profit organizations such as hospitals and universities. Accountants employed in the public and not-for-profit sectors perform functions similar to those performed by their counterparts in private organizations. The Government Accountability Office (GAO) and the regulatory agencies, such as the SEC and Federal Communications Commission (FCC), also use the services of accountants in carrying out their regulatory duties.

CHAPTER TAKE-AWAYS

1-1. Recognize the information conveyed in each of the four basic financial statements and the way that it is used by different decision makers (investors, creditors, and managers). **p. 6**

The **balance sheet** is a statement of financial position that reports dollar amounts for the assets, liabilities, and stockholders' equity at a specific point in time.

The **income statement** is a statement of operations that reports revenues, expenses, and net income for a stated period of time.

The **statement of stockholders' equity** explains changes in stockholders' equity accounts (common stock and retained earnings) that occurred during a stated period of time.

The **statement of cash flows** reports inflows and outflows of cash for a stated period of time.

The statements are used by investors and creditors to evaluate different aspects of the firm's financial position and performance.

1-2. Identify the role of generally accepted accounting principles (GAAP) in determining financial statement content and managers', directors', and auditors' responsibilities for ensuring accuracy of the financial statements. **p. 17**

GAAP refers to the measurement rules used to develop the information in financial statements. Knowledge of GAAP is necessary for accurate interpretation of the numbers in financial statements.

Management has primary responsibility for the accuracy of a company's financial information. Auditors are responsible for expressing an opinion on the fairness of the financial statement presentations based on their examination of the reports and records of the company.

Users will have confidence in the accuracy of financial statement numbers only if the people associated with their preparation and audit have reputations for ethical behavior and competence. Management and auditors also can be held legally liable for fraudulent financial statements.

In this chapter, we studied the basic financial statements that communicate financial information to external users. Chapters 2, 3, and 4 provide a more detailed look at financial statements and examine how to translate data about business transactions into these statements. Learning how to translate back and forth between business transactions and financial statements is the key to using financial statements in planning and decision making. Chapter 2 begins our discussion of the way that the accounting function collects data about business transactions and processes the data to provide periodic financial statements, with emphasis on the balance sheet. To accomplish this purpose, Chapter 2 discusses key accounting concepts, the accounting model, transaction analysis, and analytical tools. We examine the typical business activities of an actual service-oriented company to demonstrate the concepts in Chapters 2, 3, and 4.

FINDING FINANCIAL INFORMATION

Balance Sheet

Assets = Liabilities + Stockholders' Equity

Income Statement

Revenues
− Expenses
Net Income

Statement of Stockholders' Equity

Beginning balance
+ Increases
− Decreases
Ending balance

Statement of Cash Flows

+/− Cash Flows from Operating Activities
+/− Cash Flows from Investing Activities
+/− Cash Flows from Financing Activities
Net Change in Cash

KEY TERMS

Accounting A system that collects and processes (analyzes, measures, and records) financial information about an organization and reports that information to decision makers. **p. 4**

Accounting Entity The organization for which financial data are to be collected. **p. 7**

Accounting Period The time period covered by the financial statements. **p. 10**

Audit An examination of the financial reports to ensure that they represent what they claim and conform with generally accepted accounting principles. **p. 21**

Balance Sheet (Statement of Financial Position) Reports the amount of assets, liabilities, and stockholders' equity of an accounting entity at a point in time. **p. 6**

Basic Accounting Equation (Balance Sheet Equation) Assets = Liabilities + Stockholders' Equity. **p. 8**

Faithful Representation Requires that the information be complete, neutral, and free from error. **p. 19**

Generally Accepted Accounting Principles (GAAP) The measurement and disclosure rules used to develop the information in financial statements. **p. 17**

Income Statement (Statement of Income, Statement of Earnings, Statement of Operations) Reports the revenues less the expenses of the accounting period. **p. 10**

Internal Controls Processes by which a company provides reasonable assurance regarding the reliability of the company's financial reporting, the effectiveness and efficiency of its operations, and its compliance with applicable laws and regulations. **p. 21**

Notes (Footnotes) Provide supplemental information about the financial condition of a company, without which the financial statements cannot be fully understood. **p. 17**

Primary Objective of Financial Reporting to External Users To provide financial information about the reporting entity that is useful to existing and potential investors, lenders, and other creditors in making decisions about providing resources to the entity. **p. 18**

Relevant Information Information that can influence a decision; it has predictive and/or feedback value. **p. 19**

Statement of Cash Flows (Cash Flow Statement) Reports inflows and outflows of cash during the accounting period in the categories of operating, investing, and financing. **p. 15**

Statement of Stockholders' Equity The statement reports the changes in each of the company's stockholders' equity accounts during the period. **p. 12**

QUESTIONS

1. Define **accounting.**
2. Briefly distinguish financial accounting from managerial accounting.
3. The accounting process generates financial reports for both internal and external users. Identify some of the groups of users.
4. Briefly distinguish investors from creditors.
5. What is an accounting entity? Why is a business treated as a separate entity for accounting purposes?
6. Complete the following:

Name of Statement	Alternative Title
a. Income statement	*a.* ____________
b. Balance sheet	*b.* ____________
c. Cash Flow Statement	*c.* ____________

7. What information should be included in the heading of each of the four primary financial statements?
8. What are the purposes of (*a*) the income statement, (*b*) the balance sheet, (*c*) the statement of cash flows, and (*d*) the statement of stockholders' equity?
9. Explain why, for companies whose fiscal years end on December 31, the income statement and the statement of cash flows are dated "For the Year Ended December 31," whereas the balance sheet is dated "At December 31."
10. Briefly explain the importance of assets and liabilities to the decisions of investors and creditors.
11. Briefly define **net income** and **net loss**.
12. Explain the equation for the income statement. What are the three major items reported on the income statement?
13. Explain the equation for the balance sheet. Define the three major components reported on the balance sheet.
14. Explain the equation for the statement of cash flows. Explain the three major components reported on the statement of cash flows.
15. Explain the equation for retained earnings. Explain the four major items reported on the statement of stockholders' equity related to retained earnings.
16. The financial statements discussed in this chapter are aimed at **external** users. Briefly explain how a company's **internal** managers in different functional areas (e.g., marketing, purchasing, human resources) might use financial statement information from their own and other companies.
17. Briefly describe the way that accounting measurement rules (generally accepted accounting principles) are determined in the United States.
18. Briefly explain the responsibility of company management and the independent auditors in the accounting communication process.
19. (Supplement A) Briefly differentiate between a sole proprietorship, a partnership, and a corporation.
20. (Supplement B) List and briefly explain the three primary services that CPAs in public practice provide.

MULTIPLE-CHOICE QUESTIONS

1. Which of the following is **not** one of the four basic financial statements?
   a. Balance sheet.
   b. Audit report.
   c. Income statement.
   d. Statement of cash flows.
2. As stated in the audit report, or **Report of Independent Accountants**, the primary responsibility for a company's financial statements lies with
   a. The owners of the company.
   b. Independent financial analysts.
   c. The auditors.
   d. The company's management.
3. Which of the following is true?
   a. FASB creates SEC.
   b. GAAP creates FASB.
   c. SEC creates AICPA.
   d. FASB creates U.S. GAAP.
4. Which of the following regarding retained earnings is false?
   a. Retained earnings is increased by net income and decreased by a net loss.
   b. Retained earnings is a component of stockholders' equity on the balance sheet.

c. Retained earnings is an asset on the balance sheet.
d. Retained earnings represents earnings not distributed to stockholders in the form of dividends.

5. Which of the following is **not** one of the four items required to be shown in the heading of a financial statement?
   a. The financial statement preparer's name.
   b. The title of the financial statement.
   c. The unit of measure in the financial statement.
   d. The name of the business entity.
6. Which of the following statements regarding the statement of cash flows is true?
   a. The statement of cash flows separates cash inflows and outflows into three major categories: operating, investing, and financing.
   b. The ending cash balance shown on the statement of cash flows must agree with the amount shown on the balance sheet for the same fiscal period.
   c. The total increase or decrease in cash shown on the statement of cash flows must agree with the "bottom line" (net income or net loss) reported on the income statement.
   d. Both (a) and (b) are true.
   e. All of the above are true.
7. Which of the following is **not** a typical note included in an annual report?
   a. A note describing the auditor's opinion of the management's past and future financial planning for the business.
   b. A note providing more detail about a specific item shown in the financial statements.
   c. A note describing the accounting rules applied in the financial statements.
   d. A note describing financial disclosures about items not appearing in the financial statements.
8. Which of the following is true regarding the income statement?
   a. The income statement is sometimes called the statement of operations.
   b. The income statement reports revenues, expenses, and liabilities.
   c. The income statement reports only revenue for which cash was received at the point of sale.
   d. The income statement reports the financial position of a business at a particular point in time.
9. Which of the following is false regarding the balance sheet?
   a. The accounts shown on a balance sheet represent the basic accounting equation for a particular business entity.
   b. The retained earnings balance shown on the balance sheet must agree with the ending retained earnings balance shown on the statement of stockholders' equity.
   c. The balance sheet reports the changes in specific account balances over a period of time.
   d. The balance sheet reports the amount of assets, liabilities, and stockholders' equity of an accounting entity at a point in time.
10. Which of the following regarding GAAP is true?
    a. U.S. GAAP is the body of accounting knowledge followed by all countries in the world.
    b. Changes in GAAP can affect the interests of managers and stockholders.
    c. GAAP is the abbreviation for generally accepted auditing procedures.
    d. Changes to GAAP must be approved by the Senate Finance Committee.

MINI-EXERCISES

M1-1 Matching Elements with Financial Statements

LO1-1

Match each element with its financial statement by entering the appropriate letter in the space provided.

Element	Financial Statement
___ (1) Expenses	A. Balance sheet
___ (2) Cash flow from investing activities	B. Income statement
___ (3) Assets	C. Statement of stockholders' equity
___ (4) Dividends	D. Statement of cash flows
___ (5) Revenues	
___ (6) Cash flow from operating activities	
___ (7) Liabilities	
___ (8) Cash flow from financing activities	

Matching Financial Statement Items to Financial Statement Categories

M1-2
LO1-1

Mark each item in the following list as an asset (A), liability (L), or stockholders' equity (SE) item that would appear on the balance sheet or a revenue (R) or expense (E) item that would appear on the income statement.

___ (1) Retained earnings
___ (2) Accounts receivable
___ (3) Sales revenue
___ (4) Property, plant, and equipment
___ (5) Cost of goods sold
___ (6) Inventories
___ (7) Interest expense
___ (8) Accounts payable
___ (9) Land

Identifying Important Accounting Abbreviations

M1-3
LO1-2

The following is a list of important abbreviations used in the chapter. These abbreviations also are used widely in business. For each abbreviation, give the full designation. The first one is an example.

Abbreviation	Full Designation
(1) CPA	Certified Public Accountant
(2) GAAP	___
(3) SEC	___
(4) FASB	___

connect

EXERCISES

Matching Definitions with Terms or Abbreviations

E1-1
LO1-1, 1-2

Match each definition with its related term or abbreviation by entering the appropriate letter in the space provided.

Term or Abbreviation	Definition
___ (1) SEC	A. A system that collects and processes financial information about an organization and reports that information to decision makers.
___ (2) Audit	B. Information that helps evaluate the company's past behavior and predict its future.
___ (3) Sole proprietorship	C. An unincorporated business owned by two or more persons.
___ (4) Corporation	D. The organization for which financial data are to be collected (separate and distinct from its owners).
___ (5) Accounting	E. An incorporated entity that issues shares of stock as evidence of ownership.
___ (6) Accounting entity	F. An examination of the financial reports to ensure that they represent what they claim and conform with generally accepted accounting principles.
___ (7) Audit report	G. Certified public accountant.
___ (8) Publicly traded	H. An unincorporated business owned by one person.
___ (9) Partnership	I. A report that describes the auditor's opinion of the fairness of the financial statement presentations and the evidence gathered to support that opinion.
___ (10) FASB	J. Securities and Exchange Commission.
___ (11) CPA	K. Financial Accounting Standards Board.
___ (12) Relevant information	L. A company with stock that can be bought and sold by investors on established stock exchanges.
___ (13) GAAP	M. Generally accepted accounting principles.

Matching Financial Statement Items to Financial Statement Categories

E1-2
LO1-1
P&G

According to its annual report, **P&G**'s billion-dollar brands include Pampers, Tide, Ariel, Always, Pantene, Bounty, Charmin, Downy, Olay, Crest, Vicks, Gillette, and others. The following are items taken from its recent balance sheet and income statement. Note that different companies use slightly different titles for the same item. Mark each item in the following list as an asset (A), liability (L), or stockholders' equity

(SE) item that would appear on the balance sheet or a revenue (R) or expense (E) item that would appear on the income statement.

___	(1) Accounts receivable	___	(9) Income taxes
___	(2) Cash and cash equivalents	___	(10) Accounts payable
___	(3) Net sales	___	(11) Trademarks and other intangible assets
___	(4) Debt due within one year	___	(12) Property, plant, and equipment
___	(5) Taxes payable	___	(13) Long-term debt
___	(6) Retained earnings	___	(14) Inventories
___	(7) Cost of products sold	___	(15) Interest expense
___	(8) Selling, general, and administrative expense		

E1-3
LO1-1
Tootsie Roll Industries

Matching Financial Statement Items to Financial Statement Categories

Tootsie Roll Industries is engaged in the manufacture and sale of candy. Major products include Tootsie Rolls, Tootsie Roll Pops, Tootsie Pop Drops, Tootsie Flavor Rolls, Charms, and Blow-Pop lollipops. The following items were listed on Tootsie Roll's recent income statement and balance sheet. Mark each item from the balance sheet as an asset (A), liability (L), or shareholders' equity (SE) and mark each item from the income statement as a revenue (R) or expense (E) item.

___	(1) Bank loans	___	(10) Machinery and equipment
___	(2) Selling, marketing, and administrative expenses	___	(11) Net product sales
___	(3) Accounts payable	___	(12) Inventories
___	(4) Dividends payable	___	(13) Trademarks
___	(5) Retained earnings	___	(14) Buildings
___	(6) Cash and cash equivalents	___	(15) Land
___	(7) Accounts receivable	___	(16) Income taxes payable
___	(8) Provision for income taxes*	___	(17) Rental and royalty costs
___	(9) Product cost of goods sold	___	(18) Investments (in other companies)

*In the United States, "provision for income taxes" is most often used as a synonym for "income tax expense."

E1-4
LO1-1
Honda Motor Corporation

Preparing a Balance Sheet

Honda Motor Corporation of Japan is a leading international manufacturer of automobiles, motorcycles, all-terrain vehicles, and personal watercraft. As a Japanese company, it follows Japanese GAAP and reports its financial statements in billions of yen (the sign for yen is ¥). A simplified version of its recent balance sheet contained the following items (in billions). Prepare a balance sheet as of March 31, current year, solving for the missing amount. (**Hint:** Exhibit 1.2 in the chapter provides a good model for completing this exercise.)

Cash and cash equivalents	¥ 2,106
Common stock	231
Accounts payable and other current liabilities	5,429
Inventories	1,364
Investments	597
Long-term debt	4,022
Net property, plant, and equipment	3,200
Other assets	8,606
Other liabilities	1,938
Retained earnings	7,338
Total assets	18,958
Total liabilities and stockholders' equity	?
Trade accounts, notes, and other receivables	3,085

Source: Honda Motor Corporation

E1-5
LO1-1

Completing a Balance Sheet and Inferring Net Income

Bennett Griffin and Chula Garza organized Cole Valley Book Store as a corporation; each contributed $80,000 cash to start the business and received 4,000 shares of common stock. The store completed its first year of operations on December 31, current year. On that date, the following financial items for the year were determined: December 31, current year, cash on hand and in the bank, $75,600; December 31, current year, amounts due from customers from sales of books, $39,000; unused portion of store and office equipment, $73,000; December 31, current year, amounts owed to publishers for books purchased, $12,000; one-year note payable to a local bank for $3,000. No dividends were declared or paid to the stockholders during the year.

Required:

1. Complete the following balance sheet as of the end of the current year.
2. What was the amount of net income for the year? (**Hint:** Use the retained earnings equation [Beginning Retained Earnings + Net Income − Dividends = Ending Retained Earnings] to solve for net income.)

Assets		**Liabilities**	
Cash	$ ____	Accounts payable	$ ____
Accounts receivable	____	Note payable	____
Store and office equipment	____	Interest payable	300
		Total liabilities	____
		Stockholders' Equity	
		Common stock	____
		Retained earnings	$12,300
		Total stockholders' equity	____
Total assets	$ ____	Total liabilities and stockholders' equity	$ ____

Analyzing Revenues and Expenses and Preparing an Income Statement

E1-6
LO1-1

Assume that you are the owner of Campus Connection, which specializes in items that interest students. At the end of January of the current year, you find (for January only) this information:

a. Sales, per the cash register tapes, of $150,000, plus one sale on credit (a special situation) of $2,500.
b. With the help of a friend (who majored in accounting), you determine that all of the goods sold during January cost $70,000 to purchase.
c. During the month, according to the checkbook, you paid $37,000 for salaries, rent, supplies, advertising, and other expenses; however, you have not yet paid the $900 monthly utilities for January.

Required:
On the basis of the data given (disregard income taxes), what was the amount of net income for January? Show computations. (**Hint:** A convenient form to use has the following major side captions: Revenues, Expenses, and the difference–Net Income.)

Preparing an Income Statement

E1-7
LO1-1
Sysco Corp.

Sysco Corp. is one of the nation's leading distributors of food and related products to restaurants, universities, hotels, and other customers. A simplified version of its recent income statement contained the following items (in millions). Prepare an income statement for the year ended June 30, current year. (**Hint:** First order the items as they would appear on the income statement and then confirm the values of the subtotals and totals. Exhibit 1.3 in the chapter provides a good model for completing this exercise.)

Cost of sales	$44,814
Income taxes	371
Interest expense	303
Net earnings	1,395
Sales	55,371
Earnings before income taxes	1,766
Selling, general, and administration expense	8,504
Other revenues	16
Total expenses (excluding income taxes)	53,621
Total revenues	55,387

Source: Sysco Corp.

E1-8 Analyzing Revenues and Expenses and Completing an Income Statement

LO1-1

Neighborhood Realty, Incorporated, has been operating for three years and is owned by three investors. S. Bhojraj owns 60 percent of the total outstanding stock of 9,000 shares and is the managing executive in charge. On December 31, current year, the following financial items for the entire year were determined: commissions earned and collected in cash, $150,900, plus $16,800 uncollected; rental service fees earned and collected, $20,000; salaries expense paid, $62,740; commissions expense paid, $35,330; payroll taxes paid, $2,500; rent paid for January through November, $2,475 (not including December rent yet to be paid); utilities expense paid, $1,600; promotion and advertising paid, $7,750; income taxes paid, $15,660; and miscellaneous expenses paid, $500. There were no other unpaid expenses at December 31. Also during the year, the company paid the owners "out-of-profit" cash dividends amounting to $12,000. Complete the following income statement:

________________		
________________		
________________		
Revenues		
Commissions earned	$ ______	
Rental service fees	______	
Total revenues		$ ______
Expenses		
Salaries expense	______	
Commissions expense	______	
Payroll tax expense	______	
Rent expense	______	
Utilities expense	______	
Promotion and advertising expense	______	
Miscellaneous expenses	______	
Total expenses (excluding income taxes)		______
Pretax income		______
Income tax expense		______
Net income		$58,920

E1-9 Inferring Values Using the Income Statement and Balance Sheet Equations

LO1-1

Review the chapter explanations of the income statement and the balance sheet equations. Apply these equations in each independent case to compute the two missing amounts for each case. Assume that it is the end of the first full year of operations for the company. (**Hint:** Organize the listed items as they are presented in the balance sheet and income statement equations and then compute the missing amounts.)

Independent Cases	Total Revenues	Total Expenses	Net Income (Loss)	Total Assets	Total Liabilities	Stockholders' Equity
A	$93,500	$75,940	$	$140,200	$56,500	$
B		75,834	14,740	107,880		77,500
C	68,120	76,430		98,200	69,850	
D	55,804		21,770		20,300	78,680
E	84,840	75,320			25,520	80,000

E1-10 Inferring Values Using the Income Statement and Balance Sheet Equations

LO1-1

Review the chapter explanations of the income statement and the balance sheet equations. Apply these equations in each independent case to compute the two missing amounts for each case. Assume that it is the end of the first full year of operations for the company. (**Hint:** Organize the listed items as they are presented in the balance sheet and income statement equations and then compute the missing amounts.)

Independent Cases	Total Revenues	Total Expenses	Net Income (Loss)	Total Assets	Total Liabilities	Stockholders' Equity
A	$242,300	$196,700	$	$253,500	$ 75,000	$
B		186,500	29,920	590,000		350,600
C	73,500	91,890		260,400	190,760	
D	35,840		9,840		190,430	97,525
E	224,130	209,500			173,650	360,100

Preparing an Income Statement and Balance Sheet

E1-11
LO1-1

Painter Corporation was organized by five individuals on January 1 of the current year. At the end of January of the current year, the following monthly financial data are available:

Total revenues	$305,000
Total expenses (excluding income taxes)	189,000
Income tax expense (all unpaid as of January 31)	25,000
Cash balance, January 31	65,150
Receivables from customers (all considered collectible)	44,700
Merchandise inventory (by inventory count at cost)	94,500
Payables to suppliers for merchandise purchased from them (will be paid during February of the current year)	25,950
Common stock	62,400

No dividends were declared or paid during January.

Required:
Complete the following two statements:

PAINTER CORPORATION
Income Statement
For the Month of January, Current Year

Total revenues	$
Less: Total expenses (excluding income tax)	
Pretax income	
Less: Income tax expense	
Net income	$

PAINTER CORPORATION
Balance Sheet
At January 31, Current Year

Assets	
Cash	$
Receivables from customers	
Merchandise inventory	
Total assets	$
Liabilities	
Payables to suppliers	$
Income taxes payable	
Total liabilities	
Stockholders' Equity	
Common stock	
Retained earnings	
Total stockholders' equity	
Total liabilities and stockholders' equity	$

E1-12 Preparing an Income Statement and Balance Sheet

LO1-1

Analytics Corporation was organized on January 1, current year. At the end of the current year, the following financial data are available:

Total revenues	$299,000
Total expenses (excluding income taxes)	184,000
Income tax expense (all unpaid as of December 31)	34,500
Cash	70,150
Receivables from customers (all considered collectible)	34,500
Merchandise inventory (by inventory count at cost)	96,600
Payables to suppliers for merchandise purchased from them (will be paid during the following year)	26,450
Common stock	59,800

No dividends were declared or paid during the first year.

Required:
Complete the following two statements:

ANALYTICS CORPORATION **Income Statement** **For the Year Ended December 31, Current Year**	
Total revenues	$ ____
Less: Total expenses (excluding income tax)	____
Pretax income	____
Less: Income tax expense	
Net income	$ ____

ANALYTICS CORPORATION **Balance Sheet** **At December 31, Current Year**	
Assets	
Cash	$ ____
Receivables from customers	____
Merchandise inventory	____
Total assets	$ ____
Liabilities	
Payables to suppliers	$ ____
Income taxes payable	____
Total liabilities	____
Stockholders' Equity	
Common stock	____
Retained earnings	____
Total stockholders' equity	____
Total liabilities and stockholders' equity	$ ____

E1-13 Preparing a Statement of Stockholders' Equity

LO1-1

Plummer Stonework Corporation was organized on January 1, 2022. For its first two years of operations, it reported the following:

Net income for 2022	$ 31,000
Net income for 2023	42,000
Dividends for 2022	14,200
Dividends for 2023	18,700
Total assets at the end of 2022	130,000
Total assets at the end of 2023	250,000
Common stock at the end of 2022	100,000
Common stock at the end of 2023	100,000

Required:
On the basis of the data given, prepare a statement of stockholders' equity for 2023. Show computations.

Preparing a Summarized Income Statement, Statement of Stockholders' Equity, and Balance Sheet

E1-14
LO1-1

Bennett Inc. was organized four years ago. At the end of the current year, the following financial data are available:

Beginning retained earnings	$ 193	Common stock	$ 120
Cash	281	Ending retained earnings	?
Other assets	443	Expenses	1,301
Revenues	1,401	Liabilities	331
Dividends	20		

Required:
Complete the following three statements:

BENNETT INC.
Income Statement
For the Year Ended December 31, current year

Revenues	$
Expenses	
Net income	$

BENNETT INC.
Statement of Stockholders' Equity
For the Year Ended December 31, current year

	Common Stock	Retained Earnings
Beginning	$	$
+ Net income		
– Dividends		
Ending	$	$

BENNETT INC.
Balance Sheet
December 31, current year

Cash	$
Other assets	
Total assets	$
Liabilities	$
Common stock	
Retained Earnings	
Total liabilities and stockholders' equity	$

E1-15 Focus on Cash Flows: Matching Cash Flow Statement Items to Categories

LO1-1

The following items were taken from a recent cash flow statement. Note that different companies use slightly different titles for the same item. Mark each item in the list as a cash flow from operating activities (O), investing activities (I), or financing activities (F). Place parentheses around the letter if it is a cash outflow.

___ (1) Purchases of property, plant, and equipment
___ (2) Cash received from customers
___ (3) Cash paid for dividends to stockholders
___ (4) Cash paid to suppliers
___ (5) Income taxes paid
___ (6) Cash paid to employees
___ (7) Cash proceeds received from sale of investment in another company
___ (8) Repayment of borrowings

PROBLEMS

P1-1 Preparing an Income Statement, Statement of Stockholders' Equity, and Balance Sheet (AP1-1)

LO1-1

Assume that you are the president of Highlight Construction Company. At the end of the first year of operations (December 31), the following financial data for the company are available:

Cash	$ 25,600
Receivables from customers (all considered collectible)	10,800
Inventory of merchandise (based on physical count and priced at cost)	81,000
Equipment owned, at cost less used portion	42,000
Accounts payable owed to suppliers	46,140
Salary payable (on December 31, this was owed to an employee who will be paid on January 10)	2,520
Total sales revenue	128,400
Expenses, including the cost of the merchandise sold (excluding income taxes)	80,200
Income tax expense at 30% × Pretax income; all paid during the current year	?
Common stock (December 31)	87,000
Dividends declared and paid during the current year	10,000
(Note: The beginning balances in Common Stock and Retained Earnings are zero because it is the first year of operations.)	

Required:

Using the financial statement exhibits in the chapter as models and showing computations:

1. Prepare a summarized income statement for the year.
2. Prepare a statement of stockholders' equity for the year.
3. Prepare a balance sheet at December 31.

P1-2 Analyzing a Student's Business and Preparing an Income Statement (AP1-2)

LO1-1

During the summer between his junior and senior years, James Cook needed to earn sufficient money for the coming academic year. Unable to obtain a job with a reasonable salary, he decided to try the lawn care business for three months. After a survey of the market potential, James bought a used pickup truck on June 1 for $1,800. On each door he painted "James Cook Lawn Service, Phone 471-4487." He also spent $900 for mowers, trimmers, and tools. To acquire these items, he borrowed $3,000 cash by signing a note payable promising to pay the $3,000 plus interest of $78 at the end of the three months (ending August 31).

By the end of the summer, James had done a lot of work and his bank account looked good. This prompted him to wonder how much profit the business had earned.

A review of the check stubs showed the following: Bank deposits of collections from customers totaled $15,000. The following checks had been written: gas, oil, and lubrication, $1,050; pickup repairs, $250; mower repair, $110; miscellaneous supplies used, $80; helpers, $5,400; payroll taxes, $190; payment for assistance in preparing payroll tax forms, $25; insurance, $125; telephone, $110; and $3,078 to pay off the note including interest (on August 31). A notebook kept in the pickup, plus some unpaid bills, reflected that customers still owed him $700 for lawn services rendered and that he owed $180 for gas and oil (credit card charges). He estimated that the cost for use of the truck and the other equipment (called **depreciation**) for three months amounted to $600.

Required:

1. Prepare a quarterly income statement for James Cook Lawn Service for the months June, July, and August. Use the following main captions: Revenues from Services, Expenses, and Net Income. Assume that the company will not be subject to income tax.
2. Do you see a need for one or more additional financial reports for this company for the quarter and thereafter? Explain.

Comparing Income with Cash Flow (Challenging) (AP1-3)

P1-3
LO1-1

Huang Trucking Company was organized on January 1. At the end of the first quarter (three months) of operations, the owner prepared a summary of its activities as shown in item (*a*) of the following table:

	Computation of	
Summary of Transactions	Income	Cash
a. Services performed for customers, $66,000, of which $11,000 remained uncollected at the end of the quarter.	+$66,000	+$55,000
b. Cash borrowed from the local bank, $56,000 (one-year note).		
c. Small service truck purchased at the end of the quarter to be used in the business for two years starting the next quarter: Cost, $12,500 cash.		
d. Wages earned by employees, $25,000, of which one-half remained unpaid at the end of the quarter.		
e. Service supplies purchased for use in the business, $3,800 cash, of which $900 were unused (still on hand) at the end of the quarter.		
f. Other operating expenses, $38,000, of which $6,500 remained unpaid at the end of the quarter.		
g. Based only on these transactions, compute the following for the quarter: Income (or loss) Cash inflow (or outflow)		

Required:

1. For items (*b*) through (*g*), enter what you consider to be the correct amounts. Enter a zero when appropriate. The first transaction is illustrated.
2. For each transaction, explain the basis for your response in requirement (1).

ALTERNATE PROBLEMS

Preparing an Income Statement, Statement of Stockholders' Equity, and Balance Sheet (P1-1)

AP1-1
LO1-1

Assume that you are the president of Influence Corporation. At the end of the first year (December 31) of operations, the following financial data for the company are available:

Cash	$ 13,150
Receivables from customers (all considered collectible)	10,900
Inventory of merchandise (based on physical count and priced at cost)	27,000
Equipment owned, at cost less used portion	66,000
Accounts payable owed to suppliers	31,500
Salary payable (on December 31, this was owed to an employee who will be paid on January 10)	1,500
Total sales revenue	100,000
Expenses, including the cost of the merchandise sold (excluding income taxes)	68,500
Income tax expense at 30% × Pretax income; all paid during December of the current year	?
Common stock at the end of the current year	62,000

No dividends were declared or paid during the current year. The beginning balances in Common Stock and Retained Earnings are zero because it is the first year of operations.

Required:

Using the financial statement exhibits in the chapter as models and showing computations:

1. Prepare a summarized income statement for the year.
2. Prepare a statement of stockholders' equity for the year.
3. Prepare a balance sheet at year end.

AP1-2 Analyzing a Student's Business and Preparing an Income Statement (P1-2)

LO1-1

Upon graduation from high school, Sam List immediately accepted a job as an electrician's assistant for a large local electrical repair company. After three years of hard work, Sam received an electrician's license and decided to start his own business. He had saved $12,000, which he invested in the business. First, he transferred this amount from his savings account to a business bank account for List Electric Repair Company, Incorporated. His lawyer had advised him to start as a corporation. He then purchased a used panel truck for $9,000 cash and secondhand tools for $1,500; rented space in a small building; inserted an ad in the local paper; and opened the doors on October 1. Immediately, Sam was very busy; after one month, he employed an assistant.

Although Sam knew practically nothing about the financial side of the business, he realized that a number of reports were required and that costs and collections had to be controlled carefully. At the end of the year, prompted in part by concern about his income tax situation (previously he had to report only salary), Sam recognized the need for financial statements. His assistant developed some financial statements for the business. On December 31, with the help of a friend, she gathered the following data for the three months just ended. Bank account deposits of collections for electric repair services totaled $32,000. The following checks had been written: electrician's assistant, $7,500; payroll taxes, $175; supplies purchased and used on jobs, $9,500; oil, gas, and maintenance on truck, $1,200; insurance, $700; rent, $500; utilities and telephone, $825; and miscellaneous expenses (including advertising), $600. Also, uncollected bills to customers for electric repair services amounted to $3,500. The $250 rent for December had not been paid. Sam estimated the cost of using the truck and tools (depreciation) during the three months to be $1,200. Income taxes for the three-month period were $3,930.

Required:

1. Prepare a quarterly income statement for List Electric Repair for the three months October through December. Use the following main captions: Revenues from Services, Expenses, Pretax Income, and Net Income.
2. Do you think that Sam may need one or more additional financial reports for the quarter and thereafter? Explain.

AP1-3 Comparing Income with Cash Flow (Challenging) (P1-3)

LO1-1

Choice Chicken Company was organized on January 1. At the end of the first quarter (three months) of operations, the owner prepared a summary of its activities as shown in transaction (*a*) of the following table:

	Computation of	
Summary of Transactions	Income	Cash
a. Services performed for customers, $85,000, of which $15,000 remained uncollected at the end of the quarter.	+$85,000	+$70,000
b. Cash borrowed from the local bank, $25,000 (one-year note).		
c. Small service truck purchased at the end of the quarter to be used in the business for two years starting the next quarter: Cost, $8,000 cash.		
d. Wages earned by employees, $36,000, of which one-sixth remained unpaid at the end of the quarter.		
e. Service supplies purchased for use in the business, $4,000 cash, of which $1,000 were unused (still on hand) at the end of the quarter.		
f. Other operating expenses, $31,000, of which one-half remained unpaid at the end of the quarter.		
g. Based only on these transactions, compute the following for the quarter: Income (or loss) Cash inflow (or outflow)		

Required:

1. For items (*b*) through (*g*), enter what you consider to be the correct amounts. Enter a zero when appropriate. The first transaction is illustrated.
2. For each transaction, explain the basis for your response in requirement (1).

CONTINUING PROBLEM

Financial Statements for a New Business Plan

CON1-1

Penny Cassidy is considering forming her own pool service and supply company, Penny's Pool Service & Supply, Inc. She has decided to incorporate the business to limit her legal liability. She expects to invest $20,000 of her own savings and receive 1,000 shares of common stock. Her plan for the first year of operations forecasts the following amounts at December 31, the end of the current year: cash in bank, $2,900; amounts due from customers for services rendered, $2,300; pool supplies inventory, $4,600; equipment, $28,000; amounts owed to **Pool Corporation, Inc.**, a pool supply wholesaler, $3,500; note payable to the bank, $5,000. Penny forecasts first-year sales of $60,000, wages of $24,000, cost of supplies used of $8,200, other administrative expenses of $4,500, and income tax expense of $4,000. She expects to pay herself a $10,000 dividend as the sole stockholder of the company.

Required:

If Penny's estimates are correct, what would the following first-year financial statements look like for Penny's Pool Service & Supply (use Exhibits 1.2, 1.3, and 1.4 as models)?

1. Income statement
2. Statement of stockholders' equity
3. Balance sheet

CASES AND PROJECTS

Annual Report Cases

Finding Financial Information

CP1-1
LO1-1, 1-2
Target Corporation

Refer to the financial statements of **Target Corporation** in Appendix B at the end of this book.

Required:

Skim the annual report. Look at the income statement, balance sheet, and cash flow statement closely and attempt to infer what kinds of information they report. Then answer the following questions based on the report.

1. What best describes the types of products Target sells?
   a. Electronics
   b. Sporting goods
   c. General merchandise and food
   d. Mexican food
2. On what date does Target's most recent reporting year end?
   a. February 1, 2020
   b. December 31, 2020
   c. January 30, 2021
   d. December 31, 2021

3. For how many years does it present complete balance sheets, income statements, and cash flow statements?
   a. 3 balance sheets, 3 income statements, and 3 cash flow statements.
   b. 2 balance sheets, 3 income statements, and 3 cash flow statements.
   c. 2 balance sheets, 2 income statements, and 3 cash flow statements.
4. Are its financial statements audited by independent CPAs? How do you know?
   a. Yes, as indicated in the "Report of Independent Registered Public Accounting Firm."
   b. No, as indicated in the "Report of Management."
5. Did its total assets increase or decrease over the last year?
   a. Increase
   b. Decrease
6. How much inventory (in dollars) did the company have as of January 30, 2021, in millions (accountants would call this the ending balance)?
   a. $66,177
   b. $8,992
   c. $8,511
   d. $10,653
7. Write out the basic accounting (balance sheet) equation and provide the values in millions of dollars reported by the company as of January 30, 2021.
   a. $51,248 = $36,808 + $14,440
   b. $93,561 – $89,193 = $4,368

CP1-2
LO1-1, 1-2
Walmart Inc.

Finding Financial Information

Refer to the financial statements of **Walmart Inc.** in Appendix C at the end of this book. All dollar amounts are in millions.

Required:
1. What is the amount of "Consolidated net income" for the most recent year? ______________
2. What amount of revenue was earned in the most recent year? ______________
3. How much does the company report for inventories as of January 31, 2021? ______________
4. By what amount did cash and cash equivalents* change during the most recent year? ______________
5. Who is the auditor for the company? ______________

***Cash equivalents** are short-term investments readily convertible to cash whose value is unlikely to change.

CP1-3
LO1-1
Target Corporation
Walmart Inc.

Comparing Companies within an Industry

Refer to the financial statements of **Target Corporation** in Appendix B and **Walmart Inc.** in Appendix C.

Required:
1. Total assets is a common measure of the size of a company. Which company had the higher total assets at the end of the most recent year? (Note: Some companies will label a year that has a January 30 year-end as having a fiscal year-end dated one year earlier. For example, a January 30, 2021, year-end may be labeled as Fiscal 2020 because the year actually has more months that fall in the 2020 calendar year than in the 2021 calendar year.)
   a. Target
   b. Walmart
2. Net sales (or net revenue) is also a common measure of the size of a company. Which company had the higher net sales for the most recent year?
   a. Target
   b. Walmart
3. Both companies sell a wide variety of general merchandise and food. In what account would you find the general merchandise and food in the companies' stores and warehouses at year end?
   a. Property and equipment
   b. Cost of sales
   c. Accounts payable
   d. Inventory or Inventories

Financial Reporting and Analysis Cases

Evaluating Data to Support a Loan Application (Challenging)

CP1-4
LO1-1

On January 1 of the current year, three individuals organized Northwest Company as a corporation. Each individual invested $10,000 cash in the business. On December 31 of the current year, they prepared a list of resources owned (assets) and debts owed (liabilities) to support a company loan request for $70,000 submitted to a local bank. None of the three investors had studied accounting. The two lists prepared were as follows:

Company Resources	
Cash	$ 12,000
Service supplies inventory (on hand)	7,000
Service trucks (four, practically new)	57,000
Personal residences of organizers (three houses)	190,000
Service equipment used in the business (practically new)	30,000
Bills due from customers (for services already completed)	15,000
Total	$311,000
Company Obligations	
Unpaid wages to employees	$ 19,000
Unpaid taxes	8,000
Owed to suppliers	10,000
Owed on service trucks and equipment (to a finance company)	45,000
Loan from organizer	10,000
Total	$ 92,000

Required:

Prepare a short memo in which you discuss the following:

1. Which of these items do not belong on the balance sheet? (Bear in mind that the company is considered to be separate from the owners.)
2. What additional questions would you raise about the measurement of items on the list? Explain the basis for each question.
3. If you were advising the local bank on its loan decision, which amounts on the lists would create special concerns? Explain the basis for each concern and include any recommendations that you have.
4. In view of your responses to (1) and (2), what do you think the amount of stockholders' equity (i.e., assets minus liabilities) of the company would be? Show your computations.

Using Financial Reports: Identifying and Correcting Deficiencies in an Income Statement and Balance Sheet

CP1-5
LO1-1

Precision Corporation was organized on January 1, 2021. At the end of 2021, the company had not yet employed an accountant; however, an employee who was "good with numbers" prepared the following statements at that date:

PRECISION CORPORATION
December 31, 2021

Income from sales of merchandise	$ 180,000
Total amount paid for goods sold during 2021	(90,000)
Selling costs	(25,000)
Depreciation (on service vehicles used)	(12,000)
Income from services rendered	52,000
Salaries and wages paid	(62,000)

PRECISION CORPORATION
December 31, 2021

Resources		
Cash		$ 32,000
Merchandise inventory (held for resale)		42,000
Service vehicles		50,000
Retained earnings (profit earned in 2021)		32,250
Grand total		$156,250
Debts		
Payables to suppliers		$ 17,750
Note owed to bank		25,000
Due from customers		13,000
Total		55,750
Supplies on hand (to be used in rendering services)	$15,000	
Accumulated depreciation* (on service vehicles)	12,000	
Common stock, 6,500 shares	65,000	
Total		92,000
Grand total		$ 147,750

*This represents the portion of the service vehicles that has been used up to date.

Required:

1. List all deficiencies that you can identify in these statements. Give a brief explanation of each one.
2. Prepare a proper income statement (correct net income is $32,250 and income tax expense is $10,750) and balance sheet (correct total assets are $140,000).

Critical Thinking Cases

CP1-6 LO1-2 Making Decisions as an Owner: Deciding about a Proposed Audit

You are one of three partners who own and operate Mary's Maid Service. The company has been operating for seven years. One of the other partners has always prepared the company's annual financial statements. Recently you proposed that the statements be audited each year because it would benefit the partners and preclude possible disagreements about the division of profits. The partner who prepares the statements proposed that his Uncle Ray, who has a lot of financial experience, can do the job and at little cost. Your other partner remained silent.

Required:

1. What position would you take on the proposal? Justify your response.
2. What would you strongly recommend? Give the basis for your recommendation.

CP1-7 LO1-2 Evaluating an Ethical Dilemma: Ethics and Auditor Responsibilities

A key factor that an auditor provides is independence. The **AICPA Code of Professional Conduct** states that "a member in public practice should be independent in fact and appearance when providing auditing and other attestation services."

Required:

Do you consider the following circumstances to suggest a lack of independence? Justify your position. (Use your imagination. Specific answers are not provided in the chapter.)

1. Jack Jones is a partner with a large audit firm and is assigned to the **Ford** audit. Jack owns 10 shares of Ford.
2. Melissa Chee has invested in a mutual fund company that owns 500,000 shares of **Target** stock. She is the auditor of Sears.

3. Bob Franklin is a clerk/typist who works on the audit of **AT&T**. He has just inherited 50,000 shares of AT&T stock. (Bob enjoys his work and plans to continue despite his new wealth.)
4. Nancy Sodoma worked on weekends as the controller for a small business that a friend started. Nancy quit the job in midyear and now has no association with the company. She works full time for a large CPA firm and has been assigned to do the audit of her friend's business.
5. Mark Jacobs borrowed $100,000 for a home mortgage from First City National Bank. The mortgage was granted on normal credit terms. Mark is the partner in charge of the First City audit.

You as Analyst: Online Company Research

Examining an Annual Report (an Individual or Team Project)

CP1-8
LO1-1, 1-2

In your web browser, search for the investor relations page of a public company you are interested in (e.g., Papa John's investor relations). Select SEC Filings or Annual Report or Financials to obtain the 10-K for the most recent year available.*

Required:
Answer the following questions based on the annual report (10-K) that you have downloaded:

1. What types of products or services does it sell?
2. On what day of the year does its fiscal year end?
3. For how many years does it present complete:
   a. Balance sheets?
   b. Income statements?
   c. Cash flow statements?
4. Are its financial statements audited by independent CPAs? If so, indicate who performs the audit.
5. Did its total assets increase or decrease over last year? By what percentage? (Percentage change is calculated as [Current year − Last year] ÷ Last year. Show supporting computations.)
6. Did its net income increase or decrease over last year? By what percentage?

*Alternatively, you can go to sec.gov, click on Company Filings (under the search box), and type the name of the public company you want to find. Once at the list of filings, type 10-K in the Filing Type box. The most recent 10-K annual report will be at the top of the list. Click on Interactive Data for a list of the parts or the entire report to examine.

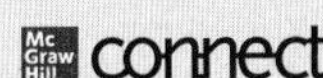

BUSINESS ANALYTICS AND DATA VISUALIZATION WITH EXCEL AND TABLEAU

Connect offers a variety of exercises to assess Excel skills, data visualization, interpretation, and analysis, including auto-graded Tableau Dashboard Activities, Applying Excel problems, and Integrated Excel problems.

Tip Most companies make data-driven decisions for most aspects of their businesses, such as, where to open a new store, understanding customer preferences, which mix of products to produce, and trends. These exercises will introduce you to current analytical tools.

Images used throughout chapter: Question of ethics: mushmello/Shutterstock; Pause for feedback: McGraw Hill; Guided help: McGraw Hill; Financial analysis: McGraw Hill; Focus on cash flows: Hilch/Shutterstock; Key ratio analysis: guillermain/123RF; Data analytics: Hilch/Shutterstock; Tip: McGraw Hill; ESG reporting: McGraw Hill; International perspective: Hilch/Shutterstock; Internal control alert icon: McGraw Hil

chapter 2

Investing and Financing Decisions and the Accounting System

Entrepreneur and chef Steve Ells had a vision for a restaurant that serves food fast but uses higher-quality fresh ingredients and classic cooking techniques found in finer restaurants. In 1993, he borrowed $85,000 cash from his family to open his first **Chipotle Mexican Grill** in a former Dolly Madison ice cream store in Denver, Colorado. Chipotle Mexican Grill soon became a leader in the "fast-casual" segment of the restaurant industry. As of March 31, 2020, the Chipotle chain operated nearly 2,600 restaurants in the United States, 40 internationally, and three non-Chipotle restaurants called Pizzeria Locale following a similar business model.

How did Chipotle grow so fast? First, Chipotle's mission to provide "Food with Integrity" jump-started its tremendous growth. It was committed to making meals with fresh food, using responsibly raised meat, and purchasing organic produce and dairy products from local farmers, which appealed to customers who were beginning to demand healthier food options. Then, in 1999, **McDonald's Corporation** became the majority stockholder by investing about $360 million in Chipotle. This provided funding for its early growth from 19 stores to nearly 490 restaurants by the end of 2005. In January 2006, Chipotle "went public." In its IPO, or initial public offering, it issued stock to the public for the first time (listed on the New York Stock Exchange as CMG). Then, McDonald's spun off (sold its ownership in) Chipotle for nearly $1.4 billion—a handsome profit of over $1 billion.

LEARNING OBJECTIVES

After studying this chapter, you should be able to:

FOCUS COMPANY

Chipotle Mexican Grill

EXPANDING ONE OF THE HOTTEST CHAINS BUILT ON SUSTAINABILITY

chipotle.com

Robert Evans Alamy Stock Photo

Learn more about Chipotle from founder, Steve Ells, by listening to the NPR podcast

Chipotle: Steve Ells: How I Built This.

How I Built This NPR podcasts are about innovators, entrepreneurs, idealists, and the movements they built.

The $173 million Chipotle raised from its IPO along with its operating profits funded additional store growth. It also has invested in enhancing information technology to meet the increasing need for digital engagement, including mobile and artificial intelligence (AI) ordering and marketing. The company uses the AI information, for example, to add new assembly lines for processing online and delivery orders when needed. It announced in June 2020 that it is partnering with **GrubHub** to expand its delivery footprint, and, in July 2020, it said that 60 percent of its new restaurants will feature a drive-through, or "Chipotlane"—Chipotle continues to invest in its buildings, equipment, and technology for future growth.

UNDERSTANDING THE BUSINESS

The "fast-casual" segment of the $4 trillion global restaurant industry generates approximately $60 billion in sales annually. What identifies a restaurant as fast-casual? Typically, customers can order online, use the digital app, or order in person. However, unlike fast food restaurants, the food is made to order, typically in view of the customers and without full table service, and is served in modern and upscale surroundings, with checks typically ranging between $8 and $16. Chipotle Mexican Grill has been a leader in this segment, although competition has increased and growth in this industry segment has slowed in recent years.

Franchising is common in chain restaurants. The largest restaurant to use franchising is **Subway**, with nearly 42,000 restaurants—all franchised. Franchising involves selling the right to use or sell a product or service to another. This is an easy way for someone to start his or her own business because the franchisor (the seller, such as **Noodles & Company**) often provides site location, design, marketing, and management training support in exchange for initial franchise fees and ongoing royalty fees usually based on weekly sales. At Noodles & Company, for example, only 85 percent of the stores are company-owned.

Unlike most restaurant chains, however, Chipotle does not franchise the business. All restaurants are company-owned. Developing a new site, usually on rented or leased property, costs on average about $835,000. In 2019, Chipotle spent nearly $334 million on new and renovated property and equipment. The creation of new restaurants to meet consumer demand for healthier food options explains most of the changes in Chipotle's assets and liabilities from year to year. To understand how the result of Chipotle Mexican Grill's growth strategy is communicated in the balance sheet, we must answer the following questions:

- What business activities cause changes in the balance sheet amounts from one period to the next?
- How do specific business activities affect each of the balance sheet amounts?
- How do companies keep track of the balance sheet amounts?

Tip Focus on learning the material well in Chapters 2, 3, and 4 since it is essential to understanding the rest of the chapters in the text. Commit your time now. It will pay off later.

In the first chapter, you learned about the importance of accounting in business decisions and the structure of basic financial statements, their relationships, and key terms. The next three chapters build on Chapter 1 as we use Chipotle's activities to illustrate new tools and concepts necessary to develop, report, and use real financial statements. In this chapter, we focus on some common asset acquisition activities (often called **investing activities**), along with related **financing activities**, such as borrowing funds from creditors or selling stock to investors to provide the cash necessary to acquire the assets. Operating activities that affect both the income statement and the balance sheet are covered in Chapters 3 and 4. Let's begin with the basic concepts related to measuring and reporting these activities.

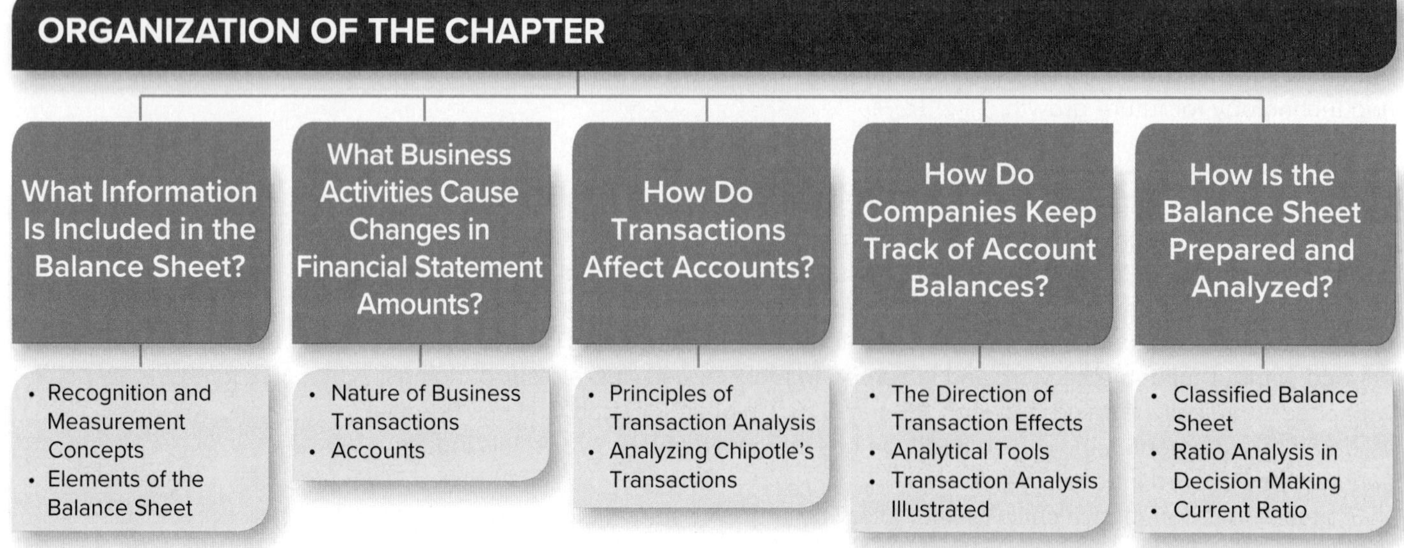

WHAT INFORMATION IS INCLUDED IN THE BALANCE SHEET?

LEARNING OBJECTIVE 2-1

Define the key accounting assumptions, principles, and elements related to the balance sheet.

Recognition and Measurement Concepts

Before we discuss accountants' definitions for the elements of the balance sheet, we should consider three assumptions and a measurement concept that underlie much of our application of these definitions. First, the separate entity assumption states that each business's activities must be accounted for separately from the personal activities of its owners, all other persons, and other entities. This means, for example, that, when an owner purchases property for personal use, the property is not an asset of the business. Second, under the going concern assumption (also called the **continuity assumption**), unless there is evidence to the contrary, we assume that the business will continue operating into the foreseeable future, long enough to meet its contractual commitments and plans. This means, for example, that if there was a high likelihood of bankruptcy, then its assets should be valued and reported on the balance sheet as if the company were to be liquidated (that is, discontinued, with all of its assets sold and all debts paid). Under the monetary unit assumption, each business entity accounts for and reports its financial results primarily in terms of the national monetary unit (e.g., dollars in the United States, yen in Japan, and euros in Germany), without any adjustment for changes in purchasing power (e.g., inflation).

Finally, accountants measure the elements of the balance sheet initially at their cost (historical cost), which is the cash-equivalent value on the date of the transaction. For example, assets are initially recorded on the exchange date at the cash paid plus the dollar value of all noncash considerations, such as the trade-in value of a used asset. We will discuss the conditions under which these values are adjusted to other amounts, such as their market value, starting in Chapter 6 of this text. With these assumptions in mind, we are now ready to discuss accountants' definitions of the elements of the balance sheet.

Elements of the Balance Sheet

The four financial statements–balance sheet, income statement, statement of stockholders' (shareholders' or owners') equity, and statement of cash flows–along with the notes to the statements provide the structure for the information communicated to users. As we learned in Chapter 1, assets, liabilities, and stockholders' equity are the elements of a corporation's balance sheet. The conceptual framework defines them as follows.

Assets

Assets are economic resources owned or controlled by a company; they have measurable value and are expected to benefit the company by producing cash inflows or reducing cash outflows in the future. As shown in **Chipotle**'s balance sheet presented in Exhibit 2.1, most companies list assets **in order of liquidity**, or how soon an asset is expected by management to be turned into cash or used. Notice that several of Chipotle's assets are categorized as current assets. Current assets are those resources that Chipotle will use or turn into cash within one year (the next 12 months). Chipotle's current assets include Cash, Short-Term Investments (in the stocks and bonds of other companies), Accounts Receivable (due from customers and others), Supplies (to make and serve the food), and Prepaid Expenses (for rent, insurance, and advertising paid in advance of use). For manufacturers that produce and sell goods and merchandisers who sell already-completed goods, Inventory (for goods to be sold) also would be listed after Accounts Receivable. Inventory is always considered a current asset, regardless of how long it takes to produce and sell the inventory. Another common account title is Other Current Assets, which is a summary of several smaller accounts. These are typical titles used by most entities.

All other assets are considered long term (or noncurrent). That is, they are to be used or turned into cash after the coming year. For Chipotle, that includes property and equipment (Land, Buildings, and Equipment), Operating lease right-of-use assets (for rented facilities, primarily stores in shopping centers), and Intangibles (nonphysical assets such as trademarks and patents) used over several years. Chipotle also may acquire the stocks and bonds of other companies as Long-Term Investments, discussed in detail in Appendix A.

Ben Margot/AP Photo

EXHIBIT 2.1

Chipotle Mexican Grill, Inc., Balance Sheet

Section	CHIPOTLE MEXICAN GRILL, INC. **Consolidated Balance Sheet*** **December 31, 2019** **(in millions of dollars, except per share data)**		**EXPLANATIONS**
			"Consolidated" means all subsidiaries are combined
			Point in time for which the balance sheet was prepared
	ASSETS		
	Current Assets:		
Current Assets	Cash	$ 481	
Current Assets	Short-term investments	400	*Ownership of other companies' stocks and bonds*
Current Assets	Accounts receivable	81	*Amounts due from customers and others*
Current Assets	Supplies	26	*Food, beverage, and packaging supplies on hand*
Current Assets	Prepaid expenses	85	*Rent, advertising, and insurance paid in advance*
	Total current assets	1,073	*Summary of assets to be used or turned into cash within one year*
Noncurrent Assets	Property and Equipment:		
Noncurrent Assets	Land	13	
Noncurrent Assets	Buildings	1,811	*Buildings owned*
Noncurrent Assets	Equipment	836	*Includes furniture and fixtures*
Noncurrent Assets	Total cost	2,660	*Cost of property and equipment at date of acquisition*
Noncurrent Assets	Accumulated depreciation	(1,201)	*Amount of cost used in past operations*
Noncurrent Assets	Net property and equipment	1,459	
Noncurrent Assets	Operating lease right-of-use assets	2,505	*Facilities rented under leases with right to use the assets*
Noncurrent Assets	Intangible assets	69	*Rights, such as patents, trademarks, and licenses*
	Total assets	$5,106	
	LIABILITIES AND STOCKHOLDERS' EQUITY		
	Current Liabilities:		
Current Liabilities	Accounts payable	$ 116	*Amount due to suppliers*
Current Liabilities	Unearned revenue	95	*Unredeemed gift cards*
Current Liabilities	Accrued expenses payable:		
Current Liabilities	Wages payable	127	*Amount due to employees*
Current Liabilities	Utilities payable	156	*Amount due for electric, gas, and telephone utilities*
Current Liabilities	Current lease liabilities	173	*Amount due on rented facilities within the next year*
	Total current liabilities	667	*Summary of liabilities to be settled within one year*
Noncurrent Liabilities	Notes payable	77	*Amount owed on loans from banks*
Noncurrent Liabilities	Long-term lease liabilities	2,678	*Amount due on rented facilities after one year*
	Total liabilities	3,422	
	Stockholders' Equity:		
Stockholders' Equity	Common stock ($0.01 par value)	1	*Total par value of stock issued by company to investors*
Stockholders' Equity	Additional paid-in capital	1,466	*Excess amount received from investors over par*
Stockholders' Equity	Treasury stock	(2,699)	*Amount paid to repurchase its own stock from investors*
Stockholders' Equity	Retained earnings	2,916	*Undistributed earnings reinvested in the company*
	Total stockholders' equity	1,684	
	Total liabilities and stockholders' equity	$5,106	

*The information has been adapted from actual statements and simplified for this chapter.

Liabilities

Liabilities are defined as measurable obligations resulting from a past transaction; they are expected to be settled in the future by transferring assets or providing services. Entities that a company owes money to are called **creditors**.

Similar to how assets are reported in order of liquidity, liabilities are usually listed on the balance sheet **in order of maturity** (how soon an obligation is to be paid). Liabilities that Chipotle will need to pay or settle within the coming year (with cash, goods, other current assets, or services) are classified as current liabilities. Chipotle's current liabilities include Accounts Payable (to suppliers), Unearned Revenue (for unredeemed gift cards that have been purchased by customers), Accrued Expenses Payable (more specifically, Wages Payable and Utilities Payable, although additional accrued liabilities may include Interest Payable, among others) and Current Lease Liabilities representing the current amount owed on leases from renting facilities, for example, in shopping centers. Companies may also include Income Taxes Payable (due to federal, state, and local governments) and Other Current Liabilities (a summary of several smaller accounts). Distinguishing current assets and current liabilities assists external users of the financial statements in assessing the amounts and the timing of future cash flows.

Chipotle's noncurrent liabilities include Notes Payable (written promises to pay the amount borrowed and interest as specified in the signed agreement) and Long-term Lease Liabilities (the amount owed beyond the next 12 months for rent of buildings).

Stockholders' Equity

Stockholders' equity (also called shareholders' equity or owners' equity) is the residual interest in the assets of the entity after subtracting liabilities. It is a combination of the financing provided by the owners and by business operations.

- **Financing Provided by Owners** is referred to as **contributed capital**. Owners invest in the business by providing cash and sometimes other assets, receiving in exchange shares of stock as evidence of ownership. The largest investors in Chipotle's stock are financial institutions (mutual funds, pension funds, etc.). The directors and executive officers also own stock, as do other corporate employees and the general public. Common Stock and Additional Paid-in Capital are the accounts used to represent the amount investors paid to Chipotle when they purchased the stock from the company. Note, however, that the Treasury Stock account **reduces** stockholders' equity. Treasury Stock represents the amount Chipotle paid to its investors when the company repurchased from investors a portion of previously issued common stock. Treasury Stock will be discussed in more detail in Chapter 11.
- **Financing Provided by Operations** is referred to as **earned capital** or retained earnings.[1] When companies earn profits, they can be distributed to owners as dividends or reinvested in the business. The portion of profits reinvested in the business is called Retained Earnings. Companies with a growth strategy, such as Chipotle, often pay little or no dividends to retain funds for expansion. A look at Chipotle's balance sheet (Exhibit 2.1) indicates that its growth has been financed by substantial reinvestment of earnings ($2,916 million).

PAUSE FOR FEEDBACK

We just learned the elements of the balance sheet (assets, liabilities, and stockholders' equity) and how assets and liabilities are usually classified (current or noncurrent). Current assets (including inventory) are expected to be used or turned into cash within the next 12 months and current liabilities are expected to be paid or satisfied within the next 12 months with cash, services, or other current assets.

---

[1]Retained earnings can increase only from profitable operations, but they decrease when a firm has a loss or pays dividends.

SELF-STUDY QUIZ

The following is a list of items from a recent balance sheet of **McDonald's Corporation**. Indicate on the line provided whether each of the following is usually categorized on the balance sheet as a current asset (CA), noncurrent asset (NCA), current liability (CL), noncurrent liability (NCL), or stockholders' equity (SE).

____	*a.* Retained Earnings	____	*d.* Prepaid Expenses	____	*g.* Accounts Payable
____	*b.* Inventories	____	*e.* Additional Paid-in Capital	____	*h.* Property and Equipment
____	*c.* Accounts Receivable	____	*f.* Long-Term Debt	____	*i.* Accrued Payroll

After you have completed your answers, check them below.

Related Homework: M2-4, M2-5, E2-3, P2-1

FINANCIAL ANALYSIS

Unrecorded but Valuable Assets and Liabilities

Many very valuable intangible **assets**, such as trademarks, patents, and copyrights that are developed inside a company (not purchased), are **not reported** on the balance sheet. For example, **Facebook**'s balance sheet reveals no listing for the Facebook trademark because it was developed internally over time through research, development, and advertising (it was not purchased). Likewise, the **Coca-Cola Company** does not report any asset for its patented Coke formula, although it does report more than $9.2 billion in various trademarks that it has purchased.

Many large companies have some form of off-balance-sheet financing–obligations **not reported** as **liabilities** on the balance sheet. For example, Chipotle's recent 10-K states that "leases with an initial term of 12 months or less . . . are not recorded on the consolidated balance sheets." The notes to the financial statements indicated that the company incurred about $3 million in short-term lease cost out of about $345 million. This illustrates the importance of reading the notes, not just the financial statements, when analyzing a company's financial information and predicting future cash flows.

Now that we have reviewed the basic elements of the balance sheet and related recognition and measurement concepts as part of the conceptual framework, let's see what economic activities cause changes in the amounts reported on the balance sheet.

LEARNING OBJECTIVE 2-2

Identify what constitutes a business transaction and recognize common balance sheet account titles used in business.

WHAT BUSINESS ACTIVITIES CAUSE CHANGES IN FINANCIAL STATEMENT AMOUNTS?

Nature of Business Transactions

Accounting focuses on certain events that have an economic impact on the entity. Those events that are recorded as part of the accounting process are called transactions. The first step in translating the results of business events to financial statement numbers is determining which events to include. As the definitions of assets and liabilities indicate, only economic resources and obligations **resulting from past transactions** are recorded on the balance sheet. Transactions include two types of events:

1. **External events:** These are **exchanges** of assets, goods, or services by one party for assets, services, or promises to pay (liabilities) from one or more other parties. Examples include the purchase of a machine from a supplier for cash, sale of merchandise to customers on account (store credit), borrowing of cash from a bank and signing a promissory note for repayment, and investment of cash in the business by the owners in exchange for ownership shares.

Solutions to SELF-STUDY QUIZ

a. SE *b.* CA *c.* CA *d.* CA *e.* SE *f.* NCL *g.* CL *h.* NCA *i.* CL

2. **Internal events:** These include certain events that are not exchanges between the business and other parties but nevertheless have a direct and measurable effect on the entity. Examples include using up insurance paid in advance and using buildings and equipment over several years.

Throughout this textbook, the word transaction is used in the broad sense to include both types of events.

Some important events that have a future economic impact on a company, however, are **not** reflected in the financial statements. In most cases, signing a contract is not considered to be an accounting transaction because it involves **only the exchange of promises**, not of assets such as cash, goods, services, or property. For example, assume that **Chipotle** signs an employment contract with a new regional manager. From an accounting perspective, no transaction has occurred because no exchange of assets, goods, or services has been made. Each party to the contract has exchanged promises–the manager agrees to work; Chipotle agrees to pay the manager for the work. For each day the new manager works, however, the exchange of services for pay results in a transaction that Chipotle must record. Because of their importance, long-term employment contracts and other commitments may need to be disclosed in notes to the financial statements.

Tip A recordable transaction occurs when assets, goods, or services are either received or given. **An exchange of two promises does not make a transaction.**

Accounts

To accumulate the dollar effect of transactions on each financial statement item, organizations use a standardized format called an account. The resulting balances are kept separate for financial statement purposes. To facilitate the recording of transactions, each company establishes a **chart of accounts**, a list of all account titles and their unique numbers. The accounts are usually organized by financial statement element, with asset accounts listed first, followed by liability, stockholders' equity, revenue, and expense accounts in that order. Exhibit 2.2 lists various account titles that are quite common and are used by most companies. The exhibit also provides special notes to help you in learning account titles. When you are completing assignments and are unsure of an account title, refer to this listing for help.

Every company creates its own chart of accounts to fit the nature of its business activities. For example, a small lawn care service may have an asset account titled Lawn Mowing Equipment, but

EXHIBIT 2.2

Typical Account Titles

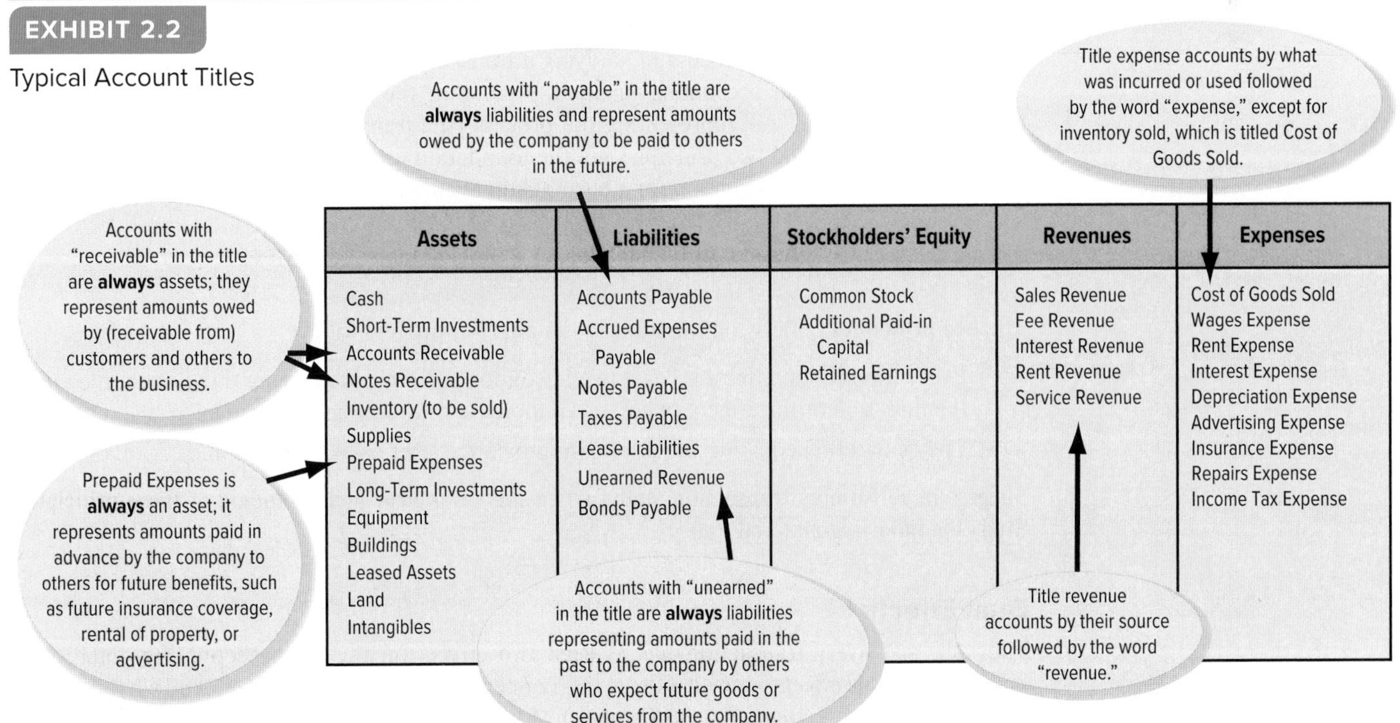

Assets	Liabilities	Stockholders' Equity	Revenues	Expenses
Cash	Accounts Payable	Common Stock	Sales Revenue	Cost of Goods Sold
Short-Term Investments	Accrued Expenses Payable	Additional Paid-in Capital	Fee Revenue	Wages Expense
Accounts Receivable	Notes Payable	Retained Earnings	Interest Revenue	Rent Expense
Notes Receivable	Taxes Payable		Rent Revenue	Interest Expense
Inventory (to be sold)	Lease Liabilities		Service Revenue	Depreciation Expense
Supplies	Unearned Revenue			Advertising Expense
Prepaid Expenses	Bonds Payable			Insurance Expense
Long-Term Investments				Repairs Expense
Equipment				Income Tax Expense
Buildings				
Leased Assets				
Land				
Intangibles				

a large corporation such as **Dell** is unlikely to report such an account on its balance sheet. These differences in accounts will become more apparent as we examine the balance sheets of various companies. Because each company has its own chart of accounts, you should **not** try to memorize a typical chart of accounts, but focus instead on understanding the nature of each typical account **by where it is located in the financial statements.** Then when you see a company that uses a slightly different title, you will understand what it means. For example, some companies use the terms Trade Accounts Receivable (same as Accounts Receivable) or Merchandise Inventory (same as Inventory). In homework problems, you will either be given the account names or be expected to select appropriate names, similar to the ones in Exhibit 2.2. Once you select a name for an account, you must use that exact name in all transactions affecting that account.

The accounts you see in the financial statements of most large corporations are actually summations (or aggregations) of a number of specific accounts in their recordkeeping system. For example, **Chipotle** keeps separate accounts for food, beverage, and packaging supplies but combines them under Supplies on the balance sheet. Wages Payable under Accrued Expenses Payable summarizes several accounts with smaller balances related to workers' compensation liability and other benefits owed to employees such as medical, dental, and vision health insurance, paid meal breaks, tuition reimbursement, life insurance, and free burritos.

LEARNING OBJECTIVE 2-3

Apply transaction analysis to simple business transactions in terms of the accounting model: Assets = Liabilities + Stockholders' Equity.

HOW DO TRANSACTIONS AFFECT ACCOUNTS?

Managers' business decisions often result in transactions that affect the financial statements. For example, decisions to expand the number of stores, advertise a new product, change an employee benefit package, and invest excess cash all would affect the financial statements. Sometimes these decisions have unintended consequences as well. The decision to purchase additional inventory for cash in anticipation of a major sales initiative, for example, will increase inventory and decrease cash. But if there is no demand for the additional inventory, the lower cash balance also will reduce the company's ability to pay its other obligations.

Because business decisions often involve an element of risk, managers should understand exactly how transactions impact the financial statements. The process for determining the effects of transactions is called **transaction analysis.**

Principles of Transaction Analysis

Transaction analysis is the process of studying a transaction to determine its economic effect on the entity in terms of the **accounting equation**. We outline the process in this section of the chapter and create a visual tool representing the process (the **transaction analysis model**). The basic accounting equation and two principles are the foundation for this model. Recall from Chapter 1 that the basic accounting equation for a business that is organized as a corporation is as follows:

Assets (A) = Liabilities (L) + Stockholders' Equity (SE)

The two principles underlying the transaction analysis process follow:

- Every transaction affects at least two accounts; correctly identifying those accounts and the direction of the effects (whether an increase or a decrease) is critical.
- The accounting equation must remain in balance after each transaction.

Success in performing transaction analysis depends on a clear understanding of these principles. Study the following material well.

Dual Effects

The idea that every transaction has **at least two effects** on the basic accounting equation is known as the **dual effects** concept. (From this concept, accountants have developed what is known as the *double-entry system of recordkeeping.*) Most transactions with external parties involve an **exchange** by which the business **entity both receives something and gives up something in return.**

For example, suppose **Chipotle** purchased tomatoes (supplies) and paid cash. In this exchange, Chipotle would receive food supplies (an increase in an asset) and in return would give up cash (a decrease in an asset).

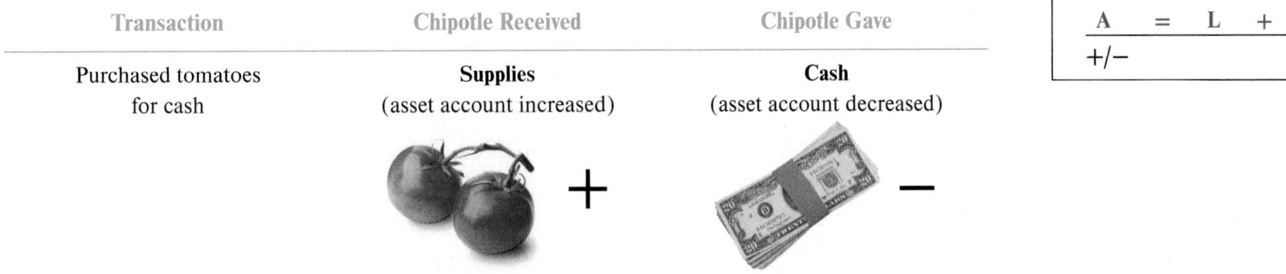

Transaction	Chipotle Received	Chipotle Gave
Purchased tomatoes for cash	**Supplies** (asset account increased) +	**Cash** (asset account decreased) −

A	=	L	+	SE
+/−				

In analyzing this transaction, we determined that the accounts affected were Supplies and Cash. However, most supplies are purchased on credit (that is, money is owed to suppliers). In that case, Chipotle would engage in **two** separate transactions at different points in time:

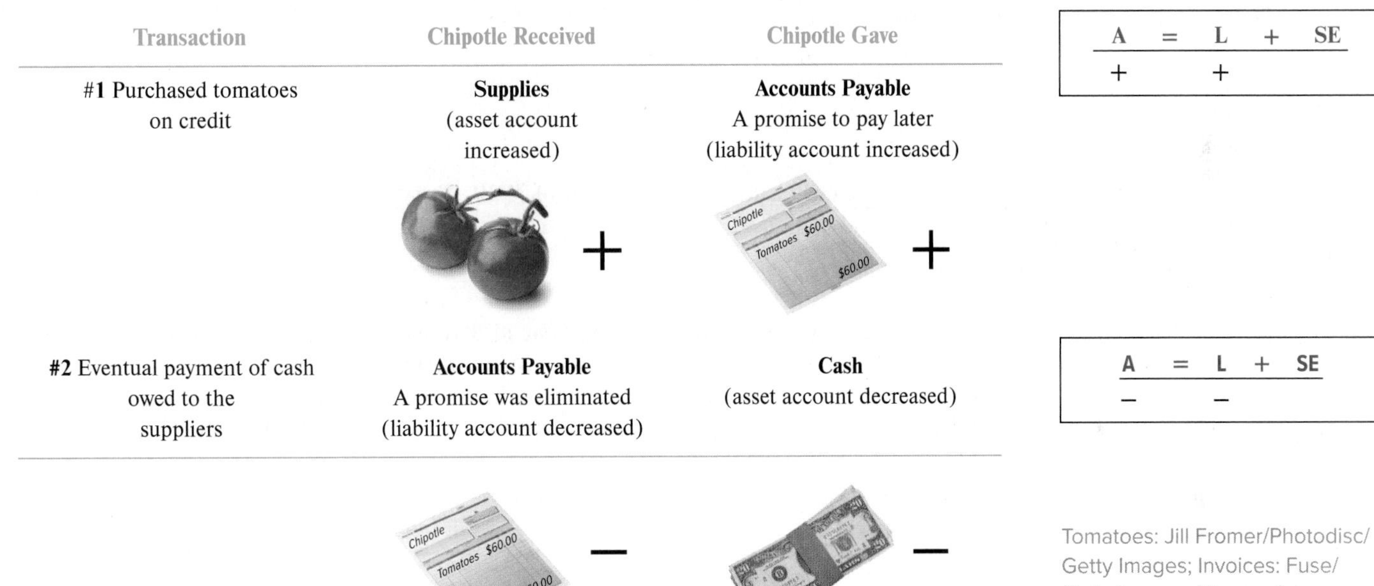

Transaction	Chipotle Received	Chipotle Gave
#1 Purchased tomatoes on credit	**Supplies** (asset account increased) +	**Accounts Payable** A promise to pay later (liability account increased) +
#2 Eventual payment of cash owed to the suppliers	**Accounts Payable** A promise was eliminated (liability account decreased) −	**Cash** (asset account decreased) −

A	=	L	+	SE
+		+		

A	=	L	+	SE
−		−		

Tomatoes: Jill Fromer/Photodisc/Getty Images; Invoices: Fuse/Getty Images; Money: Jules Frazier/Photodisc/Getty Images

Balancing the Accounting Equation

Notice in the previous tomato purchase illustrations that the accounting equation for each transaction remained in balance. **The accounting equation must remain in balance after each transaction.** That is, total assets (resources) must equal total liabilities and stockholders' equity (claims to resources). If all correct accounts have been identified and the appropriate direction of the effect on each account has been determined, the equation should remain in balance. Exhibit 2.3 lists the steps to follow in analyzing investing and financing transactions, with an example of applying the steps. Follow these steps in all illustrations and assignments in this chapter.

Analyzing Common Transactions

To illustrate the use of the transaction analysis process, let's consider hypothetical transactions of **Chipotle** that are also common to most businesses. Remember that this chapter presents investing and financing transactions that affect only the balance sheet accounts. "Investing" does not just mean buying other companies' stocks and bonds. Investing activities by a company are those in which the company typically buys or sells its noncurrent assets (growing or shrinking its productive capacity) as well as investments (current or noncurrent). Financing activities are those in which the company borrows or repays loans (typically from banks) and sells or repurchases its common stock and pays dividends (activities with stockholders).

EXHIBIT 2.3 Analyzing Investing and Financing Transactions

Steps to follow in analyzing investing and financing transactions:

Step 1: Ask → What was received?

- Identify the account(s) affected
- Classify the account(s) by type of element:
  - Asset (A)
  - Liability (L)
  - Stockholders' Equity (SE)
- Determine the direction and amount of the effect(s):
  - The account increased (+)
  - The account decreased (−)

Step 2: Ask → What was given?

- Repeat–Identify, Classify, and Determine effect

Step 3: Verify → Is the accounting equation in balance? (Does **A = L + SE?**)

Example: **A company borrows $100 from a bank**

Step 1: What was **received?** Cash (+A) 100

Step 2: What was **given?** A written promise to repay the loan called Notes Payable (+L) 100

Step 3: Is the **accounting equation** in balance? A 100 = L 100 + SE 0

A	=	L	+	SE
+100	=	+100		

Assume that Chipotle engages in the following events during the first quarter of 2020, the first three months following the balance sheet in Exhibit 2.1. Account titles are from that balance sheet, and remember that, for simplicity, **all amounts are in millions, except per share data:**

(a) **Chipotle issued (sold) 100 additional shares of common stock with a par value of $0.01 per share at a market value of $0.17 per share, receiving $17 in cash from investors**–a financing activity. Each share of common stock usually has a nominal (low) par value printed on the face of the certificate. Par value is a legal amount per share established by the board of directors; it has no relationship to the market price of the stock (additional discussion in Chapter 11). Chipotle's common stock has a par value of $0.01 per share, and in this transaction, each share sold for $0.17 per share. When a corporation issues common (capital) stock, the transaction affects separate accounts:

- **Received** from shareholders: **Cash** or other considerations for the market value of the shares given (100 shares × $0.17 market value per share = $17).
- **Given** to shareholders: Common Stock for the number of shares issued times the par value per share (100 shares × $0.01 par value per share = $1) and Additional Paid-in Capital (or Paid-in Capital or Contributed Capital in Excess of Par) for the excess received above par (100 shares × $0.16 per share in excess over par value per share [that is, $0.17 market value per share − $0.01 par value per share] = $16).

Step 1: What was **received?**
Received: Cash (+A) 17

Step 2: What was **given?**
Given: Additional stock shares → Common Stock (+SE) 1 *(100 shares × $0.01 per share)*
Additional Paid-in Capital (+SE) 16 *(100 shares × $0.16 per share)*

Step 3: Verify that the accounting equation balances: A 17 = L 0 + SE 17

Assets	=	Liabilities	+	Stockholders' Equity	
Cash				**Common Stock**	**Additional Paid-in Capital**
+17				**+1**	**+16**

***(b)* Chipotle borrowed $4 from its local bank, signing a note to be paid in three years (a noncurrent liability)**—a financing activity.

Step 1: What was **received?**
Received: Cash (+A) 4

Step 2: What was **given?**
Given: Written promises to pay the bank: Notes Payable (+L) 4 *(noncurrent)*

Step 3: Verify that the accounting equation balances: A 4 = L 4 + SE 0

Assets	=	Liabilities	+	Stockholders' Equity
Cash		**Notes Payable**		
+4		+4		

Companies that need cash to buy or build additional facilities often seek funds by selling stock to investors as in transaction (*a*) or by borrowing from creditors as in transaction (*b*). Any transactions with stockholders (usually issuing additional stock and paying dividends) and transactions with banks (borrowing and repaying loans) are **financing** activities.

***(c)* Chipotle purchased for cash $26 in new equipment and $5 in additional intangible assets**—an investing activity.

Step 1: What was **received?**
Received: Equipment (+A) 26
Intangible Assets (+A) 5

Step 2: What was **given?**
Given: Cash (−A) 31

Step 3: Verify that the accounting equation balances: A 0 = L 0 + SE 0

Assets			=	Liabilities	+	Stockholders' Equity
Cash	**Equipment**	**Intangible Assets**				
−31	+26	+5				

***(d)* Chipotle acquired $20 in additional land and $40 in new buildings, signed leases for $86 for right-of-use (ROU) assets, paid $29 in cash, and signed $6 in current leases and $111 in long-term leases to rent facilities**—an investing activity.

Step 1: What was **received?**
Received: Land (+A) 20
Buildings (+A) 40
Operating Lease Right-of-Use Assets (+A) 86

Step 2: What was **given?**
Given: Cash (−A) 29
Current Lease Liabilities (+L) 6
Long-Term Lease Liabilities (+L) 111

Step 3: Verify that the accounting equation balances: A 117 = L 117 + SE 0

Assets				=	Liabilities		+	Stockholders' Equity
Cash	**Land**	**Buildings**	**Operating Lease ROU Assets**		**Current Lease Liabilities**	**Long-Term Lease Liabilities**		
−29	+20	+40	+86		+6	+111		

Purchasing and selling property, equipment, and investments in the stock of other companies are **investing** activities. In the investing transactions in *(c)* and *(d),* notice that more than two accounts were affected.

***(e)* Chipotle sold $19 in its short-term investments for $19 cash**–an investing activity.

Step 1: What was **received**?
Received: Cash (+A) 19

Step 2: What was **given**?
Given: Short-Term Investments (−A) 19

Step 3: Verify that the accounting equation balances: A 0 = L 0 + SE 0

Assets		=	Liabilities	+	Stockholders' Equity
Cash	**Short-Term Investments**				
+19	**−19**				

***(f)* Within the quarter, assume Chipotle paid $1 on the note payable in (*b*) above (ignore any interest on the loan in this chapter)**–a financing activity.

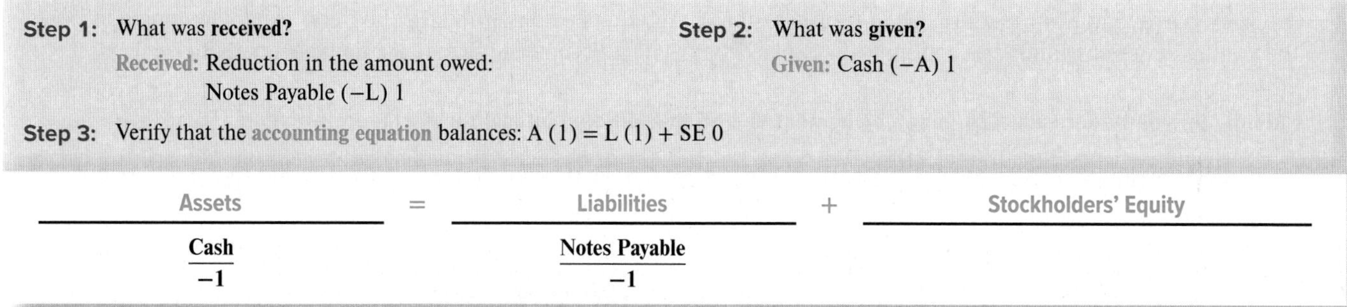

***(g)* Chipotle repurchased a portion of its issued common stock from investors for $103 cash**–a financing activity. When a company buys back its stock, it is accounted for in a new type of account called a **contra-account**. A contra-account reduces an account or section of a financial statement it is related to. In this case, the account is called **Treasury Stock** and it reduces total stockholders' equity. Treasury Stock accounting and reporting are discussed in more depth in Chapter 11.

Step 1: What was **received**?
Received: Reduction in stockholders' equity (the owners' claims to the company's assets):
Treasury Stock (−SE) 103

Step 2: What was **given**?
Given: Cash (−A) 103

Step 3: Verify that the accounting equation balances: A (103) = L 0 + SE (103)

Assets	=	Liabilities	+	Stockholders' Equity
Cash				**Treasury Stock**
−103				**−103**

(h) Chipotle does not pay dividends, but instead reinvests profits into growing the business. However, for illustration purposes, **assume Chipotle's board of directors declared that the Company will pay a total of $2 in cash as dividends to shareholders next quarter**. Dividends are a distribution of profits (from Retained Earnings) to shareholders. When cash dividends are declared, a liability, Dividends Payable, is created until the cash is distributed to shareholders. This is a financing activity, but it does not yet involve paying cash until next quarter.

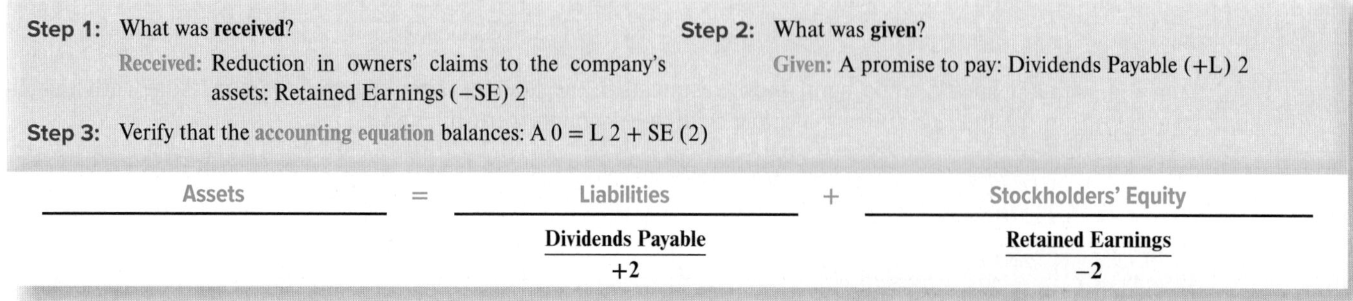

PAUSE FOR FEEDBACK

Transaction analysis involves identifying accounts affected in a transaction (by title), recognizing that at least two accounts are affected, classifying the accounts (asset, liability, or stockholders' equity), and determining the direction of the effect on the account (increase or decrease). If all accounts and effects are correct, then the fundamental accounting equation (A = L + SE) will remain in balance. **Practice is the most effective way to develop your transaction analysis skills.**

SELF-STUDY QUIZ

For the following transactions:

1. Analyze each using the three-step process in Exhibit 2.3 (what was received, what was given, and verify that the accounting equation balances). Including account names, direction of effects, type of accounts, and amounts.
2. Indicate the effects on the accounting equation in the chart below. Answer from the standpoint of the business.
   (a) Paul Knepper contributes $50,000 cash to establish Florida Flippers, Inc., a new scuba business organized as a corporation; in exchange, he receives 25,000 shares of common stock with a par value of $0.10 per share.
   (b) Florida Flippers buys a small building near the ocean for $250,000, paying $25,000 cash and signing a 10-year note payable for the rest.
   (c) Florida Flippers purchased $10,000 in short-term investments for $10,000 cash.

	Assets			=	Liabilities	+	Stockholders' Equity	
	Cash	Short-Term Investments	Building		Notes Payable		Common Stock	Additional Paid-in Capital
(a)								
(b)								
(c)								

After you have completed your answers, check them below. If your answers did not agree with ours, we recommend that you go back to each event to make sure that you have completed each of the steps of transaction analysis.

GUIDED HELP 2-1

For additional step-by-step video instruction on analyzing transaction effects, go to mhhe.com/libby_gh2-1.

Related Homework: M2-6, E2-4, E2-5, P2-2

Solutions to SELF-STUDY QUIZ

	Step 1: Received	Step 2: Given	Step 3: Accounting Equation
(a)	Cash (+A) 50,000	25,000 shares × $0.10 par value ↓ Common Stock (+SE) 2,500 and Additional Paid-in Capital (+SE) 47,500	A 50,000 = L 0 + SE 50,000
(b)	Building (+A) 250,000	Cash (−A) 25,000 and Notes Payable (+L) 225,000	A 225,000 = L 225,000 + SE 0
(c)	Short-term Investments (+A) 10,000	Cash (−A) 10,000	A 0 = L 0 + SE 0

	Assets			=	Liabilities	+	Stockholders' Equity	
	Cash	Short-Term Investments	Building		Notes Payable		Common Stock	Additional Paid-in Capital
(a)	+50,000						+2,500	+47,500
(b)	−25,000		+250,000		+225,000			
(c)	−10,000	+10,000						

LEARNING OBJECTIVE 2-4

Determine the impact of business transactions on the balance sheet using two basic tools: Journal entries and T-accounts.

HOW DO COMPANIES KEEP TRACK OF ACCOUNT BALANCES?

For most organizations, recording transaction effects and keeping track of account balances in the manner just presented is impractical. To handle the multitude of daily transactions that a business generates, companies establish accounting systems, usually computerized, that follow a cycle. Exhibit 2.4 presents the primary activities of the accounting cycle performed **during the accounting period** separately from those that occur at the **end of the accounting period**. In Chapters 2 and 3, we will illustrate hypothetical transactions **during Chipotle**'s **first quarter** of 2020 (following steps 1-3 in Exhibit 2.4). In Chapter 4, we will complete the accounting cycle by discussing and illustrating activities at the end of the period to adjust the records, prepare financial statements, and finally close the accounting records.

During the accounting period, transactions that result in exchanges between the company and external parties are first analyzed to determine the accounts and effects. The effects are then recorded in the **general journal**, a listing in chronological order of each transaction's effects. To determine account balances, the accounts are updated by posting the effects listed in the general journal to the respective accounts in the **general ledger**, a record of effects to and balances of each account.

Tip **As future business managers**, you should develop your understanding and use of these tools in financial analysis.

For those studying accounting, this knowledge is the foundation for an understanding of the accounting system and future accounting coursework.

These formal records are based on two very important tools used by accountants: **journal entries** and **T-accounts**. From the standpoint of accounting systems design, these analytical tools are a more efficient way to reflect the effects of transactions, determine account balances, and prepare financial statements. After we explain how to perform transaction analysis using these tools, we illustrate their use in financial analysis.

The Direction of Transaction Effects

As we saw earlier in this chapter, transaction effects increase and decrease assets, liabilities, and stockholders' equity accounts. To reflect these effects efficiently, we need to structure the transaction analysis model in a manner that shows the **direction** of the effects. As shown in Exhibit 2.5, each account is set up as a "T" with the following structure:

- **Increases in asset accounts are on the left** because assets are on the left side of the accounting equation (**A = L + SE**).
- **Increases in liability and stockholders' equity accounts are on the right** because they are on the right side of the accounting equation (**A = L + SE**).

Also notice that

- The term debit (dr for short) always refers to the **left** side of the T.
- The term credit (cr for short) always refers to the **right** side of the T.

EXHIBIT 2.4 The Accounting Cycle

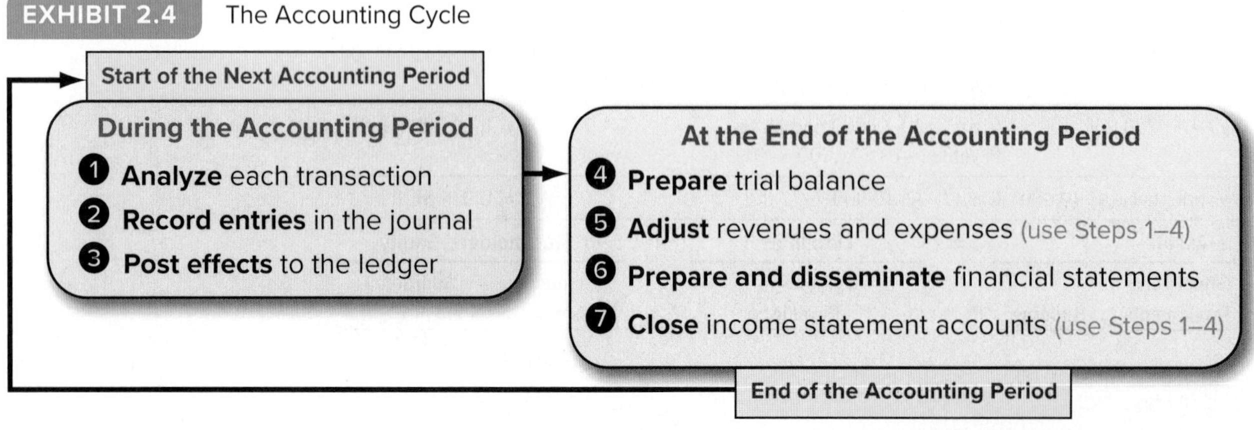

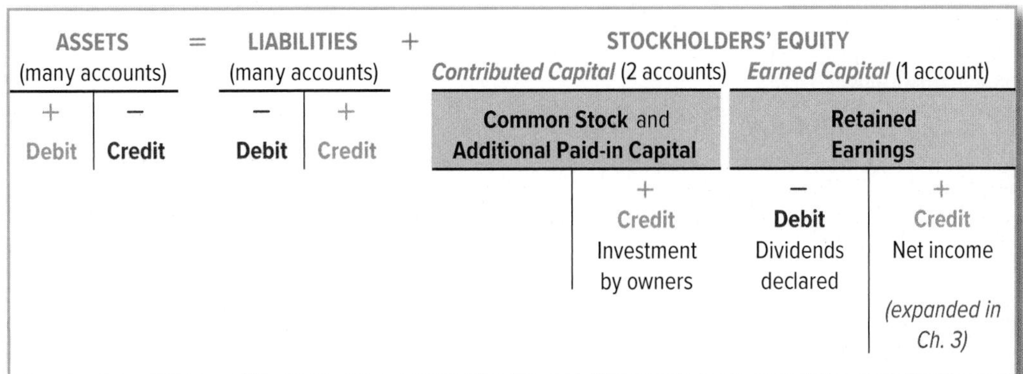

EXHIBIT 2.5

Basic Transaction Analysis Model

As a consequence:

- Asset accounts increase on the left (debit) side and normally have debit balances. It would be highly unusual for an asset account, such as Inventory, to have a negative (credit) balance.
- Liability and stockholders' equity accounts increase on the right (credit) side and normally have credit balances.

In summary:

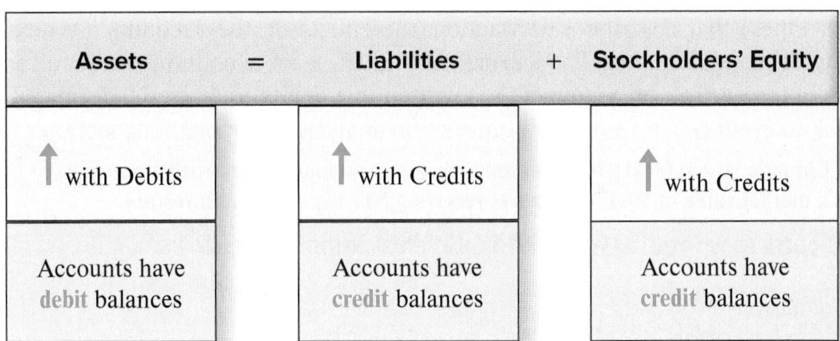

In Chapter 3, we will add revenue and expense account effects to Retained Earnings in our model. Until then, as you are learning to perform transaction analysis, **you should refer to the transaction analysis model in Exhibit 2.5 often until you can construct it on your own without assistance.**

Many students have trouble with accounting because they forget that the term **debit** is simply the **left** side of an account and the term **credit** is simply the **right** side of an account. Perhaps someone once told you that you were a credit to your school or your family. As a result, you may think that credits are good and debits are bad. Such is not the case. Just remember that **debit is on the left** and **credit is on the right.**

> **Tip** **Reminder:** Debit is on the left side and Credit is on the right side of a T-account. And that's it!

If you have identified the correct accounts and effects through transaction analysis, the accounting equation will remain in balance. **The total dollar value of all debits will equal the total dollar value of all credits** in a transaction. For an extra measure of assurance, add this equality check (Debits = Credits) to the transaction analysis process.

PAUSE FOR FEEDBACK

From Exhibit 2.5, we learned that each account can increase and decrease. In the transaction analysis model, the effect of a transaction on each element can be represented with a T with one side increasing and the other side decreasing. Asset accounts on the left side of the accounting equation increase their balances on the left side of the T. Liability and stockholders' equity accounts are on the right side of the accounting equation and increase their balances on the right side of the T. In accounting, the left side of the T is called the debit side and the right is called the credit side. Most accounts have a balance on the positive side.

SELF-STUDY QUIZ

The following is a list of accounts from a balance sheet of **The Wendy's Company**. Indicate on the line provided whether each of the following usually has a debit (DR) or credit (CR) balance.

(a) _____ Accounts Payable	*(d)* _____ Properties (land, buildings, and equipment)	*(g)* _____ Cash
(b) _____ Retained Earnings	*(e)* _____ Inventories	*(h)* _____ Long-Term Debt
(c) _____ Accrued Expenses Payable	*(f)* _____ Notes Receivable (due in five years)	*(i)* _____ Accounts Receivable

After you have completed your answers, check them below.

Related Homework: M2-7, M2-8, E2-3, P2-1

Tip When accountants look at a correct journal entry, they can tell you what the transaction was. You should be able to do this, too!

Analytical Tools

The Journal Entry

In an accounting system, transactions are recorded in chronological order in a **general journal** (or, simply, journal). After analyzing the business documents (such as purchase invoices, receipts, and cash register tapes) that describe a transaction, the effects on the accounts are recorded in the journal using debits and credits. The journal entry, then, is an accounting method for expressing the effects of a transaction on accounts. It is written in a debits-equal-credits format. To illustrate, we refer back to event (*a*) in **Chipotle**'s transaction analysis in the previous section.

***(a)* Assume Chipotle issued (sold) 100 additional shares of common stock with a par value of $0.01 per share at a market value of $0.17 per share, receiving $17 in cash from investors.**

The journal entry for event (*a*) in the Chipotle illustration is as follows:

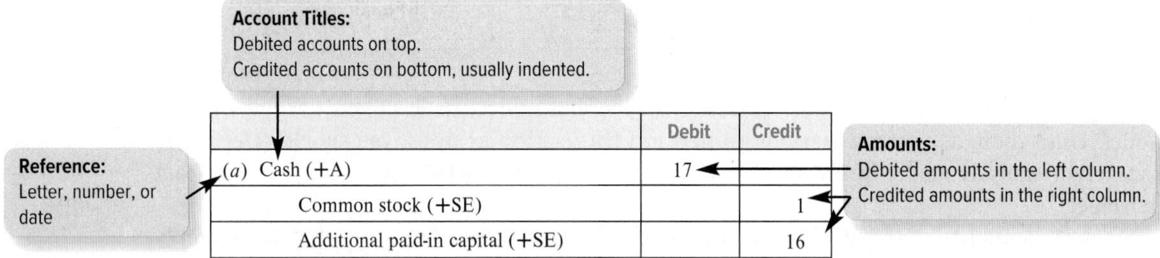

	Debit	Credit
(*a*) Cash (+A)	17	
Common stock (+SE)		1
Additional paid-in capital (+SE)		16

Notice the following:

- It is useful to include a date or some form of reference for each transaction. The debited accounts are written first (on top) with the amounts recorded in the left (debit) column. The credited accounts are written below the debits and are usually indented in manual records; the credited amounts are written in the right column. **The order of the debited accounts or credited accounts does not matter, as long as the debits are on top and the credits are on the bottom and indented to the right.**
- Dollar signs are not needed.
- Total debits ($17) equal total credits ($1 + $16 = $17).
- Three accounts are affected by this transaction. Any journal entry that affects more than two accounts is called a **compound entry.** Many transactions in this and subsequent chapters require a compound journal entry.

Tip The debited accounts (on top) represent what was received. The **credited** accounts (on bottom) represent what was **given**.

Solutions to SELF-STUDY QUIZ

(a) CR; *(b)* CR; *(c)* CR; *(d)* DR; *(e)* DR; *(f)* DR; *(g)* DR; *(h)* CR; *(i)* DR

- As you can see in the illustration of a formal bookkeeping system in Exhibit 2.6, an additional line is written below the journal entry as an explanation of the transaction. For simplicity, explanations will not be included in this text.

While you are learning to perform transaction analysis, use the symbols A, L, and SE next to each account title in journal entries, as is illustrated in the journal entry for event (*a*). Specifically identifying an account as an asset (A), a liability (L), or a stockholders' equity account (SE) clarifies the transaction analysis and makes journal entries easier to write. For example, if Cash is to be increased, we write Cash (+A). Throughout subsequent chapters, we include the direction of the effect along with the symbol to help you understand the effects of each transaction on the financial statements. By using the symbols in event (*a*), we can easily see that assets are affected by +$17 and stockholders' equity accounts are affected by +$17. The accounting equation A = L + SE remains in balance.

A note of caution: Many students try to memorize journal entries without understanding or using the transaction analysis model. As more detailed transactions are presented in subsequent chapters, the task becomes increasingly more difficult. In the long run, **memorizing, understanding, and using the transaction analysis model** presented here will save you time and prevent confusion.

Tip Memorize and use the transaction analysis model for all transactions.

The T-Account

By themselves, journal entries do not provide the balances in accounts. After the journal entries have been recorded, the dollar amounts to each account affected by the transaction are **posted** (transferred) to determine the new account balances. (In most computerized accounting systems, this happens automatically.)

As a group, the accounts are called a **general ledger.** In the manual accounting system used by some small businesses, the ledger is often a three-ring binder with a separate page for each account. In a computerized system, accounts are stored on the computer's memory or in the cloud. See Exhibit 2.6 for an illustration of a journal page and the related ledger pages. Note

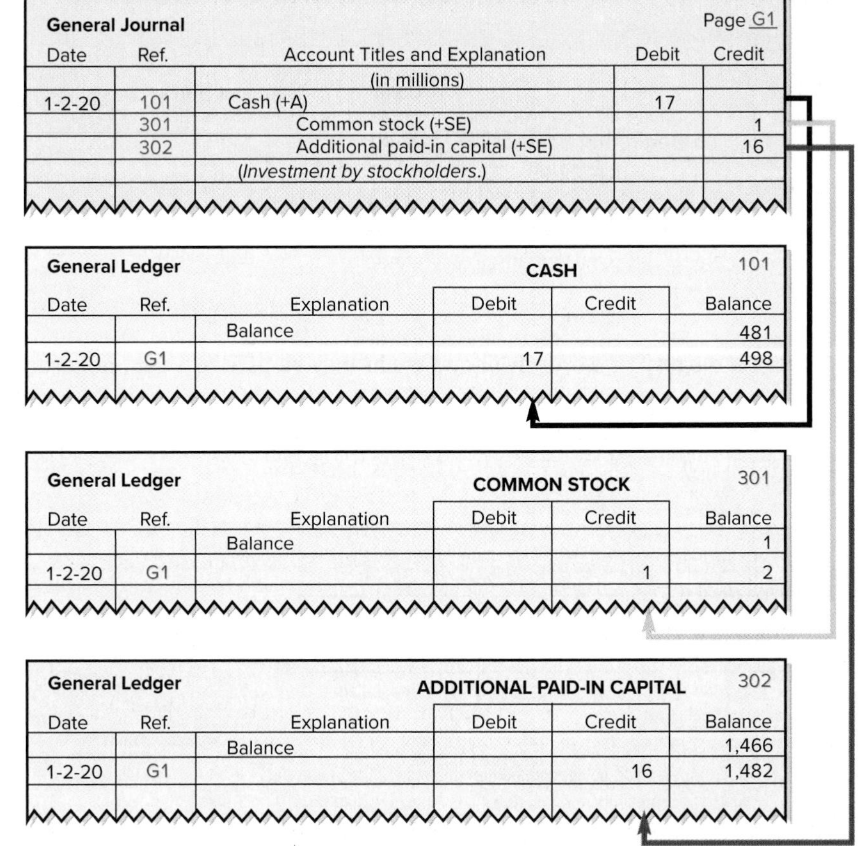

General Journal — Page G1

Date	Ref.	Account Titles and Explanation	Debit	Credit
		(in millions)		
1-2-20	101	Cash (+A)	17	
	301	Common stock (+SE)		1
	302	Additional paid-in capital (+SE)		16
		(Investment by stockholders.)		

General Ledger — CASH — 101

Date	Ref.	Explanation	Debit	Credit	Balance
		Balance			481
1-2-20	G1		17		498

General Ledger — COMMON STOCK — 301

Date	Ref.	Explanation	Debit	Credit	Balance
		Balance			1
1-2-20	G1			1	2

General Ledger — ADDITIONAL PAID-IN CAPITAL — 302

Date	Ref.	Explanation	Debit	Credit	Balance
		Balance			1,466
1-2-20	G1			16	1,482

EXHIBIT 2.6

Posting Transaction Effects from the Journal to the Ledger

that the debit amount of $17 to Cash from the journal entry for event (*a*) has been posted to the debit column on the Cash ledger page. Likewise, the credit amounts of $1 and $16 in the journal entry have been posted to the credit columns on the respective Common Stock and Additional Paid-in Capital ledger pages. Again, dollar signs are not needed.

One very useful tool for summarizing the transaction effects and determining the balances for individual accounts is a **T-account**, a simplified representation of a ledger account. Exhibit 2.7 shows the T-accounts for Chipotle's Cash and Common Stock accounts based on event (*a*) (the same would also be done for the Additional Paid-in Capital T-account). Notice the following:

- For Cash, which is classified as an asset, increases are shown on the left and decreases appear on the right side of the T-account. For Common Stock, however, increases are shown on the right and decreases on the left because Common Stock is a stockholders' equity account.
- Every T-account starts with a beginning balance.
- It is important to include the reference to the journal entry next to the debit or credit in each T-account. In our illustration, it is (*a*). For companies, it would be a date. This cross-referencing allows the transactions to be traced between the journal entries and T-accounts.
- When all of the transactions have been posted to a T-account, a horizontal line is drawn across it, similar to the line that is drawn in a mathematical problem, to signify that a balance is to be determined.
- An ending balance is written on the appropriate side of the T-account.

Some small businesses still use handwritten or manually maintained accounts in this T-account format. Computerized systems retain the concept but not the format of the T-account (that is, a positive number is written on the positive side of the T-account).

To find the account balances, we can express the T-accounts as equations:

	Cash	Common Stock
Beginning balance	$ 481	$ 1
+ "+" side	+ 17	+ 1
− "−" side	− 0	− 0
Ending balance	$ 498	$ 2

A word on terminology: The words **debit** and **credit** may be used as verbs, nouns, and adjectives. For example, we can say that Chipotle's Cash account was debited (verb) when stock was

EXHIBIT 2.7 T-Accounts Illustrated

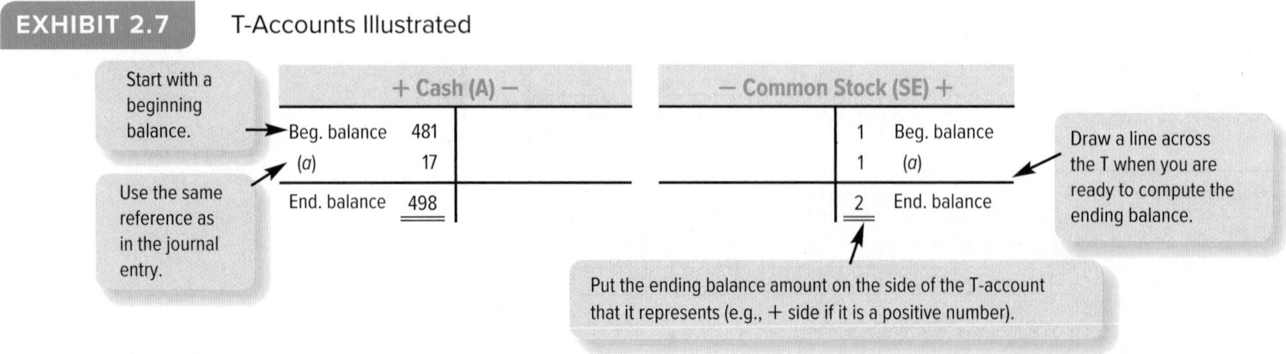

issued to investors, meaning that the amount was entered on the left side of the T-account. Or we can say that a credit (noun) was entered on the right side of an account. Common Stock may be described as a credit account (adjective). These terms will be used instead of **left** and **right** throughout the rest of this textbook. The next section illustrates the steps to follow in analyzing the effects of transactions, recording the effects in journal entries, and determining account balances using T-accounts.

FINANCIAL ANALYSIS

Inferring Business Activities from T-Accounts

T-accounts are useful primarily for instructional and analytical purposes. In many cases, we will use T-accounts to determine what transactions a company engaged in during a period. For example, the primary transactions affecting Accounts Payable for a period are purchases of assets on account from suppliers (increasing the account) and cash payments to suppliers (decreasing the account). If we know the beginning and ending balances of Accounts Payable and the amount of purchases on account (for credit) during a period, we can determine the amount of cash paid. A T-account analysis would include the following:

− Accounts Payable (L) +		
	600	Beg. bal.
Cash payments to suppliers?	1,500	Purchases on account
	300	End. bal.

Solution:

Beginning Balance	+	Purchases on Account	−	Cash Payments to Suppliers	=	Ending Balance
$600	+	$1,500	−	?	=	$ 300
				?	=	**$1,800**

Transaction Analysis Illustrated

In this section, we will use the hypothetical quarterly investing and financing transactions for **Chipotle Mexican Grill** (events [*a*] to [*h*]) that were analyzed earlier to demonstrate recording journal entries and posting effects to the relevant T-accounts. Note that the accounting equation remains in balance and that debits equal credits after each entry. In the T-accounts, the amounts from Chipotle's December 31, 2019, balance sheet (Exhibit 2.1) have been inserted as the beginning balances.

Tip **Don't memorize entries.** Instead, apply transaction analysis to determine journal entries and T-account effects . . . and **Practice! Practice! Practice!**

Study the following illustration carefully, including the explanations of transaction analysis. Careful study is **essential** to an understanding of (1) the accounting model, (2) transaction analysis, (3) the dual effects of each transaction, and (4) the system of balancing the debits and credits and the accounting equation for each transaction. The most effective way to learn these critical concepts, which are basic to material throughout the rest of the text, is to **practice, practice, practice.**

(a) **Assume Chipotle issued (sold) 100 additional shares of common stock with a par value of $0.01 per share at a market value of $0.17 per share, receiving $17 in cash from investors–**an financing activity. Common stock is recorded at par (100 shares × $0.01 par value per share) and Additional Paid-in Capital is recorded for the excess over par value (100 shares × $0.16 per share).

	Debit	Credit
(a) Cash (+A)	17	
Common stock (+SE)		1
Additional paid-in capital (+SE)		16

Assets		=	Liabilities		+	Stockholders' Equity	
Cash	+17					Common stock	+1
						Additional paid-in capital	+16

+ Cash (A) −

	Debit	Credit
1/1/20	481	
(a)	**17**	

− Common Stock (SE) +

Debit	Credit	
	1	1/1/20
	1	*(a)*

− Additional Paid-in Capital (SE) +

Debit	Credit	
	1,466	1/1/20
	16	*(a)*

The effects reflected in the journal entry have been posted to the appropriate T-accounts. Notice that if an account was debited such as Cash, that effect was written in the debit column of the Cash T-account. Similarly, if an account was credited such as Common Stock, that effect was written in the credit column of the T-account. Also notice that the January 1, 2020, beginning balances are the same as the ending balances at December 31, 2019 (see Exhibit 2.1), and are indicated on the respective positive side of the account—assets have debit balances and liabilities and stockholders' equity accounts have credit balances.

(b) **Chipotle borrowed $4 from its local bank, signing a note to be paid in three years (a noncurrent liability)**—a financing activity.

	Debit	Credit
(b) Cash (+A)	4	
Notes payable (+L)		4

Assets		=	Liabilities		+	Stockholders' Equity
Cash	+4		Notes payable	+4		

+ Cash (A) −

	Debit	Credit
1/1/20	481	
(a)	17	
(b)	**4**	

− Notes Payable (L) +

Debit	Credit	
	77	1/1/20
	4	***(b)***

(c) **Chipotle purchased for cash $26 in new equipment and $5 in additional intangible assets**—an investing activity.

	Debit	Credit
(c) Equipment (+A)	26	
Intangible assets (+A)	5	
Cash (− A)		31

Assets		=	Liabilities	+	Stockholders' Equity
Equipment	+26				
Intangible assets	+5				
Cash	-31				

+ Cash (A) −

	Debit	Credit	
1/1/20	481		
(a)	17	**31**	**(c)**
(b)	4		

+ Equipment (A) −

	Debit	Credit
1/1/20	836	
(c)	**26**	

+ Intangible Assets (A) −

	Debit	Credit
1/1/20	69	
(c)	**5**	

(d) **Chipotle acquired $20 in additional land and $40 in new buildings, signed leases for $86 for right-of-use (ROU) assets, paid $29 in cash, and signed $6 in current leases and $111 in long-term leases to rent facilities**—a financing activity.

	Debit	Credit
(d) Land (+A)	20	
Buildings (+A)	40	
Operating lease right-of-use assets (+A)	86	
Cash (−A)		29
Current lease liabilities (+L)		6
Long-term lease liabilities (+L)		111

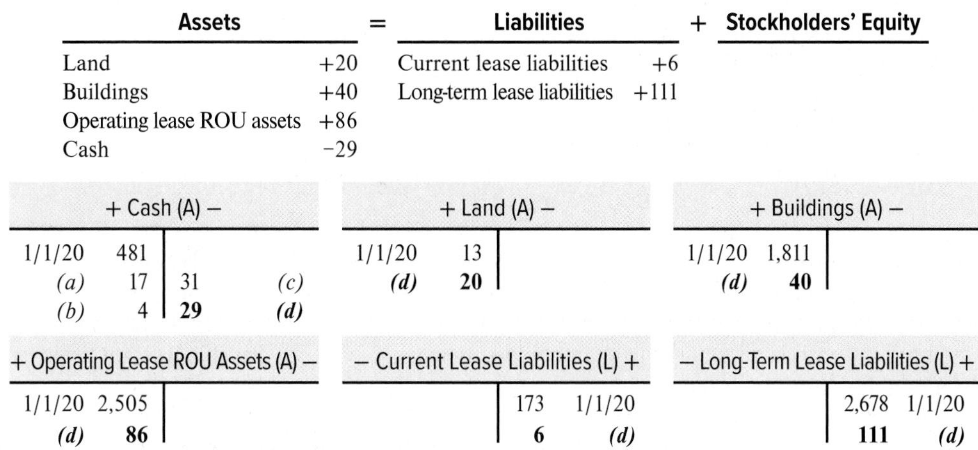

***(e)* Chipotle sold $19 in its short-term investments for $19 cash**—an investing activity.

	Debit	Credit
(e) Cash (+A)	19	
Short-term investments (−A)		19

Assets		=	Liabilities	+	Stockholders' Equity
Cash	+19				
Short-term investments	−19				

+ Cash (A) −

1/1/20	481		
(a)	17	31	*(c)*
(b)	4	29	*(d)*
(e)	**19**		

+ Short-Term Investments (A) −

1/1/20	400		
		19	***(e)***

***(f)* Within the quarter, assume Chipotle paid $1 on the note payable in *(b)* above (ignore any interest on the loan in this chapter)**—a financing activity.

	Debit	Credit
(f) Notes payable (−L)	1	
Cash (−A)		1

Assets		=	Liabilities		+	Stockholders' Equity
Cash	−1		Notes payable	−1		

+ Cash (A) −

1/1/20	481		
(a)	17	31	*(c)*
(b)	4	29	*(d)*
(e)	19	**1**	***(f)***

− Notes Payable (L) +

		77	1/1/20
(f)	**1**	4	*(b)*

***(g)* Chipotle repurchased a portion of its issued common stock from investors for $103 cash**—a financing activity. When a company buys back its stock, it is accounted for in a new type of account called a **contra-account.** A contra-account reduces an account or section of a financial statement it is related to. In this case, the account is called **Treasury Stock** and it reduces total stockholders' equity. Treasury Stock accounting and reporting are discussed in more depth in Chapter 11.

	Debit	Credit
(g) Treasury stock (−SE)	103	
Cash (−A)		103

Assets		=	Liabilities	+	Stockholders' Equity	
Cash	−103				Treasury Stock	−103

Tip **Reminder:** Debiting Treasury Stock increases the account, but it has a negative effect on stockholders' equity.

+ Cash (A) –			
1/1/20	481		
(a)	17	31	*(c)*
(b)	4	29	*(d)*
(e)	19	1	*(f)*
		103	*(g)*

+ Treasury Stock (SE) –			
1/1/20	2,699		
(g)	**103**		

(h) Chipotle does not pay dividends, but instead reinvests profits into growing the business. However, for illustration purposes, **assume Chipotle's board of directors declared that the Company will pay a total of $2 in cash as dividends to shareholders next quarter.** Dividends are a distribution of profits (from Retained Earnings) to shareholders. When cash dividends are declared, a liability is created until the cash is distributed to shareholders. Because Dividends Payable was not listed on the December 31, 2019, balance sheet (see Exhibit 2.1), it has a $0 balance on January 1, 2020.

	Debit	Credit
(h) Retained earnings (–SE)	2	
Dividends payable (+L)		2

Assets	=	Liabilities		+	Stockholders' Equity	
		Dividends payable	+2		Retained earnings	–2

– Dividends Payable (L) +			
		0	1/1/20
		2	*(h)*

– Retained Earnings (SE) +			
		2,916	1/1/20
(h)	**2**		

Now we can **determine the balances in the T-accounts that changed** during the quarter based on the hypothetical transactions. As shown in Exhibit 2.8, each T-account is listed with the beginning balances and transaction effects with references. Then a line is drawn across the T-account after the last transaction effect with the balance indicated below the summation line on the positive side.

EXHIBIT 2.8

T-Accounts

+ Cash (A) –			
1/1/20	481		
(a)	17	31	*(c)*
(b)	4	29	*(d)*
(e)	19	1	*(f)*
		103	*(g)*
	357		

+ Short-Term Investments (A) –			
1/1/20	400		
		19	*(e)*
	381		

+ Land (A) –			
1/1/20	13		
(d)	20		
	33		

+ Buildings (A) –			
1/1/20	1,811		
(d)	40		
	1,851		

+ Equipment (A) –			
1/1/20	836		
(c)	26		
	862		

+ Operating Lease ROU Assets (A) –			
1/1/20	2,505		
(d)	86		
	2,591		

+ Intangible Assets (A) –			
1/1/20	69		
(c)	5		
	74		

– Dividends Payable (L) +			
		0	1/1/20
		2	*(h)*
		2	

– Current Lease Liabilities (L) +			
		173	1/1/20
		6	*(d)*
		179	

– Notes Payable (L) +			
		77	1/1/20
(f)	1	4	*(b)*
		80	

– Long-Term Lease Liabilities (L) +			
		2,678	1/1/20
		111	*(d)*
		2,789	

– Common Stock (SE) +			
		1	1/1/20
		1	*(a)*
		2	

– Additional Paid-in Capital (SE) +			
		1,466	1/1/20
		16	*(a)*
		1,482	

+ Treasury Stock (SE) –			
1/1/20	2,699		
(g)	103		
	2,802		

– Retained Earnings (SE) +			
		2,916	1/1/20
(h)	2		
		2,914	

PAUSE FOR FEEDBACK

Accountants analyze and then record transactions in the general journal in chronological order in journal entry form. Debited accounts are written on top with amounts in the left column and credited accounts are written on the bottom with amounts in the right column. Then the effects are posted in the general ledger (similar to a T-account). Each page of the ledger represents a different account that has a debit (left) side and a credit (right) side. To post transaction effects, the amount for each account in a journal entry is written in the appropriate debit or credit column on the ledger page to obtain account balances. Refer to Exhibit 2.5 for the transaction analysis model.

SELF-STUDY QUIZ

Record the following transactions in good journal entry form and post the effects to the T-accounts. Because this is a new company, all T-accounts start with a beginning balance of $0.

(a) Paul Knepper contributes $50,000 cash to establish Florida Flippers, Inc., a new scuba business organized as a corporation; he receives in exchange 25,000 shares of stock with a $0.10 per share par value.
(b) Florida Flippers buys a small building near the ocean for $250,000, paying $25,000 in cash and signing a 10-year note payable for the rest.
(c) Florida Flippers purchased $10,000 in short-term investments for $10,000 cash.

After you have completed your answers, check them below.

GUIDED HELP 2-2

For additional step-by-step video instruction on analyzing, recording, and posting transaction effects and classifying accounts, go to mhhe.com/libby_gh2-2.

Related Homework: M2-9, M2-10, E2-6, E2-7, E2-8, E2-9, E2-10, E2-13, E2-14, E2-15, E2-16, P2-3, P2-5, CON2-1

Solutions to SELF-STUDY QUIZ

	Account	Debit	Credit	
(a)	Cash (+A)	50,000		
	Common stock (+SE)		2,500	[25,000 shares × $0.10 par]
	Additional paid-in capital (+SE)		47,500	
(b)	Buildings (+A)	250,000		
	Cash (−A)		25,000	
	Notes payable (+L)		225,000	
(c)	Short-term investments (+A)	10,000		
	Cash (−A)		10,000	

+ Cash −

	Debit	Credit	
Beg.	0		
(a)	50,000	25,000	*(b)*
		10,000	*(c)*
	15,000		

+ Short-Term Investments −

	Debit	Credit
Beg.	0	
(c)	10,000	
	10,000	

+ Buildings −

	Debit	Credit
Beg.	0	
(b)	250,000	
	250,000	

− Notes Payable +

Debit	Credit	
	0	Beg.
	225,000	*(b)*
	225,000	

− Common Stock +

Debit	Credit	
	0	Beg.
	2,500	*(a)*
	2,500	

− Additional Paid-in Capital +

Debit	Credit	
	0	Beg.
	47,500	*(a)*
	47,500	

DATA ANALYTICS

Using Data Analytics for Business Expansion

Data Analytics (also called Business Intelligence and Big Data) has exploded in the past several years, but what is it? SAS (a world leader in business analytics software and services) describes it as follows:

> Big data analytics examines large amounts of data to uncover hidden patterns, correlations and other insights. With today's technology, it's possible to analyze your data and get answers from it almost immediately. . . .[2]

By collecting structured data from various sources inside the business (from accounting, human resources, supply chain, and sales) and unstructured data from outside the business (from social media, customers, and weather and traffic patterns), companies worldwide are now making more data-driven business decisions. These decisions can be aimed at decreasing costs, identifying new innovative opportunities, launching new products and services, and transforming the business for the future.

Beginning in 2017, **Chipotle** increased its investment in technological innovations, such as digital/mobile ordering, which provides more information about its customers. Chipotle also uses data analytics for new restaurant site selection. The company gathers demographic and business information about each area, as well as information on competitors and other restaurants, and uses a predictive model to project sales and return on investment for each potential restaurant site. Chipotle, like most companies, understands the importance of creating a data-driven culture to change the way it thinks.

What does this shift to a data-driven culture mean for students? Competition for talented individuals with strong analytical skills is extreme. Zoher Karu, vice president, global customer optimization and data at **eBay**, stated it this way:

> Talent is critical along any data and analytics journey. And analytics talent by itself is no longer sufficient, in my opinion. We cannot have people with singular skills. And the way I build out my organization is I look for people with a major and a minor. You can major in analytics, but you can minor in marketing strategy. Because if you don't have a minor, how are you going to communicate with other parts of the organization? Otherwise, the pure data scientist will not be able to talk to the database administrator, who will not be able to talk to the market-research person, who which [sic] will not be able to talk to the email-channel owner, for example. You need to make sound business decisions, based on analytics, that can scale.[3]

LEARNING OBJECTIVE 2-5

Prepare a trial balance and simple classified balance sheet and analyze the company using the current ratio.

HOW IS THE BALANCE SHEET PREPARED AND ANALYZED?

Although no operating activities occurred yet (they will be illustrated in Chapter 3), it is possible to create a balance sheet based solely on the investing and financing activities recorded previously. Usually, businesses first will create a **trial balance** spreadsheet for internal purposes before preparing statements for external users. A trial balance lists the names of the T-accounts in one column, usually in financial statement order (assets, liabilities, stockholders' equity, revenues, and expenses), with their ending debit or credit balances in the next two columns. Debit balances are indicated in the left column and credit balances are indicated in the right column. Then the two columns are totaled **to provide a check on the equality of the debits and credits**. Errors in a computer-generated trial balance may exist if wrong accounts and/or amounts are used in the journal entries.[4]

---

[2]Source: sas.com/en_us/insights/analytics/big-data-analytics.html#

[3]Quoted in "How companies are using big data and analytics." Interview, April 2016. McKinsey & Company. mckinsey.com/business-functions/mckinsey-analytics/our-insights/how-companies-are-using-big-data-and-analytics

[4]In homework assignments, if you have an error in your trial balance (the two column totals are not equal), errors can be traced and should be corrected before adjusting the records. To find errors, reverse your steps. Check that:

- You copied the ending balances in all of the T-accounts (both amount and whether a debit or credit) correctly to the trial balance.
- You computed the ending balances in the T-accounts correctly.
- You posted the transaction effects correctly from the journal entries to the T-accounts (amount, account, and whether a debit or credit).
- You prepared the journal entries correctly (amount, account, and whether a debit or credit).

File Home Insert Page Layout Formulas Data Review View Help

L22

	A	B	C	D	E
1		**CHIPOTLE MEXICAN GRILL -- TRIAL BALANCE**			
2		**March 31, 2020**			
3			**Debit**	**Credit**	
4		Cash	357		*
5		Short-term investments	381		*
6		Accounts receivable	81		
7		Supplies	26		
8		Prepaid expenses	85		
9		Land	33		*
10		Buildings and leased assets	1,851		*
11		Equipment	862		*
12		Accumulated depreciation		1,201	
13		Operating lease right-of-use assets	2,591		*
14		Intangible assets	74		*
15		Accounts payable		116	
16		Unearned revenue		95	
17		Wages payable		127	
18		Utilities payable		156	
19		Dividends payable		2	*
20		Current lease liabilities		179	*
21		Notes payable		80	*
22		Long-term lease liabilities		2,789	*
23		Common stock		2	*
24		Additional paid-in capital		1,482	*
25		Treasury stock	2,802		*
26		Retained earnings		2,914	*
27					
28		**Total**	**9,143**	**9,143**	← Debits = Credits!
29					
30	*	**Balance changed due to hypothetical investing and financing**			
31		**transactions during the first quarter of 2020.**			

Microsoft Corporation

Chipotle's trial balance based on hypothetical quarterly transactions follows. The account balances that did not change are taken from the December 31, 2019, balance sheet in Exhibit 2.1. The accounts that did change due to the transactions illustrated in this chapter are noted with an asterisk (*); their balances are taken from the T-accounts in Exhibit 2.8.

Classified Balance Sheet

The balance sheet in Exhibit 2.9 was prepared from the trial balance shown above based on hypothetical quarterly transactions. As a formal statement for external users, it needs a good

EXHIBIT 2.9

Chipotle Mexican Grill's First Quarter 2020 Balance Sheet (based on hypothetical investing and financing activities)

CHIPOTLE MEXICAN GRILL, INC.
Consolidated Balance Sheets*
(in millions of dollars, except per share data)

	March 31, 2020	December 31, 2019
ASSETS		
Current Assets:		
Cash	$ 357	$ 481
Short-term investments	381	400
Accounts receivable	81	81
Supplies	26	26
Prepaid expenses	85	85
Total current assets	930	1,073
Property and Equipment:		
Land	33	13
Buildings	1,851	1,811
Equipment	862	836
Total cost	2,746	2,660
Accumulated depreciation	(1,201)	(1,201)
Net property and equipment	1,545	1,459
Operating lease right-of-use assets	2,591	2,505
Intangible assets	74	69
Total assets	**$5,140**	**$5,106**
LIABILITIES AND STOCKHOLDERS' EQUITY		
Current Liabilities:		
Accounts payable	$ 116	$ 116
Unearned revenue	95	95
Accrued expenses payable:		
Wages payable	127	127
Utilities payable	156	156
Dividends payable	2	
Current lease liabilities	179	173
Total current liabilities	675	667
Notes payable	80	77
Long-term lease liabilities	2,789	2,678
Total liabilities	3,544	3,422
Stockholders' Equity:		
Common stock ($0.01 par value per share)	2	1
Additional paid-in capital	1,482	1,466
Treasury stock	(2,802)	(2,699)
Retained earnings	2,914	2,916
Total stockholders' equity	1,596	1,684
Total liabilities and stockholders' equity	**$5,140**	**$5,106**

*Reflects simplified December 31, 2019, figures and hypothetical March 31, 2020, information.

heading (name of the company, title of the statement, date, and if the dollars are in thousands or millions). Notice in Exhibit 2.9 several additional features:

- The assets and liabilities are **classified** into two categories: **current** and **noncurrent**. Current assets are those to be used or turned into cash within the upcoming year, whereas noncurrent assets are those that will last longer than one year. Current liabilities are those obligations to be paid or settled within the next 12 months with current assets.
- Dollar signs are indicated at the top and bottom of the asset section and top and bottom of the liabilities and shareholders' equity section. More than that tends to look messy.
- The statement includes **comparative data**. That is, it compares the actual but simplified account balances at December 31, 2019, with those at March 31, 2020, based on assumed quarterly transactions. When multiple periods are presented, the most recent balance sheet amounts are usually listed on the left, but not always (look carefully).
- Unlike **Chipotle**, most companies do not provide a total liabilities line on the balance sheet. To determine total liabilities on those statements, add total current liabilities and each of the noncurrent liabilities.

INTERNATIONAL PERSPECTIVE

Understanding Foreign Financial Statements

Although IFRS (International Financial Reporting Standards) differ from U.S. GAAP (Generally Accepted Accounting Principles), it uses the same system of analyzing, recording, and summarizing the results of business activities that you have learned in this chapter. One place where IFRS differs from GAAP is in the formatting of financial statements.

Financial statements prepared using GAAP and IFRS include the same elements (assets, liabilities, revenues, expenses, etc.). However, a single, consistent format has not been mandated. Consequently, various formats have evolved over time, with those in the United States differing from those typically used internationally. The formatting differences include

	GAAP	IFRS
Balance Sheet Order	**Assets:**	**Assets:**
Similar accounts are	Current	Noncurrent
shown, but the order of	Noncurrent	Current
liquidity (for assets) and	**Liabilities:**	**Stockholders' Equity**
the order of maturity (for	Current	**Liabilities:**
liabilities) differ	Noncurrent	Noncurrent
	Stockholders' Equity	Current

On the balance sheet, GAAP begins with current items, whereas IFRS begins with noncurrent items. Consistent with this, **assets are listed in decreasing order of liquidity under GAAP, but, internationally, assets are usually listed in increasing order of liquidity.** IFRS similarly emphasizes longer-term financing sources by listing equity before liabilities and, within liabilities, by listing noncurrent liabilities before current liabilities (**decreasing time to maturity**). The key to avoiding confusion is to be sure to **pay attention to the subheadings** in the statement. Any account under the heading "liabilities" must be a liability.

Ratio Analysis in Decision Making

Why do the classifications of current and noncurrent on the balance sheet matter? Users of financial information compute a number of ratios in analyzing a company's past performance and financial condition as input in predicting its future potential. How ratios change over time and how they compare to the ratios of the company's competitors or industry averages provide valuable information about a company's strategies for its operating, investing, and financing activities. We introduce here the first of many ratios that will be presented throughout the rest of this textbook, with a final summary of ratio analysis in Chapter 13.

KEY RATIO ANALYSIS

Current Ratio

ANALYTICAL QUESTION

Does the company have the short-term resources to pay its short-term obligations?

RATIO AND COMPARISONS

$$\textbf{Current Ratio} = \frac{\textbf{Current Assets}}{\textbf{Current Liabilities}}$$

The 2019 ratio for **Chipotle** is (dollars in millions):

$$\frac{\$1,073}{\$667} = 1.609$$

COMPARISONS OVER TIME		
Chipotle Mexican Grill, Inc.		
2017	**2018**	**2019**
1.944	1.811	1.609

COMPARISONS WITH COMPETITORS	
El Pollo Loco Holdings, Inc.	Shake Shack, Inc.
2019	**2019**
0.334	0.882
Offers Mexican-inspired grilled chicken and entrees	Offers a classic American menu of premium burgers, hot dogs, crispy chicken, crinkle cut fries, shakes, and more

INTERPRETATIONS

In General

The current ratio is a very common ratio. Creditors and security analysts use the current ratio **to measure the ability of the company to pay its short-term obligations with short-term assets.** Generally, the higher the ratio, the more cushion a company has to pay its current obligations if future economic conditions take a downturn. Many industries, such as retail companies and manufacturers, historically face difficult times with sustained dips in the economy. They often have a current ratio at 2.0 (twice as many current economic resources as current obligations) or higher to be able to pay employees, suppliers, and other current obligations until the economy recovers.

While a ratio above 1.0 normally suggests good liquidity, today, many strong companies use sophisticated management techniques to minimize funds invested in current assets and, as a result, have current ratios below 1.0. Many businesses with strong inflows of cash from customers, like Chipotle and its competitors, also may have a current ratio below 1.0. Likewise, when compared to others in the industry, too high of a ratio may suggest inefficient use of resources.

Focus Company Analysis

Over time, the current ratio for Chipotle shows a high level of liquidity of 1.609, although the ratio has decreased each year since 2017. In 2019, nearly half of its current assets was in cash, which the company uses to fund its rapid growth strategy of opening or renovating over 130 new restaurants annually, many with Chipotlanes for drive-through service.

Compared with competitors in the fast-casual restaurant industry, Chipotle reports a much higher current ratio than Shake Shack and El Pollo Loco. Shake Shack operates over 275 restaurants worldwide, all company owned. Its strategy is to open a significant portion of new stores in airports. The approximately 480 El Pollo Loco restaurants are located primarily in the southwest United States and are approximately 40 percent company-owned and 60 percent franchised. El Pollo Loco's plans are to grow its loyalty program and expand franchising opportunities. Franchising does not typically require the higher cash flow levels needed for expanding company-owned facilities. Companies in the restaurant industry tend to have high cash inflows from customers as well as sophisticated cash management systems that enable them to maintain lower cash balances, and thus lower current ratios.

Selected Focus Companies' Current Ratios

Company	Current Ratio
Skechers	2.28
Harley-Davidson	1.31
FedEx	1.58

A Few Cautions

The current ratio may be a misleading measure of liquidity if significant funds are tied up in assets that cannot be easily converted into cash. A company with a high current ratio still might have liquidity problems if the majority of its current assets consists of slow-moving inventory. Analysts also recognize that managers can manipulate the current ratio by engaging in certain transactions just before the close of the fiscal year. In most cases, for example, the current ratio can be improved by paying creditors immediately prior to the preparation of financial statements.

PAUSE FOR FEEDBACK

We just learned that the current ratio measures a company's ability to pay short-term obligations with short-term assets–a liquidity measure. It is computed by dividing current assets by current liabilities. A ratio above 1.0 is normally considered good, although some may need a higher ratio and others with good cash management systems and/or strong cash flows can have a ratio below 1.0 (i.e., more current liabilities than current assets).

SELF-STUDY QUIZ

Yum! Brands, Inc., is the world's largest quick-service restaurant company that develops, franchises, and operates over 50,000 units in more than 150 countries and territories through three restaurant concepts (KFC, Pizza Hut, and Taco Bell). The company reported the following balances on its recent balance sheets (in millions). Compute Yum! Brands' current ratio for the three years presented. Round your answers to three decimal places.

(dollars in millions)	CURRENT ASSETS	CURRENT LIABILITIES
2019	$1,527	$1,541
2018	1,207	1,301
2017	2,507	1,512

What do these results suggest about Yum! Brands' liquidity in the current year and over time?

After you have completed your answers, check them on the next page.

GUIDED HELP 2-3

For additional step-by-step video instruction on computing and interpreting the current ratio, go to mhhe.com/libby_gh2-3.

Related Homework: M2-12, E2-16

FOCUS ON CASH FLOWS

LEARNING OBJECTIVE 2-6

Identify investing and financing transactions and demonstrate how they impact cash flows.

Investing and Financing Activities

As discussed in Chapter 1, companies report cash inflows and outflows over a period in their **statement of cash flows,** which is divided into three categories: operating, investing, and financing activities:

- Operating activities are covered in Chapter 3.
- Investing activities include buying and selling noncurrent assets and short- and long-term investments.
- Financing activities include borrowing and repaying debt, including short-term bank loans; issuing and repurchasing stock; and paying dividends.

Tip You must see CASH in the transaction for it to affect the statement of cash flows.

Only transactions affecting cash are reported on the statement. An important step in constructing and analyzing the statement of cash flows is identifying the various transactions as operating (**O**), investing (**I**), or financing (**F**). Let's analyze the Cash T-account for **Chipotle**'s transactions in this chapter. Refer to transactions *(a)*-*(h)* illustrated earlier in this chapter.

			+ Cash (A) –				
		1/1/20	481				
From investors	+F	*(a)*	17	31	*(c)*	−I	**For noncurrent assets**
From the bank	+F	*(b)*	4	29	*(d)*	−I	**For noncurrent assets**
From sale of investments	+I	*(e)*	19	1	*(f)*	−F	**To repay notes payable to the bank**
				103	*(g)*	−F	**To repurchase common stock**
			357				

PAUSE FOR FEEDBACK

As we discussed, every transaction affecting cash can be classified as an operating (discussed in Chapter 3), investing, or financing effect. Investing effects relate to purchasing/selling investments or noncurrent assets such as property and equipment or lending funds to/receiving repayment from others. Financing effects relate to borrowing or repaying banks, issuing stock to investors, repurchasing stock from investors, or paying dividends to investors.

SELF-STUDY QUIZ

Indicate whether the following transactions from a recent annual statement of cash flows for **Apple Inc.** were investing (I) or financing (F) activities and the direction of their effects on cash (+ for increases; – for decreases):

Solutions to SELF-STUDY QUIZ

Current Ratio:

2019	$1,527	÷	$1,541	=	0.991
2018	1,207	÷	1,301	=	0.928
2017	2,507	÷	1,512	=	1.658

Yum! Brands' most recent current ratio hovers near 1.0, although it has fluctuated over the past three years. The 0.991 ratio suggests that the company currently has sufficient current assets to settle short-term obligations. There is no concern about liquidity because Yum! Brands is a cash-oriented business and maintains a strong cash management system.

Transactions	Type Of Activity (I Or F)	Effect On Cash Flows (+ Or −)
1. Purchased investments	______	______
2. Issued common stock	______	______
3. Acquired property, plant, and equipment	______	______
4. Sold investments	______	______
5. Purchased intangible assets (e.g., patents)	______	______

After you have completed your answers, check them below.

Related Homework: M2-14, E2-19, E2-20, P2-4, CON2-1

DEMONSTRATION CASE

On April 1, 2023, three ambitious college students started Terrific Lawn Maintenance Corporation. A summary of transactions completed through April 7, 2023, for Terrific Lawn Maintenance Corporation follows:

a. To each of the three investors, issued 500 shares of stock (1,500 shares in total) with a par value of $0.10 per share in exchange for a total of $9,000 cash.

b. Acquired rakes and other hand tools (equipment) with a list price of $690 for $600; paid the hardware store $200 cash and signed a three-month note for the balance.

c. Ordered three lawn mowers and two edgers from XYZ Lawn Supply, Inc., for $4,000.

d. Purchased four acres of land for the future site of a storage garage; paid cash, $5,000.

e. Received the mowers and edgers that had been ordered, signing a note to pay XYZ Lawn Supply in full in 18 months.

f. Sold for $1,250 one acre of land to the city for a park. Accepted a note from the city for payment by the end of the month.

g. One of the owners borrowed $3,000 from a local bank for personal use.

Required:

1. Set up T-accounts for Cash, Notes Receivable (from the city), Equipment (hand tools and mowing equipment), Land, Short-Term Notes Payable (to the hardware store), Long-Term Notes Payable (to the equipment supply company), Common Stock, and Additional Paid-in Capital. Beginning balances are $0; indicate these beginning balances in the T-accounts. Analyze each transaction using the transaction analysis model and the process outlined in the chapter and prepare journal entries in chronological order. Enter the effects of the transactions in the appropriate T-accounts; identify each amount with its letter in the preceding list. Compute ending balances for each T-account.

ASSETS = LIABILITIES + STOCKHOLDERS' EQUITY

ASSETS (many accounts)		LIABILITIES (many accounts)		Contributed Capital (2 accounts): Common Stock and Additional Paid-in Capital		Earned Capital (1 account): Retained Earnings	
+ Debit	− Credit	− Debit	+ Credit	−	+ Credit	+ Debit	+ Credit
					Investment by owners	Dividends declared	Netcome *(expanded in Ch. 3)*

1. I− 2. F+ 3. I− 4. I+ 5. I−

Solutions to SELF-STUDY QUIZ

2. Use the balances in the T-accounts developed in the previous requirement to prepare a classified balance sheet for Terrific Lawn Maintenance Corporation at April 7, 2023.
3. Identify transactions (*a*)–(*g*) as investing or financing activities affecting cash flows and the direction of each effect. Use +I for investing inflow, −I for investing outflow, +F for financing inflow, and −F for financing outflow.

   Check your answers with the solution in the following section.

SUGGESTED SOLUTION

1. Transaction Analysis:

Received:	Given:
a. Cash (+A) $9,000	Common Stock (+SE) $150 *(1,500 shares × $0.10 par value per share)* Additional Paid-in Capital (+SE) $8,850 *($9,000 − $150)*
b. Equipment (+A) $600	Cash (−A) $200 Short-Term Notes Payable (+L) $400
c. Not a transaction–a promise to pay for a promise to deliver from the supplier	
d. Land (+A) $5,000	Cash (−A) $5,000
e. Equipment (+A) $4,000	Long-Term Notes Payable (+L) $4,000
f. Notes Receivable (+A) $1,250	Land (−A) $1,250 *(1/4 of the $5,000 cost of the land)*
g. Not a transaction of the business–separate-entity assumption	

Journal Entries	Debit	Credit
(a) Cash (+A)	9,000	
Common stock (+SE)		150
Additional paid-in capital (+SE)		8,850
(b) Equipment (+A)	600	
Cash (−A)		200
Short-term notes payable (+L)		400
(c) No transaction		
(d) Land (+A)	5,000	
Cash (−A)		5,000
(e) Equipment (+A)	4,000	
Long-term notes payable (+L)		4,000
(f) Notes receivable (+A)	1,250	
Land (−A)		1,250
(g) No transaction		

Equality Checks:
All debits = credits
Each equation balances

	A	=	L	+	SE
(a)	+9,000				+9,000
(b)	+400		+400		
(d)	+/−5,000				
(e)	+4,000		+4,000		
(f)	+/−1,250				

T-Accounts:

+ Cash (A) –			
4/1/23	0		
(a)	9,000	200	*(b)*
		5,000	*(d)*
	3,800		

+ Notes Receivable (A) –		
4/1/23	0	
(f)	1,250	
	1,250	

+ Equipment (A) –		
4/1/23	0	
(b)	600	
(e)	4,000	
	4,600	

+ Land (A) –			
4/1/23	0		
(d)	5,000	1,250	*(f)*
	3,750		

– Short-Term Notes Payable (L) +		
	0	4/1/23
	400	*(b)*
	400	

– Long-Term Notes Payable (L) +		
	0	4/1/23
	4,000	*(e)*
	4,000	

– Common Stock (SE) +		
	0	4/1/23
	150	*(a)*
	150	

– Additional Paid-in Capital (SE) +		
	0	4/1/23
	8,850	*(a)*
	8,850	

2. Classified Balance Sheet:

TERRIFIC LAWN MAINTENANCE CORPORATION
Balance Sheet
April 7, 2023

Assets	
Current Assets:	
Cash	$ 3,800
Notes receivable	1,250
Total current assets	5,050
Equipment	4,600
Land	3,750
Total assets	**$13,400**
Liabilities and Stockholders' Equity	
Current Liabilities:	
Short-term notes payable	$ 400
Total current liabilities	400
Long-term notes payable	4,000
Total liabilities	4,400
Stockholders' Equity:	
Common stock ($0.10 par)	150
Additional paid-in capital	8,850
Total stockholders' equity	9,000
Total liabilities and stockholders' equity	**$13,400**

3. Cash Flows:

+ Cash (A) –			
4/1/23 0			
(a) 9,000		200	*(b)*
		5,000	*(d)*
3,800			

Only transactions *(a)*, *(b)*, and *(d)* affect cash flows (as shown in the Cash T-account).

(a) +F for $9,000

(b) –I for $200

(d) –I for $5,000

CHAPTER TAKE-AWAYS

2-1. Define the key accounting assumptions, principles, and elements related to the balance sheet. **p. 47**

Assumptions:

- Separate entity assumption–Transactions of the business are accounted for separately from transactions of the owner.
- Going concern assumption–A business is expected to continue to operate into the foreseeable future.
- Monetary unit assumption–Financial information is reported in the national monetary unit without adjustment for changes in purchasing power.

Principles:

- Historical cost principle–Financial statement elements should be recorded at the cash-equivalent cost on the date of the transaction; however, these values may be adjusted to other amounts, such as market value, depending on certain conditions.

Elements of the balance sheet:

- Assets–Economic resources owned or controlled by a company; they have measurable value and are expected to benefit the company by producing cash inflows or reducing cash outflows in the future.
- Liabilities–Measurable obligations resulting from a past transaction; they are expected to be settled in the future by transferring assets or providing services.
- Stockholders' equity–Residual interest of owners in the assets of the entity after settling liabilities; the financing provided by the owners (contributed capital) and by business operations (earned capital).

2-2. Identify what constitutes a business transaction and recognize common balance sheet account titles used in business. **p. 50**

- An exchange of cash, goods, or services for cash, goods, services, or promises between a business and one or more external parties to a business (not the exchange of a promise for a promise),

or

- A measurable internal event, such as adjustments for the use of assets in operations.

An account is a standardized format that organizations use to accumulate the dollar effects of transactions related to each financial statement item. Typical balance sheet account titles include the following:

- *Assets:* Cash, Accounts Receivable, Inventory, Prepaid Expenses, Investments, Property (buildings and land) and Equipment, and Intangibles (rights without physical substance).
- *Liabilities:* Accounts Payable, Notes Payable, Accrued Expenses Payable, Unearned Revenues, and Taxes Payable.
- *Stockholders' Equity:* Common Stock, Additional Paid-in Capital, and Retained Earnings.

2-3. Apply transaction analysis to simple business transactions in terms of the accounting model: Assets = Liabilities + Stockholders' Equity. **p. 52**

To determine the economic effect of a transaction on an entity in terms of the accounting equation, each transaction must be analyzed to determine the accounts (at least two) that are affected. In an exchange, the company receives something and gives up something. If the accounts, direction of the effects, and amounts are correctly analyzed, the accounting equation will stay in balance.

Systematic transaction analysis includes (1) determining the accounts that were received and were given in the exchange, including the type of each account (A, L, or SE), the amounts, and the direction of the effects, and (2) determining that the accounting equation remains in balance.

2-4. Determine the impact of business transactions on the balance sheet using two basic tools: journal entries and T-accounts. **p. 58**

- Journal entries express the effects of a transaction on accounts in a debits-equal-credits format. The accounts and amounts to be debited are listed first. Then the accounts and amounts to be credited are listed below the debits and indented, resulting in debit amounts on the left and credit amounts on the right. Each entry needs a reference (date, number, or letter).
- T-accounts summarize the transaction effects for each account. These tools can be used to determine balances and draw inferences about a company's activities.

2-5. Prepare a trial balance and simple classified balance sheet and analyze the company using the current ratio. **p. 68**

A trial balance lists all accounts and their balances, with debit balances in the left column and credit balances in the right column. The two columns are totaled to determine if debits equal credits.

Classified balance sheets are structured as follows:

- Assets are categorized as current assets (those to be used or turned into cash within the year, with inventory always considered a current asset) and noncurrent assets, such as long-term investments, property and equipment, and intangible assets.
- Liabilities are categorized as current liabilities (those that will be paid with current assets) and long-term liabilities.
- Stockholders' equity accounts are listed as Common Stock (number of shares × par value per share) and Additional Paid-in Capital (number of shares × excess of issue price over par value per share) first, followed by Retained Earnings (earnings reinvested in the business).

The current ratio (Current Assets ÷ Current Liabilities) measures a company's liquidity, that is, the ability of the company to pay its short-term obligations with current assets.

2-6. Identify investing and financing transactions and demonstrate how they impact cash flows. **p. 74**

A statement of cash flows reports the sources and uses of cash for the period by the type of activity that generated the cash flow: operating, investing, and financing. Investing activities include purchasing and selling investments and long-term assets, and making loans and receiving principal repayments from others. Financing activities include borrowing from and repaying to banks the principal amount on loans, issuing and repurchasing stock, and paying dividends.

In this chapter, we discussed the accounting model and transaction analysis. Journal entries and T-accounts were used to record the results of transaction analysis for investing and financing decisions that affect balance sheet accounts. In Chapter 3, we continue our detailed look at the financial statements, in particular the income statement. The purpose of Chapter 3 is to build on your knowledge by discussing the measurement of revenues and expenses and illustrating the transaction analysis of operating decisions.

KEY RATIO

Current ratio measures the ability of the company to pay its short-term obligations with current assets. Although a ratio above 1.0 indicates sufficient current assets to meet obligations when they come due, many companies with sophisticated cash management systems have ratios below 1.0 (see Key Ratio Analysis on p. 72.)

$$\text{Current Ratio} = \frac{\text{Current Assets}}{\text{Current Liabilities}}$$

FINDING FINANCIAL INFORMATION

Balance Sheet

Current Assets
- Cash
- Short-term investments
- Accounts receivable
- Notes receivable
- Inventory
- Prepaid expenses

Noncurrent Assets
- Long-term investments
- Property and equipment
- Accumulated depreciation (reduces property and equipment)
- Operating lease right-of-use assets
- Intangibles

Current Liabilities
- Accounts payable
- Accrued expenses payable
- Short-term notes payable
- Unearned revenue
- Current lease liabilities

Noncurrent Liabilities
- Long-term debt (notes payable)
- Long-term lease liabilities

Stockholders' Equity
- Common stock
- Additional paid-in capital
- Retained earnings
- Treasury stock (reduces stockholders' equity)

Income Statement

To be presented in Chapter 3

Statement of Cash Flows

Operating Activities
To be presented in Chapter 3

Investing Activities
- \+ Sales of noncurrent assets and investments for cash
- − Purchases of noncurrent assets and investments for cash
- − Loans to others
- \+ Receipt of loan principal payments from others

Financing Activities
- \+ Borrowing from banks
- − Repayment of loan principal to banks
- \+ Issuance of stock
- − Repurchasing stock
- − Dividends paid

Notes

To be discussed in future chapters

KEY TERMS

Account A standardized format that organizations use to accumulate the dollar effect of transactions on each financial statement item **p. 51**

Accounting Cycle The process used by entities to analyze and record transactions, adjust the records at the end of the period, prepare financial statements, and prepare the records for the next cycle **p. 58**

Additional Paid-in Capital (Paid-in Capital, Contributed Capital in Excess of Par) The amount of contributed capital less the par value of the stock **p. 54**

Assets Economic resources owned or controlled by a company; they have measurable value and are expected to benefit the company by producing cash inflows or reducing cash outflows in the future **p. 47**

Common Stock The basic voting stock issued by a corporation **p. 54**

Cost (Historical Cost) The cash-equivalent value of an asset on the date of the transaction **p. 47**

Credit The right side of an account **p. 59**

Current Assets Assets that will be used or turned into cash within one year **p. 47**

Current Liabilities Short-term obligations that will be paid or settled within the coming year in cash, goods, other current assets, or services **p. 49**

Debit The left side of an account **p. 59**

Going Concern Assumption Businesses are assumed to continue to operate into the foreseeable future (also called the continuity assumption) **p. 47**

Journal Entry The accounting method for expressing the effects of a transaction on accounts in a debits-equal-credits format **p. 60**

Liabilities Measurable obligations resulting from a past transaction; they are expected to be settled in the future by transferring assets or providing services **p. 48**

Monetary Unit Assumption Accounting information should be measured and reported in the national monetary unit without any adjustments for changes in purchasing power **p. 47**

Par Value
(1) The nominal value per share of stock as specified in the corporate charter
(2) Also, another name for bond principal, or the maturity amount of a bond (in Chapter 10) **p. 54**

Retained Earnings Cumulative earnings of a company that are not distributed to the owners and are reinvested in the business **p. 49**

Separate Entity Assumption Business transactions are separate from the transactions of owners **p. 47**

Stockholders' Equity (Shareholders' or Owners' Equity) The financing provided by the owners and the operations of the business **p. 49**

T-Account A tool for summarizing transaction effects for each account, determining balances, and drawing inferences about a company's activities **p. 62**

Transaction
(1) An exchange between a business and one or more external parties to a business or
(2) A measurable internal event such as the use of assets in operations **p. 50**

Transaction Analysis The process of studying a transaction to determine its economic effect on the business in terms of the accounting equation **p. 52**

Trial Balance A list of all accounts with their balances to provide a check on the equality of the debits and credits **p. 68**

QUESTIONS

1. Explain what the following accounting terms mean:
   a. Separate entity assumption
   b. Monetary unit assumption
   c. Going concern assumption
   d. Historical cost principle
2. Why are accounting assumptions necessary?
3. Define the following:
   a. Asset
   b. Current asset
   c. Liability
   d. Current liability
   e. Additional paid-in capital
   f. Retained earnings
4. For accounting purposes, what is an account? Explain why accounts are used in an accounting system.
5. What is the accounting equation?
6. Define a business transaction in the broad sense and give an example of two different kinds of transactions.
7. Explain what *debit* and *credit* mean.
8. Briefly explain what is meant by *transaction analysis.* What are the three steps in transaction analysis?
9. What two accounting equalities must be maintained in transaction analysis?
10. What is a journal entry?
11. What is a T-account? What is its purpose?
12. How is the current ratio computed and interpreted?
13. What transactions are classified as investing activities in a statement of cash flows? What transactions are classified as financing activities?

MULTIPLE-CHOICE QUESTIONS

1. If a publicly traded company is trying to maximize its perceived value to decision makers external to the corporation, the company is most likely to understate which of the following on its balance sheet?
   a. Assets
   b. Common Stock
   c. Retained Earnings
   d. Liabilities
2. Which of the following is not an asset?
   a. Investments
   b. Land
   c. Prepaid Expense
   d. Additional Paid-in Capital

3. Total liabilities on a balance sheet at the end of the year are $150,000, retained earnings at the end of the year are $80,000, net income for the year is $60,000, common stock is $40,000, and additional paid-in capital is $20,000. What amount of total assets would be reported on the balance sheet at the end of the year?
   a. $290,000
   b. $270,000
   c. $205,000
   d. $15,000
4. The dual-effects concept can best be described as follows:
   a. When one records a transaction in the accounting system, at least two effects on the basic accounting equation will result.
   b. When an exchange takes place between two parties, both parties must record the transaction.
   c. When a transaction is recorded, both the balance sheet and the income statement must be impacted.
   d. When a transaction is recorded, one account will always increase and one account will always decrease.
5. The T-account is a tool commonly used for analyzing which of the following?
   a. Increases and decreases to a single account in the accounting system.
   b. Debits and credits to a single account in the accounting system.
   c. Changes in specific account balances over a time period.
   d. All of the above describe how T-accounts are used by accountants.
6. Which of the following describes how assets are listed on the balance sheet?
   a. In alphabetical order.
   b. In order of magnitude, lowest value to highest value.
   c. From most liquid to least liquid.
   d. From least liquid to most liquid.
7. The Cash T-account has a beginning balance of $21,000. During the year, $100,000 was debited and $110,000 was credited to the account. What is the ending balance of Cash?
   a. $11,000 debit balance
   b. $11,000 credit balance
   c. $31,000 credit balance
   d. $31,000 debit balance
8. Which of the following statements are true regarding the balance sheet?
   1. One cannot determine the true fair market value of a company by reviewing its balance sheet.
   2. Certain internally generated assets, such as a trademark, are not reported on a company's balance sheet.
   3. A balance sheet shows only the ending balances, in a summarized format, of all balance sheet accounts in the accounting system as of a particular date.
   a. None are true.
   b. Statements 1 and 2 only are true.
   c. Statements 2 and 3 only are true.
   d. Statements 1, 2, and 3 are true.
9. At the end of a recent year, **The Gap, Inc.**, reported total assets of $13,679 million, current assets of $4,516 million, total liabilities of $10,363 million, current liabilities of $3,209 million, and stockholders' equity of $3,316 million. What is its current ratio and what does this suggest about the company?
   a. The ratio of 1.32 suggests that The Gap has liquidity problems.
   b. The ratio of 1.41 suggests that The Gap has sufficient liquidity.
   c. The ratio of 1.32 suggests that The Gap has greater current assets than current liabilities.
   d. The ratio of 1.41 suggests that The Gap is not able to pay its short-term obligations with current assets.
10. Which of the following is *not* a financing activity on the statement of cash flows?
   a. When the company lends money.
   b. When the company borrows money.
   c. When the company pays dividends.
   d. When the company issues stock to shareholders.

MINI-EXERCISES

Matching Definitions with Terms

M2-1
LO2-1, 2-4

Match each definition with its related term by entering the appropriate letter in the space provided. There should be only one definition per term (that is, there are more definitions than terms).

Term	Definition
___ (1) Going concern assumption	A. = Liabilities + Stockholders' Equity.
___ (2) Historical cost principle	B. Reports assets, liabilities, and stockholders' equity.
___ (3) Credits	C. Accounts for a business separate from its owners.
___ (4) Assets	D. Increase assets; decrease liabilities and stockholders' equity.
___ (5) Account	E. An exchange between an entity and other parties.
	F. The concept that businesses will operate into the foreseeable future.
	G. Decrease assets; increase liabilities and stockholders' equity.
	H. The concept that assets should be recorded at the amount paid on the date of the transaction.
	I. A standardized format used to accumulate data about each item reported on financial statements.

Matching Definitions with Terms

M2-2
LO2-1, 2-2, 2-3, 2-4

Match each definition with its related term by entering the appropriate letter in the space provided. There should be only one definition per term (that is, there are more definitions than terms).

Term	Definition
___ (1) Journal entry	A. Accounting equation.
___ (2) A = L + SE, and Debits = Credits	B. Four periodic financial statements.
___ (3) Assets = Liabilities + Stockholders' Equity	C. The two equalities in accounting that aid in providing accuracy.
___ (4) Liabilities	D. The results of transaction analysis in accounting format.
___ (5) Income statement, balance sheet, statement of stockholders' equity, and statement of cash flows	E. The account that is debited when money is borrowed from a bank.
	F. Economic resources owned or controlled by a company, with measurable value and expected future benefits.
	G. Cumulative earnings of a company that are not distributed to the owners.
	H. Every transaction has at least two effects.
	I. Measurable obligations from a past transaction that are expected to be settled in the future by transferring assets or providing services.

Identifying Events as Accounting Transactions

M2-3
LO2-2

For each of the following events, which ones result in an exchange transaction for Dittman Company (Y for yes and N for no)?

___ (1) Six investors in Dittman Company sold their stock to another investor.
___ (2) The founding owner, Megan Dittman, purchased additional stock in another company.
___ (3) The company borrowed $2,500,000 from a local bank.
___ (4) Dittman Company leased a machine for two years.
___ (5) The company lent $300,000 to a supplier.
___ (6) Dittman Company ordered supplies from **Staples** to be delivered next week.

M2-4 LO2-1, 2-2 Classifying Accounts on a Balance Sheet

The following are the accounts of Rosa-Perez Company:

___ (1) Accounts Payable
___ (2) Accounts Receivable
___ (3) Buildings
___ (4) Cash
___ (5) Common Stock
___ (6) Land
___ (7) Merchandise Inventory
___ (8) Income Taxes Payable
___ (9) Long-Term Investments
___ (10) Notes Payable (due in three years)
___ (11) Notes Receivable (due in six months)
___ (12) Prepaid Rent
___ (13) Retained Earnings
___ (14) Supplies
___ (15) Utilities Payable
___ (16) Wages Payable

In the space provided, classify each as it would be reported on a balance sheet. Use:

CA for current asset
NCA for noncurrent asset
CL for current liability
NCL for noncurrent liability
SE for stockholders' equity

M2-5 LO2-1, 2-2 Classifying Accounts on a Balance Sheet

The following are the accounts of Woods-Michelson Corporation:

___ (1) Additional Paid-in Capital
___ (2) Buildings and Leased Assets
___ (3) Current Lease Liabilities
___ (4) Dividends Payable
___ (5) Equipment
___ (6) Intangible Assets
___ (7) Long-Term Lease Liabilities
___ (8) Notes Payable (due in six months)
___ (9) Prepaid Insurance
___ (10) Short-Term Investments
___ (11) Trade Accounts Receivable
___ (12) Treasury Stock
___ (13) Unearned Revenue

In the space provided, classify each as it would be reported on a balance sheet. Use:

CA for current asset
NCA for noncurrent asset
CL for current liability
NCL for noncurrent liability
SE for stockholders' equity

M2-6 LO2-3 Determining Financial Statement Effects of Several Transactions

For each of the following transactions of JonesSpa Corporation for the month of January, indicate the accounts, the amounts, and the direction of the effects on the accounting equation. A sample is provided.

a. *(Sample)* Borrowed $30,000 from a local bank; the loan is due in nine months.
b. Lent $10,000 to an affiliate; accepted a note due in one year.
c. Sold to investors 100 additional shares of stock with a par value of $0.10 per share and a market price of $5 per share; received cash.
d. Purchased $15,000 of equipment, paying $5,000 cash and signing a note for the rest due in one year.
e. Declared $2,000 in cash dividends to stockholders, to be paid in February.

Assets		=	Liabilities		+	Stockholders' Equity
a. Sample: Cash	+30,000		Notes payable	+30,000		

M2-7 LO2-4 Identifying Increase and Decrease Effects on Balance Sheet Elements

Complete the following table by entering either the word *increase* or *decrease* in each column.

	Debit	Credit
Assets	______	______
Liabilities	______	______
Stockholders' equity	______	______

Identifying Debit and Credit Effects on Balance Sheet Elements

M2-8
LO2-4

Complete the following table by entering either the word *debit* or *credit* in each column.

	Increase	Decrease
Assets	________	________
Liabilities	________	________
Stockholders' equity	________	________

Recording Simple Transactions

M2-9
LO2-4

For each transaction in M2-6 (including the sample), write the journal entry in the proper form.

Remember: Debits are on top and credits are on the bottom and indented.

Completing T-Accounts

M2-10
LO2-4

For each transaction in M2-6 (including the sample), post the effects to the appropriate T-accounts and determine ending account balances. Beginning balances are provided.

Cash	
Beg. bal. 900	
═	

Notes Receivable	
Beg. bal. 1,000	
═	

Equipment	
Beg. bal. 15,100	
═	

Notes Payable	
	3,000 Beg. bal.
	═

Dividends Payable	
	0 Beg. bal.
	═

Common Stock	
	1,000 Beg. bal.
	═

Additional Paid-in Capital	
	3,000 Beg. bal.
	═

Retained Earnings	
	10,000 Beg. bal.
	═

Preparing a Trial Balance

M2-11
LO2-5

Complete M2-10 and then prepare a trial balance for JonesSpa Corporation as of January 31.

Preparing a Simple Classified Balance Sheet

M2-12
LO2-5

Starting with the beginning balances in M2-10 and given the transactions in M2-6 (including the sample), prepare a balance sheet for JonesSpa Corporation as of January 31, classified into current and noncurrent assets and liabilities.

Computing and Interpreting the Current Ratio

M2-13
LO2-5
Chipotle

Calculate the current ratio for Matteo's Taco Company at the end of 2018 and 2019, based on the following data:

	Current Assets	Current Liabilities
End of 2018	$280,000	$155,000
End of 2019	$270,000	$250,000

What does the result suggest about the company over time? What can you say about the ratio for Matteo's Taco Company when compared to **Chipotle**'s 2019 ratio of 1.609?

M2-14 LO2-6

Identifying Transactions as Investing or Financing Activities on the Statement of Cash Flows

For the transactions in M2-6 (including the sample), identify each as an investing (I) activity or financing (F) activity on the statement of cash flows for January.

EXERCISES

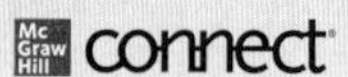

E2-1 LO2-1, 2-2, 2-3, 2-4

Matching Definitions with Terms

Match each definition with its related term by entering the appropriate letter in the space provided. There should be only one definition per term (that is, there are more definitions than terms).

Term	Definition
___ (1) Transaction	A. Economic resources to be used or turned into cash within one year.
___ (2) Going concern assumption	B. Reports assets, liabilities, and stockholders' equity.
___ (3) Balance sheet	C. Business transactions are accounted for separately from the transactions of the owners.
___ (4) Liabilities	D. Increase assets; decrease liabilities and stockholders' equity.
___ (5) Assets = Liabilities + Stockholders' Equity	E. An exchange between an entity and one or more external parties to a business.
___ (6) Notes payable	F. The concept that businesses will operate into the foreseeable future.
___ (7) Common stock	G. Decrease assets; increase liabilities and stockholders' equity.
___ (8) Historical cost principle	H. The concept that assets should be recorded at the cash-equivalent value on the exchange date.
___ (9) Account	I. A standardized format used to accumulate the dollar effect of transactions on each financial statement item.
___ (10) Dual effects	J. Amounts owed from customers.
___ (11) Retained earnings	K. The accounting equation.
___ (12) Current assets	L. Represents the shares issued at par value.
___ (13) Separate entity assumption	M. The account that is credited when money is borrowed from a bank.
___ (14) Par value	N. Accounting information should be measured and reported in the national monetary unit without adjustment for changes in purchasing power.
___ (15) Debits	O. Cumulative earnings of a company that are not distributed to the owners.
___ (16) Accounts receivable	P. Measurable obligations resulting from a past transaction that are expected to be settled in the future by transferring assets or providing services.
___ (17) Monetary unit assumption	Q. Every transaction has at least two effects on the accounting equation.
___ (18) Stockholders' equity	R. Financing provided by owners and by business operations.
	S. The concept to exercise care not to overstate assets and revenues or understate liabilities and expenses.
	T. Useful information has predictive and feedback value.
	U. Relatively small amounts not likely to influence users' decisions are to be recorded in the most cost-beneficial way.
	V. Measurable economic resources expected to be used or turned into cash beyond the next 12 months.
	W. Useful information should be complete, neutral, and free from error.
	X. A legal amount per share.

Identifying Account Titles

E2-2
LO2-1, 2-2

The following are independent situations.

a. A new company is formed and sells 100 shares of $1 par value stock for $12 per share to investors.
b. A company purchases for $18,000 cash a new delivery truck that has a list, or sticker, price of $21,000.
c. A women's clothing retailer orders 30 new display stands for $300 each for future delivery.
d. A company orders and receives 10 personal computers for office use for which it signs a note promising to pay $25,000 within three months.
e. A construction company signs a contract to build a new $500,000 warehouse for a corporate customer. At the signing, the corporation writes a check for $50,000 to the construction company as the initial payment for the construction (receiving construction in progress). Answer from the standpoint of the corporation (not the construction company).
f. A publishing firm purchases for $40,000 cash the copyright (an intangible asset) to a manuscript for an introductory accounting text.
g. A manufacturing firm declares a $100,000 cash dividend to be distributed to stockholders next period.
h. A company purchases a piece of land for $50,000 cash. An appraiser for the buyer values the land at $52,500.
i. A manufacturing company acquires the patent (an intangible asset) on a new digital satellite system for television reception, paying $500,000 cash and signing a $400,000 note payable due in one year.
j. A local company is a sole proprietorship (one owner); its owner buys a car for $10,000 for personal use. Answer from the local company's point of view.
k. A company purchases 100 shares of **Apple Inc.** common stock as an investment for $5,000 cash.
l. A company borrows $1,000 from a local bank and signs a six-month note for the loan.
m. A company pays $1,500 principal on its note payable (ignore interest).

Required:

1. Indicate the appropriate account titles, if any, affected in each of the preceding events. Consider what is received and what is given.
2. At what amount would you record the truck in (*b*)? The land in (*h*)? What measurement principle are you applying?
3. For (*c*), what accounting concept did you apply? For (*j*), what accounting concept did you apply?

Classifying Accounts and Their Usual Balances

E2-3
LO2-1, 2-2, 2-4
Verizon Communications

As described in a recent annual report, **Verizon Communications** provides wireless voice and data services across one of the most extensive wireless networks in the United States. Verizon now serves more than 100 million customers, making it the largest wireless service provider in the United States in terms of the total number of customers. The following are accounts from a recent balance sheet for Verizon:

(1) Accounts Receivable	(6) Long-Term Investments	(11) Inventories
(2) Retained Earnings	(7) Plant, Property, and Equipment	(12) Additional Paid-in Capital
(3) Accrued Expenses Payable	(8) Accounts Payable	(13) Current Lease Obligations
(4) Prepaid Expenses	(9) Short-Term Investments	(14) Operating Lease Right-of-Use Assets
(5) Common Stock	(10) Long-Term Debt	(15) Treasury Stock

Required:
For each account, indicate (1) whether the account is usually classified as a current asset (CA), noncurrent asset (NCA), current liability (CL), noncurrent liability (NCL), or stockholders' equity (SE) item and (2) whether the account usually has a debit or credit balance.

Determining Financial Statement Effects of Several Transactions

E2-4
LO2-3

The following events occurred for Johnson Company:

a. Received investment of cash by organizers and distributed to them 1,000 shares of $1 par value common stock with a market price of $40 per share.
b. Leased $15,000 of equipment, paying $3,000 in cash and signing a long-term right-of-use lease for the rest owed.
c. Borrowed $10,000 cash from a bank.
d. Loaned $800 to an employee who signed a note due in six months.
e. Purchased $13,000 of land; paid $4,000 in cash and signed a note for the balance.

Required:
For each of the events *(a)* through *(e),* perform transaction analysis and indicate the account, amount, and direction of the effect (+ for increase and – for decrease) on the accounting equation. Check that the accounting equation remains in balance after each transaction. Use the following headings:

Event	Assets	=	Liabilities	+	Stockholders' Equity

E2-5 Determining Financial Statement Effects of Several Transactions

LO2-1, 2-3
Nike, Inc.

Nike, Inc., with headquarters in Beaverton, Oregon, is one of the world's leading manufacturers of athletic shoes and sports apparel. The following activities occurred during a recent year. The amounts are rounded to millions, except for par value.

a. Purchased additional buildings for \$303 and equipment for \$1,202; paid \$432 in cash and signed a long-term note for the rest.
b. Issued 10 shares of \$1 par value common stock for \$885 cash.
c. Declared \$1,491 in dividends to be paid in the following year.
d. Purchased additional short-term investments for \$2,426 cash.
e. Several Nike investors sold their own stock to other investors on the stock exchange for \$7,150.
f. Sold \$2,379 in short-term investments for \$2,379 in cash.
g. Borrowed \$6,134 from a bank; signed a note due in 20 years.
h. Repurchased its common stock for \$3,067 in cash.

Required:
1. For each of the events (*a*) through (*h*), perform transaction analysis and indicate the account, amount in millions, and direction of the effect on the accounting equation. Check that the accounting equation remains in balance after each transaction. Use the following headings:

Event	Assets	=	Liabilities	+	Stockholders' Equity

2. Explain your response to event (*e*).

E2-6 Recording Investing and Financing Activities

LO2-4

Refer to E2-4.

Tip **Remember:** Debits go on the top and credits go on the bottom indented.

Required:
For each of the events (*a*) through (*e*) in E2-4, prepare journal entries, checking that debits equal credits.

E2-7 Recording Investing and Financing Activities

LO2-1, 2-4

Refer to E2-5.

Required:
1. For each of the events (*a*) through (*h*) in E2-5, prepare journal entries, checking that debits equal credits.
2. Explain your response to event (*e*).

E2-8 Recording Investing and Financing Activities

LO2-4

Kelsey Baker founded GolfDeals.com at the beginning of February. GolfDeals.com sells new and used golf equipment online. The following events occurred in February:

a. Borrowed \$30,000 cash from a bank, signing a note due in three years.
b. Received investment of cash by organizers and distributed to them 500 shares of \$0.10 par value common stock with a market price of \$30 per share.
c. Leased a warehouse for \$115,000, paying \$3,000 in cash and signing a 10-year right-of-use lease for the balance.
d. Purchased computer and office equipment for \$20,000, paying \$4,000 in cash and signing a note payable to the manufacturer for the rest.
e. Loaned \$1,000 to an employee who signed a note due in three months.

f. Paid $2,000 to the manufacturers in (*d*) above.
g. Purchased short-term investments for $10,000 cash.

Required:
For each of the events (*a*) through (*g*), prepare journal entries, checking that debits equal credits.

Analyzing the Effects of Transactions in T-Accounts

E2-9
LO2-4

Griffin Service Company, Inc., was organized by Bennett Griffin and five other investors (that is, six in total). The following activities occurred during the year:

a. Received $70,000 cash from the six investors; each investor was issued 8,400 shares of common stock with a par value of $0.10 per share.
b. Signed a five-year lease for $150,000 for the right to use a building each year.
c. Purchased equipment for use in the business at a cost of $18,000; one-fourth was paid in cash and the company signed a note for the balance (due in six months).
d. Signed an agreement with a cleaning service to pay $120 per week for cleaning the corporate offices next year.
e. Received an additional contribution from investors who provided $3,000 in cash and land valued at $15,000 in exchange for 1,000 shares of stock in the company.
f. Lent $2,500 to one of the investors, who signed a note due in six months.
g. Bennett Griffin borrowed $7,000 for personal use from a local bank, signing a one-year note.

Required:
1. Create T-accounts for the following accounts: Cash, Notes Receivable, Equipment, Land, Operating Lease Right-of-Use Assets, Notes Payable, Long-Term Lease Liabilities, Common Stock, and Additional Paid-in Capital. Beginning balances are $0. For each of the transactions (*a*) through (*g*), record the effects of the transaction in the appropriate T-accounts. Include good referencing and totals for each T-account.
2. Using the balances in the T-accounts, fill in the following amounts for the accounting equation:

   Assets $________ = Liabilities $________ + Stockholders' Equity $________

3. Explain your responses to events (*d*) and (*g*).

Analyzing the Effects of Transactions in T-Accounts

E2-10
LO2-4
Precision Builders

Precision Builders construction company was incorporated by Chris Stoscheck. Assume the following activities occurred during the year:

a. Received from three investors $60,000 cash and land valued at $35,000; each investor was issued 1,000 shares of common stock with a par value of $0.10 per share.
b. Purchased construction equipment for use in the business at a cost of $36,000; one-fourth was paid in cash and the company signed a note for the balance (due in six months).
c. Lent $2,500 to one of the investors, who signed a note due in six months.
d. Chris Stoscheck purchased a truck for personal use; paid $5,000 down and signed a one-year note for $22,000.
e. Paid $12,000 on the note for the construction equipment in (*b*) (ignore interest).

Required:
1. Create T-accounts for the following accounts: Cash, Notes Receivable, Equipment, Land, Notes Payable, Common Stock, and Additional Paid-in Capital. Beginning balances are $0. For each of the transactions (*a*) through (*e*), record the effects of the transaction in the appropriate T-accounts. Include good referencing and totals for each T-account.
2. Using the balances in the T-accounts, fill in the following amounts for the accounting equation:

   Assets $________ = Liabilities $________ + Stockholders' Equity $________

3. Explain your response to event (*d*).
4. Compute the market value per share of the stock issued in (*a*).

E2-11 Inferring Investing and Financing Transactions and Preparing a Balance Sheet
LO2-4, 2-5

During its first week of operations ending January 7, FastTrack Sports Inc. completed six transactions with the dollar effects indicated in the following schedule:

	DOLLAR EFFECT OF EACH OF THE SIX TRANSACTIONS						Ending Balance
Accounts	1	2	3	4	5	6	
Cash	$15,000	$75,000	$(5,000)	$(1,000)	$(9,500)	$(4,000)	
Notes receivable (short-term)				1,000			
Store fixtures					9,500		
Operating lease right-of-use assets			135,000				
Notes payable (due in three months)		75,000				(4,000)	
Long-term lease liabilities			130,000				
Common stock (15,000 shares)	1,500						
Additional paid-in capital	13,500						

Required:
1. Write a brief explanation of transactions (1) through (6). Explain any assumptions that you made.
2. Compute the ending balance in each account and prepare a classified balance sheet for FastTrack Sports Inc. on January 7.

E2-12 Inferring Investing and Financing Transactions and Preparing a Balance Sheet
LO2-4, 2-5

During its first month of operations in March, Volz Cleaning, Inc., completed six transactions with the dollar effects indicated in the following schedule:

	DOLLAR EFFECT OF EACH OF THE SIX TRANSACTIONS						Ending Balance
Accounts	1	2	3	4	5	6	
Cash	$45,000	$(8,000)	$(2,000)	$(7,000)	$3,000	$(4,000)	
Investments (short-term)				7,000	(3,000)		
Notes receivable (due in six months)			2,000				
Computer equipment						$4,000	
Delivery truck		35,000					
Notes payable (due in 10 years)		27,000					
Common stock (3,000 shares)	6,000						
Additional paid-in capital	39,000						

Required:
1. Write a brief explanation of transactions (1) through (6). Explain any assumptions that you made.
2. Compute the ending balance in each account and prepare a classified balance sheet for Volz Cleaning, Inc., at the end of March.

E2-13 Recording Journal Entries
LO2-4

Jameson Corporation was organized on May 1. The following events occurred during the first month.

a. Received $70,000 cash and a building valued at $250,000 from the five investors who organized Jameson Corporation. Each investor received 100 shares of $10 par value common stock.
b. Ordered store fixtures costing $15,000.
c. Borrowed $18,000 cash and signed a note due in two years.
d. Purchased $11,000 of equipment, paying $1,500 in cash and signing a six-month note for the balance.
e. Lent $2,000 to an employee who signed a note to repay the loan in three months.
f. Received and paid for the store fixtures ordered in (*b*).

Required:
Prepare journal entries for transactions (*a*) through (*f*). Be sure to use good referencing and categorize each account as an asset (A), liability (L), or stockholders' equity (SE) item. If a transaction does not require a journal entry, explain the reason.

Recording Journal Entries

E2-14
LO2-4
Alphabet Inc.
Google

Alphabet Inc. is the parent company for a collection of businesses–the largest of which is **Google**. The following activities were adapted from a recent annual report of Alphabet Inc. Dollars are in millions; shares are as shown.

a. Issued 8,000 shares of $0.001 par value stock for $202.
b. Ordered $6,540 of equipment.
c. Collected $1,419 cash on a note receivable.
d. Borrowed $4,291 from banks, signing long-term notes.
e. Sold short-term investments at their cost of $73,959.
f. Received equipment ordered in *(b)*; paid cash.
g. Repurchased its common stock for $4,846 cash.
h. Repaid $4,377 cash on bank borrowings (ignore interest).

Required:
Prepare journal entries for transactions (*a*) through (*h*). Show your answers in millions of dollars. Be sure to use good referencing and categorize each account as an asset (A), liability (L), or stockholders' equity (SE) item. If a transaction does not require a journal entry, explain the reason.

Analyzing the Effects of Transactions Using T-Accounts and Interpreting the Current Ratio as a Manager of the Company

E2-15
LO2-4, 2-5

Higgins Company began operations last year. You are a member of the management team investigating expansion ideas that will require borrowing funds from banks. On January 1, the start of the current year, Higgins' T-account balances were as follows:

Assets:

Cash		Short-Term Investments		Property and Equipment	
5,000		2,500		3,000	

Liabilities:

Notes Payable *(current)*		Notes Payable *(noncurrent)*	
	2,200		800

Stockholders' Equity:

Common Stock		Additional Paid-in Capital		Retained Earnings	
	500		4,000		3,000

Required:
1. Using the data from these T-accounts, determine the amounts for the following on January 1 of the current year:

   Assets $________ = Liabilities $________ + Stockholders' Equity $________

2. Prepare journal entries for transactions (*a*) through (*e*) for the current year. Be sure to use good referencing and categorize each account as an asset (A), a liability (L), or a stockholders' equity (SE) account. If the transaction does not require a journal entry, explain the reason.
   a. Borrowed $4,000 from a local bank, signing a note due in three years.
   b. Sold $1,500 of the investments for $1,500 cash.
   c. Sold one-half of the property and equipment for $1,500 in cash.
   d. Declared $800 in cash dividends to stockholders.
   e. Paid dividends to stockholders.

3. Enter the effects of the transactions in 2. above in the T-accounts. You will need to create a new T-account for Dividends Payable as well, with a $0 beginning balance. Be sure to use good referencing.
4. Prepare a trial balance at December 31.
5. Prepare a classified balance sheet at December 31 of the current year in good form.
6. Calculate the current ratio at December 31 of the current year, rounding your answer to two decimal places. If the industry average for the current ratio is 1.50, what does your computation suggest to you about Higgins Company? Would you suggest that Higgins Company increase its short-term liabilities? Why or why not?

E2-16 LO2-4, 2-5 Analyzing the Effects of Transactions Using T-Accounts, Preparing a Balance Sheet, and Evaluating the Current Ratio over Time as a Bank Loan Officer

Bailey Delivery Company, Inc., was organized in 2021 in Wisconsin. The following transactions occurred during the year:

a. Received cash from investors in exchange for 10,000 shares of stock (par value of $1.00 per share) with a market value of $4 per share.
b. Purchased land in Wisconsin for $16,000, signing a one-year note (ignore interest).
c. Bought two used delivery trucks for operating purposes at the start of the year at a cost of $10,000 each; paid $4,000 cash and signed a note due in three years for the rest (ignore interest).
d. Paid $1,000 cash to a truck repair shop for a new motor for one of the trucks. (Increase the account you used to record the purchase of the trucks because the productive life of the truck has been improved.)
e. Sold one-fourth of the land for $4,000 to Pablo Development Corporation, which signed a six-month note.
f. Stockholder Helen Bailey paid $27,600 cash for a vacant lot (land) in Canada for her personal use.

Required:

1. Set up appropriate T-accounts with beginning balances of zero for Cash, Short-Term Notes Receivable, Land, Equipment, Short-Term Notes Payable, Long-Term Notes Payable, Common Stock, and Additional Paid-in Capital.
   a. Using the T-accounts, record the effects of transactions (*a*) through (*f*) by Bailey Delivery Company.
   b. Explain your analysis of transaction (*f*).
2. Prepare a trial balance at December 31, 2021.
3. Prepare a classified balance sheet for Bailey Delivery Company at December 31, 2021.
4. At the end of the next two years, Bailey Delivery Company reported the following amounts on its balance sheets:

	December 31, 2022	December 31, 2023
Current Assets	$52,000	$ 47,000
Long-Term Assets	38,000	73,000
Total Assets	**90,000**	**120,000**
Short-Term Notes Payable	23,000	40,000
Long-Term Notes Payable	17,000	20,000
Total Liabilities	**40,000**	**60,000**
Stockholders' Equity	**50,000**	**60,000**

   Compute the company's current ratio for 2021, 2022, and 2023. What is the trend and what does this suggest about the company?
5. At the beginning of year 2024, Bailey Delivery Company applied to your bank for a $50,000 short-term loan to expand the business. The vice president of the bank asked you to review the information and make a recommendation on lending the funds based solely on the results of the current ratio. What recommendation would you make to the bank's vice president about lending the money to Bailey Delivery Company?

E2-17 LO2-4 Explaining the Effects of Transactions on Balance Sheet Accounts Using T-Accounts

Waldman Furniture Repair Service, a company with two stockholders, began operations on June 1. The following T-accounts indicate the activities for the month of June.

Cash (A)

	Debit	Credit	
6/1	0		
a.	20,000	1,800	*b.*
d.	900	10,000	*c.*

Notes Receivable (A)

	Debit	Credit
6/1	0	
b.	1,800	

Tools and Equipment (A)

	Debit	Credit	
6/1	0		
a.	5,000	900	*d.*

Building (A)

	Debit	Credit
6/1	0	
c.	40,000	

Notes Payable (L)

Debit	Credit	
	0	6/1
	30,000	*c.*

Common Stock (100,000 shares) (SE)

Debit	Credit	
	0	6/1
	2,000	*a.*

Additional Paid-in Capital (SE)

Debit	Credit	
	0	6/1
	23,000	*a.*

Required:
Explain events (*a*) through (*d*) that resulted in the entries in the T-accounts.

Inferring Typical Investing and Financing Activities in Accounts

E2-18
LO2-4

The following T-accounts indicate the effects of normal business transactions:

Equipment

	Debit	Credit
1/1	500	
	250	?
12/31	100	

Notes Receivable

	Debit	Credit
1/1	150	
	?	225
12/31	170	

Notes Payable

Debit	Credit	
	100	1/1
?	170	
	160	12/31

Required:
1. Describe the typical investing and financing transactions that affect each T-account. That is, what economic events occur to make each of these accounts increase and decrease?
2. For each T-account, compute the missing amount.

Identifying Investing and Financing Activities Affecting Cash Flows

E2-19
LO2-6
Foot Locker, Inc.

Foot Locker, Inc., is a large global retailer of athletic footwear and apparel selling directly to customers and through the Internet. It includes the Foot Locker family of stores, Champs Sports, Footaction, Runners Point, and Sidestep. The following are a few of Foot Locker's investing and financing activities as reflected in a recent annual statement of cash flows.

a. Capital expenditures (for the purchase of property, plant, and equipment).
b. Repurchases of common stock from investors.
c. Sale of short-term investments.
d. Issuance of common stock.
e. Purchases of short-term investments.
f. Dividends paid on common stock.

Required:
For activities (*a*) through (*f*), indicate whether the activity is investing (I) or financing (F) and the direction of the effect on cash flows (+ for increases cash; − for decreases cash).

Identifying Investing and Financing Activities Affecting Cash Flows

E2-20
LO2-6
Marriott International, Inc.

Marriott International, Inc., is a leading global lodging company, with more than 7,000 properties in 134 countries. Information adapted from the company's recent annual statement of cash flows indicates the following investing and financing activities during that year (simplified, in millions of dollars):

a. Additional borrowing from banks	$1,397
b. Purchase of investments	47
c. Sale of assets and investments (assume sold at cost)	395
d. Issuance of stock	7
e. Purchases of property, plant, and equipment	653
f. Payment of debt principal	835
g. Dividends paid	612
h. Receipt of principal payment on a note receivable	51

Required:
For activities (*a*) through (*h*), indicate whether the activity is investing (I) or financing (F) and the direction of the effects on cash flows (+ for increases cash; − for decreases cash).

E2-21
LO2-1, 2-2, 2-5, 2-6

Finding Financial Information as a Potential Investor

You are considering investing the cash you inherited from your grandfather in various stocks. You have received the annual reports of several major companies.

Required:
For each of the following items, indicate where you would locate the information in an annual report. The information may be in more than one location.

1. Total current assets.
2. Amount of debt principal repaid during the year.
3. Summary of significant accounting policies.
4. Cash received from sales of noncurrent assets.
5. Amount of dividends paid during the year.
6. Short-term obligations.
7. Date of the statement of financial position.

PROBLEMS

P2-1
LO2-1, 2-2, 2-4
Exxon Mobil Corporation

Identifying Accounts on a Classified Balance Sheet and Their Normal Debit or Credit Balances (AP2-1)

Exxon Mobil Corporation explores, produces, refines, markets, and supplies crude oil, natural gas, and petroleum products in the United States and around the world. The following are accounts from a recent balance sheet of Exxon Mobil Corporation:

	Balance Sheet Classification	Debit or Credit Balance
(1) Notes and Loans Payable (short-term)	______	______
(2) Materials and Supplies	______	______
(3) Common Stock	______	______
(4) Intangible Assets	______	______
(5) Income Taxes Payable	______	______
(6) Long-Term Debt	______	______
(7) Property, Plant, and Equipment	______	______
(8) Retained Earnings	______	______
(9) Notes and Accounts Receivable (short-term)	______	______
(10) Investments (long-term)	______	______
(11) Cash and Cash Equivalents	______	______
(12) Accounts Payable and Accrued Liabilities	______	______
(13) Crude Oil, Products and Merchandise	______	______
(14) Additional Paid-in Capital	______	______

Required:
For each account, indicate how it normally should be categorized on a classified balance sheet. Use CA for current asset, NCA for noncurrent asset, CL for current liability, NCL for noncurrent liability, and SE for stockholders' equity. Also indicate whether the account normally has a debit or credit balance.

P2-2
LO2-2, 2-3, 2-5

Determining Financial Statement Effects of Various Transactions (AP2–2)

East Hill Home Healthcare Services was organized five years ago by four friends who each invested \$10,000 in the company and, in turn, were issued in total 8,000 shares of \$1.00 par value common stock. To date, they are the only stockholders. At the end of last year, the accounting records reflected total assets of \$700,000 (\$50,000 cash; \$500,000 land; \$50,000 equipment; and \$100,000 buildings), total liabilities of \$200,000 (short-term notes payable \$100,000 and long-term notes payable \$100,000), and stockholders' equity of $500,000 ($20,000 common stock; $80,000 additional paid-in capital; and $400,000 retained earnings). During the current year, the following summarized events occurred:

a. Sold 9,000 additional shares of stock to the original organizers for a total of $90,000 cash.
b. Purchased a building for $60,000, equipment for $15,000, and four acres of land for $14,000; paid $9,000 in cash and signed a note for the balance (due in 15 years). (**Hint:** Five different accounts are affected.)
c. Sold one acre of land acquired in (*b*) for $3,500 cash to another company.
d. Purchased short-term investments for $18,000 cash.
e. One stockholder reported to the company that 300 shares of his East Hill stock had been sold and transferred to another stockholder for $3,000 cash.
f. Lent one of the shareholders $5,000 for moving costs and received a signed, six-month note from the shareholder.
g. Borrowed $8,000 from a local bank; signed a note due in six months.

Required:

1. Was East Hill Home Healthcare Services organized as a sole proprietorship, a partnership, or a corporation? Explain the basis for your answer.
2. During the current year, the records of the company were inadequate. You were asked to prepare the summary of transactions shown above. To develop a quick assessment of their economic effects on East Hill Home Healthcare Services, you have decided to complete the tabulation that follows and to use plus (+) for increases and minus (−) for decreases for each account. The first event is used as an example.

	ASSETS						=	LIABILITIES		+	STOCKHOLDERS' EQUITY		
	Cash	Short-Term Investments	Notes Receivable	Land	Buildings	Equipment		Short-Term Notes Payable	Long-Term Notes Payable		Common Stock	Additional Paid-in Capital	Retained Earnings
Beg.	50,000			500,000	100,000	50,000	=	100,000	100,000		20,000	80,000	400,000
(*a*)	+90,000						=				+9,000	+81,000	

3. Did you include the transaction between the two stockholders—event (*e*)—in the tabulation? Why?
4. Based only on the completed tabulation, provide the following amounts (show computations):
   a. Total assets at the end of the year.
   b. Total liabilities at the end of the year.
   c. Total stockholders' equity at the end of the year.
   d. Cash balance at the end of the year.
   e. Total current assets at the end of the year.
5. Compute the current ratio for the current year. Round your answer to two decimal places. What does this suggest about the company?

Recording Transactions in T-Accounts, Preparing the Balance Sheet from a Trial Balance, and Evaluating the Current Ratio (AP2-3)

P2-3
LO2-2, 2-4, 2-5

Jaguar Plastics Company has been operating for three years. At December 31 of last year, the accounting records reflected the following:

Cash	$22,000	Accounts payable	$15,000
Investments (short-term)	3,000	Accrued liabilities payable	4,000
Accounts receivable	3,000	Notes payable *(current)*	7,000
Inventory	20,000	Notes payable *(noncurrent)*	87,000
Notes receivable (long-term)	1,000	Long-term lease liabilities	63,000
Equipment	50,000	Common stock	10,000
Factory building	90,000	Additional paid-in capital	117,000
Operating lease right-of-use assets	140,000	Retained earnings	31,000
Intangible assets	5,000		

During the current year, the company had the following summarized activities:

a. Purchased short-term investments for $10,000 cash.
b. Lent $5,000 to a supplier, who signed a two-year note.
c. Leased equipment that cost $18,000; paid $5,000 cash and signed a five-year right-of-use lease for the balance.

d. Hired a new president at the end of the year. The contract was for $85,000 per year plus options to purchase company stock at a set price based on company performance. The new president begins her position on January 1 of next year.
e. Issued an additional 2,000 shares of $0.50 par value common stock for $11,000 cash.
f. Borrowed $9,000 cash from a local bank, payable in three months.
g. Purchased a patent (an intangible asset) for $3,000 cash.
h. Built an addition to the factory for $24,000; paid $8,000 in cash and signed a three-year note for the balance.
i. Returned defective equipment to the manufacturer, receiving a cash refund of $1,000.

Required:
1. Create T-accounts for each of the accounts taken from the accounting records shown above and enter the end-of-year balances as the beginning balances for the current year.
2. Record each of the events for the current year in T-accounts (including referencing) and determine the ending balances.
3. Explain your response to event (*d*).
4. Prepare a trial balance at December 31 of the current year.
5. Prepare a classified balance sheet at December 31 of the current year. Include a good heading.
6. Compute the current ratio for the current year. Round to two decimal places. What does this suggest about Jaguar Plastics?

P2-4 LO2-6

Identifying Effects of Transactions on the Statement of Cash Flows (AP2-4)

Refer to P2-3.

Required:
Using events (*a*) through (*i*) in P2-3, indicate whether each is an investing (I) or financing (F) activity for the year and the direction of the effect on cash flows (+ for increase and – for decrease). If there is no effect on cash flows, write NE.

P2-5 LO2-2, 2-4, 2-5 **Apple Inc.**

Recording Transactions, Preparing Journal Entries, Posting to T-Accounts, Preparing the Balance Sheet, and Evaluating the Current Ratio (AP2-5)

Apple Inc., headquartered in Cupertino, California, designs, manufactures, and markets smartphones, personal computers, tablets, wearables, and accessories, and sells a variety of related services. The following is Apple's (simplified) balance sheet from a recent year (fiscal year ending on the last Saturday of September).

APPLE INC.
Consolidated Balance Sheet
September 28, 2019
(dollars in millions)

ASSETS	
Current assets:	
Cash	$ 48,844
Short-term investments	51,713
Accounts receivable	22,926
Inventories	4,106
Other current assets	35,230
Total current assets	162,819
Long-term investments	105,341
Property, plant, and equipment, net	37,378
Other noncurrent assets	32,978
Total assets	$338,516

(Continued)

APPLE INC. **Consolidated Balance Sheet** **September 28, 2019** **(dollars in millions)**	
LIABILITIES AND STOCKHOLDERS' EQUITY	
Current liabilities:	
Accounts payable	$ 46,236
Accrued expenses	43,700
Unearned revenue	5,522
Short-term debt	10,260
Total current liabilities	105,718
Long-term debt	91,807
Other noncurrent liabilities	50,503
Total liabilities	248,028
Shareholders' equity:	
Common stock ($0.00001 par value)	1
Additional paid-in capital	45,173
Retained earnings	45,314
Total shareholders' equity	90,488
Total liabilities and shareholders' equity	$338,516

Source: Apple Inc.

Assume that the following transactions (in millions) occurred during the next fiscal year (ending on September 26, 2020):

a. Borrowed $18,266 from banks due in two years.
b. Purchased additional investments for $21,000 cash; one-fifth were long term and the rest were short term.
c. Purchased property, plant, and equipment; paid $9,571 in cash and signed a short-term note for $1,410.
d. Issued additional shares of common stock for $1,469 in cash; total par value was $1 and the rest was in excess of par value.
e. Sold short-term investments costing $18,810 for $18,810 cash.
f. Declared $11,126 in dividends to be paid at the beginning of the next fiscal year.

Required:

1. Prepare a journal entry for each transaction. Use the account titles in the Apple balance sheet and show answers in millions of dollars.
2. Create T-accounts for each balance sheet account and include the September 28, 2019, balances; create a new account, Dividends Payable, with a $0 beginning balance. Post each journal entry to the appropriate T-accounts.
3. Prepare a trial balance at September 26, 2020.
4. Prepare a classified balance sheet for Apple at September 26, 2020, based on these transactions. Include a good heading.
5. Compute Apple's current ratio on September 26, 2020. Round your answer to two decimal places. What does this suggest about the company?

Mc Graw Hill connect

ALTERNATE PROBLEMS

Identifying Accounts on a Classified Balance Sheet and Their Normal Debit or Credit Balances (P2-1)

AP2-1
LO2-1, 2-2, 2-4
Mattel, Inc.

According to a recent Form 10-K report of **Mattel, Inc.**, the company "designs, manufactures, and markets a broad variety of toy products worldwide." Mattel's brands include Barbie, Hot Wheels, Fisher-Price toys, Matchbox, and American Girl brand dolls and accessories. The following are several of the accounts from a recent balance sheet:

	Balance Sheet Classification	Debit or Credit Balance
(1) Prepaid Expenses	______	______
(2) Inventories	______	______
(3) Accounts Receivable	______	______
(4) Long-Term Debt	______	______
(5) Treasury Stock	______	______
(6) Right-of-Use Assets	______	______
(7) Accounts Payable	______	______
(8) Income Taxes Payable	______	______
(9) Property, Plant, and Equipment	______	______
(10) Retained Earnings	______	______
(11) Additional Paid-in Capital	______	______
(12) Noncurrent Lease Liabilities	______	______
(13) Accrued Liabilities	______	______
(14) Common Stock	______	______

Required:
Indicate how each account normally should be categorized on a classified balance sheet. Use CA for current asset, NCA for noncurrent asset, CL for current liability, NCL for noncurrent liability, and SE for stockholders' equity. Also indicate whether the account normally has a debit or credit balance.

AP2-2 Determining Financial Statement Effects of Various Transactions (P2-2)

LO2-2, 2-3, 2-5

Russeck Incorporated is a small manufacturing company that makes model trains to sell to toy stores. It has a small service department that repairs customers' trains for a fee. The company has been in business for five years. At the end of the company's prior fiscal year ending on December 31, the accounting records reflected total assets of $500,000 (cash, $120,000; equipment, $70,000; buildings, $310,000), total liabilities of $200,000 (all long-term notes payable), and total stockholders' equity of $300,000 (common stock with a par value of $1.00 per share, $20,000; additional paid-in capital, $200,000; retained earnings, $80,000). During the current year, the following summarized events occurred:

a. Borrowed $11,000 cash from the bank and signed a 10-year note.
b. Purchased model train molding equipment for $30,000, paying $3,000 in cash and signing a note due in six months for the balance.
c. Issued an additional 10,000 shares of common stock for $20,000 cash.
d. Purchased a delivery truck (equipment) for $10,000; paid $5,000 cash and signed a short-term note payable for the remainder.
e. Lent $2,000 cash to the company president, Kal Russeck, who signed a note with terms showing the principal plus interest due in six months.
f. Purchased $85,000 in long-term investments.
g. A stockholder sold $5,000 of his common stock in Russeck Incorporated to his neighbor.

Required:
1. Was Russeck Incorporated organized as a sole proprietorship, a partnership, or a corporation? Explain the basis for your answer.
2. During the current year, the records of the company were inadequate. You were asked to prepare the summary of transactions shown above. To develop a quick assessment of their economic effects on Russeck Incorporated, you have decided to complete the tabulation that follows and to use plus (+) for increases and minus (−) for decreases for each account. The first transaction is used as an example.

	ASSETS					=	LIABILITIES		+	STOCKHOLDERS' EQUITY		
	Cash	Short-Term Notes Receivable	Long-Term Investments	Equipment	Buildings		Short-Term Notes Payable	Long-Term Notes Payable		Common Stock	Additional Paid-in Capital	Retained Earnings
Beg.	120,000			70,000	310,000	=		200,000		20,000	200,000	80,000
(*a*)	+11,000					=		+11,000				

3. Did you include event (*g*) in the tabulation? Why?
4. Based on beginning balances plus the completed tabulation, provide the following amounts (show computations):
   a. Total assets at the end of the year.
   b. Total liabilities at the end of the year.
   c. Total stockholders' equity at the end of the year.
   d. Cash balance at the end of the year.
   e. Total current assets at the end of the year.
5. Compute the current ratio for the current year. Round your answer to two decimal places. What does this suggest about the company?

AP2-3
LO2-2, 2-4, 2-5
Ethan Allen Interiors Inc.

Recording Transactions in T-Accounts, Preparing the Balance Sheet, and Evaluating the Current Ratio (P2-3)

Ethan Allen Interiors Inc. is a leading interior design company and manufacturer and retailer of home furnishings in the United States and abroad. The following is adapted from Ethan Allen's recent annual financial statements for fiscal year ending on June 30. Dollar amounts are in thousands.

Cash	$ 20,824	Accounts payable	$ 35,485
Accounts receivable	14,247	Unearned revenue	56,714
Inventories	162,389	Accrued expenses payable	30,077
Prepaid expenses and other current assets	18,830	Long-term debt (includes the current portion of $550)	1,066
Property, plant, and equipment	245,246	Other long-term liabilities	23,080
Intangible assets	45,128	Common stock ($0.01 par value)	491
Long-term investments	2,108	Additional paid-in capital	377,913
Other assets	1,579	Treasury stock	656,597
		Retained earnings	642,122

Assume that the following events occurred in the first quarter ended September 30 of the next fiscal year:

a. Issued 1,600 additional shares of stock for $1,020 in cash.
b. Purchased $3,400 in additional intangibles for cash.
c. Ordered $43,500 in wood and other raw materials for the manufacturing plants.
d. Sold equipment at its cost for $4,020 cash.
e. Purchased $2,980 in long-term investments for cash.
f. Purchased property, plant, and equipment; paid $1,830 in cash and signed additional long-term notes for $9,400.
g. Sold at cost other assets for $310 cash.
h. Declared $300 in dividends.

Required:
1. Create T-accounts for each of the accounts listed above, including a new account Dividends Payable. Enter the balances at June 30 as the beginning balances for the quarter (in thousands of dollars). The account Treasury Stock reduces stockholders' equity; its balance is on the debit side of the T-account.
2. Record each of the transactions for the first quarter ended September 30 in the T-accounts (including referencing) and determine the ending balances.
3. Explain your response to event (*c*).
4. Prepare a trial balance at September 30.
5. Prepare a classified balance sheet at September 30.
6. Compute the current ratio for the quarter ended September 30. Round your answer to three decimal places. What does this suggest about Ethan Allen Interiors Inc.?

AP2-4
LO2-6

Identifying Effects of Transactions on the Statement of Cash Flows (P2-4)

Required:
Using the events (*a*) through (*h*) in AP2-3, indicate whether each transaction is an investing (I) or financing (F) activity for the quarter and the direction and amount of the effect on cash flows (+ for increase and − for decrease). If there is no effect on cash flows, write NE.

AP2-5 Recording Transactions, Preparing Journal Entries, Posting to T-Accounts, Preparing the Balance Sheet, and Evaluating the Current Ratio (P2-5)

LO2-2, 2-4, 2-5

Kiwi, Inc., headquartered in Boston, Massachusetts, designs, manufactures, and markets headphones and other audio components. The following is Kiwi's (simplified) balance sheet from a recent fiscal year ending on June 30.

KIWI, INC. **CONSOLIDATED BALANCE SHEET** **June 30, 2022** **(dollars in thousands)**	
ASSETS	
Current assets:	
Cash	$ 14,004
Short-term investments	11,361
Accounts receivable	17,656
Inventories	2,131
Other current assets	24,107
Total current assets	69,259
Long-term investments	131,546
Property, plant, and equipment, net	20,844
Other noncurrent assets	12,658
Total assets	$234,307
LIABILITIES AND STOCKHOLDERS' EQUITY	
Current liabilities:	
Accounts payable	$ 30,520
Accrued expenses	18,653
Unearned revenue	8,587
Short-term notes payable	6,376
Total current liabilities	64,136
Long-term debt	29,303
Other noncurrent liabilities	28,157
Total liabilities	121,596
Stockholders' equity:	
Common stock ($0.01 par value)	1
Additional paid-in capital	25,112
Retained earnings	87,598
Total stockholders' equity	112,711
Total liabilities and shareholders' equity	$234,307

Assume that the following transactions (in thousands) occurred during the next fiscal year (ending on June 30, 2023):

a. Borrowed $18,296 from banks due in two years.
b. Purchased additional investments for $23,800 cash; one-fifth were long term and the rest were short term.
c. Purchased property, plant, and equipment; paid $9,603 in cash and signed a short-term note for $1,440.
d. Issued additional shares of common stock for $1,500 in cash; total par value was $1 and the rest was in excess of par value.
e. Sold short-term investments costing $19,038 for $19,038 cash.
f. Declared $11,156 in dividends to be paid at the beginning of the next fiscal year.

Required:

1. Prepare a journal entry for each transaction. Use the account titles on the Kiwi balance sheet and show answers in thousands of dollars.
2. Create T-accounts for each balance sheet account and include the June 30, 2022, balances; create a new account, Dividends Payable, with a $0 beginning balance. Post each journal entry to the appropriate T-accounts.
3. Prepare a trial balance at June 30, 2023.
4. Prepare a classified balance sheet for Kiwi at June 30, 2023, based on these transactions.
5. Compute Kiwi's current ratio on June 30, 2023. (Round your answer to two decimal places.) What does this suggest about the company?

CONTINUING PROBLEM

Accounting for the Establishment of a New Business (the Accounting Cycle)

CON2-1
LO2-4, 2-5, 2-6

Penny Cassidy has decided to start her business, Penny's Pool Service & Supply, Inc. (PPSS). There is much to do when starting a new business. Here are some transactions that have occurred in PPSS in March.

a. Received $25,000 cash and a large delivery van with a value of $36,000 from Penny, who was given 4,000 shares of $0.05 par value common stock in exchange.
b. Purchased land with a small office and warehouse by paying $10,000 cash and signing a 10-year note payable to the local bank for $80,000. The land has a value of $18,000 and the building's value is $72,000. Use separate accounts for land and buildings.
c. Purchased new computer equipment from **Dell** for $2,500 cash, and purchased other office equipment for $4,000, signing a note payable due in six months to the office equipment manufacturer.
d. Hired a receptionist for the office at a salary of $1,500 per month; the receptionist will begin working for PPSS starting in April.
e. Paid $1,000 on the note payable to the bank [in (*b*) above] at the end of March (ignore interest).
f. Purchased short-term investments in the stock of other companies for $5,000 cash.
g. Ordered $10,000 in inventory from **Pool Corporation, Inc.**, a pool supply wholesaler, to be received in April.

Required:

1. For each of the events (*a*) through (*g*), prepare journal entries if a transaction of the business exists, checking that debits equal credits. If a transaction does not exist, explain why there is no transaction for the business.
2. Create T-accounts and post each of the transactions to determine balances at March 31. Because this is a new business, beginning balances are $0.
3. Prepare a trial balance on March 31 to check that debits equal credits after the transactions are posted to the T-accounts.
4. From the trial balance, prepare a classified balance sheet (with current assets and current liabilities sections) at March 31 (before the beginning of operations in April).
5. For each of the events (*a*) through (*g*), indicate if it is an investing activity (I) or financing activity (F) and the direction (+ for increases; − for decreases) and amount of the effect on cash flows using the following structure. Write NE if there is no effect on cash flows.

	Type of Activity (I, F, or NE)	Effect on Cash Flows (+ or − and amount)
(*a*)	________	________
(*b*) etc.	________	________

6. Calculate the current ratio at March 31. Round your answer to three decimal places. What does this ratio indicate about the ability of PPSS to pay its current liabilities?

CASES AND PROJECTS

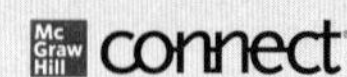

Annual Report Cases

CP2-1
LO2-1, 2-2, 2-5, 2-6
Target Corporation

Finding Financial Information

Refer to the financial statements of **Target Corporation** in Appendix B at the end of this book. All dollar amounts are in millions. (Note: Fiscal year 2019 for Target runs from February 2, 2019 to February 1, 2020.)

1. What is the title used by Target for its balance sheets?
   a. Consolidated Balance Sheets
   b. Consolidated Statements of Financial Position
   c. Consolidated Statements of Balances
   d. Consolidated Statements of Operations
2. On the balance sheets, what is the most recent fiscal year reported?
   a. Fiscal year 2020, ending on February 1, 2020
   b. Fiscal year 2021, ending on January 30, 2021
   c. Fiscal year 2021, ending on February 1, 2020
   d. Fiscal year 2020, ending on January 30, 2021
3. What amount does the company report for inventory at the end of the most recent year?
   a. $8,992, which represents the expected selling price for the inventory
   b. $10,653, which represents the cost of the inventory
   c. $10,653, which represents the expected selling price for the inventory
   d. $8,992, which represents the cost of the inventory
4. Which of the following is **not** a component of property and equipment?
   a. Computer hardware and software
   b. Land
   c. Inventory
   d. Fixtures and equipment
5. What is the current ratio for the most recent fiscal year and what does this suggest about the company?
   a. 1.40, suggesting that Target is highly liquid.
   b. 0.89, suggesting that Target is not able to pay its short-term obligations.
   c. 1.03, suggesting that Target has sufficient current assets to pay current liabilities.
   d. 2.55, suggesting that Target is doing very well.

CP2-2
LO2-1, 2-2, 2-5, 2-6
Walmart Inc.

Finding Financial Information

Refer to the financial statements of **Walmart Inc.** in Appendix C at the end of this book. All dollar amounts are in millions.

1. What amount does the company report for common stock for the most recent year (in millions)?
   ____
2. What is the amount of total liabilities at the end of the most recent year? ____________________
3. What is the company's current ratio for the most recent year (round to two decimal places)?
   ____
4. If the company were liquidated at the end of the most recent year, are the shareholders guaranteed to receive $87,531 (total equity)? ____________________
5. Regarding your answer to 4. above, why or why not?
   a. By law, shareholders are entitled to receive the amount in Retained Earnings of $88,763.
   b. Total equity is a residual balance; shareholders will receive what remains in cash and assets after the creditors have been satisfied.
   c. Shareholders are entitled to receive the total equity because that amount represents the residual interest to shareholders.
   d. Walmart shareholders are guaranteed to receive $80,925 and those with a noncontrolling interest are entitled to receive $6,606.

Comparing Companies within an Industry

CP2-3
LO2-2, 2-5, 2-6
Target Corporation
Walmart Inc.

Refer to the following:

- **Target Corporation** in Appendix B,
- **Walmart Inc.** in Appendix C, and the
- **Industry Ratio Report** in Appendix D at the end of this book.

All dollar amounts are in millions of dollars.

1. Compute the current ratio for both companies (round your answers to two decimal places).

   Target = ______ **Walmart** = ______

2. Compared to each other, are these two companies more or less able to satisfy short-term obligations with current assets?
   a. Target is less able than Walmart to satisfy short-term obligations with current assets.
   b. Target is more able than Walmart to satisfy short-term obligations with current assets.
   c. Both companies' ratios suggest they are each likely to satisfy short-term obligations with current assets.
3. How does each company compare to the industry regarding the current ratio?
   a. Target and Walmart are both less liquid than the industry average.
   b. Target and Walmart are more liquid than the industry average.
   c. Target is less liquid and Walmart is more liquid than the industry average.
   d. Target is more liquid and Walmart is less liquid than the industry average.
4. How is the current ratio influenced by these companies' choice to lease space instead of buying facilities?
   a. Current lease liabilities will increase the current ratio.
   b. Leasing facilities instead of buying space has no effect on the current ratio.
   c. Current lease liabilities increase the denominator in the ratio, reducing the ratio.
   d. Operating lease assets decrease the current ratio.
5. Which company's current ratio increased from the year ended in 2020 to the year ended in 2021?
   a. Target's current ratio increased between 2020 and 2021.
   b. Walmart's current ratio increased between 2020 and 2021.
   c. Neither company's current ratio increased between 2020 and 2021.
   d. Both company's current ratio increased between 2020 and 2021.

Financial Reporting and Analysis Cases

Broadening Financial Research Skills: Locating Financial Information on the SEC's Database

CP2-4
LO2-2, 2-5, 2-6
Chipotle Mexican Grill

The Securities and Exchange Commission (SEC) regulates companies that issue stock on the stock market. It receives financial reports from public companies electronically under a system called EDGAR (Electronic Data Gathering and Retrieval Service). Using the Internet, anyone may search the database for the reports that have been filed.

Using your Web browser, access the EDGAR database at sec.gov. To search the database, click on "Filings" in the menu bar near the top of the page and then select "Company Filing Search" in the drop-down menu. Then type in "**Chipotle Mexican Grill**" for the company name in the search window and press enter.

Required:
To look at SEC filings, type in "10-Q" in the space indicating "Filing Type" and press enter. All of the Form 10-Q quarterly reports will be listed in reverse chronological order. Skim down the "Filing Date" column until you locate the Form 10-Q filed July 29, 2020. Click on the "Documents" for that report, click on the 10-Q document (first item), and skim to the Table of Contents.

1. Click on "Financial Statements" and locate the "Condensed Consolidated Balance Sheets."
   a. What was the amount in thousands of dollars of Chipotle's total assets at the end of the most recent quarter reported?
   b. Did current liabilities increase or decrease since December 31, 2019?
   c. Compute the current ratio (round your answer to three decimal places). How does it compare to the ratio indicated for Chipotle Mexican Grill in the chapter at December 31, 2019? What does this suggest about the company?

2. Skim to the Chipotle "Consolidated Statements of Cash Flows."
   a. What amount in thousands of dollars did Chipotle spend on "leasehold improvements, property and equipment" for the six months ended June 30, 2020? (Leasehold improvements are major renovations, such as adding elevators, to rented property.)
   b. What was the total amount in thousands of dollars of cash flows used in financing activities?

CP2-5 Using Financial Reports: Evaluating the Reliability of a Balance Sheet

LO2-1, 2-5

Frances Sabatier asked a local bank for a $50,000 loan to expand her small company. The bank asked Frances to submit a financial statement of the business to supplement the loan application. Frances prepared the following balance sheet.

FS COMPUTING **Balance Sheet** **June 30, 2023**	
Assets	
Cash and investments	$ 9,000
Inventory	30,000
Equipment	46,000
Personal residence (monthly payments, $2,800)	300,000
Remaining assets	20,000
Total assets	$405,000
Liabilities	
Short-term debt to suppliers	$ 62,000
Long-term debt on equipment	38,000
Total debt	100,000
Stockholders' equity	305,000
Total liabilities and stockholders' equity	$405,000

Required:

The balance sheet has several flaws. However, there is one major deficiency. Identify it and explain its significance.

CP2-6 Using Financial Reports: Analyzing the Balance Sheet

LO2-2, 2-4, 2-5
Twitter, Inc.

Recent balance sheets are provided for **Twitter, Inc.**, a global platform for real-time public self-expression and conversation. Show your answers in thousands of dollars.

TWITTER, INC. **CONSOLIDATED BALANCE SHEETS*** **(In thousands, unless otherwise specified)**	Dec. 31, 2019	Dec. 31, 2018
ASSETS		
Current assets:		
Cash and cash equivalents	$ 1,799,082	$ 1,894,444
Short-term investments	4,839,970	4,314,957
Accounts receivable	850,184	788,700
Prepaid expenses and other current assets	130,839	112,935
Total current assets	7,620,075	7,111,036
Property and equipment, net	1,031,781	885,078
Operating lease right-of-use assets	697,095	-
Intangible assets	1,311,805	1,272,294
Other noncurrent assets	2,042,633	894,164
Total assets	$12,703,389	$ 10,162,572

(Continued)

TWITTER, INC.
CONSOLIDATED BALANCE SHEETS*
(In thousands, unless otherwise specified)

	Dec. 31, 2019	Dec. 31, 2018
LIABILITIES AND STOCKHOLDERS' EQUITY		
Current liabilities:		
Accounts payable	$ 161,148	$ 145,186
Accrued and other current liabilities	500,893	1,303,079
Operating lease liabilities, short-term	146,959	-
Finance lease liabilities, short-term	23,476	68,046
Total current liabilities	832,476	1,516,311
Notes payable	2,508,800	1,730,922
Operating lease liabilities, long-term	609,245	-
Finance lease liabilities, long-term	205	24,394
Other long-term liabilities	48,277	85,351
Total liabilities	3,999,003	3,356,978
Stockholders' equity:		
Common stock, $0.000005 par value	4	4
Additional paid-in capital	8,692,796	8,259,663
Retained earnings (accumulated deficit)	11,586	(1,454,073)
Total stockholders' equity	8,704,386	6,805,594
Total liabilities and stockholders' equity	$12,703,389	$10,162,572

*These statements have been simplified for instructional purposes.

Source: Twitter, Inc.

Required:

1. Is Twitter a corporation, sole proprietorship, or partnership? Explain the basis of your answer.
2. Use the company's balance sheet to determine the amounts in the accounting equation (A = L + SE) at the end of the most recent year.
3. Calculate the company's current ratio on December 31, 2019, and on December 31, 2018 (round your answers to three decimal places). Interpret the ratios that you calculated. What other information would make your interpretation more useful?
4. Prepare the journal entry the company will make in 2020 assuming it pays its December 31, 2019, accounts payable balance in full.
5. Does the company appear to have been profitable over its years in business? On what account are you basing your answer? Assuming no dividends were paid, how much was net income (or net loss) in thousands of dollars in the most recent year? If it is impossible to determine without an income statement, state so.

Critical Thinking Cases

Making a Decision as a Financial Analyst: Preparing and Analyzing a Balance Sheet

CP2-7
LO2-1, 2-5

Your best friend from home writes you a letter about an investment opportunity that has come her way. A company is raising money by issuing shares of stock and wants her to invest $20,000 (her recent inheritance from her great-aunt's estate). Your friend has never invested in a company before and, knowing that you are a financial analyst, asks that you look over the balance sheet and send her some advice. An **unaudited** balance sheet, in only moderately good form, is enclosed with the letter.

There is only one disclosure note, and it states that the building was purchased for $65,000, has been depreciated by $5,000 on the books, and still carries a mortgage (shown in the liability section). The note also states that, in the opinion of the company president, the building is "easily worth $98,000."

LETTUCEDOTHIS.COM, INC. **Balance Sheet** **For the Most Recent Year Ending December 31**	
Accounts receivable	$ 8,000
Cash	1,000
Inventory	8,000
Furniture and fixtures	52,000
Delivery truck	12,000
Buildings (estimated market value)	98,000
Total assets	**$179,000**
Accounts payable	$ 16,000
Payroll taxes payable	13,000
Notes payable (due in three years)	15,000
Mortgage payable	50,000
Total liabilities	**$ 94,000**
Contributed capital (issued 2,000 shares, $2 par value per share)	$ 80,000
Retained earnings	5,000
Total stockholders' equity	**$ 85,000**

Required:

1. Draft a new balance sheet for your friend, correcting any errors you note. (If any of the account balances need to be corrected, you may need to adjust the retained earnings balance correspondingly.) If there are no errors or omissions, so state.
2. Write a letter to your friend explaining the changes you made to the balance sheet, if any, and offer your comments on the company's apparent financial condition based only on this information. Suggest other information your friend might want to review before coming to a final decision on whether to invest.

CP2-8 Evaluating an Ethical Dilemma: Analyzing Management Incentives

LO2-1

Celadon Group, Inc.

On December 5, 2019, the Securities and Exchange Commission (SEC) charged two top executives of **Celadon Group, Inc.**, an Indiana-based trucking company, for their participation in an accounting fraud. The SEC alleged that "they sought to conceal losses by engaging in a scheme to buy and sell trucks at inflated prices, in some cases double or triple their fair market value . . . As alleged in our complaint, these members of Celadon's C-suite lied to its auditor and investors to try to conceal millions of dollars of overvalued trucks," said Joel R. Levin, Director of the SEC's Chicago Regional Office. "The SEC will continue to pursue corporate officers who employ schemes to inflate financial statements and defraud investors." (Source: sec.gov/news/press-release/2019-253)

Epilogue: On December 9, 2019, Celadon Group, Inc., filed for bankruptcy and in March 2020, it auctioned off assets as part of the bankruptcy agreement.

Required:

1. Describe the parties who were harmed or helped by this fraud.
2. Explain how greed may have contributed to the fraud.

You As Analyst: Online Company Research

CP2-9 Analysis of Investing and Financing Activities of a Public Company (an Individual or Team Project)

LO2-2, 2-5, 2-6

In your web browser, search for the investor relations page of a public company you are interested in (e.g., Papa John's investor relations). Select SEC Filings or Annual Report or Financials to obtain the 10-K for the most recent year available.*

Required:

1. Go to the Balance Sheet. For the most recent year:
   a. What is the date of the balance sheet?
   b. What are the top three asset accounts by size?
   c. What is the percentage of each to total assets? (Calculated as Asset A/Total Assets)
   d. What are the top three liability accounts by size?
   e. What is the percentage of each to total liabilities? (Calculated as Liability A/Total Liabilities)
   f. What are the significant changes, if any, in stockholders' equity?
   g. Does the company's investment in assets come primarily from liabilities or stockholders' equity?
2. Ratio Analysis:
   a. What does the current ratio measure in general?
   b. Compute the current ratio for each of the last three years. (You will need to look at the prior year's 10-K for the third year of numbers.)
   c. What do your results suggest about the company over time?
3. Go to the Statement of Cash Flows. For the most recent year:
   a. What are the major investing activities (by dollar size)?
   b. Was total cash flow from investing activities positive or negative?
   c. What are the major financing activities (by dollar size)?
   d. Was total cash flow from financing activities positive or negative?

---

*Alternatively, you can go to sec.gov, click on Company Filings (under the search box), type in the name of the public company you want to find. Once at the list of filings, type 10-K in the Filing Type box. The most recent 10-K annual report will be at the top of the list. Click on Interactive Data for a list of the parts or the entire report to examine.

BUSINESS ANALYTICS AND DATA VISUALIZATION WITH EXCEL AND TABLEAU

Connect offers a variety of exercises to assess Excel skills, data visualization, interpretation, and analysis, including auto-graded Tableau Dashboard Activities, Applying Excel problems, and Integrated Excel problems.

Tip Most companies make data-driven decisions for most aspects of their businesses, such as, where to open a new store, understanding customer preferences, which mix of products to produce, and trends. These exercises will introduce you to current analytical tools.

Images used throughout chapter: Question of ethics: mushmello/Shutterstock; Pause for feedback: McGraw Hill; Guided help: McGraw Hill; Financial analysis: McGraw Hill; Focus on cash flows: Hilch/Shutterstock; Key ratio analysis: guillermain/123RF; Data analytics: Hilch/Shutterstock; Tip: McGraw Hill; ESG reporting: McGraw Hill; International perspective: Hilch/Shutterstock

chapter 3

Operating Decisions and the Accounting System

Chipotle Mexican Grill keeps operations simple, offering a few menu items (burritos, burrito bowls, tacos, and salads). Within these items, customers can choose from a variety of meats, tofu, veggies beans, rice, and additional items such as salsa, guacamole, cheese, lettuce, and queso—creating hundreds of options. The focused menu allows Chipotle to concentrate on the source of the food items, a challenging activity given the smaller and often costlier market for organic meats, produce, and dairy products. Anticipating changes in these food costs and sources is critical to determining menu prices and controlling costs.

To control quality and increase efficiency, the company purchases key ingredients such as meat, beans, rice, cheese, and tortillas from a small number of suppliers and other raw materials from approved sources. Twenty-three independently owned and operated regional distribution centers purchase from these suppliers and then deliver the items as needed to the Chipotle restaurants in each region. To ensure food safety, Chipotle provides training for local farmers, utilizes advanced technology to trace the source of the food from suppliers to the restaurants, uses the sous vide (slow-cooking in hot water bath) method to control any pathogens or bacteria in meat, and provides bonuses to crew teams who meet specific food safety goals, among other measures.

The second highest cost for Chipotle, as with most restaurants, is hiring and developing its over 91,000 employees. The food is prepared from scratch on stoves and grills, not with microwaves and other automated cooking techniques. Each employee

LEARNING OBJECTIVES

After studying this chapter, you should be able to:

3-1 Describe a typical business operating cycle and explain the necessity for the time period assumption. p. 110

3-2 Explain how business activities affect the elements of the income statement. p. 112

3-3 Explain the accrual basis of accounting and apply the revenue and expense recognition principles to measure income. p. 116

3-4 Apply transaction analysis to examine and record the effects of operating activities on the financial statements. p. 121

3-5 Prepare a classified income statement. p. 129

3-6 Compute and interpret the net profit margin ratio. p. 131

3-7 Identify operating transactions and demonstrate how they affect cash flows. p. 133

FOCUS COMPANY

Luke Sharrett/Bloomberg via Getty Images

Chipotle Mexican Grill

IT'S MORE THAN MEAT, GUACAMOLE, AND TORTILLAS

chipotle.com

Learn more about Chipotle from founder, Steve Ells, by listening to the NPR podcast

Chipotle: Steve Ells: How I Built This.

How I Built This NPR podcasts are about innovators, entrepreneurs, idealists, and the movements they built.

is cross-trained in all aspects of preparing the food—from grilling, to making fresh salsa and guacamole, to cooking rice—and creating a positive interactive experience for customers. The company has a strong culture of employee professional and personal development with numerous incentives to build and retain strong leadership. Chipotle's Cultivate Education program provides tuition reimbursement and has a Debt-Free Degree program at selected colleges, including Paul Quinn College, one of the oldest historically black colleges in the country. These programs contribute to retention, with about 80 percent of its general managers promoted from within Chipotle.

Chipotle also competes using marketing strategies. In 2018, Chipotle began to utilize more aggressive marketing efforts, including "addressable TV" ads (targeting selective segments of on-demand or live TV shows), digital marketing, online ordering, and a loyalty program. Having these initiatives in place allowed Chipotle to respond rapidly to the Covid-19 pandemic, resulting in a surge in on-line ordering and deliveries.

UNDERSTANDING THE BUSINESS

Over **Chipotle**'s history since 1993, the restaurant industry has become extremely competitive with many established as well as new concept restaurants adopting service and sourcing formats similar to Chipotle's. For example, in 2012, **McDonald's Corporation** announced a requirement that suppliers need to phase out stalls that restrict the movement of pregnant pigs, a change made in direct response to Chipotle's TV video on its ethical stance aired at the Grammy Awards. **Taco Bell** created its urban Taco Bell Cantina model with a menu featuring "gourmet" food items. **Jack in the Box, Inc.**, expanded its **Qdoba Mexican Grill** chain to compete in the fast-casual segment of the restaurant industry. The newer concepts feature Mediterranean, Indian, farm-to-table, fish-to-table, and vegetarian cuisine, with many more popping up every day that focus on selective food sourcing, food prepared on-site, and a service model that allows customers to choose exactly what they want to eat. For example, the fast-growing, fast-casual concepts include **City Barbecue** offering smoked in-house meats and sides, **Sweetgreen** with seasonal salads and grain bowls, and **Bibibop Asian Grill** with Korean flavors using healthy ingredients.

Restaurants have to manage economic downturns and shifts in consumer tastes for healthier food choices while facing the competition. The Covid-19 pandemic, for example, created tremendous upheaval in the restaurant industry. To respond, most of the fast-casual restaurants began offering drive-through or curbside pick-up, digital ordering, and delivery service, supported by digital technology. Based on their projections of these forces, companies set goals for their performance. Published income statements provide the primary basis for comparing projections to the actual results of operations. To understand how business plans and the results of operations are reflected on the income statement, we need to answer the following questions:

1. How do business activities affect the income statement?
2. How are business activities measured?
3. How are business activities reported on the income statement?

In Chapter 2, we illustrated the use of transaction analysis, journal entries, and T-accounts for investing and financing activities. In this chapter, we apply these tools for operating activities, as illustrated with hypothetical quarterly transactions for Chipotle that involve the sale of food to the public. The results of these activities are reported on the income statement.

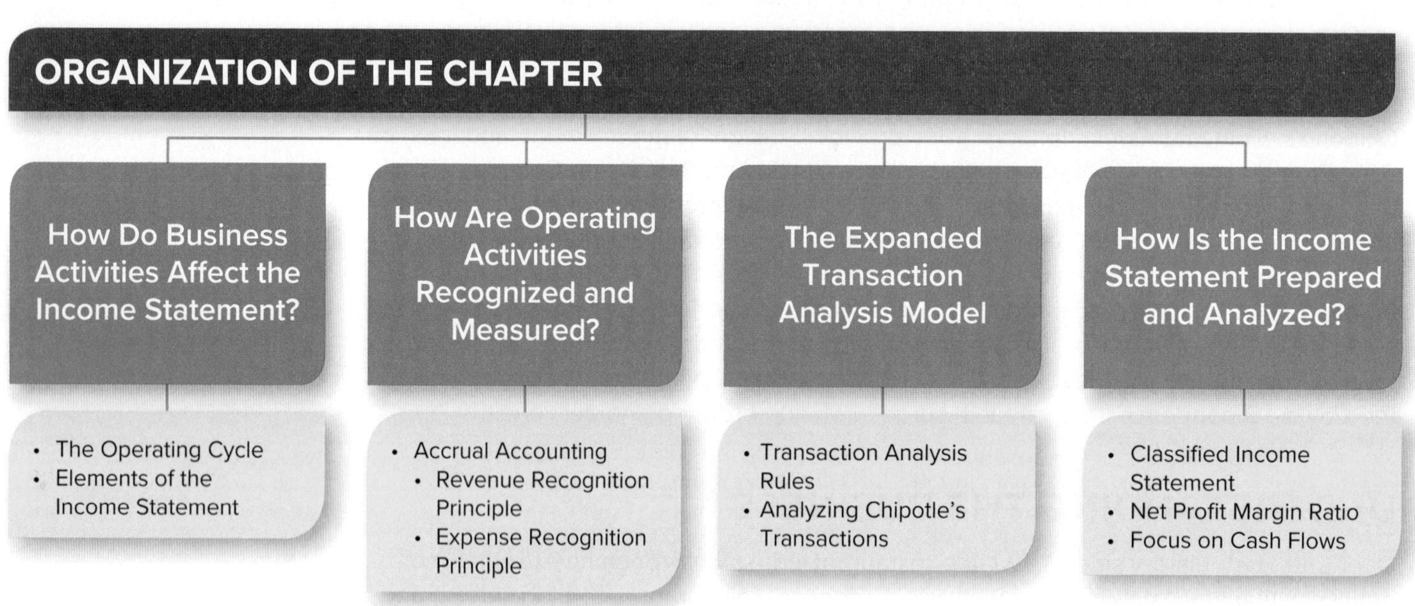

LEARNING OBJECTIVE 3-1

Describe a typical business operating cycle and explain the necessity for the time period assumption.

HOW DO BUSINESS ACTIVITIES AFFECT THE INCOME STATEMENT?

The Operating Cycle

The long-term objective for any business is to **turn cash into more cash**. If a company is to stay in business, this excess cash must be generated from operations (that is, from the activities for which the business was established), not from borrowing money or selling long-lived assets.

Companies (1) acquire inventory and the services of employees and (2) sell inventory or services to customers. The **operating (cash-to-cash) cycle** begins when a company receives goods to sell, then continues when the company pays for them and sells the goods to customers (or, in the case of a service company, has employees work to provide services to customers). It ends when customers pay cash to the company. The length of time for completion of the operating cycle depends on the nature of the business.

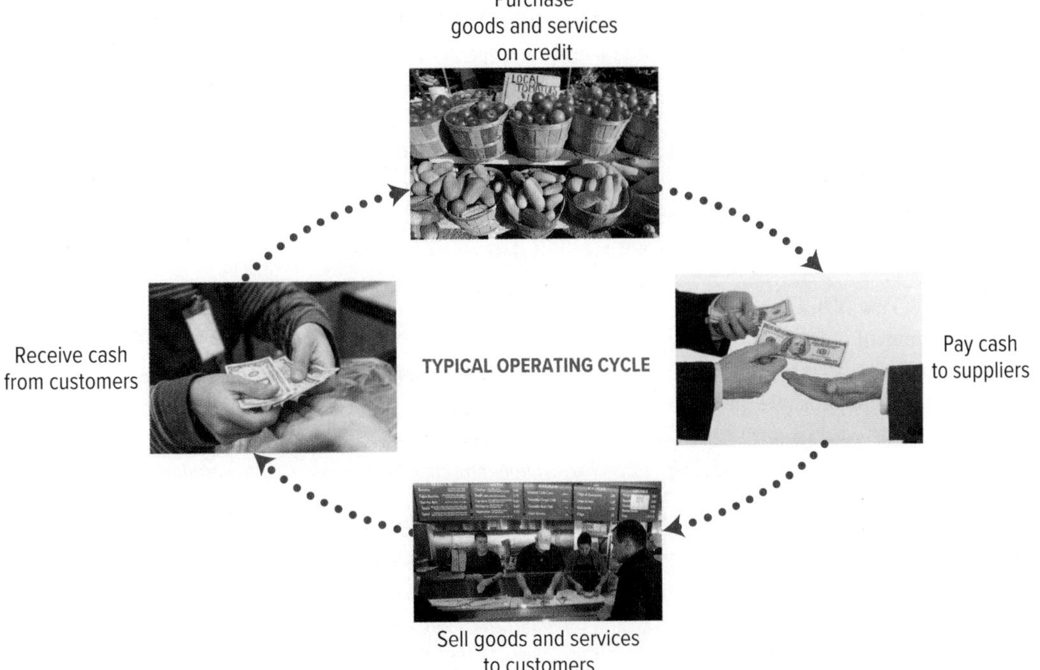

Left: Digital Vision/Getty Images; Top: Juanmonino/Getty Images; Right: Tetra Images/Getty Images; Bottom: Jeff Kowalsky/Bloomberg/Getty Images

The operating cycle for **Chipotle** is relatively short. It spends cash to purchase fresh ingredients, prepares the food, and sells it to customers for cash. In some companies, inventory is paid for well before it is sold. **Amazon.com**, for example, builds its inventory for months preceding the year-end holiday season. It may borrow funds from banks to pay for the inventory, and then it repays the loans with interest when it receives cash from customers. In other companies, cash is received from customers well after a sale takes place. For example, furniture retailers such as **Ethan Allen** often allow customers to make monthly payments over several years. Shortening the operating cycle by creating incentives that encourage customers to buy sooner and/or pay faster improves a company's cash flows.

Until a company ceases its activities, the operating cycle is repeated continuously. However, decision makers require information periodically about the company's financial condition and performance. To measure income for a specific period of time, accountants follow the **time period assumption**, which assumes that the long life of a company can be reported in shorter time periods, such as months, quarters, and years.[1] Two types of issues arise in reporting periodic income to users:

1. Recognition issues: **When** should the effects of operating activities be recognized (recorded)?
2. Measurement issues: **What amounts** should be recognized?

[1] In addition to the audited annual statements, most businesses prepare quarterly financial statements (also known as **interim reports** covering a three-month period) for external users. The Securities and Exchange Commission requires public companies to do so.

LEARNING OBJECTIVE 3-2

Explain how business activities affect the elements of the income statement.

Before we examine the rules accountants follow in resolving these issues, however, let's examine the elements of the income statement that are affected by operating activities.

Elements of the Income Statement

Exhibit 3.1 shows a recent income statement for **Chipotle**, simplified for the purposes of this chapter. It has multiple subtotals, such as **income from operations** and **income before income taxes**. This format is known as **multiple step** and is very common.[2] In fact, you can tell if a company uses the multiple-step format if you see the Income from Operations subtotal (also called Operating Income).

Operating Activities

Revenues are the amounts earned and recorded from a company's day-to-day business activities, mostly when a company sells products or provides services to customers or clients (the central

EXHIBIT 3.1

Chipotle Mexican Grill's Income Statement

CHIPOTLE MEXICAN GRILL, INC.
Consolidated Statement of Income*
For the Year ended December 31, 2019
(in millions of dollars, except per share data)

Section	Item	Amount	EXPLANATIONS
			Period of time that financial performance was measured
Operating section (central focus of business)	Restaurant sales revenue	$5,586	*Earned from providing food service to customers during the year*
	Restaurant operating expenses:		
	Supplies expense	1,848	*Cost of food, drink, and packaging supplies used during the year*
	Wages expense	1,472	*Cost of employee wages and salaries for work during the year*
	Rent expense	363	*Cost of renting facilities used during the year*
	Insurance expense	201	*Cost of insurance coverage used during the year*
	Utilities expense	102	*Cost of electric and gas used during the year*
	Repairs expense	73	*Cost of repairing buildings and equipment during the year*
	Other operating expenses	384	*Summary of other operating costs used during the year*
	General and administrative expenses:		
	Training expense	321	*Cost of training employees and managers during the year*
	Advertising expense	142	*Cost of advertising done during the year*
	Depreciation expense	213	*Portion of cost of buildings and equipment used during the year*
	Loss on disposal of assets	23	*Cost of assets sold during the year minus exchange price*
	Total operating expenses	5,142	
	Income from operations	444	*Subtraction of operating expenses from operating revenues*
Other Items section (not central focus of business)	Other items:		*Revenues/expenses/gains/losses from investments/debt during the year*
	Interest revenue	17	*Earned from investments during the year*
	Interest expense	(3)	*Incurred on debt owed during the year*
	Income before income taxes	458	
	Income tax expense	108	*Also called Provision for Income Taxes for the year*
	Net income	$ 350	*Difference between all revenues and expenses for the year*
	Earnings per share	$12.62	*= $350 million ÷ 27.74 million weighted average shares of stock outstanding (from Chipotle's 10-K)*

*The information has been adapted from actual statements and simplified for this chapter.

Source: Chipotle Mexican Grill, Inc.

[2]Another common format, **single step**, reorganizes all accounts from the multiple-step format. All revenues and gains are listed together and all expenses and losses except taxes are listed together. The expense subtotal is then subtracted from the revenue subtotal to arrive at income before income taxes, the same subtotal as on the multiple-step statement. In the single-step format, **there is no subtotal for income from operations or a separate section for other items.**

focus of the business). When Chipotle sells salad bowls to consumers, it has **earned** revenue. When revenue is earned, usually Cash or Accounts Receivable (amounts due from customers) increases. Sometimes if a customer pays for goods or services in advance, for example, when buying a Chipotle gift card, the company creates a liability account, usually Unearned (or Deferred) Revenue. At this point, no revenue has been earned. There is simply a receipt of cash in exchange for a promise to provide a good or service in the future. Later, when the company provides the promised goods or services to the customer paying with the gift card, then the revenue is recognized and the liability is eliminated.

Many companies generate revenues from a variety of sources. For example, **General Motors** reports revenues from its automotive sales as well as from providing financing to customers. In the restaurant industry, many companies, such as **McDonald's Corporation**, have company-owned stores but also sell franchise rights. The franchisor (seller) reports revenues from both the sales of food in company-owned stores and the fees from franchisees. Chipotle does not sell franchises. Therefore, the company generates revenue from one source–sales of food orders to customers–that is reported in the **Restaurant Sales Revenue** account.

Tip Some students confuse the terms **expenditure** and **expense**. An expenditure is an **outlay of cash for any purpose**—including to buy equipment, pay off a bank loan, and pay for equipment repair. Not all expenditures are for expenses.

Expenses, on the other hand, are costs incurred to generate revenue during the period—**most expenses are not paid in cash when incurred**.

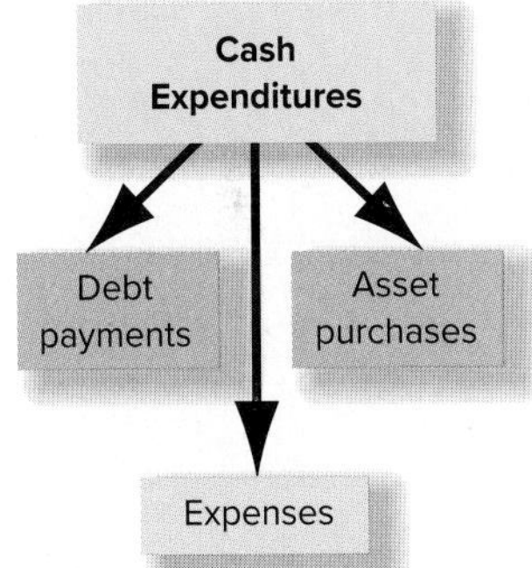

Expenses are the costs of operating the business that are incurred to generate revenues during the period. Usually, many expenses are incurred (that is, the resources or services of others that are used) in making a sale or providing a service. When Chipotle's employees prepare and serve food to customers, Chipotle incurs an expense for **using** employee labor to generate revenue. The company **uses** electric service to operate equipment and light its facilities, and it **uses** food and paper supplies. Without incurring these expenses, Chipotle could not generate revenues. Expenses may be incurred before, after, or at the same time as they are paid in cash. When an expense is incurred, assets such as Supplies decrease (are used up) **or** liabilities such as Wages Payable or Utilities Payable increase. The following are Chipotle's primary expenses:

Restaurant Operating Expenses:

- **Supplies Expense**. In Chipotle's restaurant operations, any food ingredients or beverage and packaging supplies that are used to produce and sell meals are expensed as they are used. For Chipotle, this is its largest expense at $1,848 million in 2019. In companies with a manufacturing or merchandising focus, the most significant expense is usually Cost of Sales (or Cost of Goods Sold), representing the cost of inventory used in generating sales.
- **Wages Expense**. When salaried and hourly employees work and generate sales for Chipotle, the company incurs an expense, although wages and salaries will be paid later. Wages Expense of $1,472 million is Chipotle's second largest expense. In purely service-oriented companies in which no products are produced or sold, the cost of having employees generate revenues is usually the largest expense. For example, **Federal Express** reported over $25,031 million in salaries expense for the year ended May 31, 2020.
- **Rent Expense, Insurance Expense, Utilities Expense, and Repairs Expense**. Renting facilities, insuring property and equipment at the stores, using utilities, and repairing and maintaining facilities and equipment are typical expenses related to operating stores. Usually, rent and insurance are paid before occupying the facilities, but utilities and repairs are paid after occupying the facilities.
- **Other Operating Expenses**. These expenses include a wide variety of accounts with smaller dollar balances.

General and Administrative Expenses: General and Administrative Expenses include costs of training employees and managers, advertising, and other expenses not directly related to operating stores. These often include expenses such as renting headquarters facilities and paying executive salaries.

Depreciation Expense: When a company uses buildings and equipment to generate revenues, a part of the cost of these assets is reported as an expense called Depreciation Expense. Chapter 8 discusses methods for estimating the amount of depreciation expense.

Tip Note that **selling** short- or long-term **investments** above or below cost also results in gains or losses, but these are **reported in the Other Items section of the multiple-step income statement** (they are not operating activities).

Losses (Gains) on Disposal of Assets: Companies sell property, plant, and equipment from time to time to maintain modern facilities. When assets **other than investments** are sold or disposed of for more than their cost minus the amount of cost depreciated in the past, gains result. If they are sold or disposed of for less than their cost minus the amount of cost depreciated in the past, losses result. In 2019, Chipotle reported a loss on disposal of assets of $23 million.

Revenues minus expenses from operating activities equals Income from Operations (also called Operating Income)–a measure of the profit from central ongoing operations.

Other Items

Not all activities affecting an income statement are central to ongoing operations. Any revenues, expenses, gains, or losses that result from these other activities are not included as part of income from operations but are instead categorized as Other Items. Typically, these include the following:

- **Interest Revenue (also Investment Revenue, Investment Income, or Dividend Revenue).** Using excess cash to purchase stocks or bonds in other companies is not a part of Chipotle's central operation of making and selling fresh Mexican food. Therefore, any interest or dividends earned on investments in other companies is not included as operating revenue.
- **Interest Expense.** Likewise, for most businesses, borrowing money is not central to ongoing operations. Thus, the cost of using that money (called interest) is not an operating expense. Financial institutions such as banks are the exception where incurring interest expense and earning interest revenue are central to their operations.
- **Losses (Gains) on Sale of Investments.** When investments are sold for less (or more) than the original cost, a loss (or gain) results and is reported as an Other Item on the income statement. In 2019, Chipotle did not report any gain or loss from selling investments.

Income Tax Expense

Operating expenses are subtracted from operating revenues to determine Income before Income Taxes (also called Pretax Income). From this subtotal, **Income Tax Expense** (also called **Provision for Income Taxes**) is calculated by applying the tax rates of the federal, state, local, and foreign taxing authorities. Chipotle's effective tax rate in 2019 was 23.6 percent ($108 million in income tax expense divided by $458 million in income before income taxes). This indicates that, for every dollar of income before taxes that Chipotle made in 2019, the company paid nearly $0.24 to taxing authorities.

Earnings per Share

Corporations are required to disclose earnings per share on the income statement or in the notes to the financial statements. This ratio is widely used in evaluating the operating performance and profitability of a company. At this introductory level, we can compute earnings per share simply as:

$$\text{Earnings per Share}^* = \frac{\text{Net Income}}{\text{Weighted average number of shares of common stock outstanding}}$$

*As you will learn in Chapter 11: (1) If there are preferred stock dividends, the amount is subtracted from net income in the numerator, (2) the denominator for weighted average shares is a complex computation, and (3) outstanding shares are those that are currently held by the shareholders.

Please note, however, that the calculation of the ratio is actually much more complex and beyond the scope of this course. For simplicity, we use the $350 million net income in Exhibit 3.1 as the numerator and approximately 27.74 million weighted average number of shares as computed by Chipotle for the denominator. For 2019, Chipotle reported $12.62 in earnings for each share of stock owned by investors.

DATA ANALYTICS

Using Data Analytics in the Restaurant Industry to Increase Revenues and Decrease Costs

Restaurants are using a variety of technologies including kiosks, mobile apps, and tableside tablets from which ordering data can be mined to analyze purchasing profiles. Data analytics also facilitates monitoring employee performance, improving scheduling, boosting customer loyalty, and maximizing marketing efficiency. Here are a few examples of restaurants that use data analytics to optimize performance, make better and faster decisions, reduce costs, and improve the customer experience:

Raymond Deleon/Alamy Stock Photo

- **Panera Bread** was one of the first restaurants to install ordering kiosks to (1) encourage menu browsing, (2) capture customer preferences, (3) fine-tune the menu based on preferences, (4) produce shorter lines for a better customer experience, (5) ensure better order accuracy to improve operational efficiency and reduce waste, and (6) save and/or redeploy labor costs.
- **McDonald's** uses data to predict customer demand in drive-thru sales. By ensuring adequate staffing and alerting staff to the spike in demand, the efficiency of operations is improved along with enhancing the customer experience.
- **Wendy's** analyzes big data on past sales and customer demographics to identify the most profitable new restaurant locations.
- **Pizza Hut** uses software to track customer eye movements on digital, interactive menus in some of its restaurants to discover what customers subconsciously want.
- **Dunkin'** mines data from its mobile loyalty program called DD Perks to send customers targeted offers at specific times.

SOURCES: hotschedules.com/blog/biggest-restaurant-brands-use-big-data-stay-competitive/; delltechnologies.com/en-us/video-collateral/panera_case_study_in_big_data_analytics_and_data_science_bluedata.htm; michiganstateuniversityonline.com/resources/business-analytics/dining-on-big-data/; pymnts.com/mobile-order-ahead/2019/how-dunkin-uses-ai-for-order-ahead-analytics/.

HOW ARE OPERATING ACTIVITIES RECOGNIZED AND MEASURED?

There is more than one way to recognize and measure operating activities. Many sole proprietors and small partnerships, such as dental and doctors' offices, choose to use the **cash basis accounting** method[3] to determine performance. It is simple and is permitted for tax purposes. With cash basis accounting, owners record each transaction as money changes hands–paying a vendor in cash is a cash outflow and receiving cash from a customer or client is a cash inflow. This basis produces net cash flow information that is often quite adequate for organizations that do not need to report to external users.

Using cash basis accounting may lead to an incorrect interpretation of company performance and financial position:

- Revenues and expenses are often postponed or accelerated long before or after goods and service are delivered, and
- Other than cash, assets and liabilities of the company are not reported in financial statements.

[3]For more information on businesses that can use cash basis accounting, a couple of sources are patriotsoftware.com/blog/accounting/when-is-cash-basis-accounting-acceptable/ and irs.gov/newsroom/irs-issues-guidance-on-small-business-accounting-method-changes-under-tax-cuts-and-jobs-act. (Note: These are applicable as of the writing of this text. IRS regulations can change over time, so check with irs.gov for the up-to-date information.)

For these reasons, cash basis financial statements are not very useful to external decision makers. Therefore, generally accepted accounting principles require **accrual basis accounting** for financial reporting.

LEARNING OBJECTIVE 3-3

Explain the accrual basis of accounting and apply the revenue and expense recognition principles to measure income.

Accrual Accounting

In accrual basis accounting, **revenues are recognized when goods and services are provided to customers** (they are earned)**, and expenses are recognized in the same period as the revenues to which they relate** (resources are used or debts are incurred to generate revenues)**, regardless of when cash is received or paid**. The two basic accounting principles that determine when revenues and expenses are recorded under accrual basis accounting are the **revenue recognition principle** and the **expense recognition principle** (also called the **matching principle**).

Accrual Accounting, in short:

- **Recognize Revenues when EARNED** (performed, delivered)
- **Recognize Expenses when INCURRED** (resources used or debts incurred) to generate revenues in the same period

Revenue Recognition Principle

The core revenue recognition principle specifies both the timing and amount of revenue to be recognized during an accounting period. It requires that a company **recognize revenue (1) when the company transfers promised goods or services to customers (2) in the amount it expects to be entitled to receive.**

The five steps to follow for recognizing revenue, especially when a sales contract is more complex,[4] are:

Step 1. Identify the contract (written, verbal, or implied agreement) between the company and customer.

Example: A contract is created when **Chipotle** agrees to sell you a sofritas burrito.

Step 2. Identify the seller's performance obligations (promised goods and services).

Example: Some contracts involve one performance obligation–to deliver a sofritas burrito. However, other contracts include multiple obligations. **Apple Inc.** has identified up to three performance obligations involving the sale of certain products such as the iPhone: (1) to deliver the iPhone and its software; (2) to provide product-related bundled services including iCloud, Siri, and Maps; and (3) to provide future unspecified software upgrades for the iPhone.

Step 3. Determine the transaction price (the amount the seller expects to be entitled to receive from the customer).

Example: For Chipotle, the transaction price is the amount shown on the menu minus any discounts, coupons, and loyalty program awards–$9 from the Chipotle customer, for example. For Apple, the transaction price is the total price for the iPhone to be paid by the customer–$750, for example.

Step 4. Allocate the transaction price to the performance obligations.

Example: For a single performance obligation, the full price relates to the delivery to the customer. However, when Apple sells (1) an iPhone, (2) product-related bundled services, and (3) a promise to provide future software upgrades, the transaction price is split among the three obligations by referring to the prices of each part sold separately.

Step 5. Recognize revenue when each performance obligation is satisfied (or over time if a service is provided over time).

Example: Chipotle recognizes revenue upon delivery of the burrito to the customer. Apple will recognize as revenue a substantial portion of the allocated transaction price of the iPhone itself when it is delivered. Then, it will recognize a portion of the second and third obligations as they are provided to customers.

For most contracts discussed in this text, the revenue recognition steps are easy to apply. For example, Chipotle (1) agrees to (2) deliver a burrito that has been ordered by a customer for (3) the menu price with (4) the entire menu price (5) recognized on delivery of the burrito to the customer. **The critical point for revenue recognition under the five-step model is when goods or services are delivered**, not when cash is received from customers. Cash may be received before, after, or at the time of delivery as illustrated in Exhibit 3.2. Let's see how to handle each of these cases.

---

[4]Accounting for bundled sales transactions is discussed in Chapter 6, with additional detailed coverage in intermediate accounting courses.

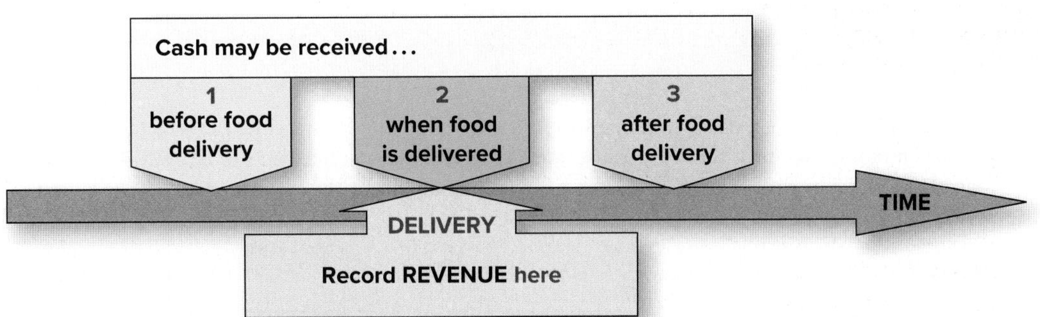

EXHIBIT 3.2

Recording Revenues versus Cash Receipts

1 **Cash is received *before* the goods or services are delivered.** Chipotle sells gift cards to customers for cash in exchange for the promise to provide future food orders. Because Chipotle has not delivered food at that point, it records **no revenue**. Instead, it creates a liability account called Unearned Revenue (or Deferred Revenue), representing the amount of food service owed to the customers. Later, when customers redeem their gift cards and Chipotle delivers the food, it earns and records the revenue while reducing the liability account because it has satisfied its promise to deliver.

2 **Cash is received *in the same period as* the goods or services are delivered.** As is a typical timing of cash receipts and revenue recognition in the restaurant industry, Chipotle receives cash from most customers within a few minutes of them receiving their food. Chipotle delivers the food to the customer as ordered in exchange for cash, earning revenue in the process.

3 **Cash is received *after* the goods or services are delivered.** When a business sells goods or services on account (creating Accounts Receivable due from customers), the revenue is earned when the goods or services are delivered, not when cash is received at a later date. Let's assume that, to boost business, Chipotle agrees to deliver food ordered by select customers, such as departments at area colleges or local businesses. These customers pay for the food order when Chipotle bills them at the end of the month, rather than when they receive the food. When delivered, Chipotle records both Restaurant Sales Revenue and the asset Accounts Receivable, representing the customer's promise to pay in the future for past food deliveries. When the customer pays its monthly bill, Chipotle will increase its Cash account and decrease the asset Accounts Receivable.

Companies usually disclose their revenue recognition practices in the financial statement note titled Significant Accounting Policies or in a separate note. The following excerpt from Note 1 to recent financial statements describes how Chipotle recognizes its revenue:

1. **Description of Business and Summary of Significant Accounting Policies**

Revenue Recognition

We generally recognize revenue, net of discounts and incentives, when payment is tendered at the point of sale. . . .

Delivery

We offer our customers delivery in almost all of our geographic regions. . . . We . . . recognize revenue, including delivery fees, when the delivery partner transfers food to the customer. . .

Gift Cards

. . . Gift card balances are initially recorded as unearned revenue. We recognize revenue from gift cards when the gift card is redeemed by the customer. . .

CHIPOTLE MEXICAN GRILL
REAL WORLD EXCERPT:
2019 Annual Report

Source: Chipotle Mexican Grill, Inc.

PAUSE FOR FEEDBACK

We just learned the **revenue recognition principle's** criteria: Recognize revenue (1) when the company transfers promised goods or services to customers (2) in the amount it expects to be entitled to receive. Regardless of when cash is paid by customers, revenue is recognized upon delivery (satisfaction of performance obligations).

SELF-STUDY QUIZ

Complete this quiz now to make sure you can apply the revenue recognition principle. The following transactions are samples of typical monthly operating activities of **Papa John's International, Inc.** (dollars in thousands), a company that makes and delivers pizza and sells franchises.

(a) In January, Papa John's company-owned restaurants sold food to customers for $32,000 cash.
(b) In January, Papa John's sold new franchises for $625 cash, providing $400 in services to these new franchisees during January; the remainder of the services will be provided over the next three months.
(c) In January, Papa John's received $210 in cash from customers as deposits on large orders to be delivered in February.
(d) In January, Papa John's delivered $1,630 in pizza to select customers on account; the customers will pay when billed at the end of January.
(e) In January, customers paid $1,200 on account to Papa John's from December deliveries of pizza.
(f) In January, Papa John's delivered $385 in pizza to customers who provided deposits in December.

Required:
Creating a table with headings as shown below, if revenue is to be recognized in **January**, indicate the title of the revenue account and the amount of revenue to be recognized. For account titles, name the revenue account based on the nature of the transaction. For example, sales to customers are Restaurant Sales Revenue and sales of franchises are Franchise Fee Revenue.

Transaction	Revenue Account Title	Amount of Revenue Recognized In January
(a)		

After you have completed your answers, check them below.

GUIDED HELP 3-1

For additional video instruction on identifying revenues in the proper period and the amount, go to mhhe.com/libby_gh3-1.

Related Homework: M3-2, E3-2

Solutions to SELF-STUDY QUIZ

Revenue Account Title	Amount of Revenue Recognized in January
(a) Restaurant Sales Revenue	$32,000
(b) Franchise Fee Revenue	$ 400
(c) No revenue earned in January	–
(d) Restaurant Sales Revenue	$ 1,630
(e) No revenue earned in January	–
(f) Restaurant Sales Revenue	$ 385

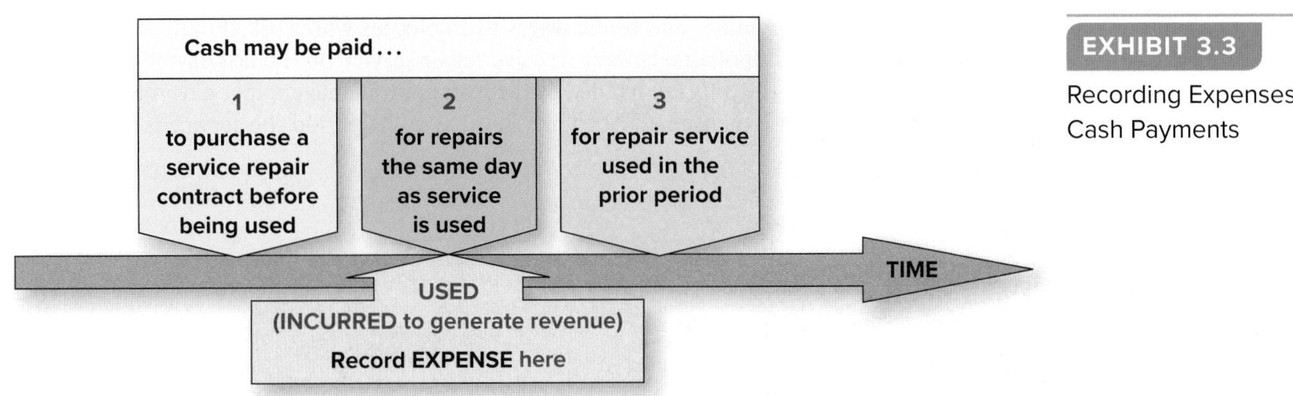

EXHIBIT 3.3

Recording Expenses versus Cash Payments

Expense Recognition Principle

The expense recognition principle (also called the **matching principle**) requires that costs incurred to generate revenues be recognized in the same period–a matching of costs with benefits. For example, when Chipotle's restaurants provide food service to customers, revenue is earned. The costs of generating the revenue include expenses incurred such as these:

- Salaries and wages to employees who worked **during the period**.
- Utilities for the electricity used **during the period.**
- Food, beverage, and packaging supplies used **during the period.**
- Facilities rented **during the period.**
- Grills and other equipment used **during the period.**

As with revenues and cash receipts, expenses are recorded as incurred, **regardless of when cash is paid.** Cash may be paid (1) **before**, (2) **during**, or (3) **after** an expense is incurred (see Exhibit 3.3). An entry will be made on the date the expense is incurred and another on the date the cash is paid, if they occur at different times. Let's see how to handle each of these cases related to the expense recognition principle.

1 **Cash is paid *before* the expense is incurred to generate revenue.** Companies purchase many assets that are used to generate revenues in future periods. Examples include buying insurance for future coverage, paying rent for future use of space, and acquiring supplies and equipment for future use. When revenues are generated in the future, the company records an expense for the portion of the cost of the assets used–costs are matched with the benefits. As an example, assume Chipotle signs a two-year contract with a repair company for service any time over the contracted years at no additional cost in exchange for a cash prepayment. When acquired, the service contract is recorded as an asset called Prepaid Expenses that will benefit future periods. When the service is used the following month, Repairs Expense is recorded for the month and the asset Prepaid Expenses is reduced to the balance yet to be used. Similarly, rent, insurance, and advertising that are prepaid are often recorded in an asset account called Prepaid Expenses and expensed when used.

2 **Cash is paid *in the same period* as the expense is incurred to generate revenue.** Expenses are sometimes incurred and paid for in the period in which they arise. An example is paying for repairs on grills the day of the service. If Chipotle spends $275 cash to repair grills so that food can be prepared to sell, an expense is incurred and recorded (Repairs Expense).

3 **Cash is paid *after* the cost is incurred to generate revenue.** Although rent and supplies are typically purchased before they are used, many costs are paid after goods or services have been received and used, including using utilities in the current period that are not paid for until the following period, using borrowed funds and incurring Interest Expense

to be paid in the future, and owing wages to employees who worked in the current period. When Chipotle restaurants receive repair service on the last day of the accounting period, and the bills are handed to the restaurant managers that day, the company records Repairs Expense and Accounts Payable in the period the service is used, not when cash is paid.

PAUSE FOR FEEDBACK

The **expense recognition principle** (or matching principle) requires that costs incurred to generate revenues be recognized in the same period—that costs are matched with the revenues they generate. Regardless of when cash is paid, expense is recorded when incurred.

SELF-STUDY QUIZ

Complete this quiz now to make sure you can apply the expense recognition principle. The following transactions are samples of typical monthly operating activities of **Papa John's International, Inc.** (dollars in thousands).

(a) At the beginning of January, Papa John's restaurants paid $3,000 in rent for the months of January, February, and March.
(b) In January, Papa John's paid suppliers $10,000 on account for supplies received in December.
(c) In January, the food and paper products supplies used in making and selling pizza products to customers were $9,500. The supplies were purchased in December on account.
(d) In late January, Papa John's received a $400 utility bill for electricity used in January. The bill will be paid in February.

Required:
Creating a table with headings as shown below, if an expense is to be recognized in **January**, indicate the title of the expense account and the amount of expense to be recognized.

Transaction	Expense Account Title	Amount of Expense Recognized In January
(a)		

After you have completed your answers, check them below.

GUIDED HELP 3-2

For additional step-by-step video instruction on identifying revenue and expense accounts and amounts for a given period, go to mhhe.com/libby11e_gh3-2.

Related Homework: M3-3, E3-3

Solutions to SELF-STUDY QUIZ

Expense Account Title	Amount of Expense Recognized in January
(a) Rent Expense	$1,000 ($3,000 ÷ 3 months)
(b) No expense in January	Supplies will be expensed when used.
(c) Supplies Expense	$9,500
(d) Utilities Expense	$ 400

A QUESTION OF ETHICS

Management's Incentives to Violate Accounting Rules

Investors in the stock market base their decisions on their expectations of a company's future earnings. When companies announce quarterly and annual earnings information, investors evaluate how well the companies have met expectations and adjust their investing decisions accordingly. Companies that fail to meet expectations often experience a decline in stock price. Thus, managers are motivated to produce earnings results that meet or exceed investors' expectations to bolster stock prices. Greed may lead some managers to make unethical accounting and reporting decisions, often involving falsifying revenues and expenses. While this sometimes fools people for a short time, it rarely works in the long run and often leads to very bad consequences.

Fraud is a criminal offense for which managers may be sentenced to jail. A couple of historic fraud cases involving faulty revenue and expense accounting are discussed briefly below:

- In 2002, **WorldCom,** the second largest long-distance telephone company in the United States at the time (now merged into **Verizon**), **violated the expense recognition principle** by recording $11 billion in expenses as assets, thus overstating assets and overstating net income. This act to inflate earnings was perpetrated to boost WorldCom's sagging stock price. Bernie Ebbers, age 65 and former CEO of WorldCom, was convicted and found guilty in 2005 and subsequently sentenced to 25 years in prison. At the time, this was the largest accounting fraud in U.S. history. [*Post-script:* Ebbers was released from prison in December 2019 due to declining health and died in February 2020.]
- **ZZZZ Best** was a carpet cleaning company started by teenager Barry Minkow who took the company public in 1986 when he was 20. However, the company was one of the largest accounting and investments frauds ever perpetrated by a single person. Among numerous criminal or questionable activities, Minkow **violated the revenue recognition principle** by creating fictitious sales to boost the company's earnings and stock price and appear strong to attract large investment deals. But the company was a sham, one that its auditing firm failed to discover. At the age of 23, Minkow was convicted and sentenced to 25 years in prison and ordered to pay $26 million in restitution. The audit firm paid $35 million for failing to uncover the fraud. Investors and lenders reportedly lost $100 million. [*Post-script:* After early release in 1995, Minkow pursued numerous fraudulent activities and was sentenced to federal prison two additional times before being released in 2019 and ordered to pay over $580 million in restitution.]

Many others are affected by accounting fraud. Shareholders lose stock value, employees may lose their jobs (and pension funds, as in the case of **Enron**), and customers and suppliers may become wary of dealing with a company operating under the cloud of fraud. As a manager, you may face an ethical dilemma in the workplace. The ethical decision to make is the one you will be proud of 20 years later.

THE EXPANDED TRANSACTION ANALYSIS MODEL

LEARNING OBJECTIVE 3-4

Apply transaction analysis to examine and record the effects of operating activities on the financial statements.

We have discussed the variety of business activities affecting the income statement and how they are measured. Next, we need to determine how these business activities are recorded in the accounting system and reflected in the financial statements. Chapter 2 covered investing and financing activities that affect assets, liabilities, and stockholders' equity. We now expand the transaction analysis model to include operating activities that also affect revenues and expenses.

Transaction Analysis Rules

The complete transaction analysis model presented in Exhibit 3.4 includes **all five elements: assets, liabilities, stockholders' equity, revenues,** and **expenses.** Recall that the Retained Earnings account is the accumulation of all past revenues and expenses minus any income distributed to

EXHIBIT 3.4 Expanded Transaction Analysis Model

ASSETS (many accounts) = LIABILITIES (many accounts) + STOCKHOLDERS' EQUITY

ASSETS (many accounts)		LIABILITIES (many accounts)	
+	−	−	+
Debit	Credit	Debit	Credit

STOCKHOLDERS' EQUITY

Contributed Capital (2 accounts)

Common Stock and Additional Paid-in Capital	
−	+
Debit	Credit
	Issuance of stock

Earned Capital (1 account)

Retained Earnings	
−	+
Debit	Credit
Dividends declared	Net income

Net income = REVENUES (many accounts) − EXPENSES (many accounts)

REVENUES	
	+
	Credit

EXPENSES	
+	
Debit	

Note: *As expenses increase (are debited), net income, retained earnings, and stockholders' equity decrease.*

Tip **DO** memorize and use the **transaction analysis model** for all transactions.

DON'T memorize journal entries—there are just too many throughout the text and they can be complex.

stockholders as dividends (that is, earnings not retained in the business).[5] When net income is positive, Retained Earnings increases; a net loss decreases Retained Earnings.

To aid your learning, you should be able to **construct the transaction analysis model in Exhibit 3.4 on your own without assistance and use it to analyze transactions.** It will be very beneficial in future chapters when completing assignments and analyzing more complex transactions. Now let's study Exhibit 3.4 carefully to remember how the model is constructed and to understand the impact of operating activities on both the balance sheet and income statement:

- All accounts can increase or decrease, although revenues and expenses mostly tend to increase throughout a period. For accounts on the left side of the accounting equation, the increase symbol + is written on the left side of the T-account. For accounts on the right side of the accounting equation, the increase symbol + is written on the right side of the T-account, **except for expenses, which increase on the left side of the T-account. That is because, as expenses increase, they have an opposite effect on net income, the Retained Earnings account (which increases on the credit side), and thus Stockholders' Equity.**
- Debits (dr) are written on the left of each T-account and credits (cr) are written on the right.
- Every transaction affects at least two accounts.
- When a revenue or expense is recorded, either an asset or a liability will be affected as well:
  - Revenues increase stockholders' equity through the account Retained Earnings and therefore have **credit** balances (the positive side of Retained Earnings). Recording revenue requires either increasing an asset (such as Accounts Receivable when selling goods on account to customers) or decreasing a liability (such as Unearned Revenue that was recorded in the past when cash was received from customers before being earned).
  - Expenses decrease stockholders' equity through Retained Earnings. As expenses increase, they have the opposite effect on net income, which affects Retained Earnings. Therefore, they have **debit** balances (opposite of the positive credit side in Retained Earnings). That is, to increase an expense, you debit it, thereby decreasing net income and Retained Earnings. Recording an expense requires either decreasing an asset (such as Supplies when used) or increasing a liability (such as Wages Payable when money is owed to employees).
- When revenues exceed expenses, the company reports net income, increasing Retained Earnings and stockholders' equity. However, when expenses exceed revenues, a net loss results that decreases Retained Earnings and thus stockholders' equity.

A	=	L	+	SE
+ or −				+ (+ revenue ↑ RE)

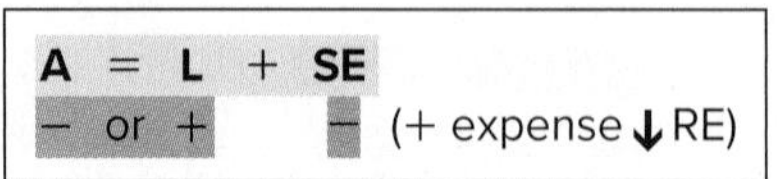

[5] Instead of reducing Retained Earnings directly when dividends are declared, companies may use the account Dividends Declared, which has a debit balance.

EXHIBIT 3.5 Steps for Analyzing Any Transaction

Step 1: Was a revenue earned by delivering goods or services?

- If so, **debit the account for what was received (+A, −L)** and **credit the revenue account (+R, +SE)**

OR Was an expense incurred to generate revenue in the current period?

- If so, **debit the expense account (+E, −SE)** and **credit the account for what was given (−A, +L)**

OR, if neither a revenue was earned or an expense was incurred, what was received and given?

debit the account for what was received (+A, −L)
credit the account for what was given (−A, +L)

Step 2: Verify → Is the accounting equation in balance? (Does A = L + SE?)
Do debits = credits?

Example: **Chipotle delivers a food order for $25 and receives cash from the customer.**

Step 1: Was a revenue earned? Yes

Cash (received) (+A)	**25**	
Restaurant sales revenue (+R, +SE)		**25**

Step 2: Is the accounting equation in balance? Yes

A 25 = L 0 + SE 25

A	=	L	+	SE
+25	=			+25

Do debits = credits? Yes **Debits 25; Credits 25**

In summary:

REVENUES	EXPENSES
• Increase net income and stockholders' equity	• Decrease net income and stockholders' equity
• ↑ with Credits	• ↑ with Debits
• Accounts have credit balances	• Accounts have debit balances

Tip **Expenses** increase on the left side (the **debit side**) of the T-account to reduce net income, retained earnings, and stockholders' equity.

The steps to follow in analyzing transactions presented in Chapter 2 are now modified to determine the effects of earning revenues and incurring expenses as well. Now, as shown in Exhibit 3.5, when a transaction occurs, the questions to ask are (1) was a revenue earned or expense incurred and (2) is the accounting equation in balance based on the analysis.

Analyzing Common Transactions

Next, we continue our discussion with hypothetical operating activities for **Chipotle Mexican Grill,** building on the company's trial balance presented in Exhibit 2.8 (in Chapter 2) that included only investing and financing transactions assumed to have occurred during the first quarter of 2020.

Using the transaction analysis steps in Exhibit 3.5, we now analyze, record, and post to the T-accounts the effects of this chapter's operating activities that we assume occurred during the first quarter. The T-accounts begin with the **trial balance amounts** in Exhibit 2.8. All amounts are in millions of dollars, except per share information. You should notice, in each journal entry, that:

- When a revenue or expense is recorded, we insert (+R, +SE) for revenues and (+E, −SE) for expenses to emphasize the effect of the transaction on the accounting equation and to help you see that the equation remains in balance.
- Debits equal credits–another check you should make when preparing journal entries.

In Chapter 4, we complete the accounting cycle with the activities at the end of the quarter.

(1) **During the first quarter, assume Chipotle sold food and beverages to customers for $1,359; $44 was sold to universities on account** (to be paid by the universities next quarter) **and the rest was received in cash from customers. NOTE:** To measure revenues and expenses in a new period, these accounts begin with $0 balances.

	Debit	Credit
(1) Cash (+A)	1,315	
Accounts receivable (+A)	44	
Restaurant sales revenue (+R, +SE)		1,359

Assets		=	Liabilities	+	Stockholders' Equity	
Cash	+1,315				Restaurant sales revenue (+R)	+1,359
Accounts receivable	+44					

+ Cash (A) −				+ Accounts Receivable (A) −				− Restaurant Sales Revenue (R) +	
Bal.	357			Bal.	81			0	Bal.
(1)	**1,315**			*(1)*	**44**			**1,359**	*(1)*

(2) **Assume Chipotle purchased food, beverage, and packaging supplies costing $459 during the quarter, paying $379 in cash, and owing the rest on account to the suppliers.**

	Debit	Credit
(2) Supplies (+A)	459	
Cash (−A)		379
Accounts payable (+L)		80

Assets		=	Liabilities		+	Stockholders' Equity
Supplies	+459		Accounts payable	+80		
Cash	−379					

+ Cash (A) −				+ Supplies (A) −			− Accounts Payable (L) +	
Bal.	357			Bal.	26		116	Bal.
(1)	1,315	**379**	*(2)*	*(2)*	**459**		**80**	*(2)*

(3) **At the beginning of January, Chipotle paid $207 cash for rent, insurance, and advertising to be used in the future** (all included in the account Prepaid Expenses until used).

	Debit	Credit
(3) Prepaid expenses (+A)	207	
Cash (−A)		207

Assets		=	Liabilities	+	Stockholders' Equity
Prepaid expenses	+207				
Cash	−207				

+ Cash (A) −				+ Prepaid Expenses (A) −		
Bal.	357			Bal.	85	
(1)	1,315	379	*(2)*	*(3)*	**207**	
		207	*(3)*			

(4) **Chipotle paid $65 as training expense for management during the quarter.**

Tip **Reminder:** In debiting the expense, the account increases, but it has a negative effect on net income, Retained Earnings and thus stockholders' equity.

	Debit	Credit
(4) Training expense (+E, −SE)	65	
Cash (−A)		65

Assets		=	Liabilities	+	Stockholders' Equity	
Cash	−65				Training expense (+E)	−65

+ Cash (A) −			
Bal.	357		
(1)	1,315	379	*(2)*
		207	*(3)*
		65	***(4)***

+ Training Expense (E) −			
Bal.	0		
(4)	**65**		

(5) **Chipotle paid employees $342 for work this quarter and $47 for work last quarter** (recorded last quarter as Wages Expense and Wages Payable for the amount owed to employees who worked then).

	Debit	Credit
(5) Wages expense (+E, −SE)	342	
Wages payable (−L)	47	
Cash (−A)		389

Assets		=	Liabilities		+	Stockholders' Equity	
Cash	−389		Wages payable	−47		Wages expense (+E)	−342

+ Cash (A) −			
Bal.	357		
(1)	1,315	379	*(2)*
		207	*(3)*
		65	*(4)*
		389	***(5)***

− Wages Payable (L) +			
		127	Bal
(5)	**47**		

+ Wages Expense (E) −			
Bal.	0		
(5)	**342**		

(6) **Chipotle sold land costing $21 for $12 cash, resulting in a loss of $9 on the disposal of the asset.**

	Debit	Credit
(6) Cash (+A)	12	
Loss on disposal of assets (+E, −SE)	9	
Land (−A)		21

Tip Losses on asset disposals are treated similarly to expenses. **Use +E for losses and +R for gains.**

Assets		=	Liabilities	+	Stockholders' Equity	
Cash	+12				Loss on disposal of assets (+E)	−9
Land	−21					

+ Cash (A) −			
Bal.	357		
(1)	1,315	379	*(2)*
(6)	**12**	207	*(3)*
		65	*(4)*
		389	*(5)*

+ Land (A) −			
Bal.	33		
		21	***(6)***

+ Loss on Disposal of Assets (E) −			
Bal.	0		
(6)	**9**		

(7) **Chipotle received $61 cash from customers paying on their accounts.**

	Debit	Credit
(7) Cash (+A)	61	
Accounts receivable (−A)		61

Assets		=	Liabilities	+	Stockholders' Equity
Cash	+61				
Accounts receivable	−61				

+ Cash (A) −			
Bal.	357		
(1)	1,315	379	*(2)*
(6)	12	207	*(3)*
(7)	**61**	65	*(4)*
		389	*(5)*

+ Accounts Receivable (A) −			
Bal.	81		
(1)	44	**61**	***(7)***

(8) **During the quarter, assume Chipotle paid $66 on accounts payable to suppliers and paid $25 on utilities payable** (recorded last quarter as Utilities Expense and Utilities Payable for the amount owed for utility service used last year).

	Debit	Credit
(8) Accounts payable (−L)	66	
Utilities payable (−L)	25	
Cash (−A)		91

Assets		=	Liabilities		+	Stockholders' Equity
Cash	−91		Accounts payable	−66		
			Utilities payable	−25		

+ Cash (A) −

Bal.	357		
(1)	1,315	379	*(2)*
(6)	12	207	*(3)*
(7)	61	65	*(4)*
		389	*(5)*
		91	***(8)***

− Accounts Payable (L) +

		116	Bal.
(8)	**66**	80	*(2)*

− Utilities Payable (L) +

		156	Bal.
(8)	**25**		

(9) **Chipotle paid $117 for utilities used during the quarter and paid $35 for repairs of its buildings and equipment during the quarter.**

	Debit	Credit
(9) Utilities expense (+E, −SE)	117	
Repairs expense (+E, −SE)	35	
Cash (−A)		152

Assets		=	Liabilities	+	Stockholders' Equity	
Cash	−152				Utilities expense (+E)	−117
					Repairs expense (+E)	−35

+ Cash (A) −

Bal.	357		
(1)	1,315	379	*(2)*
(6)	12	207	*(3)*
(7)	61	65	*(4)*
		389	*(5)*
		91	*(8)*
		152	***(9)***

+ Utilities Expense (E) −

Bal.	0	
(9)	**117**	

+ Repairs Expense (E) −

Bal.	0	
(9)	**35**	

(10) **During the quarter, Chipotle sold gift cards to customers for $35 in cash** (expected to be redeemed for food next quarter).

	Debit	Credit
(10) Cash (+A)	35	
Unearned revenue (+L)		35

Assets		=	Liabilities		+	Stockholders' Equity
Cash	+35		Unearned revenue	+35		

+ Cash (A) −

Bal.	357		
(1)	1,315	379	*(2)*
(6)	12	207	*(3)*
(7)	61	65	*(4)*
(10)	**35**	389	*(5)*
		91	*(8)*
		152	*(9)*

− Unearned Revenue (L) +

		95	Bal.
		35	***(10)***

***(11)* Assume Chipotle received $3 cash as interest revenue earned during the quarter.**

	Debit	Credit
(11) Cash (+A)	3	
Interest revenue (+R, +SE)		3

	Assets		=	Liabilities	+	Stockholders' Equity	
Cash		+3				Interest revenue (+R)	+3

+ Cash (A) −

Bal.	357		
(1)	1,315	379	*(2)*
(6)	12	207	*(3)*
(7)	61	65	*(4)*
(10)	35	389	*(5)*
(11)	**3**	91	*(8)*
		152	*(9)*

− Interest Revenue (R) +

		0	Bal.
		3	***(11)***

Next, we determine the balances in all of the T-accounts, especially those affected by the operating activities this quarter, by adding the positive side and subtracting the negative side in each T-account. The beginning balances in the T-accounts in Exhibit 3.6 are taken from Exhibit 2.8.

EXHIBIT 3.6 T-Accounts Summary

Balance Sheet Accounts:

+ Cash (A) −

Bal.	357		
(1)	1,315	379	*(2)*
(6)	12	207	*(3)*
(7)	61	65	*(4)*
(10)	35	389	*(5)*
(11)	3	91	*(8)*
		152	*(9)*
	500		

+ Short-Term Investments (A) −

Bal.	381		
	381		

+ Accounts Receivable (A) −

Bal.	81		
(1)	44	61	*(7)*
	64		

+ Supplies (A) −

Bal.	26		
(2)	459		
	485		

+ Prepaid Expenses (A) −

Bal.	85		
(3)	207		
	292		

+ Land (A) −

Bal.	33		
		21	*(6)*
	12		

+ Buildings (A) −

Bal.	1,851		
	1,851		

+ Equipment (A) −

Bal.	862		
	862		

− Accumulated Depreciation (A) +

		1,201	Bal.
		1,201	

+ Operating Lease ROU Assets (A) −

Bal.	2,591		
	2,591		

+ Intangible Assets (A) −

Bal.	74		
	74		

− Accounts Payable (L) +

		116	Bal.
(8)	66	80	*(2)*
		130	

− Unearned Revenue (L) +

		95	Bal.
		35	*(10)*
		130	

− Wages Payable (L) +

		127	Bal.
(5)	47		
		80	

− Utilities Payable (L) +

		156	Bal.
(8)	25		
		131	

− Dividends Payable (L) +

		2	Bal.
		2	

− Current Lease Liabilities (L) +

		179	Bal.
		179	

− Notes Payable (L) +

		80	Bal.
		80	

− Long-Term Lease Liabilities (L) +

		2,789	Bal.
		2,789	

− Common Stock (SE) +

		2	Bal.
		2	

− Additional Paid-in Capital (SE) +

		1,482	Bal.
		1,482	

+ Treasury Stock (SE) −

Bal.	2,802		
	2,802		

− Retained Earnings (SE) +

		2,914	Bal.
		2,914	

(*Continued*)

EXHIBIT 3.6 T-Accounts Summary (*Concluded*)

Income Statement Accounts:

– Restaurant Sales Revenue (R) +		
	0	Bal.
	1,359	*(1)*
	1,359	

– Interest Revenue (R) +		
	0	Bal.
	3	*(11)*
	3	

+ Wages Expense (E) –		
Bal.	0	
(5)	342	
	342	

+ Utilities Expense (E) –		
Bal.	0	
(9)	117	
	117	

+ Repairs Expense (E) –		
Bal.	0	
(9)	35	
	35	

+ Training Expense (E) –		
Bal.	0	
(4)	65	
	65	

+ Loss on Disposal of Assets (E) –		
Bal.	0	
(6)	9	
	9	

PAUSE FOR FEEDBACK

We just illustrated the steps in analyzing and recording transactions, including those involving earning revenue and incurring expenses.

Transaction Analysis Steps:

Step 1: **Ask** → Was a revenue earned by delivering goods or services?

- If so, **debit the account for what was received (+A, –L)** and **credit the revenue account (+R, +SE)**

OR Was an expense incurred to generate revenue in the current period?

- If so, **debit the expense account (+E, –SE)** and **credit the account for what was given (–A, +L)**

OR, if neither a revenue was earned or an expense was incurred, what was received and given?

debit the account for what was received (+A, –L)
credit the account for what was given (–A, +L)

Step 2: **Verify** → Is the accounting equation in balance? (Does **A = L + SE?**)
Do debits = credits?

SELF-STUDY QUIZ

Now it's your turn. Analyze and record in good form the journal entries for each of the selected **June** transactions for Florida Flippers, Inc., a scuba diving and instruction business. Then post the effects to the T-accounts. Account titles and beginning balances are provided in the T-accounts that follow. Be sure to check that debits equal credits in each journal entry and that the accounting equation remains in balance.

a. In June, new customers paid Florida Flippers $8,200 in cash for diving trips; $5,200 was for trips made in June and the rest is for trips that will be provided in July.
b. In June, customers paid $3,900 in cash for instruction they received in May.
c. At the beginning of June, Florida Flippers paid a total of $6,000 cash for insurance to cover the months of June, July, and August.
d. In June, Florida Flippers paid $4,000 in wages to employees who worked in June.

+ Cash (A) −	
Beg. 25,000	
End.	

+ Accounts Receivable (A) −	
Beg. 4,500	
End.	

+ Prepaid Insurance (A) −	
Beg. 0	
End.	

− Unearned Revenue (L) +	
	0 Beg.
	End.

− Diving Trip Revenue (R) +	
	0 Beg.
	End.

+ Wages Expense (E) −	
Beg. 0	
End.	

After you have completed your answers, check them below.

GUIDED HELP 3-3

For additional step-by-step video instruction on analyzing, recording, and posting transaction effects, go to mhhe.com/libby11e_gh3-3.

Related Homework: M3-4, M3-5, E3-6, E3-7, E3-8, E3-9, E3-12, E3-14, E3-17, P3-2, P3-4, P3-6, P3-7, CON3-1, COMP3-1

HOW IS THE INCOME STATEMENT PREPARED AND ANALYZED?

LEARNING OBJECTIVE 3-5

Prepare a classified income statement.

As we discussed in Chapter 2, companies can prepare financial statements at any point in time. Before we consider creating any statements for **Chipotle,** however, we must first determine that the debits equal credits by generating a trial balance. Accounts are listed in financial statement order: assets, liabilities, stockholders' equity, revenues/gains, and expenses/losses. The balances are taken from the T-accounts in Exhibit 3.6.

Solutions to SELF-STUDY QUIZ

	Debit	Credit
a. Cash (+A)	8,200	
Diving trip revenue (+R, +SE)		5,200
Unearned revenue (+L)		3,000
b. Cash (+A)	3,900	
Accounts receivable (−A)		3,900
c. Prepaid insurance (+A)	6,000	
Cash (−A)		6,000
d. Wages expense (+E, −SE)	4,000	
Cash (−A)		4,000

+ Cash (A) −	
Beg. 25,000	
(a) 8,200	6,000 *(c)*
(b) 3,900	4,000 *(d)*
End. 27,100	

+ Accounts Receivable (A) −	
Beg. 4,500	
	3,900 *(b)*
End. 600	

+ Prepaid Insurance (A) −	
Beg. 0	
(c) 6,000	
End. 6,000	

− Unearned Revenue (L) +	
	0 Beg.
	3,000 *(a)*
	3,000 End.

− Diving Trip Revenue (R) +	
	0 Beg.
	5,200 *(a)*
	5,200 End.

+ Wages Expense (E) −	
Beg. 0	
(d) 4,000	
End. 4,000	

File Home Insert Page Layout Formulas Data

B42

	A	B	C	D	E
1		**CHIPOTLE MEXICAN GRILL**			
2		**UNADJUSTED TRIAL BALANCE***			
3		**March 31, 2020**			
4		*(in millions of dollars)*	**Debit**	**Credit**	
5		Cash	500		
6		Short-term investments	381		
7		Accounts receivable	64		
8		Supplies	485		
9		Prepaid expenses	292		
10		Land	12		
11		Buildings	1,851		
12		Equipment	862		
13		Accumulated depreciation		1,201	
14		Operating lease right-of-use assets	2,591		
15		Intangible assets	74		
16		Accounts payable		130	
17		Unearned revenue		130	
18		Wages payable		80	
19		Utilities payable		131	
20		Dividends payable		2	
21		Current lease liabilities		179	
22		Notes payable		80	
23		Long-term lease liabilities		2,789	
24		Common stock		2	
25		Additional paid-in capital		1,482	
26		Treasury stock	2,802		
27		Retained earnings		2,914	
28		Restaurant sales revenue		1,359	
29		Interest revenue		3	
30		Wages expense	342		
31		Utilities expense	117		
32		Repairs expense	35		
33		Training expense	65		
34		Loss on disposal of assets	9		
35		**Total**	**10,482**	**10,482**	
36					
37		* **Based on hypothetical transactions for the first quarter ended**			
38		**March 31, 2020; balances are not yet adjusted.**			

Debits = Credits!

Microsoft Corporation

Although debits do equal credits, why is the trial balance labeled "unadjusted"? Does it make sense that supplies were purchased during the quarter, but no Supplies Expense was recorded to show the amount of supplies used? How likely is it that gift cards were sold, but none were redeemed by customers during the quarter? And didn't Chipotle use property and equipment during the quarter to generate revenues? The answer to all of these questions is that **no end-of-period adjustments**

have been made yet to reflect all revenues earned and expenses incurred during the quarter. Therefore, the trial balance is **unadjusted** until all adjustments are made, as we illustrate in Chapter 4.

Classified Income Statement

Exhibit 3.7 presents the classified income statement. Classified means it is categorized into Operating activities and Other items, **but note that, because it is based on unadjusted balances, it would not be presented to external users.**

When comparing this statement with **Chipotle**'s 2019 income statement in Exhibit 3.1, we notice that the income from operations for the first quarter ($794) exceeds income from operations for all of 2019 ($444). Because a more representative amount for one quarter would be about 25 percent, obviously, numerous adjustments are necessary to revenues and expenses, such as providing food service to customers with gift cards (earning a revenue) and using food, packaging, and beverage supplies, renting facilities, and using buildings and equipment during the quarter to generate revenue (incurring expenses). We would not want to use the information for analysis until it has been adjusted. Instead, we use the 2019 income statement in Exhibit 3.1 to determine how effective Chipotle's management is at generating profit.

KEY RATIO ANALYSIS

Net Profit Margin Ratio

LEARNING OBJECTIVE 3-6

Compute and interpret the net profit margin ratio.

ANALYTICAL QUESTION

How effective is management at generating profit (that is, at generating revenue and controlling costs) on every dollar of sales?

EXHIBIT 3.7

Unadjusted Income Statement

CHIPOTLE MEXICAN GRILL, INC.
Consolidated Statement of Income*
UNADJUSTED
For the Quarter ended March 31, 2020
(in millions of dollars)

Restaurant sales revenue	$1,359
Restaurant operating expenses:	
Wages expense	342
Utilities expense	117
Repairs expense	35
General and administrative expenses:	
Training expense	65
Loss on disposal of assets	9
Total operating expenses	568
Income from operations	791
Other items:	
Interest revenue	3
Income before income taxes	794
Income tax expense	0
Net income	$ 794

*Based on hypothetical activities for the quarter.

RATIO AND COMPARISONS

$$\textbf{Net Profit Margin} = \frac{\textbf{Net Income}}{\textbf{Net Sales (or Operating Revenues)*}}$$

*Net sales is sales revenue less any returns from customers and other reductions. For companies in the service industry, total operating revenues is equivalent to net sales.

The 2019 ratio for **Chipotle** using reported amounts (from Exhibit 3.1) is (dollars in millions):

$$\frac{\$350}{\$5,586} = 0.0627 \text{ or } 6.27\%$$

COMPARISONS OVER TIME			COMPARISONS WITH COMPETITORS	
Chipotle Mexican Grill, Inc.			El Pollo Loco Holdings	Shake Shack Inc.
2017	2018	2019	2019	2019
0.0394	0.0363	0.0627	0.0563	0.041

INTERPRETATIONS

In General Net profit margin measures how much of every sales dollar generated during the period is profit. **Over time, a rising net profit margin signals more efficient management of sales and expenses.** Differences among industries result from the nature of the products or services provided and the intensity of competition. Differences among competitors in the same industry reflect how each company responds to changes in competition (and demand for the product or service) and changes in managing sales volume, sales price, and costs. Financial analysts expect well-run businesses to maintain or improve their net profit margin over time.

Selected Focus Companies' Net Profit Margin Ratios for 2019

Apple 21.2%

Harley-Davidson 7.9%

FedEx 1.9%

Focus Company Analysis Chipotle's net profit margin varied over the three-year period. The 2017 and 2018 ratios were below $0.04 in net income for every dollar of sales revenue. Management reported that, although sales revenue increased both of those years, costs increased as well. In March 2018, Chipotle hired Brian Niccol as Chief Executive Officer, with great hopes of re-energizing the company after a string of food safety issues in prior years. Under his leadership, in 2018, the company undertook a corporate restructuring, including a move of its headquarters to Newport Beach, CA, consolidation or closure of other corporate offices, and incurred additional costs as a result (such as, employee severance and transition costs, relocation costs, and lease termination costs among others). The company also started equipping restaurants with second food "make lines" to address the growing delivery and pick-up orders. In 2019, the net profit margin jumped to 6.27 percent, as sales revenue continued to increase (much of that due to a 7.1 percent increase in digital sales) and operating costs as a percentage of revenues decreased, despite its continuing investment in improved digital platforms and expanded delivery capabilities. This suggests that, **from 2018 to 2019, Chipotle's management was more effective at generating revenues and controlling costs.**

El Pollo Loco and **Shake Shack** each had a lower net profit margin than Chipotle, suggesting that **Chipotle was more effective at generating revenue while controlling costs than those competitors in 2019.** El Pollo Loco had a 2 percent increase in restaurant sales, opened only two company-operated and two franchised restaurants, and had an increase in labor, delivery, utility, and repair costs. Shake Shack also expanded its number of restaurant openings and partnered with **Grubhub** to expand delivery service. Revenue increased over 29 percent, but operating costs grew faster which included one-time costs for upgrading financial and operational systems to support growth initiatives. Differences in business strategies, size, and locations explain some of the variation in ratio analysis across competitors.

A Few Cautions The decisions that management makes to maintain the company's net profit margin in the current period may have negative long-run implications. Analysts should perform additional analysis of the ratio to identify trends in each component of revenues and expenses. This involves dividing each line on the income statement by net sales. Statements presented with these percentages are called **common-sized income statements.** Changes in the percentages of the individual components of net income provide information on shifts in management's strategies.

FOCUS ON CASH FLOWS

Operating Activities

LEARNING OBJECTIVE 3-7

Identify operating transactions and demonstrate how they affect cash flows.

In this chapter, we focus on cash flows from operating activities: **cash from** operating sources, primarily customers, and **cash to** suppliers and others involved in operations. The accounts most often associated with operating activities are current assets, such as Accounts Receivable, Inventories, and Prepaid Expenses, and current liabilities, such as Accounts Payable, Wages Payable, and Unearned Revenue.

As discussed in Chapter 2, companies report cash inflows and outflows over a period of time in their **statement of cash flows.** This statement is divided into three categories:

- O – Operating activities include those primarily with customers and suppliers, and interest payments on debt and earnings on investments.
- I – Investing activities include buying and selling noncurrent assets and investments.
- F – Financing activities include borrowing and repaying debt, including short-term bank loans; issuing and repurchasing stock; and paying dividends.

Only transactions affecting cash are reported on the statement. An important step in constructing and analyzing the statement of cash flows (discussed in Chapter 12) is identifying the various transactions as operating, investing, or financing. Let's analyze the Cash T-account for **Chipotle**'s assumed transactions in this chapter, adding to transactions *(a)–(g)* from Chapter 2. Refer to transactions *(1)–(11)* illustrated earlier in the chapter and remember, **if you see Cash in a transaction, it will be reflected on the statement of cash flows.**

			+ Cash (A)	–			
		1/1/20	481				
From investors	+ F	*(a)*	17	31	*(c)*	–I	**For noncurrent assets**
From the bank	+ F	*(b)*	4	29	*(d)*	–I	**For noncurrent assets**
From sale of investments	+ I	*(e)*	19	1	*(f)*	–F	**To repay notes payable to bank**
From customers	+ O	*(1)*	1,315	103	*(g)*	–F	**To repurchase common stock**
From sale of land	+ I	*(6)*	12	379	*(2)*	–O	**To suppliers for food and paper products**
From customers	+ O	*(7)*	61	207	*(3)*	–O	**To suppliers of rental facilities, insurance, and advertising**
From customers	+ O	*(10)*	35	65	*(4)*	–O	**To train employees**
From investment earnings	+ O	*(11)*	3	389	*(5)*	–O	**To pay employees for working**
				91	*(8)*	–O	**To pay suppliers of products and utilities**
				152	*(9)*	–O	**To pay suppliers of utilities and repair service**
			500				

PAUSE FOR FEEDBACK

As we discussed, every transaction affecting cash can be classified either as an operating, investing, or financing effect.

Operating effects relate to receipts of cash from customers, payments to suppliers (employees, utilities, and other suppliers of goods and services for operating the business), and any interest paid or investment income received.

Investing effects relate to purchasing/selling investments or property and equipment or lending funds to/receiving repayment from others.

Financing effects relate to borrowing or repaying banks, issuing stock to investors, repurchasing stock from investors, or paying dividends to investors.

SELF-STUDY QUIZ

Mattel, Inc., designs, manufactures, and markets a broad variety of toys (e.g., Barbie, Hot Wheels, Fisher-Price brands, and American Girl dolls) worldwide. Indicate whether these transactions from a recent statement of cash flows were operating (O), investing (I), or financing (F) activities and the direction of their effects on cash (+ for increases in cash; – for decreases in cash):

TRANSACTIONS	TYPE OF ACTIVITY (O, I, OR F)	EFFECT ON CASH FLOWS (+ OR –)
1. Purchases of property, plant, and equipment		
2. Receipts from customers		
3. Payments of dividends		
4. Payments to employees		
5. Receipts of investment income		

After you have completed your answers, check them below.

Related Homework: M3-10, E3-11, E3-15, P3-3, P3-5, P3-8

DEMONSTRATION CASE

This case is a continuation of the Terrific Lawn Maintenance Corporation transactions introduced in Chapter 2. In that chapter, the company was established and supplies, property, and equipment were purchased. Terrific Lawn is now ready for business. The balance sheet at April 7, 2023, based on the first week of investing and financing activities (from Chapter 2) is as follows:

TERRIFIC LAWN MAINTENANCE CORPORATION
Balance Sheet
April 7, 2023

Assets	
Current Assets:	
Cash	$ 3,800
Notes receivable	1,250
Total current assets	5,050
Equipment	4,600
Land	3,750
Total assets	**$13,400**
Liabilities and Stockholders' Equity	
Current Liabilities:	
Short-term notes payable	$ 400
Total current liabilities	400
Long-term notes payable	4,000
Total liabilities	4,400
Stockholders' Equity:	
Common stock ($0.10 par)	150
Additional paid-in capital	8,850
Total stockholders' equity	9,000
Total liabilities and stockholders' equity	**$13,400**

Solutions to SELF-STUDY QUIZ

1. I – 2. O + 3. F – 4. O – 5. O +

The following additional activities occurred during the rest of April 2023:

a. Purchased and used during April gasoline for mowers and edgers, paying $90 in cash at a local gas station.

b. In early April, received from the city $1,600 cash in advance for lawn maintenance service for April through July ($400 each month). (Record the entire amount as Unearned Revenue.)

c. In early April, purchased $300 of insurance covering six months, April through September. (Record the entire payment as Prepaid Expenses.)

d. Mowed lawns for residential customers who are billed every two weeks. A total of $5,200 of service was billed in April.

e. Residential customers paid $3,500 on their accounts.

f. Paid wages every two weeks. Total cash paid in April was $3,900.

g. Received a bill for $320 from the local gas station for additional gasoline purchased on account and used in April. The bill will be paid in May.

h. Paid $700 principal and $40 interest on note owed to XYZ Lawn Supply.

i. Paid $100 on accounts payable.

j. Collected $1,250 principal and $12 interest on the note owed by the city to Terrific Lawn Maintenance Corporation.

Required:

1. *a.* On a separate sheet of paper, set up T-accounts for Cash, Accounts Receivable, Notes Receivable, Prepaid Expenses, Equipment, Land, Accounts Payable, Short-Term Notes Payable, Unearned Revenue (same as deferred revenue), Long-Term Notes Payable, Common Stock, Additional Paid-in Capital, Retained Earnings, Mowing Revenue, Interest Revenue, Wages Expense, Fuel Expense, and Interest Expense. Beginning balances for the balance sheet accounts should be taken from the preceding balance sheet. Beginning balances for operating accounts are $0. Indicate these balances on the T-accounts.

b. Analyze each transaction, referring to the expanded transaction analysis model presented in this chapter.

c. On a separate sheet of paper, prepare journal entries in chronological order and indicate their effects on the accounting model (Assets = Liabilities + Stockholders' Equity). Include the equality checks: (1) Debits = Credits and (2) the accounting equation is in balance.

d. Enter the effects of each transaction in the appropriate T-accounts. Identify each amount with its letter in the preceding list of activities.

e. Compute balances in each of the T-accounts.

2. Use the amounts in the T-accounts to prepare an unadjusted classified income statement for Terrific Lawn Maintenance Corporation for the month ended April 30, 2023. (Adjustments to accounts will be presented in Chapter 4.)

3. On the Cash T-account, identify each transaction as O for operating activity, I for investing activity, or F for financing activity.

Now check your answers with the following suggested solution.

SUGGESTED SOLUTION

1. ***b.* and *c.*** Transaction analysis, journal entries, and the effect on the accounting model:

Journal Entries	Debit	Credit	Equality Checks for All — Debits = Credits • Equation balances: A	= L	+ SE
(a) Fuel expense (+E, −SE)	90				
Cash (−A)		90	**−90**		**+E −90**
(b) Cash (+A)	1,600				
Unearned revenue (+L)		1,600	**+1,600**	**+1,600**	
(c) Prepaid expenses (+A)	300		**+300**		
Cash (−A)		300	**−300**		
(d) Accounts receivable (+A)	5,200				
Mowing revenue (+R, +SE)		5,200	**+5,200**		**+R +5,200**
(e) Cash (+A)	3,500		**+3,500**		
Accounts receivable (−A)		3,500	**−3,500**		
(f) Wages expense (+E, −SE)	3,900				
Cash (−A)		3,900	**−3,900**		**+E −3,900**
(g) Fuel expense (+E, −SE)	320				
Accounts payable (+L)		320		**+320**	**+E −320**
(h) Interest expense (+E, −SE)	40				
Long-term notes payable (−L)	700				
Cash (−A)		740	**−740**	**−700**	**+E −40**
(i) Accounts payable (−L)	100				
Cash (−A)		100	**−100**	**−100**	
(j) Cash (+A)	1,262				
Notes receivable (−A)		1,250	**+1,262**		**+R +12**
Interest revenue (+R, +SE)		12	**−1,250**		

1. ***a.*, *d.*, and *e.* T-Accounts:**

Assets

+ Cash (A) −

	Debit	Credit	
Beg.	3,800		
(b)	1,600	90	*(a)*
(e)	3,500	300	*(c)*
(j)	1,262	3,900	*(f)*
		740	*(h)*
		100	*(i)*
	5,032		

+ Accounts Receivable (A) −

	Debit	Credit	
Beg.	0		
(d)	5,200	3,500	*(e)*
	1,700		

+ Notes Receivable (A) −

	Debit	Credit	
Beg.	1,250		
		1,250	*(j)*
	0		

+ Prepaid Expenses (A) −

	Debit	Credit
Beg.	0	
(c)	300	
	300	

+ Equipment (A) −

	Debit	Credit
Beg.	4,600	
	4,600	

+ Land (A) −

	Debit	Credit
Beg.	3,750	
	3,750	

Liabilities

− Accounts Payable (L) +			
		0	Beg.
(i)	100	320	*(g)*
		220	

− Short-Term Notes Payable (L) +			
		400	Beg.
		400	

− Unearned Revenue (L) +			
		0	Beg.
		1,600	*(b)*
		1,600	

− Long-Term Notes Payable (L) +			
		4,000	Beg.
(h)	700		
		3,300	

Stockholders' Equity

− Common Stock (SE) +			
		150	Beg.
		150	

− Additional Paid-in Capital (SE) +			
		8,850	Beg.
		8,850	

− Retained Earnings (SE) +			
		0	Beg.
		0	

Revenues

− Mowing Revenue (R) +			
		0	Beg.
		5,200	*(d)*
		5,200	

− Interest Revenue (R) +			
		0	Beg.
		12	*(j)*
		12	

Expenses

+ Wages Expense (E) −		
Beg.	0	
(f)	3,900	
	3,900	

+ Fuel Expense (E) −		
Beg.	0	
(a)	90	
(g)	320	
	410	

+ Interest Expense (E) −		
Beg.	0	
(h)	40	
	40	

2. Income Statement:

TERRIFIC LAWN MAINTENANCE CORPORATION
Unadjusted Income Statement
For the Month Ended April 30, 2023

Mowing revenue	$5,200
Operating expenses:	
Wages expense	3,900
Fuel expense	410
Total operating expenses	4,310
Income from operations	890
Other items:	
Interest revenue	12
Interest expense	(40)
Income before taxes	862
Income tax expense	0
Net income	$ 862

To be computed and recorded after adjustments are made to revenue and expense accounts (Chapter 4)

3. Cash flow activities identified (O = operating, I = investing, and F = financing):

		+ Cash (A) –				
	Beg.	3,800				
From customers **+O**	*(b)*	1,600	90	*(a)*	**–O**	To suppliers of fuel
From customers **+O**	*(e)*	3,500	300	*(c)*	**–O**	To suppliers of insurance coverage
$12 for interest **+O**; $1,250 for principal **+I**	*(j)*	1,262	3,900	*(f)*	**–O**	To employees
			740	*(h)*	**–O**	$40 for interest; **–F** $700 for principal
			100	*(i)*	**–O**	To suppliers
		5,032				

CHAPTER TAKE-AWAYS

3-1. Describe a typical business operating cycle and explain the necessity for the time period assumption. **p. 110**

- The operating cycle, or cash-to-cash cycle, is the time needed to purchase goods or services from suppliers, sell the goods or services to customers, and collect cash from customers.
- Time period assumption–to measure and report financial information periodically, we assume the long life of a company can be cut into shorter periods.

3-2. Explain how business activities affect the elements of the income statement. **p. 112**

- Elements of the income statement:
  a. Revenues–the amounts earned and recorded from a company's day-to-day business activities, mostly when a company sells products or provides services to customers or clients (the central focus of the business).
  b. Expenses–the costs of operating the business that are incurred to generate revenues during the period.
  c. Gains–result primarily from the disposal of assets for more than their cost minus the amount of cost depreciated in the past.
  d. Losses–result primarily from the disposal of assets for less than their cost minus the amount of cost depreciated in the past.

3-3. Explain the accrual basis of accounting and apply the revenue and expense recognition principles to measure income. **p. 116**

In accrual basis accounting, revenues are recognized when earned and expenses are recognized when incurred.

- Revenue recognition principle–recognize revenues (1) when the company transfers promised goods or services to customers (2) in the amount it expects to be entitled to receive. The five-step model for determining when and the amount to recognize revenue is:
  (1) identify the contract,
  (2) identify the seller's performance obligations (promised goods and services),
  (3) determine the transaction price,
  (4) allocate the transaction price to the performance obligations, and
  (5) recognize revenue when each performance obligation is satisfied.
- Expense recognition principle (matching)–recognize expenses when they are incurred in generating revenue (a matching of costs with benefits).

3-4. Apply transaction analysis to examine and record the effects of operating activities on the financial statements. **p. 121**

The expanded transaction analysis model includes revenues and expenses:

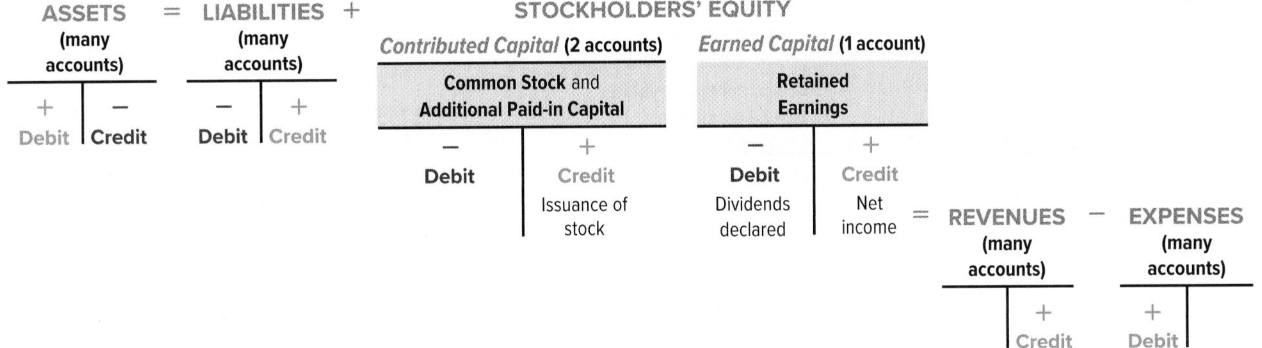

3-5. Prepare a classified income statement. **p. 129**

Until the accounts have been updated to include all revenues earned and expenses incurred in the period (due to a difference in the timing of when cash is received or paid), the financial statements are **unadjusted:**

- Income Statement–net income is needed to determine ending Retained Earnings; classifications include Operating Revenues, Operating Expenses (to determine Income from Operations), Other Items (to determine Pretax Income), Income Tax Expense, Net Income (or Net Loss), and Earnings per Share [Net income (or loss) ÷ Weighted average number of shares of common stock outstanding].

3-6. Compute and interpret the net profit margin ratio. **p. 131**

The net profit margin ratio (Net Income [or Net Loss] ÷ Net Sales [or Operating Revenues]) measures the profit generated per dollar of sales (operating revenues). The higher the ratio when compared to competitors or over time, the more effective the company is at generating revenues and/or controlling costs.

3-7. Identify operating activities and demonstrate how they affect cash flows. **p. 133**

On the Statement of Cash Flows, operating activities include those primarily with customers and suppliers, but interest payments and earnings on investments are also included, unlike how these are reported on the income statement (under Other Items). Only when cash is received or paid in an operating activity is the statement of cash flows affected.

In this chapter, we discussed the operating cycle and accounting concepts relevant to income determination: the time period assumption, definitions of the income statement elements (revenues, expenses, gains, and losses), the revenue recognition principle, and the expense recognition principle. The accounting principles are defined in accordance with the accrual basis of accounting, which requires revenues to be recorded when earned and expenses to be recorded when incurred in the process of generating revenues. We expanded the transaction analysis model introduced in Chapter 2 by adding revenues and expenses and prepared an unadjusted classified income statement. In Chapter 4, we discuss the activities that occur at the end of the accounting period: the adjustment process, the preparation of adjusted financial statements, and the closing process.

KEY RATIO

Net profit margin ratio measures the profit generated per dollar of sales (operating revenues). A high ratio as compared to competitors or over time suggests that a company is generating revenues and/or controlling expenses more effectively. The ratio is computed as follows (see the "Key Ratio Analysis" box on pages 131–132):

$$\text{Net Profit Margin Ratio} = \frac{\text{Net Income}}{\text{Net Sales (or Operating Revenues)}}$$

FINDING FINANCIAL INFORMATION

Balance Sheet

Current Assets
- Cash
- Short-term investments
- Accounts receivable
- Inventory (goods to be sold)
- Supplies
- Prepaid expenses

Noncurrent Assets
- Long-term investments
- Land
- Buildings
- Equipment
- (Accumulated depreciation)
- Operating lease right-of-use assets
- Intangible assets

Current Liabilities
- Accounts payable
- Short-term notes payable
- Accrued expenses payable (e.g., wages, taxes)
- Unearned revenue
- Current lease liabilities

Noncurrent Liabilities
- Long-term notes payable
- Long-term debt
- Long-term lease liabilities

Stockholders' Equity
- Common stock
- Additional paid-in capital
- (Treasury stock)
- Retained earnings

Income Statement

Revenues (operating)
- Sales (from various operating activities)

Expenses (operating)
- Cost of goods sold (used inventory)
- Rent, wages, depreciation, insurance, etc.
- Losses (gains) on disposal of assets

Operating Income

Other Items
- Interest expense
- Interest revenue
- Losses (gains) on sale of investments

Pretax Income
- Income tax expense

Net Income

Earnings per Share

Statement of Cash Flows

Operating Activities
- \+ Cash from customers
- \+ Cash from interest and dividends
- − Cash to suppliers
- − Cash to employees
- − Interest paid
- − Income taxes paid

Notes

Under Summary of Significant Accounting Policies
Description of the company's revenue recognition policy.

KEY TERMS

Accrual Basis Accounting Revenues are recognized when goods and services are provided to customers, and expenses are recognized in the same period as the revenues to which they relate, regardless of when cash is received or paid **p. 116**

Expense Recognition Principle (or Matching Principle) Expenses are recorded in the same time period when incurred to generate revenue **p. 119**

Expenses The costs of operating the business that are incurred to generate revenues during the period **p. 113**

Gains Result primarily from the disposal of assets for more than their cost minus the amount of cost depreciated in the past **p. 114**

Losses Result primarily from the disposal of assets for less than their cost minus the amount of cost depreciated in the past **p. 118**

Operating (Cash-to Cash) Cycle The time it takes for a company to pay cash to suppliers, sell goods and service to customers, and collect cash from customers **p. 111**

Operating Income (Income from Operations) Net sales (operating revenues) less operating expenses (including cost of goods sold) **p. 114**

Revenue Recognition Principle Revenues are recognized when the company transfers promised goods or service to customers in the amount it expects to receive **p. 116**

Revenues The amounts earned and recorded from a company's day-to-day business activities, mostly when a company sells products or provides services to customers or clients **p. 112**

Time Period Assumption The long life of a company can be reported in shorter time periods, such as months, quarters, and years **p. 111**

QUESTIONS

1. Describe a typical business operating cycle.
2. Explain what the time period assumption means.
3. Write the income statement equation and define each element.

4. Explain the difference between
   a. Revenues and gains.
   b. Expenses and losses.
5. Define **accrual accounting** and contrast it with cash basis accounting.
6. For revenue to be recognized under accrual basis accounting:
   a. What are the steps for determining the amount and timing of revenue recognition?
   b. What is the critical point for when to record revenue?
7. Explain the expense recognition principle.
8. Explain why stockholders' equity is increased by revenues and decreased by expenses.
9. Explain why revenues are recorded as credits and expenses are recorded as debits.
10. Complete the following matrix by entering either **debit** or **credit** in each cell:

Item	Increase	Decrease
Revenues		
Losses		
Gains		
Expenses		

11. Complete the following matrix by entering either **increase** or **decrease** in each cell:

Item	Debit	Credit
Revenues		
Losses		
Gains		
Expenses		

12. Identify whether the following transactions affect cash flow from operating, investing, or financing activities and indicate the effect of each on cash (+ for increase and – for decrease). If there is no cash flow effect, write "None."

Transaction	Operating, Investing, or Financing Effect on Cash	Direction of the Effect on Cash
Cash paid to suppliers		
Sale of goods on account		
Cash received from customers		
Purchase of investments		
Cash paid for interest		
Issuance of stock for cash		

13. State the equation for the net profit margin ratio and explain how it is interpreted.

MULTIPLE-CHOICE QUESTIONS

1. Which of the following is **not** a specific account in a company's chart of accounts?
   a. Gain on Sale of Assets
   b. Interest Revenue
   c. Net Income
   d. Unearned Revenue

2. Which of the following is **not** one of the criteria that normally must be met for revenue to be recognized according to the revenue recognition principle for accrual basis accounting?
   a. Cash has been collected.
   b. Services have been performed.
   c. Goods have been transferred.
   d. The amount the company expects to be entitled to receive is determinable.
3. The expense recognition principle controls
   a. Where on the income statement expenses should be presented.
   b. When costs are recognized as expenses on the income statement.
   c. The ordering of current assets and current liabilities on the balance sheet.
   d. How costs are allocated between Cost of Sales (sometimes called Cost of Goods Sold) and general and administrative expenses.
4. When expenses exceed revenues in a given period,
   a. Retained earnings are not impacted.
   b. Retained earnings are decreased.
   c. Retained earnings are increased.
   d. One cannot determine the impact on retained earnings without additional information.
5. On January 1, 2023, Anson Company started the year with a $300,000 credit balance in Retained Earnings, a $50,000 balance in Common Stock, and a $300,000 balance in Additional Paid-in Capital. During 2023, the company earned net income of $45,000, declared a dividend of $15,000, and issued 900 additional shares of stock (par value of $1 per share) for $10,000. What is total stockholders' equity on December 31, 2023?
   a. $692,500.
   b. $695,000.
   c. $690,000.
   d. None of the above.
6. During 2023, CliffCo Inc. incurred operating expenses of $250,000, of which $150,000 was paid in cash; the balance will be paid in January 2024. Transaction analysis of operating expenses for 2023 should reflect only the following:
   a. Decrease stockholders' equity, $150,000; decrease assets, $150,000.
   b. Decrease assets, $250,000; decrease stockholders' equity, $250,000.
   c. Decrease stockholders' equity, $250,000; decrease assets, $150,000; increase liabilities, $100,000.
   d. Decrease assets, $250,000; increase liabilities, $100,000; decrease stockholders' equity, $150,000.
   e. None of the above is correct.
7. Which of the following is the entry to be recorded by a law firm when it receives a $2,000 retainer from a new client at the initial client meeting?
   a. Debit to Cash, $2,000; credit to Legal Fees Revenue, $2,000.
   b. Debit to Accounts Receivable, $2,000; credit to Legal Fees Revenue, $2,000.
   c. Debit to Unearned Revenue, $2,000; credit to Legal Fees Revenue, $2,000.
   d. Debit to Cash, $2,000; credit to Unearned Revenue, $2,000.
   e. Debit to Unearned Revenue, $2,000; credit to Cash, $2,000.
8. You have observed that the net profit margin ratio for a retail chain has increased steadily over the last three years. The **most likely** explanation is which of the following?
   a. Salaries for upper management as a percentage of total expenses have decreased over the last three years.
   b. A successful advertising campaign increased sales companywide, but with no increases in operating expenses.
   c. New stores were added throughout the last three years and sales increased as a result of the additional new locations.
   d. The company began construction of a new, larger main office location three years ago that was put into use at the end of the second year.
9. Cash payments for salaries are reported in what section of the statement of cash flows?
   a. Operating.
   b. Investing.
   c. Financing.
   d. None of the above.

10. This period a company collects $100 cash on an account receivable from a customer for a sale last period. How would the receipt of cash impact the following two financial statements this period?

	Income Statement	Statement of Cash Flows
a.	Revenue + $100	Inflow from investing
b.	No impact	Inflow from operations
c.	Revenue − $100	Inflow from operations
d.	No impact	Inflow from financing

MINI-EXERCISES

Matching Definitions with Terms

M3-1
LO3-1, 3-2, 3-3

Match each definition with its related term by entering the appropriate letter in the space provided. There should be only one definition per term (that is, there are more definitions than terms).

Term

___ (1) Losses
___ (2) Expense recognition principle
___ (3) Revenues
___ (4) Time period assumption
___ (5) Operating cycle

Definition

A. Record revenues when earned and measurable (when the company transfers promised goods or services to customers, it should record the amount it expects to be entitled to receive).
B. The time it takes to purchase goods or services from suppliers, sell goods or services to customers, and collect cash from customers.
C. Record expenses when incurred in earning revenue.
D. The costs of operating the business that are incurred to generate revenues during the period.
E. Report the long life of a company in shorter time periods.
F. The amounts earned and recorded from a company's day-to-day business activities, mostly when a company sells products or provides services to customers or clients.
G. Result primarily from the disposal of assets for less than their cost minus the amount of cost depreciated in the past.

Identifying Revenues

M3-2
LO3-2, 3-3

The following transactions are July activities of Bennett's Bowling, Inc., which operates several bowling centers, offering customers lanes for games, snack bar service, and merchandise for sale from the pro shop. If revenue is to be recognized in **July,** indicate the revenue account title and amount. If revenue is not to be recognized in July, explain why.

Activity	Revenue Account Title	Amount of Revenue
a. Bennett's collected $15,000 from customers for games played in July.		
b. Bennett's served customers food from its snack bar; received $800 in cash.		
c. Bennett's received $400 from customers who purchased merchandise from the pro shop in June on account.		
d. The men's and ladies' bowling leagues gave Bennett's a deposit of $2,500 for the upcoming fall season.		

Tip Use account titles that represent the source. For example, providing games to customers would be Games Revenue.

M3-3 Identifying Expenses
LO3-2, 3-3

The following transactions are July activities of Bennett's Bowling, Inc., which operates several bowling centers, offering customers lanes for games, snack bar service, and merchandise for sale from the pro shop. If expense is to be recognized in **July,** indicate the expense account title and amount. If expense is not to be recognized in July, explain why.

Activity	Expense Account Title	Amount of Expense
e. Bennett's purchased $680 in food supplies for the snack bar; paid $590 in cash and owed the rest on account with the supplier.		
f. Bennett's paid $500 on the electricity bill for June (recorded as an expense in June).		
g. Bennett's paid $3,600 to employees for work in July.		
h. Bennett's purchased $1,500 in insurance for coverage from August 1 to November 1.		
i. Bennett's paid $700 to plumbers for repairing a broken pipe in the restrooms.		
j. Bennett's received the July electricity bill for $900 to be paid in August.		

M3-4 Recording Revenues
LO3-4

For each of the transactions in M3-2, write the journal entry in good form.

M3-5 Recording Expenses
LO3-4

For each of the transactions in M3-3, write the journal entry in good form.

M3-6 Determining the Financial Statement Effects of Operating Activities Involving Revenues
LO3-4

The following transactions are July activities of Bennett's Bowling, Inc., which operates several bowling centers, offering customers lanes for games, snack bar service, and merchandise for sale from the pro shop. For each of the following transactions, complete the tabulation, indicating the amount and effect (+ for increase and – for decrease) of each transaction. (Remember that A = L + SE; R – E = NI; and NI affects SE through Retained Earnings.) Write NE if there is no effect. The first transaction is provided as an example.

Tip **How to answer equation effects questions:**

- Following transaction analysis steps in Exhibit 3.5, if **revenue** was earned, indicate that on the schedule (with +)
- Indicate what was **received:** An asset (with +) or a reduction of a liability (with –)
- Fill in what the effects were for determining net income
- Whatever the effect is on net income is also the effect on stockholders' equity
- All other elements would have no effect
- Check that the accounting equation balances

	BALANCE SHEET			INCOME STATEMENT		
Transaction	Assets	Liabilities	Stockholders' Equity	Revenues	Expenses	Net Income
a. Bennett's collected $15,000 from customers for games played in July.	+15,000	NE	+15,000	+15,000	NE	+15,000
b. Bennett's served customers food from its snack bar; received $800 in cash.						
c. Bennett's received $400 from customers who purchased merchandise in June from the pro shop on account.						
d. The men's and ladies' bowling leagues gave Bennett's a deposit of $2,500 for the upcoming fall season.						

Determining the Financial Statement Effects of Operating Activities Involving Expenses

M3-7
LO3-4

The following transactions are July activities of Bennett's Bowling, Inc., which operates several bowling centers, offering customers lanes for games, snack bar service, and merchandise for sale from the pro shop. For each of the following transactions, complete the tabulation, indicating the amount and effect (+ for increase and – for decrease) of each transaction. (Remember that A = L + SE; R – E = NI; and NI affects SE through Retained Earnings.) Write NE if there is no effect. The first transaction is provided as an example.

Tip **How to answer equation effects questions:**

- Following transaction analysis steps in Exhibit 3.5, if **expense** was incurred, indicate that on the schedule (with +)
- Indicate what was **given:** A reduction of an asset (with –) or a liability (with +)
- Fill in what the effects were for determining net income [NOTE: Increasing expenses decreases net income!]
- Whatever the effect is on net income is also the effect on stockholders' equity
- All other elements would have no effect
- Check that the accounting equation balances

	BALANCE SHEET			INCOME STATEMENT		
Transaction	Assets	Liabilities	Stockholders' Equity	Revenues	Expenses	Net Income
e. Bennett's purchased $680 in food supplies for the snack bar; paid $590 in cash and owed the rest on account with the supplier.	+680 –590	+90	NE	NE	NE	NE
f. Bennett's paid $500 on the electricity bill for June (recorded as an expense in June).						
g. Bennett's paid $3,600 to employees for work in July.						
h. Bennett's purchased $1,500 in insurance for coverage from August 1 to November 1.						
i. Bennett's paid $700 to plumbers for repairing a broken pipe in the restrooms.						
j. Bennett's received the July electricity bill for $900 to be paid in August.						

Preparing a Simple Income Statement

M3-8
LO3-5

Given the transactions in M3-6 and M3-7 (including the examples), prepare an unadjusted income statement for Bennett's Bowling, Inc., for the month of July.

Computing and Explaining the Net Profit Margin Ratio

M3-9
LO3-6

The following data are from annual reports of Jen's Jewelry Company:

	2024	2023	2022
Total assets	$ 60,000	$ 53,000	$ 41,000
Total liabilities	14,000	11,000	6,000
Total stockholders' equity	46,000	42,000	35,000
Sales revenue	163,000	151,000	132,000
Net income	51,000	45,000	25,000

Compute Jen's net profit margin ratio for each year. What do these results suggest to you about Jen's Jewelry Company?

Identifying the Operating Activities in a Statement of Cash Flows

M3-10
LO3-7

Given the transactions in M3-6 and M3-7 (including the examples), indicate how the transactions will affect the statement of cash flows for Bennett's Bowling, Inc., for the month of July. Create a table similar to the one below for transactions (*a*) through (*j*). Use O for operating, I for investing, and F for financing activities and indicate the direction of their effects on cash (+ for increases in cash; – for decreases in cash). Also include the amount of cash to be reported on the statement. If there is no effect on the statement of cash flows, write NE.

Transaction	Type of Activity (O, I, or F)	Effect on Cash Flows (+ or – and amount)
a.		
b.		
etc.		

EXERCISES

E3-1 Matching Definitions with Terms
LO3-1, 3-2, 3-3

Match each definition with its related term by entering the appropriate letter in the space provided. There should be only one definition per term (that is, there are more definitions than terms).

Term

___ (1) Expenses
___ (2) Gains
___ (3) Revenue recognition principle
___ (4) Cash basis accounting
___ (5) Unearned revenue
___ (6) Operating cycle
___ (7) Accrual basis accounting
___ (8) Prepaid expenses
___ (9) Revenues – Expenses = Net Income
___ (10) Ending Retained Earnings = Beginning Retained Earnings + Net Income – Dividends Declared

Definition

A. Report the long life of a company in shorter periods.
B. Record expenses in the same time period as incurred in earning revenue.
C. The time it takes to purchase goods or services from suppliers, sell goods or services to customers, and collect cash from customers.
D. Record revenues when earned and expenses when incurred.
E. Result primarily from the disposal of assets for more than their cost minus the amount of cost depreciated in the past.
F. An asset account used to record cash paid before expenses have been incurred.
G. Revenues are recognized when the company transfers promised goods or services to customers in the amount it expects to receive.
H. Result primarily from the disposal of assets for less than their cost minus the amount of cost depreciated in the past.
I. Record revenues when received and expenses when paid.
J. The income statement equation.
K. The costs of operating the business that are incurred to generate revenues during the period.
L. The retained earnings equation.
M. A liability account used to record cash received before revenues have been earned.

E3-2 Identifying Revenues
LO3-2, 3-3

Revenues are normally recognized when the company transfers promised goods or services in the amount the company expects to be entitled to receive. Assume that the following transactions occurred in **September**:

a. A popular ski magazine company receives a total of $12,345 today from subscribers. The subscriptions begin in the next fiscal year. Answer from the magazine company's standpoint.

b. On September 1 of the current year, a bank lends $15,000 to a company; the note principal and $1,500 ($15,000 × 10 percent) annual interest are due in one year. Answer from the bank's standpoint.

c. **Fucillo Automotive Group** (offering a wide variety of car and truck brands) sells a Ford F-150 truck with a list, or "sticker," price of $34,050 for $32,000 cash.

d. **Macy's** department store orders 1,000 men's shirts for $21 each for future delivery from **PVH Corp.**, manufacturer of IZOD, ARROW, Van Heusen, Calvin Klein, and Tommy Hilfiger and other brand-name apparel. The terms require payment in full within 30 days of delivery. Answer from PVH Corp.'s standpoint.

e. PVH Corp. completes production of the shirts described in (*d*) and delivers the order. Answer from PVH's standpoint.

f. PVH Corp. receives payment from Macy's for the events described in (*d*) and (*e*). Answer from PVH's standpoint.

g. A customer purchases a ticket from **American Airlines** for $780 cash to travel the following January. Answer from American Airlines's standpoint.

h. **Ford Motor Company** issues $15 million in new common stock.

i. **Michigan State University** receives $27,440,000 cash for 80,000 seven-game season football tickets to be played in the upcoming season.

j. Michigan State plays the first football game referred to in (*i*).

k. **Precision Builders** signs a contract with a customer for the construction of a new $1,500,000 warehouse. At the signing, Precision receives a check for $200,000 as a deposit on the future construction. Answer from Precision's standpoint.

l. **Best Buy** receives inventory of 100 laptop computers from **Dell**; Best Buy promises to pay $60,000 within three months. Answer from Dell's standpoint.

m. **Amazon.com** delivers a $300 lamp to a customer who charges the purchase on his Amazon Store Card. Answer from Amazon's standpoint.

Required:
For each of the transactions, if revenue is to be recognized in September, indicate the revenue account title and amount. If revenue is not to be recognized in September, explain why.

Identifying Expenses

E3-3
LO3-2, 3-3

Revenues are normally recognized when a company transfers promised goods or services to customers in the amount the company expects to be entitled to receive. Expense recognition is guided by an attempt to match the costs associated with the generation of those revenues to the same time period. Assume that the following transactions occurred in **January**:

a. **McGraw-Hill Education** uses $3,800 worth of electricity and natural gas in its headquarters building for which it has not yet been billed.

b. At the beginning of January, **Turner Construction Company** pays $1,350 for magazine advertising to run in monthly publications each of the first three months of the year.

c. **Dell** pays its computer service technicians $403,000 in salaries for the two weeks ended January 7. Answer from Dell's standpoint.

d. **Iowa State University** orders 200,000 football tickets from its printer and prepays $8,340 for the custom printing. The first game will be played in September. Answer from the university's standpoint.

e. The campus bookstore receives 500 accounting texts at a cost of $210 each. The terms indicate that payment is due within 30 days of delivery.

f. During the last week of January, the campus bookstore sold 400 accounting texts received in (*e*) at a sales price of $280 each.

g. **Fucillo Automotive Group** pays its salespersons $63,800 in commissions related to December automobile sales. Answer from Fucillo's standpoint.

h. On January 31, Fucillo Automotive Group determines that it will pay its salespersons $55,560 in commissions related to January sales. The payment will be made in early February. Answer from Fucillo's standpoint.

i. A new grill is received and installed at a **Wendy's** restaurant at the end of the day on January 31; a $12,750 cash payment is made on that day to the grill supply company. Answer from Wendy's standpoint.

j. **Mall of America** (in Bloomington, MN) had janitorial supplies costing $3,500 in storage. An additional $2,600 worth of supplies was purchased during January. At the end of January, $1,400 worth of janitorial supplies remained in storage.

k. An **Emory University** employee works eight hours, at $23 per hour, on January 31; however, payday is not until February 3. Answer from the university's point of view.

l. Wang Company paid $4,800 for a fire insurance policy on January 1. The policy covers 12 months beginning on January 1. Answer from Wang's point of view.

m. Derek Incorporated has its delivery van repaired in January for $600 and charges the amount on account.

n. Hass Company, a farm equipment company, receives its phone bill at the end of January for $154 for January calls. The bill has not been paid to date.

o. Martin Company receives and pays in January a $2,034 invoice (bill) from a consulting firm for services received in January. Answer from Martin's standpoint.

p. Parillo's Taxi Company pays a $595 invoice from a consulting firm for services received and recorded in December.

q. **PVH Corp.**, manufacturer of IZOD, ARROW, Van Heusen, Calvin Klein, and Tommy Hilfiger apparel among other brands, completes production of 450 men's shirts ordered by **Macy's** department stores at a cost of $21 each and delivers the order in January. Answer from PVH Corp.'s standpoint.

Required:

For each of the transactions, if an expense is to be recognized in January, indicate the expense account title and the amount. If an expense is not to be recognized in January, indicate why.

E3-4 Determining Financial Statement Effects of Various Transactions

LO3-4

Amazon.com, Inc.

Amazon.com, Inc., headquartered in Seattle, WA, started its electronic commerce business in 1995 and expanded rapidly. The following transactions occurred during a recent year (dollars in millions):

a. Issued stock for $623 cash (example).

b. Purchased equipment costing $6,320, paying $4,893 in cash and charging the rest on account.

c. Paid $5,000 in principal and $300 in interest expense on long-term debt.

d. Earned $280,522 in sales revenue; collected $223,949 in cash with the customers owing the rest on their Amazon credit card accounts.

e. Incurred $25,249 in shipping expenses, all on credit.

f. Paid $118,241 cash on accounts owed to suppliers.

g. Incurred $18,878 in marketing expenses; paid cash.

h. Collected $38,200 in cash from customers paying on their Amazon credit card accounts.

i. Borrowed $16,231 in cash as long-term debt.

j. Used inventory costing $165,536 when sold to customers. (The expense title for the using up of inventory sold to customers is Cost of Goods Sold.)

k. Paid $830 in income tax recorded as an expense in the prior year.

Tip For problem-solving help, see the marginal tips in M3-6 and M3-7.

Required:

For each of the transactions, complete the tabulation, indicating the effect (+ for increase and − for decrease) of each transaction. (Remember that A = L + SE; R − E = NI; and NI affects SE through Retained Earnings.) Write NE if there is no effect. The first transaction is provided as an example.

	BALANCE SHEET			INCOME STATEMENT		
Transaction	Assets	Liabilities	Stockholders' Equity	Revenues	Expenses	Net Income
(a) (example)	+623	NE	+623	NE	NE	NE

E3-5 Determining Financial Statement Effects of Various Transactions

LO3-4

Wolverine World Wide, Inc.

Wolverine World Wide, Inc., designs, markets, and licenses casual, industrial, performance outdoor, and athletic footwear and apparel under a variety of brand names, such as Hush Puppies, Wolverine, Merrell, Sperry, and Saucony, to a global market. The following transactions occurred during a recent year. Dollars are in millions.

a. Issued common stock to investors for $21.4 cash (example).
b. Purchased $1,626.6 of additional inventory on account.
c. Paid $40.1 on long-term debt principal and $3.7 in interest on the debt.
d. Sold $2,350.0 of products to customers on account.
e. Cost of the products sold was $1,426.6.
f. Paid cash dividends of $23.0 to shareholders.
g. Purchased for cash $32.4 in additional property, plant, and equipment.
h. Incurred $713.6 in selling expenses, paying three-fourths in cash and owing the rest on account.
i. Earned $0.50 of interest on investments, receiving 80 percent in cash.
j. Incurred $35.0 in interest expense to be paid at the beginning of next year.

Required:
For each of the transactions, complete the tabulation, indicating the effect (+ for increase and − for decrease) of each transaction. (Remember that A = L + SE; R − E = NI; and NI affects SE through Retained Earnings.) Write NE if there is no effect. The first transaction is provided as an example.

Tip For problem-solving help, see the marginal tips in M3-6 and M3-7.

	BALANCE SHEET			INCOME STATEMENT		
Transaction	Assets	Liabilities	Stockholders' Equity	Revenues	Expenses	Net Income
(*a*) (example)	+ 21.4	NE	+ 21.4	NE	NE	NE

Recording Journal Entries

E3-6
LO3-4
Sysco Corporation

Sysco Corporation, formed in 1969, is the largest global distributor of food service products, serving restaurants, hotels, schools, hospitals, and other institutions. The following summarized transactions are typical of those that occurred in a recent year (dollars are in millions).

a. Purchased buildings costing $432 and equipment costing $254 for cash.
b. Borrowed $119 from a bank, signing a short-term note.
c. Provided $55,371 in service to customers during the year, with $28,558 on account and the rest received in cash.
d. Paid $132,074 cash on accounts payable.
e. Purchased $41,683 of inventory on account.
f. Paid payroll, $6,540 during the year.
g. Received $22,043 on account paid by customers.
h. Purchased and used fuel of $1,750 in delivery vehicles during the year (paid for in cash).
i. Declared $698 in dividends at the end of the year to be paid the following year.
j. Incurred $121 in utility usage during the year; paid $110 in cash and owed the rest on account.

Required:
For each of the transactions, prepare journal entries. Determine whether the accounting equation remains in balance and debits equal credits after each entry.

Recording Journal Entries

E3-7
LO3-4
Vail Resorts, Inc.

Vail Resorts, Inc., owns and operates over 30 premier ski resort properties (located in the Colorado Rocky Mountains, the Lake Tahoe area, the upper midwest, the northeast, mid-Atlantic states, and Australia). The company also owns a collection of luxury hotels, resorts, and lodging properties. The company sells lift tickets, ski and snowboard lessons, and ski equipment. The following hypothetical **December** transactions are typical of those that occur at the resorts.

a. Borrowed $2,300,000 from the bank on December 1, signing a note payable due in six months.
b. Purchased a new snowplow for $98,000 cash on December 31.
c. Purchased ski equipment inventory for $35,000 on account to sell in the ski shops.
d. Incurred $62,000 in routine repairs expense for the chairlifts; paid cash.
e. Sold $390,000 of January through March season passes and received cash.

f. Sold a pair of skis from inventory in a ski shop to a customer for $700 on account.
g. The cost of the skis sold in (*f*) was $400.
h. Sold daily lift passes in December for a total of $320,000 in cash.
i. Received a $3,500 deposit on a townhouse to be rented for five days in January.
j. Paid half the charges incurred on account in (*c*).
k. Received $400 on account from the customer in (*f*).
l. Paid $245,000 in wages to employees for the month of December.

Required:

1. Prepare journal entries for each transaction. (Remember to check that debits equal credits and that the accounting equation is in balance after each transaction.)
2. Assume that Vail Resorts had a $1,000 balance in Accounts Receivable at the beginning of December. Determine the ending balance in the Accounts Receivable account at the end of December based on transactions (*a*) through (*l*). Show your work in T-account format.

E3-8 Recording Journal Entries

LO3-4

Griffin Air Transport Service, Inc., providing air delivery service for businesses, has been in operation for three years. The following transactions occurred in February:

February 1	Paid $275 for rent of hangar space in February.
February 2	Purchased fuel costing $490 on account for the next flight to Dallas.
February 4	Received customer payment of $820 to ship several items to Philadelphia next month.
February 7	Flew cargo from Denver to Dallas; the customer paid $910 for the air transport.
February 10	Paid $175 for an advertisement in the local paper to run on February 19.
February 14	Paid pilot $2,300 in wages for flying in January (recorded as expense in January).
February 18	Flew cargo for two customers from Dallas to Albuquerque for $3,800; one customer paid $1,600 cash and the other asked to be billed.
February 25	Purchased on account $2,550 a supply of spare parts for the planes.
February 27	Declared a $200 cash dividend to be paid in March.

Required:

Prepare journal entries for each transaction. Be sure to categorize each account as an asset (A), liability (L), stockholders' equity (SE), revenue (R), or expense (E).

E3-9 Analyzing the Effects of Transactions in T-Accounts

LO3-3, 3-4

Stacey's Piano Rebuilding Company has been operating for one year. At the start of the second year, its income statement accounts had zero balances and its balance sheet account balances were as follows:

Cash	$ 6,400	Accounts payable	$ 9,600
Accounts receivable	32,000	Unearned revenue	3,840
Supplies	1,500	Long-term note payable	48,500
Equipment	9,500	Common stock	1,600
Land	7,400	Additional paid-in capital	7,000
Building	25,300	Retained earnings	11,560

Required:

1. Create T-accounts for the balance sheet accounts and for these additional accounts: Rebuilding Fees Revenue, Rent Revenue, Wages Expense, Utilities Expense, and Interest Expense. Enter the beginning balances.
2. Enter the following transactions for January of the second year into the T-accounts, using the letter of each transaction as the reference:
   a. Rebuilt and delivered five pianos in January to customers who paid $19,000 in cash.
   b. Received a $600 deposit from a customer who wanted her piano rebuilt.
   c. Rented a part of the building to a bicycle repair shop; received $850 for rent in January.
   d. Received $7,200 from customers as payment on their accounts.
   e. Received an electric and gas utility bill for $400 to be paid in February.
   f. Ordered $960 in supplies.

g. Paid $2,300 on account in January.
h. Received from the home of Stacey Eddy, the major shareholder, a $920 tool (equipment) to use in the business in exchange for 100 shares of $1 par value stock.
i. Paid $16,500 in wages to employees who worked in January.
j. Declared and paid a $2,200 dividend (reduce Retained Earnings and Cash).
k. Received and paid cash for the supplies in (*f*).
l. Paid $320 in interest expense incurred this year on the long-term note payable.

3. Using the data from the T-accounts, amounts for the following at the end of January of the second year were

Revenues $ _____ – Expenses $ _____ = Net Income $ _____
Assets $ _____ = Liabilities $ _____ + Stockholders' Equity $ _____

Preparing an Income Statement

E3-10
LO3-5

Refer to E3-9.

Required:
Use the ending balances in the T-accounts in E3-9 to prepare an unadjusted classified income statement for January of the second year (ignore income taxes).

Identifying Activities Affecting the Statement of Cash Flows

E3-11
LO3-7

Refer to E3-9.

Required:
Use the transactions in E3-9 to identify the operating (O), investing (I), and financing (F) activities and the direction (+ for increase, – for decrease) and amount of the effect. If there is no effect, use NE.

Recording Journal Entries and Posting Effects to T-Accounts

E3-12
LO3-3, 3-4

At January 1 (beginning of its fiscal year), Freeman Inc., a financial services consulting firm, reported the following account balances (in thousands, except for par and market value per share):

Cash	$1,900	Accounts payable	$ 210
Short-term investments	410	Unearned revenue	1,320
Accounts receivable	3,570	Salaries payable	870
Supplies	150	Short-term note payable	780
Prepaid expenses	4,720	Common stock ($1 par value)	50
Office equipment	1,050	Additional paid-in capital	6,560
		Retained earnings	2,010

Required:
1. Prepare journal entries for the following transactions for the current year. Use the balance sheet account titles above and the revenue or expense account titles mentioned in requirement (2):
   a. Received $9,500 cash for consulting services rendered.
   b. Issued 10 additional shares of common stock at a market price of $120 per share.
   c. Purchased $640 of office equipment, paying 25 percent in cash and owing the rest on a short-term note.
   d. Received $890 from clients for consulting services to be performed in the next year.
   e. Bought $470 of supplies on account.
   f. Incurred and paid $1,800 in utilities for the current year.
   g. Consulted for clients in the current year for fees totaling $1,620, due from clients in the next year.
   h. Received $2,980 from clients paying on their accounts.
   i. Incurred $6,210 in salaries in the current year, paying $5,300 and owing the rest (to be paid next year).
   j. Purchased $1,230 in short-term investments and paid $800 for insurance coverage beginning in the next fiscal year.
   k. Received $10 in interest revenue earned in the current year on short-term investments.

2. Create T-accounts for the balance sheet accounts and for these additional accounts: Consulting Fees Revenue, Interest Revenue, Salaries Expense, and Utilities Expense. Enter the beginning balances of the balance sheet accounts. Freeman's income statement accounts had zero balances. Post the journal entry effects in requirement (1) above into the T-accounts, using the letter of each transaction as the reference.
3. Using the data from the T-accounts, amounts for the following at the end of the current year were

Revenues $ _____ − Expenses $ _____ = Net Income $ _____
Assets $ _____ = Liabilities $ _____ + Stockholders' Equity $ _____

E3-13 Preparing an Income Statement
LO3-5

Refer to E3-12.

Required:
Use the ending balances in the T-accounts in E3-12 to prepare in good form an unadjusted classified income statement for the current year ended December 31. (Ignore income taxes.)

E3-14 Analyzing the Effects of Transactions in T-Accounts
LO3-4

J. Kamas and G. Charrier have been operating a catering business for several years. In March, the partners plan to expand by opening a retail sales shop. They have decided to form the business as a corporation called Traveling Gourmet, Inc. The following transactions occurred in March:

a. Received $80,000 cash from each of the two shareholders to form the corporation, in addition to $2,000 in accounts receivable, $5,300 in equipment, a van (equipment) appraised at a fair value of $13,000, and $1,200 in supplies. Gave the two owners each 500 shares of common stock with a par value of $1 per share.
b. Purchased a vacant store for sale in a good location for $360,000, making a $72,000 cash down payment and signing a 10-year mortgage note from a local bank for the rest.
c. Borrowed $50,000 from the local bank on a 10 percent, one-year note.
d. Purchased food and paper supplies costing $10,200 in March; paid cash.
e. Catered four parties in March for $4,200; $1,600 was billed and the rest was received in cash.
f. Sold food at the retail store for $16,900 cash.
g. Used food and paper supplies costing $10,830.
h. Received a $420 telephone bill for March to be paid in April.
i. Paid $363 in gas for the van in March.
j. Paid $6,280 in wages to employees who worked in March.
k. Paid a $300 dividend from the corporation to each owner.
l. Purchased $50,000 of equipment (refrigerated display cases, cabinets, tables, and chairs) and renovated and decorated the new store for $20,000 (added to the cost of the building); paid cash.

Required:
1. Set up appropriate T-accounts for Cash, Accounts Receivable, Supplies, Equipment, Building, Accounts Payable, Note Payable, Mortgage Payable, Common Stock, Additional Paid-in Capital, Retained Earnings, Food Sales Revenue, Catering Sales Revenue, Supplies Expense, Utilities Expense, Wages Expense, and Fuel Expense.
2. Record in the T-accounts the effects of each transaction for Traveling Gourmet, Inc., in March. Identify the amounts with the letters starting with (*a*). Compute ending balances.

E3-15 Preparing an Income Statement, Identifying Cash Flow Effects, and Analyzing Results
LO3-5, 3-7

Refer to E3-14.

Required:
Use the balances and activity in the completed T-accounts in E3-14 to respond to the following:
1. Prepare an unadjusted classified income statement in good form for the month of March.
2. Identify operating (O), investing (I), and financing (F) activities affecting cash flows. Include the direction and amount of the effect. If there is no effect on cash flows, use NE for both the effect and the amount.
3. What do you think about the success of this company based on the results of the first month of operations? (**Hint:** Compare net income to cash flows from operations.)

Inferring Operating Transactions and Preparing an Income Statement and Balance Sheet

E3-16
LO3-2, 3-3, 3-4, 3-5

Kate's Kite Company (a corporation) sells and repairs kites from manufacturers around the world. Its stores are located in rented space in malls and shopping centers. During its first month of operations ended April 30, Kate's Kite Company completed eight transactions with the dollar effects indicated in the following schedule:

Accounts	DOLLAR EFFECT OF EACH OF THE EIGHT TRANSACTIONS								Ending Balance
	(a)	(b)	(c)	(d)	(e)	(f)	(g)	(h)	
Cash	$82,000	$(15,400)	$(6,200)	$ 9,820		$(1,300)	$(2,480)	$3,960	
Accounts Receivable				4,180					
Inventory			24,800	(7,000)					
Prepaid Expenses							1,860		
Store Fixtures		15,400							
Accounts Payable			18,600		$ 1,480				
Unearned Revenue								2,510	
Common Stock ($1 par value)	10,000								
Additional Paid-in Capital	72,000								
Sales Revenue				14,000				1,450	
Cost of Sales				7,000					
Wages Expense						1,300			
Rent Expense							620		
Utilities Expense					1,480				

Required:

1. Write a brief explanation of transactions (*a*) through (*h*). Include any assumptions that you made.
2. Compute the ending balance in each account and prepare an unadjusted classified income statement and a classified balance sheet for Kate's Kite Company on April 30.

Analyzing the Effects of Transactions Using T-Accounts and Interpreting the Net Profit Margin Ratio as a Financial Analyst

E3-17
LO3-4, 3-6

Massa Company, which has been operating for three years, provides marketing consulting services worldwide for dot-com companies. You are a financial analyst assigned to report on the Massa management team's effectiveness at managing its assets efficiently. At the start of 2024 (its fourth year), Massa's account balances were as follows. Dollars are in thousands.

Accounts payable	$2,400	Long-term investments	$6,400
Accounts receivable	8,000	Long-term notes payable	1,600
Additional paid-in capital	4,000	Rent expense	0
Cash	3,200	Retained earnings	3,200
Common stock ($0.10 par value)	800	Travel expense	0
Consulting fee revenue	0	Wages expense	0
Interest revenue	0	Unearned revenue	5,600
		Utilities expense	0

Required:

1. Using the data from this list, amounts for the following on January 1, 2024, were

Assets $ _____ = Liabilities $ _____ + Stockholders' Equity $ _____

2. Create T-accounts and start with the list above as beginning balances. Then, enter in the T-accounts the following transactions for 2024:
   a. Provided $58,000 in services to clients who paid $48,000 in cash and owed the rest on account.
   b. Received $5,600 cash from clients on account.
   c. Received $400 in cash as interest revenue on investments.
   d. Paid $36,000 in wages, $12,000 in travel, $7,600 in rent, and $1,600 on accounts payable.
   e. Received $1,600 in cash from clients in advance of services Massa will provide next year.
   f. Received a utility bill for $800 for 2024 services.
   g. Declared and immediately paid $480 in dividends to stockholders.
3. Compute ending balances in the T-accounts to determine amounts for the following on December 31, 2024:

   Revenues $ _____ − Expenses $ _____ = Net Income $ _____
   Assets $ _____ = Liabilities $ _____ + Stockholders' Equity $ _____

4. Calculate the net profit margin ratio for 2024. If the company had a net profit margin ratio of 2.9 percent in 2023 and 2.5 percent in 2022, what does your computation suggest to you about Massa Company? What would you say in your report?

E3-18 Inferring Transactions and Computing Effects Using T-Accounts

LO3-4
Gannett Co., Inc.

Gannett Co., Inc., states in a recent annual report that it is "an innovative, digitally focused media and marketing solutions company committed to fostering the communities in our network and helping them build relationships with their local businesses." Gannett owns media assets including "USA TODAY, local media organizations in 46 states in the United States and Guam, and Newsquest" (in the United Kingdom with over 140 local media brands). Gannett also owns digital marketing services companies ReachLocal, UpCurve, WordStream, and runs the largest U.S. media-owned events business Gatehouse Live. Gannett's annual report included the following accounts. Dollars are in millions:

Accounts Receivable		
1/1	174	
	1,394	?
12/31	439	

Prepaid Expenses		
1/1	50	
	1,142	?
12/31	129	

Unearned Subscriptions Revenue		
	105	1/1
?	795	
	219	12/31

Required:
1. For each T-account, describe the typical transactions that affect each account (that is, the economic events that occur to make these accounts increase and decrease).
2. For each T-account, compute the missing amounts.

E3-19 Finding Financial Information as an Investor

LO3-5, 3-6

You are evaluating your current portfolio of investments to determine those that are not performing to your expectations. You have all of the companies' most recent annual reports.

Required:
For each of the following, indicate where you would locate the information in an annual report. (**Hint:** The information may be in more than one location.)
1. Description of a company's primary business(es).
2. Income taxes paid.
3. Accounts receivable.
4. Cash flow from operating activities.
5. Description of a company's revenue recognition policy.
6. The inventory sold during the year.
7. The data needed to compute the net profit margin ratio.

PROBLEMS

Recording Nonquantitative Journal Entries (AP3-1)

P3-1
LO3-4

The following is a list of accounts for Sanjeev Corporation, which has been operating for three years. These accounts are listed and numbered for identification. Following the accounts is a series of transactions. For each transaction, indicate the account(s) that should be debited and credited by entering the appropriate account number(s) to the right of each transaction. If no journal entry is needed, write **none** after the transaction. The first transaction is used as an example.

Account No.	Account Title	Account No.	Account Title
1	Cash	10	Income Taxes Payable
2	Accounts Receivable	11	Common Stock
3	Supplies	12	Additional Paid-in Capital
4	Prepaid Expenses	13	Retained Earnings
5	Equipment	14	Service Revenue
6	Patents	15	Operating Expenses (wages, supplies)
7	Accounts Payable	16	Income Tax Expense
8	Note Payable	17	Interest Expense
9	Wages Payable		

Transactions	Debit	Credit
a. *Example:* Purchased equipment for use in the business; paid one-third cash and signed a note payable for the balance.	5	1, 8
b. Paid cash for salaries and wages earned by employees this period.	______	______
c. Paid cash on accounts payable for expenses incurred last period.	______	______
d. Purchased supplies to be used later; paid cash.	______	______
e. Performed services this period on credit.	______	______
f. Collected cash on accounts receivable for services performed last period.	______	______
g. Issued stock to new investors for cash greater than par value.	______	______
h. Paid operating expenses incurred this period.	______	______
i. Incurred operating expenses this period to be paid next period.	______	______
j. Purchased a patent (an intangible asset); paid cash.	______	______
k. Collected cash for services performed this period.	______	______
l. Used some of the supplies on hand for operations.	______	______
m. Paid three-fourths of the income tax expense incurred for the year; the balance will be paid next year.	______	______
n. Made a payment on the equipment note in (*a*); the payment was part principal and part interest expense.	______	______
o. On the last day of the current period, paid cash for an insurance policy covering the next two years.	______	______

Recording Journal Entries (AP3-2)

P3-2
LO3-4

Ryan Terlecki organized a new Internet company, CapUniverse, Inc. The company specializes in baseball-type caps with logos printed on them. Ryan, who is never without a cap, believes that his target market is college and high school students. You have been hired to record the transactions occurring in the first month of operations.

a. Issued 2,000 shares of $0.01 par value common stock to investors for cash at $20 per share.
b. Borrowed $60,000 from the bank to provide additional funding to begin operations; the note is due in two years.
c. Paid $3,000 cash for rent of a warehouse: $1,500 for the current month's rent and another $1,500 for next month's rent.
d. Paid $2,400 for a one-year fire insurance policy on the warehouse (recorded as a prepaid expense).

e. Purchased furniture and fixtures for the warehouse for $15,000, paying $3,000 cash and the rest on account. The amount is due within 30 days.
f. Purchased for $2,800 cash **Indiana University**, **University of Washington**, **Notre Dame**, **The University of Texas at Austin**, **The Ohio State University**, and **Michigan State University** baseball caps as inventory to sell online.
g. Placed advertisements on **Google** for a total of $350 cash; the ads were run immediately.
h. Sold caps totaling $1,700, half of which was charged on account.
i. The cost of the caps sold in (*h*) was $900.
j. Made full payment for the furniture and fixtures purchased on account in (*e*).
k. Received $210 from a customer on account.

Required:
For each of the transactions, prepare journal entries. Be sure to categorize each account as an asset (A), liability (L), stockholders' equity (SE), revenue (R), or expense (E).

P3-3 Determining Financial Statement Effects of Various Transactions and Identifying Cash Flow Effects (AP3-3)

LO3-4, 3-7

The Wendy's Company

According to a recent annual report of **The Wendy's Company**, it "is the world's third largest quick-service restaurant company in the hamburger sandwich segment" with more than 6,700 restaurants worldwide. The company owns and operates about 5 percent of the restaurants and sells franchises for the other 95 percent. The following activities were inferred from a recent annual report.

a. Purchased food and paper products; paid part in cash and the rest on account.
b. Purchased additional investments.
c. Incurred restaurant operating costs in company-owned facilities; paid part in cash and the rest on account.
d. Served food to customers for cash.
e. Used food and paper products.
f. Paid cash dividends.
g. Sold franchises, receiving part in cash and the rest in notes due from franchisees.
h. Paid interest on debt incurred and due during the period.

Required:
1. For each of the transactions, complete the tabulation, indicating the effect (+ for increase and − for decrease) of each transaction. (Remember that A = L + SE; R − E = NI; and NI affects SE through Retained Earnings.) Write NE if there is no effect. The first transaction is provided as an example.

	BALANCE SHEET			INCOME STATEMENT		
Transaction	Assets	Liabilities	Stockholders' Equity	Revenues	Expenses	Net Income
(*a*)	+/−	+	NE	NE	NE	NE

2. Where, if at all, would each transaction be reported on the statement of cash flows? Use O for operating activities, I for investing activities, F for financing activities, and NE if the transaction would not be included on the statement.

P3-4 Analyzing the Effects of Transactions Using T-Accounts, Preparing an Income Statement, and Evaluating the Net Profit Margin Ratio as a Manager (AP3-4)

LO3-4, 3-5, 3-6

Kaylee James, a connoisseur of fine chocolate, opened Kaylee's Sweets in Collegetown on February 1. The shop specializes in a selection of gourmet chocolate candies and a line of gourmet ice cream. You have been hired as manager. Your duties include maintaining the store's financial records. The following transactions occurred in February, the first month of operations.

a. Received four shareholders' contributions totaling $30,200 cash to form the corporation; issued 400 shares of $0.10 par value common stock.

b. Paid three months' rent for the store at $1,750 per month (recorded as prepaid expenses).
c. Purchased and received candy inventory for $6,000 on account, due in 60 days.
d. Purchased supplies for $1,560 cash.
e. Negotiated and signed a two-year $11,000 loan at the bank, receiving cash at the time.
f. Used the money from (*e*) to purchase a computer for $2,750 (for recordkeeping and inventory tracking); used the balance for furniture and fixtures for the store.
g. Placed a grand opening advertisement in the local paper for $400 cash; the ad ran in the current month.
h. Made sales on Valentine's Day totaling $3,500; $2,675 was in cash and the rest on accounts receivable.
i. The cost of the candy sold in (*h*) above was $1,600. (*Reminder:* Used inventory is an expense called Cost of Goods Sold.)
j. Made a $550 payment on accounts payable.
k. Incurred and paid employee wages of $1,300.
l. Collected accounts receivable of $600 from customers.
m. Made a repair to one of the display cases for $400 cash.
n. Made cash sales of $1,200 during the rest of the month.
o. The cost of the candy sold in (*n*) above was $600.

Required:

1. Set up appropriate T-accounts for Cash, Accounts Receivable, Supplies, Inventory, Prepaid Expenses, Equipment, Furniture and Fixtures, Accounts Payable, Notes Payable, Common Stock, Additional Paid-in Capital, Sales Revenue, Cost of Goods Sold (expense), Repair Expense, Advertising Expense, and Wage Expense. All accounts begin with zero balances.
2. Record in the T-accounts the effects of each transaction for Kaylee's Sweets in February, referencing each transaction in the accounts with the transaction letter. Show the ending balances in the T-accounts.
3. Prepare an unadjusted income statement at the end of the first month of operations ended February 28.
4. Write a short memo to Kaylee offering your opinion on the results of operations during the first month of business.
5. After three years in business, you are being evaluated for a promotion. One measure is how effectively you managed the sales and expenses of the business. The following data are available:

	2025*	2024	2023
Total assets	$88,000	$58,500	$52,500
Total liabilities	49,500	22,000	18,500
Total stockholders' equity	38,500	36,500	34,000
Net sales revenue	93,500	82,500	55,000
Net income	22,000	11,000	4,400

*At the end of 2025, Kaylee decided to open a second store, requiring loans and inventory purchases prior to the store's opening in early 2026.

Compute the net profit margin ratio for each year and evaluate the results, including if you think you should be promoted. Why?

Identifying Cash Flow Effects (AP3-5)

P3-5
LO3-7

Refer to P3-4.

Required:
For the transactions listed in P3-4, indicate the type of effect on cash flows (O for operating, I for investing, and F for financing) and the direction (+ for increase and – for decrease) and amount of the effect. If there is no effect, write NE for both the effect and amount.

Analyzing the Effects of Transactions Using T-Accounts, Preparing an Income Statement, and Evaluating the Net Profit Margin Ratio (AP3-6)

P3-6
LO3-4, 3-5, 3-6
United Parcel Service

Following are selected account balances (in millions of dollars) from a recent **United Parcel Service** (UPS) annual report, followed by several typical transactions. Assume that the following are account balances on December 31 (end of the prior fiscal year):

Account	Balance	Account	Balance
Property, plant, and equipment (net)	$30,482	Receivables	$9,552
Retained earnings	9,105	Other current assets	809
Accounts payable	5,555	Cash	5,238
Prepaid expenses	108	Spare parts, supplies, and fuel	511
Accrued expenses payable	2,552	Other non-current liabilities	1,437
Long-term notes payable	21,320	Other current liabilities	1,641
Other non-current assets	1,082	Additional paid-in capital	150
Common stock ($0.01 par value)	9		

These accounts are not necessarily in good order and have normal debit or credit balances. (Note: Because these are not all of UPS's accounts, these will not balance in a trial balance.) Assume the following transactions (in millions, except for par value) occurred the next fiscal year beginning January 1 (the current year):

a. Provided delivery service to customers, who paid $1,390 in cash and owed $24,704 on account.
b. Purchased new equipment costing $3,434; signed a long-term note.
c. Paid $7,864 cash to rent equipment and aircraft, with $3,136 for rent this year and the rest for rent next year (a prepaid expense).
d. Spent $864 cash to repair facilities and equipment during the year.
e. Collected $24,285 from customers on account.
f. Repaid $150 on a long-term note (ignore interest).
g. Issued 200 million additional shares of $0.01 par value stock for $16 (that's $16 million).
h. Paid employees $9,276 for work during the year.
i. Purchased spare parts, supplies, and fuel for the aircraft and equipment for $6,564 cash.
j. Used $6,450 in spare parts, supplies, and fuel for the aircraft and equipment during the year.
k. Paid $784 on accounts payable.
l. Ordered $88 in spare parts and supplies.

Required:

1. Prepare journal entries for each transaction. Use the account titles that UPS uses as listed above for balance sheet account effects.
2. Prepare T-accounts for the current year from the preceding list; enter the ending balances from December 31 as the respective beginning balances for January 1 of the current year. You will need additional T-accounts for income statement accounts; enter zero for beginning balances. Post the effects of the transactions in the T-accounts, and compute ending balances.
3. Prepare an unadjusted income statement for the current year ended December 31.
4. Compute the company's net profit margin ratio for the current year ended December 31. Round your answer to two decimal places. What do the results suggest to you about UPS?

P3-7 Recording Journal Entries (AP3-7)

LO3-4
Cedar Fair, L.P.

Cedar Fair, L.P. (Limited Partnership), is one of the largest regional amusement park operators in the world, owning 11 amusement parks, two water parks, and four hotels. The parks include Cedar Point in Ohio; Valleyfair near Minneapolis/St. Paul; Dorney Park and Wildwater Kingdom near Allentown, Pennsylvania; Worlds of Fun in Kansas City; Great America in Santa Clara, California; Canada's Wonderland near Toronto, Canada, Schlitterbahn Waterpark & Resort New Braunfels in New Braunfels, Texas; and Schlitterbahn Waterpark Galveston in Galveston, Texas, among several others. The following are summarized transactions similar to those that occurred in a recent year. Dollars are in thousands.

a. Guests at the parks paid $795,271 cash in admissions.
b. The primary operating expenses for the year were employee wages of $433,416, with $401,630 paid in cash and the rest to be paid to employees in the following year.
c. Cedar Fair paid $47,100 principal on long-term notes payable.
d. The parks sell merchandise in park stores. The cash received during the year for sales was $365,693.
e. The cost of the merchandise inventory sold during the year was $92,057.
f. Cedar Fair purchased and built additional rides and other equipment during the year, paying $90,190 in cash.

g. Guests may stay in the parks at accommodations owned by the company. During the year, accommodations revenue was $82,994; $81,855 was paid by the guests in cash and the rest was owed on account.

h. Interest incurred and paid on long-term debt was $153,326.

i. The company purchased $147,531 in inventory for the park stores during the year, paying $119,431 in cash and owing the rest on account.

j. Advertising costs for the parks were $140,426 for the year; $134,044 was paid in cash and the rest was owed on account.

k. Cedar Fair paid $11,600 on accounts payable during the year.

Required:
For each of these transactions, record journal entries. Use the letter of each transaction as its reference.

Identifying Cash Flow Effects (AP3-8)

P3-8
LO3-7

Refer to P3-7.

Required:
For the transactions listed in P3-7, use the following chart to identify whether each transaction results in a cash flow effect from operating (O), investing (I), or financing (F) activities and indicate the direction and amount of the effect on cash (+ for increase and – for decrease). If there is no cash flow effect, write **NE** in each column. The first transaction is provided as an example.

Transaction	Operating, Investing, or Financing Effect	Direction and Amount of the Effect (in thousands)
(*a*)	O	+795,271

ALTERNATE PROBLEMS

Recording Nonquantitative Journal Entries (P3-1)

AP3-1
LO3-4

The following is a series of accounts for Kruger & Laurenzo, Incorporated, which has been operating for two years. The accounts are listed and numbered for identification. Following the accounts is a series of transactions. For each transaction, indicate the account(s) that should be debited and credited by entering the appropriate account number(s) to the right of each transaction. If no journal entry is needed, write **none** after the transaction. The first transaction is given as an example.

Account No.	Account Title	Account No.	Account Title
1	Cash	9	Wages Payable
2	Accounts Receivable	10	Income Taxes Payable
3	Supplies	11	Common Stock
4	Prepaid Expenses	12	Additional Paid-in Capital
5	Buildings	13	Retained Earnings
6	Land	14	Service Revenue
7	Accounts Payable	15	Other Expenses (wages, supplies, interest)
8	Mortgage Payable	16	Income Tax Expense

Transactions	Debit	Credit
a. *Example:* Issued stock to new investors.	1	11, 12
b. Incurred and recorded operating expenses on credit to be paid next period.	____	____
c. Purchased on credit but did not use supplies this period.	____	____
d. Performed services for customers this period on credit.	____	____
e. Prepaid a fire insurance policy this period to cover the next 12 months.	____	____
f. Purchased a building this period by making a 20 percent cash down payment and signing a mortgage loan for the balance.	____	____
g. Collected cash this year for services rendered and recorded in the prior year.	____	____
h. Collected cash for services rendered this period.	____	____
i. Paid cash this period for wages earned and recorded last period.	____	____
j. Paid cash for operating expenses charged on accounts payable in the prior period.	____	____
k. Paid cash for operating expenses incurred in the current period.	____	____
l. Made a payment on the mortgage loan, which was part principal repayment and part interest.	____	____
m. This period a shareholder sold some shares of her stock to another person for an amount above the original issuance price.	____	____
n. Used supplies on hand to clean the offices.	____	____
o. Recorded income taxes for this period to be paid at the beginning of the next period.	____	____
p. Declared and paid a cash dividend this period.	____	____

AP3-2 Recording Journal Entries (P3-2)

LO3-4

Jimmy Langenberger is the president of TemPro, Inc., a company that provides temporary employees for not-for-profit companies. TemPro has been operating for five years; its revenues are increasing with each passing year. You have been hired to help Jimmy analyze the following transactions for the first two weeks of April:

a. Billed the local **United Way** office $23,500 for temporary services provided.
b. Paid $3,005 for supplies purchased and recorded on account last period.
c. Purchased supplies for the office for $2,600 on account.
d. Purchased a new computer for the office costing $3,800 cash.
e. Placed an advertisement in the local paper for $1,400 cash.
f. Paid employee wages of $11,900. Of this amount, $3,800 had been earned by employees and recorded in the Wages Payable account in the prior period.
g. Issued 3,000 additional shares of common stock for cash at $45 per share in anticipation of building a new office. The common stock had a par value of $0.50 per share.
h. Received $12,500 on account from the local United Way office for the services provided in (*a*).
i. Billed Family & Children's Services $14,500 for services rendered.
j. Purchased land as the site of a future office for $10,000. Paid $3,000 cash as a down payment and signed a note payable for the balance.
k. Received the April telephone bill for $1,950 to be paid next month.

Required:
For each of the transactions, prepare journal entries. Be sure to categorize each account as an asset (A), liability (L), stockholders' equity (SE), revenue (R), or expense (E).

AP3-3 Determining Financial Statement Effects of Various Transactions and Identifying Cash Flow Effects (P3-3)

LO3-4, 3-7

The TJX Companies, Inc.

The TJX Companies, Inc., parent company of **T.J. Maxx**, **Marshalls**, **Homegoods**, and others, is "the leading off-price apparel and home fashions retailer in the United States and worldwide," with over 4,500 stores.

a. *Example:* Incurred expenses; paid part in cash and part on credit.
b. Paid interest on long-term debt.
c. Sold merchandise to customers on account. (Indicate the effects of earning a revenue.)
d. Provided merchandise inventory to customers in (*c*) above. (Indicate the effects of using products to generate revenue.)
e. Sold equipment for cash for more than its cost.
f. Collected cash on account.
g. Used supplies.
h. Repaid long-term debt principal.
i. Received interest on investments.
j. Purchased equipment; paid part in cash and part on credit.
k. Paid cash on account to suppliers.
l. Issued additional stock for cash.
m. Paid rent to mall owners.

Required:

1. For each of the transactions, complete the tabulation, indicating the effect (+ for increase and − for decrease) of each transaction. (Remember that A = L + SE; R − E = NI; and NI affects SE through Retained Earnings.) Write NE if there is no effect. The first transaction is provided as an example.

	BALANCE SHEET			INCOME STATEMENT		
Transaction	**Assets**	**Liabilities**	**Stockholders' Equity**	**Revenues**	**Expenses**	**Net Income**
(*a*)	−	+	−	NE	+	−

2. For each transaction, indicate where, if at all, it would be reported on the statement of cash flows. Use O for operating activities, I for investing activities, F for financing activities, and NE if the transaction would not be included on the statement.

Analyzing the Effects of Transactions Using T-Accounts, Preparing an Income Statement, and Evaluating the Net Profit Margin Ratio as a Manager (P3-4)

AP3-4
LO3-4, 3-5, 3-6

Alpine Stables, Inc., is established in Denver, Colorado, on April 1, 2023, to provide stables, animal care, and grounds for riding and showing horses. You have been hired as the new assistant controller. The following transactions for April 2023 are provided for your review.

a. Received contributions of $60,000 in cash from five investors ($12,000 each), a barn valued at $100,000, land valued at $90,000, and supplies valued at $12,000. Each investor received 3,000 shares of stock with a par value of $0.01 per share.
b. Built a small barn for $62,000. The company paid half the amount in cash on April 1, 2023, and signed a three-year note payable for the balance.
c. Provided $35,260 in animal care services for customers, all on credit.
d. Rented stables to customers who cared for their own animals; received cash of $13,200.
e. Received from a customer $2,400 to board her horse in May, June, and July (record as unearned revenue).
f. Purchased hay and feed supplies on account for $3,810 to be used in the summer.
g. Paid $1,240 in cash for water utilities incurred in the month.
h. Paid $2,700 on accounts payable for previous purchases.
i. Received $10,000 from customers on accounts receivable.
j. Paid $6,000 in wages to employees who worked during the month.
k. At the end of the month, purchased a two-year insurance policy for $3,600.
l. Received an electric utility bill for $1,800 for usage in April; the bill will be paid next month.
m. Paid $100 cash dividend to each of the five investors at the end of the month.

Required:

1. Set up appropriate T-accounts. All accounts begin with zero balances.
2. Record in the T-accounts the effects of each transaction for Alpine Stables in April, referencing each transaction in the accounts with the transaction letter. Show the ending balances in the T-accounts.
3. Prepare an unadjusted income statement for April.

4. Write a short memo to the five owners offering your opinion on the results of operations during the first month of business.
5. After three years in business, you are being evaluated for a promotion to chief financial officer. One measure is how effectively you have managed the revenues and expenses of the business. The following annual data are available:

	2025*	2024	2023
Total assets	$480,000	$320,000	$300,000
Total liabilities	125,000	28,000	30,000
Total stockholders' equity	355,000	292,000	270,000
Operating revenue	450,000	400,000	360,000
Net income	50,000	30,000	(10,000)

*At the end of 2025, Alpine Stables decided to build an indoor riding arena for giving lessons year-round. The company borrowed construction funds from a local bank in 2025 and the arena was opened in early 2026.

Compute the net profit margin ratio for each year and evaluate the results, including if you think you should be promoted. Why?

Identifying Cash Flow Effects (P3-5)

AP3-5
LO3-7

Refer to AP3-4.

Required:

For the transactions listed in AP3-4, indicate the type of activity (O for operating, I for investing, and F for financing) and the direction (+ for increase, – for decrease) and amount of the effect. If the transaction had no effect on cash flows, write NE for both the effect and amount.

Analyzing the Effects of Transactions Using T-Accounts, Preparing an Income Statement, and Evaluating the Net Profit Margin Ratio (P3-6)

AP3-6
LO3-4, 3-5, 3-6
Exxon Mobil Corporation

The following are selected account balances from a recent balance sheet of **Exxon Mobil Corporation**. The accounts have normal debit or credit balances, but they are not necessarily listed in good order. The amounts are shown in millions of dollars for the end of the prior year. Assume the year-end is December 31.

Cash	$ 3,089	Short-term investments	$ 985
Long-term notes payable	26,342	Retained earnings	421,341
Accounts receivable	26,966	Accounts payable	41,831
Inventories	18,528	Income taxes payable	1,580
Other long-term debt	21,416	Prepaid expenses	484
Property and equipment, net	253,018	Long-term investments	43,164
Common stock	15,637	Other assets and intangibles	16,363
Other current assets	1,469	Short-term notes payable	20,578

Source: Exxon Mobil Corp.

The following is a list of hypothetical transactions for January of the current year (in millions of dollars):

a. Purchased new equipment for $1,610 on account.
b. Received $3,100 on accounts receivable.
c. Received and paid $3 for utility bills for utility usage during January.
d. Earned $39,780 in sales of fuel to gas station franchisee customers, all on account.
e. Used $5,984 of fuel inventory in the sales to customers in (*d*). [Title the account Cost of Sales.]
f. Paid employees $1,238 for wages earned during the month.
g. Paid three-fourths of the income taxes payable (rounded to the nearest million).
h. Purchased $23 in supplies on account (include in Inventories).
i. Prepaid $82 to rent a warehouse next month.
j. Paid $10 of other long-term debt principal and $1 in interest expense on the debt.
k. Purchased a patent (an intangible asset) for $6 cash.

Required:

1. Prepare journal entries for each transaction. Use the account titles that Exxon Mobil uses in the list above when a balance sheet account is affected.

2. Prepare T-accounts for the current year from the preceding list; enter the beginning balances based on the prior year's December 31 ending balances. You will need additional T-accounts for income statement accounts; enter zero for beginning balances. Post the effects of the transactions in the T-accounts, and compute ending balances.
3. Prepare an unadjusted income statement for January of the current year.
4. Compute the company's net profit margin ratio for the month ended January 31 of the current year. What does it suggest to you about Exxon Mobil Corporation?

Recording Journal Entries (P3-7)

AP3-7
LO3-4

Waterfun Park, Inc., is a large regional waterpark operator in the southern United States. The following are summarized transactions similar to those that occurred in a recent year. Dollars are in thousands.

a. Guests at the parks paid $641,042 cash in admissions.
b. Waterfun Park paid $49,800 principal on long-term notes payable.
c. Waterfun Park purchased and built additional water rides and other equipment during the year, paying $98,290 in cash.
d. Guests may stay in the parks at accommodations owned by the company. During the year, accommodations revenue was $90,194; $88,605 was paid by the guests in cash and the rest was owed on account.
e. The primary operating expenses for the year were employee wages of $469,416, with $437,630 paid in cash and the rest to be paid to employees in the following year.
f. The park sells merchandise in park stores. The cash received during the year for sales was $401,693.
g. The cost of the merchandise inventory sold during the year was $101,057.
h. Interest incurred and paid on long-term debt was $171,326.
i. The company purchased $161,031 in inventory for the park stores during the year, paying $130,231 in cash and owing the rest on account.
j. Waterfun Park paid $13,400 on accounts payable during the year.
k. Advertising costs for the parks were $153,926 for the year; $143,944 was paid in cash and the rest was owed on account.

Required:
For each of these transactions, record journal entries. Use the letter of each transaction as its reference.

Identifying Cash Flow Effects (P3-8)

AP3-8
LO3-7

Refer to AP3-7.

Required:
For the transactions listed in AP3-7, use the following chart to identify whether each transaction results in a cash flow effect from operating (O), investing (I), or financing (F) activities and indicate the direction and amount of the effect on cash (+ for increase and – for decrease). If there is no cash flow effect, write **NE** in each column. The first transaction is provided as an example.

Transaction	Operating, Investing, or Financing Effect	Direction and Amount of the Effect
(*a*)	O	+641,042

CONTINUING PROBLEM

Accounting for Operating Activities in a New Business (the Accounting Cycle)

CON3-1
LO3-4, 3-5, 3-6

Penny's Pool Service & Supply, Inc. (PPSS), had the following transactions related to operating the business in its first year's busiest quarter ended September 30:

a. Placed and paid for $2,600 in advertisements with several area newspapers (including the online versions), all of which ran in the newspapers during the quarter.
b. Cleaned pools for customers for $19,200, receiving $16,000 in cash with the rest owed by customers who will pay when billed in October.

c. Paid **Pool Corporation, Inc.**, a pool supply wholesaler, $10,600 for inventory received by PPSS in May.
d. As an incentive to maintain customer loyalty, PPSS offered customers a discount for prepaying next year's pool cleaning service. PPSS received $10,000 from customers who took advantage of the discount.
e. Paid the office receptionist $4,500, with $1,500 owed from work in the prior quarter and the rest from work in the current quarter. Last quarter's amount was recorded as an expense and a liability, Wages Payable.
f. Had the company van repaired, paying $310 to the mechanic.
g. Paid $220 for phone, water, and electric utilities used during the quarter.
h. Received $75 cash in interest earned during the current quarter on short-term investments.
i. Received a property tax bill for $600 for use of the land and building in the quarter; the bill will be paid next quarter.
j. Paid $2,400 for the next quarter's insurance coverage.

Required:

1. For each of the events, prepare journal entries, checking that debits equal credits.
2. Based only on these quarterly transactions, prepare a classified income statement (with income from operations determined separately from other items) for the quarter ended September 30.
3. Calculate the net profit margin ratio at September 30. What does this ratio indicate about the ability of PPSS to control operations?

COMPREHENSIVE PROBLEM (CHAPTERS 1–3)

COMP3-1 Recording Journal Entries, Posting Effects to T-Accounts, Preparing Unadjusted Financial Statements, and Performing Ratio Analysis

LO1-1, 2-4, 2-5, 3-4, 3-5, 3-6

In April 2023, Sarah Jones created a new business, IthacaDeep, Inc., offering therapeutic deep tissue massage for stress reduction, pain management, injury recovery, and relief from muscle strains and tightness experienced by anyone, especially athletes, fitness enthusiasts, runners, and physical laborers. You have been hired to record the transactions occurring in the first month of operations.

a. Received investment of cash by three organizers and issued to them a total of 200 shares of $0.01 par value stock with a market price of $40 per share.
b. Borrowed $20,000 from a local bank, signing a note due in three years.
c. Signed a one-year lease for a space near a health club, paying $600 for April rent and $1,800 for rent for May, June, and July.
d. Purchased equipment costing $15,200, paying 20 percent in cash and owing the rest on account to the supplier, due in 60 days.
e. Ordered a business computer and printer from **Dell** for $2,900.
f. Loaned $1,000 to an employee who signed a note due in three months.
g. Purchased supplies for $2,600 on account.
h. Paid **Facebook** $2,000 as a budget for advertising. (Facebook charges the advertiser's account per click, drawing down the balance. The average click is $0.27.)
i. Paid $2,400 for 12 months of insurance coverage, with one-twelfth covering April and the rest covering the remainder of the fiscal year (end of March next year).
j. Purchased short-term investments for $10,000 cash.
k. Along with her four other licensed massage therapists, Sarah and her team provided $42,000 of deep tissue service to clients in April who paid half in cash and agreed to pay the rest in May.
l. Paid employees $18,000 in wages for work in April.
m. At the end of April, received a $310 utility bill for the use of gas and electric in April. The bill will be paid in May.
n. Paid $1,500 on the long-term note owed to the bank (ignore interest).
o. Earned and received $35 in interest on the short-term investments.
p. Sent the team to Boston in April to receive additional specialty training, costing IthacaDeep $2,100 cash.
q. Received $1,400 from clients for a series of services to be performed beginning in May.

Required:

1. Prepare journal entries for each transaction, using the letter next to each as a reference.
2. Create T-accounts and post the effects of the transactions to the T-accounts.
3. Prepare an unadjusted trial balance for IthacaDeep, Inc., at the end of April.
4. Prepare an unadjusted classified income statement (include a line for income tax expense and earnings per share), statement of stockholders' equity, and classified balance sheet from the trial balance created in requirement (3) above.
5. Compute the following ratios: (1) current ratio and (2) net profit margin ratio. Round your answers to two decimal points. What do your results suggest about IthacaDeep, Inc.?

CASES AND PROJECTS

Annual Report Cases

Finding Financial Information

CP3-1
LO3-2, 3-4, 3-6
Target Corporation

Refer to the financial statements of **Target Corporation** in Appendix B at the end of this book. All dollar amounts are in millions.

1. What is the format of Target's income statement and how do you know this?
   a. Single-step format because Other Revenue is included in Total revenue.
   b. Multiple-step format because the company reports interest expense separately from operating expenses.
   c. Single-step format because the statement is condensed.
   d. Multiple-step format because the company separates continued operations from discontinued operations.
2. How much did Target's sales revenue increase or decrease in the most recent year?
   a. Decreased $15,270
   b. Increased $15,449
   c. Increased $15,270
   d. Decreased $15,449
3. What is the largest expense on the income statement for the most recent year, and how much did it change from the previous year (in millions)?
   a. Selling, general and administrative expenses, which increased $2,382
   b. Cost of sales, which decreased $1,565
   c. Depreciation and amortization, which increased $133
   d. Cost of sales, which increased $11,313
4. A Target shareholder has complained that "more dividends should be paid because the company had net earnings of $4,368 million. Since this amount is all cash, more of it should go to the owners." Is this a valid assumption and why?
   a. The assumption is not valid, because the reported amount of net earnings is based on applying accrual accounting principles in which revenues are recorded when earned and expenses are recorded when incurred, regardless of when cash is received or paid.
   b. The assumption is valid, because the income statement is based on applying the cash accounting principles in which cash received is revenue and cash paid is an expense.
   c. The assumption is valid because Target has $8,511 in cash to distribute.
   d. The assumption is not valid, because, over the life of the business, total earnings will not equal total net cash flow.
5. What is Target's net profit margin ratio for the most recent year based on total revenue and what does is suggest about Target?
   a. 0.0390, suggesting that Target earned $3.90 for every dollar of total revenue.
   b. 0.0699, suggesting that Target is doing very well.
   c. 0.0467, suggesting that Target earned $4.67 for every dollar of total revenue.
   d. 0.0473, suggesting that Target earned $4.73 for every dollar of sales.

CP3-2
LO3-2, 3-4, 3-6
Walmart Inc.

Finding Financial Information

Refer to the financial statements of **Walmart Inc.** in Appendix C at the end of this book. All dollar amounts are in millions.

1. What amount does the company report for consolidated net income for the most recent year (in millions)?
2. What is the amount of income tax expense for the most recent year?
3. What is the company's net profit margin percentage for the most recent year based on consolidated net income (round to two decimal places)?
4. How much did Walmart pay in cash dividends for the most recent year? (***Hint:*** Look at the Statements of Cash Flows.)
5. Total revenues were higher in fiscal year ending in 2021 than in fiscal year ending in 2020. Why was consolidated net income lower?
   a. Operating costs and expenses were 6.19% higher in fiscal year ending 2021 than in 2020.
   b. Operating income increased by 9.63%, but the largest change was a 39.5% increase in the provision for income taxes in fiscal year ending in 2021, causing the lower consolidated net income.
   c. The membership and other income total was 11.56% lower in fiscal year ending 2021 than in the previous year.

CP3-3
LO3-2, 3-4, 3-6
Target Corporation
Walmart Inc.

Comparing Companies within an Industry

Refer to the following:

- **Target Corporation** in Appendix B,
- **Walmart Inc.** in Appendix C, and the
- **Industry Ratio Report** in Appendix D at the end of this book.

All dollar amounts are in millions of dollars.

> **Tip** Percentage change = (This year's amount – Last year's amount) divided by Last year's amount

1. What was each company's percentage change in total revenues between the fiscal year ending in 2020 and the fiscal year ending in 2021? Round to three decimal places and indicate whether the amount increased or decreased.

Target's percentage change in total revenues =	
Walmart's percentage change in total revenues =	

2. Compute the net profit margin ratio for both companies (round your answers to three decimal places.) for the fiscal years ending:

January 30, 2021 Target =		**January 31, 2021 Walmart =**	
February 1, 2020 Target =		**January 31, 2020 Walmart =**	

3. Compared over time and with each other, how effective was management at generating revenues and controlling expenses from the previous year to the current year?
   a. Both companies' ratios suggest their managements are effective at generating revenues and/or controlling costs over time.
   b. Target is more effective over time, while Walmart is less effective over time at generating revenues and/or controlling costs.
   c. Target is less effective over time at generating revenues and/or controlling costs as compared to Walmart which was more effective at generating revenues and/or controlling costs over time.
   d. Walmart's management is doing poorly at generating revenues and controlling costs over time.
4. How does each company compare to the industry regarding the net profit margin ratio?
   a. Target and Walmart are both less effective at generating revenues and/or controlling costs than the industry average.
   b. Target and Walmart are more effective at generating revenues and/or controlling costs than the industry average.
   c. Target is less effective at generating revenues and/or controlling costs and Walmart is more effective at generating revenues and/or controlling costs than the industry average.
   d. Target is more effective at generating revenues and/or controlling costs and Walmart is less effective at generating revenues and/or controlling costs than the industry average.

5. How is the net profit margin ratio influenced by these companies' choice to take on more debt?
   a. Debt will increase the net profit margin ratio.
   b. Increasing debt has no effect on the net profit margin ratio.
   c. The interest on increased debt obligations decreases the numerator in the ratio, decreasing the ratio.
   d. Operating lease assets decrease the current ratio.

Financial Reporting and Analysis Case

Analyzing a Company over Time

CP3-4
LO3-6
Dollar General Corporation

Below is five years of Statement of Income data for **Dollar General Corporation**, one of the largest discount retailers in the United States:

	YEAR ENDED				
(Amounts in millions)	**January 29, 2021**	**January 31, 2020**	**February 1, 2019**	**February 2, 2018**	**February 3, 2017**
Net sales	$33,746.8	$27,754.0	$25,625.0	$23,471.0	$21,986.6
Cost of goods sold	23,027.9	19,264.9	17,821.1	16,249.6	15,204.0
Gross profit	10,718.9	8,489.1	7,803.9	7,221.4	6,782.6
Selling, general and administrative expenses	7,164.1	6,186.8	5,687.6	5,213.6	4,719.2
Operating profit	3,554.8	2,302.3	2,116.3	2,007.8	2,063.4
Interest expense	150.4	100.6	99.9	97.0	97.8
Other (income) expense	0.0	0.0	1.0	3.5	0.0
Income before income taxes	3,404.4	2,201.7	2,015.4	1,907.3	1,965.6
Income tax expense	749.3	489.1	425.9	368.3	714.5
Net income	$ 2,655.1	$ 1,712.6	$ 1,589.5	$ 1,539.0	$ 1,251.1

1. Compute the net profit margin ratio for each of the years presented, rounding your answers to three decimal places.
2. What trends do you observe over time and what do the trends suggest about Dollar General?

Critical Thinking Cases

Making a Decision as a Bank Loan Officer: Analyzing and Restating Financial Statements That Have Major Deficiencies (Challenging)

CP3-5
LO3-3, 3-4, 3-5

Julio Estela started a small boat repair service company during the current year. He is interested in obtaining a $100,000 loan from your bank to build a dry dock to store boats for customers. At the end of the year, he prepared the following statements based on information stored in a large filing cabinet:

ESTELA COMPANY **Profit for the Current Year**		
Service fees collected in cash during the current year		$ 55,000
Cash dividends received		10,000
Total		65,000
Expense for operations paid during the current year	$22,000	
Cash stolen	500	
New tools purchased during the current year (cash paid)	1,000	
Supplies purchased for use on service jobs (cash paid)	3,200	
Total		26,700
Profit		$ 38,300

(Continued)

ESTELA COMPANY	
Assets Owned at the End of the Current Year	
Cash in checking account	$ 29,300
Building (at current market value)	32,000
Tools and equipment	18,000
Land (at current market value)	30,000
Stock in ABC Industrial	130,000
Total	$239,300

The following is a summary of completed transactions:

a. Received the following contributions (at fair value) to the business from the owner when it was started in exchange for 1,000 shares of $1 par value common stock in the new company:

Building	$21,000	Land	$20,000
Tools and equipment	17,000	Cash	1,000

b. Earned service fees during the current year of $87,000; of the cash collected, $20,000 was for deposits from customers on work to be done by Julio in the next year.
c. Received the cash dividends on shares of ABC Industrial stock purchased by Julio Estela six years earlier (the stock was not owned by the company).
d. Incurred operating expenses during the current year of $61,000.
e. Determined amount of supplies on hand (unused) at the end of the current year as $700.
f. A temporary employee, subsequently fired, stole $500 cash from the business. There was no insurance coverage for theft.
g. Purchased tools and equipment during the year.

Required:

1. Did Julio prepare the income statement on a cash basis or an accrual basis? Explain how you can tell. Which basis should be used? Explain why.
2. Reconstruct the correct entries under accrual accounting principles and post the effects to T-accounts.
3. Prepare an accrual-based income statement, statement of stockholder's equity (only one shareholder), and a classified balance sheet. Explain (using footnotes) the reason for each change that you make to the income statement.
4. What additional information would assist you in formulating your decision regarding the loan to Julio?
5. Based on the revised financial statements and any additional information needed, write a letter to Julio explaining your decision at this time regarding the loan.

CP3-6 LO3-3

Evaluating an Ethical Dilemma

Mike Lynch is the manager of an upstate New York regional office for an insurance company. As the regional manager, his compensation package comprises a base salary, commissions, and a bonus when the region sells new policies in excess of its quota. Mike has been under enormous pressure lately, stemming largely from two factors. First, he is experiencing a mounting personal debt due to a family member's illness. Second, compounding his worries, the region's sales of new policies have dipped below the normal quota for the first time in years.

You have been working for Mike for two years, and like everyone else in the office, you consider yourself lucky to work for such a supportive boss. You also feel great sympathy for his personal problems over the last few months. In your position as accountant for the regional office, you are only too aware of the drop in new policy sales and the impact this will have on the manager's bonus. While you are working late at year-end, Mike stops by your office.

Mike asks you to change the manner in which you have accounted for a new property insurance policy for a large local business. A substantial check for the premium came in the mail on December 31, the last day of the reporting year. The premium covers a period beginning on January 5. You deposited the check and correctly debited Cash and credited an **unearned revenue** account. Mike says, "Hey, we have the money this year, so why not count the revenue this year? I never did understand why you accountants are so picky about these things anyway. I'd like you to change the way you have recorded the transaction. I want you to credit a *revenue* account. And anyway, I've done favors for you in the past, and I am asking for such a small thing in return." With that, he leaves for the day.

Required:

1. How should you handle this situation?
2. What are the ethical implications of Mike's request?
3. Who are the parties who would be helped or harmed if you complied with the request?
4. If you fail to comply with his request, how will you explain your position to him in the morning?

You As Analyst: Online Company Research

Examining Operating Activities of a Public Company (an Individual or Team Project)

CP3-7
LO3-2, 3-3, 3-6

In your web browser, search for the investor relations page of a public company you are interested in (e.g., Papa John's investor relations). Select SEC Filings or Annual Report or Financials to obtain the 10-K for the most recent year available.*

Required:

1. Go to the Income Statement (Statement of Income, Statement of Earnings, Statement of Operations). For the most recent year:
   a. What is (are) the major revenue accounts(s)?
   b. What percentage is each to total operating revenues? (Calculated as Revenue A/Total Operating Revenues)
   c. What is (are) the three top expense account(s) by size?
   d. What is the percentage of each to total operating expenses? (Calculated as Expense A/Total Operating Expenses)
2. Describe the company's revenue recognition policy, if reported (usually in the Significant Accounting Policies note to the financial statements), and how it has followed the conditions of the revenue recognition principle.
3. Ratio Analysis:
   a. What does the net profit margin ratio measure in general?
   b. Compute the net profit margin ratio for each of the last three years.
   c. What do your results suggest about the company over time?

*Alternatively, you can go to sec.gov, click on Company Filings (under the search box), type in the name of the public company you want to find. Once at the list of filings, type 10-K in the Filing Type box. The most recent 10-K annual report will be at the top of the list. Click on Interactive Data for a list of the parts or the entire report to examine.

BUSINESS ANALYTICS AND DATA VISUALIZATION WITH EXCEL AND TABLEAU

Connect offers a variety of exercises to assess Excel skills, data visualization, interpretation, and analysis, including auto-graded Tableau Dashboard Activities, Applying Excel problems, and Integrated Excel problems.

Images used throughout chapter: Question of ethics: mushmello/Shutterstock; Pause for feedback: McGraw Hill; Guided help: McGraw Hill; Financial analysis: McGraw Hill; Focus on cash flows: Hilch/Shutterstock; Key ratio analysis: guillermain/123RF; Data analytics: Hilch/Shutterstock; Tip: McGraw Hill; ESG reporting: McGraw Hill; International perspective: Hilch/Shutterstock

4

chapter

Adjustments, Financial Statements, and the Closing Process

The end of the accounting period is a very busy time for **Chipotle Mexican Grill.** Although the last day of the fiscal year for Chipotle falls on the last day of December each year, the financial statements are not distributed to users until management and the external auditors (independent CPAs) make many critical evaluations.

- Management at the corporate headquarters must ensure that the correct amounts are reported on the balance sheet and income statement. This often requires estimations, assumptions, and judgments about the timing of revenue and expense recognition and values for assets and liabilities.
- The auditors have to (1) assess the strength of the controls established by management to safeguard the company's assets and ensure the accuracy of the financial records and (2) evaluate the appropriateness of estimates and accounting principles used by management in determining revenues and expenses.

Managers of most companies understand the need to present financial information fairly so as not to mislead users. However, because end-of-period adjustments are the most complex portion of the annual recordkeeping process, they are prone to error. External auditors examine the company's records on a test, or sample, basis. To maximize the chance of detecting any errors significant enough to affect users' decisions, CPAs allocate more of their testing to transactions most likely to be in error.

Several accounting research studies have documented the most error-prone transactions for medium-size manufacturing companies. End-of-period adjustment errors,

LEARNING OBJECTIVES

After studying this chapter, you should be able to:

4-1 Explain the purpose of adjustments and analyze the adjustments necessary at the end of the period to update revenues and expenses and related balance sheet accounts. p. 172

4-2 Present an income statement with earnings per share, a statement of stockholders' equity, and a balance sheet. p. 183

4-3 Compute and interpret the total asset turnover ratio. p. 188

4-4 Explain the closing process. p. 190

Richard Drew/AP Photo

FOCUS COMPANY

Chipotle Mexican Grill

ESTIMATING REVENUES AND EXPENSES AT YEAR-END

chipotle.com

Learn more about Chipotle from founder, Steve Ells, by listening to the NPR podcast

Chipotle: Steve Ells: How I Built This.

How I Built This NPR podcasts are about innovators, entrepreneurs, idealists, and the movements they built.

such as failure to provide adequate product warranty liability, failure to include items that should be expensed, and end-of-period transactions recorded in the wrong period (called cut-off errors), are in the top category and thus receive a great deal of attention from auditors.

For 2019, Chipotle's year-end estimation and auditing process took until February 4, 2020, the date on which the auditor Ernst & Young LLP completed the audit work and signed its audit opinion. At that point, the financial statements were made available to the public and submitted to the U.S. Securities and Exchange Commission, about five weeks after the end of the year.

UNDERSTANDING THE BUSINESS

Managers are responsible for preparing financial statements that will be useful to investors, creditors, and others. Financial information is most useful for analyzing the past and predicting the future when it is considered by users to be of **high quality.** High-quality information is information that is relevant (that is, material and able to influence users' decisions) and a faithful representation of what is being reported (that is, complete, free from error, and unbiased in portraying economic reality).

Users expect revenues and expenses to be reported in the proper period based on the revenue and expense recognition principles discussed in Chapter 3. Revenues are to be recorded when earned, and expenses are to be recorded when incurred, regardless of when cash receipts or payments occur. Many operating activities take place over a period of time or over several periods, such as using insurance that has been prepaid or owing wages to employees for past work. Because recording these and similar activities daily is often very costly, most companies wait until the end of the period (annually, but monthly and quarterly as well) to make **adjustments** to record related revenues and expenses in the correct period. These entries update the records and are the focus of this chapter.

Tip If you find this material to be challenging, study this chapter well, review prior chapters when unsure (especially revenue and expense recognition in Chapter 3), and **PRACTICE, PRACTICE, PRACTICE!**

In this chapter, we emphasize the use of the same analytical tools illustrated in Chapters 2 and 3 (journal entries and T-accounts) and the application of the revenue and expense recognition principles discussed in Chapter 3 to understand how common **adjustments** are analyzed and recorded at the end of the accounting period. These tools provide the foundation for understanding adjustments that require additional estimation and judgments by management, which we discuss in future chapters. Then, in this chapter, we prepare financial statements using adjusted accounts, and finally, we illustrate how to prepare the accounting records for the next period by performing a process called **closing the books.**

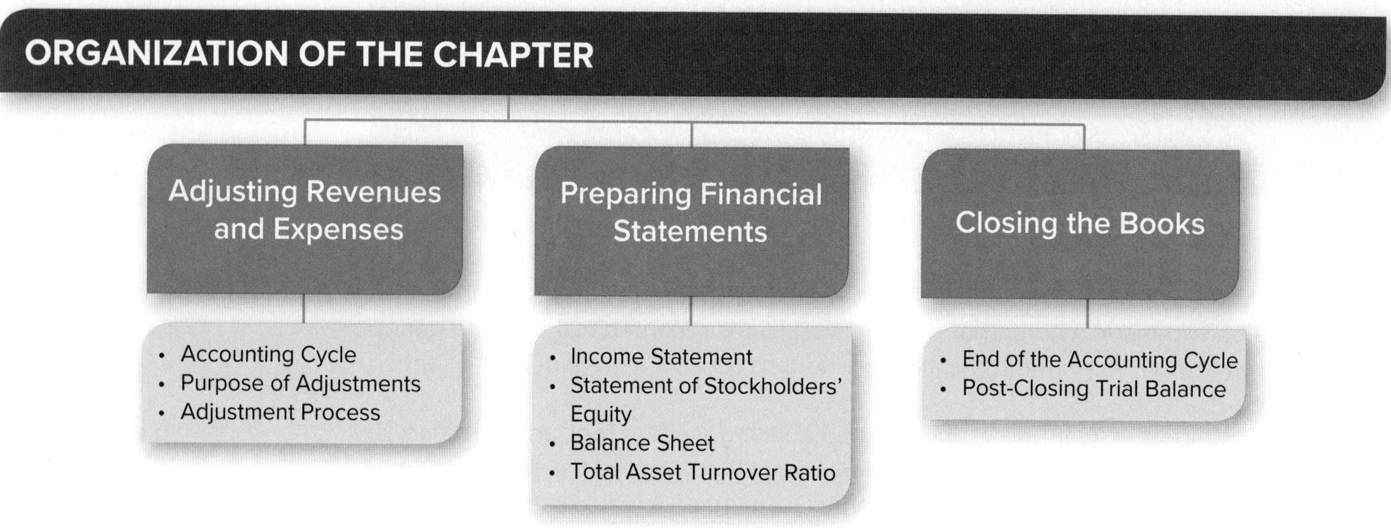

LEARNING OBJECTIVE 4-1

Explain the purpose of adjustments and analyze the adjustments necessary at the end of the period to update revenues and expenses and related balance sheet accounts.

ADJUSTING REVENUES AND EXPENSES

Accounting Cycle

Exhibit 4.1 presents the basic steps in the **accounting cycle.** As initially discussed in Chapter 2, the accounting cycle is the process followed by entities to analyze and record transactions, adjust the records at the end of the period, prepare financial statements, and prepare the records for the next cycle. **During** the accounting period, transactions that result in exchanges between the company and other external parties are analyzed and recorded in the general journal in chronological order (journal entries), and the related accounts are updated in the general ledger (T-accounts), similar to our **Chipotle** illustrations in Chapters 2 and 3. In this chapter, we examine the **end-of-period** steps that focus primarily on adjustments to record revenues and expenses in the proper period and to update the balance sheet accounts for reporting purposes.

Purpose of Adjustments

Accounting systems are designed to record most recurring daily transactions, particularly those involving cash. As cash is received or paid, it is recorded in the accounting system. In general, this focus on cash works well, especially when cash receipts and payments occur in the same period as the activities that produce revenues and expenses. However, as illustrated in Exhibit 4.2, cash is not always received in the period in which the company earns revenue; likewise, cash is not always paid in the period in which the company incurs an expense.

EXHIBIT 4.1 The Accounting Cycle

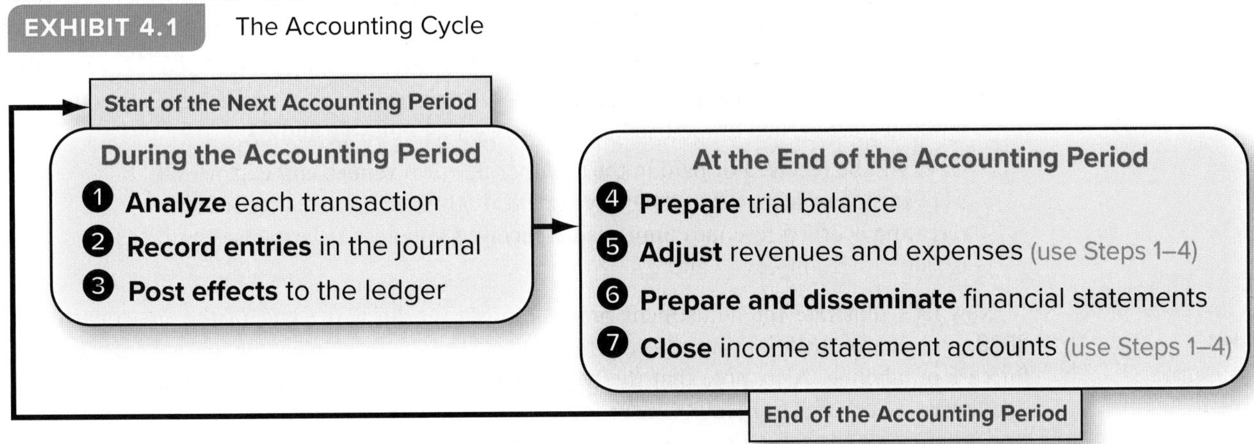

How does the accounting system record revenues and expenses when one transaction is needed to record a cash receipt or payment and another transaction is needed to record revenue when it is earned or an expense when it is incurred? The solution to the problem created by such differences in timing is to record adjusting entries at the end of every accounting period, so that:

- Revenues are recorded when they are earned (the **revenue recognition principle**),
- Expenses are recorded when they are incurred to generate revenue (the **expense recognition principle**),
- **Assets** are reported at amounts that represent the probable future benefits remaining at the end of the period, and
- **Liabilities** are reported at amounts that represent the probable future sacrifices of assets or services owed at the end of the period.

Companies wait until the **end of the accounting period** to adjust their accounts because adjusting the records daily would be very costly and time-consuming. Adjusting entries are required every time a company wants to prepare financial statements for external users.

Exhibit 4.2 provides a list of the deferral and accrual balance sheet accounts that are affected by adjusting entries at the end of the accounting period. In practice, almost every account, **except Cash,** could require an adjustment. We will illustrate the process involved in analyzing and recording **Chipotle Mexican Grill**'s adjustments, common to most companies, before preparing Chipotle's financial statements for the first quarter of 2020 based on adjusted balances.

EXHIBIT 4.2

Types of Adjustments

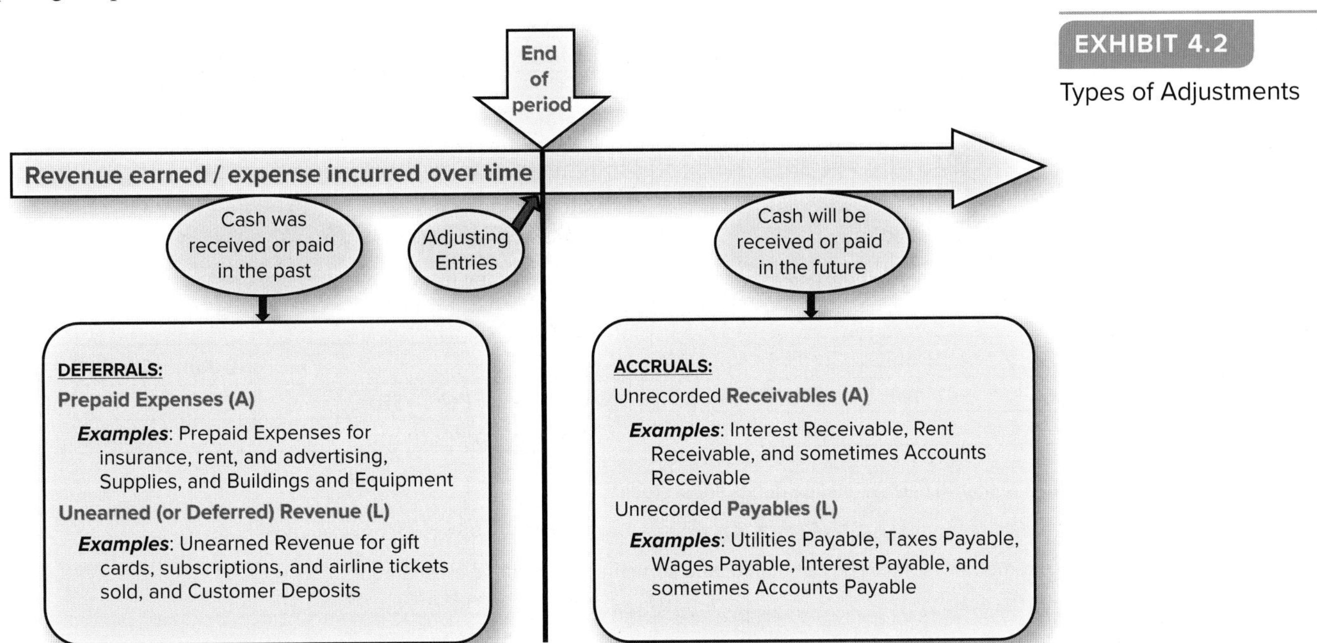

Adjustment Process

Exhibit 4.3 describes the process for analyzing and recording adjusting entries when:

- Cash was received or paid in the past (creating deferred revenue and expense accounts until they are earned or incurred over time) → Examples ❶ and ❸.
- Cash will be received or paid in the next period for revenues and expenses that were earned or incurred in the current period but have not been recorded (creating accrued revenues until cash is received and accrued expenses until cash is paid) → Examples ❷ and ❹.

Tip **Reminder:**

- Revenues and expenses are increased in adjusting entries.
- Cash is never in an adjusting entry.

Now let's illustrate the adjustment process for **Chipotle** at the end of the first quarter of 2020. For each of the following adjustments, we shorten the term **adjusting journal entry** to AJE for ease of labeling. Also, note that the beginning balance in each T-account is taken from the unadjusted T-accounts in Exhibit 3.6. Finally, as you learned in Chapters 2 and 3, it is important to continue to check that debits equal credits in each entry and that the accounting equation remains in balance. In the following adjustments, all amounts are in millions of dollars, and all entries and the accounting equation are in balance.

Deferred Revenues (❶ in Exhibit 4.3)

When a customer pays for goods or services before the company delivers them, the company records the amount of cash received in a **deferred (unearned) revenue** account. This unearned revenue is a liability representing the company's promise to perform or deliver the goods or services in the future. Recognition of (recording) the revenue is postponed (deferred) until the company meets its obligation.

EXHIBIT 4.3 Adjustment Process

Ask: **Was revenue earned that is not yet recorded and . . .**

❶ **Cash was received in the past?** ***Deferral***

Debit the account recorded when cash was received in the past

Credit the revenue account for what was earned*

Example:

	Debit	Credit
Unearned revenue (−L)	600	
Gift card revenue (+R, +SE)		600

❷ **Cash will be received in the future?** ***Accrual***

Debit the account for what is owed to the company

Credit the revenue account for what was earned*

Example:

	Debit	Credit
Interest receivable (+A)	60	
Interest revenue (+R, +SE)		60

OR

Was an expense incurred that has not yet been recorded and . . .

❸ **Cash was paid in the past?** ***Deferral***

Debit the expense account for what was incurred*

Credit the account recorded when cash was paid in the past

Example:

	Debit	Credit
Rent expense (+E, −SE)	100	
Prepaid rent expense (−A)		100

❹ **Cash will be paid in the future?** ***Accrual***

Debit the expense account for what was incurred*

Credit the account for what the company owes

Example:

	Debit	Credit
Wages expense (+E, −SE)	1,000	
Wages payable (+L)		1,000

Verify: Does the accounting equation remain in balance and do debits equal credits?

NOTE: Cash is never included in an adjusting entry because either it was recorded in the past or it will be recorded in the future.

*Sometimes the amount is given, sometimes it must be calculated, and sometimes it must be estimated.

AJE 1 **Unearned Revenue** Chipotle had an unadjusted balance of $130 in Unearned Revenue at the end of the quarter, representing gift card purchases by customers in the past. However, during the quarter, customers redeemed a portion of the gift cards for $52 in food service. If no adjustment has been made at the end of the quarter, the liability is overstated, and the revenue is understated. An adjusting entry is needed to correct the balances → **Reduce Unearned Revenue and increase Restaurant Sales Revenue for $52.**

	Debit	Credit
(AJE 1) Unearned revenue (−L)	52	
Restaurant sales revenue (+R, +SE)		52

Assets	=	Liabilities		+	Stockholders' Equity	
		Unearned revenue	−52		Restaurant sales revenue (+R)	+52

− Unearned Revenue (L) +			
		130	Bal.
(AJE 1)	52		
		78	

− Restaurant Sales Revenue (R) +			
		1,359	Bal.
		52	*(AJE 1)*
		1,411	

TIP

Reminder: The beginning balance in each account is the unadjusted balance from Exhibit 3.6.

Additional examples of deferred revenues include magazine subscription sales by publishing companies; season tickets sold in advance to sporting events, plays, and concerts by these types of organizations; air flight tickets sold in advance by airlines; and rent received in advance by landlords. Each of these requires an adjusting entry at the end of the accounting period to report the amount of revenue earned during the period.

Accrued Revenues (❷ in Exhibit 4.3)

Sometimes companies perform services or provide goods (i.e., earn revenue) before customers pay. Because cash is owed, the revenue that was earned may not have been recorded. Revenues that have been earned but have not yet been recorded at the end of the accounting period are called **accrued revenues**.

AJE 2 **Interest on Investments** Assume that the short-term investments owned by Chipotle earned $1 in additional interest revenue for the current quarter, but the cash will be received in the next quarter. Because no entry was recorded yet, the asset to reflect what is owed to Chipotle and the revenue are both understated. An adjusting entry is needed to correct the balances → **Increase Interest Receivable and Increase Interest Revenue for $1.**

	Debit	Credit
(AJE 2) Interest receivable (+A)	1	
Interest revenue (+R, +SE)		1

Assets		=	Liabilities	+	Stockholders' Equity	
Interest receivable	+1				Interest revenue (+R)	+1

+ Interest Receivable (A) −			
Bal.	0		
(AJE 2)	1		
	1		

− Interest Revenue (R) +			
		3	Bal.
		1	*(AJE 2)*
		4	

Tip Interest Receivable is a new account. **When creating a new account title, call it what it is**—This would not be called Notes Receivable, for example.

Deferred Expenses (❸ in Exhibit 4.3)

Assets represent resources with probable future benefits to the company. Many assets are used over time to generate revenues, including supplies, prepaid expenses for insurance, advertising, and rent, and buildings and equipment. These assets are **deferred expenses** (that is, recording the expenses for using these assets is deferred to the future). At the end of every period, an adjustment must be made to record the amount of the asset that was used during the period.

AJE 3 **Supplies** The Supplies account includes food, beverage, and paper products that Chipotle purchased throughout the quarter. At the end of the quarter, the Supplies account has a balance of $485, but Chipotle counted $23 of supplies on hand, indicating supplies were used. Since no adjustment has been made yet, the asset is overstated and the expense is understated by the amount that has been used during the quarter. An adjusting entry is needed to correct the balances → **Increase Supplies Expense and decrease Supplies for $462 ($485 available for use − $23 remaining at the end = $462 used during the quarter).**

	Debit	Credit
(AJE 3) Supplies expense (+E, −SE)	462	
Supplies (−A)		462

Assets		=	Liabilities	+	Stockholders' Equity	
Interest receivable	+1				Interest revenue (+R)	+1

+ Supplies (A) −			
Bal.	485		
		462	*(AJE 3)*
	23		

+ Supplies Expense (E) −		
Bal.	0	
(AJE 3)	**462**	
	462	

AJE 4 **Prepaid Expenses** Among other things, the Prepaid Expenses unadjusted account balance of $292 includes

- $128 paid at the end of last quarter for rental of facilities at $32 per month,
- $96 for insurance coverage for six months beginning January 1, 2020, and
- $41 for advertising during the quarter.

By the end of the quarter, each of these prepaid expenses has been used for **three months.** Since no adjustment has been made yet, the asset is overstated and the expense is understated by the amount that has been used during the quarter. An adjusting entry is needed to correct the balances → **Increase the appropriate expense accounts and decrease Prepaid Expenses for the following amount:**

Rent expense:	$32 per month × 3 months =	$ 96
Insurance expense:	$96 prepaid × (3 out of 6 months of coverage) =	48
Advertising expense:	$41 all used during the quarter =	41
	Total prepaid expenses used during the quarter	**$185**

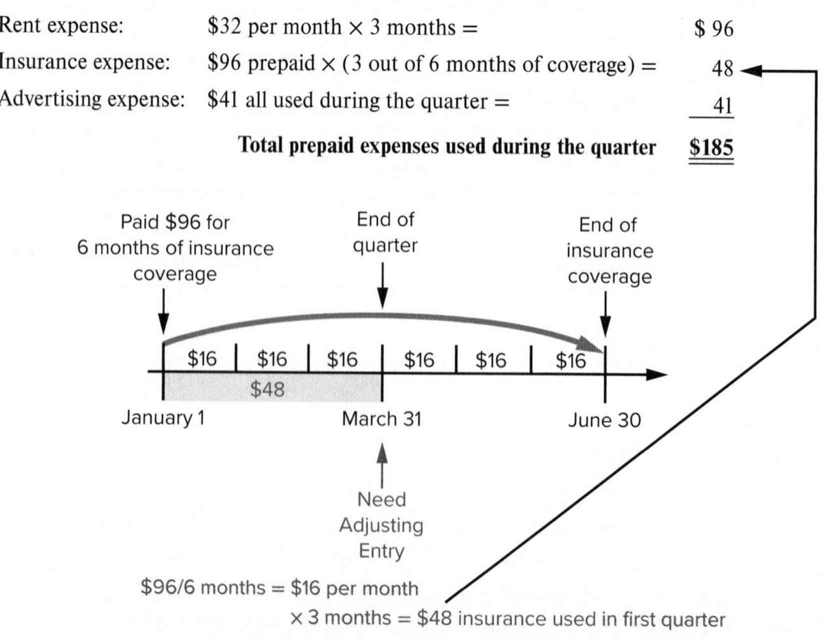

Tip Draw a timeline when you need to visualize the number of months, etc., for computations.

	Debit	Credit
(AJE 4) Rent expense (+E, −SE)	96	
Insurance expense (+E, −SE)	48	
Advertising expense (+E, −SE)	41	
Prepaid expenses (−A)		185

Assets		=	Liabilities	+	Stockholders' Equity	
Prepaid expenses	−185				Rent expense (+E)	−96
					Insurance expense (+E)	−48
					Advertising expense (+E)	−41

+ Prepaid Expenses (A) −

	Debit	Credit	
Bal.	292		
		185	*(AJE 4)*
	107		

+ Rent Expense (E) −

	Debit	Credit
Bal.	0	
(AJE 4)	**96**	
	96	

+ Insurance Expense (E) −

	Debit	Credit
Bal.	0	
(AJE 4)	**48**	
	48	

+ Advertising Expense (E) −

	Debit	Credit
Bal.	0	
(AJE 4)	**41**	
	41	

AJE 5 **Buildings and Equipment** Chipotle's Buildings and Equipment accounts are listed at **cost.** The accounts increase by the cost of the assets when they are **acquired** and decrease by the cost of the assets when they are **sold** or disposed of. However, these assets also are **used** over time to generate revenue. A part of their cost should be recorded as an expense in the same period (following the expense recognition principle). Accountants say that buildings and equipment, but not land, **depreciate** over time as they are used. In accounting, **depreciation is an allocation of the cost of buildings and equipment over their estimated useful lives to the organization.**

To keep track of the asset's historical cost, the amount that has been used is not subtracted directly from the asset account. Instead, it is accumulated in a new kind of account called a **contra-account**. Contra-accounts are accounts that are **directly linked to another account or financial statement section, but with an opposite balance.** For Buildings and Equipment, the contra-account for the total cost used to date is called **Accumulated Depreciation.** Accumulated Depreciation increases with the amount of depreciation expense for the period and decreases when an asset is sold for the portion used in prior periods. We will designate contra-accounts with an X in front of the type of account to which it is related. For example, this contra-account will be shown as Accumulated Depreciation (XA).

Because assets have debit balances, Accumulated Depreciation has a credit balance. On the balance sheet, the amount that is reported for property and equipment is its **net book value** (also called the **book value** or **carrying value**), which equals the ending balance in the property and equipment accounts (total cost of property and equipment) minus the ending balance in the Accumulated Depreciation account (used cost of buildings and equipment).

> **Tip** **Land does not depreciate in an accounting sense:** Buildings and equipment wear away and will need to be replaced at some time in the future, but land will not.

> **Tip** **Treasury Stock** is also a contra-account and reduces stockholders' equity. This and **Accumulated Depreciation** are the first two of several **contra-accounts** you will learn throughout the text.

COST + Property and Equipment (A) −		−	USED COST − Accumulated Depreciation (XA) +		= UNUSED COST = **NET BOOK VALUE**
Beg. Bal. **Asset purchases (at cost)**	**Asset disposals (at cost)**		**Asset disposals (for assets' used cost)**	Beg. Bal. **Depreciation expense (used in current period)**	↑ **Amount reported on the balance sheet**
End. Bal.				End. Bal.	

Tip When we say that something is **"net,"** we mean that **two accounts or totals have been subtracted.** For example, Net Income is the result of subtracting expenses from revenues. You will see this term used throughout the text.

For Chipotle, based on unadjusted balances (from Exhibit 3.6 with dollars in millions), Land, Buildings, and Equipment (property and equipment) have a total cost of $2,725 and Accumulated Depreciation has a credit balance of $1,201. On the balance sheet, property and equipment would be reported **net** of those two amounts and written as follows:

Property and equipment (net of accumulated depreciation of $1,201)	$1,524

Depreciation is discussed in much greater detail in Chapter 8. Until then, we will give you the amount of depreciation estimated by the company. Assume Chipotle estimates depreciation to be $232 per year. For the quarter, depreciation expense would be **$58** ($232 × 3 months/12 months).

At the end of the quarter, since no adjustment has been made yet, the net assets (property and equipment minus accumulated depreciation) are overstated, and the expense is understated by the amount that has been used during the quarter. An adjusting entry is needed to correct the balances → **Increase Depreciation Expense and increase Accumulated Depreciation for $58.**

	Debit	Credit
(AJE 5) Depreciation expense (+E, −SE)	58	
Accumulated depreciation (+XA, −A)		58

Assets		=	Liabilities	+	Stockholders' Equity	
Accumulated depreciation (+XA)	−58				Depreciation expense (+E)	−58

+ Depreciation Expense (E) −

	Debit	Credit
Bal.	0	
(AJE 5)	**58**	
	58	

− Accumulated Depreciation (XA) +

Debit	Credit	
	1,201	Bal.
	58	*(AJE 5)*
	1,259	

Accrued Expenses (❹ in Exhibit 4.3)

Numerous expenses are incurred in the current period without being paid until the next period. Common examples include Wages Expense for the wages owed to employees who worked during the period, Interest Expense incurred on debt owed during the period, and Utilities Expense for the water, gas, and electricity used during the period. These **accrued expenses** accumulate (accrue) over time but are not recognized as expenses with the related liability until the end of the period through an adjusting entry.

AJE 6 **Wages** Assume that Chipotle's employees worked two days at the end of the quarter, earning $26 per day, but they will not be paid until next quarter. The $26 per day accrues (grows) until paid. Because no entry was recorded yet, the liability to reflect what is owed by Chipotle and the related expense are both understated. An adjusting entry is needed to correct the balances → **Increase Wages Expense and Increase Wages Payable for $52 ($26 per day × 2 days).**

	Debit	Credit
(AJE 6) Wages expense (+E, −SE)	52	
Wages payable (+L)		52

Assets	=	Liabilities		+	Stockholders' Equity	
		Wages payable	+52		Wages expense (+E)	−52

+ Wages Expense (E) −

	Debit	Credit
Bal.	342	
(AJE 6)	**52**	
	394	

− Wages Payable (L) +

Debit	Credit	
	80	Bal.
	52	*(AJE 6)*
	132	

AJE 7 **Interest on Debt** There are two components when borrowing (or lending) money:

- **Principal** → the amount borrowed (or loaned) and
- **Interest** → the cost of borrowing (or lending)–that is, the cost of **using** another's money.

Principal on debt remains due until paid, but interest on the borrowing accrues over time and is paid according to the debt contract. Based on the assumed transactions in Chapters 2 and 3, Chipotle had a **principal balance of $80** in long-term notes payable at the end of the current quarter. There is no adjustment needed for the Notes Payable account (the principal).

However, interest expense is incurred by Chipotle for the quarter and it will be paid in the future. Assume that the **annual** interest rate on Chipotle's borrowings is 5.0 percent. Because no entry for interest expense was recorded yet this quarter, the liability to reflect what interest is owed by Chipotle and the related expense are both understated. An adjusting entry is needed to correct the balances → **Increase Interest Expense and Increase Interest Payable** determined by the following formula:

Tip Two important points:

- The interest rate we give you will always be the **annual rate.**
- In short, the formula is:

P × R × T/12

P is principal.

R is annual interest rate.

T/12 is time—the number of months out of 12 since the last accrual.

Interest Formula:

$$\text{Principal} \times \text{Annual Interest Rate} \times \text{Time: } \frac{\#\text{ of months}}{12\text{ months}} = \text{Interest for the Period}$$

$$\$80 \times 0.05 \times 3/12 = \$1$$

	Debit	Credit
(AJE 7) Interest expense (+E, −SE)	1	
Interest payable (+L)		1

Assets	=	Liabilities		+	Stockholders' Equity	
		Interest payable	+1		Interest expense (+E)	−1

+ Interest Expense (E) −		
Bal.	0	
(AJE 7)	1	
	1	

− Interest Payable (L) +		
	0	Bal.
	1	*(AJE 7)*
	1	

AJE 8 **Utilities** Most organizations receive utility bills after using utility services such as electricity, natural gas, and telephone. At the end of the period, managers estimate what the expense should be based on prior bills, or the company receives a bill soon after the end of the period but before the financial statements are completed. In either case, the usage of utility services accrues throughout the period. Assume Chipotle received a utility bill for $15 for utility service near the end of the quarter. Because no entry was recorded yet, the liability to reflect what is owed by Chipotle and the related expense are both understated. An adjusting entry is needed to correct the balances → **Increase Utilities Expense and Increase Utilities Payable for $15.**

	Debit	Credit
(AJE 8) Utilities expense (+E, −SE)	15	
Utilities payable (+L)		15

Assets	=	Liabilities		+	Stockholders' Equity	
		Utilities payable	+15		Utilities expense (+E)	−15

+ Utilities Expense (E) –		
Bal.	117	
(AJE 8)	**15**	
	132	

– Utilities Payable (L) +		
	131	Bal.
	15	*(AJE 8)*
	146	

AJE 9 **Income Taxes** The final adjusting entry is to record the accrual of income taxes that will be paid in the next quarter. This requires computing adjusted pretax income and applying the appropriate tax rate:

	Revenues and Gains	–	Expenses and Losses		
Summary from Exhibit 3.7	$1,362		$ 568		
AJE 1	52				
AJE 2	1				
AJE 3			462		
AJE 4			185		
AJE 5			58		
AJE 6			52		
AJE 7			1		
AJE 8			15		
	$ 1,415	–	$1,341	=	**$74 Pretax Income**

Then, compute income tax expense. Assume Chipotle estimated a tax rate of 20.0 percent for the quarter, with the taxes due next quarter. Computation of the quarterly income tax expense is

Tip There are many other kinds of taxes companies pay.

Examples:

Sales taxes, property taxes, payroll taxes, and state and local income taxes.

Pretax income	×	Income tax rate	=	Income tax expense
$74	×	**0.20**	=	**$15 for the quarter (rounded to the nearest dollar—which is in millions)**

Because no entry was recorded yet, the liability to reflect the income taxes owed by Chipotle and the related expense are both understated. An adjusting entry is needed to correct the balances → **Increase Income Tax Expense and Increase Income Taxes Payable for $15.**

	Debit	Credit
(AJE 9) Income tax expense (+E, −SE)	15	
Income taxes payable (+L)		15

Assets	=	Liabilities		+	Stockholders' Equity	
		Income taxes payable	+15		Income tax expense (+E)	−15

+ Income Tax Expense (E) –		
Bal.	0	
(AJE 9)	**15**	
	15	

– Income Taxes Payable (L) +		
	0	Bal.
	15	*(AJE 9)*
	15	

In all of the above adjustments, you may have noticed that **the Cash account was never adjusted.** The cash has already been received or paid by the end of the period, or it will be received or paid in the next period. Adjustments are required to record revenues and expenses in the proper period because the cash part of the transaction is at a different point in time. In addition, **each adjusting entry always included at least one income statement account and at least one balance sheet account.** Now it's your turn to practice the adjustment process.

PAUSE FOR FEEDBACK

Adjustments are necessary at the end of the accounting cycle to record all revenues and expenses in the proper period and to reflect the proper valuation for assets and liabilities.

- **Deferred revenues** (liabilities) have balances at the end of the period because cash was received before it was earned. If all or part of the liability has been satisfied by the end of the period, revenue needs to be recorded and the liability reduced.
- **Accrued revenue** adjustments are necessary when the company has earned revenue but the cash will be received in the next period. Because nothing has been recorded yet, revenue needs to be recognized and an asset (a receivable) increased.
- **Deferred expenses** (assets) have balances at the end of the period because cash was paid in the past by the company for the assets. If all or part of the asset has been used to generate revenues in the period, an expense needs to be recorded and the asset reduced.
- **Accrued expense** adjustments are necessary when the company has incurred an expense but the cash will be paid in the next period. Because nothing has been recorded yet, an expense needs to be recognized and a liability (a payable) increased.

SELF-STUDY QUIZ

For practice, complete the following adjustments using the process outlined in Exhibit 4.3:

Ask

(1) Was revenue earned that is not yet recorded and cash was received in the past–a Deferred Revenue? **Increase revenue; decrease liability**

(2) Was revenue earned that is not yet recorded and cash will be received in the future–an Accrued Revenue? **Increase revenue; increase asset (a receivable)**

(3) Was an expense incurred that has not yet been recorded and cash was paid in the past–a Deferred Expense? **Increase expense; decrease asset**

(4) Was an expense incurred that has not yet been recorded and cash will be paid in the future–an Accrued Expense? **Increase expense; increase liability (a payable)**

Florida Flippers, a scuba diving and instruction business, completed its first year of operations on December 31.

AJE 1: Florida Flippers received $6,000 from customers on November 15 for diving trips to the Bahamas in December and January of the next year. The $6,000 was recorded in Unearned Revenue on that date. By the end of December, one-third of the diving trips had been completed.

AJE 2: On December 31, Florida Flippers provided advanced diving instruction to 10 customers who will pay the business $800 in January of next year. No entry was made when the instruction was provided.

AJE 3: On September 1, Florida Flippers paid $24,000 for insurance for the 12 months beginning on September 1. The amount was recorded as Prepaid Insurance on September 1.

AJE 4: On March 1, Florida Flippers borrowed $300,000 at 12 percent. Interest is payable each March 1 for three years.

Required:
Answer (1), (2), and (3) using the following chart headings and record the adjusting journal entry.

	(1) Title of revenue earned or expense incurred	(2) Title of asset or liability account to offset cash received/paid in the past or cash to be received/paid in the future	(3) Amount	Adjusting Journal Entry		
				Accounts	Debit	Credit
AJE 1						

After you have completed your answers, check them at the bottom of page below.

GUIDED HELP 4-1

For additional step-by-step video instruction on recording adjusting entries, go to mhhe.com/libby_gh4-1.

Related Homework: M4-4, M4-6, E4-2, E4-3, E4-4, E4-5, E4-6, E4-8, E4-9, E4-12, E4-14, E4-16, E4-18, E4-19, E4-20, P4-2, P4-3, P4-6, P4-7, CON4-1, COMP4-1, COMP4-2, CP4-9

A QUESTION OF ETHICS

Adjustments and Incentives

Owners and managers of companies are most directly affected by the information presented in financial statements. If the financial performance and condition of the company appear strong, the company's stock price rises. Shareholders usually receive dividends and increase their investment value. Managers often receive bonuses based on the strength of a company's financial performance, and many in top management are compensated with options to buy their company's stock at prices below market value. The higher the market value, the more compensation they earn.

Solutions to SELF-STUDY QUIZ

	(1)	(2)	(3) Amount	Adjusting Journal Entry		
				Accounts	Debit	Credit
AJE 1	Diving Trip Revenue	Unearned Revenue	$\$6,000 \times \frac{1}{3} =$ $2,000 earned	Unearned revenue (−L) Diving trip revenue (+R, +SE)	2,000	 2,000
AJE 2	Instruction Revenue	Accounts Receivable	$800 earned (given)	Accounts receivable (+A) Instruction revenue (+R, +SE)	800	 800
AJE 3	Insurance Expense	Prepaid Expense	$24,000 × 4 months/ 12 months = $8,000 used	Insurance expense (+E, −SE) Prepaid expense (−A)	8,000	 8,000
AJE 4	Interest Expense	Interest Payable	$\$300,000 \times 0.12 \times \frac{10}{12} = \$30,000$ incurred and owed	Interest expense (+E, −SE) Interest payable (+L)	30,000	 30,000

When actual performance lags behind expectations, managers and owners may be tempted to manipulate accruals and deferrals to make up part of the difference. For example, managers may record cash received in advance of being earned as revenue in the current period or may fail to accrue certain expenses at year-end. Evidence from studies of large samples of companies indicates that some managers do engage in such fraudulent behavior. This research is borne out by enforcement actions, against companies and sometimes against their auditors, by the U.S. Securities and Exchange Commission (SEC), the independent, federal agency responsible for overseeing the fair functioning of the securities markets and for protecting investors. From 2015 through 2020, the SEC brought an annual average of over 800 enforcement actions against corporations and executives for reasons including financial reporting and disclosure issues. In 2020 alone, the SEC obtained over $4.5 billion in monetary remedies for ill-gotten gains and penalties.*

In many of these cases, the firms involved, their managers, and their auditors are penalized for such actions. Furthermore, owners suffer because news of an SEC investigation negatively affects the company's stock price.

**U.S. Securities and Exchange Commission Division of Enforcement 2020 Annual Report* (November 2, 2020). Available at sec.gov/reports.

PREPARING FINANCIAL STATEMENTS

LEARNING OBJECTIVE 4-2

Present an income statement with earnings per share, a statement of stockholders' equity, and a balance sheet.

As you learned in Chapter 1, the financial statements are interrelated—that is, the numbers from one statement flow into the next statement. Exhibit 4.4 highlights the interconnections among the statements using the fundamental accounting equation, followed by a summary structure of each statement demonstrating relationships.

EXHIBIT 4.4 Interrelationships of Financial Statements

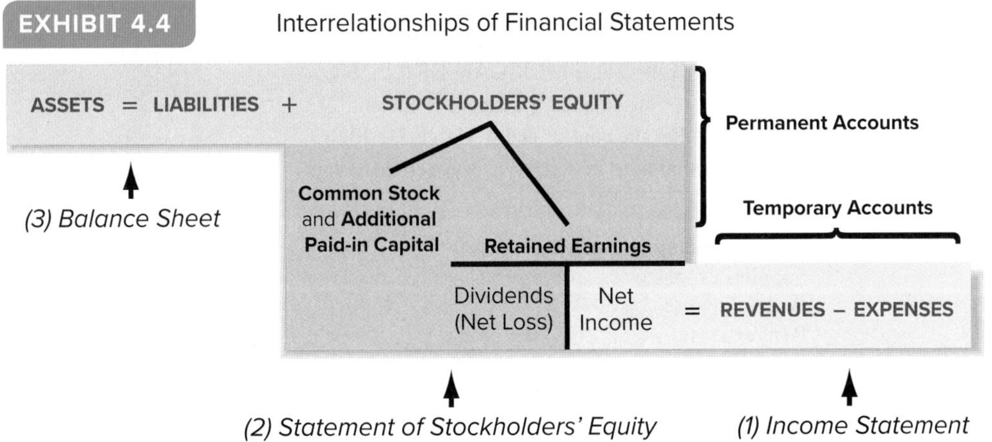

Another way of presenting the relationships among the statements follows.

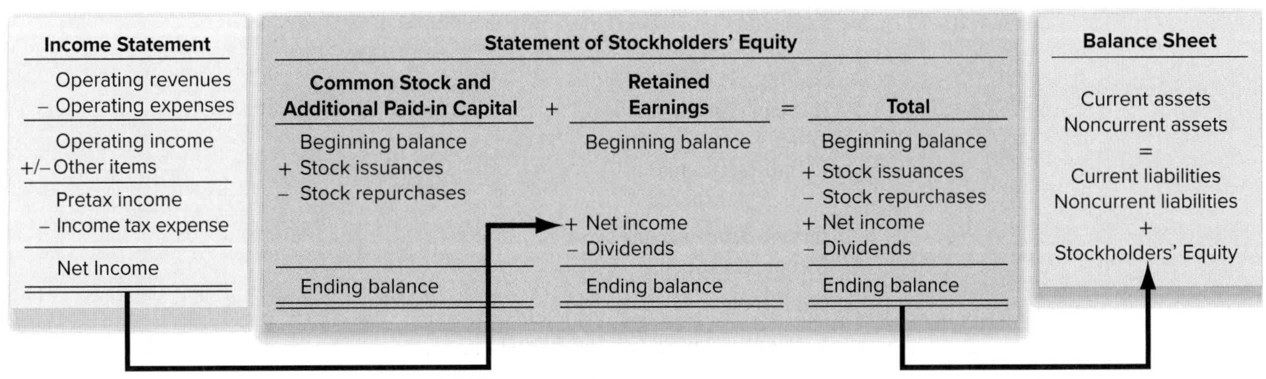

Notice that:

(1) The first statement to prepare is the **Income Statement** which reports that revenues minus expenses yields net income.

(2) Net income is a component in determining total stockholders' equity. Net income (or net loss) and dividends declared to stockholders affect Retained Earnings and any additional issuances or repurchases of stock during the period affect the balances in Common Stock and Additional Paid-in Capital, all of which appear on the **Statement of Stockholders' Equity.**

(3) Stockholders' Equity is a component of the **Balance Sheet.**

Thus, if a number on the income statement changes or is in error, it will impact the other statements.

Before we prepare a complete set of financial statements, let's update Chipotle's trial balance to reflect the adjustments assumed in this chapter, providing us with the adjusted balances needed for the statements. The spreadsheet in Exhibit 4.5 has three sets of debit-credit columns: one for the unadjusted balances from the T-accounts in Exhibit 3.6, then the effects of the adjustments AJE 1 through AJE 9, and finally, the adjusted balances that are determined by adding or subtracting the adjustment across each row. Again, we note that the total debits equal the total credits in each of the sets. Also notice that nearly every revenue and expense account was adjusted and several new accounts were created during the adjustment process at the end of the period (e.g., Interest Receivable and Depreciation Expense). It is from these adjusted balances that we will prepare an income statement, a statement of stockholders' equity (which includes a column for Retained Earnings), and a balance sheet. Only Retained Earnings is yet to be updated with the effects of the adjustments on net income. It will be updated during the closing process discussed after financial statements are prepared and disseminated.

Income Statement

The income statement is prepared first because net income is a component of Retained Earnings. The first quarter 2020 income statement for **Chipotle** based on the adjusted trial balance follows.

CHIPOTLE MEXICAN GRILL, INC.
Consolidated Statement of Income*
For the quarter ended March 31, 2020
(in millions of dollars, except per share data)

Restaurant sales revenue	$1,411
Restaurant operating expenses:	
Supplies expense	462
Wages expense	394
Rent expense	96
Insurance expense	48
Utilities expense	132
Repairs expense	35
General and administrative expenses:	
Training expense	65
Advertising expense	41
Depreciation expense	58
Loss on disposal of assets	9
Total operating expenses	1,340
Income from operations	71
Other items:	
Interest revenue	4
Interest expense	(1)
Income before income taxes	74
Income tax expense	15
Net income	$ 59
Earnings per share (for the quarter)	$ 0.39

*Based on hypothetical transactions in Chapters 2, 3, and 4.

Chipotle Mexican Grill's Trial Balance Spreadsheet

EXHIBIT 4.5

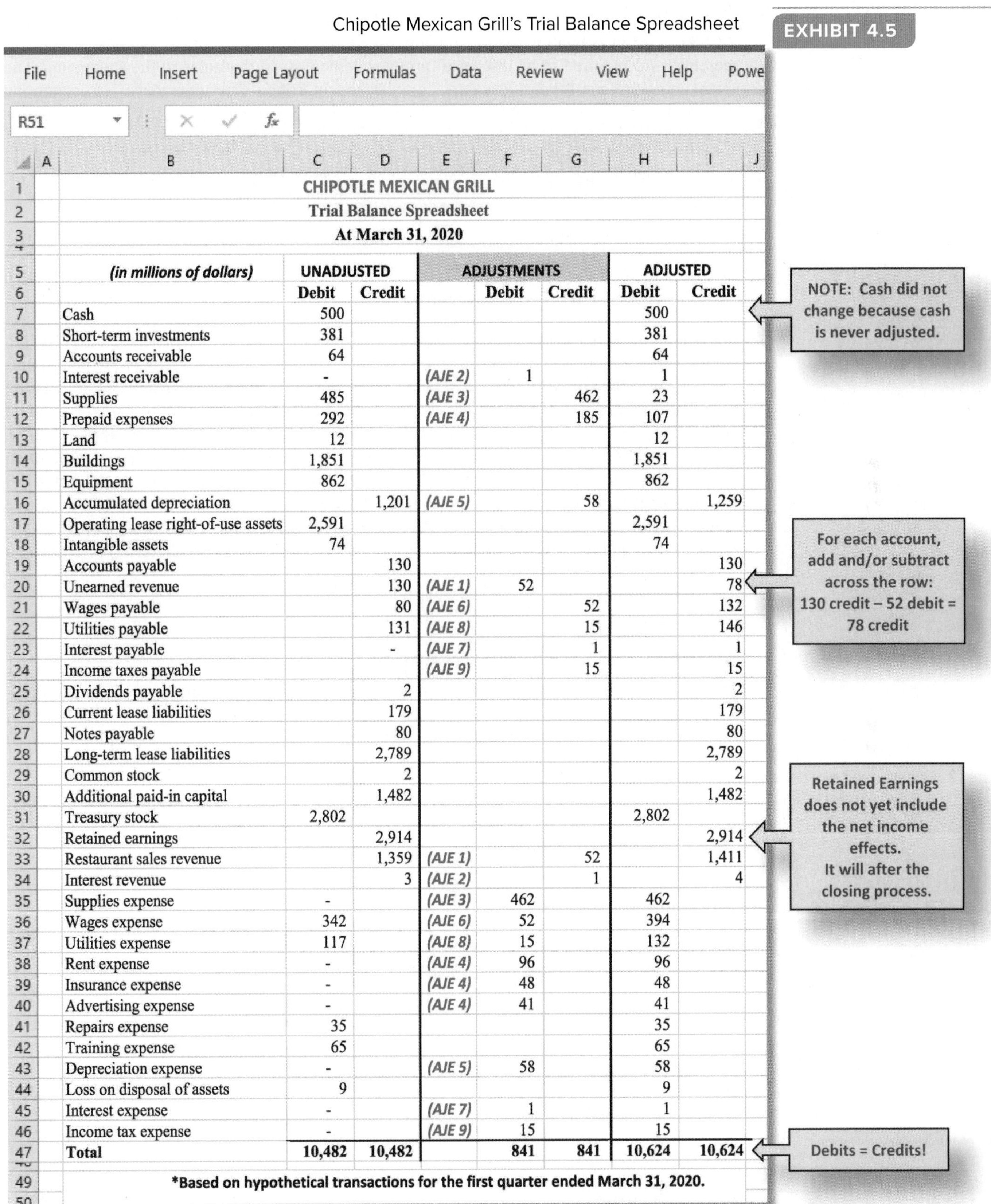

CHIPOTLE MEXICAN GRILL
Trial Balance Spreadsheet
At March 31, 2020

(in millions of dollars)	UNADJUSTED		ADJUSTMENTS			ADJUSTED	
	Debit	**Credit**		**Debit**	**Credit**	**Debit**	**Credit**
Cash	500					500	
Short-term investments	381					381	
Accounts receivable	64					64	
Interest receivable	-		*(AJE 2)*	1		1	
Supplies	485		*(AJE 3)*		462	23	
Prepaid expenses	292		*(AJE 4)*		185	107	
Land	12					12	
Buildings	1,851					1,851	
Equipment	862					862	
Accumulated depreciation		1,201	*(AJE 5)*		58		1,259
Operating lease right-of-use assets	2,591					2,591	
Intangible assets	74					74	
Accounts payable		130					130
Unearned revenue		130	*(AJE 1)*	52			78
Wages payable		80	*(AJE 6)*		52		132
Utilities payable		131	*(AJE 8)*		15		146
Interest payable		-	*(AJE 7)*		1		1
Income taxes payable			*(AJE 9)*		15		15
Dividends payable		2					2
Current lease liabilities		179					179
Notes payable		80					80
Long-term lease liabilities		2,789					2,789
Common stock		2					2
Additional paid-in capital		1,482					1,482
Treasury stock	2,802					2,802	
Retained earnings		2,914					2,914
Restaurant sales revenue		1,359	*(AJE 1)*		52		1,411
Interest revenue		3	*(AJE 2)*		1		4
Supplies expense	-		*(AJE 3)*	462		462	
Wages expense	342		*(AJE 6)*	52		394	
Utilities expense	117		*(AJE 8)*	15		132	
Rent expense	-		*(AJE 4)*	96		96	
Insurance expense	-		*(AJE 4)*	48		48	
Advertising expense	-		*(AJE 4)*	41		41	
Repairs expense	35					35	
Training expense	65					65	
Depreciation expense	-		*(AJE 5)*	58		58	
Loss on disposal of assets	9					9	
Interest expense	-		*(AJE 7)*	1		1	
Income tax expense	-		*(AJE 9)*	15		15	
Total	**10,482**	**10,482**		**841**	**841**	**10,624**	**10,624**

***Based on hypothetical transactions for the first quarter ended March 31, 2020.**

Microsoft Excel

You will note that the earnings per share (EPS) ratio is reported on the income statement. It is widely used in evaluating the operating performance and profitability of a company, and it is the only ratio required to be disclosed on the statement or in the notes to the statements. The actual computation of the ratio is quite complex and appropriate for more advanced accounting courses. In this text, we simplify the earnings per share computation as:

$$\textbf{Earnings per Share*} = \frac{\textbf{Net Income}}{\textbf{Weighted average number of shares of common stock outstanding}}$$

*As you will learn in Chapter 11: (1) If there are preferred stock dividends, the amount is subtracted from net income in the numerator, (2) the denominator for weighted average shares is a complex computation, and (3) outstanding shares are those that are currently held by the shareholders.

The denominator in the EPS ratio is the weighted average number of shares outstanding (NOTE: Until Chapter 11, we compute a simple average–the number at the beginning of the period plus the number at the end of the period, divided by 2). For our Chipotle Mexican Grill illustration, the number of shares at the beginning of 2020 (end of 2019) was 100 million shares [computed by dividing the $1 (in millions) Common Stock amount reported on the December 31, 2019, balance sheet in Exhibit 2.1 by the $0.01 par value per share (listed next to Common Stock in Exhibit 2.1)]. During the first quarter of 2020, we illustrated an issuance of an additional 100 million shares for a total of 200 million shares at the end of the quarter. Therefore, the average number of shares outstanding was 150 million for the quarter [(Beg. 100 + End. 200)/2 = 150 average]. The quarterly EPS for Chipotle in our illustration is $0.39 per share:

$$\text{EPS} = \frac{\$59 \text{ net income for the quarter}}{150 \text{ average number of shares outstanding}} = \$0.39 \text{ for the quarter}$$

Statement of Stockholders' Equity

The final total from the income statement, net income, is carried forward to the Retained Earnings column of the statement of stockholders' equity. To this, the additional elements of the statement are added. Dividends declared and an additional stock issuance (from Chapter 2) also are included in the statement:

CHIPOTLE MEXICAN GRILL, INC.
Consolidated Statement of Stockholders' Equity*
For the quarter ended March 31, 2020
(in millions of dollars)

	Common Stock	Additional Paid-in Capital	Treasury Stock	Retained Earnings	Total Stockholders' Equity	
Balance on December 31, 2019	$ 1	$1,466	$(2,699)	$2,916	$1,684	
Additional stock issuance	1	16			17	← From transaction (*a*) in Ch. 2
Stock repurchase			(103)		(103)	← From transaction (*g*) in Ch. 2
Net income				59	59	← From the income statement
Dividends declared				(2)	(2)	← From transaction (*h*) in Ch. 2
Balance on March 31, 2020	$ 2	$1,482	$(2,802)	$2,973	$1,655	← On the balance sheet

*Based on hypothetical transactions in Chapter 2, 3, and 4.

Balance Sheet

The ending balances for Common Stock, Additional Paid-in Capital, Treasury Stock, and Retained Earnings from the statement of stockholders' equity are included on the balance sheet that follows. You will notice that the contra-asset account Accumulated Depreciation (used cost) has been subtracted from the total of the land, buildings, and equipment accounts (at cost) to reflect **net book value** (or carrying value) at period-end for balance sheet purposes. Also recall that assets are listed in order of liquidity and liabilities are listed in order of due dates. Current assets are those used or turned into cash within one year (as well as inventory). Current liabilities are obligations to be paid with current assets within one year. We present a comparative balance sheet that shows the amounts at two points in time: December 31, 2019 and March 31, 2020.

CHIPOTLE MEXICAN GRILL, INC.
Consolidated Balance Sheets*
(in millions of dollars, except per share data)

	March 31, 2020	December 31, 2019
ASSETS		
Current Assets:		
Cash	$ 500	$ 481
Short-term investments	381	400
Accounts receivable	64	81
Interest receivable	1	–
Supplies	23	26
Prepaid expenses	107	85
Total current assets	1,076	1,073
Property and Equipment:		
Land	12	13
Buildings	1,851	1,811
Equipment	862	836
Total cost	2,725	2,660
Accumulated depreciation	(1,259)	(1,201)
Net property and equipment	1,466	1,459
Operating least right-of-use assets	2,591	2,505
Intangible assets	74	69
Total assets	$ 5,207	$ 5,106
LIABILITIES AND STOCKHOLDERS' EQUITY		
Current Liabilities:		
Accounts payable	$ 130	$ 116
Unearned revenue	78	95
Accrued expenses payable:		
Wages payable	132	127
Utilities payable	146	156
Interest payable	1	-
Income taxes payable	15	-
Dividends payable	2	-
Current lease liabilities	179	173
Total current liabilities	683	667
Notes payable	80	77
Long-term lease liabilities	2,789	2,678
Total liabilities	3,552	3,422
Stockholders' Equity:		
Common stock ($0.01 par value per share)	2	1
Additional paid-in capital	1,482	1,466
Treasury stock	(2,802)	(2,699)
Retained earnings	2,973	2,916
Total stockholders' equity	1,655	1,684
Total liabilities and stockholders' equity	$ 5,207	$ 5,106

* Reflects simplified December 31, 2019, figures and hypothetical March 31, 2020, information

FOCUS ON CASH FLOWS

Cash Flows from Operations, Net Income, and the Quality of Earnings

As presented in the previous chapters, the statement of cash flows explains the difference between the ending and beginning balances in the Cash account on the balance sheet during the accounting period. Put simply, the cash flow statement is a categorized list of all transactions of the period that affected the Cash account. The three categories are operating, investing, and financing activities. **Because no adjustments made in this chapter affected cash, the cash flow categories identified on the Cash T-account at the end of Chapter 3 remain the same.**

Many standard financial analysis texts warn analysts to look for unusual deferrals and accruals when they attempt to predict future periods' earnings. They often suggest that wide disparities between net income and cash flow from operations are a useful warning sign. For example, Subramanyan suggests the following:

> Accounting accruals determining net income rely on estimates, deferrals, allocations, and valuations. These considerations sometimes allow more subjectivity than do the factors determining cash flows. For this reason we often relate cash flows from operations to net income in assessing its quality. **Some users consider earnings of higher quality when the ratio of cash flows from operations divided by net income is greater.** This derives from a concern with revenue recognition or expense accrual criteria yielding high net income but low cash flows (emphasis added).*

The cash flows from operations to net income ratio is illustrated and discussed in more depth in Chapter 12.

*Source: K. Subramanyan, *Financial Statement Analysis,* New York: McGraw-Hill Education, 2014, 428.

KEY RATIO ANALYSIS

LEARNING OBJECTIVE 4-3

Compute and interpret the total asset turnover ratio.

Total Asset Turnover Ratio

ANALYTICAL QUESTION

How efficient is management in using assets (its resources) to generate sales?

RATIO AND COMPARISONS

$$\text{Total Asset Turnover Ratio} = \frac{\text{Net Sales (or Operating Revenues)}}{\text{Average Total Assets*}}$$

*To compute "average": (Beginning balance + Ending balance) ÷ 2

The 2019 ratio for **Chipotle** is (dollars in millions):

$$\frac{\$5{,}586}{\$3{,}686^*} = 1.516$$

*($2,266 + $5,106) ÷ 2 (from 2019 10-K)

Comparisons Over Time		
Chipotle Mexican Grill, Inc.		
2017	2018	2019
2.198	2.257	1.516

Comparisons With Competitors	
El Pollo Loco Holdings, Inc.	Shake Shack Inc.
2019	2019
0.823	0.753

Selected Focus Companies' Total Asset Turnover Ratios

FedEx	1.082
Harley-Davidson	0.506
Starbucks	0.968

INTERPRETATIONS

In General The total asset turnover ratio measures how efficient management is at using assets to generate sales. Over time or compared to competitors, the higher the asset turnover is, the more efficient assets are being utilized to generate revenues. A company's products or services and business strategy contribute significantly to its asset turnover ratio. However, when competitors are similar, management's ability to control the firm's assets is vital in determining its success. Stronger financial performance improves the asset turnover ratio.

Creditors and security analysts use this ratio to assess a company's effectiveness at controlling both current and noncurrent assets. In a well-run business, creditors expect the ratio on a quarterly basis to fluctuate due to seasonal upswings and downturns. For example, as inventory is built up prior to a heavy sales season, companies need to borrow funds. The asset turnover ratio declines with this increase in assets. Eventually, the season's high sales provide the cash needed to repay the loans. The asset turnover ratio then rises with the increased sales.

Focus Company Analysis Chipotle's total asset turnover ratio decreased from 2018 to 2019, primarily due to a reporting requirement change in 2019. The total assets in 2019 more than doubled because operating lease right-of-use assets (the majority of the Chipotle's facilities) are now required to be included on the balance sheet in assets along with the lease liabilities. Previously, these were reported in the notes to the financial statements. If we exclude the leased assets from the 2019 total assets amount, then the ratio becomes 2.296. Using this revised ratio, asset turnover increased over time. This suggests that **Chipotle's management used assets more efficiently over time to generate operating revenues.**

Chipotle's total asset turnover ratio is higher than that for both **El Pollo Loco** and **Shake Shack** in 2019. This is due in part to differences in business strategies. Chipotle has been one of the largest fast-casual and fastest-growing restaurant chains, and it is significantly larger (with over $5 billion in total assets at the end of 2019) than its two competitors (each with under $1 billion in total assets at the end of 2019). In addition, approximately 60 of El Pollo Loco restaurants are franchised and 12 percent of Shake Shack's are licensed, whereas Chipotle's restaurants are all company-owned. Also, Chipotle's much larger size enhances its efficiency.

A Few Cautions While the total asset turnover ratio may decrease due to seasonal fluctuations, a declining ratio also may be caused by changes in corporate policies leading to a rising level of assets. Examples include relaxing credit policies for new customers or reducing collection efforts in accounts receivable. And, as we noted above, a change in accounting and reporting requirements can also have an impact. A detailed analysis of the changes in the key components of assets and a review of the notes to the financial statements to identify accounting and reporting changes are needed to determine the causes of a change in the asset turnover ratio and thus management's decisions.

DATA ANALYTICS

The SEC Uses Data Analytics

The U.S. Securities and Exchange Commission formed the Financial Reporting and Audit (FRAud) Group under the Division of Enforcement, which concentrates on detecting fraud and prosecuting corporations and individuals for violations involving false or misleading financial statements and disclosures. The SEC uses data analytics to build a more proactive enforcement program. The FRAud Group relies on statistical modeling and other data tools, for example, to analyze narratives in financial statements submitted to the SEC by public corporations to identify subtle differences in the tone and language that provide quantifiable measures of risk (and potential fraud). Also, the Division's Earnings Per Share Initiative uses risk-based data analytics to uncover potential accounting and disclosure violations often caused by earnings management practices to hide weak performances that were not expected.

LEARNING OBJECTIVE 4-4

Explain the closing process.

CLOSING THE BOOKS

End of the Accounting Cycle

As shown in the steps of the accounting cycle in Exhibit 4.1, all adjusting entries are recorded and posted to update the accounts and then the financial statements are prepared and disseminated to users. A **closing process** is needed as the last step in the accounting cycle to mark the end of the current period and the beginning of the next.

First, before illustrating the process, notice special labels for the accounts in Exhibit 4.4:

- Balance sheet accounts (assets, liabilities, and stockholders' equity) are considered permanent accounts, indicating that they **retain their balances** from the end of one period to the beginning of the next. For example, Chipotle's December 31, 2019 Cash balance of $481 million is the beginning Cash balance of the first quarter of 2020. The only time a permanent account has a zero balance is when the item it represents is no longer owned or owed.
- Income statement accounts (revenues, expenses, gains, and losses accounts) are temporary accounts because **their balances accumulate** during a period to determine financial performance for the period. However, the accounts must start with a zero balance at the beginning of the next period to determine next period's financial performance. For example, notice in the T-accounts for *AJE 4* that the three expense accounts begin with $0 balances and accumulate amounts through the transaction. A process is needed to return these income statement accounts to a $0 balance for the beginning of the next quarter.

Another issue is that the Retained Earnings account balance is not correct until the closing process is complete. Retained Earnings increases with the period's net income and decreases with dividends declared (and net losses) for the period. You can see in Chipotle's Statement of Stockholders' Equity on page 186 that Retained Earnings should have an ending balance of $2,973 million. However, the trial balance spreadsheet in Exhibit 4.5 shows a balance for Retained Earnings of $2,914. The Retained Earnings T-account does not yet include the effects of net income. The closing process is needed to move net income (a subtotal) to Retained Earnings.

The final step in the accounting cycle, **closing the books**, is done by recording a closing journal entry and posting the effects to the appropriate accounts. A closing entry has two purposes:

1. To transfer the balances in the temporary accounts (income statement accounts) to Retained Earnings.[1]
2. To establish a zero balance in each of the temporary accounts to start the accumulation in the next accounting period.

The closing entry is dated the last day of the accounting period, entered in the usual debits-equal-credits format (in the journal), and immediately posted to the ledger (or T-accounts). **The income statement (temporary) accounts with debit balances are credited and the income statement (temporary) accounts with credit balances are debited.** The net amount, equal to net income, affects Retained Earnings.

To illustrate the process, we create an example using just a few accounts. Assume Ashley Company had the following partial adjusted trial balance and related T-accounts:

Tip **Quick Closing Entry Tip:**

- Revenue and gain accounts **(R)** are debited.
- Expense and loss accounts **(E)** are credited.
- **Retained Earnings** is credited if there is net income (R > E) **or** debited if there is net loss (R < E) for the difference: R – E = net income or net loss.

[1] Companies may close income statement accounts to a special temporary summary account, called **Income Summary**, which is then closed to Retained Earnings.

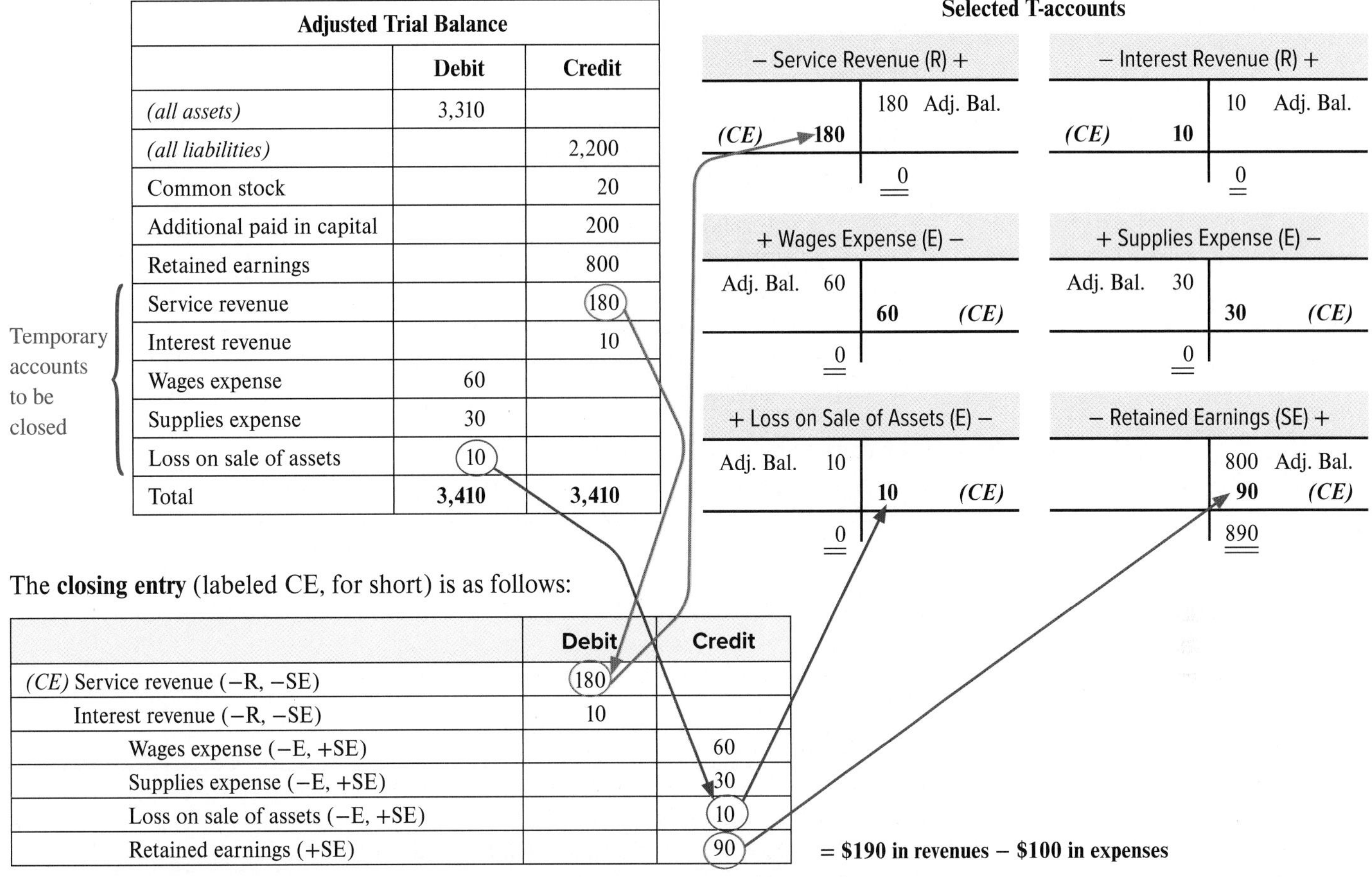

Adjusted Trial Balance		
	Debit	Credit
(all assets)	3,310	
(all liabilities)		2,200
Common stock		20
Additional paid in capital		200
Retained earnings		800
Service revenue		180
Interest revenue		10
Wages expense	60	
Supplies expense	30	
Loss on sale of assets	10	
Total	**3,410**	**3,410**

The **closing entry** (labeled CE, for short) is as follows:

	Debit	Credit
(CE) Service revenue (−R, −SE)	180	
Interest revenue (−R, −SE)	10	
Wages expense (−E, +SE)		60
Supplies expense (−E, +SE)		30
Loss on sale of assets (−E, +SE)		10
Retained earnings (+SE)		90

= $190 in revenues − $100 in expenses

Follow the examples from (1) the trial balance to (2) the closing entry to (3) the postings to the T-accounts:

- Every revenue account (with a credit balance) was debited to make the ending balances $0 (e.g., see the **green** arrow example) .
- Every expense and loss account (with a debit balance) was credited to make the ending balances $0 (e.g., see the **red** arrow example).
- The revenues and expenses were "closed" (zeroed out by moving the balances) to Retained Earnings - equal to net income of $90. This is also the number that makes the debits equal to the credits (see the **blue** arrow).

We will now prepare the closing entry (CE) for **Chipotle** at March 31, 2020, although companies close their records usually only at the end of the fiscal year. These amounts are taken from the adjusted trial balance spreadsheet in Exhibit 4.5. The effects on the accounting equation and the posting of the effects to the income statement and Retained Earnings T-accounts follow the closing entry. Notice that the $59 increase in Retained Earnings equals net income and all income statement accounts have $0 balances.

Tip Most companies use computerized accounting applications (from desktop to cloud-based packages) to record journal entries, produce trial balances and financial statements, and close the books. As an example, for small- to medium-sized businesses, QuickBooks® is a popular accounting software package that offers advanced and cloud capabilities.

	Debit	Credit
(CE) Restaurant sales revenue (−R, −SE)	1,411	
Interest revenue (−R, −SE)	4	
Supplies expense (−E, +SE)		462
Wages expense (−E, +SE)		394

(Continued)

	Debit	Credit
Utilities expense (−E, +SE)		132
Rent expense (−E, +SE)		96
Insurance expense (−E, +SE)		48
Advertising expense (−E, +SE)		41
Repairs expense (−E, +SE)		35
Training expense (−E, +SE)		65
Depreciation expense (−E, +SE)		58
Loss on disposal of assets (−E, +SE)		9
Interest expense (−E, +SE)		1
Income tax expense (−E, +SE)		15
Retained earnings (+SE)		59

Beginning balances are from the adjusted trial balance in Exhibit 4.5:

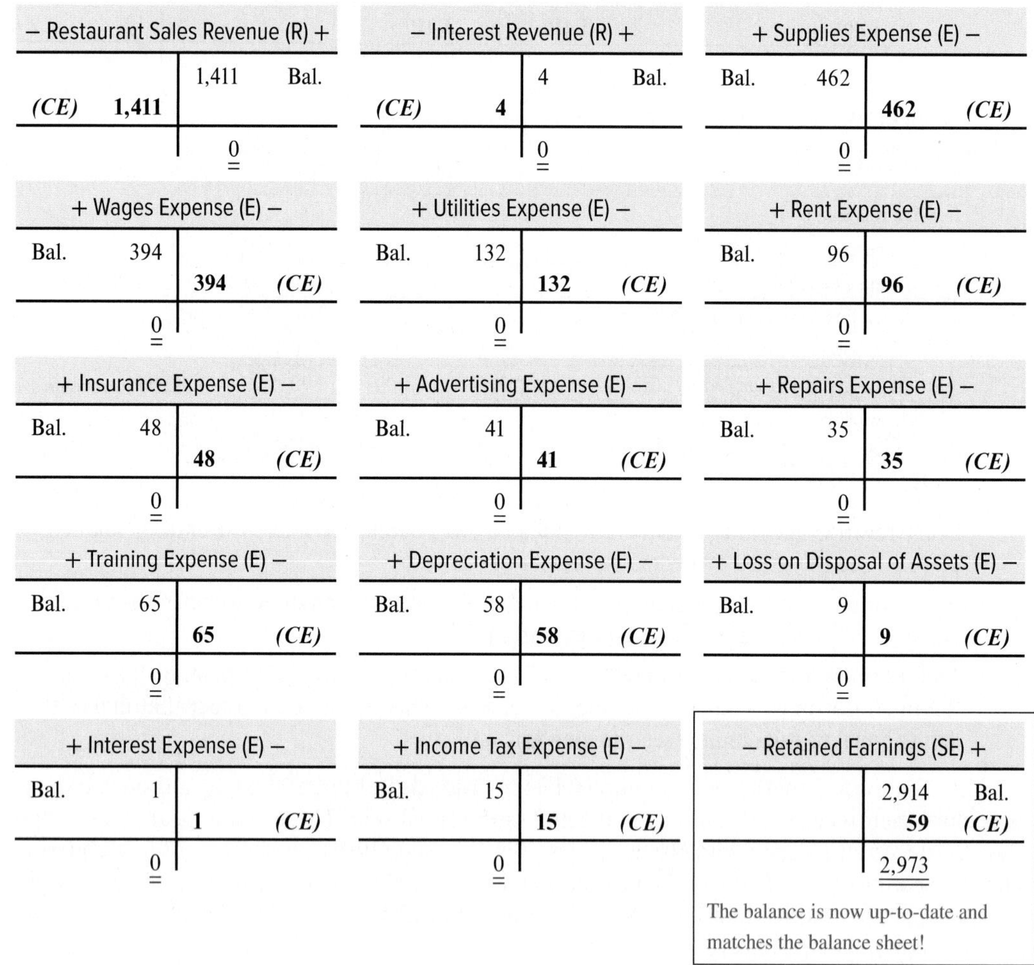

PAUSE FOR FEEDBACK

The process of closing the books (after adjustments) includes making all temporary account balances (from the income statement) zero and transferring the difference (net income) to Retained Earnings.

SELF-STUDY QUIZ

The following is an adjusted trial balance from a recent year for **Mattel, Inc.** (designer, manufacturer, and marketer of popular toys including American Girl and Barbie dolls, Fisher-Price toys, and Hot Wheels). Record the closing journal entry at the end of the accounting cycle to close the books for Mattel.

	A	B	C	D
1		MATTEL, INC. -- **ADJUSTED TRIAL BALANCE**		
2		**At a recent year-end**		
3		***(in millions)***	**Debit**	**Credit**
4		Cash and cash equivalents	1,079	
5		Accounts receivable	1,129	
6		Inventories	601	
7		Prepaid expenses	303	
8		Land	49	
9		Buildings	517	
10		Machinery and equipment	1,790	
11		Software	385	
12		Accumulated depreciation		1,956
13		Other assets	2,342	
14		Accounts payable		572
15		Accrued expenses payable		802
16		Long-term debt		3,123
17		Other liabilities		484
18		Common stock		441
19		Additional paid-in capital		1,809
20		Treasury stock	2,390	
21		Retained earnings		2,452
22		Sales revenue		4,882
23		Interest revenue		7
24		Cost of sales	3,061	
25		Advertising expenses	642	
26		Other selling and administrative expenses	1,521	
27		Interest expense	105	
28		Loss on disposal of assets	65	
29		Income tax expense	549	
30		**Total**	**16,528**	**16,528**

Source: Mattel, Inc.

After you have completed your answers, check them with the solutions at the bottom of the next page.

GUIDED HELP 4-2

For additional step-by-step video instruction on recording a closing entry at the end of a given period, go to mhhe.com/libby_gh4-2.

Related Homework: M4-13, E4-12, E4-22, P4-6, P4-7, CON4-1, COMP 4-1, COMP4-2, CP4-5

Post-Closing Trial Balance

As an additional step of the accounting information processing cycle, a **post-closing trial balance** should be prepared as a check that debits still equal credits and that all temporary accounts have been closed. It would have the structure of the trial balance shown in Exhibit 4.5 with only balance sheet accounts having balances. The income statement accounts should be $0. The accounting cycle for the period is now complete.

DEMONSTRATION CASE

We take our final look at the accounting activities of Terrific Lawn Maintenance Corporation by illustrating the activities at the end of the accounting cycle: the adjustment process, financial statement preparation, and the closing process. No adjustments had been made to the accounts to reflect all revenues earned and expenses incurred in April. The trial balance for Terrific Lawn on April 30, 2023, based on the unadjusted balances in Chapter 3, is as follows:

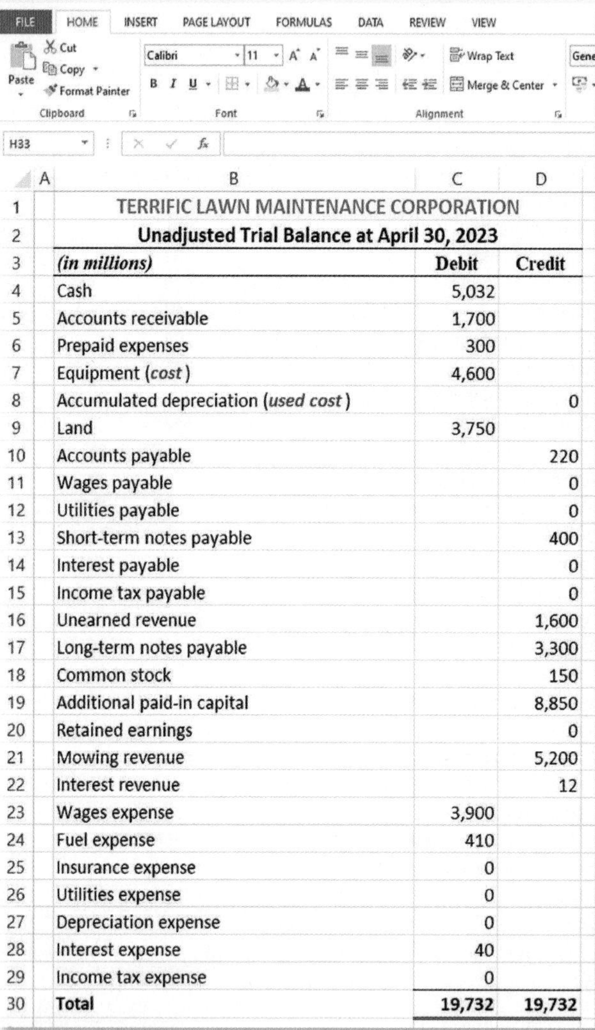

	B	C	D
1	TERRIFIC LAWN MAINTENANCE CORPORATION		
2	**Unadjusted Trial Balance at April 30, 2023**		
3	***(in millions)***	**Debit**	**Credit**
4	Cash	5,032	
5	Accounts receivable	1,700	
6	Prepaid expenses	300	
7	Equipment (*cost*)	4,600	
8	Accumulated depreciation (*used cost*)		0
9	Land	3,750	
10	Accounts payable		220
11	Wages payable		0
12	Utilities payable		0
13	Short-term notes payable		400
14	Interest payable		0
15	Income tax payable		0
16	Unearned revenue		1,600
17	Long-term notes payable		3,300
18	Common stock		150
19	Additional paid-in capital		8,850
20	Retained earnings		0
21	Mowing revenue		5,200
22	Interest revenue		12
23	Wages expense	3,900	
24	Fuel expense	410	
25	Insurance expense	0	
26	Utilities expense	0	
27	Depreciation expense	0	
28	Interest expense	40	
29	Income tax expense	0	
30	**Total**	**19,732**	**19,732**

Solutions to SELF-STUDY QUIZ

Closing Entry	Debit	Credit
Sales revenue (−R, −SE)	4,882	
Interest revenue (−R, −SE)	7	
Retained earnings (−SE)	1,054	
Cost of sales (−E, +SE)		3,061
Advertising expenses (−E, +SE)		642
Other selling and administrative expenses (−E, +SE)		1,521
Interest expense (−E, +SE)		105
Loss on disposal of assets (−E, +SE)		65
Income tax expense (−E, +SE)		549

NOTE: Since expenses exceed revenues, Mattel had a net loss which reduced stockholders' equity.

Additional information follows:

a. The $1,600 in Unearned Revenue represents four months of service from April through July.

b. Prepaid Expenses includes insurance costing $300 for coverage for six months (April through September).

c. Mowers, edgers, rakes, and hand tools (equipment) have been used in April to generate revenues. The company estimates $300 in depreciation each year.

d. Wages have been paid through April 28. Employees worked the last two days of April and will be paid in May. Wages accrue at $200 per day.

e. An extra telephone line was installed in April at an estimated cost of $50, including hookup and usage charges. No entry has yet been recorded. The utility bill will be received and paid in May.

f. Interest accrues on the outstanding short-term and long-term notes payable at an annual rate of 12 percent. The $3,700 total in principal has been outstanding all month.

g. The estimated income tax rate for Terrific Lawn is 25 percent. Round to the nearest dollar.

Adjusting Entry Analysis

Answer and then prepare the appropriate entry for one of the following:

(1) Was revenue earned and cash received in the past?
(increase revenue; decrease liability)—*deferral*

(2) Was revenue earned and will cash be received in the future?
(increase revenue; increase asset)—*accrual*

(3) Was an expense incurred and cash paid in the past?
(increase expense; decrease asset)—*deferral*

(4) Was an expense incurred and will cash be paid in the future?
(increase expense; increase liability)—*accrual*

Required:

1. Prepare the adjusting journal entries for April, using the account titles shown in the trial balance. In your analysis, be sure to use the process outlined in Exhibit 4.3.

2. Prepare an adjusted trial balance.

3. Prepare an income statement, statement of stockholders' equity, and balance sheet from the amounts in the adjusted trial balance. Include earnings per share on the income statement. The company issued 1,500 shares.

4. Prepare the closing entry for the month ended April 30, 2023.

5. Compute the following ratios for the month (round to three decimal places):
   a. Current ratio
   b. Net profit margin
   c. Total asset turnover

Now you can check your answers with the following solutions.

SUGGESTED SOLUTION

1. Adjusting entries

AJE	Debit	Credit
a. Unearned revenue (−L)	400	
Mowing revenue (+R, +SE)		400
$1,600 × 1/4 = $400 earned in April		
b. Insurance expense (+E, −SE)	50	
Prepaid expenses (−A)		50
$300 × 1/6 = $50 insurance used in April		
c. Depreciation expense (+E, −SE)	25	
Accumulated depreciation (+XA, −A)		25
$300 × 1/12 = $25 depreciation in April		

(Continued)

	Revenues	–	Expenses	
Unadjusted balances	$ 5,212		$4,350	← From trial balance
AJE (a)	400			
AJE (b)			50	
AJE (c)			25	
AJE (d)			400	
AJE (e)			50	
AJE (f)			37	
Adjusted balances	$ 5,612	–	$4,912	= $700 Pretax income
				× 0.25 Tax rate
	Income tax expense			**$175** → g.

AJE	Debit	Credit
d. Wages expense (+E, −SE)	400	
Wages payable (+L)		400
$200 per day × 2 days = $400 incurred in April		
e. Utilities expense (+E, −SE)	50	
Utilities payable (+L)		50
$50 is estimated as incurred in April		
f. Interest expense (+E, −SE)	37	
Interest payable (+L)		37
$3,700 principal × 0.12 annual rate × 1/12 = $37 interest incurred in April		
g. Income tax expense (+E, −SE)	175	
Income tax payable (+L)		175

2. Adjusted trial balance

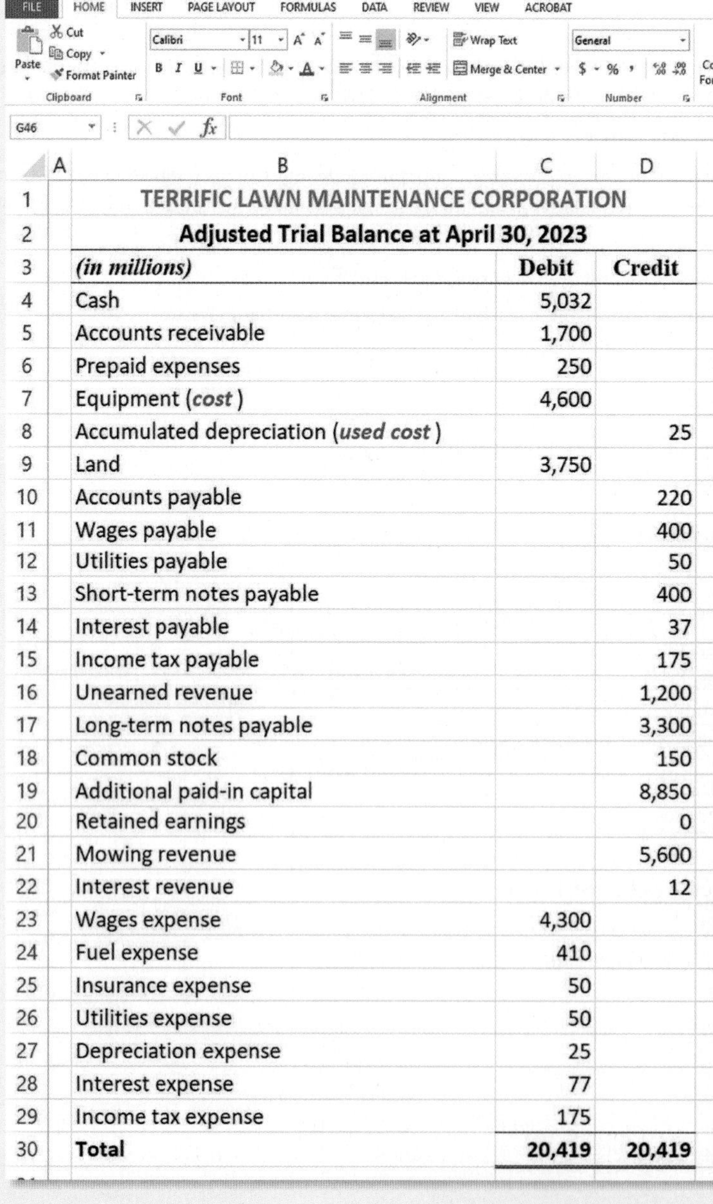

	A	B	C	D
1		TERRIFIC LAWN MAINTENANCE CORPORATION		
2		**Adjusted Trial Balance at April 30, 2023**		
3		***(in millions)***	**Debit**	**Credit**
4		Cash	5,032	
5		Accounts receivable	1,700	
6		Prepaid expenses	250	
7		Equipment (***cost***)	4,600	
8		Accumulated depreciation (***used cost***)		25
9		Land	3,750	
10		Accounts payable		220
11		Wages payable		400
12		Utilities payable		50
13		Short-term notes payable		400
14		Interest payable		37
15		Income tax payable		175
16		Unearned revenue		1,200
17		Long-term notes payable		3,300
18		Common stock		150
19		Additional paid-in capital		8,850
20		Retained earnings		0
21		Mowing revenue		5,600
22		Interest revenue		12
23		Wages expense	4,300	
24		Fuel expense	410	
25		Insurance expense	50	
26		Utilities expense	50	
27		Depreciation expense	25	
28		Interest expense	77	
29		Income tax expense	175	
30		**Total**	**20,419**	**20,419**

3. Financial statements:

TERRIFIC LAWN MAINTENANCE CORPORATION
Income Statement
For the Month Ended April 30, 2023

Operating revenues:	
Mowing revenue	$5,600
Operating expenses:	
Wages expense	4,300
Fuel expense	410
Insurance expense	50
Utilities expense	50
Depreciation expense	25
Total operating expenses	4,835
Operating income	765
Other items:	
Interest revenue	12
Interest expense	(77)
Pretax income	700
Income tax expense	175
Net Income	$ 525
Earnings per share (for the month) ($525 ÷ 1,500 shares)	$ 0.35

TERRIFIC LAWN MAINTENANCE CORPORATION
Statement of Stockholders' Equity
For the Month Ended April 30, 2023

	Common Stock	Additional Paid-in Capital	Retained Earnings	Total
Balance, April 1, 2023	$ 0	$ 0	$ 0	$ 0
Stock issuance	150	8,850		9,000
Net income			525	525
Dividends declared			0	0
Balance, April 30, 2023	$150	$8,850	$525	$9,525

TERRIFIC LAWN MAINTENANCE CORPORATION
Balance Sheet
April 30, 2023

Assets		**Liabilities and Stockholders' Equity**	
Current Assets:		Current Liabilities:	
Cash	$ 5,032	Accounts payable	$ 220
Accounts receivable	1,700	Wages payable	400
Prepaid expenses	250	Utilities payable	50
Total current assets	6,982	Short-term notes payable	400
		Interest payable	37
		Income taxes payable	175
		Unearned revenue	1,200
Equipment (net of $25 accumulated depreciation)	4,575	Total current liabilities	2,482
		Long-term notes payable	3,300
Land	3,750	Total liabilities	5,782
		Stockholders' Equity:	
		Common stock	150
		Additional paid-in capital	8,850
		Retained earnings	525
		Total stockholders' equity	9,525
Total assets	**$15,307**	**Total liabilities and stockholders' equity**	**$15,307**

4. Closing entry:

CE	Debit	Credit
Mowing revenue (−R, −SE)	5,600	
Interest revenue (−R, −SE)	12	
Wages expense (−E, +SE)		4,300
Fuel expense (−E, +SE)		410
Insurance expense (−E, +SE)		50
Utilities expense (−E, +SE)		50
Depreciation expense (−E, +SE)		25
Interest expense (−E, +SE)		77
Income tax expense (−E, +SE)		175
Retained earnings (+SE)		525

5. Ratios:

a. $\text{Current Ratio} = \dfrac{\text{Current Assets}}{\text{Current Liabilities}} = \dfrac{\$6{,}982}{\$2{,}482} = 2.813$

b. $\text{Net Profit Margin for April} = \dfrac{\text{Net Income}}{\text{Net Sales (or Operating Revenues)}} = \dfrac{\$525}{\$5{,}600} = 0.094 \text{ or } 9.4\%$

c. $\text{Total Asset Turnover for April} = \dfrac{\text{Net Sales (or Operating Revenues)}}{\text{Average Total Assets}} = \dfrac{\$5{,}600}{\$7{,}653.50^*} = 0.732$

*(Beginning $0 + Ending $15,307) ÷ 2 = $7,653.50

CHAPTER TAKE-AWAYS

4-1. Explain the purpose of adjustments and analyze the adjustments necessary at the end of the period to update revenues and expenses and related balance sheet accounts. **p. 172**

- Adjusting entries are necessary at the end of the accounting period to measure income properly, correct errors, and provide for adequate valuation of balance sheet accounts. These are the types:
  - Deferrals:
    - Revenue earned and cash received in the past (recorded as a liability)—Increase revenue, decrease liability
    - Expense incurred and cash paid in the past (recorded as an asset)—Increase expense, decrease asset
  - Accruals:
    - Revenue earned and cash to be received in the future (not yet recorded)—Increase revenue, increase asset (receivable)
    - Expense incurred and cash to be paid in the future (not yet recorded)—Increase expense, increase liability (payable)
  - Recording adjusting entries has no effect on the Cash account.

4-2. Present an income statement with earnings per share, a statement of stockholders' equity, and a balance sheet. **p. 183**

Adjusted account balances are used in preparing the following financial statements:

- **Income Statement:**
  - Operating revenues
  - − Operating expenses
  - Operating income (or loss)
  - +/− Other items
  - Pretax income
  - − Income tax expense
  - Net income
  - Earnings per share
- **Statement of Stockholders' Equity:**
  - Beg. Common stock + New issuances
  - Beg. Additional paid-in capital + New issuances
  - −Beg. Treasury stock + New stock repurchases
  - Beg. Retained Earnings + Net income − Dividends declared
  - Ending stockholders' equity
- **Balance Sheet**
  - Current assets
  - Noncurrent assets
  - Total assets
  - Current liabilities
  - Noncurrent liabilities
  - Stockholders' equity
  - Total liabilities and stockholders' equity

4-3. Compute and interpret the total asset turnover ratio. **p. 188**

The total asset turnover ratio (Net Sales (or Operating Revenues) ÷ Average Total Assets) measures sales generated per dollar of assets. A rising total asset turnover signals more efficient management of assets.

4-4. Explain the closing process. **p. 190**

Temporary accounts (revenues, expenses, gains, and losses) are closed to a zero balance at the end of the accounting period to allow for the accumulation of income statement items in the following period and to update Retained Earnings for the period's net income. To close these accounts, debit each revenue and gain account, credit each expense and loss account, and record the difference (equal to net income) to Retained Earnings.

		Debit	Credit
(CE)	Each revenue (−R, −SE)	xx	
	Each gain (−R, −SE)	xx	
	Each expense (−E, +SE)		xx
	Each loss (−E, +SE)		xx
	Retained earnings (+SE)*		xx

Tip * The credit to Retained Earnings assumes net income is positive. If the total of expenses/losses exceeds the total of revenues/gains, Retained Earnings would be debited (reduced) for the amount of the net loss.

This chapter discussed the important steps in the accounting cycle that take place at year-end. These include the adjustment process, the preparation of the basic financial statements, and the closing process that prepares the records for the next accounting period. This end to the internal portions of the accounting cycle, however, is just the beginning of the process of communicating accounting information to external users.

In the next chapter, we take a closer look at more sophisticated financial statements and related disclosures. We also examine the process by which financial information is disseminated to professional analysts, investors, the Securities and Exchange Commission, and the public, and the role each plays in analyzing and interpreting the information. These discussions will help you consolidate much of what you have learned about the financial reporting process from previous chapters. It also will preview many of the important issues we address in later chapters. These later chapters include many other adjustments that involve difficult and complex estimates about the future, such as estimates of customers' ability to make payments to the company for purchases on account, the useful lives of new machines, and future amounts that a company may owe on warranties of products sold in the past. Each of these estimates and many others can have significant effects on the stream of net earnings that companies report over time.

KEY RATIO

Total asset turnover measures the sales generated per dollar of assets. A high or rising ratio suggests that the company is managing its assets more efficiently. It is computed as follows (see the "Key Ratio Analysis" box in the Preparing Financial Statements section) (p. 188):

$$\text{Total Asset Turnover} = \frac{\text{Net Sales (or Operating Revenues)}}{\text{Average Total Assets}}$$

FINDING FINANCIAL INFORMATION

Balance Sheet

Current Assets
Accrued revenues include:
- Accounts receivable
- Interest receivable
- Rent receivable

Deferred expenses include:
- Supplies
- Prepaid expenses (insurance, rent, and advertising)

Noncurrent Assets
Deferred expenses include:
- Buildings
- Equipment
- Operating lease right-of-use assets
- Intangible assets

Current Liabilities
Accrued expenses include:
- Interest payable
- Wages payable
- Utilities payable
- Income tax payable

Deferred revenues include:
- Unearned revenue

Income Statement

Revenues
Increased by adjusting entries

Expenses
Increased by adjusting entries

Pretax Income
Income tax expense

Net Income

Statement of Cash Flows

Adjusting Entries Do Not Affect Cash

Notes

In Various Notes (if not on the balance sheet)
Details of accrued expenses payable
Interest paid and income taxes paid

KEY TERMS

Accrued Expenses Liabilities (payables) created when expenses are incurred, but cash will be paid in the future; created at end of period during the adjustment process to reflect the amount of expense incurred that the company will pay in the future **p. 178**

Accrued Revenues Assets (receivables) created when revenues are earned, but cash will be collected from customers in the future; created at end of period during the adjustment process to reflect the amount of revenue earned by providing goods or services over time to customers who will pay in the future **p. 175**

Adjusting Entries Entries necessary at the end of the accounting period to measure all revenues and expenses of that period and update assets and liabilities **p. 173**

Closing Entries Made at the end of the accounting period to transfer balances in temporary (income statement) accounts to Retained Earnings and to establish a zero balance in each of the temporary accounts for beginning the next accounting period **p. 190**

Contra-Account An account that is an offset to, or reduction of, the primary account or financial statement section **p. 177**

Deferred Expenses Assets created when purchased in the past before being used to generate revenues; need to be adjusted at the end of the period to reflect the amount of expense incurred by using the assets over time **p. 175**

Deferred (Unearned) Revenues Liabilities created from collecting cash from customers before providing goods or services to customers; need to be adjusted at the end of the period to reflect the amount of revenue earned by providing goods or services over time to customers **p. 174**

Net Book Value (Carrying Value or Book Value) The acquisition cost of an asset less its accumulated depreciation, depletion (of natural resources), or amortization (of intangible assets) **p. 177**

Permanent Accounts The balance sheet accounts that carry their ending balances into the next accounting period **p. 190**

Post-Closing Trial Balance Prepared as an additional step in the accounting cycle to check that debits equal credits and all temporary accounts have been closed (have zero balances) **p. 193**

Temporary Accounts Income statement (and sometimes Dividends Declared) accounts that are closed to Retained Earnings at the end of the accounting period **p. 190**

QUESTIONS

1. What is the purpose of recording adjusting entries?
2. List the four types of adjusting entries and give an example of each type.
3. What is a contra-asset? Give an example of one.
4. Explain how the financial statements relate to each other.

5. What is the equation for each of the following statements: (*a*) income statement, (*b*) balance sheet, and (*c*) statement of stockholders' equity?
6. Explain the effect of adjusting entries on cash.
7. How is earnings per share computed and interpreted?
8. How is the total asset turnover ratio computed and interpreted?
9. What are the purposes for closing the books?
10. Differentiate between permanent and temporary accounts.
11. Explain why the income statement accounts are closed but the balance sheet accounts are not.
12. What is a post-closing trial balance? Is it a useful part of the accounting information processing cycle? Explain.

MULTIPLE-CHOICE QUESTIONS

1. Which of the following accounts would **not** appear in a closing entry?
   a. Salary Expense
   b. Interest Income
   c. Accumulated Depreciation
   d. Retained Earnings
2. Which account is least likely to appear in an adjusting journal entry?
   a. Cash
   b. Interest Receivable
   c. Property Tax Expense
   d. Salaries Payable
3. On October 1, 2023, the $12,000 premium on a one-year insurance policy for the building was paid and recorded as Prepaid Insurance Expense. On December 31, 2023 (end of the accounting period), what adjusting entry is needed?

a. Insurance expense (+E)	2,000	
Prepaid insurance expense (−A)		2,000
b. Insurance expense (+E)	3,000	
Prepaid insurance expense (−A)		3,000
c. Prepaid insurance expense (+A)	3,000	
Insurance expense (−E)		3,000
d. Prepaid insurance expense (+A)	9,000	
Insurance expense (−E)		9,000

4. On June 1, 2022, Oakcrest Company signed a three-year $110,000 note payable with 9 percent interest. Interest is due on June 1 of each year beginning in 2023. What amount of interest expense should be reported on the income statement for the year ended December 31, 2022?
   a. $5,250
   b. $9,900
   c. $4,950
   d. $5,775
5. Failure to make an adjusting entry to recognize accrued salaries payable would cause which of the following? (***Hint:*** See Tip for how to analyze the effects.)
   a. An understatement of expenses, liabilities, and stockholders' equity.
   b. An understatement of expenses and liabilities and an overstatement of stockholders' equity.
   c. An overstatement of assets and stockholders' equity.
   d. An overstatement of assets and liabilities.
6. An adjusted trial balance
   a. Shows the ending account balances in a "debit" and "credit" format before posting the adjusting journal entries.
   b. Is prepared after closing entries have been posted.
   c. Shows the ending account balances resulting from the adjusting journal entries in a "debit" and "credit" format.
   d. Is a tool used by financial analysts to review the performance of publicly traded companies.

For "effects" questions such as this, do the following:

1. Write out what **the entry should have been**, then
2. Put the **effects of NOT doing the entry** (O—overstated, U—understated) in the equations (see table below) [or the effects of doing the entry (+ for increase, – for decrease)], and
3. Determine the **rest of the equation effects** starting with the income statement (and remember—whatever the effect is on net income, it is also the effect on stockholders' equity).

Example:

Failed to record $5 of supplies used:

1. **Supplies expense (+E, −SE) 5**
   Supplies (− A) 5

2. and 3.

A	L	SE	R	E	NI
O5	NE	O5	NE	U5	O5

The answer is:

Assets, stockholders' equity, and net income are overstated by $5, and expenses are understated by $5.

7. JJ Company owns a building. Which of the following statements regarding depreciation as used by accountants is **false?**
   a. As depreciation is recorded, stockholders' equity is reduced.
   b. Depreciation is an estimated expense to be recorded over the building's estimated useful life.
   c. As depreciation is recorded, the net book value of the asset is reduced.
   d. As the value of the building decreases over time, it "depreciates."
8. At the beginning of the current year, Donna Company had $1,000 of supplies on hand. During the current year, the company purchased supplies amounting to $6,400 (paid for in cash and debited to Supplies). At the end of the current year, a count of supplies reflected $2,000. The adjusting entry Donna Company would record at the end of the current year to adjust the Supplies account would include a
   a. Debit to Supplies for $2,000.
   b. Credit to Supplies Expense for $5,400.
   c. Credit to Supplies for $5,400.
   d. Debit to Supplies Expense for $4,400.
9. According to GAAP, what ratio must be reported on the financial statements or in the notes to the statements?
   a. Earnings per share ratio.
   b. Return on equity ratio.
   c. Net profit margin ratio.
   d. Current ratio.
10. If a company is successful in acquiring several large buildings at the end of the year, what is the effect on the total asset turnover ratio?
    a. The ratio will increase.
    b. The ratio will not change.
    c. The ratio will decrease.
    d. Either (a) or (c).

MINI-EXERCISES

M4-1 Preparing a Trial Balance
LO4-1

Nash Company has the following adjusted accounts and balances at year-end (June 30):

Accounts payable	$ 250	Interest expense	$ 70
Accounts receivable	420	Interest income	60
Accrued expenses payable	160	Inventories	710
Accumulated depreciation	250	Land	300
Additional paid-in capital	300	Long-term debt	1,360
Buildings and equipment	1,300	Prepaid expenses	30
Cash	175	Rent expense	460
Common stock	100	Retained earnings	150
Cost of sales	780	Salaries expense	640
Depreciation expense	150	Sales revenue	2,400
Income taxes expense	135	Unearned fees	90
Income taxes payable	50		

Prepare an adjusted trial balance in good form for the Nash Company at June 30.

M4-2 Matching Definitions with Terms
LO4-1

Match each definition with its related term by entering the appropriate letter in the space provided.

Definition	Term
____ (1) A revenue not yet earned; collected in advance.	A. Accrued expense
____ (2) Rent not yet collected; already earned.	B. Deferred expense
____ (3) Property taxes incurred; not yet paid.	C. Accrued revenue
____ (4) Rent revenue collected; not yet earned.	D. Deferred revenue
____ (5) An expense incurred; not yet paid or recorded.	
____ (6) Office supplies on hand to be used next accounting period.	
____ (7) An expense not yet incurred; paid in advance.	
____ (8) A revenue earned; not yet collected.	

Matching Definitions with Terms

M4-3
LO4-1

Match each item with its related term by entering the appropriate letter in the space provided.

Item	Term
___ (1) At year-end, service revenue of $1,000 was collected in cash but was not yet earned.	A. Accrued expense
___ (2) Interest of $550 on a note receivable was earned at year-end, although collection of the interest is not due until the following year.	B. Deferred expense
___ (3) At year-end, wages payable of $5,600 had not been recorded or paid.	C. Accrued revenue
___ (4) Office supplies were purchased during the year for $700, and $100 of them remained on hand (unused) at year-end.	D. Deferred revenue
___ (5) $8,000 of the equipment's cost was used during the year, but not yet recorded.	
___ (6) A $720 bill for utility usage for the last month of the year was received, but not yet paid or recorded.	

Recording Adjusting Entries (Deferred Accounts)

M4-4
LO4-1

In each of the following transactions (*a*) through (*c*) for Catena's Marketing Company, use the process illustrated in the chapter to record the adjusting entry at the end of the current year, December 31. The process includes (1) determining if revenue was earned or an expense was incurred and (2) determining whether cash was received or paid in the past or will be received or paid in the future.

a. Collected $1,200 rent for the period December 1 of the current year to April 1 of next year, which was credited to Unearned Rent Revenue on December 1.
b. Purchased a machine for $32,000 cash on January 1. The company estimates annual depreciation at $3,200.
c. Paid $5,000 for a two-year insurance premium on July 1 of the current year; debited Prepaid Insurance for that amount.

Determining Financial Statement Effects of Adjusting Entries (Deferred Accounts)

M4-5
LO4-1

For each of the transactions in M4-4, indicate the amounts and the direction of effects of the adjusting entry on the elements of the balance sheet and income statement. Using the following format, indicate + for increase, – for decrease, and NE for no effect.

Tip When asked to determine effects, see the tip next to Multiple Choice Question 5.

	BALANCE SHEET			INCOME STATEMENT		
Transaction	Assets	Liabilities	Stockholders' Equity	Revenues	Expenses	Net Income
a.						

Recording Adjusting Entries (Accrued Accounts)

M4-6
LO4-1

In each of the following transactions (*a*) through (*c*) for Catena's Marketing Company, use the process illustrated in the chapter to record the adjusting entry at the end of the current year, December 31. The process includes (1) determining if revenue was earned or an expense was incurred and (2) determining whether cash was received or paid in the past or will be received or paid in the future.

a. Estimated electricity usage at $450 for December; to be paid in January of next year.
b. On September 1 of the current year, loaned $6,000 to an officer who will repay the loan principal and interest in one year at an annual interest rate of 14 percent.
c. Owed wages to 10 employees who worked four days at $200 each per day at the end of the current year. The company will pay employees at the end of the first week of next year.

M4-7 Determining Financial Statement Effects of Adjusting Entries (Accrued Accounts)

LO4-1

For each of the transactions in M4-6, indicate the amounts and the direction of effects of the adjusting entry on the elements of the balance sheet and income statement. Using the following format, indicate + for increase, – for decrease, and NE for no effect.

	BALANCE SHEET			INCOME STATEMENT		
Transaction	**Assets**	**Liabilities**	**Stockholders' Equity**	**Revenues**	**Expenses**	**Net Income**
a.						

M4-8 Reporting an Income Statement with Earnings per Share

LO4-2

Catena's Marketing Company has the following adjusted trial balance at the end of the current year. Cash dividends of $600 were declared at the end of the year, and 500 additional shares of common stock ($0.10 par value per share) were issued at the end of the year for $3,000 in cash (for a total at the end of the year of 800 shares). These effects are included below:

CATENA'S MARKETING COMPANY		
Adjusted Trial Balance at the End of the Current Year		
(in millions)	**Debit**	**Credit**
Cash	1,500	
Accounts receivable	2,200	
Interest receivable	100	
Prepaid insurance	1,600	
Long-term notes receivable	2,800	
Equipment	15,290	
Accumulated depreciation		3,000
Accounts payable		2,400
Dividends payable		600
Accrued expenses payable		3,920
Income taxes payable		1,680
Unearned rent revenue		500
Common stock (800 shares)		80
Additional paid-in capital		3,620
Retained earnings		1,400
Sales revenue		38,500
Rent revenue		800
Interest revenue		100
Wages expense	19,500	
Depreciation expense	1,800	
Utilities expense	380	
Insurance expense	750	
Rent expense	9,000	
Income tax expense	1,680	
Total	**56,600**	**56,600**

Prepare a multistep income statement in good form for the current year. Include the operating income subtotal and earnings per share (rounded to two decimal places).

Reporting a Statement of Stockholders' Equity

M4-9
LO4-2

Refer to M4-8. Prepare a statement of stockholders' equity in good form for the current year. Beginning balances for stockholders' equity accounts are: Common stock, $30; Additional paid-in capital, $670; and Retained earnings, $2,000.

Reporting a Balance Sheet

M4-10
LO4-2

Refer to M4-8. Prepare a classified balance sheet in good form for the end of the current year.

Effects of Adjustments on the Statement of Cash Flows

M4-11
LO4-2

Refer to M4-4 and M4-6. Explain how the year-end **adjustments** affect the operating, investing, and financing activities on the statement of cash flows for Catena's Marketing Company.

Analyzing Total Asset Turnover

M4-12
LO4-3

Compute total assets for Catena's Marketing Company based on the adjusted trial balance in M4-8. Then compute the company's total asset turnover (rounded to two decimal places) for the current year, assuming total assets at the end of the prior year were $16,050.

Recording a Closing Entry

M4-13
LO4-4

Refer to the adjusted trial balance for Catena's Marketing Company in M4-8. Prepare the closing entry at the end of the current year.

EXERCISES

Preparing a Trial Balance

E4-1
LO4-1

Jameson Consultants, Inc., provides marketing research for clients in the retail industry. At the end of the current year, the company had the following unadjusted accounts with normal debit and credit balances:

Depreciation expense	$ 8,000	Travel expense	$ 23,990
Cash	153,000	Gain on sale of land	6,000
Salaries expense	1,610,000	Accounts payable	96,830
Accounts receivable	225,400	Additional paid-in capital	220,000
Income taxes payable	3,030	Rent expense (on leased computers)	152,080
Utilities expense	25,230	Salaries payable	25,650
Investment income	10,800	Supplies	12,200
Common stock	3,370	Interest expense	17,200
Notes payable	160,000	Retained earnings	?
Accumulated depreciation	18,100	Buildings and equipment	623,040
Supplies expense	21,050	Unearned consulting fees	32,500
Prepaid expenses	10,200	Land	60,000
Consulting fees revenue	2,564,200	Professional development expense	18,600
		Investments	325,000

Required:
Prepare in good form an unadjusted trial balance for Jameson Consultants, Inc., at the end of the current year.

E4-2
LO4-1, 4-4
Facebook, Inc.

Identifying Adjusting Entries from Unadjusted Trial Balance

Facebook, Inc., which also owns Instagram, Messenger, WhatsApp, and Oculus (virtual reality products), generates substantially all of its revenue from selling advertising placements to marketers. Following is a trial balance listing accounts that Facebook uses. Assume that the balances are unadjusted at the end of a recent fiscal year ended December 31.

File Home Insert Page Layout Formulas Data Review View

G9

	A	B	C	D
1		**FACEBOOK, INC.**		
2		**Unadjusted Trial Balance (in millions of dollars)**		
3		**At December 31**		
4			Debit	Credit
5		Cash	17,576	
6		Marketable securities *(short-term investments)*	44,378	
7		Accounts receivable	11,335	
8		Prepaid expenses and other current assets	2,381	
9		Land	1,326	
10		Buildings	35,264	
11		Network, computer, and office equipment	24,461	
12		Accumulated depreciation		15,418
13		Operating lease right-of-use assets	9,348	
14		Intangible assets	19,673	
15		Other assets	2,758	
16		Accounts payable		1,331
17		Operating lease liabilities, current		1,023
18		Accrued expenses and other current liabilities		11,152
19		Deferred revenue and deposits		382
20		Other current liabilities		1,093
21		Operating lease liabilities, noncurrent		9,631
22		Other liabilities		6,414
23		Common stock		1
24		Additional paid-in capital		50,017
25		Retained earnings		42,892
26		Revenue		85,965
27		Interest and other income		509
28		Cost of revenue	16,692	
29		Research and development expense	18,447	
30		Marketing and sales	11,591	
31		General and administrative	6,564	
32		Provision for income taxes *(income tax expense)*	4,034	
33		**Totals**	**225,828**	**225,828**
34				

Microsoft Excel

Required:

1. Based on the information in the unadjusted trial balance, list types of adjustments on the balance sheet that may need to be adjusted at December 31 and the related income statement account for each (no computations are necessary). You may need to make assumptions.
2. Which accounts should be closed at the end of the year? Why?

Recording Adjusting Entries

E4-3
LO4-1

Dodie Company completed its first year of operations on December 31. All of the year's entries have been recorded except for the following:

a. At year-end, employees earned wages of $4,000, which will be paid on the next payroll date in January of next year.
b. At year-end, the company had earned interest revenue of $1,500. The cash will be collected March 1 of the next year.

Required:

1. What is the annual reporting period for this company?
2. Identify whether each transaction results in adjusting a deferred or an accrued account. Using the process illustrated in the chapter, prepare the required adjusting entry for transactions (*a*) and (*b*). Include appropriate dates and write a brief explanation of each entry.
3. Why are these adjustments made?

Recording Adjusting Entries

E4-4
LO4-1

Elana's Traveling Veterinary Services, Inc., completed its first year of operations on December 31. All of the year's entries have been recorded except for the following:

a. On March 1 of the current year, the company borrowed $60,000 at a 10 percent interest rate to be repaid in five years.
b. On the last day of the current year, the company received a $360 utility bill for utilities used in December. The bill will be paid in January of next year.

Required:

1. What is the annual reporting period for this company?
2. Identify whether each transaction results in adjusting a deferred or an accrued account. Using the process illustrated in the chapter, prepare the required adjusting entry for transactions (*a*) and (*b*). Include appropriate dates and write a brief explanation of each entry.
3. Why are these adjustments made?

Recording Adjusting Entries and Reporting Balances in Financial Statements

E4-5
LO4-1, 4-2

A + T Williamson Company is making adjusting entries for the year ended December 31 of the current year. In developing information for the adjusting entries, the accountant learned the following:

a. A two-year insurance premium of $4,800 was paid on October 1 of the current year for coverage beginning on that date. The bookkeeper debited the full amount to Prepaid Insurance on October 1.
b. At December 31 of the current year, the following data relating to Shipping Supplies were obtained from the records and supporting documents.

Shipping supplies on hand, January 1 of the current year	$13,000
Purchases of shipping supplies during the current year	75,000
Shipping supplies on hand, counted on December 31 of the current year	20,000

Required:

1. Using the process illustrated in the chapter, record the adjusting entry for insurance at December 31 of the current year.
2. Using the process illustrated in the chapter, record the adjusting entry for supplies at December 31 of the current year, assuming that the shipping supplies purchased during the current year were debited in full to the account Shipping Supplies.

3. What amount should be reported on the current year's income statement for Insurance Expense? For Shipping Supplies Expense?
4. What amount should be reported on the current year's balance sheet for Prepaid Insurance? For Shipping Supplies?

E4-6 LO4-1, 4-2 Recording Adjusting Entries and Reporting Balances in Financial Statements

Gauge Construction Company is making adjusting entries for the year ended March 31 of the current year. In developing information for the adjusting entries, the accountant learned the following:

a. The company paid $1,800 on January 1 of the current year to have advertisements placed in the local monthly neighborhood paper. The ads were to be run from January through June. The bookkeeper debited the full amount to Prepaid Advertising on January 1.

b. At March 31 of the current year, the following data relating to Construction Equipment were obtained from the records and supporting documents.

Construction equipment (at cost)	$340,000
Accumulated depreciation (through March 31 of the prior year)	132,000
Estimated annual depreciation for using the equipment	34,000

Required:
1. Using the process illustrated in the chapter, record the adjusting entry for advertisements at March 31 of the current year.
2. Using the process illustrated in the chapter, record the adjusting entry for the use of construction equipment during the current year.
3. What amount should be reported on the current year's income statement for Advertising Expense? For Depreciation Expense?
4. What amount should be reported on the current year's balance sheet for Prepaid Advertising? For Construction Equipment (at net book value)?

E4-7 LO4-1 Determining Financial Statement Effects of Adjusting Entries

Refer to E4-3 and E4-5.

Required:
For each of the transactions in E4-3 and E4-5, indicate the amount and the direction of effects of the adjusting entry on the elements of the balance sheet and income statement. Using the following format, indicate + for increase, – for decrease, and NE for no effect.

Tip When asked to determine effects, see the tip next to Multiple Choice Question 5.

	BALANCE SHEET			INCOME STATEMENT		
Transaction	**Assets**	**Liabilities**	**Stockholders' Equity**	**Revenues**	**Expenses**	**Net Income**
E4-3 *a.*						
E4-3 *b.*						
E4-5 *a.*						
E4-5 *b.*						

E4-8 LO4-1 Recording Seven Typical Adjusting Entries

Trotman's Variety Store is completing the accounting process for the current year just ended, December 31. The transactions during the year have been journalized and posted. The following data with respect to adjusting entries are available:

a. Wages earned by employees during December, unpaid and unrecorded at December 31, amounted to $2,700. The last payroll was December 28; the next payroll will be January 6.

b. Office supplies on hand at January 1 of the current year totaled $450. Office supplies purchased and debited to Office Supplies during the year amounted to $500. The year-end count showed $275 of supplies on hand.

c. One-fourth of the basement space is rented to Kathy's Specialty Shop for $560 per month, payable monthly. At the end of the current year, the rent for November and December had not been collected or recorded. Collection is expected in January of the next year.

d. The store used delivery equipment all year that cost $60,500; $12,100 was the estimated annual depreciation.

e. On July 1 of the current year, a two-year insurance premium amounting to $2,400 was paid in cash and debited in full to Prepaid Insurance. Coverage began on July 1 of the current year.

f. The remaining basement of the store is rented for $1,600 per month to another merchant, M. Carlos, Inc. Carlos sells compatible, but not competitive, merchandise. On November 1 of the current year, the store collected six months' rent in the amount of $9,600 in advance from Carlos; it was credited in full to Unearned Rent Revenue when collected.

g. Trotman's Variety Store operates a repair shop to meet its own needs. The shop also does repairs for M. Carlos. At the end of the current year, Carlos had not paid $800 for completed repairs. This amount has not yet been recorded as Repair Shop Revenue. Collection is expected during January of next year.

Required:
Prepare the adjusting entries that should be recorded for Trotman's Variety Store at December 31 of the current year.

Recording Seven Typical Adjusting Entries

E4-9
LO4-1

Johnson's Boat Yard, Inc., repairs, stores, and cleans boats for customers. It is completing the accounting process for the year just ended on November 30. The transactions for the past year have been journalized and posted. The following data with respect to adjusting entries at year-end are available:

a. Johnson's winterized (cleaned and covered) three boats for customers at the end of November but did not record the service for $3,300.

b. On October 1, Johnson's paid $2,200 to the local newspaper for an advertisement to run every Thursday for 12 weeks. All ads have been run except for three Thursdays in December to complete the 12-week contract.

c. Johnson's borrowed $300,000 at an 11 percent annual interest rate on April 1 of the current year to expand its boat storage facility. The loan requires Johnson's to pay the interest quarterly until the note is repaid in three years. Johnson's paid quarterly interest on July 1 and October 1.

d. The Sanjeev family paid Johnson's $4,500 on November 1 to store its sailboat for the winter until May 1 of the next fiscal year. Johnson's credited the full amount to Unearned Storage Revenue on November 1.

e. Johnson's used boat-lifting equipment that cost $180,000; $18,000 was the estimated depreciation for the current year.

f. Boat repair supplies on hand at the beginning of the current year totaled $18,900. Repair supplies purchased and debited to Supplies during the year amounted to $45,200. The year-end count showed $15,600 of the supplies on hand.

g. Wages of $5,600 earned by employees during November were unpaid and unrecorded at November 30. The next payroll date will be December 5 of the next fiscal year.

Required:
Prepare the adjusting entries that should be recorded for Johnson's at November 30, end of the current year.

Determining Financial Statement Effects of Seven Typical Adjusting Entries

E4-10
LO4-1

Refer to E4-8.

Required:
For each of the transactions in E4-8, indicate the amount and the direction of effects of the adjusting entry on the elements of the balance sheet and income statement. Using the following format, indicate + for increase, – for decrease, and NE for no effect.

	BALANCE SHEET			INCOME STATEMENT		
Transaction	**Assets**	**Liabilities**	**Stockholders' Equity**	**Revenues**	**Expenses**	**Net Income**
a.						

E4-11 Determining Financial Statement Effects of Seven Typical Adjusting Entries
LO4-1

Refer to E4-9.

Required:
For each of the transactions in E4-9, indicate the amount and the direction of effects of the adjusting entry on the elements of the balance sheet and income statement. Using the following format, indicate + for increase, – for decrease, and NE for no effect.

	BALANCE SHEET			INCOME STATEMENT		
Transaction	Assets	Liabilities	Stockholders' Equity	Revenues	Expenses	Net Income
a.						

E4-12 Recording Transactions Including Adjusting and Closing Entries
LO4-1, 4-4

The following accounts are used by Emily Consultants Company, with a fiscal year ending December 31.

Codes	Accounts	Codes	Accounts
A	Cash	M	Common Stock and Additional Paid-in Capital
B	Short-term Investments	N	Retained Earnings
C	Office Supplies	O	Service Revenue
D	Accounts Receivable	P	Interest Revenue
E	Office Equipment	Q	Gain on Sale of Investments
F	Accumulated Depreciation	R	Wage Expense
G	Notes Payable	S	Depreciation Expense
H	Wages Payable	T	Interest Expense
I	Interest Payable	U	Supplies Expense
J	Unearned Service Revenue	V	Income tax expense
K	Dividends Payable	W	None of the above
L	Income Taxes Payable		

Required:
For each of the following independent situations, prepare the journal entry by entering the appropriate code(s) and amount(s). The first transaction is used as an example.

	DEBIT		CREDIT	
Independent Situations	Code	Amount	Code	Amount
a. Accrued wages, unrecorded and unpaid at year-end, $400 (example).	R	400	H	400
b. Service revenue earned but not yet collected at year-end, $600.				
c. Dividends declared during the year, $900, to be paid next year.				
d. Office supplies on hand during the year, $400; supplies on hand at year-end, $160.				
e. Service revenue collected from customers in advance during the year, $1,500.				
f. Depreciation expense for the year, $1,000.				
g. Earned all but $800 of (*e*) by the end of the year.				
h. Sold $2,000 in investments at a gain of $150.				
i. Interest on $5,000, 8 percent note payable (borrowed on October 1 of this year); not yet recorded or paid at year end.				

Independent Situations	DEBIT		CREDIT	
	Code	Amount	Code	Amount
j. Balance at year-end in the following accounts: • Service revenue, $186,000 • Interest revenue, $35 • Gain on sale of investments, $150 • Wage expense, $130,000 • Depreciation expense, $1,000 • Interest expense, $100 • Supplies expense, $240 • Dividends payable, $900 • Income tax expense, $1,100 Prepare the closing entry.				

Determining Financial Statement Effects of Three Adjusting Entries

E4-13
LO4-1, 4-2

Gordon Company started operations on January 1 of the current year. It is now December 31, the end of the current annual accounting period. The part-time bookkeeper needs your help to analyze the following three transactions:

a. During the year, the company purchased office supplies that cost $3,000. At the end of the year, office supplies of $800 remained on hand.
b. On January 1 of the current year, the company purchased a special machine for cash at a cost of $25,000. The machine's cost is estimated to depreciate at $2,500 per year.
c. On July 1, the company paid cash of $1,000 for a two-year premium on an insurance policy on the machine; coverage began on July 1 of the current year.

Required:
Complete the following schedule with the amounts that should be reported for the current year:

Selected Balance Sheet Accounts at December 31	Amount to Be Reported
Assets	
Equipment	$ ________
Accumulated depreciation	________
Net book value of equipment	________
Office supplies	________
Prepaid insurance	________
Selected Income Statement Accounts for the Year Ended December 31	
Expenses	
Depreciation expense	$ ________
Office supplies expense	________
Insurance expense	________

Recording Journal Entries for Two Notes (Challenging)

E4-14
LO4-1

Warren Corporation had the following transactions in Year 1:

1. On April 1, Warren received a $30,000, 10 percent note from a customer in settlement of a $30,000 account receivable. According to the terms, the principal and interest on the note are payable at the end of 12 months on March 31.
2. On August 1, to meet a cash shortage, Warren obtained a $20,000, 12 percent loan from a local bank. The principal and interest on the note are payable at the end of six months on January 31.

Required:

Warren Corporation's year-end is December 31. Record all the entries related to the notes in Years 1 and 2. The relevant dates are:

Year 1:	Year 2:
April 1	January 31
August 1	March 31
December 31	

E4-15 LO4-1 **Campbell Soup Company**

Inferring Transactions

Campbell Soup Company is a manufacturer and marketer of branded food and beverages including familiar products such as *Campbell's* soups, *Swanson* broths, *Prego* pasta sauce, *V8* juices, and *Pepperidge Farm* baked goods. The following information is from a recent annual report (in millions of dollars):

Accrued Income Taxes Payable

		15	Beg. bal.
(*a*)	?	174	(*b*)
		24	End. bal.

Accrued Compensation and Benefits Payable

		234	Beg. bal.
(*c*)	?	429	(*d*)
		252	End. bal.

Accrued Interest Payable

		97	Beg. bal.
(*e*)	363	?	(*f*)
		79	End. bal.

Source: Campbell Soup Company

Required:

1. Identify the nature of each of the transactions (*a*) through (*f*). Specifically, what activities cause the accounts to increase and decrease?
2. For transactions (*a*), (*c*), and (*f*), compute the amount.

E4-16 LO4-1

Analyzing the Effects of Errors on Financial Statement Items

Kinney-Harvey, Inc., publishers of movie and song trivia books, made the following errors in adjusting the accounts at year-end (December 31):

a. Did not accrue $1,400 owed to the company by another company renting part of the building as a storage facility.
b. Recorded $15,000 depreciation on the equipment costing $115,000; should have recorded $20,000.
c. Failed to adjust the Unearned Fee Revenue account to reflect that $1,500 was earned by the end of the year.
d. Recorded a full year of accrued interest expense on a $17,000, 9 percent note payable that has been outstanding only since November 1.
e. Failed to adjust Prepaid Insurance to reflect that $650 of insurance coverage had been used.

Required:

1. For each error, prepare (*a*) the adjusting journal entry that was made, if any, and (*b*) the adjusting journal entry that should have been made at year-end.
2. Using the following headings, indicate the effect of each error and the amount of the effect (that is, the difference between the entry that was or was not made and the entry that should have been made). Use O if the effect overstates the item, U if the effect understates the item, and NE if there is no effect. (**Reminder:** Assets = Liabilities + Stockholders' Equity; Revenues − Expenses = Net Income; and Net Income accounts are closed to Retained Earnings, a part of Stockholders' Equity.)

	BALANCE SHEET			INCOME STATEMENT		
Transaction	**Assets**	**Liabilities**	**Stockholders' Equity**	**Revenues**	**Expenses**	**Net Income**
a.						

Analyzing the Effects of Adjusting Entries on the Income Statement and Balance Sheet

E4-17
LO4-1, 4-2

On December 31, Fawzi Company prepared an income statement and balance sheet and failed to take into account four adjusting entries. The income statement, prepared on this incorrect basis, reflected pretax income of $65,000. The balance sheet (before the effect of income taxes) reflected total assets, $185,000; total liabilities, $90,000; and stockholders' equity, $95,000. The data for the four adjusting entries follow:

a. Wages amounting to $37,000 for the last three days of December were not paid and not recorded (the next payroll will be at the beginning of next year).
b. Depreciation of $19,000 for the year on equipment that cost $190,000 was not recorded.
c. Rent revenue of $10,500 was collected on December 1 of the current year for office space for the period December 1 to February 28 of the next year. The $10,500 was credited in full to Unearned Rent Revenue when collected.
d. Income taxes were not recorded. The income tax rate for the company is 21 percent.

Required:
Complete the following tabulation to correct the financial statements for the effects of the four errors (indicate deductions with parentheses):

Items	Net Income	Total Assets	Total Liabilities	Stockholders' Equity
Balances reported	$65,000	$185,000	$90,000	$95,000
Additional adjustments:				
a. Wages				
b. Depreciation				
c. Rent revenue				
Adjusted balances				
d. Income taxes				
Correct balances				

Recording the Effects of Adjusting Entries and Reporting a Corrected Income Statement and Balance Sheet

E4-18
LO4-1, 4-2

On December 31, the bookkeeper for Grillo Company prepared the following income statement and balance sheet summarized here but neglected to consider three adjusting entries.

	As Prepared	Effects of Adjusting Entries	Corrected Amounts
Income Statement			
Revenues	$ 97,000		
Expenses	(73,000)		
Income tax expense			
Net income	$ 24,000		
Balance Sheet			
Assets			
Cash	$ 20,000		
Accounts receivable	22,000		
Rent receivable			
Equipment	50,000		
Accumulated depreciation	(10,000)		
	$ 82,000		
Liabilities			
Accounts payable	$ 10,000		
Income taxes payable			
Stockholders' Equity			
Common stock	10,000		
Additional paid-in capital	30,000		
Retained earnings	32,000		
	$ 82,000		

Data on the three adjusting entries follow:

a. Rent revenue of $2,500 earned in December of the current year was neither collected nor recorded.
b. Depreciation of $4,500 on the equipment for the current year was not recorded.
c. Income tax expense of $5,100 for the current year was neither paid nor recorded.

Required:

1. Prepare the three adjusting entries that were omitted. Use the account titles shown in the income statement and balance sheet data.
2. Complete the two columns to the right in the preceding tabulation to show the effects of the adjusting entries and the corrected amounts on the income statement and balance sheet.

E4-19 Reporting a Correct Income Statement with Earnings per Share to Include the Effects of Adjusting Entries and Evaluating Total Asset Turnover as an Auditor

LO4-1, 4-2, 4-3

Jay, Inc., a party rental business, completed its third year of operations on December 31. Because this is the end of the annual accounting period, the company bookkeeper prepared the following tentative income statement:

Income Statement	
Rent revenue	$109,000
Expenses:	
Salaries and wages expense	26,500
Maintenance expense	12,000
Rent expense	8,800
Utilities expense	4,300
Gas and oil expense	3,000
Miscellaneous expenses (items not listed elsewhere)	1,000
Total expenses	55,600
Income	$ 53,400

You are an independent CPA hired by the company to audit the company's accounting systems and review the financial statements. In your audit, you developed additional data as follows:

a. Salaries and wages for the last three days of December amounting to $730 were not recorded or paid.
b. Jay estimated telephone usage at $440 for December, but nothing has been recorded or paid.
c. Depreciation on rental autos, amounting to $24,000 for the current year, was not recorded.
d. Interest on a $15,000, one-year, 8 percent note payable dated October 1 of the current year was not recorded. The 8 percent interest is payable on the maturity date of the note.
e. Maintenance expense excludes $1,100, representing the cost of maintenance supplies used during the current year.
f. The Unearned Rent Revenue account includes $4,100 of revenue to be earned in January of next year.
g. The income tax expense is $5,800. Payment of income tax will be made next year.

Required:

1. For items (*a*) through (*g*), what adjusting entry should Jay record at December 31? If none is required, explain why.
2. Prepare a corrected income statement for the current year in good (with subheadings for income from Operations and Other Item), including earnings per share (rounded to two decimal places). Assume that 7,000 shares of stock are outstanding all year. Show computations.
3. Assume the beginning-of-the-year balance for Jay's total assets was $58,020 and its ending balance for total assets was $65,180. Compute the total asset turnover ratio (rounded to two decimal places) based on the corrected information. What does this ratio suggest? If the average total asset turnover ratio for the industry is 2.31, what might you infer about Jay, Inc.?

Recording Four Adjusting Entries and Completing the Trial Balance Worksheet

E4-20
LO4-1

Green Valley Company prepared the following trial balance at the end of its first year of operations ending December 31. To simplify the case, the amounts given are in thousands of dollars. The "Ref." column is for the reference letter of the adjusting entry effect.

	A	B	C	D	E	F	G	H
1	GREEN VALLEY COMPANY							
2	**Trial Balance Spreadsheet on December 31 (the end of the first year of operations)**							
3	*(dollars in thousands)*	**UNADJUSTED**		**ADJUSTMENTS**			**ADJUSTED**	
4		**Debit**	**Credit**	**Ref.**	**Debit**	**Credit**	**Debit**	**Credit**
5	Cash	20						
6	Accounts receivable	13						
7	Prepaid insurance	8						
8	Machinery	85						
9	Accumulated depreciation		-					
10	Accounts payable		11					
11	Wages payable		-					
12	Income taxes payable		-					
13	Common stock (4,000 shares)		4					
14	Additional paid-in capital		67					
15	Retained earnings	6						
16	Revenues (*not detailed*)		82					
17	Expenses (*not detailed*)	32						
18	**Total**	**164**	**164**					

Other data not yet recorded at December 31 include

a. Insurance expired during the current year, $6.
b. Wages payable, $4.
c. Depreciation expense for the current year, $9.
d. Income tax expense, $7.

Required:

1. Prepare the adjusting entries for the current year.
2. Complete the trial balance Adjustments and Adjusted columns.

Reporting an Income Statement, Statement of Stockholders' Equity, and Balance Sheet

E4-21
LO4-2

Refer to E4-20.

Required:
Using the adjusted balances for Green Valley Company in E4-20, prepare an income statement, statement of stockholders' equity, and balance sheet for the current year.

Recording A Closing Entry

E4-22
LO4-4

Refer to E4-20.

Required:

1. What are the purposes for "closing the books" at the end of the accounting period?
2. Using the adjusted balances for Green Valley Company in E4-20, prepare the closing entry for the current year.

PROBLEMS

P4-1 LO4-1 Papa John's International Inc.

Preparing a Trial Balance (AP4-1)

Papa John's International Inc. operates and franchises pizza delivery and carryout restaurants worldwide. The following is an alphabetical list of accounts and amounts reported in a recent year's set of financial statements. The accounts have normal debit or credit balances and the dollars are rounded to the nearest million.

Accounts payable	$ 32	Interest expense	$ 11
Accounts receivable	65	Interest revenue	1
Accrued expenses payable	68	Inventories	31
Accumulated depreciation	406	Land	34
Additional paid-in capital	184	Lease right-of-use assets	158
Advertising expense	72	Long-term debt	470
Buildings and leasehold improvements	228	Long-term lease liabilities	133
Cash	22	Long-term notes receivable	16
Common stock	1	Loss on impairment of assets	2
Cost of sales	1,059	Other assets	48
Current lease liabilities	25	Other long-term liabilities	73
Depreciation expense	44	Prepaid expenses and other current assets	45
Equipment	379	Rent and utilities expense	62
General and administrative expenses	78	Restaurant and franchise sales revenue	1,784
Income tax expense	34	Retained earnings	?
Income tax receivable	4	Salaries and benefits expense	240
Income taxes payable	11	Short-term notes receivable	4
Intangible assets	87	Treasury stock	597
		Unearned revenue	6

Source: Papa John's International Inc.

Required:

1. Prepare an adjusted trial balance.
2. How did you determine the amount for retained earnings?

P4-2 LO4-1

Recording Adjusting Entries (AP4-2)

All of the current year's entries for Zimmerman Company have been made, except the following adjusting entries. The company's annual accounting year ends on December 31.

a. On September 1 of the current year, Zimmerman collected six months' rent of $9,600 on storage space. At that date, Zimmerman debited Cash and credited Unearned Rent Revenue for $9,600.

b. On October 1 of the current year, the company borrowed $18,000 from a local bank and signed a one-year, 12 percent note for that amount. The principal and interest are payable on the maturity date.

c. Depreciation of $4,400 must be recognized on a service truck purchased in July of the current year at a cost of $22,000.

d. Cash of $3,000 was collected on November 1 of the current year for services to be rendered evenly over the next year beginning on November 1 of the current year. Unearned Service Revenue was credited when the cash was received.

e. On November 1 of the current year, Zimmerman paid a one-year premium for property insurance, $8,400, for coverage starting on that date. Cash was credited and Prepaid Insurance was debited for this amount.

f. The company earned service revenue of $4,000 on a special job that was completed December 29 of the current year. Collection will be made during January of the next year. No entry has been recorded.

g. At December 31 of the current year, wages earned by employees totaled $14,000. The employees will be paid on the next payroll date in January of the next year.

h. On December 31 of the current year, the company estimated it owed $400 for this year's property taxes on land. The tax will be paid when the bill is received in January of next year.

Tip **Reminder:** When you need to create a new account title, be as specific as possible. For example, property taxes would not be called income taxes.

Required:

1. Indicate whether each transaction relates to a deferred revenue, deferred expense, accrued revenue, or accrued expense.
2. Give the adjusting entry required for each transaction at December 31 of the current year.

Recording Adjusting Entries (AP4-3)

P4-3
LO4-1

Mellor Towing Company provides hauling and delivery services for other businesses. It is at the end of its accounting year ending December 31. The following data that must be considered were developed from the company's records and related documents:

a. On January 1 of the current year, the company purchased a new hauling van at a cash cost of $38,000. Depreciation estimated at $3,800 for the year has not been recorded for the current year.

b. During the current year, office supplies amounting to $1,000 were purchased for cash and debited in full to Supplies. At the end of last year, the count of supplies remaining on hand was $400. The inventory of supplies counted on hand at the end of the current year was $180.

c. On December 31 of the current year, Lanie's Garage completed repairs on one of Mellor Towing's trucks at a cost of $2,600; the amount is not yet recorded by Mellor Towing and by agreement will be paid during January of next year.

d. On December 31 of the current year, property taxes on land owned during the current year were estimated at $1,900. The taxes have not been recorded and will be paid in the next year when billed.

e. On December 31 of the current year, the company completed towing service for an out-of-state company for $4,000 payable by the customer within 30 days. No cash has been collected, and no journal entry has been made for this transaction.

f. On July 1 of the current year, a three-year insurance premium on equipment in the amount of $900 was paid and debited in full to Prepaid Insurance on that date. Coverage began on July 1 of the current year.

g. On October 1 of the current year, the company borrowed $25,000 from the local bank on a two-year, 10 percent note payable. The principal plus interest is payable at the end of 24 months.

h. The income before any of the adjustments or income taxes was $30,000. The company's income tax rate is 21 percent. (**Hint:** Compute adjusted pre-tax income based on (*a*) through (*g*) to determine income tax expense.) Round the income tax computation to the nearest dollar.

Required:

1. Indicate whether each transaction relates to a deferred revenue, deferred expense, accrued revenue, or accrued expense.
2. Prepare the adjusting entry required for each transaction at December 31 of the current year.

Determining Financial Statement Effects of Adjusting Entries (AP4-4)

P4-4
LO4-1

Refer to the information regarding Zimmerman Company in P4-2.

Required:

1. Indicate whether each transaction relates to a deferred revenue, deferred expense, accrued revenue, or accrued expense.
2. Using the following headings, indicate the effect of each adjusting entry and the amount of the effect. Use + for increase, – for decrease, and NE for no effect. (**Reminder:** Assets = Liabilities + Stockholders' Equity; Revenues – Expenses = Net Income; and Net Income accounts are closed to Retained Earnings, a part of Stockholders' Equity.)

	BALANCE SHEET			INCOME STATEMENT		
Transaction	**Assets**	**Liabilities**	**Stockholders' Equity**	**Revenues**	**Expenses**	**Net Income**
a.						

P4-5 Determining Financial Statement Effects of Adjusting Entries (AP4-5)

LO4-1

Refer to the information regarding Mellor Towing Company in P4-3.

Required:

1. Indicate whether each transaction relates to a deferred revenue, deferred expense, accrued revenue, or accrued expense.
2. Using the following headings, indicate the effect of each adjusting entry and the amount of each. Use + for increase, – for decrease, and NE for no effect. (**Reminder:** Assets = Liabilities + Stockholders' Equity; Revenues – Expenses = Net Income; and Net Income accounts are closed to Retained Earnings, a part of Stockholders' Equity.)

	BALANCE SHEET			INCOME STATEMENT		
Transaction	**Assets**	**Liabilities**	**Stockholders' Equity**	**Revenues**	**Expenses**	**Net Income**
a.						

P4-6 Inferring Year-End Adjustments, Computing Earnings per Share and Total Asset Turnover, and Recording Closing Entries (AP4-6)

LO4-1, 4-3, 4-4

Ramirez Company is completing the information processing cycle at its fiscal year-end on December 31. Following are the correct balances at December 31 for the accounts both before and after the adjusting entries.

RAMIREZ COMPANY

Trial Balance Spreadsheet on December 31 of the Current Year

	UNADJUSTED		ADJUSTMENTS			ADJUSTED	
	Debit	**Credit**	**Ref.**	**Debit**	**Credit**	**Debit**	**Credit**
Cash	13,500					13,500	
Accounts receivable						1,820	
Prepaid insurance	850					720	
Equipment	162,280					168,280	
Accumulated depreciation, equipment		42,100					48,100
Income taxes payable							1,155
Common stock and additional paid-in capital		112,000					112,000
Retained earnings, January 1		19,600					19,600
Service revenue		64,400					66,220
Salary expense	55,470					55,470	
Depreciation expense						6,000	
Insurance expense						130	
Income tax expense						1,155	
Total	**232,100**	**238,100**				**247,075**	**247,075**

Required:

1. Compare the amounts in the columns before and after the adjusting entries to reconstruct the adjusting entries made in the current year. Provide an explanation of each.
2. Compute the amount of net income assuming that it is based on the amounts (*a*) before adjusting entries and (*b*) after adjusting entries. Which net income amount is correct? Explain why.
3. Compute earnings per share (rounded to two decimal places), assuming that 3,000 shares of stock are outstanding all year.

4. Compute the total asset turnover ratio (rounded to two decimal places), assuming total assets at the beginning of the year were $110,000. If the industry average is 0.49, what does this suggest to you about Ramirez Company?
5. Record the closing entry at December 31 of the current year.

Recording Adjusting and Closing Entries and Preparing a Balance Sheet and Income Statement Including Earnings per Share (AP4-7)

P4-7
LO4-1, 4-2, 4-4

Tunstall, Inc., a small service company, keeps its records without the help of an accountant. After much effort, an outside accountant prepared the following unadjusted trial balance as of the end of the annual accounting period on December 31:

	A	B	C	D
1		TUNSTALL, INC.		
2		Undjusted Trial Balance at December 31		
3			Debit	Credit
4		Cash	42,000	
5		Accounts receivable	11,600	
6		Supplies	900	
7		Prepaid insurance	800	
8		Service trucks	19,000	
9		Accumulated depreciation		9,200
10		Other assets	8,300	
11		Accounts payable		3,000
12		Wages payable		
13		Income taxes payable		
14		Note payable (*3 years; 10% interest due each September 30*)		17,000
15		Common stock (5,000 shares outstanding)		400
16		Additional paid-in capital		19,000
17		Retained earnings		6,000
18		Service revenue		61,360
19		Wages expense	16,200	
20		Remaining expenses (*not detailed; excludes income tax*)	17,160	
21		Income tax expense		
22		**Total**	**115,960**	**115,960**

Data not yet recorded at December 31 included

a. The supplies count on December 31 reflected $300 in remaining supplies on hand to be used in the next year.
b. Insurance expired during the current year, $800.
c. Depreciation expense for the current year, $3,700.
d. Wages earned by employees not yet paid on December 31, $640.
e. Three months of interest expense (for the note payable borrowed on October 1 of the current year) was incurred in the current year.
f. Income tax expense, $5,540.

Required:

1. Record the adjusting entries.
2. Prepare an income statement (with Operating Income and Other Items sections) and a classified balance sheet that include the effects of the preceding six transactions.
3. Record the closing entry.

ALTERNATE PROBLEMS

AP4-1 Preparing a Trial Balance (P4-1)

LO4-1

Tesla, Inc.

Tesla, Inc., designs, develops, manufactures, sells, and leases fully electric vehicles, energy generation and storage systems, and service related to its products. The following is a simplified list of accounts and amounts reported in recent financial statements. The accounts have normal debit or credit balances, and the dollars are rounded to the nearest million. The fiscal year ends on December 31.

Accounts payable	$ 3,771	Equipment	$ 9,747
Accounts receivable	1,324	Intangible assets	537
Accrued liabilities	3,222	Interest expense	685
Accumulated deficit (*from net losses*)	?	Interest income	89
Accumulated depreciation	3,734	Inventory	3,552
Additional paid-in capital	14,228	Land and buildings	3,788
Automotive cost of revenues	16,398	Long-term lease liabilities	11,634
Automotive revenues	20,821	Operating lease right-of-use assets	3,665
Cash	6,514	Other assets	9,662
Common stock	1	Other long-term liabilities	3,898
Computer equipment	595	Other operating expenses	149
Current lease liabilities	1,785	Prepaid expenses and other current assets	713
Customer deposits	726	Provision for income taxes (*income tax expense*)	110
Customer notes receivable (*noncurrent*)	393	Research and development expenses	1,343
Deferred revenue	1,163	Selling, general, and administrative expenses	2,646
Energy generation cost of revenues	1,341	Services cost of revenues	2,770
Energy generation revenues	1,531	Services revenues	2,226

Source: Tesla, Inc.

Required:

1. Prepare an adjusted trial balance at December 31.
2. How did you determine the amount for accumulated deficit (from net losses)?

AP4-2 Recording Adjusting Entries (P4-2)

LO4-1

Hannah Company's annual accounting year ends on June 30. All of the entries for the current year have been made, except the following adjusting entries:

a. On March 30 of the current year, Hannah paid a six-month premium for property insurance, $3,200, for coverage starting on that date. Cash was credited and Prepaid Insurance was debited for this amount.

b. On June 1 of the current year, Hannah collected two months' maintenance revenue of $450. At that date, Hannah debited Cash and credited Unearned Maintenance Revenue for $450.

c. At June 30 of the current year, wages of $900 were earned by employees but not yet paid. The employees will be paid on the next payroll date in July, the beginning of the next fiscal year.

d. Depreciation of $3,000 must be recognized on a service truck that cost $15,000 when purchased on July 1 of the current year.

e. Cash of $4,200 was collected on May 1 of the current year for services to be rendered evenly over the next year beginning on May 1 of the current year. Unearned Service Revenue was credited when the cash was received.

f. On February 1 of the current year, the company borrowed $18,000 from a local bank and signed a one-year, 9 percent note for that amount, with the principal and interest payable on the maturity date.

g. On June 30 of the current year, the company estimated that it owed $500 in property taxes on land it owned in the second half of the current fiscal year. The taxes will be paid when billed in August of the next fiscal year.

h. The company earned service revenue of $2,000 on a special job that was completed June 29 of the current year. Collection will be made during July and no entry has been recorded.

Required:

1. Indicate whether each transaction relates to a deferred revenue, deferred expense, accrued revenue, or accrued expense.
2. Prepare the adjusting entry required for each transaction at June 30.

Recording Adjusting Entries (P4-3)

AP4-3
LO4-1

Bill's Catering Company is at its accounting year-end on December 31. The following data that must be considered were developed from the company's records and related documents:

a. During the current year, office supplies amounting to $1,200 were purchased for cash and debited in full to Supplies. At the beginning of the year, the count of supplies on hand was $450; at the end of the year, the count of supplies on hand was $400.
b. On December 31 of the current year, the company catered an evening gala for a local celebrity. The $7,440 bill is due from the customer by the end of January of next year. No cash has been collected, and no journal entry has been made for this transaction.
c. On October 1 of the current year, a one-year insurance premium on equipment in the amount of $1,200 was paid and debited in full to Prepaid Insurance on that date. Coverage began on November 1 of the current year.
d. On December 31 of the current year, repairs on one of the company's delivery vans were completed at a cost estimate of $600; the amount has not yet been paid or recorded by Bill's. The repair shop will bill Bill's Catering at the beginning of January of next year.
e. In November of the current year, Bill's Catering signed a lease for a new retail location, providing a down payment of $2,100 for the first three months' rent that was debited in full to Prepaid Rent. The lease began on December 1 of the current year.
f. On July 1 of the current year, the company purchased new refrigerated display counters at a cash cost of $18,000. Depreciation of $2,570 has not been recorded for the current year.
g. On November 1 of the current year, the company loaned $4,000 to one of its employees on a one-year, 12 percent note. The principal plus interest is payable by the employee at the end of 12 months.
h. The income before any of the adjustments or income taxes was $22,400. The company's income tax rate is 25 percent. (**Hint:** Compute adjusted pretax income based on (*a*) through (*g*) to determine income tax expense.)

Required:

1. Indicate whether each transaction relates to a deferred revenue, deferred expense, accrued revenue, or accrued expense.
2. Prepare the adjusting entry required for each transaction at December 31 of the current year.

Determining Financial Statement Effects of Adjusting Entries (P4-4)

AP4-4
LO4-1

Refer to the information regarding Hannah Company in AP4-2.

Required:

1. Indicate whether each transaction relates to a deferred revenue, deferred expense, accrued revenue, or accrued expense.
2. Using the following headings, indicate the effect of each adjusting entry and the amount of the effect. Use + for increase, − for decrease, and NE for no effect. (**Reminder:** Assets = Liabilities + Stockholders' Equity; Revenues − Expenses = Net Income; and Net Income accounts are closed to Retained Earnings, a part of Stockholders' Equity.)

	BALANCE SHEET			INCOME STATEMENT		
Transaction	**Assets**	**Liabilities**	**Stockholders' Equity**	**Revenues**	**Expenses**	**Net Income**
a.						

Determining Financial Statement Effects of Adjusting Entries (P4-5)

AP4-5
LO4-1

Refer to the information regarding Bill's Catering Company in AP4-3.

Required:

1. Indicate whether each transaction relates to a deferred revenue, deferred expense, accrued revenue, or accrued expense.

2. Using the following headings, indicate the effect of each adjusting entry and the amount of each. Use + for increase, – for decrease, and NE for no effect. (**Reminder:** Assets = Liabilities + Stockholders' Equity; Revenues – Expenses = Net Income; and Net Income accounts are closed to Retained Earnings, a part of Stockholders' Equity.)

	BALANCE SHEET			INCOME STATEMENT		
Transaction	**Assets**	**Liabilities**	**Stockholders' Equity**	**Revenues**	**Expenses**	**Net Income**
a.						

AP4-6
LO4-1, 4-3, 4-4

Inferring Year-End Adjustments, Computing Earnings per Share and Total Asset Turnover, and Recording Closing Entries (P4-6)

Taos Company is completing the information processing cycle at the end of its fiscal year on December 31. Following are the correct balances at December 31 of the current year for the accounts both before and after the adjusting entries for the current year.

FILE HOME INSERT PAGE LAYOUT FORMULAS DATA REVIEW VIEW

K23

	A	B	C	D	E	F	G	H	I
1		RAMIREZ COMPANY							
2		Trial Balance Spreadsheet on December 31 of the Current Year							
3			**UNADJUSTED**		**ADJUSTMENTS**			**ADJUSTED**	
4			**Debit**	**Credit**	**Ref.**	**Debit**	**Credit**	**Debit**	**Credit**
5		Cash	18,000					18,000	
6		Accounts receivable						1,500	
7		Prepaid rent	1,200					800	
8		Property, plant, and equipment	208,000					208,000	
9		Accumulated depreciation		52,500					70,000
10		Income taxes payable							4,650
11		Unearned revenue		16,000					8,000
12		Common stock and additional paid-in capital		110,000					110,000
13		Retained earnings, January 1		21,700					21,700
14		Service revenue		83,000					92,500
15		Salary expense	56,000					56,000	
16		Depreciation expense						17,500	
17		Rent expense						400	
18		Income tax expense						4,650	
19		**Total**	**283,200**	**283,200**				**306,850**	**306,850**

Required:

1. Compare the amounts in the columns before and after the adjusting entries to reconstruct the adjusting entries made in the current year. Provide an explanation of each.
2. Compute the amount of net income, assuming that it is based on the amount (*a*) before adjusting entries and (*b*) after adjusting entries. Which net income amount is correct? Explain why.
3. Compute earnings per share (rounded to two decimal places), assuming that 5,000 shares of stock are outstanding.
4. Assuming total assets were $136,000 at the beginning of the year, compute the total asset turnover ratio (rounded to two decimal places). What does this tell you about Taos Company?
5. Record the closing entry at December 31 of the current year.

Recording Adjusting and Closing Entries and Preparing a Balance Sheet and Income Statement Including Earnings per Share (P4-7)

AP4-7
LO4-1, 4-2, 4-4

South Bend Repair Service Co. keeps its records without the help of an accountant. After much effort, an outside accountant prepared the following **unadjusted trial balance** as of the end of the annual accounting period on December 31:

	A	B	C	D
1		SOUTH BEND REPAIR SERVICE CO.		
2		**Undjusted Trial Balance at December 31**		
3			**Debit**	**Credit**
4		Cash	19,600	
5		Accounts receivable	7,000	
6		Supplies	1,300	
7		Prepaid insurance	900	
8		Equipment	27,000	
9		Accumulated depreciation		12,000
10		Other assets	5,100	
11		Accounts payable		2,500
12		Wages payable		
13		Income taxes payable		
14		Note payable (2 *years; 12% interest due each December 31*)		5,000
15		Common stock (3,000 shares outstanding all year)		300
16		Additional paid-in capital		15,700
17		Retained earnings		10,300
18		Service revenue		48,000
19		Wages expense	25,200	
20		Remaining expenses (*not detailed; excludes income tax*)	7,700	
21		Income tax expense		
22		**Total**	**93,800**	**93,800**

Data not yet recorded at December 31 of the current year include

a. Depreciation expense for the current year, $3,000.
b. Insurance expired during the current year, $450.
c. Wages earned by employees but not yet paid on December 31 of the current year, $2,100.
d. The supplies count at the end of the current year reflected $800 in remaining supplies on hand to be used in the next year.
e. Seven months of interest expense (on the note payable borrowed on June 1 of the current year) was incurred in the current year.
f. Income tax expense was $1,914.

Required:

1. Record the adjusting entries.
2. Prepare an income statement (with Operating Income and Other Items sections, and earnings per share) and a classified balance sheet for the current year to include the effects of the preceding six transactions. Round earnings per share to the nearest penny.
3. Record the closing entry.

connect

CONTINUING PROBLEM

End of the Accounting Cycle: Recording Adjustments, Preparing Statements, and Closing the Books

CON4-1
LO4-1, 4-2, 4-4

Penny's Pool Service & Supply, Inc. (PPSS) is completing the accounting process for the first year of operations ended on December 31. Transactions during the year have been journalized and posted. The following trial balance spreadsheet reflects the unadjusted balances on December 31:

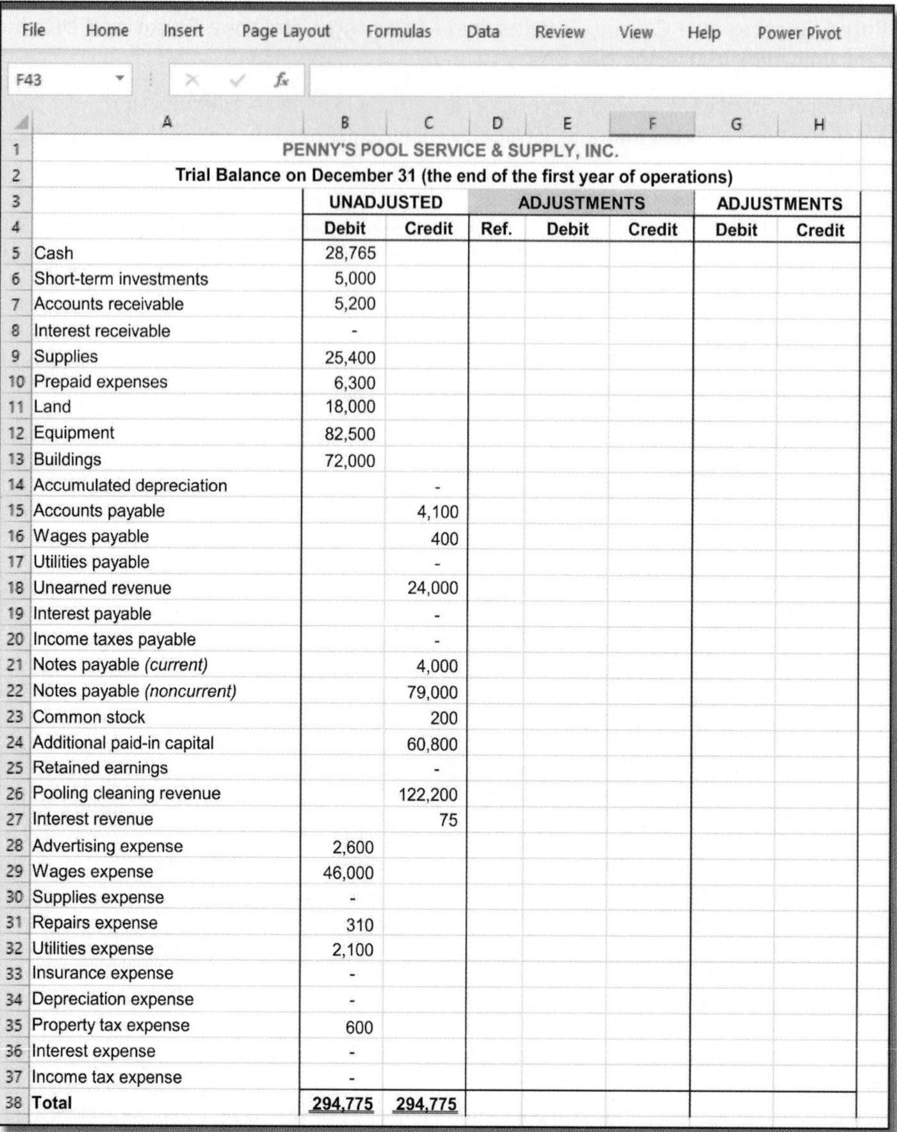

File Home Insert Page Layout Formulas Data Review View Help Power Pivot

F43

	A	B	C	D	E	F	G	H
1	PENNY'S POOL SERVICE & SUPPLY, INC.							
2	Trial Balance on December 31 (the end of the first year of operations)							
3		UNADJUSTED		ADJUSTMENTS			ADJUSTMENTS	
4		Debit	Credit	Ref.	Debit	Credit	Debit	Credit
5	Cash	28,765						
6	Short-term investments	5,000						
7	Accounts receivable	5,200						
8	Interest receivable	-						
9	Supplies	25,400						
10	Prepaid expenses	6,300						
11	Land	18,000						
12	Equipment	82,500						
13	Buildings	72,000						
14	Accumulated depreciation		-					
15	Accounts payable		4,100					
16	Wages payable		400					
17	Utilities payable		-					
18	Unearned revenue		24,000					
19	Interest payable		-					
20	Income taxes payable		-					
21	Notes payable *(current)*		4,000					
22	Notes payable *(noncurrent)*		79,000					
23	Common stock		200					
24	Additional paid-in capital		60,800					
25	Retained earnings		-					
26	Pooling cleaning revenue		122,200					
27	Interest revenue		75					
28	Advertising expense	2,600						
29	Wages expense	46,000						
30	Supplies expense	-						
31	Repairs expense	310						
32	Utilities expense	2,100						
33	Insurance expense	-						
34	Depreciation expense	-						
35	Property tax expense	600						
36	Interest expense	-						
37	Income tax expense	-						
38	**Total**	294,775	294,775					

Microsoft Excel

The data for the adjusting entries follows:

a. PPSS owed $7,500 in wages to the office receptionist and three assistants for working the last 10 days in December. The employees will be paid early next year.

b. On October 1 of the current fiscal year, PPSS received $24,000 from customers who prepaid pool cleaning service for one year beginning on November 1 of the current year.

c. The company received a $520 utility bill for December utility usage. It will be paid early next year.

d. PPSS borrowed $79,000 from a local bank on August 1, signing a one-year, 12 percent note. The note and interest are due on August 1 next year. Round to the nearest dollar.

e. On December 31, PPSS cleaned and winterized a customer's pool for $800, but the service was not yet recorded on December 31.

f. On November 1 of the current fiscal year, PPSS purchased a two-year insurance policy for $4,200, with coverage beginning on that date. The amount was recorded as Prepaid Expenses when paid.

g. On December 31, PPSS had $3,100 of pool cleaning supplies on hand after purchasing supplies costing $25,400 during the year from **Pool Corporation, Inc.**

h. PPSS estimated that depreciation on its buildings and equipment was $8,300 for the year.

i. At December 31, $110 of interest on investments was earned that will be received in the next year.

j. The company's income tax rate for the year was 22 percent. Round to the nearest dollar.

Required:

1. Prepare adjusting entries for Penny's Pool Service & Supply, Inc., on December 31, of the current year.
2. Complete the trial balance spreadsheet (enter adjustments and determine the adjusted balances).

3. Prepare a multiple-step income statement (with a subtotal for Income from Operations, a section on Other Items) and earnings per share (Note: 4,000 shares outstanding at end of the year), a statement of stockholder's equity, and a classified balance sheet (with current assets and liabilities). Round earnings per share to two decimal places.
4. Prepare the closing entry.

COMPREHENSIVE PROBLEMS (CHAPTERS 1–4)

Recording Transactions (Including Adjusting and Closing Entries), Preparing Financial Statements, and Performing Ratio Analysis

COMP4-1
LO4-1, 4-2, 4-3, 4-4
H & H Tool

Brothers Herm and Steve Hargenrater began operations of their tool and die shop **(H & H Tool)** on January 1, 1987, in Meadville, PA. The annual reporting period ends December 31. Assume that the trial balance on January 1, 2023, was as follows:

	H & H TOOL Trial Balance at January 1, 2023		
	(dollars in millions, except number of shares and par value)	**Debit**	**Credit**
4	Cash	6	
5	Accounts receivable	5	
6	Supplies	13	
7	Land		
8	Equipment	78	
9	Accumulated depreciation (*on equipment*)		8
10	Other noncurrent assets (*not detailed to simplify*)	7	
11	Accounts payable		
12	Wages payable		
13	Interest payable		
14	Dividends payable		
15	Income taxes payable		
16	Long-term notes payable		
17	Common stock (8 million shares, $0.50 par value) all year)		4
18	Additional paid-in capital		80
19	Retained earnings		17
20	Service revenue		
21	Depreciation expense		
22	Supplies expense		
23	Wages expense		
24	Interest expense		
25	Income tax expense		
26	Miscellaneous expenses (*not detailed to simplify*)		
27	**Total**	**109**	**109**

Transactions during 2023 follow. All dollars are in millions, except number of shares and per share amounts:

a. Borrowed $15 cash on a five-year, 8 percent note payable, dated March 1, 2023.
b. Sold 4 million additional shares of common stock for cash at $1 market value per share on January 1, 2023.
c. Purchased land for a future building site; paid cash, $13.
d. Earned $215 in revenues for 2023, including $52 on credit and the rest in cash.
e. Incurred $89 in wages expense and $25 in miscellaneous expenses for 2023, with $20 on credit and the rest paid in cash.
f. Collected accounts receivable, $34.
g. Purchased other noncurrent assets, $15 cash.
h. Purchased supplies on account for future use, $27.
i. Paid accounts payable, $26.
j. Declared cash dividends on December 1, $25.
k. Signed a three-year $33 service contract to start February 1, 2024.
l. Paid the dividends in *(j)* on December 31.

Data for adjusting entries (amounts in millions):

m. Supplies counted on December 31, 2023, $18.
n. Depreciation for the year on the equipment, $10.
o. Interest accrued on notes payable (to be computed).
p. Wages earned by employees since the December 24 payroll but not yet paid, $16.
q. Income tax expense, $11, payable in 2024.

Required:

1. Set up T-accounts for the accounts on the trial balance and enter beginning balances.
2. Prepare journal entries for transactions (*a*) through (*l*) and post them to the T-accounts.
3. Journalize and post the adjusting entries (*m*) through (*q*).
4. Prepare an income statement (including earnings per share rounded to two decimal places), statement of stockholders' equity, and balance sheet.
5. Identify the type of transaction for (*a*) through (*l*) for the statement of cash flows (O for operating, I for investing, F for financing) and the direction and amount of the effect.
6. Journalize and post the closing entry.
7. Compute the following ratios (rounded to two decimal places) for 2023 and explain what the results suggest about the company:
   a. Current ratio
   b. Total asset turnover
   c. Net profit margin

COMP4-2 LO4-1, 4-2, 4-3, 4-4 Recording Transactions (Including Adjusting and Closing Entries), Preparing Financial Statements, and Performing Ratio Analysis

Aubrae and Tylor Williamson began operations of their furniture repair shop (Furniture Refinishers, Inc.) on January 1, 2019. The annual reporting period ends December 31. The trial balance on January 1, 2024, was as follows:

	B	C	D
1	**FURNITURE REFINISHERS, INC.**		
2	**Trial Balance at January 1, 2024**		
3		**Debit**	**Credit**
4	Cash	5,000	
5	Accounts receivable	4,000	
6	Supplies	2,000	
7	Small tools	6,000	
8	Equipment		
9	Accumulated depreciation (*on equipment*)		
10	Other noncurrent assets (*not detailed to simplify*)	9,000	
11	Accounts payable		7,000
12	Dividends payable		
13	Notes payable		
14	Wages payable		
15	Interest payable		
16	Income taxes payable		
17	Unearned revenue		
18	Common stock (60,000 shares, $0.10 par value) all year)		6,000
19	Additional paid-in capital		9,000
20	Retained earnings		4,000
21	Service revenue		
22	Depreciation expense		
23	Wages expense		
24	Interest expense		
25	Income tax expense		
26	Miscellaneous expenses (*not detailed to simplify*)		
27	**Total**	**26,000**	**26,000**

Transactions during 2024 follow:

a. Sold 10,000 additional shares of capital stock for cash at $0.50 market value per share at the beginning of the year.
b. Borrowed $20,000 cash on July 1, 2024, signing a one-year, 10 percent note payable.
c. Purchased equipment for $18,000 cash on July 1, 2024.
d. Earned $70,000 in revenues for 2024, including $14,000 on credit and the rest in cash.
e. Incurred $27,000 in wages expense and $8,000 in miscellaneous expenses for 2024, with $7,000 on credit and the rest paid with cash.
f. Purchased additional small tools, $3,000 cash.
g. Collected accounts receivable, $8,000.
h. Paid accounts payable, $11,000.
i. Purchased $10,000 of supplies on account.
j. Declared a cash dividend on December 1, $10,000.
k. Received a $3,000 deposit on work to start January 15, 2025.
l. Paid the dividends in (*j*) on December 31.

Data for adjusting entries:
m. Supplies of $4,000 and small tools of $8,000 were counted on December 31, 2024 (debit Miscellaneous Expenses).
n. Depreciation for 2024, $2,000.
o. Interest accrued on notes payable (to be computed).
p. Wages earned since the December 24 payroll but not yet paid, $3,000.
q. Income tax expense was $4,000, payable in 2025.

Required:
1. Set up T-accounts for the accounts on the trial balance and enter beginning balances.
2. Prepare journal entries for transactions (*a*) through (*l*) and post them to the T-accounts.
3. Journalize and post the adjusting entries (*m*) through (*q*).
4. Prepare an income statement (including earnings per share rounded to two decimal places), statement of stockholders' equity, and balance sheet.
5. Identify the type of transaction for (*a*) through (*l*) for the statement of cash flows (O for operating, I for investing, F for financing) and the direction and amount of the effect.
6. Journalize and post the closing entry.
7. Compute the following ratios (rounded to two decimal places) for 2024 and explain what the results suggest about the company:
   a. Current ratio
   b. Total asset turnover
   c. Net profit margin

CASES AND PROJECTS

Annual Report Cases

Finding Financial Information

CP4-1
LO4-1, 4-3, 4-4
Target Corporation

Refer to the financial statements of **Target Corporation** in Appendix B at the end of this book. All dollar amounts are in millions.

1. Did the company accrue more or pay more for wages and benefits in the most recent fiscal year and by how much?
   a. Target accrued more by $519.
   b. Target accrued more by $1,677.
   c. Target paid more by $1,158.
   d. Target paid more by $1,716.
   e. Cannot determine the effect or amount by the information provided.

2. Did the company receive more or accrue more for accounts and other receivables in the most recent fiscal year and by how much?
   a. Target received more by $133.
   b. Target accrued more by $259.
   c. Target accrued more by $133.
   d. Target received more by $259.
   e. Cannot determine the effect or amount by the information provided.
3. Of the $935 balance in gift card liability on February 1, 2020, what adjusting entry did Target make to recognize revenue during the most recent year for gift cards redeemed by customers?

	Debit		Credit	
a.	Cash	1,035	Gift card liability	1,035
b.	Cash	739	Sales revenue	739
c.	Sales revenue	739	Gift card liability	739
d.	Gift card liability	639	Sales revenue	639

4. What is(are) Target's revenue recognition policy(ies) for merchandise sales?
   a. Target records Target gift card sales upon redemption, which is typically within one year of issuance.
   b. Target records almost all retail store revenues at the point of sale.
   c. Target records digital sales upon delivery to the customer.
   d. All of the above are revenue recognition policies for Target.
5. Which of the following is included in the closing entry for Target for the most recent year?
   a. Debit to Cost of Sales, $66,177
   b. Credit to Selling, General and Administrative expenses, $18,615
   c. Debit to Accumulated Depreciation, $20,278
   d. Credit to Sales Revenue, $92,400
   e. Debit to Retained Earnings, $4,368
6. What is the total asset turnover ratio for the most recent fiscal year and what does this suggest about the company?
   a. 1.99, suggesting that Target's management generates $1.99 in operating revenues for every dollar of assets.
   b. 0.51, suggesting that Target generates $0.51 for every dollar of sales revenue.
   c. 0.09, suggesting that Target's management is not effective at utilizing assets to generate earnings.
   d. 2.47, suggesting that Target's management is effective at balancing the ratio of current assets to total assets.

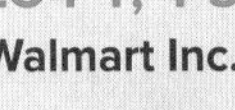

CP4-2
LO4-1, 4-3
Walmart Inc.

Finding Financial Information

Refer to the financial statements of **Walmart Inc.** in Appendix C at the end of this book. All dollar amounts are in millions.

1. Did the company accrue more or pay more in income taxes during the most recent year? By how much?
2. By what percentage did Accrued liabilities increase from the prior year to the most recent year (round the percentage to two decimal places)?
3. If Walmart sold $3,620 in gift cards to customers during the most recent year, what adjusting entry did Walmart record for the gift cards that were redeemed for merchandise?
4. What is Walmart's total asset turnover on total operating revenues for the most recent fiscal year ended in 2021 (round to two decimal places)?
5. In the fiscal year ended in 2020, Walmart's total asset turnover ratio was 2.28 and, in the fiscal year ended in 2019, total asset turnover ratio was 2.41. Between 2019 and 2020, what does this suggest about Walmart over time?
   a. Walmart's management generated fewer sales over time.
   b. Walmart was less liquid, but the company is still able to pay short-term obligations with current assets.
   c. Walmart's management was less effective at generating revenues or controlling costs over time.
   d. Walmart's management was less effective at utilizing assets to generate sales over time.

Comparing Companies within an Industry

CP4-3
LO4-1, 4-3
Target Corporation
Walmart Inc.

Refer to the following:

- **Target Corporation** in Appendix B,
- **Walmart Inc.** in Appendix C, and the
- **Industry Ratio Report** in Appendix D at the end of this book.

All dollar amounts are in millions of dollars.

1. Compute the total asset turnover ratio on total operating revenues for both companies (round your answers to two decimal places).

   Target = ______ **Walmart** = ______

2. Compared to each other, is the management of these two companies more or less effective at utilizing assets to generate sales?
   a. Target's management is less effective than Walmart's management at utilizing assets to generate sales.
   b. Target's management is less effective at controlling expenses than Walmart's management.
   c. Both companies' ratios suggest that their management teams are each likely to generate revenues with current assets.
   d. Target's management is doing poorly.
3. How does each company's management compare to the industry regarding the total asset turnover ratio?
   a. Target's and Walmart's managements are both more effective at utilizing assets to generate revenues than the average company in the industry.
   b. Target's management is less effective and Walmart's management is more effective at utilizing assets to generate revenues than the average company in the industry.
   c. Target's management is more effective and Walmart's management is less effective at generating sales and controlling costs with assets compared to the industry average.
   d. Target's management is weaker than Walmart's management because of its smaller size.
4. If both companies failed to record the adjusting entry for depreciation expense for the most recent year, what impact will that have on the total asset turnover ratio?
   a. There will be no effect on either company's total asset turnover ratio.
   b. Failure to record the adjusting entry for depreciation expense understates expenses, resulting in higher net income and a higher asset turnover ratio for the year.
   c. Failure to record depreciation expense overstates assets, resulting in a higher denominator and lower total asset turnover ratio for the year.
   d. Target's ratio will be closer to Walmart's ratio.
5. For each company, calculate the **percentage change** from fiscal year ended in 2020 to the fiscal year ended in 2021 for each of the following accounts (round your percentage to two decimal places):

Percentage Change in:	Target	Walmart
Total operating revenues		
Cost of sales		

   Which company's management was more effective at controlling costs between fiscal years ended 2020 and 2021? _____

Financial Reporting and Analysis Cases

Computing Amounts on Financial Statements and Finding Financial Information

CP4-4
LO4-1, 4-2

The following information was provided by the records of Dupont Circle Apartments (a corporation) at the end of the current annual fiscal period, December 31:

Rent

a. Rent revenue collected in cash during the current year for occupancy in the current year, $500,000.
b. Rent revenue earned for occupancy in December of the current year; not collected until the following year, $10,000.
c. In December of the current year, rent revenue collected in advance for January of the following year, $14,000.

Salaries

d. Cash payment in January of the current year to employees for work in December of the prior year (accrued in the prior year), $6,000.

e. Salaries incurred and paid during the current year, $70,000.

f. Salaries earned by employees during December of the current year that will be paid in January of the next year, $3,000.

g. Cash advances to employees in December of the current year for salaries that will be earned in January of the next year, $2,000.

Supplies

h. Maintenance supplies on January 1 of the current year (balance on hand), $7,000.

i. Maintenance supplies purchased for cash during the current year, $8,000.

j. Maintenance supplies counted on December 31 of the current year, $2,000.

Required:

For each of the following accounts, compute the balance to be reported in the current year, the statement the account will be reported on, and the effect (direction and amount) on cash flows (+ for increases cash and − for decreases cash). (**Hint:** Create T-accounts to determine balances.)

Account	Current Year Balance	Financial Statement	Effect on Cash Flows
1. Rent revenue			
2. Salary expense			
3. Maintenance supplies expense			
4. Rent receivable			
5. Receivables from employees			
6. Maintenance supplies			
7. Unearned rent revenue			
8. Salaries payable			

CP4-5 Using Financial Reports: Inferring Adjusting Entries and Information Used in Computations and Recording Closing Entries

LO4-1, 4-4

The pre-closing balances in the T-accounts of Chang Company at the end of the third year of operations follow. The current year's adjusting entries are identified by letters.

Cash

Bal. 25,000	

Note Payable (6% interest rate)

	Bal. 10,000

Common Stock (10,000 shares)

	Bal. 10,000

Maintenance Supplies

Bal. 800	(*a*) 500

Interest Payable

	(*b*) 600

Additional Paid-in Capital

	Bal. 40,000

Service Equipment

Bal. 90,000	

Income Taxes Payable

	(*f*) 13,020

Retained Earnings

	Bal. 12,000

Accumulated Depreciation

	Bal. 21,000
	(*d*) 9,000

Wages Payable

	(*e*) 400

Service Revenue

	Bal. 214,000
	(*c*) 10,000

Remaining Assets

Bal. 44,800	

Unearned Revenue

(*c*) 10,000	Bal. 13,600

Expenses

Bal. 160,000	
(*a*) 500	
(*b*) 600	
(*d*) 9,000	
(*e*) 400	
(*f*) 13,020	

Required:

1. Develop three trial balances for Chang Company using the following format:

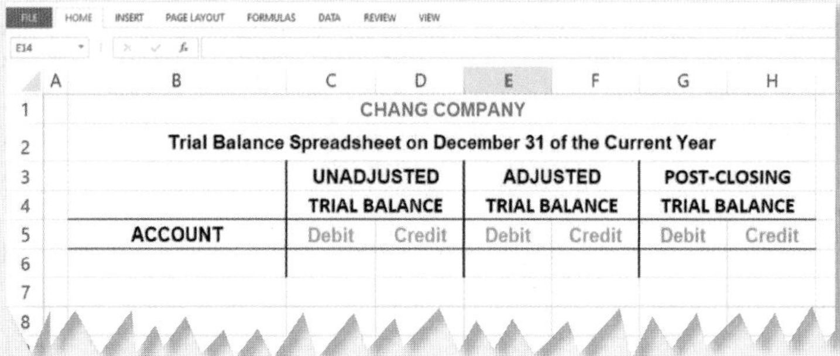

	UNADJUSTED TRIAL BALANCE		ADJUSTED TRIAL BALANCE		POST-CLOSING TRIAL BALANCE	
ACCOUNT	Debit	Credit	Debit	Credit	Debit	Credit

2. Write an explanation for each adjusting entry.
3. Record the closing journal entry at the end of the current year.
4. What was the average income tax rate for the current year?
5. What was the average issue (sale) price per share of the common stock?

Using Financial Reports: Analyzing the Effects of Adjustments

CP4-6
LO4-1, 4-2

Carey Land Company, a closely held corporation, invests in commercial rental properties. Carey's annual accounting period ends on December 31. At the end of each year, numerous adjusting entries must be made because many transactions completed during current and prior years have economic effects on the financial statements of the current and future years. Assume that the current year is 2024.

Required:

This case concerns four transactions that have been selected for your analysis. Answer the questions for each.

Transaction (*a*): On January 1, 2023, the company purchased office equipment costing $14,000 for use in the business. The company estimates that the equipment's cost should be allocated at $1,000 annually.

1. Over how many accounting periods will this transaction directly affect Carey's financial statements? Explain.
2. How much depreciation expense was reported on the 2023 and 2024 income statements?
3. How should the office equipment be reported on the December 31, 2025 balance sheet?
4. Would Carey make an adjusting entry at the end of each year during the life of the equipment? Explain your answer.

Transaction (*b*): On September 1, 2024, Carey collected $30,000 rent on office space. This amount represented the monthly rent in advance for the six-month period September 1, 2024, through February 28, 2025. Unearned Rent Revenue was increased (credited) and Cash was increased (debited) for $30,000.

1. Over how many accounting periods will this transaction affect Carey's financial statements? Explain.
2. How much rent revenue on this office space should Carey report on the 2024 income statement? Explain.
3. Did this transaction create a liability for Carey as of the end of 2024? Explain. If yes, how much?
4. Should Carey make an adjusting entry on December 31, 2025? Explain why. If your answer is yes, prepare the adjusting entry.

Transaction (*c*): On December 31, 2024, Carey owed employees unpaid and unrecorded wages of $7,500 because the employees worked the last three days in December 2024. The next payroll date is January 5, 2025.

1. Over how many accounting periods will this transaction affect Carey's financial statements? Explain.
2. How will this $7,500 affect Carey's 2024 income statement and balance sheet?
3. Should Carey make an adjusting entry on December 31, 2024? Explain why. If your answer is yes, prepare the adjusting entry.

Transaction (*d*): On January 1, 2024, Carey agreed to supervise the planning and subdivision of a large tract of land for a customer, J. Cirba. This service job that Carey will perform involves four separate phases. By December 31, 2024, three phases had been completed to Cirba's satisfaction. The remaining phase will be performed during 2025. The total price for the four phases (agreed on in advance by both parties) was $60,000. Each phase involves about the same amount of services. On December 31, 2024, Carey had collected no cash for the services already performed.

1. Should Carey record any service revenue on this job for 2024? Explain why. If yes, how much?
2. If your answer to part (1) is yes, should Carey make an adjusting entry on December 31, 2024? If yes, prepare the entry. Explain.
3. What entry will Carey make when it completes the last phase, assuming that the full contract price is collected on the completion date, February 15, 2025?

CP4-7 Using Financial Reports: Analyzing Financial Information in a Sale of a Business (Challenging)

LO4-1, 4-2

Lisa Knight owns and operates Lisa's Day Spa and Salon, Inc. She has decided to sell the business and retire, and is in discussions with Helen Bailey, the owner of a regional chain of day spas. The discussions are at the complex stage of agreeing on a price. Among the important factors have been the financial statements of the business. Lisa's secretary, Alisha, under Lisa's direction, maintained the records. Each year they developed a statement of profits on a cash basis; no balance sheet was prepared. Upon request, Lisa provided the Helen with the following statement for 2023 prepared by Alisha:

LISA'S DAY SPA AND SALON, INC.
Statement of Profits 2023

Spa fees collected		$1,215,000
Expenses paid:		
Rent for office space	$130,000	
Utilities expense	43,600	
Telephone expense	12,200	
Salaries expense	562,000	
Supplies expense	31,900	
Miscellaneous expenses	12,400	
Total expenses		792,100
Profit for the year		$ 422,900

Upon agreement of the parties, you have been asked to examine the financial figures for 2023. Helen said, "I question the figures because, among other things, they appear to be on a 100 percent cash basis." Your investigations revealed the following additional data at December 31, 2023:

a. Of the $1,215,000 in spa fees collected in 2023, $142,000 was for services performed prior to 2023.
b. At the end of 2023, spa fees of $29,000 for services performed during the year were uncollected.
c. Office equipment owned and used by Lisa cost $205,000. Depreciation was estimated at $20,500 annually.
d. A count of supplies at December 31, 2023, reflected $5,200 worth of items purchased during the year that were still on hand. Also, the records for 2022 indicated that the supplies on hand at the end of that year were $3,125.
e. At the end of 2023, the secretary whose salary is $24,000 per year had not been paid for December because of a long trip that extended to January 15, 2024.
f. The December 2023 telephone bill for $1,400 has not been recorded or paid. In addition, the $12,200 amount on the statement of profits includes payment of the December 2022 bill of $1,800 in January 2023.
g. The $130,000 office rent paid was for 13 months (it included the rent for January 2024).

Required:

1. On the basis of this information, prepare a corrected income statement for 2023 (ignore income taxes). Show your computations for any amounts changed from those in the statement prepared by Lisa's secretary. (**Suggestion:** Format solution with four column headings: Items; Cash Basis per Lisa's Statement, $; Explanation of Changes; and Corrected Basis, $.)
2. Write a memo to Lisa Knight and Helen Bailey to support your schedule prepared in requirement (1). The purpose should be to explain the reasons for your changes and to suggest other important items that should be considered in the pricing decision.

Critical Thinking Cases

Using Financial Reports: Evaluating Financial Information as a Bank Loan Officer

CP4-8
LO4-1, 4-2, 4-3

Zoltar Moving Co. has been in operation for over 30 years providing moving services for local households and businesses. It is now December 31, 2024, the end of the annual accounting period. Assume that the company has not done well financially during the year, although revenue has been fairly good. The two stockholders manage the company, but they have not given much attention to recordkeeping. In view of a serious cash shortage, they have applied to your bank for a $30,000 loan. You requested a complete set of financial statements. The following 2024 annual financial statements were prepared by a clerk and then were given to your bank.

ZOLTAR MOVING CO. **Balance Sheet** **At December 31, 2024**	
Assets	
Cash	$ 2,000
Receivables	3,000
Supplies	4,000
Equipment	40,000
Prepaid insurance	6,000
Remaining assets	27,000
Total assets	$82,000
Liabilities	
Accounts payable	$ 9,000
Stockholders' Equity	
Common stock (10,000 shares outstanding)	30,000
Retained earnings	43,000
Total liabilities and stockholders' equity	$82,000

ZOLTAR MOVING CO. **Income Statement** **For the Period Ended December 31, 2024**	
Transportation revenue	$85,000
Expenses:	
Salaries expense	17,000
Supplies expense	12,000
Other expenses	18,000
Total expenses	47,000
Net income	$38,000

After briefly reviewing the statements and "looking into the situation," you requested that the statements be redone (with some expert help) to "incorporate depreciation, accruals, inventory counts, income taxes, and so on." As a result of a review of the records and supporting documents, the following additional information was developed:

a. The Supplies of $4,000 shown on the balance sheet has not been adjusted for supplies used during 2024. A count of the supplies on hand on December 31, 2024, showed $1,800 worth of supplies remaining.
b. The insurance premium paid in 2024 was for years 2024 and 2025. The total insurance premium was debited in full to Prepaid Insurance when paid in 2024 and no adjustment has been made.
c. The equipment cost $40,000 when purchased January 1, 2024. It has an estimated annual depreciation of $8,000. No depreciation has been recorded for 2024.
d. Unpaid (and unrecorded) salaries at December 31, 2024, amounted to $3,200.
e. At December 31, 2024, transportation revenue collected in advance amounted to $7,000. This amount was credited in full to Transportation Revenue when the cash was collected earlier during 2024.
f. The income tax rate is 25 percent.

Required:

1. Record the six adjusting entries required on December 31, 2024, based on the preceding additional information.

2. Recast the preceding statements after taking into account the adjusting entries. You do not need to use classifications on the statements. Suggested form for the solution:

Items	Amounts Reported	CHANGES		Corrected Amounts
		Debit	Credit	
(List here each item from the two statements)				

3. Omission of the adjusting entries caused:
   a. Net income to be overstated or understated (select one) by $__________.
   b. Total assets on the balance sheet to be overstated or understated (select one) by $__________.
   c. Total liabilities on the balance sheet to be overstated or understated (select one) by $__________.
4. For both the unadjusted and adjusted balances, calculate these ratios for the company: (*a*) earnings per share (rounded to two decimal places) and (*b*) total asset turnover (rounded to three decimal places), assuming the correct amount of total assets at the beginning of the year was $46,400. There were 10,000 shares outstanding all year. Explain the causes of the differences and the impact of the changes on financial analysis.
5. Write a letter to the company explaining the results of the adjustments, your analysis, and your decision regarding the loan.

CP4-9 Evaluating the Effect of Adjusting Unearned Subscriptions on Cash Flows and Performance as a Manager

LO4-1

You are the regional sales manager for Jackie Branco News Company. Jackie is making adjusting entries for the year ended March 31, 2024. On September 1, 2023, customers in your region paid $36,000 cash for three-year magazine subscriptions beginning on that date. The magazines are published and mailed to customers monthly. These were the only subscription sales in your region during the year.

Required:

1. What amount should be reported as cash from operations on the statement of cash flows for the year ended March 31, 2024?
2. What amount should be reported on the income statement for subscriptions revenue for the year ended March 31, 2024.
3. What amount should be reported on the March 31, 2024, balance sheet for unearned subscriptions revenue?
4. Prepare the adjusting entry at March 31, 2024, assuming that the subscriptions received on September 1, 2023, were recorded for the full amount in Unearned Subscriptions Revenue.
5. The company expects your region's annual revenue target to be $9,000.
   a. Evaluate your region's performance, assuming that the revenue target is based on cash sales.
   b. Evaluate your region's performance, assuming that the revenue target is based on accrual accounting.

You As Analyst: Online Company Research

CP4-10 Analyzing Accruals, Earnings per Share, and Net Profit Margin of a Public Company (an Individual or Team Project)

LO4-1, LO4-2, LO4-3

In your web browser, search for the investor relations page of a public company you are interested in (e.g., Papa Johns investor relations). Select SEC Filings or Annual Report or Financials (whichever the website provides) to obtain the 10-K for the most recent year available.*

Required:

1. Go to the Income Statement (Statement of Income, Statement of Earnings, Statement of Operations). For the most recent year, what is the company's basic earnings per share for each of the three years reported?

2. Go to the Balance Sheet for the most recent year:
   a. List the accounts and amounts of accrued expenses payable on the most recent balance sheet. You may need to search the notes to the statements for detail.
   b. What is the ratio of the total accrued expenses payable to total liabilities?
3. Ratio Analysis:
   a. What does the total asset turnover ratio measure in general?
   b. Using *Item 6. Selected Financial Data* in the 10-K (or prior 10-K reports, if there is no Item 6 information), what is the company's total asset turnover ratio (rounded to three decimal places) for the last three years?
   c. What do your results suggest about the company? (You may refer to *Item 7. Management's Discussion and Analysis of Financial Condition and Results of Operations*. It provides information on why numbers changed.)

*Alternatively, you can go to sec.gov, click on Company Filings (under the search box), and type the name of the public company you want to find. Once at the list of filings, type 10-K in the Filing Type box. The most recent 10-K annual report will be at the top of the list. Click on Interactive Data for a list of the parts or the entire report to examine.

BUSINESS ANALYTICS AND DATA VISUALIZATION WITH EXCEL AND TABLEAU

Connect offers a variety of exercises to assess Excel skills, data visualization, interpretation, and analysis, including auto-graded Tableau Dashboard Activities, Applying Excel problems, and Integrated Excel problems.

Images used throughout chapter: Question of ethics: mushmello/Shutterstock; Pause for feedback: McGraw Hill; Guided help: McGraw Hill; Financial analysis: McGraw Hill; Focus on cash flows: Hilch/Shutterstock; Key ratio analysis: guillermain/123RF; Data analytics: Hilch/Shutterstock; Tip: McGraw Hill; ESG reporting: McGraw Hill; International perspective: Hilch/Shutterstock

chapter 5

Communicating and Analyzing Accounting Information

It is the rare person today who has not been affected by **Apple** products and services. From the first commercially viable personal computer, the Apple II introduced in 1977, to the raft of mobile communication and media devices, personal computers, software, and App Store content that we all use today, Apple has fundamentally changed the way we work, play, and interact. Apple Inc. the company is a far cry from the startup incorporated by Steve Jobs, Steve Wozniak, and a group of venture capitalists in 1977. Its 1977 sales of $1 million rose to $1 billion by 1982 and exceeded $274 billion in 2020. To accomplish this feat, Apple didn't just invent new products; it created whole new product categories such as the personal music player, the smartphone, and the tablet. And its laserlike focus on superior ease-of-use; seamless integration of hardware, software, and content; innovative design; and frequent updating make it very difficult for others to compete.

Apple's financial statements reflect its phenomenal sales and profit growth and convey this information to the stock market. Apple's stock price more than tripled over the last five years in response to news of its success.

Financial statement information will only affect a company's stock price if the market believes in the integrity of the financial communication process. As a publicly traded company, Apple Inc. is required to provide detailed information in regular filings with the Securities and Exchange Commission. As the certifying officers of the company, current President and CEO Timothy Cook and Senior Vice President and Chief Financial

LEARNING OBJECTIVES

After studying this chapter, you should be able to:

5-1 Recognize the people involved in the accounting communication process (regulators, managers, directors, auditors, information intermediaries, and users), their roles in the process, and the guidance they receive from legal and professional standards. p. 239

5-2 Identify the steps in the accounting communication process, including the issuance of press releases, annual reports, quarterly reports, and SEC filings, as well as the role of online information services in this process. p. 244

5-3 Recognize and apply the different financial statement and disclosure formats used by companies in practice and analyze the gross profit percentage. p. 247

5-4 Analyze a company's performance based on return on assets and its components and the effects of transactions on financial ratios. p. 257

grinvalds/iStock Editorial/Getty Images

Apple Inc.

COMMUNICATING FINANCIAL INFORMATION AND CORPORATE STRATEGY

apple.com

Officer Luca Maestri are responsible for the accuracy of the filings. The board of directors and auditors monitor the integrity of the system that produces the disclosures. Integrity in communication with investors and other users of financial statements is key to maintaining relationships with suppliers of capital.

UNDERSTANDING THE BUSINESS

Apple Inc.'s best-known products and services are the iPhone®, iPad®, Mac®, AirPods®, iCloud®, and the App Store®. The company sells its products and services worldwide through its own Apple Store retail and online stores, as well as through third-party cellphone companies such as **AT&T** and **Verizon** and retailers such as **Best Buy.** Components for its products are produced and final assembly is performed by outsourcing partners, primarily located in Asia. Apple invests considerable sums in research and development, marketing, and advertising and is known for introducing new and innovative products long before the end of existing products' life cycles.

Apple also invests in **corporate governance**: procedures designed to ensure that the company is managed in the interests of the shareholders. Much of its corporate governance system is aimed at ensuring integrity in the financial reporting process. Good corporate governance eases the company's access to capital, lowering both the costs of borrowing (interest rates) and the perceived riskiness of Apple's stock.

Apple knows that when investors lose faith in the truthfulness of a firm's accounting numbers, they also normally punish the company's stock. Disclosure of an accounting fraud causes, on average, a 20 percent drop in the price of a company's stock. The extreme accounting scandals at **Le-Nature's Inc.** (discussed in Chapter 1), **Enron**, and **WorldCom** caused their stock to become worthless. U.S. securities laws require that companies maintain and report that they have internal controls that ensure the accuracy of their financial reports.

A QUESTION OF ETHICS

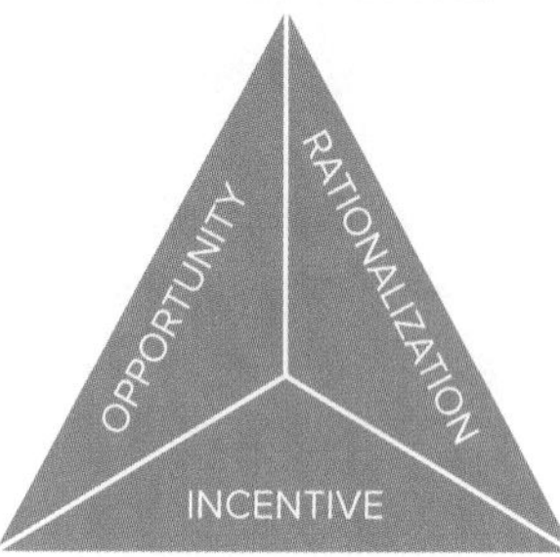

The Fraud Triangle

Three conditions are necessary for financial statement fraud to occur. There must be (1) an incentive to commit fraud, (2) the opportunity to commit fraud, and (3) the ability to rationalize the misdeed. These conditions make up what antifraud experts call the fraud triangle. A good system of corporate governance is designed to address these conditions. Clear lines of responsibility and sure and severe punishment counteract incentives to commit fraud. Strong internal controls and oversight by directors and auditors reduce opportunity to commit fraud. A strong code of ethics, ethical actions by those at the top of the organization, fair dealings with employees, and rewards for whistle-blowing make it more difficult for individuals to rationalize fraud. Financial statement users also have a role to play in preventing fraud. While even the savviest user can still be surprised by fraudulent reports in some cases, accounting knowledge and healthy skepticism are the best protection from such surprises.

Chapters 2 through 4 focused on the mechanics of preparing the income statement, balance sheet, statement of stockholders' equity, and cash flow statement. Based on your better understanding of financial statements, we will next take a closer look at the people involved and the regulations that govern the process that conveys accounting information to statement users in the Internet age. We also will take a more detailed look at statement formats and additional disclosures provided in financial reports to help you learn how to find relevant information. Finally, we will examine a general framework for assessing a company's business strategy and performance based on these reports.

ORGANIZATION OF THE CHAPTER

Players in the Accounting Communication Process

- Regulators (SEC, FASB, PCAOB, Stock Exchanges)
- Managers (CEO, CFO, and Accounting Staff)
- Boards of Directors (Audit Committee)
- Auditors
- Information Intermediaries: Information Services and Financial Analysts
- Users: Institutional and Private Investors, Creditors, and Others

The Disclosure Process

- Press Releases
- Annual Reports and Form 10-K
- Quarterly Reports and Form 10-Q
- Other SEC Reports

A Closer Look at Financial Statement Formats and Notes

- Classified Balance Sheet
- Classified Income Statement
- Gross Profit Percentage
- Statement of Stockholders' Equity
- Statement of Cash Flows
- Notes to Financial Statements
- Voluntary Disclosures

ROA Analysis: A Framework for Evaluating Company Performance

- Return on Assets (ROA)
- ROA Profit Driver Analysis and Business Strategy
- How Transactions Affect Ratios

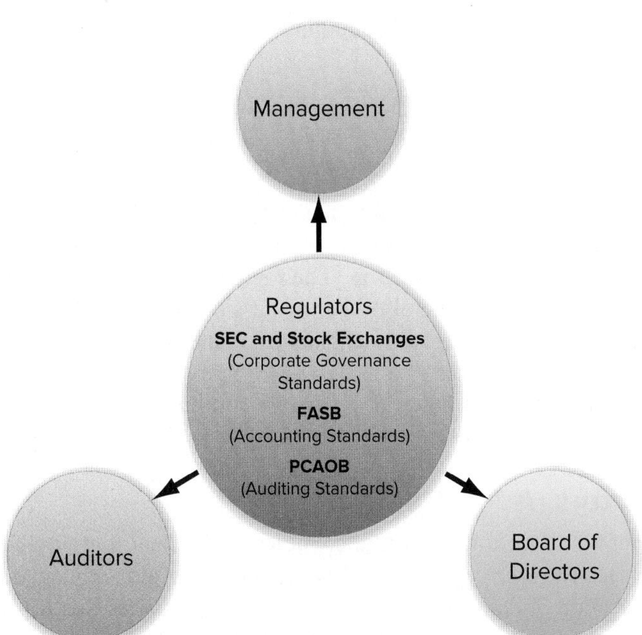

EXHIBIT 5.1

Ensuring the Integrity of Financial Information

PLAYERS IN THE ACCOUNTING COMMUNICATION PROCESS

LEARNING OBJECTIVE 5-1

Recognize the people involved in the accounting communication process (regulators, managers, directors, auditors, information intermediaries, and users), their roles in the process, and the guidance they receive from legal and professional standards.

Exhibit 5.1 summarizes the major actors involved and the regulations designed to ensure the integrity of the financial reporting process.

Regulators (SEC, FASB, PCAOB, Stock Exchanges)

The mission of the U.S. Securities and Exchange Commission (SEC) is to protect investors and maintain the integrity of the securities markets. As part of this mission, the SEC oversees the work of the Financial Accounting Standards Board (FASB), which sets generally accepted accounting principles (GAAP), and the Public Company Accounting Oversight Board (PCAOB), which sets auditing standards for independent auditors (CPAs) of public companies.

The SEC staff also reviews the reports filed with it for compliance with its standards, investigates irregularities, and punishes violators. During 2019 and 2020, the SEC brought 154 enforcement actions related to issuer financial reporting.[1] As a consequence, a number of company officers and auditors have been fined and lost their rights to appear before the SEC. In prior years, a number of high-profile company officers have been sentenced to jail for their actions. Consequences to the company can include large financial penalties as well as bankruptcy, as in the cases of **Le-Nature's**, **Enron**, and **WorldCom**. You can read about recent SEC enforcement actions at: sec.gov/divisions/enforce/friactions.shtml

Managers (CEO, CFO, and Accounting Staff)

The primary responsibility for the information in **Apple**'s financial statements and related disclosures lies with management, specifically the highest officer in the company, often called the **chief executive officer** (CEO), and the highest officer associated with the financial and accounting side of the business, often called the **chief financial officer** (CFO). At Apple and all public companies, these two officers must personally certify that

- Each report filed with the Securities and Exchange Commission does not contain any untrue material statement or omit a material fact and fairly presents in all material respects the financial condition, results of operations, and cash flows of the company.

[1]Source: sec.gov/files/enforcement-annual-report-2020.pdf.

Internal Control Alert

- There are no significant deficiencies and material weaknesses in the internal controls over financial reporting.
- They have disclosed to the auditors and audit committee of the board any weaknesses in internal controls or any fraud involving management or other employees who have a significant role in financial reporting.

An example of management's report on the financial statements and internal controls can be found in Appendix B. Executives who knowingly certify false financial reports are subject to a fine of $5 million and a 20-year prison term. The members of the **accounting staff,** who actually prepare the details of the reports, also bear professional responsibility for the accuracy of this information, although their legal responsibility is smaller. Their future professional success depends heavily on their reputation for honesty and competence. Accounting managers responsible for financial statements with material errors are routinely fined and fired and often have difficulty finding other employment.

Board of Directors (Audit Committee)

As **Apple**'s statement on corporate governance indicates, the **board of directors** (elected by the stockholders) oversees the chief executive officer and other senior management in the competent and ethical operation of Apple on a day-to-day basis and assures that the long-term interests of shareholders are being served. The **audit committee** of the board, which must be composed of nonmanagement (independent) directors with financial knowledge, is responsible for ensuring that processes are in place for maintaining the integrity of the company's accounting, financial statement preparation, and financial reporting. It is responsible for hiring the company's independent auditors. Members of the audit committee meet separately with the auditors to discuss management's compliance with their financial reporting responsibilities.

Auditors

The SEC requires publicly traded companies to have their **financial statements and related disclosures** and their **control systems over the financial reporting process** audited by an independent registered public accounting firm (independent auditor) following auditing standards established by the PCAOB. Many privately owned companies also have their statements audited. By signing an **unqualified (clean) audit opinion**, a CPA firm assumes part of the financial responsibility for the fairness of the financial statements and related presentations. This opinion, which adds credibility to the statements, also is often required by agreements with lenders and private investors. Subjecting the company's statements to independent verification reduces the risk that the company's financial condition is misrepresented in the statements. As a result, rational investors and lenders should lower the rate of return (interest) they charge for providing capital.

An example of an unqualified audit opinion is presented under Report of Independent Registered Public Accounting Firm in Appendix B of this text.

Ernst & Young (EY) is currently **Apple**'s auditor. Ernst & Young, **Deloitte, KPMG,** and **PricewaterhouseCoopers (PwC)** make up what are referred to as the "Big 4" CPA firms. Each of these firms employs thousands of CPAs in offices scattered throughout the world. They audit the great majority of publicly traded companies as well as many that are privately held. Some public companies and most private companies are audited by smaller CPA firms. A list of the auditors for selected focus companies follows.

sakkmesterke/123RF

Focus Company	Industry	Auditor
Starbucks	Coffee	Deloitte
Skechers	Footwear	BDO
Walt Disney	Entertainment	PricewaterhouseCoopers

DATA ANALYTICS

How Data Analytics Are Affecting What Auditors Do

Modern data analytics are changing the world of auditing. The availability of more data from clients' enterprisewide accounting systems, which combine the various record-keeping functions within an organization, has allowed access now to entire populations of transactions instead of smaller statistical samples as in the past. This eases identification of trends, patterns, and outliers, which become the focus for further investigation. For example, deliberate or unintentional mistakes in manual journal entries (such as the adjusting entries you learned about in Chapter 4) are often a source of financial statement error. Even for a large multinational client, auditors can now examine the whole population of manual entries to determine particular locations and types of transactions generating unexpected numbers of entries, which the auditor then examines further.

Data analytics also make it easier to correlate information from various parts of the clients' accounting systems such as sales invoices, shipping records, and cash receipts to identify areas where undetected misstatements may exist (audit risks). As companies digitize more data sources for their own decision making such as call center records, search tracking and shopping cart data, and social media feeds, this same information will help auditors better anticipate potential areas of high audit risk such as inventory obsolescence and warranty liabilities. The ability to understand client accounting systems and to apply predictive models and data visualization tools to data extracted from client systems is fast becoming a key part of the auditor's skill set.

Information Intermediaries: Information Services and Financial Analysts

Students sometimes view the communication process between companies and financial statement users as a simple process of mailing the report to individual shareholders who read the report and then make investment decisions based on what they have learned. This simple picture is far from today's reality. Now most investors rely on company websites, information services, and financial analysts to gather and analyze information.

Companies actually file their SEC forms electronically through the EDGAR (Electronic Data Gathering, Analysis, and Retrieval) Service, which is sponsored by the SEC. Each fact in the report is now tagged to identify its source and meaning using a language called **iXBRL.** Users can retrieve information from EDGAR within 24 hours of its submission, long before it is available through the mail. EDGAR is a free service available on the web under "Filings" at: sec.gov

Most companies also provide direct access to their financial statements and other information over the web. You can view this information for **Apple** at: investor.apple.com

Information services allow investors to gather their own information about the company and monitor the recommendations of a variety of analysts. Financial analysts and other sophisticated users obtain much of the information they use from the wide variety of commercial online information services. Fee-based services such as **S&P Global Market Intelligence** provide broad access to financial statements and news information. A growing number of other resources offering a mixture of free and fee-based information exist on the web. These include: finance.google.com, finance.yahoo.com, and marketwatch.com.

Exhibit 5.2 suggests the wide range of information about Apple available on the Yahoo! Finance website. It includes stock price and financial statement information, news accounts, and important future events related to Apple. To see what has happened to Apple since this chapter was written, go to finance.yahoo.com and search for AAPL to see how Apple has fared compared to its competitors.

Financial analysts receive accounting reports and other information about the company from online information services. They also gather information through conversations with company executives and visits to company facilities and competitors. The results of their analyses are combined into analysts' reports. Analysts' reports normally include forecasts of future quarterly and annual earnings per share and share price; a buy, hold, or sell recommendation for the

EXHIBIT 5.2

Yahoo! Finance Information about Apple

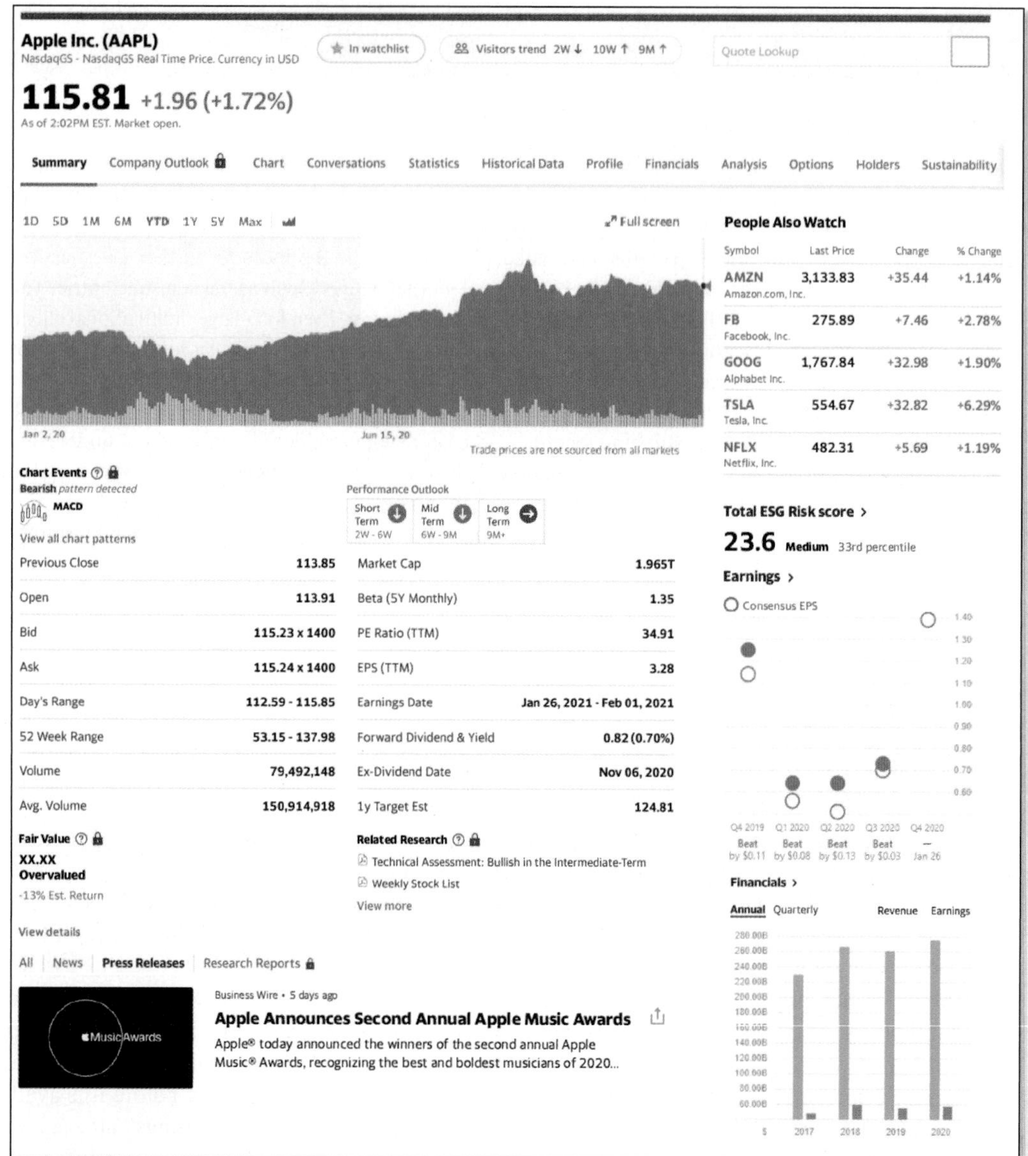

Source: Yahoo! Finance

company's shares; and explanations for these judgments. In making their **earnings forecasts**, the analysts rely heavily on their knowledge of the way the accounting system translates business events into the numbers on a company's financial statements, which is the subject matter of this text. Individual analysts often specialize in particular industries (such as sporting goods or energy companies). Analysts are regularly evaluated based on the accuracy of their forecasts, as well as the profitability of their stock picks. A sample of these forecasts and stock recommendations for Apple at the time this chapter was written follow:

Firm	Stock Recommendation	Earnings per Share Forecast for 2021	Earnings per Share Forecast for 2022
Credit Suisse	Neutral	3.72	4.13
Wells Fargo	Overweight	3.98	4.42
RBC Capital	Outperform	4.07	4.35
Deutsche Bank	Buy	4.01	4.42
Consensus of 38 analysts	Buy	3.94	4.28

Analysts often work in the research departments of brokerage and investment banking houses such as **Credit Suisse**, mutual fund companies such as **Fidelity Investments**, and investment advisory services such as **Value Line** that sell their advice to others. Through their reports and recommendations, analysts are transferring their knowledge of accounting, the company, and the industry to customers who lack this expertise.

FINANCIAL ANALYSIS

Information Services and Your Job Search

Information services have become the primary tool for professional analysts who use them to analyze competing firms. Information services are also an important source of information for job seekers. Potential employers expect job applicants to demonstrate knowledge of their companies during an interview, and online information services are an excellent source of company information. The best place to begin learning about potential employers is to visit their websites. Be sure to read the material in the employment section and the investor relations section of the site. To learn more about online information services, contact the business or reference librarian at your college or university or explore the websites discussed in this section.

Users: Institutional and Private Investors, Creditors, and Others

Institutional investors include pension funds (associated with companies, unions, or government agencies); mutual funds; and endowment, charitable foundation, and trust funds (such as the endowment of your college or university). These institutional stockholders usually employ their own analysts, who also rely on the information intermediaries just discussed. Institutional shareholders control the majority of publicly traded shares of U.S. companies. For example, at the time this chapter was written, institutional investors own 59 percent of **Apple** stock. Apple's three largest institutional investors follow:

Institution	Approximate Ownership
Vanguard Group Inc.	7.53%
Blackrock Inc.	6.29%
Berkshire Hathaway Inc.	5.55%

Most small investors own stock in companies such as Apple indirectly through mutual and pension funds.

Private investors include large individual investors such as the venture capitalists who originally invested directly in Apple, as well as small retail investors who buy shares of publicly traded companies through brokers such as **Fidelity.** Retail investors often lack the expertise to understand financial statements and the resources to gather data efficiently. They often rely on the advice of information intermediaries or turn their money over to the management of mutual and pension funds (institutional investors).

Lenders, or **creditors**, include suppliers, banks, commercial credit companies, and other financial institutions that lend money to companies. Lending officers and financial analysts in these organizations use the same public sources of information. They also use additional financial information (e.g., monthly statements) that companies often agree to provide as part of the lending contract. Lenders are the primary external user group for financial statements of private companies. Institutional and private investors also become creditors when they buy a company's publicly traded bonds.

Financial statements also play an important role in the relationships between suppliers and customers. Customers evaluate the financial health of suppliers to determine whether they will be reliable, up-to-date sources of supply. Suppliers evaluate their customers to estimate their future needs and ability to pay debts. Competitors also attempt to learn useful information about a company from its statements. The potential loss of competitive advantage is one of the costs of public financial disclosures. Small amounts do not have to be reported separately or accounted for precisely according to GAAP if they would not influence users' decisions. Accountants usually designate such items and amounts as **immaterial.** Determining material amounts is often very subjective.

PAUSE FOR FEEDBACK

In this section, we learned the roles of different parties in the accounting communication process and the guidance they receive from legal and professional standards. Management of the reporting company decides the appropriate format and level of detail to present in its financial reports. Independent audits increase the credibility of the information. Directors monitor managers' compliance with reporting standards and hire the auditor. The SEC staff reviews public financial reports for compliance with legal and professional standards and punishes violators. Financial statement announcements from public companies usually are first transmitted to users through online information services. Analysts play a major role in making financial statement and other information available to average investors through their stock recommendations and earnings forecasts. Before you move on, complete the following exercise to test your understanding of these concepts.

SELF-STUDY QUIZ

Match the key terms in the left column with their definitions in the right column.

1. Material amount
2. CEO and CFO
3. Financial analyst
4. Auditor
5. Institutional investors

a. Management primarily responsible for accounting information.
b. An independent party who verifies financial statements.
c. Amount large enough to influence users' decisions.
d. Managers of pension, mutual, endowment, and other funds who invest on the behalf of others.
e. An individual who analyzes financial information and provides advice.

After you have completed your answers, check them below.

Related Homework: M5-1, E5-1

LEARNING OBJECTIVE 5-2

Identify the steps in the accounting communication process, including the issuance of press releases, annual reports, quarterly reports, and SEC filings, as well as the role of online information services in this process.

THE DISCLOSURE PROCESS

As noted in our discussion of information services and information intermediaries, the accounting communication process includes more steps and participants than one might imagine. SEC regulation FD, for "Fair Disclosure," requires that companies provide all investors equal access to all important company news. Managers and other insiders also are prohibited from trading their company's shares based on nonpublic (insider) information so that no party benefits from early access.

Press Releases

To provide timely information to external users and to limit the possibility of selective leakage of information, **Apple** and other public companies announce quarterly and annual earnings through a press release as soon as the verified figures (audited for annual and reviewed for

Solution to SELF-STUDY QUIZ

1. *c;* 2. *a;* 3. *e;* 4. *b;* 5. *d.*

quarterly earnings) are available. Apple normally issues its earnings press releases within four weeks of the end of the accounting period. The announcements are sent electronically to the major print and electronic news services, including Dow Jones and Bloomberg, which make them immediately available to subscribers. Exhibit 5.3 shows an excerpt from a typical earnings press release for Apple that includes key financial figures. This excerpt is followed by management's discussion of the results and condensed income statements and balance sheets, which will be included in the formal report to shareholders, distributed after the press release.

EXHIBIT 5.3

Earnings Press Release Excerpt for Apple Inc.

APPLE

REAL WORLD EXCERPT:

Press Release

APPLE REPORTS FOURTH QUARTER RESULTS

Company revenue sets September quarter record, Services and Mac revenue reach new all-time high

Cupertino, California–October 29, 2020–Apple today announced financial results for its fiscal 2020 fourth quarter ended September 26, 2020. The Company posted record September quarter revenue of $64.7 billion and quarterly earnings per diluted share of $0.73. International sales accounted for 59 percent of the quarter's revenue.

. . .

"Our outstanding September quarter performance concludes a remarkable fiscal year, where we established new all-time records for revenue, earnings per share, and free cash flow, in spite of an extremely volatile and challenging macro environment," said Luca Maestri, Apple's CFO. "Our sales results and the unmatched loyalty of our customers drove our active installed base of devices to an all-time high in all of our major product categories. We also returned nearly $22 billion to shareholders during the quarter, as we maintain our target of reaching a net cash neutral position over time."

Source: Apple press release, October 29, 2020.

Many companies, including Apple, follow these press releases with a **conference call** during which senior managers answer analysts' questions about the quarterly results. These calls are open to the investing public. (Go to apple.com/investor/earnings-call/ to listen to Apple's most recent conference call.) Listening to these recordings is a good way to learn about a company's business strategy and its expectations for the future, as well as key factors that analysts consider when they evaluate a company.

Companies such as Apple also issue press releases concerning other important events such as new product announcements. Press releases related to annual earnings and quarterly earnings often precede the issuance of the quarterly or annual report by 15 to 45 days. This time is necessary to prepare the additional detail and to distribute those reports.

Annual Reports and Form 10-K

For privately held companies, **annual reports** are relatively simple documents. They normally include only the following:

1. Four basic financial statements: income statement, balance sheet, stockholders' equity or retained earnings statement, and cash flow statement.
2. Related notes (footnotes).
3. Report of Independent Accountants (Auditor's Opinion) if the statements are audited.

The annual reports of public companies filed on Form 10-K are significantly more elaborate mainly because of additional SEC reporting requirements. SEC reports are normally referred to by number (for example, the "10-K"). The principal components of the financial disclosures in the 10-K include:

Item 1. Business: Description of business operations and company strategy.

Item 7. Management's Discussion and Analysis of Financial Condition and Results of Operations: Management's views on the causes of its successes and failures during the reporting period and the risks it faces in the future.

Item 8. Financial Statements and Supplemental Data: The four basic financial statements and related notes, the report of management, and the auditor's report (Report of Independent Registered Public Accounting Firm).

Except for the Management's Discussion and Analysis (MD&A), most of these elements have been covered in earlier chapters. MD&A includes an explanation of key figures on the financial statements and the risks the company faces in the future. The Form 10-K also provides a more detailed description of the business, including its products, product development, sales and marketing, manufacturing, and competitors. It also lists properties owned or leased, any legal proceedings it is involved in, and significant contracts it has signed.

Quarterly Reports and Form 10-Q

Quarterly reports for private companies include condensed financial statements providing fewer details than annual statements and only key notes to the statements. They are not audited and so are marked **unaudited.** Private companies normally prepare quarterly reports for their lenders. Public companies file their quarterly reports on **Form 10-Q** with the SEC. The Form 10-Q contains most of the information items provided in the financial section of the 10-K and some additional items.

Other SEC Reports

Public companies must file other reports with the SEC. These include the current events report **Form 8-K**, which is used to disclose any material event not previously reported that is important to investors (e.g., auditor changes, mergers). Other filing requirements for public companies are described on the SEC website.

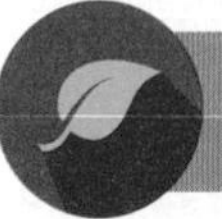

ENVIRONMENTAL, SOCIAL, & GOVERNANCE (ESG) REPORTING

Performance Beyond the Bottom Line

In the last decade, most large public companies have started to publish a report on the sustainability of their operations, often called a corporate social responsibility (CSR) or environmental, social, and governance (ESG) report. Why the big change? Managers today are increasingly aware that the way they did business in the past might not work tomorrow. ESG reports help investors assess the long-term consequences of the company's broader business strategy.

According to the Center for Audit Quality*:

- The E (for environmental) component of ESG information encompasses how a company manages risks and opportunities related to climate, pollution, waste, and other environmental factors.
- The S (for social) component of ESG includes labor and supply-chain standards, employee health and safety, product quality and safety, privacy and data security, and diversity and inclusion policies and efforts.
- The G (for governance) component of ESG incorporates information about a company's corporate governance including the board structure and diversity; executive compensation; and policies on lobbying, political contributions, and bribery and corruption.

These reports can range in coverage from a single paragraph dealing with key environmental impacts to Apple's reporting of its ESG Index which is 22 pages long. You can find the Apple ESG Index 2020 at: **investor.apple.com/esg/default.aspx**

*See Center for Audit Quality, *The Role of Auditors in Company Prepared ESG Information: Present and Future* (June 2020).

A CLOSER LOOK AT FINANCIAL STATEMENT FORMATS AND NOTES

LEARNING OBJECTIVE 5-3

Recognize and apply the different financial statement and disclosure formats used by companies in practice and analyze the gross profit percentage.

The financial statements shown in previous chapters provide a good introduction to their content and structure. In this section, we will discuss three additional characteristics of financial statements and the related disclosures that are designed to make them more useful to investors, creditors, and analysts:

- **Comparative financial statements.** To allow users to compare performance from period to period, companies report financial statement values for the current period and one or more prior periods. Apple and most U.S. companies present two years' balance sheets and three years' income statements, cash flow statements, and statements of stockholders' equity.
- **Additional subtotals and classifications in financial statements.** You should not be confused when you notice slightly different statement formats used by different companies. In this section, we will focus on similarities and differences in the classifications and line items presented on Apple's and Chipotle's balance sheet, income statement, and cash flow statement.
- **Additional disclosures.** Most companies present voluminous notes that are necessary to understand a company's performance and financial condition. In addition, certain complex transactions require additional statement disclosures. We take a closer look at some of Apple's note disclosures to prepare you for more detailed discussions in the remaining chapters in this text.

Classified Balance Sheet

Exhibit 5.4 shows the September 26, 2020, balance sheet for Apple. This balance sheet looks very similar in structure to the balance sheet for Chipotle presented in Chapter 4, but it is presented for two years as it is in Apple's annual report on Form 10-K. The statement classifications (current vs. noncurrent assets and current vs. noncurrent liabilities) play a major role in our discussion of ratio analysis (e.g., the current ratio in Chapter 2).

The specific accounts listed on a company's balance sheet will differ depending on the nature of the company's business. For example, nearly 65 percent of FedEx Corporation's assets are its property and equipment which include its owned and leased aircraft, handling equipment, and vehicles. Consequently, FedEx reports separately the cost of its land, buildings, and equipment on the face of the balance sheet, as well as the accumulated depreciation on the total property and equipment. On the other hand, property, plant, and equipment makes up less than 12 percent of Apple's assets, and Apple reports it on a single line. Companies also have the option to disaggregate balance sheet line items in the notes to the financial statements. We will illustrate that type of note later in the chapter.

When you first look at a new set of financial statements, try not to be confused by differences in terminology. When interpreting line items you have never seen before, be sure to consider their description **and their classification.**

Classified Income Statement

Apple's 2020 consolidated income statement is reprinted in Exhibit 5.5. It presents the income statement followed by earnings per share for three years, as required by the SEC. Apple's income statement includes one subtotal not included in Chipotle's. Like many manufacturing and merchandising (retail and wholesale) companies that sell goods, Apple reports the subtotal Gross Profit (also called Gross Margin), which is the difference between net sales and cost of goods sold (also called cost of sales). **It is important to note that regardless of whether a company reports a gross profit subtotal, the income statement presents the same information.** Apple also separately reports revenues and cost of sales for its sales of its products (iPhones, etc.) and its services (AppleCare, digital content, iCloud storage, etc.). This disaggregation

EXHIBIT 5.4 Balance Sheet of Apple Inc.

APPLE
REAL WORLD EXCERPT:
Annual Report

APPLE INC.
Consolidated Balance Sheets
(In millions, except number of shares which are reflected in thousands and par value)

		September 26, 2020	September 28, 2019
	ASSETS		
	Current assets:		
Assets that will be used or turned into cash within one year	Cash and cash equivalents	$ 39,789	$ 50,224
	Short-term marketable securities	52,927	51,713
	Accounts receivable, net	16,120	22,926
	Inventories	4,061	4,106
	Vendor non-trade receivables	21,325	22,878
	Other current assets	11,228	12,329
	Total current assets	145,450	164,176
	Non-current assets:		
Assets that will be used or turned into cash beyond one year	Long-term marketable securities	100,887	105,341
	Property, plant and equipment, net	36,766	37,378
	Other non-current assets	40,785	31,621
	Total non-current assets	178,438	174,340
	Total assets	$323,888	$338,516
	LIABILITIES AND SHAREHOLDERS' EQUITY		
	Current liabilities:		
Obligations that will be paid or settled within one year	Accounts payable	$ 42,296	$ 46,236
	Other current liabilities	42,684	37,720
	Deferred revenue	6,643	5,522
	Commercial paper	4,996	5,980
	Current portion of long-term debt	8,773	10,260
	Total current liabilities	105,392	105,718
	Non-current liabilities:		
Obligations that will be paid or settled after one year	Long-term debt	98,667	91,807
	Other non-current liabilities	54,490	50,503
	Total non-current liabilities	153,157	142,310
	Total liabilities	258,549	248,028
	Shareholders' equity:		
Capital contributed by shareholders	Common stock and additional paid-in capital, $0.00001 par value: 50,400,000 shares authorized; 16,976,763 and 17,772,945 shares issued and outstanding, respectively	50,779	45,174
Earnings reinvested in the company	Retained earnings	14,966	45,898
	Accumulated other comprehensive income/(loss)	(406)	(584)
	Total shareholders' equity	65,339	90,488
	Total liabilities and shareholders' equity	$323,888	$338,516

*Apple's statements have been simplified for purposes of our discussion.

Source: Apple Inc.

Balance Sheet of Apple Inc. **EXHIBIT 5.5**

APPLE
REAL WORLD EXCERPT:
Annual Report

APPLE INC.
Consolidated Statement of Operations
(In millions, except number of shares which are reflected in thousands and per share amounts)

	Years ended			
	September 26, 2020	**September 28, 2019**	**September 29, 2018**	
Net sales:				
Products	$220,747	$213,883	$225,847	
Services	53,768	46,291	39,748	
Total net sales	274,515	260,174	265,595	
Cost of sales:				
Products	151,286	144,996	148,164	
Services	18,273	16,786	15,592	*Operating activities (central focus of the business)*
Total cost of sales	169,559	161,782	163,756	
Gross margin	104,956	98,392	101,839	
Operating expenses:				
Research and development	18,752	16,217	14,236	
Selling, general and administrative	19,916	18,245	16,705	
Total operating expenses	38,668	34,462	30,941	
Operating income	66,288	63,930	70,898	
Other income/(expense), net	803	1,807	2,005	} *Other items (not the main focus of the business)*
Income before provision for income taxes	67,091	65,737	72,903	
Provision for income taxes	9,680	10,481	13,372	} *Income tax expense*
Net income	$ 57,411	$ 55,256	$ 59,531	
Earnings per share:				
Basic	$ 3.31	$ 2.99	$ 3.00	} *= Net Income/Weighted Average Number of Shares of Common Stock Outstanding*
Shares used in computing earnings per share:				
Basic	17,352,119	18,471,336	19,821,510	

*Apple's statements have been simplified for purposes of our discussion.

Source: Apple Inc.

highlights the growing role of services in Apple's sales portfolio. Another subtotal–**Operating Income** (also called Income from Operations)–is computed by subtracting operating expenses from gross profit.

Nonoperating (other) Items are revenues, expenses, gains, and losses that do not relate to the company's primary operations. Examples include interest income, interest expense, and gains and losses on the sale of investments. These nonoperating items are added to or subtracted from income from operations to obtain **Income before Income Taxes,** also called Pretax Earnings. At this point, Provision for Income Taxes (Income Tax Expense) is subtracted to obtain Net Income. Some companies show fewer subtotals on their income statements. No difference exists in the revenue, expense, gain, and loss items reported using the different formats. Only the categories and subtotals differ.

When a major component of a business is sold or abandoned, income or loss from that component earned before the disposal, as well as any gain or loss on disposal, is included as **Discontinued Operations.** The item is presented separately because it is not useful in predicting the future income of the company given its nonrecurring nature. If discontinued operations are reported, an additional subtotal is presented before this item for **Income from Continuing Operations**.

Finally, **Earnings per Share** is reported. Simple computations of earnings per share (EPS) are as follows:

$$\text{Earnings per Share*} = \frac{\text{Net Income}}{\text{Weighted Average Number of Shares of Common Stock Outstanding}}$$

*As you will learn in Chapter 11: (1) If there are preferred stock dividends, the amount is subtracted from net income in the numerator, (2) the denominator for weighted average shares is a complex computation, and (3) outstanding shares are those that are currently held by the shareholders.

FINANCIAL ANALYSIS

Statement of Comprehensive Income

Both the FASB and the IASB require an additional statement entitled the Statement of Comprehensive Income, which can be presented separately or in combination with the income statement. When presented separately, the statement starts with Net Income, the bottom line of the income statement. Following this total would be the components of other comprehensive income. The Net Income and Other Comprehensive Income items are then combined to create a total called Comprehensive Income (the bottom line for this statement). The following summarizes the information **Apple** presented in a recent quarterly report. Other Comprehensive Income items include fair value changes on certain marketable securities, which are discussed in Appendix A, as well as other items discussed in more advanced accounting classes.

APPLE INC.
Consolidated Statement of Comprehensive Income
Three months ended June 27, 2020

Net income	$11,253
Other comprehensive income/(loss):	
Change in foreign currency translation	194
Change in unrealized gains/losses on derivative instruments	(1,042)
Change in unrealized gains/losses on marketable debt securities	3,087
Total comprehensive income	$13,492

PAUSE FOR FEEDBACK

As **Apple**'s statements suggest, most statements are classified and include subtotals that are relevant to analysis. On the balance sheet, the most important distinctions are between current and noncurrent assets and liabilities. On the income statement, the subtotals gross profit and income from operations are most important. So the next step in preparing to analyze financial statements is to see if you understand the effects of transactions you already have studied on these subtotals. The following questions will test your ability to do so.

SELF-STUDY QUIZ

1. Complete the following tabulation, indicating the **direction** (+ for increase, − for decrease, and NE for no effect) **and amount** of the effect of each transaction. Consider each item independently. (**Hint:** Prepare journal entries for each transaction. Then consider the balance sheet or income statement classification of each account affected to come up with your answers.)

   a. Recorded and paid rent expense of $200.

   b. Recorded the sale of services on account for $400.

Transaction	Current Assets	Gross Profit	Income from Operations
a.			
b.			

Tip Even if companies use different subtotals, information services such as **Yahoo! Finance** put companies' statements into a standard format to allow for easier comparisons. Consequently, experienced analysts often rely on the services for financial statement data.

After you have completed your answers, check them at the bottom of this page.

GUIDED HELP 5-1 

For additional step-by-step video instruction on preparing the balance sheet and income statement from a trial balance, go to mhhe.com/libby_gh5-1.

Related Homework: M5-4, M5-5, E5-14, E5-15, P5-5, CON5-1

KEY RATIO ANALYSIS

Gross Profit Percentage

The key subtotals on the income statement we just discussed also play a major role in financial ratio analysis. As we noted above, net sales less cost of goods sold equals the subtotal **gross profit** or **gross margin.** Analysts often examine gross profit as a percentage of sales (the gross profit or gross margin percentage).

ANALYTICAL QUESTION

How effective is management in selling goods and services for more than the costs to purchase or produce them?

RATIO AND COMPARISONS

The gross profit percentage ratio is computed as follows:

$$\textbf{Gross Profit Percentage} = \frac{\textbf{Gross Profit*}}{\textbf{Net Sales}}$$

*Gross Profit = Net Sales − Cost of Sales

The ratio for 2020 for **Apple** is:

$$\frac{\$104{,}956}{\$274{,}515} = 0.382\ (38.2\%)$$

Comparisons Over Time		
Apple		
2018	2019	2020
38.3%	37.8%	38.2%

Comparison With Competitor
HP
2020
18.4%

Selected Focus Companies' Gross Profit Percentage Ratios

Apple	38.2%
Harley-Davidson	25.4%
Skechers	47.7%

INTERPRETATIONS

In General The gross profit percentage measures a company's ability to charge premium prices and produce goods and services at low cost. All other things equal, a higher gross profit results in higher net income.

Business strategy, as well as competition, affects the gross profit percentage. Companies pursuing a product-differentiation strategy use research and development and product promotion activities to convince customers of the superiority or distinctiveness of the company's products. This allows them to charge premium prices, producing a higher gross profit percentage. Companies following a low-cost strategy rely

Solution to SELF-STUDY QUIZ

1. *a.* Rent expense (+E, −SE) 200
   Cash (−A) 200
   −200, NE, −200

   b. Accounts receivable (+A) 400
   Sales revenue (+R, +SE) 400
   +400, +400, +400

on more efficient management of production to reduce costs and increase the gross profit percentage. Managers, analysts, and creditors use this ratio to assess the effectiveness of the company's product development, marketing, and production strategy.

Focus Company Analysis Apple's gross profit percentage has remained fairly steady over the past three years and remains well above that of its competitor, **HP**. At the beginning of the chapter, we discussed key elements of Apple's business strategy that focused on introducing new integrated technologies, product lines, and styles, as well as managing production and inventory costs. Each of these elements can have a large effect on gross profit. Its Form 10-K indicates that its various product lines have different gross profit percentages so that product mix can affect the overall gross profit percentage. Introducing new products with higher initial cost structures can decrease gross profit percentage.

A Few Cautions To assess the company's ability to sustain its gross profits, you must understand the sources of any change in the gross profit percentage. For example, an increase in margin resulting from increased sales of high-margin new products can be eroded by actions of competitors or increases in component costs for popular products. Also, higher prices must often be sustained with higher R&D and advertising costs, which reduce net income and can offset any increase in gross profit. This has not been the case for Apple in recent years as we will see later in the chapter. Apple's astonishing gross profit results in an industry-leading net profit margin and return on assets.

Statement of Stockholders' Equity

The statement of stockholders' (shareholders') equity reports the changes in each of the company's stockholders' equity accounts during the accounting period. Exhibit 5.6 presents **Apple**'s 2020 consolidated statement of stockholders' equity. The statement has a column for each stockholders' equity account and one for the effect on total stockholders' equity. (Apple combines the common stock account and additional paid-in capital accounts.) The first row of the statement starts with the beginning balances in each account, which correspond to the prior year's ending balances on the balance sheet. Each row that follows lists each event that occurred during the period that affected any stockholders' equity accounts. Apple reported net income of $57,411 for the year, which increases retained earnings. Apple declared dividends of $14,087, which is subtracted from retained earnings. Apple issued shares of common stock during the year. Apple also repurchased and retired shares. This topic is discussed in Chapter 11. The final row lists the ending balances in the accounts, which correspond to the ending balances on the balance sheet. Public companies must present information for the prior three years in their statements of stockholders' equity. So Apple's 2018 and 2019 statements would be presented above the information shown in Exhibit 5.6.

EXHIBIT 5.6 Statement of Stockholders' Equity of Apple Inc.

APPLE INC.
Consolidated Statements of Shareholders' Equity
(in millions)

	Common Stock and Additional Paid-In Capital	Retained Earnings	Accumulated Other Comprehensive Income/(Loss)	Total Shareholders' Equity
Balances as of September 28, 2019	$ 45,174	$ 45,898	$ (584)	$ 90,488
Net income	-	57,411	-	57,411
Other comprehensive income/(loss)	-	-	178	178
Dividends and dividend equivalents declared	-	(14,087)	-	(14,087)
Stock issued	5,605	-	-	5,605
Stock repurchased	-	(74,256)	-	(74,256)
Balances as of September 26, 2020	$50,779	$ 14,966	$ (406)	$65,339

*Apple's statements have been simplified for purposes of our discussion.

Source: Apple Inc.

Statement of Cash Flows

We introduced the three cash flow statement classifications in prior chapters:

Cash Flows from Operating Activities. This section reports cash flows associated with earning income (primarily related to dealings with customers, suppliers, interest, and earnings on investments).

Cash Flows from Investing Activities. Cash flows in this section are associated with the purchase and sale of (1) productive assets (other than inventory) and (2) investments in other companies.

Cash Flows from Financing Activities. These cash flows are related to financing the business through borrowing and repaying loans from financial institutions, stock (equity) issuances and repurchases, and dividend payments.

Exhibit 5.7 presents **Apple**'s 2020 consolidated statement of cash flows. The first section (Cash Flows from Operating Activities) can be reported using either the **direct** or **indirect** method. For Apple, this first section is reported using the indirect method, which presents a reconciliation of net income on an accrual basis to cash flows from operations.

The Operating Activities section prepared using the indirect method helps the analyst understand the **causes of differences** between a company's net income and its cash flows. Net income and cash flows from operating activities can be quite different. Remember that the income statement is prepared under the accrual concept. Revenues are recorded when earned without regard to when the related cash flows occur. Likewise, expenses are matched with revenues and recorded in the same period without regard to when the related cash flows occur.

In the indirect method, the Operating Activities section starts with net income computed under the accrual concept and then eliminates noncash items, leaving cash flow from operating activities:

Net income (loss)
+/−Adjustments for noncash items
Cash provided by operating activities

The items listed between these two amounts explain the reasons they differ. For example, because no cash is paid during the current period for Apple's depreciation expense reported on the income statement, this amount is added back to net income to eliminate its effect. Similarly, increases and decreases in certain assets and liabilities (called operating assets and liabilities) also account for some of the difference between net income and cash flow from operations. For example, sales on account increase net income as well as the current asset accounts receivable, but sales on account do not increase cash. As we cover different portions of the income statement and balance sheet in more detail in Chapters 6 through 11, we also will discuss the relevant sections of the cash flow statement. Then we discuss the complete cash flow statement in detail in Chapter 12.

Notes to Financial Statements

While the numbers reported on the various financial statements provide important information, users require additional details to facilitate their analysis. All financial reports include additional information in notes that follow the statements. **Apple**'s 2020 notes include three types of information:

1. Descriptions of the key accounting rules applied in the company's statements.
2. Additional detail supporting reported numbers.
3. Relevant financial information not disclosed on the statements.

EXHIBIT 5.7 Cash Flow Statement of Apple Inc.

APPLE
REAL WORLD EXCERPT:
Annual Report

APPLE INC.
Consolidated Statements of Cash Flows
(in millions)

	Years ended September 26, 2020	September 28, 2019	September 29, 2018
Cash and cash equivalents, beginning balances	$ 50,224	$ 25,913	$ 20,289
Operating activities:			
Net income	57,411	55,256	59,531
Adjustments to reconcile net income to cash generated by operating activities:			
Depreciation and amortization	11,056	12,547	10,903
Other noncash items	6,517	5,076	(27,694)
Changes in operating assets and liabilities:	5,690	(3,488)	34,694
Cash generated by operating activities	80,674	69,391	77,434
Investing activities:			
Purchases of marketable securities	(114,938)	(39,630)	(71,356)
Proceeds from maturities of marketable securities	69,918	40,102	55,881
Proceeds from sales of marketable securities	50,473	56,988	47,838
Payments for acquisition of property, plant, and equipment	(7,309)	(10,495)	(13,313)
Payments made in connection with business acquisitions, net	(1,524)	(624)	(721)
Purchases of non-marketable securities	(210)	(1,001)	(1,871)
Proceeds from non-marketable securities	92	1,634	353
Other	(791)	(1,078)	(745)
Cash generated by/(used in) investing activities	(4,289)	45,896	16,066
Financing activities:			
Proceeds from issuance of common stock	880	781	669
Proceeds from issuance of term debt, net	16,091	6,963	6,969
Repayments of term debt	(12,629)	(8,805)	(6,500)
Payments for dividends	(14,081)	(14,119)	(13,712)
Repurchases of common stock	(72,358)	(66,897)	(72,738)
Other financing activities	(4,723)	(8,899)	(2,564)
Cash used in financing activities	(86,820)	(90,976)	(87,876)
Increase/(Decrease) in cash and cash equivalents	(10,435)	24,311	5,624
Cash and cash equivalents, ending balances	$ 39,789	$ 50,224	$ 25,913
Supplemental cash flow disclosure:			
Cash paid for income taxes, net	$ 9,501	$ 15,263	$ 10,417
Cash paid for interest	$ 3,002	$ 3,423	$ 3,022

*Apple's statements have been simplified for purposes of our discussion.

Cash flows associated with earning income computed by eliminating noncash items from net income

Cash flows associated with purchase and sale of productive assets and investments

Cash flows associated with borrowing and repaying loans, issuing and repurchasing stock, and paying dividends

Total change in cash

End of year cash on balance sheet

Source: Apple Inc.

Accounting Rules Applied in the Company's Statements

One of the first notes is typically a summary of significant accounting policies. As you will see in your study of subsequent chapters, generally accepted accounting principles (GAAP) permit companies to select from alternative methods for measuring the effects of transactions.

The summary of significant accounting policies tells the user which accounting methods the company has adopted. Apple's accounting policy for property, plant, and equipment is as follows:

NOTE 1 – SUMMARY OF SIGNIFICANT ACCOUNTING POLICIES

Property, Plant, and Equipment

Depreciation on property, plant, and equipment is recognized on a straight-line basis over the estimated useful lives of the assets, which for buildings is the lesser of 40 years or the remaining life of the building; between one and five years for machinery and equipment, including product tooling and manufacturing process equipment; and the shorter of lease term or useful life for leasehold improvements. Capitalized costs related to internal-use software are amortized on a straight-line basis over the estimated useful lives of the assets, which range from three to seven years.

APPLE
REAL WORLD EXCERPT:
Annual Report

We will discuss alternative depreciation methods in Chapter 8. Without an understanding of the various accounting methods used, it is impossible to analyze a company's financial results effectively.

Additional Detail Supporting Reported Numbers

The second category of notes provides supplemental information concerning the data shown on the financial statements. Among other information, these notes may show revenues broken out by geographic region or business segment, describe unusual transactions, and/or offer expanded detail on a specific classification. For example, in Note 4, Apple indicates the makeup of property, plant, and equipment presented on the balance sheet.

NOTE 4 – CONSOLIDATED FINANCIAL STATEMENT DETAILS

Property, Plant, and Equipment, Net

	2020	2019
Land and buildings	$ 17,952	$ 17,085
Machinery, equipment, and internal-use software	75,291	69,797
Leasehold improvements	10,283	9,075
Gross property, plant, and equipment	103,526	95,957
Accumulated depreciation and amortization	(66,760)	(58,579)
Total property, plant, and equipment, net	$ 36,766	$ 37,378

APPLE
REAL WORLD EXCERPT:
Annual Report

Relevant Financial Information Not Disclosed on the Statements

The final category includes information that impacts the company financially but is not shown on the statements. Examples include information on legal matters and contractual agreements that do not result in an asset or liability on the balance sheet. In Note 10, Apple disclosed the details of its commitments under supply agreements, which total over $8 billion and are not shown as a liability on the balance sheet.

APPLE
REAL WORLD EXCERPT:
Annual Report

NOTE 10 – COMMITMENTS AND CONTINGENCIES

Unconditional Purchase Obligations

The Company has entered into certain off-balance sheet commitments that require the future purchase of goods or services ("unconditional purchase obligations"). The Company's unconditional purchase obligations primarily consist of payments for supplier arrangements, Internet and telecommunication services, intellectual property licenses, and content creation. Future payments under noncancelable unconditional purchase obligations having a remaining term in excess of one year as of September 26, 2020, are as follows (in millions):

2021	$ 3,476
2022	2,885
2023	1,700
2024	357
2025	104
Thereafter	130
Total	$ 8,652

Voluntary Disclosures

GAAP and SEC regulations set only the minimum level of required financial disclosures. Many companies provide important disclosures beyond those required. For example, in its annual report, 10-K, and recent earnings press release, **Apple** discloses sales by major product category, which helps investors track the success of new products.

APPLE
REAL WORLD EXCERPT:
Annual Report

Net sales by product for 2020, 2019, and 2018 were as follows (in millions):

Net sales by product:	2020	2019	2018
iPhone	$137,781	$142,381	$164,888
Mac	28,622	25,740	25,198
iPad	23,724	21,280	18,380
Wearables, Home, and Accessories	30,620	24,482	17,381
Services	53,768	46,291	39,748
Total net sales	$274,515	$260,174	$265,595

INTERNATIONAL PERSPECTIVE

Differences in Accounting Methods Acceptable under IFRS and U.S. GAAP

Financial accounting standards and disclosure requirements are adopted by national regulatory agencies. Many countries, including the members of the European Union, have adopted International Financial Reporting Standards (IFRS) issued by the International Accounting Standards Board (IASB). IFRS are similar to U.S. GAAP, but there are several important differences. A partial list of the differences at the time this chapter was written is presented below, along with the chapter in which these issues will be addressed:

Difference	U.S. GAAP	IFRS	Chapter
Last-in first-out (LIFO) method for inventory	Permitted	Prohibited	7
Reversal of inventory write-downs	Prohibited	Required	7
Basis for property, plant, and equipment	Historical cost	Fair value or historical cost	8
Development costs	Expensed	Capitalized	8
Debt to be refinanced	Current	Noncurrent	9
Recognition of contingent liabilities	Probable	More likely than not	9
Stockholders' equity accounts	Common stock	Share capital	11
	Paid-in capital	Share premium	
Interest received on cash flow statement	Operating	Operating or investing	12
Interest paid on cash flow statement	Operating	Operating or financing	12

The FASB and IASB are working together to eliminate some of these differences.

RETURN ON ASSETS ANALYSIS: A FRAMEWORK FOR EVALUATING COMPANY PERFORMANCE

LEARNING OBJECTIVE 5-4

Analyze a company's performance based on return on assets and its components and the effects of transactions on financial ratios.

Evaluating company performance is the primary goal of financial statement analysis. Company managers, as well as competitors, use financial statements to better understand and evaluate a company's business strategy. Analysts, investors, and creditors use these same statements to judge company performance when they estimate the value of the company's stock and its creditworthiness. Our discussion of the financial data contained in accounting reports has now reached the point where we can develop an overall framework for using those data to evaluate company performance. The most general framework for evaluating company performance is called return on assets (ROA) analysis.

KEY RATIO ANALYSIS

Return on Assets (ROA)

ANALYTICAL QUESTION

During the period, how well has management used the company's total investment in assets financed by both debt holders and stockholders?

RATIO AND COMPARISONS

$$\textbf{Return on Assets} = \frac{\textbf{Net Income*}}{\textbf{Average Total Assets}^{\dagger}}$$

*In more complex return on assets analyses, interest expense (net of tax) and noncontrolling interest are added back to net income in the numerator of the ratio because the measure assesses return on capital independent of its source.

†Average Total Assets = (Beginning Total Assets + Ending Total Assets) ÷ 2.

The 2020 ratio for **Apple:**

$$\frac{\$57{,}411}{(\$323{,}888 + 338{,}516)/2} = 0.173\ (17.3\%)$$

Comparisons Over Time		
Apple		
2018	2019	2020
16.1%	15.7%	17.3%

Comparison With Competitor
HP
2020
8.3%

Selected Focus Companies' Return on Assets Ratios

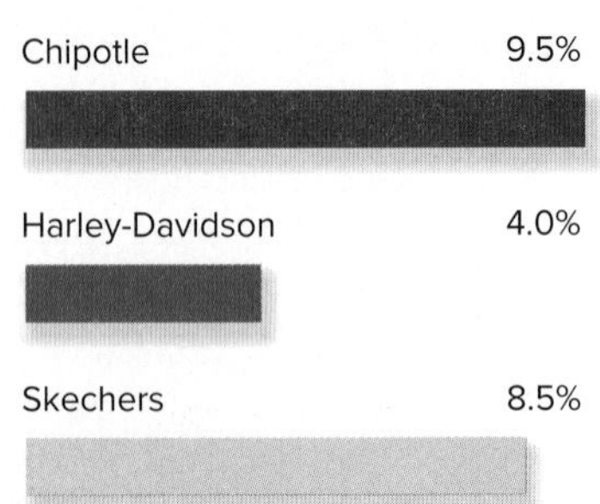

INTERPRETATIONS

In General ROA measures how much the firm earned for each dollar of investment in assets. It is the broadest measure of profitability and management effectiveness, independent of financing strategy. Firms with higher ROA are doing a better job of selecting and managing investments, all other things equal. Because it is independent of the source of financing (debt vs. equity), it can be used to evaluate performance at any level within the organization. It is often computed on a division-by-division or product line basis and used to evaluate division or product line managers' relative performance.

Focus Company Analysis After a relatively consistent return on assets in 2018 and 2019, the increase in Apple's return on assets in 2020 was mainly due to a decrease in average assets accompanied by consistent net income. Specifically, marketable securities have decreased dramatically over the last three years. Apple has issued dividends and continued a stock buyback program to return the excess assets to shareholders.

A Few Cautions Like all ratios, the key to interpreting change is to dig deeper to understand the reason for each change. Our next topic, ROA Profit Driver Analysis and Business Strategy, is aimed at doing just that.

ROA Profit Driver Analysis and Business Strategy

Effective analysis of **Apple**'s performance also requires understanding **why** its ROA differs both from prior levels and from those of its competitors. ROA profit driver analysis (also called **ROA decomposition** or **DuPont analysis**) breaks down ROA into the two factors shown in Exhibit 5.8. These factors are often called **profit drivers** or **profit levers** because they describe the two ways that management can improve ROA. They are measured by the key ratios you learned in Chapters 3 and 4.

1. **Net profit margin = Net Income ÷ Net Sales***. It measures how much of every sales dollar is profit. It can be increased by
   a. Increasing sales volume.
   b. Increasing sales price.
   c. Decreasing cost of goods sold and operating expenses.
2. **Total asset turnover = Net Sales* ÷ Average Total Assets.** It measures how many sales dollars the company generates with each dollar of assets (efficiency of use of assets). It can be increased by
   a. Centralizing distribution to reduce inventory kept on hand.
   b. Consolidating production facilities in fewer factories to reduce the amount of assets necessary to generate each dollar of sales.
   c. Increasing sales volume or sales price without a proportionate increase in inventories kept on hand or production facilities.

EXHIBIT 5.8

ROA Profit Driver Analysis

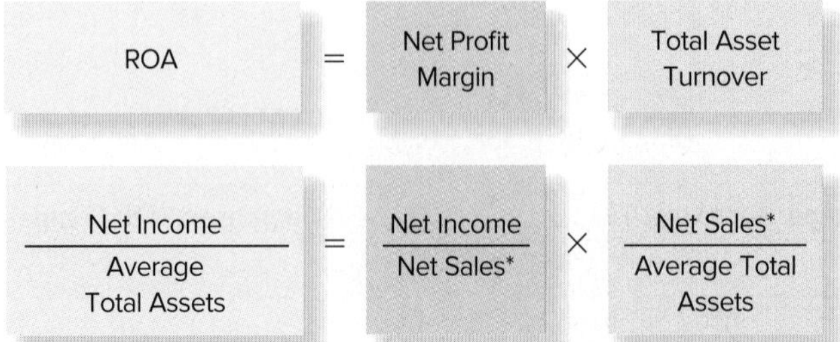

*or Operating Revenues.

These two ratios report on the effectiveness of the company's operating and investing activities, respectively.

Successful manufacturers often follow one of two business strategies. The first is a **high-value** or **product-differentiation** strategy. Companies following this strategy rely on research and development and product promotion to convince customers of the superiority or distinctiveness of their products. This allows the company to charge higher prices and earn a higher net profit margin. The second is a **low-cost strategy,** which relies on efficient management of accounts receivable, inventory, and productive assets to produce high asset turnover.

The ROA profit driver analysis presented in Exhibit 5.9 indicates the sources of Apple's ROA and compares them to the same figures for **HP. Apple** follows a classic **high-value strategy,** developing a reputation for the most innovative products in its markets. The success of this strategy is evident in its market-leading **net profit margin** of 0.209 or **20.9**%. This means that 20.9 cents of every sales dollar is net profit. This compares with HP's 5.0% net profit margin.

HP primarily follows a **low-cost strategy** by offering excellent products and service at competitive prices. The efficiency of HP's operations is evident in its higher **total asset turnover** of **1.662** compared to Apple's 0.829. Apple has produced a much higher ROA than HP because its phenomenal net profit margin more than offsets its lower total asset turnover, and its stock price has responded accordingly.

If Apple follows the same strategy it has in the past, the secret to maintaining its ROA must be continued product development to support premium selling prices. In 2020, Apple made major strides in new product development and the success of its new product introductions bodes well for a high ROA in the longer term. As the preceding discussion indicates, a company can take many different actions to try to affect its profit drivers. To understand the impact of these actions, financial analysts disaggregate each of the profit drivers into more detailed ratios. For example, the total asset turnover ratio is further disaggregated into turnover ratios for specific assets such as accounts receivable, inventory, and fixed assets. We will develop our understanding of these more specific ratios in the next seven chapters of the book. Then, in Chapter 13, we will combine the ratios in a comprehensive review.

How Transactions Affect Ratios

Apple and other companies know that investors and creditors follow their key financial ratios closely. Changes in ROA and its components can have a major effect on a company's stock price and interest rates that lenders charge. As a consequence, company managers closely follow the effects of their actual and planned transactions on these same key financial ratios. We already have learned how to determine the effects of transactions on key subtotals on the income statement and balance sheet (gross profit, current assets, etc.). So we are only one step away from being able to compute the effects of transactions on ratios. The following three-step process will help you do so:

Tip Determining the effects of transactions on a financial ratio requires that you separately determine the effects on the numerator and denominator. When only one of the two is affected, the answer is simple. When both are affected, the effect will depend on whether they are affected by the same or different amounts.

1. **Journalize the transaction to determine its effects on various accounts,** just as we did in Chapters 2 through 4.
2. **Determine which accounts belong to the financial statement subtotals or totals in the numerator (top) and denominator (bottom) of the ratio and the direction of their effects.**
3. **Evaluate the combined effects from step 2 on the ratio.**

Let's try a few examples to get a feel for the process. What would be the effect of the following transactions on the ratios indicated (ignoring taxes)? The examples we will consider illustrate that the effect depends on what part of the ratio, numerator (top) and/or denominator (bottom), is affected. We need to consider three cases.

EXHIBIT 5.9

Apple vs. HP ROA Profit Driver Analysis

ROA Profit Drivers	Formulas	Apple	HP
Net Profit Margin	Net Income/Net Sales*	0.209	0.050
× Total Asset Turnover	× Net Sales*/Average Total Assets	0.829	1.662
= Return on Assets	= Net Income/Average Total Assets	0.173	0.083

* or Operating Revenues.

What if only the numerator or denominator is affected?

Example 1: Assume Apple incurred an additional $1,000 in research and development expense paid for in cash (all numbers in millions). What would be the effect on the **net profit margin** ratio? The entry would be:

	Debit	Credit
Research and development expense (+E, −SE)	1,000	
Cash (−A)		1,000

Note that the transaction would decrease the numerator Net Income and have no effect on the denominator Net Sales. The ratio was 0.209 (using numbers from Exhibit 5.5). It would decrease to 0.205 as follows.

	Net Income	÷	Net Sales	=	Net Profit Margin
As reported:	$57,411		$274,515		0.209
Transaction effect:	(1,000)		–		
After transaction:	$56,411		$274,515		0.205

This example illustrates a general point about the effect of transactions on ratios. If a transaction **only** affects the numerator **or** denominator of the ratio, it will have the following effects on the ratio:

Ratio Changes Given Changes in Numerator *or* Denominator	
Numerator	**Ratio**
Increases	Increases
Decreases	Decreases
Denominator	
Increases	Decreases
Decreases	Increases

What if both the numerator and denominator are affected but by different amounts?

Example 2: Consider the same transaction as in Example 1. What would be the effect on the **return on assets** ratio? Note that the transaction would decrease the numerator Net Income by $1,000. It also would **decrease the ending** total assets by $1,000 but have **no effect on beginning** total assets. So the denominator, **average** total assets, would decrease by only $500:

$$\text{Avg. Total Assets} = (\$323{,}888 + \$338{,}516 - \$1{,}000)/2 = \$330{,}702$$

The ratio was 0.173 in Exhibit 5.9. It would decrease as follows:

	Net Income	÷	Avg. Total Assets	=	Return on Assets
As reported:	$ 57,411		$331,202		0.173
Transaction effect:	(1,000)		(500)		
After transaction:	$ 56,411		$330,702		0.171

This example illustrates a second general point about the effect of transactions on ratios. If a transaction affects the numerator by more than it affects the denominator, or if it affects the denominator by more than it affects the numerator, you must compute the effect with the numbers given.

What if the numerator and denominator are affected by the same amount?

Example 3: Assume Apple paid $4,000 of accounts payable in cash (all numbers in millions). What would be the effect on the **current ratio?** The entry would be

	Debit	Credit
Accounts payable (−L)	4,000	
Cash (−A)		4,000

Note that the transaction would decrease the numerator, Current Assets, and the denominator, Current Liabilities, by the same amount. The ratio was 1.38 (using numbers from Exhibit 5.4). It would increase as follows.

	Current Assets	÷	Current Liabilities	=	Current Ratio
As reported:	$145,450		$105,392		1.38
Transaction effect:	(4,000)		(4,000)		
After transaction:	$141,450		$101,392		1.40

This example illustrates a third general point about the effect of transactions on ratios. **If a transaction affects the numerator and denominator of the ratio by the same amount, the effect will depend on whether the original ratio value was greater or less than 1.00:**

Ratio Changes Given *Same* Change in Numerator *and* Denominator		
Numerator and Denominator	**Ratio < 1**	**Ratio > 1**
Increase both	Increases	Decreases
Decrease both	Decreases	Increases

PAUSE FOR FEEDBACK

ROA measures how well management used the company's invested capital during the period. Its two determinants, net profit margin and asset turnover, indicate why ROA differs from prior levels or the ROAs of competitors. They also suggest strategies to improve ROA in future periods. The effect of an individual transaction on a financial ratio depends on its effects on both the numerator and denominator of the ratio.

SELF-STUDY QUIZ

1. We used profit driver analysis in Exhibit 5.9 to explain why a company has an ROA different from its competitors at a single point in time. This type of analysis is called **cross-sectional analysis.** Profit driver analysis also can be used to explain how changes in net profit margin (Net Income/Net Sales) and total asset turnover (Net Sales/Average Total Assets) changed **Apple**'s ROA over time. This type of analysis often is called **time-series analysis.** Following is the recent year's ROA analysis for Apple Inc. Using profit driver analysis, explain why Apple's ROA has increased.

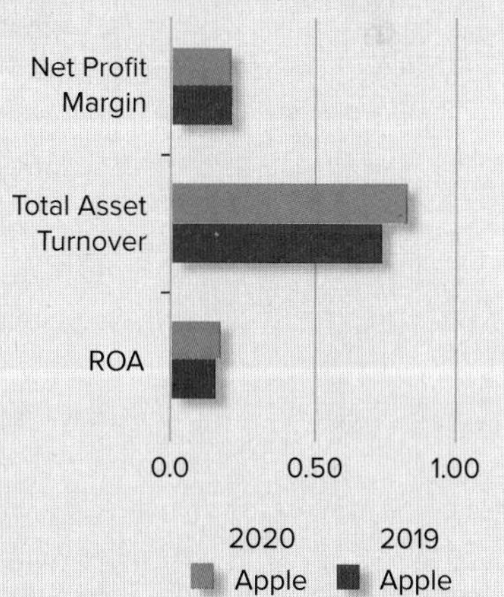

ROA Profit Drivers	2020	2019
Net Income/Net Sales	0.209	0.212
× Net Sales/Average Total Assets	0.829	0.739
= Net Income/Average Total Assets	0.173	0.157

2. What would be the **direction** of the effect of the following transactions on the following ratios (+ for increase, − for decrease, and NE for no effect)? Consider each item independently.

   a. Recorded and paid rent expense of $200.
   b. Recorded the sale of services on account for $400.

Transaction	Gross Profit Percentage	Return on Assets	Current Ratio
a.			
b.			

After you have completed your answers, check them at the bottom of the next page.

GUIDED HELP 5-2

For additional step-by-step video instruction on conducting ROA profit driver analysis, go to mhhe.com/libby_gh5-2

Related homework: M5-7; E5-17, E5-18, E5-19, P5-6

DEMONSTRATION CASE

(Complete the following requirements before proceeding to the suggested solution.) **Microsoft Corporation** is the developer of a broad line of computer software, including the Windows operating systems and Word (word processing) and Excel (spreadsheet) applications. Following is a list of the financial statement items and amounts adapted from a recent Microsoft income statement and balance sheet. These items have normal debit and credit balances and are reported in millions of dollars. For that year, 7,568 million (weighted average) shares of stock were outstanding. The company closed its books on June 30, 2020.

Accounts payable	$ 12,530	Other current liabilities	$ 13,776
Accounts receivable (net)	32,011	Other income (expense), net	77
Accrued compensation	7,874	Other investments	2,965
Cash and short-term investments	136,527	Other noncurrent assets	72,280
Common stock and paid-in capital	80,552	Property, plant, and equipment (net)	$ 44,151
Cost of goods sold	46,078	Provision for income taxes	8,755
General and administrative	5,111	Research and development	19,269
Income taxes payable	2,130	Retained earnings	37,752
Long-term liabilities	110,697	Sales and marketing	19,598
Net revenue	143,015	Unearned revenue	36,000
Other current assets	13,377		

Required:

1. Prepare in good form a classified (multiple-step) income statement (showing gross profit, operating income, income before income taxes, net income, and earnings per share) and a classified balance sheet for the year.
2. Compute the company's ROA. Briefly explain its meaning using ROA profit driver analysis. (Microsoft's total assets at the beginning of the year were $286,556 million.)
3. If Microsoft had an additional $1,500 in general and administrative expenses (paid for in cash), what would be the effect on its ROA (increase, decrease, or no effect)?

Solution to SELF-STUDY QUIZ

1. Apple's 1.6 percent increase (17.3% − 15.7%) in ROA resulted from an increase in its total asset turnover. The balance sheet presented in Exhibit 5.4 indicates that much of this increase in asset turnover resulted from the decrease in cash and accounts receivable.
2. *a.* Rent expense (+E, −SE) 200
   Cash (−A) 200
   NE, −, −,

   b. Accounts receivable (+A) 400
   Sales revenue (+R, +SE) 400
   +, +, +

SUGGESTED SOLUTION

1.

MICROSOFT CORPORATION
Income Statements
(In millions, except per share amounts)

Year Ended June 30, 2020	
Net revenue	$143,015
Cost of goods sold	46,078
Gross profit	96,937
Research and development	19,269
Sales and marketing	19,598
General and administrative	5,111
Operating income	52,959
Nonoperating income and expenses:	
Other income (expense), net	77
Income before income taxes	53,036
Provision for income taxes	8,755
Net income	$ 44,281
Earnings per share	$ 5.85

MICROSOFT CORPORATION
Balance Sheet
June 30, 2020
(in millions)

ASSETS	
Current assets:	
Cash and short-term investments	$136,527
Accounts receivable (net)	32,011
Other current assets	13,377
Total current assets	181,915
Noncurrent assets:	
Property and equipment, net	44,151
Other investments	2,965
Other noncurrent assets	72,280
Total assets	$301,311
LIABILITIES AND STOCKHOLDERS' EQUITY	
Current liabilities:	
Accounts payable	$ 12,530
Accrued compensation	7,874
Income taxes payable	2,130
Unearned revenue	36,000
Other current liabilities	13,776
Total current liabilities	72,310
Long-term liabilities	110,697
Total liabilities	183,007
Stockholders' equity:	
Common stock and paid-in capital	80,552
Retained earnings	37,752
Total stockholders' equity	118,304
Total liabilities and stockholders' equity	$301,311

2.

Fiscal Year Ending June 30, 2020	
Net Income/Net Sales	0.31
× Net Sales/Average Total Assets	0.49
= Net Income/Average Total Assets	0.15

For the year ended June 30, Microsoft earned an ROA of 15 percent. Microsoft maintains high net profit margins, earning $0.31 of net income for every $1 of net sales, and asset efficiency of $0.49 in sales generated for each $1 of assets. The analysis also indicates Microsoft's dominance of the computer software business, which allows the company to charge premium prices for its products.

3.

General and administrative expenses (+E, −SE)	1,500	
Cash (−A)		1,500

The numerator Net Income would decrease by $1,500 and the denominator Average Total Assets would decrease by $750. As a consequence, ROA would decrease.

CHAPTER TAKE-AWAYS

5-1. Recognize the people involved in the accounting communication process (regulators, managers, directors, auditors, information intermediaries, and users), their roles in the process, and the guidance they receive from legal and professional standards. p. 239

Management of the reporting company must decide on the appropriate format (categories) and level of detail to present in its financial reports. Independent audits increase the credibility of the information. Directors monitor managers' compliance with reporting standards and hire the auditor. Financial statement announcements from public companies usually are first transmitted to users through online information services. The SEC staff reviews public financial reports for compliance with legal and professional standards, investigates irregularities, and punishes violators. Analysts play a major role in making financial statement and other information available to average investors through their stock recommendations and earnings forecasts.

5-2. Identify the steps in the accounting communication process, including the issuance of press releases, annual reports, quarterly reports, and SEC filings, as well as the role of online information services in this process. p. 244

Earnings are first made public in press releases. Companies follow these announcements with annual and quarterly reports containing statements, notes, and additional information. Public companies must file additional reports with the SEC, including the 10-K, 10-Q, and 8-K, which contain more details about the company. Online information services are the key source of dissemination of this information to sophisticated users.

5-3. Recognize and apply the different financial statement and disclosure formats used by companies in practice and analyze the gross profit percentage. p. 247

Most statements are classified and include subtotals that are relevant to analysis. On the balance sheet, the most important distinctions are between current and noncurrent assets and liabilities. On the income and cash flow statements, the distinction between operating and nonoperating items is most important. The notes to the statements provide descriptions of the accounting rules applied, add more information about items disclosed on the statements, and present information about economic events not included in the statements.

5-4. Analyze a company's performance based on return on assets and its components and the effects of transactions on financial ratios. p. 257

ROA measures how well management used the company's invested capital during the period. Its two determinants, net profit margin and asset turnover, indicate why ROA differs from prior levels or the ROAs of competitors. They also suggest strategies to improve ROA in future periods. The effect of an individual transaction on a financial ratio depends on its effects on both the numerator and denominator of the ratio.

In Chapter 6, we will begin our in-depth discussion of individual items presented in financial statements. We will start with two of the most liquid assets, cash and accounts receivable, and transactions that involve revenues and certain selling expenses. Accuracy in revenue recognition and the related recognition of cost of goods sold (discussed in Chapter 7) are the most important determinants of the accuracy–and, thus, the usefulness–of financial statements. We will also introduce concepts related to the management and control of cash and receivables, a critical business function. A detailed understanding of these topics is crucial to future managers, accountants, and financial analysts.

KEY RATIOS

Gross profit percentage measures the excess of sales prices over the costs to purchase or produce the goods or services sold as a percentage. It is computed as follows (see the "Key Ratio Analysis" box in the A Closer Look at Financial Statement Formats and Notes section):

$$\text{Gross Profit Percentage} = \frac{\text{Gross Profit}}{\text{Net Sales}}$$

Return on assets (ROA) measures how much the firm earned for each dollar of investment. It is computed as follows (see the "Key Ratio Analysis" box in the Return on Assets section):

$$\text{Return on Assets} = \frac{\text{Net Income}}{\text{Average Total Assets}}$$

FINDING FINANCIAL INFORMATION

Balance Sheet

Assets (by order of liquidity)
  Current assets (short-term)
  Noncurrent assets
    Total assets
Liabilities (by order of time to maturity)
  Current liabilities (short-term)
  Long-term liabilities
    Total liabilities
Stockholders' equity (by source)
  Common stock and Additional paid-in capital (by owners)
  Retained earnings (accumulated earnings minus accumulated dividends declared)
    Total stockholders' equity
    Total liabilities and stockholders' equity

Income Statement

Net sales
– Cost of goods sold
Gross profit
– Operating expenses
Income from operations
+/– Nonoperating revenues/expenses and gains/losses
Income before income taxes
– Income tax expense
Net income
Earnings per share

Statement of Stockholders' Equity

	Common Stock	Add'l Paid-in Capital	Retained Earnings	Total Stockholders' Equity
Beginning balance	xx	xx	xx	xx
Net income			xx	xx
Dividends declared			(xx)	(xx)
Stock issued	xx	xx		xx
Stock retired	(xx)	(xx)		(xx)
Ending balance	xx	xx	xx	xx

Statement of Cash Flows

Operating activities:
  Net income
  +/–Adjustments for noncash items
  Cash provided by operating activities
Investing activities:
Financing activities:

Notes

Key Classifications
  Descriptions of accounting rules applied in the statements
  Additional detail supporting reported numbers
  Relevant financial information not disclosed on the statements

KEY TERMS

Board of Directors Elected by the shareholders to represent their interests; its audit committee is responsible for maintaining the integrity of the company's financial reports. **p. 240**

Corporate Governance The procedures designed to ensure that the company is managed in the interests of the shareholders. **p. 237**

Earnings Forecasts Predictions of earnings for the future accounting period, prepared by financial analysts. **p. 242**

Financial Accounting Standards Board (FASB) The private sector body given the primary responsibility to work out the detailed rules that become generally accepted accounting principles. **p. 239**

Form 8-K The report used by publicly traded companies to disclose any material event not previously reported that is important to investors. **p. 246**

Form 10-K The annual report that publicly traded companies must file with the SEC. **p. 245**

Form 10-Q The quarterly report that publicly traded companies must file with the SEC. **p. 246**

Gross Profit (Gross Margin) Net sales less cost of goods sold. **p. 247**

Institutional Investors Managers of pension, mutual, endowment, and other funds that invest of the behalf of others. **p. 243**

Lenders (Creditors) Suppliers and financial institutions that lend money to companies. **p. 243**

Material Amounts Amounts that are large enough to influence a user's decision. **p. 244**

Press Release A written public news announcement normally distributed to major news services. **p. 244**

Private Investors Individuals who purchase shares in companies. **p. 243**

Public Company Accounting Oversight Board (PCAOB) The private sector body given the primary responsibility to work out detailed auditing standards. **p. 239**

Securities and Exchange Commission (SEC) The U.S. government agency that determines the financial statements and other disclosures that public companies must provide to stockholders and the measurement rules that they must use in producing those statements. **p. 239**

Unqualified (Clean) Audit Opinion Auditor's statement that the financial statements are fair presentations in all material respects in conformity with GAAP and that the company maintained effective internal controls over financial reporting. **p. 240**

QUESTIONS

1. Describe the roles and responsibilities of management and independent auditors in the financial reporting process.
2. Define the following three users of financial accounting disclosures and the relationships among them: (*a*) financial analysts, (*b*) private investors, and (*c*) institutional investors.
3. Briefly describe the role of information services in the communication of financial information.
4. Explain what a material amount is.
5. What basis of accounting (cash or accrual) does GAAP require on the (*a*) income statement, (*b*) balance sheet, and (*c*) statement of cash flows?
6. Briefly explain the normal sequence and form of financial reports produced by private companies in a typical year.
7. Briefly explain the normal sequence and form of financial reports produced by public companies in a typical year.
8. What are the four major subtotals or totals on the income statement?
9. List the six major classifications reported on a balance sheet.
10. For property, plant, and equipment, as reported on the balance sheet, explain (*a*) cost, (*b*) accumulated depreciation, and (*c*) net book value.
11. Briefly explain the major classifications of stockholders' equity for a corporation.
12. What are the three major classifications on a statement of cash flows?
13. What are the three major categories of notes or footnotes presented in annual reports? Cite an example of each.
14. Briefly define return on assets and what it measures.

MULTIPLE-CHOICE QUESTIONS

1. If average total assets increase, but net income, net sales, and average stockholders' equity remain the same, what is the impact on the return on assets ratio?
   a. Increases.
   b. Decreases.
   c. Remains the same.
   d. Cannot be determined without additional information.

2. If a company plans to differentiate its products by offering low prices and discounts for items packaged in bulk (like a discount retailer that requires memberships for its customers), which component in the ROA profit driver analysis is the company attempting to boost?
   a. Net profit margin.
   b. Asset turnover.
   c. Financial leverage.
   d. All of the above.
3. If a company reported the following items on its income statement (cost of goods sold $6,000, income tax expense $2,000, interest expense $500, operating expenses $3,500, sales revenue $14,000), what amount would be reported for the subtotal "income from operations"?
   a. $8,000
   b. $2,000
   c. $4,500
   d. $4,000
4. Which of the following is one of the possible nonrecurring items that must be shown in a separate line item **below** the Income from Continuing Operations subtotal in the income statement?
   a. Gains and losses from the sale of fixed assets.
   b. Discontinued operations.
   c. Extraordinary items.
   d. Both a and b.
5. Which of the following reports is filed annually with the SEC?
   a. Form 10-Q
   b. Form 10-K
   c. Form 8-K
   d. Press release
6. Which of the following would normally **not** be found in the notes to the financial statements?
   a. Accounting rules applied in the company's financial statements.
   b. Additional detail supporting numbers reported in the company's financial statements.
   c. Relevant financial information not presented in the company's financial statements.
   d. All of the above would be found in the notes to the financial statements.
7. Which of the following is **not** a normal function of a financial analyst?
   a. Issue earnings forecasts.
   b. Examine the records underlying the financial statements to certify their conformance with GAAP.
   c. Make buy, hold, and sell recommendations on companies' stock.
   d. Advise institutional investors on their securities holdings.
8. The classified balance sheet format allows one to ascertain quickly which of the following?
   a. The most valuable asset of the company.
   b. The specific due date for all liabilities of the company.
   c. What liabilities must be paid within the upcoming year.
   d. None of the above.
9. When a company issues stock with a par value, what columns are typically presented in the statement of stockholders' equity?
   a. Common Stock; Additional Paid-In Capital; and Property, Plant, and Equipment, Net.
   b. Cash; and Property, Plant, and Equipment, Net.
   c. Common Stock; Additional Paid-In Capital; and Retained Earnings.
   d. Common Stock; Additional Paid-In Capital; and Cash.
10. Net income was $850,000. Beginning and ending assets were $8,500,000 and $9,600,000, respectively. What was the return on assets (ROA)?
   a. 9.39%
   b. 10.59%
   c. 9.94%
   d. 10.41%

connect

MINI-EXERCISES

Matching Players in the Accounting Communication Process with Their Definitions

M5-1
LO5-1

Match each player with the related definition by entering the appropriate letter in the space provided.

Players	Definitions
___ (1) Independent auditor	A. Adviser who analyzes financial and other economic information to form forecasts and stock recommendations.
___ (2) CEO and CFO	B. Institutional and private investors and creditors (among others).
___ (3) Users	C. Chief executive officer and chief financial officer who have primary responsibility for the information presented in financial statements.
___ (4) Financial analyst	D. Independent CPA who examines financial statements and attests to their fairness.

M5-2 LO5-2 Identifying the Disclosure Sequence

Indicate the order in which the following disclosures or reports are normally issued by public companies.

No.	Title
_____	Form 10-K
_____	Earnings press release
_____	Annual report

M5-3 LO5-3 Finding Financial Information: Matching Financial Statements with the Elements of Financial Statements

Match each financial statement with the items presented on it by entering the appropriate letter in the space provided.

Elements of Financial Statements	Financial Statements
___ (1) Expenses	A. Income statement
___ (2) Cash from operating activities	B. Balance sheet
___ (3) Losses	C. Cash flow statement
___ (4) Assets	D. None of the above
___ (5) Revenues	
___ (6) Cash from financing activities	
___ (7) Gains	
___ (8) Owners' equity	
___ (9) Liabilities	
___ (10) Assets personally owned by a stockholder	

M5-4 LO5-3 Determining the Effects of Transactions on Balance Sheet and Income Statement Categories

Complete the following tabulation, indicating the sign of the effect (+ for increase, – for decrease, and NE for no effect) of each transaction. Consider each item independently.

a. Recorded sales on account of $300 and related cost of goods sold of $200.
b. Recorded advertising expense of $10 incurred but not paid for.

Transaction	Current Assets	Gross Profit	Current Liabilities
a.			
b.			

M5-5 LO5-3 Determining Financial Statement Effects of Sales and Cost of Goods Sold and Issuance of Stock

Using the following categories, indicate the effects of the following transactions. Use + for increase and – for decrease and indicate the accounts affected and the amounts.

a. Sales on account were $1,800 and related cost of goods sold was $1,200.
b. Issued 5,000 shares of $1 par value stock for $60,000 cash.

Event	Assets	=	Liabilities	+	Stockholders' Equity
a.					
b.					

M5-6 LO5-3 Recording Sales and Cost of Goods Sold and Issuance of Stock

Prepare journal entries for each transaction listed in M5-5.

Computing and Interpreting Return on Assets

M5-7
LO5-4

Saunders, Inc., recently reported the following December 31 amounts in its financial statements (dollars in thousands):

	Current Year	Prior Year
Gross profit	$ 200	$120
Net income	100	40
Total assets	1,000	800
Total shareholders' equity	800	600

Compute return on assets for the current year. What does this ratio measure?

connect EXERCISES

Matching Players in the Accounting Communication Process with Their Definitions

E5-1
LO5-1

Match each player with the related definition by entering the appropriate letter in the space provided.

Players

___ (1) Financial analyst
___ (2) Creditor
___ (3) Independent auditor
___ (4) Private investor
___ (5) SEC
___ (6) Information service
___ (7) Institutional investor
___ (8) CEO and CFO

Definitions

A. Financial institution or supplier that lends money to the company.
B. Chief executive officer and chief financial officer who have primary responsibility for the information presented in financial statements.
C. Manager of pension, mutual, and endowment funds that invest on the behalf of others.
D. Securities and Exchange Commission, which regulates financial disclosure requirements.
E. A company that gathers, combines, and transmits (paper and electronic) financial and related information from various sources.
F. Adviser who analyzes financial and other economic information to form forecasts and stock recommendations.
G. Individual who purchases shares in companies.
H. Independent CPA who examines financial statements and attests to their fairness.

Matching Definitions with Information Releases Made by Public Companies

E5-2
LO5-2

Following are the titles of various information releases. Match each definition with the related release by entering the appropriate letter in the space provided.

Information Release

___ (1) Form 10-Q
___ (2) Quarterly report
___ (3) Press release
___ (4) Annual report
___ (5) Form 10-K
___ (6) Form 8-K

Definitions

A. Report of special events (e.g., auditor changes, mergers) filed by public companies with the SEC.
B. Brief unaudited report for quarter normally containing summary income statement and balance sheet.
C. Quarterly report filed by public companies with the SEC that contains additional unaudited financial information.
D. Written public news announcement that is normally distributed to major news services.
E. Annual report filed by public companies with the SEC that contains additional detailed financial information.
F. Report containing the four basic financial statements for the year, related notes, and often statements by management and auditors.

E5-3 LO5-2 Finding Financial Information: Matching Information Items to Financial Reports

Following are information items included in various financial reports. Match each information item with the report(s) where it would most likely be found by entering the appropriate letter(s) in the space provided.

Information Item	Report
___ (1) Summarized financial data for five-year period.	A. Form 10-Q
___ (2) Notes to financial statements.	B. Annual report
___ (3) The four basic financial statements for the year.	C. Form 8-K
___ (4) Summarized income statement information for the quarter.	D. Press release
___ (5) Detailed discussion of the company's competition.	E. Quarterly report
___ (6) Initial announcement of hiring of new vice president for sales.	F. Form 10-K
___ (7) Initial announcement of quarterly earnings.	G. None of the above
___ (8) Description of those responsible for the financial statements.	
___ (9) Complete quarterly income statement, balance sheet, and cash flow statement.	
___ (10) Announcement of a change in auditors.	

E5-4 LO5-3 Ordering the Classifications on a Typical Balance Sheet

Following is a list of classifications on the balance sheet. Number them in the order in which they normally appear on a balance sheet.

No.	Title
___	Long-term liabilities
___	Current liabilities
___	Long-term investments
___	Intangible assets
___	Common stock and additional paid-in capital
___	Current assets
___	Retained earnings
___	Property, plant, and equipment
___	Other noncurrent assets

E5-5 LO5-3 Preparing a Classified Balance Sheet

Campbell Soup Company

Campbell Soup Company is the world's leading maker and marketer of soup and sells other well-known brands of food in 160 countries. Presented here are the items listed on a simplified version of its recent balance sheet (dollars in millions) presented in alphabetical order:

Accounts payable	$1,049	Other assets	$ 283
Accounts receivable	575	Other current assets	80
Accrued expenses	693	Other current debt	1,333
Cash and cash equivalents	859	Other noncurrent liabilities	6,728
Common stock, $0.0375 par value	406	Property, plant, and equipment, net	2,368
Intangible assets	7,336	Retained earnings	2,163
Inventories	871		

Source: Campbell Soup Company

Required:
Prepare a classified consolidated balance sheet for Campbell Soup for the current year (ended July 31) using the categories presented in the chapter.

E5-6 LO5-3 Preparing and Interpreting a Classified Balance Sheet with Discussion of Terminology (Challenging)

The Hershey Company

The Hershey Company is a global confectionery leader known for its branded portfolio of chocolate, sweets, mints, and other great-tasting snacks. The Company has more than 80 brands worldwide including such iconic brand names as Hershey's, Reese's, Kisses, Jolly Rancher, and Ice Breakers, which are sold in approximately 85 countries worldwide. Presented here are the items listed on a simplified version of its recent balance sheet (dollars in thousands) in alphabetical order:

Accounts payable	$ 550,828	Other assets (noncurrent)	$ 543,033
Accounts receivable, net	568,509	Other intangibles, net	1,341,166
Accrued short-term liabilities	702,372	Other long-term liabilities	855,795
Additional paid-in capital	1,142,210	Other payables	19,921
Cash and cash equivalents	493,262	Prepaid expenses and other current assets	240,080
Common stock (221,553,025 shares outstanding)	221,553	Property, plant, and equipment, net	2,153,139
Goodwill	1,985,955	Retained earnings	381,231
Inventories	815,251	Short-term debt	735,672
Long-term debt	3,530,813		

Source: The Hershey Company

Required:
1. Prepare a classified consolidated balance sheet for The Hershey Company for the current year (ended December 31) using the categories presented in the chapter.
2. Three of the items end in the term **net.** Explain what this term means in each case.

Preparing a Classified (Multiple-Step) Income Statement

E5-7
LO5-3
Macy's, Inc.

Macy's, Inc., operates the two best-known high-end department store chains in North America: Macy's and Bloomingdale's. The following simplified data (in millions) were taken from its recent annual report for the year ended February 1:

Cost of sales	$15,171
Federal, state, and local income tax expense	164
Interest expense	205
Interest income	20
Net sales	25,331
Other operating expenses	249
Selling, general, and administrative expenses	8,998

Source: Macy's, Inc.

Required:
Prepare a complete classified (multiple-step) consolidated statement of income for the company (showing gross margin, operating income, and income before income taxes).

Preparing a Classified (Multiple-Step) Income Statement and Computing the Gross Profit Percentage

E5-8
LO5-3

The following data were taken from the records of Township Corporation at December 31 of the current year:

Sales revenue	$85,000
Gross profit	30,000
Selling (distribution) expense	7,000
Administrative expense	?
Pretax income	13,000
Income tax rate	35%
Shares of stock outstanding	2,500

Required:
Prepare a complete classified (multiple-step) income statement for the company (showing both gross profit and income from operations). Show all computations. (**Hint:** Set up the side captions or rows starting with sales revenue and ending with earnings per share; rely on the amounts and percentages given to infer missing values.) What is the gross profit percentage?

E5-9 LO5-3 Salesforce.com, inc.

Preparing a Classified (Multiple-Step) Income Statement (Challenging)

Salesforce.com, inc., is a leading provider of enterprise software, delivered through the cloud, with a focus on customer relationship management, or CRM. The Company helps its customers to connect with their customers through cloud, mobile, social, blockchain, voice, advanced analytics, and artificial intelligence ("AI") technologies. Presented below are the items adapted from its recent income statement for the year ended January 31 (in millions, except per share amounts). Net earnings per share was $0.15, and the weighted-average shares used in the computation were 829 million.

Cost of subscription and support revenues	$ 3,198	Professional services and other revenues	$1,055
Cost of professional services and other revenues	1,037	Other income	243
General and administrative expense	1,704	Marketing and sales expense	7,930
Income tax expense	580	Research and development expense	2,766
Subscription and support revenues	16,043		

Source: salesforce.com, inc.

Required:

1. Recognizing that Salesforce has two sources of operating revenues, prepare a classified (multiple-step) income statement for Salesforce following the format and using the subtotals presented in Exhibit 5.5.
2. Which source of operating revenues produces the higher gross profit?

E5-10 LO5-3

Inferring Income Statement Values

Supply the missing dollar amounts for the current year income statement of NexTech Company for each of the following independent cases. (**Hint:** Organize each case in the format of the classified or multiple-step income statement discussed in the chapter. Rely on the amounts given to infer the missing values.)

	Case A	Case B	Case C	Case D	Case E
Sales revenue	$800	$600	$500	$?	$?
Selling expense	?	50	80	350	240
Cost of goods sold	?	150	?	500	320
Income tax expense	?	30	20	50	20
Gross margin	375	?	?	?	440
Pretax income	200	300	?	200	?
Administrative expense	125	?	70	120	80
Net income	150	?	50	?	100

E5-11 LO5-3

Inferring Income Statement Values

Supply the missing dollar amounts for the current year income statement of BGT Company for each of the following independent cases. (**Hint:** Organize each case in the format of the classified or multiple-step income statement discussed in the chapter. Rely on the amounts given to infer the missing values.)

	Case A	Case B	Case C	Case D	Case E
Sales revenue	$770	$?	$?	$600	$1,050
Pretax income	?	?	150	130	370
Income tax expense	65	210	60	45	?
Cost of goods sold	?	320	125	250	?
Gross margin	?	880	?	?	630
Selling expense	90	275	45	70	?
Net income	115	275	?	?	240
Administrative expense	200	120	80	?	175

E5-12 LO5-3 Tapestry Inc.

Stock Issuances and the Statement of Stockholders' Equity

In a recent year, **Tapestry Inc.**, parent company of major fashion brands Coach New York, Kate Spade New York, and Stuart Weitzman, issued 1,300,000 shares of its $0.01 par value stock for $10,500,000 (these numbers are rounded). These additional shares were issued under an employee stock option plan. Prepare the line on the statement of stockholders' equity that would reflect this transaction. The statement has the following columns:

Common Stock		Additional Paid-in Capital	Retained Earnings	Total Stockholders' Equity
Shares	Amount			

E5-13
LO5-3
Consolidated Edison, Inc.

Inferring Stock Issuances and Cash Dividends from Changes in Stockholders' Equity

Consolidated Edison, Inc. (Con Edison), is a public utility company operating primarily in New York whose annual revenues exceed $12 billion. It reported the following December 31 simplified balances in its statement of stockholders' equity (dollars in millions):

	Current Year	Prior Year
Common stock	$ 35	$ 34
Paid-in capital	8,054	7,117
Retained earnings	11,100	10,728

Source: Consolidated Edison, Inc.

During the current year, Con Edison reported net income of $1,343.

Required:

1. How much did Con Edison declare in dividends for the year?
2. Assume that the only other transaction that affected stockholders' equity during the current year was a single stock issuance for cash. Recreate the journal entry reflecting the stock issuance (in millions).

E5-14
LO5-3
Hasbro

Determining the Effects of Transactions on Balance Sheet and Income Statement Categories

Hasbro is one of the world's leading toy manufacturers and the maker of such popular board games as Monopoly, Scrabble, and Clue, among others. Listed here are selected aggregate transactions from a recent year (dollars in millions). Complete the following tabulation, indicating the sign (+ for increase, − for decrease, and NE for no effect) and amount of the effect of each transaction. Consider each item independently.

a. Recorded sales on account of $4,720.2 and related cost of goods sold of $1,807.8.
b. Issued debt due in six months with a principal amount of $2,355.
c. Incurred research and development expense of $262.2, which was paid in cash.

Transaction	Current Assets	Gross Profit	Current Liabilities
a.			
b.			
c.			

E5-15
LO5-3

Determining the Effects of Transactions on Balance Sheet, Income Statement, and Statement of Cash Flows Categories

Listed here are selected aggregate transactions for ModernStyle Furniture Company from the first quarter of a recent year (dollars in millions). Complete the following tabulation, indicating the sign (+ for increase, − for decrease, and NE for no effect) and amount of the effect of each transaction. Consider each item independently.

a. Recorded collections of cash from customers owed on open account of $40.8.
b. Repaid $5.6 in principal on line of credit with a bank with principal payable within one year.

Transaction	Current Assets	Gross Profit	Current Liabilities	Cash Flow from Operating Activities
a.				
b.				

E5-16 Preparing a Simple Statement of Cash Flows Using the Indirect Method

LO5-3

Avalos Corporation is preparing its annual financial statements at December 31 of the current year. Listed here are the items on its statement of cash flows presented in alphabetical order. Parentheses indicate that a listed amount should be subtracted on the cash flow statement. The beginning balance in cash was $25,000 and the ending balance was $50,000.

Cash borrowed on three-year note	$30,000
Decrease in accounts payable	(3,000)
Decrease in inventory	1,000
Increase in accounts receivable	(9,000)
Land purchased	(36,000)
Net income	25,000
New delivery truck purchased for cash	(7,000)
Stock issued for cash	24,000

Required:

Prepare the current year statement of cash flows for Avalos Corporation. The section reporting cash flows from operating activities should be prepared using the indirect method discussed in the chapter.

E5-17 Analyzing and Interpreting Return on Assets

LO5-4

The TJX Companies, Inc.

The TJX Companies, Inc., which operates the T.J. Maxx, Marshalls, and HomeGoods chains, is the leading off-price apparel and home fashions retailer in the United States and worldwide. Presented here are selected recent income statement and balance sheet amounts (dollars in thousands).

	Current Year	Prior Year
Net sales	$38,972,934	$35,864,664
Net income	3,059,798	2,607,948
Average shareholders' equity	5,098,458	4,829,454
Average total assets	14,192,022	13,470,912

Source: The TJX Companies, Inc.

Required:

1. Compute ROA for the current and prior years and explain the meaning of the change.
2. Explain the major cause(s) of the change in ROA using ROA profit driver analysis.

E5-18 Analyzing and Evaluating Return on Assets from a Security Analyst's Perspective

LO5-4

Papa John's

Papa John's operates and franchises pizza delivery and carryout restaurants in 49 countries. Presented here are selected years' income statement and balance sheet amounts (dollars in thousands).

	Current Year	Prior Year
Net sales	$1,619,248	$1,662,871
Net income	4,866	2,474
Average shareholders' equity	(310,335)	(204,984)
Average total assets	663,309	595,897

Source: Papa John's International, Inc.

Required:

1. Compute ROA for the current and prior years and explain the meaning of the change.
2. Would security analysts more likely increase or decrease their estimates of share value on the basis of this change? Explain.

E5-19 Determining the Effects of Transactions on Ratios

LO5-4

What would be the **direction** of the effect of the following transactions on the following ratios (+ for increase, − for decrease, and NE for no effect)? Consider each item independently.

a. Repaid principal of $2,000 on a long-term note payable with the bank.
b. Recorded rent expense of $100 paid for in cash.

Transaction	Net Profit Margin	Return on Assets	Current Ratio
a.			
b.			

PROBLEMS

Preparing a Balance Sheet and Analyzing Some of Its Parts (AP5-1)

P5-1
LO5-3

Exquisite Jewelers is developing its annual financial statements for the current year. The following amounts were correct at December 31, current year: cash, $58,000; accounts receivable, $71,000; merchandise inventory, $154,000; prepaid insurance, $1,500; investment in stock of Z Corporation (long-term), $36,000; store equipment, $67,000; used store equipment held for disposal, $9,000; accumulated depreciation, store equipment, $19,000; accounts payable, $52,500; long-term note payable, $42,000; income taxes payable, $9,000; retained earnings, $164,000; and common stock, 100,000 shares outstanding, par value $1.00 per share (originally sold and issued at $1.10 per share).

Required:

1. Based on these data, prepare a December 31, current year, balance sheet. Use the following major subtotals, and totals (list the individual items in the appropriate locations):
   a. Total current assets and Total assets.
   b. Total current liabilities and Total liabilities.
   c. Total contributed capital, Total stockholders' equity, and Total liabilities and stockholders' equity.
2. What is the net book value of the store equipment? Explain what this value means.

Preparing a Statement of Stockholders' Equity (AP5-2)

P5-2
LO5-3

At the end of the prior annual reporting period, Barnard Corporation's balance sheet showed the following:

BARNARD CORPORATION
Balance Sheet
At December 31, Prior Year

Stockholders' Equity	
Contributed capital	
Common stock (par $15; 5,500 shares)	$ 82,500
Paid-in capital	13,000
Total contributed capital	95,500
Retained earnings	44,000
Total stockholders' equity	$139,500

During the current year, the following selected transactions (summarized) were completed:

a. Sold and issued 1,000 shares of common stock at $35 cash per share (at year-end).
b. Determined net income, $37,000.
c. Declared and paid a cash dividend of $2 per share on the beginning shares outstanding.

Required:
Prepare a statement of stockholders' equity for the year ended December 31, current year. Be sure to show both the dollar amount and number of shares of common stock.

P5-3 LO5-3 Preparing a Classified (Multiple-Step) Income Statement and Interpreting the Gross Profit Percentage (AP5-3)

Nordstrom, Inc.

Nordstrom, Inc., is a leading fashion retailer that offers customers an extensive selection of high-quality fashion brands focused on apparel, shoes, cosmetics, and accessories for women, men, young adults, and children. The items reported on its income statement for an earlier year (ended February 1) are presented here (dollars in millions) in simplified form in alphabetical order:

Cost of goods sold	$ 9,932
Interest expense	102
Net revenue	15,524
Other selling, general, and administrative expenses	4,808
Income tax expense	186
Weighted average shares outstanding	155

Source: Nordstrom, Inc.

Required:

Prepare a classified (multiple-step) consolidated income statement (showing gross profit, operating income, and income before income taxes). Include a presentation of earnings per share. What is the gross profit percentage? Explain its meaning.

P5-4 LO5-3 Preparing Both an Income Statement and a Balance Sheet from a Trial Balance (AP5-4)

Jordan Sales Company (organized as a corporation on April 1, 2021) has completed the accounting cycle for the second year, ended March 31, 2023. Jordan also has completed a correct trial balance as follows:

	A	B	C
1	JORDAN SALES COMPANY		
2	Trial Balance At March 31, 2023		
3	**Account Titles**	**Debit**	**Credit**
4	Cash	$58,000	
5	Accounts receivable	49,000	
6	Office supplies inventory	1,000	
7	Automobiles (company cars)	34,000	
8	Accumulated depreciation, automobiles		$14,000
9	Office equipment	3,000	
10	Accumulated depreciation, office equipment		1,000
11	Accounts payable		22,000
12	Income taxes payable		0
13	Salaries and commissions payable		2,000
14	Note payable, long-term		33,000
15	Capital stock (par $1; 33,000 shares)		33,000
16	Paid-in capital		5,000
17	Retained earnings (on April 1, 2022)		7,500
18	Dividends declared and paid during the current year	10,500	
19	Sales revenue		99,000
20	Cost of goods sold	33,000	
21	Operating expenses (detail omitted to conserve time)	19,000	
22	Depreciation expense (on autos and including $500 on office equipment)	8,000	
23	Interest expense	1,000	
24	Income tax expense (not yet computed)		
25	**Total**	**$216,500**	**$216,500**

Required:
Complete the financial statements as follows:

a. Classified (multiple-step) income statement for the reporting year ended March 31, 2023. Include income tax expense, assuming a 25 percent tax rate. Use the following subtotals: Gross Profit, Total Operating Expenses, Income from Operations, Income before Income Taxes, Net Income, and EPS.
b. Classified balance sheet at the end of the reporting year, March 31, 2023. Include (1) income taxes for the current year in Income Taxes Payable and (2) dividends in Retained Earnings. Use the following captions (list each item under these captions):

Assets	**Stockholders' Equity**
Current assets	Contributed capital
Noncurrent assets	Retained earnings
Liabilities	
Current liabilities	
Long-term liabilities	

Determining and Interpreting the Effects of Transactions on Income Statement Categories and Return on Assets (AP5-5)

P5-5
LO5-3, 5-4
Sonos, Inc.

Sonos, Inc., designs, develops, manufactures, and sells multi-room audio products. The Sonos sound system provides customers with an immersive listening experience created by the design of its speakers and components, a proprietary software platform, and the ability to stream content from a variety of sources over the customer's wireless network or over Bluetooth. In an earlier year, it reported the following on its income statement (dollars in millions).

Net sales	$1,326
Costs and expenses	
Cost of sales	754
Research and development	215
Selling, general, and administrative	384
Operating income (loss)	(27)
Interest and other income (expense), net	7
Loss before provision for income taxes	(20)
Provision for income taxes	0
Net loss	$ (20)

Source: Sonos, Inc.

The company's beginning and ending assets were $762 and $816, respectively.

Required:
Listed here are hypothetical **additional** transactions. Assuming that they **also** occurred during the fiscal year, complete the following tabulation, indicating the sign of the effect of each **additional** transaction (+ for increase, – for decrease, and NE for no effect). Consider each item independently and ignore taxes. (**Hint:** Construct the journal entry for each transaction before evaluating its effect.)

a. Recorded sales on account of $400 and related cost of goods sold of $300.
b. Incurred additional research and development expense of $100, which was paid in cash.
c. Issued additional shares of common stock for $260 cash.
d. Declared and paid dividends of $90.

Transaction	Gross Profit	Operating Income	Return on Assets
a.			
b.			
c.			
d.			

P5-6
LO5-4

Determining the Effects of Transactions on Ratios (AP5-6)

Mateo Inc. is a retailer of men's and women's clothing aimed at college-age customers. Listed below are additional transactions that Mateo was considering at the end of the accounting period.

Required:
Complete the following tabulation, indicating the sign of the effect of each additional transaction (+ for increase, – for decrease, and NE for no effect). Consider each item independently and ignore taxes. (**Hint:** Construct the journal entry for each transaction before evaluating its effect.)

a. Borrowed $3,000 on a line of credit with the bank.
b. Incurred salary expense of $1,000 paid for in cash.
c. Provided $2,000 of services on account.
d. Purchased $700 of inventory on account.
e. Sold $500 of goods on account. The related cost of goods sold was $300. Gross profit margin was 45 percent before this sale.

Transaction	Total Asset Turnover	Return on Assets	Gross Profit Percentage
a.			
b.			
c.			
d.			
e.			

P5-7
LO5-3
Cloud Comfort, Inc.

Preparing a Multiple-Step Income Statement with Discontinued Operations (AP5-7)

Cloud Comfort, Inc., researches, designs, manufactures, and distributes interior furnishings for use in various environments including office, health care, educational, and residential settings. The items reported on its income statement for the year ended December 31, 2020, are presented here (dollars in millions) in alphabetical order:

Cost of products sold	$1,575
Income tax expense	49
Interest expense	19
Loss on sale of discontinued operations, net of income taxes	(8)
Net sales	2,490
Other expense	20
Selling, general, and administrative expenses	643

Source: Cloud Comfort, Inc.

Required:
Using appropriate headings and subtotals, prepare a multiple-step consolidated income statement (showing gross profit, operating income, and any other subheadings you deem appropriate).

ALTERNATE PROBLEMS

AP5-1
LO5-3

Preparing a Balance Sheet and Analyzing Some of Its Parts (P5-1)

TangoCo is developing its annual financial statements for the current year. The following amounts were correct at December 31, current year: cash, $48,800; investment in stock of PIL Corporation (long-term), $36,400; store equipment, $67,200; accounts receivable, $71,820; inventory, $154,000; prepaid rent, $1,120; used store equipment held for disposal, $9,800; accumulated depreciation, store equipment,

$13,440; income taxes payable, $9,800; long-term note payable, $32,000; accounts payable, $58,800; retained earnings, $165,100; and common stock, 100,000 shares outstanding, par value $1 per share (originally sold and issued at $1.10 per share).

Required:

1. Based on these data, prepare a December 31, current year, balance sheet. Use the following major captions (list the individual items under these captions):
   a. Assets: Current Assets and Noncurrent Assets.
   b. Liabilities: Current Liabilities and Long-Term Liabilities.
   c. Stockholders' Equity: Contributed Capital and Retained Earnings.
2. What is the net book value of the store equipment? Explain what this value means.

Preparing a Statement of Stockholders' Equity (P5-2)

AP5-2
LO5-3

At the end of the prior annual reporting period, Mesa Industries' balance sheet showed the following:

MESA INDUSTRIES **Balance Sheet** **At December 31, Prior Year**	
Stockholders' Equity	
Common stock (par $15; 7,000 shares)	$105,000
Additional paid-in capital	9,000
Retained earnings	48,000
Total stockholders' equity	$162,000

During the current year, the following selected transactions (summarized) were completed:

a. Sold and issued 1,500 shares of common stock at $26 cash per share (at year-end).
b. Determined net income, $46,000.
c. Declared and paid a cash dividend of $1 per share on the beginning shares outstanding.

Required:
Prepare a statement of stockholders' equity for the year ended December 31, current year. Be sure to show both the dollar amount and number of shares of common stock.

Preparing a Classified (Multiple-Step) Income Statement and Interpreting the Gross Profit Percentage (P5-3)

AP5-3
LO5-3
Target Corporation

Target Corporation, is a general merchandise retailer that sells products through its stores and digital channels. The company offers everyday essentials and merchandise at discounted prices. The items reported on its income statement for an earlier year (ended February 1) are presented here (dollars in millions) in simplified form in alphabetical order:

Cost of goods sold	$54,864
Interest expense	468
Net revenue	78,112
Selling, general, and administrative expenses	18,590
Provision for income taxes	909
Weighted average shares outstanding	510.9

Source: Target Corporation

Required:
Prepare a classified (multiple-step) consolidated income statement (showing gross profit, operating income, and income before income taxes). Include a presentation of basic earnings per share. What is the gross profit percentage? Explain its meaning.

AP5-4 LO5-3

Preparing Both an Income Statement and a Balance Sheet from a Trial Balance (P5-4)

Dynamite Sales (organized as a corporation on September 1, 2022) has completed all but the closing process in the accounting cycle for the second year ended August 31, 2024. Dynamite's trial balance follows:

	B	C	D
1	DYNAMITE SALES		
2	**Trial Balance**		
3	**At August 31, 2024**		
4		**Debit**	**Credit**
5	Cash	47,700	
6	Accounts receivable	38,320	
7	Office supplies	270	
8	Company vehicles (delivery vans)	27,000	
9	Accumulated depreciation, company vehicles		9,000
10	Equipment	2,700	
11	Accumulated depreciation, equipment		900
12	Accounts payable		16,225
13	Income taxes payable		-
14	Salaries payable		1,350
15	Long-term debt		22,000
16	Common stock (par $1; 29,000)		29,000
17	Additional paid-in capital		4,500
18	Retained earnings *(includes $4,200 in dividends declared and paid during the year)*		2,415
19	Sales revenue		81,000
20	Cost of goods sold	27,000	
21	Operating expenses *(detail omitted to conserve time)*	16,200	
22	Depreciation expense	4,950	
23	Interest expense	2,250	
24	Income tax expense *(not yet computed)*	-	
25	Totals	166,390	166,390

Required:

Complete the financial statements, as follows:

a. Classified (multiple-step) income statement for the reporting year ended August 31, 2024. Include income tax expense, assuming a 25 percent tax rate. Use the following subtotals: Gross Profit, Total Operating Expenses, Income from Operations, Income before Income Taxes, Net Income, and EPS.

b. Classified balance sheet at the end of the reporting year, August 31, 2024. Include (1) income taxes for the current year in Income Taxes Payable and (2) dividends in Retained Earnings. Use the following captions (list each item under these captions).

Assets

Current assets
Noncurrent assets

Liabilities

Current liabilities
Long-term liabilities

Stockholders' Equity

Contributed capital
Retained earnings

Determining and Interpreting the Effects of Transactions on Income Statement Categories and Return on Assets (P5-5)

AP5-5
LO5-3, 5-4
Avon Products, Inc.

Avon Products, Inc., is a leading manufacturer and marketer of beauty products and related merchandise. The company sells its products in 79 countries through a combination of direct selling and use of individual sales representatives. Presented here is an earlier year's income statement (dollars in millions).

Net sales	$4,763.2
Costs and expenses:	
Cost of sales	2,010.1
Selling, general, and administrative	2,627.5
Operating income (loss)	125.6
Interest and other income (expenses), net	12.8
Income (loss) before provision (benefit) for income taxes	138.4
Provision (benefit) for income taxes	103.1
Net income (loss)	$ 35.3

Avon's beginning and ending total assets were $3010.1 and $3086.3, respectively.

Required:

1. Listed below are hypothetical **additional** transactions. Assuming that they **also** occurred during the fiscal year, complete the following tabulation, indicating the sign of the effect of each **additional** transaction (+ for increase, – for decrease, and NE for no effect). Consider each item independently and ignore taxes.
   a. Recorded and received additional interest income of $7.
   b. Purchased $80 of additional inventory on open account.
   c. Recorded and paid additional advertising expense of $16.
   d. Issued additional shares of common stock for $40 cash.

Transaction	Operating Income (Loss)	Net Income	Return on Assets
a.			
b.			
c.			
d.			

2. Assume that next period, Avon does not pay any dividends, does not issue or retire stock, and earns 20 percent more than during the current period. If total assets increase by 5 percent, will Avon's ROA next period be higher, lower, or the same as in the current period? Why?

Determining the Effects of Transactions on Ratios (P5-6)

AP5-6
LO5-4

HarveySafe Inc. is a provider of commercial and residential security and monitoring systems. Listed below are additional transactions that Harvey was considering at the end of the accounting period.

Required:
Complete the following tabulation, indicating the sign of the effect of each additional transaction (+ for increase, – for decrease, and NE for no effect). Consider each item independently and ignore taxes. (**Hint:** Construct the journal entry for each transaction before evaluating its effect.)

a. Borrowed $17,000 on a line of credit with the bank.
b. Incurred salary expense of $2,000 paid for in cash.
c. Provided $4,000 of services on account.
d. Purchased $1,600 of inventory on account.
e. Sold $800 of goods on account. The related cost of goods sold was $500. Gross profit margin was 40 percent before this sale.

Transaction	Total Asset Turnover	Return on Assets	Gross Profit Percentage
a.			
b.			
c.			
d.			
e.			

AP5-7
LO5-3
Newell Brands Inc.

Preparing a Multiple-Step Income Statement with Discontinued Operations (P5-7)

Newell Brands Inc. is a leading global consumer goods company with a strong portfolio of well-known brands, including Sharpie, Paper Mate, Mr. Coffee, Rubbermaid, Yankee Candle, and others. The items reported on its income statement for the year ended December 31, 2019, are presented here (dollars in millions) in alphabetical order:

Cost of Products Sold	$6,495.5
Income Tax Benefit	1,037.7
Interest and Other Nonoperating Expense	369.9
Impairment expense of goodwill, intangibles and other assets	1,223.0
Loss from discontinued operations, net of tax	(79.5)
Net Sales	9,714.9
Other Expense	27.1
Selling, General, and Administrative Expenses	2,451.0

Source: Newell Brands Inc.

Required:
Using appropriate headings and subtotals, prepare a multiple-step consolidated income statement (showing gross profit, operating income, and any other subheadings you deem appropriate). Note that the company has an income tax benefit (they are receiving money back from the government) related to its loss.

CONTINUING PROBLEMS

(CON5-1)
LO5-4

Evaluating the Impact of Transactions on Statement Categories and Ratios

After completing her first year of operations, Penny Cassidy used a number of ratios to evaluate the performance of Penny's Pool Service & Supply, Inc. She was particularly interested in the effects of the following transactions from the last quarter:

a. Paid herself a dividend of $10,000 as the sole stockholder.
b. Recorded advance payments from customers of $2,000.
c. Paid the current month's rent in cash, $500.
d. Purchased a new truck for $14,000 and signed a note payable for the whole amount. The truck was not placed in service until January of the second year of operations.
e. Recorded depreciation expense on office equipment of $600.
f. Accrued interest expense on the note payable to the bank was $400.

Required:
(**Hint:** Construct the journal entry for each transaction before evaluating its effect.)

1. Complete the following table, indicating the effects of each transaction on each financial statement category listed for the first year of operations. Indicate the amount and use + for increase, − for decrease, and NE for no effect.

Transaction	Gross Profit	Operating Income (Loss)	Current Assets
a.			
etc.			

2. Complete the following table, indicating the sign of the effects of each transaction on the financial ratio listed for the first year of operations. Use + for increase, – for decrease, and NE for no effect.

Transaction	Net Profit Margin	Total Asset Turnover	Return on Assets
a.			
etc.			

Preparing an Income Statement and Balance Sheet and Computing Gross Profit Percentage and Return on Assets for a Public Company

(CON5-2)
LO5-3, 5-4
Pool Corporation, Inc.

Pool Corporation, Inc., is the world's largest wholesale distributor of swimming pool supplies and equipment. It is a publicly traded corporation that trades on the NASDAQ exchange under the symbol POOL.

It sells these products to swimming pool repair and service businesses like Penny's Pool Service & Supply, Inc.; swimming pool builders; and retail swimming pool stores. The majority of these customers are small, family-owned businesses like Penny's. Its trial balance and additional information adapted from a recent year ended December 31 are presented below. All numbers are in thousands.

File Home Insert Page Layout Formulas Data Review View

U39

	A	B	C	D
1		POOL CORPORATION, INC.		
2		Trial Balance		
3		At December 31, Current Year		
4			Debit	Credit
5		Cash and cash equivalents	28,583	
6		Receivables, net	226,539	
7		Product inventories, net	702,274	
8		Prepaid expenses and other current assets	16,172	
9		Property and equipment, net	112,246	
10		Intangible assets	199,634	
11		Operating lease assets	176,689	
12		Other noncurrent assets, net	21,129	
13		Accounts payable		261,963
14		Accrued expenses and other current liabilities		60,813
15		Current portion of long-term debt		11,745
16		Operating lease liability, current		56,325
17		Long-term debt		499,662
18		Operating lease liability, noncurrent		122,010
19		Other long-term liabilities		60,568
20		Common stock		40
21		Additional paid-in capital		485,239
22		Retained (deficit) earnings	336,674	
23		Net sales		3,199,517
24		Cost of sales	2,274,592	
25		Selling and administrative expenses	583,679	
26		Interest expense	23,510	
27		Provision for income taxes	56,161	
28			4,757,882	4,757,882
29				

Required:

1. Prepare a classified consolidated statement of income (with earnings per share) and consolidated balance sheet for the current year. Number of shares outstanding used in computation of earnings per share was 39,833.
2. Compute gross profit percentage and return on assets. Total assets at the beginning of the year was $1,240,871.

CASES AND PROJECTS

Annual Report Cases

CP5-1
LO5-2, 5-3, 5-4
Target Corporation

Finding Financial Information

Refer to the financial statements of **Target** given in Appendix B at the end of this book. At the bottom of each statement, the company warns readers to "Refer to Notes to Consolidated Financial Statements." The following questions illustrate the types of information that you can find in the financial statements and accompanying notes. (**Hint:** Use the notes.) All dollar amounts are in millions.

Required:

1. What items were included as Noncurrent assets on the balance sheet? (Select all that apply.)
   a. Property and equipment
   b. Operating lease assets
   c. Inventory
   d. Other noncurrent assets
   e. Deferred income taxes
2. How much land did the company own at the end of the most recent reporting year?
   a. $26,879
   b. $5,914
   c. $6,141
   d. $6,036
   e. None of the above
3. What percentage of Accrued and other current liabilities was "Gift card liability" at the end of the current year (round to one decimal place)?
   a. 16.9%
   b. 11.3%
   c. 4.7%
   d. 28.2%
   e. None of the above
4. At what point were digitally originated (website) sales recognized as revenue?
   a. When the order is placed
   b. When the order is shipped
   c. When the order is paid for
   d. Upon delivery or pickup
   e. None of the above
5. The company reported cash flows from operating activities of $10,525. However, its net income was only $4,369 for the current year. What was the largest single cause of the difference?
   a. Depreciation and amortization
   b. Increase in Accounts payable
   c. Increase in Inventory
   d. Expenditures for property and equipment
   e. Deferred income taxes

6. Calculate the company's ROA for the year ended January 30, 2021. Round your percentage answer to two decimal places.
   a. 9.29%
   b. 5.61%
   c. 8.52%
   d. 29.33%
   e. None of the above

Finding Financial Information

CP5-2
LO5-2, 5-3

Walmart, Inc.

Refer to the financial statements of **Walmart** given in Appendix C at the end of this book. At the bottom of each statement, the company warns readers that "The accompanying notes are an integral part of these financial statements." The following questions illustrate the types of information that you can find in the financial statements and accompanying notes. (**Hint:** Use the notes.) All dollar amounts are in millions

Required:

1. What subtotals does Walmart report on its income statement? Select all that apply.
   a. Gross profit
   b. Income before income taxes
   c. Operating income
   d. Total current assets
   e. Cash dividends declared
2. The company spent $10,264 on purchases of Property and equipment and $180 on business acquisitions during the most recent year. Were operating activities or financing activities the major source of cash for these expenditures?
3. What was the company's largest asset (net) at the end of the most recent year?
4. What are the two largest components of the company's "Current liabilities"?
5. Over what useful lives is "Transportation equipment" depreciated?
6. What percentage of *gross* "Property and equipment" is composed of "Buildings and improvements"? Round the percentage to two decimal places.
7. *(a)* Compute the company's gross profit percentage for the most recent two years. Round the percentages to two decimal places.
   (b) Has it increased or decreased?
   (c) Explain the meaning of the change. Note that Walmart uses the term "Total revenues" in place of "Net sales."

Comparing Companies within an Industry

CP5-3
LO5-4

Target Corporation
Walmart, Inc.

Refer to the financial statements of **Target** (Appendix B) and **Walmart** (Appendix C) at the end of this book.

Required:

1. (a) Compute return on assets for the most recent year. Round the percentage to two decimal places. (b) Which company provided the highest return on invested capital during the current year?
2. (a) Compare the ROA profit driver analysis for Target and Walmart. Round the Net profit margin percentage and Total asset turnover to two decimal places. (b) Which company outperforms or underperforms the other on each ratio?
3. Which is the more important cause of the difference in ROA: Net profit margin or Total asset turnover?

Financial Reporting and Analysis Case

Using Financial Reports: Financial Statement Inferences

CP5-4
LO5-3

The following amounts were selected from the annual financial statements for Genesis Corporation at December 31, 2024 (end of the third year of operations):

From the 2024 income statement:	
Sales revenue	$ 275,000
Cost of goods sold	(170,000)
All other expenses (including income tax)	(95,000)
Net income	$ 10,000

From the December 31, 2024, balance sheet:	
Current assets	$ 90,000
All other assets	212,000
Total assets	$ 302,000
Current liabilities	$ 40,000
Long-term liabilities	66,000
Capital stock (par $10)	100,000
Paid-in capital	16,000
Retained earnings	80,000
Total liabilities and stockholders' equity	$ 302,000

Required:
Analyze the data on the 2024 financial statements of Genesis by answering the questions that follow. Show computations.

1. What was the gross margin on sales?
2. What was the amount of EPS?
3. If the income tax rate was 25 percent, what was the amount of pretax income?
4. What was the average sales price per share of the capital stock?
5. Assuming that no dividends were declared or paid during 2024, what was the beginning balance (January 1, 2024) of retained earnings?

Critical Thinking Cases

CP5-5
LO5-4
Sony

Making Decisions as a Manager: Evaluating the Effects of Business Strategy on Return on Assets

Sony is a world leader in the manufacture of consumer and commercial electronics as well as in the entertainment and insurance industries. Its ROA has decreased over the last three years.

Required:
Indicate the most likely effect of each of the changes in business strategy on Sony's ROA for the next period and future periods (+ for increase, − for decrease, and NE for no effect), assuming all other things are unchanged. Explain your answer for each. Treat each item independently.

a. Sony decreases its investment in research and development aimed at products to be brought to market in more than one year.
b. Sony begins a new advertising campaign for a movie to be released during the next year.

Strategy Change	Current Period ROA	Future Periods' ROA
a.		
b.		

CP5-6
LO5-1, 5-3

Making a Decision as an Auditor: Effects of Errors on Income, Assets, and Liabilities

Megan Company (not a corporation) was careless about its financial records during its first year of operations, the current year. It is December 31 of the current year the end of the annual accounting period. An outside CPA has examined the records and discovered numerous errors, all of which are described here. Assume that each error is independent of the others.

Required:
Analyze each error and indicate its effect on the current year's and the next year's net income, assets, and liabilities if not corrected. Do not assume any other errors. Use these codes to indicate the effect of each dollar amount: O = overstated, U = understated, and NE = no effect. Write an explanation of your analysis of each transaction to support your response. The first transaction is used as an example.

Independent Errors	Effect on					
	Net Income		Assets		Liabilities	
	Current Year	Next Year	Current Year	Next Year	Current Year	Next Year
1. Depreciation expense for the current year not recorded in the current year, $950.	O $950	NE	O $950	O $950	NE	NE
2. Wages earned by employees during the current year not recorded or paid in the current year but recorded and paid in the next year, $500.						
3. Revenue earned during the current year but not collected or recorded until the next year, $600.						
4. Amount paid in the current year and recorded as expense in the current year but not an expense until the next year, $200.						
5. Revenue collected in the current year and recorded as revenue in the current year but not earned until the next year, $900.						
6. Sale of services and cash collected in the current year. Recorded as a debit to Cash and as a credit to Accounts Receivable, $300.						
7. On December 31 of the current year, bought land on credit for $8,000; not recorded until payment was made on February 1 of the next year.						

Following is a sample explanation of the first error:

Failure to record depreciation in the current year caused depreciation expense to be too low; therefore, net income was overstated by $950. Accumulated depreciation also is too low by $950, which causes assets to be overstated by $950 until the error is corrected.

Evaluating an Ethical Dilemma: Management Incentives and Fraudulent Financial Statements

CP5-7
LO5-1, 5-3
Royal Ahold

Netherlands-based **Royal Ahold** ranked among the world's three largest food retailers. In the United States it operated the **Stop & Shop** and **Giant** supermarket chains. Its subsidiary, U.S. Foodservice, Inc. ("USF") was a leading food distributor for commercial customers. The U.S. Justice Department and Securities and Exchange Commission and its Dutch counterparts brought criminal and civil charges against the company and executives from both the Dutch parent company and its U.S. subsidiary for overstating earnings by more than $1 billion. U.S. officials also brought charges against representatives of USF's suppliers who provided outside auditors with fraudulent audit confirmations aimed at supporting the fictitious numbers. The U.S. Attorney's Office for the Southern District of New York described the U.S.-based part of the accounting fraud as follows:

> Between 2000 and early 2003, USF was one of the United States' leading distributors of food and related products, supplying customers including restaurants and cafeterias. USF typically purchased the products it resold from a variety of suppliers at full price. However, the suppliers often refunded a portion of the purchase price to USF in the form of negotiated rebates, known as "promotional allowances." Promotional allowances reduced USF's cost of sales and thereby increased the company's earnings.

During this time period, Kaiser and others falsely inflated USF's earnings by causing USF to record hundreds of millions of dollars in fictitious promotional allowances that had not been earned.

Press Release from the U.S. Attorney's Office Southern District of New York, December 7, 2011.

Required:
Using news reports and press releases from relevant regulators and prosecutors (*a Google search for "Ahold Accounting Fraud" will uncover many documents*), answer the following questions.

1. Whom did the courts and regulatory authorities hold responsible for the misstated financial statements?
2. Did the company cooperate with investigations into the fraud? How did this affect the penalties imposed against the company?
3. How might executive compensation plans that tied bonuses to accounting earnings have motivated unethical conduct in this case?

You as Analyst: Online Company Research

CP5-8
LO5-1, 5-2, 5-3, 5-4

Analyzing the Accounting Communication Process (an Individual or Team Project)

In your web browser, search for the investor relations page of a public company you are interested in (e.g., Papa John's investor relations). Select SEC Filings or Annual Report or Financials to obtain the 10-K for the most recent year available.*

Required:
Answer the following questions based on the annual report (10-K) that you have downloaded:

1. What formats are used to present the
   a. Balance Sheets?
   b. Income Statements?
   c. Operating Activities section of the Statements of Cash Flows?
2. Find one footnote for each of the following and describe its contents in brief:
   a. An accounting rule applied in the company's statements.
   b. Additional detail about a reported financial statement number.
   c. Relevant financial information but with no number reported in the financial statements.
3. Using electronic sources, find one article reporting the company's annual earnings announcement. When is it dated and how does that date compare to the balance sheet date?
4. Using electronic sources, find two analysts' reports for your company.
   a. Give the date, name of the analyst, and his or her recommendation from each report.
   b. Discuss why the recommendations are similar or different. Look at the analysts' reasoning for their respective recommendations.
5. Using the SEC EDGAR website (sec.gov), what is the most recent document filed by your company with the SEC (e.g., 8-K, S-1) and what did it say in brief?
6. Ratio analysis:
   a. What does the return on total assets ratio measure in general?
   b. Compute the ROA ratio for the last three years.
   c. What do your results suggest about the company?
   d. If available, find the industry ratio for the most recent year, compare it to your results, and discuss why you believe your company differs from or is similar to the industry ratio.
7. Use the ROA profit driver analysis to determine the cause(s) of any differences in the ROA ratio over the last three years. (Remember that you computed the three profit driver ratios in the last three chapters.)

*Alternatively, you can go to sec.gov, click on Company Filings (under the search box), and type the name of the public company you want to find. Once at the list of filings, type 10-K in the Filing Type box. The most recent 10-K annual report will be at the top of the list. Click on Interactive Data for a list of the parts or the entire report to examine.

BUSINESS ANALYTICS AND DATA VISUALIZATION WITH EXCEL AND TABLEAU

Connect offers a variety of exercises to assess Excel skills, data visualization, interpretation, and analysis, including auto-graded Tableau Dashboard Activities, Applying Excel problems, and Integrated Excel problems.

Images used throughout chapter: Question of ethics: mushmello/Shutterstock; Pause for feedback: McGraw Hill; Guided help: McGraw Hill; Financial analysis: McGraw Hill; Focus on cash flows: Hilch/Shutterstock; Key ratio analysis: guillermain/123RF; Data analytics: Hilch/Shutterstock; Tip: McGraw Hill; ESG reporting: McGraw Hill; International perspective: Hilch/Shutterstock; Internal control alert icon: McGraw Hill

chapter 6

Reporting and Interpreting Sales Revenue, Receivables, and Cash

Since its founding in 1992, **Skechers U.S.A., Inc.**, has become a major player in the active, casual, dress casual, and athletic footwear market reporting over $5.2 billion in sales for 2019. Its growth strategy requires building brand recognition by developing and introducing additional innovative footwear that satisfy the company's high standards for styling, quality, comfort, and affordability. Skechers accurately recognized changing tastes in footwear both for work and play and focuses on a price point in the largest segment of the footwear market. It also supports increased brand recognition with focused advertising relying on celebrity endorsements. But unlike athletic apparel titans such as **Nike** and **Under Armour** who contract mainly with the biggest current names in sports, Skechers celebrity endorsers are a mix of former and current athletes and entertainers including Clayton Kershaw, Brooke Henderson, Howie Long, David Ortiz, Tony Romo, Matt Kuchar, and Sugar Ray Leonard. These endorsers appeal to the broad range of customers for Skechers more than 3,000 footwear styles covering every age and activity.

Skechers currently markets more than 3,000 footwear styles for men, women, and children. To sell its footwear, it has developed a very successful multichannel distribution system. First, it sells to department and specialty stores such as **Kohl's** and **Dick's Sporting Goods** where it acts as a wholesaler. It also sells directly to consumers through more than 800 Skechers retail stores and online at skechers.com. Its wholesale and retail channels present different accounting issues that we will focus on in this chapter. Outside of the United States, it continues to penetrate new markets through its international subsidiaries and joint ventures in Asia, Canada, Europe, and elsewhere. These international ventures have been the largest source of recent sales growth.

LEARNING OBJECTIVES

After studying this chapter, you should be able to:

6-1 Analyze the impact of credit card sales, sales discounts, sales returns, and sales of bundled items on the amounts reported as net sales. p. 293

6-2 Estimate, report, and evaluate the effects of uncollectible accounts receivable (bad debts) on financial statements. p. 298

6-3 Analyze and interpret the receivables turnover ratio and the effects of accounts receivable on cash flows. p. 304

6-4 Report, control, and safeguard cash. p. 307

FOCUS COMPANY

Kevin Khoo/Shutterstock

Skechers U.S.A.

BUILDING BRANDS TO BUILD GROSS PROFIT

skechers.com

UNDERSTANDING THE BUSINESS

Planning **Skechers**' growth strategy requires careful coordination of sales activities, as well as cash collections from customers. Much of this coordination revolves around allowing consumers to use credit cards, providing business customers discounts for early payment, and allowing sales returns and allowances under certain circumstances—strategies that motivate customers to buy its products and make payment for their purchases. These activities affect **net sales** revenue, the top line on the income statement. Coordinating sales and cash collections from customers also involves managing bad debts, which affect selling, general, and administrative expenses on the income statement and **cash** and **accounts receivable** on the balance sheet. Net sales, accounts receivable, and cash are the focus of this chapter. We also will introduce the receivables turnover ratio as a measure of the efficiency of credit-granting and collection activities. Finally, because the cash collected from customers is also a tempting target for fraud and embezzlement, we will discuss how accounting systems commonly include controls to prevent and detect such misdeeds.

ORGANIZATION OF THE CHAPTER

Accounting for Net Sales Revenue

- Motivating Sales and Collections
- Credit Card Sales to Consumers
- Sales Discounts to Businesses
- Sales Returns and Allowances
- Reporting Net Sales
- Revenue Recognition for Bundled Goods and Services

Measuring and Reporting Receivables

- Classifying Receivables
- Accounting for Bad Debts
- Reporting Accounts Receivable and Bad Debts
- Estimating Bad Debts
- Control over Accounts Receivable
- Receivables Turnover Ratio

Reporting and Safeguarding Cash

- Cash and Cash Equivalents Defined
- Cash Management
- Internal Control of Cash
- Reconciliation of the Cash Accounts and the Bank Statements

ACCOUNTING FOR NET SALES REVENUE

As indicated in Chapter 3, the **revenue recognition principle** requires that revenues be recorded when the company transfers goods and services to customers, in the amount it expects to be entitled to receive. For sellers of goods, sales revenue is recorded when title and risks of ownership transfer to the buyer. The point at which title (ownership) changes hands is determined by the shipping terms in the sales contract. When goods are shipped **FOB (free on board) shipping point,** title changes hands at shipment and the buyer normally pays for shipping. When they are shipped **FOB destination,** title changes hands on delivery and the seller normally pays for shipping. **Skechers** ships its goods to retailers, such as **Kohl's** and **Dick's**, FOB shipping point. Revenues from goods shipped FOB shipping point are normally recognized at shipment. Revenues from goods shipped FOB destination are normally recognized at delivery.

Service companies most often record sales revenue when they have provided services to the buyer. Companies disclose the revenue recognition rule they follow in the footnote to the financial statements entitled Summary of Significant Accounting Policies. In that note, Skechers reports the following:

SKECHERS U.S.A.
REAL WORLD EXCERPT:
Quarterly Report

NOTES TO CONSOLIDATED FINANCIAL STATEMENTS

1. Summary of Significant Accounting Policies

Revenue Recognition

The Company recognizes revenue when control of the promised goods or services is transferred to its customers in an amount that reflects the consideration the Company expects to be entitled to in exchange for those goods or services. . . . The Company recognizes revenue on wholesale sales upon shipment as that is when the customer obtains control of the promised goods. . . . For in-store sales, the Company recognizes revenue at the point of sale. For sales made through its websites, the Company recognizes revenue upon shipment to the customer which is when the customer obtains control of the promised good. . . .

Source: Skechers U.S.A., Inc.

The appropriate **amount** of revenue to record is **the amount it expects to be entitled to receive.** Revenue recognition for more complex sales contracts with multiple performance obligations requires application of the five-step process which is discussed at the end of this section.

Motivating Sales and Collections

LEARNING OBJECTIVE 6-1

Analyze the impact of credit card sales, sales discounts, sales returns, and sales of bundled items on the amounts reported as net sales.

Some sales practices differ depending on whether sales are made to businesses or consumers. **Skechers** sells footwear and apparel to other **businesses,** which then sell the goods to consumers. It also operates its own online and physical retail stores that sell footwear directly to **consumers.**

Skechers and other companies use a variety of methods to motivate both groups of customers to buy its products and make payment for their purchases. The principal methods include (1) allowing consumers to use credit cards to pay for purchases, (2) providing business customers direct credit and discounts for early payment, and (3) allowing returns from all customers under certain circumstances. These methods, in turn, affect the way we compute **net sales revenue.**

Credit Card Sales to Consumers

Skechers accepts cash or credit card payment for its retail store and online sales. Retailers accept credit cards (mainly Visa, Mastercard, and American Express) for a variety of reasons:

1. Increasing customer traffic.
2. Avoiding the costs of providing credit directly to consumers, including recordkeeping and bad debts (discussed later).
3. Lowering losses due to bad checks.
4. Avoiding losses from fraudulent credit card sales. (As long as the retailer follows the credit card company's verification procedure, the credit card company [e.g., Visa] absorbs any losses.)
5. Receiving money faster. (Because credit card receipts can be deposited directly in its bank account, Skechers receives its money faster than it would if it provided credit directly to consumers.)

The credit card company charges a fee for the service it provides. For example, when Skechers deposits its credit card receipts in the bank, it might receive credit for only 97 percent of the sales price. The credit card company is charging a 3 percent fee (the **credit card discount**) for its services. If daily credit card sales were $3,000, Skechers would report the following:

Sales revenue	$ 3,000
Less: Credit card discounts (0.03 × $3,000)	90
Net sales (reported on the income statement)	$ 2,910

The accounting by the retailer is the same when a consumer uses a contactless mobile payment app such as Google Pay or Apple Pay to charge a purchase to one of their credit cards.

Sales Discounts to Businesses

Most of **Skechers**' sales to businesses are credit sales on open account; that is, there is no formal written promissory note or credit card. When Skechers sells footwear to retailers on credit, credit terms are printed on the sales document and invoice (bill) sent to the customer. Often credit terms are abbreviated. For example, if the full price is due within 30 days of the invoice date, the credit terms would be noted as **n/30.** Here, the **n** means the sales amount **net** of, or less, any sales returns.

Early Payment Incentive

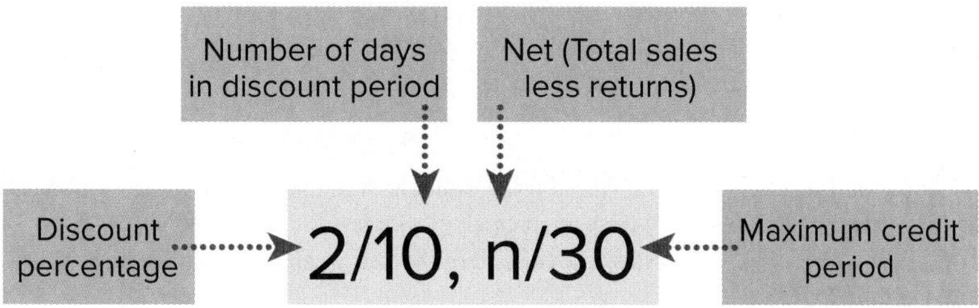

In some cases, a **sales discount** (often called a cash discount) is granted to the purchaser to encourage early payment.[1] For example, Skechers could offer terms of 2/10, n/30, which means that the customer may deduct 2 percent from the invoice price if cash payment is made within 10 days from the date of sale. If cash payment is not made within the 10-day discount period, the full sales price (less any returns) is due within a maximum of 30 days.

Companies offer this sales discount to encourage customers to pay more quickly. This provides two benefits:

1. Prompt receipt of cash from customers reduces the necessity to borrow money to meet operating needs.
2. Because customers tend to pay bills providing discounts first, a sales discount also decreases the chances that the customer will run out of funds before the company's bill is paid.

Companies commonly record sales discounts taken by subtracting the discount from sales if payment is made **within** the discount period.[2] For example, if credit sales of $1,000 are recorded with terms 2/10, n/30 and payment of $980 ($1,000 × 0.98 = $980) is made within the discount period, net sales of the following amount would be reported:

Sales revenue	$1,000
Less: Sales discounts (0.02 × $1,000)	20
Net sales (reported on the income statement)	$ 980

If payment is made after the discount period, the full $1,000 would be reported as net sales. Accounting for sales discounts is discussed in more detail in the Supplement at the end of this chapter. Any quantity discounts or rebates provided to customers also must be subtracted in the computation of net sales.

FINANCIAL ANALYSIS

To Take or Not to Take the Discount, That Is the Question

Purchasers often pay within the discount period because the savings are substantial. With terms 2/10, n/30, customers save 2 percent by paying 20 days early (on the 10th day instead of the 30th). This translates into a 37 percent annual interest rate. To calculate the annual interest rate, first compute the interest rate for the discount period. When the 2 percent discount is taken, the customer pays only 98 percent of the gross sales price. For example, on a $100 sale with terms 2/10, n/30, $2 would be saved and $98 would be paid 20 days early.

The interest rate for the 20-day discount period and the annual interest rate are computed as follows:

$$\frac{\text{Amount Saved}}{\text{Amount Paid}} = \text{Interest Rate for 20 Days} \qquad \text{Interest Rate for 20 Days} \times \frac{365 \text{ days}}{20 \text{ days}} = \text{Annual Interest Rate}$$

$$\frac{\$2}{\$98} = 2.04\% \text{ for 20 Days} \qquad 2.04\% \times \frac{365 \text{ days}}{20 \text{ days}} = 37.23\% \text{ Annual Interest Rate}$$

As long as the bank's interest rate is less than the interest rate associated with failing to take cash discounts, the customer will save by taking the cash discount. For example, even if credit customers had to borrow from the bank at a rate as high as 15 percent, they would save a great deal.

[1]It is important not to confuse a cash discount with a trade discount. Vendors sometimes use a **trade discount** for quoting sales prices; the sales price is the list or printed catalog price **less** the trade discount.

[2]Companies also estimate discounts not yet taken at the end of the year to ensure that the amounts are subtracted from sales revenue in the proper period.

Sales Returns and Allowances

Retailers and consumers have a right to return unsatisfactory or damaged merchandise and receive a refund or an adjustment to their bill. Such returns are often accumulated in a separate account called Sales Returns and Allowances and must be deducted from gross sales revenue in determining net sales. This account informs **Skechers'** managers of the volume of returns and allowances and thus provides an important measure of the quality of customer service. Assume that **Fontana's Shoes** of Ithaca, New York, buys 40 pairs of athletic shoes (at $50 each) from Skechers for $2,000 on account. Before paying for the shoes, Fontana's discovers that 10 pairs of shoes are not the color ordered and returns them to Skechers.[3] Skechers would compute net sales as follows:

Sales revenue	$2,000
Less: Sales returns and allowances (10 pairs × $50)	500
Net sales (reported on the income statement)	$1,500

Cost of goods sold related to the 10 pairs of shoes also would be reduced.

Reporting Net Sales

On the company's books, credit card discounts, sales discounts, and sales returns and allowances are accounted for separately to allow managers to monitor the costs of credit card use, sales discounts, and returns. Using the numbers in the preceding examples, the amount of net sales reported on the income statement is computed in the following manner:

Sales revenue	$6,000
Less: Credit card discounts (a contra-revenue)	90
Sales discounts (a contra-revenue)	20
Sales returns and allowances (a contra-revenue)	500
Net sales (included on the first line of the income statement)	$5,390

Tip The amount of revenue to record is the **amount it expects to be entitled to receive.** Consequently, credit card discounts, sales discounts, and sales returns and allowances must be subtracted to compute **net sales.**

Net Sales to all customers is the top line reported on **Skechers'** income statement, presented in Exhibit 6.1. Skechers indicates in its revenue recognition footnote that the appropriate subtractions are made.

EXHIBIT 6.1

Net Sales on the Income Statement

SKECHERS U.S.A.

REAL WORLD EXCERPT: Annual Report

SKECHERS U.S.A., INC. AND SUBSIDIARIES
Consolidated Statements of Earnings (partial)
Years ended December 31, 2019, 2018, 2017
(amounts in thousands)

	2019	2018	2017
Net sales	$5,220,051	$4,642,068	$4,164,160
Cost of sales	2,728,894	2,418,463	2,225,271
Gross profit	2,491,157	2,223,605	1,938,889
Royalty income	22,493	20,582	16,666
	$2,513,650	$2,244,187	$1,955,555
Operating expenses:			
Selling	369,901	350,435	327,201
General and administrative	1,625,306	1,455,987	1,245,474
	1,995,207	1,806,422	1,572,675
Earnings from operations	$ 518,443	$ 437,765	$ 382,880
. . .			

Source: Skechers U.S.A., Inc.

[3]Alternatively, Skechers might offer Fontana's a $200 allowance to keep the wrong color shoes. If Fontana's accepts the offer, Skechers reports $200 as sales returns and allowances.

SKECHERS U.S.A.
REAL WORLD EXCERPT:
Annual Report

NOTES TO CONSOLIDATED FINANCIAL STATEMENTS

1. Summary of Significant Accounting Policies

Revenue Recognition

. . . Allowances for estimated returns, discounts, . . . and chargebacks are provided for when related revenue is recorded. . . . Allowance for returns, sales allowances and customer chargebacks are recorded against revenue.

Source: Skechers U.S.A., Inc.

A QUESTION OF ETHICS

Volume Discounts/Rebates and Earnings Misstatements at Monsanto

In 2016, the SEC found that agribusiness company **Monsanto** had materially misstated company revenues and earnings by improperly accounting for volume discounts and rebates offered to retailers and distributors of its flagship product, Roundup. In an attempt to offset the effects of generic competition for Roundup, Monsanto instituted new discount and rebate programs. As we learned in Chapter 3 and in this chapter, net sales revenue should be recorded "in the amount the company expects to be entitled to receive." This rule requires that Monsanto reduce the amount of reported net sales by the expected rebates in the period of sale. Instead, Monsanto delayed recording these reductions until the following year, overstating net sales and earnings before taxes by $44.5 million and $48 million, respectively, over two years. Monsanto also improperly accounted for additional rebates of more than $56 million as selling, general, and administrative expense instead of a reduction in net sales. This practice overstated gross profit, an important measure used by analysts to assess competitive pricing pressure, but did not affect income before taxes. Monsanto agreed to pay an $80 million penalty to settle these violations and three Monsanto managers paid penalties of between $30,000 and $55,000 for their involvement in the scheme. And Monsanto's CEO and CFO returned bonuses of $3,165,852 and $728,843 they had received as a result of the earnings overstatements, though they were not found to be involved in personal misconduct.

PAUSE FOR FEEDBACK

In the last section, we learned to analyze the impact of **credit card sales, sales discounts,** and **sales returns,** all of which reduce the amounts reported as net sales. Both credit card discounts and sales or cash discounts promote faster receipt of cash. Sales returns and allowances include refunds and adjustments to customers' bills for defective or incorrect merchandise.

Before you move on, complete the following questions to test your understanding of these concepts.

SELF-STUDY QUIZ

1. Assume that **Skechers** sold $30,000 worth of footwear to various retailers with terms 1/10, n/30 and half of that amount was paid within the discount period. Gross retail store and online sales were $5,000 for the same period; 80 percent of these sales were paid for with credit cards with a 3 percent discount and the rest were paid for with cash. Compute net sales for the period.
2. During the fourth quarter of 2019, Skechers' net sales totaled $1,330,732 and cost of sales was $692,983. What was Skechers' gross profit for the fourth quarter of 2019?

After you have completed your answers, check them at the bottom of the next page.

GUIDED HELP 6-1

For additional step-by-step video instruction on computing net sales and gross profit, go to mhhe.com/libby_gh6-1

Related Homework: M6-1, M6-2, E6-1, E6-2, E6-3, E6-4

Revenue Recognition for Bundled Goods and Services: A Five-Step Process

Bundling of goods and services within one sales contract is common in a variety of industries. For example, **Verizon** sells its cell phones at a discount when purchased as part of a two-year service contract. When **Jaguar** sells its new cars to customers, it bundles a fairly complete five-year warranty and five years of scheduled maintenance "free" with the purchase. And when **Apple** sells its iPad, the contract with its customer includes not only the iPad and software essential to the functioning of the product, but future upgrades relating to the essential software.

When a seller promises to provide more than one good or service in a single sales contract, FASB standards specify a five-step process to determine the amount to be recognized as revenue. Let's assume that the total selling price for an iPad is $500, (1) $450 of which relates to the **hardware with essential software** and (2) $50 of which relates to **future software upgrades** that would be provided over **five years.** In this case, we would apply the five-step process as follows:

Step 1: Identify the contract between the company and customer.	Bundled: iPad "with essential software" **and** related **future upgrade** services
Step 2: Identify the performance obligations (promised goods and services).	#1 Hardware with essential software #2 Future software upgrades
Step 3: Determine the transaction price.	$500 total
Step 4: Allocate the transaction price to the performance obligations.	#1 Hardware with essential software → $450 #2 Future software upgrades → $50
Step 5: Recognize revenue when each performance obligation is satisfied (or over time if a service is provided over time).	#1 Hardware with essential software → $450 in year 1 #2 Future software upgrades → $50/5 = $10 each year for five years

As a result, revenue from the contract would be recognized as follows:

Year	1	2	3	4	5	Total
Revenue	$450 + $10 = $460	$10	$10	$10	$10	**$500**

MEASURING AND REPORTING RECEIVABLES

Classifying Receivables

Receivables may be classified in three common ways. First, they may be classified as either an account receivable or a note receivable. An accounts receivable is created by a credit sale on an open account. For example, an account receivable is created when **Skechers** sells shoes on

Solutions to SELF-STUDY QUIZ

1.

Gross Sales	$ 35,000
Less: Sales Discounts (0.01 × 1/2 × $30,000)	150
Credit Card Discounts (0.03 × 0.80 × $5,000)	120
Net Sales	$ 34,730

2.

Net Sales	$1,330,732
Cost of Sales	692,983
Gross Profit	$ 637,749

open account to **Dick's**. A notes receivable is a promise in writing (a formal document) to pay (1) a specified amount of money, called the **principal,** at a definite future date known as the maturity date and (2) a specified amount of **interest** at one or more future dates. The interest is the amount charged for use of the principal.

Second, receivables may be classified as trade or nontrade receivables. A **trade receivable** is created in the normal course of business when a sale of merchandise or services on credit occurs. A **nontrade receivable** arises from transactions other than the normal sale of merchandise or services. For example, if Skechers loaned money to a new vice president to help finance a home at the new job location, the loan would be classified as a nontrade receivable. Third, in a classified balance sheet, receivables also are classified as either **current** or **noncurrent** (short term or long term), depending on when the cash is expected to be collected. Skechers reports Trade Accounts Receivable from customers and classifies the asset as a current asset because the accounts receivable are all due to be paid within one year. It also reports Other Receivables in a much smaller amount, and also classifies that asset as a current asset.

INTERNATIONAL PERSPECTIVE

Selected Foreign Currency Exchange Rates (in US$)

Mexican Peso	$0.05
Singapore Dollar	$0.75
Euro	$1.21

Foreign Currency Receivables

Export (international) sales are a growing part of the U.S. economy. For example, international sales amounted to 57.9 percent of **Skechers'** net sales in 2019. Most export sales to businesses are on credit. When a buyer agrees to pay in its local currency, Skechers cannot add the resulting accounts receivable, which are denominated in foreign currency, directly to its U.S. dollar accounts receivable. Skechers' accountants first must convert them to U.S. dollars using the end-of-period exchange rate between the two currencies. For example, if a French department store owed Skechers €20,000 (euros, the common currency of the European Monetary Union) on December 31, 2019, and each euro was worth US$1.21 on that date, Skechers would add US$24,200 to its accounts receivable on the balance sheet.

LEARNING OBJECTIVE 6-2

Estimate, report, and evaluate the effects of uncollectible accounts receivable (bad debts) on financial statements.

Accounting for Bad Debts

For billing and collection purposes, **Skechers** keeps a separate accounts receivable account for each business customer (retailer) that resells its footwear (called a **subsidiary account**). The accounts receivable amount on the balance sheet represents the total of these individual customer accounts.

When Skechers extends credit to its commercial customers, it knows that some of these customers will not pay their debts. The expense recognition principle requires recording of bad debt expense in the **same** accounting period in which the related sales are made. This presents an important accounting problem. Skechers may not learn which particular customers will not pay until the **next** accounting period. So, at the end of the period of sale, it normally does not know which customers' accounts receivable are bad debts.

Skechers resolves this problem by using the allowance method to measure bad debt expense. The allowance method is based on **estimates** of the expected amount of bad debts. Two primary steps in employing the allowance method are:

1. Making the end-of-period adjusting entry to record estimated bad debt expense.
2. Writing off specific accounts determined to be uncollectible during the period.

Recording Bad Debt Expense Estimates

Bad debt expense (doubtful accounts expense, uncollectible accounts expense, provision for uncollectible accounts) is the expense associated with estimated uncollectible accounts receivable. An **adjusting journal entry at the end of the accounting period** records the bad debt estimate. For the year ended December 31, 2019, Skechers estimated bad debt expense to be $6,402 (all numbers in thousands of dollars)[4] and made the following adjusting entry:

	Debit	Credit
Bad debt expense (+E, −SE)	6,402	
Allowance for doubtful accounts (+XA, −A)		6,402

Assets		=	Liabilities	+	Stockholders' Equity	
Allowance for doubtful accounts	−6,402				Bad debt expense (+E)	−6,402

Tip An **adjusting journal entry at the end of the accounting period** records the bad debt estimate.

The Bad Debt Expense is included in the category "General and Administrative" expenses on the income statement. It decreases net income and stockholders' equity. Accounts Receivable could not be credited in the journal entry because there is no way to know which customers' accounts receivable are involved. So the credit is made, instead, to a contra-asset account called Allowance for Doubtful Accounts (Allowance for Bad Debts or Allowance for Uncollectible Accounts). As a contra-asset, the balance in Allowance for Doubtful Accounts is always subtracted from the balance of the asset Accounts Receivable. Thus, the entry decreases the net book value of Accounts Receivable and total assets.

Writing Off Specific Uncollectible Accounts

Throughout the year, when it is determined that a customer will not pay its debts (e.g., due to bankruptcy), the write-off of that individual bad debt is recorded through a journal entry. Now that the specific uncollectible customer account receivable has been identified, it can be removed with a credit. At the same time, we no longer need the related estimate in the contra-asset Allowance for Doubtful Accounts, which is removed by a debit. The journal entry summarizing **Skechers'** total write-offs of $7,912 during 2019 follows:

	Debit	Credit
Allowance for doubtful accounts (−XA, +A)	7,912	
Accounts receivable (−A)		7,912

Assets		=	Liabilities	+	Stockholders' Equity
Allowance for doubtful accounts	+7,912				
Accounts receivable	−7,912				

Tip Individual bad debts are written off **throughout the period** when it is determined that a customer won't pay its debts.

Notice that this journal entry did **not affect any income statement accounts.** It did not record a bad debt expense because the estimated expense was recorded with an adjusting entry in the period of sale. Also, the entry did **not change the net book value of accounts receivable** because the decrease in the asset account (Accounts Receivable) was offset by the decrease in the contra-asset account (Allowance for Doubtful Accounts). Thus, it also did not affect total assets.

FINANCIAL ANALYSIS

Bad Debt Recoveries

When a company receives a payment on an account that already has been written off, the journal entry to write off the account is reversed to put the receivable back on the books and then the collection of cash is recorded. For example, if the previously written-off amount was $677, it would make the following entries:

	Debit	Credit
Accounts receivable (+A)	677	
Allowance for doubtful accounts (+XA, −A)		677
Cash (+A)	677	
Accounts receivable (−A)		677

Note that these entries, like the original write-off, do not affect total assets or net income. Only the estimate of bad debts affects these amounts.

[4] Amounts have been simplified for our discussion by assuming that all sales are on open account and that the total allowances (contra-assets) to accounts receivable related to bad debts.

Summary of the Accounting Process

It is important to remember that accounting for bad debts is a two-step process:

Step	Timing	Accounts Affected		Financial Statement Effects	
1. Record estimated bad debts adjustment	End of period in which sales are made	Bad Debt Expense (E)	↑	Net Income	↓
		Allowance for Doubtful Accounts (XA)	↑	Assets (Accounts Receivable, Net)	↓
2. Identify and write off actual bad debts	Throughout period as bad debts become known	Accounts Receivable (A)	↓	Net Income	No effect
		Allowance for Doubtful Accounts (XA)	↓	Assets (Accounts Receivable, Net)	No effect

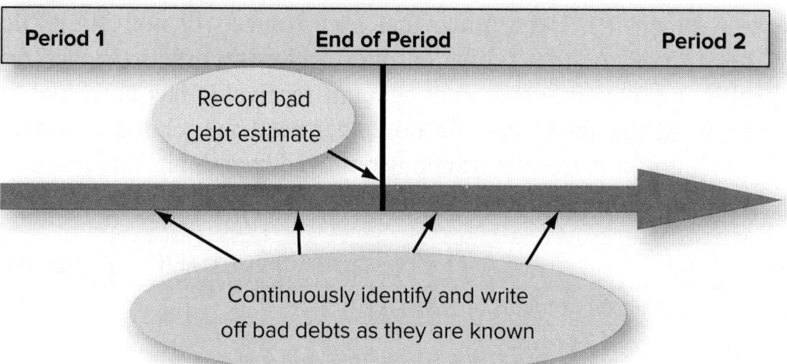

Skechers' complete 2019 accounting process for bad debts can now be summarized in terms of the changes in Accounts Receivable (Gross) and the Allowance for Doubtful Accounts:

Accounts Receivable (Gross) (A)			
Beginning balance	527,529	Collections on account	5,070,259
Sales on account	5,220,051	Write-offs	7,912
Ending balance	669,409		

Allowance for Doubtful Accounts (XA)			
		Beginning balance	25,616
Write-offs	7,912	Bad debt expense adjustment	6,402
		Ending balance	24,106

Accounts Receivable Dec. 31, 2019	
Accounts Receivable (Gross) (A)	$669,409
Allowance for Doubtful Accounts (XA)	24,106
Accounts Receivable (Net) (A)	$645,303

Accounts Receivable (Gross) includes the total accounts receivable, both collectible and uncollectible. The balance in the Allowance for Doubtful Accounts is the portion of the accounts receivable balance the company estimates to be uncollectible. Accounts Receivable (Net) reported on the balance sheet is the portion of the accounts the company expects to collect (or its estimated net realizable value).

Reporting Accounts Receivable and Bad Debts

Analysts who want information on **Skechers'** receivables will find Accounts Receivable, net of allowance for doubtful accounts (the net book value), of $645,303 and $501,913 for year-end 2019 and 2018, respectively, reported on the balance sheet (Exhibit 6.2). Skechers reports the balance in the Allowance for Doubtful Accounts ($24,106 in 2019 and $25,616 in 2018) within the account title. Other companies report the balance in the Allowance for Doubtful Accounts in a note. Accounts Receivable (Gross), the total accounts receivable, can be computed by adding the two amounts together.

EXHIBIT 6.2

Accounts Receivable on the Partial Balance Sheet

SKECHERS U.S.A.
REAL WORLD EXCERPT:
Annual Report

SKECHERS U.S.A., INC. AND SUBSIDIARIES
CONSOLIDATED BALANCE SHEETS (partial)
December 31, 2019 and 2018
(amounts in thousands)

	2019	2018
ASSETS		
Current assets:		
Cash and cash equivalents	$ 824,876	$ 872,237
Short-term investments	112,037	100,029
Trade accounts receivable, less allowances of $24,106 in 2019 and $25,616 in 2018	645,303	501,913
Other receivables	53,932	55,683
Inventories	1,069,863	863,260
Prepaid expenses and other current assets	113,580	79,018
Total current assets	$2,819,591	$2,472,140

Source: Skechers U.S.A., Inc.

The amounts of bad debt expense and accounts receivable written off for the period, if material, are reported on a schedule that publicly traded companies must include in their Annual Report Form 10-K filed with the SEC. Exhibit 6.3 presents this schedule from Skechers' 2019 filing.

EXHIBIT 6.3

Accounts Receivable Valuation Schedule (Form 10-K)

SKECHERS U.S.A.
REAL WORLD EXCERPT:
Annual Report

SCHEDULE II—VALUATION AND QUALIFYING ACCOUNTS
Years Ended December 31, 2019, 2018 and 2017
(amounts in thousands)

Allowance for Doubtful Accounts	Balance at Beginning of Year	Additions (Bad Debt Expense)	Deductions (Write Offs)	Balance at End of Year
December 31, 2017	$16,594	$12,773	$ 8,851	$20,516
December 31, 2018	20,516	15,485	10,385	25,616
December 31, 2019	25,616	6,402	7,912	24,106

Source: Skechers U.S.A., Inc.

PAUSE FOR FEEDBACK II

When receivables are material, companies must employ the allowance method to account for uncollectibles. These are the steps in the process:

a. The end-of-period adjusting entry to record the estimate of bad debt expense and *increase* the allowance for doubtful accounts.
b. Writing off specific accounts determined to be uncollectible during the period to eliminate the specific uncollectible account receivable and *decrease* the allowance for doubtful accounts.

The adjusting entry reduces net income as well as net accounts receivable. The write-off affects neither. Before you move on, complete the following questions to test your understanding of these concepts.

SELF-STUDY QUIZ

In a recent year, **Crocs™, Inc.**, a **Skechers** competitor, had a beginning credit balance in the Allowance for Doubtful Accounts of $10,959 (all numbers in thousands of dollars). It wrote off accounts receivable totaling $4,249 during the year and made a bad debt expense adjustment for the year of $1,566.

1. What adjusting journal entry did Crocs make for bad debts at the end of the year?
2. Make the journal entry summarizing Crocs's total write-off of bad debts during the year.
3. Compute the balance in the Allowance for Doubtful Accounts at the end of the year.

After you have completed your answers, check them at the bottom of this page.

GUIDED HELP 6-2

For additional step-by-step video instruction on preparing journal entries related to bad debts, go to mhhe.com/libby_gh6-2.

Related Homework: M6-3, M6-4, E6-8

Estimating Bad Debts

The bad debt expense amount recorded in the end-of-period adjusting entry often is estimated based on either (1) a percentage of total credit sales for the period or (2) an aging of accounts receivable. Both methods are acceptable under GAAP and are widely used. The percentage of credit sales method is simpler to apply, but the aging method is generally more accurate. Many companies use the simpler method on a weekly or monthly basis and use the more accurate method on a monthly or quarterly basis to check the accuracy of the earlier estimates. In our example, both methods produce exactly the same estimate, which rarely occurs in practice.

Percentage of Credit Sales Method

The **percentage of credit sales method** bases bad debt expense on the historical percentage of credit sales that result in bad debts. The average percentage of credit sales that result in bad debts can be computed by dividing total bad debt losses by total **credit** sales. A company that has been operating for some years has sufficient experience to project probable future bad debt losses. For example, if we assume that, during the year 2020, **Skechers** expected bad debt losses of 1.0 percent of credit sales, and its credit sales were $1,970,000 (all numbers in thousands), it would estimate the current year's bad debts as

Tip The **percentage of credit sales method** is a simple one-step process where the current period's bad debt expense is directly estimated.

Credit sales	$1,970,000
× **Bad debt loss rate** (1.0%)	× .01
Bad debt expense	$ 19,700

This amount would be directly recorded as Bad Debt Expense (and an increase in Allowance for Doubtful Accounts) in the current year. Our beginning balance in the Allowance for

Solutions to SELF-STUDY QUIZ

1. Bad debt expense (+E, −SE)	1,566	
Allowance for doubtful accounts (+XA, −A)		1,566
2. Allowance for doubtful accounts (−XA, +A)	4,249	
Accounts receivable (−A)		4,249

3. Beginning Balance + Bad Debt Expense Estimate − Write-Offs = Ending Balance:
$10,959 + 1,566 − 4,249 = $8,276

Doubtful Accounts for 2020 would be the ending balance for 2019. Assuming write-offs during 2020 of $14,106, the ending balance is computed as follows:

Allowance for Doubtful Accounts (XA)			
		2020 Beginning balance	24,106
2020 Write-offs	14,106	2020 Bad debt expense adjustment	19,700
		2020 Ending balance	? = 29,700

Percent of credit sales estimate

Beginning balance	$24,106
+ Bad debt expense	19,700
− Write-offs	14,106
Ending balance	$29,700

Aging of Accounts Receivable

The **aging of accounts receivable method** relies on the fact that, as accounts receivable become older and more overdue, it is less likely that they will be collected. For example, a receivable that was due in 30 days but has not been paid after 120 days is less likely to be collected, on average, than a similar receivable that remains unpaid after 45 days.

If Skechers split its assumed 2020 ending balance in accounts receivable (gross) of $670,000 into three age categories, it would first examine the individual customer accounts receivable and sort them into the three age categories. Based on prior experience, management would then estimate the probable bad debt loss rates for each category: for example, not yet due, 1 percent; 1 to 90 days past due, 6 percent; over 90 days, 30 percent.

As illustrated in the aging schedule below, this would result in an estimate of total uncollectible amounts of $29,700, the estimated ending balance that should be in the Allowance for Doubtful Accounts. From this, the adjustment to record Bad Debt Expense (and an increase in Allowance for Doubtful Accounts) for 2020 would be computed as follows:

Aging Schedule 2020

Aged accounts receivable			Estimated Percentage Uncollectible		Estimated Amount Uncollectible
Not yet due	$450,000	×	1%	=	$ 4,500
Up to 90 days past due	170,000	×	6%	=	10,200
Over 90 days past due	50,000	×	30%	=	15,000
Estimated ending balance in Allowance for Doubtful Accounts					29,700
Less: Balance in Allowance for Doubtful Accounts before adjustment ($24,106 − $14,106)					10,000
Bad Debt Expense for the year					$19,700

Allowance for Doubtful Accounts (XA)			
		2020 Beginning balance	24,106
2020 Write-offs	14,106	2020 Bad debt expense adjustment	? =19,700
		2020 Ending balance	29,700 Total estimated uncollectible accounts

Tip The **aging of accounts receivable method** is a three-step process where (1) the estimated ending balance in the allowance is calculated, (2) which is compared to the current balance, (3) to compute the bad debt expense adjustment for the period.

Comparison of the Two Methods

It is important to recognize that the approach to recording bad debt expense using the percentage of credit sales method is different from that for the aging method:

- **Percentage of credit sales.** Directly compute the amount to be recorded as **Bad Debt Expense** on the **income statement** for the period in the adjusting journal entry.
- **Aging of Accounts Receivable.** Compute the **estimated ending balance** we would like to have in the **Allowance for Doubtful Accounts** on the **balance sheet** after we make the necessary adjusting entry. The **difference** between the current balance in the account and the estimated balance is recorded as the adjusting entry for Bad Debt Expense for the period.

In either case, the balance sheet presentation for 2020 would show Accounts Receivable, less Allowance for Doubtful Accounts, of $640,300 ($670,000 – $29,700).

Actual Write-Offs Compared with Estimates

Skechers' Form 10-K provides clear information on its approach to estimating uncollectible accounts:

SKECHERS U.S.A.
REAL WORLD EXCERPT:
Form 10-K

CRITICAL ACCOUNTING POLICIES

Allowance for Bad Debts . . .

The Company provides a reserve, charged against revenue and its receivables, for estimated losses that may result from its customers' inability to pay. To minimize the likelihood of uncollectability, customers' credit-worthiness is reviewed and adjusted periodically in accordance with external credit reporting services, financial statements issued by the customer and the Company's experience with the account. When a customer's account becomes significantly past due, the Company generally places a hold on the account and discontinues further shipments to that customer, minimizing further risk of loss. The Company determines the amount of the reserve by analyzing known uncollectible accounts, aged receivables, economic conditions in the customers' countries or industries, historical losses and its customers' credit-worthiness. Amounts later determined and specifically identified to be uncollectible are charged against this reserve.

Source: Skechers U.S.A., Inc.

If uncollectible accounts actually written off differ from the estimated amount previously recorded, a higher or lower amount of bad debt expense is recorded in the next period to make up for the previous period's error in estimate. For example, Skechers reported that during the second quarter of 2020, it "recorded an incremental $10.2 million in bad debt expense, due to the expected impact of the COVID-19 pandemic on wholesale customers around the world." **When estimates are found to be incorrect, financial statement values for prior annual accounting periods are not corrected.**

Control over Accounts Receivable

Internal Control Alert

Many managers forget that extending credit will increase sales volume, but unless the related receivables are collected, they do not add to the bottom line. Companies that emphasize sales without monitoring the collection of credit sales soon find much of their current assets tied up in accounts receivable. The following practices can help minimize bad debts:

1. Require approval of customers' credit history by a person independent of the sales and collections functions.
2. Age accounts receivable periodically and contact customers with overdue payments.
3. Reward both sales and collections personnel for speedy collections so that they work as a team.

To assess the effectiveness of overall credit-granting and collection activities, managers and analysts often compute the receivables turnover ratio.

LEARNING OBJECTIVE 6-3

Analyze and interpret the receivables turnover ratio and the effects of accounts receivable on cash flows.

KEY RATIO ANALYSIS

Receivables Turnover Ratio

ANALYTICAL QUESTION

How effective are credit-granting and collection activities?

RATIO AND COMPARISONS

The receivables turnover ratio is computed as follows (see Exhibits 6.1 and 6.2):

$$\textbf{Receivables Turnover} = \frac{\textbf{Net Sales*}}{\textbf{Average Net Trade Accounts Receivable}\dagger}$$

The 2019 receivables turnover ratio for **Skechers:**

$$\frac{\$5,220,051}{(\$645,303 + \$501,913)/2} = 9.1$$

Comparisons Over Time		
Skechers U.S.A.		
2017	**2018**	**2019**
11.4	10.2	9.1

Comparisons With Competitors	
Wolverine World Wide	Crocs
2019	**2019**
6.6	12.0

INTERPRETATIONS

In General The receivables turnover ratio reflects how many times average trade receivables are recorded and collected during the period. The higher the ratio, the faster the collection of receivables. A higher ratio benefits the company because it can invest the money collected to earn interest income or reduce borrowings to reduce interest expense. Overly generous payment schedules and ineffective collection methods keep the receivables turnover ratio low. Analysts and creditors watch this ratio because a sudden decline may mean that a company is extending payment deadlines in an attempt to prop up lagging sales or is even recording sales that will later be returned by customers. Many managers and analysts compute the related number, **average collection period** or **average days sales in receivables,** which is equal to 365 ÷ Receivables Turnover Ratio. It indicates the average time it takes a customer to pay its accounts. For Skechers, the amount would be computed as follows for 2019:

$$\textbf{Average Collection Period} = \frac{\textbf{365}}{\textbf{Receivables Turnover}} = \frac{\textbf{365}}{\textbf{9.1}} = \textbf{40.1 days}$$

Focus Company Analysis Skechers' receivables turnover decreased from 11.4 in 2017 to 9.1 in 2019. This indicates that the company is taking more time to convert its receivables into cash. Compared to the receivables turnover ratios of its competitors, Skechers' ratio is below that of **Crocs** and ahead of that of **Wolverine World Wide**, which markets Merrell, Sperry, Wolverine, and Keds.

A Few Cautions Because differences across industries and between firms in the manner in which customer purchases are financed can cause dramatic differences in the ratio, a particular firm's ratio should be compared only with its prior years' figures or with other firms in the same industry following the same financing practices.

FOCUS ON CASH FLOWS

Accounts Receivable

The change in accounts receivable can be a major determinant of a company's cash flow from operations. While the income statement reflects the revenues of the period, the cash flow from operating activities reflects cash collections from customers. Because sales on account increase the balance in accounts receivable and cash collections from customers decrease the balance in accounts receivable, the change in accounts receivable from the beginning to the end of the period is the difference between sales and collections.

*Because the amount of net credit sales is normally not reported separately, most analysts use net sales in this equation.
†Average Net Trade Accounts Receivable = (Beginning Net Trade Accounts Receivable + Ending Net Trade Accounts Receivable) ÷ 2.

EFFECT ON STATEMENT OF CASH FLOWS

In General When there is a net **decrease in accounts receivable** for the period, cash collected from customers is more than revenue; thus, the decrease must be **added** in computing cash flows from operations. When a net **increase in accounts receivable** occurs, cash collected from customers is less than revenue; thus, the increase must be **subtracted** in computing cash flows from operations.*

	Effect on Cash Flows
Operating activities (indirect method)	
Net income	$ xxx
Adjusted for	
Add accounts receivable decrease	+
or	
Subtract accounts receivable increase	−

Focus Company Analysis The excerpt below shows the Operating Activities section of **Skechers**' statement of cash flows. Sales growth outpaced collections during 2019 to result in an increase in Skechers' balance in receivables. This increase is subtracted in reconciling net income to cash flow from operating activities because revenues are higher than cash collected from customers for 2019. When receivables decrease, the amount of the decrease in receivables is added in reconciling net income to cash flow from operating activities because cash collected from customers is higher than revenues.

	2019
Cash flows from operating activities	
Net earnings	$427,252
Adjustments to reconcile net income to net cash provided by operating activities:	
....	...
Changes in operating assets and liabilities:	
Receivables	(118,390)
Inventories	(171,903)
	...
	...
Net cash provided by operating activities	$426,552

PAUSE FOR FEEDBACK

When using the **percentage of sales method,** you directly compute the bad debt expense for the period by multiplying the amount of credit sales by the bad debt loss rate. With the **aging method,** you compute the estimated ending balance in the allowance and solve for the bad debt expense. This process involves multiplying the amount in each age category by the estimated percentage uncollectible to produce the estimated ending balance in the allowance for doubtful accounts. The difference between the estimated ending balance and the balance in the allowance before the adjustment becomes the bad debt expense for the year. Before you move on, try an example of the more difficult aging method computations based on **Crocs**'s numbers reported in an earlier year.

*For companies with receivables in foreign currency or business acquisitions/dispositions, the change reported on the cash flow statement will not equal the change in the accounts receivable reported on the balance sheet.

SELF-STUDY QUIZ

1. In an earlier year, **Skechers'** competitor Crocs reported a beginning balance in the Allowance for Doubtful Accounts of $5,262. It also wrote off bad debts amounting to $2,551 during the year. At the end of the year, it computed total estimated uncollectible accounts using the aging method to be $3,973 (all numbers in thousands of dollars). What amount did Crocs record as bad debt expense for the period? (**Solution approach:** Use the Allowance for Doubtful Accounts T-account or the following equation to solve for the missing value.)

Allowance for Doubtful Accounts (XA)	

Estimated ending balance in Allowance for Doubtful Accounts	______
Less: Current balance in Allowance for Doubtful Accounts	______
Bad Debt Expense for the year	______

The accounts receivable turnover ratio measures the effectiveness of credit-granting and collection activities. Faster turnover means faster receipt of cash from your customers. To test whether you understand this concept, answer the following question:

2. Indicate whether **granting later payment deadlines** (e.g., 60 days instead of 30 days) will most likely **increase** or **decrease** the accounts receivable turnover ratio. Explain.

After you have completed your answers, check them below.

GUIDED HELP 6-3

For additional step-by-step video instruction on estimating and reporting bad debts using the aging method, go to mhhe.com/libby_gh-3.

Related Homework: M6-5, E6-13, E6-14, E6-15

REPORTING AND SAFEGUARDING CASH

LEARNING OBJECTIVE 6-4

Report, control, and safeguard cash.

Cash and Cash Equivalents Defined

Cash is defined as money or any instrument that banks will accept for deposit and immediate credit to a company's account, such as a check, money order, or bank draft. Cash equivalents are investments with original maturities of three months or less that are readily convertible to cash and whose value is unlikely to change (i.e., they are not sensitive to interest rate changes).

Solutions to SELF-STUDY QUIZ

1.

Allowance for Doubtful Accounts (XA)			
		Beginning balance	5,262
Write-offs	2,551	Bad debt expense (solve)	1,262
		Ending balance	3,973

Estimated ending balance in Allowance for Doubtful Accounts	$3,973
Less: Current balance in Allowance for Doubtful Accounts ($5,262 – $2,551)	2,711
Bad Debt Expense for the year	$1,262

2. Granting later payment deadlines will most likely **decrease** the accounts receivable turnover ratio because later collections from customers will increase the average accounts receivable balance (the denominator of the ratio), decreasing the ratio.

Typical instruments included as cash equivalents are bank certificates of deposit and Treasury bills that the U.S. government issues to finance its activities.

Like most companies, **Skechers** combines all of its bank accounts and cash equivalents into one amount, Cash and Cash Equivalents, on the balance sheet. It also reports that the book values of cash equivalents on the balance sheet equal their fair market values—which we should expect given the nature of the instruments (investments whose value is unlikely to change).

Cash Management

Many businesses receive a large amount of cash, checks, and credit card receipts from their customers each day. Anyone can spend cash, so management must develop procedures to safeguard the cash it uses in the business. Effective cash management involves more than protecting cash from theft, fraud, or loss through carelessness. Other cash management responsibilities include:

1. Accurate accounting so that reports of cash flows and balances may be prepared.
2. Controls to ensure that enough cash is available to meet (*a*) current operating needs, (*b*) maturing liabilities, and (*c*) unexpected emergencies.
3. Prevention of the accumulation of excess amounts of idle cash. Idle cash earns no revenue. Therefore, it often is invested in securities to earn a return until it is needed for operations.

Internal Control of Cash

Internal Control Alert

Because cash is the asset most vulnerable to theft and fraud, a significant number of internal control procedures should focus on cash. You already have observed internal control procedures for cash, although you may not have known it at the time. At most movie theaters, one employee sells tickets and another employee collects them. Having one employee do both jobs would be less expensive, but that single employee could easily steal cash and admit a patron without issuing a ticket. If different employees perform the tasks, a successful theft requires the participation of both.

Juice Images/Alamy Stock Photo

Effective internal control of cash should include the following:

1. Separation of duties.
   a. Complete separation of the jobs of receiving cash and disbursing cash.
   b. Complete separation of the procedures of accounting for cash receipts and cash disbursements.
   c. Complete separation of the physical handling of cash and all phases of the accounting function.
2. Prescribed policies and procedures.
   a. Require that all cash receipts be deposited in a bank daily. Keep any cash on hand under strict control.
   b. Require separate approval of the purchases and the actual cash payments. Prenumbered checks should be used. Special care must be taken with payments by **electronic funds transfers** because they involve no controlled documents (checks).
   c. Assign the responsibilities for cash payment approval and check-signing or electronic funds transfer transmittal to different individuals.
   d. Require monthly reconciliation of bank accounts with the cash accounts on the company's books (discussed in detail in the next section).

A QUESTION OF ETHICS

Ethics and the Need for Internal Control

Some people are bothered by the recommendation that all well-run companies should have strong internal control procedures. These people believe that control procedures suggest that management does not trust the company's employees. Although the vast majority of employees are trustworthy, employee theft does cost businesses billions of dollars each year. Interviews with convicted felons indicate that in many cases they stole from their employers because they thought that it was easy and that no one cared (there were no internal control procedures).

Many companies have a formal code of ethics that requires high standards of behavior in dealing with customers, suppliers, fellow employees, and the company's assets. Although each employee is ultimately responsible for his or her own ethical behavior, internal control procedures can be thought of as important value statements from management.

Reconciliation of the Cash Accounts and the Bank Statements

Content of a Bank Statement

Proper use of the bank accounts can be an important internal cash control procedure. Each month, the bank provides the company (the depositor) with a **bank statement**. **Online banking provides this same information on a daily basis.** The bank statement and the online banking site list (1) each paper or electronic deposit recorded by the bank during the period, (2) each paper or electronic payment cleared by the bank during the period, (3) the bank charges or deductions (such as service charges) made directly to the company's account by the bank, and (4) the balance in the company's account. A typical bank statement for ROW.COM, Inc., is shown in Exhibit 6.4.

Exhibit 6.4 lists four items that need explanation. Notice the $500, $100, and $2,150 items listed in the Checks and Debits column and coded **EFT.**[5] This is the code for **electronic funds transfers.** ROW.COM pays its electricity, rent, and insurance bills using electronic checking. When it orders the electronic payments, it records these items on the company's books in the same manner as a paper check. So no additional entry is needed.

EXHIBIT 6.4

Example of a Bank Statement

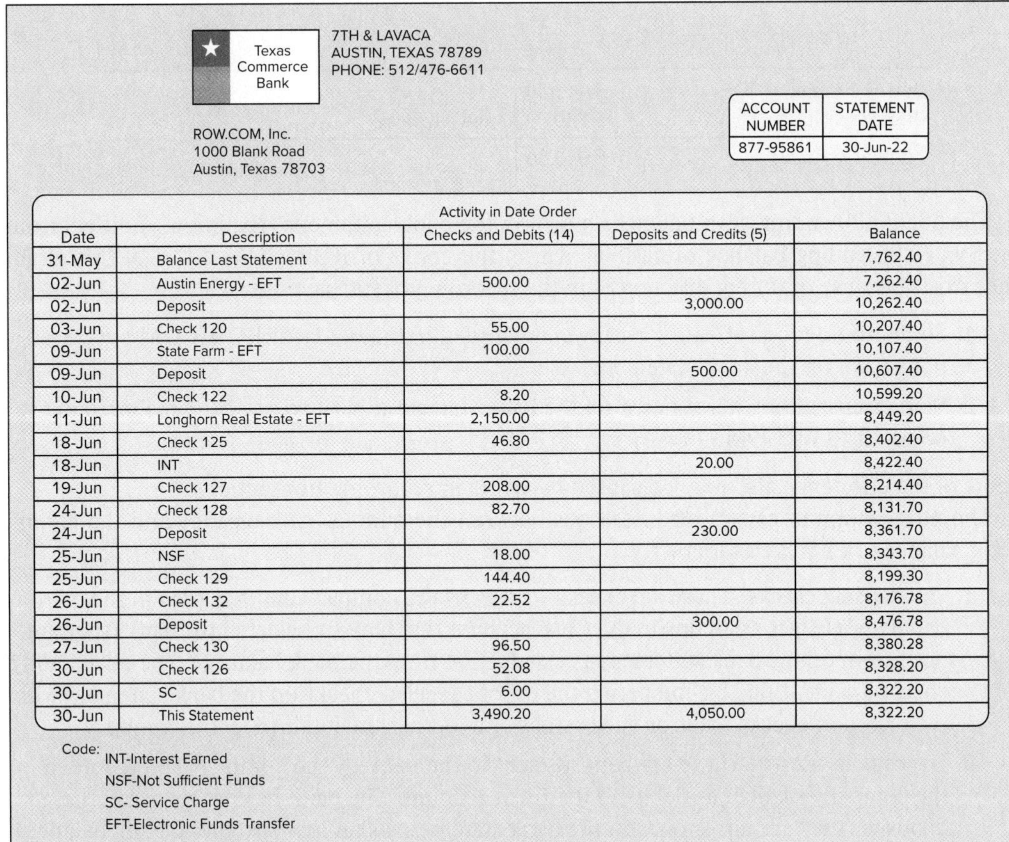

Texas Commerce Bank
7TH & LAVACA
AUSTIN, TEXAS 78789
PHONE: 512/476-6611

ROW.COM, Inc.
1000 Blank Road
Austin, Texas 78703

ACCOUNT NUMBER	STATEMENT DATE
877-95861	30-Jun-22

Activity in Date Order

Date	Description	Checks and Debits (14)	Deposits and Credits (5)	Balance
31-May	Balance Last Statement			7,762.40
02-Jun	Austin Energy - EFT	500.00		7,262.40
02-Jun	Deposit		3,000.00	10,262.40
03-Jun	Check 120	55.00		10,207.40
09-Jun	State Farm - EFT	100.00		10,107.40
09-Jun	Deposit		500.00	10,607.40
10-Jun	Check 122	8.20		10,599.20
11-Jun	Longhorn Real Estate - EFT	2,150.00		8,449.20
18-Jun	Check 125	46.80		8,402.40
18-Jun	INT		20.00	8,422.40
19-Jun	Check 127	208.00		8,214.40
24-Jun	Check 128	82.70		8,131.70
24-Jun	Deposit		230.00	8,361.70
25-Jun	NSF	18.00		8,343.70
25-Jun	Check 129	144.40		8,199.30
26-Jun	Check 132	22.52		8,176.78
26-Jun	Deposit		300.00	8,476.78
27-Jun	Check 130	96.50		8,380.28
30-Jun	Check 126	52.08		8,328.20
30-Jun	SC	6.00		8,322.20
30-Jun	This Statement	3,490.20	4,050.00	8,322.20

Code:
INT-Interest Earned
NSF-Not Sufficient Funds
SC- Service Charge
EFT-Electronic Funds Transfer

[5]These codes vary among banks.

Notice that listed in the Checks and Debits column there is a deduction for $18 coded **NSF.** This entry refers to a check for $18 received from a customer and deposited by ROW.COM with its bank. The bank processed the check through banking channels to the customer's bank, but the account did not have sufficient funds to cover the check. The customer's bank therefore returned it to ROW.COM's bank, which then charged it back to ROW.COM's account. This type of check often is called an **NSF check** (not sufficient funds). The NSF check is now a receivable; consequently, ROW.COM must make an entry to debit Receivables and credit Cash for the $18.

Notice the $6 listed on June 30 in the Checks and Debits column and coded **SC.** This is the code for bank service charges. The bank statement included a memo by the bank explaining this service charge (which was not documented by a check). ROW.COM must make an entry to reflect this $6 decrease in the bank balance as a debit to a relevant expense account, such as Bank Service Expense, and a credit to Cash.

Notice the $20 listed on June 18 in the Deposits and Credits column and coded **INT** for interest earned. The bank pays interest on checking account balances, and it increased ROW.COM's account for interest earned during the period. ROW.COM must record the interest by making an entry to debit Cash and credit Interest Income for the $20.

Need for Reconciliation

A **bank reconciliation** is the process of comparing (reconciling) the ending cash balance in the company's records and the ending cash balance reported by the bank on the monthly bank statement (or on the online banking site). A bank reconciliation should be completed at the end of each month. Usually, the ending cash balance as shown on the bank statement does not agree with the ending cash balance shown by the related Cash ledger account on the books of the company. For example, the Cash ledger account of ROW.COM showed the following at the end of June (ROW.COM has only one checking account):

Cash (A)			
June 1 balance	7,753.40		
June deposits	5,830.00	June payments	4,543.40
Ending balance	9,040.00		

The $8,322.20 ending cash balance shown on the bank statement (Exhibit 6.4) differs from the $9,040.00 ending balance of cash shown on the books of ROW.COM. Most of this difference exists because of timing differences in the recording of transactions:

1. Some transactions affecting cash were recorded in the books of ROW.COM but were not shown on the bank statement.
2. Some transactions were shown on the bank statement but had not been recorded in the books of ROW.COM.

Some of the difference also may be caused by errors in recording transactions.

The most common causes of differences between the ending bank balance and the ending book balance of cash are as follows:

1. **Outstanding checks.** These are checks written by the company and recorded in the company's ledger as credits to the Cash account that have not cleared the bank (they are not shown on the bank statement as a deduction from the bank balance). The outstanding checks are identified by comparing the list of canceled checks on the bank statement with the record of checks (such as check stubs or a journal) maintained by the company.
2. **Deposits in transit.** These are deposits sent to the bank by the company and recorded in the company's ledger as debits to the Cash account. The bank has not recorded these deposits (they are not shown on the bank statement as an increase in the bank balance). Deposits in transit usually happen when deposits are made one or two days before the close of the period covered by the bank statement. Deposits in transit are determined by comparing the deposits listed on the bank statement with the company deposit records.

3. **Bank service charges.** These are expenses for bank services listed on the bank statement but not recorded on the company's books.
4. **NSF checks.** These are "bad checks" or "bounced checks" that have been deposited but must be deducted from the company's cash account and rerecorded as accounts receivable.
5. **Interest.** This is the interest paid by the bank to the company on its bank balance.
6. **Errors.** Both the bank and the company may make errors, especially when the volume of cash transactions is large.

Bank Reconciliation Illustrated

The general format for the bank reconciliation follows:

Ending cash balance per books	$xxx	Ending cash balance per bank statement	$xxx
+ Interest paid by bank	xx	+ Deposits in transit	xx
− NSF checks/Service charges	xx	− Outstanding checks	xx
± Company errors	xx	± Bank errors	xx
Ending correct cash balance	$xxx	Ending correct cash balance	$xxx

Exhibit 6.5 shows the bank reconciliation prepared by ROW.COM for the month of June to reconcile the ending bank balance ($8,322.20) with the ending book balance ($9,040.00). On the completed reconciliation, the correct cash balance is $9,045.00. This correct balance is the amount that should be shown in the Cash account after the reconciliation. Because ROW.COM has only one checking account and no cash on hand, it is also the correct amount of cash that should be reported on the balance sheet.[6]

ROW.COM followed these steps in preparing the bank reconciliation:

1. **Identify the outstanding checks.** A comparison of the checks and electronic payments listed on the bank statement with the company's record of all checks drawn and electronic payments made showed the following checks were still outstanding (had not cleared the bank) at the end of June:

Check No.	Amount
121	$ 145.00
123	815.00
131	117.20
Total	$1,077.20

This total was entered on the reconciliation as a deduction from the bank account. These checks will be deducted by the bank when they clear the bank.

EXHIBIT 6.5

Bank Reconciliation Illustrated

ROW.COM, INC.
Bank Reconciliation
For the Month Ending June 30, 2022

Company's Books		**Bank Statement**	
Ending cash balance per books	$9,040.00	Ending cash balance per bank statement	$8,322.20
Additions		Additions	
Interest paid by the bank	20.00	Deposit in transit	1,800.00
Error in recording payment	9.00		
	9,069.00		10,122.20
Deductions		Deductions	
NSF check of R. Smith	18.00	Outstanding checks	1,077.20
Bank service charges	6.00		
Ending correct cash balance	$9,045.00	Ending correct cash balance	$9,045.00

[6]In this example, there were no outstanding checks or deposits in transit at the end of May.

2. **Identify the deposits in transit.** A comparison of the deposit slips on hand with those listed on the bank statement revealed that a deposit of $1,800 made on June 30 was not listed on the bank statement. This amount was entered on the reconciliation as an addition to the bank account. It will be added by the bank when it records the deposit.
3. **Record bank charges and credits:**
   a. Interest received from the bank, $20—entered on the bank reconciliation as an addition to the book balance; it already has been included in the bank balance.
   b. NSF check of R. Smith, $18—entered on the bank reconciliation as a deduction from the book balance; it has been deducted from the bank balance.
   c. Bank service charges, $6—entered on the bank reconciliation as a deduction from the book balance; it has been deducted from the bank balance.
4. **Determine the impact of errors.** At this point, ROW.COM found that the reconciliation did not balance by $9. Upon checking the journal entries made during the month, the electronic payment on June 9 for $100 to pay an account payable was found. The payment was recorded in the company's accounts as $109. Therefore, $9 (i.e., $109 – $100) must be added to the book cash balance on the reconciliation; the bank cleared the electronic payment for the correct amount, $100.

Note that in Exhibit 6.5 the two sections of the bank reconciliation now agree at a correct cash balance of $9,045.00.

A bank reconciliation as shown in Exhibit 6.5 accomplishes two major objectives:

1. It checks the accuracy of the bank balance and the company cash records, which involves developing the correct cash balance. The correct cash balance (plus cash on hand, if any) is the amount of cash that is reported on the balance sheet.
2. It identifies any previously unrecorded transactions or changes that are necessary to cause the company's Cash account(s) to show the correct cash balance. Any transactions or changes on the **company's books side** of the bank reconciliation need journal entries. Therefore, the following journal entries based on the company's books side of the bank reconciliation (Exhibit 6.5) must be entered into the company's records:

	Debit	Credit
(a) Cash (+A)	20	
Interest income (+R, +SE)		20
To record interest by bank.		
(b) Accounts receivable (+A)	18	
Cash (−A)		18
To record NSF check.		
(c) Bank service expense (+E, −SE)	6	
Cash (−A)		6
To record service fees charged by bank.		
(d) Cash (+A)	9	
Accounts payable (+L)		9
To correct error made in recording a check payable to a creditor.		

Assets		=	Liabilities		+	Stockholders' Equity	
Cash (+20, −18, −6, +9)	+5		Accounts payable	+9		Interest income (+R)	+20
Accounts receivable	+18					Bank service expense (+E)	−6

Notice again that all of the additions and deductions on the company's books side of the reconciliation need journal entries to update the Cash account. The additions and deductions on the bank statement side do not need journal entries because they will work out automatically when they clear the bank.

PAUSE FOR FEEDBACK

Cash is the most liquid of all assets, flowing continually into and out of a business. As a result, a number of critical control procedures, including the **reconciliation** of bank accounts, should be applied. Also, management of cash may be critically important to decision makers who must have cash available to meet current needs yet must avoid excess amounts of idle cash that produce no revenue. To see if you understand the basics of a bank reconciliation, answer the following questions:

SELF-STUDY QUIZ

Indicate which of the following items discovered while preparing a company's bank reconciliation will result in adjustment of the cash balance on the balance sheet.

1. Outstanding checks.
2. Deposits in transit.
3. Bank service charges.
4. NSF checks that were deposited.

After you have completed your answers, check them at the bottom of this page.

Related Homework: M6-6

DEMONSTRATION CASE A

(Complete the requirements before proceeding to the suggested solutions.) Wholesale Warehouse Stores sold $950,000 in merchandise during 2022. Of this amount, $400,000 was on credit with terms 2/10, n/30 (75 percent of these amounts were paid within the discount period), $500,000 was paid with credit cards (there was a 3 percent credit card discount), and the rest was paid in cash. On December 31, 2022 The Accounts Receivable balance was $80,000. The beginning balance in the Allowance for Doubtful Accounts was $9,000 and $6,000 of bad debts was written off during the year.

Required:

1. Compute net sales for 2022, assuming that sales and credit card discounts are treated as contra-revenues.

2. Assume that Wholesale uses the percentage of sales method for estimating bad debt expense and that it estimates that 2 percent of credit sales will produce bad debts. Record bad debt expense for 2022.

3. Assume instead that Wholesale uses the aging of accounts receivable method and that it estimates that $10,000 worth of current accounts is uncollectible. Record bad debt expense for 2022.

SUGGESTED SOLUTION

1. Both sales discounts and credit card discounts should be subtracted from sales revenues in the computation of net sales.

Sales revenue	$950,000
Less: Sales discounts (0.02 × 0.75 × $400,000)	6,000
Credit card discounts (0.03 × $500,000)	15,000
Net sales	$929,000

Solutions to SELF-STUDY QUIZ

3. Bank service charges are deducted from the company's account; thus, cash must be reduced and an expense must be recorded.
4. NSF checks that were deposited were recorded on the books as increases in the cash account; thus, cash must be decreased and the related accounts receivable increased if payment is still expected.

2. The percentage estimate of bad debts should be applied to credit sales. Cash sales never produce bad debts.

Bad debt expense (+E, −SE) (0.02 × $400,000)	8,000	
Allowance for doubtful accounts (+XA, −A)		8,000

Assets		=	Liabilities	+	Stockholders' Equity	
Allowance for doubtful accounts	−8,000				Bad debt expense (+E)	−8,000

3. The entry made when using the aging of accounts receivable method is the estimated balance minus the current balance.

Estimated ending balance in Allowance for Doubtful Accounts	$10,000
Less: Current balance in Allowance for Doubtful Accounts ($9,000 – $6,000)	3,000
Bad Debt Expense for the year	$ 7,000

Bad debt expense (+E, −SE)	7,000	
Allowance for doubtful accounts (+XA, −A)		7,000

Assets		=	Liabilities	+	Stockholders' Equity	
Allowance for doubtful accounts	−7,000				Bad debt expense (+E)	−7,000

DEMONSTRATION CASE B

(Complete the requirements before proceeding to the suggested solution that follows.) Laura Anne Long, a freshman at a large state university, has just received her first checking account statement. This was her first chance to attempt a bank reconciliation. She had the following information to work with:

Bank balance, September 1	$1,150
Deposits during September	650
Checks cleared during September	900
Bank service charge	25
Bank balance, October 1	875

Laura was surprised that the deposit of $50 she made on September 29 had not been posted to her account and was pleased that her rent check of $200 had not cleared her account. Her checkbook balance on October 1 was $750.

Required:

1. Complete Laura's bank reconciliation.
2. Why is it important for individuals such as Laura and businesses to do a bank reconciliation each month?

SUGGESTED SOLUTION

1. Laura's bank reconciliation:

Laura's Books		Bank Statement	
October 1 cash balance	$750	October 1 cash balance	$875
Additions		Additions	
None		Deposit in transit	50
Deductions		Deductions	
Bank service charge	(25)	Outstanding check	(200)
Correct cash balance	$725	Correct cash balance	$725

2. Bank statements, whether personal or business, should be reconciled each month. This process helps ensure that a correct balance is reflected in the account owner's books. Failure to reconcile a bank statement increases the chance that an error will not be discovered and may result in bad checks being written. Businesses must reconcile their bank statements for an additional reason: The correct balance that is calculated during reconciliation is recorded on the balance sheet.

Chapter Supplement

Recording Discounts and Returns

Credit card discounts and **cash discounts** must be recorded as contra-revenues that reduce reported net sales. For example, if the credit card company is charging a 3 percent fee for its service and **Skechers'** online credit card sales are $3,000 for January 2, Skechers will record the following:

	Debit	Credit
Cash (+A)	2,910	
Credit card discount (+XR, −R, −SE)	90	
Sales revenue (+R, +SE)		3,000

Assets		=	Liabilities	+	Stockholders' Equity	
Cash	+2,910				Sales revenue (+R)	+3,000
					Credit card discount (+XR)	−90

Similarly, if credit sales of $1,000 are recorded with terms 2/10, n/30 ($1,000 × 0.98 = $980) and payment is made within the discount period, Skechers will record the following:

	Debit	Credit
Accounts receivable (+A)	1,000	
Sales revenue (+R, +SE)		1,000

Assets		=	Liabilities	+	Stockholders' Equity	
Accounts receivable	+1,000				Sales revenue (+R)	+1,000

	Debit	Credit
Cash (+A)	980	
Sales discount (+XR, −R, −SE)	20	
Accounts receivable (−A)		1,000

Assets		=	Liabilities	+	Stockholders' Equity	
Cash	+980				Sales discount (+XR)	−20
Accounts receivable	−1,000					

Sales returns and allowances should always be treated as a contra-revenue that reduces net sales. Assume that **Dick's Sporting Goods** buys 40 pairs of shoes from Skechers for $2,000 on account. On the date of sale, Skechers makes the following journal entry:

	Debit	Credit
Accounts receivable (+A)	2,000	
Sales revenue (+R, +SE)		2,000

Assets		=	Liabilities	+	Stockholders' Equity	
Accounts receivable	+2,000				Sales revenue (+R)	+2,000

Before paying for the shoes, however, Dick's Sporting Goods discovers that 10 pairs of shoes are not the color ordered and returns them to Skechers. On that date Skechers records:

	Debit	Credit
Sales returns and allowances (+XR, −R, −SE)	500	
Accounts receivable (−A)		500

Assets		=	Liabilities	+	Stockholders' Equity	
Accounts receivable	−500				Sales returns and allowances (+XR)	−500

In addition, the related cost of goods sold entry for the 10 pairs of shoes would be reversed.

CHAPTER TAKE-AWAYS

6-1. Analyze the impact of credit card sales, sales discounts, sales returns, and sales of bundled items on the amounts reported as net sales. **p. 293**

Credit card discounts and **sales** or **cash discounts** must be recorded as contra-revenues that reduce net sales. **Sales returns and allowances,** which also should be treated as a contra-revenue, also reduce net sales. **Sales of bundled items** must be accounted for using the five-step process to allocate sales price to performance obligations.

6-2. Estimate, report, and evaluate the effects of uncollectible accounts receivable (bad debts) on financial statements. **p. 298**

When receivables are material, companies must employ the allowance method to account for uncollectibles. These are the steps in the process:

a. The end-of-period adjusting entry to record bad debt expense estimates.
b. Writing off specific accounts determined to be uncollectible during the period.

The adjusting entry reduces net income as well as net accounts receivable. The related expense must be recorded as an operating expense. The write-off affects neither net income nor net accounts receivable.

6-3. Analyze and interpret the receivables turnover ratio and the effects of accounts receivable on cash flows. **p. 303**

a. **Receivables turnover ratio**–This ratio measures the effectiveness of credit-granting and collection activities. It reflects how many times average trade receivables were recorded and collected during the period. Analysts and creditors watch this ratio because a sudden decline in it may mean that a company is extending payment deadlines in an attempt to prop up lagging sales or is recording sales that later will be returned by customers.
b. **Effects on cash flows**–When a net decrease in accounts receivable for the period occurs, cash collected from customers is always more than revenue and cash flows from operations increase. When a net increase in accounts receivable occurs, cash collected from customers is always less than revenue. Thus, cash flows from operations decline.

6-4. Report, control, and safeguard cash. **p. 307**

Cash is the most liquid of all assets, flowing continually into and out of a business. As a result, a number of critical control procedures, including the reconciliation of bank accounts, should be applied. Also, management of cash may be critically important to decision makers, who must have cash available to meet current needs yet must avoid excess amounts of idle cash that produce no revenue.

Closely related to recording revenue is recording the cost of what was sold. Chapter 7 will focus on transactions related to inventory and cost of goods sold. This topic is important because cost of goods sold has a major impact on a company's gross profit and net income, which are watched closely by investors, analysts, and other users of financial statements. Increasing emphasis on quality, productivity, and costs have further focused production managers' attention on cost of goods sold and inventory. Because inventory cost figures play a major role in product introduction and pricing decisions, they also are important to marketing and general managers. Finally, because inventory accounting has a major effect on many companies' tax liabilities, this is an important place to introduce the effect of taxation on management decision making and financial reporting.

KEY RATIO

Receivables turnover ratio measures the effectiveness of credit-granting and collection activities. It is computed as follows (see the "Key Ratio Analysis" box in the Measuring and Reporting Receivables section):

$$\text{Receivables Turnover} = \frac{\text{Net Sales}}{\text{Average Net Trade Accounts Receivable}}$$

FINDING FINANCIAL INFORMATION

Balance Sheet

Under Current Assets
- Accounts receivable (net of allowance for doubtful accounts)

Income Statement

Revenues
- Net sales (sales revenue less discounts and sales returns and allowances)

Expenses
- Selling, general, and administrative expenses (including bad debt expense)

Statement of Cash Flows

Under Operating Activities (indirect method)
- Net income
- + decreases in accounts receivable (net)
- − increases in accounts receivable (net)

Notes

Under Summary of Significant Accounting Policies
- Revenue recognition policy

Under a Separate Note on Form 10-K
- Bad debt expense and write-offs of bad debts

KEY TERMS

Accounts Receivable (Trade Receivables or Receivables) Open accounts owed to the business by trade customers. **p. 297**

Aging of Accounts Receivable Method Estimates uncollectible accounts based on the age of each account receivable. **p. 303**

Allowance for Doubtful Accounts (Allowance for Bad Debts or Allowance for Uncollectible accounts) Contra-asset account containing the estimated uncollectible accounts receivable. **p. 299**

Allowance Method Bases bad debt expense on an estimate of uncollectible accounts. **p. 298**

Bad Debt Expense (Doubtful Accounts Expense, Uncollectible Accounts Expense, or Provision for Uncollectible Accounts) Expense associated with estimated uncollectible accounts receivable. **p. 298**

Bank Reconciliation Process of verifying the accuracy of both the bank statement and the cash accounts of a business. **p. 310**

Bank Statement A monthly report from a bank that shows deposits recorded, checks cleared, other debits and credits, and a running bank balance. This same information is available on a daily basis from the bank's online banking site. **p. 309**

Cash Money or any instrument that banks will accept for deposit and immediate credit to a company's account, such as a check, money order, or bank draft. **p. 307**

Cash Equivalents Short-term investments with original maturities of three months or less that are readily convertible to cash and whose value is unlikely to change. **p. 307**

Credit Card Discount Fee charged by the credit card company for its services. **p. 293**

Net Sales The top line reported on the income statement. Net sales = Sales revenue − (Credit card discounts + Sales discounts + Sales returns and allowances). **p. 295**

Notes Receivable Written promises that require another party to pay the business under specified conditions (amount, time, interest). **p. 297**

Percentage of Credit Sales Method Bases bad debt expense on the historical percentage of credit sales that result in bad debts. **p. 302**

Sales (or Cash) Discount Cash discount offered to encourage prompt payment of an account receivable. **p. 294**

Sales Returns and Allowances A reduction of sales revenues for return of or allowances for unsatisfactory goods. **p. 295**

QUESTIONS

1. Explain the difference between sales revenue and net sales.
2. What is gross profit or gross margin on sales? In your explanation, assume that net sales revenue was $100,000 and cost of goods sold was $60,000.
3. What is a credit card discount? How does it affect amounts reported on the income statement?
4. What is a sales discount? Use 1/10, n/30 in your explanation.
5. What is the distinction between sales allowances and sales discounts?
6. Differentiate accounts receivable from notes receivable.
7. Which basic accounting principle is the allowance method of accounting for bad debts designed to satisfy?
8. Using the allowance method, is bad debt expense recognized in (*a*) the period in which sales related to the uncollectible account are made or (*b*) the period in which the seller learns that the customer is unable to pay?
9. What is the effect of the write-off of bad debts (using the allowance method) on (*a*) net income and (*b*) accounts receivable, net?
10. Does an increase in the receivables turnover ratio generally indicate faster or slower collection of receivables? Explain.
11. Define cash and cash equivalents in the context of accounting. Indicate the types of items that should be included and excluded.
12. Summarize the primary characteristics of an effective internal control system for cash.
13. Why should cash-handling and cash-recording activities be separated? How is this separation accomplished?
14. What are the purposes of a bank reconciliation? What balances are reconciled?
15. Briefly explain how the total amount of cash reported on the balance sheet is computed.

MULTIPLE-CHOICE QUESTIONS

1. Sales discounts with terms 2/10, n/30 mean:
   a. 10 percent discount for payment within 30 days.
   b. 2 percent discount for payment within 10 days or the full amount (less returns) due within 30 days.
   c. Two-tenths of a percent discount for payment within 30 days.
   d. None of the above.
2. Gross sales total $300,000, one-half of which were credit sales. Sales returns and allowances of $15,000 apply to the credit sales, sales discounts of 2 percent were taken on all of the net credit sales, and credit card sales of $100,000 were subject to a credit card discount of 3 percent. What is the dollar amount of net sales?
   a. $227,000
   b. $229,800
   c. $279,300
   d. $240,000
3. A company has been successful in reducing the amount of sales returns and allowances. At the same time, a credit card company reduced the credit card discount from 3 percent to 2 percent. What effect will these changes have on the company's net sales, all other things equal?
   a. Net sales will not change.
   b. Net sales will increase.
   c. Net sales will decrease.
   d. Either (b) or (c).
4. When a company using the allowance method writes off a specific customer's $100,000 account receivable from the accounting system, which of the following statements is/are true?
   1. Total stockholders' equity remains the same.
   2. Total assets remain the same.
   3. Total expenses remain the same.
   a. 2
   b. 1 and 3
   c. 1 and 2
   d. 1, 2, and 3

5. You have determined that Company X estimates bad debt expense with an aging of accounts receivable schedule. Company X's estimate of uncollectible receivables resulting from the aging analysis equals $250. The beginning balance in Allowance for Doubtful Accounts was $220. Write-offs of bad debts during the period were $180. What amount would be recorded as bad debt expense for the current period?
   a. $180
   b. $250
   c. $210
   d. $220
6. Upon review of the most recent bank statement, you discover that you recently received a "not sufficient funds check" from a customer. Which of the following describes the actions to be taken when preparing your bank reconciliation?

Balance per Books	Balance per Bank Statement
a. No change	Decrease
b. Decrease	Increase
c. Decrease	No change
d. Increase	Decrease

7. Which of the following is **not** a step toward effective internal control over cash?
   a. Require signatures from a manager and one financial officer on all checks.
   b. Require that cash be deposited daily at the bank.
   c. Require that the person responsible for removing the cash from the register have no access to the accounting records.
   d. All of the above are steps toward effective internal control.
8. When using the allowance method, as bad debt expense is recorded,
   a. Total assets remain the same and stockholders' equity remains the same.
   b. Total assets decrease and stockholders' equity decreases.
   c. Total assets increase and stockholders' equity decreases.
   d. Total liabilities increase and stockholders' equity decreases.
9. Which of the following best describes the proper presentation of accounts receivable in the financial statements?
   a. Gross accounts receivable plus the allowance for doubtful accounts in the asset section of the balance sheet.
   b. Gross accounts receivable in the asset section of the balance sheet and the allowance for doubtful accounts in the expense section of the income statement.
   c. Gross accounts receivable less bad debt expense in the asset section of the balance sheet.
   d. Gross accounts receivable less the allowance for doubtful accounts in the asset section of the balance sheet.
10. Which of the following is **not** a component of net sales?
   a. Sales returns and allowances
   b. Sales discounts
   c. Cost of goods sold
   d. Credit card discounts

MINI-EXERCISES

Reporting Net Sales with Sales Discounts

M6-1
LO6-1

Merchandise invoiced at $9,500 is sold on terms 1/10, n/30. If the buyer pays within the discount period, what amount will be reported on the income statement as net sales?

Reporting Net Sales with Sales Discounts, Credit Card Discounts, and Sales Returns

M6-2
LO6-1

Total gross sales for the period include the following:

Credit card sales (discount 3%)	$ 9,400
Sales on account (2/5, n/60)	$12,000

Sales returns related to sales on account were $650. All returns were made before payment. One-half of the remaining sales on account were paid within the discount period. The company treats all discounts and returns as contra-revenues. What amount will be reported on the income statement as net sales?

M6-3 Recording Bad Debts
LO6-2

Prepare journal entries for each transaction listed.

a. During the period, bad debts are written off in the amount of $14,500.
b. At the end of the period, bad debt expense is estimated to be $16,000.

M6-4 Determining Financial Statement Effects of Bad Debts
LO6-2

Using the following categories, indicate the effects of the following transactions. Use + for increase and − for decrease and indicate the accounts affected and the amounts.

a. At the end of the period, bad debt expense is estimated to be $15,000.
b. During the period, bad debts are written off in the amount of $9,500.

Assets	=	Liabilities	+	Stockholders' Equity

M6-5 Determining the Effects of Credit Policy Changes on Receivables Turnover Ratio
LO6-3

Indicate the most likely effect of the following changes in credit policy on the receivables turnover ratio (+ for increase, − for decrease, and NE for no effect).

a. Granted credit with shorter payment deadlines.
b. Increased effectiveness of collection methods.
c. Granted credit to less creditworthy customers.

M6-6 Matching Reconciling Items to the Bank Reconciliation
LO6-4

Indicate whether the following items would be added (+) or subtracted (−) from the company's books or the bank statement during the construction of a bank reconciliation.

Reconciling Item	Company's Books	Bank Statement
a. Outstanding checks		
b. Bank service charge		
c. Deposit in transit		

M6-7 (Chapter Supplement) Recording Sales Discounts
LO6-4

A sale is made for $6,000; terms are 3/10, n/30. Give the required entry to record the sale and the collection entry, assuming that it is during the discount period.

EXERCISES

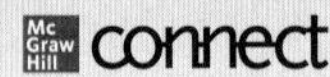

E6-1 Reporting Net Sales with Credit Sales and Sales Discounts
LO6-1

During the months of January and February, Hancock Corporation sold goods to three customers. The sequence of events was as follows:

Jan.	6	Sold goods for $1,500 to S. Green and billed that amount subject to terms 2/10, n/30.
	6	Sold goods to M. Munoz for $850 and billed that amount subject to terms 2/10, n/30.
	14	Collected cash due from S. Green.
Feb.	2	Collected cash due from M. Munoz.
	28	Sold goods for $400 to R. Reynolds and billed that amount subject to terms 2/10, n/45.

Required:
Assuming that Sales Discounts is treated as a contra-revenue, compute net sales for the two months ended February 28.

Reporting Net Sales with Credit Sales, Sales Discounts, and Credit Card Sales

E6-2
LO6-1

The following transactions were selected from the records of OceanView Company:

July	12	Sold merchandise to Customer R, who charged the $3,000 purchase on his Visa credit card. Visa charges OceanView a 2 percent credit card fee.
	15	Sold merchandise to Customer S at an invoice price of $9,000; terms 3/10, n/30.
	20	Sold merchandise to Customer T at an invoice price of $4,000; terms 3/10, n/30.
	23	Collected payment from Customer S from July 15 sale.
Aug.	25	Collected payment from Customer T from July 20 sale.

Required:
Assuming that Sales Discounts and Credit Card Discounts are treated as contra-revenues, compute net sales for the two months ended August 31.

Reporting Net Sales with Credit Sales, Sales Discounts, Sales Returns, and Credit Card Sales

E6-3
LO6-1

The following transactions were selected from among those completed by Bennett Retailers in November and December:

Nov.	20	Sold 20 items of merchandise to Customer B at an invoice price of $5,500 (total); terms 3/10, n/30.
	25	Sold two items of merchandise to Customer C, who charged the $400 (total) sales price on her Visa credit card. Visa charges Bennett Retailers a 2 percent credit card fee.
	28	Sold 10 identical items of merchandise to Customer D at an invoice price of $9,000 (total); terms 3/10, n/30.
	29	Customer D returned one of the items purchased on the 28th; the item was defective and credit was given to the customer.
Dec.	6	Customer D paid the account balance in full.
	20	Customer B paid in full for the invoice of November 20.

Required:
Assume that Sales Returns and Allowances, Sales Discounts, and Credit Card Discounts are treated as contra-revenues; compute net sales for the two months ended December 31.

Determining the Effects of Credit Sales, Sales Discounts, Credit Card Sales, and Sales Returns and Allowances on Income Statement Categories

E6-4
LO6-1

Griffin Shoe Company records Sales Returns and Allowances, Sales Discounts, and Credit Card Discounts as contra-revenues. Complete the following tabulation, indicating the effect (+ for increase, − for decrease, and NE for no effect) and amount of the effects of each transaction, including related cost of goods sold.

July	12	Sold merchandise to customer at factory store who charged the $300 purchase on her American Express card. American Express charges a 1 percent credit card fee. Cost of goods sold was $175.
July	15	Sold merchandise to Customer T at an invoice price of $5,000; terms 3/10, n/30. Cost of goods sold was $2,500.
July	20	Collected cash due from Customer T.
July	21	Before paying for the order, a customer returned shoes with an invoice price of $900; cost of goods sold was $600.

Transaction	Net Sales	Cost of Goods Sold	Gross Profit
July 12			
July 15			
July 20			
July 21			

E6-5 LO6-1

Evaluating the Annual Interest Rate Implicit in a Sales Discount with Discussion of Management Choice of Financing Strategy

Clark's Landscaping bills customers subject to terms 3/10, n/50.

Required:

1. Compute the annual interest rate implicit in the sales discount. (Round to two decimal places.)
2. If his bank charges 15 percent interest, should the customer borrow from the bank so that he can take advantage of the discount? Explain your recommendation.

E6-6 LO6-1 Dell

Determining Revenue from a Bundled Sale

Assume that on June 30, **Dell** sells a laptop computer with a one-year cloud service contract for $1,000. Its fiscal year ends September 30 of the current year. Dell estimates that the value of the hardware sold is $960 and the cloud service contract is $40.

Required:

Following the five-step process for revenue recognition, answer the following questions:

1. Identify the contract between the company and customer.
2. Identify the performance obligations (components of the bundled sale).
3. Determine the transaction price.
4. Allocate the transaction price to the performance obligations.
5. Determine the amount of revenue that should be recorded related to the bundled sale in the **current year** and in the **following year.**

E6-7 LO6-1 Verizon

Determining Revenue from a Bundled Sale

Assume that **Verizon** normally sells a Samsung S21 phone for $480 and charges $60 per month for a one-year cell service contract. Assume further that on January 1, Verizon offered a special package price combining the phone and the one-year service contract for $75 per month.

Required:

1. Identify the contract between the company and the customer.
2. Identify the performance obligations (components of the bundled sale).
3. Determine the transaction price.
4. Allocate the transaction price to the performance obligations **proportionately based on the normal retail prices of the performance obligations.**
5. Determine the amount of revenue that should be recorded related to the bundled sale in the **first quarter** (January 1 to March 31).

E6-8 LO6-2

Reporting Bad Debt Expense and Accounts Receivable

At the end of the prior year, Durney's Outdoor Outfitters reported the following information.

Accounts Receivable, Dec. 31, prior year

Accounts Receivable (Gross) (A)	$48,067
Allowance for Doubtful Accounts (XA)	8,384
Accounts Receivable (Net) (A)	$39,683

During the current year, sales on account were $304,423, collections on account were $289,850, write-offs of bad debts were $6,969, and the bad debt expense adjustment was $4,685.

Required:
Show how the amounts related to Accounts Receivable and Bad Debt Expense would be reported on the income statement and balance sheet for the current year. (**Hint:** Complete the Accounts Receivable and Allowance for Doubtful Accounts T-accounts to determine the balance sheet values.)

Recording Bad Debt Expense Estimates and Write-Offs Using the Percentage of Credit Sales Method

E6-9
LO6-2

During the current year, Witz Electric, Inc., recorded credit sales of $1,300,000. Based on prior experience, it estimates a 1 percent bad debt rate on credit sales.

Required:
Prepare journal entries for each transaction:

a. On September 29 of the current year, an account receivable for $4,000 from March of the current year was determined to be uncollectible and was written off.
b. The appropriate bad debt expense adjustment was recorded for the current year.

Recording Bad Debt Expense Estimates and Write-Offs Using the Percentage of Credit Sales Method

E6-10
LO6-2

During the current year, Sun Electronics, Incorporated, recorded credit sales of $5,000,000. Based on prior experience, it estimates a 2 percent bad debt rate on credit sales.

Required:
Prepare journal entries for each transaction:

a. On November 13 of the current year, an account receivable for $98,000 from a prior year was determined to be uncollectible and was written off.
b. At year-end, the appropriate bad debt expense adjustment was recorded for the current year.

Determining Financial Statement Effects of Bad Debts Using the Percentage of Credit Sales Method

E6-11
LO6-2

Using the following categories, indicate the effects of the transactions listed in E6-10. Use + for increase and − for decrease and indicate the accounts affected and the amounts.

Assets	=	Liabilities	+	Stockholders' Equity

Recording and Determining the Effects of Bad Debt Transactions on Income Statement Categories Using the Percentage of Credit Sales Method

E6-12
LO6-2

During the current year, Giatras Electronics recorded credit sales of $680,000. Based on prior experience, it estimates a 3.5 percent bad debt rate on credit sales.

Required:
1. Prepare journal entries for each of the following transactions.
   a. On October 28 of the current year, an account receivable for $2,800 from a prior year was determined to be uncollectible and was written off.
   b. At year-end, the appropriate bad debt expense adjustment was recorded for the current year.
2. Complete the following tabulation, indicating the amount and effect (+ for increase, − for decrease, and NE for no effect) of each transaction.

Transaction	Net Sales	Gross Profit	Income from Operations
a.			
b.			

E6-13 LO6-2 Computing Bad Debt Expense Using Aging Analysis

Lin's Dairy uses the aging approach to estimate bad debt expense. The ending balance of each account receivable is aged on the basis of three time periods as follows: (1) not yet due, $22,000; (2) up to 120 days past due, $6,500; and (3) more than 120 days past due, $2,800. Experience has shown that for each age group, the average loss rate on the amount of the receivables at year-end due to uncollectibility is (1) 3 percent, (2) 14 percent, and (3) 34 percent, respectively. At the end of the current year, the Allowance for Doubtful Accounts balance is $1,200 (credit) before the end-of-period adjusting entry is made.

Required:
What amount should be recorded as Bad Debt Expense for the current year?

E6-14 LO6-2 Recording and Reporting a Bad Debt Estimate Using Aging Analysis

Casilda Company uses the aging approach to estimate bad debt expense. The ending balance of each account receivable is aged on the basis of three time periods as follows: (1) not yet due, $50,000; (2) up to 180 days past due, $14,000; and (3) more than 180 days past due, $4,000. Experience has shown that for each age group, the average loss rate on the amount of the receivables at year-end due to uncollectibility is (1) 3 percent, (2) 12 percent, and (3) 30 percent, respectively. At December 31, the end of the current year, the Allowance for Doubtful Accounts balance is $200 (credit) before the end-of-period adjusting entry is made.

Required:
1. Prepare the appropriate bad debt expense adjusting entry for the current year.
2. Show how the various accounts related to accounts receivable should be shown on the December 31, current year, balance sheet.

E6-15 LO6-2 Recording and Reporting a Bad Debt Estimate Using Aging Analysis

Chou Company uses the aging approach to estimate bad debt expense. The ending balance of each account receivable is aged on the basis of three time periods as follows: (1) not yet due, $295,000; (2) up to 120 days past due, $55,000; and (3) more than 120 days past due, $18,000. Experience has shown that for each age group, the average loss rate on the amount of the receivables at year-end due to uncollectibility is (1) 2.5 percent, (2) 11 percent, and (3) 30 percent, respectively. At December 31, the end of the current year, the Allowance for Doubtful Accounts balance is $100 (credit) before the end-of-period adjusting entry is made.

Required:
1. Prepare the appropriate bad debt expense adjusting entry for the current year.
2. Show how the various accounts related to accounts receivable should be shown on the December 31, current year, balance sheet.

E6-16 LO6-2 SAP Interpreting Bad Debt Disclosures

SAP is a global company headquartered in Germany. SAP is a market leader in enterprise application software and also a leading experience management, analytics, and business intelligence company. In a recent annual report, it disclosed the following information concerning its allowance for doubtful accounts (euros in millions denoted as €):

Balance at Beginning of Period	Charged to Costs and Expenses	Amounts Written Off	Balance at End of Period
€99	€18	(€10)	€107

Source: SAP Financial Statements

Required:
1. Record summary journal entries related to the allowance for doubtful accounts for the current year.
2. If SAP had written off an additional €10 million of accounts receivable during the period, how would receivables, net and net income have been affected? Explain why.

Interpreting Bad Debt Disclosures

E6-17
LO6-2
Wolverine World Wide

Wolverine World Wide designs and markets Merrell, Sperry, Wolverine, and Keds shoes. Its products are sold through department stores and specialty and Internet retailers. In a recent annual report, it disclosed the following information concerning its allowance for doubtful accounts (in millions):

Balance at Beginning of Period	Charged to Costs and Expenses	Amounts Written Off	Balance at End of Period
$9.5	$16.3	$13.7	$12.1

Source: Wolverine World Wide

Required:

1. Record summary journal entries related to the allowance for doubtful accounts for the current year.
2. If Wolverine World Wide had written off $5 million less of accounts receivable during the period, how would receivables, net, and net income have been affected? Explain why.

Inferring Bad Debt Write-Offs and Cash Collections from Customers

E6-18
LO6-2

On its recent financial statements, Hassell Fine Foods reported the following information about net sales revenue and accounts receivable (amounts in thousands):

	Current Year	Prior Year
Accounts receivable, net of allowances of $153 and $117	$13,589	$11,338
Net sales revenue	60,420	51,122

According to its Form 10-K, Hassell recorded bad debt expense of $88 and there were no bad debt recoveries during the current year. (**Hint:** Refer to the summary of the effects of accounting for bad debts on the Accounts Receivable (Gross) and the Allowance for Doubtful Accounts T-accounts. Use the T-accounts to solve for the missing values.)

Required:

1. What amount of bad debts was written off during the current year?
2. Based on your answer to requirement (1), solve for cash collected from customers for the current year, assuming that all of Hassell's sales during the period were on open account.

Inferring Bad Debt Write-Offs and Cash Collections from Customers

E6-19
LO6-2
Microsoft

Microsoft develops, produces, and markets a wide range of computer software, including the Windows operating system. On its recent financial statements, Microsoft reported the following information about net sales revenue and accounts receivable (amounts in millions).

	Current Year	Prior Year
Accounts receivable, net of allowances of $411 and $377	$29,524	$26,481
Net sales revenue	66,069	64,497

Source: Microsoft Corporation

According to its Form 10-K, Microsoft recorded bad debt expense of $116 and there were no bad debt recoveries during the current year. (**Hint:** Refer to the summary of the effects of accounting for bad debts on the Accounts Receivable (Gross) and the Allowance for Doubtful Accounts T-accounts. Use the T-accounts to solve for the missing values.)

Required:

1. What amount of bad debts was written off during the current year?
2. Based on your answer to requirement (1), solve for cash collected from customers for the current year, assuming that all of Microsoft's sales during the period were on open account.

E6-20 LO6-2 CVS Inferring Bad Debt Expense and Determining the Impact of Uncollectible Accounts on Income (Including Tax Effects) and Working Capital

A recent annual report for **CVS** contained the following information (dollars in thousands) at the end of its fiscal year:

	Year 2	Year 1
Accounts receivable	$19,936,000	$17,918,000
Less: Allowance for doubtful accounts	319,000	287,000
	$19,617,000	$17,631,000

Source: CVS Health Corporation

A footnote to the financial statements disclosed that uncollectible accounts amounting to $79,000 and $37,000 were written off as bad debts during Year 2 and Year 1, respectively. Assume that the tax rate for CVS was 21 percent.

Required:

1. Determine the bad debt expense for Year 2 based on the preceding facts. (**Hint:** Use the Allowance for Doubtful Accounts T-account to solve for the missing value.)
2. **Working capital** is defined as current assets minus current liabilities. How was CVS's working capital affected by the write-off of $79,000 in uncollectible accounts during Year 2? What impact did the recording of bad debt expense have on working capital in Year 2?
3. How was net income affected by the $79,000 write-off during Year 2? What impact did recording bad debt expense have on net income for Year 2?

E6-21 LO6-2 Recording, Reporting, and Evaluating a Bad Debt Estimate Using the Percentage of Credit Sales Method

During the current year, Robby's Camera Shop had sales revenue of $170,000, of which $75,000 was on credit. At the start of the current year, Accounts Receivable showed a $16,000 debit balance and the Allowance for Doubtful Accounts showed a $900 credit balance. Collections of accounts receivable during the current year amounted to $60,000.

Data during the current year follow:

a. On December 31, an Account Receivable (J. Doe) of $1,700 from a prior year was determined to be uncollectible; therefore, it was written off immediately as a bad debt.

b. On December 31, on the basis of experience, a decision was made to continue the accounting policy of basing estimated bad debt losses on 1.5 percent of credit sales for the year.

Required:

1. Give the required journal entries for the two items on December 31, the end of the accounting period.
2. Show how the amounts related to Accounts Receivable and Bad Debt Expense would be reported on the income statement and balance sheet for the current year. Disregard income tax considerations.
3. On the basis of the data available, does the 1.5 percent rate appear to be reasonable? Explain.

E6-22 LO6-2 Recording, Reporting, and Evaluating a Bad Debt Estimate Using the Percentage of Credit Sales Method

During the current year, Bob's Ceramics Shop had sales revenue of $60,000, of which $25,000 was on credit. At the start of the current year, Accounts Receivable showed a $3,500 debit balance and the Allowance for Doubtful Accounts showed a $300 credit balance. Collections of accounts receivable during the current year amounted to $18,000.

Data during the current year follow:

a. On December 31, an Account Receivable (Toby's Gift Shop) of $550 from a prior year was determined to be uncollectible; therefore, it was written off immediately as a bad debt.

b. On December 31, on the basis of experience, a decision was made to continue the accounting policy of basing estimated bad debt losses on 2 percent of credit sales for the year.

Required:

1. Give the required journal entries for the two items on December 31, the end of the accounting period.
2. Show how the amounts related to Accounts Receivable and Bad Debt Expense would be reported on the income statement and balance sheet for the current year. Disregard income tax considerations.
3. On the basis of the data available, does the 2 percent rate appear to be reasonable? Explain.

Recording, Reporting, and Evaluating a Bad Debt Estimate Using Aging Analysis

E6-23
LO6-2

Brown Cow Dairy uses the aging approach to estimate bad debt expense. The ending balance of each account receivable is aged on the basis of three time periods as follows: (1) not yet due, $14,000; (2) up to 120 days past due, $4,500; and (3) more than 120 days past due, $2,500. Experience has shown that for each age group, the average loss rate on the amount of the receivables at year-end due to uncollectibility is (1) 2 percent, (2) 12 percent, and (3) 30 percent, respectively. At December 31 (end of the current year), the Allowance for Doubtful Accounts balance is $800 (credit) before the end-of-period adjusting entry is made.

Data during the current year follow:

a. During December, an Account Receivable (Patty's Bake Shop) of $750 from a prior sale was determined to be uncollectible; therefore, it was written off immediately as a bad debt.
b. On December 31, the appropriate adjusting entry for the year was recorded.

Required:

1. Give the required journal entries for the two items listed above.
2. Show how the amounts related to Accounts Receivable and Bad Debt Expense would be reported on the income statement and balance sheet for the current year. Disregard income tax considerations.
3. On the basis of the data available, does the estimate resulting from the aging analysis appear to be reasonable? Explain.

Computing and Interpreting the Receivables Turnover Ratio

E6-24
LO6-3
FedEx

A recent annual report for **FedEx** contained the following data:

	(dollars in thousands)	
	Current Year	Previous Year
Accounts receivable	$ 9,416,000	$8,882,000
Less: Allowances	300,000	401,000
Net accounts receivable	$ 9,116,000	$8,481,000
Net sales (assume all on credit)	$69,693,000	

Source: FedEx Corporation

Required:

1. Determine the receivables turnover ratio and average days sales in receivables for the current year.
2. Explain the meaning of each calculated number.

Computing and Interpreting the Receivables Turnover Ratio

E6-25
LO6-3
Adobe Inc.

A recent annual report for **Adobe Inc.** contained the following data:

	(dollars in thousands)	
	Current Year	Previous Year
Accounts receivable	$ 1,544,459	$1,330,559
Less: Allowances	9,650	14,981
Net accounts receivable	$ 1,534,809	$1,315,578
Net sales (assume all on credit)	$11,171,297	

Source: Adobe Inc.

Required:

1. Determine the receivables turnover ratio and average days sales in receivables for the current year.
2. Explain the meaning of each calculated number.

E6-26 LO6-3 Interpreting the Effects of Sales Declines and Changes in Receivables on Cash Flow from Operations

Tupperware Brands Corporation

Tupperware Brands Corporation is engaged in the marketing, manufacture, and sale of design-centric preparation, storage and serving solutions for the kitchen and home and beauty products through international brands. Assume that two recent years produced a combination of declining sales revenue and net income, culminating in a net income of only $12,400 (all numbers in thousands). Yet Tupperware was able to report positive cash flows from operations in the current year of $87,400. Contributing to that positive cash flow was the change in accounts receivable. The current and prior years' balance sheets reported the following:

	amounts in thousands	
	Current Year	Prior Year
Accounts receivable, net of allowances	$110,700	$144,700

Required:

1. On the current year's cash flow statement (indirect method), how would the change in accounts receivable affect cash flow from operations? Explain why it would have this effect.
2. Explain how declining sales revenue often leads to (*a*) declining accounts receivable and (*b*) cash collections from customers being higher than sales revenue.

E6-27 LO6-4 Preparing Bank Reconciliation and Entries and Reporting Cash

Bentley Company's June 30 bank statement and June ledger account for cash are summarized below:

BANK STATEMENT	Checks	Deposits	Balance
Balance, June 1			$ 6,500
Deposits during June		$16,200	22,700
Checks cleared during June	$16,600		6,100
Bank service charges	40		6,060
Balance, June 30			6,060

Cash (A)

June 1	Balance	6,500	June	Checks written	19,000
June	Deposits	18,100			

Required:

1. Reconcile the bank account. A comparison of the checks written with the checks that have cleared the bank shows outstanding checks of $2,400. A deposit of $1,900 is in transit at the end of June.
2. Give any journal entries that should be made as a result of the bank reconciliation.
3. What is the balance in the Cash account after the reconciliation entries?
4. What is the total amount of cash that should be reported on the balance sheet at June 30?

E6-28 LO6-4 Preparing Bank Reconciliation and Entries and Reporting Cash

The September 30 bank statement for Bennett Company and the September ledger account for cash are summarized here:

BANK STATEMENT	Checks	Deposits	Balance
Balance, September 1			$ 6,500
Deposits recorded during September		$26,900	33,400
Checks cleared during September	$27,400		6,000
NSF checks–Betty Brown	170		5,830
Bank service charges	60		5,770
Balance, September 30			5,770

Cash (A)					
Sept. 1	Balance	6,500	Sept.	Checks written	28,900
Sept.	Deposits	28,100			

No outstanding checks and no deposits in transit were carried over from August; however, there are deposits in transit and checks outstanding at the end of September.

Required:

1. Reconcile the bank account.
2. Give any journal entries that should be made as the result of the bank reconciliation.
3. What should the balance in the Cash account be after the reconciliation entries?
4. What total amount of cash should the company report on the September 30 balance sheet?

(Chapter Supplement) Recording Credit Sales, Sales Discounts, Sales Returns, and Credit Card Sales

E6-29

The following transactions were selected from among those completed by Hailey Retailers in the current year:

Nov.	20	Sold two items of merchandise to Customer B, who charged the $450 (total) sales price on her Visa credit card. Visa charges Hailey a 2 percent credit card fee.
	25	Sold 14 items of merchandise to Customer C at an invoice price of $2,800 (total); terms 2/10, n/30.
	28	Sold 12 identical items of merchandise to Customer D at an invoice price of $7,200 (total); terms 2/10, n/30.
	30	Customer D returned one of the items purchased on the 28th; the item was defective and credit was given to the customer.
Dec.	6	Customer D paid the account balance in full.
	30	Customer C paid in full for the invoice of November 25.

Required:

1. Give the appropriate journal entry for each of these transactions. Do not record cost of goods sold.
2. Compute Net Sales.

PROBLEMS

Reporting Net Sales and Expenses with Discounts, Returns, and Bad Debts (AP6-1)

P6-1
LO6-1, 6-2

The following data were selected from the records of Sykes Company for the year ended December 31, current year.

Balances January 1, current year	
Accounts receivable (various customers)	$120,000
Allowance for doubtful accounts	8,000

In the following order, except for cash sales, the company sold merchandise and made collections on credit terms 2/10, n/30 (assume a unit sales price of $500 in all transactions).

Transactions during current year

a. Sold merchandise for cash, $235,000.
b. Sold merchandise to R. Smith; invoice price, $11,500.
c. Sold merchandise to K. Miller; invoice price, $26,500.
d. Two days after purchase date, R. Smith returned one of the units purchased in (*b*) and received account credit.

e. Sold merchandise to B. Sears; invoice price, $24,000.
f. R. Smith paid his account in full within the discount period.
g. Collected $98,000 cash from customer sales on credit in prior year, all within the discount periods.
h. K. Miller paid the invoice in (*c*) within the discount period.
i. Sold merchandise to R. Roy; invoice price, $19,000.
j. Three days after paying the account in full, K. Miller returned seven defective units and received a cash refund.
k. After the discount period, collected $6,000 cash on an account receivable on sales in a prior year.
l. Wrote off a prior year account of $3,000 after deciding that the amount would never be collected.
m. The estimated bad debt rate used by the company was 1.5 percent of credit sales net of returns.

Required:

1. Using the following categories, indicate the effect of each listed transaction, including the write-off of the uncollectible account and the adjusting entry for estimated bad debts (ignore cost of goods sold). Indicate the sign and amount of the effect or use NE for no effect. The first transaction is used as an example.

	Sales Revenue	Sales Discounts (taken)	Sales Returns and Allowances	Bad Debt Expense
(*a*)	+235,000	NE	NE	NE

2. Show how the accounts related to the preceding sale and collection activities should be reported on the current year income statement.

P6-2 LO6-2 Recording Bad Debts and Interpreting Disclosure of Allowance for Doubtful Accounts (AP6-2)

General Mills, Inc., is a leading global manufacturer and marketer of branded consumer foods sold through retail stores. It recently disclosed the following information concerning the Allowance for Doubtful Accounts on its Form 10-K Annual Report submitted to the Securities and Exchange Commission.

A summary of the Allowance for Doubtful Accounts is as follows (dollars in millions):

	Balance at Beginning of Year	Additions (Charges) to Expense	Write-Offs	Balance At End of Year
Year 1	$24.3	$?	$22.6	$28.4
Year 2	28.4	23.9	?	28.8
Year 3	28.8	25.9	21.5	33.2

Source: General Mills, Inc.

Required:

1. Record summary journal entries related to bad debts for Year 3.
2. Supply the missing dollar amounts noted by (?) for Year 1 and Year 2.

P6-3 LO6-2 Determining Bad Debt Expense Based on Aging Analysis (AP6-3)

Blue Skies Equipment Company uses the aging approach to estimate bad debt expense at the end of each accounting year. Credit sales occur frequently on terms n/60. The balance of each account receivable is aged on the basis of three time periods as follows: (1) not yet due, (2) up to one year past due, and (3) more than one year past due. Experience has shown that for each age group, the average loss rate on the amount of the receivable at year-end due to uncollectibility is (*a*) 3 percent, (*b*) 9 percent, and (*c*) 28 percent, respectively.

At December 31, 2022 (end of the current accounting year), the Accounts Receivable balance was $48,700 and the Allowance for Doubtful Accounts balance was $920 (credit). In determining which accounts have been paid, the company applies collections to the oldest sales first. To simplify, only five customer accounts are used; the details of each on December 31, 2022, follow:

Date	Explanation	Debit	Credit	Balance
	B. Brown—Account Receivable			
3/11/2021	Sale	13,000		13,000
6/30/2021	Collection		3,000	10,000
1/31/2022	Collection		3,800	6,200
	D. Donalds—Account Receivable			
2/28/2022	Sale	21,000		21,000
4/15/2022	Collection		8,000	13,000
11/30/2022	Collection		6,000	7,000
	N. Napier—Account Receivable			
11/30/2022	Sale	8,000		8,000
12/15/2022	Collection		1,000	7,000
	S. Strothers—Account Receivable			
3/2/2020	Sale	4,000		4,000
4/15/2020	Collection		4,000	-0-
9/1/2021	Sale	9,000		9,000
10/15/2021	Collection		4,500	4,500
2/1/2022	Sale	21,000		25,500
3/1/2022	Collection		5,000	20,500
12/31/2022	Sale	4,000		24,500
	T. Thomas—Account Receivable			
12/30/2022	Sale	4,000		4,000

Required:

1. Compute the total accounts receivable in each age category.
2. Compute the estimated uncollectible amount for each age category and in total.
3. Give the adjusting entry for bad debt expense at December 31, 2022.
4. Show how the amounts related to accounts receivable should be presented on the 2022 income statement and balance sheet.

Preparing an Income Statement and Computing the Receivables Turnover Ratio with Discounts, Returns, and Bad Debts (AP6-4)

P6-4
LO6-1, 6-2, 6-3

Tungsten Company, Inc., sells heavy construction equipment. There are 10,000 shares of capital stock outstanding. The annual fiscal period ends on December 31. The following condensed trial balance was taken from the general ledger on December 31, current year:

Account Titles	Debit	Credit
Cash	$ 33,600	
Accounts receivable (net)	14,400	
Inventory, ending	52,000	
Operational assets	40,000	
Accumulated depreciation		$ 16,800
Liabilities		24,000
Capital stock		72,000
Retained earnings, January 1, current year		9,280

(Continued)

Account Titles	Debit	Credit
Sales revenue		147,100
Sales returns and allowances	5,600	
Cost of goods sold	78,400	
Selling expense	14,100	
Administrative expense	15,400	
Bad debt expense	1,600	
Sales discounts	6,400	
Income tax expense	7,680	
Totals	$269,180	$269,180

Required:

1. Beginning with the amount for net sales, prepare an income statement (showing both gross profit and income from operations).
2. The beginning balance in Accounts Receivable (net) was $16,000. Compute the receivables turnover ratio and explain its meaning.

P6-5 Preparing a Bank Reconciliation and Related Journal Entries (AP6-5)

LO6-4

The bookkeeper at Jefferson Company has not reconciled the bank statement with the Cash account, saying, "I don't have time." You have been asked to prepare a reconciliation and review the procedures with the bookkeeper.

The April 30, current year, bank statement and the April ledger account for Cash showed the following (summarized):

BANK STATEMENT			
	Checks	**Deposits**	**Balance**
Balance, April 1, current year			$31,000
Deposits during April		$37,100	68,100
Interest collected		1,180	69,280
Checks cleared during April	$43,000		26,280
NSF check–A. B. Wright	160		26,120
Bank service charges	50		26,070
Balance, April 30, current year			26,070

Cash (A)					
Apr. 1	Balance	23,500	Apr.	Checks written	41,100
Apr.	Deposits	41,500			

A comparison of checks written before and during April with the checks cleared through the bank showed outstanding checks at the end of April of $5,600 (including $3,700 written before and $1,900 written during April). No deposits in transit were carried over from March, but a deposit was in transit at the end of April.

Required:

1. Prepare a detailed bank reconciliation for April.
2. Give any required journal entries as a result of the reconciliation. Why are they necessary?
3. What was the beginning balance in the Cash account in the ledger on May 1, current year?
4. What total amount of cash should be reported on the balance sheet at the end of April?

Computing Outstanding Checks and Deposits in Transit and Preparing a Bank Reconciliation and Journal Entries (AP6-6)

P6-6
LO6-4

The August, current year, bank statement for Allison Company and the August, current year, ledger account for cash follow:

BANK STATEMENT

Date	Checks and EFTs	Deposits	Balance
Aug. 1			$17,510
2	$ 320		17,190
3		$11,700	28,890
4	430		28,460
5	270		28,190
9	880		27,310
10	250 EFT		27,060
15		4,000	31,060
21	350		30,710
24	20,400		10,310
25		6,500	16,810
30	850 EFT		15,960
30		2,350*	18,310
31	120†		18,190

*interest collected.
†Bank service charge.

Cash (A)

		Checks written and electronic funds transfers	
Aug. 1 Balance	16,490		
Deposits		Aug. 2	EFT 250
Aug. 2	11,700	4	880
12	4,000	15	280
24	6,500	17	510
31	5,200	18	EFT 850
		20	350
		23	20,400

Outstanding checks at the end of July were for $270, $430, and $320. No deposits were in transit at the end of July.

Required:

1. Compute the deposits in transit at the end of August by comparing the deposits on the bank statement to the deposits listed on the cash ledger account.
2. Compute the outstanding checks at the end of August by comparing the checks listed on the bank statement with those on the cash ledger account and the list of outstanding checks at the end of July.
3. Prepare a bank reconciliation for August.
4. Give any journal entries that the company should make as a result of the bank reconciliation. Why are they necessary?
5. What total amount of cash should be reported on the August 31, current year, balance sheet?

(Chapter Supplement) Recording Sales, Returns, and Bad Debts (AP6-7)

P6-7

Use the data presented in P6-1, which were selected from the records of Sykes Company for the year ended December 31, current year.

Required:

1. Give the journal entries for these transactions, including the write-off of the uncollectible account and the adjusting entry for estimated bad debts. Do not record cost of goods sold. Show computations for each entry.
2. Show how the accounts related to the preceding sale and collection activities should be reported on the current year income statement.

ALTERNATE PROBLEMS

AP6-1 LO6-1, 6-2

Reporting Net Sales and Expenses with Discounts, Returns, and Bad Debts (P6-1)

The following data were selected from the records of Sharkim Company for the year ended December 31, current year.

Balances January 1, current year:	
Accounts receivable (various customers)	$116,000
Allowance for doubtful accounts	5,200

In the following order, except for cash sales, the company sold merchandise and made collections on credit terms 2/10, n/30 (assume a unit sales price of $500 in all transactions).

Transactions during the current year

a. Sold merchandise for cash, $227,000.
b. Sold merchandise to Karen Corp.; invoice price, $12,000.
c. Sold merchandise to White Company; invoice price, $23,500.
d. Karen paid the invoice in (*b*) within the discount period.
e. Sold merchandise to Cavendish Inc.; invoice price, $26,000.
f. Two days after paying the account in full, Karen returned one defective unit and received a cash refund.
g. Collected $88,200 cash from customer sales on credit in prior year, all within the discount periods.
h. Three days after purchase date, White returned seven of the units purchased in (*c*) and received account credit.
i. White paid its account in full within the discount period.
j. Sold merchandise to Delta Corporation; invoice price, $18,500.
k. Cavendish (*e*) paid its account in full after the discount period.
l. Wrote off a prior year account of $2,400 after deciding that the amount would never be collected.
m. The estimated bad debt rate used by the company was 4 percent of credit sales net of returns.

Required:

1. Using the following categories, indicate the effect of each listed transaction, including the write-off of the uncollectible account and the adjusting entry for estimated bad debts (ignore cost of goods sold). Indicate the sign and amount of the effect or use NE to indicate no effect. The first transaction is used as an example.

	Sales Revenue	Sales Discounts (taken)	Sales Returns and Allowances	Bad Debt Expense
(*a*)	+227,000	NE	NE	NE

2. Show how the accounts related to the preceding sale and collection activities should be reported on the current year income statement.

AP6-2 LO6-2 **V.F. Corporation**

Recording Bad Debts and Interpreting Disclosure of Allowance for Doubtful Accounts (P6-2)

V.F. Corporation is a global leader in the design, production, procurement, marketing and distribution of branded lifestyle apparel, footwear and related products. Their largest brands are Vans®, The North Face®, Timberland®, Wrangler®, and Lee®. Assume that it recently disclosed the following information concerning the allowance for doubtful accounts on its Form 10-K Annual Report submitted to the Securities and Exchange Commission.

Schedule II Valuation and Qualifying Accounts (amounts in thousands)				
	Balance at Beginning of Year	Charged to Costs and Expenses	Write-Offs	Balance At End of Year
Year 3	$24,993	$22,553	(?)	$28,367
Year 2	26,266	(?)	3,932	24,993
Year 1	20,538	21,046	15,318	(?)

Source: V.F. Corporation

Required:

1. Record summary journal entries related to bad debts for Year 1.
2. Supply the missing dollar amounts noted by (?) for Year 1, Year 2, and Year 3.

Determining Bad Debt Expense Based on Aging Analysis (P6-3)

AP6-3
LO6-2

Assume that Witz and Steenhoven, Inc. uses the aging approach to estimate bad debt expense at the end of each accounting year. Credit sales occur frequently on terms n/45. The balance of each account receivable is aged on the basis of four time periods as follows: (1) not yet due, (2) up to 6 months past due, (3) 6 to 12 months past due, and (4) more than 1 year past due. Experience has shown that for each age group, the average loss rate on the amount of the receivable at year-end due to uncollectibility is (*a*) 1 percent, (*b*) 5 percent, (*c*) 20 percent, and (*d*) 50 percent, respectively.

At December 31, 2022 (end of the current accounting year), the Accounts Receivable balance was $39,500 and the Allowance for Doubtful Accounts balance was $1,550 (credit). In determining which accounts have been paid, the company applies collections to the oldest sales first. To simplify, only five customer accounts are used; the details of each on December 31, 2022, follow:

Date	Explanation	Debit	Credit	Balance
	R. Devens—Account Receivable			
3/13/2022	Sale	19,000		19,000
5/12/2022	Collection		10,000	9,000
9/30/2022	Collection		7,000	2,000
	C. Howard—Account Receivable			
11/01/2021	Sale	31,000		31,000
06/01/2022	Collection		20,000	11,000
12/01/2022	Collection		5,000	6,000
	D. McClain—Account Receivable			
10/31/2022	Sale	12,000		12,000
12/10/2022	Collection		8,000	4,000
	T. Skibinski—Account Receivable			
05/02/2022	Sale	15,000		15,000
06/01/2022	Sale	10,000		25,000
06/15/2022	Collection		15,000	10,000
07/15/2022	Collection		10,000	0
10/01/2022	Sale	26,000		26,000
11/15/2022	Collection		16,000	10,000
12/15/2022	Sale	4,500		14,500
	H. Wu—Account Receivable			
12/30/2022	Sale	13,000		13,000

Required:

1. Compute the total accounts receivable in each age category.
2. Compute the estimated uncollectible amount for each age category and in total.
3. Give the adjusting entry for bad debt expense at December 31, 2022.
4. Show how the amounts related to accounts receivable should be presented on the 2022 income statement and balance sheet.

AP6-4 LO6-1, 6-2, 6-3

Preparing an Income Statement and Computing the Receivables Turnover Ratio with Discounts, Returns, and Bad Debts (P6-4)

Perry Corporation is a local grocery store organized seven years ago as a corporation. At that time, a total of 10,000 shares of common stock were issued to the three organizers. The store is in an excellent location and sales have increased each year. At the end of the current year, the bookkeeper prepared the following statement (assume that all amounts are correct; note the incorrect terminology and format):

PERRY CORPORATION
Profit and Loss
December 31, current year

	Debit	Credit
Sales		$184,000
Cost of goods sold	$ 98,000	
Sales returns and allowances	9,000	
Selling expense	17,000	
Administrative and general expense	18,000	
Bad debt expense	2,000	
Sales discounts	8,000	
Income tax expense	10,900	
Net profit	21,100	
Totals	$184,000	$184,000

Required:

1. Beginning with the amount of net sales, prepare an income statement (showing both gross profit and income from operations).
2. The beginning and ending balances in accounts receivable were $16,000 and $18,000, respectively. Compute the receivables turnover ratio and explain its meaning.

AP6-5 LO6-4

Preparing a Bank Reconciliation and Related Journal Entries (P6-5)

The bookkeeper at Washington Company has not reconciled the bank statement with the Cash account, saying, "I don't have time." You have been asked to prepare a reconciliation and review the procedures with the bookkeeper.

The May 31, Current Year, bank statement and the May ledger account for cash showed the following (summarized):

BANK STATEMENT

	Checks	Deposits	Balance
Balance, May 1, Current Year			$32,600
Deposits during May		$37,600	70,200
Interest collected		1,240	71,440
Checks cleared during May	$46,200		25,240
NSF check–B. C. Wong	240		25,000
Bank service charges	50		24,950
Balance, May 31, Current Year			24,950

Cash (A)

May 1 Balance	25,500	May Checks written	42,500
May Deposits	43,200		

A comparison of checks written before and during May with the checks cleared through the bank showed outstanding checks at the end of May of $3,400 (including $2,040 written before and $1,360 written during May). No deposits in transit were carried over from March, but a deposit was in transit at the end of May.

Required:

1. Prepare a detailed bank reconciliation for May.
2. Give any required journal entries as a result of the reconciliation. Why are they necessary?
3. What was the beginning balance in the Cash account in the ledger on June 1, current year?
4. What total amount of cash should be reported on the balance sheet at the end of May?

Computing Outstanding Checks and Deposits in Transit and Preparing a Bank Reconciliation and Journal Entries (P6-6)

AP6-6
LO6-4

The December 31, current year, bank statement for Rivas Company and the December current year ledger account for cash follow.

BANK STATEMENT

Date	Checks and EFTs	Deposits	Balance
Dec. 1			$48,000
2	$400; 300	$17,000	64,300
4	7,000; 90		57,210
6	120; 180; 1,600 EFT		55,310
11	500; 1,200; 70	28,000	81,540
13	480; 700; 1,900		78,460
17	12,000; 8,000 EFT		58,460
23	60; 23,500	36,000	70,900
26	900; 2,650		67,350
28	2,200; 5,200		59,950
30	17,000; 1,890; 300*	19,000	59,760
31	1,650; 1,350; 150†	5,250‡	61,860

*NSF check, J. Left, a customer.
†Bank service charge.
‡Interest collected.

Cash (A)

			Checks written during December:		
Dec. 1	Balance	64,100			
Deposits			60	5,000	2,650
Dec. 11		28,000	17,000	5,200	1,650
23		36,000	700	1,890	2,200
30		19,000	3,500	EFT 1,600	7,000
31		13,000	1,350	120	300
			180	90	480
			12,000	23,500	EFT 8,000
			70	500	1,900
			900	1,200	

The November, current year, bank reconciliation showed the following: correct cash balance at November 30, $64,100; deposits in transit on November 30, $17,000; and outstanding checks on November 30, $400 + $500 = $900.

Required:

1. Compute the deposits in transit as of December 31, current year, by comparing the deposits on the bank statement to the deposits listed on the cash ledger account and the list of deposits in transit at the end of November.
2. Compute the outstanding checks at December 31, current year, by comparing the checks listed on the bank statement with those on the cash ledger account and the list of outstanding checks at the end of November.
3. Prepare a bank reconciliation at December 31, current year.
4. Give any journal entries that should be made as a result of the bank reconciliation made by Rivas Company. Why are they necessary?
5. What total amount of cash should be reported on the December 31, current year, balance sheet?

AP6-7 **(Chapter Supplement) Recording Sales, Returns, and Bad Debts**

Use the data presented in AP6-1, which were selected from the records of Sharkim Company for the year ended December 31, current year.

Required:

1. Give the journal entries for these transactions, including the write-off of the uncollectible account and the adjusting entry for estimated bad debts. Do not record cost of goods sold. Show computations for each entry.
2. Show how the accounts related to the preceding sale and collection activities should be reported on the current year income statement.

CONTINUING PROBLEM

CON6-1
LO6-1, 6-2
Pool Corporation, Inc.

Computing Net Sales and Recording Bad Debt Estimates and Write-Offs

Pool Corporation, Inc., is the world's largest wholesale distributor of swimming pool supplies and equipment.

Required:

1. Pool Corp. reported the following information related to bad debt estimates and write-offs for a recent year. Prepare journal entries for the bad debt expense adjustment and total write-offs of bad debts for the current year.

Allowance for doubtful accounts:	
Balance at beginning of year	$6,182
Bad debt expense	2,768
Write-offs	(3,478)
Balance at end of year	$5,472

Source: Pool Corporation

2. Pool Corp. reduces net sales by the amount of sales returns and allowances, cash discounts, and credit card fees. Bad debt expense is recorded as part of selling and administrative expense. Assume that gross sales revenue for the month was $137,256, bad debt expense was $146, sales discounts were $1,134, sales returns were $856, and credit card fees were $1,849. What amount would Pool Corp. report for net sales for the month?

CASES AND PROJECTS

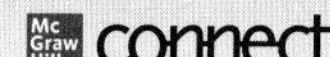

Annual Report Cases

CP6-1
LO6-1, 6-2, 6-3
Target Corporation

Finding Financial Information

Refer to the financial statements of **Target** given in Appendix B at the end of this book.

Required:

1. What does the company include in its category of cash and cash equivalents? How close do you think the disclosed amount is to actual fair market value? (**Hint:** The notes may be helpful in answering this question.)
   a. All assets with a fair value measurement.
   b. Highly liquid investments with an original maturity of three months or less from the time of purchase.
   c. Cash and accounts receivable (net).
   d. Cash and bank overdrafts.
   e. None of the above.
2. What expenses does Target subtract from Total revenue (net sales) in the computation of Operating income? (Select all that apply.)
   a. Cost of sales
   b. Selling, General, and administrative expenses

   c. Net interest expense
   d. Provision for income taxes
   e. Depreciation and amortization
3. Compute Target's receivables turnover ratio for the current year using the "Total revenue" for net sales and the account "Accounts and other receivables." Round your answer to the nearest whole number. ____________
4. What characteristic of its business is the main cause Target's receivables turnover ratio is so high?
   a. Its net profit margin is very high.
   b. Most of its sales are for cash or credit cards such as Visa and Mastercard.
   c. It sells a wide variety of merchandise and food.

Finding Financial Information

CP6-2
LO6-2, 6-3
Walmart, Inc.

Refer to the financial statements of **Walmart** given in Appendix C at the end of this book. All dollar amounts in the statements are in millions.

Required:

1. *(a)* How much cash and cash equivalents does the company report at the end of the current year? (Enter your answer in millions.) ____________
   (b) Note that Walmart is a large international company. What amount (in billions) of its cash and cash equivalents may not be freely transferable to the United States? ____________
2. *(a)* What was the change in receivables, net (in millions) between last year and the current year? ____________
   (b) What was the direction of the effect of the change in receivables, net on net cash provided by operating activities for the current year?
   - Increase
   - Decrease
3. Walmart's total receivables, net were $6.5 billion at the end of the current year. What amount (in billions) were receivables from transactions with customers? _____
4. Did Walmart disclose the amount in the "reserve for doubtful accounts?" If they did not, what is the most likely reason the amount was omitted?
   - Yes, because it is required by U.S. GAAP.
   - No, because they are not "material amounts."
5. Where does the company disclose its revenue recognition policy?
   - On the income statement beside "Total Revenue."
   - In note 1 under "Revenue Recognition."
6. When does the company record revenues for the "sale" of gift cards?
   - When the customer pays for the gift card.
   - When the card is redeemed and the customer purchases merchandise using the gift card.

Comparing Companies within an Industry

CP6-3
LO6-1, 6-3
Target Corporation
Walmart, Inc.

Refer to the financial statements of **Target** (Appendix B) and **Walmart** (Appendix C) and the Industry Ratio Report (Appendix D) at the end of this book.

Required:

1. Compute the receivables turnover ratio for both companies for the most recent year. For Target, use the "Accounts and other receivables" account for the denominator. For Walmart, use the "receivables from transactions with customers, net" account for the denominator.

	Target	**Walmart**
Receivables turnover		

2. What characteristic of their businesses causes their receivables turnover ratios to be so high?
   a. Their net profit margins are very high.
   b. Most of their sales are for cash or credit cards such as Visa and Mastercard.
   c. They sell a wide variety of merchandise and food.

3. How do Target and Walmart account for expected or estimated customer returns?
   a. They are subtracted from sales revenue in the computation of net sales.
   b. They are recorded as an increase in "Cost of sales."
   c. They are recorded as an increase in "Selling, general, and administrative" expense.

Critical Thinking Cases

CP6-4
LO6-1, 6-3
Symbol Technologies, Inc.

Evaluating an Ethical Dilemma: Management Incentives, Revenue Recognition, and Sales with the Right of Return

Symbol Technologies, Inc., was a fast-growing maker of bar-code scanners. According to the federal charges, Tomo Razmilovic, the CEO at Symbol, was obsessed with meeting the stock market's expectation for continued growth. His executive team responded by improperly recording revenue and allowances for returns, as well as a variety of other tricks, to overstate revenues by $230 million and pretax earnings by $530 million. What makes this fraud nearly unique is that virtually the whole senior management team was charged with participating in the six-year fraud. In April 2015, the SEC settled with the last of the 13 Symbol executives that were defendants in the case. Razmilovic, the former CEO, fled the country to avoid prosecution and was still at large at the time of the final settlement. The exact nature of the fraud is described in the following excerpts from the SEC civil complaint.

Concerning sales of goods, the complaint alleged that "Defendant Borghese, Symbol's former head of sales, spearheaded the revenue recognition fraud. Whenever actual sales fell short of Razmilovic's target, Borghese stuffed the distribution channel by granting resellers return rights and contingent payment terms in side agreements that he negotiated or authorized. . . . In addition, Borghese employed multiple schemes for claiming revenue before it was earned, such as shipping the wrong product when the product ordered by the customer was unavailable. . . . In a related scheme that Burke originated, Mortenson and Donlon also caused revenue to be recognized in several quarters on shipments that did not occur until the next quarter. To conceal this premature recognition of revenue, Mortenson and Donlon, acting at the direction of Borghese and others, secured backdated phony 'bill and hold' letters from the customers."

Concerning sales of service, the complaint alleged that "Defendant Heuschneider, finance director for Symbol's customer service division, artificially inflated the service revenue reported by Symbol . . . by directing subordinates to make multimillion dollar fraudulent entries that improperly accelerated revenue recognition on existing service contracts. Heuschneider also fabricated revenue by improperly 'renewing' dormant or cancelled service contracts without the customer's approval."

Source: SECURITIES AND EXCHANGE COMMISSION, Plaintiff, against SYMBOL TECHNOLOGIES, INC., TOMO RAZMILOVIC, KENNETH JAEGGI, LEONARD GOLDNER, BRIAN BURKE, MICHAEL DEGENNARO, FRANK BORGHESE, CHRISTOPHER DESANTIS, JAMES HEUSCHNEIDER, GREGORY MORTENSON, JAMES DEAN, and ROBERT DOLON, Defendants. Dated: New York, New York June 3, 2004.

Required:

1. What facts, if any, presented in the complaint suggest that Symbol violated the revenue recognition principle?
2. Assuming that Symbol did recognize revenue when goods were shipped, how could it have properly accounted for the fact that customers had a right to cancel the contracts (make an analogy with accounting for bad debts)?
3. What do you think may have motivated management to falsify the statements? Why was management concerned with reporting continued growth in net income?
4. Explain who was hurt by management's unethical conduct.
5. Assume that you are the auditor for other firms. After reading about the fraud, what types of transactions would you pay special attention to in the audit of your clients in this industry? What ratio might provide warnings about possible channel stuffing?

CP6-5
LO6-4

Evaluating Internal Control

Cripple Creek Company has one trusted employee who, as the owner said, "handles all of the bookkeeping and paperwork for the company." This employee is responsible for counting, verifying, and recording cash receipts and payments; making the weekly bank deposit; preparing checks for major expenditures (signed by the owner); making small expenditures from the cash register for daily expenses; and collecting accounts receivable. The owners asked the local bank for a $20,000 loan. The bank asked that an audit be performed covering the year just ended. The independent auditor (a local CPA), in a private conference with the owner, presented some evidence of the following activities of the trusted employee during the past year.

a. Cash sales sometimes were not entered in the cash register and the trusted employee pocketed approximately $50 per month.
b. Cash taken from the cash register (and pocketed by the trusted employee) was replaced with expense memos with fictitious signatures (approximately $12 per day).
c. A $300 collection on an account receivable of a valued out-of-town customer was pocketed by the trusted employee and was covered by making a $300 entry as a debit to Sales Returns and a credit to Accounts Receivable.
d. An $800 collection on an account receivable from a local customer was pocketed by the trusted employee and was covered by making an $800 entry as a debit to Allowance for Doubtful Accounts and a credit to Accounts Receivable.

Required:
1. What was the approximate amount stolen during the past year?
2. What would be your recommendations to the owner?

You as Analyst: Online Company Research

Analyzing the Accounting Communication Process (an Individual or Team Project)

CP6-6
LO6-2, 6-3

In your web browser, search for the investor relations page of a public company you are interested in (e.g., Papa John's investor relations). Select SEC Filings or Annual Report or Financials to obtain the 10-K for the most recent year available.*

Required:
Answer the following questions based on the annual report (10-K) that you have downloaded:
1. If your company lists receivables in its balance sheet, what percentage of total assets does receivables represent for each of the last three years? If your company does not list receivables, discuss why this is so.
2. Ratio analysis
   a. What does the receivables turnover ratio measure in general?
   b. If your company lists receivables, compute the ratio for the last three years.
   c. What do your results suggest about the company?
   d. If available, find the industry ratio for the most recent year, compare it to your results, and discuss why you believe your company differs or is similar to the industry ratio.
3. If your company lists receivables, use the 10-K to determine what additional disclosure is available concerning the allowance for doubtful accounts. (Usually the information is in a separate schedule, Item 15.) What is bad debt expense as a percentage of sales for the last three years?
4. What is the effect of the change in receivables on cash flows from operating activities for the most recent year (that is, did the change increase or decrease operating cash flows)? Explain your answer.

*Alternatively, you can go to sec.gov, click on Company Filings (under the search box), and type the name of the public company you want to find. Once at the list of filings, type 10-K in the Filing Type box. The most recent 10-K annual report will be at the top of the list. Click on Interactive Data for a list of the parts or the entire report to examine.

BUSINESS ANALYTICS AND DATA VISUALIZATION WITH EXCEL AND TABLEAU

Connect offers a variety of exercises to assess Excel skills, data visualization, interpretation, and analysis, including auto-graded Tableau Dashboard Activities, Applying Excel problems, and Integrated Excel problems.

Images used throughout chapter: Question of ethics: mushmello/Shutterstock; Pause for feedback: McGraw Hill; Guided help: McGraw Hill; Financial analysis: McGraw Hill; Focus on cash flows: Hilch/Shutterstock; Key ratio analysis: guillermain/123RF; Data analytics: Hilch/Shutterstock; Tip: McGraw Hill; ESG reporting: McGraw Hill; International perspective: Hilch/Shutterstock; Internal control alert icon: McGraw Hill

chapter 7

Reporting and Interpreting Cost of Goods Sold and Inventory

The **Harley-Davidson** eagle trademark was once known best as a popular request in tattoo parlors. Now, Harley-Davidson dominates the heavyweight motorcycle market in North America with a 49.1 percent market share. Harley is also a market leader in Japan and Australia and has captured between 9 and 11 percent of the European market in recent years.

But the heavyweight king is facing rough waters ahead. Industrywide U.S. motorcycle sales have been declining and the strong U.S. dollar has hurt international sales. Harley responded with an aggressive plan to enhance profitability through continuous improvement in manufacturing, product development, and business operations. Harley introduced the "More Roads" plan in an attempt to grow the sport and promote the experience of motorcycling to new customers, which the company sees as necessary to sustain business over the long term. In addition to expanding its customer base, Harley also hopes to grow its international business to make up 50 percent of its sales.

Controlling inventory quality, quantities, and cost is key to maintaining gross profit margin. Introducing new products to stay ahead of major competitors **Honda** and **BMW** and providing a premium dealer experience to all of Harley's customers also will increase gross margin. Finally, selecting appropriate accounting methods for inventory can have a dramatic effect on the amount Harley-Davidson pays in income taxes. Harley produced solid financial results in 2019, but continuous improvement in all of these areas will be necessary for the Harley-Davidson eagle to continue its rise.

LEARNING OBJECTIVES

After studying this chapter, you should be able to:

7-1 Apply the cost principle to identify the amounts that should be included in inventory and cost of goods sold for typical retailers, wholesalers, and manufacturers. p. 345

7-2 Report inventory and cost of goods sold using the four inventory costing methods. p. 350

7-3 Decide when the use of different inventory costing methods is beneficial to a company. p. 355

7-4 Report inventory at the lower of cost or net realizable value. p. 358

7-5 Understand methods for controlling inventory and analyze the effects of inventory errors on financial statements. p. 359

7-6 Evaluate inventory management using the inventory turnover ratio and analyze the effects of inventory on cash flows. p. 361

Diego Fiore/Shutterstock

FOCUS COMPANY

Harley-Davidson, Inc.

BUILDING A LEGEND INTO A WORLD-CLASS MANUFACTURER

harley-davidson.com

UNDERSTANDING THE BUSINESS

The cost and quality of inventory are concerns faced by all modern manufacturers and merchandisers, and so we turn our attention to **cost of goods sold** (cost of sales, cost of products sold) on the income statement and **inventory** on the balance sheet. Exhibit 7.1 presents the relevant excerpts from **Harley-Davidson**'s financial statements that include these accounts. Note that Cost of Goods Sold is subtracted from Net Sales to produce Gross Profit on its income statement. On the balance sheet, Inventory is a current asset; it is reported below cash, marketable securities, and accounts and finance receivables because it is less liquid than those assets.

The primary goals of inventory management are to have sufficient quantities of high-quality inventory available to serve customers' needs while minimizing the costs of carrying inventory (production, storage, obsolescence, and financing). Low quality leads to customer dissatisfaction, returns, and a decline in future sales. Also, purchasing or producing too few units of a hot-selling item causes stock-outs, which mean lost sales revenue and decreases in customer satisfaction. Conversely, purchasing too many units of a slow-selling item increases storage costs as well as interest costs on short-term borrowings used to finance the purchases. It even may lead to losses if the merchandise cannot be sold at normal prices.

The accounting system plays three roles in the inventory management process. First, the system must provide accurate information for preparation of periodic financial statements and tax returns. Second, it must provide up-to-date information on inventory quantities and costs to facilitate ordering and manufacturing decisions. Third, because inventories are subject to theft and other forms of misuse, the system also must provide the information needed to help protect these important assets.

EXHIBIT 7.1

Income Statement and Balance Sheet Excerpts

HARLEY-DAVIDSON, INC.

REAL WORLD EXCERPT: Annual Report

HARLEY-DAVIDSON, INC.
Consolidated Statements of Income
(In thousands)*
12 Months Ended

	Dec. 31, 2019	Dec. 31, 2018	Dec. 31, 2017
Net Sales	$5,361,789	$5,716,875	$5,647,224
Cost of Goods Sold	3,229,798	3,351,796	3,272,330
Gross Profit	$2,131,991	$2,365,079	$2,374,894

HARLEY-DAVIDSON, INC.
Consolidated Balance Sheet
(In thousands)*

	Dec. 31, 2019	Dec. 31, 2018
Assets		
Current assets:		
Cash and cash equivalents	$ 833,868	$ 1,203,766
Marketable securities	-	10,007
Accounts receivable, net	259,334	306,474
Finance receivables, net	2,272,522	2,214,424
Inventories, net	603,571	556,128
Restricted cash	64,554	49,275
Other current assets	168,974	144,368
Total current assets	$4,202,823	$4,484,442

Source: Harley-Davidson, Inc.
*Harley-Davidson's statements have been simplified for purposes of our discussion.

Harley's mix of product lines makes it a particularly good example for this chapter. Although best known as a **manufacturer** of motorcycles, Harley also purchases and resells completed products such as its popular line of Motorclothes apparel. In the second case, it acts as a **wholesaler.** Both the motorcycle and Motorclothes product lines are sold to the company's network of independent dealers. From an accounting standpoint, these independent dealers are Harley-Davidson's customers. The independent dealers are the **retailers** who sell the products to the public.

We begin this chapter with a discussion of the makeup of inventory, the important choices management must make in the financial and tax reporting process, and how these choices affect the financial statements and taxes paid. Then we discuss how managers and analysts evaluate the efficiency of inventory management. Finally, we briefly discuss how accounting systems are organized to keep track of inventory quantities and costs for decision making and control. This topic will be the principal subject matter of your managerial accounting course.

ORGANIZATION OF THE CHAPTER

Nature of Inventory and Cost of Goods Sold	Inventory Costing Methods	Valuation at Lower of Cost or Net Realizable Value	Control of Inventory	Evaluating Inventory Management
• Items Included in Inventory • Costs Included in Inventory Purchases • Flow of Inventory Costs • Cost of Goods Sold Equation • Perpetual and Periodic Inventory Systems	• Specific Identification Method • Cost Flow Assumptions (FIFO, LIFO, Average Cost) • Financial Statement Effects of Inventory Methods • Managers' Choice of Inventory Methods		• Internal Control of Inventory • Errors in Measuring Ending Inventory	• Measuring Efficiency in Inventory Management • Inventory Turnover Ratio • Inventory Methods and Financial Statement Analysis • Inventory and Cash Flows

NATURE OF INVENTORY AND COST OF GOODS SOLD

LEARNING OBJECTIVE 7-1

Apply the cost principle to identify the amounts that should be included in inventory and the cost of goods sold for typical retailers, wholesalers, and manufacturers.

Items Included in Inventory

Inventory is tangible property that is (1) held for sale in the normal course of business or (2) used to produce goods or services for sale. Inventory is reported on the balance sheet as a current asset because it normally is used or converted into cash within one year or the next operating cycle. The types of inventory normally held depend on the characteristics of the business.

Merchandisers (wholesale or retail businesses) hold the following:

Merchandise inventory Goods (or merchandise) held for resale in the normal course of business. The goods usually are acquired in a finished condition and are ready for sale without further processing.

For **Harley-Davidson**, merchandise inventory includes the Motorclothes line and the parts and accessories it purchases for sale to its independent dealers.

Manufacturing businesses hold three types of inventory:

Raw materials inventory Items acquired for processing into finished goods. These items are included in raw materials inventory until they are used, at which point they become part of work in process inventory.

Work in process inventory Goods in the process of being manufactured but not yet complete. When completed, work in process inventory becomes finished goods inventory.

Finished goods inventory Manufactured goods that are complete and ready for sale.

Inventories related to Harley-Davidson's motorcycle manufacturing operations are recorded in these accounts.

Harley-Davidson's recent inventory note reports the following:

HARLEY-DAVIDSON, INC.
REAL WORLD EXCERPT:
Annual Report

HARLEY-DAVIDSON, INC.
Notes to Consolidated Financial Statements

2. ADDITIONAL BALANCE SHEET AND CASH FLOW INFORMATION
Inventories, net (in thousands)

	2019	2018
Raw materials and work in process	$235,433	$ 177,110
Motorcycle finished goods	280,306	301,630
Parts & accessories and general merchandise	144,258	136,027
Inventory at lower of FIFO cost or net realizable value	659,997	614,767

Source: Harley-Davidson, Inc.

Note that Harley-Davidson combines the raw materials and work in process into one number. Other companies separate the two components. The parts and accessories and general merchandise category includes purchased parts and Motorclothes and other accessories that make up merchandise inventory.[1]

Costs Included in Inventory Purchases

Goods in inventory are initially recorded at cost. Inventory cost includes the sum of the costs incurred in bringing an article to usable or salable condition and location. When **Harley-Davidson** purchases raw materials and merchandise inventory, the amount recorded should include the invoice price to be paid plus other expenditures related to the purchase, such as freight charges to deliver the items to its warehouses (**freight-in**) and inspection and preparation costs. Any **purchase returns and allowances** or **purchase discounts** taken are subtracted. In general, the company should cease accumulating purchase costs when the raw materials are **ready for use** or when the merchandise inventory is **ready for shipment.** Any additional costs related to selling the inventory to the dealers, such as marketing department salaries and dealer training sessions, are incurred after the inventory is ready for use. So they should be included in selling, general, and administrative expenses in the period in which they are incurred.

FINANCIAL ANALYSIS

Applying the Materiality Constraint in Practice

Incidental costs such as inspection and preparation costs often are not material in amount (see the discussion of materiality in Chapter 5) and do not have to be assigned to the inventory cost. Thus, for practical reasons, many companies use the invoice price, less returns and discounts, to assign a unit cost to raw materials or merchandise and record other indirect expenditures as a separate cost that is reported as an expense.

Flow of Inventory Costs

The flow of inventory costs for merchandisers (wholesalers and retailers) is relatively simple, as Exhibit 7.2A shows. When merchandise is purchased, the merchandise inventory account is increased. When the goods are sold, cost of goods sold is increased and merchandise inventory is decreased.

[1]These do not add up to the balance reported in Exhibit 7.1 because they do not include the LIFO adjustment discussed later.

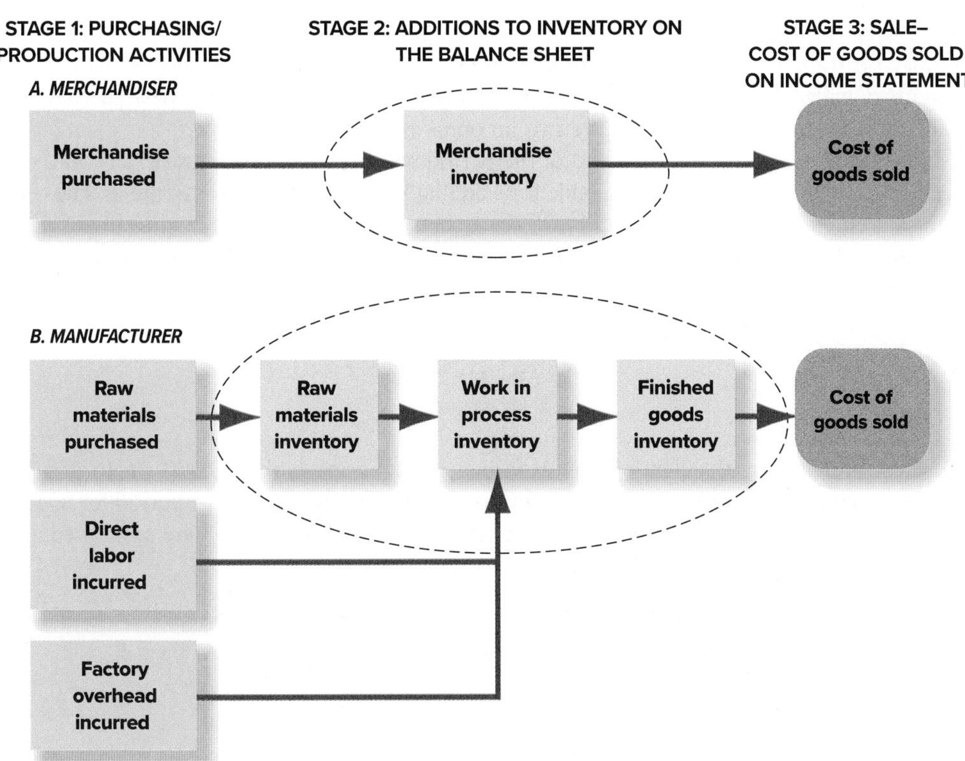

EXHIBIT 7.2

Flow of Inventory Costs

The flow of inventory costs in a manufacturing environment is more complex, as diagrammed in Exhibit 7.2B. First, **raw materials** (also called **direct materials**) must be purchased. For **Harley-Davidson**, these raw materials include steel and aluminum castings, forgings, sheet, and bars, as well as certain motorcycle component parts produced by its small network of suppliers, including electronic fuel injection systems, batteries, and tires. When they are used, the cost of these materials is removed from the raw materials inventory and added to the work in process inventory.

H. Mark Weidman Photography/Alamy Stock Photo

Two other components of manufacturing cost, direct labor and factory overhead, also are added to the work in process inventory when they are used. **Direct labor** cost represents the earnings of employees who work directly on the products being manufactured. **Factory overhead** costs include all other manufacturing costs. For example, the factory supervisor's salary and the cost of heat, light, and power to operate the factory are included in factory overhead. When the motorcycles are completed and ready for sale, the related amounts in work in process inventory are transferred to finished goods inventory. When the finished goods are sold, cost of goods sold increases, and finished goods inventory decreases.

As Exhibit 7.2 indicates, there are three stages to inventory cost flows for both merchandisers and manufacturers. The first involves purchasing and/or production activities. In the second stage, these activities result in additions to inventory accounts on the balance sheet. In the third stage, the inventory items are sold and the amounts become cost of goods sold expense on the income statement. Because the flow of inventory costs from merchandise inventory and finished goods to cost of goods sold are very similar, we will focus the rest of our discussion on merchandise inventory.

Cost of Goods Sold Equation

Cost of goods sold (CGS) expense is directly related to sales revenue. Sales revenue during an accounting period is the number of units sold multiplied by the sales price. Cost of goods sold is the same number of units multiplied by their unit costs.

Let's examine the relationship between cost of goods sold on the income statement and inventory on the balance sheet. **Harley-Davidson** starts each accounting period with a stock of inventory called **beginning inventory** (BI). During the accounting period, new **purchases** (P) are added to inventory. The sum of the two amounts is the goods available for sale during that period. What remains unsold at the end of the period becomes **ending inventory** (EI) on the balance sheet. The portion of goods available for sale that is sold becomes **cost of goods sold** on the income statement. The ending inventory for one accounting period then becomes the beginning inventory for the next period. The relationships between these various inventory amounts are brought together in the cost of goods sold equation:

BI + P − EI = CGS

Tip Be sure to include **beginning inventory** in **all** cost of goods sold calculations.

To illustrate, assume that Harley-Davidson began the period with $40,000 worth of Motorclothes in beginning inventory, purchased additional merchandise during the period for $55,000, and had $35,000 left in inventory at the end of the period. These amounts are combined as follows to compute cost of goods sold of $60,000:

Beginning inventory	$40,000
+ Purchases of merchandise during the year	55,000
Goods available for sale	95,000
− Ending inventory	35,000
Cost of goods sold	$60,000

These same relationships are illustrated in Exhibit 7.3 and can be represented in the merchandise inventory T-account as follows:

Merchandise Inventory (A)			
Beginning inventory	40,000		
Add: Purchases of inventory	55,000	Deduct: Cost of goods sold	60,000
Ending inventory	35,000		

If three of these four values are known, either the cost of goods sold equation or the inventory T-account can be used to solve for the fourth value.

EXHIBIT 7.3

Cost of Goods Sold for Merchandise Inventory

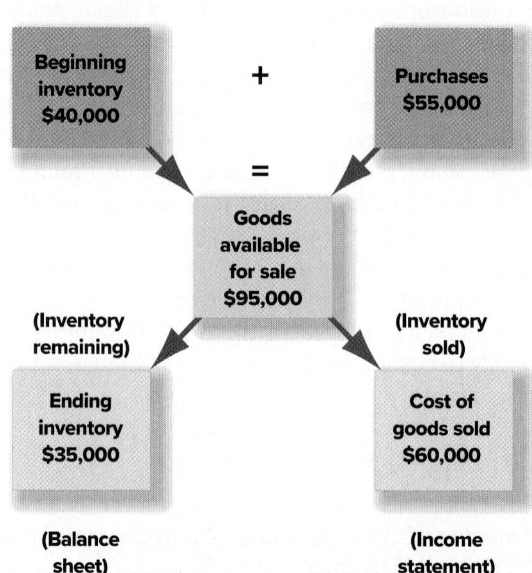

PAUSE FOR FEEDBACK

Inventory should include all items owned that are held for resale. Costs flow into inventory when goods are purchased or manufactured. They flow out (as an expense) when they are sold or disposed of. The cost of goods sold equation describes these flows.

SELF-STUDY QUIZ

1. Assume the following facts for **Harley-Davidson**'s Motorclothes leather baseball jacket product line for the year 2022.

Beginning inventory:	400 units at unit cost of $75.
Purchases:	600 units at unit cost of $75.
Sales:	700 units at a sales price of $100 (cost per unit $75).

Using the cost of goods sold equation, compute the dollar amount of **goods available for sale, ending inventory,** and **cost of goods sold** of leather baseball jackets for the period.

Beginning inventory	
+ Purchases of merchandise during the year	
Goods available for sale	
– Ending inventory	
Cost of goods sold	

2. Assume the following facts for **Harley-Davidson**'s Motorclothes leather baseball jacket product line for the year 2023.

Beginning inventory:	300 units at unit cost of $75.
Ending inventory:	600 units at unit cost of $75.
Sales:	1,100 units at a sales price of $100 (cost per unit $75).

Using the cost of goods sold equation, compute the dollar amount of **purchases** of leather baseball jackets for the period. Remember that if three of these four values are known, the cost of goods sold equation can be used to solve for the fourth value.

Beginning inventory	
+ Purchases of merchandise during the year	
– Ending inventory	
Cost of goods sold	

After you have completed your answers, check them below.

GUIDED HELP 7-1

For additional step-by-step video instruction on using the cost of goods sold equation to compute relevant income statement amounts, go to mhhe.com/libby_gh7-1.

Related Homework: M7-4, E7-2, E7-3, E7-4

Solutions to SELF-STUDY QUIZ

1. Beginning inventory (400 × $75)	$30,000
+Purchases of merchandise during the year (600 × $75)	45,000
Goods available for sale (1,000 × $75)	75,000
−Ending inventory (300 × $75)	22,500
Cost of goods sold (700 × $75)	$52,500

2. BI = 300 × $75 = $22,500	BI + P − EI = CGS
EI = 600 × $75 = $45,000	$22,500 + P − $45,000 = $82,500
CGS = 1,100 × $75 = $82,500	P = $105,000 (1,400 × $75)

Perpetual and Periodic Inventory Systems

The amount of purchases for the period is always accumulated in the accounting system. The amount of cost of goods sold and ending inventory can be determined by using one of two different inventory systems: perpetual or periodic.

Perpetual Inventory System

To this point in the text, all journal entries for purchase and sales transactions have been recorded using a perpetual inventory system. In a perpetual inventory system, purchase transactions are recorded directly in an inventory account. When each sale is recorded, a companion cost of goods sold entry is made, decreasing inventory and recording cost of goods sold. You already have experienced the starting point for that process when your purchases are scanned at the checkout counter at **Walmart** or **Target**. Not only does that process determine how much you must pay the cashier, it also removes the sold items from the store inventory records. As a result, information on cost of goods sold and ending inventory is available on a continuous (perpetual) basis.

In a perpetual inventory system, a detailed record is maintained for each type of merchandise stocked, showing (1) units and cost of the beginning inventory, (2) units and cost of each purchase, (3) units and cost of the goods for each sale, and (4) units and cost of the goods on hand at any point in time. This up-to-date record is maintained on a transaction-by-transaction basis. Most modern companies could not survive without this information. And as a consumer, you access that same information every time you search **Amazon.com** for merchandise and are told, "Only 4 left in stock–order soon" or "Out of stock."

As noted at the beginning of the chapter, cost, quality, and customer service pressures brought on by increasing competition, combined with dramatic declines in the cost of information systems, have made sophisticated perpetual inventory systems a requirement at all but the smallest companies. As a consequence, we will continue to focus on perpetual inventory systems throughout the book.

Periodic Inventory System

Under the periodic inventory system, no up-to-date record of inventory is maintained during the year. An actual physical count of the goods remaining on hand is required at the **end of each period.** The number of units of each type of merchandise on hand is multiplied by unit cost to compute the dollar amount of the ending inventory. Cost of goods sold is calculated using the cost of goods sold equation.

Because the amount of inventory is not known until the end of the period when the inventory count is taken, the amount of cost of goods sold cannot be reliably determined until the inventory count is complete. The primary disadvantage of a periodic inventory system is the lack of inventory information. Managers are not informed about low or excess stock situations.

LEARNING OBJECTIVE 7-2

Report inventory and cost of goods sold using the four inventory costing methods.

INVENTORY COSTING METHODS

In the Motorclothes example presented in the Self-Study Quiz, the cost of all units of the leather baseball jackets was the same–$75. If inventory costs normally did not change, this would be the end of our discussion. As we are all aware, however, the prices of most goods do change. In recent years, the costs of many manufactured items such as automobiles and motorcycles have risen gradually. In some industries such as computers, costs of production have dropped dramatically along with retail prices.

When inventory costs have changed, which inventory items are treated as sold or remaining in inventory can turn profits into losses and cause companies to pay or save millions in taxes. A simple example will illustrate these dramatic effects. Do not let the simplicity of our example mislead you. It applies broadly to actual company practices.

Assume that a **Harley-Davidson** dealer had the indicated inventory on hand and made purchases during January as follows:

Jan. 1	Had beginning inventory of two units of a Model A leather jacket at $70 each.
Jan. 12	Purchased four units of the Model A leather jacket at $80 each.
Jan. 14	Purchased one unit of the Model A leather jacket at $100.
Jan. 15	Sold four units of the Model A leather jacket for $120 each.

Note that the **cost of the leather jacket rose** rapidly during January. On January 15, four units are sold for $120 each and revenues of $480 are recorded. What amount is recorded as cost of goods sold? The answer depends on which specific goods we assume are sold. Four generally accepted inventory costing methods are available for determining cost of goods sold:

1. Specific identification.
2. First-in, first-out (FIFO).
3. Last-in, first-out (LIFO).
4. Average cost.

The four inventory costing methods are alternative ways to assign the total dollar amount of goods available for sale between (1) ending inventory and (2) cost of goods sold. The first method identifies individual items that remain in inventory or are sold. The remaining three methods assume that the inventory costs follow a certain flow.

Specific Identification Method

When the **specific identification method** is used, the cost of each item sold is individually identified and recorded as cost of goods sold. This method requires keeping track of the purchase cost of each item. In the leather jacket example, any four of the items could have been sold. If we assume that one of the $70 items, two of the $80 items, and the one $100 item have been sold, the cost of those items ($70 + $80 + $80 + $100) would become cost of goods sold ($330). The cost of the remaining items (two $80 items and one $70 item) would be ending inventory ($80 + $80 + $70 = $230).

The specific identification method is impractical when large quantities of similar items are stocked. On the other hand, when dealing with expensive unique items such as houses or fine jewelry, this method is appropriate. As a consequence, most inventory items are accounted for using one of three cost flow assumptions.

Cost Flow Assumptions

The **choice of an inventory costing method is NOT based on the physical flow of goods** on and off the shelves. That is why they are called **cost flow assumptions.** A useful tool for representing inventory cost flow assumptions is a bin, or container. Try visualizing these inventory costing methods as flows of inventory in and out of the bin.

First-In, First-Out Method

The **first-in, first-out method**, frequently called **FIFO**, assumes that the earliest goods purchased (the first ones in) are the first goods sold, and the last goods purchased are left in ending inventory. Under FIFO, cost of goods sold and ending inventory are computed as if the flows in and out of the FIFO inventory bin in Exhibit 7.4A had taken place. First, each purchase is treated as if it were deposited in the bin from the top in sequence (two units of beginning inventory at $70 followed by purchases of four units at $80 and one unit at $100), producing goods available for sale of $560. Each good sold is then removed from the *bottom* in sequence (two units at $70 and two at $80); **first in is first out.** These goods totaling $300 become cost of goods sold (CGS). The remaining units (two units at $80 and one unit at $100 = $260) become ending inventory. FIFO allocates the **oldest** unit costs **to cost of goods sold** and the **newest** unit costs **to ending inventory**.

Tip Regardless of the actual flow of goods to customers, firms may use any of the three cost flow assumptions described in this chapter. We discuss the rationale for managers' choices later in the chapter.

EXHIBIT 7.4

FIFO and LIFO Inventory Flows

A. FIFO

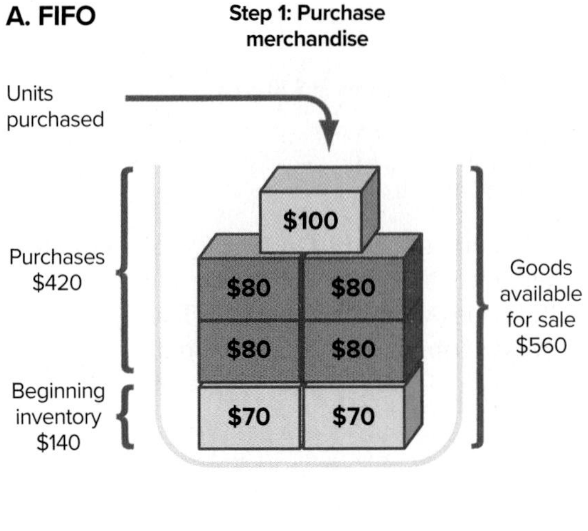

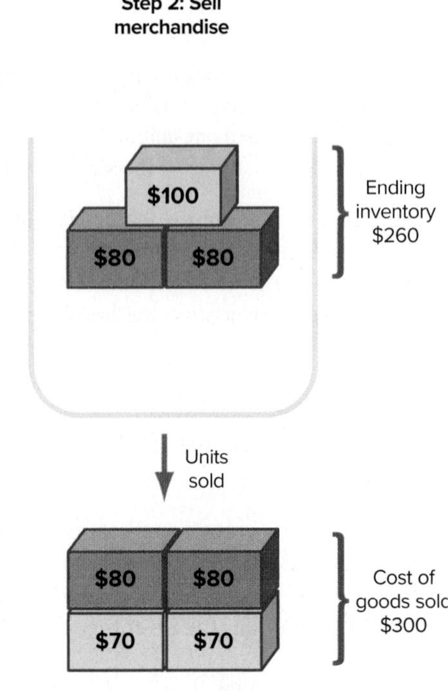

B. LIFO

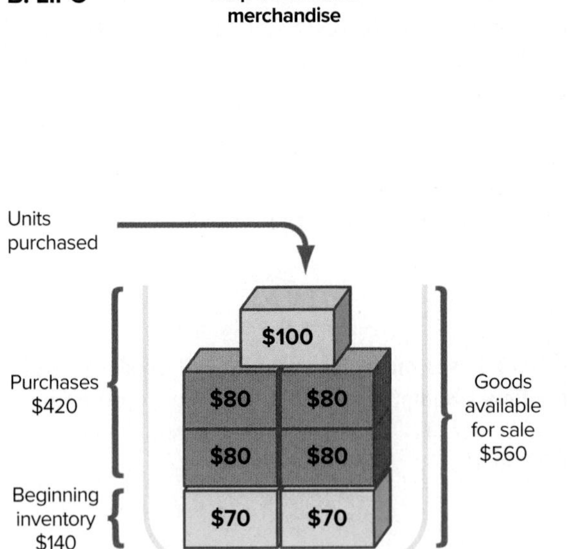

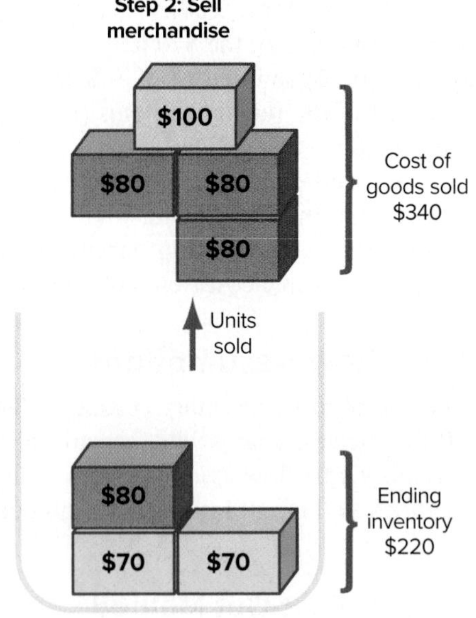

Cost of Goods Sold Calculation (FIFO)		
Beginning inventory	(2 units at $70 each)	$140
+ Purchases	(4 units at $80 each)	320
	(1 unit at $100)	100
Goods available for sale		560
− Ending inventory	(2 units at $80 each and 1 unit at $100)	260
Cost of goods sold	(2 units at $70 each and 2 units at $80 each)	$300

Last-In, First-Out Method

The **last-in, first-out method**, often called **LIFO**, assumes that the most recently purchased goods (the last ones in) are sold first and the oldest units are left in ending inventory. It is illustrated by the LIFO inventory bin in Exhibit 7.4B. As in FIFO, each purchase is treated as if it were deposited in the bin from the top (two units of beginning inventory at $70 followed by purchases of four units at $80 and one unit at $100), resulting in the goods available for sale of $560. Unlike FIFO, however, each good sold is treated as if it were removed from the *top* in sequence (one unit at $100 followed by three units at $80). These goods totaling $340 become cost of goods sold (CGS). The remaining units (one at $80 and two at $70 = $220) become ending inventory. LIFO allocates the **newest** unit costs **to cost of goods sold** and the **oldest** unit costs to ending inventory.

Cost of Goods Sold Calculation (LIFO)		
Beginning inventory	(2 units at $70 each)	$140
+ Purchases	(4 units at $80 each)	320
	(1 unit at $100)	100
Goods available for sale		560
− Ending inventory	(2 units at $70 each and 1 unit at $80)	220
Cost of goods sold	(3 units at $80 each and 1 unit at $100)	$340

The LIFO cost flow assumption is the exact opposite of the FIFO cost flow assumption:

	FIFO	LIFO
Cost of goods sold on income statement	Oldest unit costs	Newest unit costs
Inventory on balance sheet	Newest unit costs	Oldest unit costs

Average Cost Method

The **average cost method** (weighted average cost method) uses the weighted average unit cost of the goods available for sale for both cost of goods sold and ending inventory. The weighted average unit cost of the goods available for sale is computed as follows:

Number of Units	×	Unit Cost	=	Total Cost
2	×	$ 70	=	$140
4	×	$ 80	=	320
1	×	$100	=	100
7				$560

$$\text{Average cost} = \frac{\text{Cost of Goods Available for Sale}}{\text{Number of Units Available for Sale}}$$

$$\text{Average cost} = \frac{\$560}{\text{7 Units}} = \$80 \text{ per Unit}$$

Cost of goods sold and ending inventory are assigned the same weighted average cost per unit of $80.

Cost of Goods Sold Calculation (Average Cost)		
Beginning inventory	(2 units at $70 each)	$140
+ Purchases	(4 units at $80 each)	320
	(1 unit at $100)	100
Goods available for sale	(7 units at $80 average cost each)	560
− Ending inventory	(3 units at $80 average cost each)	240
Cost of goods sold	(4 units at $80 average cost each)	$320

Perpetual Inventory Systems and Cost Flow Assumptions in Practice

You should have noted that, in our example, all inventory units were purchased before a sale was made and cost of goods sold recorded. In reality, most companies make numerous purchases and sales of the same inventory item throughout the accounting period. How can we apply our simple example to these circumstances given that companies normally employ perpetual inventory systems?

In practice, firms follow a two-step process:

1. **Virtually all accounting systems that keep track of the costs of individual items do so on a FIFO or average cost basis,** regardless of the cost flow assumption used for financial reporting.
2. As a consequence, **companies that wish to report under LIFO convert the outputs of their perpetual inventory system to LIFO with an adjusting entry at the end of each period.** By waiting until the end of the period to calculate this LIFO adjustment, LIFO ending inventory and cost of goods sold are calculated as if all purchases during the period were recorded before cost of goods sold was calculated and recorded.

In other words, our simple example of how to calculate cost of goods sold applies even though a company actually tracks the number of units bought and sold on a perpetual basis.[2]

INTERNATIONAL PERSPECTIVE

LIFO and International Comparisons

While U.S. GAAP allows companies to choose between FIFO, LIFO, and average cost inventory accounting methods, International Financial Reporting Standards (IFRS) currently prohibit the use of LIFO. U.S. GAAP also allows different inventory accounting methods to be used for different types of inventory items and even for the same item in different locations. IFRS requires that the same method be used for all inventory items that have a similar nature and use. These differences can create comparability problems when one attempts to compare companies across international borders. For example, **Harley-Davidson** uses LIFO to value most U.S. inventories and FIFO for non-U.S. inventories, while **Honda** (of Japan) uses FIFO for all inventories. Each individual country's tax laws determine the acceptability of different inventory methods for tax purposes.

Financial Statement Effects of Inventory Methods

Each of the four alternative inventory costing methods is in conformity with GAAP and the tax law. To understand why managers choose different methods in different circumstances, we first must understand their effects on the income statement and balance sheet. Exhibit 7.5 summarizes the financial statement effects of the FIFO, LIFO, and average cost inventory methods in our example, assuming $80 in other expenses and a 25 percent tax rate. Remember that the methods differ only in the dollar amount of goods available for sale allocated to cost of goods sold versus ending inventory. For that reason, the method that gives the highest ending inventory amount also gives the lowest cost of goods sold and the highest gross profit, income tax expense, and net income amounts, and vice versa. The weighted average cost method generally gives net income and inventory amounts that are between the FIFO and LIFO extremes.

In our example, recall that unit costs were increasing. **When unit costs are rising, LIFO produces lower net income and a lower inventory valuation than FIFO.** Even in inflationary times, some companies' costs decline. **When unit costs are declining, LIFO produces higher net income**

[2]While it is mathematically possible to compute ending inventory and cost of goods sold on a perpetual basis using LIFO, since it never occurs in practice, we do not discuss this possibility in this text.

	FIFO	LIFO	Average Cost
Effect on the Income Statement			
Sales	$480	$480	$480
Cost of goods sold	300	340	320
Gross profit	180	140	160
Other expenses	80	80	80
Income before income taxes	100	60	80
Income tax expense (25%)	25	15	20
Net income	$ 75	$ 45	$ 60
Effect on the Balance Sheet			
Inventory	$260	$220	$240

EXHIBIT 7.5

Financial Statement Effects of Inventory Costing Methods

and higher inventory valuation than FIFO. These effects, which hold as long as inventory quantities are constant or rising, are summarized in the following table:

Increasing Costs: Normal Financial Statement Effects	FIFO	LIFO
Cost of goods sold on income statement	Lower	Higher
Net income	Higher	Lower
Income taxes	Higher	Lower
Inventory on balance sheet	Higher	Lower

Decreasing Costs: Normal Financial Statement Effects	FIFO	LIFO
Cost of goods sold on income statement	Higher	Lower
Net income	Lower	Higher
Income taxes	Lower	Higher
Inventory on balance sheet	Lower	Higher

Managers' Choice of Inventory Methods

LEARNING OBJECTIVE 7-3

Decide when the use of different inventory costing methods is beneficial to a company.

What motivates companies to choose different inventory costing methods? Most managers choose accounting methods based on two factors:

1. Net income effects (managers prefer to report higher earnings for their companies).
2. Income tax effects (managers prefer to pay the least amount of taxes allowed by law as late as possible–the **least-latest rule of thumb**).

Any conflict between the two motives is normally resolved by choosing one accounting method for external financial statements and a different method for preparing the company's tax return. The choice of inventory costing methods is a special case, however, because of what is called the **LIFO conformity rule:** If LIFO is used on the U.S. income tax return, it also must be used to calculate inventory and cost of goods sold for the financial statements.

Increasing Cost Inventories

- **For inventory with increasing costs, LIFO is used on the tax return because it normally results in lower income taxes.**

This is illustrated in Exhibit 7.5, where income before income taxes was lowered from $100 under FIFO to $60 under LIFO. On the income tax expense line, this lowers income taxes from

$25 under FIFO to $15 under LIFO, generating cash tax savings of $10 under LIFO.[3] The LIFO conformity rule leads companies to adopt LIFO for **both** tax and financial reporting purposes for increasing cost inventories located in the United States. **Harley-Davidson** is a fairly typical company facing increasing costs. Assuming an average tax rate of 25 percent, it has saved approximately $15 million in taxes from the date it adopted the LIFO method through 2019.

For inventory located in countries that do not allow LIFO for tax purposes or that do not have a LIFO conformity rule, companies with increasing costs most often use FIFO or average cost to report higher income on the income statement.

Decreasing Cost Inventories

- **For inventory with decreasing costs, FIFO is most often used for both the tax return and financial statements.**

Using this method (along with lower of cost or net realizable value, discussed later) produces the lowest tax payments for companies with decreasing cost inventories. Many high-technology companies are facing declining costs. In such circumstances, the FIFO method, in which the oldest, most expensive goods become cost of goods sold, produces the highest cost of goods sold, the lowest pretax earnings, and thus the lowest income tax liability. For example, **Apple** and **HP** account for inventories using the FIFO method.

Because most companies in the same industry face similar cost structures, clusters of companies in the same industries often choose the same accounting method.

Consistency in Use of Inventory Methods

It is important to remember that regardless of the physical flow of goods, a company can use any of the inventory costing methods. Also, a company is not required to use the same inventory costing method for all inventory items, and no particular justification is needed for the selection of one or more of the acceptable methods. Harley-Davidson, and most large companies, use different inventory methods for different inventory items. However, accounting rules require companies to apply their accounting methods on a consistent basis over time. A company is not permitted to use LIFO one period, FIFO the next, and then go back to LIFO. A change in method is allowed only if the change will improve the measurement of financial results and financial position.

Tip In the U.S., managers normally choose LIFO to account for their increasing cost inventories to reduce income taxes. They choose FIFO or average cost for their decreasing cost and non-U.S. inventories.

A QUESTION OF ETHICS

LIFO and Conflicts between Managers' and Owners' Interests

We have seen that the selection of an inventory method can have significant effects on the financial statements. Company managers may have an incentive to select a method that is not consistent with the owners' objectives. For example, during a period of rising prices, using LIFO may be in the best interests of the owners because LIFO often reduces a company's tax liability. However, if managers' compensation is tied to reported profits, they may prefer FIFO, which typically results in higher profits.

While a well-designed compensation plan should reward managers for acting in the best interests of the owners, that is not always the case. Clearly, a manager who selects an accounting method that is not optimal for the company solely to increase his or her compensation is engaging in questionable ethical behavior.

[3]In theory, LIFO cannot provide permanent tax savings because (1) when inventory levels drop or (2) costs drop, the income effect reverses and the income taxes deferred must be paid. The economic advantage of deferring income taxes in such situations is due to the fact that interest can be earned on the money that otherwise would be paid as taxes for the current year.

PAUSE FOR FEEDBACK

Four different inventory costing methods may be used to allocate costs between the units remaining in inventory and the units sold, depending on economic circumstances. The methods include specific identification, FIFO, LIFO, and average cost. Each of the inventory costing methods conforms to GAAP. Remember that the cost flow assumption need not match the physical flow of inventory. The following questions test your understanding of the FIFO and LIFO methods.

SELF-STUDY QUIZ

1. Compute cost of goods sold and pretax income for **2021** under the FIFO and LIFO accounting methods. Assume that a company's beginning inventory and purchases for 2021 included:

Beginning inventory	10 units @ $ 6 each
Purchases January	5 units @ $10 each
Purchases May	5 units @ $12 each

During 2021, 15 units were sold for $20 each, and other operating expenses totaled $100.

2. Compute cost of goods sold and pretax income for **2022** under the FIFO and LIFO accounting methods. (**Hint:** The 2021 ending inventory amount from Part 1 becomes the 2022 beginning inventory amount.) Assume that the company's purchases for 2022 included:

Purchases March	6 units @ $13 each
Purchases November	5 units @ $14 each

During 2022, 10 units were sold for $24 each, and other operating expenses totaled $70.

3. Which method would you recommend that the company adopt? Why?

After you have completed your answers, check them below.

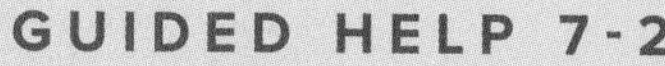

GUIDED HELP 7-2

For additional step-by-step video instruction on computing ending inventory and cost of goods sold using different cost flow assumptions, go to mhhe.com/libby_gh7-2.

Related Homework: E7-5, E7-6, E7-7, E7-8, E7-9, E7-10, E7-11, P7-2, P7-3, P7-4

Solutions to SELF-STUDY QUIZ

1.

2021	FIFO	LIFO
Beginning inventory	$ 60	$ 60
Purchases (5 × $10) + (5 × $12)	110	110
Goods available for sale	170	170
Ending inventory*	60	30
Cost of goods sold	$110	$140

	FIFO	LIFO
Sales revenue (15 × $20)	$300	$300
Cost of goods sold	110	140
Gross profit	190	160
Other expenses	100	100
Pretax income	$ 90	$ 60

*FIFO ending inventory = (5 × $12) = $60
Cost of goods sold = (10 × $6) + (5 × $10) = $110
LIFO ending inventory = (5 × $6) = $30
Cost of goods sold = (5 × $12) + (5 × $10) + (5 × $6) = $140

2.

2022	FIFO	LIFO
Beginning inventory	$ 60	$ 30
Purchases (6 × $13) + (5 × $14)	148	148
Goods available for sale	208	178
Ending inventory†	83	43
Cost of goods sold	$125	$135

	FIFO	LIFO
Sales revenue (10 × $24)	$240	$240
Cost of goods sold	125	135
Gross profit	115	105
Other expenses	70	70
Pretax income	$ 45	$ 35

†FIFO ending inventory = (5 × $14) + (1 × $13) = $83
Cost of goods sold = (5 × $12) + (5 × $13) = $125
LIFO ending inventory = (5 × $6) + (1 × $13) = $43
Cost of goods sold = (5 × $14) + (5 × $13) = $135

3. LIFO would be recommended because it produces lower pretax income and lower taxes when inventory costs are rising.

LEARNING OBJECTIVE 7-4

Report inventory at the lower of cost or net realizable value.

VALUATION AT LOWER OF COST OR NET REALIZABLE VALUE

Inventories should be measured initially at their purchase cost in conformity with the cost principle. When the **net realizable value (NRV)** (sales price less costs to sell) of goods remaining in ending inventory falls below cost, these goods must be assigned a unit cost equal to their current estimated net realizable value. This rule is known as measuring inventories at the **lower of cost or net realizable value** (lower of cost or market).

This departure from the cost principle is based on the **conservatism** constraint, which requires special care to avoid overstating assets and income. It is particularly important for two types of companies: (1) high-technology companies such as **HP** that manufacture goods for which costs of production and selling price are declining and (2) companies such as **American Eagle Outfitters** that sell seasonal goods such as clothing, the value of which drops dramatically at the end of each selling season (fall or spring).

Under lower of cost or net realizable value, companies recognize a "holding" loss in the period in which the net realizable value of an item drops, rather than in the period the item is sold. The holding loss is the difference between the purchase cost and the lower net realizable value. It is added to the cost of goods sold for the period. To illustrate, assume that HP had the following in the current period ending inventory:

Item	Quantity	Cost per Item	Net Realizable Value (NRV) per Item	Lower of Cost or NRV per Item	Total Lower of Cost or Net Realizable Value
Intel chips	1,000	$250	$200	$200	1,000 × $200 = $200,000
Disk drives	400	100	110	100	400 × $100 = 40,000

The 1,000 Intel chips should be recorded in the ending inventory at the current net realizable value ($200) because it is **lower** than the cost ($250). HP makes the following journal entry to record the write-down:

	Debit	Credit
Cost of goods sold (+E, −SE) (1,000 × $50)	50,000	
Inventory (−A)		50,000

Assets		=	Liabilities	+	Stockholders' Equity	
Inventory	−50,000				Cost of Goods Sold (+E)	−50,000

Because the net realizable value of the disk drives ($110) is higher than the original cost ($100), no write-down is necessary. The drives remain on the books at their cost of $100 per unit ($40,000 in total). Recognition of holding gains on inventory is not permitted by GAAP.

The write-down of the Intel chips to market produces the following effects on the income statement and balance sheet:

Effects of Lower of Cost or NRV Write-Down	Current Period	Next Period (if sold)
Cost of goods sold	Increase $50,000	Decrease $50,000
Pretax income	Decrease $50,000	Increase $50,000
Ending inventory on balance sheet	Decrease $50,000	Unaffected

Tip The write-down to lower of Cost or NRV **decreases pretax income in the current period** and **increases pretax income in the period of sale** by the same amount.

Note that the effects in the period of sale are the opposite of those in the period of the write-down. Lower of cost or net realizable value changes only the timing of cost of goods sold. It transfers cost of goods sold from the period of sale to the period of write-down.

Note that in the two examples that follow, both **Harley-Davidson**, which is a mixed LIFO company, and HP, which is a FIFO company, report the use of lower of cost or net realizable value for financial statement purposes.[4]

HARLEY-DAVIDSON, INC.
REAL WORLD EXCERPT:
Annual Report

HARLEY-DAVIDSON, INC.

Notes to Consolidated Financial Statements

1. SUMMARY OF SIGNIFICANT ACCOUNTING POLICIES

Inventories, net–Substantially all inventories located in the U.S. are valued using the last-in, first-out (LIFO) method. Other inventories totaling $326.5 million and $247.6 million at December 31, 2019 and 2018, respectively, are valued at the lower of cost or net realizable value using the first-in, first-out (FIFO) method.

Source: Harley-Davidson, Inc.

HP INC.
REAL WORLD EXCERPT:
Annual Report

HP INC. AND SUBSIDIARIES

Notes to Consolidated Financial Statements

NOTE 1: Overview and Summary of Significant Accounting Policies

We state our inventory at the lower of cost or market on a first-in, first-out basis. We make adjustments to reduce the cost of inventory to its net realizable value at the product group level for estimated excess or obsolescence. Factors influencing these adjustments include changes in demand, technological changes, product life cycle and development plans, component cost trends, product pricing, physical deterioration and quality issues.

Source: HP Inc.

CONTROL OF INVENTORY

LEARNING OBJECTIVE 7-5

Understand methods for controlling inventory and analyze the effects of inventory errors on financial statements.

Internal Control of Inventory

After cash, inventory is the asset second most vulnerable to theft. Efficient management of inventory to avoid the cost of stock-outs and overstock situations is also crucial to the profitability of most companies. As a consequence, a number of control features focus on safeguarding inventories and providing up-to-date information for management decisions. Key among these are:

1. Separation of responsibilities for inventory accounting and physical handling of inventory.
2. Storage of inventory in a manner that protects it from theft and damage.
3. Limiting access to inventory to authorized employees.
4. Maintaining perpetual inventory records (described earlier in this chapter).
5. Comparing perpetual records to periodic physical counts of inventory.

Internal Control Alert

[4]For tax purposes, lower of cost or net realizable value may be applied with all inventory costing methods except LIFO.

Alistair Berg/Digital Vision/Getty Images

Errors in Measuring Ending Inventory

As the cost of goods sold equation indicates, a direct relationship exists between ending inventory and cost of goods sold because items not in the ending inventory are assumed to have been sold. Thus, the measurement of ending inventory quantities and costs affects both the balance sheet (assets) and the income statement (cost of goods sold, gross profit, and net income). The measurement of ending inventory affects not only the net income for that period but also the net income for the next accounting period. This two-period effect occurs because the ending inventory for one period is the beginning inventory for the next accounting period.

Greeting card maker **Gibson Greetings** overstated its net income by 20 percent because one division overstated ending inventory for the year. You can compute the effects of the error on both the current year's and the next year's income before taxes using the cost of goods sold equation. Assume that ending inventory was overstated by $10,000 due to a clerical error that was not discovered. This would have the following effects in the current year and next year:

Current Year		Next Year	
Beginning inventory		Beginning inventory	**Overstated $10,000**
+ Purchases of merchandise during the year		+ Purchases of merchandise during the year	
− Ending inventory	**Overstated $10,000**	− Ending inventory	
Cost of goods sold	**Understated $10,000**	Cost of goods sold	**Overstated $10,000**

Because cost of goods sold was understated, **income before taxes would be overstated** by $10,000 in the **current year.** And, because the current year's ending inventory becomes next year's beginning inventory, it would have the opposite effects the next year. Because cost of goods sold was overstated, **income before taxes would be understated** by $10,000 in the **next year.**

Each of these errors would flow into retained earnings so that at the end of the current year, retained earnings would be overstated by $10,000 (less the related income tax expense). This error would be offset in the next year, and retained earnings and inventory at the end of next year would be correct.

In this example, we assumed that the overstatement of ending inventory was inadvertent, the result of a clerical error. However, inventory fraud is a common form of financial statement fraud.

PAUSE FOR FEEDBACK

An error in the measurement of ending inventory affects cost of goods sold on the current period's income statement and ending inventory on the balance sheet. Because this year's ending inventory becomes next year's beginning inventory, it also affects cost of goods sold in the following period by the same amount but in the opposite direction. These relationships can be seen through the cost of goods sold equation (BI + P − EI = CGS).

SELF-STUDY QUIZ

Assume that it is now the end of 2022 and Bennett-Griffin, Inc., is undergoing its first audit by an independent CPA. The annual income statement prepared by the company is presented here. Assume further that the independent CPA discovers that the ending inventory for 2022 was understated by $15,000. Correct and reconstruct the income statement in the space provided.

		For the Year Ended December 31		
	2022 Uncorrected		2022 Corrected	
Sales revenue		$750,000		
Cost of goods sold				
Beginning inventory	$ 45,000			
Add purchases	460,000			
Goods available for sale	505,000		___	
Less ending inventory	40,000		___	
Cost of goods sold		465,000		___
Gross margin on sales		285,000		
Operating expenses		275,000		___
Pretax income		10,000		
Income tax expense (20%)		2,000		___
Net income		$ 8,000		___

After you have completed your answers, check them below.

GUIDED HELP 7-3 

For additional step-by-step video instruction on correcting the income statement for errors in ending inventory, go to mhhe.com/libby_gh7-3

Related Homework: M7-8, E7-14, E7-15, P7-6

EVALUATING INVENTORY MANAGEMENT

LEARNING OBJECTIVE 7-6

Evaluate inventory management using the inventory turnover ratio and analyze the effects of inventory on cash flows.

Measuring Efficiency in Inventory Management

As noted at the beginning of the chapter, the primary goals of inventory management are to have sufficient quantities of high-quality inventory available to serve customers' needs while minimizing the costs of carrying inventory (production, storage, obsolescence, and financing). The inventory turnover ratio is an important measure of the company's success in balancing these conflicting goals.

Solutions to SELF-STUDY QUIZ

Sales revenue		$750,000
Cost of goods sold		
Beginning inventory	$ 45,000	
Add purchases	460,000	
Goods available for sale	505,000	
Less ending inventory	55,000	
Cost of goods sold		450,000
Gross margin on sales		300,000
Operating expenses		275,000
Pretax income		25,000
Income tax expense (20%)		5,000
Net income		$ 20,000

Note: An ending inventory error in one year affects pretax income by the amount of the error. In the next year, the ending inventory error affects pretax income again by the same amount, but in the opposite direction.

KEY RATIO ANALYSIS

Inventory Turnover

ANALYTICAL QUESTION

How efficient are inventory management activities?

RATIO AND COMPARISONS

$$\textbf{Inventory Turnover} = \frac{\textbf{Cost of Goods Sold}}{\textbf{Average Inventory}}$$

The 2019 ratio for **Harley-Davidson** (see Exhibit 7.1 for the inputs to the equation):

$$\frac{\$3{,}229{,}798}{(\$603{,}571 + \$556{,}128)/2} = 5.6$$

Comparisons Over Time		
Harley-Davidson		
2017	**2018**	**2019**
6.3	6.1	5.6

Comparisons With Competitors	
Polaris	Honda Motor
2019	**2019**
4.9	8.1

INTERPRETATIONS

In General The inventory turnover ratio reflects how many times average inventory was produced and sold during the period. A higher ratio indicates that inventory moves more quickly through the production process to the ultimate customer, reducing storage and obsolescence costs. Because less money is tied up in inventory, the excess can be invested to earn interest income or reduce borrowing, which reduces interest expense. More efficient purchasing and production techniques, such as just-in-time inventory, as well as high product demand cause this ratio to be high. Analysts and creditors also watch the inventory turnover ratio because a sudden decline may mean that a company is facing an unexpected drop in demand for its products or is becoming sloppy in its production management. Many managers and analysts compute the related number, average days to sell inventory, which, for Harley-Davidson, is equal to

Selected Focus Companies' Inventory Turnover

Company	Inventory Turnover
National Beverage	9.39
Home Depot	5.11
Skechers	2.82

$$\textbf{Average Days to Sell inventory} = \frac{\textbf{365}}{\textbf{Inventory Turnover}} = \frac{\textbf{365}}{\textbf{5.6}} = \textbf{65.2 days}$$

It indicates the average time it takes the company to produce and deliver inventory to customers.

Focus Company Analysis Harley-Davidson's inventory turnover has steadily declined from 6.3 in 2017 to 5.6 in 2019. Harley's ratio is higher than that of motorcycle, off-road vehicle, and snowmobile manufacturer **Polaris** but lower than that of giant Japanese auto and motorcycle manufacturer **Honda**.

A Few Cautions Differences across industries in purchasing, production, and sales processes cause dramatic differences in this ratio. For example, restaurants such as **Papa John's**, which must turn over their perishable inventory very quickly, tend to have much higher inventory turnover. A particular firm's ratio should be compared only with its figures from prior years or with figures for other firms in the same industry.

PAUSE FOR FEEDBACK

The inventory turnover ratio measures the efficiency of inventory management. It reflects how many times average inventory was produced and sold during the period. Analysts and creditors watch this ratio because a sudden decline may mean that a company is facing an unexpected drop in demand for its products or is becoming sloppy in its production management. Before you move on, complete the following questions to test your understanding of these concepts.

SELF-STUDY QUIZ

Refer to the Key Ratio Analysis for **Harley-Davidson**'s inventory turnover. Based on the computations for 2019, answer the following question. If Harley-Davidson had been able to manage its inventory more efficiently and decrease purchases and ending inventory by $20,000 for 2019, would its inventory turnover ratio have increased or decreased? Explain.

After you have completed your answer, check it below.

Related Homework: M7-9, E7-16, P7-7

Inventory Methods and Financial Statement Analysis

What would analysts do if they wanted to compare two companies that prepared their statements using different inventory accounting methods? Before meaningful comparisons could be made, one company's statements would have to be converted to a comparable basis. Making such a conversion is eased by the requirement that U.S. public companies using LIFO also report beginning and ending inventory on a FIFO basis in the notes if the FIFO values are materially different. We can use this information along with the cost of goods sold equation to convert the balance sheet and income statement to the FIFO basis.

Converting the Income Statement to FIFO

Recall that the choice of a cost flow assumption affects how goods available for sale are allocated to ending inventory and cost of goods sold. It does not affect the recording of purchases. Ending inventory will be different under the alternative methods, and, because last year's ending inventory is this year's beginning inventory, beginning inventory also will be different:

Beginning inventory	**Different**
+ Purchases of merchandise during the year	**Same**
− Ending inventory	**Different**
Cost of goods sold	**Different**

This equation suggests that if we know the differences between a company's inventory valued at LIFO and FIFO for both beginning and ending inventory, we can compute the difference in cost of goods sold. Exhibit 7.6 shows **Harley-Davidson**'s 2018 disclosure of the differences between LIFO and FIFO values for beginning and ending inventory. These amounts, referred to as the LIFO reserve or "Excess of FIFO over LIFO," are disclosed by LIFO users in their inventory footnotes.

Using Harley-Davidson's LIFO reserve values reported in the footnote presented in Exhibit 7.6, we see that cost of goods sold would have been $6,284 **lower** had it used FIFO.

Beginning LIFO Reserve (Excess of FIFO over LIFO)	$52,355
− Less: Ending LIFO Reserve (Excess of FIFO over LIFO)	(58,639)
Difference in Cost of Goods Sold under FIFO	($6,284)

Solutions to SELF-STUDY QUIZ

Inventory turnover would have increased because the denominator of the ratio (average inventory) would have decreased by $10,000.

$$\frac{\$3{,}229{,}798}{(\$583{,}571 + \$556{,}128)/2} = 5.7$$

EXHIBIT 7.6 Financial Statement Effects of Inventory Costing Methods

HARLEY-DAVIDSON, INC.
REAL WORLD EXCERPT:
Annual Report

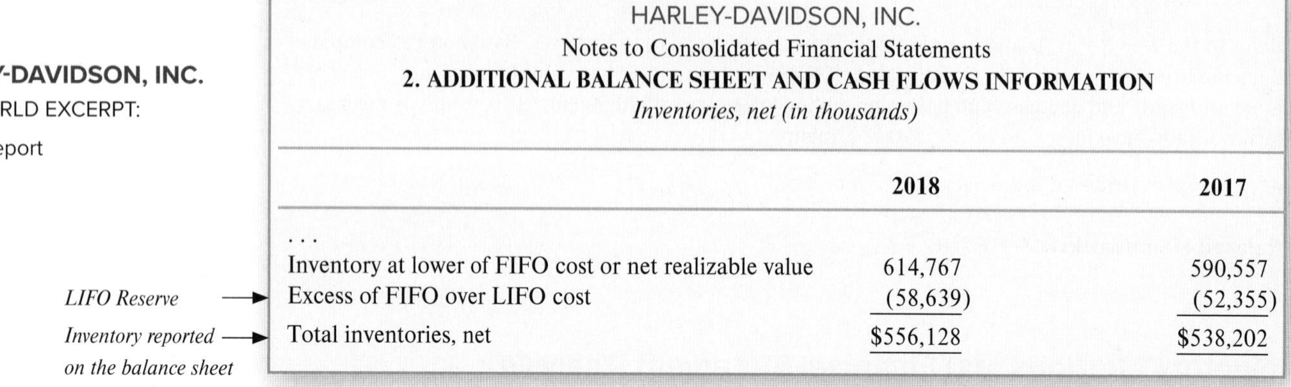

HARLEY-DAVIDSON, INC.
Notes to Consolidated Financial Statements
2. ADDITIONAL BALANCE SHEET AND CASH FLOWS INFORMATION
Inventories, net (in thousands)

		2018	2017
	. . .		
	Inventory at lower of FIFO cost or net realizable value	614,767	590,557
LIFO Reserve →	Excess of FIFO over LIFO cost	(58,639)	(52,355)
Inventory reported on the balance sheet →	Total inventories, net	$556,128	$538,202

Source: Harley-Davidson, Inc.

Because FIFO cost of goods sold expense is **lower,** income before income taxes would have been $6,284 **higher.** Income taxes would be that amount times its 2018 tax rate of 21 percent[5] **higher** had it used FIFO.

Difference in pretax income under FIFO	$ 6,284
Tax rate	× .21
Difference in taxes under FIFO	$ 1,320

Combining the two effects, net income would be increased by the change in cost of goods sold of $6,284 and decreased by the change in income tax expense of $1,320, resulting in an overall increase in net income of $4,964.

Decrease in Cost of Goods Sold Expense (Income increases)	$ 6,284
Increase in Income Tax Expense (Income decreases)	(1,320)
Increase in Net Income under FIFO	$ 4,964

These Harley-Davidson computations are for 2018. It is important to note that even companies that usually face increasing costs occasionally face decreasing costs. For example, during 2019, Harley-Davidson's costs of new inventory declined due to manufacturing efficiencies. As a result, even though LIFO usually **saves** the company taxes, Harley paid **extra** taxes in 2019.

Converting Inventory on the Balance Sheet to FIFO

You can adjust the inventory amounts on the balance sheet to FIFO by substituting the FIFO values in the note ($614,767 and $590,557 for 2018 and 2017, respectively) for the LIFO values (see Exhibit 7.6). Alternatively, you can add the LIFO reserve to the LIFO value on the balance sheet to arrive at the same numbers.

[5]Starting in 2018, the corporate tax rate in the United States is 21 percent. This rate is often changed when new federal tax laws are passed. Firms' tax rates may also be different in circumstances where foreign corporate tax rates apply or state corporate tax rates must be added.

FINANCIAL ANALYSIS

LIFO and Inventory Turnover Ratio

For many LIFO companies, the inventory turnover ratio can be deceptive. Remember that, for these companies, the beginning and ending inventory numbers that make up the denominator of the ratio will be artificially small because they reflect older, lower costs. Consider **Deere & Co.**, manufacturer of John Deere farm, lawn, and construction equipment. Its inventory note lists the following values:

DEERE & COMPANY
REAL WORLD EXCERPT:
Annual Report

DEERE & COMPANY
Notes to Consolidated Financial Statements
(dollars in millions)

	2019	2018
Inventories:		
Total FIFO value	$7,645	$7,786
Less adjustment to LIFO value	1,670	1,637
Inventories	$5,975	$6,149

Source: Deere & Company

John Deere's cost of goods sold for 2019 was $26,792 million. If the ratio were computed using the reported LIFO inventory values for the ratio, it would be

$$\text{Inventory Turnover Ratio} = \frac{\$26{,}792}{(\$5{,}975 + \$6{,}149)/2} = 4.4$$

Converting cost of goods sold (the numerator) to a FIFO basis and using the more current FIFO inventory values in the denominator, it would be

$$\text{Inventory Turnover Ratio} = \frac{\$26{,}792 - (\$1{,}670 - \$1{,}637)}{(\$7{,}645 + \$7{,}786)/2} = 3.5$$

Note that the major difference between the two ratios is in the denominator. FIFO inventory values are roughly 27 percent higher than the LIFO values. The LIFO beginning and ending inventory numbers are artificially small because they reflect older, lower costs.

PAUSE FOR FEEDBACK

The selection of an inventory costing method is important because it will affect reported income, income tax expense (and hence cash flow), and the inventory valuation reported on the balance sheet. In a period of rising prices, FIFO normally results in a higher net income and higher taxes than LIFO; in a period of falling prices, the opposite occurs. The choice of methods is normally made to minimize taxes. Answer the following question to practice converting cost of goods sold and pretax income from the LIFO to the FIFO method for a company facing increasing prices.

SELF-STUDY QUIZ

In a recent year, **Caterpillar Inc.**, a major manufacturer of farm and construction equipment, reported pretax earnings of $7,812 million. Its inventory note indicated "if the FIFO (first-in, first-out) method had been in use, inventories would have been $2,086 and $2,009 higher than reported at the end of the current and prior year, respectively."* (The amounts noted are for the LIFO reserve.) Convert pretax earnings for the current year from a LIFO to a FIFO basis.

Beginning LIFO Reserve (Excess of FIFO over LIFO)	______
Less: Ending LIFO Reserve (Excess of FIFO over LIFO)	______
Difference in cost of goods sold under FIFO	______
Pretax income (LIFO)	______
Difference in pretax income under FIFO	______
Pretax income (FIFO)	______

After you have completed your answers, check them below.

*Source: Caterpillar Inc.

GUIDED HELP 7-4

For additional step-by-step video instruction on converting ending inventory, cost of goods sold, and pretax income from LIFO to FIFO, go to mhhe.com/libby_gh7-4

Related Homework: E7-17, E7-18

Inventory and Cash Flows

When companies expand production to meet increases in demand, this increases the amount of inventory reported on the balance sheet. However, when companies overestimate demand for a product, they usually produce too many units of the slow-selling item. This increases storage costs as well as the interest costs on short-term borrowings that finance the inventory. It even may lead to losses if the excess inventory cannot be sold at normal prices. The cash flow statement often provides the first sign of such problems.

FOCUS ON CASH FLOWS

Inventory

As with a change in accounts receivable, a change in inventories can have a major effect on a company's cash flow from operations. Cost of goods sold on the income statement may be more or less than the amount of cash paid to suppliers during the period. Because most inventory is purchased on open credit (borrowing from suppliers is normally called *accounts payable*), reconciling cost of goods sold with cash paid to suppliers requires consideration of the changes in both the Inventory and Accounts Payable accounts.

The simplest way to think about the effects of changes in inventory is that buying (increasing) inventory eventually decreases cash, while selling (decreasing) inventory eventually increases cash. Similarly, borrowing from suppliers, which increases accounts payable, increases cash. Paying suppliers, which decreases accounts payable, decreases cash.

Solutions to SELF-STUDY QUIZ

Beginning LIFO Reserve	$2,009	Pretax income (LIFO)	$ 7,812
Less: Ending LIFO Reserve	2,086	Difference in pretax income	77
Difference in cost of goods sold	$ 77	Pretax income (FIFO)	$ 7,889

EFFECT ON STATEMENT OF CASH FLOWS

In General When a net **decrease in inventory** for the period occurs, sales are greater than purchases; thus, the decrease must be **added** in computing cash flows from operations.

When a net **increase in inventory** for the period occurs, sales are less than purchases; thus, the increase must be **subtracted** in computing cash flows from operations.

When a net **decrease in accounts payable** for the period occurs, payments to suppliers are greater than new purchases on account; thus, the decrease must be **subtracted** in computing cash flows from operations.

When a net **increase in accounts payable** for the period occurs, payments to suppliers are less than new purchases on account; thus, the increase must be **added** in computing cash flows from operations.

	Effect on Cash Flows
Operating activities (indirect method)	
Net income	$xxx
Adjusted for	
Add inventory **decrease**	+
or	
Subtract inventory **increase**	−
Add accounts payable **increase**	+
or	
Subtract accounts payable **decrease**	−

Focus Company Analysis When the inventory balance increases during the period, as was the case at **Harley-Davidson** in 2019, the company has purchased or produced more inventory than it has sold. Thus, the increase is subtracted in the computation of cash flow from operations. Conversely, when the inventory balance decreases during the period, the company has sold more inventory than it purchased or produced. Thus, the decrease is added in the computation of cash flow from operations. When the accounts payable balance increases during the period, the company has borrowed more from suppliers than it has paid them (or postponed payments). Thus, the increase is added in the computation of cash flow from operations.*

HARLEY-DAVIDSON, INC.
Consolidated Statement of Cash Flows
Year Ended December 31, 2019
(dollars in thousands)

Cash flows from operating activities:	
Net Income	$423,635
Adjustments to reconcile net income to net cash provided by operating activities:	
Depreciation	232,537
. . . .	
Changes in current assets and current liabilities:	
. . . .	
Inventories	(47,576)
Accounts payable and accrued liabilities	(18,462)
. . . .	
Total adjustments	444,637
Net cash (used by) provided by continuing operating activities	$868,272

Source: Harley-Davidson, Inc.

*For companies with foreign currency or business acquisitions/dispositions, the amount of the change reported on the cash flow statement will not equal the change in the accounts reported on the balance sheet.

DEMONSTRATION CASE

(Complete the requirements before proceeding to the suggested solution that follows.) This case reviews the application of the FIFO and LIFO inventory costing methods and the inventory turnover ratio.

Balent Appliances distributes a number of household appliances. One product, microwave ovens, has been selected for case purposes. Assume that the following summarized transactions were completed during the year ended December 31, 2022, in the order given (assume that all transactions are cash):

	Units	Unit Cost
a. Beginning inventory	11	$200
b. New inventory purchases	9	220
c. Sales (selling price, $420)	8	?

Required:

1. Compute the following amounts, assuming the application of the FIFO and LIFO inventory costing methods:

	Ending Inventory		Cost of Goods Sold	
	Units	Dollars	Units	Dollars
FIFO				
LIFO				

2. Assuming that inventory cost was expected to follow current trends, which method would you suggest that Balent select to account for these inventory items? Explain your answer.

3. Assuming that other operating expenses were $500 and the income tax rate is 25 percent, prepare the income statement for the period using your selected method.

4. Compute the inventory turnover ratio for the current period using your selected method. What does it indicate?

SUGGESTED SOLUTION

1.

	Ending Inventory		Cost of Goods Sold	
	Units	Dollars	Units	Dollars
FIFO	12	$2,580	8	$1,600
LIFO	12	$2,420	8	$1,760

Computations

Beginning inventory (11 units × $200)	$2,200
+ Purchases (9 units × $220)	1,980
Goods available for sale	$4,180
FIFO inventory (costed at end of period)	
Goods available for sale (from above)	$4,180
– Ending inventory [(9 units × $220) + (3 units × $200)]	2,580
Cost of goods sold (8 units × $200)	$1,600
LIFO inventory (costed at end of period)	
Goods available for sale (from above)	$4,180
– Ending inventory [(11 units × $200) + (1 unit × $220)]	2,420
Cost of goods sold (8 units × $220)	$1,760

2. LIFO should be selected. Because costs are rising, LIFO produces higher cost of goods sold, lower pretax income, and lower income tax payments. It is used on the tax return and income statement because of the LIFO conformity rule.

3.

BALENT APPLIANCES Statement of Income Year Ended December 31, 2022	
Sales	$3,360
Cost of goods sold	1,760
Gross profit	1,600
Other expenses	500
Income before income taxes	1,100
Income tax expense (25%)	275
Net income	$ 825

Computations

Sales = 8 × $420 = $3,360

4. Inventory turnover ratio = Cost of Goods Sold ÷ Average Inventory

= $1,760 ÷ [($2,200 + $2,420) ÷ 2 = $2,310]

= 0.76

The inventory turnover ratio reflects how many times average inventory was produced or purchased and sold during the period. Thus, Balent Appliances purchased and sold its average inventory less than one time during the year.

Chapter Supplement A

FIFO Cost of Goods Sold under Periodic and Perpetual Inventory Systems and End of Period Adjustments to LIFO

The purpose of this supplement is to compare the calculation of FIFO cost of goods sold under a periodic versus a perpetual inventory system. As we noted in the chapter, calculations of FIFO cost of goods sold will always be the same under both systems. Companies that wish to report under LIFO will then convert the FIFO amount of cost of goods sold to the LIFO amount with an adjusting entry. Consider the following company purchase and sales data for the month of January. Note that beginning inventory is 2,000 units, purchases are 14,000 units, and sales are 9,000 units.

	Units	Unit Cost
January 1 Beginning inventory	2,000	$20.60
January 5 Sold	1,000	
January 13 Purchased	6,000	22.00
January 17 Sold	3,000	
January 25 Purchased	8,000	25.10
January 27 Sold	5,000	

FIFO (First-in, First-out)

FIFO assumes that the oldest goods are the first ones sold. Using a **periodic inventory** calculation, the 9,000 **oldest goods available during the month** would include the 2,000 in beginning inventory, the

6,000 purchased on January 13, and 1,000 of the units purchased January 25. Cost of goods sold would be calculated as follows:

Cost of Goods Sold		
Units	**Unit Cost**	**Total Cost**
2,000	$20.60	$ 41,200
6,000	22.00	132,000
1,000	25.10	25,100
Total		$198,300

Using a **perpetual inventory** calculation, we would compute the cost of goods sold for each sale separately using the **oldest goods available at the time of each sale.**

Cost of Goods Sold			
Date of Sale	**Units**	**Unit Cost**	**Total Cost**
Jan. 5	1,000	$20.60	$ 20,600
Jan. 17	1,000	20.60	20,600
	2,000	22.00	44,000
Jan. 27	4,000	22.00	88,000
	1,000	25.10	25,100
Total			$198,300

Note that cost of goods sold is $198,300 using both computations. This is true because the oldest goods available during the month are the same as the oldest goods available at the time of each sale. This will always be true.

The summary journal entry for cost of goods sold for the month would be:

	Debit	Credit
Cost of goods sold (+E, −SE)	198,300	
Inventory (−A)		198,300

Assets		=	Liabilities	+	Stockholders' Equity	
Inventory	−198,300				Cost of Goods Sold (+E)	−198,300

Adjustments to Report Under LIFO (Last-in, First-out)

LIFO assumes that the newest goods are the first ones sold. To convert the FIFO amounts kept in the company's record keeping system to LIFO, the company would first perform a **periodic inventory** calculation where the 9,000 **newest goods available during the month** would include the 8,000 units purchased January 25 and 1,000 of the units purchased on January 13. Cost of goods sold would be calculated as follows:

Cost of Goods Sold		
Units	**Unit Cost**	**Total Cost**
8,000	$25.10	$200,800
1,000	22.00	22,000
Total		$222,800

The company would then prepare an adjusting entry to increase (debit) Cost of Goods Sold from the FIFO amount of $198,300 to the LIFO amount $222,800 and decrease (credit) Inventory by the same amount ($222,800 − $198,300 = $24,500).

	Debit	Credit
Cost of goods sold (+E, −SE)	24,500	
Inventory (−A)		24,500

Assets		=	Liabilities	+	Stockholders' Equity	
Inventory	−24,500				Cost of Goods Sold (+E)	−24,500

In actual accounting systems, the credit is often made to a contra-asset account called LIFO Reserve (or simply Excess of FIFO over LIFO Cost).

Why You Won't See LIFO Perpetual Calculations in Practice

Even if a company's perpetual inventory information system is sophisticated enough to instantaneously record the arrival of new inventory, it is unlikely that it will have sufficient information concerning invoice pricing, returns, allowances, and discounts to instantaneously compute a unit cost for those goods. Also, consider the number of calculations of goods available for sale that would have to be made by a company that has numerous sales and purchases of many different inventory items. This makes it very costly or impossible for most companies to apply LIFO using a perpetual calculation. In most cases, there is also an added tax savings that results from the simpler periodic computation.

Chapter Supplement B

Additional Issues in Measuring Inventory Purchases

Purchase Returns and Allowances

Purchased goods may be returned to the vendor if they do not meet specifications, arrive in damaged condition, or are otherwise unsatisfactory. **Purchase returns and allowances** require a reduction in the cost of inventory purchases and the recording of a cash refund or a reduction in the liability to the vendor. For example, assume that **Harley-Davidson** returned to a supplier damaged harness boots that cost $1,000. The return would be recorded as follows:

	Debit	Credit
Accounts payable (−L) (or Cash +A)	1,000	
Inventory (−A)		1,000

Assets		=	Liabilities		+	Stockholders' Equity
Inventory	−1,000		Accounts Payable	−1,000		

Purchase Discounts

Cash discounts must be accounted for by both the seller and the buyer (accounting by the seller was discussed in Chapter 6). When merchandise is bought on credit, terms such as 2/10, n/30 are sometimes specified. That is, if payment is made within 10 days from the date of purchase, a 2 percent cash discount known as the **purchase discount** is granted for prompt payment of the account. If payment is not made within the discount period, the full invoice cost is due 30 days after the purchase.

Assume that on January 17, **Harley-Davidson** bought goods that had a $1,000 invoice price with terms 2/10, n/30. The purchase would be recorded as follows (using what is called the **gross method**):

		Debit	Credit
Date of Purchase			
Jan. 17	Inventory (+A)	1,000	
	Accounts payable (+L)		1,000

Assets		=	Liabilities		+	Stockholders' Equity
Inventory	+1,000		Accounts Payable	+1,000		

		Debit	Credit
Date of Payment, within the Discount Period			
Jan. 26	Accounts payable (−L)	1,000	
	Inventory (−A)		20
	Cash (−A)		980

Assets		=	Liabilities		+	Stockholders' Equity
Inventory	−20		Accounts Payable	−1,000		
Cash	−980					

If for any reason Harley-Davidson did not pay within the 10-day discount period, the following entry would be needed:

		Debit	Credit
Date of Payment, after the Discount Period			
Feb. 1	Accounts payable (−L)	1,000	
	Cash (−A)		1,000

Assets		=	Liabilities		+	Stockholders' Equity
Cash	−1,000		Accounts Payable	−1,000		

CHAPTER TAKE-AWAYS

7-1. Apply the cost principle to identify the amounts that should be included in inventory and cost of goods sold for typical retailers, wholesalers, and manufacturers. **p. 345**

Inventory should include all items owned that are held for resale. Costs flow into inventory when goods are purchased or manufactured. They flow out (as an expense) when they are sold or disposed of. In conformity with the expense matching principle, the total cost of the goods sold during the period must be matched with the sales revenue earned during the period. A company can keep track of the ending inventory and cost of goods sold for the period using (1) the perpetual inventory system, which is based on the maintenance of detailed and continuous inventory records, and (2) the periodic inventory system, which is based on a physical count of ending inventory and use of the cost of goods sold equation to determine cost of goods sold.

7-2. Report inventory and cost of goods sold using the four inventory costing methods. **p. 350**

The chapter discussed four different inventory costing methods used to allocate costs between the units remaining in inventory and the units sold and their applications in different economic circumstances. The methods discussed were specific identification, FIFO, LIFO, and average cost. Each of the inventory costing methods conforms to GAAP. Public companies using LIFO must provide note disclosures that allow conversion of inventory and cost of goods sold to FIFO amounts. Remember that the cost flow assumption need not match the physical flow of inventory.

7-3. Decide when the use of different inventory costing methods is beneficial to a company. **p. 355**

The selection of an inventory costing method is important because it will affect reported income, income tax expense (and hence cash flow), and the inventory valuation reported on the balance sheet. In a period of rising prices, FIFO normally results in higher net income and higher taxes than LIFO; in a period of falling prices, the opposite occurs. The choice of methods is normally made to minimize taxes.

7-4. Report inventory at the lower of cost or net realizable value. **p. 358**

Ending inventory should be measured based on the lower of actual cost or net realizable value (NRV). This practice can have a major effect on the statements of companies facing declining costs. Damaged, obsolete, and out-of-season inventories also should be written down to their current estimated net realizable value if below cost. The lower of cost or NRV adjustment increases cost of goods sold, decreases income, and decreases reported inventory in the year of the write-down.

7-5 **Understand methods for controlling inventory and analyze the effects of inventory errors on financial statements.** **p. 359**

Various control procedures can limit inventory theft or mismanagement. An error in the measurement of ending inventory affects cost of goods sold on the current period's income statement and ending inventory on the balance sheet. Because this year's ending inventory becomes next year's beginning inventory, it also affects cost of goods sold in the following period by the same amount but in the opposite direction. These relationships can be seen through the cost of goods sold equation (BI + P − EI = CGS).

7-6. **Evaluate inventory management using the inventory turnover ratio and analyze the effects of inventory on cash flows.** **p. 361**

The inventory turnover ratio measures the efficiency of inventory management. It reflects how many times average inventory was produced and sold during the period. Analysts and creditors watch this ratio because a sudden decline may mean that a company is facing an unexpected drop in demand for its products or is becoming sloppy in its production management. When a net **decrease in inventory** for the period occurs, sales are more than purchases; thus, the decrease must be **added** in computing cash flows from operations. When a net **increase in inventory** for the period occurs, sales are less than purchases; thus, the increase must be **subtracted** in computing cash flows from operations.

In this and previous chapters, we discussed the current assets of a business. These assets are critical to operations, but many of them do not directly produce value. In Chapter 8, we will discuss the noncurrent assets property, plant, and equipment; intangibles; and natural resources. Many of the noncurrent assets produce value, such as a factory that manufactures cars. These assets present some interesting accounting problems because they benefit a number of accounting periods.

KEY RATIO

Inventory turnover ratio measures the efficiency of inventory management. It reflects how many times average inventory was produced and sold during the period (see the "Key Ratio Analysis" box in the Evaluating Inventory Management section):

$$\text{Inventory Turnover} = \frac{\text{Cost of Goods Sold}}{\text{Average Inventory}}$$

FINDING FINANCIAL INFORMATION

Balance Sheet

Under Current Assets
  Inventories

Income Statement

Expenses
  Cost of goods sold

Statement of Cash Flows

Under Operating Activities (indirect method):

Net income
  − increases in inventory
  + decreases in inventory
  + increases in accounts payable
  − decreases in accounts payable

Notes

Under Summary of Significant Accounting Policies
  Description of management's choice of inventory accounting policy (FIFO, LIFO, etc.)

In Separate Note
  If not listed on balance sheet, components of inventory (merchandise, raw materials, work in progress, finished goods)
  If using LIFO, LIFO reserve (excess of FIFO over LIFO)

KEY TERMS

Average Cost Method Uses the weighted average unit cost of the goods available for sale for both cost of goods sold and ending inventory. **p. 353**

Cost of Goods Sold Equation BI + P − EI = CGS. **p. 348**

Direct Labor The earnings of employees who work directly on the products being manufactured. **p. 347**

Factory Overhead Manufacturing costs that are not raw material or direct labor costs. **p. 347**

Finished Goods Inventory Manufactured goods that are complete and ready for sale. **p. 345**

First-In, First-Out (FIFO) Method An inventory costing method that assumes that the first goods purchased (the first in) are the first goods sold. **p. 351**

Goods Available for Sale The sum of beginning inventory and purchases (or transfers to finished goods) for the period. **p. 348**

Inventory Tangible property held for sale in the normal course of business or used in producing goods or services for sale. **p. 345**

Last-In, First-Out (LIFO) Method An inventory costing method that assumes that the most recently purchased units (the last in) are sold first. **p. 353**

LIFO Reserve A contra-asset for the excess of FIFO over LIFO inventory. **p. 363**

Lower of Cost or Net Realizable Value Valuation method departing from the cost principle; it serves to recognize a loss when net realizable value drops below cost. **p. 358**

Merchandise Inventory Goods held for resale in the ordinary course of business. **p. 345**

Net Realizable Value (NRV) The expected sales price less selling costs (e.g., repair and disposal costs). **p. 358**

Periodic Inventory System An inventory system in which ending inventory and cost of goods sold are determined at the end of the accounting period based on a physical inventory count. **p. 350**

Perpetual Inventory System An inventory system in which a detailed inventory record is maintained, recording each purchase and sale during the accounting period. **p. 350**

Purchase Discount Cash discount received for prompt payment of an account. **p. 371**

Purchase Returns and Allowances A reduction in the cost of purchases associated with unsatisfactory goods. **p. 371**

Raw Materials Inventory Items acquired for the purpose of processing into finished goods. **p. 345**

Specific Identification Method An inventory costing method that identifies the cost of the specific item that was sold. **p. 351**

Work in Process Inventory Goods in the process of being manufactured. **p. 345**

QUESTIONS

1. Why is inventory an important item to both internal (management) and external users of financial statements?
2. What are the general guidelines for deciding which items should be included in inventory?
3. Explain the application of the cost principle to an item in the ending inventory.
4. Define goods available for sale. How does it differ from cost of goods sold?
5. Define beginning inventory and ending inventory.
6. The chapter discussed four inventory costing methods. List the four methods and briefly explain each.
7. Explain how income can be manipulated when the specific identification inventory costing method is used.
8. Contrast the effects of LIFO versus FIFO on reported assets (i.e., the ending inventory) when (*a*) prices are rising and (*b*) prices are falling.
9. Contrast the income statement effect of LIFO versus FIFO (i.e., on pretax income) when (*a*) prices are rising and (*b*) prices are falling.
10. Contrast the effects of LIFO versus FIFO on cash outflow and inflow.
11. Explain briefly the application of the lower of cost or net realizable value concept to ending inventory and its effect on the income statement and balance sheet when net realizable value is lower than cost.
12. When a perpetual inventory system is used, unit costs of the items sold are known at the date of each sale. In contrast, when a periodic inventory system is used, unit costs are known only at the end of the accounting period. Why are these statements correct?

MULTIPLE-CHOICE QUESTIONS

1. Consider the following information: ending inventory, $24,000; sales, $250,000; beginning inventory, $30,000; selling and administrative expenses, $70,000; and purchases, $90,000. What is cost of goods sold?
   a. $86,000
   b. $94,000
   c. $96,000
   d. $84,000
2. The inventory costing method selected by a company will affect
   a. The balance sheet.
   b. The income statement.
   c. The statement of retained earnings.
   d. All of the above.
3. Which of the following is **not** a component of the cost of manufactured inventory?
   a. Administrative overhead
   b. Direct labor
   c. Raw materials
   d. Factory overhead
4. Consider the following information: beginning inventory, 10 units @ $20 per unit; first purchase, 35 units @ $22 per unit; second purchase, 40 units @ $24 per unit; 50 units were sold. What is cost of goods sold using the **FIFO** method of inventory costing?
   a. $1,090
   b. $1,060
   c. $1,180
   d. $1,200
5. Consider the following information: beginning inventory, 10 units @ $20 per unit; first purchase, 35 units @ $22 per unit; second purchase, 40 units @ $24 per unit; 50 units were sold. What is cost of goods sold using the **LIFO** method of inventory costing?
   a. $1,090
   b. $1,060
   c. $1,180
   d. $1,200
6. An increasing inventory turnover ratio
   a. Indicates a longer time span between the ordering and receiving of inventory.
   b. Indicates a shorter time span between the ordering and receiving of inventory.
   c. Indicates a shorter time span between the purchase and sale of inventory.
   d. Indicates a longer time span between the purchase and sale of inventory.
7. If the ending balance in accounts payable decreases from one period to the next, which of the following is true?
   a. Cash payments to suppliers exceeded current period purchases.
   b. Cash payments to suppliers were less than current period purchases.
   c. Cash receipts from customers exceeded cash payments to suppliers.
   d. Cash receipts from customers exceeded current period purchases.
8. Which of the following regarding the lower of cost or net realizable value (NRV) rule for inventory are true?
   (1) The lower of cost or NRV rule is an example of the historical cost principle.
   (2) When the net realizable value of inventory drops below the cost shown in the financial records, net income is reduced.
   (3) When the net realizable value of inventory drops below the cost shown in the financial records, total assets are reduced.
   a. (1)
   b. (2)
   c. (2) and (3)
   d. All three
9. Which inventory method provides a better matching of current costs with sales revenue on the income statement and outdated values for inventory on the balance sheet?
   a. FIFO
   b. Average cost
   c. LIFO
   d. Specific identification
10. Which of the following is false regarding a perpetual inventory system?
    a. Physical counts are not needed because records are maintained on a transaction-by-transaction basis.
    b. The balance in the inventory account is updated with each inventory purchase and sales transaction.
    c. Cost of goods sold is increased as sales are recorded.
    d. Managers are regularly informed about low or excess stock information.

MINI-EXERCISES

M7-1 Matching Inventory Items to Type of Business
LO7-1

Match the type of inventory with the type of business in the following matrix:

	TYPE OF BUSINESS	
Type of Inventory	**Merchandising**	**Manufacturing**
Work in process		
Finished goods		
Merchandise		
Raw materials		

M7-2 Recording the Cost of Purchases for a Merchandiser
LO7-1

Select Apparel purchased 90 new shirts and recorded a total cost of $2,258, determined as follows:

Invoice cost	$1,800
Shipping charges	185
Import taxes and duties	165
Interest (6.0%) on $1,800 borrowed from the bank to finance the purchase	108
	$2,258

Required:
Make the needed corrections in this calculation. Give the journal entry (or entries) to record this purchase in the correct amount, assuming a perpetual inventory system. Show computations.

M7-3 Identifying the Cost of Inventories for a Manufacturer
LO7-1

Operating costs incurred by a manufacturing company become either (1) part of the cost of inventory to be expensed as cost of goods sold at the time the finished goods are sold or (2) expenses at the time they are incurred. Indicate whether each of the following costs belongs in category (1) or (2).

___ *a.* Wages of factory workers
___ *b.* Costs of raw materials purchased
___ *c.* Sales salaries
___ *d.* Heat, light, and power for the factory building
___ *e.* Heat, light, and power for the headquarters office building

M7-4 Inferring Purchases Using the Cost of Goods Sold Equation
LO7-1
JCPenney Company, Inc.

JCPenney Company, Inc., is a major department store chain. The dominant portion of the company's business consists of providing merchandise and services to consumers through department stores and online. In a prior annual report, JCPenney reported cost of goods sold of $8,174 million, ending inventory for the current year of $2,762 million, and ending inventory for the previous year of $2,854 million.

Required:
Is it possible to develop a reasonable estimate of the merchandise purchases for the year? If so, prepare the estimate; if not, explain why.

Matching Financial Statement Effects to Inventory Costing Methods

M7-5
LO7-2

Indicate whether the FIFO or LIFO inventory costing method normally produces each of the following effects under the listed circumstances.

a. Declining costs
   Highest net income _____
   Highest inventory _____

b. Rising costs
   Highest net income _____
   Highest inventory _____

Matching Inventory Costing Method Choices to Company Circumstances

M7-6
LO7-3

Indicate whether the FIFO or LIFO inventory costing method would normally be selected when inventory costs are rising. Explain why.

Reporting Inventory under Lower of Cost or Net Realizable Value

M7-7
LO7-4

Wood Company had the following inventory items on hand at the end of the year:

	Quantity	Cost per Item	Net Realizable Value per Item
Item A	70	$110	$100
Item B	30	60	85

Computing the lower of cost or net realizable value on an item-by-item basis, determine what amount would be reported on the balance sheet for inventory.

Determining the Financial Statement Effects of Inventory Errors

M7-8
LO7-5

Assume the prior year ending inventory was understated by $50,000. Explain how this error would affect the prior year and current year pretax income amounts. What would be the effects if the prior year ending inventory were overstated by $50,000 instead of understated?

Determining the Effects of Inventory Management Changes on Inventory Turnover Ratio

M7-9
LO7-6

Indicate the most likely effect of the following changes in inventory management on the inventory turnover ratio (use + for increase, – for decrease, and NE for no effect).

_____ *a.* Have parts inventory delivered daily by suppliers instead of weekly.
_____ *b.* Extend payments for inventory purchases from 15 days to 30 days.
_____ *c.* Shorten production process from 10 days to 8 days.

Mc Graw Hill connect

EXERCISES

Analyzing Items to Be Included in Inventory

E7-1
LO7-1

Based on its physical count of inventory in its warehouse at year-end, December 31 of the current year, Plummer Company planned to report inventory of $34,000. During the audit, the independent CPA developed the following additional information:

a. Goods from a supplier costing $700 are in transit with UPS on December 31 of the current year. The terms are FOB shipping point (explained in the "Required" section). Because these goods had not yet arrived, they were excluded from the physical inventory count.

b. Plummer delivered samples costing $1,800 to a customer on December 27 of the current year, with the understanding that they would be returned to Plummer on January 15 of the next year. Because these goods were not on hand, they were excluded from the inventory count.

c. On December 31 of the current year, goods in transit to customers, with terms FOB shipping point, amounted to $6,500 (expected delivery date January 10 of the next year). Because the goods had been shipped, they were excluded from the physical inventory count.

d. On December 31 of the current year, goods in transit to customers, with terms FOB destination, amounted to $1,500 (expected delivery date January 10 of the next year). Because the goods had been shipped, they were excluded from the physical inventory count.

Required:

Plummer's accounting policy requires including in inventory all goods for which it has title. Note that the point where title (ownership) changes hands is determined by the shipping terms in the sales contract. When goods are shipped "FOB shipping point," title changes hands at shipment and the buyer normally pays for shipping. When they are shipped "FOB destination," title changes hands on delivery, and the seller normally pays for shipping. Begin with the $34,000 inventory amount and compute the correct amount for the ending inventory. Explain the basis for your treatment of each of the preceding items. (**Hint:** Set up three columns: Item, Amount, and Explanation.)

E7-2 Inferring Missing Amounts Based on Income Statement Relationships

LO7-1

Supply the missing dollar amounts for the income statement for each of the following independent cases. (**Hint:** In Case B, work from the bottom up.)

	Case A		Case B		Case C	
Net sales revenue		$7,500		$?		$5,050
Beginning inventory	$11,200		$ 7,000		$ 4,000	
Purchases	4,500		?		9,500	
Goods available for sale	?		15,050		13,500	
Ending inventory	9,000		11,050		?	
Cost of goods sold		?		?		4,200
Gross profit		?		800		?
Expenses		300		?		700
Pretax income (loss)		$ 500		$ (200)		$ 150

E7-3 Inferring Missing Amounts Based on Income Statement Relationships

LO7-1

Supply the missing dollar amounts for the income statement for each of the following independent cases:

Cases	Sales Revenue	Beginning Inventory	Purchases	Total Available	Ending Inventory	Cost of Goods Sold	Gross Profit	Expenses	Pretax Income (Loss)
A	$ 650	$100	$700	$?	$500	$?	$?	$200	$?
B	1,100	200	900	?	?	?	?	150	150
C	?	150	?	?	300	200	400	100	?
D	800	?	550	?	300	?	?	200	200
E	1,000	?	900	1,100	?	?	500	?	(50)

E7-4 Inferring Merchandise Purchases

LO7-1
Abercrombie and Fitch

Abercrombie and Fitch is a leading retailer of casual apparel for men, women, and children. Assume that you are employed as a stock analyst and your boss has just completed a review of the new Abercrombie annual report. She provided you with her notes, but they are missing some information that you need. Her notes show that the ending inventory for Abercrombie in the current and previous years was $424,393,000 and $399,795,000, respectively. Net sales for the current year were $3,492,690,000. Cost of goods sold was $1,408,848,000. Income before taxes was $55,161,000. For your analysis, you determine that you need to know the amount of purchases for the year.

Required:
Can you develop the information from her notes? Explain and show calculations. (**Hint:** Use the cost of goods sold equation or the inventory T-account to solve for the needed value.)

Calculating Ending Inventory and Cost of Goods Sold under FIFO, LIFO, and Average Cost

E7-5
LO7-2

Nittany Company uses a periodic inventory system. At the end of the annual accounting period, December 31 of the current year, the accounting records provided the following information for product 1:

	Units	Unit Cost
Inventory, December 31, prior year	2,000	$5
For the current year:		
Purchase, March 21	5,000	6
Purchase, August 1	3,000	8
Inventory, December 31, current year	4,000	

Required:
Compute ending inventory and cost of goods sold for the current year under FIFO, LIFO, and average cost inventory costing methods. (**Hint:** Set up adjacent columns for each case.)

Calculating Ending Inventory and Cost of Goods Sold under FIFO, LIFO, and Average Cost

E7-6
LO7-2

Hamilton Company uses a periodic inventory system. At the end of the annual accounting period, December 31 of the current year, the accounting records provided the following information for product 1:

	Units	Unit Cost
Inventory, December 31, prior year	2,000	$5
For the current year:		
Purchase, March 21	6,000	4
Purchase, August 1	4,000	2
Inventory, December 31, current year	3,000	

Required:
Compute ending inventory and cost of goods sold under FIFO, LIFO, and average cost inventory costing methods. (**Hint:** Set up adjacent columns for each case.)

Analyzing and Interpreting the Financial Statement Effects of LIFO and FIFO

E7-7
LO7-2, 7-3

Emily Company uses a periodic inventory system. At the end of the annual accounting period, December 31 of the current year, the accounting records provided the following information for product 2:

		Units	Unit Cost
Inventory, December 31, prior year		3,000	$ 9
For the current year:			
Purchase, April 11		9,000	10
Purchase, June 1		7,000	15
Sales ($50 each)		10,000	
Operating expenses (excluding income tax expense)	$190,000		

Required:
1. Prepare a separate income statement through pretax income that details cost of goods sold for (*a*) Case A: FIFO and (*b*) Case B: LIFO. For each case, show the computation of the ending inventory and cost of goods sold. (**Hint:** Set up adjacent columns for each case.)

2. Compare the pretax income and the ending inventory amounts between the two cases. Explain the similarities and differences.
3. Which inventory costing method may be preferred for income tax purposes? Explain.

E7-8 Analyzing and Interpreting the Financial Statement Effects of LIFO and FIFO
LO7-2, 7-3

Givoly Inc. uses a periodic inventory system. At the end of the annual accounting period, December 31 of the current year, the accounting records provided the following information for product 2:

		Units	Unit Cost
Inventory, December 31, prior year		7,000	$11
For the current year:			
Purchase, March 5		19,000	9
Purchase, September 19		10,000	5
Sale ($28 each)		8,000	
Sale ($30 each)		16,000	
Operating expenses (excluding income tax expense)	$400,000		

Required:
1. Prepare a separate income statement through pretax income that details cost of goods sold for (*a*) Case A: FIFO and (*b*) Case B: LIFO. For each case, show the computation of the ending inventory and cost of goods sold. (**Hint:** Set up adjacent columns for each case.)
2. Compare the pretax income and the ending inventory amounts between the two cases. Explain the similarities and differences.
3. Which inventory costing method may be preferred for income tax purposes? Explain.

E7-9 Evaluating the Choice among Three Alternative Inventory Methods Based on Cash Flow Effects
LO7-2, 7-3

Following is partial information for the income statement of Audio Solutions Company under three different inventory costing methods, assuming the use of a periodic inventory system:

	FIFO	LIFO	Average Cost
Cost of goods sold			
Beginning inventory (400 units @ $28)	$11,200	$11,200	$11,200
Purchases (475 units @ $35)	16,625	16,625	16,625
Goods available for sale			
Ending inventory (525 units)			
Cost of goods sold	$	$	$
Sales, 350 units; unit sales price, $50			
Expenses, $1,700			

Required:
1. Compute cost of goods sold under the FIFO, LIFO, and average cost inventory costing methods.
2. Prepare an income statement through pretax income for each method.
3. Rank the three methods in order of income taxes paid (favorable cash flow) and explain the basis for your ranking.

E7-10 Evaluating the Choice among Three Alternative Inventory Methods Based on Cash Flow Effects
LO7-2, 7-3

Following is partial information for the income statement of Arturo Technologies Company under three different inventory costing methods, assuming the use of a periodic inventory system:

	FIFO	LIFO	Average Cost
Cost of goods sold			
Beginning inventory (400 units @ $30)	$12,000	$12,000	$12,000
Purchases (400 units @ $20)	8,000	8,000	8,000
Goods available for sale			
Ending inventory (500 units)			
Cost of goods sold	$	$	$
Sales, 300 units; unit sales price, $50			
Expenses, $2,500			

Required:

1. Compute cost of goods sold under the FIFO, LIFO, and average cost inventory costing methods.
2. Prepare an income statement through pretax income for each method.
3. Rank the three methods in order of preference based on income taxes paid (favorable cash flow) and explain the basis for your ranking.

Evaluating the Choice among Three Alternative Inventory Methods Based on Income and Cash Flow Effects

E7-11
LO7-2, 7-3

Daniel Company uses a periodic inventory system. Data for the current year: beginning merchandise inventory (ending inventory December 31, prior year), 2,000 units at $38; purchases, 8,000 units at $40; expenses (excluding income taxes), $184,500; ending inventory per physical count at December 31, current year, 1,800 units; sales, 8,200 units; sales price per unit, $75; and average income tax rate, 20 percent.

Required:

1. Compute cost of goods sold and prepare income statements under the FIFO, LIFO, and average cost inventory costing methods. Use a format similar to the following:

		INVENTORY COSTING METHOD		
Cost of Goods Sold	Units	FIFO	LIFO	Average Cost
Beginning inventory		$	$	$
Purchases				
Goods available for sale				
Ending inventory				
Cost of goods sold		$	$	$

Income Statement	FIFO	LIFO	Average Cost
Sales revenue	$	$	$
Cost of goods sold			
Gross profit			
Expenses			
Pretax income			
Income tax expense			
Net income	$	$	$

2. Between FIFO and LIFO, which method is preferable in terms of (*a*) net income and (*b*) income taxes paid (cash flow)? Explain.
3. What would your answer to requirement (2) be, assuming that prices were falling? Explain.

E7-12 Reporting Inventory at Lower of Cost or Net Realizable Value

LO7-4

H.T. Tan Company is preparing the annual financial statements dated December 31 of the current year. Ending inventory information about the five major items stocked for regular sale follows:

	ENDING INVENTORY, CURRENT YEAR		
Item	Quantity on Hand	Unit Cost When Acquired (FIFO)	Net Realizable Value (Market) at Year-End
A	50	$15	$12
B	80	30	40
C	10	48	52
D	70	25	30
E	350	10	5

Required:
Compute the valuation that should be used for the current year ending inventory using lower of cost or net realizable value applied on an item-by-item basis. (**Hint:** Set up columns for Item, Quantity, Total Cost, Total Net Realizable Value, and Lower of Cost or NRV.)

E7-13 Reporting Inventory at Lower of Cost or Net Realizable Value

LO7-4

Sanchez Company was formed on January 1 of the current year and is preparing the annual financial statements dated December 31, current year. Ending inventory information about the four major items stocked for regular sale follows:

	ENDING INVENTORY, CURRENT YEAR		
Item	Quantity on Hand	Unit Cost When Acquired (FIFO)	Net Realizable Value (Market) at Year-End
A	30	$20	$15
B	55	40	44
C	35	52	55
D	15	27	32

Required:
1. Compute the valuation that should be used for the current year ending inventory using lower of cost or net realizable value applied on an item-by-item basis. (**Hint:** Set up columns for Item, Quantity, Total Cost, Total Net Realizable Value, and Lower of Cost or NRV.)
2. What will be the effect of the write-down of inventory to lower of cost or net realizable value on cost of goods sold for the year ended December 31, current year?

E7-14 Analyzing and Interpreting the Impact of an Inventory Error

LO7-5

Griffin Corporation prepared the following two income statements (simplified for illustrative purposes):

	FIRST QUARTER		SECOND QUARTER	
Sales revenue		$12,800		$18,300
Cost of goods sold				
Beginning inventory	$4,200		$ 3,700	
Purchases	2,800		12,200	
Goods available for sale	7,000		15,900	
Ending inventory	3,700		9,000	
Cost of goods sold		3,300		6,900
Gross profit		9,500		11,400
Expenses		4,800		5,300
Pretax income		$ 4,700		$ 6,100

During the third quarter, it was discovered that the ending inventory for the first quarter should have been $4,280.

Required:

1. What effect did this error have on the combined pretax income of the two quarters? Explain.
2. Did this error affect the EPS amounts for each quarter? (See Chapter 5 for discussion of EPS.) Explain.
3. Prepare corrected income statements for each quarter.
4. Set up a schedule with the following headings to reflect the comparative effects of the correct and incorrect amounts on the income statement:

	FIRST QUARTER			SECOND QUARTER		
Income Statement Item	Incorrect	Correct	Error	Incorrect	Correct	Error

Analyzing and Interpreting the Impact of an Inventory Error

E7-15
LO7-5

Grants Corporation prepared the following two income statements (simplified for illustrative purposes):

	FIRST QUARTER		SECOND QUARTER	
Sales revenue		$11,000		$18,000
Cost of goods sold				
Beginning inventory	$4,000		$ 3,800	
Purchases	3,000		13,000	
Goods available for sale	7,000		16,800	
Ending inventory	3,800		9,000	
Cost of goods sold		3,200		7,800
Gross profit		7,800		10,200
Expenses		5,000		6,000
Pretax income		$ 2,800		$ 4,200

During the third quarter, it was discovered that the ending inventory for the first quarter should have been $4,400.

Required:

1. What effect did this error have on the combined pretax income of the two quarters? Explain.
2. Did this error affect the EPS amounts for each quarter? (See Chapter 5 for discussion of EPS.) Explain.
3. Prepare corrected income statements for each quarter.
4. Set up a schedule with the following headings to reflect the comparative effects of the correct and incorrect amounts on the income statement:

	FIRST QUARTER			SECOND QUARTER		
Income Statement Item	Incorrect	Correct	Error	Incorrect	Correct	Error

Analyzing and Interpreting the Inventory Turnover Ratio

E7-16
LO7-6
Dell Inc.

Dell Inc. is the leading manufacturer of personal computers. In a recent year, it reported the following in millions of dollars:

Net sales revenue	$78,660
Cost of sales	58,606
Beginning inventory	2,538
Ending inventory	2,678

Source: Dell Inc.

Required:

1. Determine the inventory turnover ratio and average days to sell inventory for the current year.
2. Explain the meaning of each number.

E7-17 LO7-6 Analyzing and Interpreting the Effects of the LIFO/FIFO Choice on Inventory Turnover Ratio

The records at the end of January of the current year for Young Company showed the following for a particular kind of merchandise:

Beginning Inventory at FIFO: 19 Units @ $16 = $304
Beginning Inventory at LIFO: 19 Units @ $12 = $228

January Transactions	Units	Unit Cost	Total Cost
Purchase, January 9	25	$13	$325
Purchase, January 20	50	19	950
Sale, January 21 (at $38 per unit)	40		
Sale, January 27 (at $39 per unit)	25		

Required:
Compute the inventory turnover ratio for the month of January under the FIFO and LIFO inventory costing methods (show computations and round to the nearest dollar). Which costing method is more accurate indicator of the efficiency of inventory management? Explain.

E7-18 LO7-6 Ford Motor Company — Analyzing Notes to Adjust Inventory from LIFO to FIFO

The following note was contained in a recent **Ford Motor Company** annual report:

NOTE 8. INVENTORIES—AUTOMOTIVE SECTOR
Inventories at December 31 were as follows (dollars in millions)

	Current Year	Previous Year
Raw material, work in process, & supplies	$2,847	$2,812
Finished products	3,982	3,970
Total inventories at FIFO	6,829	6,782
Less LIFO adjustment	(928)	(865)
Total	$5,901	$5,917

About one-third of inventories were determined under the last-in, first-out method.

Source: Ford Motor Company

Required:

1. What amount of ending inventory would have been reported in the current year if Ford had used only FIFO?
2. The cost of goods sold reported by Ford for the current year was $113,345 million. Determine the cost of goods sold that would have been reported if Ford had used only FIFO for both years.
3. Explain why Ford management chose to use LIFO for certain of its inventories.

E7-19 LO7-6 BorgWarner Inc. — Analyzing Notes to Adjust Inventory from LIFO to FIFO

BorgWarner Inc. is a leading global supplier of highly engineered automotive systems and components primarily for powertrain applications. The following note was contained in its recent annual report:

NOTE 3. INVENTORIES, NET as of December 31 (in millions)		
	Current Year	**Prior Year**
Raw materials and supplies	$319.5	$279.8
Work in progress	89.0	78.0
Finished goods	115.5	116.3
FIFO inventories	524.0	474.1
LIFO reserve	(18.3)	(16.0)
Total inventories, net	$505.7	$458.1

Source: BorgWarner Inc.

Required:

1. What amount of ending inventory would have been reported in the current year if BorgWarner had used only FIFO?
2. The cost of goods sold reported by BorgWarner for the current year was $6,548.7 million. Determine the cost of goods sold that would have been reported if BorgWarner had used only FIFO for both years.
3. Explain why BorgWarner management chose to use LIFO for certain of its inventories.

Interpreting the Effect of Changes in Inventories and Accounts Payable on Cash Flow from Operations

E7-20
LO7-6
PepsiCo

In its recent annual report, **PepsiCo** included the following information in its balance sheets (dollars in millions):

CONSOLIDATED BALANCE SHEETS		
	Current Year	**Previous Year**
. . .		
Inventories	$2,947	$2,723
. . .		
Accounts payable	15,017	14,243

Source: PepsiCo

Required:
Explain the effects of the changes in inventory and accounts payable on cash flow from operating activities for the current year.

(Chapter Supplement A) FIFO and LIFO Cost of Goods Sold under Periodic versus Perpetual Inventory Systems

E7-21

Assume that a retailer's beginning inventory and purchases of a popular item during January included (1) 300 units at $7 in beginning inventory on January 1, (2) 450 units at $8 purchased on January 8, and (3) 750 units at $9 purchased on January 29. The company sold 350 units on January 12 and 550 units on January 30.

Required:

1. Calculate the cost of goods sold for the month of January under (*a*) FIFO (periodic calculation), (*b*) FIFO (perpetual calculation), and (*c*) LIFO (periodic calculation).
2. Which cost flow assumption would you recommend to management and why?

(Chapter Supplement B) Recording Sales and Purchases with Cash Discounts

E7-22

Scott's Cycles sells merchandise on credit terms of 2/15, n/30. A sale invoiced at $1,500 (cost of sales $975) was made to Shannon Allen on February 1. The company uses the gross method of recording sales discounts.

Required:

1. Give the journal entry to record the credit sale. Assume use of the perpetual inventory system.
2. Give the journal entry, assuming that the account was collected in full on February 9.
3. Give the journal entry, assuming instead that the account was collected in full on March 2.

On March 4, the company purchased bicycles and accessories from a supplier on credit, invoiced at $9,000; the terms were 3/10, n/30. The company uses the gross method to record purchases.

Required:

4. Give the journal entry to record the purchase on credit. Assume use of the perpetual inventory system.
5. Give the journal entry, assuming that the account was paid in full on March 12.
6. Give the journal entry, assuming instead that the account was paid in full on March 28.

PROBLEMS

P7-1 LO7-1 Analyzing Items to Be Included in Inventory (AP7-1)

Travis Company has just completed a physical inventory count at year-end, December 31 of the current year. Only the items on the shelves, in storage, and in the receiving area were counted and costed on a FIFO basis. The inventory amounted to $80,000. During the audit, the independent CPA developed the following additional information:

a. Goods costing $900 were being used by a customer on a trial basis and were excluded from the inventory count at December 31 of the current year.

b. Goods in transit on December 31 of the current year, from a supplier, with terms FOB destination (explained in the "Required" section), cost $900. Because these goods had not yet arrived, they were excluded from the physical inventory count.

c. On December 31 of the current year, goods in transit to customers, with terms FOB shipping point, amounted to $1,700 (expected delivery date January 10 of next year). Because the goods had been shipped, they were excluded from the physical inventory count.

d. On December 28 of the current year, a customer purchased goods for cash amounting to $2,650 and left them "for pickup on January 3 of next year." Travis Company had paid $1,750 for the goods and, because they were on hand, included the latter amount in the physical inventory count.

e. On the date of the inventory count, the company received notice from a supplier that goods ordered earlier at a cost of $3,550 had been delivered to the transportation company on December 27 of the current year; the terms were FOB shipping point. Because the shipment had not arrived by December 31 of the current year, it was excluded from the physical inventory count.

f. On December 31 of the current year, the company shipped $700 worth of goods to a customer, FOB destination. The goods are expected to arrive at their destination no earlier than January 8 of next year. Because the goods were not on hand, they were not included in the physical inventory count.

g. One of the items sold by the company has such a low volume that management planned to drop it last year. To induce Travis Company to continue carrying the item, the manufacturer-supplier provided the item on a "consignment basis." This means that the manufacturer-supplier retains ownership of the item, and Travis Company (the consignee) has no responsibility to pay for the items until they are sold to a customer. Each month, Travis Company sends a report to the manufacturer on the number sold and remits cash for the cost. At the end of December of the current year, Travis Company had six of these items on hand; therefore, they were included in the physical inventory count at $950 each.

Required:

Assume that Travis's accounting policy requires including in inventory all goods for which it has title. Note that the point where title (ownership) changes hands is determined by the shipping terms in the sales contract. When goods are shipped "FOB shipping point," title changes hands at shipment, and the buyer normally pays for shipping. When they are shipped "FOB destination," title changes hands on delivery, and the seller normally pays for shipping. Begin with the $80,000 inventory amount and compute the correct amount for the ending inventory. Explain the basis for your treatment of each of the preceding items. (**Hint:** Set up three columns: Item, Amount, and Explanation.)

Analyzing the Effects of Four Alternative Inventory Methods (AP7-2)

P7-2
LO7-2

Kirtland Corporation uses a periodic inventory system. At the end of the annual accounting period, December 31, the accounting records for the most popular item in inventory showed the following:

Transactions	Units	Unit Cost
Beginning inventory, January 1	400	$3.00
Transactions during the year:		
a. Purchase, January 30	300	3.40
b. Purchase, May 1	460	4.00
c. Sale ($5 each)	(160)	
d. Sale ($5 each)	(700)	

Required:

Compute the amount of (*a*) goods available for sale, (*b*) ending inventory, and (*c*) cost of goods sold at December 31 under each of the following inventory costing methods (show computations and round to the nearest dollar):

1. Average cost (round the average cost per unit to the nearest cent).
2. First-in, first-out.
3. Last-in, first-out.
4. Specific identification, assuming that the first sale was selected two-fifths from the beginning inventory and three-fifths from the purchase of January 30. Assume that the second sale was selected from the remainder of the beginning inventory, with the balance from the purchase of May 1.

Evaluating Four Alternative Inventory Methods Based on Income and Cash Flow (AP7-3)

P7-3
LO7-2, 7-3

At the end of January of the current year, the records of Donner Company showed the following for a particular item that sold at $16 per unit:

Transactions	Units	Amount
Inventory, January 1	500	$2,365
Purchase, January 12	600	3,600
Purchase, January 26	160	1,280
Sale	(370)	
Sale	(250)	

Required:

1. Assuming the use of a periodic inventory system, prepare a summarized income statement through gross profit for the month of January under each method of inventory: (*a*) average cost (round the average cost per unit to the nearest cent), (*b*) FIFO, (*c*) LIFO, and (*d*) specific identification. For specific identification, assume that the first sale was selected from the beginning inventory and the second sale was selected from the January 12 purchase. Show the inventory computations in detail.
2. Between FIFO and LIFO, which method results in the higher pretax income? Which method results in the higher EPS?
3. Between FIFO and LIFO, which method results in the lower income tax expense? Explain, assuming a 20 percent average tax rate.
4. Between FIFO and LIFO, which method produces the more favorable cash flow? Explain.

Evaluating the LIFO and FIFO Choice When Costs Are Rising and Falling (AP7-4)

P7-4
LO7-2, 7-3

Income is to be evaluated under four different situations as follows:

a. Prices are rising:
  (1) Situation A: FIFO is used.
  (2) Situation B: LIFO is used.

b. Prices are falling:
  (1) Situation C: FIFO is used.
  (2) Situation D: LIFO is used.

The basic data common to all four situations are sales, 500 units for $15,000; beginning inventory, 300 units; purchases, 400 units; ending inventory, 200 units; and operating expenses, $4,000. The following tabulated income statements for each situation have been set up for analytical purposes:

	PRICES RISING		PRICES FALLING	
	Situation A FIFO	Situation B LIFO	Situation C FIFO	Situation D LIFO
Sales revenue	$15,000	$15,000	$15,000	$15,000
Cost of goods sold:				
Beginning inventory	3,300	?	?	?
Purchases	4,800	?	?	?
Goods available for sale	8,100	?	?	?
Ending inventory	2,400	?	?	?
Cost of goods sold	5,700	?	?	?
Gross profit	9,300	?	?	?
Expenses	4,000	4,000	4,000	4,000
Pretax income	5,300	?	?	?
Income tax expense (30%)	1,590	?	?	?
Net income	$ 3,710	?	?	?

Required:

1. Complete the preceding tabulation for each situation. In Situations A and B (prices rising), assume the following: beginning inventory, 300 units at $11 = $3,300; purchases, 400 units at $12 = $4,800. In Situations C and D (prices falling), assume the opposite; that is, beginning inventory, 300 units at $12 = $3,600; purchases, 400 units at $11 = $4,400. Use periodic inventory procedures.
2. Analyze the relative effects on pretax income and net income as demonstrated by requirement (1) when prices are rising and when prices are falling.
3. Analyze the relative effects on the cash position for each situation.
4. Would you recommend FIFO or LIFO? Explain.

P7-5 LO7-4 Evaluating the Income Statement and Cash Flow Effects of Lower of Cost or Net Realizable Value (AP7-5)

Jaffa Company prepared its annual financial statements dated December 31 of the current year. The company applies the FIFO inventory costing method; however, the company neglected to apply lower of cost or net realizable value to the ending inventory. The preliminary current year income statement follows:

Sales revenue		$300,000
Cost of goods sold		
Beginning inventory	$ 33,000	
Purchases	184,000	
Goods available for sale	217,000	
Ending inventory (FIFO cost)	50,450	
Cost of goods sold		166,550
Gross profit		133,450
Operating expenses		62,000
Pretax income		71,450
Income tax expense (30%)		21,435
Net income		$ 50,015

Assume that you have been asked to restate the current year financial statements to incorporate lower of cost or NRV. You have developed the following data relating to the current year ending inventory:

Item	Quantity	Acquisition Cost Unit	Acquisition Cost Total	Net Realizable Value Per Unit
A	3,050	$3.00	$ 9,150	$4.00
B	1,500	5.50	8,250	3.50
C	7,100	1.50	10,650	3.50
D	3,200	7.00	22,400	4.00
			$50,450	

Required:

1. Restate the income statement to reflect lower of cost or net realizable value valuation of the current year ending inventory. Apply lower of cost or NRV on an item-by-item basis and show computations.
2. Compare and explain the lower of cost or net realizable value effect on each amount that was changed on the income statement in requirement (1).
3. What is the conceptual basis for applying lower of cost or net realizable value to merchandise inventories?
4. Thought question: What effect did lower of cost or net realizable value have on the current year cash flow? What will be the long-term effect on cash flow?

Analyzing and Interpreting the Effects of Inventory Errors (AP7-6)

P7-6
LO7-5

The income statement for Pruitt Company summarized for a four-year period shows the following:

	2016	2017	2018	2019
Sales revenue	$2,025,000	$2,450,000	$2,700,000	$2,975,000
Cost of goods sold	1,505,000	1,627,000	1,782,000	2,113,000
Gross profit	520,000	823,000	918,000	862,000
Expenses	490,000	513,000	538,000	542,000
Pretax income	30,000	310,000	380,000	320,000
Income tax expense (30%)	9,000	93,000	114,000	96,000
Net income	$ 21,000	$ 217,000	$ 266,000	$ 224,000

An audit revealed that in determining these amounts, the ending inventory for 2017 was overstated by $18,000. The company uses a periodic inventory system.

Required:

1. Recast the income statements to reflect the correct amounts, taking into consideration the inventory error.
2. Compute the gross profit percentage for each year (*a*) before the correction and (*b*) after the correction.
3. What effect would the error have had on the income tax expense assuming a 30 percent average rate?

Evaluating the Effects of Manufacturing Changes on Inventory Turnover Ratio and Cash Flows from Operating Activities (AP7-7)

P7-7
LO7-6

Mears and Company has been operating for five years as an electronics component manufacturer specializing in cellular phone components. During this period, it has experienced rapid growth in sales revenue and in inventory. Mr. Mears and his associates have hired you as Mears's first corporate controller. You have put into place new purchasing and manufacturing procedures that are expected to reduce inventories by approximately one-third by year-end. You have gathered the following data related to the changes:

	(dollars in thousands)	
	Beginning of Year	**End of Year (projected)**
Inventory	$582,500	$384,610
		Current Year (projected)
Cost of goods sold		$7,283,566

Required:

1. Compute the inventory turnover ratio based on two different assumptions:
   a. Those presented in the preceding table (a decrease in the balance in inventory).
   b. No change from the beginning-of-the-year inventory balance.
2. Compute the effect of the projected change in the inventory balance on cash flow from operating activities for the year (indicate the sign and amount of effect).
3. On the basis of the preceding analysis, write a brief memo explaining how an increase in inventory turnover can result in an increase in cash flow from operating activities. Also explain how this increase can benefit the company.

ALTERNATE PROBLEMS

AP7-1 Analyzing Items to be Included in Inventory (P7-1)

LO7-1

Sabre Company has just completed a physical inventory count at year-end, December 31 of the current year. Only the items on the shelves, in storage, and in the receiving area were counted and costed on a FIFO basis. The inventory amounted to $96,000. During the audit, the independent CPA developed the following additional information:

a. Goods costing $350 were being used by a customer on a trial basis and were excluded from the inventory count at December 31 of the current year.

b. On December 28 of the current year, a customer purchased goods for cash amounting to $3,000 and left them "for pickup on January 3 of next year." Sabre Company had paid $1,900 for the goods and, because they were on hand, included the latter amount in the physical inventory count.

c. Goods in transit on December 31 of the current year, from a supplier, with terms FOB destination (explained in the "Required" section), cost $1,400. Because these goods had not yet arrived, they were excluded from the physical inventory count.

d. On December 31 of the current year, goods in transit to customers, with terms FOB shipping point, amounted to $2,200 (expected delivery date January 10 of next year). Because the goods had been shipped, they were excluded from the physical inventory count.

e. On December 31 of the current year, the company shipped $650 worth of goods to a customer, FOB destination. The goods are expected to arrive at their destination no earlier than January 8 of next year. Because the goods were not on hand, they were not included in the physical inventory count.

f. On the date of the inventory count, the company received notice from a supplier that goods ordered earlier at a cost of $4,200 had been delivered to the transportation company on December 27 of the current year; the terms were FOB shipping point. Because the shipment had not arrived by December 31 of the current year, it was excluded from the physical inventory count.

g. One of the items sold by the company has such a low volume that management planned to drop it last year. To induce Sabre Company to continue carrying the item, the manufacturer-supplier provided the item on a "consignment basis." This means that the manufacturer-supplier retains ownership of the item, and Sabre Company (the consignee) has no responsibility to pay for the items until they are sold to a customer. Each month, Sabre Company sends a report to the manufacturer on the number sold and remits cash for the cost. At the end of December of the current year, Sabre Company had five of these items on hand; therefore, they were included in the physical inventory count at $800 each.

Required:

Assume that Sabre's accounting policy requires including in inventory all goods for which it has title. Note that the point where title (ownership) changes hands is determined by the shipping terms in the sales contract. When goods are shipped "FOB shipping point," title changes hands at shipment, and the buyer normally pays for shipping. When they are shipped "FOB destination," title changes hands on delivery, and the seller normally pays for shipping. Begin with the $96,000 inventory amount and compute the correct amount for the ending inventory. Explain the basis for your treatment of each of the preceding items. (**Hint:** Set up three columns: Item, Amount, and Explanation.)

Analyzing the Effects of Four Alternative Inventory Methods (P7-2)

AP7-2
LO7-2

Dixon Company uses a periodic inventory system. At the end of the annual accounting period, December 31, the accounting records for the most popular item in inventory showed the following:

Transactions	Units	Unit Cost
Beginning inventory, January 1	390	$32.00
Transactions during the current period:		
a. Purchase, February 20	700	34.25
b. Purchase, June 30	460	37.00
c. Sale ($50 each)	(70)	
d. Sale ($50 each)	(750)	

Required:

Compute the cost of (*a*) goods available for sale, (*b*) ending inventory, and (*c*) goods sold at December 31 under each of the following inventory costing methods (show computations and round to the nearest dollar):

1. Average cost (round average cost per unit to the nearest cent).
2. First-in, first-out.
3. Last-in, first-out.
4. Specific identification, assuming that the first sale was selected two-fifths from the beginning inventory and three-fifths from the purchase of February 20. Assume that the second sale was selected from the remainder of the beginning inventory, with the balance from the purchase of June 30.

Evaluating Four Alternative Inventory Methods Based on Income and Cash Flow (P7-3)

AP7-3
LO7-2, 7-3

At the end of January of the current year, the records of NewRidge Company showed the following for a particular item that sold at $16 per unit:

Transactions	Units	Amount
Inventory, January 1	120	$ 960
Purchase, January 12	380	3,420
Purchase, January 26	200	2,200
Sale	(100)	
Sale	(140)	

Required:

1. Assuming the use of a periodic inventory system, prepare a summarized income statement through gross profit for January under each method of inventory: (*a*) average cost, (*b*) FIFO, (*c*) LIFO, and (*d*) specific identification. For specific identification, assume that the first sale was selected from the beginning inventory and the second sale was selected from the January 12 purchase. Show the inventory computations (including for ending inventory) in detail.

2. Between FIFO and LIFO, which method results in the higher pretax income? Which method results in the higher EPS?
3. Between FIFO and LIFO, which method results in the lower income tax expense? Explain, assuming a 20 percent average tax rate.
4. Between FIFO and LIFO, which method produces the more favorable cash flow? Explain.

AP7-4 Evaluating the LIFO and FIFO Choice When Costs Are Rising and Falling (P7-4)

LO7-2, 7-3

Income is to be evaluated under four different situations as follows:

a. Prices are rising:
  (1) Situation A: FIFO is used.
  (2) Situation B: LIFO is used.

b. Prices are falling:
  (1) Situation C: FIFO is used.
  (2) Situation D: LIFO is used.

The basic data common to all four situations are sales, 510 units for $13,260; beginning inventory, 340 units; purchases, 410 units; ending inventory, 240 units; and operating expenses, $5,000. The following tabulated income statements for each situation have been set up for analytical purposes:

	PRICES RISING		PRICES FALLING	
	Situation A FIFO	Situation B LIFO	Situation C FIFO	Situation D LIFO
Sales revenue	$13,260	$13,260	$13,260	$13,260
Cost of goods sold:				
Beginning inventory	3,060	?	?	?
Purchases	4,100	?	?	?
Goods available for sale	7,160	?	?	?
Ending inventory	2,400	?	?	?
Cost of goods sold	4,760	?	?	?
Gross profit	8,500	?	?	?
Expenses	5,000	5,000	5,000	5,000
Pretax income	3,500	?	?	?
Income tax expense (30%)	1,050	?	?	?
Net income	$ 2,450	?	?	?

Required:

1. Complete the preceding tabulation for each situation. In Situations A and B (prices rising), assume the following: beginning inventory, 340 units at $9 = $3,060; purchases, 410 units at $10 = $4,100. In Situations C and D (prices falling), assume the opposite; that is, beginning inventory, 340 units at $10 = $3,400; purchases, 410 units at $9 = $3,690. Use periodic inventory procedures.
2. Analyze the relative effects on pretax income and net income as demonstrated by requirement (1) when prices are rising and when prices are falling.
3. Analyze the relative effects on the cash position for each situation.
4. Would you recommend FIFO or LIFO? Explain.

AP7-5 Evaluating the Income Statement and Cash Flow Effects of Lower of Cost or Net Realizable Value (P7-5)

LO7-4

Hadera Company prepared its annual financial statements dated December 31 of the current year. The company applies the FIFO inventory costing method; however, the company neglected to apply lower of cost or net realizable value to the ending inventory. The preliminary current year income statement follows:

Sales revenue		$500,000
Cost of goods sold:		
Beginning inventory	$ 45,000	
Purchases	202,000	
Goods available for sale	247,000	
Ending inventory	55,900	
Cost of goods sold		191,100
Gross profit		308,900
Operating expenses		174,000
Pretax income		134,900
Income tax expense (25%)		33,725
Net income		$101,175

Assume that you have been asked to restate the current year financial statements to incorporate lower of cost or NRV. You have developed the following data relating to the current year ending inventory:

		Acquisition Cost		Net Realizable Value Per
Item	**Quantity**	**Unit**	**Total**	**Unit**
A	2,900	$2.00	$ 5,800	$2.50
B	1,600	6.00	9,600	4.00
C	6,500	1.00	6,500	3.00
D	4,000	8.50	34,000	6.00

Required:

1. Restate the income statement to reflect lower of cost or net realizable value valuation of the current year ending inventory. Apply lower of cost or NRV on an item-by-item basis and show computations.
2. Compare and explain the lower of cost or net realizable value effect on each amount that was changed on the income statement in requirement (1).
3. What is the conceptual basis for applying lower of cost or net realizable value to merchandise inventories?
4. Thought question: What effect did lower of cost or net realizable value have on the current year cash flow? What will be the long-term effect on cash flow?

Analyzing and Interpreting the Effects of Inventory Errors (P7-6)

AP7-6
LO7-5

The income statements for four consecutive years for Colca Company reflected the following summarized amounts:

	2016	2017	2018	2019
Sales revenue	$ 60,000	$ 63,000	$ 65,000	$ 68,000
Cost of goods sold	39,000	43,000	44,000	46,000
Gross profit	21,000	20,000	21,000	22,000
Expenses	16,000	17,000	17,000	19,000
Pretax income	$ 5,000	$ 3,000	$ 4,000	$ 3,000

Subsequent to development of these amounts, it has been determined that the physical inventory taken on December 31, 2017, was understated by $2,000.

Required:

1. Recast the income statements to reflect the correct amounts, taking into consideration the inventory error.
2. Compute the gross profit percentage for each year (*a*) before the correction and (*b*) after the correction.
3. What effect would the error have had on the income tax expense, assuming a 30 percent average rate?

AP7-7 LO7-6

Evaluating the Effects of Manufacturing Changes on Inventory Turnover Ratio and Cash Flows from Operating Activities (P7-7)

Connors LLC has been operating for three years as a lumber producer specializing in pine, aspen, and hardwoods. During this period, it has experienced rapid growth in sales revenue and in inventory. Mr. Connors and his associates have hired you as Connors's first corporate controller. You have put into place new purchasing and manufacturing procedures that are expected to reduce inventories by approximately one-third by year-end. You have gathered the following data related to the changes:

	(dollars in thousands)	
	Beginning of Year	End of Year (projected)
Inventory	$62,035	$41,560
		Current Year (projected)
Cost of goods sold		$687,780

Required:

1. Compute the inventory turnover ratio based on two different assumptions:
   a. Those presented in the preceding table (a decrease in the balance in inventory).
   b. No change from the beginning-of-the-year inventory balance.
2. Compute the effect of the projected change in the inventory balance on cash flow from operating activities for the year (indicate the sign and amount of effect).
3. On the basis of the preceding analysis, write a brief memo explaining how an increase in inventory turnover can result in an increase in cash flow from operating activities. Also explain how this increase can benefit the company.

CONTINUING PROBLEM

CON7-1 LO7-2, 7-3 **Pool Corporation, Inc.**

Evaluating the Choice of Inventory Method When Costs Are Rising and Falling

Pool Corporation, Inc., reported in its recent annual report that "In 2010, our industry experienced some price deflation. . . . In 2011, our industry experienced more normalized price inflation of approximately 2 percent overall despite price deflation for certain chemical products." This suggests that in some years Pool's overall inventory costs rise, and in some years they fall. Furthermore, in many years, the costs of some inventory items rise while others fall. Assume that Pool has only two product items in its inventory this year. Purchase and sales data are presented below.

	Inventory Item A		Inventory Item B	
Transaction	Units	Unit Cost	Units	Unit Cost
Beginning inventory	40	$6	40	$6
Purchases, February 7	80	8	80	5
Purchases, March 16	100	9	100	3
Sales, April 28	160		160	

Required:

1. Compute cost of goods sold for each of the two items separately using the FIFO and LIFO inventory costing methods.
2. Between FIFO and LIFO, which method is preferable in terms of (*a*) net income and (*b*) income taxes paid (cash flow)? Answer the question for each item separately. Explain.

COMPREHENSIVE PROBLEM (CHAPTERS 6–7)

Computing and Reporting Net Sales, Cost of Goods Sold, Bad Debt Expense, Accounts Receivable (net), and Ending Inventory

COMP7-1
LO6-1, 6-2, 7-1, 7-2, 7-3, 7-4

Easley-O'Hara Office Equipment sells furniture and technology solutions to consumers and to businesses. Most consumers pay for their purchases with credit cards and business customers make purchases on open account with terms 1/10, net 30. Costs of furniture inventory purchases have generally been rising and costs of computer inventory purchases have generally been declining. The company's income tax rate is 20 percent. Casey Easley, the general manager, was particularly interested in the financial statement effects of the following facts related to first quarter operations.

a. Credit card sales (discount 2 percent) were $30,000.
b. Sales on account were $80,000. The company expects one-half of the accounts to be paid within the discount period.
c. The company computed cost of goods sold for the transactions in (*a*) and (*b*) above under FIFO and LIFO for its two product lines and chose the method for each product that minimizes income taxes:

	FIFO	LIFO
Furniture	$25,000	$28,000
Computer equipment	30,000	26,000

d. During the period, the company wrote off $1,000 worth of bad debts.
e. At the end of the period, the company estimated that 1.5 percent of gross sales on account would prove to be uncollectible.
f. Costs to deliver furniture to customers were $3,000.
g. Rent, utilities, salaries, and other operating expenses were $20,000.
h. At the end of the period, the company discovered that the net realizable value of ending inventory was $800 less than original cost.

Required:

Complete the following table, indicating the effects of each transaction on each income statement line item or subtotal listed. Indicate the amount and use + for increase and – for decrease; leave the space blank for no effect. (**Hint:** Remember that any item that affects revenues or expenses also affects Income Tax Expense by the amount of the revenue or expense times the income tax rate.) When you are done, sum across the columns to produce Easley-O'Hara's income statement for the quarter. (**Hint:** We recommend that you create an Excel spreadsheet in the form of the table below to complete this problem.)

	Transaction							
	a.	b.	c.	d.	e.	f.	g.	h.
Net sales								
Cost of goods sold								
Gross profit								
Selling, general, and administrative expenses								
Income before income taxes								
Income tax expense								
Net income								

CASES AND PROJECTS

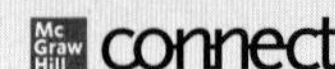

Annual Report Cases

CP7-1
LO7-1, 7-2, 7-4, 7-5
Target Corporation

Finding Financial Information

Refer to the financial statements of **Target** given in Appendix B at the end of this book. All dollar amounts in the statements and answers are in millions.

Required:

1. How much inventory does the company hold at the end of the most recent year?
   a. $44,949
   b. $8,992
   c. $20,756
   d. $10,653
   e. None of the above
2. Estimate the amount of inventory that the company purchased during the current year. (**Hint:** Use the cost of goods sold equation and ignore "certain buying, occupancy, and warehousing expenses.")
   a. $67,838
   b. $64,516
   c. $66,177
   d. $10,653
   e. None of the above
3. What method does the company use to determine the cost of its inventory?
   a. FIFO
   b. LIFO
   c. Average Cost
   d. Specific Identification
   e. None of the above
4. What is the inventory turnover ratio and average days to sell inventory for the current year and what does this suggest about the company? (Round your answer to two decimal places.)
   a. 7.36, suggesting that, on average, it takes the company 49.59 days to sell an item of inventory.
   b. 6.21, suggesting that, on average, it takes the company 58.78 days to sell an item of inventory.
   c. 6.74, suggesting that, on average, it takes the company 54.15 days to sell an item of inventory.
   d. 9.53, suggesting that, on average, it takes the company 38.30 days to sell an item of inventory.
   e. None of the above

CP7-2
LO7-2, 7-4, 7-5, 7-7
Walmart Inc.

Finding Financial Information

Refer to the financial statements of **Walmart**, given in Appendix C at the end of this book.

Required:

1. The company uses LIFO to account for its "Walmart U.S. inventory" and FIFO to account for its "Walmart International inventory." Is there anything special about U.S. GAAP that may have caused Walmart to select LIFO to account for its Walmart U.S. inventory on its financial statements?
   a. IFRS does not allow use of LIFO.
   b. The LIFO conformity rule requires that if LIFO is used on the U.S. tax return, it must be used on the financial statements.
   c. U.S. GAAP requires that the LIFO method must be used for all inventories.
   d. U.S. GAAP requires that different methods be used for domestic and foreign inventories.
2. If the company overstated ending inventory by $100 million for the year ended January 31, 2021, what would be the corrected value for Income before Income Taxes for that year (in millions)? ________
3. Compute the inventory turnover ratio for the current year. (Round your answer to two decimal places.) ________
4. If Walmart's inventory turnover ratio is higher this year than last year, what does this suggest about Walmart over time?
   a. It takes the company more days to sell an item of inventory.
   b. The selling prices that Walmart charges have increased.
   c. Inventory is moving more quickly through the process of purchasing and delivering products to the ultimate consumer.
   d. None of the above.

Comparing Companies within an Industry

CP7-3
LO7-5
Target Corporation
Walmart Inc.

Refer to the financial statements of **Target** (Appendix B) and **Walmart** (Appendix C) and the Industry Ratio Report (Appendix D) at the end of this book.

Required:

1. Compute the inventory turnover ratio for both companies for the current year.

   Target = [ ] **Walmart** = [ ]

2. What do you infer from the difference?
   a. Walmart is moving inventory more quickly through the process of purchasing and delivering products to the ultimate consumer than is Target.
   b. Target's management is less effective at controlling expenses than Walmart's management.
   c. Both companies' ratios suggest that their management teams are each likely to generate revenues from inventory sales.
   d. Walmart is collecting money from customers more quickly than Target.
3. Compare the inventory turnover ratio for both companies to the industry average. Are these two companies doing better or worse than the industry average in turning over their inventory?
   a. Target's and Walmart's managements are both more effective than the average company in the industry.
   b. Target's management is less effective and Walmart's management is more effective than the average company in the industry.
   c. Target's management is more effective and Walmart's management is less effective compared to the industry average.
   d. Target's management is weaker than Walmart's management because of its smaller size.
4. Both companies sell similar types of merchandise. Would you expect them to use the same or different inventory costing methods for their *U.S. inventories?* Why? (**Hint:** Their inventory footnotes will tell you what inventory costing methods they use.)
   a. Different because Walmart is larger than Target.
   b. Different because Walmart has a higher inventory turnover ratio than Target.
   c. Same because U.S. GAAP requires all companies to use the same costing method for inventory.
   d. Same because unit costs of inventory generally change in the same direction for both Target and Walmart.

Financial Reporting and Analysis Cases

Using Financial Reports: Interpreting the Effect of Charging Costs to Inventory as Opposed to Current Operating Expenses

CP7-4
LO7-1
Dana Incorporated

Dana Incorporated designs and manufactures component parts for the vehicular, industrial, and mobile off-highway original equipment markets. In a prior annual report, Dana's inventory note indicated the following:

> Dana changed its method of accounting for inventories effective January 1 . . . to include in inventory certain production-related costs previously charged to expense. This change in accounting principle resulted in a better matching of costs against related revenues. The effect of this change in accounting increased inventories by $23.0 and net income by $12.9.

Required:

1. Under Dana's previous accounting method, certain production costs were recognized as expenses on the income statement in the period they were incurred. When will they be recognized under the new accounting method?
2. Explain how including these costs in inventory increased both inventories and net income for the year.

Using Financial Reports: Evaluating the Choice between LIFO and FIFO Based on an Inventory Note

CP7-5
LO7-3
International Paper Company

An annual report for **International Paper Company** included the following note:

> The last-in, first-out inventory method is used to value most of International Paper's U.S. inventories . . . If the first-in, first-out method had been used, it would have increased total inventory balances by approximately $293 million and $290 million at December 31, 2017, and 2016, respectively.

For the year 2017, International Paper Company reported net income (after taxes) of $2,144 million. At December 31, 2017, the balance of International Paper Company's retained earnings account was $6,180 million.

Required:

1. Determine the amount of net income that International Paper would have reported in 2017 if it had used the FIFO method (assume a 30 percent tax rate).
2. Determine the amount of retained earnings that International Paper would have reported at the end of 2017 if it always had used the FIFO method (assume a 30 percent tax rate).
3. Use of the LIFO method reduced the amount of taxes that International Paper had to pay in 2017 compared with the amount that would have been paid if International Paper had used FIFO. Calculate the amount of this reduction (assume a 30 percent tax rate).

Critical Thinking Cases

CP7-6
LO7-3
Seneca Foods

Making a Decision as a Financial Analyst: Analysis of the Effect of a Change to LIFO

A press release for **Seneca Foods** (licensee of the **Libby's** brand of canned fruits and vegetables) included the following information:

> The current year's net earnings were $8,019,000 or $0.65 per diluted share, compared with $32,067,000 or $2.63 per diluted share, last year. These results reflect the Company's decision to implement the LIFO (last-in, first-out) inventory valuation method effective December 30, 2007 (fourth quarter). The effect of this change was to reduce annual pretax earnings by $28,165,000 and net earnings by $18,307,000 or $1.50 per share ($1.49 diluted) below that which would have been reported using the Company's previous inventory method. The Company believes that in this period of significant inflation, the use of the LIFO method better matches current costs with current revenues. This change also results in cash savings of $9,858,000 by reducing the Company's income taxes, based on statutory rates. If the Company had remained on the FIFO (first-in, first-out) inventory valuation method, the pretax results, less non-operating gains and losses, would have been an all-time record of $42,644,000, up from $40,009,000 in the prior year.

Required:

As a new financial analyst at a leading Wall Street investment banking firm, you are assigned to write a memo outlining the effects of the accounting change on Seneca's financial statements. In your report, be sure to include the following:

1. Why did management adopt LIFO?
2. By how much did the change affect pretax earnings and ending inventory? Verify that the amount of the tax savings listed in the press release is correct. At the time, the corporate tax rate was 35 percent.
3. As an analyst, how would you react to the decrease in income caused by the adoption of LIFO? Consider all of the information in the press release.

CP7-7
LO7-5
Micro Warehouse

Evaluating an Ethical Dilemma: Earnings, Inventory Purchases, and Management Bonuses

Micro Warehouse was a computer software and hardware online and catalog sales company.* A 1996 *Wall Street Journal* article disclosed the following:

> MICRO WAREHOUSE IS REORGANIZING TOP MANAGEMENT
>
> Micro Warehouse Inc. announced a "significant reorganization" of its management, including the resignation of three senior executives. The move comes just a few weeks after the Norwalk, Conn., computer catalogue sales company said it overstated earnings by $28 million since 1992 as a result of accounting irregularities. That previous disclosure prompted a flurry of shareholder lawsuits against the company. In addition, Micro Warehouse said it is cooperating with an "informal inquiry" by the Securities and Exchange Commission.
>
> Source: Stephen E. Frank, *The Wall Street Journal*, November 21, 1996, B2. Copyright © 1996 by Dow Jones & Co. Used with permission.

Its Form 10-Q quarterly report filed with the Securities and Exchange Commission two days before indicated that inaccuracies involving understatement of purchases and accounts payable in current and prior periods amounted to $47.3 million. It also indicated that, as a result, $2.2 million of executive bonuses for 1995 would be rescinded. Micro Warehouse's total tax rate is approximately 40.4 percent. Both cost of goods sold and executive bonuses are fully deductible for tax purposes.

*Micro Warehouse declared bankruptcy in 2003.

Required:

As a new staff member at Micro Warehouse's auditing firm, you are assigned to write a memo outlining the effects of the understatement of purchases and the rescinding of the bonuses. In your report, be sure to include the following:

1. The total effect on pretax and after-tax earnings of the understatement of purchases.
2. The total effect on pretax and after-tax earnings of the rescinding of the bonuses.
3. An estimate of the percentage of after-tax earnings management is receiving in bonuses.
4. A discussion of why Micro Warehouse's board of directors may have decided to tie managers' compensation to reported earnings and the possible relation between this type of bonus scheme and the accounting errors.

You as Analyst: Online Company Research

CP7-8
LO7-2, 7-3, 7-5, 7-6

Examining an Annual Report (an Individual or Team Project)

In your web browser, search for the investor relations page of a public company you are interested in (e.g., Papa John's investor relations). Select SEC Filings or Annual Report or Financials to obtain the 10-K for the most recent year available.*

Required:

Answer the following questions based on the annual report (10-K) that you have downloaded:

1. If your company lists inventories in its balance sheet, what percentage of total assets does inventories represent for each of the last three years? If your company does not list inventories, discuss why this is so.
2. If your company lists inventories, what inventory costing method is applied to U.S. inventories?
   a. What do you think motivated this choice?
   b. If the company uses LIFO, how much higher or lower would net income before taxes be if it had used FIFO or a similar method instead?
3. Ratio Analysis:
   a. What does the inventory turnover ratio measure in general?
   b. If your company reports inventories, compute the ratio for the last three years.
   c. What do your results suggest about the company?
   d. If available, find the industry ratio for the most recent year, compare it to your results, and discuss why you believe your company differs or is similar to the industry ratio.
4. What is the effect of the change in inventories on cash flows from operating activities for the most recent year (i.e., did the change increase or decrease operating cash flows)? Explain your answer.

---

*Alternatively, you can go to sec.gov, click on Company Filings (under the search box), and type the name of the public company you want to find. Once at the list of filings, type 10-K in the Filing Type box. The most recent 10-K annual report will be at the top of the list. Click on Interactive Data for a list of the parts or the entire report to examine.

BUSINESS ANALYTICS AND DATA VISUALIZATION WITH EXCEL AND TABLEAU

Connect offers a variety of exercises to assess Excel skills, data visualization, interpretation, and analysis, including auto-graded Tableau Dashboard Activities, Applying Excel problems, and Integrated Excel problems.

Images used throughout chapter: Question of ethics: mushmello/Shutterstock; Pause for feedback: McGraw Hill; Guided help: McGraw Hill; Financial analysis: McGraw Hill; Focus on cash flows: Hilch/Shutterstock; Key ratio analysis: guillermain/123RF; Data analytics: Hilch/Shutterstock; Tip: McGraw Hill; ESG reporting: McGraw Hill; International perspective: Hilch/Shutterstock

chapter 8

Reporting and Interpreting Property, Plant, and Equipment; Intangibles; and Natural Resources

FedEx Corporation is the parent holding company of a portfolio of business segments, including

- FedEx Express—the world's largest express transportation company,
- FedEx Ground—a leading North American provider of small-package ground delivery services,
- FedEx Freight—a leading North American provider of less-than-truckload freight services, and
- FedEx Office—providing document and business services and retail access to package transportation businesses.

With over 670 aircraft and 180,000 vehicles in 220 countries and territories, its over 500,000 team members handle over 250 million daily tracking requests. It is a capital-intensive company with more than $33.6 billion in net property, plant, and equipment. In the year ending May 31, 2020 alone, FedEx spent nearly $5.9 billion on capital expenditures, primarily for new aircraft and ground vehicles.

LEARNING OBJECTIVES

After studying this chapter, you should be able to:

Sundry Photography/Getty Images

FOCUS COMPANY

FedEx Corporation

MANAGING PRODUCTIVE CAPACITY FOR THE WORLD'S LEADER IN AIR CARGO SERVICES

fedex.com

UNDERSTANDING THE BUSINESS

Because the demand for package and cargo delivery is seasonal, with peak demand occurring during the November and December holidays, and because international air cargo service is dependent on trade negotiations between countries, planning for productive capacity in the cargo and package delivery services industry is very difficult. FedEx's managers must determine how many aircraft and vehicles are needed in which cities at what points in time to meet shifting demand. If a cargo plane takes off from Memphis, Tennessee (where FedEx is headquartered) en route to New York City with unused cargo space, the economic value associated with the unused space is lost for that flight. There is no way to sell the unused space to a customer once the cargo plane has left the airport. Unlike a manufacturer, a cargo and package delivery company cannot "inventory" the unused space for future sale.

With the tremendous growth in e-commerce as a fundamental part of the retail industry and an increasingly connected world, competition in this industry is fierce. The focus of retailers is to get a product to a customer in the fastest, most convenient way possible and at as low a shipping cost as possible. FedEx competes directly with United Parcel Service (UPS), the U.S. Post Office, DHL International, and many large airlines (e.g., Delta among others). Much of the battle for both residential and business-to-business customers is fought in terms of property, plant, and equipment. Managers devote considerable time and utilize data analytics to plan optimal levels of productive capacity, and financial analysts closely review a company's statements to determine the impact of management's decisions.

This chapter is organized according to the life cycle of long-lived assets—acquisition, use, and disposal. First, we will discuss the measuring and reporting issues related to land, buildings, and equipment. Then we will discuss the measurement and reporting issues for intangible assets and natural resources. Among the issues we will discuss are the maintenance, use, and disposal of property and equipment over time and the measurement and reporting of assets considered impaired in their ability to generate future cash flows.

ORGANIZATION OF THE CHAPTER

Acquisition and Maintenance of Plant and Equipment

- Classifying Long-Lived Assets
- Measuring and Recording Acquisition Cost
- Fixed Asset Turnover Ratio
- Repairs, Maintenance, and Improvements

Use, Impairment, and Disposal of Plant and Equipment

- Depreciation Concepts
- Alternative Depreciation Methods
- How Managers Choose
- Measuring Asset Impairment
- Disposal of Property, Plant, and Equipment

Intangible Assets and Natural Resources

- Acquisition and Amortization of Intangible Assets
- Acquisition and Depletion of Natural Resources

LEARNING OBJECTIVE 8-1

Define, classify, and explain the nature of long-lived productive assets and interpret the fixed asset turnover ratio.

ACQUISITION AND MAINTENANCE OF PLANT AND EQUIPMENT

Exhibit 8.1 shows the asset section of the balance sheet from **FedEx**'s annual report for the fiscal year ended May 31, 2020. Nearly 46 percent of FedEx's total assets are property and equipment. FedEx also reports other assets with probable long-term benefits. Let's begin by classifying these assets.

EXHIBIT 8.1

FedEx Corporation's Asset Section of the Balance Sheet

FEDEX CORPORATION

REAL WORLD EXCERPT:

2020 Annual Report

FEDEX CORPORATION
Consolidated Balance Sheets (partial)
(in millions)

	May 31	
	2020	**2019**
ASSETS		
CURRENT ASSETS *(summarized)*	$16,383	$13,086
PROPERTY AND EQUIPMENT, AT COST		
Aircraft and related equipment	24,518	22,793
Package handling and ground support equipment	11,382	10,409
Information technology	6,884	6,268
Vehicles and trailers	9,101	8,339
Facilities and other	13,139	11,702
Gross property and equipment	65,024	59,511
Less accumulated depreciation and amortization	31,416	29,082
Net property and equipment	33,608	30,429
OTHER LONG-TERM ASSETS		
Operating lease right-of-use assets, net	13,917	
Goodwill	6,372	6,884
Other assets	3,257	4,004
Total other long-term assets	23,546	10,888
	$73,537	$54,403

Source: FedEx Corporation

Classifying Long-Lived Assets

The resources that determine a company's productive capacity often are called long-lived assets. These assets, which are listed as noncurrent assets on the balance sheet, may be either tangible or intangible and have the following characteristics:

1. Tangible assets have physical substance; that is, they can be touched. The three kinds of long-lived tangible assets are
   a. **Land** used in operations. As is the case with **FedEx**, land often is not shown as a separate item on the balance sheet.
   b. **Buildings, fixtures, and equipment** used in operations. For FedEx, this category includes aircraft and ground equipment to service the aircraft, information technology, and vehicles and trailers. (*Note:* Land, buildings, fixtures, and equipment also are called **property, plant, and equipment** or **fixed assets.**)
   c. **Natural resources** used in operations. FedEx does not report any natural resources on its balance sheet. However, companies in other industries report natural resources such as timber tracts and silver mines.
2. Intangible assets are long-lived assets without physical substance that confer specific rights on their owner. Examples are patents, copyrights, franchises, licenses, and trademarks. FedEx also reports over $6 billion of goodwill on its balance sheet. Goodwill represents many of the intangible assets acquired through mergers and acquisitions, which we discuss briefly in this chapter.

Plant and Equipment as a Percent of Total Assets for Selected Focus Companies

Company	Percent
National Beverage	18.6%
Chipotle Mexican Grill	28.6%
Harley-Davidson	8.1%

KEY RATIO ANALYSIS

Fixed Asset Turnover

ANALYTICAL QUESTION

How effectively is management utilizing fixed assets to generate revenues?

RATIO AND COMPARISONS

$$\text{Fixed Asset Turnover} = \frac{\text{Net Sales (or Operating Revenues)}}{\text{Average Net Fixed Assets*}}$$

*[Beginning + Ending Fixed Asset Balances (net of accumulated depreciation)] ÷ 2.

The ratio for **FedEx** for the fiscal year ended May 31, 2020 is (dollars in millions):

Operating Revenues $69,217 ÷ [($30,429 + $33,608) ÷ 2] = 2.16 times

Comparisons Over Time		
FedEx Corporation		
2018	**2019**	**2020**
2.42	2.39	2.16

Comparisons With Competitor
United Parcel Service
2020
2.70

Selected Focus Companies' Fixed Asset Turnover Ratios

Company	Ratio
Chipotle Mexican Grill	3.93
Skechers	5.43
Apple	7.40

INTERPRETATIONS

In General The fixed asset turnover ratio measures the sales dollars generated by each dollar of fixed assets (land, buildings, and equipment) used. Creditors and security analysts use this ratio to assess a company's effectiveness at generating sales from its fixed assets. A high rate normally suggests effective management. An increasing rate over time signals more efficient fixed asset use.

Focus Company Analysis FedEx's fixed asset turnover ratio decreased each year between 2018 and 2020. This suggests that FedEx was less efficient in using its property, plant, and equipment over time. In 2019, FedEx and Amazon ended their express delivery contract, resulting in about a one percent reduction in operating revenues in 2019 and 2020. With the explosion in e-commerce, intensified by the Covid-19 pandemic, and Amazon's expanding commitment to build its own Amazon Air cargo service, FedEx shifted its strategy to focus on the broader retail market, such as Walmart and Target. United Parcel Service (UPS), on the other hand, picked up the capacity with Amazon that FedEx lost in those years.

A Few Cautions A lower or declining fixed asset turnover rate may indicate that a company is expanding (by acquiring additional productive assets) in anticipation of higher future sales. An increasing ratio also could signal that a firm has cut back on capital expenditures due to a downturn in business. This is not the case at FedEx, which continues to expand and upgrade its fleet of planes, vehicles, equipment, and information technology. As a consequence, appropriate interpretation of the fixed asset turnover ratio requires an investigation of related activities.

LEARNING OBJECTIVE 8-2

Apply the cost principle to measure the acquisition and maintenance of property, plant, and equipment.

Measuring and Recording Acquisition Cost

Under the cost principle, all reasonable and necessary expenditures made in acquiring and preparing an asset for use (or sale, as in the case of inventory) **should be recorded as the cost of the asset.** These include any sales taxes, legal fees, transportation costs, and installation costs to acquire and prepare the asset for use. These expenditures are **capitalized** (recorded as part of the total cost of the asset), not recorded as expenses in the current period. However, any interest charges associated with the purchase are recorded as expenses as incurred.

DaveAlan/iStock Unreleased/Getty Images

In addition to purchasing buildings and equipment, a company may acquire undeveloped land, typically with the intent to build a new factory or office building. When a company purchases land, all of the incidental costs of the purchase, such as title fees, sales commissions, legal fees, title insurance, delinquent taxes, and surveying fees, should be included in its cost.

Sometimes a company purchases an old building or used machinery for the business operations. Renovation and repair costs incurred by the company prior to the asset's use should be included as a part of its total cost. Also, when purchasing land, buildings, and equipment as a group (known as a *basket purchase*), the total cost is allocated to each asset in proportion to the asset's market value relative to the total market value of the assets as a whole [e.g., Building Cost = (Market value of building/Total market value of the basket purchase) × Total cost of the basket purchase].

In 2017, **FedEx** signed a deal with **ATR** (headquartered in Toulouse, France), the world's largest regional turbo-prop plane manufacturer, to purchase over several years 50 ATR 72-600F freighter aircraft. This fuel-efficient plane provides fast, economical services to small- and medium-sized businesses around the world, as part of FedEx Express's Feeder fleet renewal program. For illustration, assume that FedEx took delivery of a new ATR cargo plane on June 1, 2023 (the beginning of FedEx's fiscal year) with the following information:

- List price = $26.8 million
- Discount offered by ATR = $1.8 million for signing the purchase agreement
- Transportation (delivery) costs paid by FedEx = $400,000
- Preparation (e.g., detailing of FedEx logo) costs paid by FedEx = $600,000

The amount recorded for the purchase, called the **acquisition cost**, is the net cash amount paid for the asset, or when noncash assets are used as payment, the fair value of the asset given or asset received, whichever can be more clearly determined (called the **cash equivalent price**). FedEx would calculate the acquisition cost of the new aircraft as follows:

Invoice price	$26,800,000
Less: Discount from ATR	(1,800,000)
Net cash invoice price	25,000,000
Add: Transportation charges paid by FedEx	400,000
Preparation costs paid by FedEx	600,000
Cost of the aircraft (added to the asset account)	$26,000,000

For Cash

Assuming that FedEx paid cash for the aircraft and related transportation and preparation costs, the transaction is recorded as follows (in millions):

	Debit	Credit
Aircraft (+A)	26	
Cash (−A)		26

Assets		=	Liabilities		+	Stockholders' Equity
Aircraft	+26					
Cash	−26					

It might seem unusual for FedEx to pay cash to purchase new assets that cost $26 million, but this is often the case. When it acquires productive assets, a company may pay with cash that was generated from operations or cash recently borrowed. It also is possible for the seller to finance the purchase on credit.

For Debt

Now let's assume that FedEx signed a note payable for the new aircraft and paid cash for the transportation and preparation costs. In that case, FedEx would record the following journal entry (in millions):

	Debit	Credit
Aircraft (+A)	26	
Cash (−A)		1
Note payable (+L)		25

Assets		=	Liabilities		+	Stockholders' Equity
Aircraft	+26		Note payable	+25		
Cash	−1					

Instead of signing a note payable, another option is to utilize schemes that include leasing aircraft. About four in ten commercial aircraft carrying passengers are leased. FedEx owns approximately 95 percent of its aircraft, but leases a significant amount of national, regional, and metropolitan sorting facilities, retail facilities, and administrative buildings, land, and equipment. Effective in 2019, companies are required to report most types of leases on the balance sheet as **Operating Lease Right-of-Use Assets,** with the related obligations reported as debt entitled Operating Lease Liabilities. FedEx reported $13,917 million in operating lease right-of-use assets on May 31, 2020. Because leases confer right-of-use to the company using the asset, these are considered **intangible assets** and are not included in property, plant, and equipment (fixed assets). The lessee (the one using the asset) will recognize (1) depreciation of the right-of-use assets and (2) interest on the lease liability. Additional discussion of leases is provided in Chapter 9, with advanced discussion in other accounting courses.

Tip Companies widely use leasing—from office buildings and shopping centers to vehicles, farm equipment, and airplanes. Beginning in 2019 as required by new accounting standards, many companies, especially airlines and retailers, reported significant increases in assets and debt due to leases. **Remember:** Don't include the right-of-use assets in total fixed assets; they are intangible assets.

For Equity (or Other Noncash Considerations)

Noncash consideration, such as the company's common stock or a right given by the company to the seller to purchase the company's goods or services at a special price, also might be part of the transaction. When noncash consideration is included in the purchase of an asset, the cash-equivalent cost (fair value of the asset given or received) is determined.

Assume that FedEx gave ATR 1,000,000 shares of new $1.00 par value common stock with a market value of $10 per share and paid the balance of the plane plus transportation and preparation costs in cash. The journal entry and transaction effects follow (in millions):

		Debit	Credit
	Aircraft (+A)	26	
1,000,000 shares × $1 par →	Common stock (+SE)		1
1,000,000 shares × $9 excess ($10 market value − $1 par) →	Additional paid-in capital (+SE)		9
	Cash (−A)		16

Assets		=	Liabilities	+	Stockholders' Equity	
Aircraft	+26				Common stock	+1
Cash	−16				Additional paid-in capital	+9

By Construction

Tip **Remember:** All reasonable and necessary expenditures made in acquiring and **preparing an asset for its intended use** should be recorded as part of the cost of the asset—they should be **capitalized!** But, after the asset is ready to use, no other costs, such as insurance on the asset while in use, are capitalized.

In some cases, a company may construct an asset for its own use instead of buying it from a manufacturer. When a company does so, the cost of the asset includes all the necessary costs associated with construction, such as labor, materials, and, in most situations, a portion of the interest incurred during the construction period, called **capitalized interest**. The amount of interest expense that is capitalized is recorded by debiting the asset and crediting cash when the interest is paid. The amount of interest to be capitalized is a complex computation discussed in detail in other accounting courses.

Capitalizing labor, materials, and a portion of interest expense has the effect of increasing assets, decreasing expenses, and increasing net income in the current period. Let's assume FedEx constructed a new hangar, paying $8 million in labor costs and $11 million in supplies and materials. FedEx also paid $1 million in interest expense during the year related to the construction project. The company would record the following journal entry (in millions):

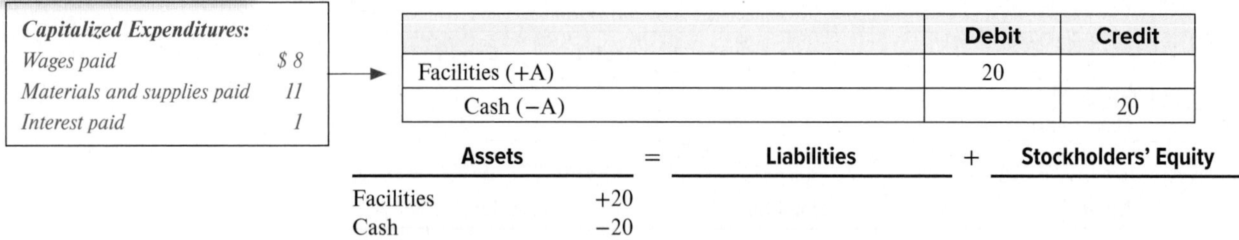

Capitalized Expenditures:	
Wages paid	*$ 8*
Materials and supplies paid	*11*
Interest paid	*1*

	Debit	Credit
Facilities (+A)	20	
Cash (−A)		20

Assets		=	Liabilities	+	Stockholders' Equity
Facilities	+20				
Cash	−20				

In a recent annual report, FedEx Corporation included a note on capitalized interest for financing aircraft purchases and modifications, construction of facilities, and software development:

FEDEX CORPORATION
REAL WORLD EXCERPT:
2020 Annual Report

Note 1

Summary of Significant Accounting Policies

CAPITALIZED INTEREST. Interest on funds used to finance the acquisition and modification of aircraft, including purchase deposits, construction of certain facilities, and development of certain software up to the date the asset is ready for its intended use, is capitalized and included in the cost of the asset if the asset is actively under construction. Capitalized interest was $54 million in 2020, $64 million in 2019 and $61 million in 2018.

Source: FedEx Corporation

PAUSE FOR FEEDBACK

We just learned how to measure the cost of operational assets acquired under various methods. In general, all necessary and reasonable costs to ready the asset for its intended use are part of the cost of the asset. Assets can be acquired with cash, with debt, and/or with the company's stock (at market value).

SELF-STUDY QUIZ

It's your turn to apply these concepts by answering the following questions. In a recent year, **McDonald's Corporation** purchased property, plant, and equipment. Assume the following for the purchase of the equipment (in millions, except share and per share amounts):

- $1,200 list price
- Suppliers gave McDonald's a 10 percent discount
- $10 for transportation costs to deliver the equipment (paid by McDonald's)
- $32 for installation and preparation of the equipment before use
- $1 in maintenance contracts to cover repairs to the equipment during use
- For payment:
  - Issued 1 million shares of $1 common stock with a market value of $40 per share
  - Signed a one-year note payable for $800 with a four percent interest rate, all due in the following year
  - Paid the remainder in cash

1. Record the journal entry for the purchase of the equipment.
2. Indicate the accounts, amounts, and effects (+ for increase; − for decrease) of the purchase on the accounting equation.
3. Was the $1 in maintenance contracts included in the cost of the equipment? Why or why not?

After you have completed your answers, check them below.

GUIDED HELP 8-1

For additional step-by-step video instruction on recording long-lived asset purchases, go to mhhe.com/libby_gh8-1.

Related Homework: E8-3, E8-4, E8-5, P8-1, P8-3

Solutions to SELF-STUDY QUIZ

1. Journal Entry:

	Debit	Credit
Equipment (+A)	1,122	
Common stock (+SE)		1
Additional paid-in capital (+SE)		39
Notes payable (+L)		800
Cash (−A)		282

$1,200	*List price*
(120)	*10% discount*
10	*Transportation costs*
32	*Installation and preparation costs*
$ 1,122	*Cost of the equipment*

2. Effects on the accounting equation:

Assets		=	Liabilities		+	Stockholders' Equity	
Equipment	+1,122		Notes payable	+800		Common stock	+1
Cash	−282					Additional paid-in capital	+39

3. The maintenance contracts were not included in the cost of the equipment because they apply to the period when the asset is in use, not to get it ready for use.

Repairs, Maintenance, and Improvements

Most assets require substantial expenditures during their lives to maintain or enhance their productive capacity. These expenditures include cash outlays for ordinary repairs and maintenance, major repairs, replacements, and additions. Expenditures that are made after an asset has been acquired are classified as follows:

1. **Ordinary repairs and maintenance** are expenditures that maintain the productive capacity of the asset during the current accounting period only. These expenditures are recurring in nature, involve relatively small amounts at each occurrence, and do not directly increase the productive life, operating efficiency, or capacity of the asset. These cash outlays are recorded as **expenses** in the current period.

   In the case of **FedEx**, examples of ordinary repairs would include changing the oil in the aircraft engines, replacing the lights in the control panels, and cleaning the sorting facilities. Although the cost of individual ordinary repairs is relatively small, in the aggregate these expenditures can be substantial. For the year ended May 31, 2020, FedEx reported $2,893 million in Maintenance and Repairs on its income statement. The following summary entry represents how these expenditures would have been recorded by FedEx (in millions):

	Debit	Credit
Maintenance and repairs expense (+E, −SE)	2,893	
Cash (−A)		2,893

Assets		=	Liabilities	+	Stockholders' Equity	
Cash	−2,893				Maintenance and repairs expense (+E)	−2,893

2. **Improvements** are expenditures that increase the productive life, operating efficiency, or capacity of the asset. These **capital expenditures** are added to the appropriate asset accounts (i.e., they are capitalized). They occur infrequently, involve large amounts of money, and increase an asset's economic usefulness in the future through either increased efficiency or longer life. Examples include additions, major overhauls, complete reconditioning, and major replacements and improvements, such as the complete replacement of an engine on an aircraft.

FedEx's annual report includes a description of what it capitalizes, which follows the accounting for capital expenditures:

FEDEX CORPORATION
REAL WORLD EXCERPT:
2020 Annual Report

Note 1

Summary of Significant Accounting Policies

PROPERTY AND EQUIPMENT. Expenditures for major additions, improvements and flight equipment modifications are capitalized when such costs are determined to extend the useful life of the asset or are part of the cost of acquiring the asset. Expenditures for equipment overhaul costs of engines or airframes prior to their operational use are capitalized as part of the cost of such assets as they are costs required to ready the asset for its intended use.

Source: FedEx Corporation

Assume that FedEx spent $300 million in 2023 to modify the cargo area of its oldest aircraft to reduce weight, resulting in 9 percent greater fuel efficiency and lower operating costs. The summary entry below represents how these expenditures would have been recorded by FedEx as capital expenditures:

	Debit	Credit
Aircraft (+A)	300	
Cash (−A)		300

Assets		=	Liabilities	+	Stockholders' Equity
Aircraft	+300				
Cash	−300				

Aviation Images Ltd/Alamy Stock Photo

In many cases, no clear line distinguishes improvements (assets) from ordinary repairs and maintenance (expenses). In these situations, managers must exercise professional judgment and make a subjective decision. **Capitalizing expenses will increase assets and net income in the current year, lowering future years' income by the amount of the annual depreciation.** On the other hand, for tax purposes, expensing the amount in the current period will lower taxes immediately. Because the decision to capitalize or expense is subjective, auditors review the items reported as capital expenditures and ordinary repairs and maintenance closely.

To avoid spending too much time classifying additions and improvements (capital expenditures) and repair expenses (revenue expenditures), some companies develop simple policies to govern the accounting for these expenditures. For example, one large computer company expenses all individual items that cost less than $1,000. Such policies are acceptable because immaterial (relatively small dollar) amounts will not affect users' decisions when analyzing financial statements.

A QUESTION OF ETHICS

WorldCom: Hiding Billions in Expenses through Capitalization

When expenditures that should be recorded as current period expenses are improperly capitalized as part of the cost of an asset, the effects on the financial statements can be enormous. In one of the largest accounting frauds in history, **WorldCom** (now part of **Verizon**) inflated its income and cash flows from operations by billions of dollars in just such a scheme. This fraud turned WorldCom's actual losses into large profits.

Over five quarters in 2001 and 2002, the company initially announced that it had capitalized $3.8 billion that should have been recorded as operating expenses. By early 2004, auditors discovered $11 billion in necessary restatements (reductions to previously reported pretax income) for 2000 and 2001.

Accounting for expenses as capital expenditures increases current income because it spreads a single period's operating expenses over many future periods as depreciation expense. It increases cash flows from operations by moving cash outflows from the operating section to the investing section of the cash flow statement.

ENVIRONMENTAL, SOCIAL, & GOVERNANCE (ESG) REPORTING

Being a Global Citizen

FedEx publishes an ESG report at sustainability.fedex.com that "covers FedEx corporate social responsibility (CSR) strategies, goals, programs, and progress." Its *2020 Global Citizenship Report,* for example, highlights its innovative technologies to focus on meeting customers' and employees' needs and being environmentally conscious. The innovations include: Using emissions-free e-bikes in high-congestion areas to reduce the company's environmental footprint; expanding its fleet of electric vehicles; replacing and modernizing older aircraft with more fuel-efficient planes (the company uses a lot of jet fuel!) such as the ATR 72-600F purchases for its FedEx Express Feeder fleet; obtaining jet fuel from alternative low-carbon renewable jet fuel sources; optimizing vehicle routes to reduce fuel usage; investing in autonomous vehicles (e.g., robots–Roxo™, the SameDay Bot and drones using **Alphabet**'s Wing technology); installing solar and fuel cell technologies; and enhancing the recycling of packaging.

Kristoffer Tripplaar/Alamy Stock Photo

The report provides metrics on CSR goals and progress. For example, ***Goal:*** Reduce aircraft emissions intensity 30 percent from 2005 baseline by 2020; ***Progress:*** 24 percent reduction (not yet achieved due to certain inefficient aircraft that had not yet been retired). As stated in the report, "Collectively, our sustainability efforts have contributed to an approximately 40% reduction in CO_2 emissions intensity across the enterprise. . ." Here is a small excerpt from the many metrics displayed in the *2020 Global Citizenship Report:*

FEDEX CORPORATION

REAL WORLD EXCERPT:

2020 Global Citizenship Report

FUEL- AND ENERGY-SAVING INITIATIVES	Energy saved (terajoules)			CO_2e emissions avoided (metric tons)		
Energy Saved (terajoules)	**FY17**	**FY18**	**FY19**	**FY17**	**FY18**	**FY19**
On-site Solar Electricity Generation	75	76	85	12,425	12,504	13,447
Facility Energy Efficiency Initiatives[(i), (ii)]	793	828	915	164,018	171,252	179,638
FedEx Fuel Sense (jet fuel)	12,510	13,436	15,571	849,183	912,023	1,054,418
FedEx Express Aircraft Fleet Modernization	12,705	15,591	19,992	862,420	1,058,368	1,355,852
FedEx Express Reduce, Replace, Revolutionize Vehicle Efficiency	3,113	3,401	3,627	219,714	240,171	255,666
FedEx Freight Intermodal Rail Usage	3,408	3,787	4,022	264,296	296,511	281,278
Total Energy Saved/Emissions Avoided	**32,604**	**37,119**	**44,211**	**2,372,056**	**2,690,828**	**3,140,299**

(i) Facility energy efficiency initiatives include building lighting retrofits and energy management systems.
(ii) CO_2e calculated using the EPA GHG Calculator. FY19 emissions uses EPA GHG Calculator's updated emission factors.

Source: FedEx Corporation

PAUSE FOR FEEDBACK

Practice these applications for operational assets as they are used over time: repairing or maintaining (expensed in current period) and adding to or improving (capitalized as part of the cost of the asset).

SELF-STUDY QUIZ

A building that originally cost $400,000 has been used over the past 10 years and needs continual maintenance and repairs. For each of the following expenditures, indicate whether it should be expensed in the current period or capitalized as part of **the cost of the asset.**

	Expense or Capitalize?
1. Major replacement of electrical wiring throughout the building.	________
2. Repairs to the front door of the building.	________
3. Annual cleaning of the filters on the building's air-conditioning system.	________
4. Significant repairs due to damage from an unusual and infrequent flood.	________

After you have completed your answers, check them below.

Related Homework: M8-3, E8-6, E8-7, E8-8, E8-24

Solutions to SELF-STUDY QUIZ

1. Capitalize 2. Expense 3. Expense 4. Capitalize

When a company acquires a new long-lived asset as illustrated above, management must ensure that sound **internal controls** are established and followed to safeguard the asset. One of the most important controls is to create a registry (a record) of each fixed asset with relevant information, such as the purchase date, serial number, acquisition date, and cost. Another useful physical control is to "tag" each asset with an identifying number. Technology simplifies tagging and tracking, especially for moveable assets such as computer monitors, by using QR codes attached to the asset paired with mobile technology (a smartphone or scanner). An annual review comparing the asset registry to the physical QR code provides a real-time snapshot of assets and their locations. In addition, management strengthens internal controls by establishing and following policies on capitalization of expenditures for fixed assets, generally accepted depreciation methods to be used, and approval procedures for acquisition and disposition of assets.

While most large companies have strong controls for acquisition, the controls surrounding disposition of assets often are lacking. When fixed assets are sold, it is important that management established procedures to segregate duties–that is, a different person is needed for each point in the sale: Approving the sale, recording the sale in the accounting system, reconciling accounting records, and physically possessing the cash from the sale. Otherwise, there is a risk of loss to the company. Now, let's discuss the use, impairment and disposal of property and equipment.

Internal Control Alert

Tip **Reminder: Establishing internal controls is the responsibility of management.** Auditors have a duty to test the internal controls for weaknesses that could impact financial information.

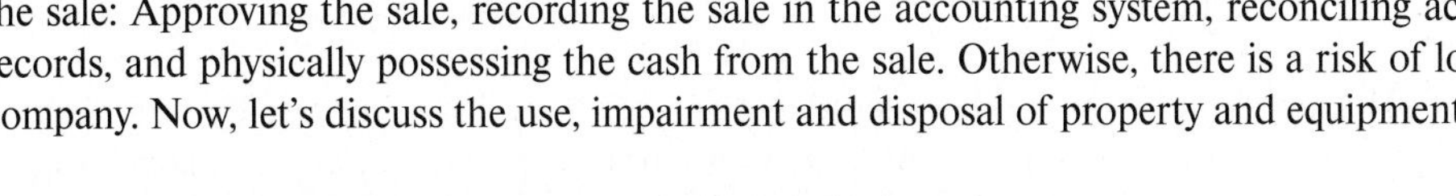

USE, IMPAIRMENT, AND DISPOSAL OF PLANT AND EQUIPMENT

LEARNING OBJECTIVE 8-3

Apply various cost allocation methods as assets are held and used over time.

Depreciation Concepts

Except for land, which is considered to have an unlimited life, a long-lived asset with a limited useful life, such as an airplane, represents the prepaid cost of a bundle of future services or benefits. The **expense recognition (matching) principle** requires that a portion of an asset's cost be allocated as an expense in the same period that revenues are generated by its use. **FedEx Corporation** earns revenue when it provides cargo and delivery service and incurs an expense when using its aircraft to generate the revenue.

The term used to identify the matching of the cost of using buildings and equipment with the revenues they generate is **depreciation**. Thus, depreciation is **the process of allocating the cost of buildings and equipment over their productive lives using a systematic and rational method.**

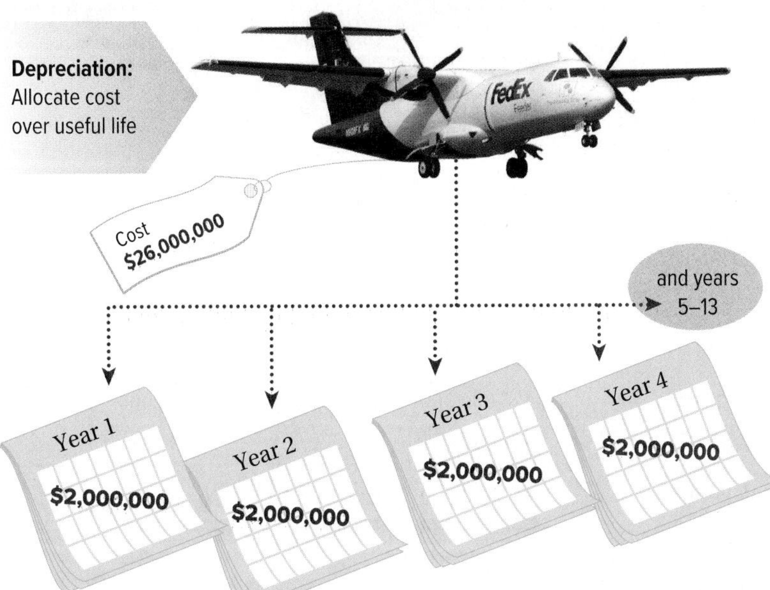

DaveAlan/iStock Unreleased/Getty Images

Tip **Again → In accounting, depreciation is simply a cost allocation concept**—net book value is reduced as the asset is used to generate revenue. It has nothing to do with an asset's market value (as if you were going to sell it) because your intent is to use it.

Students often are confused by the concept of depreciation as accountants use it. In accounting, depreciation is a process of **cost allocation,** not a process of determining an asset's current market value or worth. When an asset is depreciated, the remaining balance sheet amount **probably does not represent its current market value.** On balance sheets subsequent to acquisition, the undepreciated cost is not measured on a market or fair value basis.

As we discussed in Chapter 4, an adjusting journal entry is needed at the end of each period to reflect the use of buildings and equipment for the period:

	Debit	Credit
Depreciation expense (+E, −SE)	X,XXX	
Accumulated depreciation (+XA, −A)		X,XXX

Assets		=	Liabilities	+	Stockholders' Equity	
Accumulated depreciation (+XA)	−x,xxx				Depreciation expense (+E)	−x,xxx

Tip *On financial statements:*

Income Statement
Depreciation expense: Estimated cost used in current period

Balance Sheet

Property, Plant, and Equipment (Cost)	−	Accumulated Depreciation (Used cost)	=	Net Book Value (Unused cost)

The amount of depreciation recorded during each period is reported on the income statement as **Depreciation Expense.** The amount of depreciation expense accumulated since the acquisition date is reported on the balance sheet as a contra-account, **Accumulated Depreciation,** and deducted from the related asset's cost. The net amount on the balance sheet is called **net book value** or **carrying value.** The **net book value** (or **carrying value** or **book value**) of a long-lived asset is its acquisition cost less the accumulated depreciation from the acquisition date to the balance sheet date.

From the balance sheet excerpt in Exhibit 8.1, we see that FedEx's acquisition cost for property and equipment is $65,024 million on May 31, 2020. The accumulated depreciation and amortization on the property and equipment is $31,416 million (amortization is the name for allocating costs of intangible assets and is discussed later in the chapter). Thus, the book value is reported as net property and equipment of $33,608 million. FedEx also reported depreciation and amortization expense of $3,615 million on its income statement for the year ended May 31, 2020.

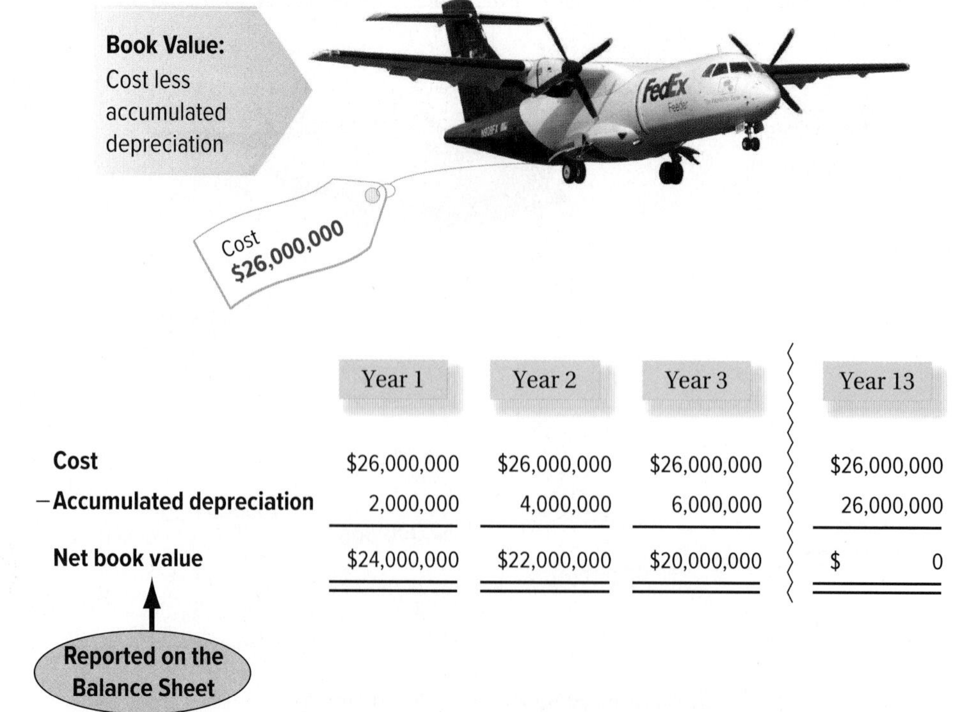

	Year 1	Year 2	Year 3	Year 13
Cost	$26,000,000	$26,000,000	$26,000,000	$26,000,000
−Accumulated depreciation	2,000,000	4,000,000	6,000,000	26,000,000
Net book value	$24,000,000	$22,000,000	$20,000,000	$ 0

Reported on the Balance Sheet

DaveAlan/iStock Unreleased/Getty Images

FINANCIAL ANALYSIS

Book Value as an Approximation of Remaining Life

Some analysts compare the book value of assets to their original cost as an approximation of their remaining life. If the book value of an asset is 100 percent of its cost, it is a new asset; if the book value is 25 percent of its cost, the asset has about 25 percent of its estimated life remaining. In **FedEx**'s case, the book value of its property and equipment ($33,608) was nearly 52 percent of its original cost ($65,024) on May 31, 2020, compared to 51 percent for **United Parcel Service** and 58 percent for German company **Deutsche Post DHL Group**.

This comparison suggests that the flight equipment of FedEx and UPS may be slightly older than the equipment at DHL. However, this comparison is only a rough approximation and is influenced by some of the accounting issues discussed in the next section, including how fast a company depreciates its buildings and equipment.

Book Value as a Percentage of Original Cost

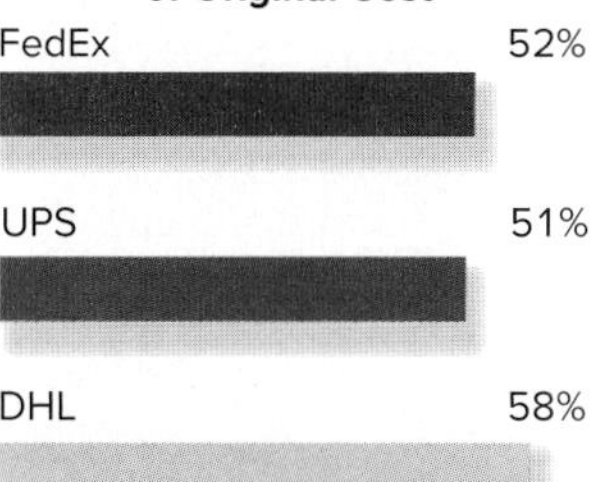

Once an asset's cost is determined, to calculate depreciation expense, three pieces of information are required for each asset:

* **Estimated** useful life to the company.
* **Estimated** residual (or salvage) value at the end of the asset's useful life to the company.
* **Depreciation method.**

Estimated useful life represents management's estimate of the asset's **useful economic life to the company** rather than its total economic life to all potential users. The asset's expected physical life is often longer than the company intends to use the asset. Economic life may be expressed in terms of years or units of capacity, such as the number of hours a machine is expected to operate or the number of units it can produce. FedEx's wide-body aircraft fleet is expected to fly for more than 30 years, but FedEx has goals of reducing fuel emissions by replacing its older aircraft with modern fuel-efficient equipment. For accounting purposes, FedEx assigns an estimated useful life range between 5 and 30 years depending on the type of cargo plane (e.g., Boeing 777F, ATR 72-600F). At the end of its useful life to FedEx, a plane may be sold. The subsequent owner of the aircraft (likely a regional or foreign airline) would use an estimated useful life based on its own policies.

Tip Notice that, since the asset's useful life and residual values are estimates, **depreciation expense is an estimate.** Companies ask equipment suppliers what the entire expected life is (say 20 years). Then, management decides, based on the company's own experience with similar assets and policies on equipment renewal, as to the estimated life and residual value to assign (say, 15 years with a 10 percent value at the end).

FINANCIAL ANALYSIS

Differences in Estimated Lives within a Single Industry

Notes to recent actual financial statements of various air cargo and package delivery companies reveal the following estimates for the useful lives of flight equipment:

Company	Estimated Useful Life (in years)
FedEx: Wide-body aircraft	15 to 30
Narrow-body aircraft	5 to 18
United Parcel Service	12 to 40
Deutsche Post DHL Group	15 to 20

The differences in the estimated lives may be attributed to a number of factors such as the type of aircraft used by each company, equipment replacement plans, operational differences, and the degree of management's conservatism. In addition, given the same type of aircraft, companies that plan to use the equipment over fewer years may estimate higher residual values than companies that plan to use the equipment longer.

Differences in estimated lives and residual values of assets can have a significant impact on a comparison of the profitability of the competing companies. Analysts must be certain to identify the causes of differences in depreciable lives.

Estimated residual (or salvage) value represents management's estimate of the amount the company **expects to recover upon disposal of the asset at the end of its estimated useful life.** The residual value may be the estimated value of the asset as salvage or scrap or its expected value if sold to another user. In the case of FedEx's aircraft, residual value may be the amount it expects to receive when it sells the asset to a small regional or foreign air cargo company that operates older equipment. The notes to FedEx's financial statements state that "Substantially all property and equipment have no material residual values."

Alternative Depreciation Methods

Because of significant differences among companies and the assets they own, accountants have not been able to agree on a single best method of depreciation. As a result, managers may choose from several acceptable depreciation methods that match depreciation expense with the revenues generated in a period. They also may choose different methods for specific assets or groups of assets. Once selected, the method should be applied consistently over time to enhance comparability of financial information. We will discuss three depreciation methods:

1. **Straight-line**—when an asset's usage is the same each period.
2. **Units-of-production**—when an asset's usage varies each period depending on activity or productivity during the period.
3. **Declining-balance**—when an asset is more efficient in its early years of usage, producing more revenue, but is less efficient over time.

To illustrate each method, let's assume that **FedEx** acquired a new delivery van on June 1, 2023, the start of its fiscal year. The relevant information is shown in Exhibit 8.2.

Straight-Line Method

The vast majority of companies, including FedEx, select the **straight-line depreciation** method **for financial reporting.** It is the simplest method, and it is used when no other cost allocation method provides a better matching of revenues and expenses. Under the straight-line method, an equal portion of an asset's **depreciable cost** is allocated to each accounting period over the asset's estimated useful life. The straight-line formula follows:

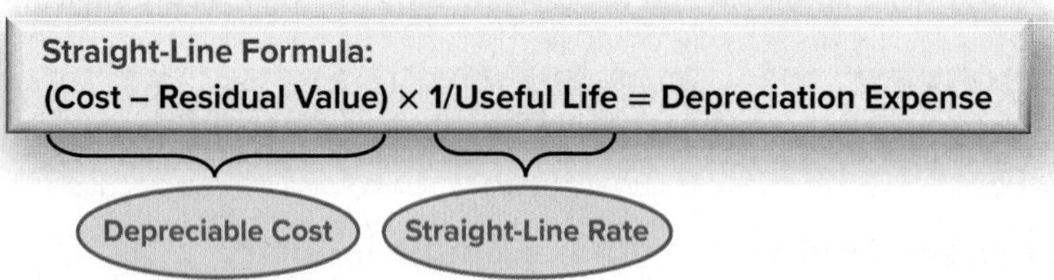

In this formula, "Cost minus Residual Value" (C - RV, for short) is the amount to be depreciated, also called the **depreciable cost**. The formula "1/Useful Life" is the **straight-line rate.** Using the data provided in Exhibit 8.2, the depreciation expense for (1/UL, for short) FedEx's new delivery van would be $20,000 per year, calculated as follows:

(C	–	RV)	×	1/UL	=	Depreciation Expense
($ 62,500	–	$2,500)	×	1/3 years	=	$20,000 per year

EXHIBIT 8.2

Data for Illustrating the Computation of Depreciation under Alternative Methods

Acquisition of New Delivery Van #91-DHH16335PA			
Cost, purchased on June 1, 2023		$62,500	
Estimated residual value		$ 2,500	
Estimated useful life		3	years **OR** 100,000 miles
Actual miles driven in:	Year ended May 31, 2024		30,000 miles
	Year ended May 31, 2025		50,000 miles
	Year ended May 31, 2026		20,000 miles

Companies often create a **depreciation schedule** that shows the computed amount of depreciation expense each year over the entire useful life of the asset. The new delivery van's depreciation schedule is created in an Excel spreadsheet using the data in Exhibit 8.2:

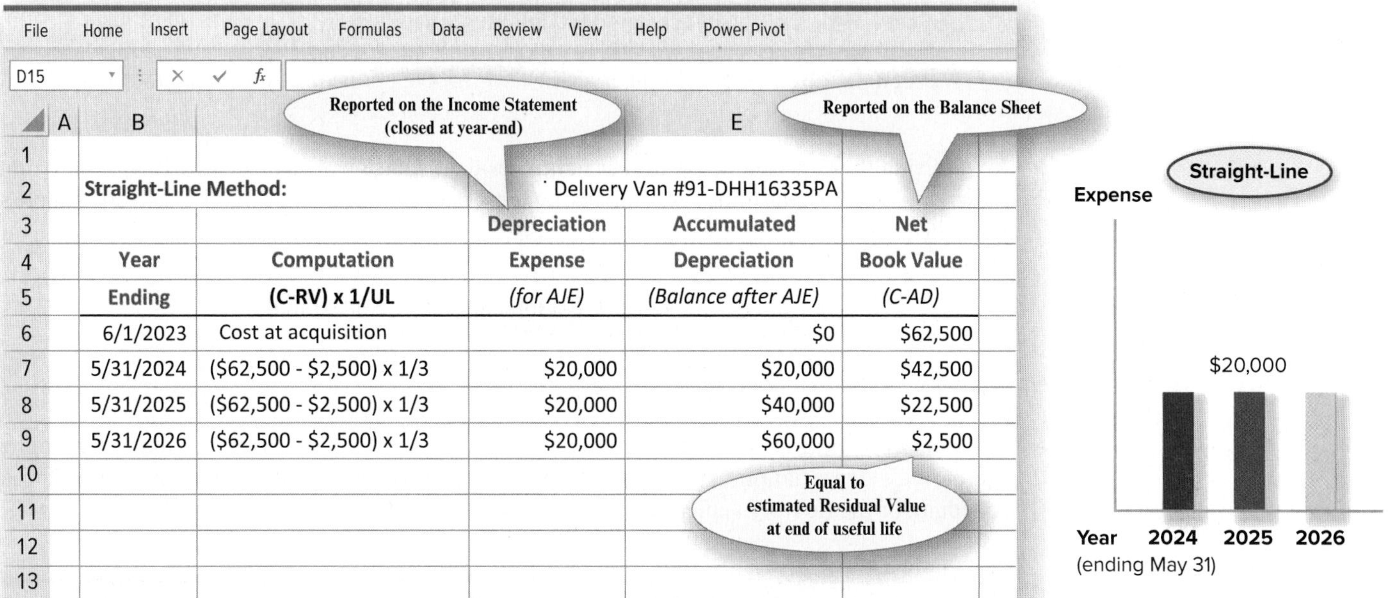

	B			E	
1					
2	**Straight-Line Method:**		Delivery Van #91-DHH16335PA		
3			**Depreciation**	**Accumulated**	**Net**
4	**Year**	**Computation**	**Expense**	**Depreciation**	**Book Value**
5	**Ending**	**(C-RV) x 1/UL**	*(for AJE)*	*(Balance after AJE)*	*(C-AD)*
6	6/1/2023	Cost at acquisition		$0	$62,500
7	5/31/2024	($62,500 - $2,500) x 1/3	$20,000	$20,000	$42,500
8	5/31/2025	($62,500 - $2,500) x 1/3	$20,000	$40,000	$22,500
9	5/31/2026	($62,500 - $2,500) x 1/3	$20,000	$60,000	$2,500
10					
11					
12					
13					

Microsoft Excel

Expense
Straight-Line
$20,000
Year 2024 2025 2026
(ending May 31)

Notice that:

- Depreciation expense is a constant amount each year.
- Accumulated depreciation increases by an equal amount each year.
- Net book value decreases by the same amount each year until it equals the estimated residual value.

This is the reason for the name **straight-line method.** Notice, too, that the adjusting entry can be prepared from this schedule, and the effects on the income statement and balance sheet are known. FedEx uses the straight-line method for all its assets as reported in the notes to recent financial statements:

NOTE 1.

. . .

PROPERTY AND EQUIPMENT. . . . For financial reporting purposes, we record depreciation and amortization of property and equipment on a straight-line basis over the asset's service life or related lease term, if shorter.

Source: FedEx Corporation

FEDEX CORPORATION
REAL WORLD EXCERPT:
2020 Annual Report

The company reported approximately $3.6 billion in depreciation (annual amount of used cost for property and equipment) and amortization expense (annual amount of used cost for intangible assets) for the year ending May 31, 2020, equal to 5.2 percent of the company's revenues for that year.

Units-of-Production Method

The **units-of-production depreciation** method relates depreciable cost to total estimated productive output or activity level. It can be used for depreciating equipment when production or activity levels vary over time, generating varying amounts of revenue–a good matching of expenses with revenues. The formula to estimate annual depreciation expense under this method is as follows:

Units-of-Production Formula:
(**C**ost − **R**esidual **V**alue)/**Est**imated **total prod**uction (or activity level) units

Unit Rate × **Actual production** or activity level for the period = **Depreciation Expense**

First, divide the depreciable cost (cost minus residual value) by the estimated total production or activity level to determine the depreciation **unit rate.** In our illustration, the delivery vehicle's unit rate is:

(C − RV)	/ Est total prod =	Unit Rate
($62,500 − $2,500)	/ 100,000 miles =	$0.60 per mile Unit Rate

Then multiply the unit rate by the actual production or activity level for the period to determine the period's depreciation expense. Based on the information in Exhibit 8.2, the depreciation schedule for the delivery vehicle under the units-of-production method follows:

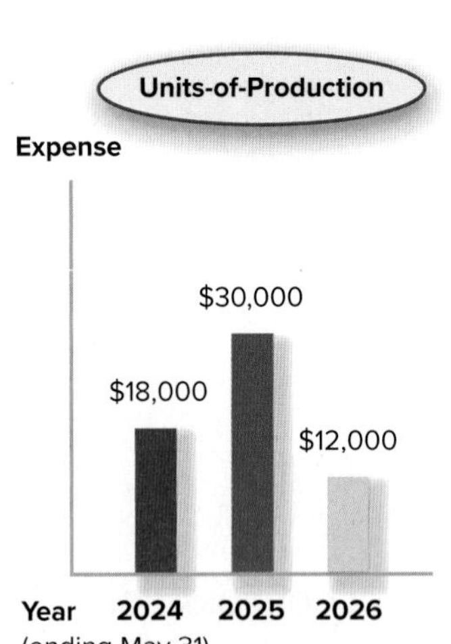

	A	B	C	D	E	F	G	H
1								
2		Units-of-Production Method:				Delivery Van #91-DHH16335PA		
3		(C-RV)/Est. total activity =			Unit Rate			
4		($62,500 - $2,500)/100,000 miles =			$0.60	Depreciation	Accumulated	Net
5			Computation			Expense	Depreciation	Book Value
6		Year ending	Unit Rate x Actual Activity			(for AJE)	(Balance after AJE)	(C-AD)
7		6/1/2023	Cost at acquisition				$0	$62,500
8		5/31/2024	$0.60	x 30,000 miles		$18,000	$18,000	$44,500
9		5/31/2025	$0.60	x 50,000 miles		$30,000	$48,000	$14,500
10		5/31/2026	$0.60	x 20,000 miles		$12,000	$60,000	$2,500
11								
12							Equal to estimated Residual Value at end of useful life	
13								
14								

Microsoft Excel

Notice that, from period to period, depreciation expense, accumulated depreciation, and book value vary directly with the miles of usage. In the units-of-production method, depreciation expense is a **variable expense** because it varies directly with production or use.

Also notice that, the net book value at the end of the vehicle's useful life equals the estimated residual value. You might wonder what happens if the total estimated productive output differs from actual total output. Remember that the estimate is management's best guess of total output. If any difference occurs at the end of the asset's life, the final adjusting entry to depreciation expense should be for the amount needed to bring the asset's net book value equal to the asset's estimated residual value. For example, if, in the year ending May 31, 2026, FedEx's delivery van ran 25,000 actual miles, the same amount of depreciation expense, $12,000, would be recorded.

Although FedEx does not use the units-of-production method, the **Exxon Mobil Corporation**, a major energy company that explores, produces, transports, and sells crude oil and natural gas worldwide, does, as a note to the company's annual report explains:

NOTES TO CONSOLIDATED FINANCIAL STATEMENTS

1. Summary of Accounting Policies

Depreciation, Depletion and Amortization. Depreciation, depletion and amortization are primarily determined under either the unit-of-production method or the straight-line method, which is based on estimated asset service life taking obsolescence into consideration.

Acquisition costs of proved properties are amortized using a unit-of-production method, computed on the basis of total proved oil and gas reserves.

Source: Exxon Mobil Corporation

EXXON MOBIL CORPORATION
REAL WORLD EXCERPT
2019 Annual Report

The units-of-production method is used when activity or production level is the best determinant of life. It is applied most commonly for depreciating and depleting natural resources and related property, based on an estimate of an asset's total future productive capacity or output, which is difficult to determine. This is another example of the degree of subjectivity inherent in accounting.

Declining-Balance Method

If an asset is considered to be more efficient or productive when it is newer, managers might choose the **declining-balance depreciation** method to match a higher depreciation expense with higher revenues in the early years of an asset's life and a lower depreciation expense with lower revenues in the later years. We say, then, that this is an **accelerated depreciation** method. Although accelerated methods are **seldom used for financial reporting purposes,** the method that is used more frequently than others is the declining-balance method.

Declining-balance depreciation is based on applying a rate exceeding the straight-line rate to the asset's net book value over time. The rate is often double (two times) the straight-line rate and is termed the **double-declining-balance rate.** For example, if the straight-line rate is 10 percent (1 ÷ 10 years) for a 10-year estimated useful life, then the declining-balance rate is 20 percent (2 × the straight-line rate). Other typical acceleration rates are 1.5 times and 1.75 times. The double-declining-balance rate is adopted most frequently by companies employing an accelerated method, so we will use it in our illustration, with information from Exhibit 8.2. The formula is:

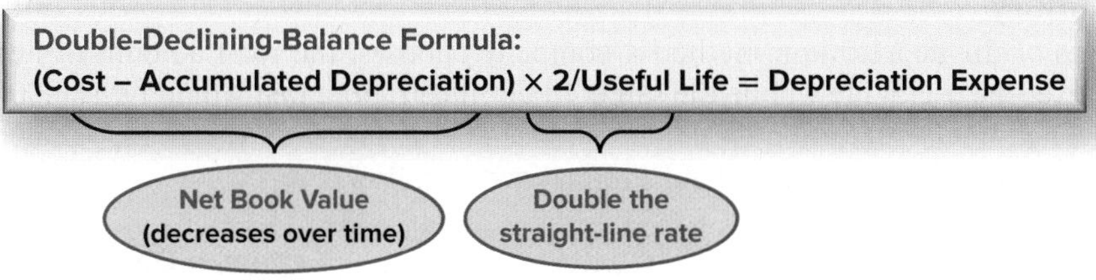

Tip Beware → Unlike the other methods, **this formula calculates depreciation expense into perpetuity—net book value decreases each period, but never reaches $0.** Check each period that the net book value does not drop below residual value!

There are two important differences between this method and the others described previously:

1. Notice that accumulated depreciation, not residual value, is included in the formula. Because accumulated depreciation increases each year, net book value (Cost minus Accumulated Depreciation) decreases. **The double-declining rate is applied to a lower net book value each year, resulting in a decline in depreciation expense over time.**

2. As with the other methods, **the net book value should not be depreciated below the residual value:**
   - Occasionally, before the end of the estimated useful life, if the annual computation reduces net book value below residual value, only the amount of depreciation expense needed to make net book value equal to residual value is recorded, and no additional depreciation expense is computed in subsequent years.
   - More likely, **in the last year of the asset's estimated useful life,** whatever amount is needed to bring net book value to residual value is recorded, regardless of the amount of the computation as shown in the following double-declining-balance depreciation schedule:

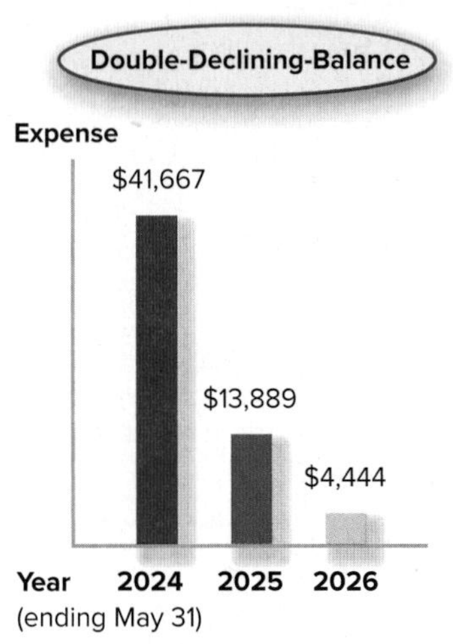

Double-Declining-Balance Method		Delivery Van #91-DHH16335PA		
		Depreciation	Accumulated	Net
Year	Computation	Expense	Depreciation	Book Value
Ending	(C-AD) x 2/UL	(for AJE)	(Balance after AJE)	(C-AD)
6/1/2023	Cost at acquisition		$0	$62,500
5/31/2024	($62,500 - $0) x 2/3	$41,667	$41,667	$20,833
5/31/2025	($62,500 - $41,667) x 2/3	$13,889	$55,556	$6,944
5/31/2026	End of useful life→	$4,444	$60,000	$2,500

3. Set Depreciation Expense equal to depreciable cost (C-RV) minus prior Accumulated Depreciation balance.

2. Set Accumulated Depreciation equal to depreciable cost (C-RV).

1. In the last year of asset's useful life, set Net Book Value equal to Residual Value. Then work backwards.

Microsoft Excel

An asset should never be depreciated below the point at which net book value equals its residual value. In the illustration, the asset owned by FedEx has an estimated residual value of $2,500. Prior to the last year, the net book value remains above $2,500. In the last year of the asset's useful life, regardless of the computation, the correct depreciation expense is the amount that will reduce the net book value to $2,500. To determine the amount to record in fiscal year 2026, work backwards from the net book value column: (1) First, indicate the amount needed for net book value ($2,500 residual value at the end of the asset's useful life); (2) then, determine what the balance in accumulated depreciation should be when fully depreciated ($62,500 cost – $2,500 residual value = $60,000); and (3) finally, compute the amount of depreciation expense necessary to increase the balance in accumulated depreciation to $60,000 ($60,000 balance needed in accumulated depreciation – $55,556 prior balance in accumulated depreciation = $4,444).

In Summary

Regardless of the depreciation method a company chooses, the total amount of depreciation expense over the useful life will be the same. In our illustration, that would be $60,000 for each method. The three depreciation methods, the formula for each, and the pattern of depreciation expense over time for each method are summarized as follows:

Method	Formula	Pattern of Depreciation Expense
Straight-line	(Cost – Residual Value) × 1/Useful Life	Equal amounts each year
Units-of-production	(Cost – Residual Value)/Estimated Total Production = Unit Rate × Annual Production	Varying amounts based on production level
Double-declining-balance	(Cost – Accumulated Depreciation) × 2/Useful Life	Declining amounts over time

FINANCIAL ANALYSIS

Impact of Alternative Depreciation Methods

Assume that you are comparing two companies that are exactly the same, except that one uses accelerated depreciation (declining-balance) and the other uses the straight-line method. Which company would you expect to report a higher net income? Actually, this question is a bit tricky. The answer is that you cannot say for certain which company's income would be higher.

The accelerated methods report higher depreciation and therefore lower net income during the early years of an asset's life. As the age of the asset increases, this effect reverses. Therefore, companies that use accelerated depreciation report lower depreciation expense and higher net income during the later years of an asset's life. The graph illustrates the pattern of depreciation over the life of an asset for the straight-line and declining-balance methods discussed in this chapter. When the curve for the accelerated declining-balance method falls below the line for the straight-line method, the accelerated method produces a higher net income than the straight-line method. However, total depreciation expense by the end of the asset's life is the same for each method.

Users of financial statements must understand the impact of alternative depreciation methods used over time. **Differences in depreciation methods rather than real economic differences can cause significant variation in reported net incomes.**

Summary Depreciation Expense

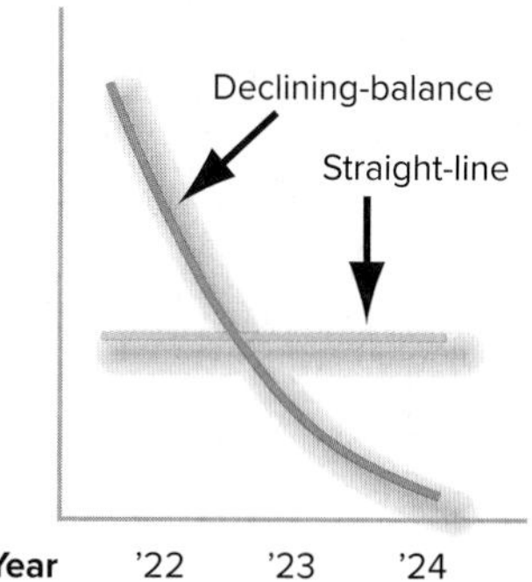

PAUSE FOR FEEDBACK

The three cost allocation methods discussed in this section are:

- Straight-line: (Cost − Residual Value) × 1/Useful Life
- Units-of-production: (Cost − Residual Value)/Estimated Total Production = Unit Rate × Actual Production
- Double-declining-balance: (Cost − Accumulated Depreciation) × 2/Useful Life

Practice these methods using the following information.

SELF-STUDY QUIZ

Assume that **Southwest Airlines** has acquired new computer equipment at a cost of $240,000. The equipment has an estimated life of six years, an estimated operating life of 50,000 hours, and an estimated residual value of $30,000. Determine depreciation expense for the first full year under each of the following methods:

1. Straight-line method.
2. Units-of-production method (assume the equipment ran for 8,000 hours in the first year).
3. Double-declining-balance method.

After you have completed your answers, check them below.

GUIDED HELP 8-2

For additional step-by-step video instruction on using the three cost allocation methods discussed in this section, go to mhhe.com/libby_gh8-2.

Related Homework: M8-4, M8-5, M8-6, E8-4, E8-5, E8-9, E8-10, E8-11, E-14, CON 8-1

Solutions to SELF-STUDY QUIZ

1. ($240,000 − $30,000) × 1/6 = $35,000
2. ($240,000 − $30,000) ÷ 50,000 hours = $4.20 per hour unit rate; $4.20 unit rate × 8,000 actual hours = $33,600
3. ($240,000 − $0) × 2/6 = $80,000

FINANCIAL ANALYSIS

Increased Profitability Due to an Accounting Adjustment? Reading the Notes

Financial analysts are particularly interested in changes in accounting estimates because they can have a large impact on a company's before-tax operating income. In 2017, **United States Steel Corporation** increased the estimated useful life of its machinery and equipment. The change reduced depreciation expense for the year by approximately $106 million and would reduce expenses by a similar amount each year over the remaining life of the assets. Analysts pay close attention to this number because it represents increased profitability due merely to an accounting adjustment.

How Managers Choose

Financial Reporting

For financial reporting purposes, corporate managers must determine which depreciation method provides the best matching of revenues and expenses for any given asset. If the asset is expected to provide benefits evenly over time or no other method is more systematic or rational, then the straight-line method is preferred. Managers also find this method to be easy to use and to explain. Also, during the early years of an asset's life, the straight-line method reports higher income than the accelerated methods do. For these reasons, the straight-line method is, by far and away, the most common.

On the other hand, certain assets produce more revenue in their early lives because they are more efficient than in later years. In this case, managers select an accelerated method to allocate cost.

Tax Reporting

FedEx Corporation, like most public companies, maintains two sets of accounting records. Both sets of records reflect the same transactions, but the transactions are accounted for using two different sets of measurement rules. One set is prepared under GAAP for reporting to stockholders. The other set is prepared to determine the company's tax obligation under the Internal Revenue Code. The reason that the two sets of rules are different is simple: The objectives of GAAP and the Internal Revenue Code differ.

Financial Reporting (GAAP)	Tax Reporting (IRC)
The objective of financial reporting is to provide economic information about a business that is useful in projecting future cash flows of the business. Financial reporting rules follow generally accepted accounting principles.	The objective of the Internal Revenue Code is to raise sufficient revenues to pay for the expenditures of the federal government. Many of the Code's provisions are designed to encourage certain behaviors that are thought to benefit society (e.g., contributions to charities are made tax deductible to encourage people to support worthy programs).

In some cases, differences between the Internal Revenue Code and GAAP leave the manager no choice but to maintain separate records. In other cases, the differences are the result of management choice. When given a choice among acceptable **tax accounting** methods, managers apply what is called the **least and the latest rule.** All taxpayers want to pay the lowest amount of tax that is legally permitted and at the latest possible date. If you had the choice of paying $100,000 to the federal government at the end of this year or at the end of next year, you would choose the end of next year. By doing so, you could invest the money for an extra year and earn a significant return on the investment.

A QUESTION OF ETHICS

Two Sets of Books

When they first learn that companies maintain two sets of books, some people question the ethics or legality of the practice. In reality, **it is both legal and ethical to maintain separate records for tax and financial reporting purposes. However, these records must reflect the same transactions.** Understating revenues or overstating expenses on a tax return can result in financial penalties and/or imprisonment. Accountants who aid tax evaders also can be fined or imprisoned and lose their professional licenses.

Most corporations use the IRS-approved Modified Accelerated Cost Recovery System (MACRS) to calculate depreciation expense for their tax returns, while choosing the straight-line method for financial reporting purposes. MACRS is similar to the declining-balance method and is applied over relatively short asset lives to yield high depreciation expense in the early years. The high depreciation expense reported under MACRS reduces a corporation's taxable income and therefore the amount it must pay in taxes. MACRS provides an incentive for corporations to invest in modern property, plant, and equipment to be competitive in world markets. However, **MACRS is not acceptable for financial reporting purposes.**

By maintaining two sets of books, corporations can defer (delay) paying millions and sometimes billions of dollars in taxes. The following companies reported significant gross deferred tax obligations in their most recent annual reports. Much of these deferrals were due to differences in their choice of asset cost allocation (depreciation) methods:

Company	Deferred Tax Liabilities	Percentage Due to Applying Different Depreciation Methods
FedEx Corporation	$9,120 million	96%
General Motors Company	$2,414 million	69
Amazon.com	$12,478 million	44
Costco Wholesale Corporation	$1,950 million	41

Measuring Asset Impairment

LEARNING OBJECTIVE 8-4

Explain the effect of asset impairment on the financial statements.

As we discussed in Chapter 2, assets are defined as economic resources owned or controlled by a company that have measurable value and are expected to provide benefits to the company by producing cash inflows or reducing cash outflows in the future. On the date of the exchange, an asset is measured at historical cost. Subsequently, corporations must review long-lived tangible and most intangible assets for possible impairment when events or changed circumstances cause the estimated future cash flows of these assets to fall below their book value. The three steps to follow are:

Step 1: Consider whether indicators of impairment are present.

Companies must look for indicators or triggers to decide when to impair assets. Factors include:

- Significant pattern of decline in the market price of the asset
- Lower demand for a medium- to long-term period due to global economic conditions
- Severe change in economic or legal factors affecting the company or its assets (e.g., regulatory or technology changes)
- Obsolescence or physical damage to the asset
- Asset is held for disposal or is part of a restructuring

Tip **Estimating future cash flows** is subjective and requires management to use significant judgment, basing future cash flow projections on reasonable and supportable assumptions for conditions that will exist over the remaining useful life of the asset. External auditors will review the assumptions for reasonableness.

Step 2: Test the recoverability of the long-lived assets.

When indicators of impairment exist, management assesses if the asset's net book value is recoverable through estimated **future cash flows** (i.e., will estimated future cash flows equal or exceed the net book value?). If net book value is recoverable, no impairment exists.

The asset is **impaired if not recoverable** when:

Net book value (NBV) > Estimated future cash flows (FCF)

Step 3: Measure the impairment of the long-lived assets.

For any asset considered to be impaired, companies recognize a loss for the difference between the asset's net book value and its **fair value** (a market concept, usually determined by discounting estimated future cash flows). *Note:* Discounting cash flows will be discussed in Chapter 9. Until then, we will give you the fair value amount.

The impaired asset is **written down** to fair value:

Net book value (NBV) − Fair value (FV) = Impairment loss

A journal entry is made to record the loss due to impairment and reduce the asset. The fair value then becomes the new book value and is not written back up if conditions change in the future.

Asset write-downs increase during tough times. To illustrate measuring impairment losses, Delta Air Lines reported the following in its 2020 10-K report (Note 2). Dollars are in millions:

Step 1 → Indicators: "The unprecedented, widespread and persistent impact of COVID-19 and the related travel restrictions and social distancing measures implemented throughout the world have significantly reduced demand for air travel. . . (T)he spread of the virus and the resulting global pandemic have significantly affected our entire network."

Step 2 → Recoverability: 383 aircraft were affected.

Net book value $4,909 > Estimated future cash flows $900 (assumed)

The assets are **impaired.**

Step 3 → Impairment measurement: The aircraft were retired from service.

Net book value $4,909 − Fair value $500 = **$4,409 impairment loss**

Journal entry to record the impairment loss:

Tip After determining that the indicators suggest asset impairment, the three numbers needed are:

	Debit	**Credit**
Loss due to impairment (+E, −SE)	4,409	
Aircraft (−A)		4,409

Assets		=	**Liabilities**	+	**Stockholders' Equity**	
Aircraft	−4,409				Loss due to impairment (+E)	−4,409

LEARNING OBJECTIVE 8-5

Analyze the disposal of property, plant, and equipment.

Disposal of Property, Plant, and Equipment

In some cases, a business may dispose of an asset **involuntarily,** as the result of a casualty such as a storm, fire, theft, or accident. Often losses for involuntary disposals are covered by insurance. However, more likely, a company may **voluntarily** decide not to hold a long-lived asset for its entire estimated life. For example, the company may drop a product from its line and no longer need the equipment that was used to produce it, or managers may want to replace a machine with a more efficient one. These disposals include sales, trade-ins, and retirements.

Disposals of long-lived assets seldom occur on the last day of the accounting period. Therefore, depreciation must be recorded on the date of disposal for the amount of cost used since the last time depreciation was recorded. Therefore, the disposal of a depreciable asset usually requires **two journal entries:**

1. An entry to update the depreciation expense and accumulated depreciation accounts.
2. An entry to record the disposal. **The cost of the asset and any accumulated depreciation at the date of disposal must be removed from the accounts.** The difference between any resources received on the disposal of an asset and its net book value on the date of disposal is treated as a gain or loss on the disposal of the asset. This gain (or loss) is reported in operations on the income statement.

Assume that at the end of year 17, FedEx sold an aircraft that was no longer needed. The aircraft was sold for $11.0 million cash. The $30.0 million original cost of the cargo plane was depreciated using the straight-line method over 25 years with no residual value ($1.2 million depreciation expense per year). The last accounting for depreciation was at the end of Year 16. The computations of the gain or loss on disposal follows (in millions):

Cash received		$11.0
Original cost of cargo plane	$ 30.0	
Less: Accumulated depreciation ($1.2 million × 17 years)	(20.4)	
Less: Net book value at date of sale		(9.6)
Gain on sale of cargo plane		$ 1.4

The entries and effects of the transaction on the date of the sale are as follows (dollars in millions):

1. Update depreciation expense for Year 17:

	Debit	Credit
Depreciation expense (+E, −SE)	1.2	
Accumulated depreciation (+XA, −A)		1.2

2. Record the sale:

	Debit	Credit
Cash (+A)	11.0	
Accumulated depreciation (−XA, +A)	20.4	
Aircraft (−A)		30.0
Gain on sale of assets (+R, +SE)		1.4

Assets		= Liabilities +	Stockholders' Equity	
(1) Accumulated depreciation (+XA)	−1.2		Depreciation expense (+E)	−1.2
(2) Cash	+11.0		Gain on sale of asset (+R)	+1.4
Aircraft	−30.0			
Accumulated depreciation (−XA)	+20.4			

PAUSE FOR FEEDBACK

We learned that, when disposing of an operational asset, you must first record depreciation expense for usage of the asset since the last time it was recorded. Then eliminate the asset at cost and its related accumulated depreciation. The difference between the cash received, if any, and the net book value of the asset is either a gain or loss on disposal.

SELF-STUDY QUIZ

Now let's assume the same facts as illustrated in the example above except that the asset was sold for $2.0 million cash.

Required:

1. Prepare the two entries on the date of the sale:
   (a) Update depreciation expense for Year 17.
   (b) Record the sale.
2. Show the effects on the accounting equation.

	Assets	=	Liabilities	+	Stockholders' Equity
(1)					
(2)					

After you have completed your answers, check them below.

GUIDED HELP 8-3

For additional step-by-step video instruction on recording a disposal of an asset, go to mhhe.com/libby_gh8-3.

Related Homework: M8-8, E8-15, E8-16, E8-17, E8-18, P8-5

LEARNING OBJECTIVE 8-6

Apply measurement and reporting concepts for intangible assets and natural resources.

INTANGIBLE ASSETS AND NATURAL RESOURCES

Acquisition and Amortization of Intangible Assets

Intangible assets are increasingly important resources for organizations. An intangible asset, like any other asset, has value because of certain rights and privileges often conferred by law on its owner. Unlike tangible assets such as land and buildings, however, an intangible asset has no material or physical substance. Instead, the majority of intangible assets usually are evidenced by a legal document. The most common types of intangible assets are the following:

- Goodwill (recognized in a business merger or acquisition).
- Trademarks.
- Copyrights.
- Technology (computer software and website).

Solutions to SELF-STUDY QUIZ

(a)	Depreciation expense (+E, −SE)	1.2	
	Accumulated Depreciation (+XA, −A)		1.2
(b)	Cash (+A)	2.0	
	Accumulated depreciation (−XA, +A)	20.4	
	Loss on sale of assets (+E, −SE)	7.6	
	Aircraft (−A)		30.0

Assets		=	Liabilities	+	Stockholders' Equity	
(a) Accumulated depreciation (+XA)	−1.2				Depreciation expense (+E)	−1.2
(b) Aircraft	−30.0				Loss on sale of asset (+E)	−7.6
Accumulated depreciation (−XA)	+20.4					
Cash	+2.0					

- Patents.
- Franchises.
- Licenses and operating rights.
- Others, including customer lists/relationships, noncompete covenants, and contracts and agreements.

As reported by FedEx in its 2020 10-K report, "Intangible assets primarily include customer relationships, technology assets and trademarks acquired in business combinations."

Accounting for intangible assets has become increasingly important due to the tremendous expansion in computer information systems, Web technologies, intellectual property development, and the frenzy in companies purchasing other companies at high prices, with the expectation that these intangible resources will provide significant future benefits to the company. Intangible assets are recorded **at historical cost only if they have been purchased.** If these assets are developed internally by the company, they are expensed when incurred.

Upon acquisition of intangible assets, managers determine whether the separate intangibles have definite or indefinite lives:

- **Definite Life.** The cost of an intangible asset with a definite life is allocated on a **straight-line basis** each period over its useful life in a process called amortization that is similar to depreciation. Most companies do not estimate a residual value for their intangible assets because they are expected to be used by the company, not sold to others. Amortization expense is included on the income statement each period, and the intangible assets are reported at cost less accumulated amortization on the balance sheet.

  Let's assume a company purchases a patent for $800,000 and intends to use it for 20 years (its legal life). The adjusting entry to record $40,000 in amortization expense ($800,000 ÷ 20 years) is as follows:

	Debit	Credit
Amortization expense (+E, −SE)	40,000	
Patents (−A)[1]		40,000

Assets		=	Liabilities	+	Stockholders' Equity	
Patents	−40,000				Amortization expense (+E)	−40,000

- **Indefinite Life.** Intangible assets with indefinite lives are **not amortized.** Instead, these assets **must be reviewed at least annually for possible impairment** of value by first using qualitative factors to determine whether it is more likely than not (i.e., it is greater than a 50 percent likelihood) that the fair value of the indefinite-life intangible is less than its carrying amount. Qualitative factors can include, for example, negative effects due to increases in costs, decreases in cash flows beyond expectations, an economic downturn, or deterioration in the industry. If it is more likely, then the company must perform a quantitative test to determine the amount of the impairment loss, which is the difference between the net book value and the fair value.

Goodwill

The term *goodwill,* as used by most business people, means the favorable reputation that a company has with its customers. Goodwill arises from factors such as customer confidence, reputation for good service or quality goods, location, outstanding management team, and financial standing. From its first day of operations, a successful business continually builds goodwill. In this context, the goodwill is said to be **internally generated** and **is not reported as an asset** (i.e., it was not purchased).

[1]Consistent with the procedure for recording depreciation, an accumulated amortization account may be used. In practice, however, most companies credit the asset account directly for periodic amortization. This procedure is also typically used for natural resources, which are discussed in the next section.

Tip Remember – **Goodwill** is only recorded as **an asset when it is purchased.**

By far, the most frequently reported intangible asset is goodwill (cost in excess of net assets acquired). **The only way to record and report goodwill as an asset is to purchase another business.** Often the purchase price of the business exceeds the fair value of all of its net assets (assets minus liabilities). Why would a company pay more for a business as a whole than it would pay if it bought the assets individually? The answer is to obtain its goodwill. You easily could buy modern bottling equipment to produce and sell a new cola drink, but you would not make as much money as you would if you acquired the goodwill associated with Coke or Pepsi brand names.

For accounting purposes, goodwill is defined as the difference between the purchase price of a company as a whole and the fair value of its net assets (assets minus liabilities) that are identifiable. For example, in 2019, **Salesforce.com, Inc.** (a leading provider of cloud-delivered enterprise software focusing on customer relationship management) bought **Tableau Software, Inc.** (an analytics platform enabling users to easily access, prepare, analyze, and present findings of their data). The total purchase price that Salesforce.com agreed to pay ($14,845 million) exceeded the fair value of Tableau's net assets ($4,039 million). As shown below, Salesforce paid the extra $10,806 million to acquire goodwill associated with Tableau's business.

Salesforce.com's Purchase of Tableau Software	In Millions
Purchase price	**$14,845**
Less: Fair value of purchased assets and assumed liabilities:	
Current assets	1,274
Operating lease right-of-use assets and other assets	664
Intangible assets (identifiable technology, customer relationships, and other)	3,252
Liabilities	(1,151)
Net assets, at fair value	**4,039**
Goodwill	**$10,806**

In many acquisitions, the amount recorded as Goodwill can be very large. For example, **Cisco Systems**, which designs, manufactures, and sells Internet-based networking and other products and services, has a long-term strategy of growth by acquisition, spending $14.2 billion buying companies just between July 2015 and January 2021 alone. Of the nearly $14.2 billion total cost of these acquisitions, $10.5 billion was recorded as Goodwill. That represents over 30 percent of the $34.7 billion in Goodwill reported on Cisco's January 23, 2021 quarterly balance sheet and the largest asset reported out of $95.6 billion in total assets.

Goodwill is considered to have an indefinite life and, as described in the previous section, must be tested for possible impairment for indefinite-life intangibles. Cisco reported the following policy:

CISCO SYSTEMS, INC.
REAL WORLD EXCERPT:
2020 Annual Report

2. Summary of Significant Accounting Policies

Goodwill and Purchased Intangible Assets

Goodwill is tested for impairment on an annual basis in the fourth fiscal quarter and, when specific circumstances dictate, between annual tests. When impaired, the carrying value of goodwill is written down to fair value.

Source: Cisco Systems, Inc.

Trademarks

A trademark is a special name, image, or slogan identified with a product or a company; it is protected by law. Trademarks are among the most valuable assets a company can own. For example, most of us cannot imagine **The Walt Disney Company** without Mickey Mouse. Similarly, you probably enjoy your favorite soft drink more because of the image that has been built up around its name than because of its taste. Many people can identify the shape of a corporate logo as quickly as they can recognize the shape of a stop sign. Although trademarks are valuable assets, they are rarely seen on balance sheets. The reason is simple: Intangible assets are not recorded unless they are purchased. Companies often spend millions of dollars developing trademarks, but most of those expenditures are recorded as expenses rather than being capitalized as an intangible asset.

D. Hurst/Alamy Stock Photo

Copyrights

A copyright gives the owner the exclusive right to publish, use, and sell a literary, musical, or artistic piece for a period not exceeding 70 years after the author's death.[2] The book you are reading has a copyright to protect the publisher and authors. It is against the law, for example, for an instructor to copy several chapters from this book and hand them out in class. A copyright that is purchased is recorded at cost.

Technology

The number of companies reporting a technology intangible asset continues to rise, with website and computer software development costs becoming increasingly significant. For website development, costs related to acquiring a domain name and developing graphics are capitalized as an intangible asset. For computer software, any costs incurred during the preliminary concept phase of a software project should be expensed. Once the software project reaches "technological feasibility" (the point at which there is a detailed program design or completion of a working model), the direct costs of the actual development, such as coding and testing the software, should be capitalized as an intangible asset.

If the software is obtained or developed for **internal use** by the company, the intangible asset is amortized usually over a short useful life with the amortization reported on the income statement as a general expense. For projects that produce a software **product that is to be sold, leased, or marketed** to customers, the amortization expense is included as a part of the cost of sales. Annually, if the unamortized cost of the software product is higher than the product's net realizable value (the selling price of the product less the selling costs related to its completion and disposal), the intangible asset is written down to the net realizable value.

At December 31, 2019, **IBM Corporation** reported $15,235 million in intangible assets, including completed technology and capitalized software. Together with $58,222 million in goodwill, total intangible assets account for over 48 percent of IBM's total assets:

Intangible assets:	**In millions**
Client relationships	$ 7,488
Completed technology	4,861
Patents/trademarks	1,856
Capitalized software	1,006
Other	24
	$ 15,235
Goodwill	$58,222

Source: International Business Machines Corporation

[2]In general, the limit is 70 years beyond the death of an author. For anonymous authors, the limit is 95 years from the first publication date. For more detail, go to copyright.gov.

IBM disclosed the following accounting policies for its technology assets:

INTERNATIONAL BUSINESS MACHINES CORPORATION
REAL WORLD EXCERPT:
2019 Annual Report

Note A.
SIGNIFICANT ACCOUNTING POLICIES
Software Costs

Costs that are related to the conceptual formulation and design of licensed software programs are expensed as incurred to research, development and engineering expense; costs that are incurred to produce the finished product after technological feasibility has been established are capitalized as an intangible asset. Capitalized amounts are amortized on a straight-line basis over periods ranging up to three years and are recorded in software cost within cost of sales. The company performs periodic reviews to ensure that unamortized program costs remain recoverable from future revenue.

The company capitalizes certain costs that are incurred to purchase or develop internal-use software. Capitalized costs are amortized on a straight-line basis over periods ranging up to three years and are recorded in selling, general and administrative expense or cost of sales.

Source: International Business Machines Corporation

Tip **Do not capitalize research and development expenses—R & D is NOT an intangible asset.**

Note in the IBM excerpt above that costs of "formulation and design of licensed software programs are **expensed** as incurred to research, development and engineering expense." If an intangible asset is developed internally, the cost of development normally is recorded as **research and development expense. Research and development costs are not capitalized** as an intangible asset under U.S. GAAP due to too much uncertainty as to future benefits. For example, one of the top ten global research-based biopharmaceutical companies is **Gilead Sciences**, which focuses on discovering, developing, and commercializing innovative medicines primarily for HIV/AIDS, liver, blood, cancer, inflammation, and respiratory diseases. Gilead Sciences recently reported it spent about $9.1 billion annually on research to discover new products. These amounts were reported as expenses on the income statement, not assets, because research and development expenditures typically do not possess sufficient probability of resulting in measurable future cash flows. If Gilead Sciences had spent an equivalent amount to purchase patents for new products from other drug companies, it would have recorded the expenditures as assets.

Patents

A patent is an exclusive right granted by the federal government for a period of 20 years, typically granted to the inventor of a new product or process.[3] The patent enables the owner to use, manufacture, and sell both the subject of the patent and the patent itself. It prevents a competitor from simply copying a new invention or discovery until the inventor has had time to earn an economic return on the new product. Without the protection of a patent, inventors likely would be unwilling to search for new products. Patents are recorded at their purchase price or, if **developed internally,** at only their registration and legal costs because GAAP requires the immediate expensing of research and development costs.

Franchises

Franchises may be granted by the government or a business for a specified period and purpose. A city may grant one company a franchise to distribute gas to homes for heating purposes, or

[3]For more details, go to uspto.gov/patents-getting-started/general-information-concerning-patents #heading-3.

a company may sell franchises, such as the right to operate a **KFC** restaurant (owned by **Yum! Brands**). Franchise agreements are contracts that can have a variety of provisions. They usually require an investment by the franchisee; therefore, they should be accounted for as intangible assets by the franchisee. The life of the franchise agreement depends on the contract. It may be a single year or an indefinite period. For example, as of December 29, 2019, **Papa John's International**, a franchisor, had 5,395 stores around the world, and about 89 percent were franchises. The franchise agreement covers a 10-year term that is renewable. In the United States, to obtain a new Papa John's franchise, an eligible franchisee pays an initial franchise fee of $5,000 to Papa John's. This amount is then recorded by the franchisee as an intangible asset. The franchise agreement also requires that monthly payments of 5 percent of net sales at each franchise be remitted to Papa John's and that at least 8 percent of net sales be spent monthly for marketing purposes (for national and/or local initiatives).

Licenses and Operating Rights

There are many types of **licenses and operating rights**, such as permission for companies to use airwaves for radio and television broadcasts or land for cable and telephone lines. For passenger and cargo airlines, a landing/takeoff slot pair (for use during a specified time period at a certain airport) is permission granted to an airline by the airport operator and authorized by the International Air Transport Association (IATA) worldwide and the Federal Aviation Administration (FAA) in the United States.

Landing slots at airports, especially those that are congested, are extremely valuable. The airline must use the slots to keep them. In June 2020, the agencies approved the transfer of one slot to FedEx for the Hong Kong–Singapore route when **UPS** decided to give up its landing slots. Airlines can also sell slots to each other. The highest price paid to-date for a slot pair was $75 million by **Oman Air** to **Air France/KLM** for the right to land at and take off from Heathrow Airport in London during peak hours. In a recent annual report, **Delta Air Lines** reported over $3.2 billion in international and domestic landing slots, classifying them as intangible assets with indefinite lives.

Acquisition and Depletion of Natural Resources

You are probably most familiar with large companies that are involved in manufacturing (**Ford Motor Company, Stanley Black & Decker**), distribution (**Macy's, Home Depot**), or services (**Marriott International, United Parcel Service**). A number of large companies, some of which are less well known, develop raw materials and products from **natural resources**, including mineral deposits such as gold or iron ore, oil wells, and timber tracts. These resources often are called **wasting assets** because they are **depleted** (i.e., physically used up). Companies that develop natural resources are critical to the economy because they produce essential items such as lumber for construction, fuel for heating and transportation, and food for consumption. Because of the significant effect they can have on the environment, these companies attract considerable public attention. Concerned citizens often read the financial statements of companies involved in the exploration for oil, coal, and various ores to determine the amount of money they spend to protect the environment.

When natural resources are acquired or developed, they are recorded using the **cost principle.** As a natural resource is used up, its acquisition cost must be apportioned among the periods in which revenues are earned in conformity with the **expense recognition principle.** The term **depletion** describes the process of allocating a natural resource's cost over the period of its exploitation.[4] The units-of-production method often is applied to compute depletion.

When a natural resource such as a timber tract is depleted, the company obtains inventory (timber). Because depleting the natural resource is necessary to obtain the inventory, the depletion computed during a period is not expensed immediately but is **capitalized** as part of the cost

[4]Consistent with the procedure for recording depreciation, an accumulated depletion account may be used. In practice, however, most companies credit the asset account directly for periodic depletion.

of the inventory. Only when the inventory is sold does the company record an expense (Cost of Sales). Consider the following illustration:

A timber tract costing $530,000 is depleted over its estimated cutting period based on a "cutting" rate of approximately 20 percent per year as in the following entry. Note that the amount of the natural resource that is depleted is capitalized as inventory, not expensed. When the inventory is sold, the cost of goods sold will be included as an expense on the income statement.

	Debit	Credit
Inventory (+A)	106,000	
Timber tract (−A)		106,000

Assets		=	Liabilities	+	Stockholders' Equity
Inventory	+106,000				
Timber tract	−106,000				

International Paper Company is a global producer of renewable fiber-based packaging, pulp, and paper products. The company owns, manages, or has harvesting rights to approximately 314,000 acres of forests in Brazil and Russia. Its December 31, 2020, balance sheet lists Forestlands of $311 million as an important natural resource. As the timber is harvested, it is recorded as Inventory, consisting of raw materials and finished pulp, paper, and packaging of $2,050 million at the end of 2020.

FOCUS ON CASH FLOWS

LEARNING OBJECTIVE 8-7

Explain how the acquisition, use, and disposal of long-lived assets impact cash flows.

Productive Long-lived Assets, Depreciation, and Amortization

EFFECT ON STATEMENT OF CASH FLOWS

The indirect method for preparing the operating activities section of the statement of cash flows (discussed in Chapter 12) involves reconciling net income on the accrual basis (reported on the income statement) to cash flows from operations. This means that, among other adjustments, (1) revenues and expenses that do not involve cash and (2) gains and losses that relate to investing or financing activities (not operations) should be eliminated.

When depreciation is recorded, no cash payment is made (i.e., there is no credit to Cash). Because depreciation expense (a noncash expense) is subtracted in calculating net income on the income statement, it must be added back to net income to eliminate its effect. Likewise, because any gain (or loss) on the sale of long-lived assets (an investing activity) is added (or subtracted) to determine net income, it must be subtracted from (or added to) net income to eliminate its effect.

In General The acquisition, sale, depreciation, and amortization of long-term assets are reflected on a company's cash flow statement as indicated in the following table:

	Effect on Cash Flows
Operating activities (indirect method)	
Net income	$xxx
Adjusted for:	
Depreciation and amortization expense	+
Gains on sale of long-lived assets	−
Losses on sale of long-lived assets	+
Losses due to asset impairment write-downs	+
Investing activities	
Purchase of long-lived assets	−
Sale of long-lived assets	+

Focus Company Analysis The following is a condensed version of **FedEx**'s statement of cash flows for the year ended May 31, 2020. Buying and selling long-lived assets are investing activities (i.e., the company is growing or shrinking itself). FedEx used $5,868 million in cash to purchase property and equipment. FedEx's cash flow statement also listed $22 million in cash received from selling property and equipment during the year. **Note:** Selling long-lived assets is not an operating activity. Therefore, any gains (losses) on sales of long-term assets that were included in net income must be deducted from (added to) net income in the operating section to eliminate the effect of the sale. Unless they are large, these gain and loss adjustments normally are not specifically highlighted on the statement of cash flows. FedEx did not list any gains or losses as adjustments on the May 31, 2020, statement of cash flows.

In capital-intensive industries such as airlines, cargo delivery companies, hotels, and automobile manufacturing companies, depreciation and amortization expenses are each a significant noncash expense. In FedEx's case, depreciation and amortization expense is usually the single largest adjustment to net income in determining cash flows from operations. For example, the adjustment for depreciation and amortization expense shown below was 71 percent of operating net cash flows of $5,097 million.

FEDEX CORPORATION
Consolidated Statement of Cash Flows (partial)
For the Year Ended May 31, 2020

(In millions)

Cash Flows from Operating Activities:	
Net income	$1,286
Adjustments to reconcile net income to cash provided by operating activities:	
Depreciation and amortization	3,615
Other (*summarized*)	196
Net cash provided by (used in) operating activities	5,097
Cash Flows from Investing Activities:	
Capital expenditures (*purchases of property and equipment*)	(5,868)
Proceeds from asset dispositions and other	22
Net cash used in investing activities	(5,846)

Source: FedEx Corporation

FINANCIAL ANALYSIS

A Misinterpretation

Some analysts misinterpret the meaning of a noncash expense, saying that "cash is provided by depreciation." Although depreciation is added in the operating section of the statement of cash flows, **depreciation is not a source of cash.** Cash from operations can be provided only by selling goods and services. A company with a large amount of depreciation expense does not generate more cash compared with a company that reports a small amount of depreciation expense, assuming that they are exactly the same in every other respect. While depreciation expense reduces the amount of reported net income for a company, it does not reduce the amount of cash generated by the company because it is a noncash expense. Remember that the effects of recording depreciation are a reduction in stockholders' equity and a reduction in fixed assets, not in cash. That is why, on the statement of cash flows, depreciation expense is added back to net income on an accrual basis to compute cash flows from operations (on a cash basis).

Although depreciation is a noncash expense, the **depreciation for tax purposes can affect a company's cash flows.** Depreciation is a deductible expense for income tax purposes. The higher the amount of depreciation recorded by a company for tax purposes, the lower the company's taxable income and the taxes it must pay. Because taxes must be paid in cash, a reduction in a company's results reduces the company's cash outflows (i.e., lower net income leads to lower tax payments).

DEMONSTRATION CASE A

(Resolve the requirements before proceeding to the suggested solution that follows.) Diversified Industries started as a residential construction company. In recent years, it has expanded into heavy construction, ready-mix concrete, construction supplies, and earth-moving services. Assume the company completed the following transactions during 2023. Amounts have been simplified.

2023

Jan. 1	The management acquired a 10-year-old building for $775,000 and the land on which it was situated for $130,000. It paid $180,000 in cash and signed a mortgage note payable for the rest.
Jan. 12	Paid $38,000 in renovation costs on the building prior to use.
July 10	Paid $4,200 for ordinary repairs on the building.
Dec. 31	Year-end adjustments:

a. The building will be depreciated on a straight-line basis over an estimated useful life of 30 years. The estimated residual value is $33,000.

b. Diversified purchased another company several years ago at $100,000 over the fair value of the net assets acquired. The goodwill has an indefinite life.

c. At the beginning of the year, the company owned equipment with a cost of $650,000 and accumulated depreciation of $150,000. The equipment is being depreciated using the double-declining-balance method, with a useful life of 20 years and no residual value.

d. At year-end, the company tested its long-lived assets for possible impairment of their value. It identified a piece of old excavation equipment with a cost of $156,000 and remaining book value of $120,000. Due to its smaller size and lack of safety features, the old equipment has limited use. The future cash flows are expected to be $40,000 and the fair value is determined to be $35,000. No other assets including goodwill were found to be impaired.

December 31 is the end of Diversified's annual accounting period.

Required:

1. Indicate the accounts affected and the amount and direction (+ for increase and – for decrease) of the effect of each of the preceding events (Jan. 1, Jan. 12, July 10, and adjustments *a* through *d*) on the financial statement categories at the end of the year. Use the following headings:

Date	Assets	=	Liabilities	+	Stockholders' Equity

2. Record the December 31, 2023, adjusting journal entries (*a*) and (*c*) only.
3. Show the December 31, 2023, balance sheet classification and amount reported for each of the following items:

   Fixed assets–land, building, and equipment

   Intangible asset–goodwill
4. Assuming that the company had operating revenues of $1,000,000 for the year and a net book value of $500,000 for fixed assets at the beginning of the year, compute the fixed asset turnover ratio. Round your answer to two decimal places. Explain its meaning.

SUGGESTED SOLUTION

1. Effects of events (with computations):

Date		Assets		=	Liabilities		+	Stockholders' Equity	
Jan. 1		Cash	−180,000		Note payable	+725,000			
		Land	+130,000						
		Building	+775,000						
Jan. 12	(1)	Cash	−38,000						
		Building	+38,000						
July 10	(2)	Cash	−4,200					Repairs expense (+E)	−4,200
Dec. 31 *a*	(3)	Accumulated depreciation (+XA)	−26,000					Depreciation expense (+E)	−26,000
Dec. 31 *b*	(4)	No entry							
Dec. 31 *c*	(5)	Accumulated depreciation (+XA)	−50,000					Depreciation expense (+E)	−50,000
Dec. 31 *d*	(6)	Equipment	−85,000					Loss due to impairment (+E)	−85,000

(1) Capitalize the $38,000 expenditure because it is necessary to prepare the asset for use.

(2) This is an ordinary repair and should be expensed.

(3)

Cost of Building		Straight-Line Depreciation
Initial purchase price	$775,000	($813,000 cost − $33,000 residual value) ×
Renovations prior to use	38,000	1/30 years = **$26,000** annual depreciation
Acquisition cost	$813,000	

(4) Goodwill has an indefinite life and is therefore not amortized. We will test for impairment later.

(5) **Double-declining-balance depreciation**
($650,000 cost − $150,000 accumulated depreciation) × 2/20 years = **$50,000** depreciation for 2023.

(6) **Asset impairment**
Impairment Test: The book value of old equipment, $120,000, exceeds expected future cash flows, $40,000. The asset is impaired.

Impairment Loss	
Book value	$120,000
Less: Fair value	−35,000
Loss due to impairment	$ 85,000

2. Adjusting entries at December 31, 2023:

		Debit	Credit
a.	Depreciation expense (+E, −SE)	26,000	
	Accumulated depreciation (+XA, −A)		26,000
c.	Depreciation expense (+E, −SE)	50,000	
	Accumulated depreciation (+XA, −A)		50,000

3. Partial balance sheet, December 31, 2023:

	Assets		
	Fixed assets		
	Land		$ 130,000
	Building	$813,000	
	Less: Accumulated depreciation	26,000	787,000
$650,000 – $85,000 →	Equipment	565,000	
$150,000 + $50,000 →	Less: Accumulated depreciation	200,000	365,000
	Total fixed assets		1,282,000
	Intangible asset		
	Goodwill		100,000

4. Fixed asset turnover ratio:

$$\frac{\textbf{Operating Revenues (Net Sales)}}{\textbf{(Beginning Net Fixed Asset Balance + Ending Net Fixed Asset Balance)} \div 2} = \frac{\textbf{\$1,000,000}}{\textbf{(\$500,000 + \$1,282,000)} \div 2} = \textbf{1.12}$$

This construction company is capital intensive. The fixed asset turnover ratio measures the company's efficiency at using its investment in property, plant, and equipment to generate sales. For 2023, Diversified generated $1.12 in operating revenues for every dollar of total net fixed assets.

DEMONSTRATION CASE B

In 2024, Diversified Industries, a residential construction company, acquired a gravel pit (designated Gravel Pit #1) to support its construction operations. The company completed the following transactions during 2024 related to the gravel pit. Amounts have been simplified and the company's fiscal year ends on December 31.

June 19 Bought Gravel Pit #1 for $50,000 cash. It was estimated that 100,000 cubic yards of gravel could be removed.

Aug. 1 Paid $10,000 for costs of preparing the new gravel pit for exploitation.

Nov. 10 12,000 cubic yards of gravel were removed from Gravel Pit #1 to be used or sold in 2025.

Required:

Record the June 19, August 1, and November 10 transactions.

SUGGESTED SOLUTION

		Debit	Credit
June 19	Gravel pit #1 (+A)	50,000	
	Cash (−A)		50,000
Aug. 1	Gravel pit #1 (+A)	10,000	
	Cash (−A)		10,000
Nov. 10*	Gravel inventory (+A)	7,200	
	Gravel pit #1 (−A)		7,200

* **Cost of Gravel Pit**

Initial purchase price	$50,000
Preparation costs	10,000
Total cost	$60,000

Units-of-Production Depletion

Depletion Rate: $60,000 cost ÷ 100,000 estimated production = $0.60 per unit

Depletion Expense: $0.60 per unit × 12,000 actual production = $7,200.

Capitalize the depletion expense to gravel inventory.

Chapter Supplement

Changes in Depreciation Estimates

Depreciation is computed using two estimates: useful life and residual value. These estimates are made at the time a depreciable asset is acquired. As experience with the asset accumulates, one or both of these initial estimates may need to be revised. In addition, any improvements that extend the asset's useful life may be added to the original acquisition cost at some time during the asset's use. When it is clear that either estimate should be revised to a material degree or that the asset's cost has changed, the undepreciated asset balance (less any residual value at that date) should be apportioned **over the remaining estimated life** from the current year into the future. This is called a prospective **change in estimate.**

To compute the new depreciation expense due to a change in estimate for any of the depreciation methods described here, substitute the net book value for the original acquisition cost, the new residual value for the original amount, and the estimated remaining life in place of the original estimated life. An illustration using the straight-line method follows.

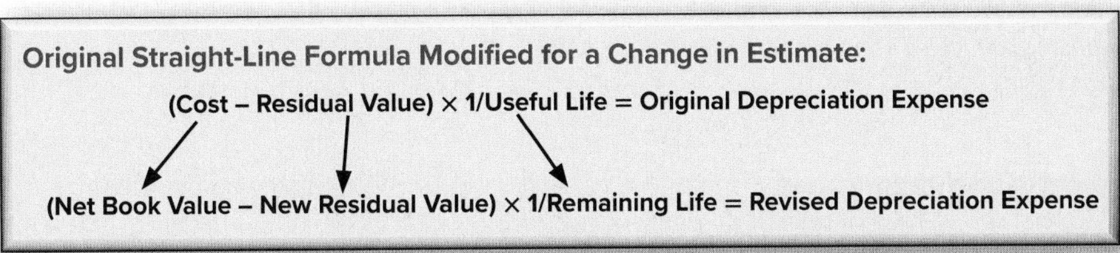

Assume **FedEx** purchased an aircraft for $60,000,000 with an estimated useful life of 20 years and estimated residual value of $3,000,000. Shortly after the start of Year 5, FedEx changed the initial estimated life to 25 years and lowered the estimated residual value to $2,400,000. At the end of Year 5, the computation of the new amount for depreciation expense is as follows:

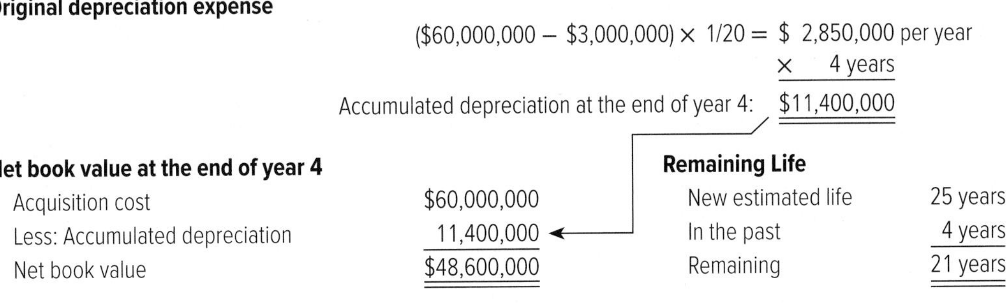

Original depreciation expense

($60,000,000 − $3,000,000) × 1/20 =	$ 2,850,000 per year
	× 4 years
Accumulated depreciation at the end of year 4:	$11,400,000

Net book value at the end of year 4		**Remaining Life**	
Acquisition cost	$60,000,000	New estimated life	25 years
Less: Accumulated depreciation	11,400,000	In the past	4 years
Net book value	$48,600,000	Remaining	21 years

Depreciation in years 5 through 25 based on changes in estimates

(Net Book Value − New Residual Value) × 1/Remaining Years = New Depreciation Expense

($48,600,000 − $2,400,000) × 1/21 years = $2,200,000 per year

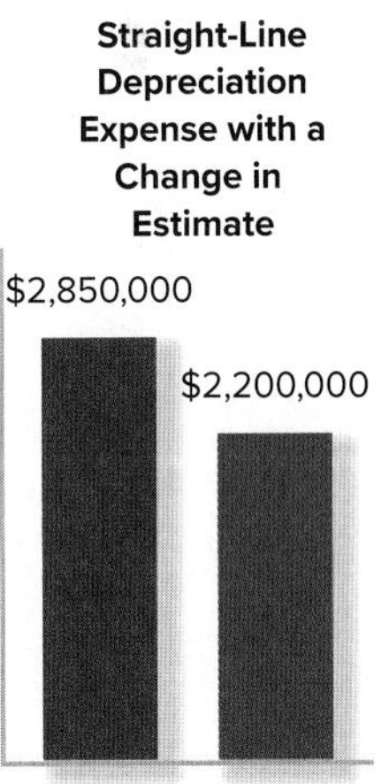

Companies also may change depreciation methods (e.g., from declining balance to straight line). Such a change requires significantly more disclosure because it violates the consistency principle, which requires that accounting information reported in the financial statements should be comparable across accounting periods. Under GAAP, changes in accounting estimates and depreciation methods should be made only when a new estimate or accounting method "better measures" the periodic income of the business.

PAUSE FOR FEEDBACK

When management changes an estimate used in a depreciation computation, the net book value at the time of the change minus any expected residual value is allocated over the remaining useful life of the asset to the company.

SELF-STUDY QUIZ

Assume that **FedEx** owned a delivery truck that originally cost \$100,000. When purchased at the beginning of 2019, the truck had an estimated useful life of 10 years with no residual value. At the beginning of 2024, after operating the truck for five years, FedEx determined that the remaining life was only two more years. FedEx uses the straight-line method.

1. What is the truck's net book value at the beginning of 2024?
2. Based on this change in estimate, what amount of depreciation should be recorded each year over the remaining life of the asset?

After you have completed your answers, check them below.

CHAPTER TAKE-AWAYS

8-1. Define, classify, and explain the nature of long-lived productive assets and interpret the fixed asset turnover ratio. p. 402

a. Productive assets are those that a business retains for long periods of time for use in the course of normal operations rather than for sale. They may be divided into tangible assets (land, buildings, equipment, natural resources) and intangible assets (including goodwill, patents, and franchises).

b. The cost allocation method utilized affects the amount of net property, plant, and equipment that is used in the computation of the fixed asset turnover ratio. Accelerated methods reduce book value and increase the turnover ratio.

8-2. Apply the cost principle to measure the acquisition and maintenance of property, plant, and equipment. p. 404

The acquisition cost of property, plant, and equipment is the cash-equivalent purchase price plus all reasonable and necessary expenditures made to acquire and prepare the asset for its intended use. These assets may be acquired using cash, debt, or stock or through self-construction. Expenditures made after the asset is in use are either additions and improvements or ordinary repairs (expenses):

a. **Ordinary repairs and maintenance** provide benefits during the current accounting period only. Amounts are debited to appropriate current expense accounts when the expenses are incurred.

b. **Improvements** provide benefits for one or more accounting periods beyond the current period. Amounts are debited to the appropriate asset accounts (they are capitalized) and depreciated, depleted, or amortized over their useful lives.

8-3. Apply various cost allocation methods as assets are held and used over time. p. 411

Cost allocation methods: In conformity with the expense matching principle, cost less any estimated residual value is allocated to expense over the periods benefited. Because of depreciation, the net book value of an asset declines over time and net income is reduced by the amount of the expense.

Solutions to SELF-STUDY QUIZ

1. (Cost \$100,000 − Residual Value \$0) × 1/10 = \$10,000 Original Annual Depreciation
   \$10,000 Annual Depreciation Expense × 5 Years = \$50,000 Accumulated Depreciation
   Net Book Value After 5 Years = Cost \$100,000 − Accumulated Depreciation \$50,000 = \$50,000
2. (Net Book Value \$50,000 − Residual Value \$0) × 1/2 (2-year remaining life) = \$25,000 Depreciation Expense per Year

Common depreciation methods include straight-line (a constant amount over time), units-of-production (a variable amount over time), and double-declining-balance (a decreasing amount over time).

a. Depreciation–buildings and equipment.
b. Amortization–intangibles.
c. Depletion–natural resources.

8-4. Explain the effect of asset impairment on the financial statements. p. 421

When events or changes in circumstances reduce the estimated future cash flows of long-lived assets below their book value, the book values should be written down (by recording a loss) to the fair value of the assets.

8-5. Analyze the disposal of property, plant, and equipment. p. 422

When assets are disposed of through sale or abandonment,

a. Record additional depreciation since the last adjustment was made.
b. Remove the cost of the old asset and its related accumulated depreciation, depletion, or amortization.
c. Recognize the cash proceeds.
d. Recognize any gain or loss when the asset's net book value is not equal to the cash received.

8-6. Apply measurement and reporting concepts for intangible assets and natural resources. p. 424

The cost principle should be applied in recording the acquisition of intangible assets and natural resources. Intangibles with definite useful lives are amortized using the straight-line method. Intangibles with indefinite useful lives, including goodwill, are not amortized but are reviewed at least annually for impairment. Report intangible assets at net book value on the balance sheet. Natural resources should be depleted (typically by the units-of-production method) with the amount of the depletion expense usually capitalized to an inventory account.

8-7. Explain how the acquisition, use, and disposal of long-lived assets impact cash flows. p. 430

Depreciation expense is a noncash expense that has no effect on cash. It is added back to net income on the statement of cash flows to determine cash from operations. Acquiring and disposing of long-lived assets are investing activities.

In previous chapters, we discussed business and accounting issues related to the assets that a company holds. In Chapters 9, 10, and 11, we shift our focus to the other side of the balance sheet to see how managers finance business operations and the acquisition of productive assets. We discuss various types of liabilities in Chapters 9 and 10 and examine stockholders' equity in Chapter 11.

KEY RATIO

The **fixed asset turnover ratio** measures how efficiently a company utilizes its investment in property, plant, and equipment over time. Its ratio can then be compared to competitors' ratios. The fixed asset turnover ratio is computed as follows (see the "Key Ratio Analysis" box in the Acquisition and Maintenance of Plant and Equipment section on p. 403):

$$\text{Fixed Asset Turnover} = \frac{\text{Net Sales (or Operating Revenues)}}{\text{Average Net Fixed Assets}}$$

FINDING FINANCIAL INFORMATION

Balance Sheet

Under Noncurrent Assets

Property, plant, and equipment (net of accumulated depreciation)

Natural resources (net of accumulated depletion)

Intangibles (net of accumulated amortization, if any)

Income Statement

Under Operating Expenses

Depreciation, depletion, and amortization expense **or** included in

Selling, general, and administrative expenses and

Cost of goods sold (with the amount for depreciation expense disclosed in a note)

Statement of Cash Flows

Under Operating Activities (indirect method)

Net income

+ Depreciation and amortization expense

− Gains on sales of assets

+ Losses on sales or impairment of assets

Under Investing Activities

+ Sales of assets for cash

− Purchases of assets for cash

Notes

Under Summary of Significant Accounting Policies

Description of management's choice for depreciation and amortization methods, including useful lives, and the amount of annual depreciation expense, if not listed on the income statement.

Under a Separate Footnote

If not specified on the balance sheet, a listing of the major classifications of long-lived assets at cost and the balance in accumulated depreciation, depletion, and amortization.

KEY TERMS

Acquisition cost The net cash equivalent amount paid or to be paid for an asset **p. 404**

Amortization The systematic and rational allocation of the acquisition cost of an intangible asset over its useful life **p. 425**

Capitalized interest Interest expenditures included in the cost of a self-constructed asset **p. 406**

Declining-balance depreciation Method that allocates the net book value (cost minus accumulated depreciation) of an asset over its useful life based on a multiple of the straight-line rate, thus assigning more depreciation to early years and less depreciation to later years of an asset's life **p. 417**

Depletion Systematic and rational allocation of the cost of a natural resource over the period of its exploitation **p. 429**

Depreciable cost Cost minus residual value; the amount to be allocated over an asset's useful life **p. 414**

Depreciation The process of allocating the cost of buildings and equipment (but not land) over their productive lives using a systematic and rational method **p. 411**

Estimated residual (or salvage) value The estimated amount to be recovered by the company, less disposal costs, at the end of an asset's estimated useful life **p. 414**

Estimated useful life The expected service life of an asset to the present owner **p. 413**

Franchise A contractual right to sell certain products or services, use certain trademarks, or perform activities in a geographical region **p. 428**

Goodwill (Cost in Excess of Net Assets Acquired) For accounting purposes, the excess of the purchase price of an acquired business over the fair value of the acquired business's assets and liabilities **p. 426**

Improvements Expenditures that increase the productive life, operating efficiency, or capacity of an asset; recorded as increases in asset accounts, not as expenses **p. 408**

Intangible assets Assets that have special rights but not physical substance **p. 403**

Licenses and operating rights Obtained through agreements with governmental units or agencies that permit owners to use public property in performing their services **p. 429**

Natural resources Assets occurring in nature, such as mineral deposits, timber tracts, oil, and gas **p. 429**

Net book value (carrying value or book value) The acquisition cost of an asset less its accumulated depreciation, amortization (for intangible assets), or depletion (for natural recourses) **p. 412**

Ordinary repairs and maintenance Expenditures that maintain the productive capacity of an asset during the current accounting period only; recorded as expenses for the period **p. 408**

Patent Granted by the federal government for an invention; gives the owner the exclusive right to use, manufacture, and sell the subject of the patent **p. 428**

Straight-line depreciation Method that allocates the depreciable cost of an asset in equal periodic amounts over its useful life **p. 414**

Tangible assets Assets that have physical substance **p. 403**

Technology Includes costs capitalized for computer software and website development **p. 427**

Trademark An exclusive legal right to use a special name, image, or slogan **p. 426**

Units-of-production depreciation Method that allocates the depreciable cost of an asset over its useful life based on the relationship of its periodic output or activity level to its total estimated output or activity level **p. 415**

QUESTIONS

1. Define **long-lived assets.** Why are they considered to be a "bundle of future services"?
2. How is the fixed asset turnover ratio computed? Explain its meaning.
3. What are the classifications of long-lived assets? Explain each.
4. Under the cost measurement concept, what amounts should be included in the acquisition cost of a long-lived asset?
5. Describe the relationship between the expense matching principle and accounting for long-lived assets.

6. Distinguish between ordinary repairs and improvements. How is each accounted for?
7. Distinguish among depreciation, depletion, and amortization.
8. In computing depreciation, three pieces of information must be known or estimated; identify and explain the nature of each.
9. The estimated useful life and residual value of a long-lived asset relate to the current owner or user rather than all potential users. Explain this statement.
10. What type of depreciation expense pattern is used under each of the following methods and when is its use appropriate?
    a. The straight-line method.
    b. The units-of-production method.
    c. The double-declining-balance method.
11. Over what period should an addition or improvement to an existing long-lived asset be depreciated? Explain.
12. What is **asset impairment?** How is it accounted for?
13. When equipment is sold for more than net book value, how is the transaction recorded? What if the equipment is sold for less than net book value? What is **net book value?**
14. Define **intangible asset.** What period should be used to amortize an intangible asset with a definite life?
15. Define **goodwill.** When is it appropriate to record goodwill as an intangible asset?
16. Why is depreciation expense added to net income (indirect method) on the statement of cash flows?

MULTIPLE-CHOICE QUESTIONS

1. Miga Company and Porter Company both bought a new delivery truck a few years ago on January 1. Both companies paid exactly the same cost, $30,000, for their respective vehicles. As of December 31 of the current year, the net book value of Miga's truck was less than Porter Company's net book value for the same vehicle. Which of the following is an acceptable explanation for the difference in net book value?
    a. Miga Company estimated a lower residual value, but both estimated the same useful life and both elected straight-line depreciation.
    b. Both companies elected straight-line depreciation, but Miga Company used a longer estimated life.
    c. Because GAAP specifies rigid guidelines regarding the calculation of depreciation, this situation is not possible.
    d. Miga Company is using the straight-line method of depreciation, and Porter Company is using the double-declining-balance method of depreciation.
2. Leslie, Inc., followed the practice of depreciating its building on a straight-line basis. A building was purchased last year and had an estimated useful life of 25 years and a residual value of $20,000. The company's depreciation expense for last year was $15,000 on the building. What was the original cost of the building?
    a. $395,000
    b. $500,000
    c. $520,000
    d. Cannot be determined from the information given.
3. Maks, Inc., uses straight-line depreciation for all of its depreciable assets. Maks sold a used piece of machinery on December 31 of this year that it purchased on January 1 of last year for $10,000. The asset had a five-year life, zero residual value, and $2,000 accumulated depreciation as of December 31 of last year. If the sales price of the used machine was $7,500, the resulting gain or loss upon the sale was which of the following amounts?
    a. Loss of $500
    b. Gain of $500
    c. Loss of $1,500
    d. Gain of $1,500
    e. No gain or loss upon the sale.
4. Under which method(s) of depreciation is an asset's **net book value** the depreciable base (the amount to be depreciated)?
    a. Straight-line method
    b. Declining-balance method
    c. Units-of-production method
    d. All of the above

5. What assets should be amortized using the straight-line method?
   a. Intangible assets with definite lives
   b. Intangible assets with indefinite lives
   c. Natural resources
   d. All of the above
6. A company wishes to report the highest earnings possible for financial reporting purposes. Therefore, when calculating depreciation,
   a. It will follow the MACRS depreciation tables prescribed by the IRS.
   b. It will select the shortest lives possible for its assets.
   c. It will select the lowest residual values for its assets.
   d. It will estimate higher residual values for its assets.
7. How many of the following statements regarding goodwill are true?
   - Goodwill is not reported unless purchased in an exchange.
   - Goodwill must be reviewed annually for possible impairment.
   - Impairment of goodwill results in a decrease in net income.
     a. Three
     b. Two
     c. One
     d. None
8. Company X is going to retire equipment that is fully depreciated with no residual value. The equipment will simply be disposed of, not sold. Which of the following statements is *true?*
   1 - Total assets will not change as a result of this transaction.
   2 - Net income will not be impacted as a result of this transaction.
   3 - This transaction will not impact cash flow.
     a. Only statement 2 is true.
     b. Only statements 1 and 2 are true.
     c. Only statement 3 is true.
     d. All of the statements are true.
9. When recording depreciation, which of the following statements is *true?*
   a. Total assets increase and stockholders' equity increases.
   b. Total assets decrease and total liabilities increase.
   c. Total assets decrease and stockholders' equity increases.
   d. None of the above are true.
10. (Chapter Supplement) Irish Industries purchased a machine for $65,000 and is depreciating it using the straight-line method over a life of 10 years, with a residual value of $3,000. At the beginning of the sixth year, a major overhaul was made costing $5,000, and the total estimated useful life was extended to 13 years with a residual value of $3,000. Depreciation expense for Year 6 is
    a. $1,885.
    b. $2,000.
    c. $3,250.
    d. $3,625.
    e. $4,500.

MINI-EXERCISES

M8-1 Classifying Long-Lived Assets and Related Cost Allocation Concepts

LO8-1, 8-3, 8-6

For each of the 10 long-lived assets shown below, indicate its nature and the related cost allocation concept. Use the following abbreviations:

Nature		Cost Allocation Concept	
L	Land	DR	Depreciation
B	Building	DP	Depletion
E	Equipment	AM	Amortization
NR	Natural resource	NO	No cost allocation
I	Intangible	O	Other
O	Other		

Asset	Nature	Cost Allocation	Asset	Nature	Cost Allocation
(1) Tractors	_____	_____	(6) Operating license	_____	_____
(2) Land in use	_____	_____	(7) Production plant	_____	_____
(3) Timber tract	_____	_____	(8) Patent	_____	_____
(4) Warehouse	_____	_____	(9) Silver mine	_____	_____
(5) New engine for old machine	_____	_____	(10) Land held for sale	_____	_____

Computing and Evaluating the Fixed Asset Turnover Ratio

M8-2
LO8-1
FedEx Corporation

The following information was reported by Young's Air Cargo Service for 2020:

Net fixed assets (beginning of year)	$1,500,000
Net fixed assets (end of year)	2,300,000
Net operating revenues for the year	3,600,000
Net income for the year	1,600,000

Compute the company's fixed asset turnover ratio (rounded to two decimal places) for the year. What can you say about Young's ratio when compared to **FedEx**'s 2020 ratio of 2.16?

Identifying Capital Expenditures and Expenses

M8-3
LO8-2

For each of the following transactions, enter the correct letter to the left to show the type of expenditure. Use the following:

Type of Expenditure		Transactions
C Capital expenditure	_____	(1) Purchased a patent, $4,300 cash.
E Expense	_____	(2) Paid $10,000 for monthly salaries.
N Neither	_____	(3) Paid cash dividends, $20,000.
	_____	(4) Purchased a machine, $7,000; gave a long-term note.
	_____	(5) Paid three-year insurance premium, $900.
	_____	(6) Paid for routine maintenance, $200, on credit.
	_____	(7) Paid $400 for ordinary repairs.
	_____	(8) Paid $6,000 for improvements that lengthened the asset's productive life.
	_____	(9) Paid $20,000 cash for addition to old building.

Computing Book Value (Straight-Line Depreciation)

M8-4
LO8-3

Calculate the book value of a three-year-old machine that has a cost of $31,000, an estimated residual value of $1,000, and an estimated useful life of five years. The company uses straight-line depreciation.

Computing Book Value (Double-Declining-Balance Depreciation)

M8-5
LO8-3

Calculate the book value of a three-year-old machine that has a cost of $55,000, an estimated residual value of $5,000, and an estimated useful life of five years. The company uses double-declining-balance depreciation. Round to the nearest dollar.

Computing Book Value (Units-of-Production Depreciation)

M8-6
LO8-3

Calculate the book value of a three-year-old machine that has a cost of $26,000, an estimated residual value of $1,000, and an estimated useful life of 50,000 machine hours. The company uses units-of-production depreciation and ran the machine 3,200 hours in Year 1; 7,050 hours in Year 2; and 7,500 hours in Year 3.

Identifying Asset Impairment

M8-7
LO8-4

For each of the following scenarios, indicate whether an asset has been impaired (Y for yes and N for no) and, if so, the amount of loss that should be recorded.

	Book Value	Estimated Future Cash Flows	Fair Value	Is Asset Impaired?	Amount of Loss
a. Machine	$ 15,500	$ 10,000	$ 9,500		
b. Copyright	31,000	41,000	37,900		
c. Factory building	58,000	29,000	27,000		
d. Building	227,000	227,000	200,000		

M8-8
LO8-5

Recording the Disposal of a Long-Lived Asset (Straight-Line Depreciation)

As part of a major renovation at the beginning of the year, Bonham's Bakery sold shelving units (store fixtures) that were 10 years old for $1,800 cash. The original cost of the shelves was $6,500 and they had been depreciated on a straight-line basis over an estimated useful life of 12 years with an estimated residual value of $800. Record the sale of the shelving units.

M8-9
LO8-6

Computing Goodwill and Patents

Elizabeth Pie Company has been in business for 50 years and has developed a large group of loyal restaurant customers. Giant Bakery Inc. has made an offer to buy Elizabeth Pie Company for $5,000,000. The book value of Elizabeth Pie's recorded assets and liabilities on the date of the offer is $4,300,000 with a fair value of $4,500,000. Elizabeth Pie also (1) holds a patent for a pie crust fluting machine that the company invented (the patent with a fair value of $300,000 was never recorded by Elizabeth Pie because it was developed internally) and (2) estimates goodwill from loyal customers to be $310,000 (also never recorded by the company). Should Elizabeth Pie Company management accept Giant Bakery's offer of $5,000,000? If so, compute the amount of goodwill that Giant Bakery should record on the date of the purchase.

M8-10
LO8-7

Preparing the Statement of Cash Flows

Garrett Company had the following activities for a recent year ended December 31: Sold land that cost $20,000 for $20,000 cash; purchased $181,000 of equipment, paying $156,000 in cash and signing a note payable for the rest; and recorded $5,500 in depreciation expense for the year. Net income for the year was $18,000. Compute (1) cash provided by operating activities and (2) cash used in investing activities for the year based on the data provided.

EXERCISES

E8-1
LO8-1
Hasbro, Inc.

Preparing a Classified Balance Sheet

The following is a list of account titles and amounts (dollars in millions) from a recent annual report of **Hasbro, Inc.**, a leading manufacturer of games, toys, and interactive entertainment software for children and families:

Buildings and improvements	$ 195	Machinery, equipment, and software	$ 493
Prepaid expenses and other current assets	310	Accumulated depreciation	534
Allowance for doubtful accounts	17	Inventories	446
Other noncurrent assets	585	Tools, dies, and molds	71
Accumulated amortization (other intangibles)	769	Other intangibles	1,415
Cash and cash equivalents	4,580	Land and improvements	3
Goodwill	495	Accounts receivable	1,428
		Lease right-of-use assets	154

Source: Hasbro, Inc.

Required:
Prepare the asset section of the balance sheet for Hasbro, Inc., classifying the assets into Current Assets; Property, Plant, and Equipment (net); and Other Assets.

Computing and Interpreting the Fixed Asset Turnover Ratio from a Financial Analyst's Perspective

E8-2
LO8-1
Apple Inc.

The following data were included in a recent **Apple Inc.** annual report ($ in millions):

In millions	2017	2018	2019	2020
Net sales	$229,234	$265,595	$260,174	$274,515
Net property, plant, and equipment	33,783	41,304	37,378	36,766

Source: Apple Inc.

Required:

1. Compute Apple's fixed asset turnover ratio for 2018, 2019, and 2020. Round your answers to two decimal points.
2. How might a financial analyst interpret the results?

Computing and Recording Cost and Depreciation of Assets (Straight-Line Depreciation)

E8-3
LO8-2, 8-3

Shahia Company bought a building for $382,000 cash and the land on which it was located for $107,000 cash. The company paid transfer costs of $9,000 ($3,000 for the building and $6,000 for the land). Renovation costs on the building before it could be used were $21,000.

Required:

1. Give the journal entry to record the purchase of the property, including all relevant expenditures. Assume that all transactions were for cash and that all purchases occurred at the start of the year.
2. Compute straight-line depreciation at the end of one year, assuming an estimated 10-year useful life and a $15,000 estimated residual value.
3. What would be the net book value of the property (land and building) at the end of Year 2?

Determining Financial Statement Effects of an Asset Acquisition and Depreciation (Straight-Line Depreciation)

E8-4
LO8-2, 8-3

During Year 1, Ashkar Company ordered a machine on January 1 at an invoice price of $21,000. On the date of delivery, January 2, the company paid $6,000 on the machine, with the balance on credit at 10 percent interest due in six months. On January 3, it paid $1,000 for freight on the machine. On January 5, Ashkar paid installation costs relating to the machine amounting to $2,500. On July 1, the company paid the balance due on the machine plus the interest. On December 31 (the end of the accounting period), Ashkar recorded depreciation on the machine using the straight-line method with an estimated useful life of 10 years and an estimated residual value of $3,000.

Required (round all amounts to the nearest dollar):

1. Indicate the effects (accounts, amounts, and + or −) of each transaction (on January 1, 2, 3, and 5 and July 1) on the accounting equation. Use the following schedule:

Date	Assets	=	Liabilities	+	Stockholders' Equity

2. Compute the acquisition cost of the machine.
3. Compute the depreciation expense to be reported for Year 1.
4. What impact does the interest paid on the 10 percent note have on the cost of the machine? Under what circumstances can interest expense be included in acquisition cost?
5. What would be the net book value of the machine at the end of Year 2?

Determining Financial Statement Effects of an Asset Acquisition and Depreciation (Straight-Line Depreciation)

E8-5
LO8-2, 8-3

Steve's Outdoor Company purchased a new delivery van on January 1 for $45,000 plus $3,800 in sales tax. The company paid $12,800 cash on the van (including the sales tax), signing an 8 percent note for the $36,000 balance due in nine months (on September 30). On January 2, the company paid cash of $700 to have the company name and logo painted on the van. On September 30, the company paid the balance due on the van plus the interest. On December 31 (the end of the accounting period), Steve's Outdoor recorded depreciation on the van using the straight-line method with an estimated useful life of five years and an estimated residual value of $4,500.

Required (round all amounts to the nearest dollar):

1. Indicate the effects (accounts, amounts, and + or −) of each transaction (on January 1, 2, and September 30) on the accounting equation. Use the following schedule:

Date	Assets	=	Liabilities	+	Stockholders' Equity

2. Compute the acquisition cost of the van.
3. Compute the depreciation expense to be reported for Year 1.
4. What impact does the interest paid on the 8 percent note have on the cost of the van? Under what circumstances can interest expense be included in acquisition cost?
5. What would be the net book value of the van at the end of Year 2?

E8-6 Recording Depreciation and Repairs (Straight-Line Depreciation)

LO8-2, 8-3

Manrow Growers, Inc., owns equipment for sowing and harvesting its organic fruit, vegetables, and tree nuts that are sold to local restaurants and grocery stores. At the beginning of this year, an asset account for the company showed the following balances:

Equipment	$350,000
Accumulated depreciation through the end of last year	165,000

During the current year, the following expenditures were incurred for the equipment:

Major overhaul of the equipment on January 1 of the current year that improved efficiency	$42,000
Routine maintenance and repairs on the equipment	5,000

The equipment is being depreciated on a straight-line basis over an estimated life of eight years with a $20,000 estimated residual value. The annual accounting period ends on December 31.

Required:

1. Give the adjusting entry that **was made at the end of last year** for depreciation on the equipment.
2. Starting at the beginning of the current year, what is the remaining estimated life?
3. Give the journal entries to record the two expenditures during the current year.

E8-7 Recording Depreciation and Repairs (Straight-Line Depreciation)

LO8-2, 8-3

Hulme Company operates a small manufacturing facility as a supplement to its regular service activities. At the beginning of the current year, an asset account for the company showed the following balances:

Manufacturing equipment	$120,000
Accumulated depreciation through the end of last year	57,600

During the current year, the following expenditures were incurred for the equipment:

Major overhaul of the equipment on January 2 the current year that improved efficiency	$13,000
Routine repairs on the equipment	1,000

The equipment is being depreciated on a straight-line basis over an estimated life of 15 years with a $12,000 estimated residual value. The annual accounting period ends on December 31.

Required:

1. Give the adjusting entry that **was made at the end of last year** for depreciation on the manufacturing equipment.
2. Starting at the beginning of the current year, what is the remaining estimated life?
3. Give the journal entries to record the two expenditures during the current year.

Determining Financial Statement Effects of Depreciation and Repairs (Straight-Line Depreciation)

E8-8
LO8-2, 8-3

Refer to the information in E8-7.

Required:
Indicate the effects (accounts, amounts, and + or −) of the items below on the accounting equation. Use the following schedule:

Date	Assets	=	Liabilities	+	Stockholders' Equity

1. The adjustment for depreciation at the end of last year.
2. The two expenditures during the current year.

Computing Depreciation under Alternative Methods

E8-9
LO8-3
Purity Ice Cream Company, Inc.

Assume **Purity Ice Cream Company, Inc.**, in Ithaca, NY, bought a new ice cream production kit (pasteurizer/homogenizer, cooler, aging vat, freezer, and filling machine) at the beginning of the year at a cost of $152,000. The estimated useful life was four years, and the residual value was $8,000. Assume that the estimated productive life of the machine was 16,000 hours. Actual annual usage was 5,500 hours in Year 1; 3,800 hours in Year 2; 3,200 hours in Year 3; and 3,500 hours in Year 4.

Required:
1. Complete a separate depreciation schedule for each of the alternative methods. A sample schedule is shown below. Round your answers to the nearest dollar.
   a. Straight-line.
   b. Units-of-production (use two decimal places for the per unit output factor).
   c. Double-declining-balance.

Method: ________				
Year	Computation	Depreciation Expense	Accumulated Depreciation	Net Book Value
At acquisition				
1				
2				
etc.				

2. Assuming that the machine was used directly in the production of one of the ice cream products that the company manufactures and sells, what factors might management consider in selecting a preferable depreciation method in conformity with the expense recognition principle?

Computing Depreciation under Alternative Methods

E8-10
LO8-3

Strong Metals Inc. purchased a new stamping machine at the beginning of the year at a cost of $950,000. The estimated residual value was $50,000. Assume that the estimated useful life was five years and the estimated productive life of the machine was 300,000 units. Actual annual production was as follows:

Year	Units
1	70,000
2	67,000
3	50,000
4	73,000
5	40,000

Required:

1. Complete a separate depreciation schedule for each of the alternative methods. A sample schedule is shown below. Round your answers to the nearest dollar.
   a. Straight-line.
   b. Units-of-production (use two decimal places for the per unit output factor).
   c. Double-declining-balance.

Method: ____________				
Year	Computation	Depreciation Expense	Accumulated Depreciation	Net Book Value
At acquisition				
1				
2				
etc.				

2. Assuming that the machine was used directly in the production of one of the products that the company manufactures and sells, what factors might management consider in selecting a preferable depreciation method in conformity with the expense recognition (matching) principle?

E8-11 Computing Depreciation under Alternative Methods

LO8-3

At the beginning of the year, Palermo Brothers, Inc., purchased a new plastic water bottle-making machine at a cost of $45,000. The estimated residual value was $5,000. Assume that the estimated useful life was four years and the estimated productive life of the machine was 400,000 units. Actual annual production was as follows:

Year	Units
1	120,000
2	90,000
3	110,000
4	80,000

Required:

1. Complete a separate depreciation schedule for each of the alternative methods. Round your answers to the nearest dollar.
   a. Straight-line.
   b. Units-of-production (use two decimal places for the per unit output factor).
   c. Double-declining-balance.

Method: ____________				
Year	Computation	Depreciation Expense	Accumulated Depreciation	Net Book Value
At acquisition				
1				
2				
etc.				

2. Assuming that the machine was used directly in the production of one of the products that the company manufactures and sells, what factors might management consider in selecting a preferable depreciation method in conformity with the expense recognition principle?

Explaining Depreciation Policy

E8-12
LO8-3
Microsoft Corporation

Microsoft Corporation is a leading technology company with products ranging from operating systems, productivity applications, server applications, business solution applications, software development tools, to devices including PCs, tablets, and gaming and entertainment consoles. Its recent quarterly report contained the following note:

NOTE 1—ACCOUNTING POLICIES

Estimates and Assumptions

In July 2020, we completed an assessment of the useful lives of our server and network equipment and determined we should increase the estimated useful life of server equipment from three years to four years and increase the estimated useful life of network equipment from two years to four years. This change in accounting estimate was effective beginning fiscal year 2021. Based on the carrying amount of server and network equipment included in property and equipment, net as of June 30, 2020, the effect of this change in estimate for the three months ended September 30, 2020, was an increase in operating income of $927 million and net income of $763 million . . .

Source: Microsoft Corporation

Required:
Why do you think Microsoft changed its depreciation method for property, plant, and equipment?

Interpreting Management's Choice of Different Depreciation Methods for Tax and Financial Reporting

E8-13
LO8-3
FedEx Corporation

A recent annual report for **FedEx** includes the following information:

For financial reporting purposes, we record depreciation and amortization of property and equipment on a straight-line basis over the asset's service life or related lease term, if shorter. For income tax purposes, depreciation is computed using accelerated methods when applicable.

Source: FedEx Corporation

Required:
Explain why FedEx uses different depreciation methods for financial reporting and tax purposes.

Computing Depreciation and Book Value for Two Years Using Alternative Depreciation Methods

E8-14
LO8-3, 8-7

Schrade Company bought a machine for $96,000 cash. The estimated useful life was four years and the estimated residual value was $6,000. Assume that the estimated useful life in productive units is 120,000. Units actually produced were 43,000 in Year 1 and 45,000 in Year 2.

Required:

1. Determine the appropriate amounts to complete the following schedule. Show computations, and round to the nearest dollar.

	Depreciation Expense for		Net Book Value at the End of	
Method of Depreciation	Year 1	Year 2	Year 1	Year 2
Straight-line				
Units-of-production				
Double-declining-balance				

2. Which method would result in the lowest Earnings per Share for Year 1? For Year 2?
3. Which method would result in the highest amount of cash outflows in Year 1? Why?

E8-15
LO8-4, 8-5
United Parcel Service

Inferring Asset Impairment and Recording Disposal of an Asset

In a recent 10-K report, **United Parcel Service** states it "is the world's largest package delivery company, a leader in the United States less-than-truckload industry, and the premier provider of global supply chain management solutions." The following note and data were reported:

NOTE 1—SUMMARY OF ACCOUNTING POLICIES

Property, Plant and Equipment

We review long-lived assets for impairment when circumstances indicate the carrying amount of an asset may not be recoverable based on the undiscounted future cash flows. If the carrying amount of the asset is determined not to be recoverable, a write-down to fair value is recorded. Fair values are determined based on quoted market values, discounted cash flows, or external appraisals, as appropriate.

Source: United Parcel Service

	Dollars in Millions
Cost of property and equipment (beginning of year)	$54,488
Cost of property and equipment (end of year)	59,727
Capital expenditures during the year	6,380
Accumulated depreciation (beginning of year)	27,912
Accumulated depreciation (end of year)	29,245
Depreciation expense during the year	2,360
Cost of property and equipment sold during the year	1,141
Accumulated depreciation on property sold	1,027
Cash received on property sold	65

Required:

1. Reconstruct the journal entry for the disposal of property and equipment during the year.
2. Compute the amount of property and equipment that United Parcel wrote off as impaired during the year, if any. (**Hint:** Set up T-accounts.)

E8-16
LO8-5
Delta Air Lines
Amazon.com

Recording the Disposal of an Asset at Three Different Sale Prices

Delta Air Lines owns hundreds of aircraft, with about 60 percent of its fleet consisting of **Boeing** aircraft, while **Airbus** aircraft make up about 40 percent. It sold seven used Boeing 767-300 jets to **Amazon.com** as Amazon plans to expand its growing Amazon Air cargo service. The average age of the jets is about 20 years old.

Assume the records of the company reflected the following for the jets that were sold:

Aircraft cost	$62,500,000
Accumulated depreciation	46,800,000

Required:

1. Give the journal entry for the disposal of the airplanes, assuming that the airplanes sold for
   a. $15,700,000 cash
   b. $16,300,000 cash
   c. $14,600,000 cash
2. Based on the three preceding situations, explain the effects of the disposal of an asset.

Recording the Disposal of an Asset at Three Different Sale Prices

E8-17
LO8-5
Marriott International

Marriott International is a worldwide operator, franchisor, and licensor of hotels, residential, and time-share properties totaling nearly $1.8 billion in net property and equipment. Assume that Marriott replaced furniture that had been used in the business for five years. The records of the company reflected the following regarding the sale of the existing furniture:

Furniture (cost)	$8,000,000
Accumulated depreciation	7,700,000

Required:

1. Give the journal entry for the disposal of the furniture, assuming that it was sold for
   a. $300,000 cash
   b. $900,000 cash
   c. $100,000 cash
2. Based on the three preceding situations, explain the effects of the disposal of an asset.

Inferring Asset Age and Recording Accidental Loss on a Long-Lived Asset (Straight-Line Depreciation)

E8-18
LO8-3, 8-5

On January 1 of the current year, the records of Khouri Corporation showed the following regarding a truck:

Equipment (estimated residual value, $9,000)	$25,000
Accumulated depreciation (straight-line, three years)	6,000

On December 31 of the current year, the delivery truck was a total loss as the result of an accident.

Required:

1. Based on the data given, compute the estimated useful life of the truck that was used for recording depreciation.
2. Give all journal entries with respect to the truck on December 31 of the current year, assuming there was no insurance coverage on the truck. Show computations.
3. Assuming Khouri had casualty insurance on the truck and received $13,000 from the insurance company for the accident, would there be a gain or loss recorded for the disposal of the asset? If so how much?

Computing the Acquisition and Depletion of a Natural Resource

E8-19
LO8-6
Freeport-McMoRan Copper & Gold, Inc.

Freeport-McMoRan Copper & Gold Inc., headquartered in Phoenix, Arizona, is a leading international mining company of copper, gold, and molybdenum. Its revenues were over $14 billion in a recent year.

Assume that in February of last year, Freeport-McMoRan paid $800,000 for a mineral deposit in Indonesia. During March, it spent $70,000 in preparing the deposit for exploitation. It was estimated that 1,000,000 total cubic yards could be extracted economically. During last year, 60,000 cubic yards were extracted. During January of the current year, the company spent another $6,000 for additional developmental work that increased the estimated productive capacity of the mineral deposit.

Required:

1. Compute the acquisition cost of the deposit in last year.
2. Compute depletion for last year.
3. Compute the net book value of the deposit in the current year after payment of the January developmental costs.

Computing and Reporting the Acquisition and Amortization of Three Different Intangible Assets

E8-20
LO8-6

Trotman Company had three intangible assets at the end of the current year:

a. Computer software and website development technology purchased on January 1 of the prior year for $70,000. The technology is expected to have a four-year useful life to the company with no residual value.
b. A patent purchased from Ian Zimmer on January 1 of the current year for a cash cost of $6,000. Zimmer had registered the patent with the U.S. Patent and Trademark Office five years ago. Trotman intends to use the patent for its remaining life.
c. A trademark purchased for $13,000 on November 1 of the current year. Management decided the trademark has an indefinite life.

Required:

1. Compute the amortization of each intangible at December 31 of the current year. The company does not use contra-accounts.
2. Show how these assets and any related expenses should be reported on the balance sheet and income statement for the current year.

E8-21 LO8-6 **Computing and Reporting the Acquisition and Amortization of Three Different Intangible Assets**

Springer Company had three intangible assets at the end of 2023 (end of the accounting year):

a. A copyright purchased on January 1, 2023, for a cash cost of $14,500. The copyright is expected to have a 10-year useful life to Springer.
b. Goodwill of $65,000 from the purchase of the Hartford Company on July 1, 2022.
c. A patent purchased on January 1, 2022, for $48,000. The inventor had registered the patent with the U.S. Patent and Trademark Office on January 1, 2018. Springer intends to use the patent for its remaining life.

Required:

1. Compute the amortization of each intangible at December 31, 2023. The company does not use contra-accounts.
2. Show how these assets and any related expenses should be reported on the balance sheet and income statement for 2023. (Assume there has been no impairment of goodwill.)

E8-22 LO8-6 Starbucks Corporation **Recording Leasehold Improvements and Related Amortization**

Starbucks Corporation is "the premier roaster, marketer and retailer of specialty coffee in the world, operating in 83 countries" with over 32,000 company-operated and licensed stores worldwide. Assume that Starbucks planned to open a new store on Beacon Street near Boston College and obtained a 10-year lease starting October 1 (the beginning of the current fiscal year). The company had to renovate the facility by installing an elevator costing $325,000. Amounts spent to enhance leased property are capitalized as intangible assets called Leasehold Improvements. The elevator will be amortized over the useful life of the lease.

Required:

1. Give the journal entry to record the installation of the new elevator.
2. Give any adjusting entries required on September 30 (the end of the current fiscal year) related to the new elevator. Show computations.

E8-23 LO8-3 **(Chapter Supplement) Recording a Change in Estimate**

Refer to E8-7.

Required:

Give the adjusting entry that should be made by Hulme Company at the end of the current year for depreciation of the manufacturing equipment, assuming no change in the original estimated life or residual value. Show computations. Round answer to the nearest dollar.

E8-24 LO8-2, 8-3 **(Chapter Supplement) Recording and Explaining Depreciation, Improvements, and Changes in Estimated Useful Life and Residual Value (Straight-Line Depreciation)**

At the end of the prior year ending on December 31, O'Connor Company's records reflected the following for Machine A:

Cost when acquired	$30,000
Accumulated depreciation	10,200

At the beginning of January of the current year, the machine was renovated at a cost of $15,500. As a result, the estimated life increased from five years to eight years, and the residual value increased from $4,500 to $6,500. The company uses straight-line depreciation.

Required:

1. Give the journal entry to record the renovation.
2. How old was the machine at the end of the prior year?
3. Give the adjusting entry at the end of the current year to record straight-line depreciation for the year.
4. Explain the rationale for your entries in requirements 1 and 3.

E8-25
LO8-3, 8-7

(Chapter Supplement) Computing the Effect of a Change in Useful Life and Residual Value on Financial Statements and Cash Flows (Straight-Line Depreciation)

Yukelson Company owns the building occupied by its administrative office. The office building was reflected in the accounts at the end of last year as follows:

Cost when acquired	$330,000
Accumulated depreciation (based on straight-line depreciation, an estimated life of 50 years, and a $30,000 residual value)	78,000

During January of this year, on the basis of a careful study, management decided that the total estimated useful life should be changed to 30 years (instead of 50) and the residual value reduced to $22,500 (from $30,000). The depreciation method will not change.

Required:

1. Compute the annual depreciation expense prior to the change in estimates.
2. Compute the annual depreciation expense after the change in estimates.
3. What will be the net effect of the change in estimates on the balance sheet, net income, and cash flows for this year?

PROBLEMS

P8-1
LO8-1, 8-2

Explaining the Nature of a Long-Lived Asset and Determining and Recording the Financial Statement Effects of Its Purchase (AP8-1)

On January 2, Summers Company received a machine that the company had ordered with an invoice price of $85,000. Freight costs of $1,000 were paid by the vendor per the sales agreement. The company exchanged the following on January 2 to acquire the machine:

a. Issued 2,000 shares of Summers Company common stock, par value $1 (market value, $3.50 per share).
b. Signed a note payable for $60,000 with an 11.5 percent interest rate (principal plus interest are due April 1 of the current year).
c. The balance of the invoice price was on account with the vendor, to be paid in cash by January 12.

On January 3, Summers Company paid $2,400 cash for installation costs to prepare the machine for use.

On January 12, Summers Company paid the balance due on its accounts payable to the vendor.

Required:

1. What are the classifications of long-lived assets? Explain their differences.
2. Record the purchase on January 2, the installation costs on January 3, and the subsequent payment on January 12. Show computations.
3. Indicate the accounts, amounts, and effects (+ for increase and − for decrease) of the purchase and subsequent cash payment on the accounting equation. Use the following structure:

Date	Assets	=	Liabilities	+	Stockholders' Equity

4. What is the cost of the machine recorded on Summers's records? Explain the basis you used for any questionable items.

P8-2 Analyzing the Effects of Repairs, an Addition, and Depreciation (AP8-2)

LO8-2, 8-3

Delta Air Lines

A recent annual report for **Delta Air Lines** included the following note:

NOTE 1. SUMMARY OF SIGNIFICANT ACCOUNTING POLICIES

Maintenance Costs

We record maintenance costs related to our fleet in aircraft maintenance materials and outside repairs. Maintenance costs are expensed as incurred, except for costs incurred under power-by-the-hour contracts, which are expensed based on actual hours flown. Modifications that enhance the operating performance or extend the useful lives of airframes or engines are capitalized and amortized over the remaining estimated useful life of the asset or the remaining lease term, whichever is shorter.

Source: Delta Air Lines

Assume that Delta made extensive repairs on an airplane engine, increasing the fuel efficiency and extending the useful life of the airplane. The existing airplane originally cost $45,000,000, and by the **end of last year,** it was half depreciated based on use of the straight-line method, a 20-year estimated useful life, and no residual value. During the **current year,** the following transactions related to the airplane were made:

a. Ordinary repairs and maintenance expenditures for the year, $7,000,000 cash.
b. Extensive and major repairs to the airplane's engine, $2,700,000 cash. These repairs were completed at the end of the current year.
c. Recorded depreciation for the current year.

Required:

1. Applying the policies of Delta, complete the following, indicating the effects for the preceding expenditures for the current year. If there is no effect on an account, write NE on the line.

	Aircraft	Accumulated Depreciation	Depreciation Expense	Repairs Expense	Cash
Balance January 1	$45,000,000	$22,500,000			
a.					
b.					
c.					
Balance December 31					

2. What was the net book value of the aircraft on December 31 of the current year?
3. Explain the effect of depreciation on cash flows.

P8-3 Computing the Acquisition Cost and Recording Depreciation under Three Alternative Methods (AP8-3)

LO8-2, 8-3

Primo Fitness

At the beginning of the year, Plummer's Sports Center bought three used fitness machines from **Primo Fitness**, an established supplier of used, new and refurbished gym equipment in Southern California. The machines immediately were overhauled and started operating. The machines were different; therefore, each had to be recorded separately in the accounts.

	Machine A	Machine B	Machine C
Invoice price paid for asset	$11,000	$30,000	$8,000
Shipping costs (paid by Plummer)	500	1,000	500
Renovation costs prior to use	2,500	1,000	1,500

By the end of the first year, each machine had been operating 4,800 hours.

Required:

1. Compute the cost of each machine.
2. Give the entry to record depreciation expense at the end of Year 1, assuming the following:

Machine	ESTIMATES Life	Residual Value	Depreciation Method
A	5 years	$1,000	Straight-line
B	60,000 hours	2,000	Units-of-production
C	4 years	1,500	Double-declining-balance

Inferring Depreciation Amounts and Determining the Effects of a Depreciation Error on Key Ratios (AP8-4)

P8-4
LO8-1, 8-3
Best Buy Co., Inc.

Best Buy Co., Inc., headquartered in Richfield, Minnesota, is one of the leading consumer electronics retailers, operating more than 1,100 stores across the globe. The following was reported in a recent annual report:

CONSOLIDATED BALANCE SHEETS (partial)

($ in millions)	Current Year	Prior Year
ASSETS		
Property and Equipment		
Land and buildings	$ 650	$ 637
Leasehold improvements	2,203	2,119
Fixtures and equipment	6,286	5,865
Property under capital and finance leases	89	579
	9,228	9,200
Less accumulated depreciation	6,900	6,690
Net property and equipment	2,328	2,510

Source: Best Buy Co., Inc.

Required:

1. Assuming that Best Buy did not sell any property, plant, and equipment in the current year, what was the amount of depreciation expense recorded during the current year?
2. Assume that Best Buy failed to record depreciation during the current year. Indicate the effect of the error (i.e., overstated, understated, or no effect) on the following ratios:
   a. Earnings per share.
   b. Fixed asset turnover.
   c. Current ratio.
   d. Return on assets.

Recording and Interpreting the Disposal of Three Long-Lived Assets (AP8-5)

P8-5
LO8-3, 8-5

During the current year, Yost Company disposed of three different assets. On January 1 of the current year, prior to the disposal of the assets, the accounts reflected the following:

Asset	Original Cost	Residual Value	Estimated Life	Accumulated Depreciation (straight line)
Machine A	$ 21,000	$ 3,000	8 years	$15,750 (7 years)
Machine B	120,000	14,000	10 years	84,800 (8 years)
Machine C	85,000	5,000	15 years	64,000 (12 years)

The machines were disposed of during the current year in the following ways:

a. Machine A: Sold on January 1 for $5,000 cash.
b. Machine B: Sold on December 31 for $30,500; received cash, $22,500, and an $8,000 interest-bearing (12 percent) note receivable due at the end of 12 months.
c. Machine C: On January 1, this machine suffered irreparable damage from an accident. On January 10, a salvage company removed the machine at no cost.

Required:

1. Give all journal entries related to the disposal of each machine in the current year.
2. Explain the accounting rationale for the way that you recorded each disposal.

P8-6 Recording Journal Entries Related to Various Long-Lived Assets (AP8-6)

LO8-2, 8-3, 8-6

During the current year ending on December 31, BSP Company completed the following transactions:

a. On January 1, purchased a patent for $28,000 cash (estimated useful life, seven years).
b. On January 1, purchased another business for $164,000 cash, including $10,000 for goodwill. The assets included accounts receivable with a fair value of $12,000 and property and equipment with a fair value of $142,000 (with a residual value of $15,000 and estimated useful life of 10 years). The company assumed no liabilities. Goodwill has an indefinite life.
c. On December 31, constructed a storage shed on land leased from D. Heald. The cost of the shed was $15,600. The company uses the straight-line amortization method. The lease will expire in three years. (Amounts spent to enhance leased property are capitalized as intangible assets called Leasehold Improvements.)
d. Total expenditures for ordinary repairs were $5,500 during the current year.
e. On December 31 of the current year, sold Machine A for $6,000 cash. Original cost was $25,000; accumulated depreciation to December 31 of the prior year was $16,000 (on a straight-line basis with a $5,000 residual value and five-year useful life).
f. On December 31 of the current year, paid $5,000 for a complete reconditioning of Machine B acquired on January 1 of the prior year. Original cost, $31,000; accumulated depreciation to December 31 of the prior year was $1,600 (on a straight-line basis with a $7,000 residual value and 15-year useful life).

Required:

1. Record journal entries for transactions (*a*) through (*f*).
2. For each of the assets involved in transactions (*a*) through (*f*), record the adjusting entry for depreciation or amortization expense at the end of the current year. If no adjusting entry is needed, explain why.

P8-7 Computing Goodwill from the Purchase of a Business and Related Depreciation and Amortization (AP8-7)

LO8-3, 8-6

The notes to a recent annual report from Suzie's Shoe Corporation indicated that the company acquired another company, Steve's Shoes, Inc.

Assume that Suzie's acquired Steve's Shoes on January 5 of the current year. Suzie's acquired the name of the company and all of its assets for $750,000 cash. Suzie's did not assume the liabilities. The transaction was closed on January 5 of the current year, at which time the balance sheet of Steve's Shoes reflected the following book values. An independent appraiser estimated the following market values for the assets.

STEVE'S SHOES, INC.		
January 5 of the Current Year	**Book Value**	**Market Value**
Accounts receivable (net)	$ 50,000	$ 50,000
Inventory	385,000	350,000
Fixed assets (net)	156,000	208,000
Other assets	4,000	10,000
Total assets	$595,000	
Liabilities	$ 75,000	
Stockholders' equity	520,000	
Total liabilities and stockholders' equity	$595,000	

Required:

1. Compute the amount of goodwill resulting from the purchase. (**Hint:** Assets are purchased at market value in conformity with the cost principle.)
2. Compute the adjustments that Suzie's Shoes Corporation would make at the end of the current year (ending December 31) for the following items acquired from Steve's Shoes:
   a. Depreciation of the fixed assets (straight line), assuming an estimated remaining useful life of 10 years and no residual value.
   b. Goodwill (an intangible asset with an indefinite life).

Computing Amortization, Book Value, and Asset Impairment Related to Different Intangible Assets (AP8-8)

P8-8
LO8-3, 8-4, 8-6
Starn Tool & Manufacturing Company

Starn Tool & Manufacturing Company, located in Meadville, PA, provides component machining for robotics, drones, vision systems, and special machines and assemblies for the aerospace, military, commercial, automotive, and medical industries. Assume the company has five different intangible assets to be accounted for and reported on the financial statements. The management is concerned about the amortization of the cost of each of these intangibles. Facts about each intangible follow:

a. **Patent.** The company purchased a patent for a new tool at a cash cost of $55,900 on January 1, 2023. The patent has an estimated useful life of 13 years.
b. **Copyright.** On January 1, 2023, the company purchased a copyright for $22,500 cash. It is estimated that the copyrighted item will have no value by the end of 10 years.
c. **Franchise.** The company obtained a franchise from H & H Tool Company to make and distribute a special item for the automotive industry. It obtained the franchise on January 1, 2023, at a cash cost of $14,400 for a 10-year period.
d. **License.** On January 1, 2022, the company secured a license from the city to operate a special service for a period of five years. Total cash expended to obtain the license was $14,000.
e. **Goodwill.** The company purchased another business in January 2020 for a cash lump sum of $400,000. Included in the purchase price was "Goodwill, $40,000." Company executives stated that "the goodwill is an important long-lived asset to us." It has an indefinite life.

Required:

1. Compute the amount of amortization that should be recorded for each intangible asset at the end of the annual accounting period, December 31, 2023.
2. Give the book value of each intangible asset on December 31, 2024.
3. Assume that on January 2, 2025, the copyrighted item was likely impaired in its ability to continue to produce strong revenues due to a legal dispute. The other intangible assets were not affected. Starn estimated that the copyright would be able to produce future cash flows of $17,000. The fair value of the copyright was determined to be $16,000. Compute the amount, if any, of the impairment loss to be recorded.

(Chapter Supplement) Analyzing and Recording Entries Related to a Change in Estimated Life and Residual Value (AP8-9)

P8-9
LO8-3
Springer International Publishing

Springer International Publishing, headquartered in Berlin, Germany, is a leading global publisher of scientific, technical, and medical journals and books for researchers in academia, scientific institutions, and corporate

R&D departments. For print publications, assume that Springer owns a Didde press (now manufactured by **Graphic Systems Services**) that was acquired at an original cost of $400,000. It is being depreciated on a straight-line basis over a 20-year estimated useful life and has a $50,000 estimated residual value. At the end of the prior year, the press had been depreciated for a full six years. At the beginning of January of the current year, a decision was made, on the basis of improved maintenance procedures, that a total estimated useful life of 25 years and a residual value of $73,000 would be more realistic. The accounting period ends December 31.

Required:

1. Compute (*a*) the amount of depreciation expense recorded in the prior year and (*b*) the book value of the printing press at the end of the prior year.
2. Give the adjusting entry for depreciation at December 31 of the current year. Show computations (round amount to the nearest dollar).

ALTERNATE PROBLEMS

AP8-1 Explaining the Nature of a Long-Lived Asset and Determining and Recording the Financial Statement Effects of Its Purchase (P8-1)

LO8-1, 8-2

On June 1, the Wallace Corp. received a machine it had ordered with an invoice price of $60,000. Freight costs of $650 were paid by the vendor per the sales agreement. The company exchanged the following on June 1 to acquire the machine:

a. Issued 2,000 shares of Wallace Corp. common stock, par value $2 (market value, $6 per share).
b. Signed a 12 percent note payable for $40,000; principal and interest are due September 1 of the current year.
c. The balance of the invoice price was on account with the vendor, to be paid in cash on July 1.

On June 3, Wallace Corp. paid $1,500 cash for installation costs.
On July 1, Wallace Corp. paid the balance due on its accounts payable to the vendor.

Required:

1. What are the classifications of long-lived assets? Explain their differences.
2. Record the purchase on June 1, the payment of the installation costs on June 3, and the subsequent payment on July 1. Show computations.
3. Indicate the accounts, amounts, and effects (+ for increase and − for decrease) of the purchase and subsequent cash payment on the accounting equation. Use the following structure:

Date	Assets	=	Liabilities	+	Stockholders' Equity

4. What was the cost of the equipment recorded by Wallace Corp.? Explain the basis you used for any questionable items.

AP8-2 Analyzing the Effects of Repairs, an Addition, and Depreciation (P8-2)

LO8-2, 8-3
AMERCO
U-Haul International, Inc.

A recent annual report for **AMERCO**, the holding company for **U-Haul International, Inc.**, included the following note:

> **NOTES TO CONSOLIDATED FINANCIAL STATEMENTS**
>
> **Note 3. Accounting Policies**
>
> ***Property, Plant and Equipment***
>
> Our Property, plant and equipment is stated at cost. Interest expense, if any, incurred during the initial construction of buildings and rental equipment is considered part of cost. Depreciation is computed for financial reporting purposes using the straight line or an accelerated method based on a declining balance formula over the following estimated useful lives: rental equipment 2–20 years and buildings and non-rental equipment 3–55 years. Routine maintenance costs are charged to operating expense as they are incurred.

Source: AMERCO

AMERCO subsidiaries own property, plant, and equipment that are utilized in the manufacture, repair, and rental of U-Haul equipment and that provide offices for U-Haul. Assume that AMERCO made extensive repairs on an existing building and added a new wing. The building is a garage and repair facility for rental trucks that serve the Seattle area. The existing building originally cost $330,000, and by the end of its fifth year, the building was one-quarter depreciated on the basis of a 20-year estimated useful life and no residual value. Assume straight-line depreciation. During the sixth year, the following transactions related to the building were made:

a. Ordinary repairs and maintenance expenditures for the year, $6,000 cash.
b. Extensive and major repairs to the roof of the building, $17,000 cash. These repairs were completed on December 31.
c. Record depreciation for the current year.

Required:
1. Applying the policies of AMERCO, complete the following, indicating the effects for the preceding expenditures for the sixth year. If there is no effect on an account, write NE on the line.

	Building	Accumulated Depreciation	Depreciation Expense	Repairs Expense	Cash
Balance January 1	$330,000	$82,500			
a.					
b.					
c.					
Balance December 31					

2. What was the book value of the building on December 31 of the sixth year?
3. Explain the effect of depreciation on cash flows.

Computing the Acquisition Cost and Recording Depreciation under Three Alternative Methods (P8-3)

AP8-3
LO8-2, 8-3

At the beginning of the year, Ramos Inc. bought three used machines from Santaro Corporation. The machines immediately were overhauled and started operating. The machines were different; therefore, each had to be recorded separately in the accounts.

	Machine A	Machine B	Machine C
Invoice price of the asset	$12,200	$32,500	$21,700
Shipping costs	1,600	1,100	1,100
Renovation costs prior to use	600	1,400	1,600

By the end of the first year, each machine had been operating 7,000 hours.

Required:
1. Compute the cost of each machine.
2. Give the entry to record depreciation expense at the end of Year 1 (with separate accumulated depreciation accounts for each machine), assuming the following:

ESTIMATES			
Machine	Life	Residual Value	Depreciation Method
A	8 years	$1,000	Straight-line
B	33,000 hours	2,000	Units-of-production
C	5 years	1,400	Double-declining-balance

AP8-4
LO8-1, 8-3
The Gap, Inc.

Inferring Depreciation Amounts and Determining the Effects of a Depreciation Error on Key Ratios (P8-4)

The Gap, Inc., is a global retailer of apparel, accessories, and personal care products for women, men, and children under the Gap, Banana Republic, Old Navy, Athleta, Intermix, Janie and Jack, and Hill City brands. The Company operates approximately 3,900 stores across the globe, as well as online. The following is a note from a recent annual report:

Note 2. Additional Financial Statement Information

Property and Equipment

Property and equipment are stated at cost less accumulated depreciation and consist of the following:

($ in millions)	**Current Year**	**Prior Year**
Leasehold improvements	$ 2,923	$ 3,104
Furniture and equipment	2,802	2,732
Software	1,626	1,525
Land, buildings, and building improvements	1,408	1,123
Construction-in-progress	202	183
Property and equipment, at cost	8,961	8,667
Less: Accumulated depreciation	(5,839)	(5,755)
Property and equipment, net of accumulated depreciation	$ 3,122	$ 2,912

Source: The Gap, Inc.

Required:

1. Assuming The Gap, Inc., had no asset impairment write-offs and sold property, plant, and equipment in the most recent year with a cost of $568 million and an accumulated depreciation of $439 million, what was the amount of depreciation expense recorded in the current year?
2. Assume that The Gap, Inc., failed to record depreciation in the current year. Indicate the effect of the error (i.e., overstated, understated, or no effect) on the following ratios:
   a. Earnings per share.
   b. Fixed asset turnover.
   c. Current ratio.
   d. Return on assets.

AP8-5
LO8-3, 8-5

Recording and Interpreting the Disposal of Three Long-Lived Assets (P8-5)

During the current year ended December 31, Rank Company disposed of three different assets. On January 1 of the current year, prior to their disposal, the asset accounts reflected the following:

Asset	Original Cost	Residual Value	Estimated Life	Accumulated Depreciation (straight line)
Machine A	$24,000	$2,000	5 years	$17,600 (4 years)
Machine B	16,500	5,000	20 years	4,025 (7 years)
Machine C	59,200	3,200	14 years	48,000 (12 years)

The machines were disposed of during the current year in the following ways:

a. Machine A: Sold on January 1 for $6,750 cash.
b. Machine B: Sold on December 31 for $8,000; received cash, $2,000, and a $6,000 interest-bearing (10 percent) note receivable due at the end of 12 months.
c. Machine C: On January 1, this machine suffered irreparable damage from an accident and was scrapped.

Required:
1. Prepare all journal entries related to the disposal of each machine.
2. Explain the accounting rationale for the way in which you recorded each disposal.

Determining Financial Statement Effects of Activities Related to Various Long-Lived Assets (P8-6)

AP8-6
LO8-2, 8-3, 8-6

During the current year ending December 31, Nguyen Corporation completed the following transactions:

a. On January 1, purchased a license for $7,200 cash (estimated useful life, four years).
b. On January 1, repaved the parking lot of the building leased from H. Lane. The cost was $17,800; the estimated useful life was five years with no residual value. The lease will expire in 10 years. (Amounts spent to enhance leased property are capitalized as intangible assets called Leasehold Improvements.)
c. On July 1, purchased another business for $120,000 cash. The fair market value of the purchased assets included $32,000 in inventory and $83,000 in equipment (with a residual value of $12,000 and estimated useful life of 10 years). Nguyen also assumed $24,000 in accounts payable. The remainder was goodwill with an indefinite life.
d. On December 31, sold Machine A for $6,000 cash. Original cost, $21,500; accumulated depreciation (straight line) to December 31 of the prior year, $13,500 ($3,500 residual value and four-year life).
e. Total expenditures during the current year for ordinary repairs were $6,700.
f. On December 31, paid $8,000 for a complete reconditioning of Machine B. Original cost, $18,000; accumulated depreciation to December 31 of the prior year, $12,000 (based on the straight-line method using a $2,000 residual value and four-year life).

Required:
1. Record the journal entries for transactions (*a*) through (*f*).
2. For each of the assets involved in transactions (*a*) through (*f*), record the adjusting entry for depreciation or amortization expense at the end of the current year on December 31.

Computing Goodwill from the Purchase of a Business and Related Depreciation and Amortization (P8-7)

AP8-7
LO8-3, 8-6

The notes to a recent annual report from Lakshmi Financial Services Corporation indicated that the company acquired another company, Sanjeev Insurance Company.

Assume that Lakshmi finalized the purchase of Sanjeev on January 2 of the current year. Lakshmi acquired all of Sanjeev's assets and assumed Sanjeev's liabilities for $1,400,000 cash. On January 2, Sanjeev Insurance Company's balance sheet reflected the following book value. An independent appraiser estimated the following fair market value for the assets.

SANJEEV INSURANCE COMPANY

On January 2 of the Current Year	Book Value	Fair Market Value
Accounts receivable	$ 370,000	$ 370,000
Short-term investments	930,000	$1,090,000
Equipment (net)	70,000	25,000
Operating lease right-of-use assets	154,000	180,000
Total assets	$1,524,000	
Accounts payable	$ 6,000	$ 6,000
Unearned revenue (*deposits from clients*)	1,002,000	1,002,000
Lease liabilities	140,000	130,000
Stockholders' equity	376,000	
Total liabilities and stockholders' equity	$1,524,000	

Required:
1. Compute the amount of goodwill resulting from the purchase. (**Hint:** Identifiable assets and liabilities are purchased at market value in conformity with the cost principle.)

2. Compute the adjustments that Lakshmi Financial Services Corporation would make at the end of the current year (ending December 31) for the following items acquired from Sanjeev's Insurance Company:
   a. Depreciation of equipment (straight-line), assuming an estimated remaining useful life of eight years and no residual value.
   b. Goodwill (an intangible asset with an indefinite life).

AP8-8
LO8-3, 8-4, 8-6

Computing Amortization, Book Value, and Asset Impairment Related to Different Intangible Assets (P8-8)

Carey Corporation has five different intangible assets to be accounted for and reported on the financial statements. The management is concerned about the amortization of the cost of each of these intangibles. Facts about each intangible follow:

a. **Goodwill.** The company started business in January 2010 by purchasing another business for a cash lump sum of $650,000. Included in the purchase price was "Goodwill, $75,000." Company executives stated that "the goodwill is an important long-lived asset to us." It has an indefinite life.
b. **Patent.** The company purchased a patent at a cash cost of $18,600 on January 1, 2023. It is amortized over its expected useful life of 10 years.
c. **Copyright.** On January 1, 2023, the company purchased a copyright for $24,750 cash. It is estimated that the copyrighted item will have no value by the end of 30 years.
d. **Franchise.** The company obtained a franchise from Cirba Company to make and distribute a special item. It obtained the franchise on January 1, 2023, at a cash cost of $19,200 for a 12-year period.
e. **License.** On January 1, 2022, the company secured a license from the city to operate a special service for a period of seven years. Total cash expended to obtain the license was $21,700.

Required:
1. Compute the amount of amortization that should be recorded for each intangible asset at the end of the annual accounting period, December 31, 2023.
2. Give the book value of each intangible asset on January 1, 2026.
3. Assume that on January 1, 2026, the franchise was likely impaired in its ability to continue to produce strong revenues due to a weakened demand for the products. The other intangible assets were not affected. Carey estimated that the franchise would be able to produce future cash flows of $13,500. The fair value of the franchise was determined to be $12,000. Compute the amount, if any, of the impairment loss to be recorded.

AP8-9
LO8-3

(Chapter Supplement) Analyzing and Recording Entries related to a Change in Estimated Life and Residual Value (P8-9)

Ramirez Foods Company acquired a corn flour milling machine for $20,000 and depreciated it on a straight-line basis over an eight-year useful life with a residual value of $3,000. At the end of the prior year, the machine had been depreciated for a full five years. At the beginning of January of the current year, based on new information, the total estimated useful life would be 13 years with a residual value of $1,375. The company's accounting period ends December 31.

Required:
1. Compute (a) the amount of depreciation expense recorded in the prior year and (b) the book value of the milling machine at the end of the prior year.
2. Give the adjusting entry for depreciation at December 31 of the current year.

CONTINUING PROBLEM

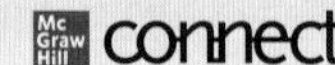

CON8-1
LO8-2, 8-3, 8-5

Asset Acquisition, Depreciation, and Disposal

Pool Corporation, Inc., is the world's largest wholesale distributor of swimming pool supplies and equipment. Assume Pool Corporation purchased for cash new loading equipment for the warehouse on January 1 of Year 1, at an invoice price of $72,000. It also paid $2,000 for freight on the equipment, $1,300 to prepare the equipment for use in the warehouse, and $800 for insurance to cover the equipment during operation in Year 1. The equipment was estimated to have a residual value of $3,300 and be used over three years or 24,000 hours.

Required:

1. Record the purchase of the equipment, freight, preparation costs, and insurance on January 1 of Year 1.
2. Create a depreciation schedule assuming Pool Corporation uses the straight-line method.
3. Create a depreciation schedule assuming Pool Corporation uses the double-declining-balance method. Round answers to the nearest dollar.
4. Create a depreciation schedule assuming Pool Corporation uses the units-of-production method, with actual production of 8,000 hours in Year 1; 7,400 hours in Year 2; and 8,600 hours in Year 3.
5. On December 31 of Year 2 before the year-end adjustments, the equipment was sold for $22,500. Record the sale of the equipment assuming the company used the straight-line method.

COMPREHENSIVE PROBLEM (CHAPTERS 6–8)

COMP8-1
LO3-6, 5-3, 6-2, 7-2, 7-4, 8-3, 8-4, 8-5, 8-6
Keurig Dr Pepper

Complete the requirements for each of the following Independent cases:

Case A. **Keurig Dr Pepper**, is a leading worldwide integrated brand owner, bottler, and distributor of non-alcoholic beverages. Key brands include Dr Pepper, Snapple, 7-UP, Mott's juices, A&W root beer, Canada Dry ginger ale, Bai antioxidant infusion drinks, and Green Mountain coffee among others, plus the innovative Keurig single-serve coffee system.

The following represents selected data from recent financial statements of Keurig Dr Pepper (dollars in millions):

KEURIG DR PEPPER

Consolidated Balance Sheets (partial)

(in millions)	December 31, 20×3	December 31, 20×2
Assets		
Current assets:		
Cash and cash equivalents	$ 240	$ 75
Accounts receivable (net of allowances of $21 and $9, respectively)	1,048	1,115

Consolidated Statements of Income (Partial)

	For the Year Ended December 31		
(in millions)	20×3	20×2	20×1
Net sales	$11,618	$11,120	$7,442
. . .			
Net income	$ 1,325	$ 1,254	$ 589

Source: Keurig Dr Pepper

The company also reported bad debt expense of $17 million in 20×3, $2 million in 20×2, and $5 million in 20×1.

1. Record the company's write-offs of uncollectible accounts for 20×3.
2. Assuming all sales were on credit, what amount of cash did Keurig Dr Pepper collect from customers in 20×3?
3. Compute the company's net profit margin (with the percentage rounded to one decimal place) for the three years presented. What does the trend suggest to you about Keurig Dr Pepper?

Case B. Samuda Enterprises uses the aging approach to estimate bad debt expense. At the end of the current year, Samuda reported a balance in accounts receivable of $620,000 and estimated that $12,400 of its accounts receivable would likely be uncollectible. The allowance for doubtful accounts has a $1,500 debit balance at year-end (i.e., more was written off during the year than the balance in the account).

1. What amount of bad debt expense should be recorded for the current year?
2. What amount will be reported on the current year's balance sheet for accounts receivable?

Case C. At the end of the current year, the unadjusted trial balance of Branco, Inc., indicated $6,530,000 in Accounts Receivable, a credit balance of $9,200 in Allowance for Doubtful Accounts, and Sales Revenue (all on credit) of $155,380,000. Based on knowledge that the current economy is in distress, Branco increased its bad debt rate estimate to 0.3 percent of credit sales.

1. What amount of bad debt expense should be recorded for the current year?
2. What amount will be reported on the current year's balance sheet for accounts receivable?

Case D. Tompkins Company reports the following inventory record for November:

INVENTORY			
Date	**Activity**	**# of Units**	**Cost/Unit**
November 1	Beginning balance	100	$16
November 4	Purchase	300	19
November 7	Sale (@ $50 per unit)	200	
November 13	Purchase	500	21
November 22	Sale (@ $50 per unit)	500	

Selling, administrative, and depreciation expenses for the month were $16,000. Tompkins's effective tax rate is 25 percent.

1. Calculate the cost of ending inventory and the cost of goods sold under each of the following methods (assume a periodic inventory system):
   a. First-in, first-out.
   b. Last-in, first-out.
   c. Weighted average (round unit cost to the nearest penny).
2. Based on your answers in requirement (1):
   a. What is the gross profit percentage under the FIFO method (round your percentage to two decimal places)?
   b. What is net income under the LIFO method?
   c. Which method would you recommend to Tompkins for tax and financial reporting purposes? Explain your recommendation.
3. Tompkins applied the lower of cost or market method to value its inventory for reporting purposes at the end of the month. Assuming Tompkins used the FIFO method and that inventory had a market replacement value of $19.50 per unit, what would Tompkins report on the balance sheet for inventory? Why?

Case E. Delso Company purchased the following on January 1, 20×1:

- Office equipment at a cost of $60,000 with an estimated useful life to the company of three years and a residual value of $15,000. The company uses the double-declining-balance method of depreciation for the equipment.
- Factory equipment at an invoice price of $880,000 plus shipping costs of $20,000. The equipment has an estimated useful life of 100,000 hours and no residual value. The company uses the units-of-production method of depreciation for the equipment.
- A patent at a cost of $330,000 with an estimated useful life of 15 years. The company uses the straight-line method of amortization for intangible assets with no residual value.

The company's year ends on December 31.

1. Prepare a partial depreciation schedule for 20×1, 20×2, and 20×3 for the following assets (round your answers to the nearest dollar):
   a. Office equipment.
   b. Factory equipment. The company used the equipment for 8,000 hours in 20×1, 9,200 hours in 20×2, and 8,900 hours in 20×3.
2. On January 1, 20×4, Delso altered its corporate strategy dramatically. The company sold the factory equipment for $700,000 in cash. Record the entry related to the sale of the factory equipment.
3. On January 1, 20×4, when the company changed its corporate strategy, the demand for one of its products produced by using the patent was significantly reduced. Its patent had estimated future cash flows of $210,000 and a fair value of $190,000. What would the company report on the income statement (account and amount) regarding the patent on January 1, 20×4? Explain your answer.

Complete the requirements for the following:

COMP8-2
LO6-1, 6-2, 7-2, 8-2, 8-3, 8-5, 8-6

Becky Olson established her corporation, Olson Sports, Inc., several years ago in Boulder, Colorado, to sell hiking and ski equipment in her store and online. The annual reporting period for the company ends December 31. Becky prepared the adjusted trial balance below at the end of 2023. However, her CPA audited the trial balance information she presented and found several items that need to be updated before financial statements can be prepared. These items are listed below Becky's trial balance. All amounts in the trial balance and in the listed items to be updated are in thousands of dollars.

OLSON SPORTS, INC. Adjusted Trial Balance December 31, 2023 (prepared by Becky Olson)		
($ in thousands)	**Debit**	**Credit**
Cash	570	
Accounts receivable	373	
Allowance for doubtful accounts		18
Inventories	539	
Prepaid expenses	59	
Land	22	
Building	189	
Equipment *(furniture, fixtures, and computers)*	360	
Accumulated depreciation		222
Software	90	
Patents	1	
Goodwill	161	
Accounts payable		252
Accrued liabilities		182
Income taxes payable		16
Long-term debt		49
Common stock		3
Additional paid-in capital		243
Retained earnings		1,107
Sale revenue		2,487
Credit card discounts	53	
Cost of sales	1,306	
Advertising expense	145	
Utilities expense	85	
Wages expense	625	
Interest expense	1	
Total	**4,579**	**4,579**

Microsoft Corporation

a. On the last day of the year, failed to record the $100 sale of hiking merchandise to a customer who paid with his Visa credit card. Visa charges Olson Sports a 3 percent fee.

b. On December 31, failed to write off a $3 bad debt.

c. Failed to record bad debt expense for the year. After the write-off in (*b*), based on an aging of the accounts receivable, Olson Sports calculated that $21 will likely be uncollectible.

d. The auditor noted that the inventory is listed on the trial balance at current cost using the first-in, first-out method. However, it should be measured using the last-in, first-out method. Beginning inventory was 15 units at $10 per unit, the April 10 purchase was 40 units at $11 per unit, the July 2 purchase was 52 units at $13 per unit, and the October 4 purchase was 28 units at $16 per unit. The count of inventory on hand at the end of the year was 35 units.

e. Failed to record $10 in new store fixtures (equipment) that arrived at Olson Sports's shipping dock during the last week of the year, with payment due to the manufacturer within 30 days. Olson Sports paid $1 cash for delivery and $3 to install the new fixtures.

f. On December 31, failed to record the sale of old computers (equipment) with a cost of $20 and a net book value of $8 for $3 cash. When they were sold, no depreciation had been recorded for the year. Olson Sports depreciates computer equipment using the straight-line method with a residual value of $4 over a four-year useful life. (**Hint:** Prepare two entries.)

g. Failed to amortize the accounting software that Olson Sports purchased at the beginning of the year. It is estimated to have a three-year useful life with no residual value. The company does not use a contra-account.

h. Failed to record the annual depreciation for the building and furniture (equipment):
- The building is depreciated using the straight-line method with a residual value of $9 over a 20-year useful life.
- Furniture costing $120 is depreciated using the double-declining-balance method with a residual value of $20 over a 10-year useful life. The accumulated depreciation of the furniture at the beginning of the year was $60.

i. Failed to record income tax expense for the year. Including the effects of the above entries, record Olson Sports's income tax expense at an effective rate of 24 percent. Round your answer to the nearest dollar.

Required:
1. Prepare journal entries to record the transactions and adjustments listed in *(a)* through *(i)*.
2. If you are completing this problem manually, create T-accounts, using the trial balance information as beginning balances, and then post the entries from requirement 1 to the T-accounts. Then prepare a revised adjusted trial balance. (If you are completing this problem in Connect, this requirement will be completed automatically for you using your responses to requirement 1.)
3. Prepare Olson Sports's annual income statement (multiple-step format with income from operations subtotal), statement of stockholders' equity, and classified balance sheet.

CASES AND PROJECTS

Annual Report Cases

CP8-1
LO8-1, 8-2, 8-3, 8-4, 8-5, 8-6, 8-7
Target Corporation

Finding Financial Information

Refer to the financial statements of **Target Corporation** in Appendix B at the end of this book. All dollar amounts are in millions. Use the notes to the financial statements for answering some of the questions.

1. How much did the company spend on property and equipment (capital expenditures) in the most recent fiscal year and where did you find this information?
   a. $26,879, found on the balance sheet.
   b. $26,283, found on the balance sheet.
   c. $2,649, found on the statement of cash flows.
   d. $3,516, found on the statement of cash flows.
   e. $1,210, determined from information on the balance sheet.
2. What is the percentage of Target's cost of computer hardware and software to its total cost of property and equipment for the most recent year? Round to the one decimal place.
   a. 5.9 percent
   b. 10.3 percent
   c. 5.4 percent
   d. 39.6 percent
   e. Cannot determine the percentage from the information provided.

3. Using information (1) on the cash received from disposal of property and equipment, (2) that all noncash losses for the most recent year related to the disposal of property and equipment, and (3) that the accumulated depreciation on the property and equipment that was sold was $1,311, what was the original cost of the property and equipment that was sold during the most recent year? (**Hints:** Review the statement of cash flows and reconstruct the journal entry made to dispose of the property and equipment.)
   a. $1,439
   b. $1,353
   c. $1,397
   d. Some other amount.
4. What method does Target use to depreciate its property and equipment?
   a. Units-of-production
   b. Declining-balance
   c. Straight-line
   d. MACRS
5. What was the amount of Goodwill reported for the most recent year?
   a. $668
   b. $663
   c. $37
   d. $631
   e. Goodwill is not disclosed in the Target 10-K report.
6. How much did Target recognize as impairment losses in fiscal year ending February 1, 2020?
   a. $92
   b. $23
   c. $62
   d. $0
7. What was Target's fixed asset turnover ratio for the most recent year presented and what does is suggest about Target?
   a. 3.48, suggesting that Target's management is efficient in utilizing fixed assets to generate sales.
   b. 3.52, suggesting that Target's management is efficient in utilizing fixed assets to generate total operating revenues.
   c. 1.97, suggesting that Target's management is not efficient in utilizing fixed assets to generate sales.
   d. 0.16, suggesting that Target's management is not efficient in utilizing assets to generate net income.

Finding Financial Information

CP8-2
LO8-1, 8-3
Walmart Inc.

Refer to the financial statements of **Walmart Inc.** in Appendix C at the end of this book. All dollar amounts are in millions.

1. What depreciation method does Walmart use for its property and equipment?
2. What was the balance of accumulated depreciation as of the end of the most recent year?
3. Record the summary adjusting journal entry that Walmart would have recorded for depreciation and amortization for the most recent year? (**Hint:** Review the statement of cash flows.)
4. What is Walmart's fixed asset turnover on total operating revenues for the most recent fiscal year ended in 2021 (round to two decimal places)?
5. In the fiscal year ended in 2020, Walmart's fixed asset turnover ratio was 5.00 and, in the fiscal year ended in 2019, fixed asset turnover ratio was 4.85. Between 2019 and 2020, what does this suggest about Walmart over time?
   a. Walmart's management was less efficient at utilizing fixed assets to generate operating revenues over time.
   b. Walmart's management sold property and equipment in 2020.
   c. Walmart's management was more effective at generating revenues or controlling costs over time.
   d. Walmart's management was more efficient at utilizing fixed assets to generate operating revenues over time.

Comparing Companies within an Industry

CP8-3
LO8-1, 8-3, 8-5
Target Corporation
Walmart Inc.

Refer to the following:

- **Target Corporation** in Appendix B,
- **Walmart Inc.** in Appendix C, and the
- **Industry Ratio Report** in Appendix D at the end of this book.

All dollar amounts are in millions of dollars.

1. Compute the fixed asset turnover ratio on total operating revenues for both companies (round your answers to two decimal places).

2. Compared to each other, is the management of these two companies more or less effective at utilizing fixed assets to generate operating revenue?
   a. Target's management is less effective than Walmart's management at utilizing fixed assets to generate sales.
   b. Target's management is less effective at controlling expenses than Walmart's management.
   c. Both companies' ratios suggest that their management teams are each likely to generate revenues with current assets.
   d. Target's management is doing poorly.
3. How does each company's management compare to the industry regarding the fixed asset turnover ratio?
   a. Target's management is less effective and Walmart's management is more effective at utilizing fixed assets to generate revenues than the average company in the industry.
   b. Target's management is more effective and Walmart's management is less effective at generating sales and controlling costs with assets compared to the industry average.
   c. Target's and Walmart's managements are both less effective at utilizing fixed assets to generate operating revenues than the average company in the industry.
   d. Target's management is weaker than Walmart's management because of its smaller size.
4. If both companies failed to record the entry for the impairment of property and equipment for the most recent year, what impact will that have on the fixed asset turnover ratio?
   a. There will be no effect on either company's fixed asset turnover ratio.
   b. Failure to record the entry for impairment understates operating expenses, resulting in higher net income and a higher fixed asset turnover ratio for the year.
   c. Target's ratio will be higher than Walmart's ratio.
   d. Failure to record the impairment of property and equipment overstates assets, resulting in a higher denominator and lower fixed asset turnover ratio for the year.
5. For each company, calculate the percentage change in property and equipment (net) from fiscal year ended in 2020 to the fiscal year ended in 2021 for Target and Walmart (round your percentage to two decimal places and use + if the percentage change increased and – if the percentage change decreased):

Percentage Change in:	Target	Walmart
Property and equipment (net)		

Both companies had capital expenditures and recorded depreciation during the most recent year. What does the percentage change result suggest about each company's activities regarding property and equipment during the most recent year?

Financial Reporting and Analysis Cases

CP8-4
LO8-3
Sysco Corporation

Using Financial Reports: Analyzing the Age of Assets

As stated in its recent annual report, "**Sysco Corporation** . . . is the largest global distributor of food and related products primarily to the foodservice or food-away-from-home industry. We provide products and related services to over 625,000 customer locations, including restaurants, healthcare and educational facilities, lodging establishments and other foodservice customers." A note in a recent annual report for Sysco contained the following information:

(in thousands)	Current Year
Land	$ 493,694
Buildings and improvements	4,854,307
Fleet and equipment	3,561,500
Computer hardware and software	1,258,980
	10,168,481
Accumulated depreciation	(5,709,914)
	$4,458,567

Source: Sysco Corporation

Depreciation expense (in thousands of dollars) charged to operations was $705,200 in the current year. Depreciation generally is computed using the straight-line method for financial reporting purposes.

Required:

1. What is your best estimate of the average expected life for Sysco's depreciable assets? Round your answer to one decimal place.
2. What is your best estimate of the average age of Sysco's depreciable assets? Round your answer to one decimal place.

Evaluating the Effect of Alternative Depreciation Methods on Key Ratios from an Analyst's Perspective

CP8-5
LO8-1, 8-3
Ford Motor Company

You are a financial analyst for **Ford Motor Company** and have been asked to determine the impact of alternative depreciation methods. For your analysis, you have been asked to compare methods based on a machine that cost $106,000. The estimated useful life is 13 years and the estimated residual value is $2,000. The machine has an estimated useful life in productive output of 200,000 units. Actual output was 20,000 in Year 1 and 16,000 in Year 2. (Round results to the nearest dollar.)

Required:

1. For years 1 and 2 only, prepare separate depreciation schedules assuming:
   a. Straight-line method.
   b. Units-of-production method.
   c. Double-declining-balance method.
2. Evaluate each method in terms of its effect on cash flow, fixed asset turnover, and earnings per share (EPS). Assuming that Ford Motor Company is most interested in reducing taxes and maintaining a high EPS for Year 1, what would you recommend to management? Would your recommendation change for Year 2? Why or why not?

Using Financial Reports: Analyzing Fixed Asset Turnover Ratio and Cash Flows

CP8-6
LO8-1, 8-6, 8-7

Karl Company operates in both the beverage and entertainment industries. In June 2013, Karl purchased Good Time, Inc., which produces and distributes motion picture, television, and home video products and recorded music; publishes books; and operates theme parks and retail stores. The purchase resulted in $2.7 billion in goodwill. Since then, Karl has undertaken a number of business acquisitions and divestitures (sales of businesses) as the company expands into the entertainment industry. Selected data from a recent annual report are as follows (amounts are in U.S. dollars in millions):

Property, Plant, Equipment, and Intangibles from the Consolidated Balance Sheet	Current Year	Prior Year
Film costs, net of amortization	$1,272	$ 991
Artists' contracts, advances, and other entertainment assets	761	645
Property, plant, and equipment, net	2,733	2,559
Excess of cost over fair value of assets acquired	3,076	3,355
From the Consolidated Statement of Income		
Total revenues	$9,714	$10,644
From the Consolidated Statement of Cash Flows		
Income from continuing operations	$ 880	$ 445
Adjustments:		
Depreciation	289	265
Amortization	208	190
Other adjustments (summarized)	(1,618)	(256)
Net cash (used in) provided by continuing operations	(241)	644
From the Notes to the Financial Statements		
Accumulated depreciation on property, plant, and equipment	$1,178	$ 1,023

Required:

1. Compute the cost of the property, plant, and equipment at the end of the current year. Explain your answer.
2. What was the approximate age of the property, plant, and equipment at the end of the current year? Round your answer to one decimal place.
3. Compute the fixed asset turnover ratio (rounded to one decimal place) for the current year. Explain your results.
4. What is "excess of cost over fair value of assets acquired?"
5. On the consolidated statement of cash flows, why are the depreciation and amortization amounts added to income from continuing operations?

CP8-7
LO8-1, 8-5, 8-7
Eastman Kodak

Using Financial Reports: Inferring the Sale of Assets

Eastman Kodak is "a global technology company focused on print and advanced materials and chemicals, which provides hardware, software, consumables and services primarily to customers in commercial print, packaging, publishing, manufacturing and entertainment." In a recent annual report, the cost of property, plant, and equipment at the end of the current year was $604 million. At the end of the previous year, it had been $611 million. During the current year, the company bought $15 million worth of new equipment. The balance of accumulated depreciation at the end of the current year was $423 million; at the end of the previous year it was $395 million. Depreciation expense for the current year was $48 million. The company reported a $13 million gain on the disposition of property, plant, and equipment. There were no impairment losses during the current year.

Required:

What amount of proceeds (in millions of dollars) did Eastman Kodak receive when it sold property, plant, and equipment during the current year? (**Hint:** Set up T-accounts.)

Critical Thinking Cases

CP8-8
LO8-1, 8-2

Evaluating an Ethical Dilemma: A Real-Life Example

Assume you work as a staff member in a large accounting department for a multinational public company. Your job requires you to review documents relating to the company's equipment purchases. Upon verifying that purchases are properly approved, you prepare journal entries to record the equipment purchases in the accounting system. Typically, you handle equipment purchases costing $100,000 or less.

This morning, you were contacted by the executive assistant to the chief financial officer (CFO). She says that the CFO has asked to see you immediately in his office. Although your boss's boss has attended a few meetings where the CFO was present, you have never met the CFO during your three years with the company. Needless to say, you are anxious about the meeting.

Upon entering the CFO's office, you are warmly greeted with a smile and friendly handshake. The CFO compliments you on the great work that you've been doing for the company. You soon feel a little more comfortable, particularly when the CFO mentions that he has a special project for you. He states that he and the CEO have negotiated significant new arrangements with the company's equipment suppliers, which require the company to make advance payments for equipment to be purchased in the future. The CFO says that, for various reasons that he didn't want to discuss, he will be processing the payments through the operating division of the company rather than the equipment accounting group. Given that the payments will be made through the operating division, they will initially be classified as operating expenses of the company. He indicates that clearly these advance payments for property and equipment should be recorded as assets, so he will be contacting you at the end of every quarter to make an adjusting journal entry to capitalize the amounts inappropriately classified as operating expenses. He advises you that a new account, called Prepaid Equipment, has been established for this purpose. He quickly wraps up the meeting by telling you that it is important that you not talk about the special project with anyone. You assume he doesn't want others to become jealous of your new important responsibility.

A few weeks later, at the end of the first quarter, you receive a voicemail from the CFO stating, "The adjustment that we discussed is $771,000,000 for this quarter." Before deleting the message, you replay it to make sure you heard it right. Your company generates over $8 billion in revenues and incurs $6 billion in operating expenses every quarter, but you've never made a journal entry for that much money. So, just to be sure there's not a mistake, you send an e-mail to the CFO confirming the amount. He phones you back immediately to abruptly inform you, "There's no mistake. That's the number." Feeling embarrassed that you may have annoyed the CFO, you quietly make the adjusting journal entry.

For each of the remaining three quarters in that year and for the first quarter in the following year, you continue to make these end-of-quarter adjustments. The "magic number," as the CFO liked to call it, was $560,000,000 for Q2, $742,745,000 for Q3, $941,000,000 for Q4, and $818,204,000 for Q1 of the following year. During this time, you've had several meetings and lunches with the CFO where he provides you the magic number, sometimes supported with nothing more than a Post-it note with the number written on it. He frequently compliments you on your good work and promises that you'll soon be in line for a big promotion.

Despite the CFO's compliments and promises, you are growing increasingly uncomfortable with the journal entries that you've been making. Typically, whenever an ordinary equipment purchase involves an advance payment, the purchase is completed a few weeks later. At that time, the amount of the advance is removed from an Equipment Deposit account and transferred to the appropriate equipment account. This hasn't been the case with the CFO's special project. Instead, the Prepaid Equipment account has continued to grow, now standing at over $3.8 billion. There's been no discussion about how or when this balance will be reduced, and no depreciation has been recorded for it.

Just as you begin to reflect on the effect the adjustments have had on your company's fixed assets, operating expenses, and operating income, you receive a call from the vice president for internal audit. She needs to talk with you this afternoon about "a peculiar trend in the company's fixed asset turnover ratio and some suspicious journal entries that you've been making."

Required:

1. Complete the following table to determine what the company's accounting records would have looked like had you not made the journal entries as part of the CFO's special project. Comment on how the decision to capitalize amounts, which were initially recorded as operating expenses, has affected the level of income from operations in each quarter.

	Q1 Year 1 (March 31)		Q2 Year 1 (June 30)		Q3 Year 1 (September 30)		Q4 Year 1 (December 31)		Q1 Year 2 (March 31)	
(amounts in millions of U.S. dollars)	**With the Entries**	**Without the Entries**	**With the Entries**	**Without the Entries**	**With the Entries**	**Without the Entries**	**With the Entries**	**Without the Entries**	**With the Entries**	**Without the Entries**
Property and equipment, net	$38,614	$	$35,982	$	$38,151	$	$38,809	$	$39,155	$
Sales revenues	8,825	8,825	8,910	8,910	8,966	8,966	8,478	8,478	8,120	8,120
Operating expenses	7,628		8,526		7,786		7,725		7,277	
Income from operations	1,197		384		1,180		753		843	

2. Using the publicly reported numbers (which include the special journal entries that you recorded), compute the fixed asset turnover ratio (rounded to two decimal places) for the periods ended Q2–Q4 of Year 1 and Q1 of Year 2. What does the trend in this ratio suggest to you? Is this consistent with the changes in operating income reported by the company?
3. Before your meeting with the vice president for internal audit, you think about the above computations and the variety of peculiar circumstances surrounding the "special project" for the CFO. What in particular might have raised your suspicion about the real nature of your work?
4. Your meeting with internal audit was short and unpleasant. The vice president indicated that she had discussed her findings with the CFO before meeting with you. The CFO claimed that he too had noticed the peculiar trend in the fixed asset turnover ratio but that he hadn't had a chance to investigate it further. He urged internal audit to get to the bottom of things, suggesting that perhaps someone might be making unapproved journal entries. Internal audit had identified you as the source of the journal entries and had been unable to find any documents that approved or substantiated the entries. She ended the meeting by advising you to find a good lawyer. Given your current circumstances, describe how you would have acted earlier had you been able to foresee where it might lead you.
5. In the real case on which this one is based, the internal auditors agonized over the question of whether they had actually uncovered a fraud or whether they were jumping to the wrong conclusion. *The Wall Street Journal* mentioned this on October 30, 2002, by stating, "it was clear . . . that their findings would be devastating for the company. They worried about whether their revelations would result in layoffs. Plus, they feared that they would somehow end up being blamed for the mess." Beyond the

personal consequences mentioned in this quote, describe other potential ways in which the findings of the internal auditors would likely be devastating for the publicly traded company and those associated with it.

Source: Susan Pulliam and Deborah Solomon, "How Three Unlikely Sleuths Exposed Fraud at WorldCom," *The Wall Street Journal*, October 30, 2012.

Epilogue: This case is based on a fraud committed at **WorldCom** (now called **Verizon**). The case draws its numbers, the nature of the unsupported journal entries, and the CFO's role in carrying out the fraud from a report issued by WorldCom's bankruptcy examiner. Year 1 in this case was actually 2001 and Year 2 was 2002. This case excludes other fraudulent activities that contributed to WorldCom's $11 billion fraud. The 63-year-old CEO was sentenced to 25 years in prison for planning and executing the biggest fraud in the history of American business. The CFO, who cooperated in the investigation of the CEO, was sentenced to five years in prison.

CP8-9
LO8-1, 8-2, 8-7
Marriott International

Evaluating the Impact of Capitalized Interest on Cash Flows and Fixed Asset Turnover from an Analyst'S Perspective

You are a financial analyst charged with evaluating the asset efficiency of companies in the hotel industry. Recent financial statements for **Marriott International** include the following note:

5. PROPERTY AND EQUIPMENT, NET

Property and equipment is stated at cost, including interest incurred during development and construction periods, less accumulated depreciation. Interest capitalized as a cost of property and equipment was $6 million, $3 million, and $4 million for the years ended December 31, 2019, December 31, 2018, and December 31, 2017, respectively.

Source: Marriott International

Required:

1. Assume that Marriott followed this policy for a major construction project this year. Explain why Marriott's policy increases, decreases, or has no effect on the following:
   a. Cash flows.
   b. Fixed asset turnover ratio.
2. Normally, how would your answer to requirement (1*b*) affect your evaluation of Marriott's effectiveness in utilizing fixed assets?
3. If the fixed asset turnover ratio decreases due to interest capitalization, does this change indicate a real decrease in efficiency? Why or why not?

You as Analyst: Online Company Research

CP8-10
LO8-1, 8-2, 8-3, 8-4, 8-5, 8-6, 8-7

Analysis of Long-Lived Assets of a Public Company (an Individual or Team Project)

In your web browser, search for the investor relations page of a public company you are interested in (e.g., Papa Johns investor relations). Select SEC Filings or Annual Report or Financials to obtain the 10-K for the three most recent years available.*

Required:

1. Go to the Balance Sheets and/or the Notes for the three most recent consecutive years:
   a. List the accounts and amounts of the company's long-lived assets (land, buildings, equipment, various intangible assets, goodwill, natural resources, and/or any other type) for the last three years.
   b. What is the percentage of each account to its respective total assets for each year (rounded to two decimal places)?
   c. What do the results of your trend analysis suggest about the strategy your company has followed with respect to investing in long-lived assets?

2. Go to the Balance Sheet and Notes for the most recent year:
   a. What cost allocation method(s) and estimates does the company disclose for each type of long-lived asset listed in (1*a.*)?
      i. What was the amount of depreciation expense?
      ii. If any, what was the amount of amortization expense?
      iii. Where did you find this information?
   b. What percentage of property, plant, and equipment (rounded to two decimal places) has been used as of the end of the most recent year? (Accumulated depreciation/Cost)
   c. What amount, if any, of interest was capitalized to property, plant, and equipment?
   d. For asset impairment:
      i. What does the company disclose regarding asset impairment policies?
      ii. What was its impairment loss, if any?
   e. What does the company report about acquisitions and mergers for the most recent year (i.e., what other companies did your company purchase or merge with and what was the acquisition price)?
3. Ratio analysis:
   a. What does the fixed asset turnover ratio measure in general?
   b. Compute the ratio for the most recent three years. Round your answers to two decimal places.
      i. What do your trend results suggest about the company?
      ii. If your company's industry ratio for the current year was 2.0, what does this comparison suggest about your company?
4. Go to the Statement of Cash Flows. For the most recent year:
   a. What were capital expenditures?
   b. What amount did the company report for the disposal (sale) of long-lived assets?
   c. In what section of the statement of cash flows–operating, investing, or financing–did you find the information for *a* and *b?*
   d. Was depreciation and/or amortization expense added back or subtracted from net income in the operating section of the statement of cash flows? Why are they added back or subtracted on the statement of cash flows?

*Alternatively, you can go to sec.gov, click on Company Filings (under the search box), and type the name of the public company you want to find. Once at the list of filings, type 10-K in the Filing Type box. The most recent 10-K annual reports will be at the top of the list. Click on Interactive Data for a list of the parts or the entire report to examine.

BUSINESS ANALYTICS AND DATA VISUALIZATION WITH EXCEL® AND TABLEAU®

Connect offers a variety of exercises to assess Excel skills, data visualization, interpretation, and analysis, including auto-graded Tableau Dashboard Activities, Applying Excel problems, and Integrated Excel problems.

Images used throughout chapter: Question of ethics: mushmello/Shutterstock; Pause for feedback: McGraw Hill; Guided help: McGraw Hill; Financial analysis: McGraw Hill; Focus on cash flows: Hilch/Shutterstock; Key ratio analysis: guillermain/123RF; Data analytics: Hilch/Shutterstock; Tip: McGraw Hill; ESG reporting: McGraw Hill; International perspective: Hilch/Shutterstock; Internal control alert icon: McGraw Hill

9

chapter

Reporting and Interpreting Liabilities

Starbucks opened its first store in Seattle's Pike Place Market in 1971. Today, the company has approximately 350,000 employees working in over 32,000 stores spread across 83 countries. In fiscal 2020, Starbucks reported global net revenues of $23.5 billion.

Starbucks has ambitious growth plans for the future, intending to grow to 55,000 stores by 2030. To be successful, management must focus on a number of critical financing activities. These activities will generate funds to finance the current operating activities of the business and the long-term assets that will permit the company to grow in the future.

UNDERSTANDING THE BUSINESS

Businesses finance the acquisition of assets from two external sources: funds supplied by creditors (debt) and funds provided by owners (equity). The mixture of debt and equity a business uses is called its **capital structure.** In addition to selecting a capital structure, management can select from a variety of sources from which to borrow money, as illustrated by the liability section of the balance sheet from Starbucks shown in Exhibit 9.1.

What factors do managers consider when they borrow money? Two key factors are risk and cost. Debt capital is risky because payments associated with debt are a company's legal obligation. If a company cannot meet a required debt payment (either principal or interest) because of a temporary cash shortage, creditors may force the company into bankruptcy and require the sale of assets to satisfy the debt. Due to the risks associated with debt financing, managers devote considerable time and effort analyzing alternative borrowing arrangements.

LEARNING OBJECTIVES

After studying this chapter, you should be able to:

9-1 Define, measure, and report current liabilities. p. 474

9-2 Compute and interpret the accounts payable turnover ratio. p. 475

9-3 Report notes payable and explain the time value of money. p. 480

9-4 Report contingent liabilities. p. 482

9-5 Explain the importance of working capital and its impact on cash flows. p. 484

9-6 Report long-term liabilities. p. 485

9-7 Compute and explain present values. p. 487

9-8 Apply the present value concept to the reporting of long-term liabilities. p. 492

thaweerat/Shutterstock

FOCUS COMPANY

Starbucks

RECORDING AND REPORTING LIABILITIES

starbucks.com

Learn more about Starbucks from owner, Howard Schultz, by listening to the NPR podcast

Starbucks: Howard Schultz: How I Built This.

How I Built This NPR podcasts are about innovators, entrepreneurs, idealists, and the movements they built.

Companies that include debt in their capital structure also must make strategic decisions concerning the balance between short-term and long-term debt. To evaluate a company's capital structure, financial analysts calculate a number of accounting ratios. In this chapter, we will discuss both short-term and long-term debt, as well as some important accounting ratios. We also will introduce present values and discuss the role present values play in how long-term liabilities are reported on a company's balance sheet. In Chapter 10, we discuss a special category of long-term debt, bond securities. We conclude our discussion of a firm's capital structure by examining stockholders' equity in Chapter 11.

ORGANIZATION OF THE CHAPTER

Liabilities Defined and Classified

Current Liabilities

- Accounts Payable
- Accounts Payable Turnover Ratio
- Accrued Liabilities
- Deferred Revenues
- Notes Payable
- Current Portion of Long-Term Debt
- Contingent Liabilities Reported on the Balance Sheet
- Contingent Liabilities Reported in the Footnotes
- Working Capital Management

Long-Term Liabilities

- Long-Term Notes Payable and Bonds
- Lease Liabilities

Computing Present Values

- Present Value of a Single Amount
- Present Value of an Annuity
- Accounting Applications of Present Values

EXHIBIT 9.1

Liability Section of Starbucks's Balance Sheets

STARBUCKS
REAL WORLD EXCERPT:
Annual Report

STARBUCKS CORPORATION
CONSOLIDATED BALANCE SHEETS
(in millions)

	Sept. 27, 2020	Sept. 29, 2019
Current liabilities:		
Accounts payable	$ 997.9	$ 1,189.7
Accrued liabilities	1,160.7	1,753.7
Accrued payroll and benefits	696.0	664.6
Income taxes payable	98.2	1,291.7
Current portion of operating lease liability	1,248.8	–
Stored value card liability and current portion of deferred revenue	1,456.5	1,269.0
Short-term debt	438.8	–
Current portion of long-term debt	1,249.9	–
Total current liabilities	7,346.8	6,168.7
Long-term debt	14,659.6	11,167.0
Operating lease liability	7,661.7	–
Deferred revenue	6,598.5	6,744.4
Other long-term liabilities	907.3	1,370.5
Total liabilities	$37,173.9	$25,450.6

Source: Starbucks Corporation

LIABILITIES DEFINED AND CLASSIFIED

LEARNING OBJECTIVE 9-1

Define, measure, and report current liabilities.

Most people have a reasonable understanding of the definition of the word *liability*. Accountants formally define liabilities as the probable future sacrifice of economic benefits that arise from past transactions. As Exhibit 9.1 shows, as of September 27, 2020 (**Starbucks**'s fiscal year ends on the Sunday closest to September 30), Starbucks had borrowed $15,909.5 million, the sum of the "current portion of long-term debt" ($1,249.9) and "long-term debt" ($14,659.6). These past transactions obligate the company to pay cash to its creditors at some time in the future, and therefore are reported as liabilities on the balance sheet.

When a liability is first recorded, it is measured in terms of its current cash equivalent, which is the cash amount a creditor would accept to settle the liability immediately. Although Starbucks borrowed $15,909.5 million, it will repay much more than that because the company also must pay interest on the debt. Interest that will be paid in the future is not included in the reported amount of the liability because it accrues and becomes a liability with the passage of time.

Like most businesses, Starbucks has several kinds of liabilities as well as a wide range of creditors. The list of liabilities on the balance sheet differs from one company to the next because different operating activities result in different types of liabilities. The liability section of Starbucks's balance sheet begins with the caption Current liabilities. **Current liabilities** are expected to be paid with current assets within the current operating cycle of the business or within one year of the balance sheet date, whichever is longer. Noncurrent liabilities include all other liabilities.

CURRENT LIABILITIES

Many current liabilities have a direct relationship to the operating activities of a business. In other words, specific operating activities are financed, in part, by a related current liability. Some examples from Starbucks's balance sheet (Exhibit 9.1) are

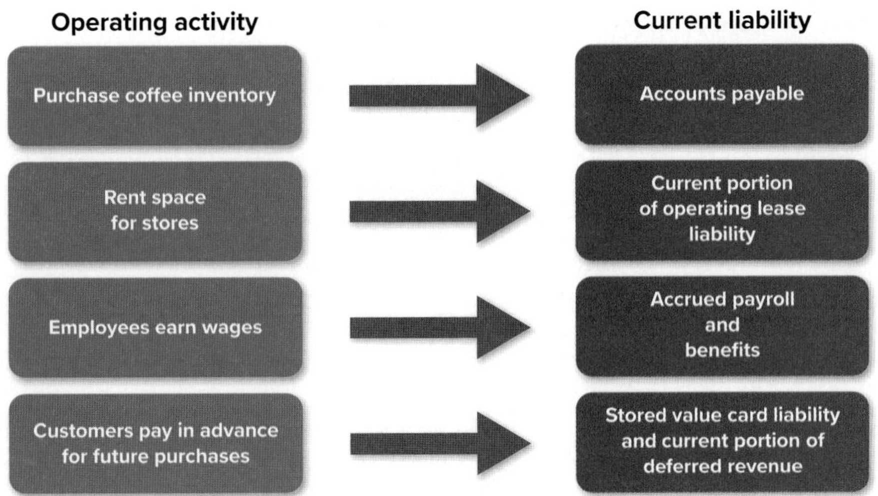

Early in this chapter, we mentioned that Starbucks is opening a lot of new stores each year. As a result, it must buy additional inventory, rent more store space, and hire more employees. By understanding the relationship between operating activities and current liabilities, an analyst can explain changes in the various current liability accounts.

We now will discuss the current liability accounts that are common to most balance sheets.

Accounts Payable

Most companies in the course of running their day-to-day operations purchase goods and services from other businesses. Typically, these purchases are made on credit with cash payments made after the goods and services have been provided. As a result, these transactions create obligations to pay suppliers in the near future. Most companies list such obligations on their balance sheets as **accounts payable** (sometimes called trade accounts payable).

For many companies, buying on credit from suppliers is a relatively inexpensive way to finance the purchase of inventory because interest does not normally accrue on accounts payable. As an incentive to encourage more sales, some suppliers offer generous credit terms that may allow buyers to resell merchandise and collect cash before payment must be made to the supplier.

Some managers may be tempted to delay payment to suppliers as long as possible to conserve cash. This strategy can create problems for suppliers, who also must pay their bills. Most successful companies develop positive working relationships with suppliers to facilitate receiving quality goods and services. A positive relationship can be destroyed by slow payments. In addition, financial analysts become concerned if a business does not meet its obligations to suppliers on a timely basis because such slowness can indicate that a company is experiencing financial difficulties. Both managers and analysts use the accounts payable turnover ratio to evaluate how effectively a company is managing its accounts payable.

KEY RATIO ANALYSIS

Accounts Payable Turnover

LEARNING OBJECTIVE 9-2

Compute and interpret the accounts payable turnover ratio.

ANALYTICAL QUESTION

How quickly does management pay its suppliers?

RATIO AND COMPARISONS

The accounts payable turnover ratio is computed as follows:

Accounts Payable Turnover = Cost of Goods Sold ÷ Average Accounts Payable

The 2020 accounts payable turnover ratio for **Starbucks** was

$7,694.9 ÷ $1,093.8* = 7.04
*($997.9 + $1,189.7) ÷ 2

COMPARISONS OVER TIME		
Starbucks		
2018	**2019**	**2020**
8.09	7.20	7.04

COMPARISONS WITH COMPETITORS	
Monster Beverages	McDonald's
2020	**2020**
6.57	8.07

INTERPRETATIONS

In General The accounts payable turnover ratio measures how quickly management pays suppliers. A high accounts payable ratio normally suggests that a company is paying its suppliers in a timely manner. To make interpreting the ratio more intuitive, analysts often divide it into the number of days in a year:

Average Days to Pay Payables = 365 Days/Accounts Payable Turnover

In 2020 the average number of days it took Starbucks to pay its accounts payable was

365 Days ÷ 7.04 = 51.85 Days

This means that, on average, Starbucks took between 51 and 52 days to pay its suppliers in 2020.

Focus Company Analysis Analyzing the average number of days payables are outstanding indicates that in 2020, Starbucks paid its suppliers more slowly than in 2018 (51.85 days versus 45.12 days), Relative to its competitors, Starbucks paid its suppliers more quickly than Monster Beverages but more slowly than McDonald's. On average, **Monster Beverages** took 55.56 days to pay its suppliers and **McDonald's** took 45.23 days. Suppliers like being paid as soon as possible and may extend benefits (e.g., faster shipments or preferential treatment when supply is limited) to companies that pay quickly.

A Few Cautions The accounts payable turnover ratio is an average based on all accounts payable. As such, the ratio does not tell us how quickly a company is paying each of its suppliers. It is possible for a company to pay some suppliers quickly and others late and yet still end up with an acceptable ratio. This is not meant to suggest that the ratio is not useful. It simply implies that the more you know about the numbers used to calculate a ratio, the more fully you can understand the ratio's implications.

Accrued Liabilities

In many situations, a business incurs an expense in one accounting period and makes the cash payment in a future period. **Accrued liabilities** are expenses that have been incurred before the end of an accounting period but have not yet been paid. These expenses include items such as insurance, rent and wages. The fiscal 2020 balance sheet for Starbucks lists accrued liabilities of $1,160.7 million. Accrued liabilities are recorded by recognizing an expense for the period and an associated liability. For example, when a company records wages expense for a period but does not immediately pay the expense, it will record an accrued wages or payroll liability on its balance sheet.

Accrued Taxes Payable

Like individuals, corporations must pay federal taxes on the income they earn. Corporations also may pay state and local income taxes and, in some cases, foreign income taxes. The notes to Starbucks's Annual Report include the following information pertaining to taxes:

STARBUCKS

REAL WORLD EXCERPT:

Notes to Financial Statements

INCOME TAXES

Note 14:

Provision for income taxes (*in millions*):

Fiscal Year Ended	Sept. 27, 2020	Sept. 29, 2019	Sept. 30, 2018
Current Taxes:			
U.S. federal	$ 49.9	$ 1,414.3	$156.2
U.S. state & local	36.9	447.8	52.0
Foreign	181.4	458.3	327.0
Total current taxes	$268.2	$2,320.4	$535.2

Source: Starbucks Corporation

For Starbucks and most other corporations, income taxes represent a major cost and are therefore carefully monitored by management and various taxing authorities (e.g., the Internal Revenue Service).

Accrued Compensation and Related Costs

At the end of each accounting period, employees usually have earned salaries that have not yet been paid. Unpaid salaries may be reported as part of a general accrued liability account on the balance sheet or as a separate item, as is the case with Starbucks. As shown in Exhibit 9.1, Starbucks reports "accrued payroll and benefits" of $696.0 million. Benefits refer to items such as retirement programs, vacation time, and health insurance that employees have earned during the reporting period but have not taken or been paid.

Let's take a closer look at vacation time as an example. Typically, a business grants employees paid vacation time based on the number of months they have worked. The cost of vacation time must be recorded in the year employees earn the vacation time by working rather than the year they actually take vacation. If Starbucks estimates the cost of earned vacation time to be $125,000, accountants make the following adjusting entry at the end of the accounting period.

	Debit	Credit
Compensation expense (+E, −SE)	125,000	
Accrued vacation liability (+L)		125,000

Assets	=	Liabilities	+	Stockholders' Equity
		Accrued vacation liability +125,000		Compensation expense (+E) −125,000

When employees take vacations (for example, next summer), the accountants record the following:

	Debit	Credit
Accrued vacation liability (−L)	125,000	
Cash (−A)		125,000

Assets	=	Liabilities	+	Stockholders' Equity
Cash −125,000		Accrued vacation liability −125,000		

Starbucks does not separately disclose the amount of accrued vacation liability. Instead, the company reports this liability as part of "accrued payroll and benefits." For most companies, the amount of accrued vacation liability is not large enough to warrant its own line item on the balance sheet.

Payroll Taxes

All payrolls are subject to a variety of taxes, including federal, state, and local income taxes; Social Security taxes; and federal and state unemployment taxes. Employees pay some of these

arfa adam/Shutterstock

taxes and employers pay others. While we will look at only the three largest taxes, reporting is similar for other types of payroll tax.

Employee Income Taxes Employers are required to withhold income taxes for each employee. The amount of income tax withheld is recorded by the employer as a current liability and remains a liability until the amount is paid to the government (usually quarterly).

Employee and Employer FICA Taxes Social Security taxes often are called **FICA taxes** because they are required by the Federal Insurance Contributions Act. These taxes are imposed in equal amounts on both employees and employers. Though employers only pay their portion of the taxes, they withhold the employees' portion from their paychecks as part of an employee's payroll deductions. The current Social Security tax rate is 6.2 percent for employees and 6.2 percent for employers, so 12.4 percent total. The Social Security tax is capped, meaning that the tax only applies to wages up to a certain amount. The capped amount for 2021 is $142,800 per employee. In addition, a separate 1.45 percent Medicare tax applies to all employee income. Therefore, the FICA tax rate is 7.65 percent (6.2 percent + 1.45 percent) on income up to and including $142,800 and 1.45 percent on income above $142,800. Employees who earn above $200,000 have withheld an "additional Medicare tax" of 0.9 percent. Unlike all other FICA taxes, this additional Medicare tax is paid only by employees, not by employers. However, employers also will withhold this additional tax as part of an employee's payroll deductions.

Employer Unemployment Taxes Employers are charged unemployment taxes through the Federal Unemployment Tax Act (FUTA) and State Unemployment Tax Acts (SUTA). These programs provide financial support to employees who lose their jobs through no fault of their own. The FUTA tax rate is 6.0 percent. The tax applies to the first $7,000 paid to each employee as wages during the year. SUTA tax rates vary by state.

Hopefully by now you have realized that the cost of hiring employees is much more than the amount that those employees actually receive in wages. To illustrate recording payroll taxes, let's assume that Starbucks accumulated the following information in its records for the first two weeks of June 2021:

Salaries earned	$1,800,000
Income taxes withheld	275,000
FICA taxes (employees' share)	137,700
FUTA taxes	2,300
SUTA taxes	8,500

Companies generally record **two journal entries to account for payroll taxes.** The first entry records the amount of cash paid to employees and the various deductions withheld from employees' paychecks:

	Debit	Credit
Compensation expense (+E, −SE)	1,800,000	
Employee income taxes withheld (+L)		275,000
FICA payable (+L)		137,700
Cash (−A)		1,387,300

Assets		=	Liabilities		+	Stockholders' Equity	
Cash	−1,387,300		FICA payable	+137,700		Compensation expense (+E)	−1,800,000
			Employee income taxes withheld	+275,000			

The second entry records the taxes that employers must pay from their own funds. Federal and state laws require these tax payments. Assuming all employees earn less than $200,000, the FICA tax amount is equal to the amount that is paid by employees:

	Debit	Credit
Compensation expense (+E, −SE)	148,500	
FICA payable (+L)		137,700
FUTA payable (+L)		2,300
SUTA payable (+L)		8,500

Assets	=	Liabilities		+	Stockholders' Equity	
		FICA payable	+137,700		Compensation expense (+E)	−148,500
		FUTA payable	+ 2,300			
		SUTA payable	+8,500			

Deferred Revenues

In most business transactions, cash is paid when a product or service is delivered, or soon thereafter. In some cases, however, cash is paid in advance of delivery. You probably have paid for an airline ticket in advance. The airline company receives cash for the ticket you purchased, but it does not provide the service (the flight) until a future date. When a company collects cash before the related revenue has been earned, the cash is called **deferred revenues,** or, occasionally, unearned revenues. Under the revenue recognition principle introduced in Chapter 3, revenue cannot be recorded until it has been earned. Deferred revenues are reported as a liability because cash has been collected from customers, but the company has not delivered a product or service, and thus the related revenue has not been earned by the end of the accounting period. The obligation to provide a product or service in the future still exists. These obligations are classified as current or long term, depending on when a company expects to provide the product or service.

A **Starbucks** card, which allows customers to pay for their purchases in advance, is an example of deferred revenues. Advantages for the customer include convenience at the point of sale and the accumulation of loyalty rewards. Advantages for Starbucks include the ability to collect and use customers' cash before they actually purchase anything, while also collecting information on the purchasing habits of individual customers. Starbucks's balance sheet shown in Exhibit 9.1 reports that the current liability at the end of fiscal 2020 associated with unused Starbucks cards totaled $1,456.5 million. Starbucks explains the amount with the following note:

Tip Deferred revenues are a liability until the company earns the revenues by delivering a good or service to customers.

STARBUCKS
REAL WORLD EXCERPT:
Notes to the Financial Statements

"Amounts loaded onto stored value cards are initially recorded as deferred revenue and recognized as revenue upon redemption."

Source: Starbucks Corporation

Starbucks has historically used the phrase "stored value cards" even though many customers today carry their balance on their mobile app and not on a physical card. Regardless, the accounting for Starbucks is the same. When the company receives cash from the customer it increases its "stored value card liability" by the amount of cash received. When the customer later places an order, Starbucks reduces its "stored value card liability" by the amount of the order and recognizes revenue. This latter entry is an example of an adjusting journal entry, which we covered in Chapter 4.

BUSINESS ANALYTICS

Using mobile app data to understand customer behavior

At the end of 2020, nearly a quarter of all transactions at Starbucks were completed using its mobile app. Were you one of them? If so, you provide data that Starbucks collects and analyzes to help them make informed operating decisions. For example, Starbucks uses artificial intelligence software to analyze how a customer's purchase history is associated with things like geographic location, weather, day of the week, and time of the day. Starbucks uses the output of this analysis to decide what products to emphasize in a given geographic location, and when to push information about these products to customers. The company uses similar software to analyze where to locate new stores. The next time you purchase a product at Starbucks pause to consider that your purchase data will be used to create the company's next annual report, and quite likely, the next special offer you receive on your phone.

LEARNING OBJECTIVE 9-3

Report notes payable and explain the time value of money.

Tip To calculate interest for a period you need: (1) the principle amount of the loan and (2) the interest rate per period.

Notes Payable

When a company borrows money, it normally signs a formal written contract with a bank and reports the amount borrowed as a **note payable.** The contract specifies the amount borrowed, the date by which it must be repaid, and the interest rate associated with the borrowing.

Banks and other creditors are willing to lend cash because they will earn interest in return. Earning interest by loaning money to others reflects the **time value of money**. To the borrower, interest reflects the cost of using someone else's money and is therefore an expense. To lenders, interest reflects the benefit of allowing someone else to use their money and is therefore revenue.

You need two pieces of information to calculate interest: (1) the **principle** (i.e., the cash that was borrowed) and (2) the **interest rate per period.** To calculate the interest rate per period you may need to adjust the annual interest rate to a monthly, weekly, or even daily rate. For example, the formula based on a monthly rate is

Principal × Annual Interest Rate × Number of Months/12 Months = Interest for the Period

To illustrate, assume that on November 1, a company with a December 31 fiscal year-end borrows $100,000 cash for six months. The annual interest rate is 12 percent. The principle and interest are payable on April 30 of the following year. The note is recorded in the accounts as follows:

	Debit	Credit
Cash (+A)	100,000	
Notes payable (+L)		100,000

Assets		=	Liabilities		+	Stockholders' Equity
Cash	+100,000		Notes Payable	+100,000		

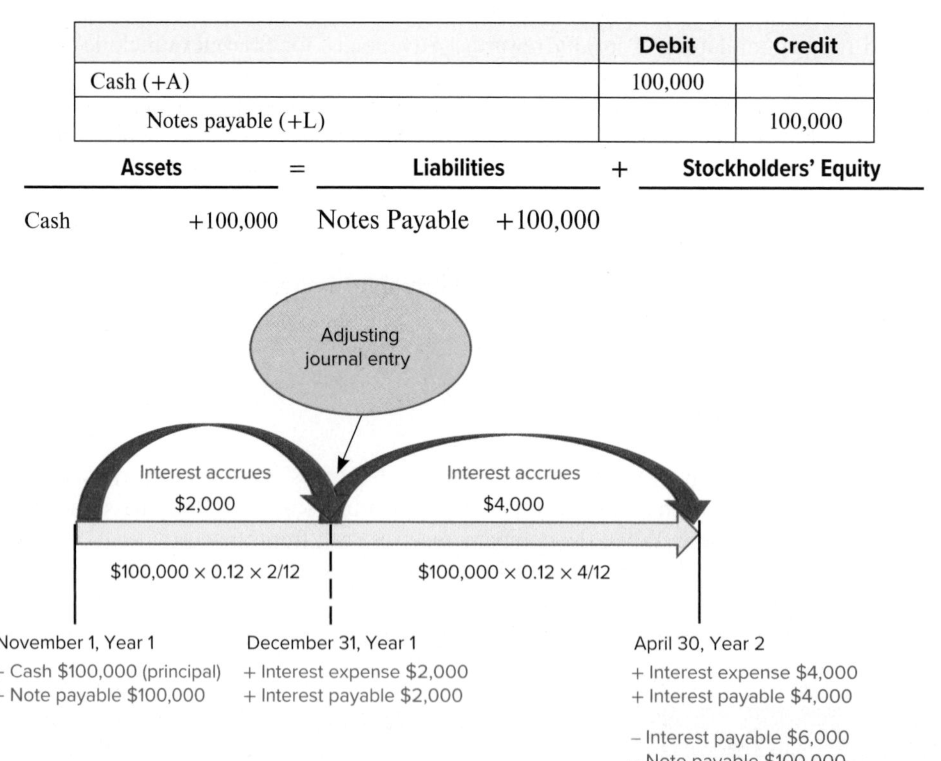

Interest is an expense incurred when companies borrow money. Companies record interest expense for a given accounting period, regardless of when they actually pay the bank cash for interest. In the above example, the company borrowed the money on November 1. By the end of the fiscal year, December 31, the company has incurred two months of interest expense. Because the company will not pay interest until April 30, it will report a current liability on its balance sheet to reflect the future obligation to the bank.

The computation to determine the amount of interest incurred during the two months and the associated liability is

Principal ×	Annual Interest Rate ×	Number of Months/12 Months	=	Interest for the Period
$100,000 ×	0.12 ×	2/12 months	=	$2,000

The entry to record interest expense and interest payable for the two months is

	Debit	Credit
Interest expense (+E, −SE)	2,000	
Interest payable (+L)		2,000

Assets	=	Liabilities		+	Stockholders' Equity	
		Interest payable	+2,000		Interest expense (+E)	−2,000

On April 30, the company has incurred an additional four months of interest expense for the period January–April. The entry to record this expense and the associated liability is

	Debit	Credit
Interest expense (+E, −SE)	4,000	
Interest payable (+L)		4,000

Assets	=	Liabilities		+	Stockholders' Equity	
		Interest payable	+4,000		Interest expense (+E)	−4,000

Also on April 30, the company pays the bank $6,000 cash for six months of interest and pays back the principal since the loan was a six-month loan. The cash payment for interest consists of the $2,000 of interest owed for November and December, plus the $4,000 of interest owed for January–April. The following journal entry reflects the cash payment to the bank to repay the principal amount and to pay for interest.

	Debit	Credit
Interest payable (−L)	6,000	
Notes payable (−L)	100,000	
Cash (−A)		106,000

Assets		=	Liabilities		+	Stockholders' Equity
Cash	−106,000		Interest payable	−6,000		
			Note payable	−100,000		

Current Portion of Long-Term Debt

The distinction between current and long-term debt is important for both managers and analysts. A company must have sufficient cash on hand to repay current debt. To provide accurate information on how much of its long-term debt is due in the current year, a company must reclassify its long-term debt as a current liability within a year of its maturity date. For example, as shown in Exhibit 9.1 and highlighted below, **Starbucks** expects to pay $1,249.9 million of its long-term debt in the current year. The remaining $14,659.6 million is due sometime after the current year.

	Sept. 27, 2020	Sept. 29, 2019
Current liabilities:		
Current portion of long-term debt	1,249.9	-
Long-term debt	14,659.6	11,167.0

In the footnotes to its 2020 Annual Report, Starbucks explains that its long-term debt consists of notes that mature on various dates out to 2050. Accounting for these long-term notes is a lot like accounting for bonds, which we will cover in Chapter 10.

FINANCIAL ANALYSIS

Refinancing Debt: Current or Long-Term Liability?

Instead of repaying a loan from current cash, a company may refinance it either by negotiating a new loan agreement with a new maturity date or by taking out a new loan and using the proceeds to pay off the old loan. If a company intends to refinance a currently maturing loan with a new *long-term* loan and has the ability to do so, the current loan should be classified as a long-term liability. It is not a current liability because current liabilities are short-term obligations that are expected to be paid with current assets within the current operating cycle or one year, whichever is longer.

LEARNING OBJECTIVE 9-4

Report contingent liabilities.

Contingent Liabilities Reported on the Balance Sheet

Some recorded liabilities are based on estimates because the exact amount will not be known until a future date. For example, a **contingent liability** is created when a company offers a warranty with a product it sells. The cost of providing future repair work must be estimated and recorded as a liability (and expense) in the period in which the product is sold.

As an example, assume **Starbucks** estimates that it will have to provide $150,000 of warranty services to customers who purchased coffee brewing equipment this year. In addition to recording the sale of the brewing equipment, Starbucks would record the following:

Thiti Sukapan/Shutterstock

	Debit	Credit
Warranty expense (+E, −SE)	150,000	
Warranty payable (+L)		150,000

Assets	=	Liabilities		+	Stockholders' Equity	
		Warranty payable	+150,000		Warranty expense (+E)	−150,000

Over time, as customers return defective equipment, Starbucks would decrease the warranty payable account and either refund the customer cash or fix the equipment and return it to the customer.

Contingent Liabilities Reported in the Footnotes

Each of the liabilities that we have discussed is reported on the balance sheet at a specific dollar amount because each involves the probable future sacrifice of economic benefits. Some transactions or events create only a reasonably possible (but not probable) future sacrifice of economic benefits. These situations create contingent liabilities that are reported in the footnotes, but not on a company's balance sheet.

Whether a contingent liability is reported on the balance sheet, in the notes to the financial statements, or not at all depends on two factors: (1) the probability of a future economic sacrifice and (2) the ability of management to estimate the amount of the liability. The following table illustrates the possibilities:

	Probable	Reasonably Possible	Remote
Amount can be reasonably estimated	Record as liability	Disclose in footnotes	Disclosure not required
Amount cannot be reasonably estimated	Disclose in footnotes	Disclose in footnotes	Disclosure not required

The probabilities of occurrence are defined in the following manner:

- Probable–The future event or events are likely to occur.
- Reasonably possible–The chance of the future event or events occurring is more than remote but less than likely.
- Remote–The chance of the future event or events occurring is slight.

Zerbor/Shutterstock; ohrim/Shutterstock

INTERNATIONAL PERSPECTIVE

It's a Matter of Degree

The assessment of future probabilities is inherently subjective, but both U.S. GAAP and IFRS provide some guidance. Under U.S. GAAP, "probable" has been defined as *likely to occur,* which is commonly interpreted to mean having a greater than 70 percent chance of occurring. Under IFRS, "probable" is defined as *more likely than not to occur,* which implies more than a 50 percent chance of occurring. This difference means that for some contingent liabilities, IFRS would require the reporting of a liability on the balance sheet whereas GAAP would simply require footnote disclosure.

In summary,

- A liability that is both probable and the amount can be reasonably estimated must be recorded and reported on the balance sheet.
- A liability that is (1) probable but the amount cannot be reasonably estimated, or (2) reasonably possible regardless of whether the amount can be estimated, must be disclosed in a footnote.
- Remote contingencies do not require any type of disclosure.

Since 2010, **Starbucks** has been fighting a lawsuit in the State of California. Below are excerpts from Starbucks's 2020 Annual Report pertaining to this lawsuit:

STARBUCKS
REAL WORLD EXCERPT:
Notes to the Financial Statements

> On April 13, 2010, an organization named Council for Education and Research on Toxics ("Plaintiff") filed a lawsuit in the Superior Court of the State of California. . .
>
> . . . Plaintiff alleges that the Company and the other defendants failed to provide warnings for their coffee products of exposure to the chemical acrylamide as required under California Health and Safety Code section 25249.5, the California Safe Drinking Water and Toxic Enforcement Act of 1986, better known as Proposition 65. . . The Plaintiff asserts that every consumed cup of coffee, absent a compliant warning, is equivalent to a violation under Proposition 65. . .
>
> The Company, as part of a joint defense group organized to defend against the lawsuit, disputes the claims of the Plaintiff. Acrylamide is not added to coffee but is present in all coffee in small amounts (parts per billion) as a byproduct of the coffee bean roasting process. . . On June 22, 2018, the California Office of Environmental Health Hazard Assessment (OEHHA) proposed a new regulation clarifying that cancer warnings are not required for coffee under Proposition 65.
>
> On June 3, 2019, the Office of Administrative Law (OAL) approved the coffee exemption regulation. . . The plaintiff has not yet filed a Notice of Appeal. Starbucks believes that the likelihood that the Company will ultimately incur a loss in connection with this litigation is ***less than reasonably possible.*** Accordingly, no loss contingency was recorded for this matter.

Source: Starbucks Corporation

Consistent with the table shown earlier, Starbucks has not recorded a liability because management deemed a loss to be "less than reasonably possible." Therefore, disclosure in a footnote was sufficient.

Working Capital Management

LEARNING OBJECTIVE 9-5

Explain the importance of working capital and its impact on cash flows.

Information about current liabilities is very important to managers and analysts because these obligations must be paid in the near future. Analysts say that a company has liquidity if it has the ability to meet its current obligations. A number of financial measures are useful in evaluating liquidity, including the current ratio (introduced in Chapter 2) and the dollar amount of **working capital.** Working capital is defined as the dollar difference between current assets and current liabilities. Working capital is important to both managers and financial analysts because it has a significant impact on the health and profitability of a company. **Starbucks's** working capital at the end of fiscal 2020 was:

Current assets	–	Current liabilities	=	Working capital
$7,806.4	–	$7,346.8	=	$459.6

Working capital reflects the amount Starbucks would have left over if it used all of its current assets to pay off all of its current liabilities.

Managers actively manage working capital accounts to achieve a balance between a company's short-term obligations and the resources to satisfy those obligations. If a business has too little working capital, it runs the risk of not being able to meet its obligations. On the other hand, too much working capital may tie up resources in unproductive assets. Excess inventory, for example, ties up dollars that could be invested more profitably elsewhere in the business and incurs additional costs associated with storage and deterioration.

Changes in working capital accounts are also important to managers and analysts because they have a direct impact on the cash flows from operating activities reported on the statement of cash flows.

FOCUS ON CASH FLOWS

Working Capital and Cash Flows

Many working capital accounts have a direct relationship to income-producing activities. Accounts receivable, for example, are related to sales revenue: Accounts receivable increase when sales are made on credit. Cash is collected when customers pay their bills. Similarly, accounts payable increase when inventory is purchased on credit. A cash outflow occurs when the account is paid. We discuss how to use changes in working capital accounts to create the operating section of the statement of cash flows in Chapter 12.

PAUSE FOR FEEDBACK

Companies classify liabilities as either current or long term. Our discussion to this point has focused on current liabilities, which are short-term obligations that will be paid in cash (or other current assets) within the current operating cycle or one year, whichever is longer. In the next section, we turn our attention to long-term liabilities. Before you move on, complete the following questions to test your understanding of the concepts we have covered.

SELF-STUDY QUIZ

For each of the following events, state whether **Starbucks**'s working capital will increase, decrease, or not change:

1. Starbucks purchases inventory on credit.
2. Starbucks borrows $1,000,000 in long-term debt.
3. Starbucks pays cash to reduce its rent payable account by $750,000.
4. Starbucks pays employee salaries with cash.

After you have completed your answers, check them below.

GUIDED HELP 9-1

For additional step-by-step video instruction, go to mhhe.com/libby_gh9-1.

Related Homework: M9-1, M9-2, M9-5, M9-6, E9-1, E9-10

LEARNING OBJECTIVE 9-6

Report long-term liabilities.

LONG-TERM LIABILITIES

Long-term liabilities include all obligations that are not classified as current liabilities, such as long-term notes payable and bonds payable. Most companies borrow money on a long-term basis in order to purchase assets, like property or equipment. In some cases, a company may pledge specific assets as security for repayment. If the company defaults on the loan, then the bank has the right to take ownership of the assets. A loan supported by this type of agreement is called **secured debt.** Agreements in which the bank relies primarily on the borrower's integrity and general earning power to repay the loan are called **unsecured debt.**

Long-Term Notes Payable and Bonds

Companies can raise capital directly from a number of financial service organizations including banks, insurance companies, and pension plans. Raising capital from one of these organizations is known as a **private placement.** The resulting liability often is called a **note payable,** which is a written promise to pay a stated sum at one or more specified future dates called the **maturity date(s).**

In many cases, a company's need for capital exceeds the financial ability of any single bank or other creditor. In these situations, the company may issue publicly traded debt called **bonds.** The opportunity to sell a bond security in established markets provides bondholders with an important benefit. Without involving the company, bondholders can sell their bond securities to other investors prior to maturity if they have an immediate need for cash. We will discuss bonds in detail in the next chapter.

Accounting for long-term debt is based on the same concepts used in accounting for short-term debt. A liability is recorded when the debt is incurred and interest expense is recorded with the passage of time.

Business operations are global in nature, with many corporations operating manufacturing facilities around the world. In order to support these foreign operations, companies sometimes borrow money from foreign banks. Borrowing money in a foreign currency raises some interesting accounting and management issues.

INTERNATIONAL PERSPECTIVE

Borrowing in Foreign Currencies

Many corporations with foreign operations elect to finance those operations with foreign debt to lessen exchange rate risk. Exchange rate risk exists because the relative value of each nation's currency varies on virtually a daily basis.

Solutions to SELF-STUDY QUIZ

1. No change	2. Increase	3. No change	4. Decrease

In attempting to mitigate exchange rate risk, **Amazon.com** states the following in the footnotes to its 2020 Annual Report:

AMAZON
REAL WORLD EXCERPT:
Notes to the Financial Statements

"Net sales and related expenses generated from our internationally-focused stores. . .are primarily denominated in the functional currencies of the corresponding stores and primarily include Euros, British Pounds, and Japanese Yen."

For reporting purposes, accountants must convert, or translate, foreign debt into U.S. dollars at the end of the accounting period in order to report the debt on a U.S. company's balance sheet. In the same footnote excerpted above, Amazon.com discusses how it does this by stating:

AMAZON
REAL WORLD EXCERPT:
Notes to the Financial Statements

"Assets and liabilities of these subsidiaries are translated into U.S. dollars at period-end exchange rates. . . ."

Lease Liabilities

Companies often lease assets rather than purchase them. We saw this reflected on Chipotle's balance sheet in Chapter 2. When a company leases an asset, it enters into a contractual agreement with the owner of the asset. In the language of contracts (and accounting), the party that owns the asset is referred to as the **lessor**. The party that pays for the right to use the asset is referred to as the **lessee**. We focus on accounting for leases from the lessee's perspective. For accounting purposes, a lessee can lease an asset by signing either a short-term lease (12 months or less) or a longer-term lease. Longer-term leases are more common and are classified as either **finance leases** or **operating leases** depending on whether effective control of the leased asset remains with the lessor or is transferred to the lessee.

Accounting for finance leases and operating leases

How do accountants determine if a longer-term lease should be recorded as a finance lease or an operating lease? GAAP helps guide them through this determination by stating that if a lease meets any of the following five criteria, it is considered a finance lease:

a. The lease transfers ownership of the underlying asset to the lessee by the end of the lease term.
b. The lease grants the lessee an option to purchase the underlying asset that the lessee is reasonably certain to exercise.
c. The lease term is for the major part of the remaining economic life of the underlying asset. . . .
d. The present value of the sum of the lease payments and any residual value guaranteed by the lessee . . . equals or exceeds substantially all of the fair value of the underlying asset.
e. The underlying asset is of such a specialized nature that it is expected to have no alternative use to the lessor at the end of the lease term.*

The five criteria are aimed at establishing whether the lessor maintains effective control of the leased asset or whether effective control has been transferred to the lessee. If any of the five

*Source: Accounting Standards Codification 842-10-25-2, Leases (February 25, 2016)

criteria are met, then effective control (i.e., substantially all of the risks and rewards of ownership) is transferred to the lessee and the lease is a finance lease. If none of the criteria are met, then effective control remains with the lessor and the lease is an operating lease.

The accounting required to initially record a finance lease and an operating lease is the same: Both require the recognition of a lease asset and a lease liability. The amount recognized is the current cash equivalent of the required future lease payments. Assume that **Starbucks** signs a four-year lease for a new delivery truck and that Starbucks's accountants have determined that the current cash equivalent of the lease is $250,000. Upon signing the lease, Starbucks records the following entry:

	Debit	Credit
Lease asset (+A)	250,000	
Lease liability (+L)		250,000

Assets		=	Liabilities		+	Stockholders' Equity
Lease asset	+250,000		Lease liability	+250,000		

Accounting for the lease over its life differs depending on whether the lease is a finance lease or an operating lease. The differences are discussed in detail in more advanced accounting courses. At this point, just keep in mind two key aspects of accounting for longer-term leases. First, regardless of whether the lease is determined to be a finance lease or an operating lease, the company must record a lease asset and a lease liability upon signing the lease agreement. Second, the amount recorded as the lease asset and the lease liability is the current cash equivalent of the required future lease payments. In the above example, you were given the current cash equivalent of the lease. In the next section, we will learn how accountants compute current cash equivalents, commonly referred to as *present values.*

Accounting for short-term leases

A **short-term lease** is a lease for 12 months or less (including expected renewals and extensions) that does not contain a purchase option that the lessee is expected to exercise. A company does not record a lease asset or a lease liability when it signs a short-term lease. Instead the company simply records lease expense over the life of the lease. As an example of a short-term lease, assume that on December 31, Starbucks signs a short-term lease agreement to rent five delivery trucks for the month of January. The agreement stipulates that Starbucks must pay $10,000 at the end of January. No entry is recorded at the time the lease is signed on December 31. The only entry recorded comes at the end of January to recognize lease expense:

	Debit	Credit
Lease expense (+E, −SE)	10,000	
Cash (−A)		10,000

Assets		=	Liabilities	+	Stockholders' Equity	
Cash	−10,000				Lease expense (+E)	−10,000

COMPUTING PRESENT VALUES

LEARNING OBJECTIVE 9-7

Compute and explain present values.

Our discussion of longer-term leases raises an interesting question about liabilities: Is the liability today the amount of cash that will be paid in the future? For example, if I agree to pay you $10,000 five years from now, should I report a liability of $10,000 on my personal balance sheet? If I can earn interest on my money, the answer is "no." To understand why, it is important for you to understand that money invested in an interest-bearing account grows over time. We briefly introduced this concept earlier in the chapter and referred to it as the time value of money. The time value of money plays an important role in how companies report long-term liabilities, such as long-term notes as well as bonds, the topic of Chapter 10.

The concept of **present value** (PV) is based on the time value of money. Quite simply, money received today is worth more than money to be received one year from today (or at any other future date) because it can be used to earn interest. If you invest $1,000 today at 10 percent, you will have $1,100 in one year. In contrast, if you receive $1,000 one year from today, you will lose the opportunity to earn the $100 in interest revenue. The difference between the $1,000 and the $1,100 is the interest that can be earned during the year, which reflects the time value of money.

In one of your math classes, you have probably already solved some problems involving the time value of money. In the typical problem, you are told a certain dollar amount has been deposited in a savings account earning a specified rate of interest. You are asked to compute the dollar amount in the savings account after a certain number of years. This is an example of a **future value** (FV) problem: How much is a given dollar amount today worth in the future if it grows at a specified interest rate? For example, if you deposited $100 today in a savings account that earns 10 percent interest, how much would you have after one year?

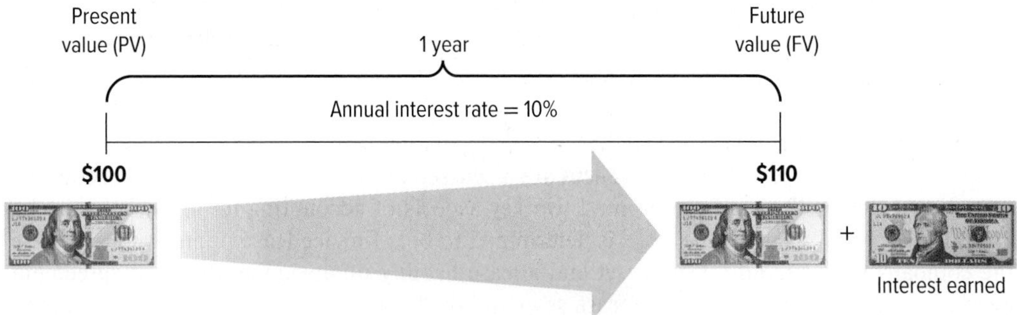

NICK FIELDING/Alamy Stock Photo; Steve Stock /Alamy Stock Photo

ANSWER: $110

In this chapter we focus on how to solve the opposite problem. In present value problems, you are asked to compute the amount you would need to deposit today at a specified interest rate to have a given dollar amount in the future. For example, if you needed $110 in one year, how much would you need to deposit in a savings account today if the savings account earns 10 percent interest?

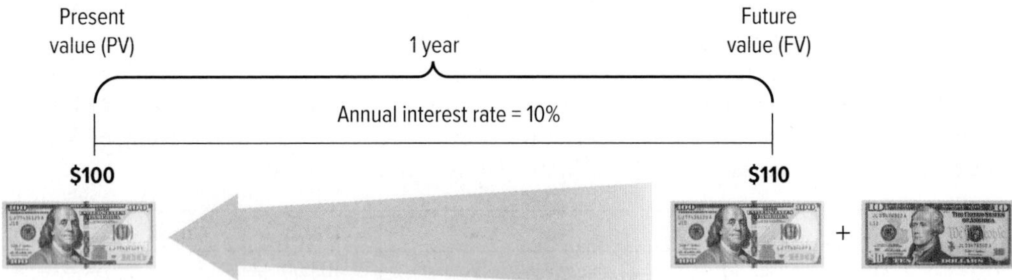

NICK FIELDING/Alamy Stock Photo; Steve Stock /Alamy Stock Photo

ANSWER: $100

There are two basic types of present value problems: those involving single amounts like the example above and those involving a stream of future amounts. Understanding and being able to compute both types is important when accounting for certain long-term liabilities.

Present Value of a Single Amount

To compute the present value of a single amount, you must discount the amount to be received or paid in the future at *i* interest rate for *n* periods. The formula to compute the present value of a single amount is

$$\text{Present value} = \frac{1}{(1 + i)^n} \times \text{Amount}$$

Tip To calculate a present value you need: (1) the amount to be received or paid in the future, (2) the interest rate per period, and (3) the number of periods.

While the formula is not difficult to use, most analysts use present value tables, calculators, or Excel. We strongly encourage you to visit Connect for tutorials on how to compute present values using each of these tools. To do so, see "Guided Help 9-2" on the next page. For the examples that follow, we provide the inputs required to compute each present value using tables, calculators, and Excel.

Assume that today is January 1, 2022, and you need to make a $1,000 cash payment on December 31, 2024. At an interest rate of 10 percent per year, how much would you need to deposit today to have exactly $1,000 on December 31, 2024? You could discount the amount year by year to figure out how much you would need to deposit today, but it is easier to use Table E.1, Appendix E, Present Value of $1. For $i = 10\%$, $n = 3$ periods, we find that the present value factor is 0.75131. The present value of $1,000 to be paid at the end of three years can be computed as follows:

$$\$1{,}000 \times 0.75131 = \$751.31$$

From Table E.1:
interest rate (i) = 10%,
periods (n) = 3:
Factor = 0.75131
Using Calculator:
rate (i) = 10,
periods (n) = 3,
pmt = $0, FV = −$1,000
Using Excel:
Rate (i) = .10,
Nper (n) = 3,
Pmt = $0, Fv = −$1,000

Once you have computed a present value amount, it is important that you understand what it means. The $751.31 is the amount you would have to deposit today in order to have exactly $1,000 three years from today, assuming an interest rate of 10 percent. Conceptually, you should be indifferent between paying $751.31 today and paying $1,000 in three years. If you had $751.31 today and did not want to worry about having to come up with $1,000 in three years, you could simply deposit the money in a savings account and at 10 percent interest it would grow to $1,000 in three years.[1] How the deposit of $751.31 grows to equal $1,000 is shown in Exhibit 9.2.

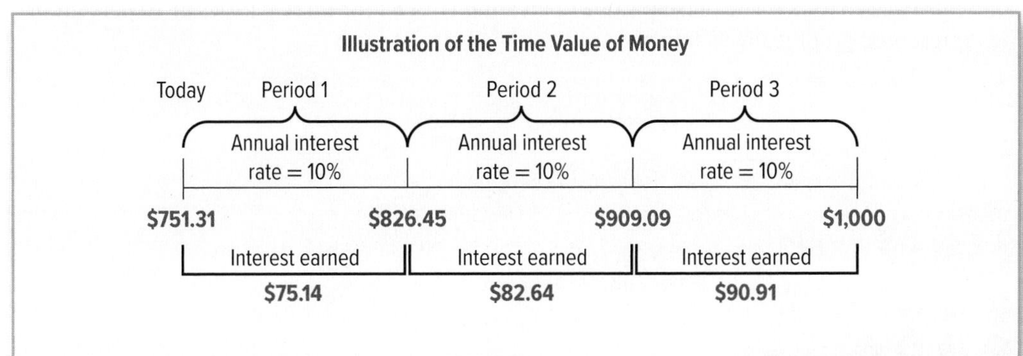

EXHIBIT 9.2

How a Deposit Grows to $1,000

PAUSE FOR FEEDBACK

So far we have discussed the first type of present value problems–those involving a single future amount. In the next section, we will discuss annuities, which involve a stream of future amounts. Before you move on, complete the following questions to test your understanding of the present value concepts we have covered so far.

SELF-STUDY QUIZ

1. If the interest rate in a present value problem increases from 8 percent to 10 percent, will the present value increase or decrease?
2. Assuming an annual interest rate of 5 percent, what amount should you deposit today if you need $10,000 in 10 years?

After you have completed your answers, check them below.

[1]Though not the focus of this chapter, we provide tables for computing future values in Appendix E. You use future value tables the same way you use present value tables. For example, to compute how much you would have after three years if you deposited $751.31 in a savings account earning 10 percent interest, you would use Table E.3 ($i = 10\%$, $n = 3$ periods) and multiply $751.31 × 1.33100. The answer: $1,000.

GUIDED HELP 9-2

For additional step-by-step video instructions on how to compute present values, go to mhhe.com/libby_gh9-2.

Related Homework: M9-9, E9-14, E9-19, P9-10

Present Value of an Annuity

Instead of a single amount, many business problems involve multiple cash payments over a number of periods. An annuity is a series of consecutive payments characterized by

1. An equal dollar amount each period.
2. Interest periods of equal length (e.g., a year, half a year, quarterly, or monthly).
3. The same interest rate each period.

Examples of annuities include monthly rent payments on an apartment or quarterly lease payments on a car.

We compute the present value of an annuity by discounting each of the equal periodic amounts back to today. The present value of an annuity of $1 for three periods at 10 percent may be represented graphically as follows:

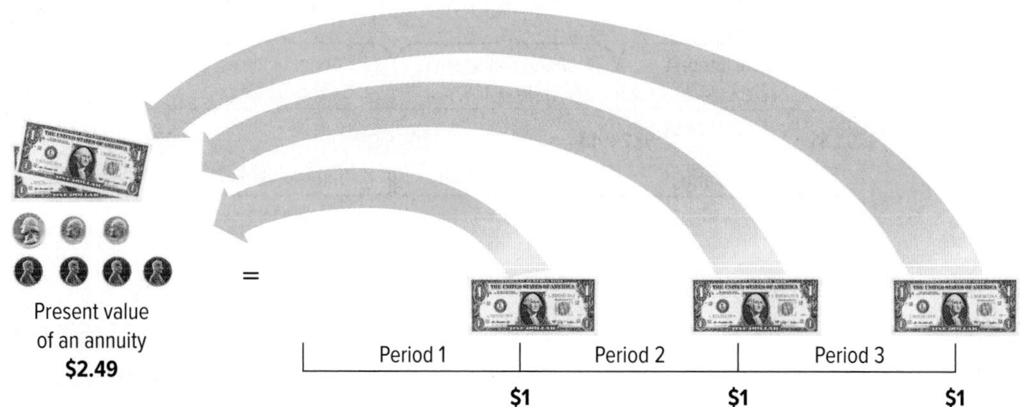

nimon/Shutterstock; Brandon Laufenberg/Getty Images

Applying this concept to a purchase decision, assume you purchase a piece of equipment and agree to pay $1,000 cash each December 31 for three years. How much would you need to deposit today at an annual interest rate of 10 percent to make each $1,000 payment? We could use Table E.1, Appendix E, to calculate the present value as follows:

Year	Amount	Factor from Table E. 1, Appendix E, i = 10%		Present Value
1	$1,000	0.90909 ($n = 1$)	=	$ 909.09
2	$1,000	0.82645 ($n = 2$)	=	$ 826.45
3	$1,000	0.75131 ($n = 3$)	=	$ 751.31
		Total present value	=	$2,486.85

Solutions to SELF-STUDY QUIZ

1. The present value will decrease.
2. $10,000 × 0.61391 = $6,139.10

We can compute the present value of this annuity more easily, however, by using Table E.2, Appendix E, as follows:

$$\$1{,}000 \times 2.48685 = \$2{,}486.85$$

From Table E.2:
interest rate (i) = 10%,
periods (n) = 3:
Factor = 2.48685
Using Calculator:
rate (i) = 10,
periods (n) = 3,
pmt = −$1,000, FV = $0
Using Excel:
Rate (i) = 0.10,
Nper (n) = 3,
Pmt = −$1,000, Fv = $0

Let's now connect the amount we computed above to the three required $1,000 payments. As shown in Exhibit 9.3, if you deposited $2,486.85 today at an interest rate of 10 percent, that amount would grow to $2,735.54 after one year ($2,486.85 + interest of $248.69). At that point you would make your first $1,000 payment and have $1,735.54 left. The $1,735.54 would grow to $1,909.09 over the next year ($1,735.54 + interest of $173.55). At that point you would make your second $1,000 payment and have $909.09 left. The $909.09 would grow to exactly $1,000 over the next year ($909.09 + interest of $90.91), and you would be able to make your last $1,000 payment. Thus, at an interest rate of 10 percent, depositing $2,486.85 today would allow you to make the three required $1,000 payments at the end of the next three years.[2]

EXHIBIT 9.3

Illustration of an Annuity over Time

Beginning of Year	+	Interest Earned During Year	=	End of Year	−	Payment	=	Remaining Balance
$2,486.85	+	$248.69	=	$2,735.54	−	$1,000.00	=	$1,735.54
1,735.54	+	173.55	=	1,909.09	−	1,000.00	=	909.09
909.09	+	90.91	=	1,000.00	−	1,000.00	=	0

Interest Rates and Interest Periods

The preceding illustrations assumed annual periods for compounding and discounting. Although interest rates are almost always quoted on an annual basis, most compounding periods encountered in business are less than one year. When interest periods are less than a year, the values of n and i must be adjusted to be consistent with the length of the interest period.

To illustrate, 12 percent interest compounded annually for five years requires the use of $n = 5$ and $i = 12\%$. If compounding is quarterly, however, the interest period is one-quarter of a year (i.e., four periods per year), and the quarterly interest rate is one-quarter of the annual rate (i.e., 3 percent per quarter). Therefore, 12 percent interest compounded quarterly for five years requires use of $n = 20$ and $i = 3\%$.

A QUESTION OF ETHICS

Truth in Advertising

Online and television advertisements are easy to misinterpret if the consumer does not understand the time value of money. For example, perhaps you have seen advertisements that promise "No payments for one year!" It is important to realize that "no payments" does not mean "no interest." In almost all cases, during the "no payments" year, interest is accruing (being added to the amount owed) and, depending on the interest rate, can add significantly to the total amount customers must pay back.

Another misleading advertisement relates to lotteries, which often promise to make winners instant millionaires. In some cases, however, the lottery amount is paid out over a long period of time, for example, $25,000 each year for 40 years. The winner will receive $1,000,000 ($25,000 × 40 years), but the present value of this annuity at 8 percent is only $298,000. While most winners are happy to get the money, they are not really millionaires.

Now that you understand the time value of money, keep an eye out for advertisements that include dollar amounts in the future. There are a lot of them out there, and knowing how to compute present values will help you more fully understand their implications.

[2]To compute the future value of an annuity, you would use Table E.4, Appendix E. For example, at an interest rate of 10 percent, if you deposited $1,000 at the end of each year for three years (with no withdrawals), you would have $3,310 ($1,000 × 3.31000, the future value factor for $n = 3$, $i = 10\%$).

LEARNING OBJECTIVE 9-8

Apply the present value concept to the reporting of long-term liabilities.

Accounting Applications of Present Values

Many business transactions that affect long-term liabilities require accountants to compute present values. We provide three brief examples below before transitioning to accounting for bonds in the next chapter.

Computing the Amount of a Liability with a Single Payment

Assume that on January 1, 2022, **Starbucks** bought new delivery trucks by signing a note and agreeing to pay $200,000 on December 31, 2023. This type of arrangement is often referred to as a "non-interest-bearing" note because no interest payments are required over the life of the note. Do not confuse "non-interest-bearing" with "no interest." The interest is simply built into the final payment, in this case the $200,000 payment on December 31, 2023. Assume that the annual market interest rate applicable to the note is 12 percent.

To record this transaction, Starbucks's accountants first must compute the present value of the single amount to be paid in the future. The problem can be shown graphically as follows:

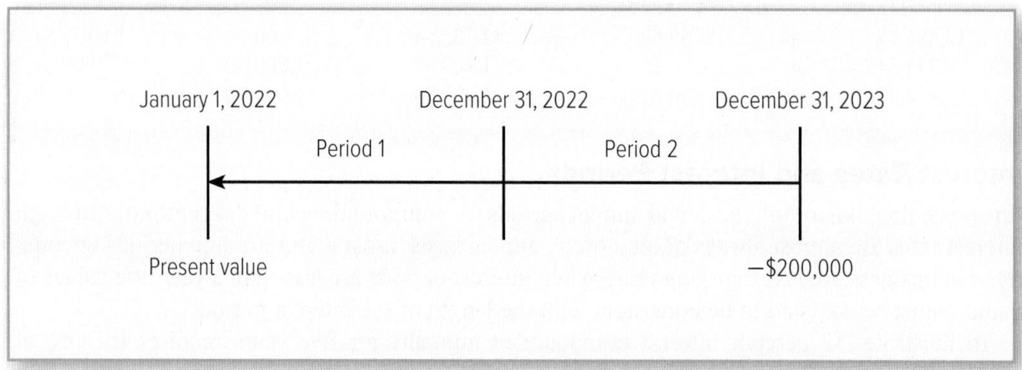

The present value of the $200,000 payment is computed as follows:

$$\$200{,}000 \times 0.79719 = \$159{,}438$$

From Table E.1:
interest rate $(i) = 12\%$,
periods $(n) = 2$:
Factor = 0.79719
Using Calculator:
rate $(i) = 12$,
periods $(n) = 2$,
pmt = $0, FV = −$200,000
Using Excel:
Rate $(i) = 0.12$,
Nper $(n) = 2$,
Pmt = $0, Fv = −$200,000

After computing the present value, Starbucks records the following journal entry:

	Debit	Credit
Delivery trucks (+A)	159,438	
Note payable (+L)		159,438

Assets		=	Liabilities		+	Stockholders' Equity
Delivery trucks	+159,438		Note payable	+159,438		

At the end of each year, Starbucks must record the implied interest expense.

December 31, 2022	Debit	Credit
Interest expense (+E, −SE)	19,133*	
Note payable (+L)		19,133

*$159,438 note payable balance × 0.12 annual interest rate = $19,133. When added to $159,438, the note payable balance is now $178,571.

Assets	=	Liabilities		+	Stockholders' Equity	
		Note payable	+19,133		Interest expense (+E)	−19,133

December 31, 2023	Debit	Credit
Interest expense (+E, −SE)	21,429*	
Note payable (+L)		21,429

*$178,571 note payable balance × 0.12 annual interest rate = $21,429. When added to $178,571, the note payable balance is now $200,000.

Assets	=	Liabilities		+	Stockholders' Equity	
		Note payable	+21,429		Interest expense (+E)	−21,429

At the end of two years, Starbucks must repay the loan amount. The amount owed is the balance in the note payable account, which started at $159,438 and grew as we added interest over the two-year period to now equal exactly $200,000 ($159,438 + $19,133 + $21,429). To repay the loan, Starbucks would record the following journal entry:

December 31, 2023	Debit	Credit
Note payable (−L)	200,000	
Cash (−A)		200,000

Assets		=	Liabilities		+	Stockholders' Equity
Cash	−200,000		Note payable	−200,000		

Computing the Amount of a Liability with an Annuity

On January 1, 2022, assume Starbucks bought several new espresso machines. The company elected to finance the purchase with a note payable to be paid off in three end-of-year payments of $163,685. Each payment includes principal plus interest on any unpaid balance. The annual interest rate is 11 percent. Payments are due on December 31, 2022, 2023, and 2024. This problem can be shown graphically as follows:

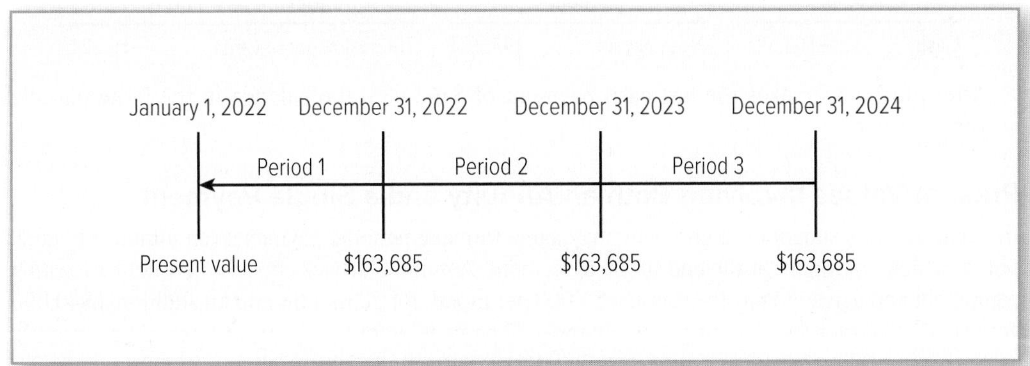

The present value of the note is the amount Starbucks would have to deposit today at 11 percent interest to cover the three $163,685 payments. This is an annuity because payments are made in three equal installments. The present value of the note is computed as follows:

$$\$163,685 \times 2.44371 = \$399,999$$

From Table E.2:
interest rate (i) = 11%,
periods (n) = 3:
Factor = 2.44371
Using Calculator:
rate (i) = 11,
periods (n) = 3,
pmt = −$163,685, FV = $0
Using Excel:
Rate (i) = 0.11,
Nper (n) = 3,
Pmt = −$163,685, Fv = $0

When Starbucks purchases the new espresso machines on January 1, 2022, it records the following journal entry:

January 1, 2022	Debit	Credit
Espresso machines (+A)	399,999	
Note payable (+L)		399,999

Assets		=	Liabilities		+	Stockholders' Equity
Espresso machines	+399,999		Note payable	+399,999		

At the end of each year over the three-year life of the note, Starbucks records the following journal entries:

December 31, 2022	Debit	Credit
Note payable (−L)	119,685	
Interest expense (+E, −SE)	44,000*	
Cash (−A)		163,685

*$399,999 note payable balance × 0.11 annual interest rate = $44,000. The remaining payable balance after recording this entry is $280,314.

Assets		=	Liabilities		+	Stockholders' Equity	
Cash	−163,685		Note payable	−119,685		Interest expense (+E)	−44,000

December 31, 2023	Debit	Credit
Note payable (−L)	132,850	
Interest expense (+E, −SE)	30,835*	
Cash (−A)		163,685

*$280,314 note payable balance × 0.11 annual interest rate = $30,835. The remaining payable balance after recording this entry is $147,464.

Assets		=	Liabilities		+	Stockholders' Equity	
Cash	−163,685		Note payable	−132,850		Interest expense (+E)	−30,835

December 31, 2024	Debit	Credit
Note payable (−L)	147,464	
Interest expense (+E, −SE)	16,221*	
Cash (−A)		163,685

*$147,464 note payable balance × 0.11 annual interest rate = $16,221.

Assets		=	Liabilities		+	Stockholders' Equity	
Cash	−163,685		Note payable	−147,464		Interest expense (+E)	−16,221

After Starbucks makes the last cash payment of $163,685, the balance in the Note payable account is zero.

Present Values Involving Both an Annuity and a Single Payment

In some business situations, a company may agree to make periodic payments (an annuity) in addition to a single payment at the end of the agreement. Assume Starbucks bought new coffee roasting equipment and agreed to pay the supplier $1,000 per month for 20 months and an additional $40,000 at the end of 20 months. The supplier is charging 12 percent interest per year, or 1 percent per month.

In this type of problem, you can determine the present value of the total obligation by **computing the present value of each part.** In other words, you compute the present value of the annuity and the present value of the single payment and add the two amounts together, as follows:

Step 1: Compute the present value of the annuity using Table E.2, Appendix E:

$$\$1{,}000 \times 18.04555 = \$18{,}046$$

From Table E.2:
interest rate (i) = 1%,
periods (n) = 20:
Factor = 18.04555
Using Excel or a Calculator:
see single calculation below

Step 2: Compute the present value of the single payment using Table E.1, Appendix E:

$$\$40{,}000 \times 0.81954 = \$32{,}782$$

From Table E.1:
interest rate (i) = 1%,
periods (n) = 20:
Factor = 0.81954
Using Excel or a Calculator:
see single calculation below

Step 3: Add the two amounts to determine the present value of the total obligation:

	$18,046	(present value of 20 months of annuity payments)
+	32,782	(present value of single sum at the end of 20 months)
	$50,828	(present value of the total obligation)

The $50,828 is the present value of all the cash payments that Starbucks must make under this agreement. Starbucks would record this amount as a liability. This amount can be computed as a single calculation using a calculator or Excel.

In the next chapter, we will use the present value techniques you have just learned to understand how to account for bonds.

Using Calculator:
rate (i) = 1,
periods (n) = 20,
pmt = −$1,000,
FV = −$40,000
Using Excel:
Rate (i) = 0.01,
Nper (n) = 20,
Pmt = −$1,000,
Fv = −$40,000

DEMONSTRATION CASE

(Try to answer the questions before proceeding to the suggested solutions that follow.) **Patagonia** completed several transactions during the year. In each case, decide if a liability (or liabilities) should be recorded and, if so, determine the amount. Assume the current date is December 31 and all transactions occurred over the last year.

1. Employees earned salaries of $100,000, which have not been paid at year-end.
2. Patagonia borrowed $100,000 on June 30 at an annual interest rate of 7 percent. As of December 31, no payments associated with this loan have been made.
3. A customer prepaid $250 for a custom waterproof jacket. The customer will pick up the jacket next month.
4. The company lost a lawsuit for $250,000 but plans to appeal.
5. A new truck was leased for a period equal to 95 percent of the expected life of the truck.
6. On December 31, a bank loaned money to Patagonia. Patagonia agreed to repay the bank $100,000 on December 31 next year. The annual interest rate is 5 percent.
7. Patagonia signed a loan agreement that requires it to pay $50,000 per year for 20 years. The annual interest rate is 8 percent.

SUGGESTED SOLUTION

1. A liability of $100,000 should be recorded.
2. The amount borrowed ($100,000) should be recorded as a liability on June 30. In addition, interest accrued but not paid should be recorded as a liability at year-end. This amount is $100,000 × 7% × 6/12 = $3,500.
3. The amount the customer paid ($250) is a liability (deferred revenue) until the customer picks up the jacket, at which point the $250 becomes revenue.
4. Unless Patagonia can make a convincing argument that it is not probable it will have to pay the $250,000, the company should record the amount as a liability.
5. The lease covers 95 percent of the estimated life of the truck, which would be considered a major part of the remaining economic life of the asset. It therefore should be accounted for as a finance lease, and a lease asset and lease liability should be recorded. The amount is the present value of the lease payments (which were not given in the problem).
6. Patagonia should record a liability equal to the present value of the obligation. Using Table E.1, Appendix E (i = 5%, n = 1), the amount is $100,000 × 0.95238 = $95,238.
7. Patagonia should record a liability for the present value of the obligation. Using Table E.2, Appendix E (i = 8%, n = 20), the amount is $50,000 × 9.81815 = $490,908.

Chapter Supplement A

Present Value Computations Using a Calculator or Excel

While the present value tables at the end of this book are useful for educational purposes, most present value problems in business are solved using a financial calculator or Excel. To review how to use a financial calculator or Excel to solve present value problems, use the instructions below or go to the videos posted to the Additional Student Resources on Connect.

Calculating Present Values Using the HP 10bII+

SAMPLE PROBLEM INPUTS:

N = Number of periods:	3
I/YR = Interest rate/period:	10%
PMT = Payments/period:	−$500
FV = Future value:	−$1,000

Step 1: Turn on, set payments per year to 1, and clear prior inputs:

- Turn your calculator on by pressing the "ON" button (**A**).
- Press "1".
- Press the orange-colored shift key (**B**).
- Press the "P/YR" key (**C**).
- To confirm the change, press the orange-colored shift key (**B**), then press "C ALL" (**D**). You should briefly see "1 P_Yr" on your screen. This step also will clear all prior inputs from your calculator.

Step 2: Enter the number of periods:

- Press "3", then press "N" (**E**).

Step 3: Enter the interest rate per period:

- Press "10", then press "I/YR" (**F**).
- *NOTE: When using an HP 10bII+, you should enter the whole number "10" for 10%, not the decimal 0.10.*

Step 4: Enter the amount of any annuity payments:

- Press "500", then press "+/−" (**G**), then press "PMT" (**C**).
- *NOTE: If you are calculating the present value of a single amount, there are no annuity payments. When there are no annuity payments, skip STEP 4 or press "0" then press "PMT"* (**C**).

Step 5: Enter the future amount:

- Press "1,000", then press "+/−" (**G**), then press "FV" (**H**).

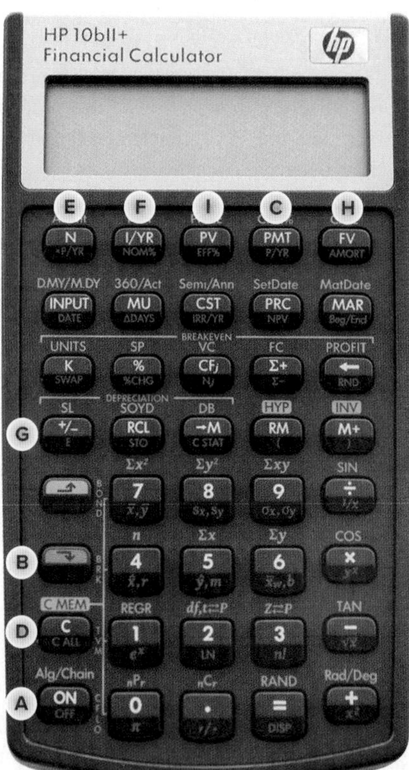

Courtesy of Weili Ge

Step 6: Compute the present value:

- Press "PV" (**I**).

ANSWER: $1,994.74

NOTE: If you omit the annuity payment of $500 in STEP 4 and solve for the present value of a single amount ($1,000), the answer is $751.31.

Calculating Present Values Using the TI BA II Plus

SAMPLE PROBLEM INPUTS:

N = Number of periods:	3
I/YR = Interest rate/period:	10%
PMT = Payments/period:	−$500
FV = Future value:	−$1,000

Step 1: Turn on and clear prior inputs:

- Turn your calculator on by pressing the "ON/OFF" button (**A**).
- Clear prior inputs by pressing the yellow "2ND" key (**B**), then "CLR TVM" (**C**).

Step 2: Enter the number of periods:

- Press "3", then press "N" (**D**).

Step 3: Enter the interest rate per period:

- Press "10", then press "I/Y" (**E**).
- *NOTE: When using a TI BA II Plus, you should enter the whole number "10" for 10%, not the decimal 0.10.*

Step 4: Enter the amount of any annuity payments:

- Press "500", then press "+/−" (**F**), then press "PMT" (**G**).
- *NOTE: If you are calculating the present value of a single amount, there are no annuity payments. When there are no annuity payments, skip STEP 4 or press "0" then press "PMT"* (**G**).

Step 5: Enter the future amount:

- Press "1,000", then press "+/−" (**F**), then press "FV" (**C**).

Step 6: Compute the present value:

- Press "CPT" (**H**), then "PV" (**I**).

ANSWER: $1,994.74

NOTE: If you omit the annuity payment of $500 in STEP 4 and solve for the present value of a single amount ($1,000), the answer is $751.31.

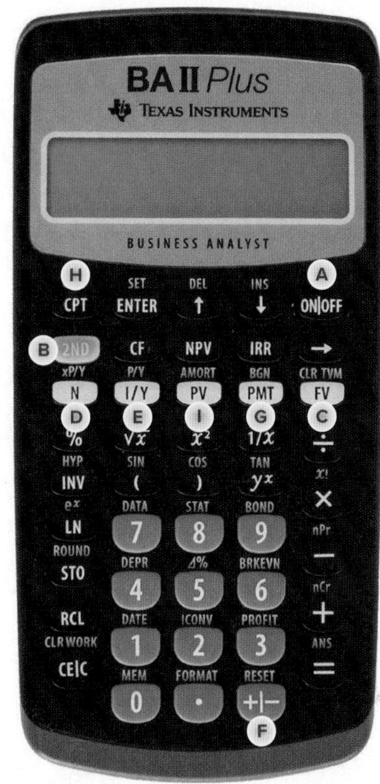

Courtesy of Weili Ge

Calculating Present Values Using the HP 12C

SAMPLE PROBLEM INPUTS:

N = Number of periods:	3
I/YR = Interest rate/period:	10%
PMT = Payments/period:	− $500
FV = Future value:	− $1,000

Step 1: Turn on and clear prior inputs:

- Turn your calculator on by pressing the "ON" button (**A**).
- Clear prior inputs by pressing the orange-colored shift key (**B**), then "CLEAR FIN" (**C**).

Step 2: Enter the number of periods:

- Press "3", then press "n" (**D**).

Step 3: Enter the interest rate per period:

- Press "10", then press "i" (**E**).
- *NOTE: When using an HP 12C, you should enter the whole number "10" for 10%, not the decimal 0.10.*

Step 4: Enter the amount of any annuity payments:

- Press "500", then press "CHS" (**F**), then press "PMT" (**G**).
- *NOTE: If you are calculating the present value of a single amount, there are no annuity payments. When there are no annuity payments, skip STEP 4 or press "0", then press "PMT"* (**G**).

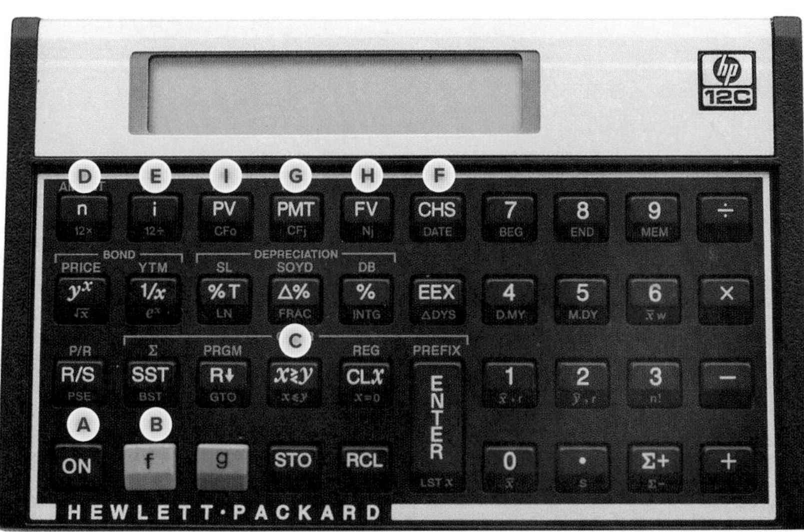

Courtesy of Weili Ge

Step 5: Enter the future amount:

- Press "1,000", then press "CHS" (**F**), then press "FV" (**H**).

Step 6: Compute the present value:

- Press "PV" (**I**).

ANSWER: $1,994.74

NOTE: If you omit the annuity payment of $500 in STEP 4 and solve for the present value of a single amount ($1,000), the answer is $751.31.

Calculating Present Values Using Excel

SAMPLE PROBLEM INPUTS:

N =	Number of periods:	3
I/YR =	Interest rate/period:	10%
PMT =	Payments/period:	– $500
FV =	Future value:	– $1,000

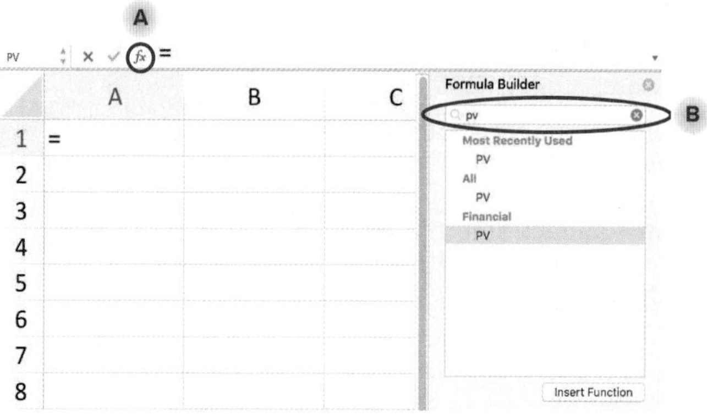

Source: Microsoft Corporation

A1 fx =PV(0.1,3,-500,-1000)

	A	B	C
1	$1,994.74		
2			
3			
4			
5			
6			
7			
8			

Formula Builder
Show All Functions
PV
Rate = 0.1
0.1
Nper = 3
3
Pmt = -500
-500
Fv = -1000
-1000
Type = number
Result: 1994.740796
Done
C

Source: Microsoft Corporation

Step 1: Opening the Formula Builder:

- Open Excel on your computer.
- Click the "*fx*" function symbol (**A**) in the menu bar to open the Formula Builder.

Step 2: Locate the present value (PV) formula:

- In the Formula Builder search bar (**B**), type in "PV".
- Double-click on "PV" shown in the search results.

Step 3: Enter the interest rate:

- You will enter inputs directly into boxes in the Formula Builder (**C**).
- In the "Rate" box enter .10.
- *NOTE: When using Excel, you should enter the decimal .10 and not the whole number "10" for 10%.*

Step 4: Enter the number of periods:

- In the "Nper" box enter "3".

Step 5: Enter the amount of any annuity payments:

- In the "Pmt" box enter "– 500".
- *NOTE: If you are calculating the present value of a single amount, there are no annuity payments. When there are no annuity payments, you would leave the "Pmt" box empty or enter "0".*

Step 6: Enter the future amount:

- In the "Fv" box enter "– 1000".

Step 7: The last box:

- Leave the "Type" box empty
- *NOTE: Entering "1" here tells Excel to assume that payments are at the beginning of the period. Entering "0" or leaving this box blank tells Excel to assume that payments are at the end of the period (which is what we want).*

ANSWER: $1,994.74

NOTE: If you omit the annuity payment of $500 in STEP 5 and solve for the present value of a single amount ($1,000), the answer is $751.31.

Chapter Supplement B

Deferred Taxes

In Chapter 8 you learned that companies follow GAAP for financial reporting but the Internal Revenue Code when creating their tax returns. Following different rules can create what are called **temporary tax differences**. Temporary tax differences are the result of a company reporting revenues and expenses on its income statement *in a different time period* than it reports them on its tax return. If the difference between financial reporting and tax reporting will result in a lower tax bill in the future, it results in the creation of an asset. If the difference will result in a higher tax bill in the future, it results in the creation of a liability. We call these assets and liabilities deferred tax assets and deferred tax liabilities. In this chapter supplement, we focus on understanding deferred tax liabilities.

A company creates a **deferred tax liability** when it:

- Reports revenue on this period's income statement that it *does not* report on its tax return until a future period or
- Reports an expense on this period's tax return that it *does not* report on its income statement until a future period.

Both circumstances result in this period's accounting income reported on the income statement being *higher* than this period's tax income reported on the company's tax return. An example is when a company pays expenses in advance. In certain situations, the company includes the advance payment as an expense on its tax return in the period it pays the cash. For financial reporting purposes, the company is required to recognize the advance payment as an asset on its balance sheet until it actually incurs the expense in a future period. When this happens, the company then uses the asset to satisfy the expense.

Another accounting area that often results in a deferred tax liability is depreciation. Many companies use straight-line depreciation for financial reporting purposes and an accelerated depreciation method for tax purposes. Let's consider a simple example. Assume that in the current year, **Starbucks** owns a piece of equipment that originally cost $10 million. The current book value (cost less accumulated depreciation) on the balance sheet is $8.5 million. For tax purposes, the book value is $6.5 million. The $2 million difference is a result of Starbucks using straight-line depreciation for financial reporting and accelerated depreciation for tax purposes. Starbucks has been able to delay or defer paying federal income taxes by reporting more depreciation on its tax return than it reports on its income statement.

The amount of deferred tax liability is computed by multiplying the timing difference by the corporate tax rate (21 percent):

Deferred Tax Liability = \$2 million × 0.21 = \$420,000

If there are no other deferred tax items, Starbucks will report a deferred tax liability on its balance sheet of \$420,000.

At the end of the following year, Starbucks again would compare the GAAP book value of the piece of equipment to the tax book value. Assume that the GAAP book value is \$8.2 million and the tax book value is \$6 million. The timing difference is \$2.2 million, resulting in a deferred tax liability of \$462,000 (\$2.2 million × 0.21).

The Income tax expense reported under GAAP is the amount needed to complete a journal entry once the company has computed the amount it will pay the IRS for taxes and the change in its deferred taxes. Based on our example, the change in the deferred tax liability for Starbucks is \$42,000 (\$462,000 – \$420,000). Assume the company completes its tax return and determines it owes the IRS \$550,000 for taxes. The company would record the following:

	Debit	Credit
Income tax expense (+E, −SE)	592,000	
Deferred taxes (+L)		42,000
Income taxes payable (+L)		550,000

Assets	=	Liabilities		+	Stockholders' Equity	
		Deferred taxes	+42,000		Income tax expense (+E)	−592,000
		Income taxes payable	+550,000			

The computation of deferred taxes involves some complexities that are discussed in advanced accounting courses. At this point, you need to understand only that deferred tax assets and liabilities are the result of temporary differences between a company's income statement and its tax return. Each temporary difference has an impact on the income statement in one accounting period and the tax return in another.

CHAPTER TAKE-AWAYS

9-1. Define, measure, and report current liabilities. **p. 476**

Accountants define liabilities as probable future sacrifices of economic benefits that arise from past transactions. Liabilities are classified on the balance sheet as either current or long term. Current liabilities are short-term obligations that will be paid within the current operating cycle of the business or within one year of the balance sheet date, whichever is longer. Long-term liabilities are all obligations not classified as current.

9-2. Compute and interpret the accounts payable turnover ratio. **p. 477**

To compute this ratio, divide cost of goods sold by average accounts payable. This ratio reflects how quickly management is paying its suppliers and is considered to be a measure of liquidity. Liquidity is a company's ability to meet its current obligations.

9-3. Report notes payable and explain the time value of money. **p. 482**

Companies sign a note when they borrow money. The note specifies the amount borrowed, when it must be repaid, and the interest rate associated with the loan. Accountants report the amount borrowed, and any unpaid interest, as liabilities. The time value of money refers to the principle that a given amount of money deposited in an interest-bearing account increases over time.

9-4. Report contingent liabilities. **p. 484**

A contingent liability is a potential liability that has arisen as the result of a past event. An example is a warranty. The past event is the sale of the item. The potential liability is the possibility that the company will have to honor the warranty. Contingent liabilities are reported on the balance sheet if they are probable and the amount can be estimated. If they are probable but the amount cannot be estimated, or if they are only reasonably possible regardless of whether the amount can be estimated, then they are reported in the footnotes.

9-5. Explain the importance of working capital and its impact on cash flows. p. 486

Working capital is defined as current assets minus current liabilities. Working capital is used to fund the operating activities of a business. Changes in working capital accounts are important to managers and analysts because they have a direct impact on the cash flows from operating activities reported on a company's cash flow statement.

9-6. Report long-term liabilities. p. 487

Any liability that is not a current liability is a long-term liability. Many long-term liabilities are reported on the balance sheet at their present value, which is the amount a company would have to pay today at a given interest rate to satisfy the obligation.

9-7. Compute and explain present values. p. 489

The present value concept is based on the time value of money. Money received today is worth more than the same amount of money to be received in the future because of interest rates. We can compute the present value of a single amount or the present value of a stream of amounts (called an annuity) using present value tables, a financial calculator, or Excel.

9-8. Apply the present value concept to the reporting of long-term liabilities. p. 494

A liability involves the payment of some amount at a future date. With long-term liabilities, the reported liability is not the dollar value of the future payment(s), but rather the present value of the future payment(s).

In this chapter, we focused on the reporting of current liabilities and introduced how to compute and interpret present values. In the next chapter, we discuss a company's capital structure and how long-term liabilities, like bonds, fit into that structure.

KEY RATIO

Accounts payable turnover is a measure of how quickly a company pays its suppliers. It is computed as follows (see the "Key Ratio Analysis" box in the Current Liabilities section):

$$\text{Accounts Payable Turnover} = \frac{\text{Costs of Goods Sold}}{\text{Average Accounts Payable}}$$

FINDING FINANCIAL INFORMATION

Balance Sheet

Under Current Liabilities
- Accounts payable
- Accrued liabilities
- Deferred revenues
- Notes payable
- Current portion of long-term debt

Under Noncurrent Liabilities
- Long-term debt
- Leases
- Deferred taxes
- Bonds

Income Statement

Liabilities are shown only on the balance sheet, never on the income statement. Transactions affecting liabilities often also affect income statement accounts. For example, employee salaries earned but not yet paid affect an income statement account (salary expense) and a balance sheet account (salaries payable).

Statement of Cash Flows

Under Operating Activities
Cash inflows and outflows associated with a company's operations, which often involve working capital accounts (current assets and current liabilities).

Under Financing Activities
Cash inflows and outflows associated with equity and debt, including long-term liabilities like notes and bonds.

Notes

Under Summary of Significant Accounting Policies
A brief description of the accounting for certain liabilities.

Under Separate Notes
Additional details about both short-term liabilities (e.g., deferred revenue) and long-term liabilities (e.g., notes).
Additional details about contingent liabilities, especially legal issues.

KEY TERMS

Accrued Liabilities Expenses that have been incurred but have not been paid at the end of the accounting period. **p. 478**

Annuity A series of periodic cash receipts or payments that are equal in amount each interest period. **p. 492**

Contingent Liability A potential liability that has arisen as the result of a past event; it is not a definitive liability until some future event occurs. **p. 484**

Deferred Tax Liability Created when differences in financial reporting and tax reporting cause accounting income to be higher than tax income in a given period. **p. 502**

Finance Lease Effective control of the leased asset is transferred to the lessee. **p. 488**

Future Value The sum to which an amount will increase as the result of compound interest. **p. 490**

Lessee The party that pays for the right to use the leased asset. **p. 488**

Lessor The party that owns a leased asset. **p. 488**

Liquidity The ability to pay current obligations. **p. 486**

Long-Term Liabilities All of the entity's obligations that are not classified as current liabilities. **p. 487**

Operating Lease Effective control of the leased asset remains with the lessor. **p. 488**

Present Value The current value of an amount to be received in the future; a future amount discounted for compound interest. **p. 490**

Short-Term Lease A lease for 12 months or less (including expected renewals and extensions) that does not contain a purchase option that the lessee is expected to exercise. **p. 489**

Temporary Tax Differences Result from companies reporting revenues and expenses on their income statements in a different time period than they report them on their tax returns. **p. 502**

Time Value of Money Principle that a given amount of money deposited in an interestbearing account increases over time. **p. 482**

Working Capital The dollar difference between total current assets and total current liabilities. **p. 486**

QUESTIONS

1. Define *liability.* Differentiate between a current liability and a long-term liability.
2. What financial statement is the primary source of information about the liabilities of a company?
3. In their balance sheets, what do companies call obligations to pay suppliers in the near future?
4. What does the *accounts payable turnover ratio* tell you about a company? How is the ratio computed?
5. Define *accrued liability.* What is an example of an accrued liability?
6. Define *note payable.* When must a company reclassify a long-term note payable as a current liability?
7. On April 1 of the current year, a company borrowed $4,000 from a bank. The annual interest rate was 12 percent. When the company prepares its year-end financial statements on December 31, how much will it report as interest expense associated with this note?
8. Define *deferred revenue.* Why is it a liability?
9. Define *contingent liability.* What conditions must be met in order for a contingent liability to be reported on a company's balance sheet?

10. Define *working capital.* How is working capital computed?
11. When a company signs a finance lease, does it record an asset and a liability on its balance sheet?
12. Explain the concept of the time value of money.
13. If you hold a valid contract that will pay you $8,000 cash in 10 years and the going annual rate of interest is 10 percent, what is the contract's present value? Show your computations.
14. Define *annuity.*
15. Using Table E.1 in Appendix E, fill in the present value factors for the following interest rates and periods:

	Present Value Factors		
	$i = 5\%$	$i = 10\%$	$i = 14\%$
	$n = 4$	$n = 7$	$n = 10$
PV of $1			
PV of annuity of $1			

16. You purchased a new car and promised to pay the dealership five payments of $8,000 at the end of each of the next five years. The applicable annual interest rate is 8 percent. What is the present value of this annuity?

MULTIPLE-CHOICE QUESTIONS

1. What is the present value factor for an annuity of five periods and an interest rate of 10 percent?
   a. 0.62092
   b. 4.32948
   c. 3.79079
   d. 7.72173
2. The university golf team needs to buy a car to travel to tournaments. A dealership in Bellevue has agreed to the following terms: $4,000 down plus 20 monthly payments of $750. A dealership in Seattle will agree to $1,000 down plus 20 monthly payments of $850. The local bank is currently charging an annual interest rate of 12 percent for car loans. Which is the better deal, *and why*?
   a. The Seattle offer is better because the total payments of $18,000 are less than the total payments of $19,000 to be made to the Bellevue dealership.
   b. The Bellevue offer is better because the cost in terms of present value is less than the present value cost of the Seattle offer.
   c. The Bellevue offer is better because the monthly payments are less.
   d. The Seattle offer is better because the cash down payment is less.
   e. The Seattle offer is better because the cost in terms of present value is less than the present value cost of the Bellevue offer.
3. Which of the following best describes *accrued liabilities?*
   a. Long-term liabilities.
   b. Current amounts owed to suppliers of inventory.
   c. Current liabilities to be recognized as revenue in a future period.
   d. Current amounts owed, but not yet paid, to various parties at the end of an accounting period.
4. Brad & Kelly Company has borrowed $100,000 from the bank to be repaid over the next five years, with payments beginning next month. Which of the following best describes the presentation of this debt in the balance sheet as of today (the date of borrowing)?
   a. $100,000 in the Long-Term Liability section.
   b. $100,000 plus the interest to be paid over the five-year period in the Long-Term Liability section.
   c. A portion of the $100,000 in the Current Liability section and the remainder of the principal in the Long-Term Liability section.
   d. A portion of the $100,000 plus interest in the Current Liability section and the remainder of the principal plus interest in the Long-Term Liability section.

5. A company is facing a lawsuit from a customer. It is possible, but not probable, that the company will have to pay a settlement that management estimates to be $2,000,000. How would this fact be reported in the financial statements to be issued at the end of the current month?
   a. $2,000,000 in the Current Liability section.
   b. $2,000,000 in the Long-Term Liability section.
   c. In a descriptive narrative in the footnote section.
   d. None because disclosure is not required.
6. Which of the following transactions would usually cause accounts payable turnover to increase?
   a. Payment of cash to a supplier for merchandise previously purchased on credit.
   b. Collection of cash from a customer.
   c. Purchase of merchandise on credit.
   d. None of the above.
7. How is working capital calculated?
   a. Current assets multiplied by current liabilities.
   b. Current assets plus current liabilities.
   c. Current assets minus current liabilities.
   d. Current assets divided by current liabilities.
8. The present value of an annuity of $10,000 per year for 10 years discounted at 8 percent is what amount?
   a. $5,002
   b. $67,101
   c. $53,349
   d. $80,000
9. Phoebe Company borrowed $100,000 at 8 percent interest for three months. How much interest does the company owe at the end of three months?
   a. $8,000
   b. $2,000
   c. $800
   d. $200
10. Raija received a gift from his grandmother of $100,000. She has promised to pay Raija the $100,000 in equal installments at the end of each year for the next 10 years. Raija wants to know how much the $100,000 is worth in today's dollars. Which of the following will Raija need to calculate this amount?
    a. The anticipated interest rate and the present value of $1 table.
    b. The anticipated interest rate and the future value of $1 table.
    c. The anticipated interest rate and the future value table for annuities.
    d. The anticipated interest rate and the present value table for annuities.

MINI-EXERCISES

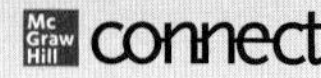

M9-1 Understanding Current Liabilities
LO9-1

Which of the following will increase a company's current liabilities?
1. A company purchases a new truck with cash.
2. A company receives cash from taking out a long-term loan.
3. A company collects half of its accounts receivable balance.
4. A company purchases inventory on credit.
5. A company purchases new manufacturing equipment with cash.

M9-2 Computing and Interpreting Accounts Payable Turnover
LO9-2

Nelson Company reported cost of goods sold of $690,000 last year and $720,000 this year. Nelson also reported accounts payable of $250,000 last year and $230,000 this year. Compute this year's accounts payable turnover ratio for Nelson. Interpret the number.

M9-3 Computing Interest Expense
LO9-3

Rainier Company borrowed $600,000 for three months. The annual interest rate on the loan was 11 percent. Rainiers fiscal year ends on December 31. Rainier borrowed the $600,000 one month prior to the end of its current fiscal year and paid back the $600,000 plus interest two months into its current fiscal year. In regards to this loan, how much interest expense, if any, would Rainier report at the end of its last fiscal year? At the end of its current fiscal year?

Recording a Note Payable

M9-4
LO9-3

Danali Corporation borrowed $290,000 on October 1. The note carried a 10 percent interest rate with the principal and interest payable on May 1 of next year. Prepare the journal entry to record the note on October 1. Prepare the adjusting entry to record accrued interest on December 31, the end of Danali's fiscal year.

Reporting Contingent Liabilities

M9-5
LO9-4

Buzz Coffee Shops is famous for its large servings of hot coffee. Last year a customer spilled a cup of hot coffee on himself and decided to file a lawsuit against Buzz for $1,000,000. Buzz's management thinks the chances of the company having to pay anything to the customer are remote. The case went to trial this year, and Buzz was found guilty of serving hot coffee in the wrong type of cup. The judge ordered Buzz to pay the customer $200,000. What is the proper reporting of the lawsuit in each year?

Computing Working Capital

M9-6
LO9-5

The balance sheet for Yakima Corporation reported the following: noncurrent assets, $240,000; total assets, $360,000; noncurrent liabilities, $176,000; total stockholders' equity, $94,000. Compute Stevenson's working capital.

Analyzing the Impact of Transactions on Working Capital

M9-7
LO9-5

Ospry Company has working capital in the amount of $1,240,000. For each of the following transactions, determine whether working capital will increase, decrease, or remain the same.

a. Paid accounts payable in the amount of $50,000.
b. Recorded accrued salaries in the amount of $100,000.
c. Borrowed $250,000 from a local bank, to be repaid in 90 days.
d. Purchased $20,000 of new inventory on credit.

Accounting for Long-Term Liabilities: Leases

M9-8
LO9-6

StarGaze Company leased a truck for three months. Accounting guidance classifies the lease as a short-term lease. StarGaze makes lease payments of $800 at the end of each month. What journal entry will StarGaze enter upon signing the lease? What journal entry will StarGaze enter when it makes its first lease payment of $800 cash to the leasing company?

Computing the Present Value of a Single Payment

M9-9
LO9-7

What is the present value of $500,000 to be paid in 10 years? The annual interest rate is 8 percent.

Computing the Present Value of an Annuity

M9-10
LO9-7

What is the present value of 10 equal payments of $15,000 to be made at the end of each year for the next 10 years? The annual interest rate is 10 percent.

Computing the Present Value of a Complex Contract

M9-11
LO9-7

Global Stores is downsizing and must let some employees go. Employees volunteering to leave are being offered a severance package of $118,000 cash, another $129,000 to be paid in one year, and an annuity of $27,500 to be paid each year for six years with the first payment coming at the end of this year. What is the present value of the total severance package, assuming an annual interest rate of 5 percent?

Computing Present Values and Recording Long-Term Liabilities

M9-12
LO9-8

Mukilteo Company signed a note to purchase a new piece of equipment. The note requires Mukilteo to pay $50,000 to the equipment manufacturer at the end of two years. Using a discount rate of 6 percent, compute the present value of this long-term liability, and provide the journal entry Mukilteo will record on the day it purchases the piece of equipment and signs the note.

EXERCISES

E9-1 Identifying Current Liabilities, Computing Working Capital, and Explaining Working Capital

LO9-1, 9-4, 9-5

Cauce Corporation is preparing its year-end balance sheet. The company records show the following selected amounts at the end of the year:

Total assets	$530,000
Total noncurrent assets	362,000
Liabilities:	
Notes payable (8%, due in 5 years)	15,000
Accounts payable	56,000
Income taxes payable	14,000
Liability for withholding taxes	3,000
Rent revenue collected in advance	7,000
Bonds payable (due in 15 years)	90,000
Wages payable	7,000
Property taxes payable	3,000
Note payable (10%, due in 6 months)	12,000
Interest payable	400
Common stock	100,000

Required:

1. Identify current liabilities and compute working capital. Why is working capital important to management?
2. Would your computation be different if the company reported $250,000 worth of contingent liabilities in the notes to its financial statements? Explain.

E9-2 Recording Payroll Costs

LO9-1

Palouse Company completed the salary and wage payroll for the month of March. The payroll provided the following details:

Salaries and wages earned by employees	$200,000
Employee income taxes withheld	40,000
Employee government insurance premiums withheld	1,000
FICA payroll taxes*	15,000

**Assessed on both employer and employee (i.e., $15,000 each).*

Required:

1. Provide the journal entry to record the payroll for March, including employee deductions. Assume employees have been paid but that Palouse has yet to transfer any withholdings to the government.
2. Provide the journal entry to record the employer's payroll taxes, which have not yet been paid to the government.
3. Provide a combined journal entry to show the payment of all amounts owed to governmental agencies.

E9-3 Computing Payroll Costs; Discussion of Labor Costs

LO9-1

Oaks Company has completed the payroll for the month of January, reflecting the following data:

Salaries and wages earned	$86,000
Employee income taxes withheld	10,000
FICA payroll taxes*	6,000

**Assessed on both employer and employee (i.e., $6,000 each).*

Required:

1. What was the total labor cost to the company? What was the amount of the employees' take-home pay?
2. List the liabilities and their amounts reported on the company's January 31 balance sheet, assuming the employees have been paid but that no transfers have been made to government agencies.
3. A junior accountant at Oaks stated in a meeting that giving all employees a 5 percent raise would have cost Oaks $4,300 ($86,000 × 0.05) in the month of January. Do you agree?

E9-4
LO9-1, 9-3
Nordstrom, Inc.
Bank of America

Recording a Note Payable through Its Time to Maturity with Strategy Discussion

Many businesses borrow money during periods of increased business activity to finance inventory and accounts receivable. **Nordstrom, Inc.**, is one of America's most prestigious retailers. Each Christmas season, Nordstrom builds up its inventory to meet the needs of Christmas shoppers. A large portion of these Christmas sales are on credit. As a result, Nordstrom often collects cash from the sales several months after Christmas. Assume that on November 1 of this year, Nordstrom borrowed $4.8 million cash from **Bank of America** to meet short-term obligations. Nordstrom signed an interest-bearing note and promised to repay the $4.8 million in six months. The annual interest rate was 8 percent. All interest will accrue and be paid when the note is due in six months. Nordstrom's accounting period ends December 31.

Required:

1. Provide the journal entry to record the note on November 1.
2. Provide any adjusting entry required at the end of the annual accounting period on December 31.
3. Provide the journal entry to record payment of the note and interest on the maturity date, April 30.
4. If Nordstrom needs extra cash during every Christmas season, should management borrow money on a long-term basis to avoid the necessity of negotiating a new short-term loan each year?

E9-5
LO9-1, 9-3

Determining Financial Statement Effects of Transactions Involving Notes Payable

Using the data from the previous exercise, complete the following requirements.

Required:

Determine the financial statement effects for each of the following: (*a*) the issuance of the note on November 1, (*b*) the impact of the adjusting entry at the end of the accounting period, and (*c*) payment of the note and interest on April 30. Indicate the effects (e.g., Cash + or −) using the format below. You do not need to include amounts, just accounts and the direction in which they are affected.

Date	Assets	Liabilities	Stockholders' Equity

E9-6
LO9-1, 9-3, 9-5

Determining the Impact of Transactions, Including Analysis of Cash Flows

Jose Company sells a wide range of goods through two retail stores operated in adjoining cities. Jose purchases most of the goods it sells in its stores on credit, promising to pay suppliers later. Occasionally, a short-term note payable is used to obtain cash for current use. The following transactions were selected from those occurring during the fiscal year, which ends on December 31:

a. Purchased merchandise on credit for $18,000 on January 10.

b. Borrowed $45,000 cash on March 1 from City Bank by signing an interest-bearing note payable. The note is due at the end of six months (August 31) and has an annual interest rate of 10 percent payable at maturity.

Required:

1. Describe the impact of each transaction on the balance sheet equation. Indicate the effects (e.g., Cash + or −) using the format below. You do not need to include amounts, just accounts and the direction in which they are affected.

Date	Assets	Liabilities	Stockholders' Equity

2. What amount of cash is paid on the maturity date of the note?
3. Discuss the impact of each transaction on Vernon's cash flows.

E9-7
LO9-2
Skullcandy

Calculating and Explaining the Accounts Payable Turnover Ratio

Skullcandy designs, markets, and distributes audio and gaming headphones, earbuds, and speakers. Assume that last year, Skullcandy reported cost of goods sold of $158 million. Assume that this year, cost of goods sold was $117 million. Accounts payable was $23 million at the end of last year and $17 million at the end of this year.

Required:
1. For this year, compute the average number of days that Skullcandy's accounts payable are outstanding.
2. Assume Skullcandy's closest competitor reports that the average number of days that its accounts payable are outstanding is 30. Comment on Skullcandy's number relative to its competitor's number.

E9-8
LO9-3
North Face
U.S. Bank

Reporting Notes Payable and Calculating Interest Expense

North Face is one of the world's most popular outdoor apparel companies. Assume that North Face borrows $2 million from **U.S. Bank** and signs a note promising to pay back the $2 million in nine months, at which time North Face also will pay any accrued interest. The interest rate on the note is 8 percent.

Required:
1. Prepare the journal entry North Face will record when it signs the note and receives the cash.
2. Prepare the journal entry that North Face will record when it pays off the note and any accrued interest after nine months.

E9-9
LO9-4

Reporting Contingent Liabilities

James Soda is a regional soda manufacturer. James is currently facing three lawsuits, summarized below:

a. A customer is suing James for $1 million because he claims to have found a piece of glass in his soda. Management deems the probability that James will lose the lawsuit and have to pay $1 million as reasonably possible.
b. An employee is suing James for $500,000 for an injury she incurred in the parking lot while walking to work. Management deems the probability that James will lose the lawsuit as probable but estimates that a reasonable payout will be $100,000, not $500,000.
c. A customer is suing James for $300,000 because her last name is James and she claims James stole her name. Management deems the probability that James will lose the lawsuit and have to pay $300,000 as remote.

Required:
How should James report each of the lawsuits in its financial statements and footnotes?

E9-10
LO9-5
Saks Fifth Avenue

Using Working Capital

Saks Fifth Avenue's balance sheet for a recent year revealed the following information:

Current assets	$750,000
Noncurrent assets	450,000
Noncurrent liabilities	400,000
Stockholders' equity	380,000

Determine the amount of working capital reported in the balance sheet.

E9-11
LO9-6
Peloton Corporation

Reporting a Long-Term Liability

Peloton Corporation sells fitness products and associated subscription services. Effective management of its properties is a key to its success. As the following note in a recent annual report indicates, Peloton leases various types of property:

> The Company leases facilities under operating leases with various expiration dates through 2039. The Company leases space for its corporate headquarters and the operation of its production studio facilities, retail showrooms, microstores, distribution centers, warehouses, factories, and other office spaces.

Required:
Should Peloton report lease liabilities on its balance sheet? Explain. If the obligation should be reported as a liability, how should the amount be measured?

Evaluating Lease Alternatives

E9-12
LO9-6
Whole Foods

As the new vice president for consumer products at **Whole Foods**, you are attending a meeting to discuss a serious problem associated with delivering merchandise to customers. Bob Smith, director of logistics, summarized the problem: "It's easy to understand; we just don't have enough delivery trucks given our recent growth." Barb Bader from the accounting department responded: "Maybe it's easy to understand, but it's impossible to do anything. Because of Wall Street's concern about the amount of debt on our balance sheet, we're under a freeze and can't borrow money to acquire new assets. There's nothing we can do."

On the way back to your office after the meeting, your assistant offers a suggestion: "Why don't we just lease the trucks we need using short-term leases that we'll renew each year? That way we can get the assets we want without having to record a liability on the balance sheet."

How would you respond to this suggestion?

Computing Four Present Value Problems

E9-13
LO9-7

On January 1 of this year, Skamania Company completed the following transactions (assume a 10 percent annual interest rate):

a. Bought a delivery truck and agreed to pay $60,000 at the end of three years.
b. Rented an office building and was given the option of paying $10,000 at the end of each of the next three years or paying $28,000 immediately.
c. Established a savings account by depositing a single amount that will increase to $90,000 at the end of seven years.
d. Decided to deposit a single sum in the bank that will provide 10 equal annual year-end payments of $40,000 to a retired employee (payments starting December 31 of this year).

Required (show computations and round to the nearest dollar):

1. In (*a*), what is the cost of the truck that should be recorded at the time of purchase?
2. In (*b*), which option for the office building results in the lowest present value?
3. In (*c*), what single amount must be deposited in this account on January 1 of this year?
4. In (*d*), what single sum must be deposited in the bank on January 1 of this year?

Computing a Present Value

E9-14
LO9-7

An investment will pay $20,000 at the end of the first year, $30,000 at the end of the second year, and $50,000 at the end of the third year. Determine the present value of this investment using a 10 percent annual interest rate.

Computing a Present Value Involving an Annuity and a Single Payment

E9-15
LO9-7

An investment will pay $15,000 at the end of each year for eight years and a one-time payment of $150,000 at the end of the eighth year. Determine the present value of this investment using a 7 percent annual interest rate.

Computing a Present Value Involving an Annuity and a Single Payment

E9-16
LO9-8

The Jenkins Corporation has purchased an executive jet. The company has agreed to pay $200,000 per year for the next 10 years and an additional $1,000,000 at the end of the 10th year. The seller of the jet is charging 6 percent annual interest. Determine the liability that would be recorded by Jenkins.

Computing a Present Value Involving an Annuity and a Single Payment

E9-17
LO9-7

You have decided to buy a used car. The dealer has offered you two options:

a. Pay $500 per month for 20 months and an additional $12,000 at the end of 20 months. The dealer is charging an annual interest rate of 24 percent.
b. Make a one-time payment of $14,906, due when you purchase the car.

In present value terms, which offer is a better deal?

E9-18 LO9-7

Using Present Value Concepts for Decision Making

You have just won the state lottery and have two choices for collecting your winnings. You can collect $100,000 today or receive $20,000 at the end of each year for the next seven years. A financial analyst has told you that you can earn 10 percent on your investments. Which alternative should you select?

E9-19 LO9-7

Calculating a Retirement Fund

You are a financial adviser working with a client who wants to retire in eight years. The client has a savings account with a local bank that pays 9 percent annual interest. The client wants to deposit an amount that will provide her with $1,000,000 when she retires. Currently, she has $300,000 in the account. How much additional money should she deposit now to provide her with $1,000,000 when she retires?

E9-20 LO9-7

Determining an Educational Fund

Judge Drago has decided to set up an educational fund for his favorite granddaughter, Emma, who will start college in one year. The judge plans to deposit an amount in a savings account that pays 9 percent annual interest. He wants to deposit an amount that is sufficient to permit Emma to withdraw $20,000 for tuition starting in one year and continuing each year for a total of four years. How much should he deposit today to provide Emma with a fund to pay for her college tuition?

E9-21 LO9-6

(Chapter Supplement B) Computing Deferred Income Tax

The following information pertains to the Lanina Corporation.

	Year 1	Year 2
Income taxes payable	$250,000	$290,000
Increase in deferred tax liability	54,000	58,000

Required:

1. For each year, compute income tax expense (assume that no taxes have been paid).
2. Explain why tax expense is not simply the amount of cash paid during the year.

E9-22 LO9-6

(Chapter Supplement B) Recording Deferred Income Tax

The balance sheet for Nair Corporation provided the following summarized pretax data:

	Year 1	Year 2
Deferred tax liability	$355,000	$463,000

The income statement reported tax expense for Year 2 in the amount of $580,000.

Required:

1. What was the amount of income taxes payable for Year 2?
2. Explain why management incurs the cost of maintaining separate tax and financial accounting records.

E9-23 LO9-7, FUTURE VALUES

Computing Future Values: Deposit Required and Accounting for a Single-Sum Savings Account

On January 1, Steph Grant decided to deposit $58,800 in a savings account that will provide funds four years later to send his son to college. The savings account will earn 8 percent annually. Any interest earned will be added to the fund at year-end (rather than withdrawn).

Required (show computations and round to the nearest dollar):

1. How much will be available in four years?
2. Assume that Steph Grant follows GAAP. Provide the journal entry that Steph Grant should make on January 1.

3. What is the total interest for the four years?
4. Assume that Steph Grant follows GAAP. Provide the journal entry that Steph Grant should make on (*a*) December 31 of the first year and (*b*) December 31 of the second year.

Computing Future Values: Recording Growth in a Savings Account with Equal Periodic Payments

E9-24
LO9-7, FUTURE VALUES

At the end of each year, you plan to deposit $2,000 in a savings account. The account will earn 9 percent annual interest, which will be added to the fund balance at year-end. The first deposit will be made at the end of Year 1.

Required (show computations and round to the nearest dollar):

1. Assume you follow GAAP. Provide the journal entry you should enter at the end of Year 1.
2. What will be the balance in the savings account at the end of the 10th year (i.e., after 10 deposits)?
3. What is the interest earned on the 10 deposits?
4. How much interest revenue did the fund earn in the second year? In the third year?
5. Assume you follow GAAP. Provide the journal entries you should enter at the end of the second and third years.

PROBLEMS

Recording and Reporting Current Liabilities (AP9-1)

P9-1
LO9-1

Vigeland Company completed the following transactions during Year 1. Vigeland's fiscal year ends on December 31.

Jan. 15	Purchased and paid for merchandise. The invoice amount was $26,500; assume a perpetual inventory system.
Apr. 1	Borrowed $700,000 from Summit Bank for general use; signed a 10-month, 6 percent annual interest-bearing note for the money.
June 14	Received a $15,000 customer deposit for services to be performed in the future.
July 15	Performed $3,750 of the services paid for on June 14.
Dec. 12	Received electric bill for $27,860. Vigeland plans to pay the bill in early January.
31	Determined wages of $15,000 were earned but not yet paid on December 31 (disregard payroll taxes).

Required:

1. Prepare journal entries for each of these transactions.
2. Prepare all adjusting entries required on December 31.

Recording and Reporting Current Liabilities and identifying Cash Flow Effects (AP9-2)

P9-2
LO9-1, 9-5

Roger Company completed the following transactions during Year 1. Roger's fiscal year ends on December 31.

Jan. 8	Purchased merchandise for resale on account. The invoice amount was $14,860; assume a perpetual inventory system.
17	Paid January 8 invoice.
Apr. 1	Borrowed $35,000 from National Bank for general use; signed a 12-month, 8 percent annual interest-bearing note for the money.
June 3	Purchased merchandise for resale on account. The invoice amount was $17,420.
July 5	Paid June 3 invoice.
Aug. 1	Rented office space in one of Roger's buildings to another company and collected six months' rent in advance amounting to $6,000.
Dec. 20	Received a $100 deposit from a customer as a guarantee to return a trailer borrowed for 30 days.
31	Determined wages of $9,500 were earned but not yet paid on December 31 (disregard payroll taxes).

Required:

1. Prepare journal entries for each of these transactions.
2. Prepare all adjusting entries required on December 31.
3. What is the total amount of liabilities arising from these transactions that will be reported on the fiscal year-end balance sheet?
4. For each transaction state whether operating cash flows increase, decrease, or are not affected.

P9-3
LO9-1, 9-5

Determining Financial Effects of Transactions Affecting Current Liabilities (AP9-3)

Use the data from Problem P9-2 to complete this problem.

Required:
For each transaction (including adjusting entries) listed in Problem P9-2, indicate the effects (e.g., Cash + or −) using the format below. You do not need to include amounts, just accounts and the direction in which they are affected.

Date	Assets	Liabilities	Stockholders' Equity

P9-4
LO9-1

Recording and Reporting Accrued Liabilities and Deferred Revenue with Discussion of Accrual versus Cash Accounting (AP9-4)

During its first year of operations, Walnut Company completed the following two transactions. The annual accounting period ends December 31.

a. Paid and recorded wages of $130,000 during Year 1; however, at the end of Year 1, three days' wages are unpaid and have not yet been recorded because the weekly payroll will not be paid to employees until January 6 of Year 2. Wages for the three days are $4,000.
b. Collected rent revenue of $2,400 on December 12 of Year 1 for office space that Walnut rented to another company. The rent collected was for 30 days from December 12 of Year 1 to January 10 of Year 2.

Required:

1. With respect to wages, provide the adjusting entry required at the end of Year 1 and the journal entry required on January 6 of Year 2.
2. With respect to rent revenue, provide the journal entry for the collection of rent on December 12 and the adjusting entry required on December 31.
3. What is the total amount of liabilities arising from these transactions that will be reported on the balance sheet on December 31 of Year 1?
4. Explain why the accrual method of accounting provides more useful information to financial analysts than the cash method of accounting.

P9-5
LO9-1

Determining Financial Statement Effects of Transactions Involving Accrued Liabilities and Deferred Revenue (AP9-5)

Use the data from Problem P9-4 to complete this problem.

Required:
For each transaction (including adjusting entries) listed in Problem P9-4, indicate the effects (e.g., Cash + or −) using the format below. You do not need to include amounts, just accounts and the direction in which they are affected.

Date	Assets	Liabilities	Stockholders' Equity

P9-6
LO9-1, 9-4
Dell Computers
Walt Disney

Determining Financial Statement Effects of Various Liabilities (AP9-6)

Dell Computers is a leader in the computer industry with over $90 billion in sales each year. A recent annual report for Dell contained the following note:

Warranty

The Company records warranty liabilities for estimated costs of fulfilling its obligations under standard limited hardware and software warranties at the time of sale. The liability for standard warranties is included in accrued and other current and other non-current liabilities in the Consolidated Statements of Financial Position.

1. Assume that estimated warranty costs for the current year are $500 million and that $400 million of warranty work was performed during the year. Provide the journal entries required to recognize warranty expense and the warranty services provided during the year. Assume that all warranty services were paid for with cash.

Walt Disney is a well-recognized brand in the entertainment industry with products ranging from broadcast media to parks and resorts. The following note is from a recent annual report:

Revenue Recognition

Sales of theme park tickets are recognized when the tickets are used. Sales of annual passes are recognized ratably over the period for which the pass is available for use.

2. Assume that in the current year, Disney collected $90 million in tickets that have not yet been used. Also in the current year, Disney estimates that $5 million worth of tickets that have been sold in the past will not be used in the current year or in the future. Provide the journal entries required to recognize (*a*) the receipt of the $90 million in cash and (*b*) the $5 million that Disney estimates will not be used.

Calculating and Explaining the Accounts Payable Turnover Ratio (AP9-7)

P9-7
LO9-2
Columbia Sportswear

Columbia Sportswear is an outdoor and active lifestyle apparel and footwear company. Assume that last year, Columbia reported cost of goods sold of $941 million. This year, cost of goods sold was $1,146 million. Accounts payable was $174 million at the end of last year and $214 million at the end of this year.

Required:

1. For this year, compute the average number of days that Columbia's accounts payable are outstanding.
2. Assume the apparel and footwear industry reports an average number of days that accounts payable are outstanding of 72. Comment on Columbia's number relative to the industry average.

Making Decisions about Contingent Liabilities (AP9-8)

P9-8
LO9-4

For each of the following situations, determine whether the company should (*a*) report a liability on the balance sheet, (*b*) disclose a contingent liability in the footnotes, or (*c*) not report the situation. Justify your conclusions.

1. An automobile company introduces a new car. Past experience demonstrates that lawsuits will be filed as soon as the new model is involved in any accidents. The company believes it is highly probable that at least one jury will award damages to people injured in an accident, but it is unable to estimate the amount of any payout.
2. A research scientist determines that the company's best-selling product may infringe on another company's patent. If the other company discovers the infringement and files suit, which is unlikely, your company could lose millions.
3. As part of land development for a new housing project, your company has polluted a natural lake. Under state law, you must clean up the lake once you complete development. The development project will take five to eight years to complete. Current estimates indicate that it will cost $3 million to clean up the lake.
4. Your company has just been notified that it is being sued by a customer. The probability of the customer winning is deemed to be probable, but the amount of any loss cannot be reliably estimated.
5. A key customer is unhappy with the quality of a major construction project. The company believes that the customer is being unreasonable but, to maintain goodwill, has decided to do $250,000 in repairs next year.

Determining Cash Flow Effects (AP9-9)

P9-9
LO9-5

For each of the following transactions, determine whether cash flows from operating activities will increase, decrease, or remain the same:

a. Purchased merchandise on credit.
b. Paid an account payable in cash.
c. Accrued payroll for the month but did not pay it.
d. Borrowed money from the bank. The term of the note is 90 days.
e. Reclassified a long-term note as a current liability.
f. Paid accrued interest expense.
g. Disclosed a contingent liability based on a pending lawsuit.

h. Paid back the bank for money borrowed in (*d*). Ignore interest.
i. Collected cash from a customer for services that will be performed in the next accounting period (i.e., deferred revenues are recorded).

P9-10
LO9-7, 9-8

Computing Present Values (AP9-10)

On January 1, Boston Company completed the following transactions (use a 7 percent annual interest rate for all transactions):

a. Promised to pay a fixed amount of $6,000 at the end of each year for seven years and a one-time payment of $115,000 at the end of the 7th year.
b. Established a plant remodeling fund of $490,000 to be available at the end of Year 8. A single sum that will grow to $490,000 will be deposited on January 1 of this year.
c. Agreed to pay a severance package to a discharged employee. The company will pay $75,000 at the end of the first year, $112,500 at the end of the second year, and $150,000 at the end of the third year.
d. Purchased a $170,000 machine on January 1 of this year for $34,000 cash. A five-year note is signed for the balance. The note will be paid in five equal year-end payments starting on December 31 of this year.

Required (show computations and round to the nearest dollar):

1. In transaction (*a*), determine the present value of the debt.
2. In transaction (*b*), what single sum amount must the company deposit on January 1 of this year? What is the total amount of interest revenue that will be earned?
3. In transaction (*c*), determine the present value of this obligation.
4. In transaction (*d*), what is the amount of each of the equal annual payments that will be paid on the note? What is the total amount of interest expense that will be incurred?

P9-11
LO9-7

Comparing Options Using Present Value Concepts (AP9-11)

After hearing a knock at your front door, you are surprised to see the Prize Patrol from your state's online lottery agency. Upon opening your door, you learn you have won the lottery of $12.5 million. You discover that you have three options: (1) you can receive $1.25 million per year for the next 10 years, (2) you can have $10 million today, or (3) you can have $4 million today and receive $1 million for each of the next eight years. Your lawyer tells you that it is reasonable to expect to earn an annual return of 10 percent on investments. All else equal, which option do you prefer? What factors influence your decision?

P9-12
LO9-6

(Chapter Supplement B) Recording and Reporting Deferred Income Tax: Depreciation (AP9-12)

Wapato Corporation purchased a new piece of equipment at the beginning of Year 1 for $1,000,000. The expected life of the asset is 20 years with no residual value. The company uses straight-line depreciation for financial reporting purposes and accelerated depreciation for tax purposes (the accelerated method results in $120,000 of depreciation in Year 1 and $100,000 of depreciation in Year 2). The company's federal income tax rate is 21 percent. The company determined its income tax obligations for Year 1 and Year 2 were $400,000 and $625,000, respectively.

Required:

1. Compute the deferred income tax amount reported on the balance sheet for each year. Explain why the deferred income tax is a liability.
2. Compute income tax expense for each year.

P9-13
LO9-7, FUTURE VALUES

Computing Future Values of a Single Amount and an Annuity (AP9-13)

a. A friend of yours, Grace, wants to purchase a house in five years. To save for the house, Grace decides to deposit $112,000 in a savings account on January 1 of this year. The savings account will earn 6 percent annually. Any interest earned will be added to the fund at year-end (rather than withdrawn).
b. At the end of each year, a different friend, Claire, plans to deposit $9,000 in a savings account. The account will earn 9 percent annual interest, which will be added to the fund balance at year-end. Claire will make her first deposit at the end of this year.

Required (show computations and round to the nearest dollar):

1. In (*a*), how much will be available at the end of five years? What is the total interest earned over the five years?
2. In (*b*), what will be the balance in the savings account at the end of the 8th year (i.e., after 8 deposits)? What is the interest earned on the 8 deposits?

ALTERNATE PROBLEMS

Recording and Reporting Current Liabilities (P9-1)

AP9-1
LO9-1

Chukanut Company completed the following transactions during Year 1. Chukanut's fiscal year ends on December 31.

Jan. 20	Paid cash for office supplies (held as office supplies inventory). The invoice amount was $17,900.
Apr. 1	Borrowed $458,000 from Royal Bank for general use; signed an 12-month, 4 percent annual interest-bearing note for the money.
June 18	Received a $17,000 customer deposit for services to be performed in the future.
July 22	Performed $6,240 of the services paid for on June 18.
Dec. 17	Received utility bill for $8,900. Chukanut plans to pay the bill in early February.
31	Determined wages of $12,000 were earned but not yet paid on December 31 (disregard payroll taxes).

Required:

1. Prepare journal entries for each of these transactions.
2. Prepare all adjusting entries required on December 31. Assume that $10,000 of the office supplies purchased were used and expensed during the year.

Recording and Reporting Current Liabilities and identifying Cash Flow Effects (P9-2)

AP9-2
LO9-1, 9-5

Sturgis Company completed the following transactions during Year 1. Sturgis's fiscal year ends on December 31.

Jan. 15	Recorded tax expense for the year in the amount of $125,000 and recognized a tax liability for the same amount.
31	Paid previously accrued interest expense in the amount of $52,000.
Apr. 30	Borrowed $550,000 from Commerce Bank; signed a 12-month, 12 percent annual interest-bearing note for the money.
June 3	Purchased merchandise for resale on account. The invoice amount was $75,820.
July 5	Paid June 3 invoice in full.
Aug. 31	Signed contract to provide security service to a small apartment complex and collected six months' fees in advance amounting to $12,000.
Dec. 31	Reclassified a long-term liability in the amount of $100,000 as a current liability.
31	Determined salary and wages of $85,000 earned but not yet paid December 31 (disregard payroll taxes).

Required:

1. Prepare journal entries for each of these transactions.
2. Prepare all adjusting entries required on December 31.
3. What is the total amount of liabilities arising from these transactions that will be reported on the fiscal year-end balance sheet?
4. For each transaction, state whether operating cash flows increase, decrease, or are not affected.

Determining Financial Effects of Transactions Affecting Current Liabilities (P9-3)

AP9-3
LO9-1, 9-5

Use data from Problem AP9-2 to complete this problem.

Required:
For each transaction (including adjusting entries) listed in Problem AP9-1, indicate the effects (e.g., Cash + or −) using the format below. You do not need to include amounts, just accounts and the direction in which they are affected.

Date	Assets	Liabilities	Stockholders' Equity

AP9-4
LO9-1

Recording and Reporting Accrued Liabilities and Deferred Revenue with Discussion of Accrual versus Cash Accounting (P9-4)

During its first year of operations, Chestnut Company completed the following two transactions. The annual accounting period ends December 31.

a. Paid and recorded wages of $89,000 during Year 1; however, at the end of Year 1, three days' wages are unpaid and have not yet been recorded because the weekly payroll will not be paid to employees until January 9 of Year 2. Wages for the three days are $7,000.

b. Collected rent revenue of $7,900 on December 14 of Year 1 for office space that Chestnut rented to another company. The rent collected was for 30 days from December 14 of Year 1 to January 12 of Year 2.

Required:

1. With respect to wages, provide the adjusting entry required at the end of Year 1 and the journal entry required on January 9 of Year 2.
2. With respect to rent revenue, provide the journal entry for the collection of rent on December 14 and the adjusting entry required on December 31.
3. What is the total amount of liabilities arising from these transactions that will be reported on the balance sheet on December 31 of Year 1?
4. Explain why the accrual method of accounting provides more useful information to decision makers than the cash method of accounting.

AP9-5
LO9-1

Determining Financial Statement Effects of Transactions Involving Accrued Liabilities and Deferred Revenue (P9-5)

Use the data from Alternate Problem AP9-4 to complete this problem.

Required:

For each transaction (including adjusting entries) listed in Alternate Problem AP9-4, indicate the effects (e.g., Cash + or −) using the format below. You do not need to include amounts, just accounts and the direction in which they are affected.

Date	Assets	Liabilities	Stockholders' Equity

AP9-6
LO9-1, 9-4
Ford Motor Company
Beyond Meats

Determining Financial Statement Effects of Various Liabilities (P9-6)

Ford Motor Company is one of the world's largest companies, with annual sales of cars and trucks in excess of $155 billion. A recent annual report for Ford contained the following note:

Warranties

We accrue obligations for warranty costs at the time of sale using a patterned estimation model that includes historical information regarding the nature, frequency, and average cost of claims for each vehicle line by model year.

1. Assume that this year Ford paid cash to service warranty claims in the amount of $4.0 billion. Ford also accrued expenses for warranties in the amount of $3.9 billion. If Ford had a balance in its accrued warranties account of $1.0 billion to start the year, what is the balance at the end of the year?

Beyond Meats is a plants-based food company. The company reported the following in a recent annual report:

Revenue Recognition

Revenue is recognized at the point in which the performance obligation under the terms of a contract with the customer have been satisfied and control has transferred.

2. Assume that Beyond Meats collected $23 million in December for sales that will be completed in January, the first month of the company's next fiscal year. What is the amount of unearned revenue that should be reported on this year's balance sheet and next year's balance sheet associated with the $23 million?

AP9-7
LO9-2
Tootsie Roll Industries, Inc.

Calculating and Explaining the Accounts Payable Turnover Ratio (P9-7)

Tootsie Roll Industries, Inc., is engaged in the manufacture and sale of confectionery products. Assume that last year, Tootsie Roll reported cost of goods sold of $352 million. This year, cost of goods sold was $342 million. Accounts payable was $9 million at the end of last year and $12 million at the end of this year.

Required:

1. For this year, compute the average number of days that Tootsie Roll's accounts payable are outstanding.
2. Assume the confectionery products industry reports an average number of days that accounts payable are outstanding of 30. Comment on Tootsie Roll's number relative to the industry average.

Making Decisions about Contingent Liabilities (P9-8)

AP9-8
LO9-4

For each of the following situations, determine whether the company should (*a*) report a liability on the balance sheet, (*b*) disclose a contingent liability in the footnotes, or (*c*) not report the situation. Justify your conclusions.

1. A company that manufactures mountain climbing equipment introduces a new type of climbing rope. Past experience demonstrates that lawsuits will be filed as soon as the new rope is involved in any serious climbing accidents. The company believes it is highly probable that at least one jury will award damages to climbers injured in an accident, but it is unable to estimate the amount of any payout.
2. An analyst puts out a report that claims a company's best-selling product may infringe on another company's patent. If the other company discovers the infringement and files suit, which is deemed to be highly unlikely, the company could lose millions.
3. As part of a large construction project to build a new dam, your company has polluted a nearby river. Under state law, you must clean up the river once the dam project is complete. The dam project will take eight to ten years to complete. Current estimates indicate that it will cost $7 million to clean up the river.
4. Your company sells coffee and is being sued by a customer who spilled hot coffee on her lap while driving. Due to a faulty lid issue that you are aware of, the probability of the customer winning is deemed to be probable, but the amount of any loss cannot be reliably estimated.
5. A patient is unhappy with the quality of a hip replacement he received. The hospital believes that the patient is being unreasonable but has informed the patient that it will do additional procedures on the hip at no charge to the patient. The procedures will cost the hospital $50,000.

Determining Cash Flow Effects (P9-9)

AP9-9
LO9-5

For each of the following transactions, determine whether cash flows from operating activities will increase, decrease, or remain the same:

a. Purchased merchandise for cash.
b. Paid salaries and wages that were earned last period, but not paid last period.
c. Paid taxes to the federal government.
d. Borrowed money from the bank. The term of the note is two years.
e. Withheld FICA taxes from employees' paychecks and immediately paid the government.
f. Recorded accrued interest expense.
g. Paid cash as the result of losing a lawsuit. A contingent liability associated with the liability had been recorded.
h. Paid salaries and wages for the current month in cash.
i. Performed services for a customer who had paid for them in the previous accounting period (i.e., deferred revenue is earned).

Computing Present Values (P9-10)

AP9-10
LO9-7, 9-8

On January 1, Ellsworth Company completed the following transactions (use an 8 percent annual interest rate for all transactions):

a. Borrowed $2,000,000 to be repaid in five years. Agreed to pay a fixed amount of $150,000 at the end of each year for five years and a one-time payment of $2,000,000 at the end of the 5th year.
b. Established a plant remodeling fund of $1,000,000 to be available at the end of Year 10. A single sum that will grow to $1,000,000 will be deposited on January 1 of this year.
c. Purchased a $750,000 machine on January 1 of this year and paid cash, $400,000. A four-year note is signed for the balance. The note will be paid in four equal year-end payments starting on December 31 of this year.

Required (show computations and round to the nearest dollar):

1. In transaction (*a*), determine the present value of the debt.
2. In transaction (*b*), what single amount must the company deposit on January 1 of this year? What is the total amount of interest revenue that will be earned?
3. In transaction (*c*), what is the amount of each of the equal annual payments that will be paid on the note? What is the total amount of interest expense that will be incurred?

AP9-11
LO9-7

Comparing Options Using Present Value Concepts (P9-11)

After completing a long and successful career as senior vice president for a large bank, you are preparing for retirement. Visiting the human resources office, you find that you have several retirement options: (1) you can receive an immediate cash payment of $750,000, (2) you can receive $60,000 per year for life (you have a life expectancy of 20 years), or (3) you can receive $50,000 per year for 10 years and then $80,000 per year for life (this option is intended to give you some protection against inflation). You have determined that you can earn 6 percent annual interest on your investments. All else equal, which option do you prefer and why?

AP9-12
LO9-6

(Chapter Supplement B) Recording and Reporting Deferred Income Tax: Depreciation (P9-12)

Gig Harbor Company purchased a new piece of shipping equipment at the beginning of Year 1 for $1,800,000. The expected life of the asset is 15 years with no residual value. The company uses straight-line depreciation for financial reporting purposes and accelerated depreciation for tax purposes (the accelerated method results in $220,000 of depreciation in Year 1 and $200,000 of depreciation in Year 2). The company's federal income tax rate is 21 percent. The company determined its income tax obligations for Year 1 and Year 2 were $600,000 and $825,000, respectively.

Required:

1. Compute the deferred income tax amount reported on the balance sheet for each year. Explain why the deferred income tax is a liability.
2. Compute income tax expense for each year.

AP9-13
LO9-7, FUTURE VALUES
Tesla, Inc.

Computing Future Values (P9-13)

Assume that on January 1 of Year 1, **Tesla, Inc.**, decided to start a fund to build an addition to its plant. Tesla will deposit $320,000 in the fund at each year-end, starting on December 31 of Year 1. The fund will earn 9 percent annual interest, which will be added to the balance at each year-end. The accounting period ends December 31 of each year.

Required:
Complete the following fund accumulation schedule:

Date	Cash Payment	Interest Earned	Fund Increase	Fund Balance
Dec. 31, Year 1				
Dec. 31, Year 2				
Dec. 31, Year 3				
Total				

CONTINUING PROBLEM

connect

CON9-1
LO9-1, 9-3
Pool Corporation, Inc.

Recording and Reporting Liabilities

Pool Corporation, Inc., sells swimming pool supplies and equipment. It is a publicly traded corporation that trades on the NASDAQ exchange. The majority of Pool's customers are small, family-owned businesses. Assume Pool Corporation completed the following transactions during the current year. Pool's fiscal year ends on December 31.

Sept. 15 Paid a supplier $125,000 for inventory previously purchased on credit.
Oct. 1 Borrowed $900,000 from Southwest Bank for general use; signed an 11-month, 5 percent annual interest-bearing note for the money.
Oct. 5 Received a $40,000 customer deposit from Joe Lipscomb for services to be performed in the future.
Oct. 15 Performed $18,000 of the services paid for by Mr. Lipscomb.
Dec. 12 Received electric bill for $12,000. Pool plans to pay the bill in early January.
31 Determined wages of $52,000 earned but not yet paid on December 31 (disregard payroll taxes).

Required:

1. Prepare journal entries for each of these transactions.
2. Prepare all adjusting entries required on December 31.

connect

CASES AND PROJECTS

Annual Report Cases

Finding Financial Information

CP9-1
LO9-1, 9-2, 9-6
Target

Refer to the financial statements and footnotes of **Target** given in Appendix B at the end of this book. All dollar amounts are in millions.

Required:

1. What is the amount of accrued wages and benefits at the end of the most recent fiscal year?
   a. $1,931
   b. $1,677
   c. $6,122
   d. $169
   e. $2,382
2. In Chapter 9, we have used the term "deferred revenue." What term does Target use to reflect cash that it has received for goods or services that it will provide in the future?
   a. Unearned Revenue
   b. Deferred Sales
   c. Other Revenue
   d. Gift Card Liability
   e. None of the above
3. What is the amount of "deferred revenue" Target reports at the end of the most recent fiscal year?
   a. $935
   b. $1,161
   c. $1,035
   d. $1,939
   e. $4,368
4. For the most recent fiscal year, compute the accounts payable turnover ratio for Target.
   a. 5.81
   b. 8.11
   c. 3.82
   d. 5.14
   e. 6.67
5. What is the amount of long-term liabilities at the end of the most recent fiscal year?
   a. $51,248
   b. $16,683
   c. $11,536
   d. $20,125
   e. $14,440

Finding Financial Information

CP9-2
LO9-1, 9-2, 9-3, 9-6
Walmart

Refer to the financial statements and footnotes of **Walmart** given in Appendix C at the end of this book. All dollar amounts are in millions.

1. What is the amount of accrued wages and benefits at the end of the most recent fiscal year? __________
2. What is the gift card liability balance at the end of the most recent fiscal year? __________
3. Where is the gift card liability reported on the balance sheet?
   a. Short-term Borrowings
   b. Accounts Payable
   c. Unearned Revenue
   d. Accrued Liabilities
   e. None of the above

4. For the most recent fiscal year, compute the accounts payable turnover ratio for Walmart. (Round your answer to two decimal places.) ___________
5. What is the amount of long-term liabilities at the end of the most recent fiscal year? ___________
6. What is the amount of its long-term debt that Walmart expects to pay within one year? ___________

CP9-3
LO9-2, 9-5

Comparing Companies within an Industry

Refer to the financial statements of Target (Appendix B) and Walmart (Appendix C) and the Industry Ratio Report (Appendix D) at the end of this book.

Required:

1. Compute the accounts payable turnover ratio for both companies for the most recent fiscal year. (Round your answer to two decimal places.)

   Target = ___________ **Walmart** = ___________

2. What do you infer from the difference?
   a. Walmart is paying its suppliers more quickly than Target.
   b. Target's management is less effective at controlling expenses than Walmart's management.
   c. Target is paying its suppliers more quickly than Walmart.
   d. Walmart is collecting money from customers more quickly than Target.
3. Compare the accounts payable turnover ratios for Target and Walmart to the average accounts payable turnover ratio for the retail industry. Are Target and Walmart paying suppliers more quickly or more slowly than the industry average?
   a. Target is paying its suppliers more quickly than the industry average, but Walmart is paying its suppliers more slowly.
   b. Both Walmart and Target are paying their suppliers more slowly than the industry average.
   c. Walmart is paying its suppliers more quickly than the industry average, but Target is paying its suppliers more slowly.
   d. Both Walmart and Target are paying their suppliers more quickly than the industry average.
4. Compute working capital for both companies for the most recent fiscal year.

   Target = ___________ **Walmart** = ___________

5. How would you interpret the working capital amounts you calculated for Target and Walmart?
   a. Target's current assets are sufficient to cover its current liabilities, but Walmart's current assets are insufficient to cover its current liabilities.
   b. Both Walmart and Target have current assets that are sufficient to cover their current liabilities.
   c. Walmart's current assets are sufficient to cover its current liabilities, but Target's current assets are insufficient to cover its current liabilities.
   d. Both Walmart and Target have current assets that are insufficient to cover their current liabilities.

Financial Reporting and Analysis Case

CP9-4
LO9-7

Analyzing Hidden Interest in a Real Estate Deal: Present Value

You are researching the housing market in Bloomington, Indiana, and you come upon an advertisement offering to sell a house for $240,000 with a zero interest rate mortgage. All you have to do is agree to make $4,000 payments ($240,000 ÷ 60 months) at the end of each month for five years. If you do so, the advertisement says you will not be charged any interest. When you see the offer, mortgages are typically being granted at a 6 percent annual interest rate.

Required:

1. If the builder demands a 6 percent return on investment, what is the actual value of the house? How much "implied" interest will you pay over the five years as you are paying off the house? The present value factor for an annuity with 60 periods and an interest rate of 0.5 percent (6 percent/12 months) is 51.72556.
2. If the builder is actually demanding a 6 percent return on investment, why would she advertise the mortgage as a "zero interest rate mortgage"?

Critical Thinking Case

Evaluating an Ethical Dilemma: Fair Advertising

CP9-5
LO9-7

A State Lottery Commission ran the following advertisement:

> The Lotto jackpot for this month's drawing is $10 million, which will be paid out to the winning ticket in equal installments at the end of each year over the next 20 years.

Do you agree that the lottery winner has won $10 million? If not, what amount is more accurate? State any assumptions you make.

You as Analyst: Online Company Research

CP9-6
LO9-1, 9-2, 9-3, 9-4, 9-5, 9-6

Examining a Company's Liabilities

In your web browser, search for the investor relations page of a public company you are interested in (e.g., Nike investor relations). Select SEC Filings or Annual Report or Financials to obtain the 10-K for the most recent year available.*

Required:

1. In the most recent fiscal year, what is the company's largest current liability? What current liability has increased the most since last year? What current liability has decreased the most since last year? Provide your answers in dollar amounts and percentages.
2. Compute the accounts payable turnover ratio for the last two years.
3. Does the company report any notes payable? If so, is the interest rate on the notes payable reported in the footnotes? What does the interest rate tell you about the risk of loaning funds to the company?
4. Does the company report any contingent liabilities on the balance sheet or in the footnotes? If so, what does the way the company reports its contingent liabilities tell you about management's beliefs about probable payment?
5. What is the company's working capital for the last two years? Any concerns?
6. In the most recent fiscal year, what is the company's largest long-term liability? What long-term liability has increased the most since last year? What long-term liability has decreased the most since last year? Provide your answers in dollar amounts and percentages.

*Alternatively, you can go to sec.gov, click on Company Filings (under the search box), type in the name of the public company you want to find. Once at the list of filings, type 10-K in the Filing Type box. The most recent 10-K annual report will be at the top of the list. Click on Interactive Data for a list of the parts or the entire report to examine.

BUSINESS ANALYTICS AND DATA VISUALIZATION WITH EXCEL® AND TABLEAU®

Connect offers a variety of exercises to assess Excel skills, data visualization, interpretation, and analysis, including auto-graded Tableau Dashboard Activities, Applying Excel problems, and Integrated Excel problems.

Images used throughout chapter: Question of ethics: mushmello/Shutterstock; Pause for feedback: McGraw Hill; Guided help: McGraw Hill; Financial analysis: McGraw Hill; Focus on cash flows: Hilch/Shutterstock; Key ratio analysis: guillermain/123RF; Data analytics: Hilch/Shutterstock; Tip: McGraw Hill; ESG reporting: McGraw Hill; International perspective: Hilch/Shutterstock

10 chapter

Reporting and Interpreting Bond Securities

In 1995, **Amazon.com** opened its virtual doors and began selling books online out of a garage in Bellevue, Washington. The company grew rapidly and went public two years later. Today, Amazon does much, much more than sell books. Amazon has over a million full-time and part-time employees worldwide and reported sales of $386 billion in fiscal 2020. The technology and infrastructure necessary to support Amazon's growth could not have been developed without billions of dollars of investment. One of the strengths of our economic system is the ability of companies to raise large amounts of money from investors. In this chapter, we will discuss how companies raise money from investors by issuing debt securities in the bond markets. The bond markets are where companies go to sell debt securities and where investors go to purchase and trade debt securities. The debt securities purchased and traded in the bond markets are generically referred to as "bonds" by the press and investors. The companies issuing debt securities in the bond markets, however, almost always refer to these securities as "notes" in their financial statements. You will see this distinction in the Real World Excerpts in this chapter. In the next chapter, Chapter 11, we will continue our discussion of a company's capital structure by discussing money raised from shareholders through the issuance of stock in the equity markets.

LEARNING OBJECTIVES

After studying this chapter, you should be able to:

10-1 Describe the characteristics of bond securities. p. 525

10-2 Report bonds payable and interest expense for bond securities issued at par. p. 531

10-3 Compute and analyze the times interest earned ratio. p. 533

10-4 Report bonds payable and interest expense for bond securities issued at a discount. p. 534

10-5 Report bonds payable and interest expense for bond securities issued at a premium. p. 538

10-6 Compute and analyze the debt-to-equity ratio. p. 544

10-7 Report the early retirement of bond securities. p. 544

10-8 Explain how bond securities are reported on the statement of cash flows. p. 545

FOCUS COMPANY

Polaris/Newscom

Amazon

ISSUING AND
REPORTING BONDS

amazon.com

For Amazon to maintain its position as an industry leader, it must reinvest large amounts of money in its business. Last year alone, the company spent almost $40 billion purchasing property, equipment, and software. Like most large companies, Amazon has raised capital to support its operations by both selling debt securities in the bond markets and issuing stock in the equity markets. Amazon has disclosed detailed information concerning its long-term debt in the note shown in Exhibit 10.1. Some of the terminology in this note will be new to you. After studying this chapter, you will understand each of the terms used in the note.

UNDERSTANDING THE BUSINESS

As we learned in Chapter 9, a company's capital structure is the mixture of debt and equity it uses to finance its operations. Almost all companies employ some debt in their capital structure, with large companies often borrowing billions of dollars. Borrowing such a large amount from an individual bank is often impractical, so companies issue bond securities (bonds) to the investing public instead. Companies are not the only entities that go to the bond markets to raise capital; governments around the world also issue bonds for the same reason.

After bond securities have been issued, they are traded on established exchanges such as the New York Bond Exchange. The ability to sell a bond on the bond exchange is a significant advantage for investors because it provides them with liquidity, or the ability to convert their investments into cash. If you lend money directly to a corporation for 20 years, you must wait 20 years before you will get your principal back. In contrast,

EXHIBIT 10.1

Excerpts from Amazon's Long-Term Debt Note

AMAZON

REAL WORLD EXCERPT:

Notes to Financial Statements

NOTE 5 - Debt

	Maturities	December 31, 2019	December 31, 2020
2012 Notes issuance of $3.0 billion	2022	1,250	1,250
2014 Notes issuance of $6.0 billion	2021-2044	5,000	5,000
2017 Notes issuance of $17.0 billion	2023-2057	17,000	16,000
2020 Notes issuance of $10.0 billion	2023-2060	–	10,000
Credit Facility		740	338
Other long-term debt		830	586
Total face value of long-term debt		24,820	33,174
Unamortized discount and issuance costs, net		(101)	(203)
Less current portion of long-term debt		(1,305)	(1,155)
Long-term debt reported on the balance sheet		$23,414	$31,816

Source: Amazon Corporation

if you lend money by purchasing a bond in the bond markets, you can always sell it to another investor if you need cash before the bond matures.

The liquidity associated with being able to trade debt securities in the bond markets offers an important advantage to corporations. Most investors are reluctant to lend money for long periods with no opportunity to receive cash prior to maturity. If they do so, they demand a higher interest rate to compensate for the illiquidity. By issuing more liquid debt that investors can easily buy and sell in the bond markets, companies are able to reduce the cost of long-term borrowing.

This chapter begins with a basic overview of the characteristics of bonds before moving on to discuss accounting for bonds from issuance to maturity. The chapter closes with a discussion of the early retirement of bonds.

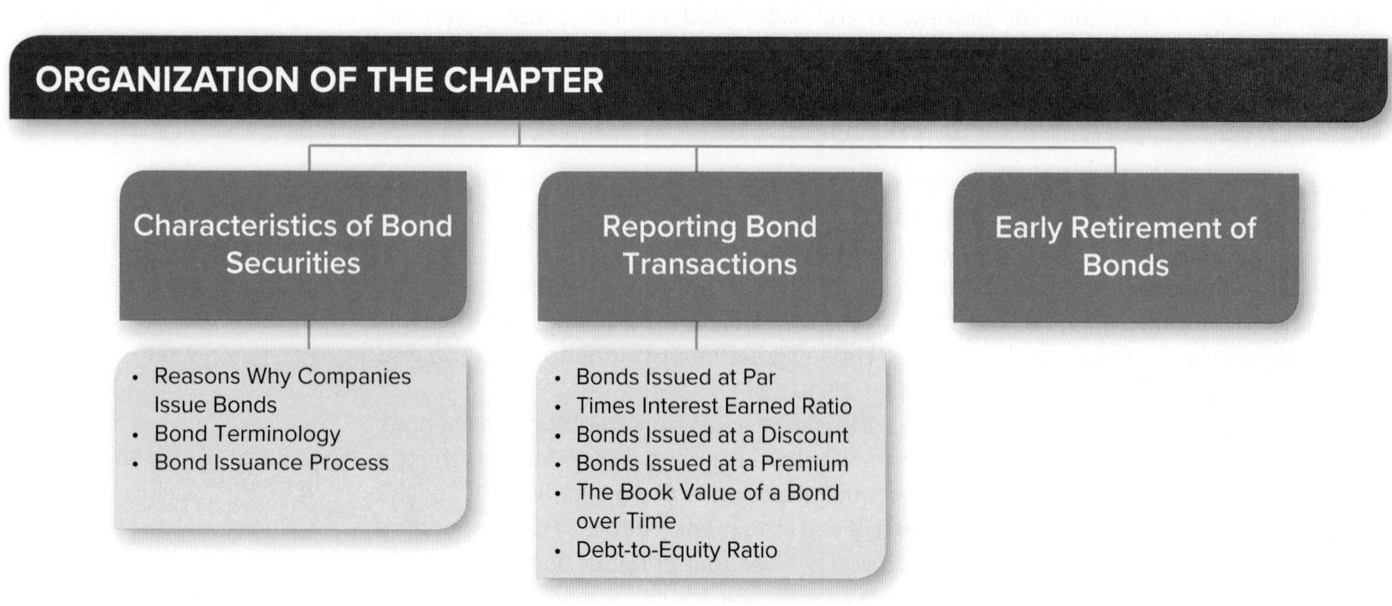

CHARACTERISTICS OF BOND SECURITIES

Reasons Why Companies Issue Bonds

LEARNING OBJECTIVE 10-1

Describe the characteristics of bond securities.

Companies issue both stock and bonds to raise capital. Several reasons why a company might choose to issue bonds instead of stock include:

1. **Stockholders maintain control.** Issuing bonds allows shareholders to maintain their current level of control. Bondholders do not vote or share in any dividend payments made to shareholders.
2. **A portion of interest expense is tax deductible.** The new tax law passed in late 2017 caps, but does not eliminate, the tax deductibility of interest associated with bonds. The tax deductibility of interest reduces the net cost of borrowing. In contrast, dividends are not tax deductible.
3. **Issuing bonds can increase the return to shareholders.** If a company can borrow at a low interest rate and invest in projects that earn a high rate of return it can increase the return to shareholders. For example, assume that Drone Delivery Company delivers critical medical supplies to search-and-rescue operations in remote locations. The company has shareholders' equity of $100,000 invested in various types of drone equipment and earns net income of $20,000 per year. Management plans to purchase new drones that will cost $100,000 and are expected to earn an additional $20,000 per year. To fund the purchase of the new drones should management issue new stock or borrow the money at an interest rate of 8 percent? Assuming that Drone has not yet met its tax deductibility cap, the following analysis shows borrowing the money will increase the return to the company's shareholders:

	Option 1	Option 2
Income Statement Impact:	Issue Stock	Borrow
Income before interest & taxes	$ 40,000	$ 40,000
Interest expense (8% × $100,000)	–	8,000
Income before taxes	40,000	32,000
Income taxes expense (21%)	8,400	6,720
Net income	$ 31,600	$ 25,280
Balance Sheet Impact:		
Stockholders' equity	$200,000	$100,000
Ratio Impact:		
Return on equity (net income/stockholders' equity)	**15.80%**	**25.28%**

$100,000 (existing)
+ $100,000 (new)
= $200,000 (total)

The above example illustrates why a company might choose to issue bonds instead of stock. So what are the potential disadvantages to issuing bonds? Here are two:

1. **Risk of bankruptcy.** Interest payments to bondholders are fixed charges that must be paid each period whether the corporation earns income or incurs a loss.
2. **Negative impact on cash flows.** Bonds must be repaid at a specified time in the future. Management must be able to generate sufficient cash to repay the debt or have the ability to refinance it.

Bond Terminology

A bond usually requires the payment of interest over its life with repayment of principal on the maturity date. The **bond principal** is (1) the amount a company must pay to bondholders at the maturity date and (2) the amount used to compute the bond's periodic cash interest payments. The bond principal also is called the **face value, par value,** or **maturity value.** All bonds have a face value. For most individual bonds, the face value is $1,000, but it can be any amount.

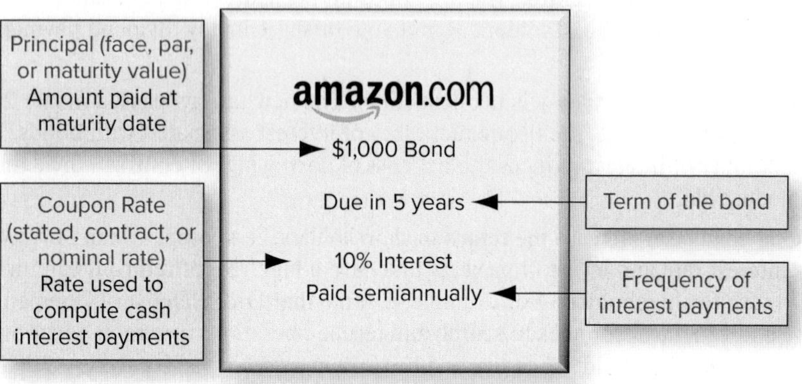

A bond always specifies a **coupon rate** (also called the **stated rate, contract rate,** or **nominal rate**) and the frequency of periodic cash interest payments. These interest payments are sometimes called coupon payments. A bond's coupon rate is always stated in annual terms. This means that if interest is paid annually, or once per year, the periodic cash interest payment is computed simply as the bond's face value times its coupon rate. If the interest payment is made more frequently, computing the cash interest payment requires that the coupon rate be converted to a rate per interest period before it is multiplied by the bond's face value. For example, the following table reflects how a bond's cash interest payment is calculated when interest is paid annually, semiannually, and quarterly. The face value of the bond is $1,000 and the coupon rate is 8 percent.

Frequency of Interest Payment	Interest Rate per Interest Period	Cash Payment per Interest Period
Annual (once per year)	8% × 1 = 8%	$1,000 × 8% = $80
Semiannual (twice per year)	8% × 1/2 = 4%	$1,000 × 4% = $40
Quarterly (four times per year)	8% × 1/4 = 2%	$1,000 × 2% = $20

As shown above, if the bond pays interest annually, bondholders will receive one interest payment of $80 during the year. If the bond pays interest semiannually, bondholders will receive a $40 interest payment every six months, for a total of $80 a year. If the bond pays interest quarterly, bondholders will receive a $20 interest payment every three months, for a total of $80 a year. Note that in all cases, $80 in interest is paid per year.

Different types of bonds have different characteristics to appeal to investors with different risk and return preferences. A retired person may be willing to receive a lower interest rate in return for greater security. This type of investor might want a **secured bond** that pledges a specific asset as security in case the company cannot repay the bond. Another type of investor might be willing to accept a low interest rate and a bond that is not backed by a specific asset (an unsecured bond) in return for the opportunity to convert the bond into common stock at some point in the future. These types of bonds are called **convertible bonds**. Companies try to design bond features that are attractive to different groups of investors just as automobile manufacturers try to design cars that appeal to different groups of consumers. Some common types of bonds are shown in the illustration below.

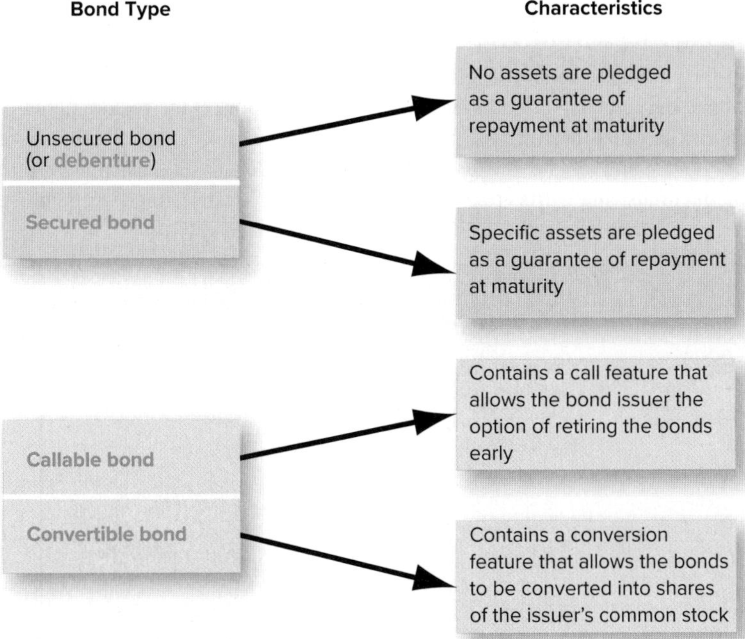

Bond Issuance Process

When **Amazon** decides to issue securities in the bond markets, it prepares a bond indenture and a bond prospectus. The indenture is a legal document that specifies all the details of the bond offering. The prospectus is a regulatory document that is filed with the Securities and Exchange Commission. It also specifies all the details of the bond offering. These details include the maturity date, the rate of interest to be paid, the date of each interest payment, and other characteristics of the bonds, such as whether the bonds are callable or convertible. The prospectus also describes any covenants designed to protect bondholders. Typical covenants include limitations on new debt that the company might issue in the future, limitations on the payment of dividends to shareholders, or requirements that the company maintain certain minimum accounting ratios, such as the debt-to-equity ratio, discussed later in this chapter. Management prefers covenants that are not overly restrictive. Bondholders, however, prefer more restrictive covenants, which lessen the risk of the investment.

Besides being described in the prospectus, bond covenants also are typically reported in the notes to the financial statements. Amazon's note states:

AMAZON
REAL WORLD EXCERPT:
Notes to Financial Statements

"We are not subject to any financial covenants under the Notes."

Charles Brutlag/Alamy Stock Photo

A company's prospectus and annual report also describe to potential investors how the proceeds from the bond issuance will be used. Amazon states in its annual report that it used the money for general corporate purposes and the acquisition of **Whole Foods Market**.

When a bond is issued to an investor, the investor receives a bond certificate. All bond certificates for the same bond issuance, whether an actual paper certificate or an electronic certificate, contain the same information. The certificates show the maturity date, coupon rate, interest dates, and other characteristics. An independent party, called the trustee, is usually appointed to represent the bondholders. A trustee's duties are to ascertain whether the issuing company has fulfilled all provisions of the bond contract.

FINANCIAL ANALYSIS

Bond Rating Agencies and Their Assessments of Default Risk

Because of the large amount of money involved and the complexities associated with bonds, several agencies exist to evaluate the risk that a bond issuer will not be able to meet the requirements specified in the prospectus. This risk is called **default risk.** Standard & Poor's, Moody's, and Fitch use letter ratings to specify the quality of a bond. Higher-quality bonds have lower default risk, as shown in the table below. Many banks, mutual funds, and trusts are permitted to invest only in investment-grade bonds.

Standard & Poor's	Moody's	Fitch	Description	Risk
AAA	Aaa	AAA	Highest investment grade	Low risk
AA	Aa	AA		↓
A	A	A		↓
BBB	Baa	BBB	Lowest investment grade	↓
BB	Ba	BB	Highest junk bond grade	↓
B	B	B		↓
CCC	Caa	CCC		↓
CC	Ca	CC		↓
C	C	C		↓
D	C	DDD	In default or unrated	High risk

REPORTING BOND TRANSACTIONS

When **Amazon** issued its bonds, it specified two types of cash payments in the bond contract:

1. **Principal.** As noted in the previous section, this amount is usually a single payment that is made when the bonds are retired at the end of their life. It is also called the **face value, par value**, or **maturity value**. We will use the term face value throughout the rest of the chapter.
2. **Cash interest payments.** These payments, which are sometimes referred to as **coupon payments**, represent an annuity and are computed by multiplying the bond's face value times the coupon rate. The bond contract specifies whether the interest payments are made quarterly, semiannually, or annually. When you are asked to work problems in which interest payments are made more frequently than once a year, be sure and **use the interest rate per period** in your calculations. For example, consider a bond with the following characteristics:

- Face value: $1,000
- Term: 10 years
- Coupon rate: 6% (annual)
- Interest paid: Semiannually (twice a year)

If you are asked to compute the cash interest payment for this bond, you will need to use an interest rate per period of 3 percent (the semiannual coupon rate). The calculation is

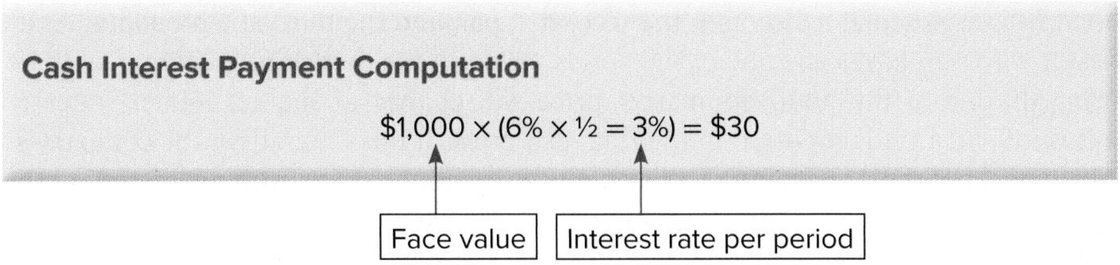

The issuing company does not determine the price at which the bonds sell. Instead, the market determines the price using the present value concepts introduced in the last chapter. To determine the present value of the bond, simply compute the present value of the principal (a single payment) and the present value of the interest payments (an annuity) and add the two amounts together.

Investors demand a certain rate of return to compensate them for the risks related to a particular company's bond offering. The demanded rate of return is called the **market interest rate** (also known as the **yield** or **effective interest rate**). Because the market rate is the interest rate investors demand on the day a bond is issued, it is the rate that should be used in computing the present value of a bond. The relationship between the market interest rate and the price of a bond is shown in the following figure. Note that as market interest rates rise the price of a bond falls and vice versa. This is because of the important role the market interest rate plays in determining the present value of a bond.

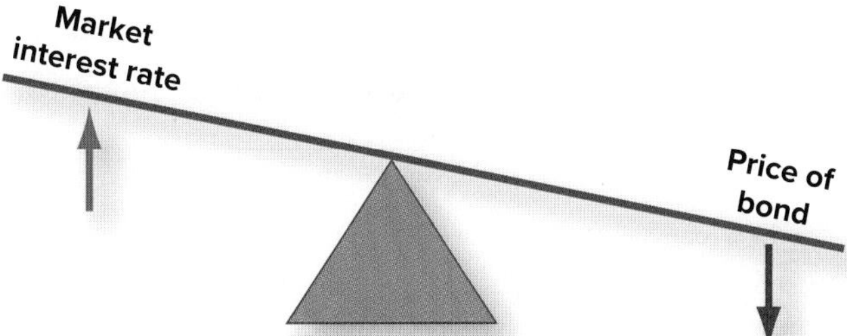

On the day a company issues a bond, the market interest rate will be either the same as the coupon rate, greater than the coupon rate, or less than the coupon rate. The relationship between the market interest rate and the bond's coupon rate determines whether the bond is issued at par, at a **premium**, or at a **discount**. When the market interest rate equals the coupon rate, the bond sells at par; when the market interest rate is greater than the coupon rate, the bond sells at a discount; and when the market interest rate is less than the coupon rate, the bond sells at a premium. This relationship can be shown graphically as follows:

Tip A bond's coupon rate relative to the market interest rate determines if a bond is issued at a premium, a discount, or at par.

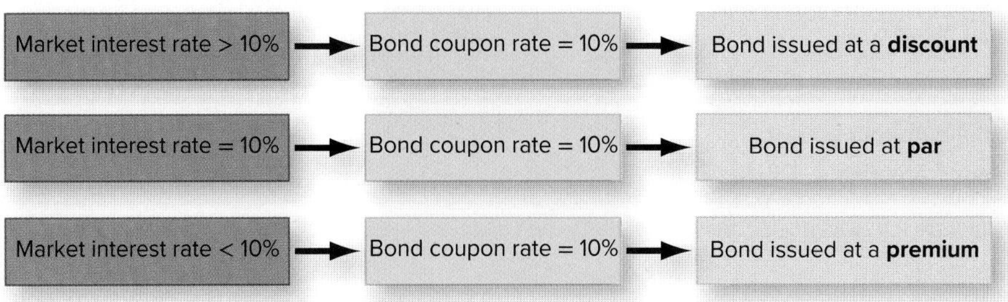

In commonsense terms, when a bond's coupon rate is less than the rate investors demand, investors will not buy the bond unless its price is reduced (i.e., a discount must be provided). When a bond's coupon rate is more than investors demand, investors will be willing to pay a premium to buy the bond.

It is important to keep in mind that regardless of whether a bond is issued at par, at a discount, or at a premium, investors always will earn the market rate of return. To illustrate, consider a company that issues three separate bonds on the same day. The bonds are the same except that one has a coupon rate of 8 percent, another a rate of 10 percent, and a third a rate of 12 percent. If the market rate of interest is 10 percent on the date all three bonds are issued, the first bond will be issued at a discount, the second at par, and the third at a premium. As a result, an investor who purchases any one of the bonds will earn the market interest rate of 10 percent.

During the life of the bond, its market price will change as market interest rates change. While this information is reported in the financial press, it does not affect the company's financial statements and the way its interest payments are accounted for from one period to the next. The interest rates that matter for accounting purposes are the bond's **coupon rate** (which does not change over time) and the **market interest rate on the day the bond is issued.**

DATA ANALYTICS

Using Artificial Intelligence (AI) to Invest in Bonds

Individuals who invest in bonds often spend considerable time and effort gathering and assessing vast amounts of market information (e.g., market interest rates, general economic conditions) as well as company-specific information. Using technology to expand and expedite this process would allow investors to make more informed, quicker decisions. Companies are stepping in to help. For example, AllianceBernstein, a global investment-management and research firm, has created Abbie, a virtual assistant based on artificial intelligence that helps investors make bond investing decisions. You can read more about Abbie's abilities here: **alliancebernstein.com/fixed-income/bonds/abbie.htm**

In the next section of this chapter, we will see how to account for bonds issued at par, at a discount, and at a premium.

PAUSE FOR FEEDBACK

There are a lot of definitions associated with accounting for bonds. Before we move on, it is important that you understand these new terms. Let's review them.

SELF-STUDY QUIZ

Define the following:

1. Market interest rate.
2. Synonyms for *market interest rate.*
3. Coupon rate.
4. Synonyms for *coupon rate.*
5. Bond discount.
6. Bond premium.

After you have completed your answers, check them below.

Solutions to SELF-STUDY QUIZ

1. The market interest rate is the interest rate demanded by investors for a bond at the time the bond is issued. It is the rate investors use in their present value computations to determine how much they will pay for the bond.
2. The market interest rate also is called a bond's *yield* or its *effective interest rate.*
3. Coupon rate is specified on the bond and is the rate used to compute the cash interest payment.
4. Coupon rate is also called the *stated rate, contract rate,* or *nominal rate.*
5. A bond that sells for less than its face value is sold at a discount. This occurs when the coupon rate is less than the market interest rate.
6. A bond that sells for more than its face value is sold at a premium. This occurs when the coupon rate is greater than the market interest rate.

Bonds Issued at Par

LEARNING OBJECTIVE 10-2

Report bonds payable and interest expense for bond securities issued at par.

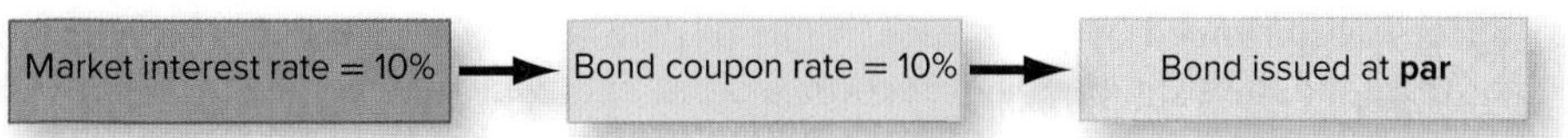

Bonds sell at their face (par) value when the market interest rate that investors demand is equal to the interest rate stated in the bond contract (the **coupon rate**). To illustrate, let's assume that on January 1, 2022, **Amazon** issues bonds with a coupon rate of 10 percent and a face value of \$100,000. On the date of issuance, investors are willing to pay Amazon \$100,000 in cash (which means that the bonds are being sold at par). The bonds start accruing interest on January 1, 2022, and will pay interest each June 30 and December 31. The bonds mature in two years on December 31, 2023.

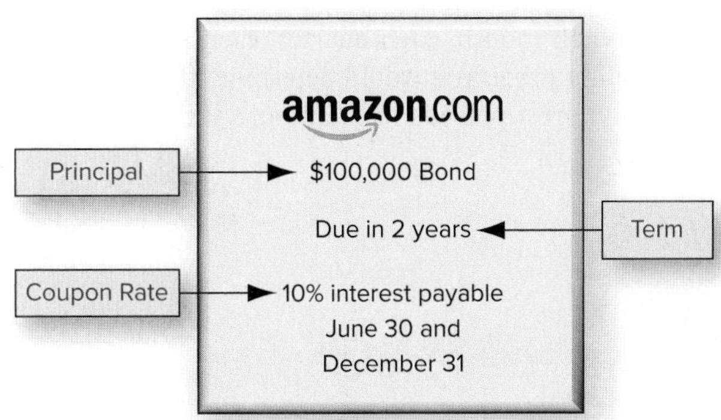

The amount of money a company receives when it sells bonds is the present value of the future cash flows associated with the bonds. In issuing the bonds described above, Amazon agrees to make two types of payments in the future: a single payment of \$100,000 when the bond matures in two years and an annuity of \$5,000 [\$100,000 × (10% × ½ year)] payable twice a year for two years. The 10 percent in the equation is the bond's coupon rate. The bond payments can be shown graphically as follows:

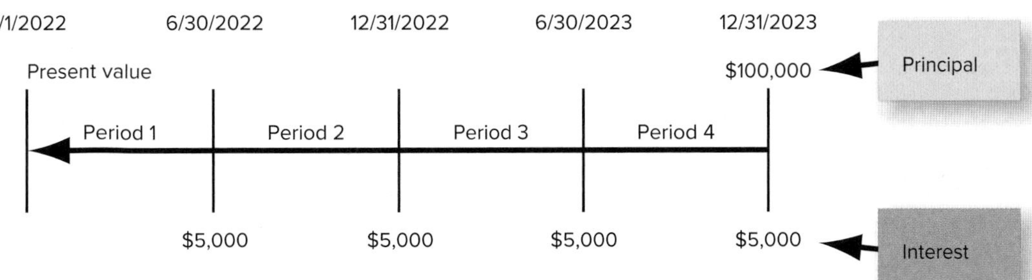

From Table E.1:
interest rate (i) = 5%
periods (n) = 4
Factor = 0.82270
From Table E.2:
interest rate (i) = 5%
periods (n) = 4
Factor = 3.54595
Using Calculator:
rate (i) = 5
periods (n) = 4
pmt = −\$5,000,
FV = −\$100,000
Using Excel:
Rate (i) = 0.05
Nper (n) = 4
Pmt = −\$5,000,
Fv = −\$100,000

We use the bond's market interest rate per period (in this case 10% ÷ 2 = 5%) to compute the bond's present value. As we discussed in the previous chapter, the present value of the bond payments can be computed using the tables in Appendix E, a financial calculator, or Excel:

	Present Value
Single principal payment at maturity: \$100,000 × 0.82270	\$ 82,270
+ Annuity cash interest payment: \$5,000 × 3.54595	17,730
= Issue price (proceeds from sale) of the bonds	\$100,000

When the market rate of interest equals the coupon rate, the present value of the future cash flows associated with a bond always equals the bond's face value amount. Remember a bond's selling price is determined by the present value of its future cash flows, not the face value. On the date Amazon issues the bonds, it records a bond liability equal to the amount investors are willing to pay for the bonds:

January 1, 2022	Debit	Credit
Cash (+A)	100,000	
Bonds payable (+L)		100,000

Assets		=	Liabilities		+	Stockholders' Equity
Cash	+100,000		Bonds payable	+100,000		

Bonds may pay interest each month, each quarter, each half-year, or each year. In all cases, to determine the bond's selling price, you would determine the present value of the bond's cash flows using the number of interest periods in the bond's life as well as the market interest rate per period.

PAUSE FOR FEEDBACK

Calculating the issuance price of a bond requires an investor to know the market rate of interest, the number of periods until the bond matures, and the bond's face value. Let's practice calculating the issuance price of a bond before we move on.

SELF-STUDY QUIZ

Assume that **Amazon** issues bonds with a face value of $500,000 that will mature in two years. The bonds pay interest at the end of each year. On the date of issuance, the coupon rate and market rate of interest are the same: 8 percent. Compute the issuance price of the bonds.

After you have completed your answer, check it below.

GUIDED HELP 10-1

For additional step-by-step instruction, go to mhhe.com/libby_gh10-1.

Related Homework: M10-2, E10-3, E10-4, P10-2, P10-3, P10-4

Reporting Interest Expense for Bonds Issued at Par

Continuing with our example, the investors who bought the Amazon bonds did so with the expectation that they would earn interest over the life of the bond. Amazon will pay interest at 10 percent per year on the face value of the bonds each June 30 and December 31 until the

Solutions to SELF-STUDY QUIZ

$500,000 × 0.85734 = $428,670
($500,000 × 0.08) × 1.78326 = 71,330
= $500,000

bond's maturity date. The amount of interest each period will be $5,000 ($100,000 × 0.10 × ½ year). The entry to record each interest payment is as follows:

June 30 and December 31 of each year	Debit	Credit
Interest expense (+E, −SE)	5,000	
Cash (−A)		5,000

Assets		=	Liabilities	+	Stockholders' Equity	
Cash	−5,000				Interest expense (+E)	−5,000

Interest expense is reported on the income statement. Because interest is related to financing activities rather than operating activities, it is normally not included in operating expenses on the income statement. Instead, interest expense is typically reported just below "income from operations" on the income statement. A portion of the income statement for Amazon shows how interest expense is usually reported.

AMAZON

REAL WORLD EXCERPT:

Partial Income Statement

AMAZON.COM, INC.
CONSOLIDATED STATEMENTS OF OPERATIONS
(in millions)

	Year Ended December 31		
	2018	2019	2020
. . .			
Operating income	$12,421	$14,541	$22,899
Interest income	440	832	555
Interest expense	(1,417)	(1,600)	(1,647)
Other income (expense), net	(183)	203	2,371
Total non-operating income (expense)	(1,160)	(565)	1,279
Income before income taxes	11,261	13,976	24,178
. . .			

Source: Amazon.com, Inc.

Mark HertzbergZUMA Wire/ Alamy

Bond interest payment dates rarely coincide with the last day of a company's fiscal year. Under the expense recognition principle introduced in Chapter 3, interest expense that has been incurred but not paid must be accrued at the end of the accounting period. If Amazon's fiscal year ended on May 31 instead of December 31, the company would accrue interest for five months and report that amount as interest expense on its income statement and the same amount as interest payable on its balance sheet.

Because interest payments are a legal obligation of the company, financial analysts want to be certain that the company is generating sufficient resources to meet its interest obligations. The times interest earned ratio is useful when making this assessment.

KEY RATIO ANALYSIS

LEARNING OBJECTIVE 10-3

Compute and analyze the times interest earned ratio.

Times Interest Earned

ANALYTICAL QUESTION

Is **Amazon** generating sufficient resources from its profit-making activities to meet its current interest obligations?

RATIO AND COMPARISONS

The times interest earned ratio is computed as follows:

$$\text{Times Interest Earned} = \frac{\text{Net Income} + \text{Interest Expense} + \text{Income Tax Expense}}{\text{Interest Expense}}$$

The 2020 ratio for Amazon (dollars in millions):

[$21,331 + $1,647 + $2,863]/$1,647 = 15.69

Comparisons Over Time		
Amazon		
2018	2019	2020
8.95	9.73	15.69

Comparisons With Competitors	
eBay	Walmart
2020	2020
22.46	8.62

INTERPRETATIONS

In General Analysts view a high times interest earned ratio more favorably than a low one. The ratio shows the amount of income earned for each dollar of interest expense. A high ratio indicates an extra margin of protection in case profitability deteriorates. Analysts are particularly interested in a company's ability to meet its required interest payments because failure to do so could result in bankruptcy.

Focus Company Analysis In 2020, profit-making activities for Amazon generated $15.69 for each dollar of interest. The ratio has fluctuated over time from a low of $8.95 in 2018 to a high of $15.69 in 2020. The large increase in 2020 is mainly due to a large jump in net income in 2020, eBay has an even higher ratio ($22.46) while Walmart's ratio is considerably lower ($8.62).

A Few Cautions The times interest earned ratio is often misleading for new or rapidly growing companies, which tend to invest considerable resources to build their capacity for future operations. In such cases, the times interest earned ratio will reflect significant amounts of interest expense associated with borrowing to support expansion plans but not the future income that likely will come from expanding. For this reason, analysts should consider the company's long-term strategy when interpreting this ratio.

LEARNING OBJECTIVE 10-4

Report bonds payable and interest expense for bond securities issued at a discount.

Bonds Issued at a Discount

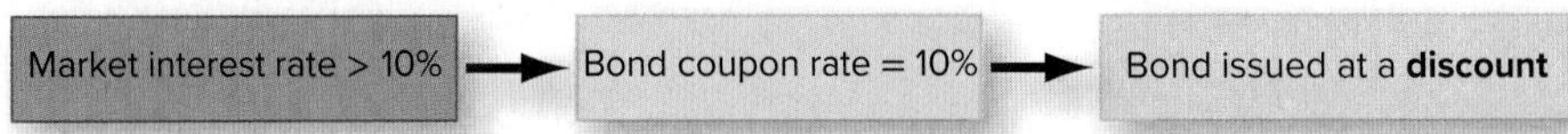

Bonds sell at a discount when the market interest rate is greater than the coupon rate. To illustrate, let's assume that the market interest rate is 12 percent on January 1, 2022, when **Amazon** sells its bonds (which have a face value of $100,000). The bonds mature in two years and have a coupon rate of 10 percent. Interest is payable twice a year on June 30 and December 31. Because the coupon rate (10 percent) is less than the market interest rate (12 percent) on the date of issuance, the bonds sell at a discount.

To compute what investors will be willing to pay for the bonds given the difference in interest rates, we can use the tables in Appendix E. As in the previous example, the number of periods is four and the interest rate is the market interest rate per period; in this case, 6 percent (12% × ½ year). With this information, we can compute the cash issue price of the Amazon bonds as follows:

From Table E.1:
interest rate (i) = 6%
periods (n) = 4
Factor = 0.79209
From Table E.2:
interest rate (i) = 6%
periods (n) = 4
Factor = 3.46511
Using Calculator:
rate (i) = 6
periods (n) = 4
pmt = −$5,000,
FV = −$100,000
Using Excel:
Rate (i) = 0.06
Nper (n) = 4
Pmt = −$5,000,
Fv = −$100,000

	Present Value
Single principal payment at maturity: $100,000 × 0.79209	$79,209
+ Annuity cash interest payment: $5,000 × 3.46511	17,326
Issue (sale) price of bonds	$96,535

Thus, if the market interest rate is 12 percent on the date of issuance, investors will be willing to pay Amazon $96,535 for the bonds. Some people refer to this price as 96.5, which indicates the selling price was 96.5 percent of the bond's face value (96.5 = $96,535 ÷ $100,000).

There are two acceptable methods for recording a bond that is sold at a discount; both result in the same dollar value being reported on a company's balance sheet. The first method ***explicitly*** keeps track of the bond discount by incorporating it into the journal entries. The second method ***implicitly*** keeps track of the bond discount but does not incorporate it into the journal entries. Regardless of the method used, the dollar value reported on the balance sheet (the bond payable book value) is identical, as shown in the example below. Using both methods, the journal entries to record the sale of Amazon's bonds issued at a discount are:

WITH DISCOUNT ACCOUNT

January 1, 2022	Debit	Credit
Cash (+A)	96,535	
Bond discount (−L)	3,465	
Bonds payable (+L)		100,000

Assets		=	Liabilities		+	Stockholders' Equity
Cash	+96,535		Bonds payable	+100,000		
			Bond discount	−3,465		

Bonds payable book value: **$96,535**
($100,000 − $3,465)

WITHOUT DISCOUNT ACCOUNT

January 1, 2022	Debit	Credit
Cash (+A)	96,535	
Bonds payable (+L)		96,535

Assets		=	Liabilities		+	Stockholders' Equity
Cash	+96,535		Bonds payable	+96,535		

Bonds payable book value: **$96,535**

Bond discount is sometimes referred to as a contra-liability account since it is debited when the bonds are issued and shown as a negative number under liabilities. This account is not separately disclosed on Amazon's balance sheet. Instead, the balance sheet reports the bonds payable at their book value ($96,535), which is the face value of the bonds less the unamortized discount ($100,000 − $3,465). Note that reporting bonds payable at their book value results in the same amount being reported on the balance sheet ($96,535), regardless of whether a bond discount is explicitly recorded in the journal entry.

Tip Regardless of whether a bond discount account is used, the dollar amounts reported on a company's balance sheet are the same.

While Amazon received only $96,535 when it sold the bonds, it must repay $100,000 when the bonds mature. The $3,465 of additional cash that Amazon must pay at maturity is incrementally reflected in interest expense and added to the book value of the liability each period over the life of the bond. This causes interest expense to reflect the **market interest rate** (also referred to as the **effective interest rate**), while the cash being paid to bondholders each period reflects the **coupon rate.** The accounting method used to record interest expense is referred to as the **effective-interest amortization** method.

Throughout the remainder of Chapter 10 we use the bond discount account in all journal entries. **We duplicate the text and show all journal entries *without the bond discount account* in the Chapter Supplement at the end of the chapter.**

Reporting Interest Expense on Bonds Issued at a Discount Using Effective-Interest Amortization (with Discount Account)

Under the effective-interest amortization method, a company computes interest expense in a given period by multiplying the bonds payable book value times the market rate of interest on the date of issuance. When bonds are issued at a discount, using a market interest rate that is greater than the coupon rate results in interest expense each period being greater than the cash owed for interest each period. The difference between interest expense and the cash owed for interest is the amount of the bond discount amortized during the period. This process can be summarized as follows:

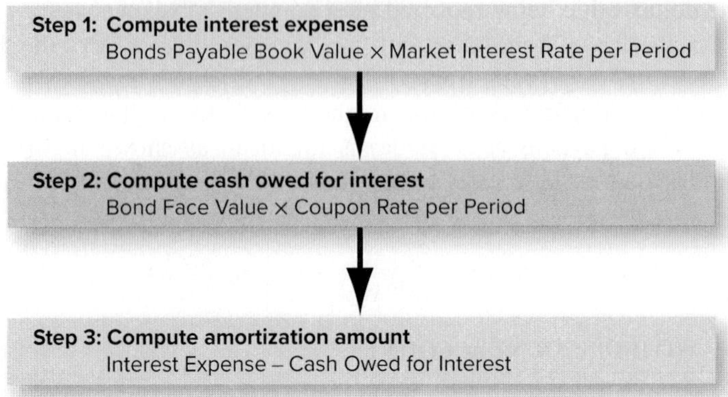

Recall that the cash owed for interest is computed by multiplying the bond's face value ($100,000) by the coupon rate per period (10% × ½ year). Thus, Amazon owes bondholders cash of $5,000 each June 30 and again on December 31. The first interest payment on the bonds is made on June 30, 2022. Following the three steps outlined above, interest expense and the amount of the bond discount amortized are:

Step 1: **Interest expense:** $96,535 × (0.12 × ½ year) = **$5,792**

Step 2: **Cash owed for interest:** $100,000 × (0.10 × ½ year) = **$5,000**

Step 3: **Amortized amount:** $5,792 – $5,000 = **$792**

The journal entry Amazon would enter is:

June 30, 2022	**Debit**	**Credit**
Interest expense (+E, −SE)	5,792	
Bond discount (+L)		792
Cash (−A)		5,000

Effective-interest amortization causes these amounts to change each period because the book value of the bonds changes each period.

Assets		=	**Liabilities**		+	**Stockholders' Equity**	
Cash	−5,000		Bond discount	+792		Interest expense (+E)	−5,792

Bonds payable book value: **$97,327** ($100,000 − $3,465 + $792)

Each period, the amortization of the bond discount increases the bond's book value, bringing it closer to the $100,000 that is due at maturity. The amortization of the bond discount can be thought of as the amount of interest earned by the bondholders in a given period that will be paid to them when the bonds mature. During the first interest period, Amazon's bondholders earned interest of $5,792 but received only $5,000 in cash. The additional $792 was added to the book value of the bond and will be paid to bondholders when the bonds mature and investors receive the full face value ($100,000).

Interest expense for the next interest period must reflect the change in the bonds payable book value. Amazon calculates interest expense for the second half of 2022 by multiplying the bonds payable book value on June 30, 2022 ($97,327) by the market rate of interest per period [$97,327 × (12% × ½ year) = $5,840]. With interest expense equal to $5,840 and cash owed for interest equal to $5,000, the amount of the bond discount amortized on December 31, 2022, is $840:

December 31, 2022	Debit	Credit
Interest expense (+E, − SE)	5,840	
Bond discount (+L)		840
Cash (− A)		5,000

Assets		=	Liabilities		+	Stockholders' Equity	
Cash	−5,000		Bond discount	+840		Interest expense (+E)	−5,840

Bonds payable book value: **$98,167**
($100,000 − $3,465 + $792 + $840)

Notice that interest expense for December 31, 2022, is more than interest expense for June 30, 2022. Amazon effectively borrowed more money during the second half of the year because of the unpaid interest accrued during the first half of the year. Because of the amortization of the bond discount, the book value of the bond and interest expense **increase** each year during the life of the bond. This process can be illustrated with the amortization schedule shown below:

BOND AMORTIZATION SCHEDULE: ISSUED AT A DISCOUNT

	(a)	(b)	(c)	(d)
	Face × Coupon Rate/Period	Beginning of Period Book Value × Market Rate/Period	Absolute Difference between (a) and (b)	Beginning of Period Book Value + (c)
Date	Cash Owed for Interest	Interest Expense	Amortization of Bond Discount	Bonds Payable (book value)
01/01/2022				$ 96,535
06/30/2022	$5,000	$5,792	$792	97,327
12/31/2022	5,000	5,840	840	98,167
06/30/2023	5,000	5,890	890	99,057
12/31/2023	5,000	5,943	943	100,000

Note that:

- Cash owed for interest (column a) is computed by multiplying the bond's face value by the coupon rate per period.
- Interest expense (column b) is computed by multiplying the book value of the bonds at the beginning of the period (column d) by the market interest rate. Note that the book value of a bond at the beginning of a period is the book value of the bond at the end of the previous period.
- Amortization of the bond discount is computed by subtracting cash owed for interest (column a) from interest expense (column b).
- The new book value of the bonds (column d) is computed by adding amortization of the bond discount (column c) to the book value at the beginning of the period.

In summary, under the effective-interest amortization method, interest expense changes each accounting period as the book value of the bonds changes each accounting period.

PAUSE FOR FEEDBACK

Calculating the cash paid to investors each period and interest expense each period requires investors to know the coupon rate, the market rate of interest, and the carrying value of the bonds at the beginning of each period. Let's practice calculating the cash paid to investors and interest expense before we move on.

SELF-STUDY QUIZ

Assume that **Amazon** issued bonds with a face value of $100,000 and a coupon rate of 5 percent. The bonds mature in 10 years and pay interest annually. The bonds were sold when the annual market interest rate was 6 percent at a price of $92,640.

1. What amount of cash was owed for interest at the end of the first year?
2. Using the effective-interest amortization method, what amount of interest expense would Amazon report at the end of the first year?

After you have completed your answers, check them below.

GUIDED HELP 10-2

For additional step-by-step instruction on how to account for a bond issued at a discount, go to mhhe.com/libby_gh10-2.

Related Homework: M10-6, E10-3, E10-4, E10-7, E10-8, E10-10, P10-3, P10-4, P10-6, P10-7

LEARNING OBJECTIVE 10-5

Report bonds payable and interest expense for bond securities issued at a premium.

Bonds Issued at a Premium

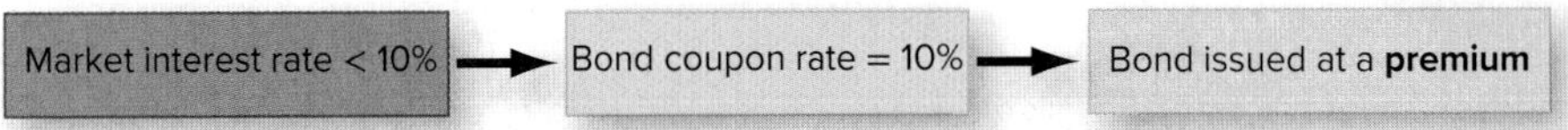

Recall that bonds sell at a **discount** when the market interest rate is greater than the bond's coupon rate. When the market interest rate is less than the bond's coupon rate, the bonds sell at a premium. To demonstrate how to account for bonds issued at a **premium**, let's use the same **Amazon** example as before but assume that the market interest rate is now 8 percent while the coupon rate remains the same, at 10 percent. Like before, the bonds are issued on January 1, 2022; pay interest semiannually; and mature in two years.

The present value of the bonds described above can be computed from the tables contained in Appendix E using the factor for four periods and an interest rate of 4 percent per period (8% × ½ year):

	Present Value
Single principal payment at maturity: $100,000 × 0.85480	$ 85,480
+ Annuity cash interest payment: $5,000 × 3.62990	18,150
Issue (sale) price of bonds	$103,630

From Table E.1:
interest rate (i) = 4%
periods (n) = 4
Factor = 0.85480
From Table E.2:
interest rate (i) = 4%
periods (n) = 4
Factor = 3.62990
Using Calculator:
rate (i) = 4
periods (n) = 4
pmt = −$5,000,
FV = −$100,000
Using Excel:
Rate (i) = 0.04
Nper (n) = 4
Pmt = −$5,000,
Fv = −$100,000

Solutions to SELF-STUDY QUIZ

1. Cash owed for interest: $100,000 × 5% = **$5,000**
2. Interest expense: $92,640 × 6% = **$5,558**

Accounting for bonds issued at a premium is similar to accounting for bonds issued at a discount. Companies can explicitly use a bond premium account in their journal entries or implicitly keep track of the premium amount. We show both side-by-side below, and then, as we did with bond discounts, we present all subsequent journal entries using a bond premium account. **We duplicate the text and show all journal entries *without the bond premium account* in the Chapter Supplement at the end of the chapter.** The January 1, 2022, issuance of Amazon's bonds at a premium would be recorded as follows:

WITH PREMIUM ACCOUNT

January 1, 2022	Debit	Credit
Cash (+A)	103,630	
Bond premium (+L)		3,630
Bonds payable (+L)		100,000

Assets		=	Liabilities		+	Stockholders' Equity
Cash	+103,630		Bonds payable	+100,000		
			Bond premium	+3,630		

Bonds payable book value: **$103,630**
($100,000 + $3,630)

WITHOUT PREMIUM ACCOUNT

January 1, 2022	Debit	Credit
Cash (+A)	103,630	
Bonds payable (+L)		103,630

Assets		=	Liabilities		+	Stockholders' Equity
Cash	+103,630		Bonds payable	+103,630		

Bonds payable book value: **$103,630**

Bond premium is sometimes referred to as an adjunct-liability account. Like the bond discount account, the bond premium account is not separately disclosed on Amazon's balance sheet. Instead, the balance sheet reports the bonds payable at their book value ($103,630), which is their face value plus the unamortized premium ($100,000 + $3,630). Note that reporting bonds payable at their book value results in the same amount being reported on the balance sheet ($103,630) regardless of whether a bond premium is explicitly recorded in the journal entry.

Tip Regardless of whether a bond premium account is used, the dollar amounts reported on a company's balance sheet are the same.

Reporting Interest Expense on Bonds Issued at a Premium Using Effective-Interest Amortization (with Premium Account)

As with the discount account, the recorded premium of $3,630 must be apportioned to each interest period so that interest expense reflects the market (effective) interest rate that Amazon is actually paying. To compute interest expense and the amount of the premium to be amortized each period, we follow the same three steps that we followed to compute these amounts when the bonds were issued at a discount:

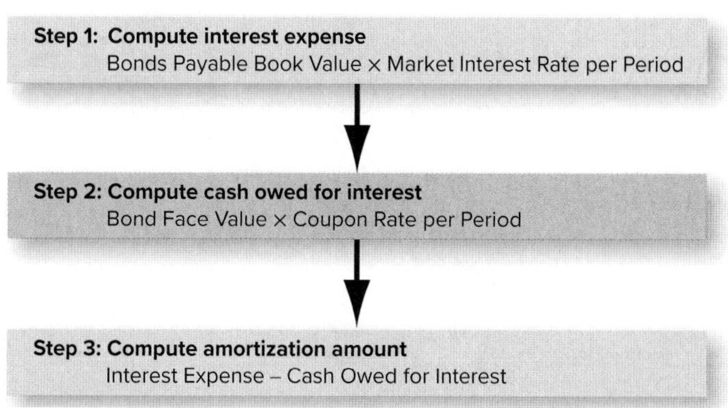

Step 1: Interest expense: \$103,630 × (0.08 × ½ year) = \$4,145

Step 2: Cash owed for interest: \$100,000 × (0.10 × ½ year) = \$5,000

Step 3: Amortized amount: \$4,145 − \$5,000 = − \$855

The journal entry Amazon would enter is:

June 30, 2022	Debit	Credit
Interest expense (+E, −SE)	4,145	
Bond premium (−L)	855	
Cash (−A)		5,000

Assets		=	Liabilities		+	Stockholders' Equity	
Cash	−5,000		Bond premium	−855		Interest expense (+E)	−4,145

Bonds payable book value: **\$102,775**
(\$100,000 + \$3,630 − \$855)

The basic difference between effective-interest amortization of a bond discount and a bond premium is that the amortization of a discount **increases** the book value of the liability and the amortization of a premium **decreases** it. Both serve the same purpose: to bring the liability to the bond's face value at the maturity date. This is illustrated in Exhibit 10.2.

EXHIBIT 10.2

The Change in the Book Value of a Bond Over Time

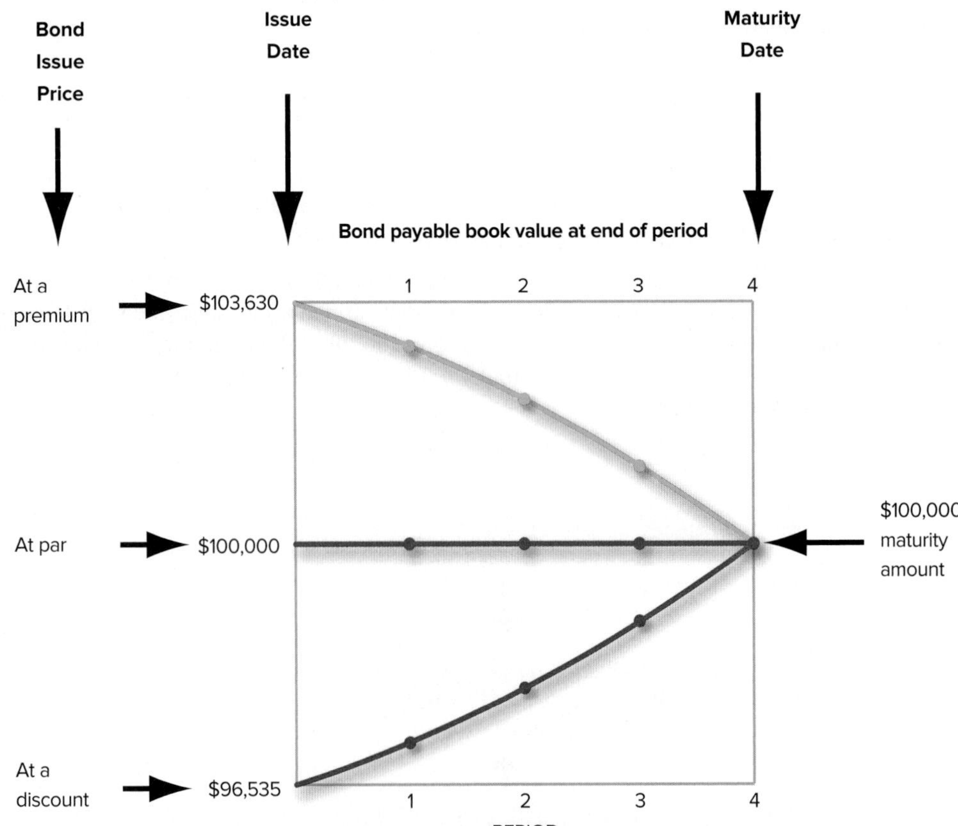

The following schedule illustrates the amortization of a premium over the life of a bond.

BOND AMORTIZATION SCHEDULE: ISSUED AT A PREMIUM				
	(a)	(b)	(c)	(d)
	Face × Coupon Rate/Period	Beginning of Period Book Value × Market Rate/Period	Absolute Difference between (a) and (b)	Beginning of Period Book Value – (c)
Date	Cash Owed for Interest	Interest Expense	Amortization of Bond Premium	Bonds Payable (book value)
01/01/2022				$103,630
06/30/2022	$5,000	$4,145	$855	102,775
12/31/2022	5,000	4,111	889	101,886
06/30/2023	5,000	4,075	925	100,962
12/31/2023	5,000	4,038	962	100,000

Regardless of whether a company issues bonds at par, at a discount, or at a premium, the company will enter the same journal entry when it retires the bonds at maturity. For our Amazon example, the journal entry would be

December 31, 2023	Debit	Credit
Bonds payable (−L)	100,000	
Cash (−A)		100,000

Assets		=	Liabilities		+	Stockholders' Equity
Cash	−100,000		Bonds payable	−100,000		

PAUSE FOR FEEDBACK

Calculating the cash paid to investors each period and interest expense each period requires investors to know the coupon rate, the market rate of interest, and the carrying value of the bonds at the beginning of each period. Let's practice calculating the cash paid to investors and interest expense before we move on.

SELF-STUDY QUIZ

Assume that **Amazon** issued bonds with a face value of $100,000 and a coupon rate of 9 percent. The bonds mature in 10 years and pay interest annually. The bonds were sold when the annual market interest rate was 8 percent at a price of $106,710.

1. What amount of cash was owed for interest at the end of the first year?
2. Using the effective-interest amortization method, what amount of interest expense would Amazon report at the end of the first year?

Answers are on the next page.

GUIDED HELP 10-3

For additional step-by-step instruction on how to account for a bond issued at a premium, go to mhhe.com/libby_gh10-3.

Related Homework: M10-9, E10-3, E10-4, E10-13, E10-15, E10-16, P10-3, P10-4, P10-9, P10-10, P10-11

FINANCIAL ANALYSIS

Zero Coupon Bonds

So far, we have discussed bonds that pay interest over their life and have a principal payment due at the end of their life, which are the most common type of bond issued by companies to raise capital. For a number of reasons, companies may choose to issue bonds that have unique features. The concepts you have learned will help you understand these bonds. For example, a company might issue a bond that does not pay periodic cash interest. These bonds are typically called *zero coupon bonds.* Why would an investor buy a bond that did not pay interest? Our discussion of bond discounts has probably given you a good idea of the answer. The coupon interest rate on a bond can be virtually any amount (including zero) and investors will price the bond so that they earn the market rate of interest. A bond with a zero coupon interest rate is simply a deeply discounted bond that will sell for substantially less than the amount due at maturity (its face value).

Let's use the $100,000 **Amazon** bond to illustrate a zero coupon rate. Assume that the market interest rate is 10 percent and the bond does not make any cash interest payments to bondholders over its life. The bond matures in five years. The selling price of the bond is the present value of the maturity amount because no other cash payments will be made over the life of the bond. We can compute the present value with the tables contained in Appendix E, using the factor for five periods and an interest rate of 10 percent:

From Table E.1:
interest rate (i) = 10%
periods (n) = 5
Factor = 0.62092
Using Calculator:
rate (i) = 10
periods (n) = 5
pmt = −$0,
FV = −$100,000
Using Excel:
Rate (i) = 0.10
Nper (n) = 5
Pmt = −$0,
Fv = −$100,000

	Present Value
Single principal payment at maturity: $100,000 × 0.62092	

Accounting for a zero coupon bond is no different from accounting for other bonds issued at a discount. However, the amount of the discount is much larger. For example, the bond discount in the above example is $37,908 ($100,000 − $62,092). Over the five-year life of the bond, this amount will decrease until it is zero at the end of the bond's life.

While zero coupon bonds do not pay cash interest, they have been priced to provide investors with a market rate of interest. Notice that the bonds payable book value in our example ($62,092) is much lower than the maturity value ($100,000). This is because the price investors are willing to pay has been discounted such that when they receive the $100,000 at the end of the five years, they will have earned an interest rate of 10 percent, the market rate of interest on the issue date.

Solutions to SELF-STUDY QUIZ

1. Cash owed for interest: $100,000 × 9% = **$9,000**
2. Interest expense: $106,710 × 8% = **$8,537**

Accounting for Issuance Costs

For the sake of simplicity, the examples in this chapter assume that the company issuing bonds does not incur any issuance costs. This is not typically the case in the business world. When companies issue bonds, they almost always hire another company (or companies) to help them with the offering. These companies are called underwriters, and they charge a fee. Accounting for this fee is quite simple. The amount of the fee is deducted from the proceeds of the bond issuance. If after deducting fees the total amount received is less than the face value of the bonds, the bonds are issued at a discount. If after deducting fees the amount received is greater than the face value of the bonds, the bonds are issued at a premium.

Reporting Interest Expense Using Straight-Line Amortization

GAAP requires that companies use the effective-interest method to amortize bond discounts and bond premiums. However, GAAP permits companies to use straight-line amortization when results do not materially differ from results computed using the effective-interest method. With **straight-line amortization**, a company simply takes the total amount of the discount or the premium at issuance, divides it by the number of periods in the bond's life, and amortizes that amount each period. For example, the total amount of the premium in the **Amazon** example above was $3,630 and the bonds paid interest over four periods. Using straight-line amortization, Amazon would amortize $907.50 each period over the life of the bonds. The amortization schedule would reflect:

BOND AMORTIZATION SCHEDULE: ISSUED AT A PREMIUM – STRAIGHT–LINE AMORTIZATION

	(a)	(b)	(c)	(d)
	Face × Coupon Rate/Period	(a) – (c)	Bond Premium/ Number of Periods	Beginning of Period Book Value – (c)
Date	Cash Owed for Interest	Interest Expense	Amortization of Bond Premium	Bonds Payable (book value)
01/01/2022				$ 103,630.00
06/30/2022	$5,000	$4,092.50	$907.50	102,722.50
12/31/2022	5,000	4,092.50	907.50	101,815.00
06/30/2023	5,000	4,092.50	907.50	100,907.50
12/31/2023	5,000	4,092.50	907.50	100,000.00

Other than the amounts, the journal entries using straight-line amortization and effective-interest amortization are the same. Because straight-line amortization is only permitted by GAAP under specific circumstances, we focus on the effective-interest method in this chapter.

KEY RATIO ANALYSIS

LEARNING OBJECTIVE 10-6

Compute and analyze the debt-to-equity ratio.

Debt-to-Equity

ANALYTICAL QUESTION

What is the relationship between the amount of capital provided by owners and the amount of capital provided by creditors?

RATIO AND COMPARISONS

The debt-to-equity ratio is computed as follows:

Debt-to-Equity = Total Liabilities ÷ Total Stockholders' Equity

The 2020 ratio for **Amazon** is

\$227,791 ÷ \$93,404 = 2.44

Comparisons Over Time		
Amazon		
2018	2019	2020
2.73	2.63	2.44

Comparisons With Competitors	
eBay	Walmart
2020	2020
4.42	1.90

INTERPRETATIONS

In General A high ratio indicates that a company relies heavily on debt financing relative to equity financing. Heavy reliance on debt financing increases the risk that a company may not be able to meet its contractual financial obligations (e.g., principal and interest payments) during a business downturn.

Focus Company Analysis The debt-to-equity ratio for Amazon has remained relatively constant over the past three years. The 2020 ratio reflects that for each dollar of stockholders' equity, Amazon has \$2.44 of liabilities. eBay's debt-to-equity ratio (4.42) is higher than Amazon's ratio while Walmart's debt-to-equity ratio. is lower (1.90).

A Few Cautions The debt-to-equity ratio tells only part of the story with respect to the risks associated with a company's debt. It does not help the analyst understand whether the company's operations can support its debt. As a result, most analysts would evaluate the debt-to-equity ratio within the context of the amount of cash the company can generate from operating activities.

LEARNING OBJECTIVE 10-7

Report the early retirement of bond securities.

EARLY RETIREMENT OF BONDS

Bonds often are issued for long periods, such as 20 or 30 years. Some bonds have a **call** feature that allows the issuing company to call (retire) the bonds early. A call feature most often requires the issuing company to pay investors an amount greater than the bond's face value to retire the bonds before their maturity date. The amount often is stated as a percentage of the bond's face value and is described in the bond indenture or bond prospectus.

Assume that several years ago, **Amazon** issued callable bonds with a face value of \$100,000. The bonds were issued at a premium, and the call feature allows Amazon to retire the bonds early by paying bondholders 102 percent of face value. If Amazon decides to call the bonds early, it will pay bondholders \$102,000 cash and remove the bond liability from its balance sheet. Any difference between the cash paid to retire the bonds and the book value of the bond liability is recorded as a gain or loss on the income statement. For example, if the book value of Amazon's bonds was \$101,000 at the time the bonds were retired, Amazon would recognize a loss on early retirement of \$1,000 on its income statement; Amazon had to pay bondholders \$102,000 cash to remove a \$101,000 liability from its balance sheet. The journal entry would be:

WITH PREMIUM ACCOUNT

Date bonds are retired	Debit	Credit
Bonds payable (−L)	100,000	
Bond premium (−L)	1,000	
Loss on bond call (+E, −SE)	1,000	
Cash (−A)		102,000

Assets	=	Liabilities	+	Stockholders' Equity
Cash −102,000		Bonds payable −100,000 Bond premium −1,000		Loss on bond call (+E) −1,000

WITHOUT PREMIUM ACCOUNT

Date bonds are retired	Debit	Credit
Bonds payable (−L)	101,000	
Loss on bond call (+E, −SE)	1,000	
Cash (−A)		102,000

Assets	=	Liabilities	+	Stockholders' Equity
Cash −102,000		Bonds payable −101,000		Loss on bond call (+E) −1,000

In some cases, a company may elect to retire bonds early by purchasing them on the open market, just as an investor would. This approach is necessary when the bonds do not have a call feature. Even when the bonds have a call feature, retiring them by purchasing them on the open market is attractive when the cost of doing so is less than the cost of paying the call premium. What could cause the price of a bond to fall? The most common cause is a rise in interest rates. As you may have noticed during our discussion of present values, **bond prices move in the opposite direction of interest rates.** If interest rates go up, bond prices fall, and vice versa. If interest rates go up enough, a company may decide that it makes good economic sense to retire its bonds early by purchasing them on the open market regardless of whether the bonds have a call feature.

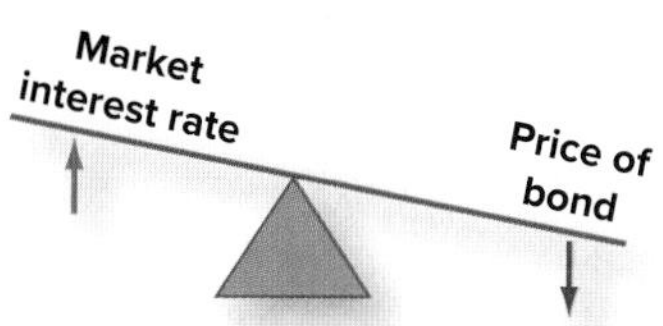

FOCUS ON CASH FLOWS

Bond Transactions and the Statement of Cash Flows

LEARNING OBJECTIVE 10-8

Explain how bond securities are reported on the statement of cash flows.

The cash a company receives when it issues bonds is reported as a cash inflow from financing activities on the statement of cash flows. The repayment of principal is reported as a cash outflow from financing activities. Many students are surprised to learn that the payment of interest is not reported as a financing activity on the statement of cash flows. Interest expense is reported on the income statement and is considered a cost of doing business during each accounting period. As a result, and as discussed further in Chapter 12, GAAP requires that cash paid for interest payments be reported as an operating activity on the statement of cash flows.

Transaction	Where Reported on Cash Flow Statement
Cash paid for interest	− Operating Activities
Cash received when bonds are issued	+ Financing Activities
Cash paid when bonds mature or are retired	− Financing Activities

Focus Company Analysis Below is an excerpt from **Amazon**'s cash flow statement showing its financing activities. The excerpt reflects the cash inflows and outflows Amazon experienced during the period associated with issuing and paying back debt. Analysts are particularly interested in the financing activities section of the statement of cash flows because it provides important insights about the capital structure of a company.

MariaX/Shutterstock

AMAZON

REAL WORLD EXCERPT:
Statement of Cash Flows

AMAZON.COM, INC.
CONSOLIDATED STATEMENTS OF CASH FLOWS
(in millions)

	Year Ended December 31,		
	2018	**2019**	**2020**
FINANCING ACTIVITIES:			
Proceeds from short-term debt, and other	$ 886	$ 1,402	$ 6,796
Repayments of short-term debt, and other	(813)	(1,518)	(6,177)
Proceeds from long-term debt	182	871	10,525
Repayments of long-term debt	(155)	(1,166)	(1,553)
Principal repayments of finance leases	(7,449)	(9,628)	(10,642)
Principal repayments of financing obligations	(337)	(27)	(53)
Net cash provided by (used in) financing activities	(7,686)	(10,066)	(1,104)

DEMONSTRATION CASE

(*Try to answer the questions below before reading the suggested solution that follows.*) To raise funds to build a new plant, the managers of Zeus Company decide to issue bonds. The bond prospectus states the following:

Face value of the bonds: $100,000.
Date of issue: January 1, 2022; due in 10 years.
Coupon rate: 12 percent per year, payable semiannually on June 30 and December 31.

The bonds were sold on January 1, 2022, at 106 percent of face value. Assume the annual market rate of interest on the date of issue was 11 percent.

Required:

1. How much cash did Zeus Company receive from the sale of the bonds? Show computations.
2. Were the bonds issued at a discount or a premium? What was the amount of the discount or premium?
3. How much cash does Zeus owe bondholders for interest on June 30, 2022?
4. Assume Zeus uses the effective-interest amortization method. What amount of interest expense will Zeus recognize on June 30, 2022?

SUGGESTED SOLUTION

1. Sale price of the bonds: $100,000 × 1.06 = $106,000.
2. The bonds were issued at a premium. The amount of the premium was $6,000 ($106,000 – $100,000).
3. Cash paid for interest on June 30, 2022: $100,000 × (12% × ½ year) = $6,000.
4. Interest expense recognized on June 30, 2022: $106,000 × (11% × ½ year) = $5,830.

LEARNING OBJECTIVE 10-4

Report bonds payable and interest expense for bond securities issued at a discount.

Chapter Supplement

Accounting for Bonds without a Discount Account or Premium Account

In this chapter supplement we duplicate the text from Chapter 10 but show all journal entries without the bond discount or bond premium accounts.

Bonds Issued at a Discount

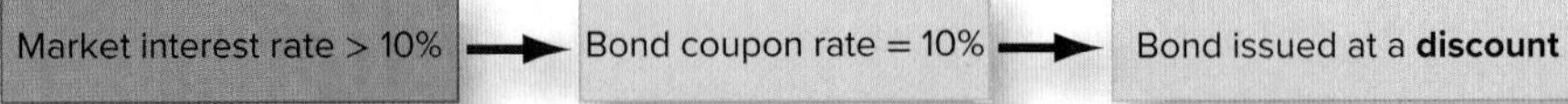

Bonds sell at a discount when the market interest rate is greater than the coupon rate. To illustrate, let's assume that the market interest rate is 12 percent on January 1, 2022, when **Amazon** sells its bonds (which have a face value of $100,000). The bonds mature in two years and have a coupon rate of 10 percent. Interest is payable twice a year on June 30 and December 31. Because the coupon rate (10 percent) is less than the market interest rate (12 percent) on the date of issuance, the bonds sell at a discount.

To compute what investors will be willing to pay for the bonds given the difference in interest rates, we can use the tables in Appendix E. The number of periods is four and the interest rate is the market interest rate per period; in this case, 6 percent (12% × ½ year). With this information, we can compute the cash issue price of the Amazon bonds as follows:

From Table E.1:
interest rate (i) = 6%
periods (n) = 4
Factor = 0.79209
From Table E.2:
interest rate (i) = 6%
periods (n) = 4
Factor = 3.46511
Using Calculator:
rate (i) = 6
periods (n) = 4
pmt = −$5,000,
FV = −$100,000
Using Excel:
Rate (i) = 0.06
Nper (n) = 4
Pmt = −$5,000,
Fv = −$100,000

	Present Value
Single principal payment at maturity: $100,000 × 0.79209	$79,209
+ Annuity cash interest payment: $5,000 × 3.46511	17,326
Issue (sale) price of bonds	$96,535

Thus, if the market interest rate is 12 percent on the date of issuance, investors will be willing to pay Amazon $96,535 for the bonds. Some people refer to this price as 96.5, which indicates the selling price was 96.5 percent of the bond's face value (96.5 = $96,535 ÷ $100,000).

There are two acceptable methods for recording a bond that is sold at a discount; both result in the same dollar value being reported on a company's balance sheet. The first method ***explicitly*** keeps track of the bond discount by incorporating it into the journal entries. The second method ***implicitly*** keeps track of the bond discount but does not incorporate it into the journal entries. Regardless of the method used, the dollar value reported on the balance sheet (the bond payable book value) is identical, as shown in the example below. Using both methods, the journal entries to record the sale of Amazon's bonds issued at a discount are:

Tip Regardless of whether a bond discount account is used, the dollar amounts reported on a company's balance sheet are the same.

WITH DISCOUNT ACCOUNT

January 1, 2022	Debit	Credit
Cash (+A)	96,535	
Bond discount (−L)	3,465	
Bonds payable (+L)		100,000

Assets		=	Liabilities		+	Stockholders' Equity
Cash	+96,535		Bonds payable	+100,000		
			Bond discount	−3,465		

Bonds payable book value: **$96,535**
($100,000 − $3,465)

WITHOUT DISCOUNT ACCOUNT

January 1, 2022	Debit	Credit
Cash (+A)	96,535	
Bonds payable (+L)		96,535

Assets		=	Liabilities		+	Stockholders' Equity
Cash	+96,535		Bonds payable	+96,535		

Bonds payable book value: **$96,535**

Bond discount is sometimes referred to as a contra-liability account since it is debited when the bonds are issued and shown as a negative number under liabilities. This account is not separately disclosed on Amazon's balance sheet. Instead, the balance sheet reports the bonds payable at their book value ($96,535), which is the face value of the bonds less the unamortized discount ($100,000 − $3,465). Note that reporting bonds payable at their book value results in the same amount being reported on the balance sheet ($96,535), regardless of whether a bond discount is explicitly recorded in the journal entry.

While Amazon received only $96,535 when it sold the bonds, it must repay $100,000 when the bonds mature. The $3,465 of additional cash that Amazon must pay at maturity is incrementally reflected in interest expense and added to the book value of the liability each period over the life of the bond. This causes interest expense to reflect the **market interest rate** (also referred to as the **effective interest rate**), while the cash being paid to bondholders each period reflects the **coupon rate.** The accounting method used to record interest expense is referred to as the **effective-interest amortization** method.

Reporting Interest Expense on Bonds Issued at a Discount Using Effective-Interest Amortization (without Discount Account)

Under the effective-interest amortization method, a company computes interest expense in a given period by multiplying the bonds payable book value times the market rate of interest on the date of issuance. When bonds are issued at a discount, using a market interest rate that is greater than the coupon rate results in interest expense each period being greater than the cash owed for interest each period. The difference between interest expense and the cash owed for interest is the amount of the bond discount amortized during the period. This process can be summarized as follows:

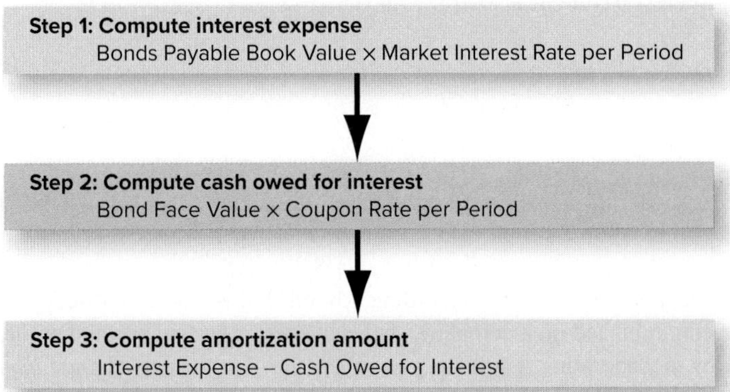

Recall that the cash owed for interest is computed by multiplying the bond's face value ($100,000) by the coupon rate per period (10% × ½ year). Thus, **Amazon** owes bondholders cash of $5,000 each June 30 and again on December 31. The first interest payment on the bonds is made on June 30, 2022. Following the three steps outlined above, interest expense and the amount of the bond discount amortized are:

Step 1: **Interest expense:** $96,535 × (0.12 × ½ year) = **$5,792**

Step 2: **Cash owed for interest:** $100,000 × (0.10 × ½ year) = **$5,000**

Step 3: **Amortized amount:** $5,792 – $5,000 = **$792**

The journal entry Amazon would enter is:

June 30, 2022	Debit	Credit
Interest expense (+E, –SE)	5,792	
Bonds payable (+L)		792
Cash (–A)		5,000

Effective-interest amortization causes these amounts to change each period because the book value of the bonds changes each period.

Assets		=	Liabilities		+	Equity	
Cash	–5,000		Bonds payable	+792		Interest expense (+E)	–5,792

Bonds payable book value: **$97,327** ($96,535 + $792)

Each period, the amortization of the bond discount increases the bond's book value, bringing it closer to the $100,000 that is due at maturity. The amortization of the bond discount can be thought of as the amount of interest earned by the bondholders in a given period that will be paid to them when the bonds mature. During the first interest period, Amazon's bondholders earned interest of $5,792 but received only $5,000 in cash. The additional $792 was added to the book value of the bond and will be paid to bondholders when the bonds mature and investors receive the full face value ($100,000).

Interest expense for the next interest period must reflect the change in the bonds payable book value. Amazon calculates interest expense for the second half of 2022 by multiplying the bonds payable book value on June 30, 2022 ($97,327) by the market rate of interest per period [$97,327 × (12% × ½ year) = $5,840]. With interest expense equal to $5,840 and cash owed for interest equal to $5,000, the amount of the bond discount amortized on December 31, 2022, is $840:

December 31, 2022	Debit	Credit
Interest expense (+E, −SE)	5,840	
Bonds payable (+L)		840
Cash (−A)		5,000

Assets		=	Liabilities		+	Stockholders' Equity	
Cash	−5,000		Bonds payable	+840		Interest expense (+E)	−5,840

Bonds payable book value: **$98,167**
($96,535 + $792 + $840)

Notice that interest expense for December 31, 2022, is more than interest expense for June 30, 2022. Amazon effectively borrowed more money during the second half of the year because of the unpaid interest accrued during the first half of the year. Because of the amortization of the bond discount, the book value of the bond and interest expense **increase** each year during the life of the bond. This process can be illustrated with the amortization schedule shown below:

BOND AMORTIZATION SCHEDULE: ISSUED AT A DISCOUNT

	(a)	(b)	(c)	(d)
	Face × Coupon Rate/Period	Beginning of Period Book Value × Market Rate/Period	Absolute Difference between (a) and (b)	Beginning of Period Book Value + (c)
Date	Cash Owed for Interest	Interest Expense	Amortization of Bond Discount	Bonds Payable (book value)
01/01/2022				$ 96,535
06/30/2022	$5,000	$5,792	$792	97,327
12/31/2022	5,000	5,840	840	98,167
06/30/2023	5,000	5,890	890	99,057
12/31/2023	5,000	5,943	943	100,000

Note that:

- Cash owed for interest (column a) is computed by multiplying the bond's face value by the coupon rate per period.
- Interest expense (column b) is computed by multiplying the book value of the bonds at the beginning of the period (column d) by the market interest rate. Note that the book value of a bond at the beginning of a period is the book value of the bond at the end of the previous period.
- Amortization of the bond discount is computed by subtracting cash owed for interest (column a) from interest expense (column b).
- The new book value of the bonds (column d) is computed by adding amortization of the bond discount (column c) to the book value at the beginning of the period.

In summary, under the effective-interest amortization method, interest expense changes each accounting period as the book value of the bonds changes each accounting period.

PAUSE FOR FEEDBACK

Calculating the cash paid to investors each period and interest expense each period requires investors to know the coupon rate, the market rate of interest, and the carrying value of the bonds at the beginning of each period. Let's practice calculating the cash paid to investors and interest expense before we move on.

SELF-STUDY QUIZ

Assume that **Amazon** issued bonds with a face value of $100,000 and a coupon rate of 5 percent. The bonds mature in 10 years and pay interest annually. The bonds were sold when the annual market interest rate was 6 percent at a price of $92,640.

1. What amount of cash was owed for interest at the end of the first year?
2. Using the effective-interest amortization method, what amount of interest expense would Amazon report at the end of the first year?

After you have completed your answers, check them below.

GUIDED HELP 10-4

For additional step-by-step instruction on how to account for a bond issued at a discount, go to mhhe.com/libby_gh10-4.

Related Homework: M10-5, E10-3, E10-4, E10-7, E10-9, E10-10, P10-3, P10-4, P10-6, P10-8

LEARNING OBJECTIVE 10-5

Report bonds payable and interest expense for bond securities issued at a premium.

Bonds Issued at a Premium

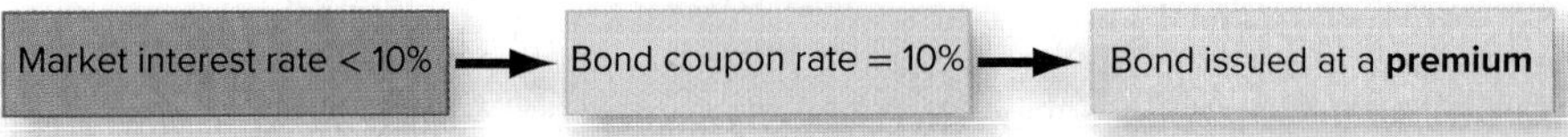

Recall that bonds sell at a **discount** when the market interest rate is greater than the bond's coupon rate. When the market interest rate is less than the bond's coupon rate, the bonds sell at a premium. To demonstrate how to account for bonds issued at a **premium,** let's use the same **Amazon** example as before but assume that the market interest rate is now 8 percent while the coupon rate remains the same, at 10 percent. Like before, the bonds are issued on January 1, 2022; pay interest semiannually; and mature in two years.

The present value of the bonds described above can be computed from the tables contained in Appendix E using the factor for four periods and an interest rate of 4 percent per period (8% × ½ year):

	Present Value
Single principal payment at maturity: $100,000 × 0.85480	$ 85,480
+ Annuity cash interest payment: $5,000 × 3.62990	18,150
Issue (sale) price of bonds	$103,630

From Table E.1:
interest rate (i) = 4%
periods (n) = 4
Factor = 0.85480
From Table E.2:
interest rate (i) = 4%
periods (n) = 4
Factor = 3.62990
Using Calculator:
rate (i) = 4
periods (n) = 4
pmt = −$5,000,
FV = −$100,000
Using Excel:
Rate (i) = 0.04
Nper (n) = 4
Pmt = −$5,000,
Fv = −$100,000

Solutions to SELF-STUDY QUIZ

1. Cash owed for interest: $100,000 × 5% = **$5,000**
2. Interest expense: $92,640 × 6% = **$5,558**

Accounting for bonds issued at a premium is similar to accounting for bonds issued at a discount. Companies can explicitly use a bond premium account in their journal entries or implicitly keep track of the premium amount. We show both side-by-side below, and then, as we did with bond discounts, we present all subsequent journal entries without using a bond premium account. The January 1, issuance of Amazon's bonds at a premium would be recorded as follows:

Tip Regardless of whether a bond premium account is used, the dollar amounts reported on a company's balance sheet are the same.

WITH PREMIUM ACCOUNT

January 1, 2022	Debit	Credit
Cash (+A)	103,630	
Bond premium (+L)		3,630
Bonds payable (+L)		100,000

Assets		=	Liabilities		+	Stockholders' Equity
Cash	+103,630		Bonds payable	+100,000		
			Bond premium	+3,630		

Bonds payable book value: **$103,630** ($100,000 + $3,630)

WITHOUT PREMIUM ACCOUNT

January 1, 2022	Debit	Credit
Cash (+A)	103,630	
Bonds payable (+L)		103,630

Assets		=	Liabilities		+	Stockholders' Equity
Cash	+103,630		Bonds payable	+103,630		

Bonds payable book value: **$103,630**

Bond premium is sometimes referred to as an adjunct-liability account. Like the bond discount account, the bond premium account is not separately disclosed on Amazon's balance sheet. Instead, the balance sheet reports the bonds payable at their book value ($103,630), which is their face value plus the unamortized premium ($100,000 + $3,630). Note that reporting bonds payable at its book value results in the same amount being reported on the balance sheet ($103,630) regardless of whether a bond premium is explicitly recorded in the journal entry.

Reporting Interest Expense on Bonds Issued at a Premium Using Effective-Interest Amortization (without Premium Account)

The recorded premium of $3,630 must be apportioned to each interest period so that interest expense reflects the market (effective) interest rate that Amazon is actually paying. To compute interest expense and the amount of the premium to be amortized each period, we follow the same three steps that we followed to compute these amounts when the bonds were issued at a discount:

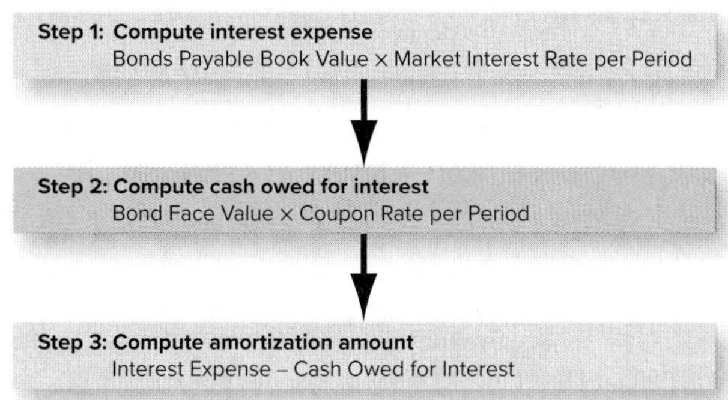

Step 1: **Interest expense:** $103,630 × (0.08 × ½ year) = $4,145

Step 2: **Cash owed for interest:** $100,000 × (0.10 × ½ year) = $5,000

Step 3: **Amortized amount:** $4,145 – $5,000 = –$855

The journal entry Amazon would enter is:

June 30, 2022	Debit	Credit
Interest expense (+E, –SE)	4,145	
Bonds payable (–L)	855	
Cash (–A)		5,000

Assets		=	Liabilities		+	Stockholders' Equity	
Cash	–5000		Bonds payable	–855		Interest expense (+E)	–4,145

Bonds payable book value: **$102,775** ($103,630 – $855)

The basic difference between effective-interest amortization of a bond discount and a bond premium is that the amortization of a discount **increases** the book value of the liability and the amortization of a premium **decreases** it. Both serve the same purpose: to bring the liability to the bond's face value at the maturity date. This is illustrated in the figure below.

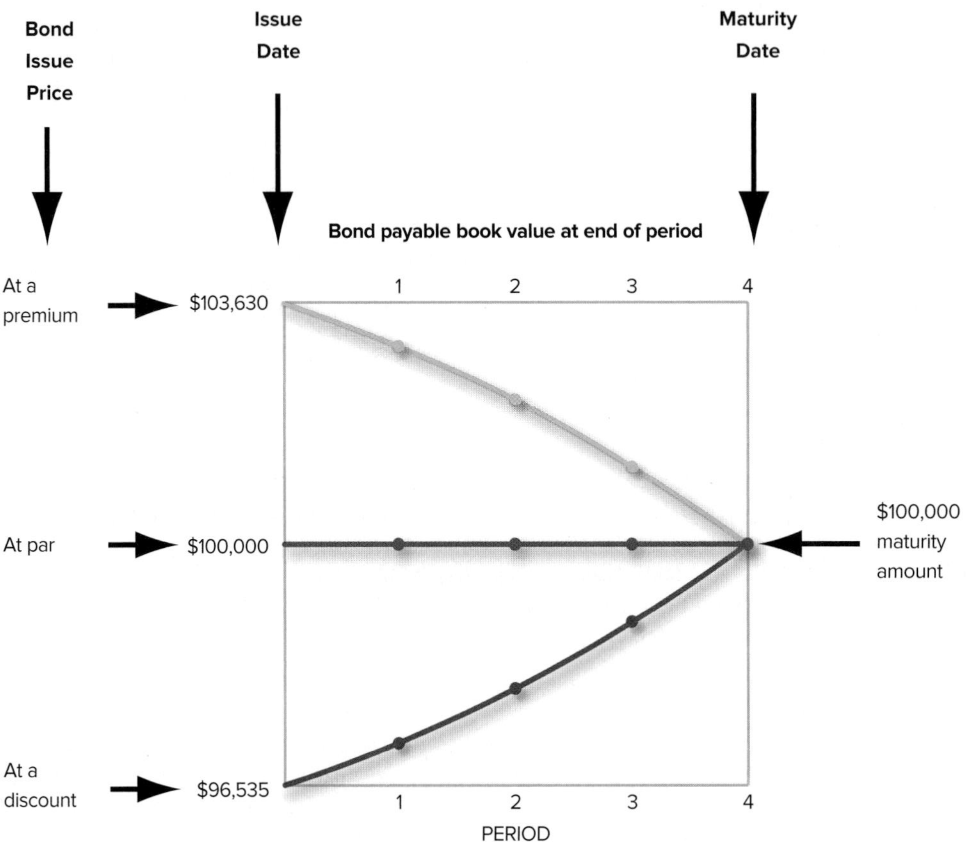

The following schedule illustrates the amortization of a premium over the life of a bond.

BOND AMORTIZATION SCHEDULE: ISSUED AT A PREMIUM

	(a)	(b)	(c)	(d)
	Face × Coupon Rate/Period	Beginning of Period Book Value × Market Rate/Period	Absolute Difference between (a) and (b)	Beginning of Period Book Value – (c)
Date	Cash Owed for Interest	Interest Expense	Amortization of Bond Premium	Bonds Payable (book value)
01/01/2022				$103,630
06/30/2022	$5,000	$4,145	$855	102,775
12/31/2022	5,000	4,111	889	101,886
06/30/2023	5,000	4,075	925	100,962
12/31/2023	5,000	4,038	962	100,000

Coupon rate/period (10% × 1/2)

Market rate/period (8% × 1/2)

Book value moves toward face value

Regardless of whether a company issues bonds at par, at a discount, or at a premium, the company will enter the same journal entry when the bonds mature. For our Amazon example, the journal entry would be:

December 31, 2023	Debit	Credit
Bonds payable (−L)	100,000	
Cash (−A)		100,000

Assets		=	Liabilities		+	Stockholders' Equity
Cash	−100,000		Bonds payable	−100,000		

PAUSE FOR FEEDBACK

Calculating the cash paid to investors each period and interest expense each period requires investors to know the coupon rate, the market rate of interest, and the carrying value of the bonds at the beginning of each period. Let's practice calculating the cash paid to investors and interest expense before we move on.

SELF-STUDY QUIZ

Assume that **Amazon** issued bonds with a face value of $100,000 and a coupon rate of 9 percent. The bonds mature in 10 years and pay interest annually. The bonds were sold when the annual market interest rate was 8 percent at a price of $106,710.

1. What amount of cash was owed for interest at the end of the first year?
2. Using the effective-interest amortization method, what amount of interest expense would Amazon report at the end of the first year?

After you have completed your answers, check them below.

GUIDED HELP 10-5

For additional step-by-step instruction on how to account for a bond issued at a premium without a premium account, go to mhhe.com/libby_gh10-5.

Related Homework: M10-8, E10-3, E10-4, E10-14, E10-15, E10-16, P10-3, P10-4, P10-9, P10-10, P10-12

CHAPTER TAKE-AWAYS

10-1. Describe the characteristics of bond securities. p. 525

Bond securities are commonly referred to as just "bonds." Companies issue bonds to raise long-term capital. Bonds offer a number of advantages compared to stock, including the tax deductibility of interest up to a cap and the fact that control of a company is not diluted when it issues bonds instead of stock. Bonds do carry additional risk, however, because interest and principal payments are not discretionary.

10-2. Report bonds payable and interest expense for bond securities issued at par. p. 531

Three types of events must be recorded over the life of a typical bond: (1) the receipt of cash when the bond is sold, (2) the periodic payment of interest, and (3) the repayment of the bond's face value at maturity. The amount of cash a company receives when it issues a bond is the present value of the future cash flows associated with the bond. When the market interest rate and the coupon rate are the same, the bond will sell at par (face value).

Solutions to SELF-STUDY QUIZ

1. Cash owed for interest: $100,000 × 9% = **$9,000**
2. Interest expense: $106,710 × 8% = **$8,537**

10-3. Compute and analyze the times interest earned ratio. **p. 533**

The times interest earned ratio reflects the amount of income earned for each dollar of interest expense. It is a measure of a company's ability to meet its interest obligations. It is computed by comparing interest expense to net income after adding back interest expense and income tax expense.

10-4. Report bonds payable and interest expense for bond securities issued at a discount. **p. 534**

Bonds are sold at a discount whenever the coupon rate is less than the market interest rate. A discount is the difference between the selling price of a bond and the bond's face value when the bond is sold for less than its face amount. Companies have the option of explicitly keeping track of the bond discount by incorporating it into journal entries or implicitly keeping track of the bond discount and not including it in journal entries. Regardless, the same amount is reported as bonds payable on a company's balance sheet.

10-5. Report bonds payable and interest expense for bond securities issued at a premium. **p. 538**

Bonds are sold at a premium whenever the coupon rate is greater than the market interest rate. A premium is the difference between the selling price of a bond and the bond's face value when the bond is sold for more than its face value. Companies have the option of explicitly keeping track of the bond premium by incorporating it into journal entries or implicitly keeping track of the bond premium and not including it in journal entries. Regardless, the same amount is reported as bonds payable on a company's balance sheet.

10-6. Compute and analyze the debt-to-equity ratio. **p. 544**

The debt-to-equity ratio compares the amount of debt to the amount of equity on a company's balance sheet. It is an important ratio because of the high risk associated with debt capital; debt capital requires interest and principal payments.

10-7. Report the early retirement of bond securities. **p. 544**

A company may retire a bond before its maturity date, by either purchasing the bond in the open market or activating a call feature if the bond contains such a feature. The difference between the book value of the bond and the amount paid to retire the bond is reported as a gain or loss on the company's income statement.

10-8. Explain how bond securities are reported on the statement of cash flows. **p. 545**

Cash received from issuing a bond and cash paid to retire a bond at maturity are financing cash flows. Cash paid for interest is an operating cash flow.

KEY RATIOS

Times interest earned ratio reflects the amount of income earned for each dollar of interest expense. It is a measure of a company's ability to meet its interest obligations. The ratio is computed as follows (see the "Key Ratio Analysis" box in the Reporting Bond Transactions section):

$$\text{Times Interest Earned} = \frac{\text{Net Income} + \text{Interest Expense} + \text{Income Tax Expense}}{\text{Interest Expense}}$$

Debt-to-equity ratio compares the amount of debt on a company's balance sheet to the amount of equity. The ratio is computed as follows (see the "Key Ratio Analysis" box in the Reporting Bond Transactions section):

$$\text{Debt-to-Equity} = \frac{\text{Total Liabilities}}{\text{Stockholders' Equity}}$$

FINDING FINANCIAL INFORMATION

Balance Sheet

Bonds are normally listed as long-term liabilities. An exception occurs when the bonds are within one year of maturity, in which case they are reported as current liabilities with the title "Current Portion of Long-Term Debt."

Income Statement

Issuing bonds and retiring bonds do not affect the income statement. Recognizing interest expense and any gain or loss from early retirement does affect the income statement. Most companies report interest expense in a separate category on the income statement.

Statement of Cash Flows

Under Operating Activities
− Cash outflows for interest payments

Under Financing Activities
+ Cash inflows from issuing bonds
− Cash outflows from retiring bonds

Notes

Under Summary of Significant Accounting Policies
A brief description of how a company accounts for long-term liabilities, including bonds.

Under a Separate Note
Most companies include a separate note where they describe in more detail their accounting for long-term debt, including the type of debt, maturity dates, and interest rates. The note also typically describes any special features associated with the debt, such as whether bonds can be called early. Typically in a company's financial statements and footnotes, bonds are referred to as "notes."

KEY TERMS

Bond Certificate The document investors receive when they purchase bond securities. **p. 527**

Bond Discount The difference between the selling price of a bond and the bond's face value when the bond is sold for less than par. **p. 529**

Bond Premium The difference between the selling price of a bond and the bond's face value when the bond is sold for more than par. **p. 529**

Bond Principal (Face Value, Par Value, Maturity Value) The amount a company pays bondholders on the maturity date and the amount used to compute the bond's periodic cash interest payments. **p. 525**

Callable Bonds Bonds containing a call feature that allows the bond issuer the option of retiring the bonds early. **p. 527**

Convertible Bonds Bonds that may be converted to other securities of the issuer (usually common stock). **p. 526**

Coupon Rate (Stated Rate, Contract Rate, Nominal Rate) The interest rate specified on a bond, and the rate used to compute the bond's periodic cash interest payment. **p. 526**

Covenants Legally binding agreements between a bond issuer and a bondholder. **p. 527**

Debenture Unsecured bonds; no assets are pledged as guarantee of repayment at maturity. **p. 527**

Effective-Interest Amortization A method of amortizing a bond discount or bond premium that reflects the effective interest rate a company pays bondholders over the life of a bond. **p. 535, 548**

Indenture A legal document that describes all the details of a debt security to potential buyers. **p. 527**

Market Interest Rate (Yield, Effective Interest Rate) The rate of return investors demand for a company's bonds on the date the bonds are issued, and the rate used to compute the bond's interest expense each period. **p. 529**

Prospectus A regulatory filing that describes all the details of a debt or equity security to potential buyers. **p. 527**

Secured Bond Specific assets are pledged as a guarantee of repayment at maturity. **p. 526**

Straight-Line Amortization An alternative method of amortizing bond discounts and premiums that allocates an equal dollar amount to each interest period. It is only permitted by GAAP under specific circumstances. **p. 543**

Trustee An independent party appointed to represent the bondholders. **p. 527**

QUESTIONS

1. From the perspective of the issuer, what are some advantages of issuing bonds instead of stock?
2. What are the primary characteristics of a bond? For what purposes are bonds usually issued?
3. What is the difference between an unsecured and a secured bond?
4. Differentiate between a bond indenture and a bond prospectus.
5. What is a bond covenant?
6. Differentiate between a bond's coupon rate and the market rate of interest.
7. Explain what determines whether a bond is issued at a discount or a premium.
8. When calculating the present value of a bond's future cash flows, do investors use the coupon rate or market interest rate as the discount rate?
9. What is the book value of a bond?
10. What is the formula used for calculating the cash payment bond investors will receive for interest each period? What is the formula used to calculate interest expense each period?
11. How is the debt-to-equity ratio computed? What does the debt-to-equity ratio tell you?
12. When market interest rates increase, do bond prices increase or decrease?

MULTIPLE-CHOICE QUESTIONS

1. Annual interest expense for a bond continues to increase over the life of the bonds. Which of the following explains this?
   a. The market rate of interest has increased since the bonds were sold.
   b. The coupon rate has increased since the bonds were sold.
   c. The bonds were sold at a discount.
   d. The bonds were sold at a premium.
2. Which of the following is an advantage of issuing bonds when compared to issuing additional shares of stock in order to raise capital?
   a. When the bonds are issued, bondholders obtain voting rights.
   b. Bonds pay smaller dividends than stock.
   c. Up to a cap, interest expense is tax deductible.
   d. All of the above are advantages associated with bonds.
3. A bond with a face value of $100,000 has a coupon rate of 8 percent. The bond matures in 10 years and pays interest annually. When the bond is issued, the market rate of interest is 10 percent. What amount will investors pay for this bond when it is issued?
   a. $100,000
   b. $87,711
   c. $49,157
   d. $113,421
4. Which account would **not** be included in the debt-to-equity ratio calculation?
   a. Unearned Revenue.
   b. Retained Earnings.
   c. Income Taxes Payable.
   d. All of the above are included.
5. Which of the following is **false** when a bond is issued at a premium?
   a. The bond will issue for an amount above its face value.
   b. The bond's book value will be greater than the bond's face value.
   c. Interest expense will exceed the cash interest payments.
   d. All of the above are false.
6. A bond with a face value of $100,000 was issued for $93,500 on January 1 of this year. The stated rate of interest was 8 percent and the market rate of interest was 10 percent when the bond was sold. Interest is paid annually. How much interest will be paid on December 31 of this year?
   a. $10,000
   b. $8,000
   c. $7,480
   d. $9,350
7. To determine whether a bond will be sold at a premium, at a discount, or at face value, one must know which of the following pairs of information?
   a. Face value and the coupon rate on the date the bond is issued.
   b. Face value and the market rate of interest on the date the bond is issued.
   c. The coupon rate and the market rate of interest on the date the bond is issued.
   d. The coupon rate and the stated rate on the date the bond is issued.
8. When using the effective-interest method of amortization, interest expense reported in the income statement is impacted by the
   a. Face value of the bonds.
   b. Coupon rate stated in the bond certificate.
   c. Market rate of interest on the date the bonds were issued.
   d. Both (a) and (b).
9. A bond with a face value of $100,000 is sold on January 1. The bond has a coupon rate of 10 percent and matures in 10 years. When the bond was issued, the market rate of interest was 10 percent. On December 31, the market rate of interest increased to 11 percent. What amount should be reported on December 31 as the bond liability on the balance sheet?
   a. $100,000
   b. $94,112
   c. $94,460
   d. $87,562
10. When using the effective-interest method of amortization, the book value of a bond changes by what amount on each interest payment date?
    a. Interest expense.
    b. Cash interest payment.
    c. The difference between interest expense and the cash interest payment.
    d. None of the above.

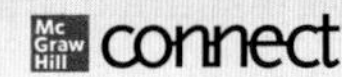

MINI-EXERCISES

Finding Financial Information

M10-1
LO10-1, 10-2, 10-8

For each of the following items, specify whether the information would most likely be found on the balance sheet, the income statement, the statement of cash flows, or in the notes to the statements.

1. The amount of a bond liability.
2. A description of any bond covenants.
3. The coupon rates associated with bond issuances.
4. Interest expense for the period.
5. The maturity dates associated with bond issuances.
6. Cash interest paid for the period.

Computing the Price of a Bond Issued at Par

M10-2
LO10-2

Williams Company plans to issue bonds with a face value of $600,000 and a coupon rate of 8 percent. The bonds will mature in 10 years and pay interest semiannually every June 30 and December 31. All of the bonds are sold on January 1 of this year. Determine the issuance price of the bonds assuming an annual market rate of interest of 8 percent.

Understanding Financial Ratios

M10-3
LO10-3, 10-6

The debt-to-equity and times interest earned ratios were discussed in this chapter. Which is a better indicator of a company's ability to meet its required interest payments? Explain.

Computing the Times Interest Earned Ratio

M10-4
LO10-3

Oak Corporation's financial statements for the current year showed the following:

Income Statement	
Revenues	$800,000
Expenses	(620,000)
Interest expense	(12,600)
Pretax income	167,400
Income tax (21%)	(35,154)
Net income	$132,246

Compute Oak's times interest earned ratio.

Computing the Price of a Bond Issued at a Discount

M10-5
LO10-4

Trew Company plans to issue bonds with a face value of $900,000 and a coupon rate of 6 percent. The bonds will mature in 10 years and pay interest semiannually every June 30 and December 31. All of the bonds are sold on January 1 of this year. Determine the issuance price of the bonds assuming an annual market rate of interest of 8.5 percent.

Recording the Issuance and Interest Payments of a Bond Issued at a Discount (with Discount Account)

M10-6
LO10-4

Coffman Company sold bonds with a face value of $1,000,000 for $940,248. The bonds have a coupon rate of 10 percent, mature in 10 years, and pay interest semiannually every June 30 and December 31. All of the bonds were sold on January 1 of this year. Using a discount account, record the sale of the bonds on January 1 and the payment of interest on June 30 of this year. Coffman uses the effective-interest amortization method. Assume an annual market rate of interest of 11 percent.

M10-7 LO10-4

(Chapter Supplement) Recording the Issuance and Interest Payments of a Bond Issued at a Discount (without Discount Account)

Coffman Company sold bonds with a face value of $1,000,000 for $940,248. The bonds have a coupon rate of 10 percent, mature in 10 years, and pay interest semiannually every June 30 and December 31. All of the bonds were sold on January 1 of this year. Record the sale of the bonds on January 1 and the payment of interest on June 30 of this year, without the use of a discount account. Coffman uses the effective-interest amortization method. Assume an annual market rate of interest of 11 percent.

M10-8 LO10-5

Computing the Price of a Bond Issued at a Premium

Waterhouse Company plans to issue bonds with a face value of $500,000 and a coupon rate of 10 percent. The bonds will mature in 10 years and pay interest semiannually every June 30 and December 31. All of the bonds are sold on January 1 of this year. Determine the issuance price of the bonds assuming an annual market rate of interest of 8 percent.

M10-9 LO10-5

Recording the Issuance and Interest Payments of a Bond Issued at a Premium (with Premium Account)

Wapato Company sold bonds with a face value of $850,000 for $909,701. The bonds have a coupon rate of 8 percent, mature in 10 years, and pay interest annually every December 31. All of the bonds were sold on January 1 of this year. Using a premium account, record the sale of the bonds on January 1 and the payment of interest on December 31 of this year. Wapato uses the effective-interest amortization method. Assume an annual market rate of interest of 7 percent.

M10-10 LO10-5

(Chapter Supplement) Recording the Issuance and Interest Payments of a Bond Issued at a Premium (without Premium Account)

Wapato Company sold bonds with a face value of $850,000 for $909,701. The bonds have a coupon rate of 8 percent, mature in 10 years, and pay interest annually every December 31. All of the bonds were sold on January 1 of this year. Record the sale of the bonds on January 1 and the payment of interest on December 31 of this year, without the use of a premium account. Wapato uses the effective-interest amortization method. Assume an annual market rate of interest of 7 percent.

M10-11 LO10-4

Recording the Issuance and Interest Payments of a Bond Issued at a Discount (Straight-Line Amortization with a Discount Account)

Alana Company sold bonds with a face value of $600,000 for $580,000. The bonds have a coupon rate of 10 percent, mature in 10 years, and pay interest semiannually every June 30 and December 31. All of the bonds were sold on January 1 of this year. Using a discount account, record the sale of the bonds on January 1 and the payment of interest on June 30 of this year. Alana uses the straight-line amortization method.

M10-12 LO10-4

(Chapter Supplement) Recording the Issuance and Interest Payments of a Bond Issued at a Discount (Straight-Line Amortization without a Discount Account)

Alana Company sold bonds with a face value of $600,000 for $580,000. The bonds have a coupon rate of 10 percent, mature in 10 years, and pay interest semiannually every June 30 and December 31. All of the bonds were sold on January 1 of this year. Record the sale of the bonds on January 1 and the payment of interest on June 30 of this year, without the use of a discount account. Alana uses the straight-line amortization method.

M10-13 LO10-7

Interest Rates and the Early Retirement of Debt

If interest rates fell after the issuance of a bond and the company decided to retire the debt early, would you expect the company to report a gain or loss on debt retirement? How would the company's balance sheet and income statement be affected?

M10-14 LO10-8

The Cash Flow Effects of Retiring Bonds and Paying Interest

In what section of the statement of cash flows would you find cash paid for principal when a bond matures? In what section would you find cash paid for interest each period?

EXERCISES

Interpreting Information Reported in the Business Press

E10-1
LO10-1
Apple

Apple recently issued a series of bonds with various maturity dates. The information below pertains to one of Apple's bonds:

Issuer	Coupon (%)	Maturity	Yield (%)
Apple	3.05	2029	3.29

Explain why investors would care about knowing the coupon rate and yield percentages. Assume that over the next several weeks the yield went down to 3.10. How would this decrease affect Apple's financial statements?

Evaluating Bond Features

E10-2
LO10-1
PepsiCo
Walt Disney

You are a personal financial planner working with a married couple in their early 40s who have decided to invest $100,000 in corporate bonds. You have found two bonds that you think will interest your clients. One is a zero coupon bond issued by **PepsiCo** with an effective interest rate of 9 percent and a maturity date of 2031. It is callable at par. The other is a **Walt Disney** bond that matures in 2093. It has an effective interest rate of 9.5 percent and is callable at 102 percent of par. Which of the two bonds is less likely to be called if interest rates fall over the next few years?

Computing Issue Prices of Bonds Sold at Par, at a Discount, and at a Premium

E10-3
LO10-2, 10-4, 10-5

LaTanya Corporation is planning to issue bonds with a face value of $100,000 and a coupon rate of 8 percent. The bonds mature in seven years. Interest is paid annually on December 31. All of the bonds will be sold on January 1 of this year.

Required:
Compute the issue (sales) price on January 1 of this year for each of the following independent cases (show computations):

a. **Case A:** Market interest rate (annual): 8 percent.
b. **Case B:** Market interest rate (annual): 6 percent.
c. **Case C:** Market interest rate (annual): 9 percent.

Computing Issue Prices of Bonds Sold at Par, at a Discount, and at a Premium

E10-4
LO10-2, 10-4, 10-5

Kalani Corporation is planning to issue bonds with a face value of $500,000 and a coupon rate of 6 percent. The bonds mature in 10 years and pay interest semiannually every June 30 and December 31. All of the bonds will be sold on January 1 of this year.

Required:
Compute the issue (sales) price on January 1 of this year for each of the following independent cases (show computations):

a. **Case A:** Market interest rate (annual): 4 percent.
b. **Case B:** Market interest rate (annual): 6 percent.
c. **Case C:** Market interest rate (annual): 8.5 percent.

Determining the Effects of Issuing Bonds on the Debt-to-Equity Ratio

E10-5
LO10-2, 10-6

On January 1 of this year, Denver Corporation sold bonds with a face value of $300,000 and a coupon rate of 6 percent. The bonds mature in 10 years and pay interest annually every December 31. At the time the bonds were issued, the annual market rate of interest was 6 percent. The company uses the effective-interest amortization method.

Required:

1. When the bonds were issued, did Denver's debt-to-equity ratio increase, decrease, or stay the same?
2. At the end of the first year, when Denver made its first interest payment to investors and recorded interest expense, did its debt-to-equity ratio increase, decrease, or stay the same?

E10-6 LO10-3, 10-6

Analyzing Financial Ratios

You have just started your first job as a financial analyst for a large stock brokerage company. Your boss, a senior analyst, has finished a detailed report evaluating bonds issued by two different companies. She stopped by your desk to ask for help and said: "I have compared two ratios for the companies and found something interesting." She went on to explain that the debt-to-equity ratio for Applied Engineering is much lower than the industry average and that the one for Innovative Engineering is much higher. On the other hand, the times interest earned ratio for Applied Engineering is much higher than the industry average, and the ratio for Innovative Engineering is much lower. Your boss then asked you to think about what the ratios indicate about the two companies so that she could include the explanation in her report. How would you respond to your boss?

E10-7 LO10-4 General Motors Corporation

Computing the Price of a Bond Issued at a Discount

Assume **General Motors Corporation** is planning to issue bonds with a face value of $250,000 and a coupon rate of 6 percent. The bonds mature in five years and pay interest semiannually every June 30 and December 31. All of the bonds were sold on January 1 of this year. Determine the issuance price of the bonds assuming an annual market rate of interest of 8 percent.

E10-8 LO10-4

Recording and Reporting a Bond Issued at a Discount (with Discount Account)

Denzel Corporation is planning to issue bonds with a face value of $600,000 and a coupon rate of 7.5 percent. The bonds mature in four years and pay interest semiannually every June 30 and December 31. All of the bonds were sold on January 1 of this year. Denzel uses the effective-interest amortization method and also uses a discount account. Assume an annual market rate of interest of 8.5 percent.

Required:

1. Provide the journal entry to record the issuance of the bonds.
2. Provide the journal entry to record the interest payment on June 30 of this year.
3. What bonds payable amount will Denzel report on its June 30 balance sheet?

E10-9 LO10-4

(Chapter Supplement) Recording and Reporting a Bond Issued at a Discount (without Discount Account)

Denzel Corporation is planning to issue bonds with a face value of $600,000 and a coupon rate of 7.5 percent. The bonds mature in four years and pay interest semiannually every June 30 and December 31. All of the bonds were sold on January 1 of this year. Denzel uses the effective-interest amortization method and does not use a discount account. Assume an annual market rate of interest of 8.5 percent.

Required:

1. Provide the journal entry to record the issuance of the bonds.
2. Provide the journal entry to record the interest payment on June 30 of this year.
3. What bond payable amount will Denzel report on its June 30 balance sheet?

E10-10 LO10-4

Preparing a Bond Amortization Schedule for a Bond Issued at a Discount and Determining Reported Amounts

On January 1 of this year, Ikuta Company issued a bond with a face value of $100,000 and a coupon rate of 5 percent. The bond matures in three years and pays interest every December 31. When the bond was issued, the annual market rate of interest was 6 percent. Ikuta uses the effective-interest amortization method.

Required:

1. Complete a bond amortization schedule for all three years of the bond's life.
2. What amounts will be reported on the income statement and balance sheet at the end of Year 1 and Year 2?

Interpreting a Bond Amortization Schedule

E10-11
LO10-4

Santa Corporation issued a bond on January 1 of this year with a face value of $1,000. The bond's coupon rate is 6 percent and interest is paid once a year on December 31. The bond matures in three years. The annual market rate of interest was 8 percent at the time the bond was sold. The following amortization schedule pertains to the bond issued:

Date	Cash Paid	Interest Expense	Amortization	Balance
1/1/20x1				948
12/31/20x1	60	76	16	964
12/31/20x2	60	77	17	981
12/31/20x3	60	79	19	1,000

Required:

1. What was the bond's issue price?
2. Did the bond sell at a discount or a premium? How much was the premium or discount?
3. What amount(s) should be shown on the balance sheet for bonds payable at 12/31/20×1 and 12/31/20x2.
4. Show how the following amounts were computed for Year 2: (*a*) $60, (*b*) $77, (*c*) $17, and (*d*) $981.

Explaining Why Debt Is Issued at a Price Other Than Par

E10-12
LO10-4, 10-5
American Airlines

A prior annual report of **American Airlines** contained the following note:

> The Company recorded the issuance of $775 million in bonds (net of $25 million discount) as long-term debt on the consolidated balance sheet. The bonds bear interest at fixed rates, with an average effective rate of 8.06 percent, and mature over various periods of time, with a final maturity in 2031.

After reading this note, an investor asked her financial advisor why the company didn't simply sell the notes for an effective yield that equaled the coupon rate, thereby avoiding the need to account for a small discount over the next 20 years. Prepare a written response to this question.

Recording and Reporting a Bond Issued at a Premium (with Premium Account)

E10-13
LO10-5

Park Corporation is planning to issue bonds with a face value of $2,000,000 and a coupon rate of 10 percent. The bonds mature in 10 years and pay interest semiannually every June 30 and December 31. All of the bonds were sold on January 1 of this year. Park uses the effective-interest amortization method and also uses a premium account. Assume an annual market rate of interest of 8.5 percent.

Required:

1. Provide the journal entry to record the issuance of the bonds.
2. Provide the journal entry to record the interest payment on June 30 of this year.
3. What bonds payable amount will Park report on its June 30 balance sheet?

(Chapter Supplement) Recording and Reporting a Bond Issued at a Premium (without Premium Account)

E10-14
LO10-5

Park Corporation is planning to issue bonds with a face value of $2,000,000 and a coupon rate of 10 percent. The bonds mature in 10 years and pay interest semiannually every June 30 and December 31. All of the bonds were sold on January 1 of this year. Park uses the effective-interest amortization method and does not use a premium account. Assume an annual market rate of interest of 8.5 percent.

Required:

1. Provide the journal entry to record the issuance of the bonds.
2. Provide the journal entry to record the interest payment on June 30 of this year.
3. What bonds payable amount will Park report on its June 30 balance sheet?

E10-15 LO10-5 **Preparing a Bond Amortization Schedule for a Bond Issued at a Premium and Determining Reported Amounts**

On January 1 of this year, Houston Company issued a bond with a face value of $10,000 and a coupon rate of 5 percent. The bond matures in three years and pays interest every December 31. When the bond was issued, the annual market rate of interest was 4 percent. Houston uses the effective-interest amortization method.

Required:

1. Complete a bond amortization schedule for all three years of the bond's life.
2. What amounts will be reported on the income statement and balance sheet at the end of Year 1 and Year 2?

E10-16 LO10-5, 10-8 **Recording and Analyzing the Cash Flow Effects of a Bond Issued at a Premium (with Premium Account)**

On January 1 of this year, LeBron Company issued bonds with a face value of $1 million and a coupon rate of 9 percent. The bonds mature in 10 years and pay interest semiannually every June 30 and December 31. When the bonds were issued, the annual market rate of interest was 8 percent. Lebron uses the effective-interest amortization method. Record the issuance of the bonds on January 1 of this year. How will LeBron's statement of cash flows be affected on January 1, June 30, and December 31 of this year?

E10-17 LO10-7 **Recording the Early Retirement of a Bond**

Several years ago, Tamika Company issued bonds with a face value of $1,000,000 at par. As a result of declining interest rates, the company has decided to call the bond at a call premium of 5 percent over par. Record the retirement of the bonds.

E10-18 LO10-7 **Recording the Early Retirement of a Bond Issued at a Discount (with Discount Account)**

Several years ago, Nicole Company issued bonds with a face value of $1,000,000 for $945,000. As a result of declining interest rates, the company has decided to call the bond at a call premium of 5 percent over par. The bonds have a current book value of $984,000. Record the retirement of the bonds, using a discount account.

E10-19 LO10-7 **(Chapter Supplement) Recording the Early Retirement of a Bond Issued at a Discount (without Discount Account)**

Several years ago, Nicole Company issued bonds with a face value of $1,000,000 for $945,000. As a result of declining interest rates, the company has decided to call the bond at a call premium of 5 percent over par. The bonds have a current book value of $984,000. Record the retirement of the bonds without using a discount account.

E10-20 LO10-4 **Recording and Reporting a Bond Issued at a Discount (Straight-Line Amortization with Discount Account)**

On January 1 of this year, Clearwater Corporation sold bonds with a face value of $750,000 and a coupon rate of 8 percent. The bonds mature in 10 years and pay interest annually every December 31. Clearwater uses the straight-line amortization method and also uses a discount account. Assume an annual market rate of interest of 9 percent.

Required:

1. Provide the journal entry to record the issuance of the bonds.
2. Provide the journal entry to record the interest payment on December 31 of this year.
3. What bonds payable amount will Clearwater report on its December 31 balance sheet?

E10-21 LO10-4 **(Chapter Supplement) Recording and Reporting a Bond Issued at a Discount (Straight-Line Amortization without Discount Account)**

On January 1 of this year, Clearwater Corporation sold bonds with a face value of $750,000 and a coupon rate of 8 percent. The bonds mature in 10 years and pay interest annually every December 31. Clearwater uses the straight-line amortization method and does not use a discount account. Assume an annual market rate of interest of 9 percent.

Required:
1. Provide the journal entry to record the issuance of the bonds.
2. Provide the journal entry to record the interest payment on December 31 of this year.
3. What bonds payable amount will Clearwater report on its December 31 balance sheet?

Recording and Reporting a Bond Issued at a Premium (Straight-Line Amortization with Premium Account)

E10-22
LO10-5

On January 1 of this year, Kona Corporation sold bonds with a face value of $1,400,000 and a coupon rate of 8 percent. The bonds mature in four years and pay interest semiannually every June 30 and December 31. Kona uses the straight-line amortization method and also uses a premium account. Assume an annual market rate of interest of 6 percent.

Required:
1. Provide the journal entry to record the issuance of the bonds.
2. Provide the journal entry to record the interest payment on June 30 of this year.
3. What bonds payable amount will Victor report on its June 30 balance sheet?

(Chapter Supplement) Recording and Reporting a Bond Issued at a Premium (Straight-Line Amortization without a Premium Account)

E10-23
LO10-5

On January 1 of this year, Kona Corporation sold bonds with a face value of $1,400,000 and a coupon rate of 8 percent. The bonds mature in four years and pay interest semiannually every June 30 and December 31. Kona uses the straight-line amortization method and does not use a premium account. Assume an annual market rate of interest of 6 percent.

Required:
1. Provide the journal entry to record the issuance of the bonds.
2. Provide the journal entry to record the interest payment on June 30 of this year.
3. What bonds payable amount will Victor report on its June 30 balance sheet?

Determining How Bond Transactions Affect the Statement of Cash Flows

E10-24

Determine whether each of the following events results in an inflow or outflow of cash. For those that affect cash, state whether the inflow or outflow would be considered an operating, investing, or financing cash flow under GAAP.

Required:
1. A bond with a face value of $1,000,000 is issued for $960,000.
2. At year-end, $45,000 accrued interest payable is recorded and $1,000 of the bond discount is amortized.
3. Early in the second year, the accrued interest recorded in requirement (2) is paid.
4. The debt matures at the end of the fifth year.

PROBLEMS

Analyzing the Use of Debt (AP10-1)

P10-1
LO10-1, 10-6

Last year, Arbor Corporation reported the following:

Balance Sheet	
Total Assets	$800,000
Total Liabilities	500,000
Total Shareholders' Equity	300,000

This year, Arbor is considering whether to issue more debt to fund a $100,000 project or to issue additional shares of common stock. Both options will bring in exactly $100,000. Arbor's current debt contracts contain a debt covenant that requires it to maintain a debt-to-equity ratio of 2.0 or less.

Required:

1. Calculate Arbor's current debt-to-equity ratio.
2. Calculate Arbor's debt-to-equity ratio assuming it funds the project using additional debt.
3. Calculate Arbor's debt-to-equity ratio assuming it funds the project by issuing common stock.
4. How do you recommend Arbor fund the project?

P10-2 Reporting Bonds Issued at Par (AP10-2)

LO10-2

On January 1 of this year, Nowell Company issued bonds with a face value of $100,000 and a coupon rate of 8 percent. The bonds mature in five years and pay interest semiannually every June 30 and December 31. When the bonds were sold, the annual market rate of interest was 8 percent.

Required:

1. What was the issue price on January 1 of this year?
2. What amount of interest expense should be recorded on June 30 and December 31 of this year?
3. What amount of cash is owed to investors on June 30 and December 31 of this year?
4. What is the book value of the bonds on December 31 of this year? December 31 of next year?

P10-3 Comparing Bonds Issued at Par, at a Discount, and at a Premium (AP10-3)

LO10-2, 10-4, 10-5

On January 1 of this year, Barnett Corporation sold bonds with a face value of $500,000 and a coupon rate of 7 percent. The bonds mature in 10 years and pay interest annually on December 31. Barnett uses the effective-interest amortization method. Ignore any tax effects. Each case is independent of the other cases.

Required:

Complete the following table. The interest rates provided are the annual market rate of interest on the date the bonds were issued.

	Case A (7%)	Case B (8%)	Case C (6%)
a. Cash received at issuance	_____	_____	_____
b. Interest expense recorded in Year 1	_____	_____	_____
c. Cash paid for interest in Year 1	_____	_____	_____
d. Cash paid at maturity for bond principal	_____	_____	_____

P10-4 Computing Issue Prices of Bonds Sold at Par, at a Discount, and at a Premium (AP10-4)

LO10-2, 10-4, 10-5

Rosh Corporation is planning to issue bonds with a face value of $800,000 and a coupon rate of 8 percent. The bonds mature in four years and pay interest semiannually every June 30 and December 31. All of the bonds will be sold on January 1 of this year.

Required:

Compute the issue (sales) price on January 1 of this year for each of the following independent cases (show computations):

a. **Case A:** Market interest rate (annual): 8 percent.
b. **Case B:** Market interest rate (annual): 6 percent.
c. **Case C:** Market interest rate (annual): 10 percent.

P10-5 Recording a Bond Issued at a Discount and Determining How the Issuance Affects Ratios (AP10-5)

LO10-3, 10-4, 10-6

On January 1 of this year, Cunningham Corporation issued bonds with a face value of $200,000 and a coupon rate of 6 percent. The bonds mature in 10 years and pay interest annually every December 31. When the bonds were sold, the annual market rate of interest was 8 percent. The company uses the effective-interest amortization method. By December 31 of this year, the annual market rate of interest had increased to 10 percent.

Required:
1. What is the issuance price of the bonds on January 1?
2. What amount of interest expense is recorded on December 31 of this year?
3. Determine whether the company's debt-to-equity ratio and times interest earned ratio increase, decrease, or stay the same when (*a*) the bonds are issued and (*b*) interest expense is recorded and cash is paid to investors for interest.

Recording and Reporting Bonds Issued at a Discount (AP10-6)

P10-6
LO10-4

PowerTap Utilities is planning to issue bonds with a face value of $1,000,000 and a coupon rate of 10 percent. The bonds mature in 10 years and pay interest semiannually every June 30 and December 31. All of the bonds were sold on January 1 of this year. PowerTap uses the effective-interest amortization method. Assume an annual market rate of interest of 12 percent.

Required:
1. What was the issue price on January 1 of this year?
2. What amount of interest expense should be recorded on June 30 and December 31 of this year?
3. What amount of cash should be paid to investors June 30 and December 31 of this year?
4. What is the book value of the bonds on June 30 and December 31 of this year?

Recording and Reporting a Bond Issued at a Discount (with Discount Account) (AP10-7)

P10-7
LO10-4

Claire Corporation is planning to issue bonds with a face value of $100,000 and a coupon rate of 8 percent. The bonds mature in two years and pay interest quarterly every March 31, June 30, September 30, and December 31. All of the bonds were sold on January 1 of this year. Claire uses the effective-interest amortization method and also uses a discount account. Assume an annual market rate of interest of 12 percent.

Required:
1. Provide the journal entry to record the issuance of the bonds.
2. Provide the journal entry to record the interest payment on March 31, June 30, September 30, and December 31 of this year.
3. What bonds payable amount will Claire report on this year's December 31 balance sheet?

(Chapter Supplement) Recording and Reporting a Bond Issued at a Discount (without Discount Account) (AP10-8)

P10-8
LO10-4

Claire Corporation is planning to issue bonds with a face value of $100,000 and a coupon rate of 8 percent. The bonds mature in two years and pay interest quarterly every March 31, June 30, September 30, and December 31. All of the bonds were sold on January 1 of this year. Claire uses the effective-interest amortization method and does not use a discount account. Assume an annual market rate of interest of 12 percent.

Required:
1. Provide the journal entry to record the issuance of the bonds.
2. Provide the journal entry to record the interest payment on March 31, June 30, September 30, and December 31 of this year.
3. What bonds payable amount will Claire report on this year's December 31 balance sheet?

Recording and Reporting Bonds Issued at a Premium (AP10-9)

P10-9
LO10-5

Cron Corporation is planning to issue bonds with a face value of $700,000 and a coupon rate of 13 percent. The bonds mature in five years and pay interest semiannually every June 30 and December 31. All of the bonds were sold on January 1 of this year. Cron uses the effective-interest amortization method. Assume an annual market rate of interest of 12 percent.

Required:
1. What was the issue price on January 1 of this year?
2. What amount of interest expense should be recorded on June 30 and December 31 of this year?
3. What amount of cash should be paid to investors June 30 and December 31 of this year?
4. What is the book value of the bonds on June 30 and December 31 of this year?

P10-10 LO10-5 Preparing a Bond Amortization Schedule for a Bond Issued at a Premium (AP10-10)

On January 1 of this year, Olive Corporation issued bonds. Interest is payable once a year on December 31. The bonds mature at the end of four years. Olive uses the effective-interest amortization method. The partially completed amortization schedule below pertains to the bonds:

Date	Cash	Interest	Amortization	Balance
1/1/20x1				48,813
12/31/20x1	3,600	3,417	183	48,630
12/31/20x2	?	?	?	48,434
12/31/20x3	?	?	210	?
12/31/20x4	?	3,376	?	48,000

Required:

1. Complete the amortization schedule.
2. When the bonds mature at the end of 20×4, what amount of principal will Olive pay investors?
3. How much cash was received on the day the bonds were issued (sold)?
4. Were the bonds issued at a premium or a discount? If so, what was the amount of the premium or discount?
5. How much cash will be disbursed for interest each period and in total over the life of the bonds?
6. What is the coupon rate?
7. What was the annual market rate of interest on the date the bonds were issued?
8. What amount of interest expense will be reported on the income statement for 20×2 and 20×3?
9. What amount will be reported on the balance sheet for bonds payable at the end of 20×2 and 20×3?

P10-11 LO10-5 Recording and Reporting a Bond Issued at a Premium (with Premium Account) (AP10-11)

Serotta Corporation is planning to issue bonds with a face value of $300,000 and a coupon rate of 12 percent. The bonds mature in two years and pay interest quarterly every March 31, June 30, September 30, and December 31. All of the bonds were sold on January 1 of this year. Serotta uses the effective-interest amortization method and also uses a premium account. Assume an annual market rate of interest of 8 percent.

Required:

1. Provide the journal entry to record the issuance of the bonds.
2. Provide the journal entry to record the interest payment on March 31, June 30, September 30, and December 31 of this year.
3. What bonds payable amount will Serotta report on this year's December 31 balance sheet?

P10-12 LO10-5 (Chapter Supplement) Recording and Reporting a Bond Issued at a Premium (without Premium Account) (AP10-12)

Serotta Corporation is planning to issue bonds with a face value of $300,000 and a coupon rate of 12 percent. The bonds mature in two years and pay interest quarterly every March 31, June 30, September 30, and December 31. All of the bonds were sold on January 1 of this year. Serotta uses the effective-interest amortization method and does not use a premium account. Assume an annual market rate of interest of 8 percent.

Required:

1. Provide the journal entry to record the issuance of the bonds.
2. Provide the journal entry to record the interest payment on March 31, June 30, September 30, and December 31 of this year.
3. What bonds payable amount will Serotta report on this year's December 31 balance sheet?

Recording the Early Retirement of a Bond Issued at a Premium (with Premium Account) (AP10-13)

P10-13
LO10-7

Several years ago, Cyclop Company issued bonds with a face value of $1,000,000 for $1,045,000. As a result of declining interest rates, the company has decided to call the bonds at a call premium of 5 percent over par. The bonds have a current book value of $1,010,000. Record the retirement of the bonds, using a premium account.

(Chapter Supplement) Recording the Early Retirement of a Bond Issued at a Premium (without Premium Account) (AP10-14)

P10-14
LO10-7

Several years ago, Cyclop Company issued bonds with a face value of $1,000,000 for $1,045,000. As a result of declining interest rates, the company has decided to call the bonds at a call premium of 5 percent over par. The bonds have a current book value of $1,010,000. Record the retirement of the bonds and do not use a premium account.

ALTERNATE PROBLEMS

Analyzing the Use of Debt (P10-1)

AP10-1
LO10-1, 10-6

Last year, Spruce Company reported the following:

BALANCE SHEET	
Total Assets	$900,000
Total Liabilities	600,000
Total Shareholders' Equity	300,000

This year, Spruce is considering whether to issue more debt to fund a $200,000 project or to issue additional shares of common stock. Both options will bring in exactly $200,000. Spruce's current debt contracts contain a debt covenant that requires it to maintain a debt-to-equity ratio of 2.5 or less.

Required:

1. Calculate Spruce's current debt-to-equity ratio.
2. Calculate Spruce's debt-to-equity ratio assuming it funds the project using additional debt.
3. Calculate Spruce's debt-to-equity ratio assuming it funds the project by issuing common stock.
4. How do you recommend Spruce fund the project?

Reporting Bonds Issued at Par (P10-2)

AP10-2
LO10-2

On January 1 of this year, Keshon Corporation issued bonds with a face value of $2,000,000 and a coupon rate of 10 percent. The bonds mature in five years and pay interest semiannually every June 30 and December 31. When the bonds were sold, the annual market rate of interest was 10 percent.

Required:

1. What was the issue price on January 1 of this year?
2. What amount of interest expense should be recorded on June 30 and December 31 of this year?
3. What amount of cash interest should be paid on June 30 and December 31 of this year?
4. What is the book value of the bonds on December 31 of this year? December 31 of next year?

Comparing Bonds Issued at Par, at a Discount, and at a Premium (P10-3)

AP10-3
LO10-2, 10-4, 10-5

On January 1 of this year, Diego Corporation sold bonds with a face value of $500,000 and a coupon rate of 5 percent. The bonds mature in 10 years and pay interest annually on December 31. Diego uses the effective-interest amortization method. Ignore any tax effects. Each case is independent of the other cases.

Required:
Complete the following table. The interest rates provided are the annual market rate of interest on the date the bonds were issued.

	Case A (5%)	Case B (7%)	Case C (4%)
a. Cash received at issuance	____	____	____
b. Interest expense recorded in Year 1	____	____	____
c. Cash paid for interest in Year 1	____	____	____
d. Cash paid at maturity for bond principal	____	____	____

AP10-4 Computing Issue Prices of Bonds Sold at Par, at a Discount, and at a Premium (P10-4)

LO10-2, 10-4, 10-5

Enchantment Corporation is planning to issue bonds with a face value of $400,000 and a coupon rate of 4 percent. The bonds mature in four years and pay interest semiannually every June 30 and December 31. All of the bonds will be sold on January 1 of this year.

Required:
Compute the issue (sales) price on January 1 of this year for each of the following independent cases (show computations):

a. **Case A:** Market interest rate (annual): 4 percent.
b. **Case B:** Market interest rate (annual): 2 percent.
c. **Case C:** Market interest rate (annual): 6 percent.

AP10-5 Recording a Bond Issued at a Discount and Determining How the Issuance Affects Ratios (P10-5)

LO10-3, 10-4, 10-6

On January 1 of this year, Yellowstone Corporation issued bonds with a face value of $400,000 and a coupon rate of 6 percent. The bonds mature in 10 years and pay interest annually every December 31. When the bonds were sold, the annual market rate of interest was 8 percent. The company uses the effective-interest amortization method. By December 31 of this year, the annual market rate of interest had increased to 10 percent.

Required:
1. What is the issuance price of the bonds on January 1?
2. What amount of interest expense is recorded on December 31 of this year?
3. Determine whether the company's debt-to-equity ratio and times interest earned ratio increase, decrease, or stay the same when (*a*) the bonds are issued and (*b*) interest expense is recorded and cash is paid to investors for interest.

AP10-6 Recording and Reporting Bonds Issued at a Discount (P10-6)

LO10-4

On January 1 of this year, Avaya Corporation issued bonds with a face value of $2,000,000 and a coupon rate of 6 percent. The bonds mature in five years and pay interest annually on December 31. When the bonds were sold, the annual market rate of interest was 7 percent. Avaya uses the effective-interest amortization method.

Required:
1. What was the issue price on January 1 of this year?
2. What amount of interest expense should be recorded on December 31 of this year? December 31 of next year?
3. What amount of cash interest should be paid on December 31 of this year? December 31 of next year?
4. What is the book value of the bonds on December 31 of this year? December 31 of next year?

AP10-7 Recording and Reporting a Bond Issued at a Discount (with Discount Account) (P10-7)

LO10-4

Zues Corporation is planning to issue bonds with a face value of $800,000 and a coupon rate of 4 percent. The bonds mature in two years and pay interest semiannually every June 30 and December 31. All of the bonds were sold on January 1 of this year. Zues uses the effective-interest amortization method and also uses a discount account. Assume an annual market rate of interest of 6 percent.

Required:

1. Provide the journal entry to record the issuance of the bonds.
2. Provide the journal entry to record the interest payment on June 30 and December 31 of this year.
3. What bonds payable amount will Zues report on this year's December 31 balance sheet?

(Chapter Supplement) Recording and Reporting a Bond Issued at a Discount (without Discount Account) (P10-8)

AP10-8
LO10-4

Makani Corporation is planning to issue bonds with a face value of $800,000 and a coupon rate of 4 percent. The bonds mature in two years and pay interest semiannually every June 30 and December 31. All of the bonds were sold on January 1 of this year. Makani uses the effective-interest amortization method and does not use a discount account. Assume an annual market rate of interest of 6 percent.

Required:

1. Provide the journal entry to record the issuance of the bonds.
2. Provide the journal entry to record the interest payment on June 30 and December 31 of this year.
3. What bonds payable amount will Makani report on this year's December 31 balance sheet?

Recording and Reporting Bonds Issued at a Premium (P10-9)

AP10-9
LO10-5

On January 1 of this year, Pablo Insurance Corporation issued bonds with a face value of $4,000,000 and a coupon rate of 9 percent. The bonds mature in five years and pay interest annually every December 31. When the bonds were sold, the annual market rate of interest was 6 percent. Thomas uses the effective-interest amortization method.

Required:

1. What was the issue price on January 1 of this year?
2. What amount of interest expense should be recorded on December 31 of this year? December 31 of next year?
3. What amount of cash interest should be paid on December 31 of this year? December 31 of next year?
4. What is the book value of the bonds on December 31 of this year? December 31 of next year?

Preparing a Bond Amortization Schedule for a Bond Issued at a Premium (P10-10)

AP10-10
LO10-5

On January 1 of this year, Phoebe Corporation issued bonds. Interest is payable once a year on December 31. The bonds mature at the end of four years. Phoebe uses the effective-interest amortization method. The partially completed amortization schedule below pertains to the bonds:

File Home Insert Page Layout Formulas Data Review View

N6

	A	B	C	D	E	F	G
1							
2		Date	Cash	Interest	Amortization	Balance	
3		1/1/20×1				$48,851	
4		12/31/20×1	$2,640	$2,443	$197	48,654	
5		12/31/20×2	?	?	?	48,446	
6		12/31/20×3	?	?	218	?	
7		12/31/20×4	?	2,411	?	48,000	
8							

Required:

1. Complete the amortization schedule.
2. When the bonds mature at the end of 20×4, what amount of principal will Phoebe pay investors?
3. How much cash was received on the day the bonds were issued (sold)?
4. Were the bonds issued at a premium or a discount? If so, what was the amount of the premium or discount?
5. How much cash will be disbursed for interest each period and in total over the life of the bonds?
6. What is the coupon rate?

7. What was the annual market rate of interest on the date the bonds were issued?
8. What amount of interest expense will be reported on the income statement for 20x2 and 20x3?
9. What amount will be reported on the balance sheet for bonds payable at the end of 20x2 and 20x3?

AP10-11 LO10-5 Recording and Reporting a Bond Issued at a Premium (with Premium Account) (P10-11)

Lemond Corporation is planning to issue bonds with a face value of $200,000 and a coupon rate of 10 percent. The bonds mature in three years and pay interest semiannually every June 30 and December 31. All the bonds were sold on January 1 of this year. Lemond uses the effective-interest amortization method and also uses a premium account. Assume an annual market rate of interest of 8.5 percent.

Required:
1. Provide the journal entry to record the issuance of the bonds.
2. Provide the journal entry to record the interest payment on June 30 and December 31 of this year.
3. What bonds payable amount will Lemond report on this year's December 31 balance sheet?

AP10-12 LO10-5 (Chapter Supplement) Recording and Reporting a Bond Issued at a Premium (without Premium Account) (P10-12)

Lemond Corporation is planning to issue bonds with a face value of $200,000 and a coupon rate of 10 percent. The bonds mature in three years and pay interest semiannually every June 30 and December 31. All of the bonds were sold on January 1 of this year. Lemond uses the effective-interest amortization method and does not use a premium account. Assume an annual market rate of interest of 8.5 percent.

Required:
1. Provide the journal entry to record the issuance of the bonds.
2. Provide the journal entry to record the interest payment on June 30 and December 31 of this year.
3. What bonds payable amount will Lemond report on this year's December 31 balance sheet?

AP10-13 LO10-7 Recording the Early Retirement of a Bond Issued at a Premium (with Premium Account) (P10-13)

Several years ago, Ben & John Company issued bonds with a face value of $2,000,000 for $2,090,000. As a result of declining interest rates, the company has decided to call the bonds at a call premium of 5 percent over par. The bonds have a current book value of $2,020,000. Record the retirement of the bonds, using a premium account.

AP10-14 LO10-7 (Chapter Supplement) Recording the Early Retirement of a Bond Issued at a Premium (without Premium Account) (P10-14)

Several years ago, Max Company issued bonds with a face value of $2,000,000 for $2,090,000. As a result of declining interest rates, the company has decided to call the bonds at a call premium of 5 percent over par. The bonds have a current book value of $2,020,000. Record the retirement of the bonds and do not use a premium account.

CONTINUING PROBLEM

CON10-1 LO10-2, 10-5 Pool Corporation, Inc. Recording and Reporting Liabilities

Pool Corporation, Inc., sells swimming pool supplies and equipment. It is a publicly traded corporation that trades on the NASDAQ exchange. The majority of Pool's customers are small, family-owned businesses. Assume that Pool issued bonds with a face value of $750,000,000 on January 1 of this year and that the coupon rate is 5 percent. At the time of the borrowing, the annual market rate of interest was 4 percent. The debt matures in 10 years, and Pool makes interest payments semiannually on June 30 and December 31.

Required:
1. What was the issue price on January 1 of this year?
2. What amount of interest expense should be recorded on June 30 and December 31 of this year?
3. What amount of cash interest should be paid on June 30 and December 31 of this year?
4. What is the book value of the bonds on June 30 and December 31 of this year?

connect

CASES AND PROJECTS

Annual Report Cases

Finding Financial Information

CP10-1
LO10-1, 10-2, 10-6, 10-8
Target

Refer to the financial statements and footnotes of **Target** given in Appendix B at the end of this book. All dollar amounts are in millions.

Required:

1. Where does Target report the amount of cash paid for interest during the most recent fiscal year?
   a. Statement of Operations
   b. Statement of Shareholders' Investment
   c. Statement of Cash Flows
   d. Statement of Financial Position
   e. None of the above
2. What is the amount of cash Target paid for interest during the most recent fiscal year?
   a. $939
   b. $1,031
   c. $2,480
   d. $1,343
   e. $977
3. What is the amount of long-term debt that Target added during the most recent fiscal year?
   a. $4,250
   b. $2,480
   c. $3,250
   d. $1,770
   e. $3,607
4. Target has an agreement to borrow money if needed. What is the total amount the company can borrow under what it calls its "unsecured revolving credit facility"?
   a. $2,500
   b. $3,607
   c. $11,536
   d. $1,939
   e. None of the above
5. For the most recent fiscal year, compute the debt-to-equity ratio for Target.
   a. 1.39
   b. 2.55
   c. 0.39
   d. 1.16
   e. 3.55

Finding Financial Information

CP10-2
LO10-1, 10-2, 10-6, 10-8
Walmart

Refer to the financial statements and footnotes of **Walmart** given in Appendix C at the end of this book. All dollar amounts are in millions.

Required:

1. What is the amount of cash Walmart paid for interest during the most recent fiscal year? ________
2. What is the amount of long-term debt that Walmart issued during the most recent fiscal year? ________
3. What is the amount of Walmart's long-term debt that will mature in fiscal year 2024? ________
4. What is the amount of cash Walmart paid to retire long-term debt during the most recent fiscal year? ________
5. For the most recent fiscal year, compute the debt-to-equity ratio for Walmart. (Round your answer to two decimal places) ________

Comparing Companies within an Industry

CP10-3
LO10-3, 10-6

Refer to the financial statements of Target (Appendix B) and Walmart (Appendix C) and the Industry Ratio Report (Appendix D) at the end of this book.

Required:

1. Compute the debt-to-equity ratio for both companies for the most recent fiscal year. (Round your answer to two decimal places)

   Target = ________ **Walmart** = ________

2. Which company relied more heavily on debt financing relative to equity financing during the most recent fiscal year?
   a. Target
   b. Walmart
3. Compare the debt-to-equity ratios for Target and Walmart to the average debt-to-equity ratio for the retail industry. Do Target and Walmart rely more or less heavily on debt financing relative to equity financing compared to the industry average?
   a. Target relies more heavily on debt financing relative to equity financing compared to the industry average, but Walmart relies less heavily.
   b. Both Target and Walmart rely less heavily on debt financing relative to equity financing compared to the industry average.
   c. Walmart relies more heavily on debt financing relative to equity financing compared to the industry average, but Target relies less heavily.
   d. Both Target and Walmart rely more heavily on debt financing relative to equity financing compared to the industry average.
4. Compute the times interest earned ratio for both companies for the most recent fiscal year. Round your answer to two decimal places. (**Hint**: Include any interest expense related to capital leases and financing obligations when calculating the times interest earned ratio for Walmart.)

   Target = ☐ **Walmart =** ☐

5. Which company generated a greater amount of income relative to interest expense during the most recent fiscal year?
   a. Target
   b. Walmart

CP10-4
LO10-4
Apple

Analyzing Zero Coupon Bonds from an Actual Company

Apple recently issued a zero coupon bond. The zero coupon bond has a face value of $1 billion and matures in six years. Assume that when the bonds were sold to the public, the annual market rate of interest was 3 percent.

Required:

1. Explain why an investor would buy a bond with a zero coupon (interest) rate.
2. How much did Apple receive when it issued the bonds with a face value of $1 billion?
3. How much would Apple have received if the annual market rate of interest remained at 3 percent, and the bonds matured in 10 years?

Critical Thinking Cases

CP10-5
LO10-1

Evaluating an Ethical Dilemma

You work for a small company that is considering investing in a new artificial intelligence business. Financial projections suggest that the company will be able to earn in excess of $40 million per year on an investment of $100 million. The company president suggests borrowing the money by issuing bonds that will carry a 7 percent interest rate. He says, "This is better than printing money! We won't have to invest a penny of our own money, and we get to keep $33 million per year after we pay interest to the bondholders." As you think about the proposed transaction, you feel a little uncomfortable about taking advantage of the creditors in this fashion. You feel that it must be wrong to earn such a high return by using money that belongs to other people. Is this an ethical business transaction?

CP10-6
LO10-1

Evaluating an Ethical Dilemma

Assume that you are a portfolio manager for a large money management company. The majority of the money you manage is from retired school teachers who depend on the income you earn on their investments. You have invested a significant amount of money in the bonds of a large corporation and have just received a call from the company's president explaining that it is unable to meet its current interest obligations because of deteriorating business operations related to a global pandemic. The president has a recovery plan that will take at least two years. During that time, the company will not be able to pay interest on the bonds and, she admits, if the plan does not work, bondholders will probably lose more than half of their money. As a creditor, you can force the company into immediate bankruptcy and probably get back at least 90 percent of the bondholders' money. You also know that your decision will cause at least 10,000 people to lose their jobs if the company ceases operations. Given only these two options, what should you do?

You as Analyst: Online Company Research

Examining a Company's Long-term Liabilities

CP10-7
LO10-1, 10-2, 10-3, 10-4, 10-5, 10-6, 10-8

In your web browser, search for the investor relations page of a public company you are interested in (e.g., Zoom investor relations). Select SEC Filings or Annual Report or Financials to obtain the 10-K for the most recent year available.*

Required:

1. Has the company issued any long-term debt, either bonds or notes? If so, read the footnote and list any unusual features (e.g., callable, convertible, secured by specific collateral).
2. If the company issued any bond securities (which may be referred to as "notes" in the footnotes), were they issued at par, a premium, or a discount? If they were issued at a premium or discount, does the company use the straight-line or effective-interest amortization method?
3. Ratio analysis:
   a. What does the debt-to-equity ratio measure in general?
   b. Compute the ratio for the company for the last three years.
   c. What do your results suggest about the company?
   d. If available, find the industry ratio for the most recent year, compare it to your results, and discuss why you believe the company differs from or is similar to the industry ratio.
4. Ratio analysis:
   a. What does the times interest earned ratio measure in general?
   b. Compute the ratio for the company for the last three years. If interest expense is not separately disclosed, you will not be able to compute the ratio. If so, state why you think it is not separately disclosed.
   c. What do your results suggest about the company?
   d. If available, find the industry ratio for the most recent year, compare it to your results, and discuss why you believe the company differs from or is similar to the industry ratio.
5. Examine the company's statement of cash flows for the most recent year. Were there any cash inflows or outflows associated with the issuance of debt, payment of interest, or repayment of principal reported on the statement of cash flows? In what section were these inflows and/or outflows reported in the statement of cash flows?

*Alternatively, you can go to sec.gov, click on Company Filings (under the search box), type in the name of the public company you want to find. Once at the list of filings, type 10-K in the Filing Type box. The most recent 10-K annual report will be at the top of the list. Click on Interactive Data for a list of the parts or the entire report to examine.

BUSINESS ANALYTICS AND DATA VISUALIZATION WITH EXCEL AND TABLEAU

Connect offers a variety of exercises to assess Excel skills, data visualization, interpretation, and analysis, including auto-graded Tableau Dashboard Activities, Applying Excel problems, and Integrated Excel problems.

Images used throughout chapter: Question of ethics: mushmello/Shutterstock; Pause for feedback: McGraw Hill; Guided help: McGraw Hill; Financial analysis: McGraw Hill; Focus on cash flows: Hilch/Shutterstock; Key ratio analysis: guillermain/123RF; Data analytics: Hilch/Shutterstock; Tip: McGraw Hill; ESG reporting: McGraw Hill; International perspective: Hilch/Shutterstock

chapter 11

Reporting and Interpreting Stockholders' Equity

Microsoft Corporation's mission is to empower every person and every organization on the planet to achieve more. To do so, Microsoft focuses on helping companies reinvent and improve their business processes, by building on being one of the two largest providers of cloud computing services, and by expanding the use of personal computers around the world. Microsoft has also stated ambitious sustainability goals. The first goal is for its operations to be carbon negative by 2030. The second goal is for the company to have removed from the environment all the carbon it has emitted since it was founded almost 50 years ago. Can the company achieve these goals? Time will tell, but with revenues in 2020 of $143 billion and total assets of $301 billion, the company has the resources to be ambitious and the desire to drive change. Microsoft discusses its commitment to building a more sustainable future in the ESG Reporting box below.

In this chapter, we study the role that stockholders' equity plays in funding a business and the strategies that managers use to maximize stockholders' wealth.

UNDERSTANDING THE BUSINESS

To some people, the words *corporation* and *business* are almost synonymous. You've probably heard friends refer to a career in business as "the corporate world." Equating business with corporations is understandable because corporations are the dominant form of business organization in terms of volume of operations. If you were to write the names of 10 familiar businesses on a piece of paper, probably all of them would be corporations.

LEARNING OBJECTIVES

After studying this chapter, you should be able to:

11-1 Explain the role of stock in the capital structure of a corporation. p. 577

11-2 Compute and analyze the earnings per share ratio. p. 579

11-3 Describe the characteristics of common stock and report common stock transactions. p. 579

11-4 Discuss and report dividends. p. 584

11-5 Compute and analyze the dividend yield ratio. p. 584

11-6 Discuss and report stock dividends and stock splits. p. 588

11-7 Describe the information reported on the statement of stockholders' equity. p. 591

11-8 Describe the characteristics of preferred stock and report preferred stock transactions. p. 593

11-9 Discuss the impact of stock transactions on cash flows. p. 594

JeanLuclchard/Shutterstock

FOCUS COMPANY

Microsoft

ISSUING AND REPORTING STOCK

microsoft.com

ENVIRONMENTAL, SOCIAL, & GOVERNANCE (ESG) REPORTING

On its official blog, Microsoft publicly commits to a more sustainable future by stating "Solving our planet's carbon issues will require technology that does not exist today. That's why a significant part of our endeavor involves putting Microsoft's balance sheet to work to stimulate and accelerate the development of carbon removal technology. Our new Climate Innovation Fund will commit to invest $1 billion over the next four years into new technologies and expand access to capital around the world to people working to solve this problem. We understand that this is just a fraction of the investment needed, but our hope is that it spurs more governments and companies to invest in new ways as well."

Microsoft's stock is traded on the National Association of Securities Dealers Automated Quotations (NASDAQ) Stock Market under the symbol MSFT. As of July 27, 2020, Microsoft had just under 92,000 registered holders of its common stock.

The popularity of the corporate form can be attributed to a critical advantage that corporations have over sole proprietorships and partnerships: They can raise large amounts of capital because both large and small investors easily can participate in their ownership. This ease of participation is related to several factors.

- Shares of stock can be purchased in small amounts. You could buy a single share of Microsoft stock for about $220 and become one of the owners of this successful company.
- Ownership interests can be transferred easily through the sale of shares on established markets such as the New York Stock Exchange or the NASDAQ Stock Exchange, where Microsoft's stock is traded.

EXHIBIT 11.1

Excerpt from Consolidated Balance Sheets for Microsoft

MICROSOFT
REAL WORLD EXCERPT:
Annual Report

MICROSOFT CORPORATION
Consolidated Balance Sheets
($ in millions)

	June 30, 2020	June 30, 2019
Stockholders' equity:		
Common stock and paid-in capital - shares authorized 24,000; outstanding **7,571** and 7,643	**$ 80,552**	$ 78,520
Retained earnings	**34,566**	24,150
Accumulated other comprehensive income (loss)	**3,186**	(340)
Total stockholders' equity	**$118,304**	$102,330

Source: Microsoft Corporation

- Stock ownership provides investors with limited liability. In the event of bankruptcy, creditors have claims against only the corporation's assets, not the assets of the individual owners.

Many Americans own stock either directly or indirectly through a mutual fund or pension program. Stock ownership offers them the opportunity to earn higher returns than they could depositing money in a bank account or investing in corporate bonds. Unfortunately, stock ownership also involves risks. The appropriate balance between risk and the expected return on an investment depends on individual preferences.

Exhibit 11.1 presents financial information from **Microsoft**'s annual report.

Notice that the stockholders' equity section of Microsoft's balance sheet lists two primary sources of equity:

1. Contributed capital from the sale of stock. This is the amount of money stockholders invested through the purchase of shares. For Microsoft, contributed capital is the amount in the Common Stock and paid-in capital accounts ($80,552 million for fiscal 2020).
2. Earned capital generated by the company's profit-making activities. Earned capital is kept track of in the Retained Earnings account (referred to as an "accumulated deficit" when negative). Retained earnings is the cumulative amount of net income the corporation has earned since it organized as a corporation, less the cumulative amount of dividends paid since it organized.

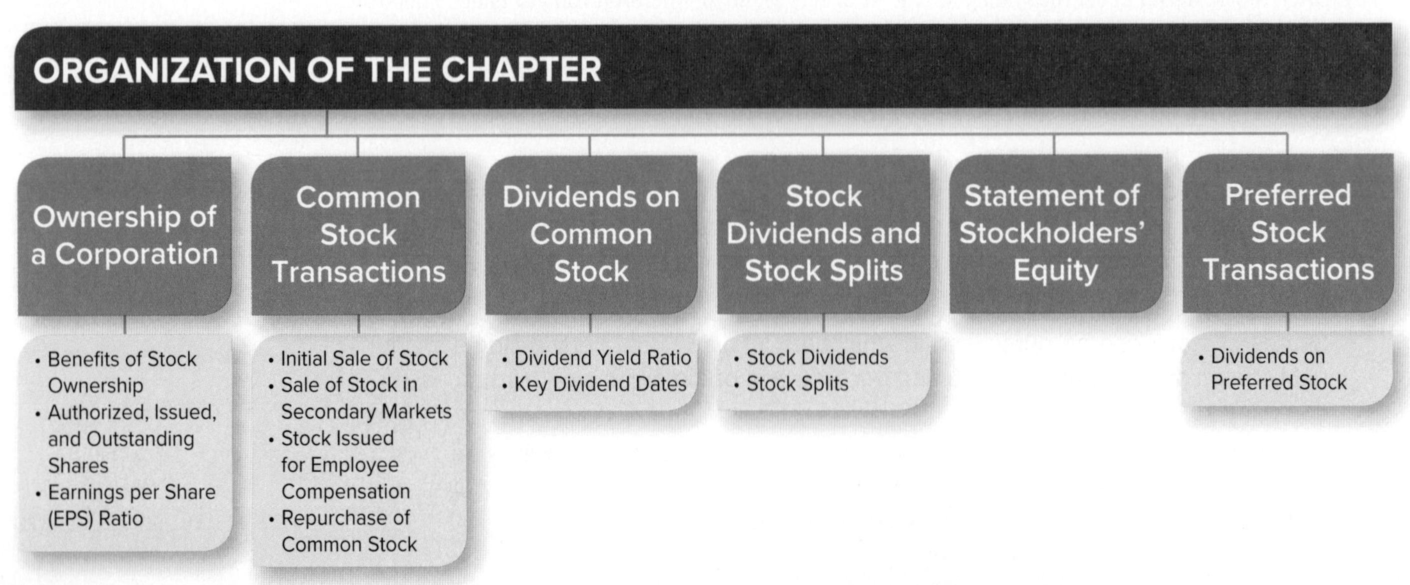

OWNERSHIP OF A CORPORATION

The corporation is the only business form the law recognizes as a separate entity. As a distinct entity, the corporation enjoys a continuous existence separate and apart from its owners. It may own assets, incur liabilities, expand and contract in size, sue others, be sued, and enter into contracts independently of its stockholder owners.

To protect everyone's rights, the creation and governance of corporations are tightly regulated by law. Corporations are created by application to a state government (not the federal government). Corporations are governed by a board of directors elected by the stockholders.

Each state has different laws governing the organization of corporations created within its boundaries. **Microsoft** incorporated in the state of Washington and has its headquarters in Redmond, Washington. You will find that an unusually large number of corporations are incorporated in Delaware even though their headquarters are located in a different state. Companies choose Delaware for incorporation because the state has some of the most favorable tax laws for corporations.

Benefits of Stock Ownership

LEARNING OBJECTIVE 11-1

Explain the role of stock in the capital structure of a corporation.

When you invest in a corporation, you are known as a stockholder or shareholder. As a stockholder, you receive shares of stock that you subsequently can sell on established stock exchanges. Owners of common stock receive a number of benefits:

- **A voice in management.** You may vote in the stockholders' meeting on major issues concerning management of the corporation.
- **Dividends.** If a company pays dividends, you receive a proportional share of the distribution of profits.
- **Residual claim.** You will receive a proportional share of the distribution of remaining assets upon the liquidation of the company.

Stockholders, unlike creditors, are able to vote at the annual stockholders' meeting. Each share of stock typically represents one vote. The following notice of the annual meeting of stockholders, referred to as a proxy statement, was recently sent to all owners of Microsoft stock:

MICROSOFT

REAL WORLD EXCERPT:

Notice of Stockholders' Meeting

NOTICE OF ANNUAL MEETING OF STOCKHOLDERS

Date	December 2, 2020
Time	8:00 a.m. Pacific Time
Virtual Meeting	This year's meeting is a virtual shareholders meeting
Record Date	October 8, 2020. Only shareholders of record at the close of business on the record date are entitled to receive notice of, and to vote at, the Annual Meeting.
Proxy Voting	**Make your vote count.** Please vote your shares promptly to ensure the presence of a quorum during the Annual Meeting. Voting your shares now via the Internet, by telephone, or by signing, dating, and returning the enclosed proxy card or voting instruction form will save the expense of additional solicitation. We are requesting your vote to:
Items of Business	• Elect the 12 director nominees named in this Proxy Statement • Approve, on a nonbinding advisory basis, the compensation paid to our named executive officers ("say-on-pay vote") • Ratify the selection of Deloitte & Touche LLP as our independent auditor for fiscal year 2021 • Vote on Shareholder Proposal: Report on Employee Representation on Board of Directors • Transact other business that may properly come before the Annual Meeting

Source: Microsoft Corporation

The proxy statement also contained information concerning the people who were nominated to be members of the board of directors as well as detailed information about executive compensation and the audit fees charged by **Deloitte & Touche**. Because most stockholders do not actually attend the annual meeting, the notice included information about how absentee stockholders can mail their votes in or cast their votes using the Internet or a telephone.

Stockholders have ultimate authority in a corporation. The board of directors and, indirectly, all employees are accountable to the stockholders.

Authorized, Issued, and Outstanding Shares

A company's corporate charter specifies the maximum number of shares the company is authorized to sell to the public. This maximum is referred to as the number of **authorized shares**. The shares a company has actually sold to the public represent the number of **issued shares**. For reasons we discuss later, a company might want to buy back shares that have already been sold to the public. Shares that have been bought back can be retired or held as **treasury stock**. Shares held as treasury stock are considered issued shares but not **outstanding shares**. Outstanding shares represent the total number of shares owned by stockholders on any particular date. Thus, when a company buys back shares and holds them as treasury stock, it creates a difference between the number of issued shares and the number of outstanding shares of its stock. Shares that are retired resume a status of being authorized but not issued.

Recall that **Microsoft** is incorporated in Washington State. Washington State is one of a small number of states that do not allow treasury stock, so Microsoft retires all shares that it repurchases each year. In fiscal 2020, Microsoft reports in its notes to its financial statements that it repurchased and retired 126 million shares of common stock. Since those shares are not listed as treasury stock, Microsoft's number of outstanding shares is equal to its number of issued shares. When this is the case, companies typically only list the number of outstanding shares on their balance sheets. You can see this for Microsoft in Exhibit 11.1. The information reported in Exhibit 11.1 is summarized below:

VDB Photos/Shutterstock

MICROSOFT CORPORATION
Common Stock Shares
June 30, 2020 (in millions)

Authorized shares	24,000
Issued shares	7,571
Less: Treasury shares	0
Outstanding shares	7,571

Knowing the number of shares outstanding is important because this number is used in the calculation of various ratios, including the earnings per share ratio.

KEY RATIO ANALYSIS

Earnings per Share (EPS)

LEARNING OBJECTIVE 11-2

Compute and analyze the earnings per share ratio.

ANALYTICAL QUESTION

How well is a company performing?

RATIO AND COMPARISONS

Earnings per share is computed as follows:

Earnings per Share = Net Income* ÷ Weighted Average Number of Common Shares Outstanding

*Any preferred dividends (discussed later in this chapter) should be subtracted from net income.

The 2020 ratio for **Microsoft**:

$44,281 million ÷ 7,610 million shares† = $5.82

†The weighted average number of common shares outstanding is reported on the income statement.

COMPARISONS OVER TIME		
Microsoft		
2018	**2019**	**2020**
$2.15	$5.11	$5.82

COMPARISONS WITH COMPETITORS	
IBM	Intel
2020	**2020**
$6.28	$4.98

INTERPRETATIONS

In General You probably have seen newspaper headlines announcing a company's earnings. Notice that those news stories normally report earnings on an earnings per share (EPS) basis. EPS is a popular measure because it emphasizes the amount of earnings attributable to a single share of outstanding common stock. Because the number of outstanding shares of common stock changes over time, and is different across firms, using EPS rather than just net income allows analysts and investors to make "profitability per share" comparisons across time and across firms. Companies are required to report EPS on their income statements.

Focus Company Analysis For Microsoft, net income has increased over the last three years while the weighted average number of common shares outstanding has remained relatively constant. This has caused the company's EPS to increase over the three years. Relative to its competitors, Microsoft's 2020 EPS ratio is less than IBM's ratio but greater than Intel's ratio. We can compare EPS numbers across firms of different sizes because EPS captures the amount of earnings attributable to a single share of outstanding common stock, regardless of the size of a company or the number of shares of stock outstanding.

A Few Cautions While EPS is an effective and widely used measure of profitability per share, it does not necessarily indicate how a company will perform in the future. Stock price is a better indication of expected future performance. For example, if two companies have identical EPS numbers, but the stock price of one company is double that of the other company, investors expect greater future performance from the firm with the higher stock price. EPS is a measure of performance per share of stock over a prior period, while stock price is an indication of expected performance over future periods. It is important to keep this in mind when analyzing EPS numbers across time and across firms.

COMMON STOCK TRANSACTIONS

LEARNING OBJECTIVE 11-3

Describe the characteristics of common stock and report common stock transactions.

All corporations issue common stock, and some elect to issue a second type of stock called preferred stock. In this section, we discuss common stock. Near the end of the chapter, we discuss preferred stock.

Common stock is held by investors who are the "owners" of a corporation. Though stockholders are owners and have the right to vote and share in the profitability of the business through dividends, they do not actively participate in managing the business. Instead, they elect a board of directors and it is the board's role to hire and monitor executives who manage a company's activities on a day-to-day basis.

Depending on state law, a company's common stock may be required to have a **par value**, a nominal value per share established in the corporate charter. Par value has no relationship to the market value of a stock. For example, **Microsoft**'s common stock has a par value of $0.00000625 per share while its stock price is over $220 per share.

The original purpose of assigning a par value to a share of common stock was to protect creditors by specifying a permanent amount of capital that owners could not withdraw before a bankruptcy, which would leave creditors with something in the event that a company did not succeed. This permanent amount of capital is called **legal capital**. Though the requirement to assign a par value and maintain legal capital is embedded in state law, in today's business world it does little to protect creditors. Like Microsoft, companies have simply transitioned to assigning an extremely low par value. Many companies assign a par value of $0.01 per share, which means that any legal capital requirements are too low to meaningfully protect creditors. As a result, creditors have adopted other protection mechanisms, like the debt covenants we discussed in Chapter 10, to provide some protection in the event that a company performs poorly.

There are some states that require the issuance of **no-par value stock**. When a corporation issues no-par stock, legal capital is defined by state law.

Initial Sale of Stock

An **initial public offering,** or IPO, involves the very first sale of a company's stock to the public (i.e., when the company first "goes public"). You have probably heard stories of a new company's stock price increasing dramatically the day of its IPO. While investors sometimes earn significant returns on IPOs, they also take significant risks. Once a company's stock has been traded on established markets, additional sales of new stock to the public are called **seasoned offerings.**

Most sales of stock to the public are cash transactions. To illustrate the accounting for an initial sale of stock, assume that Microsoft sold 1 million shares of its $0.00000625 par value stock for $220 per share. The company would record the following journal entry:

	Debit	Credit
Cash (+A) (1,000,000 × $220)	220,000,000	
Common stock (+SE) (1,000,000 × $0.00000625)		6
Additional paid-in capital (+SE)		219,999,994

Assets		=	Liabilities	+	Stockholders' Equity	
Cash	+220,000,000				Common stock	+6
					Additional paid-in capital	+219,999,994

Notice that the Common Stock account is credited for the number of shares sold times the par value per share. The Additional Paid-in Capital account is credited for the remainder, which is the amount "in addition" to par value that the company received when it issued the shares. In rare cases, a corporate charter may specify a "stated value" rather than a "par value." For accounting purposes, the two values are used in the same way. If there is no par or stated value, the entire proceeds from the sale will be entered in the Common Stock account.

Sale of Stock in Secondary Markets

Tip The sale of a company's stock from one investor to another *does not* involve the company and therefore *does not* require the company to record the transaction.

When a company sells stock to the public, the transaction is between the issuing corporation and the investor. Subsequent to the initial sale, investors can sell shares to other investors without directly affecting the corporation. For example, if investor Ed deHaan sold 1,000 shares of Microsoft stock to investor Amanda Winn, Microsoft would not record a journal entry. Mr. deHaan received cash for the shares he sold, and Ms. Winn received stock for the cash she paid. Microsoft was not a part of the transaction and therefore did not receive or pay anything.

Each business day, *The Wall Street Journal* reports the results of thousands of transactions between investors in secondary markets, such as the New York Stock Exchange (NYSE) and the NASDAQ market. Stockholders expect to earn money on their investments through dividends if a company pays dividends and through increases in a company's stock price. In many instances, senior management has been replaced because of a stock's poor performance in the stock market.

Cash

Ms. Winn

Mr. deHaan

Stock

Top: Roman Malanchuk/123RF; Left: Image Source, all rights reserved.; Right: Ariel Skelley/Blend Images LLC; Bottom: tupungato/Getty Images

Stock Issued for Employee Compensation

One of the advantages of the corporate form is the ability to separate the management of a business from its ownership. Separation also can be a disadvantage because some managers may not act in the owners' best interests. This potential problem can be addressed in a number of ways. For example, compensation packages can be developed to reward employees for meeting goals that are important to stockholders. Another strategy is to offer employees stock, either directly through stock awards or indirectly through stock options. Stock awards grant shares of stock to employees that vest on future dates. Stock options give employees the right to buy stock in the future at a fixed price. Both stock awards and stock options provide an incentive for employees to take actions that increase a company's stock price, thereby aligning their interests with the interests of stockholders. Microsoft uses equity compensation to incentivize its executives and explains why in the following disclosure:

MICROSOFT

REAL WORLD EXCERPT

Equity Compensation

PAY MIX

At least 70 percent of the annual target compensation opportunity for our Named Executives is equity-based to incentivize a long-term focus and align their interests with those of our shareholders. Our Compensation Committee structures the pay mix for our annual target total compensation opportunities to place a higher proportion in equity awards than the companies in our compensation peer group.

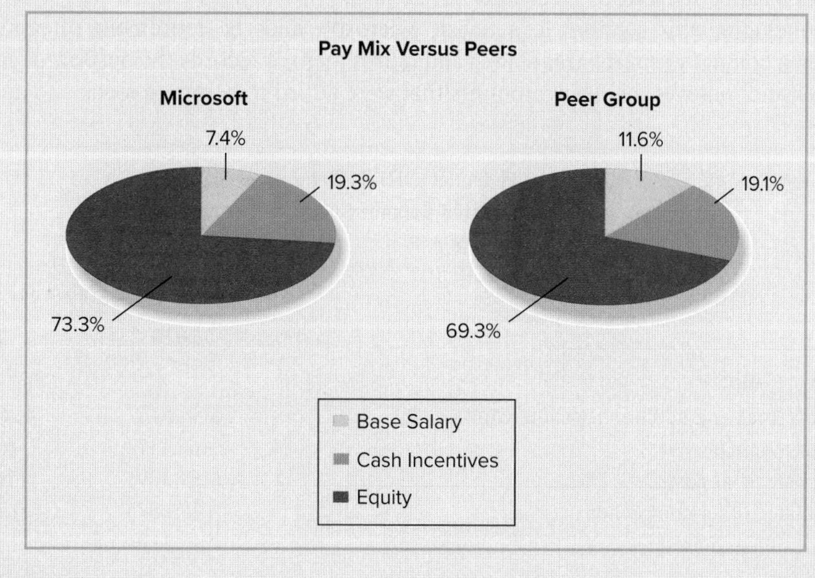

Source: Microsoft Corporation 2020 Proxy Statement

Repurchase of Stock

A corporation may want to repurchase its stock from existing stockholders for a number of reasons. One common reason is the existence of an employee bonus plan that provides workers with shares of the company's stock as part of their compensation. Because of Securities and Exchange Commission regulations concerning newly issued shares, most companies find it less costly to give employees repurchased shares than to issue new ones. In addition, if a company were to pay bonuses with newly issued shares each period, it would increase the number of shares in the market, which would decrease the company's stock price. Increasing the number of shares also would dilute existing stockholders' investments, as each share of stock they own would be worth less. By repurchasing shares to fulfill bonus obligations, companies avoid this dilutive effect. As discussed earlier, stock that has been repurchased and is held by the issuing corporation is called *treasury stock.* Treasury shares have no voting, dividend, or other stockholder rights while they are held as treasury stock.

When companies repurchase shares from the market, they pay cash and receive their own stock. Since **Microsoft** is required by Washington State law to retire shares it repurchases, let's assume that a competitor, **IBM**, repurchased 100,000 shares of its stock in the open market when it was selling for $140 per share. To reflect the repurchase, the company would record the following journal entry:

	Debit	Credit
Treasury stock (+XSE, −SE) (100,000 × $140)	14,000,000	
Cash (−A)		14,000,000

Assets		=	Liabilities	+	Stockholders' Equity	
Cash	−14,000,000				Treasury stock	−14,000,000

Intuitively, many students expect the Treasury Stock account to be reported as an asset. Such is not the case because a company cannot own itself. The Treasury Stock account is therefore a contra-equity account, which is why Treasury Stock is shown as a negative number on a company's balance sheet. This practice makes sense because treasury stock is considered issued but not outstanding. Thus, when stock is repurchased and held in treasury, it is not removed from the Common Stock account but rather is shown as its own separate account within stockholders' equity, and because repurchasing the shares reduced assets (cash), it reduces equity. As the information in Exhibit 11.2 indicates, IBM reported treasury stock in the amount of $169,339 million on its balance sheet as of December 31, 2020.

Before concluding this section, let's revisit Microsoft and the retirement of repurchased shares. When a company repurchases shares and retires them, it records the outflow of cash paid for the shares and removes the exact amounts that were added to common stock and additional

EXHIBIT 11.2

Excerpt from Consolidated Balance Sheets for IBM

IBM

REAL WORLD EXCERPT:

Annual Report

IBM CORPORATION
Consolidated Balance Sheets
($ in millions)

	December 31,	
	2020	**2019**
Stockholders' Equity		
Common stock and additional paid-in capital	$ 56,556	$ 55,895
Retained earnings	162,717	162,954
Treasury stock, at cost	(169,339)	(169,413)
Accumulated other comprehensive loss	(29,337)	(28,597)
Noncontrolling interest	129	144
Total stockholders' equity	$ 20,727	$ 20,985

**Amounts may not add due to rounding.*

paid-in capital when the stock was originally issued. The journal entry also involves increasing an additional paid-in capital account or decreasing retained earnings, depending on whether the shares were repurchased at a price lower or higher than the original share price. Accounting for share retirements is covered in more detail in advanced accounting courses.

When a company sells its treasury stock, it does not report an accounting profit or loss on the transaction, even if it sells the stock for more or less than it originally cost to repurchase the shares. GAAP does not permit a corporation to report income or losses from investments in its own stock because transactions with the owners are not considered normal profit-making activities. Based on the previous example, assume that IBM reissues 10,000 shares of treasury stock for $150 per share. Remember that the company had repurchased the shares for $140 per share. Because the reissue price ($150 per share) is higher than the repurchase price ($140 per share), stockholders' equity would increase by $10 per reissued share, or $100,000 total (10,000 shares × $10). IBM would record the following journal entry when it reissues the shares:

	Debit	Credit
Cash (+A) (10,000 × $150)	1,500,000	
Treasury stock (−XSE, +SE) (10,000 × $140)		1,400,000
Additional paid-in capital (+SE)		100,000

Assets		=	Liabilities	+	Stockholders' Equity	
Cash	+1,500,000				Treasury stock	+1,400,000
					Additional paid-in capital	+100,000

If the treasury stock had been reissued at $130 per share, stockholders' equity would decrease by $10 per reissued share, or $100,000 total (10,000 shares × $10). The $10 is the difference between the reissue price ($130 per share) and the repurchase price ($140 per share). The journal entry IBM would record if the reissue price were $130 per share is:

	Debit	Credit
Cash (+A) (10,000 × $130)	1,300,000	
Additional paid-in capital (−SE)	100,000	
Treasury stock (−XSE, +SE) (10,000 × $140)		1,400,000

Assets		=	Liabilities	+	Stockholders' Equity	
Cash	+1,300,000				Treasury stock	+1,400,000
					Additional paid-in capital	−100,000

PAUSE FOR FEEDBACK

We have looked at several transactions involving the sale and repurchase of common stock. In the next section, we will discuss dividends. Before we move on, complete the following questions to test your understanding of the concepts we have covered so far.

SELF-STUDY QUIZ

1. Assume that Apple Produce issued 10,000 shares of its common stock for $150,000 cash. The stock has a par value of $2 per share. Prepare the journal entry to record this transaction.

2. Assume that Apple Produce repurchased 5,000 shares of its stock in the open market when the stock was selling for $12 per share. Record this transaction.
3. If Apple Produce's common stock did not have a par value, how would the journal entries in (1) and (2) change?

After you have completed your answers, check them below.

GUIDED HELP 11-1

For additional step-by-step video instruction, go to mhhe.com/libby_gh11-1.

Related Homework: M11-4, E11-1, E11-2, E11-15, E11-16, P11-4

LEARNING OBJECTIVE 11-4

Discuss and report dividends.

DIVIDENDS ON COMMON STOCK

The return from investing in a company's common stock can come from two sources: stock price appreciation and dividends. Some investors prefer to buy stocks that pay little or no dividends because companies that reinvest the majority of their earnings back into their operations tend to increase their future earnings potential, along with their stock price. Wealthy investors in high tax brackets prefer to receive their return in the form of higher stock prices because capital gains may be taxed at a lower rate than dividend income. Other investors, such as those who are retired and need a steady income, prefer to receive their return in the form of dividends. These investors often seek stocks that will pay relatively high dividends, such as utility stocks. Because of the importance of dividends to many investors, analysts often compute the dividend yield ratio to evaluate a company's dividend policy.

KEY RATIO ANALYSIS

LEARNING OBJECTIVE 11-5

Compute and analyze the dividend yield ratio.

Dividend Yield

ANALYTICAL QUESTION

How much does a company pay out in dividends each year relative to its share price?

RATIO AND COMPARISONS

The dividend yield ratio is computed as follows:

Dividend Yield = Dividends per Share ÷ Market Price per Share

The 2020 ratio for **Microsoft**: $2.04 ÷ $202.49 = 1.01%

COMPARISONS OVER TIME		
Microsoft		
2018	2019	2020
1.76%	1.40%	1.01%

COMPARISONS WITH COMPETITORS	
IBM	Intel
2020	2020
5.24%	2.82%

Solutions to SELF-STUDY QUIZ

1. Cash (+A)	150,000	
Common stock (+SE) ($2 × 10,000)		20,000
Additional paid-in capital (+SE) (remainder)		130,000
2. Treasury stock (+XSE, −SE)	60,000	
Cash (−A)		60,000

3. In journal entry (1), you would credit Common stock for 150,000. There would be no "Additional paid-in capital" account in the transaction. Journal entry (2) would not change.

INTERPRETATIONS

In General Individuals who invest in the common stock of a company can earn a return from both dividends and capital appreciation (increases in the market price of the stock). The dividend yield ratio reflects the return on investment absent any capital appreciation or, said differently, the return attributed solely to the dividends a company pays.

Focus Company Analysis Microsoft's stock price at the end of fiscal 2020 was $202.49. If you had invested this amount in Microsoft and received the dividends that Microsoft paid out during 2020, your return attributable to dividends would have been 1.01 percent. Even though Microsoft has increased its dividend over the last three years (from $1.68 in 2018 to $2.04 in 2020), its dividend yield ratio has declined. This decline is driven by the significant increase in Microsoft's stock price from $95.37 at the end of fiscal 2018 to $202.49 at the end of fiscal 2020. In addition to a declining dividend yield ratio over time, Microsoft's dividend yield ratio falls below that of two of its competitors: IBM's dividend yield ratio is 5.24 percent and Intel's dividend yield ratios is 2.82 percent.

A Few Cautions Remember that the dividend yield ratio tells only part of the return on investment story; it does not reflect capital appreciation as reflected in the increase in a company's stock price over time. Often potential capital appreciation is a much more important consideration for investors. Though Microsoft pays a dividend, it also reinvests a portion of each year's earnings back into operations to fuel growth. Analysts should consider a company's dividend yield ratio in conjunction with other return measures when assessing a company's performance.

Key Dividend Dates

The declaration and payment of a dividend involve several key dates. Let's review these dates based on information reported on **Microsoft**'s Investor Relations website.

MICROSOFT
REAL WORLD EXCERPT:
Investor Relations Website

Dividend per Common Share		Date of Declaration	Date of Record	Date of Payment
Q1:	$0.51	September 18, 2019	November 21, 2019	December 12, 2019
Q2:	$0.51	December 4, 2019	February 20, 2020	March 12, 2020
Q3:	$0.51	March 9, 2020	May 21, 2020	June 11, 2020
Q4:	$0.51	June 17, 2020	August 20, 2020	September 10, 2020
	$2.04			

Source: Microsoft Corporation

This excerpt contains three important dates:

1. **Declaration date.** The declaration date is the date on which the board of directors officially approves the dividend. As soon as the board declares a dividend, a liability is created and must be recorded.
2. **Date of record.** The record date follows the declaration date; it is the date on which the corporation prepares the list of current stockholders who will receive the dividend payment. The dividend is payable only to those names listed on the record date. No journal entry is made on this date.
3. **Date of payment.** The payment date is the date on which cash is disbursed to pay the dividend liability.

Tip A company records a journal entry on the declaration date and the date of payment. No journal entry is recorded on the date of record.

These three dates apply to all cash dividends and can be shown graphically as follows:

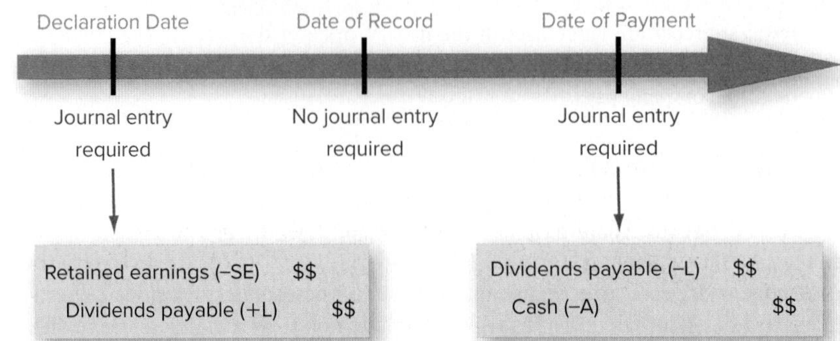

On the declaration date, a company records a liability related to the dividend. To illustrate, on September 18, 2019, Microsoft records the following journal entry. The $3,886 million was reported by Microsoft in its second-quarter earnings press release.

	Debit	Credit
Retained earnings (−SE)	3,886,000,000	
Dividends payable (+L)		3,886,000,000

Assets	=	Liabilities	+	Stockholders' Equity
		Dividends payable +$3,886,000,000		Retained earnings −$3,886,000,000

The payment of the liability on December 12 is recorded as follows:

	Debit	Credit
Dividends payable (−L)	3,886,000,000	
Cash (−A)		3,886,000,000

Assets	=	Liabilities	+	Stockholders' Equity
Cash −$3,886,000,000		Dividends payable −$3,886,000,000		

Notice that the declaration and payment of a cash dividend reduce assets (cash) and stockholders' equity (retained earnings) by the same amount. This observation explains the two fundamental requirements for payment of a cash dividend:

1. **Sufficient retained earnings or net income.** The corporation must have accumulated a sufficient amount of retained earnings, or earned a sufficient amount of income during the period, to cover the amount of the dividend.
2. **Sufficient cash.** The corporation must have sufficient cash to pay the dividend and meet the operating needs of the business. The mere fact that the Retained Earnings account has a large credit balance does not mean that the board of directors can declare and pay a cash dividend. The cash generated in the past by earnings represented in the Retained Earnings account may have been spent to acquire inventory, buy operational assets, and pay liabilities. Consequently, no necessary relationship exists between the balance of retained earnings and the balance of cash on any particular date. Quite simply, retained earnings is not cash.

Investors should be careful to research a company's dividend policy before investing. In the United States, regardless of how profitable a company is, there is no legal obligation for companies to declare dividends. Many very successful companies have never paid dividends while other equally successful companies pay out a large percentage of their earnings each year as a dividend.

The dividend policy for a company is determined by the board of directors. In some other countries, dividend payments are not discretionary and are required by law. In Brazil, for example, companies are legally required to pay out at least 25 percent of their net income in dividends each year.

While U.S. companies are under no legal obligation to declare dividends, once the board of directors declares a dividend (i.e., creates a dividend payable), there is a legal obligation to pay that dividend. In the case of a corporate bankruptcy, dividends payable would be a legally enforceable claim against the company.

FINANCIAL ANALYSIS

Impact of Dividends on Stock Price

Gorodenkoff/Shutterstock

Another date that is important in understanding dividends has no accounting implications. The date one business day before the date of record is known as the *ex-dividend date.* This date is established by the stock exchanges to account for the fact that it takes time to officially transfer stock from a seller to a buyer. If you buy stock before the ex-dividend date, you will be listed as the owner on the date of record and will receive the dividend. If you buy stock on the ex-dividend date or later, the previous owner will be listed as the owner on the date of record and will therefore receive the dividend.

If you follow stock prices, you will notice that they often fall on the ex-dividend date. The stock is worth less on that date because it no longer includes the right to receive the next dividend.

PAUSE FOR FEEDBACK

One of the reasons that investors buy common stock is to earn dividends. We have discussed dividends paid with cash. In the next section, we will look at dividends paid with stock. Before we move on, complete the following questions to test your understanding of the concepts we have covered so far.

SELF-STUDY QUIZ

1. On which dividend date is a liability created?
2. A cash outflow occurs on which dividend date?
3. Which dividend date does not require a journal entry?

After you have completed your answers, check them below.

GUIDED HELP 11-2

For additional step-by-step video instruction, go to mhhe.com/libby_gh11-2.

Related Homework: M11-7, M11-8, E11-20, E11-21, P11-9, P11-10

Solutions to SELF-STUDY QUIZ

1. Date of declaration.
2. Date of payment.
3. Date of record.

LEARNING OBJECTIVE 11-6

Discuss and report stock dividends and stock splits.

STOCK DIVIDENDS AND STOCK SPLITS

Stock Dividends

Unless stated otherwise, the term *dividend* means a cash dividend. Though cash dividends are by far the most common type of dividend, companies also can distribute additional shares of stock as a dividend. A **stock dividend** is a distribution of additional shares of a company's own stock to its stockholders on a pro rata basis at no cost to the stockholder.

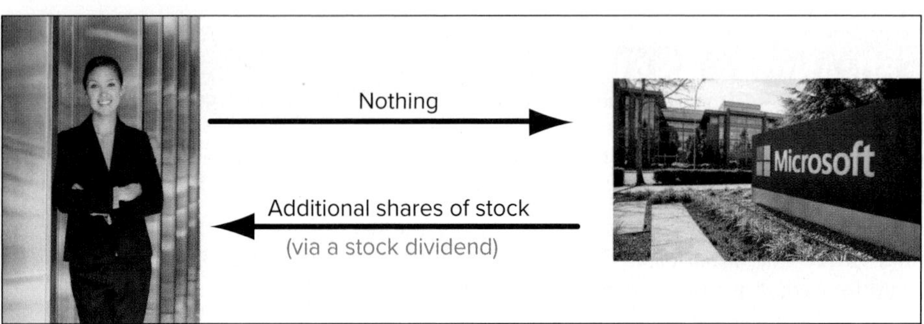

Left: Dave and Les Jacobs/Blend Images LLC; Right: VDB Photos/Shutterstock

The phrase *pro rata basis* means that each stockholder receives additional shares equal to the percentage of shares held. A stockholder with 10 percent of the outstanding shares would receive 10 percent of any additional shares issued as a stock dividend.

The economic value of a stock dividend is the subject of much debate. In reality, a stock dividend by itself has no economic value. All stockholders receive a pro rata distribution of shares, which means that each stockholder owns exactly the same portion of the company as before. The value of an investment is determined by the percentage of the company a stockholder owns, not by the number of shares held. If you get change for a dollar, you do not have more wealth because you hold four quarters instead of one dollar. Similarly, if you own 10 percent of a company, you are not wealthier simply because the company declares a stock dividend and gives you (and all other stockholders) more shares of stock. Both before and after the stock dividend, you own 10 percent of the company.

The stock market reacts immediately when a stock dividend is issued, and the stock price falls. Theoretically, if the stock price was $60 before a stock dividend and the company doubles the number of shares outstanding by issuing a stock dividend, the price of the company's stock should fall to $30. In reality, the fall in price may not be exactly proportional to the number of new shares issued. In some cases, the stock dividend makes the stock more attractive to new investors. Many investors prefer to buy stock in round lots, typically in multiples of 100 shares. An investor with $10,000 might not buy a stock selling for $150, for instance, because she cannot afford to buy 100 shares. However, she might buy the stock if the price were less than $100 as the result of a stock dividend. In such cases, the stock price decrease at the time of a stock dividend will likely not be exactly proportional to the number of new shares issued.

When a company's board of directors declares a stock dividend, the company transfers an amount from the Retained Earnings account (or the Additional Paid-in Capital account) into the Common Stock account to reflect the additional shares issued. The amount transferred depends on whether the stock dividend is classified as a large stock dividend or a small stock dividend.

A large stock dividend involves the distribution of additional shares that amount to more than 20–25 percent of currently outstanding shares. A small stock dividend involves the distribution of shares that amount to less than 20–25 percent of currently outstanding shares. Because a large stock dividend significantly decreases a company's stock price, GAAP requires the amount transferred to the Common Stock account to be based on the par value of the stock. In the case of a small stock dividend, GAAP requires the amount transferred to be based on the market price of the stock, with the par value amount being transferred to the Common Stock account and the excess transferred to the Additional Paid-in Capital account.

To demonstrate how the accounting for stock dividends works, assume **Microsoft** declared a large stock dividend that resulted in an additional 40,000,000 shares of $0.00000625 par value stock being distributed to stockholders. On the date of declaration, Microsoft would record the following journal entry:

	Debit	Credit
Retained earnings (−SE) ($0.00000625 × 40,000,000)	250	
Common stock (+SE) ($0.00000625 × 40,000,000)		250

Assets	=	Liabilities	+	Stockholders' Equity	
				Retained earnings	−$250
				Common stock	+$250

Now assume Microsoft declared a small stock dividend that resulted in an additional 4,000,000 shares being distributed to stockholders. On the date of declaration, Microsoft's stock was trading at $220 per share. The journal entry Microsoft would enter is:

	Debit	Credit
Retained earnings (−SE) ($220 market price × 4,000,000)	880,000,000	
Common stock (+SE) ($0.00000625 par value × 4,000,000)		25
Additional paid-in capital (+SE) (remainder)		879,999,975

Assets	=	Liabilities	+	Stockholders' Equity	
				Retained earnings	−880,000,000
				Common stock	25
				Additional paid-in capital	+879,999,975

It is important to note that regardless of whether a stock dividend is classified as large or small, there is no change in the total amount of stockholders' equity. Both large and small stock dividends merely redistribute amounts within the stockholders' equity section of the balance sheet.

Stock Splits

Stock splits are not dividends. While they are similar to a stock dividend in the sense that they distribute additional shares of stock to stockholders, they are quite different in terms of how they impact accounts in the stockholders' equity section of the balance sheet.

Whether a company distributes additional shares of stock by declaring a stock dividend or by initiating a stock split often is determined by state law. In a **stock split**, a company commits to giving stockholders a specified number of additional shares for each share that they currently hold. For example, when a company declares a two-for-one stock split, a stockholder who owned one share of stock before the split will own two shares of stock after the split. In essence, the one share has been "split" into two shares. A company's footnotes will state whether the stock split applies to all authorized, issued, and outstanding shares.

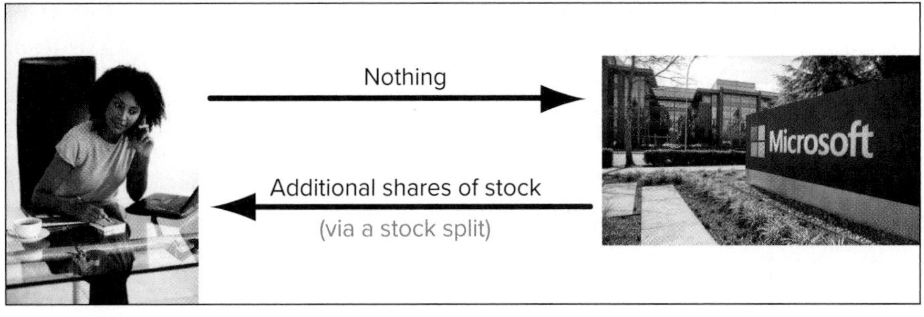

Left: Image Source, all rights reserved; Right: VDB Photos/Shutterstock

When a company initiates a stock split, it also reduces the par value of its stock so that the total dollar amount in the Common Stock account remains unchanged. For instance, if **Microsoft** executes a two-for-one stock split, thereby doubling the number of shares issued, it would reduce the par value of its stock from $0.00000625 to $0.000003125. Microsoft has executed many stock splits since it went public in 1981, which is one of the reasons its par value is so small. In contrast to a stock dividend, a stock split does not change any account balances in the stockholders' equity section of the balance sheet.

In both a stock dividend and a stock split, the stockholder receives more shares of stock without having to invest additional resources to acquire the shares. A stock dividend requires a journal entry; a stock split does not but is disclosed in the notes to the financial statements. The comparative effects of a large stock dividend versus a stock split may be summarized as follows:

STOCKHOLDERS' EQUITY			
	Before	After a 100% Stock Dividend	After a 2-for-1 Stock Split
Number of shares outstanding	300,000	600,000	600,000
Par value per share	$ 1.00	$ 1.00	$ 0.50
Common stock	300,000	600,000	300,000
Retained earnings	650,000	350,000	650,000
Total stockholders' equity	$950,000	$950,000	$950,000

It is quite common for companies to announce a "stock split" but to account for the distribution of additional shares as a large stock dividend. Companies typically do this to avoid changing the par value of their common stock. Such announcements are referred to as initiating a "stock split effected in the form of a stock dividend." Whenever you see this phrase, know that the company has accounted for the transaction as a large stock dividend.

PAUSE FOR FEEDBACK

We have concluded our discussion of common stock by looking at stock dividends and stock splits. In the next section, we will provide a brief introduction to the statement of stockholders' equity and then discuss preferred stock. Before you move on, complete the following questions to test your understanding of the concepts we have covered so far.

SELF-STUDY QUIZ

Barton Corporation issued 100,000 shares of common stock (par value $0.10) by declaring a stock dividend. At the time the dividend was declared, Barton's stock was trading at $30 per share.

1. Record this transaction, assuming it is classified as a small stock dividend.
2. Record this transaction, assuming that it is classified as a large stock dividend.
3. If Barton were to distribute the same number of shares by announcing a stock split, what journal entry would be required?

After you have completed your answers, check them below.

GUIDED HELP 11-3

For additional step-by-step video instruction, go to mhhe.com/libby_gh11-3.

Related Homework: M11-10, E11-17, E11-22, E11-23, E11-24, P11-11

Solutions to SELF-STUDY QUIZ

1. Retained earnings (−SE) ($30 × 100,000)	3,000,000	
Common stock (+SE) ($0.10 × 100,000)		10,000
Additional paid-in capital (+SE) (remainder)		2,990,000
2. Retained earnings (−SE) ($0.10 × 100,000)	10,000	
Common stock (+SE) ($0.10 × 100,000)		10,000
3. No journal entry is required in the case of a stock split.		

STATEMENT OF STOCKHOLDERS' EQUITY

LEARNING OBJECTIVE 11-7

Describe the information reported on the statement of stockholders' equity.

The purpose of the statement of stockholders' equity is to show how accounts in the stockholders' equity section of the balance sheet have changed over the accounting period. Common accounts shown are common stock, additional paid-in capital, treasury stock or repurchased stock, and retained earnings. The statement of stockholders' equity for **Microsoft** is shown in Exhibit 11.3.

As you review Exhibit 11.3, you will observe many of the issues discussed in this chapter. Notice for example that in fiscal 2020 Microsoft:

1. Issued common stock totaling $1,343 million.
2. Repurchased common stock totaling $4,599 million.
3. Granted stock-based compensation totaling $5,289 million.
4. Reported net income of $44,281 million, which increased retained earnings.
5. Issued a common stock cash dividend totaling $15,483 million, which decreased retained earnings.

At the bottom of the statement is a section entitled "Accumulated other comprehensive income (loss)." This section captures several important items that are reported as a part of comprehensive income, but not net income. Examples of items that are not included in the computation of net income include:

1. *Unrealized holding gains or losses from certain types of debt securities.* Under GAAP, gains and losses from holding certain types of debt securities are reported on the income statement only when the securities are sold. Unrealized gains and losses that occur before the securities are sold are included in comprehensive income.

EXHIBIT 11.3

Excerpt from Statement of Stockholders' Equity for Microsoft

MICROSOFT

REAL WORLD EXCERPT: Annual Report

STOCKHOLDERS' EQUITY STATEMENTS

(in millions)

Year Ended June 30,	2020	2019	2018
Common stock and paid-in capital			
Balance, beginning of period	**$ 78,520**	$ 71,223	$69,315
Common stock issued	**1,343**	6,829	1,002
Common stock repurchased	**(4,599)**	(4,195)	(3,033)
Stock-based compensation expense	**5,289**	4,652	3,940
Other, net	**(1)**	11	(1)
Balance, end of period	**80,552**	78,520	71,223
Retained earnings			
Balance, beginning of period	**24,150**	13,682	17,769
Net income	**44,281**	39,240	16,571
Common stock cash dividends	**(15,483)**	(14,103)	(12,917)
Common stock repurchased	**(18,382)**	(15,346)	(7,699)
Cumulative effect of accounting changes	**0**	677	(42)
Balance, end of period	**34,566**	24,150	13,682
Accumulated other comprehensive income (loss)			
Balance, beginning of period	**(340)**	(2,187)	627
Other comprehensive income (loss)	**3,526**	1,914	(2,856)
Cumulative effect of accounting changes	**0**	(67)	42
Balance, end of period	**3,186**	(340)	(2,187)
Total stockholders' equity	**$118,304**	$102,330	$82,718
Cash dividends declared per common share	**$ 2.04**	$ 1.84	$ 1.68

Amounts may not add due to rounding.

Source: Microsoft Corporation

2. *Foreign currency translation gains and losses.* Many U.S. companies have foreign subsidiaries that conduct business using foreign currencies. Incorporating the financial statements of these foreign subsidiaries into a U.S. company's financial statements requires the use of a foreign currency exchange rate. Changes in exchange rates from year to year result in foreign currency translation gains and losses. These gains and losses are included in comprehensive income.

The above list is not comprehensive. If you choose to take a more advanced accounting course, you will learn a great deal more about the components of comprehensive income.

PAUSE FOR FEEDBACK

We just covered the statement of stockholders' equity, and in previous chapters you learned about the accounts included in a company's balance sheet. Before we transition to discussing preferred stock, test your knowledge of where information is reported in the financial statements by completing the quiz below.

SELF-STUDY QUIZ

Identify whether the following information is reported in a company's balance sheet and/or its statement of stockholders' equity.

SELF-STUDY QUIZ

1. Ending balance of accounts receivable
2. Common stock repurchased during the year
3. Ending balance of long-term debt
4. Cash dividends declared during the year
5. Net income earned during the year
6. Ending balance of retained earnings

GUIDED HELP 11-4

For additional step-by-step video instruction on how to create an income statement, statement of stockholders' equity, and balance sheet, go to mhhe.com/libby_gh11-4.

Related Homework: M11-6, E11-4, E11-6, E11-8, E11-9, E11-14, P11-2, P11-5, P11-10

Solutions to SELF-STUDY QUIZ

1. Balance sheet
2. Statement of stockholders' equity
3. Balance sheet
4. Statement of stockholders' equity
5. Statement of stockholders' equity
6. Balance sheet and statement of stockholders' equity

PREFERRED STOCK TRANSACTIONS

LEARNING OBJECTIVE 11-8

Describe the characteristics of preferred stock and report preferred stock transactions.

In addition to common stock, some corporations issue preferred stock. The journal entries required to record the issuance and repurchase of preferred stock are the same as the journal entries required to record the issuance and repurchase of common stock. Preferred stock, however, differs from common stock in a number of ways. The most significant differences are:

- **Preferred stock typically does not have voting rights.** Without voting rights, preferred stock does not appeal to investors who want some control over the operations of a corporation. The lack of voting rights is one of the reasons some corporations issue preferred stock to raise capital: Issuing preferred stock permits them to raise money without issuing additional common shares with voting rights.
- **Preferred stock is less risky.** Generally, preferred stock is less risky than common stock because holders receive priority payment of dividends and distribution of assets if the corporation goes out of business. Usually a specified amount per share must be paid to preferred stockholders before any remaining assets can be distributed to the common stockholders.
- **Preferred stock typically has a fixed dividend rate.** For example, "6 percent preferred stock, par value $10 per share," pays an annual dividend of 6 percent of par value, or $0.60 per share. If preferred stock had no par value, the preferred dividend would be specified as $0.60 per share. The fixed dividend is attractive to certain investors who want stable income from their investments.

Dividends on Preferred Stock

Preferred stock offers several dividend preferences over common stock. The two most common preferences are a current dividend preference and a cumulative dividend preference.

Current Dividend Preference

The current dividend preference requires a company to pay dividends to preferred stockholders before paying dividends to common stockholders. This preference is always a feature of preferred stock. After the current dividend preference has been met and if no other preference is operative, dividends can be paid to the common stockholders. To illustrate, assume Wally Company has the following stock outstanding:

WALLY COMPANY
Preferred stock: 6%, $20 par value, 2,000 shares outstanding = $40,000
Common stock: $10 par value, 5,000 shares outstanding = $50,000

Assuming a current dividend preference only, dividends would be allocated as follows:

Example	Total Dividends	6% Preferred Stock*	Common Stock
No. 1	$ 3,000	$2,400	$ 600
No. 2	18,000	2,400	15,600

*Preferred dividend calculation: $20 par value × 0.06 × 2,000 shares = $2,400.

Cumulative Dividend Preference

The cumulative dividend preference requires any unpaid dividends on preferred stock to accumulate. This cumulative unpaid amount, known as dividends in arrears, must be paid before any common dividends can be paid. Of course, if the preferred stock is noncumulative, dividends can never be in arrears, and therefore any dividend that is not declared is permanently lost. Preferred stock is usually cumulative.

To illustrate the cumulative dividend preference, assume that Wally Company's preferred stock in the above example is cumulative and that dividends have been in arrears for two years.

Example	Total Dividends	6% Preferred Stock*	Common Stock
No. 1	$ 8,000	$7,200	$ 800
No. 2	30,000	7,200	22,800

*Preferred dividend calculation:
–Current dividend preference: $20 par value × 0.06 × 2,000 shares = $2,400
–Dividends in arrears: $2,400 × 2 years = $4,800
–Total preferred dividend: $2,400 + $4,800 = $7,200

The existence of dividends in arrears on preferred stock can limit a company's ability to pay dividends to common stockholders and can affect a company's future cash flows. Because dividends are never an actual liability until the board of directors declares them, dividends in arrears are not reported on the balance sheet. Instead, they are disclosed in the notes to the financial statements.

FINANCIAL ANALYSIS

Preferred Stock and Limited Voting Rights

Though not typical, some preferred stock has special voting rights. For example, the excerpt below is from **Public Storage**'s 2020 Annual Report:

PUBLIC STORAGE
REAL WORLD EXCERPT:
2020 Annual Report

> The holders of our Preferred Shares have general preference rights with respect to liquidation, quarterly distributions and any accumulated unpaid distributions. Except as noted below, holders of the Preferred Shares do not have voting rights. In the event of a cumulative arrearage equal to six quarterly dividends, holders of all outstanding series of preferred shares . . . will have the right to elect two additional members to serve on our board of trustees (our "Board") until the arrearage has been cured. At December 31, 2020, there were no dividends in arrears.

Source: Public Storage

This special voting right allows preferred stockholders to have some say in operational matters if the company has had difficulty paying dividends for an extended period of time.

FOCUS ON CASH FLOWS

LEARNING OBJECTIVE 11-9

Discuss the impact of stock transactions on cash flows.

Financing Activities

Transactions involving stock have a direct impact on the capital structure of a business. The cash inflows and outflows associated with these transactions are reported in the Financing Activities section of the statement of cash flows.

EFFECT ON STATEMENT OF CASH FLOWS

In General As reflected in the following table on the next page, cash receipts from investors are reported as cash inflows, and cash payments to investors are reported as cash outflows:

	Effect on Cash Flows
Financing activities	
Issuance of common or preferred stock	+
Common stock repurchased (treasury stock)	−
Sale of treasury stock	+
Payment of cash dividends	−

Focus Company Analysis The Financing Activities section of **Microsoft**'s Statement of Cash Flows is shown in Exhibit 11.4. Notice that for each of the last three years, Microsoft has paid out a significant amount of cash to repurchase common stock and to pay dividends.

EXHIBIT 11.4

Excerpt from Statement of Cash Flows for Microsoft

MICROSOFT

REAL WORLD EXCERPT: Annual Report

MICROSOFT CORPORATION
Cash Flows Statements
(In millions)

Year Ended June 30	**2020**	**2019**	**2018**
Financing			
Repayments of short-term debt, maturities of 90 days of less, net	**$ 0**	$ 0	$ (7,324)
Proceeds from issuance of debt	**0**	0	7,183
Cash premium on debt exchange	**(3,417)**	0	0
Repayments of debt	**(5,518)**	(4,000)	(10,060)
Common stock issued	**1,343**	1,142	1,002
Common stock repurchased	**(22,968)**	(19,543)	(10,721)
Common stock cash dividends paid	**(15,137)**	(13,811)	(12,699)
Other, net	**(334)**	(675)	(971)
Net cash used in financing	**$(46,031)**	$(36,887)	$(33,590)

Source: Microsoft Corporation

DEMONSTRATION CASE

(Try to answer the questions before proceeding to the suggested solutions that follow.) This case focuses on the organization and operations for the first year of Chap 6 Corporation. Chap 6 became a corporation on January 1 of this year. The corporate charter authorized the following stock:

Common stock, no-par value, 20,000 shares
Preferred stock, 5 percent, $100 par value, 5,000 shares

The following summarized transactions, selected from Chap 6's first year of operations, were completed on the dates indicated:

a. January Sold a total of 8,000 shares of common stock to investors for $50 cash per share.
b. February Sold 2,000 shares of preferred stock to investors for $102 cash per share.
c. March Declared, but has yet to pay, a cash dividend of $1 per share of common stock.
d. July Repurchased 100 shares of preferred stock, that were initially sold in February, for $104 cash per share. The repurchased shares are being held as treasury shares.
e. August Resold 20 shares of the preferred treasury stock for $105 per share.

Required:

1. Provide the appropriate journal entries with a brief explanation for each transaction.
2. Prepare the stockholders' equity section of the balance sheet for Chap 6 at the end of Year 1. Assume retained earnings at the end of Year 1 equals $23,000.

SUGGESTED SOLUTION

1. Journal entries:

a. Cash (+A)	400,000	
Common stock (+SE)		400,000
Sale of no-par common stock ($50 × 8,000 shares = $400,000).		
b. Cash (+A)	204,000	
Preferred stock (+SE)		200,000
Additional paid in capital, preferred stock (+SE)		4,000
Sale of $100 par value preferred stock ($102 × 2,000 shares = $204,000).		
c. Retained earnings (−SE)	8,000	
Dividends payable (+L)		8,000
Declared cash dividend ($1 × 8,000 shares = $8,000).		
d. Treasury stock (+XSE, −SE)	10,400	
Cash (−A)		10,400
Repurchased 100 shares of preferred stock ($104 × 100 shares = $10,400).		
e. Cash (+A)	2,100	
Treasury stock (−XSE, +SE)		2,080
Additional paid-in capital, preferred stock (+SE)		20
Resold 20 shares of the preferred treasury stock at $105 ($105 × 20 shares = $2,100).		

2. Stockholders' equity section of the balance sheet:

CHAP 6 CORPORATION
Partial Balance Sheet
At End of Year 1

Stockholders' Equity		
Preferred stock, 5% ($100 par value; 5,000 shares authorized, 2,000 shares issued, 1,920 shares outstanding)	$200,000	
Additional paid-in capital, preferred stock	4,020	
Common stock (no-par value; 20,000 shares authorized, 8,000 shares issued and outstanding)	400,000	
Retained earnings	23,000	
Preferred treasury stock (80 shares)	(8,320)	
Total stockholders' equity		$618,700

Chapter Supplement

Accounting for the Equity of Sole Proprietorships and Partnerships

Owner's Equity for a Sole Proprietorship

A *sole proprietorship* is an unincorporated business owned by one person. Only two owner's equity accounts are typically used. The first is a capital account for the proprietor (e.g., Hans Solo, capital). The second is a drawing or withdrawal account for the proprietor (e.g., Hans Solo, drawing).

The capital account of a sole proprietorship serves two purposes: to record investments by the owner and to accumulate the income or loss each accounting period. The drawing account is used to record the owner's withdrawals of cash or other assets from the business during an accounting period. The drawing account is a temporary account that is closed to the owner's capital account at the end of each accounting period. Thus, the capital account reflects the cumulative total of all investments by the owner and all earnings of the entity less all withdrawals by the owner.

In most respects, the accounting for a sole proprietorship is the same as for a corporation. Exhibit 11.5 presents the recording of selected transactions of Hans Solo Aviation and the Statement of owner's Equity.

EXHIBIT 11.5

Accounting for Owner's Equity for a Sole Proprietorship

Selected Entries during Year 1

January 1, Year 1

Hans Solo started an aviation business by investing $150,000 of personal savings.

	Debit	Credit
Cash (+A)	150,000	
Hans Solo, capital (+OE)		150,000

Assets		=	Liabilities	+	Owner's Equity	
Cash	+150,000				Hans Solo, capital	+150,000

During Year 1

Each month during the year, (so 12 times total) Hans withdrew $1,000 cash from the business for personal living costs.

Each Month	Debit	Credit
Hans Solo, drawing (−OE)	1,000	
Cash (−A)		1,000

Assets		=	Liabilities	+	Owner's Equity	
Cash	−1,000				Hans Solo, drawing	−1,000

Note: At the end of Year 1, after the last withdrawal, the drawing account reflected a debit balance of $12,000.

December 31, Year 1

At the end of Year 1, $418,000 of revenues and $400,000 of expenses were closed to the owner's capital account.

	Debit	Credit
Revenue accounts (−R, closing entry)	418,000	
Expense accounts (−E, closing entry)		400,000
Hans Solo, capital (+OE)		18,000

Assets	=	Liabilities	+	Owner's Equity	
				Close revenue accounts	−418,000
				Close expense accounts	+400,000
				Hans Solo, capital	+18,000

(Continued)

EXHIBIT 11.5

Concluded

At the end of Year 1, the drawing account was closed.

	Debit	Credit
Hans Solo, capital (−OE)	12,000	
Hans Solo, drawing (+OE, closing entry)		12,000

Assets	=	Liabilities	+	Owner's Equity	
				Hans Solo, drawing	+12,000
				Hans Solo, capital	−12,000

HANS SOLO AVIATION

Statement of Owner's Equity

For the Year Ended December 31, Year 1

Owner's Equity	
Hans Solo, capital, January 1, Year 1	$ 0
Add: Investments during Year 1	150,000
Add: Net income for Year 1	18,000
Total	168,000
Less: Drawings for Year 1	(12,000)
Hans Solo, capital, December 31, Year 1	$156,000

Because a sole proprietorship does not pay income taxes, its financial statements do not reflect income tax expense or income taxes payable. Instead, the net income of a sole proprietorship is taxed when it is included on the owner's personal income tax return. Likewise, any withdrawal by the sole proprietor is not recognized as an expense but rather is accounted for as a distribution of capital.

Owners' Equity for a Partnership

The Uniform Partnership Act, which most states have adopted, defines a partnership as "an association of two or more persons to carry on as co-owners of a business for profit." Small businesses and professionals such as accountants, doctors, and lawyers often use the partnership form of business.

A partnership is formed by two or more persons reaching mutual agreement about the terms of the relationship. The agreement between the partners constitutes a partnership contract and specifies matters such as division of periodic income, management responsibilities, transfer or sale of partnership interests, disposition of assets upon liquidation, and procedures to be followed in case of the death of a partner or disagreements. If the partnership agreement does not specify these matters, the laws of the resident state take precedence.

The primary advantages of a partnership are (1) ease of formation, (2) complete control by the partners, and (3) lack of income taxes on the business itself. The primary disadvantage is the unlimited liability of each partner for the partnership's debts. If the partnership does not have sufficient assets to satisfy outstanding debt, creditors of the partnership can seize the partners' personal assets.

As with a sole proprietorship, accounting for a partnership follows the same underlying principles as any other form of business organization, except for those entries that directly affect owners' equity. Accounting for partners' equity follows the same pattern as for a sole proprietorship, except that separate capital and drawing accounts are established for each partner. The net income of a partnership is divided among the partners in accordance with the partnership agreement.

Exhibit 11.6 presents selected journal entries and a Statement of Owners' Equity for Mirror Image Partners to illustrate the accounting for partnerships.

EXHIBIT 11.6

Accounting for Owners' Equity for a Partnership

Selected Entries during Year 1

January 1, Year 1

Serena and Venus organized Mirror Image Partners on January 1. Serena and Venus contributed cash to the partnership in the amount of $60,000 and $40,000, respectively.

	Debit	Credit
Cash (+A)	100,000	
Serena, capital (+OE)		60,000
Venus, capital (+OE)		40,000

Assets		=	Liabilities	+	Owners' Equity	
Cash	+100,000				Serena, capital	+60,000
					Venus, capital	+40,000

During Year 1

Each month during the year (so 12 times total), Serena withdrew $1,000 cash and Venus withdrew $650 cash for personal use.

Each Month	Debit	Credit
Serena, drawing (−OE)	1,000	
Venus, drawing (−OE)	650	
Cash (−A)		1,650

Assets		=	Liabilities	+	Owners' Equity	
Cash	−1,650				Serena, drawing	−1,000
					Venus, drawing	−650

Note: At the end of Year 1, after the last withdrawal, the drawing accounts for Serena and Venus reflected debit balances of $12,000 and $7,800, respectively.

December 31, Year 1

At the end of Year 1, $630,000 of revenues and $600,000 of expenses were closed to the owners' capital accounts. The partnership agreement specified Serena would receive 60 percent of earnings and Venus would receive 40 percent.

	Debit	Credit
Revenue accounts (−R, closing entry)	630,000	
Expense accounts (−E, closing entry)		600,000
Serena, capital (+OE) ($30,000 × 0.60)		18,000
Venus, capital (+OE) ($30,000 × 0.40)		12,000

Assets	=	Liabilities	+	Owners' Equity	
				Close revenue accounts	−630,000
				Close expense accounts	+600,000
				Serena, capital	+18,000
				Venus, capital	+12,000

(Continued)

EXHIBIT 11.6

Concluded

At the end of Year 1, the drawing accounts were closed.

	Debit	Credit
Serena, capital (−OE)	12,000	
Venus, capital (−OE)	7,800	
Serena, drawing (+OE, closing entry)		12,000
Venus, drawing (+OE, closing entry)		7,800

Assets	=	Liabilities	+	Owners' Equity	
				Serena, drawing	+12,000
				Venus, drawing	+7,800
				Serena, capital	−12,000
				Venus, capital	−7,800

MIRROR IMAGE PARTNERS
Statement of Owners' Equity
For the Year Ended December 31, Year 1

	Serena	Venus	Total
Investment, January 1, Year 1	$ 0	$ 0	$ 0
Add: Investments during Year 1	60,000	40,000	100,000
Add: Net income for Year 1	18,000	12,000	30,000
Totals	78,000	52,000	130,000
Less: Drawings during Year 1	(12,000)	(7,800)	(19,800)
Owner's equity, December 31, Year 1	$66,000	$44,200	$110,200

Like a sole proprietorship, a partnership does not report income tax expense on its income statement. Partners must report their share of the partnership profits on their individual tax returns. Also like sole proprietorships, withdrawals by the partners are not recorded as expenses but rather are treated as distributions of capital.

CHAPTER TAKE-AWAYS

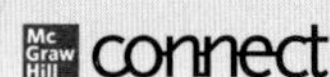

11-1. Explain the role of stock in the capital structure of a corporation. **p. 577**

Issuing stock is one way corporations raise capital. Corporations issue stock by selling shares to investors, who then become owners of the corporation. Investors can trade their stock on established stock exchanges.

11-2. Compute and analyze the earnings per share ratio. **p. 579**

The earnings per share (EPS) ratio is computed by dividing net income by the weighted average number of common shares outstanding. The EPS ratio facilitates the comparison of companies based on how much they earn per share of common stock outstanding.

11-3. Describe the characteristics of common stock and report common stock transactions. **p. 579**

Common stock is the basic voting stock issued by a corporation. Many states require common stock to have a par value. Common stock transactions consist of (1) the initial sale of shares, (2) repurchasing shares, (3) declaring and paying cash dividends, and (4) initiating stock dividends and stock splits.

11-4. Discuss and report dividends. **p. 584**

Investors earn a return on their stock investment through stock price appreciation, the receipt of cash dividends, or both. Cash dividends are payments to stockholders, typically on a per share basis. A company records a dividend as a liability when its board of directors declares the dividend (i.e., on the date of declaration). The liability is satisfied when the company pays the cash dividend to stockholders (i.e., on the date of payment).

11-5. Compute and analyze the dividend yield ratio. **p. 584**

The dividend yield ratio is computed by dividing dividends per share by a stock's market price per share. The dividend yield ratio measures an investor's return on investment attributed to the dividends a company pays.

11-6. Discuss and report stock dividends and stock splits. **p. 588**

Stock dividends and stock splits are both ways for companies to distribute additional shares of stock to existing stockholders. When a company initiates a stock dividend, it records a journal entry that transfers the dividend amount from the retained earnings account to the common stock account and, if applicable, the additional paid-in capital account. When a company initiates a stock split, no journal entry is required; rather, the company simply increases the number of shares issued and decreases the par value per share.

11-7. Describe the information reported on the statement of stockholders' equity. **p. 591**

The statement of stockholders' equity is one of the four financial statements required by GAAP. It shows how accounts that affect the stockholders' equity section of the balance sheet have changed over the accounting period. Examples of accounts reported are common stock, preferred stock, repurchased shares or treasury stock, retained earnings, and components of comprehensive income.

11-8. Describe the characteristics of preferred stock and report preferred stock transactions. **p. 593**

The purpose of preferred stock is the same as that of common stock: to raise capital. Preferred stock differs from common stock in that it is issued on a more selective basis, typically does not have voting rights, has a current dividend preference, and may have a cumulative dividend preference. A current dividend preference specifies that preferred stockholders will receive dividends before common stockholders. A cumulative dividend preference specifies that preferred stockholders will receive any past unpaid dividends before common stockholders receive current dividends.

11-9. Discuss the impact of stock transactions on cash flows. **p. 594**

Any cash inflows or outflows associated with a company's stock are reported in the Financing Activities section of the company's statement of cash flows. Typical inflows are the issuance of stock and the reselling of treasury shares. Typical outflows are the repurchase of common stock and the payment of dividends.

This chapter concludes a major section of the book. In the previous five chapters, we have discussed individual sections of the balance sheet. We will now shift our focus to the statement of cash flows. In the next chapter, you will learn how companies report cash transactions on the statement of cash flows and how companies use information from the balance sheet and income statement to create the statement of cash flows.

KEY RATIOS

The **earnings per share ratio** reflects how much a company earned per share of common stock outstanding. The ratio is computed as follows (see the "Key Ratio Analysis" box in the Ownership of a Corporation section):

$$\text{Earnings per Share} = \frac{\text{Net Income*}}{\text{Weighted Average Number of Common Shares Outstanding}}$$

*Any preferred dividends should be subtracted from net income.

The **dividend yield ratio** measures the return on investment attributable to the dividends a company pays. The ratio is computed as follows (see the "Key Ratio Analysis" box in the Dividends on Common Stock section):

$$\text{Dividend Yield} = \frac{\text{Dividends per Share}}{\text{Market Price per Share}}$$

FINDING FINANCIAL INFORMATION

Balance Sheet

Under Current Liabilities

Dividends, once declared by the board of directors, are reported as a current liability until paid.

Under Stockholders' Equity

Typical accounts include:
- Common stock
- Preferred stock
- Repurchased shares or treasury stock
- Additional paid-in capital
- Retained earnings

Statement of Stockholders' Equity

This statement reports detailed information concerning stockholders' equity, including
- Beginning and ending balances in each equity account,
- Impact of transactions such as issuing stock, repurchasing stock, earning income and paying dividends,
- Information concerning any gains or losses that affect comprehensive income.

Income Statement

Capital stock transactions do not affect the income statement. Dividends paid are not an expense. They are a distribution of income and are, therefore, taken directly out of stockholders' equity by reducing retained earnings.

Statement of Cash Flows

Under Financing Activities
- + Cash inflows from initial sale of stock
- + Cash inflows from sale of treasury stock
- − Cash outflows for repurchasing stock
- − Cash outflows for dividends

Notes

Under Summary of Significant Accounting Policies

Capital stock is typically not discussed in detail in the summary footnote.

Under a Separate Note

Most companies report information about their employee stock option plans and information about stock transactions that occurred during the period. Information about dividends declared and paid and any dividends in arrears on preferred stock are also reported in the notes.

KEY TERMS

Authorized Shares The maximum number of shares of stock a corporation can issue as specified in its charter. **p. 578**

Common Stock The basic voting stock issued by a corporation. **p. 579**

Cumulative Dividend Preference Requires any unpaid dividends on preferred stock to accumulate. These cumulative preferred dividends must be paid before any common dividends can be paid. **p. 593**

Current Dividend Preference Requires that dividends be paid to preferred stockholders before any dividends are paid to common stockholders. **p. 593**

Declaration Date The date on which the board of directors officially approves a dividend. **p. 585**

Dividends in Arrears Dividends on cumulative preferred stock that have not been paid in prior years. **p. 593**

Issued Shares The total number of shares of stock that have been sold. **p. 578**

Legal Capital The permanent amount of capital defined by state law that must remain invested in the business; serves as a cushion for creditors. **p. 580**

No-Par Value Stock Capital stock that has no par value as specified in the corporate charter. **p. 580**

Outstanding Shares The total number of shares of stock that are owned by stockholders on any particular date. **p. 578**

Par Value The nominal value per share of stock as specified in the corporate charter. **p. 580**

Payment Date The date on which a cash dividend is paid to the stockholders of record. **p. 585**

Preferred Stock Stock that has specified rights over common stock. **p. 593**

Record Date The date on which the corporation prepares the list of current stockholders who will receive the dividend when paid. **p. 585**

Stock Dividend A distribution of additional shares of a corporation's own stock on a pro rata basis at no cost to existing stockholders. **p. 588**

Stock Split Gives stockholders a specified number of additional shares for each share that they currently hold. **p. 589**

Treasury Stock A corporation's own stock that has been repurchased. Shares held as treasury stock are considered issued shares but not outstanding shares. **p. 578**

QUESTIONS

1. Define the term *corporation* and identify the primary advantages of organizing as a corporation.
2. What is a corporate charter?
3. Explain each of the following terms: (*a*) *authorized shares,* (*b*) *issued shares,* and (*c*) *outstanding shares.*
4. Differentiate between common stock and preferred stock.
5. Explain the distinction between par value and no-par value stock.
6. Define *additional paid-in capital.*
7. Explain the difference between contributed capital and earned capital. How is each represented in the stockholders' equity section of a company's balance sheet?
8. Define *treasury stock.* Why do corporations repurchase common stock?
9. How is treasury stock reported on the balance sheet? If a corporation resells treasury stock at a price above or below the price paid to originally acquire the treasury shares, how does it record this difference?
10. What are the two basic requirements to support the declaration of a cash dividend? What are the effects of a cash dividend on assets and stockholders' equity?
11. Define *stock dividend.* How does a stock dividend differ from a cash dividend?
12. Define *stock split.* How does a stock split differ from a stock dividend?
13. Identify and explain the three important dates with respect to dividends.
14. How does preferred stock differ from common stock?
15. Differentiate between cumulative and noncumulative preferred stock.

MULTIPLE-CHOICE QUESTIONS

1. Katz Corporation has issued 400,000 shares of common stock and holds 20,000 shares of treasury stock. Katz's charter authorized the issuance of 500,000 shares. The company has declared and paid a dividend of $1 per share on outstanding common stock. What is the total amount of the dividend paid to common stockholders?
   a. $400,000
   b. $20,000
   c. $380,000
   d. $500,000
2. Which statement regarding treasury stock is false?
   a. Treasury stock is considered to be issued but not outstanding.
   b. Treasury stock has no voting, dividend, or liquidation rights.
   c. Treasury stock reduces total equity on the balance sheet.
   d. None of the above are false.
3. Which of the following statements about stock dividends is true?
   a. Stock dividends are reported on the statement of cash flows.
   b. Stock dividends are reported on the statement of stockholders' equity.
   c. Stock dividends increase total equity.
   d. Stock dividends decrease total equity.
4. Which order best describes the largest number of shares to the smallest number of shares?
   a. Shares authorized, shares issued, shares outstanding.
   b. Shares issued, shares outstanding, shares authorized.
   c. Shares outstanding, shares issued, shares authorized.
   d. Shares in the treasury, shares outstanding, shares issued.
5. A company issued 100,000 shares of common stock with a par value of $1 per share. The stock sold for $20 per share. By what amount will stockholders' equity increase?
   a. $100,000
   b. $1,900,000
   c. $2,000,000
   d. Stockholders' equity will not change.

6. Which of the following dates does not require a journal entry?
   a. Date of declaration.
   b. Date of record.
   c. Date of payment.
   d. A journal entry is recorded on all of these dates.
7. A company has net income of $225,000 and declares and pays dividends in the amount of $75,000. What is the net impact on retained earnings?
   a. Increase of $225,000
   b. Decrease of $75,000
   c. Increase of $150,000
   d. Decrease of $150,000
8. Which statement regarding dividends is false?
   a. Dividends represent a distribution of corporate profits to owners.
   b. Both stock and cash dividends reduce retained earnings.
   c. Cash dividends paid to stockholders reduce net income.
   d. None of the above statements are false.
9. When treasury stock is purchased with cash, what is the impact on the balance sheet equation?
   a. No change: The reduction of the asset cash is offset with the addition of the asset treasury stock.
   b. Assets decrease and stockholders' equity increases.
   c. Assets increase and stockholders' equity decreases.
   d. Assets decrease and stockholders' equity decreases.
10. Conceptually, does a 2-for-1 stock split immediately increase an investor's personal wealth?
    a. No, because the stock price per share drops by half when the number of shares doubles.
    b. Yes, because the investor has more shares.
    c. Yes, because the investor acquired additional shares without paying a brokerage fee.
    d. Yes, because the investor will receive more in cash dividends by owning more shares.

MINI-EXERCISES

M11-1 Sources of Equity and Retained Earnings

LO11-1

There are two primary sources of equity reported in the stockholders' equity section of a company's balance sheet: contributed capital and earned capital. Earned capital is kept track of in the retained earnings account. What increases retained earnings and what decreases retained earnings?

M11-2 Computing the Number of Issued Shares

LO11-1

The balance sheet for Ronlad Corporation reported 168,000 shares outstanding, 268,000 shares authorized, and 10,000 shares of treasury stock. How many shares have been issued?

M11-3 Earnings per Share Ratio

LO11-2

How is the earnings per share (EPS) ratio calculated? On what financial statement will an investor find EPS for a given company?

M11-4 Recording the Sale of Common Stock

LO11-3

To expand operations, Aragon Consulting issued 170,000 shares of previously unissued stock with a par value of $1. Investors purchased the stock for $21 per share. Record the sale of this stock. Would your journal entry be different if the par value was $2 per share? If so, record the sale of stock with a par value of $2.

M11-5 Comparing Common Stock and Preferred Stock

LO11-3, 11-8
Microsoft

Your parents have just retired and have asked you for some financial advice. They have decided to invest $100,000 in a company very similar to **Microsoft**. The company has issued both common and preferred stock. Describe the differences between common stock and preferred stock to your parents.

M11-6 Determining the Effects of Treasury Stock Transactions

LO11-3

Skykomish Corporation purchased 20,000 shares of its own stock from investors for $45 per share. The next year, the company resold 5,000 of the repurchased shares for $50 per share, and the following year it resold 10,000 of the repurchased shares for $37 per share. Determine the impact (increase, decrease, or no change) of each of these transactions on the following:

1. Total assets
2. Total liabilities
3. Total stockholders' equity
4. Net income

Determining the Amount of a Dividend

M11-7
LO11-4

Cole Company has 288,000 shares of common stock authorized, 260,000 shares issued, and 60,000 shares of treasury stock. The company's board of directors has declared a dividend of 65 cents per share. What is the total amount of the dividend that will be paid?

Recording Dividends

M11-8
LO11-4

On April 15 of this year, the board of directors for Jedi Company declared a cash dividend of 65 cents per share payable to stockholders of record on May 20. The dividends will be paid on June 14. The company has 100,000 shares of stock outstanding. Prepare any necessary journal entries for each date.

Dividend Yield Ratio

M11-9
LO11-5

How is the dividend yield ratio calculated? Explain what the dividend yield ratio tells you about a company.

Determining the Impact of Stock Dividends and Stock Splits

M11-10
LO11-6

Reliable Tools Corporation announced a 100 percent stock dividend. Determine the impact (increase, decrease, no change) of this dividend on the following:

1. Total assets
2. Total liabilities
3. Common stock
4. Total stockholders' equity
5. Market value per share of common stock

Assume that instead of announcing a stock dividend, the company announced a 2-for-1 stock split. Determine the impact of the stock split on each of the above.

Reporting Stock Transactions on the Statement of Cash Flows

M11-11
LO11-9

During the year, University Food Systems issued stock, repurchased stock, declared a cash dividend, and declared a 2-for-1 stock split. How will each of these transactions affect University's statement of cash flows?

Mc Graw Hill connect

EXERCISES

Computing Shares Outstanding

E11-1
LO11-1

In a recent annual report, Rosh Corporation disclosed that 60,000,000 shares of common stock have been authorized. At the beginning of the fiscal year, a total of 36,356,357 shares had been issued and the number of shares in treasury stock was 7,171,269. During the year, 558,765 additional shares were issued, and the number of treasury shares increased by 3,034,188. Determine the number of shares outstanding at the end of the year.

Computing Number of Shares

E11-2
LO11-1, 11-3

The charter of Vista West Corporation specifies that it is authorized to issue 300,000 shares of common stock. Since the company was incorporated, it has sold a total of 160,000 shares (at $16 per share) to the public. It has bought back a total of 25,000. The par value of the stock is $3. When the stock was bought back from the public, the market price was $40.

Required:
1. Determine the authorized shares.
2. Determine the issued shares.
3. Determine the outstanding shares.

E11-3
LO11-1, 11-3, 11-7, 11-8

Determining the Effects of the Issuance of Common and Preferred Stock

Lucas Company was issued a charter by the state of Indiana on January 15 of this year. The charter authorized the following:

Common stock, $10 par value, 103,000 shares authorized
Preferred stock, 9 percent, par value $8 per share, 4,000 shares authorized

During the year, the following transactions took place in the order presented:

a. Sold and issued 20,000 shares of common stock at $16 cash per share.
b. Sold and issued 3,000 shares of preferred stock at $20 cash per share.
c. At the end of the year, the company reported net income of $60,000. No dividends were declared.

Required:
1. Prepare the stockholders' equity section of the balance sheet at the end of the year.
2. Assume that you are a common stockholder. If Lucas needed additional capital, would you prefer to have it issue additional common stock or additional preferred stock? Explain.

E11-4
LO11-1, 11-2, 11-3

Reporting Stockholders' Equity

The financial statements for Highland Corporation included the following selected information:

Common stock	$1,600,000
Retained earnings	$ 900,000
Net income	$1,000,000
Shares issued	90,000
Shares outstanding	80,000
Dividends declared and paid	$ 800,000

The common stock was sold at a price of $30 per share.

Required:
1. What is the amount of additional paid-in capital?
2. What was the amount of retained earnings at the beginning of the year?
3. How many shares are in treasury stock?
4. Compute earnings per share (assume the weighted average shares outstanding is equal to the shares outstanding).

E11-5
LO11-1, 11-3, 11-4, 11-7

Reporting Stockholders' Equity and Determining Dividend Policy

Tarrant Corporation was organized this year to operate a financial consulting business. The charter authorized the following stock: common stock, $10 par value, 11,500 shares authorized. During the year, the following selected transactions were completed:

a. Sold 5,600 shares of common stock for cash at $20 per share.
b. Sold 1,000 shares of common stock for cash at $25 per share.
c. At year-end, the company reported net income of $12,000. No dividends were declared.

Required:
1. Provide the journal entries required to record the sale of common stock in (*a*) and (*b*).
2. Prepare the stockholders' equity section of the balance sheet at the end of the year.

E11-6
LO11-1, 11-3, 11-7
Dillard's

Finding Amounts Missing from the Stockholders' Equity Section

Assume that the stockholders' equity section on the balance sheet of **Dillard's**, a popular department store, is shown below. During the year, the company reported net income of $463,909,000 and declared and paid dividends of $10,002,000.

Stockholders' Equity:	Current Year	Last Year
Common stock, Class A–118,529,925 and 117,706,523 shares issued; ? and ? shares outstanding	$ 118,530	$ 117,707
Common stock, Class B (convertible)–4,010,929 shares issued and outstanding	40,000	40,000
Additional paid-in capital	828,796,000	805,422,000
Retained earnings	3,107,344,000	?
Less treasury stock, at cost, Class A–73,099,319 and 61,740,439 shares	(1,846,312,000)	(1,355,526,000)

Required:
Answer the following questions. Show your computations.
1. What is the par value of Dillard's Class A common stock?
2. How many shares of Class A Common Stock were outstanding at the end of last year and the end of the current year?
3. What amount was reported in the Retained Earnings account at the end of last year?
4. How is the dollar amount in the treasury stock account at the end of the current year reflected on the asset side of the balance sheet?
5. During the current year, by what amount did treasury stock transactions increase or decrease stockholders' equity?
6. At the end of the current year, what was the average price paid per share for shares held in treasury stock?

Reporting Stockholders' Equity

E11-7
LO11-1, 11-3, 11-7

Williamson Corporation was organized to operate a tax preparation business. The charter authorized the following stock: common stock, $2 par value, 80,000 shares authorized. During the first year, the following selected transactions were completed:

a. Sold 50,000 shares of common stock for cash at $50 per share.
b. Repurchased 2,000 shares at $52 per share.

Required:
1. Provide the journal entries required for the transactions in (*a*) and (*b*).
2. Prepare the stockholders' equity section of the balance sheet at the end of the year. Assume retained earnings at the end of the year was $200,000.

Reporting Stockholders' Equity

E11-8
LO11-1, 11-3, 11-7
Ruth's Chris Steakhouse

Ruth's Chris Steakhouse is the largest upscale steakhouse company in the United States, based on total company- and franchisee-owned restaurants. The company's menu features a broad selection of high-quality steaks and other premium offerings. Assume that the following information is from a recent annual report:

a. Common stock, $0.01 par value; 100,000,000 shares authorized; 34,990,170 issued and outstanding at the end of the current year; 34,333,858 issued and outstanding at the end of last year.
b. Additional paid-in capital: $169,107,000 at the end of the current year and $155,455,000 at the end of last year.
c. Accumulated deficit: ($68,804,000) at the end of last year.
d. In the current year, net income was $16,455,000 and a cash dividend of $7,138,000 was paid.

Required:
Prepare the stockholders' equity section of the balance sheet to reflect the above information for the current year and last year.

Determining the Effects of Transactions on Stockholders' Equity

E11-9
LO11-1, 11-3, 11-7, 11-8

Quick Fix-It Corporation was organized at the beginning of this year to operate several car repair businesses in a large metropolitan area. The charter issued by the state authorized the following stock:

Common stock, $10 par value, 98,000 shares authorized
Preferred stock, $50 par value, 8 percent, 59,000 shares authorized

During January and February of this year, the following stock transactions were completed:

a. Sold 78,000 shares of common stock at $20 cash per share.
b. Sold 20,000 shares of preferred stock at $80 cash per share.
c. Repurchased 4,000 shares of common stock for $20 cash per share.

Required:
Net income for the year was $210,000; cash dividends declared and paid at year-end were $50,000. Prepare the stockholders' equity section of the balance sheet at the end of the year.

E11-10 Computing Earnings per Share
LO11-2

Below is select information from DC United Company's income statement. At the end of the current year, the weighted average number of common shares outstanding was 132,000.

Select Data from Income Statement, End of Current Year	
Sales	$942,000
Cost of goods sold	800,000
Operating expenses	80,000
Tax expense	15,000

Required:
Calculate EPS for DC United.

E11-11 Recording Stockholders' Equity Transactions
LO11-3, 11-8

On-Line Learning Corporation obtained a charter at the beginning of this year that authorized 52,000 shares of no-par common stock and 23,000 shares of preferred stock, $10 par value. The corporation was organized by four individuals who purchased a total of 20,000 shares of the common stock. The remaining shares were to be sold to other individuals. During the year, the following selected transactions occurred:

a. Issued 5,000 shares of common stock to each of the four organizers for $20 cash per share.
b. Sold 6,000 shares of common stock to an outside investor at $40 cash per share.
c. Sold 7,000 shares of preferred stock to an outside investor at $30 cash per share.

Required:
1. Provide the journal entries required to record transactions (*a*) through (*c*).
2. Is it ethical to sell stock to outsiders at a higher price than the amount paid by the organizers?

E11-12 Finding Information Missing from an Annual Report
LO11-1, 11-3, 11-4
Procter & Gamble (P&G)

Procter & Gamble (P&G) sells products that are part of most of our daily lives, including Crest, Duracell, Olay, Gillette, Tide, and Vicks. A recent annual report for P&G contained the following information:

a. Retained earnings at the end of last year totaled $80,197 million.
b. Net income for the current year was $11,643 million.
c. Par value of the stock is $1 per share.
d. Cash dividends declared in the current year were $6,850 million.
e. The Common Stock account totaled $4,009 million at the end of the current year and $4,009 million at the end of last year.

Required (assume that no other information concerning stockholders' equity is relevant):
1. Calculate the number of shares issued at the end of the current year.
2. Calculate the amount of retained earnings at the end of the current year.

E11-13 Recording and Analyzing Treasury Stock Transactions
LO11-3

Rock Bottom Gold Company recently repurchased 7 million shares of its common stock for $47 per share and is holding the shares as treasury stock. The intent of the repurchase was to increase earnings per share to be more in line with competitors.

Required:

1. Determine the impact of the stock repurchase on total assets, total liabilities, and total stockholders' equity.
2. Prepare the journal entry to record the repurchase.
3. How will this transaction affect the cash flow statement?

Preparing the Stockholders' Equity Section of the Balance Sheet and Evaluating Dividend Policy

E11-14
LO11-1, 11-3, 11-4, 11-5, 11-7

The following information was extracted from the records of TAC Corporation at the end of the fiscal year after all adjusting entries were completed:

Common stock ($20 par value; 100,000 shares authorized, 34,000 shares issued, 32,000 shares outstanding)	$680,000
Additional paid-in capital	163,000
Dividends declared and paid during the year	16,000
Retained earnings at the beginning of the year	75,000
Treasury stock at cost (2,000 shares)	(25,000)
Net income	$ 30,000
Current stock price per share	$ 22.29

Required:

1. Prepare the stockholders' equity section of the balance sheet at the end of the fiscal year.
2. Compute and evaluate the dividend yield ratio. Determine the number of shares of stock that received dividends.

Recording and Analyzing Treasury Stock Transactions

E11-15
LO11-3

During the year the following selected transactions affecting stockholders' equity occurred for Orlando Corporation:

a.	Apr. 1	Repurchased 200 shares of the company's common stock at $20 cash per share.
b.	June 14	Sold 40 of the shares purchased on April 1 for $25 cash per share.
c.	Sept. 1	Sold 30 of the shares purchased on April 1 for $15 cash per share.

Required:

1. Provide the journal entries to record each of the transactions in (*a*) through (*c*).
2. Describe the impact, if any, that these transactions have on the income statement.

Recording and Analyzing Treasury Stock Transactions

E11-16
LO11-3, 11-4, 11-9

During the year, the following selected transactions affecting stockholders' equity occurred for Navajo Corporation:

a.	Feb. 1	Repurchased 160 shares of the company's common stock at $20 cash per share.
b.	July 15	Sold 80 of the shares purchased on February 1 for $21 cash per share.
c.	Sept. 1	Sold 50 of the shares purchased on February 1 for $19 cash per share.

Required:

1. Provide the journal entries to record each of the transactions in (*a*) through (*c*).
2. What impact does repurchasing common stock and holding it as treasury stock have on dividends paid?
3. What impact does the sale of treasury stock for an amount higher than the purchase price have on net income and the statement of cash flows?

Analyzing the Impact of Dividend Policy

E11-17
LO11-2, 11-4, 11-6, 11-9

Peters and Associates is a small manufacturer of electronic connections for local area networks. Consider the three cases below as independent situations.

Case 1: Peters increases its cash dividend by 50 percent, but no other changes occur in the company's operations.

Case 2: The company's income and operating cash flows increase by 50 percent, but this does not change its dividends.

Case 3: Peters issues a 50 percent stock dividend, but no other changes occur.

Required:

1. How will each case affect Peters's statement of cash flows?
2. How will each case affect Peters's earnings per share ratio?

E11-18
LO11-4, 11-8, 11-9

Computing Dividends on Preferred Stock and Analyzing Differences

The records of Seahawks Company reflected the following balances in the stockholders' equity accounts at the end of the current year:

Common stock, $12 par value, 50,000 shares outstanding
Preferred stock, 10 percent, $10 par value, 5,000 shares outstanding
Retained earnings, $216,000

On September 1 of the current year, the board of directors was considering the distribution of an $85,000 cash dividend. No dividends were paid during the previous two years. You have been asked to determine dividend amounts under two independent assumptions (show computations):

a. The preferred stock is noncumulative.
b. The preferred stock is cumulative.

Required:

1. Determine the total and per share amounts that would be paid to the common stockholders and the preferred stockholders under the two independent assumptions.
2. Will the statement of cash flows be affected differently under the two independent assumptions?

E11-19
LO11-4, 11-6, 11-8

Determining the Impact of Dividends

Kraken Corporation has the following capital stock outstanding at the end of the current year:

Preferred stock, 6 percent, $15 par value, 8,000 outstanding shares
Common stock, $8 par value, 30,000 outstanding shares

On October 1 of the current year, the board of directors declared dividends as follows:

Preferred stock: Cash dividend, payable December 20 of the current year
Common stock: 50 percent common stock dividend issuable December 20 of the current year

On October 1 of the current year, the market price of Kraken's preferred stock was $40 per share, and the market price of its common stock was $32 per share.

Required:
Explain how the preferred stock dividend and common stock dividend affect the company's total assets, total liabilities, and total stockholders' equity.

E11-20
LO11-3, 11-4
Nordstrom Inc.

Recording the Payment of Dividends

A recent annual report for **Nordstrom Inc.** disclosed that the company declared and paid dividends on common stock in the amount of $1.20 per share. During the year, Nordstrom had 1,000,000,000 authorized shares of common stock and 191,200,000 issued shares. There is no treasury stock.

Required:
Assume Nordstrom declared the entire dividend ($1.20 per share) on February 20 and subsequently paid the dividend on March 1. Provide the journal entries to record the declaration and payment of dividends.

E11-21
LO11-3, 11-4
Procter & Gamble (P&G)

Recording Dividends

Procter & Gamble (P&G) brands touch the lives of people around the world. Assume that in the current year the company had 10 billion shares of common stock authorized, 4 billion shares issued, and 3 billion shares outstanding. Par value is $1 per share. P&G has been paying a dividend for over 100 years.

Required:
Assume that P&G declared a dividend of $2.45 per share on October 1 to stockholders of record on October 15. P&G paid the dividend on October 20. Prepare journal entries as appropriate for each date.

Analyzing Stock Dividends and Comparing to Stock Splits

E11-22
LO11-6

At the beginning of the year, the stockholders' equity section of the balance sheet of Solutions Corporation reflected the following:

Common stock ($12 par value; 65,000 shares authorized, 30,000 shares outstanding)	$360,000
Additional paid-in capital	120,000
Retained earnings	580,000

On February 1, the board of directors declared a 60 percent stock dividend to be issued April 30. The market value of the stock on February 1 was $15 per share. The market value of the stock on April 30 was $18 per share.

Required:

1. Fill in the follow table.

	Stockholders' Equity	
	Before Stock Dividend	**After Stock Dividend**
Common stock, $12 par value; 65,000 shares authorized; 30,000 shares issued and outstanding (before) 48,000 shares issued and outstanding (after)	____	____
Additional paid-in capital	____	____
Retained earnings	____	____
Total stockholders' equity	____	____

2. Show how the stock dividend affects total assets, total liabilities, and total stockholders' equity.
3. If instead of declaring a stock dividend the company had announced a 3-for-1 stock split for all authorized, issued, and outstanding shares, how would the accounts in the stockholders' equity section of the balance sheet change?

Comparing Stock Dividends and Stock Splits

E11-23
LO11-6

On July 1, Davidson Corporation had the following capital structure:

Common stock ($1 par value)	$600,000
Additional paid-in capital	900,000
Retained earnings	700,000
Treasury stock	–0–

Required:
Complete the table below for each of the two following independent cases:

Case 1: The board of directors declared and issued a 50 percent stock dividend when the stock was selling at $12 per share.

Case 2: The board of directors announced a 6-for-5 stock split. The market price prior to the split was $12 per share.

Items	Before Dividend or Split	After Stock Dividend	After Stock Split
Common stock account	$	$	$
Par value per share	$1	$	$
Shares outstanding	#	#	#
Additional paid-in capital	$900,000	$	$
Retained earnings	$700,000	$	$
Total stockholders' equity	$	$	$

E11-24 LO11-4, 11-6, 11-9

Comparing Cash Dividends and Stock Dividends

Weili Corporation has 80,000 shares of common stock outstanding with a par value of $8.

Required:

1. Complete the table below for each of the two following independent cases:

Case 1: The board of directors declared and issued a 40 percent stock dividend when the stock was selling at $25 per share.

Case 2: The board of directors declared and paid a cash dividend of $2 per share.

Items	Before Dividend	After Stock Dividend	After Cash Dividend
Common stock account	$	$	$
Par value per share	$8	$	$
Shares outstanding	#	#	#
Additional paid-in capital	$280,000	$	$
Retained earnings	$2,100,000	$	$
Total stockholders' equity	$	$	$

2. Explain how Case 1 and Case 2 will be reported on the statement of cash flows.

E11-25 LO11-7

(Chapter Supplement) Accounting for Equity Transaction for Sole Proprietorships and Partnerships

Case 1: Matsumoto Training Academies is a sole proprietorship. To start the business, the owner, Mr. Tanaka, contributed $500,000 cash. During the year the owner withdrew $30,000 cash. Net income for the year was $45,000.

Case 2: Galaxy Robotics is a partnership with two partners. To start the business, the owners, Mrs. Curtis and Mr. Wilson, each contributed $300,000 cash and agreed to split all earnings 50/50. During the year, Mrs. Curtis withdrew $15,000 cash and Mr. Wilson withdrew $25,000 cash. Net income for the year was $60,000.

Required:

1. Create the statement of owner's equity for Matsumoto Training at the end of the year.
2. Create the statement of Owner's equity for Galaxy Robotics at the end of the year.

PROBLEMS

Mc Graw Hill connect 

P11-1 LO11-1, 11-2, 11-3, 11-4, 11-6

Finding Missing Amounts (AP11-1)

At the end of the year, the records of Kwan Corporation provided the following selected and incomplete data:

Common stock ($10 par value); no changes in account during the year.
Shares authorized: 200,000.
Shares issued: ____________ (all shares were issued at $17 per share; $2,125,000 total cash collected).
Treasury stock: 3,000 shares (repurchased at $20 per share).
The treasury stock was acquired after a stock split was announced.
Net income: $240,340.
Dividends declared and paid: $123,220.
Retained earnings beginning balance: $555,000.

Required:

1. Determine:
   a. The number of authorized shares.
   b. The number of issued shares.
   c. The number of outstanding shares.
2. What is the balance in the Additional paid-in capital account?
3. What is earnings per share (EPS)?
4. What was the dividend paid per share?
5. In what section of the balance sheet should treasury stock be reported? What is the amount of treasury stock that should be reported?
6. Assume that the board of directors voted a 2-for-1 stock split. After the stock split, what will be the par value per share? How many shares will be outstanding?
7. Provide the journal entry associated with the stock split above. If no journal entry is required, explain why.
8. Disregard the stock split in (7). Assume instead that a 10 percent stock dividend was declared before any treasury stock was acquired. The market price of the common stock at the time the dividend was declared was $21. Provide the journal entry associated with the stock dividend. If no journal entry is required, explain why.

Preparing the Stockholders' Equity Section of the Balance Sheet (AP11-2)

P11-2
LO11-1, 11-3, 11-7, 11-8

Witt Corporation received its charter during January of this year. The charter authorized the following stock:

Preferred stock: 10 percent, $10 par value, 21,000 shares authorized
Common stock: $8 par value, 50,000 shares authorized

During the year, the following transactions occurred in the order given:

a. Issued 40,000 shares of the common stock for $12 per share.
b. Issued 5,500 shares of the preferred stock for $16 per share.
c. Issued 3,000 shares of the common stock for $15 per share and 1,000 shares of the preferred stock for $26 per share.
d. Net income for the year was $96,000.

Required:
Prepare the stockholders' equity section of the balance sheet at the end of the year.

Recording Transactions Affecting Stockholders' Equity (AP11-3)

P11-3
LO11-1, 11-3, 11-8

King Corporation began operations in January of the current year. The charter authorized the following stock:

Preferred stock: 10 percent, $10 par value, 40,000 shares authorized
Common stock: $5 par value, 85,000 shares authorized

During the current year, the following transactions occurred in the order given:

a. Issued 66,000 shares of common stock for $9 per share.
b. Issued 9,000 shares of the preferred stock for $20 per share.
c. Issued 1,000 shares of the preferred stock for $20 per share and 2,500 shares of common stock for $10 per share.

Required:
Provide the journal entries required to record each of the transactions in (*a*) through (*c*).

Recording Transactions and Comparing Par and No-Par Stock (AP11-4)

P11-4
LO11-1, 11-3
GoDaddy Corporation

The following was in the financial press pertaining to **GoDaddy Corporation**:

> GoDaddy's (GDDY) stock was sold for $26 per share during its opening day of trading. GoDaddy sold 23 million shares at its IPO.

Required:

1. Record the issuance of stock, assuming the stock was no-par value common stock.
2. Record the issuance of stock, assuming the common stock had a par value of $2 per share.
3. Should a stockholder care whether a company issues par or no-par value stock? Explain.

P11-5 Preparing the Stockholders' Equity Section after Selected Transactions (AP11-5)

LO11-1, 11-3, 11-7

United Resources Company obtained a charter from the state in January of this year. The charter authorized 200,000 shares of common stock with a par value of $1. During the year, the company earned $590,000. Also during the year, the following selected transactions occurred in the order given:

a. Sold 100,000 shares of the common stock in an initial public offering for $12 per share.
b. Repurchased 20,000 shares of the previously issued shares for $15 per share and is holding them as treasury stock.
c. Resold 5,000 shares of treasury stock for $18 per share.

Required:
Prepare the stockholders' equity section of the balance sheet at the end of the year.

P11-6 Analyzing Stockholders' Equity Transactions, Including Treasury Stock (AP11-6)

LO11-3, 11-4, 11-6, 11-9

1. Explain how a stock dividend differs from a cash dividend.
2. Explain how a large stock dividend differs from a small stock dividend.
3. Explain how reselling treasury stock for more than it was purchased affects the income statement and the statement of cash flows.
4. Explain why a company might purchase treasury stock.

P11-7 Analyzing Treasury Stock Transactions (AP11-7)

LO11-3, 11-9
Apple

Apple designs, manufactures, and markets smartphones, personal computers, tablets, wearables and accessories, and sells a variety of related services. Apple employs over 135,000 people in the United States. A recent statement of cash flows contained the following information (in millions):

	Year 3	Year 2	Year 1
Cash flows from financing activities:			
Repurchases of common stock	(66,897)	(72,738)	(32,900)

Required:
1. Prepare the journal entry to record the repurchase of common stock in Year 3.
2. Assume that Apple resold some of the treasury stock. The shares were originally purchased for $9 million and were resold for $10 million. Prepare the journal entry to record the sale of the treasury shares.

P11-8 Comparing Stock and Cash Dividends (AP11-8)

LO11-4, 11-6, 11-8

Chicago Company reported the following information at the end of the current year:

Common stock ($8 par value; 35,000 shares outstanding)	$280,000
Preferred stock, 10% ($15 par value; 8,000 shares outstanding)	120,000
Retained earnings	281,000

The board of directors is considering the distribution of a cash dividend to the two groups of stockholders. No dividends were declared during the previous two years. Assume the three cases below are independent of each other.

Case A: The preferred stock is noncumulative; the total amount of all dividends is $31,000.
Case B: The preferred stock is cumulative; the total amount of all dividends is $36,000.
Case C: The preferred stock is cumulative; the total amount of all dividends is $90,000.

Required:
1. Compute the amount of dividends, in total and per share, that would be payable to each class of stockholders for each case. Show computations.
2. Assume Chicago Company issued a 30 percent common stock dividend on the outstanding shares when the market value per share was $24. Fill in the table below to show how the stock dividend and Case C would affect total assets, total liabilities, and total stockholders' equity.

Item	AMOUNT OF DOLLAR INCREASE (DECREASE)	
	Cash Dividend–Case C	Stock Dividend
Total assets	$	$
Total liabilities	$	$
Total stockholders' equity	$	$

Analyzing Dividend Policy (AP11-9)

P11-9
LO11-4, 11-9
Google

Heather and Scott, two young financial analysts, were reviewing financial statements for **Google**, one of the world's largest technology companies. Scott noted that the company did not report any dividends in the financing activity section of the statement of cash flows and said, "I have heard that Google is a very profitable company. If it's so profitable, why isn't it paying any dividends?" Heather wasn't convinced that Scott was looking in the right place for dividends but didn't say anything.

Scott continued the discussion by noting, "Sales for Google are up nearly 46 percent over the previous two years, while net income is up over $3 billion compared to last year, and cash flows from operating activities are up over $6 billion to a total of $54 billion."

At that point, Heather noted that the statement of cash flows reported that Google had spent $23 billion in capital expenditures and $1 billion paying back debt. She was confused about whether Google was in a good position to pay dividends or not.

Required:

1. Is Heather's concern that Scott is looking at the wrong section of the statement of cash flows justified?
2. Is there a right time for a company like Google to start paying a dividend?

Preparing the Stockholders' Equity Section of the Balance Sheet and Evaluating Dividend Policy (AP11-10)

P11-10
LO11-1, 11-3, 11-4, 11-5, 11-7

The following information was extracted from the records of Cascade Company at the end of the fiscal year after all adjusting entries were completed:

Common stock ($0.01 par value; 200,000 shares authorized, 54,000 shares issued, 52,000 shares outstanding)	$ 540
Additional paid-in capital	456,000
Dividends declared and paid during the year	22,000
Retained earnings at the end of the year	312,000
Treasury stock at cost (2,000 shares)	(15,000)
Net income	$ 95,000
Current stock price per share	$ 10.00

Required:

1. Prepare the stockholders' equity section of the balance sheet at the end of the fiscal year.
2. Compute and evaluate the dividend yield ratio. Determine the number of shares of stock that received dividends.

Comparing Cash Dividends, Stock Dividends, and Stock Splits (AP11-11)

P11-11
LO11-4, 11-6, 11-9

Just prior to the end of the fiscal year, Biofuel Corporation reported the following information:

Common stock ($0.10 par value)	$ 60,000
Additional paid-in capital	1,900,000
Retained earnings	800,000
Treasury stock	-0-
Cash flows from financing activities	19,000

Required:
Complete the table below for each of the three following independent cases:

Case 1: The board of directors declared a cash dividend of $0.02 per share.
Case 2: The board of directors declared and issued a 100 percent stock dividend when the stock was selling at $10 per share.
Case 3: The board of directors announced a 2-for-1 stock split. The market price prior to the split was $10 per share.

Items	Before Any Dividends	After Cash Dividend	After Stock Dividend	After Stock Split
Common stock account	$ 60,000	$	$	$
Par value per share	$ 0.10	$	$	$
Shares outstanding	#	#	#	#
Additional paid-in capital	$1,900,000	$	$	$
Retained earnings	$ 800,000	$	$	$
Total stockholders' equity	$	$	$	$
Cash flows from financing activities	$ 19,000	$	$	$

P11-12 (Chapter Supplement) Comparing the Equity Sections for Alternative Forms of Organization (AP11-12)
LO11-1, 11-7

Assume for each of the following independent cases that the annual accounting period ends on December 31. Revenues for the year were $144,000. Expenses for the year were $164,000.

Case A: Assume that RiseUp Company is a *sole proprietorship* owned by Mrs. Rise. Prior to the closing entries, the capital account reflects a balance of $52,000 and the drawing account shows a balance of $9,000.
Case B: Assume that RiseUp Company is a *partnership* owned by Mrs. Rise and Mr. Up. Prior to the closing entries, the owners' equity accounts reflect the following balances: Rise, Capital, $43,000; Up, Capital, $43,000; Rise, Drawings, $5,000; and Up, Drawings, $7,000. Profits and losses are divided equally.
Case C: Assume that RiseUp Company is a *corporation.*

Required:
1. Provide all the closing entries required at December 31 for each of the separate cases.
2. Show how the statement of equity would appear at December 31 for Case A and Case B.

ALTERNATE PROBLEMS

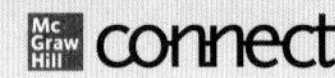

AP11-1 Finding Missing Amounts (P11-1)
LO 11-1, 11-2, 11-3, 11-4

At the end of the year, the records of Duo Corporation provided the following selected and incomplete data:

Common stock: $1,500,000 ($1 par value; no changes in account during the year).
Shares authorized: 5,000,000.
Shares issued: _____ (all shares were issued at $80 per share).
Shares held as treasury stock: 100,000 shares (repurchased at $60 per share).
Net income: $4,800,000.
Dividends declared and paid: $2 per share.
Retained earnings beginning balance: $82,900,000.

Required:
1. Answer the following:
   a. How many issued shares are there?
   b. How many outstanding shares are there?

2. What is the balance in the Additional Paid-in Capital account?
3. What is earnings per share (EPS)?
4. What was the total dividend paid during the year?
5. In what section of the balance sheet should treasury stock be reported? What is the amount of treasury stock that should be reported?

Preparing the Stockholders' Equity Section of the Balance Sheet (P11-2)

AP11-2
LO11-1, 11-3, 11-7, 11-8

Salish Corporation received its charter during January of this year. The charter authorized the following stock:

Preferred stock: 10 percent, $10 par value, 31,000 shares authorized
Common stock: $8 par value, 60,000 shares authorized

During the year, the following transactions occurred in the order given:

a. Issued 25,000 shares of the common stock for $12 per share.
b. Issued 10,000 shares of the preferred stock for $16 per share.
c. Issued 5,000 shares of the common stock for $15 per share and 2,000 shares of the preferred stock for $26 per share.
d. Net income for the year was $106,000.

Required:
Prepare the stockholders' equity section of the balance sheet at the end of the year.

Recording Transactions Affecting Stockholders' Equity (P11-3)

AP11-3
LO 11-1, 11-3, 11-8

Kameamea Company was granted a charter on January 1 that authorized the following stock:

Common stock: $40 par value; 100,000 shares authorized
Preferred stock: 8 percent; $5 par value; 20,000 shares authorized

During the year, the following transactions occurred in the order given:

a. Issued 30,000 shares of the common stock for $40 per share and 5,000 shares of the preferred stock for $26 per share.
b. Issued 2,000 shares of preferred stock when the stock was selling for $32.
c. Repurchased 3,000 shares of the common stock issued earlier. Paid $38 per share.

Required:
Provide the journal entries required to record each of the transactions in (*a*) through (*c*).

Recording Transactions and Comparing Par and No-Par Stock (P11-4)

AP11-4
LO11-1, 11-3
Zoom Video Communications

The following was in the financial press pertaining to **Zoom Video Communications**:

Zoom's (ZM) stock was sold for $65 per share during its opening day of trading. Zoom sold 21 million shares at its IPO.

Required:
1. Record the issuance of stock, assuming the stock was no-par value common stock.
2. Record the issuance of stock, assuming the common stock had a par value of $1 per share.
3. Should a stockholder care whether a company issues par or no-par value stock? Explain.

Preparing the Stockholders' Equity Section after Selected Transactions (P11-5)

AP11-5
LO 11-1, 11-3, 11-7

Mulkilteo Company obtained a charter from the state in January of this year. The charter authorized 1,000,000 shares of common stock with a $5 par value. During the year, the company earned $429,000. Also during the year, the following selected transactions occurred in the order given:

a. Sold 700,000 shares of the common stock for $54 per share.
b. Repurchased 25,000 shares for $50 per share.

Required:
Prepare the stockholders' equity section of the balance sheet at the end of the year.

AP11-6
LO11-3, 11-4, 11-6, 11-9

Analyzing Stockholders' Equity Transactions, including Treasury Stock (P11-6)

1. Explain how a stock dividend differs from a cash dividend.
2. Explain how a large stock dividend differs from a small stock dividend.
3. Explain how reselling treasury stock for less than it was purchased affects the income statement and the statement of cash flows.
4. Explain why a company might purchase treasury stock and then reissue those treasury shares as part of an employee bonus plan.

AP11-7
LO11-3, 11-9

Analyzing Treasury Stock Transactions (P11-7)

IBM recently redefined its strategy to focus the company on cloud computing and artificial intelligence. IBM employs over 345,000 people across more than 175 countries. Assume a recent statement of cash flows contained the following information (in millions):

	Year 3	Year 2	Year 1
Cash flows from financing activities:			
Repurchases of common stock	(45,000)	(22,860)	-0-

Required:
1. Prepare the journal entry to record the repurchase of common stock in Year 2.
2. Assume that IBM resold some of the treasury stock. The shares were originally purchased for $8 million and were resold for $9 million. Prepare the journal entry to record the sale of the treasury shares.

AP11-8
LO 11-4, 11-6, 11-8

Comparing Stock and Cash Dividends (P11-8)

Kainen Company reported the following information at the end of the year:

Common stock ($1 par value; 500,000 shares outstanding)	$500,000
Preferred stock, 8% ($10 par value; 21,000 shares outstanding)	210,000
Retained earnings	900,000

The board of directors is considering the distribution of a cash dividend to the two groups of stockholders. No dividends were declared during the previous two years. Assume the three cases below are independent of each other.

Case A: The preferred stock is noncumulative; the total amount of all dividends is $25,000.
Case B: The preferred stock is cumulative; the total amount of all dividends is $25,000.
Case C: The preferred stock is cumulative; the total amount of all dividends is $75,000.

Required:
1. Compute the amount of dividends, in total and per share, that would be payable to each class of stockholders for each case. Show computations.
2. Assume Kainen Company issued a 40 percent common stock dividend on the outstanding shares when the market value per share was $50. Fill in the table below to show how the stock dividend and Case C would affect total assets, total liabilities, and total stockholders' equity.

	AMOUNT OF DOLLAR INCREASE (DECREASE)	
Item	**Cash Dividend–Case C**	**Stock Dividend**
Total assets	$	$
Total liabilities	$	$
Total stockholders' equity	$	$

AP11-9
LO11-4, 11-9
Facebook

Analyzing Dividend Policy (P11-9)

Alonzo and Mika, two students in a financial statement analysis class, were reviewing financial statements for **Facebook**, one of the world's largest social-media companies. Alonzo noted that the company did not report any dividends in the financing activity section of the statement of cash flows and said, "I have heard that Facebook is a very profitable company. If it's so profitable, why isn't it paying any dividends?" Mika wasn't convinced that Alonzo was looking in the right place for dividends but didn't say anything.

Alonzo continued his analysis and noted, "Revenues for Facebook are up nearly $15 billion over the previous year, while net income is up almost $2 billion compared to last year, and the company reported over $38 billion in operating cash flows."

At that point, Mika noted that the statement of cash flows reported that Facebook had spent almost $34 billion to purchase marketable securities and $6 billion to repurchase stock. She was confused about whether Facebook was in a good position to pay dividends or not.

Required:

1. Is Mika's concern that Alonzo is looking at the wrong section of the statement of cash flows justified?
2. Is there a right time for a company like Facebook to start paying a dividend?

Preparing the Stockholders' Equity Section of the Balance Sheet and Evaluating Dividend Policy (P11-10)

AP11-10
LO11-1, 11-3, 11-4, 11-5, 11-7

The following information was extracted from the records of Olympic Company at the end of the fiscal year after all adjusting entries were completed:

Common stock ($0.05 par value; 400,000 shares authorized, 108,000 shares issued, 106,000 shares outstanding)	$ 5,400
Additional paid-in capital	756,000
Dividends declared and paid during the year	36,000
Retained earnings at the end of the year	215,000
Treasury stock at cost (2,000 shares)	(16,000)
Net income	$105,000
Current stock price per share	$ 8.00

Required:

1. Prepare the stockholders' equity section of the balance sheet at the end of the fiscal year.
2. Compute and evaluate the dividend yield ratio. Determine the number of shares of stock that received dividends.

Comparing Cash Dividends, Stock Dividends, and Stock Splits (P11-11)

AP11-11
LO11-4, 11-6, 11-9

Just prior to the end of the fiscal year, Climate Corporation reported the following information:

Common stock ($0.20 par value)	$120,000
Additional paid-in capital	820,000
Retained earnings	680,000
Treasury stock	-0-
Cash flows from financing activities	33,000

Required:

Complete the table below for each of the three following independent cases:

Case 1: The board of directors declared a cash dividend of $0.04 per share.

Case 2: The board of directors declared and issued a 100 percent stock dividend when the stock was selling at $15 per share.

Case 3: The board of directors announced a 2-for-1 stock split. The market price prior to the split was $16 per share.

Items	Before Any Dividends	After Cash Dividend	After Stock Dividend	After Stock Split
Common stock account	$120,000	$	$	$
Par value per share	$ 0.20	$	$	$
Shares outstanding	#	#	#	#
Additional paid-in capital	$820,000	$	$	$
Retained earnings	$680,000	$	$	$
Total stockholders' equity	$	$	$	$
Cash flows from financing activities	$ 33,000	$	$	$

AP11-12
LO11-1, 11-7

(Chapter Supplement) Comparing the Equity Sections for Alternative Forms of Organization (P11-12)

Assume for each of the following independent cases that the annual accounting period ends on December 31. Revenues for the year were $288,000. Expenses for the year were $328,000.

Case A: Assume that Weather Company is a *sole proprietorship* owned by Mrs. Snow. Prior to the closing entries, the capital account reflects a balance of $104,000 and the drawing account shows a balance of $18,000.

Case B: Assume that Weather Company is a *partnership* owned by Mrs. Snow and Mr. Rain. Prior to the closing entries, the owners' equity accounts reflect the following balances: Snow, Capital, $86,000; Rain, Capital, $86,000; Snow, Drawings, $10,000; and Rain, Drawings, $14,000. Profits and losses are divided equally.

Case C: Assume that Weather Company is a *corporation.*

Required:

1. Provide all the closing entries required at December 31 for each of the separate cases.
2. Show how the statement of equity would appear at December 31 for Case A and Case B.

CONTINUING PROBLEM

CON11-1
LO11-3, 11-4
Pool Corporation, Inc.

Recording and Reporting Stockholders' Equity Transactions

Pool Corporation, Inc., sells swimming pool supplies and equipment. It is a publicly traded corporation that trades on the NASDAQ exchange. The majority of Pool's customers are small, family-owned businesses. The company issued the following press release:

COVINGTON, La., Oct. 30, 2020 (GLOBE NEWSWIRE)–Pool Corporation (Nasdaq: POOL) announced today that its Board of Directors declared a quarterly cash dividend of $0.58 per share. The dividend will be payable on November 25, 2020, to holders of record on November 12, 2020.

The Company also announced in its 2020 Annual Report that it had repurchased $23.2 million of its common stock in the open market.

Required:

1. Record the repurchase of shares by Pool assuming all shares were repurchased at one time and Pool is holding the shares as treasury stock.
2. Prepare all necessary entries associated with the dividend. Assume that at the time of the dividend, Pool was authorized to issue 100 million shares and had 43 million shares outstanding.

COMPREHENSIVE PROBLEM (CHAPTERS 9–11)

Answer the questions below. Treat each case as being independent from the other cases.

Case A: The charter for Tazlina Corporation authorized the following stock:

Common stock, $10 par value, 103,000 shares authorized
Preferred stock (noncumulative), 9 percent, $8 par value, 4,000 shares authorized

The company sold 40,000 shares of common stock and 3,000 shares of preferred stock. During the year, the following selected transactions were completed in the order given:

1. Tazlina declared and paid dividends in the amount of $10,000. How much was paid to the holders of preferred stock? How much was paid to the common stockholders?
2. Tazlina repurchased 5,000 shares of common stock and is holding the shares as treasury stock. After this transaction, how many shares of common stock were outstanding?
3. Provide the journal entry if Tazlina sold 1,000 shares of treasury stock for $25 per share. The treasury stock was repurchased at $20 per share.
4. Describe how the balance sheet equation (assets = liabilities + stockholders' equity) would be affected if Tazlina declared a 2-for-1 stock split.

Case B: Ospry, Corporation has working capital in the amount of $960,000. For each of the following transactions, determine whether working capital will increase, decrease, or remain the same.

1. Paid accounts payable in the amount of $10,000.
2. Recorded rent payable in the amount of $22,000.
3. Collected $5,000 in accounts receivable.
4. Purchased $20,000 of new inventory for cash.

Case C: Eyak Corporation is planning to issue $1,000,000 worth of bonds with a coupon rate of 5 percent. The bonds mature in 10 years and pay interest annually. All of the bonds were sold on January 1 of this year.

Required:
Compute the issue (sale) price on January 1 under each independent assumption below (show computations):
1. Assume an annual market interest rate of 5 percent.
2. Assume an annual market interest rate of 4 percent.
3. Assume an annual market interest rate of 6 percent.

Case D: Miller Bikes is a national chain of upscale bicycle shops. The company has followed a successful strategy of locating near major universities. Miller has the opportunity to expand into several new markets but must raise additional capital. The company has engaged in the following transactions:
- Issued 45,000 additional shares of common stock. The stock has a $1 par value. The shares sold for $25 per share.
- Issued bonds. These bonds have a face value of $1,000,000 and a coupon rate of 10 percent. The bonds mature in 10 years and pay interest semiannually. When the bonds were issued, the annual market rate of interest was 8 percent.

Required:
1. Record the sale of the bonds.
2. Record the issuance of the stock.

connect

CASES AND PROJECTS

Annual Report Cases

Finding Financial Information

CP11-1
LO11-1, 11-3, 11-4, 11-7, 11-9
Target

Refer to the financial statements and footnotes of **Target** given in Appendix B at the end of this book. All dollar amounts are in millions.

Required:
1. What is the amount of cash Target paid to repurchase shares of their own stock during the most recent fiscal year?
   a. $1,343
   b. $745
   c. $23
   d. $1,343
   e. $977
2. What is the total par value (not par value per share) of the common stock Target reported at the end of the most recent fiscal year?
   a. $42
   b. $500
   c. $6,329
   d. $14,440
   e. None of the above
3. How many shares of common stock did Target have outstanding at the end of the most recent fiscal year?
   a. 504,198,962
   b. 6,000,000,000
   c. 500,877,129
   d. 5,000,000
   e. None of the above

4. What is the amount of shareholders' equity Target reported at the end of the most recent fiscal year?
   a. $14,440
   b. $6,329
   c. $11,833
   d. $8,825
   e. None of the above
5. What is the amount of dividends per share Target declared during the most recent fiscal year?
   a. $2.54
   b. $1.95
   c. $2.70
   d. $2.62
   e. None of the above

CP11-2 Finding Financial Information

LO11-1, 11-3, 11-4, 11-7, 11-9

Walmart

Refer to the financial statements and footnotes of **Walmart** given in Appendix C at the end of this book. All dollar amounts are in millions.

Required:

1. What is the amount of cash Walmart paid to repurchase shares of their own stock during the most recent fiscal year? ______________
2. What is the total par value (not par value per share) of the common stock Walmart reported at the end of the most recent fiscal year? ______________
3. How many shares of common stock did Walmart have outstanding at the end of the most recent fiscal year? ______________
4. What is the amount of shareholders' equity Walmart reported at the end of the most recent fiscal year? ______________
5. What is the amount of dividends per share Walmart declared during the most recent fiscal year? ______________

CP11-3 Comparing Companies within an Industry

LO11-2, 11-3, 11-4, 11-5

Refer to the financial statements of Target (Appendix B) and Walmart (Appendix C) and the Industry Ratio Report (Appendix D) at the end of this book.

Required:

1. Compare basic earnings per share for Target and Walmart.

   Target = ☐ **Walmart =** ☐

2. How would repurchasing treasury stock influence the basic earnings per share ratios for Target and Walmart?
   a. Increase the basic earnings per share ratios for both Target and Walmart.
   b. Increase the basic earnings per share ratio for Walmart but decrease the ratio for Target.
   c. Decrease the basic earnings per share ratios for both Target and Walmart.
   d. Increase the basic earnings per share ratio for Target but decrease the ratio for Walmart.
3. Compare the amount of dividends per share Target and Walmart declared during the most recent fiscal year.

   Target = ☐ **Walmart =** ☐

4. Compute the dividend yield ratio for both companies for the most recent fiscal year. Round your answer to two decimal places. (*Note:* Target and Walmart's stock price at the end of the most recent fiscal year was $181.17 and $139.27, respectively.)

   Target = ☐ **Walmart =** ☐

5. Which company paid out a greater amount of dividends relative to its share price during the most recent fiscal year?
   ☐ Target
   ☐ Walmart

Financial Reporting and Analysis Case

Computing Dividends for an Actual Company

CP11-4
LO11-4
Apple Inc.

A recent annual report for **Apple Inc.** contained the following information (dollars in millions):

Stockholders' Equity	2020
Common stock and additional paid-in capital, \$0.00001 par value, 50.4 billion shares authorized, 17.0 billion shares issued and outstanding	\$50,779
Retained earnings	14,966

Source: Apple, Inc.

In 2020, Apple declared dividends equal to \$0.795 per share. Assume all of the dividends were paid with cash by year end. Approximately how much cash in total did Apple pay to stockholders for dividends in 2020?

Critical Thinking Cases

Evaluating an Ethical Dilemma

CP11-5
LO11-4, 11-6

You are a member of the board of directors of a large company that has been in business for more than 100 years. The company is proud of the fact that it has paid dividends every year it has been in business. Because of this stability, many retired people have invested large portions of their savings in your common stock. Unfortunately, the company has struggled for the past few years as it tries to introduce new products and is considering not paying a dividend this year. The president wants to skip the dividend in order to have more cash to invest in product development: "If we don't invest this money now, we won't get these products to market in time to save the company. I don't want to risk thousands of jobs." One of the most senior board members speaks next: "If we don't pay the dividend, thousands of retirees will be thrown into financial distress. Even if you don't care about them, you have to recognize our stock price will crash when they all sell." The company treasurer proposes an alternative: "Let's skip the cash dividend and pay a stock dividend. We can still say we've had a dividend every year." The entire board now turns to you for your opinion. What should the company do?

Evaluating an Ethical Dilemma

CP11-6
LO11-4

You are the president of a very successful biotech company that has had a remarkably profitable year. You have determined that the company has more than \$10 million in excess cash that was generated by operating activities during the year. You are thinking about paying it out to stockholders as a special dividend. You discuss the idea with your vice president, who reacts angrily to your suggestion:

> Our stock price has gone up by 200 percent in the last year alone. What more do we have to do for the owners? The people who really earned that money are the employees who have been working 12 hours a day, 6 or 7 days a week, to make the company successful. Most of them didn't even take vacations last year. I say we have to pay out bonuses and nothing extra for the stockholders.

As president, you know that you are hired by the board of directors, which is elected by the stockholders. What is your responsibility to both groups? How would you recommend allocating the \$10 million?

You as Analyst: Online Company Research

CP11-7
LO11-1, 11-3, 11-4, 11-6, 11-8

Examining a Company's Stockholders' Equity

In your web browser, search for the investor relations page of a public company you are interested in (e.g., Zoom investor relations). Select SEC Filings or Annual Report or Financials to obtain the 10-K for the most recent year available.*

Required:

1. *a.* Assess the company's capital structure. Does the company tend to favor issuing equity or borrowing to support its business?
   b. From the notes to the financial statements, identify any additional information about the stockholders' equity accounts that you feel would be important to someone analyzing the company as a potential investment.
2. Examine the statement of cash flows and the statement of stockholders' equity.
   a. What amount of stock, if any, was issued in the most recent year?
   b. How much cash did the issuance generate for the company?
   c. What was the average market value per share of the issuance?
3. What amount of treasury stock, if any, did the company repurchase during the year? Did it resell any of its treasury stock?
4. What types of dividends, if any, did the company declare during the year? If declared, how much was paid out in cash for dividends during the year?

*Alternatively, you can go to sec.gov, click on Company Filings (under the search box), type in the name of the public company you want to find. Once at the list of filings, type 10-K in the Filing Type box. The most recent 10-K annual report will be at the top of the list. Click on Interactive Data for a list of the parts or the entire report to examine.

BUSINESS ANALYTICS AND DATA VISUALIZATION WITH EXCEL AND TABLEAU

Connect offers a variety of exercises to assess Excel skills, data visualization, interpretation, and analysis, including auto-graded Tableau Dashboard Activities, Applying Excel problems, and Integrated Excel problems.

Images used throughout chapter: Question of ethics: mushmello/Shutterstock; Pause for feedback: McGraw Hill; Guided help: McGraw Hill; Financial analysis: McGraw Hill; Focus on cash flows: Hilch/Shutterstock; Key ratio analysis: guillermain/123RF; Data analytics: Hilch/Shutterstock; Tip: McGraw Hill; ESG reporting: McGraw Hill; International perspective: Hilch/Shutterstock

chapter 12

Statement of Cash Flows

While once best known for its Shasta and Faygo carbonated soft drinks, **National Beverage** now focuses on its innovative LaCroix sparkling waters, Rip It energy products, and Everfresh juices. These products bring its well-known reputation for flavor variety to the growing number of health-conscious consumers. "Healthy Transformation" and "Flavor Innovation" combined with attractive packaging are its key points of differentiation from its much larger competitors. And its diverse product lines can meet all of the beverage needs of a wide variety of consumers and retailers. However, for its strategy to earn profits for shareholders, National Beverage also must be a cost-effective producer and distributor. It maintains product quality and cost discipline through centralized purchasing and by owning and operating all of its production and bottling facilities. Its 12 plants, strategically located near customer distribution centers in different markets, reduce distribution costs and allow National Beverage to tailor its products and media promotions to regional tastes.

Although it may seem puzzling, growing profitable operations do not always ensure positive cash flow. As we have seen in earlier chapters, this occurs because the timing of revenues and expenses does not always match cash inflows and outflows. As a consequence, National Beverage must carefully manage cash flows as well as profits. For the same reasons, financial analysts must consider the information provided in National Beverage's cash flow statement in addition to its income statement and balance sheet.

LEARNING OBJECTIVES

After studying this chapter, you should be able to:

12-1 Classify cash flow statement items as part of net cash flows from operating, investing, and financing activities. p. 628

12-2 Report and interpret cash flows from operating activities using the indirect method. p. 635

12-3 Analyze and interpret the quality of income ratio. p. 641

12-4 Report and interpret cash flows from investing activities. p. 642

12-5 Analyze and interpret the capital acquisitions ratio. p. 644

12-6 Report and interpret cash flows from financing activities. p. 645

12-7 Understand the format of the cash flow statement and additional cash flow disclosures. p. 647

The Washington Post/Getty Images

FOCUS COMPANY

National Beverage Corporation

PRODUCING HEALTHIER BEVERAGES FOR CUSTOMERS AND CASH FLOWS FOR SHAREHOLDERS

nationalbeverage.com

UNDERSTANDING THE BUSINESS

Clearly, net income is important, but cash flow is also critical to a company's success. Cash flow permits a company to expand operations, replace worn assets, take advantage of new investment opportunities, and pay dividends to its owners. Some Wall Street analysts go so far as to say "Cash flow is king." Both managers and analysts need to understand the various sources and uses of cash that are associated with business activity.

The cash flow statement focuses attention on a firm's ability to generate cash internally, its management of operating assets and liabilities, and the details of its investments and its external financing. It is designed to help both managers and analysts answer important cash-related questions such as these:

- Will the company have enough cash to pay its short-term debts to suppliers and other creditors without additional borrowing?
- Is the company adequately managing its accounts receivable and inventory?
- Has the company made necessary investments in new productive capacity?
- Did the company generate enough cash flow internally to finance necessary investments, or did it rely on external financing?
- Is the company changing the makeup of its external financing?

We begin our discussion with an overview of the statement of cash flows. Then we examine the information reported in each section of the statement in depth. The chapter ends with a discussion of additional cash flow disclosures.

ORGANIZATION OF THE CHAPTER

Classifications of the Statement of Cash Flows	Reporting and Interpreting Cash Flows from Operating Activities	Reporting and Interpreting Cash Flows from Investing Activities	Reporting and Interpreting Cash Flows from Financing Activities	Completing the Statement and Additional Disclosures
• Cash Flows from Operating Activities • Cash Flows from Investing Activities • Cash Flows from Financing Activities • Net Increase (Decrease) in Cash • Relationships to the Balance Sheet and Income Statement • Preliminary Steps in Preparing the Cash Flow Statement	• Reporting Cash Flows from Operating Activities—Indirect Method • Interpreting Cash Flows from Operating Activities • Quality of Income Ratio	• Reporting Cash Flows from Investing Activities • Interpreting Cash Flows from Investing Activities • Capital Acquisitions Ratio	• Reporting Cash Flows from Financing Activities • Interpreting Cash Flows from Financing Activities	• Statement Structure • Supplemental Cash Flow Information

LEARNING OBJECTIVE 12-1

Classify cash flow statement items as part of net cash flows from operating, investing, and financing activities.

CLASSIFICATIONS OF THE STATEMENT OF CASH FLOWS

Basically, the statement of cash flows explains how the amount of cash on the balance sheet at the beginning of the period has become the amount of cash reported at the end of the period. For purposes of this statement, the definition of cash includes cash and cash equivalents. **Cash equivalents** are short-term, highly liquid investments that are both

1. Readily convertible to known amounts of cash and
2. So near to maturity there is little risk that their value will change if interest rates change.

Generally, only investments with original maturities of three months or less qualify as a cash equivalent under this definition.[1] Examples of cash equivalents are Treasury bills (a form of short-term U.S. government debt), money market funds, and commercial paper (short-term notes payable issued by large corporations).

As you can see in Exhibit 12.1, the statement of cash flows reports cash inflows and outflows in three broad categories: (1) operating activities, (2) investing activities, and (3) financing activities. Together, these three cash flow categories explain the change in cash from the beginning balance to the ending balance on the balance sheet.

---

[1]**Original maturity** means original maturity to the entity holding the investment. For example, both a three-month Treasury bill and a three-year Treasury note purchased three months from maturity qualify as cash equivalents. A Treasury note purchased three years ago, however, does not become a cash equivalent when its remaining maturity is three months.

EXHIBIT 12.1

Consolidated Statement of Cash Flows

NATIONAL BEVERAGE CORP.

REAL WORLD EXCERPT: Annual Report

NATIONAL BEVERAGE CORP.
Consolidated Statement of Cash Flows*
Year Ended April 27, 2019
(dollars in thousands)

Cash flows from operating activities:	
Net income	$140,853
Adjustments to reconcile net income to net cash provided by (used in) operating activities:	
Depreciation and amortization	13,444
Changes in operating assets and liabilities:	
Accounts receivable	(481)
Inventories	(9,782)
Prepaid expenses	5,676
Accounts payable	(8,651)
Accrued expenses	1,018
Net cash provided by operating activities	142,077
Cash flows from investing activities:	
Purchases of property, plant, and equipment	(38,333)
Proceeds from disposal of property, plant, and equipment	18
Purchase of short-term investments	(1,252)
Proceeds from sale of short-term investments	3,685
Net cash used by investing activities	(35,882)
Cash flows from financing activities:	
Repayment of principal on long-term debt	–
Proceeds from issuance of long-term debt	825
Repurchase of stock	–
Proceeds from issuance of stock	1,576
Payment of cash dividends	(141,391)
Net cash used by financing activities	(138,990)
Net Increase (Decrease) in Cash and Equivalents	(32,795)
Cash and Equivalents–Beginning of Year	189,864
Cash and Equivalents–End of Year	$157,069

**Certain amounts have been adjusted for pedagogical purposes*

Source: National Beverage Corp.

Cash Flows from Operating Activities

Cash flows from operating activities (cash flows from operations) are the cash inflows and outflows that relate directly to revenues and expenses reported on the income statement. There are two alternative approaches for presenting the operating activities section of the statement:

1. The direct method reports the components of cash flows from operating activities as gross receipts and gross payments.

Inflows	Outflows
Cash received from:	**Cash paid for:**
Customers	Purchase of services (electricity, etc.) and goods for resale
Dividends and interest on investments	Salaries and wages
	Income taxes
	Interest on liabilities

The difference between the inflows and outflows is called **net cash provided by (used by) operating activities. National Beverage** experienced a net cash inflow of $142,077 (all amounts in thousands) from its operations for the fiscal year ended April 27, 2019 (hereafter 2019). Though the FASB recommends the direct method, it is rarely used in the United States. Many financial executives have reported that they do not use it because it is more expensive to implement than the indirect method. Both the FASB and the IASB are considering a proposal to require this method, but intense opposition from the preparer community continues.

2. The **indirect method** starts with net income from the income statement and then eliminates noncash items to arrive at net cash inflow (outflow) from operating activities.

Net income
+/− Adjustments for noncash items
Net cash inflow (outflow) from operating activities

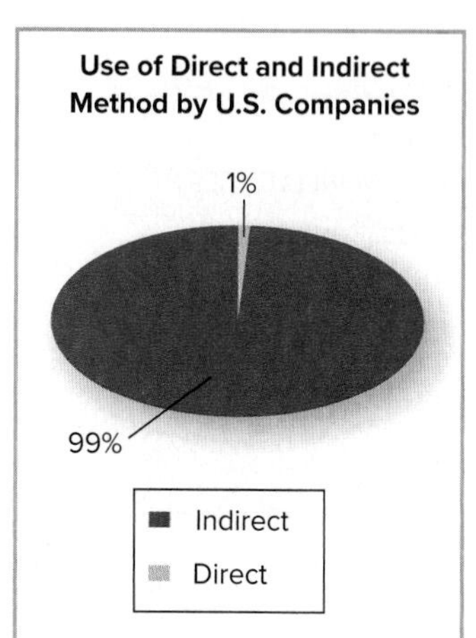

Ninety-nine percent of large U.S. companies, including National Beverage, use the indirect method.[2] Notice in Exhibit 12.1 that in 2019 National Beverage reported positive net income of $140,853 but generated positive cash flows from operating activities of $142,077. Why would income and cash flows from operating activities differ? Remember that on the income statement, revenues are recorded when they are earned, without regard to when the related cash inflows occur. Similarly, expenses are matched with revenues and recorded without regard to when the related cash outflows occur.

For now, the most important thing to remember about the two methods is that they are simply alternative ways to arrive at the same number. The total amount of **cash flows from operating activities is always the same** (an inflow of $142,077 in National Beverage's case), **regardless of whether it is computed using the direct or indirect method,** as illustrated below.

Tip Cash flow from operating activities is the same regardless of whether it is computed using the direct or indirect method.

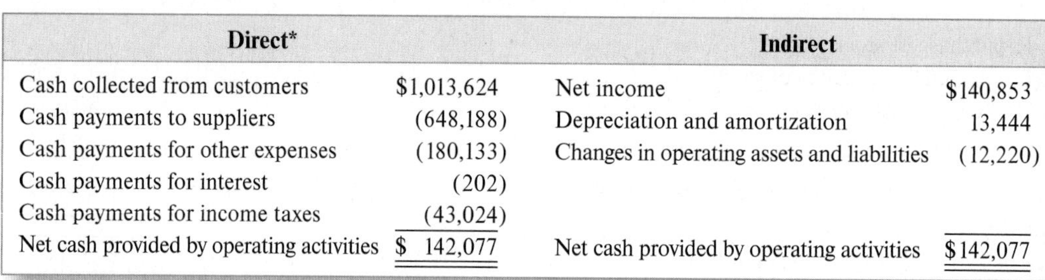

Direct*		Indirect	
Cash collected from customers	$1,013,624	Net income	$140,853
Cash payments to suppliers	(648,188)	Depreciation and amortization	13,444
Cash payments for other expenses	(180,133)	Changes in operating assets and liabilities	(12,220)
Cash payments for interest	(202)		
Cash payments for income taxes	(43,024)		
Net cash provided by operating activities	$ 142,077	Net cash provided by operating activities	$142,077

*The direct amounts are estimated from National Beverage's disclosures.

Cash Flows from Investing Activities

Cash flows from investing activities are cash inflows and outflows related to the purchase and disposal of long-lived productive assets and investments in the securities of other companies. Typical cash flows from investing activities include

Inflows	Outflows
Cash received from:	**Cash paid for:**
Sale or disposal of property, plant, and equipment	Purchase of property, plant, and equipment
Sale or maturity of investments in securities	Purchase of investments in securities

The difference between these cash inflows and outflows is called **net cash provided by (used by) investing activities.**

[2] *Accounting Trends & Techniques* (New York: American Institute of CPAs, 2012).

For **National Beverage,** this amount was an outflow of $35,882 for 2019. All of the activity was related to purchases and sales of short-term investments and the purchase and sale of property, plant, and equipment. Because total purchases exceeded cash collected from sales, there was a net cash outflow.

Cash Flows from Financing Activities

Cash flows from financing activities include exchanges of cash with creditors (debtholders) and owners (stockholders). Usual cash flows from financing activities include the following:

Inflows	Outflows
Cash received from:	**Cash paid for:**
Borrowing on notes, mortgages, bonds, etc., from creditors	Repayment of principal to creditors (excluding interest, which is an operating activity)
Issuing stock to owners	Repurchasing stock from owners
	Dividends to owners

The difference between these cash inflows and outflows is called **net cash provided by (used by) financing activities.**

National Beverage experienced a net cash outflow from financing activities of $138,990 for 2019. The Financing Activities section of its statement shows that National Beverage received proceeds in the amount of $825 from issuing long-term debt and $1,576 from issuing stock and paid $141,391 in dividends.[3]

Net Increase (Decrease) in Cash

The combination of **the net cash flows from operating activities, investing activities, and financing activities must equal the net increase (decrease) in cash** for the reporting period. For the year 2019, **National Beverage** reported a net decrease in cash of $32,795, which explains the change in cash on the balance sheet from the beginning balance of $189,864 to the ending balance of $157,069.

Net cash provided by operating activities	$142,077	
Net cash used in investing activities	(35,882)	
Net cash used in financing activities	(138,990)	
Net decrease in cash and equivalents	(32,795)	
Cash – Beginning of year	189,864	*Beginning and ending balances*
Cash – End of year	$157,069	*from the balance sheet*

PAUSE FOR FEEDBACK

We just discussed the three main sections of the cash flow statement: Cash Flows from Operating Activities, which are related to earning income from normal operations; Cash Flows from Investing Activities, which are related to the acquisition and sale of productive assets; and Cash Flows from Financing Activities, which are related to external financing of the enterprise. The net cash inflow or outflow for the year is the same amount as the increase or decrease in cash and cash equivalents for the year on the balance sheet. To make sure you understand the appropriate classifications of the different cash flows, answer the following questions before you move on.

[3]This description was simplified to eliminate discussion of stock options.

SELF-STUDY QUIZ

A listing of some typical cash flows reported on a direct method statement of cash flows follows. Indicate whether each item is disclosed in the Operating Activities (O), Investing Activities (I), or Financing Activities (F) section of the statement of cash flows.

_____ 1. Proceeds from issuance of long-term debt.

_____ 2. Collections from customers.

_____ 3. Payment of interest on debt.

_____ 4. Purchase of property, plant, and equipment.

_____ 5. Proceeds from disposal of investment securities.

After you have completed your answers, check them below.

Related Homework: M12-3, E12-3

To give you a better understanding of the statement of cash flows, we now discuss National Beverage's statement in more detail, including the way in which it relates to the balance sheet and income statement. Then we examine how each section of the statement describes a set of important decisions made by National Beverage's management. Last, we examine how financial analysts use each section to evaluate the company's performance.

Relationships to the Balance Sheet and Income Statement

Preparing and interpreting the cash flow statement requires an analysis of the balance sheet and income statement accounts that relate to the three sections of the cash flow statement. In previous chapters, we emphasized that companies record transactions as journal entries that are posted to T-accounts, which are used to prepare the income statement and the balance sheet. But companies cannot prepare the statement of cash flows using the amounts recorded in the T-accounts because those amounts are based on accrual accounting. Instead, they must analyze the numbers recorded under the accrual method and adjust them to a cash basis. To prepare the statement of cash flows, they need the following data:

1. **Comparative balance sheets** used in calculating the cash flows from all activities (operating, investing, and financing).
2. A **complete income statement** used primarily in calculating cash flows from operating activities.
3. **Additional details** concerning selected accounts where the total change in an account balance during the year does not reveal the underlying nature of the cash flows.

Our approach to preparing and understanding the cash flow statement focuses on the changes in the balance sheet accounts. It relies on a simple manipulation of the balance sheet equation:

$$\text{Assets} = \text{Liabilities} + \text{Stockholders' Equity}$$

First, assets can be split into cash and noncash assets:

$$\text{Cash} + \text{Noncash Assets} = \text{Liabilities} + \text{Stockholders' Equity}$$

If we move the noncash assets to the right side of the equation, then

$$\text{Cash} = \text{Liabilities} + \text{Stockholders' Equity} - \text{Noncash Assets}$$

Solutions to SELF-STUDY QUIZ

1. F 2. O 3. O 4. I 5. I

Category	Transaction	Cash Effect	Other Account Affected
Operating	Collect accounts receivable	+Cash	−Accounts Receivable (A)
	Pay accounts payable	−Cash	−Accounts Payable (L)
	Prepay rent	−Cash	+Prepaid Rent (A)
	Pay interest	−Cash	−Retained Earnings (SE)
	Sale for cash	+Cash	+Retained Earnings (SE)
Investing	Purchase equipment for cash	−Cash	+Equipment (A)
	Sell investment securities for cash	+Cash	−Investments (A)
Financing	Pay back debt to bank	−Cash	−Notes Payable–Bank (L)
	Issue stock for cash	+Cash	+Common Stock and Additional Paid-in Capital (SE)

EXHIBIT 12.2

Selected Cash Transactions and Their Effects on Other Balance Sheet Accounts

Given this relationship, the changes (Δ) in cash between the beginning and the end of the period must equal the changes (Δ) in the amounts on the right side of the equation between the beginning and the end of the period:

$$\triangle \text{ Cash} = \triangle \text{ Liabilities} + \triangle \text{ Stockholders' Equity} - \triangle \text{ Noncash Assets}$$

Thus, **any transaction that changes cash must be accompanied by a change in liabilities, stockholders' equity, or noncash assets.** Exhibit 12.2 illustrates this concept for selected cash transactions.

Preliminary Steps in Preparing the Cash Flow Statement

Based on this logic, we use the following preliminary steps to prepare the cash flow statement:

1. Determine the change in each balance sheet account. From this year's ending balance, subtract this year's beginning balance (i.e., last year's ending balance).
2. Classify each change as relating to operating (O), investing (I), or financing (F) activities by marking them with the corresponding letter. Use Exhibit 12.3 as a guide.

The balance sheet accounts related to earning income (operating items) should be marked with an O. These accounts are often called **operating assets and liabilities.** The accounts that should be marked with an O include the following:

- Most current assets (other than short-term investments, which relate to investing activities, and cash).[4]
- Most current liabilities (other than amounts owed to investors and financial institutions,[5] all of which relate to financing activities).
- Retained Earnings, because it increases by the amount of net income, which is the starting point for the operating section. (Retained Earnings also decreases by dividends declared and paid, which is a financing outflow noted by an F.)

[4]Certain noncurrent assets, such as long-term receivables from customers, and noncurrent liabilities, such as postretirement obligations to employees, are considered to be operating items. These items are covered in more advanced accounting classes.

[5]Examples of the accounts excluded are Dividends Payable, Short-Term Debt to Financial Institutions, and Current Maturities of Long-Term Debt. Current maturities of long-term debt are amounts of debt with an original term of more than one year that are due within one year of the statement date. Certain noncurrent liabilities involving payables to suppliers, to employees, or for taxes also are considered to be operating liabilities. These items are covered in more advanced accounting classes.

EXHIBIT 12.3

Comparative Balance Sheets and Current Income Statement

NATIONAL BEVERAGE CORP.

REAL WORLD EXCERPT:

Annual Report

NATIONAL BEVERAGE CORP.
Consolidated Balance Sheets*
(dollars in thousands)

Related Cash Flow Section		April 27 2019	April 28, 2018	*Change*
	Assets			
	Current assets:			
Change in Cash	Cash and equivalents	$ 157,069	$189,864	−32,795
I	Short-term investments	2,914	5,347	−2,433
O	Accounts receivable	84,841	84,360	+481
O	Inventories	70,702	60,920	+9,782
O	Prepaid expenses	6,800	12,476	−5,676
	Total current assets	322,326	352,967	
I†	Property, plant, and equipment–net	130,736	105,865	+24,871
	Total assets	$453,062	$458,832	
	Liabilities and Stockholders' Equity			
	Current liabilities:			
O	Accounts payable	$ 66,202	$ 74,853	−8,651
O	Accrued expenses	30,835	29,817	+1,018
	Total current liabilities	97,037	104,670	
F	Long-term debt	23,547	22,722	+825
	Stockholders' equity:			
F	Common stock	658	657	+1
F	Additional paid-in capital	19,933	18,358	+1,575
O and F	Retained earnings	311,887	312,425	−538
	Total stockholders' equity	332,478	331,440	
	Total liabilities and stockholders' equity	$453,062	$458,832	

†The Accumulated Depreciation account also is related to operations because it relates to depreciation.

NATIONAL BEVERAGE CORP.
Consolidated Statement of Income*
For the Fiscal Year Ended April 27, 2019
(dollars in thousands)

Net sales	$1,014,105
Cost of sales	629,755
Gross profit	384,350
Operating expenses:	
Selling, general, and administrative expenses	186,827
Depreciation and amortization expense	13,444
Total operating expenses	200,271
Operating Income	184,079
Interest expense	202
Income before provision for income taxes	183,877
Provision for income taxes	43,024
Net income	$ 140,853

**Certain amounts have been adjusted for pedagogical purposes.*

Source: National Beverage Corp.

In Exhibit 12.3, all of the operating assets and liabilities have been marked with an O. These items include

- Accounts Receivable
- Inventories
- Prepaid Expenses
- Accounts Payable
- Accrued Expenses

As we have noted, retained earnings are also relevant to operations.

The balance sheet accounts related to investing activities should be marked with an I. These include all of the remaining assets on the balance sheet. In Exhibit 12.3 these items include

- Short-Term Investments
- Property, Plant, and Equipment, Net

The balance sheet accounts related to financing activities should be marked with an F. These include all of the remaining liability and stockholders' equity accounts on the balance sheet. In Exhibit 12.3 these items include

- Long-Term Debt
- Common Stock
- Additional Paid-in Capital
- Retained Earnings (for decreases resulting from dividends declared and paid)

Next, we use this information to prepare each section of the statement of cash flows.

REPORTING AND INTERPRETING CASH FLOWS FROM OPERATING ACTIVITIES

LEARNING OBJECTIVE 12-2

Report and interpret cash flows from operating activities using the indirect method.

As noted earlier, the operating section can be prepared in two formats, and nearly all U.S. companies choose the indirect method. As a result, we discuss the indirect method here and the direct method in Supplement A at the end of the chapter.

Recall that

1. Cash flow from operating activities is always the **same** regardless of whether it is computed using the direct or indirect method.
2. The investing and financing sections are always presented in the **same** manner regardless of the format of the operating section.

Reporting Cash Flows from Operating Activities—Indirect Method

Exhibit 12.3 shows **National Beverage**'s comparative balance sheets and income statement. Remember that the indirect method starts with net income and converts it to cash flows from operating activities. This involves adjusting net income for the differences in the timing of accrual basis net income and cash flows. The general structure of the operating activities section is

Operating Activities
Net income
Adjustments to reconcile net income to cash flow from operating activities:
+ Depreciation and amortization expense
− Gain on sale of investing assets
+ Loss on sale of investing assets
+ Decreases in operating assets
+ Increases in operating liabilities
− Increases in operating assets
− Decreases in operating liabilities
Net Cash Flow from Operating Activities

Tip The indirect method operating activities section starts with net income and removes revenues and expenses that do not affect cash.

EXHIBIT 12.4

National Beverage Corp.: Schedule for Net Cash Flow from Operating Activities, Indirect Method (dollars in thousands)

CONVERSION OF NET INCOME TO NET CASH FLOW FROM OPERATING ACTIVITIES

Items	Amount	Explanation
Net income, accrual basis	$140,853	From income statement.
Add (subtract) to convert to cash basis:		
Depreciation and amortization	13,444	Add back because depreciation and amortization expense does not affect cash.
Accounts receivable increase	(481)	Subtract because cash collected from customers is less than accrual basis revenues.
Inventory increase	(9,782)	Subtract because purchases are more than cost of goods sold expense.
Prepaid expenses decrease	5,676	Add because cash prepayments for expenses are less than accrual basis expenses.
Accounts payable decrease	(8,651)	Subtract because cash payments to suppliers are more than amounts purchased on account (borrowed from suppliers).
Accrued expenses increase	1,018	Add because cash payments for expenses are less than accrual basis expenses.
Net cash provided by operating activities	$142,077	Subtotal on the statement of cash flows.

To keep track of all the additions and subtractions made to convert net income to cash flows from operating activities, it is helpful to set up a schedule to record the computations. We will construct a schedule for National Beverage in Exhibit 12.4.

We begin our schedule presented in Exhibit 12.4 with net income of $140,853 taken from National Beverage's income statement (Exhibit 12.3). Completing the operating section using the indirect method involves two steps:

Step 1: **Adjust net income for depreciation and amortization expense and gains and losses on sale of investing assets such as property, plant, and equipment and investments.** Recording depreciation and amortization expense does not affect the cash account (or any other operating asset or liability). It affects a noncurrent investing asset (Property, plant, and equipment, net). **Because depreciation and amortization expense is subtracted in computing net income but does not affect cash, we always add it back** to convert net income to cash flow from operating activities. In the case of National Beverage, we need to remove the effect of depreciation and amortization expense by adding back $13,444 to net income (see Exhibit 12.4).

If National Beverage had sold property, plant, and equipment at a gain or loss, the amount of cash received would be classified as an investing cash inflow. Because all of the cash received is an investing cash flow, an adjustment also must be made in the operating activities section to avoid double counting the gain or loss. **Gains on sales of property, plant, and equipment are subtracted and losses on such sales are added** to convert net income to cash flow from operating activities. We illustrate the relevant computations and adjustments for gains and losses on the sale of long-term assets in Supplement B at the end of the chapter.[6]

Step 2: **Adjust net income for changes in assets and liabilities marked as operating (O).** Each **change** in operating assets (other than cash and short-term investments) and liabilities (other than amounts owed to owners and financial institutions) causes a difference between net income and cash flow from operating activities.[7] When converting net income to cash flow from operating activities, apply the following general rules:

- Add the change when an operating asset decreases or an operating liability increases.
- Subtract the change when an operating asset increases or an operating liability decreases.

[6] Other similar additions and subtractions are discussed in more advanced accounting courses.

[7] As noted earlier, certain noncurrent assets, such as long-term receivables from customers, and noncurrent liabilities, such as postretirement obligations to employees, are considered to be operating items. These items are covered in more advanced accounting classes.

Understanding what makes these assets and liabilities increase and decrease is the key to understanding the logic of these additions and subtractions.

Change in Accounts Receivable

We illustrate this logic with the first operating item (O) listed on National Beverage's balance sheet (Exhibit 12.3), accounts receivable. Remember that the income statement reflects sales revenue, but the cash flow statement must reflect cash collections from customers. As the following accounts receivable T-account illustrates, when sales revenues are recorded, accounts receivable increases, and when cash is collected from customers, accounts receivable decreases.

	Accounts Receivable (A)			
Change $481	Beginning balance	84,360		
	Sales revenue (on account)	1,014,105	Collections from customers	1,013,624
	Ending balance	84,841		

In the National Beverage example, cash collections from customers are less than sales revenue reported on the income statement by $1,014,105 – $1,013,624 = $481. Because less money was collected from customers, this amount must be subtracted from net income to convert to cash flows from operating activities. Note that this amount is also the same as the **change** in the accounts receivable account:

Ending balance	$84,841
– Beginning balance	84,360
Change	$ 481

This same underlying logic is used to determine adjustments for the other operating assets and liabilities.

To summarize, the income statement reflects revenues of the period, but cash flow from operating activities must reflect cash collections from customers. Sales on account increase the balance in accounts receivable, and collections from customers decrease the balance.

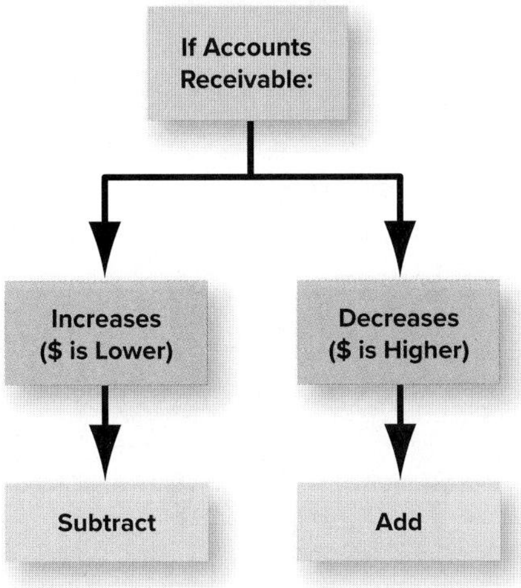

Accounts Receivable (A)		
Beginning	84,360	
Increase	481	
Ending	84,841	

If Accounts Receivable:

Increases ($ is Lower)	Decreases ($ is Higher)
Subtract	Add

The balance sheet for National Beverage Corp. (Exhibit 12.3) indicates an **increase** in accounts receivable of $481 for the period, which means that cash collected from customers is lower than revenue. To convert to cash flows from operating activities, the amount of the increase (the amount of sales over and above collections) must be **subtracted** in Exhibit 12.4. (A decrease is added.)

Change in Inventory

The income statement reflects merchandise sold for the period, whereas cash flow from operating activities must reflect cash purchases. As shown in the Inventories T-account, purchases of goods increase the balance in inventory, and recording merchandise sold decreases the balance in inventory.

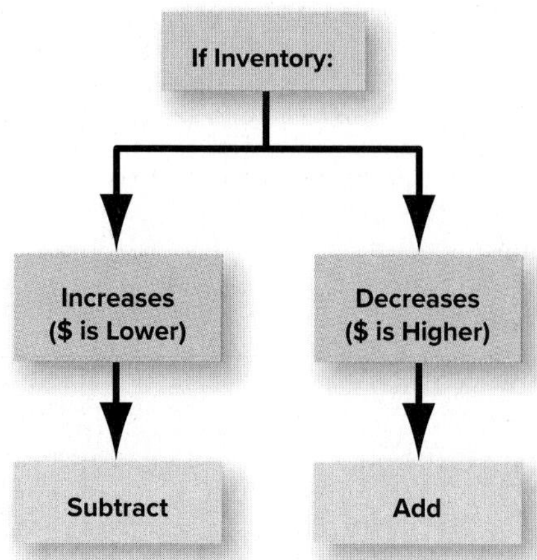

Inventories (A)	
Beg. balance	
Purchases	Costs of goods sold
End. bal.	

Inventories (A)			
Beg.	60,920		
Increase	9,782		
End.	70,702		

National Beverage's balance sheet (Exhibit 12.3) indicates that inventory **increased** by $9,782, which means that the amount of purchases is more than the amount of merchandise sold. The increase (the extra goods purchased) must be **subtracted** from net income to convert to cash flow from operating activities in Exhibit 12.4. (A decrease is added.)

Change in Prepaid Expenses

The income statement reflects expenses of the period, but cash flow from operating activities must reflect the cash payments. Cash prepayments increase the balance in prepaid expenses, and recording of expenses decreases the balance in prepaid expenses.

If Prepaid Expenses:
Increases ($ is Lower) → Subtract
Decreases ($ is Higher) → Add

Prepaid Expenses (A)	
Beg. bal.	
Cash prepayments	Services used (expense)
End. bal.	

Prepaid Expenses (A)			
Beg.	12,476		
		Decrease	5,676
End.	6,800		

The National Beverage balance sheet (Exhibit 12.3) indicates a $5,676 **decrease** in prepaid expenses, which means that new cash prepayments are less than the amount of expenses. The decrease (the extra expenses) must be **added** to net income in Exhibit 12.4.

Change in Accounts Payable

Cash flow from operations must reflect cash purchases, but not all purchases are for cash. Purchases on account increase accounts payable and cash paid to suppliers decreases accounts payable.

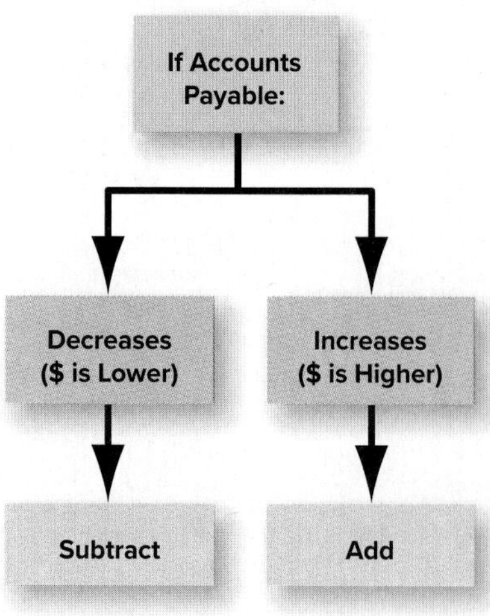

Accounts Payable (L)	
Beg. bal.	
Cash payments	Purchases on account
End. bal.	

Accounts Payable (L)			
		Beg.	74,853
Decrease	8,651		
		End.	66,202

National Beverage's accounts payable decreased by $8,651, which means that cash payments were more than purchases on account. This decrease (the extra cash payments) must be subtracted in Exhibit 12.4. (An increase is added.)

Change in Accrued Expenses

The income statement reflects all accrued expenses, but the cash flow statement must reflect actual payments for those expenses. Recording accrued expenses increases the balance in the liability accrued expenses and cash payments for the expenses decrease accrued expenses.

Accrued Expenses (L)	
	Beg. bal.
Pay off accruals	Accrued expenses
	End. bal.

Accrued Expenses (L)			
		Beg.	29,817
		Increase	1,018
		End.	30,835

National Beverage's accrued expenses (Exhibit 12.3) **increased** by $1,018 which indicates that cash paid for the expenses is less than accrual basis expenses. The increase (the lower cash paid) must be **added** in Exhibit 12.4. (A decrease is subtracted.)

If Accrued Expenses:
Decreases ($ is Lower) → Subtract
Increases ($ is Higher) → Add

Summary

We can summarize the typical additions and subtractions that are required to reconcile net income with cash flow from operating activities as follows:

	ADDITIONS AND SUBTRACTIONS TO RECONCILE NET INCOME TO CASH FLOW FROM OPERATING ACTIVITIES	
Item	When Item Increases	When Item Decreases
Depreciation and amortization	+	NA
Gain on sale of long-term assets	−	NA
Loss on sale of long-term assets	+	NA
Accounts receivable	−	+
Inventory	−	+
Prepaid expenses	−	+
Accounts payable	+	−
Accrued expense liabilities	+	−

Notice again in this table that to reconcile net income to cash flow from operating activities, you must:

- **Add the change when an operating asset decreases or an operating liability increases.**
- **Subtract the change when an operating asset increases or an operating liability decreases.**

The cash flow statement for National Beverage (Exhibit 12.1) shows the same additions and subtractions to reconcile net income to cash flow from operating activities described in Exhibit 12.4.

Tip When preparing the indirect method operating section, (1) add operating asset decreases and operating liability increases, and (2) subtract operating asset increases and operating liability decreases.

INTERNATIONAL PERSPECTIVE

Classification of Interest on the Cash Flow Statement

U.S. GAAP and IFRS differ in the cash flow statement treatment of interest received and interest paid as follows:

	Interest Received	Interest Paid
U.S. GAAP	Operating	Operating
IFRS	Operating or Investing	Operating or Financing

Under U.S. GAAP, interest paid and received are both classified as operating cash flows because the related revenue and expense enter into the computation of net income. This makes it easier to compare net income to cash flow from operations. It also benefits the financial statement user by ensuring comparability across companies. IFRS, on the other hand, allows interest received to be classified as either operating or investing and interest paid to be classified as either operating or financing. This recognizes that interest received results from investing activities, whereas interest paid, like dividends paid, involves payments to providers of financing. However, the alternative classifications may be confusing to financial statement readers.

PAUSE FOR FEEDBACK

The indirect method for reporting cash flows from operating activities reports a conversion of net income to net cash flow from operating activities. The conversion involves additions and subtractions for (1) expenses (such as depreciation expense) and revenues that do not affect current assets or current liabilities and (2) changes in each of the individual current assets (other than cash and short-term investments) and current liabilities (other than short-term debt to financial institutions, current maturities of long-term debt, and dividends payable, which relate to financing), which reflect differences in the timing of accrual basis net income and cash flows. To test whether you understand these concepts, answer the following questions before you move on.

SELF-STUDY QUIZ

Indicate which of the following items taken from **Coca-Cola Company**'s cash flow statement would be added (+), subtracted (−), or not included (NA) in the reconciliation of net income to cash flow from operations.

_____ 1. Increase in inventories.
_____ 2. Issuances of stock.
_____ 3. Amortization expense.
_____ 4. Decrease in accounts receivable.
_____ 5. Increase in accounts payable.
_____ 6. Increase in prepaid expenses.

After you have completed your answers, check them below.

GUIDED HELP 12-1

For additional step-by-step video instruction on preparing the operating section of the statement of cash flows using the indirect method, go to mhhe.com/libby_gh12-1.

Related Homework: M12-1, M12-2, E12-1

Interpreting Cash Flows from Operating Activities

mauritius images GmbH/Alamy Stock Photo

The operating activities section of the cash flow statement focuses attention on the firm's ability to generate cash internally through operations and its management of operating assets and operating liabilities (also called **operating working capital**). Most analysts believe that this is the most important section of the statement because, in the long run, operations are the only source of cash. That is, investors will not invest in a company if they do not believe that cash generated from operations will be available to pay them dividends or expand the company. Similarly, creditors will not lend money if they do not believe that cash generated from operations will be available to pay back the loan. For example, many dot-com companies crashed when investors lost faith in their ability to turn business ideas into cash flows from operations.

A common rule of thumb followed by financial and credit analysts is to avoid firms with rising net income but falling cash flow from operations. Rapidly rising inventories or receivables often predict a slump in profits and the need for external financing. A true understanding of the meaning of the difference requires a detailed understanding of its causes.

In 2019, **National Beverage** reported that cash flow from operations was higher than net income. What caused this relationship? To answer these questions, we must carefully analyze how National Beverage's operating activities are reported in its cash flow statement. To properly interpret this information, we also must learn more about the beverage industry. National Beverage normally reports higher cash flow from operations than net income because of the effect of depreciation and amortization, which reduces income but is not a cash outflow. At the same time, it carefully manages the assets and liabilities that enter into the operating cash flow calculation, keeping those total changes to a minimum. Many analysts compute the quality of income ratio as a general sign of the ability to generate cash through operations.

Solutions to SELF-STUDY QUIZ

1. − 2. NA 3. + 4. + 5. + 6. −

KEY RATIO ANALYSIS

LEARNING OBJECTIVE 12-3

Analyze and interpret the quality of income ratio.

Quality of Income Ratio

ANALYTICAL QUESTION

How much cash does each dollar of net income generate?

RATIO AND COMPARISONS

$$\text{Quality of Income Ratio} = \frac{\text{Cash Flow from Operating Activities}}{\text{Net Income}}$$

National Beverage Corp.'s ratio for the year 2019 was

$$\frac{\$142{,}077}{\$140{,}853} = 1.01\ (101\%)$$

COMPARISONS OVER TIME		
National Beverage		
2019	2018	2017
1.01	1.03	1.07

COMPARISONS WITH COMPETITORS	
Coca-Cola	PepsiCo
2019	2019
1.17	1.31

Selected Focus Company Comparisons

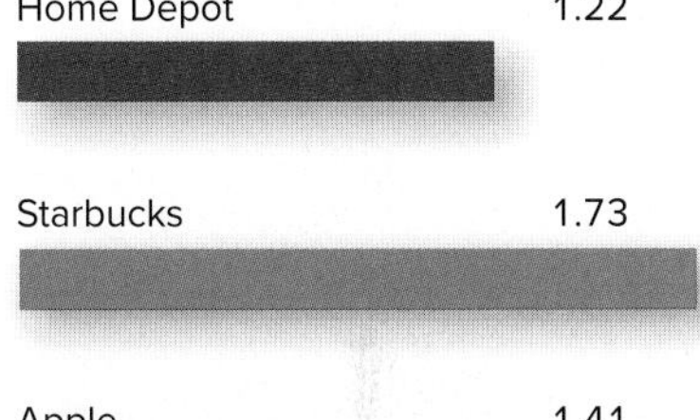

INTERPRETATIONS

In General The quality of income ratio measures the portion of income that was generated in cash. All other things equal, a higher quality of income ratio indicates greater ability to finance operating and other cash needs from operating cash inflows. A higher ratio also indicates that it is less likely that the company is using aggressive revenue recognition policies to increase net income, and therefore is less likely to experience a decline in earnings in the future. When this ratio does not equal 1.0, analysts must establish the sources of the difference to determine the significance of the findings. There are four potential causes of any difference:

1. **The corporate life cycle (growth or decline in sales).** When sales are increasing, receivables and inventory normally increase faster than accounts payable. This often reduces operating cash flows below income, which, in turn, reduces the ratio. When sales are declining, the opposite occurs, and the ratio increases.
2. **Seasonality.** Seasonal (from quarter to quarter) variations in sales and purchases of inventory can cause the ratio to deviate from 1.0 during particular quarters.
3. **Changes in revenue and expense recognition.** Aggressive revenue recognition or failure to accrue appropriate expenses will inflate net income and reduce the ratio.
4. **Changes in management of operating assets and liabilities.** Inefficient management will increase operating assets and decrease liabilities, reducing operating cash flows and the quality of income ratio. More efficient management, such as shortening of customer payment terms, will have the opposite effect.

Focus Company Analysis During the past three years, National Beverage's quality of income ratio has stayed relatively stable. Its ratio is below those of **Coca-Cola** and **PepsiCo**. National Beverage's lower ratio generally would be judged negatively by analysts and would prompt them to read the management's discussion and analysis section of the annual report to determine its causes.

A Few Cautions The quality of income ratio can be interpreted based only on an understanding of the company's business operations and strategy. For example, a low ratio for a quarter can be due simply to normal seasonal changes. However, it also can indicate obsolete inventory, slowing sales, or failed expansion plans. To test for these possibilities, analysts often analyze this ratio in tandem with the accounts receivable turnover and inventory turnover ratios.

A QUESTION OF ETHICS

Fraud and Cash Flows from Operations

The cash flow statement often gives outsiders the first hint that financial statements may contain errors and irregularities. The importance of this indicator as a predictor is receiving more attention in the United States and internationally. *Investors Chronicle* reported on an accounting fraud at a commercial credit company, suggesting the following.

INVESTORS CHRONICLE
REAL WORLD EXCERPT

. . . a look at **Versailles**'s cash flow statement—an invaluable tool in spotting creative accounting—should have triggered misgivings. In the company's last filed accounts . . . Versailles reported operating profits of . . . $25 million but a cash outflow from operating activities of $24 million . . . such figures should . . . have served as a warning. After all, what use is a company to anyone if it reports only accounting profits which are never translated into cash?

Source: James Chapman, "Creative Accounting: Exposed!," *Investors Chronicle,* March 2, 2001.

As noted in earlier chapters, unethical managers sometimes attempt to reach earnings targets by manipulating accruals and deferrals of revenues and expenses to inflate income. Because these adjusting entries do not affect the cash account, they have no effect on the cash flow statement. A growing difference between net income and cash flow from operations can be a sign of such manipulations. This early warning sign has signaled some famous bankruptcies, such as that of **W. T. Grant** in 1975. The company had inflated income by failing to make adequate accruals of expenses for uncollectible accounts receivable and obsolete inventory. The more astute analysts noted the growing difference between net income and cash flow from operations and recommended selling the stock long before the bankruptcy.

LEARNING OBJECTIVE 12-4

Report and interpret cash flows from investing activities.

REPORTING AND INTERPRETING CASH FLOWS FROM INVESTING ACTIVITIES

Reporting Cash Flows from Investing Activities

Preparing this section of the cash flow statement requires an analysis of the accounts related to property, plant, and equipment; intangible assets; and investments in the securities of other companies. Normally, the relevant balance sheet accounts include Short-Term Investments and long-term asset accounts such as Long-Term Investments and Property, Plant, and Equipment. The following relationships are the ones that you will encounter most frequently:

Tip Remember that the investing and financing activities are always presented using the "direct method." That is, they list the gross receipts and payments due to each activity.

Related Balance Sheet Account(s)	Investing Activity	Cash Flow Effect
Property, plant, and equipment and intangible assets (patents, etc.)	Purchase of property, plant, and equipment or intangible assets for cash	Outflow
	Sale of property, plant, and equipment or intangible assets for cash	Inflow
Short- or long-term investments (stocks and bonds of other companies)	Purchase of investment securities for cash	Outflow
	Sale (maturity) of investment securities for cash	Inflow

Remember that:

- **Only purchases paid for with cash or cash equivalents are included.**
- **The amount of cash that is received from the sale of assets is included, regardless of whether the assets are sold at a gain or loss.**

Items	Cash Inflows (Outflows)	Explanation
Cash flows from investing activities:		
Purchases of property, plant, and equipment	$(38,333)	Payment in cash for equipment
Proceeds from disposal of property, plant, and equipment	18	Receipt of cash from sale of equipment
Purchase of short-term investments	(1,252)	Payment in cash for new investments
Proceeds from sale of short-term investments	3,685	Receipt of cash from sale of investments
Net cash used by investing activities	$(35,882)	

EXHIBIT 12.5

National Beverage Corp.: Schedule for Net Cash Flow from Investing Activities (dollars in thousands)

In **National Beverage**'s case, the balance sheet (Exhibit 12.3) shows two investing assets (noted with an I) that have changed during the period: Property, Plant, and Equipment, Net, and Short-Term Investments. To determine the causes of these changes, accountants need to search the related company records.

Property, Plant, and Equipment, Net

Analysis of National Beverage Corp.'s records reveals that the company purchased new property, plant, and equipment for $38,333 in cash, which is a cash outflow. The company also sold old equipment for $18 in cash, an amount equal to its net book value. This is a cash inflow. These investing items are listed in the schedule of investing activities in Exhibit 12.5. These items, less the amount of depreciation and amortization expense added back in the Operations section ($13,444), explain the increase in property, plant, and equipment, net, of $24,871.

Property, Plant, and Equipment, Net (A)			
Beginning	105,865	Sold	18
Purchased	38,333	Depreciation and amortization	13,444
Ending	130,736		

Investments

National Beverage's records indicate that it purchased $1,252 in short-term investments during the year for cash, which is an investing cash outflow. The company also sold short-term investments for $3,685, an amount equal to their net book value. These investing items are listed in the schedule of investing activities in Exhibit 12.5. They explain the $2,433 decrease in short-term investments reported on the balance sheet. Changes in long-term investments would be treated in the same fashion.

Short-Term Investments (A)			
Beginning	5,347		
Purchased	1,252	Sold	3,685
Ending	2,914		

The net cash flow from investing activities resulting from these four items is a $35,882 outflow (see Exhibit 12.5).

Interpreting Cash Flows from Investing Activities

Two common ways to assess a company's ability to internally finance its expansion needs are the capital acquisitions ratio and free cash flow.

KEY RATIO ANALYSIS

LEARNING OBJECTIVE 12-5

Analyze and interpret the capital acquisitions ratio.

Capital Acquisitions Ratio

ANALYTICAL QUESTION

To what degree was the company able to finance purchases of property, plant, and equipment with cash provided by operating activities?

RATIO AND COMPARISONS

$$\text{Capital Acquisitions Ratio} = \frac{\text{Cash Flow from Operating Activities}}{\text{Cash Paid for Property, Plant, and Equipment}}$$

National Beverage's ratio for 2019 was

$$\frac{\$142{,}077}{\$38{,}333} = 3.71$$

Examine the ratio using two techniques:

COMPARISONS OVER TIME		
National Beverage		
2019	2018	2017
3.71	4.84	8.15

COMPARISONS WITH COMPETITORS	
Coca-Cola	PepsiCo
2019	2019
5.10	2.28

Selected Focus Company Comparisons

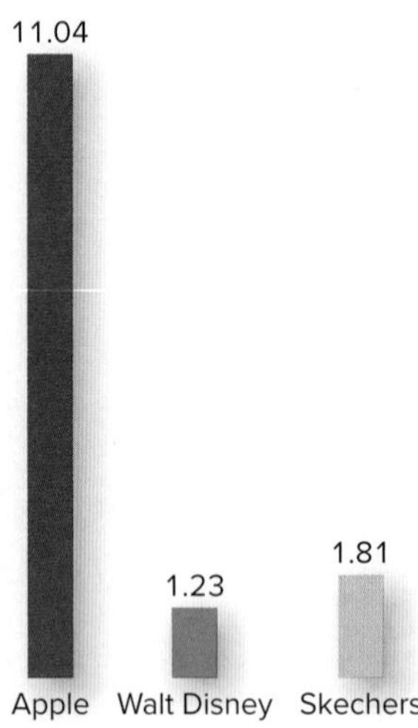

INTERPRETATIONS

In General The capital acquisitions ratio reflects the portion of purchases of property, plant, and equipment financed from operating activities (without the need for outside debt or equity financing or the sale of other investments or fixed assets). A high ratio indicates less need for outside financing for current and future expansion. It benefits the company because it provides the company opportunities for strategic acquisitions, avoids the cost of additional debt, and reduces the risk of bankruptcy that comes with additional leverage (see Chapter 10).

Focus Company Analysis National Beverage's capital acquisitions ratio has decreased from 8.15 to 3.71 in recent years. It still generates more than sufficient cash to meet its investing needs. As a consequence, when credit markets tighten during a financial downturn, National Beverage's investment plans are unaffected. National Beverage also has maintained a ratio that is higher than one of its larger competitors, **PepsiCo**, but lower than **Coca-Cola's**.

A Few Cautions Because the needs for investment in plant and equipment differ dramatically across industries (e.g., airlines versus pizza delivery restaurants), a particular firm's ratio should be compared only with its prior years' figures or with other firms in the same industry. Also, a high ratio may indicate a failure to update plant and equipment, which can limit a company's ability to compete in the future.

FINANCIAL ANALYSIS

Free Cash Flow

Managers and analysts often calculate free cash flow[8] as a measure of a firm's ability to pursue long-term investment opportunities. Free cash flow is normally calculated as follows:

$$\text{Free Cash Flow} = \text{Cash Flow from Operating Activities} - \text{Dividends} - \text{Capital Expenditures}$$

[8]An alternative definition that does not subtract dividends and interest is often called the **total cash flow of the firm** in finance.

Any positive free cash flow is available for additional capital expenditures, investments in other companies, and mergers and acquisitions without the need for external financing or reductions in dividends to shareholders. While free cash flow is considered a positive sign of financial flexibility, it also can represent a hidden cost to shareholders. Sometimes managers use free cash flow to pursue unprofitable investments just for the sake of growth or to obtain perquisites (such as fancy offices and corporate jets) that do not benefit the shareholders. In these cases, the shareholders would be better off if free cash flow were paid as additional dividends or used to repurchase the company's stock on the open market.

REPORTING AND INTERPRETING CASH FLOWS FROM FINANCING ACTIVITIES

LEARNING OBJECTIVE 12-6

Report and interpret cash flows from financing activities.

Reporting Cash Flows from Financing Activities

Financing activities are associated with generating capital from creditors and owners. This section of the cash flow statement reflects changes in two current liabilities, Notes Payable to Financial Institutions (often called short-term debt) and Current Maturities of Long-Term Debt, as well as changes in long-term liabilities and stockholders' equity accounts. These balance sheet accounts relate to the issuance and retirement of debt and stock and the payment of dividends. The following relationships are the ones that you will encounter most frequently:

Related Balance Sheet Account(s)	Financing Activity	Cash Flow Effect
Short-term debt (notes payable)	Borrowing cash from banks or other financial institutions	Inflow
	Repayment of loan principal	Outflow
Long-term debt	Issuance of bonds for cash	Inflow
	Repayment of bond principal	Outflow
Common stock and additional paid-in capital	Issuance of stock for cash	Inflow
	Repurchase (retirement) of stock with cash	Outflow
Retained earnings	Payment of cash dividends	Outflow

Remember that:

- **Cash repayments of principal are cash flows from financing activities.**
- **Interest payments are cash flows from operating activities.** Because interest expense is reported on the income statement, the related cash flow is shown in the operating section.
- **Dividend payments are cash flows from financing activities.** Dividend payments are not reported on the income statement because they represent a distribution of income to owners. Therefore, they are shown in the financing section.
- **If debt or stock is issued for other than cash, it is not included in this section.**

Tip Interest payments are operating cash flows while dividend payments are financing cash flows.

To compute cash flows from financing activities, you should review changes in debt and stockholders' equity accounts. In the case of **National Beverage Corp.**, the analysis of changes in the balance sheet (Exhibit 12.3) finds that only long-term debt, common stock, and additional paid-in capital changed during the period (noted with an F) and retained earnings changed (noted with an F and an O).

Short- and Long-Term Debt

When there is additional borrowing or principal repayments on long-term debt owed to financial institutions and investors, those amounts are financing cash flows. The appropriate amounts are determined by analyzing the long-term debt account. For 2019 the company repaid zero

EXHIBIT 12.6

National Beverage Corp.: Schedule for Net Cash Flow from Financing Activities (dollars in thousands)

Items	Cash Inflows (Outflows)	Explanation
Cash flows from financing activities:		
Repayment of principal on long-term debt	–	Cash payments of principal on long-term debt
Proceeds from issuance of long-term debt	$ 825	Cash proceeds from issuing long-term debt
Repurchase of stock	–	Cash payments to repurchase common stock
Proceeds from issuance of stock	1,576	Cash proceeds from issuing common stock
Payment of cash dividends	(141,391)	Cash payments of dividends to shareholders
Net cash used by financing activities	($138,990)	Subtotal on the statement of cash flows

in principal on long-term debt. This amount is listed in the schedule of financing activities in Exhibit 12.6. There were no additional borrowings on long-term debt.

Long-Term Debt (L)			
		Beginning	22,722
Retire (repay)	0	Issue (borrow)	825
		Ending	23,547

If the company had borrowed or repaid short-term debt to financial institutions, it would be treated in the same fashion.

Common Stock and Additional Paid-in Capital

National Beverage's change in common stock and additional paid-in capital resulted from two decisions. National Beverage decided not to repurchase any outstanding stock during the year. But the company did issue common stock for $1,576 in cash, which is a financing cash inflow.[9] This accounts for the $1,576 increase in common stock and additional paid-in capital. The amount is listed as an inflow in the schedule of financing activities in Exhibit 12.6.

Common Stock (SE)			
		Beginning	657
Repurchase		Issue	1
		Ending	658

Additional Paid-in Capital (SE)			
		Beginning	18,358
Repurchase		Issue	1,575
		Ending	19,933

Retained Earnings

Finally, retained earnings should be analyzed. Retained earnings rise when income is earned and fall when dividends are declared and paid. National Beverage earned $140,853 in income and paid $141,391 in dividends during 2019. National Beverage's dividend payment is listed on the schedule of financing activities in Exhibit 12.6.

Retained Earnings (SE)			
		Beginning	312,425
Dividends	141,391	Net Income	140,853
		Ending	311,887

Interpreting Cash Flows from Financing Activities

The long-term growth of a company is normally financed from three sources: internally generated funds (cash from operating activities), the issuance of stock, and money borrowed on a long-term

[9]This description was simplified to eliminate discussion of stock options and cash flow hedges.

basis. As we discussed in Chapter 10, companies can adopt a number of different capital structures (the balance of debt and equity). The financing sources that management uses to fund growth will have an important impact on the firm's risk and return characteristics. The statement of cash flows shows how management has elected to fund its growth. This information is used by analysts who wish to evaluate the capital structure and growth potential of a business.

PAUSE FOR FEEDBACK

As we discussed, the investing section of the statement of cash flows includes cash payments to acquire fixed assets and short- and long-term investments and cash proceeds from the sale of fixed assets and short- and long-term investments. Cash inflows from financing activities include cash proceeds from the issuance of short- and long-term debt and common stock. Cash outflows include cash principal payments on short- and long-term debt, cash paid for the repurchase of the company's stock, and cash dividend payments. Check your understanding of these concepts by answering the following questions before you move on.

SELF-STUDY QUIZ

Indicate which of the following items taken from the cash flow statement of **Coca-Cola Company** would be reported in the Investing section (I) or the Financing section (F) and whether the amount would be an inflow (+) or an outflow (−).

_____ 1. Purchases of investments.
_____ 2. Proceeds from issuance of debt (to bank).
_____ 3. Cash dividends paid.
_____ 4. Proceeds from issuance of common stock.
_____ 5. Proceeds from disposals of property, plant, and equipment.

After you have completed your answers, check them below.

GUIDED HELP 12-2

For additional step-by-step video instruction on preparing the investing and financing sections of the statement of cash flows, go to mhhe.com/libby_gh12-2.

Related Homework: M12-1, E12-1, E12-2

COMPLETING THE STATEMENT AND ADDITIONAL DISCLOSURES

LEARNING OBJECTIVE 12-7

Understand the format of the cash flow statement and additional cash flow disclosures.

Statement Structure

Refer to the formal statement of cash flows for **National Beverage Corp.** shown in Exhibit 12.1. As you can see, it is a simple matter to construct the statement after the detailed analysis of the accounts and transactions has been completed (shown in Exhibits 12.4, 12.5, and 12.6). Exhibit 12.7 summarizes the general structure of the statement for companies that use the indirect method for the operating section. When the **net increase or decrease in cash and cash equivalents** is added to the cash and cash equivalents taken from the beginning-of-period amount on the balance sheet, it equals the end-of-period cash and cash equivalents amount reported on the balance sheet. Companies also must provide two other disclosures related to the cash flow statement.

Solutions to SELF-STUDY QUIZ

1. I− 2. F+ 3. F− 4. F+ 5. I+

EXHIBIT 12.7

Structure of the Statement of Cash Flows (Indirect Method)

Statement of Cash Flows (Indirect Method)
Operating Activities:
Net Income
+ Depreciation and amortization expense
− Gain on sale of long-term assets
+ Loss on sale of long-term assets
+ Decreases in operating assets
+ Increases in operating liabilities
− Increases in operating assets
− Decreases in operating liabilities
Net Cash Flow from Operating Activities
Investing Activities:
− Purchase of property, plant, and equipment or intangible assets
+ Sale of property, plant, and equipment or intangible assets
− Purchase of investment securities
+ Sale (maturity) of investment securities
Net Cash Flow from Investing Activities
Financing Activities:
+ Borrowing from bank or other financial institution
− Repayment of loan principal
+ Issuance of bonds for cash
− Repayment of bond principal
+ Issuance of stock
− Repurchase (retirement) of stock
− Payment of (cash) dividends
Net Cash Flow from Financing Activities
Net increase or decrease in cash and cash equivalents
Cash and cash equivalents at beginning of period
Cash and cash equivalents at end of period

Supplemental Cash Flow Information

Two additional required cash flow disclosures are normally listed at the bottom of the statement or in the notes.

Noncash Investing and Financing Activities

Certain transactions are important investing and financing activities but have no cash flow effects. These are called **noncash investing and financing activities**. For example, the purchase of a $100,000 building with a $100,000 mortgage given by the former owner does not cause either an inflow or an outflow of cash. As a result, these noncash activities are not listed in the three main sections of the cash flow statement. However, supplemental disclosure of these transactions is required, in either narrative or schedule form. **National Beverage**'s statement of cash flows does not list any noncash investing and financing activities.

Cash Paid for Interest and Income taxes

Companies that use the indirect method of presenting cash flows from operations also must provide two other figures: **cash paid for interest** and **cash paid for income taxes.**

DEMONSTRATION CASE

During an earlier year (ended April 30), **National Beverage Corp.** reported net income of $24,742 (all numbers in thousands of dollars). The company also reported the following activities:

a. Purchased equipment for $6,658 in cash.

b. Disposed of equipment for $167 in cash, its net book value on the date of sale.

c. Purchased short-term investments for $109,450.

d. Sold short-term investments for $112,450, their net book value on the date of sale.

e. Issued stock for $950 in cash.

f. Repurchased treasury stock for $305 in cash.

g. Depreciation of equipment was $8,891 for the year.

Its comparative balance sheets are presented below.

NATIONAL BEVERAGE CORP.
Balance Sheets*
April 30

(dollars in thousands)	Current Year	Prior Year
Assets		
Current assets:		
Cash and cash equivalents	$ 84,140	$ 51,497
Short-term investments	–	3,000
Accounts receivable	53,735	49,186
Inventories	39,612	38,754
Prepaid expenses	5,552	12,009
Total current assets	183,039	154,446
Equipment, net	79,381	81,781
Total assets	$262,420	$236,227
Liabilities and Stockholders' Equity		
Current liabilities:		
Accounts payable	$ 48,005	$ 49,803
Accrued expenses	44,403	41,799
Total current liabilities	92,408	91,602
Stockholders' equity:		
Common stock and additional paid-in capital	9,803	9,158
Retained earnings	160,209	135,467
Total stockholders' equity	170,012	144,625
Total liabilities and stockholders' equity	$262,420	$236,227

*This statement has been modified for instructional purposes.

Source: National Beverage Corp.

Required:

Based on this information, prepare the cash flow statement using the indirect method. Evaluate cash flows reported in the statement.

SUGGESTED SOLUTION

NATIONAL BEVERAGE CORP.
Statement of Cash Flows*
Year ended April 30
(dollars in thousands)

Cash flows from operating activities:	
Net income	$ 24,742
Adjustments to reconcile net income to cash flow from operating activities:	
Depreciation and amortization	8,891
Changes in assets and liabilities:	
Accounts receivable	(4,549)
Inventory	(858)
Prepaid expenses	6,457
Accounts payable	(1,798)
Accrued expenses	2,604
Net cash provided by operating activities	35,489
Cash flows from investing activities:	
Purchases of property, plant, and equipment	(6,658)
Proceeds from disposal of property, plant, and equipment	167
Purchase of short-term investments	(109,450)
Proceeds from sale of short-term investments	112,450
Net cash used in investing activities	(3,491)
Cash flows from financing activities:	
Purchase of treasury stock	(305)
Proceeds from issuance of stock	950
Net cash provided by financing activities	645
Net increase in cash and cash equivalents	32,643
Cash and cash equivalents at beginning of period	51,497
Cash and cash equivalents at end of period	$ 84,140

*This statement has been modified for instructional purposes.

Source: National Beverage Corp.

National Beverage reported positive profits and even higher cash flows from operations for the year. This difference between the two is caused primarily by decreases in prepaid expenses and depreciation. This also suggests that National Beverage is carefully managing its current assets and current liabilities so that it has more than sufficient cash on hand to cover the costs of purchases of additional equipment without the need to borrow additional funds. This cash can be used for future expansion or to pay future dividends to stockholders.

Chapter Supplement A

Reporting Cash Flows from Operating Activities—Direct Method

The **direct method** presents a summary of all operating transactions that result in either a debit or a credit to cash. It is prepared by adjusting each item on the income statement from an accrual basis to a cash basis. We will complete this process for all of the revenues and expenses reported in **National Beverage**'s income statement in Exhibit 12.3 and accumulate them in a new schedule in Exhibit 12.8.

Cash flows from operating activities (Direct method)	
Cash collected from customers	$1,013,624
Cash payments to suppliers	(648,188)
Cash payments for other expenses	(180,133)
Cash payments for interest	(202)
Cash payments for income taxes	(43,024)
Net cash provided by operating activities	$ 142,077

EXHIBIT 12.8

National Beverage Corp.: Schedule for Net Cash Flow from Operating Activities, Direct Method (dollars in thousands)

Converting Revenues to Cash Inflows

When sales are recorded, accounts receivable increases, and when cash is collected, accounts receivable decreases. Thus, the following formula will convert sales revenue amounts from the accrual basis to the cash basis:

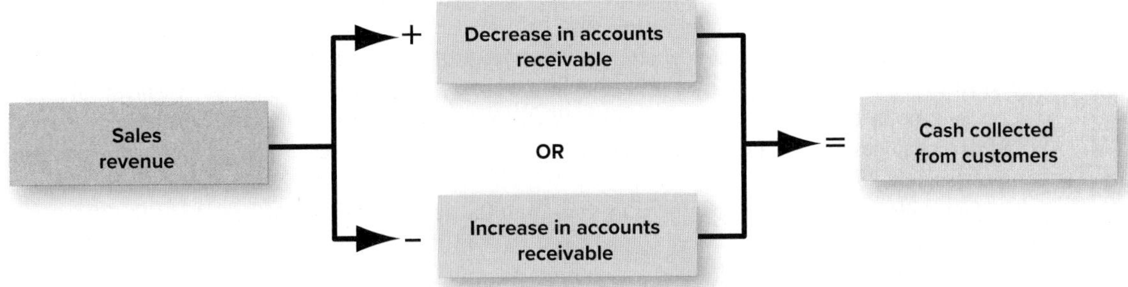

Using information from **National Beverage**'s income statement and balance sheet presented in Exhibit 12.3, we can compute cash collected from customers as follows:

Net sales	$1,014,105
−Increase in accounts receivable	481
Cash collected from customers	$1,013,624

Accounts Receivable (A)		
Beg. bal.	84,360	
Increase	481	
End. bal.	84,841	

Converting Cost of Goods Sold to Cash Paid to Suppliers

Cost of goods sold represents the cost of merchandise sold during the accounting period. It may be more or less than the amount of cash paid to suppliers during the period. In **National Beverage**'s case, inventory increased during the year because the company bought more merchandise from suppliers than it sold to customers. If the company paid cash to suppliers of inventory, it must have paid more cash to suppliers than the amount of cost of goods sold, so the increase in inventory must be added to compute cash paid to suppliers.

Typically, companies owe their suppliers money (an accounts payable balance will appear on the balance sheet). To convert cost of goods sold to cash paid to suppliers, the borrowing and repayments represented by the accounts payable also must be considered. Borrowing increases cash and accounts payable and repayment decreases cash and accounts payable, so National Beverage's increase in accounts payable also must be subtracted in the computation. Cost of goods sold can therefore be converted to a cash basis in the following manner:

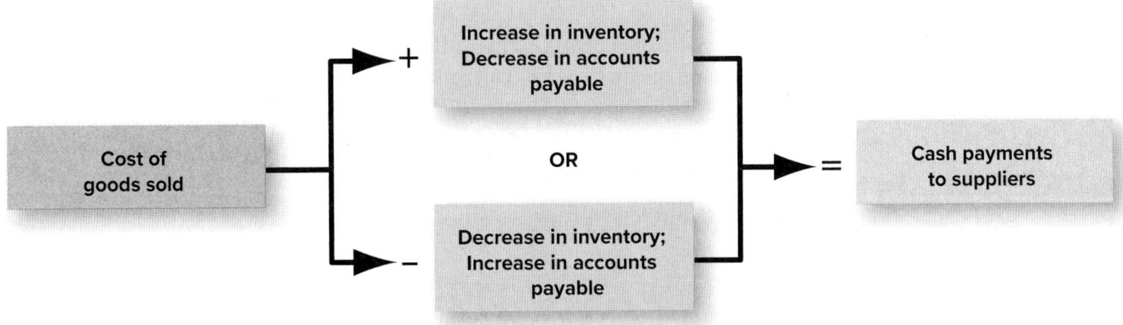

Using information from Exhibit 12.3, we can compute cash paid to suppliers as follows:

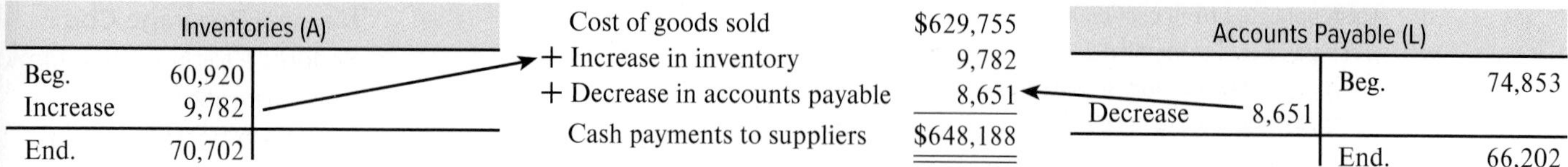

Converting Operating Expenses to a Cash Outflow

The total amount of an expense on the income statement may differ from the cash outflow associated with that activity. Some expenses are paid before they are recognized as expenses (e.g., prepaid rent). When prepayments are made, the balance in the asset prepaid expenses increases; when expenses are recorded, the balance in prepaid expenses decreases. When **National Beverage**'s prepaid expenses decreased by $5,676 during the period, it paid less cash than it recorded as operating expenses. The decrease must be subtracted in computing cash paid for expenses.

Some other expenses are paid for after they are recognized (e.g., accrued expenses). In this case, when expenses are recorded, the balance in the liability accrued expenses increases; when payments are made, the balance in accrued expenses decreases. When National Beverage's accrued expenses increased by $1,018 it paid less cash than it recorded as operating expenses. The increase must be subtracted in computing cash paid for expenses.

Generally, other expenses can be converted from the accrual basis to the cash basis in the following manner:

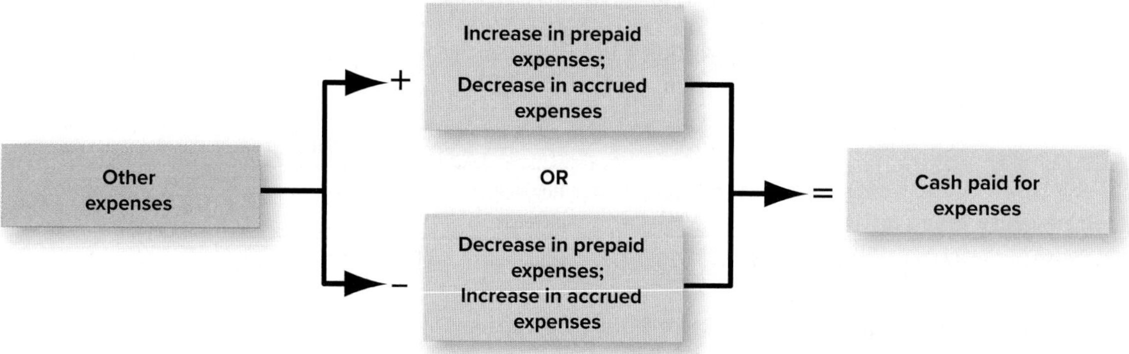

Using information from Exhibit 12.3, we can compute cash paid for expenses for National Beverage as follows:

Prepaid Expenses (A)			
Beg.	12,476		
		Decrease	5,676
End.	6,800		

SG&A Expense	$186,827
− Decrease in prepaid expenses	(5,676)
− Increase in accrued expenses	(1,018)
Cash payments for other expenses	$180,133

Accrued Expenses (L)			
		Beg.	29,817
		Increase	1,018
		End.	30,835

National Beverage also reports $202 of interest expense.[10] Because there is no interest payable balance, we can see that interest expense must be equal to cash payments for interest expense.

Interest expense	$202
No changes in interest payable	0
Cash payments for interest	$202

[10]Certain amounts have been adjusted to simplify the presentation.

The same logic can be applied to income taxes. National Beverage presents income tax expense of $43,024. Because there is no balance in Income Taxes Payable (or change in Deferred Taxes), income taxes paid must be the same as income tax expense.

Income tax expense	$43,024
No change in taxes payable	0
Cash payments for income taxes	$43,024

The amounts from all the operating cash inflows and outflows computed above are accumulated in Exhibit 12.8.

To summarize, the following adjustments must commonly be made to convert income statement items to the related operating cash flow amounts:

Income Statement Account	+/− Change in Balance Sheet Account(s)	= Operating Cash Flow
Sales revenue	+Decrease in Accounts Receivable (A) −Increase in Accounts Receivable (A)	= Collections from customers
Interest/Dividend revenue	+Decrease in Interest/Dividends Receivable (A) −Increase in Interest/Dividends Receivable (A)	= Collections of interest/dividends on investments
Cost of goods sold	+Increase in Inventory (A) −Decrease in Inventory (A) −Increase in Accounts Payable (L) +Decrease in Accounts Payable (L)	= Payments to suppliers of inventory
Other expenses	+Increase in Prepaid Expenses (A) −Decrease in Prepaid Expenses (A) −Increase in Accrued Expenses (L) +Decrease in Accrued Expenses (L)	= Payments to suppliers of services (e.g., rent, utilities, wages, interest)
Income tax expense	+Increase in Prepaid Income Taxes (Deferred Taxes) (A) −Decrease in Prepaid Income Taxes (Deferred Taxes) (A) −Increase in Income Taxes Payable (Deferred Taxes) (L) +Decrease in Income Taxes Payable (Deferred Taxes) (L)	= Payments of income taxes

It is important to note again that the net cash inflow or outflow is the same regardless of whether the direct or indirect method of presentation is used (in National Beverage's case, an inflow of $142,077). The two methods differ only in terms of the details reported on the statement.

PAUSE FOR FEEDBACK

SELF-STUDY QUIZ

Indicate which of the following line items taken from the cash flow statement would be added (+), subtracted (−), or not included (NA) in the cash flow from operations section when the **direct method** is used.

_____ 1. Increase in inventories.

_____ 2. Payment of dividends to stockholders.

_____ 3. Cash collections from customers.

_____ 4. Purchase of plant and equipment for cash.

_____ 5. Payments of interest to debtholders.

_____ 6. Payment of taxes to the government.

After you have completed your answers, check them below.

Related Homework: M12-3, E12-3

Solutions to SELF-STUDY QUIZ

1. NA 2. NA 3. + 4. NA 5. − 6. −

Chapter Supplement B

Adjustment for Gains and Losses on Sale of Long-Term Assets—Indirect Method

As noted earlier, the Operating Activities section of the cash flow statement prepared using the indirect method may include an adjustment for gains and losses on the sale of long-term assets reported on the income statement. As discussed in Chapter 8, when property, plant, and equipment is sold for more (less) than its net book value, a gain (loss) on disposal results. If property, plant, and equipment with an original cost of $10,000 and accumulated depreciation of $4,000 is sold for $8,000 cash, the following entry is made.

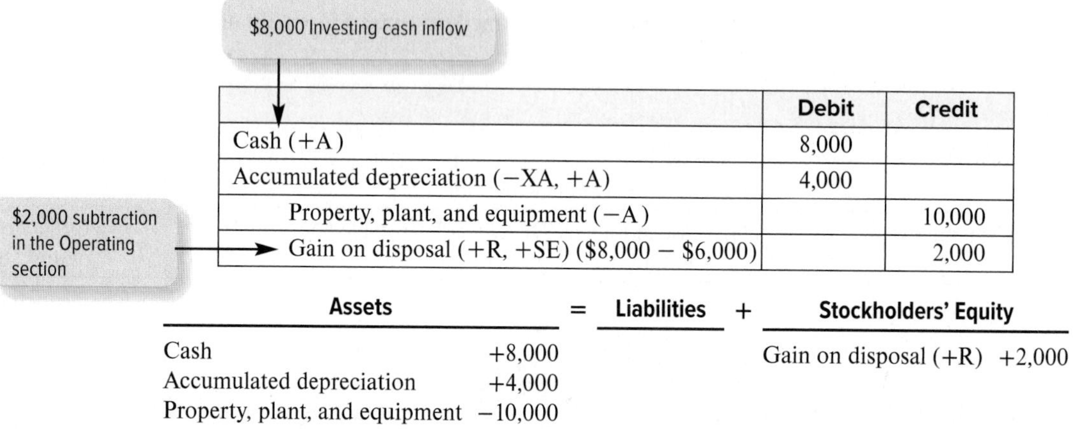

	Debit	Credit
Cash (+A)	8,000	
Accumulated depreciation (−XA, +A)	4,000	
Property, plant, and equipment (−A)		10,000
Gain on disposal (+R, +SE) ($8,000 − $6,000)		2,000

Assets		=	Liabilities	+	Stockholders' Equity	
Cash	+8,000				Gain on disposal (+R)	+2,000
Accumulated depreciation	+4,000					
Property, plant, and equipment	−10,000					

The whole $8,000 inflow of cash is an investing cash inflow, but the reported gain of $2,000 also is shown on the income statement. Because the gain is included in the computation of income, it is necessary to remove (subtract) the $2,000 gain from the Operating Activities section of the statement to avoid double counting.

Cash flows from operating activities	
Net income	$140,853
Adjustments to reconcile net income to cash flow from operating activities:	
Gain on disposal of property, plant, and equipment	(2,000)
. . .	. . .
Net cash provided by operating activities	. . .
Cash flows from investing activities	
Purchases of property, plant, and equipment	. . .
Proceeds from disposal of property, plant, and equipment	8,000
. . .	. . .
Net cash used in investing activities	. . .

If the company had sold the same asset for $5,000 cash, the following entry would be made:

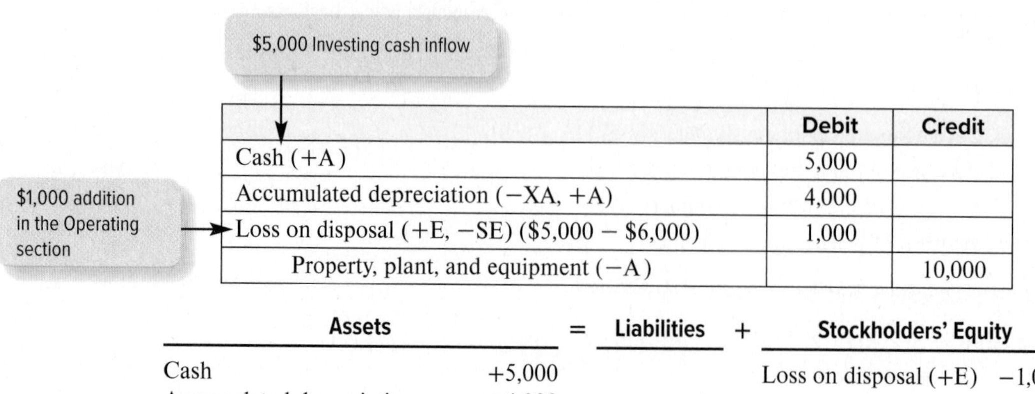

	Debit	Credit
Cash (+A)	5,000	
Accumulated depreciation (−XA, +A)	4,000	
Loss on disposal (+E, −SE) ($5,000 − $6,000)	1,000	
Property, plant, and equipment (−A)		10,000

Assets		=	Liabilities	+	Stockholders' Equity	
Cash	+5,000				Loss on disposal (+E)	−1,000
Accumulated depreciation	+4,000					
Property, plant, and equipment	−10,000					

On the cash flow statement, the loss of $1,000 must be removed (added back) in the computation of cash from operating activities, and the total cash collected of $5,000 must be shown in the investing activities section of the statement.

Cash flows from operating activities	
Net income	$ 140,853
Adjustments to reconcile net income to cash flow from operating activities:	
Loss on disposal of property, plant, and equipment	1,000
...	...
Net cash provided by operating activities	...
Cash flows from investing activities	
Purchases of property, plant, and equipment	...
Proceeds from disposal of property, plant, and equipment	5,000
...	...
Net cash used in investing activities	...

Chapter Supplement C

T-Account Approach (Indirect Method)

When we began our discussion of preparing the statement of cash flows, we noted that changes in cash must equal the sum of the changes in all other balance sheet accounts. Based on this idea, we used the following three steps to prepare the statement of cash flows:

1. Determine the change in each balance sheet account. From this year's ending balance, subtract this year's beginning balance (i.e., last year's ending balance).
2. Identify the cash flow category or categories to which each account relates.
3. Create schedules that summarize operating, investing, and financing cash flows.

Instead of creating separate schedules for each section of the statement, many accountants prefer to prepare a single large T-account to represent the changes that have taken place in cash subdivided into the three sections of the cash flow statement. Such an account is presented in Panel A of Exhibit 12.9. The

EXHIBIT 12.9 T-Approach to Preparing the Statement of Cash Flows (Indirect Method)

Panel A: Changes in Cash Account

Cash (A)			
Operating			
(1) Net Income	140,853	481	(3) Accounts Receivable
(2) Depreciation and Amortization	13,444	9,782	(4) Inventory
(5) Prepaid Expenses	5,676	8,651	(6) Accounts Payable
(7) Accrued Expenses	1,018		
Net cash provided by operating activities	142,077		
Investing			
(9) Disposals of Property, Plant, and Equipment	18	38,333	(8) Purchases of Property, Plant, and Equipment
(11) Sales of Short-Term Investments	3,685	1,252	(10) Purchases of Short-Term Investments
		35,882	Net cash used in investing activities
Financing			
(12) Issuance of Long-Term Debt	825	141,391	(14) Payment of Dividends
(13) Issuance of Stock	1,576		
		138,990	Net cash used in financing activities
Net decrease in cash and cash equivalents		32,795	

(Continued)

EXHIBIT 12.9 *(Concluded)*

Panel B: Changes in Noncash Accounts

Accounts Receivable (A)			
Beg. bal.	84,360		
(3) Increase	481		
End. bal.	84,841		

Inventory (A)			
Beg. bal.	60,920		
(4) Increase	9,782		
End. bal.	70,702		

Prepaid Expenses (A)			
Beg. bal.	12,476		
		(5) Decrease	5,676
End. bal.	6,800		

Accounts Payable (L)			
		Beg. bal.	74,853
(6) Decrease	8,651		
		End. bal.	66,202

Accrued Expenses (L)			
		Beg. bal.	29,817
		(7) Increase	1,018
		End. bal.	30,835

Property, Plant & Equipment, Net (A)			
Beg. bal.	105,865	(2) Depreciation	13,444
(8) Purchases	38,333	(9) Disposals	18
End. bal.	130,736		

Short-Term Investments (A)			
Beg. bal.	5,347		
(10) Purchases	1,252	(11) Disposals	3,685
End. bal.	2,914		

Long-Term Debt (L)			
		Beg. bal.	22,722
		(12) Borrowings	825
		End. bal.	23,547

Common Stock (SE)			
		Beg. bal.	657
		(13) Stock issued	1
		End. bal.	658

Additional Paid-In Capital (SE)			
		Beg. bal.	18,358
		(13) Stock issued	1,575
		End. bal.	19,933

Retained Earnings (SE)			
		Beg. bal.	312,425
(14) Dividends	141,391	(1) Net income	140,853
		End. bal.	311,887

cash account in Panel A shows increases in cash as debits and decreases in cash as credits. Note how each section matches the three schedules that we prepared for **National Beverage**'s cash flows presented in Exhibits 12.4, 12.5, and 12.6. Panel B includes the same T-accounts for the noncash balance sheet accounts we used in our discussion of each cash flow statement section in the body of the chapter. Note how each change in the noncash balance sheet accounts has a number referencing the change in the cash account that it accompanies. The statement of cash flows presented in Exhibit 12.1 can be prepared in proper format based on the information in the cash flow T-account.

CHAPTER TAKE-AWAYS

12-1. Classify cash flow statement items as part of net cash flows from operating, investing, and financing activities. p. 628

The cash flow statement has three main sections: Cash Flows from Operating Activities, which are related to earning income from normal operations; Cash Flows from Investing Activities, which are related to the acquisition and sale of productive assets; and Cash Flows from Financing Activities, which are related to external financing of the enterprise. The net cash inflow or outflow for the year is the same amount as the increase or decrease in cash and cash equivalents for the year on the balance sheet. Cash equivalents are highly liquid investments with original maturities of three months or less.

12-2. Report and interpret cash flows from operating activities using the indirect method. p. 635

The indirect method for reporting cash flows from operating activities reports a conversion of net income to net cash flow from operating activities. The conversion involves additions and subtractions for (1) noncurrent accruals, including expenses (such as depreciation expense) and revenues that do not affect operating assets or operating liabilities, and (2) changes in each of the individual operating assets (other than cash) and operating liabilities, which reflect differences in the timing of accrual basis net income and cash flows.

12-3. Analyze and interpret the quality of income ratio. **p. 641**

The quality of income ratio (Cash Flow from Operating Activities ÷ Net Income) measures the portion of income that was generated in cash. A higher quality of income ratio indicates greater ability to finance operating and other cash needs from operating cash inflows. A higher ratio also indicates that it is less likely that the company is using aggressive revenue recognition policies to increase net income.

12-4. Report and interpret cash flows from investing activities. **p. 642**

Investing activities reported on the cash flow statement include cash payments to acquire fixed assets, intangibles, and short- and long-term investments and cash proceeds from the sale of fixed assets, intangibles, and short- and long-term investments.

12-5. Analyze and interpret the capital acquisitions ratio. **p. 644**

The capital acquisitions ratio (Cash Flow from Operating Activities ÷ Cash Paid for Property, Plant, and Equipment) reflects the portion of purchases of property, plant, and equipment financed from operating activities without the need for outside debt or equity financing or the sale of other investments or fixed assets. A high ratio benefits the company because it provides the company with opportunities for strategic acquisitions.

12-6. Report and interpret cash flows from financing activities. **p. 645**

Cash inflows from financing activities include cash proceeds from the issuance of short- and long-term debt and common stock. Cash outflows include cash principal payments on short- and long-term debt, cash paid for the repurchase of the company's stock, and cash dividend payments. Cash payments associated with interest are a cash flow from operating activities.

12-7. Understand the format of the cash flow statement and additional cash flow disclosures. **p. 647**

The statement of cash flows splits transactions that affect cash into three categories: Operating, Investing, and Financing Activities. The operating section is most often prepared using the indirect method that begins with Net Income and adjusts the amount to eliminate noncash transactions. Noncash investing and financing activities are investing and financing activities that do not involve cash. They include, for example, purchases of fixed assets with long-term debt or stock, exchanges of fixed assets, and exchanges of debt for stock. These transactions are disclosed only as supplemental disclosures to the cash flow statement, along with cash paid for taxes and interest when using the indirect method.

Throughout the preceding chapters, we emphasized the conceptual basis of accounting. An understanding of the rationale underlying accounting is important for both preparers and users of financial statements. In Chapter 13, we bring together our discussion of the major users of financial statements and how they analyze and use these statements. We discuss and illustrate many widely used analytical techniques discussed in earlier chapters, as well as additional techniques. As you study Chapter 13, you will see that an understanding of accounting rules and concepts is essential for effective analysis of financial statements.

KEY RATIOS

The **quality of income ratio** indicates what portion of income was generated in cash. It is computed as follows (see the "Key Ratio Analysis" box in the Reporting and Interpreting Cash Flows from Operating Activities section):

$$\text{Quality of Income Ratio} = \frac{\text{Cash Flow from Operating Activities}}{\text{Net Income}}$$

The **capital acquisitions ratio** measures the ability to finance purchases of plant and equipment from operations. It is computed as follows (see the "Key Ratio Analysis" box in the Reporting and Interpreting Cash Flows from Investing Activities section):

$$\text{Capital Acquisitions Ratio} = \frac{\text{Cash Flow from Operating Activities}}{\text{Cash Paid for Property, Plant, and Equipment}}$$

FINDING FINANCIAL INFORMATION

Balance Sheet

Changes in Assets, Liabilities, and Stockholders' Equity

Income Statement

Net Income and Noncurrent Accruals

Statement of Cash Flows

Cash Flows from Operating Activities

Cash Flows from Investing Activities

Cash Flows from Financing Activities

Separate Schedule (or note):
Noncash investing and financing activities
Interest and taxes paid

Notes

Under Summary of Significant Accounting Policies
Definition of cash equivalents

Under Separate Note (if not listed on cash flow statement)
Noncash investing and financing activities
Interest and taxes paid

KEY TERMS

Cash Equivalents Short-term investments with original maturities of three months or less that are readily convertible to cash and whose value is unlikely to change. **p. 628**

Cash Flows from Financing Activities Cash inflows and outflows related to external sources of financing (owners and creditors) for the enterprise. **p. 631**

Cash Flows from Investing Activities Cash inflows and outflows related to the acquisition or sale of productive facilities and investments in the securities of other companies. **p. 630**

Cash Flows from Operating Activities (Cash Flows from Operations) Cash inflows and outflows directly related to earnings from normal operations. **p. 629**

Direct Method A method of presenting the operating activities section of the statement of cash flows that reports components of cash flows from operating activities as gross receipts and gross payments. **p. 629**

Free Cash Flow Cash Flows from Operating Activities less Dividends less Capital Expenditures. **p. 644**

Indirect Method A method of presenting the operating activities section of the statement of cash flows that adjusts net income to compute cash flows from operating activities. **p. 630**

Noncash Investing and Financing Activities Transactions that do not have direct cash flow effects; reported as a supplement to the statement of cash flows in narrative or schedule form. **p. 648**

QUESTIONS

1. Compare the purposes of the income statement, the balance sheet, and the statement of cash flows.
2. What information does the statement of cash flows report that is not reported on the other required financial statements?
3. What are cash equivalents? How are purchases and sales of cash equivalents reported on the statement of cash flows?
4. What are the major categories of business activities reported on the statement of cash flows? Define each of these activities.
5. What are the typical cash inflows from operating activities? What are the typical cash outflows from operating activities?
6. Under the indirect method, depreciation expense is added to net income to report cash flows from operating activities. Does depreciation cause an inflow of cash?
7. Explain why cash payments during the period for purchases and for salaries are not specifically reported as cash outflows on the statement of cash flows, under the indirect method.
8. Explain why a $50,000 increase in inventory during the year must be included in developing cash flows from operating activities under both the direct and indirect methods.
9. Compare the two methods of reporting cash flows from operating activities in the statement of cash flows.

10. What are the typical cash inflows from investing activities? What are the typical cash outflows from investing activities?
11. What are the typical cash inflows from financing activities? What are the typical cash outflows from financing activities?
12. What are noncash investing and financing activities? Give two examples. How are they reported on the statement of cash flows?
13. How is the sale of equipment reported on the statement of cash flows under the indirect method?

MULTIPLE-CHOICE QUESTIONS

1. In what order do the three sections of the statement of cash flows usually appear when reading from top to bottom?
   a. Financing, Investing, Operating
   b. Investing, Operating, Financing
   c. Operating, Financing, Investing
   d. Operating, Investing, Financing
2. Total cash inflow in the operating section of the statement of cash flows should include which of the following?
   a. Cash received from customers at the point of sale.
   b. Cash collections from customer accounts receivable.
   c. Cash received in advance of revenue recognition (unearned revenue).
   d. All of the above.
3. If the balance in prepaid expenses has increased during the year, what action should be taken on the statement of cash flows when following the indirect method, and why?
   a. The change in the account balance should be subtracted from net income because the net increase in prepaid expenses did not impact net income but did reduce the cash balance.
   b. The change in the account balance should be added to net income because the net increase in prepaid expenses did not impact net income but did increase the cash balance.
   c. The net change in prepaid expenses should be subtracted from net income to reverse the income statement effect that had no impact on cash.
   d. The net change in prepaid expenses should be added to net income to reverse the income statement effect that had no impact on cash.
4. Consider the following: Net income = $10,000, depreciation expense = $2,000, accounts receivable increased by $800, inventory decreased by $100, and accounts payable increased by $500. Based on this information alone, what is cash flow from operating activities?
   a. $12,000
   b. $11,600
   c. $11,800
   d. $13,400
5. Which of the following would **not** appear in the investing section of the statement of cash flows?
   a. Purchase of inventory.
   b. Sale of obsolete equipment used in the factory.
   c. Purchase of land for a new office building.
   d. All of the above would appear in the investing section.
6. Which of the following items would **not** appear in the financing section of the statement of cash flows?
   a. The repurchase of the company's own stock.
   b. The receipt of dividends.
   c. The repayment of debt.
   d. The payment of dividends.
7. Which of the following is **not** added to net income when computing cash flows from operations under the indirect method?
   a. The net increase in accounts payable.
   b. The net decrease in accounts receivable.
   c. Depreciation expense reported on the income statement.
   d. All of the above are added to net income.

8. Consider the following: Issued common stock for $18,000, sold office equipment for $1,200, paid cash dividends of $4,000, purchased investments for $2,000, and paid accounts payable of $4,000. What was the net cash inflow (outflow) from financing activities?
   a. $20,000
   b. $14,000
   c. ($20,000)
   d. ($14,000)
9. Consider the following: Issued common stock for $18,000, sold office equipment for $1,200, paid cash dividends of $4,000, purchased investments for $2,000, and purchased new equipment for $4,000. What was the net cash inflow (outflow) from investing activities?
   a. $20,200
   b. ($2,800)
   c. ($10,800)
   d. ($4,800)
10. The **total** change in cash as shown near the bottom of the statement of cash flows for the year should agree with which of the following?
   a. The difference in retained earnings when reviewing the comparative balance sheet.
   b. Net income or net loss as found on the income statement.
   c. The difference in cash when reviewing the comparative balance sheet.
   d. None of the above.

MINI-EXERCISES

connect

M12-1 LO12-1 Matching Items Reported to Cash Flow Statement Categories (Indirect Method)

MolsonCoors Beverage Company

MolsonCoors Beverage Company is the world's fifth largest brewer. In the United States, its tie to the magical appeal of the Rocky Mountains is one of its most powerful trademarks. Some of the items included in its recent annual consolidated statement of cash flows presented using the **indirect method** are listed here. Indicate whether each item is disclosed in the Operating Activities (O), Investing Activities (I), or Financing Activities (F) section of the statement or use (NA) if the item does not appear on the statement. (**Note:** This is the exact wording used on the actual statement.)

_____ 1. Purchase of stock. [This involves repurchase of the company's own stock.]
_____ 2. Principal payment on long-term debt.
_____ 3. Proceeds from sale of properties.
_____ 4. Inventories (decrease).
_____ 5. Accounts payable (decrease).
_____ 6. Depreciation and amortization.

M12-1 LO12-2 Determining the Effects of Account Changes on Cash Flow from Operating Activities (Indirect Method)

Indicate whether each item would be added (+) or subtracted (−) in the computation of cash flow from operating activities using the indirect method.

_____ 1. Accrued expenses (increase).
_____ 2. Inventories (increase).
_____ 3. Accounts receivable (decrease).
_____ 4. Accounts payable (decrease).
_____ 5. Depreciation, depletion, and amortization.

M12-3 LO12-1 Matching Items Reported to Cash Flow Statement Categories (Direct Method)

Telstra

Telstra, Australia's largest telecommunications and media company, has net revenue of more than $26 billion (Australian). Some of the items included in its recent annual consolidated statement of cash flows presented using the **direct method** are listed here. Indicate whether each item is disclosed in the Operating Activities (O), Investing Activities (I), or Financing Activities (F) section of the statement or use (NA) if the item does not appear on the statement. (**Note:** This is the exact wording used on the actual statement.)

_____ 1. Receipts from customers.
_____ 2. Dividends paid.
_____ 3. Payment for share buy-back (repurchase of company stock).

_____ 4. Proceeds from sale of property, plant, and equipment.
_____ 5. Repayments of borrowings (bank debt).
_____ 6. Income taxes paid.

Analyzing the Quality of Income Ratio

M12-4
LO12-3

Casey Corporation reported net income of $102,000, depreciation expense of $2,000, and cash flow from operations of $86,500. Compute the quality of income ratio. What does the ratio tell you about the company's ability to finance operating and other cash needs from operating cash inflows?

Computing Cash Flows from Investing Activities

M12-5
LO12-4

Based on the following information, compute cash flows from investing activities.

Cash collections from customers	$550
Sale of used equipment	400
Depreciation expense	200
Purchase of short-term investments	635

Computing Cash Flows from Financing Activities

M12-6
LO12-6

Based on the following information, compute cash flows from financing activities.

Purchase of short-term investments	$ 500
Dividends paid	700
Interest paid	300
Additional short-term borrowing from bank	1,200

Reporting Noncash Investing and Financing Activities

M12-7
LO12-7

Which of the following transactions qualify as noncash investing and financing activities (select all that apply)?
_____ Purchase of building with mortgage payable.
_____ Additional short-term borrowing from bank.
_____ Dividends paid in cash.
_____ Purchase of equipment with short-term investments.

connect

EXERCISES

Matching Items Reported to Cash Flow Statement Categories (Indirect Method)

E12-1
LO12-1
Adidas AG

Adidas AG is a global company that designs and markets sports and fitness products, including footwear, apparel, and accessories. Some of the items included in its recent annual consolidated statement of cash flows presented using the **indirect method** are listed here.

Indicate whether each item is disclosed in the Operating Activities (O), Investing Activities (I), or Financing Activities (F) section of the statement or use (NA) if the item does not appear on the statement. (**Note:** This is the exact wording used on the actual statement.)

_____ 1. Dividends paid.
_____ 2. Repayments of short-term borrowings.
_____ 3. Depreciation and amortization.
_____ 4. Proceeds from reissuance of treasury shares to employees.
_____ 5. [Change in] Accounts payable and other liabilities.
_____ 6. Cash collections from customers.
_____ 7. Purchase of investments.
_____ 8. Net income.
_____ 9. Purchase of property, plant, and equipment.
_____ 10. Increase in receivables and other assets.

E12-2 Matching Items Reported to Cash Flow Statement Categories (Indirect Method)

LO12-1

Dell Technologies Inc.

Dell Technologies Inc. is a global technology provider that brings together hardware, software, and services. Some of the items included in its recent annual consolidated statement of cash flows presented using the **indirect method** are listed here.

Indicate whether each item is disclosed in the Operating Activities (O), Investing Activities (I), or Financing Activities (F) section of the statement or use (NA) if the item does not appear on the statement. (**Note:** This is the exact wording used on the actual statement.)

_____ 1. [Change in] Accounts payable.
_____ 2. Depreciation and amortization.
_____ 3. [Change in] Inventories.
_____ 4. Maturities and sales of investments.
_____ 5. Proceeds from debt.
_____ 6. Payments to suppliers and employees.
_____ 7. Proceeds from sale of facilities, land, and other assets.
_____ 8. [Change in] Deferred revenue.
_____ 9. Repurchases of Dell Common Stock.
_____ 10. Net income.

E12-3 Matching Items Reported to Cash Flow Statement Categories (Direct Method)

LO12-1

Woolworths Group

Woolworths Group is one of the largest retailers in Australia and New Zealand. Some of the items included in its recent annual consolidated statement of cash flows presented using the **direct method** are listed here.

Indicate whether each item is disclosed in the Operating Activities (O), Investing Activities (I), or Financing Activities (F) section of the statement or use (NA) if the item does not appear on the statement. (**Note:** This is the exact wording used on the actual statement.)

_____ 1. Proceeds from the sale of property, plant, and equipment.
_____ 2. Net interest paid.
_____ 3. Payments for intangible assets.
_____ 4. Payments to suppliers and employees.
_____ 5. Proceeds from borrowings.
_____ 6. Dividends paid.
_____ 7. Income tax paid.
_____ 8. Receipts from customers.
_____ 9. Payments for the purchase of investments.
_____ 10. Proceeds from the issue of equity securities.

E12-4 Determining Cash Flow Statement Effects of Transactions

LO12-1

Caterpillar

Caterpillar is the world's leading manufacturer of construction and mining equipment. For each of the following transactions, indicate whether **net cash inflows (outflows)** from operating activities (NCFO), investing activities (NCFI), or financing activities (NCFF) are affected and whether the effect is an inflow (+) or outflow (−), or use (NE) if the transaction has no effect on cash. (**Hint:** Determine the journal entry recorded for the transaction. The transaction affects net cash flows *if and only if* the account Cash is affected.)

_____ 1. Recorded an adjusting entry to record accrued salaries expense.
_____ 2. Paid cash to purchase new equipment.
_____ 3. Collected payments on account from customers.

_____ 4. Recorded and paid interest on debt to creditors.
_____ 5. Declared and paid cash dividends to shareholders.
_____ 6. Sold used equipment for cash at book value.
_____ 7. Prepaid rent for the following period.
_____ 8. Repaid principal on revolving credit loan from bank.
_____ 9. Purchased raw materials inventory on account.
_____ 10. Made payment to suppliers on account.

Determining Cash Flow Statement Effects of Transactions

E12-5
LO12-1
Harley-Davidson

Harley-Davidson is a leading manufacturer of heavy-weight motorcycles. For each of the following recent transactions, indicate whether **net cash inflows (outflows)** from operating activities (NCFO), investing activities (NCFI), or financing activities (NCFF) are affected and whether the effect is an inflow (+) or outflow (−), or use (NE) if the transaction has no effect on cash. (**Hint:** Determine the journal entry recorded for the transaction. The transaction affects net cash flows *if and only if* the account Cash is affected.)

_____ 1. Purchased raw materials inventory on account.
_____ 2. Prepaid rent for the following period.
_____ 3. Purchased new equipment by signing a three-year note.
_____ 4. Recorded an adjusting entry for expiration of a prepaid expense.
_____ 5. Recorded and paid income taxes to the federal government.
_____ 6. Purchased investment securities for cash.
_____ 7. Issued common stock for cash.
_____ 8. Collected payments on account from customers.
_____ 9. Sold equipment for cash equal to its net book value.
_____ 10. Issued long-term debt for cash.

Comparing the Direct and Indirect Methods

E12-6
LO12-1

To compare statement of cash flows reporting under the direct and indirect methods, enter check marks to indicate which items are used with each method.

	STATEMENT OF CASH FLOWS METHOD	
Cash Flows (and Related Changes)	Direct	Indirect
1. Accounts payable, increase or decrease		
2. Payments to employees		
3. Cash collections from customers		
4. Accounts receivable, increase or decrease		
5. Payments to suppliers		
6. Inventory, increase or decrease		
7. Wages payable, increase or decrease		
8. Depreciation expense		
9. Net income		
10. Cash flows from operating activities		
11. Cash flows from investing activities		
12. Cash flows from financing activities		
13. Net increase or decrease in cash during the period		

E12-7 Reporting Cash Flows from Operating Activities (Indirect Method)
LO12-2

The following information pertains to Peak Heights Company:

Income Statement for Current Year		
Sales		$93,000
Expenses		
Cost of goods sold	$51,875	
Depreciation expense	6,000	
Salaries expense	12,000	69,875
Net income		$23,125
Partial Balance Sheet	**Current Year**	**Prior Year**
Accounts receivable	$10,500	$12,000
Inventory	13,000	8,000
Salaries payable	2,250	800

Required:
Present the operating activities section of the statement of cash flows for Peak Heights Company using the indirect method.

E12-8 Reporting and Interpreting Cash Flows from Operating Activities from an Analyst's Perspective (Indirect Method)
LO12-2

Rodriguez Company completed its income statement and comparative balance sheet for the current year and provided the following information:

Income Statement for Current Year		
Service revenue		$54,000
Expenses		
Salaries	$46,000	
Depreciation	4,500	
Amortization of copyrights	200	
Other expenses	9,700	60,400
Net loss		$ (6,400)
Partial Balance Sheet	**Current Year**	**Prior Year**
Accounts receivable	$ 8,000	$13,000
Salaries payable	12,000	1,000
Other accrued liabilities	1,000	2,800

In addition, Rodriguez bought a small service machine for $5,000.

Required:
1. Present the operating activities section of the statement of cash flows for Rodriguez Company using the indirect method.
2. What were the major reasons that Rodriguez was able to report a net loss but positive cash flow from operations? Explain why the reasons for the difference between cash flow from operations and net income are important to financial analysts.

E12-9 Reporting and Interpreting Cash Flows from Operating Activities from an Analyst's Perspective (Indirect Method)
LO12-2

A number of years ago, a leading media company's annual report contained the following information (dollars in millions):

Net loss	$(13,402)
Depreciation, amortization, and impairments	34,790
Decrease in receivables	1,245
Increase in inventories	5,766
Decrease in accounts payable	445
Additions to equipment	4,377

Required:

1. Based on this information, compute cash flow from operating activities using the indirect method.
2. What were the major reasons that the media company was able to report a net loss but positive cash flow from operations? Explain why the reasons for the difference between cash flow from operations and net income are important to financial analysts.

Reporting and Interpreting Cash Flows from Operating Activities with Loss on Sale of Equipment (Indirect Method)

E12-10
LO12-2

Parra Company completed its income statement and comparative balance sheet for the current year and provided the following information:

Service revenue		$125,000
Expenses:		
Salaries	$92,000	
Depreciation	8,500	
Utilities	8,000	
Loss on sale of equipment	2,500	111,000
Net income		$ 14,000
Partial Balance Sheet	**Current Year**	**Prior Year**
Accounts receivable	$14,000	$24,000
Salaries payable	19,000	8,000
Other accrued liabilities	7,000	9,000
Land	52,000	57,000

Required:
Present the operating activities section of the statement of cash flows for Parra Company using the indirect method.

Inferring Balance Sheet Changes from the Cash Flow Statement (Indirect Method)

E12-11
LO12-2
Colgate-Palmolive

A recent statement of cash flows for **Colgate-Palmolive** reported the following information (dollars in millions):

OPERATING ACTIVITIES	
Net income	$2,554
Depreciation	421
Cash effect of changes in	
Receivables	(130)
Inventories	(130)
Other current assets	54
Payables	199
Other	(72)
Net cash provided by operations	$2,896

Source: Colgate-Palmolive

Required:
Based on the information reported on the statement of cash flows for Colgate-Palmolive, determine whether the following accounts increased or decreased during the period: Receivables, Inventories, Other Current Assets, and Payables.

E12-12 LO12-2 **Apple**

Inferring Balance Sheet Changes from the Cash Flow Statement (Indirect Method)

A recent statement of cash flows for **Apple** contained the following information (dollars in millions):

OPERATIONS	
Net income	$57,411
Depreciation and amortization	17,573
Changes in operating assets and liabilities:	
Accounts receivable, net	8,470
Inventories	(127)
Other current assets	(9,588)
Accounts payable	(4,062)
Deferred revenue	2,081
Other current liabilities	8,916
Cash generated by operating activities	$80,674

Source: Apple

Required:
For each of the asset and liability accounts listed on the statement of cash flows, determine whether the account balances increased or decreased during the period.

E12-13

(Chapter Supplement B) Computing and Reporting Cash Flow Effects of Sale of Plant and Equipment

During two recent years, Perez Construction, Inc., disposed of the following plant and equipment:

	Year 1	Year 2
Plant and equipment (at cost)	$75,000	$13,500
Accumulated depreciation on equipment disposed of	40,385	3,773
Cash received	17,864	12,163
Gain (loss) on sale	(16,751)	2,436

Required:
1. Determine the cash flow from the sale of property for each year that would be reported in the investing activities section of the cash flow statement.
2. Perez uses the indirect method for the operating activities section of the cash flow statement. What amounts related to the sales would be added or subtracted in the computation of Net Cash Flows from Operating Activities for each year?

E12-14

(Chapter Supplement B) Computing and Reporting Cash Flow Effects of the Sale of Equipment

During the period, Sanchez Company sold some excess equipment at a loss. The following information was collected from the company's accounting records:

From the Income Statement	
Depreciation expense	$ 1,500
Loss on sale of equipment	2,300
From the Balance Sheet	
Beginning equipment	82,500
Ending equipment	72,000
Beginning accumulated depreciation	43,000
Ending accumulated depreciation	41,000

No new equipment was bought during the period.

Required:

1. For the equipment that was sold, determine its original cost, its accumulated depreciation, and the cash received from the sale. (Use the equipment and accumulated depreciation T-accounts to infer the book value of the equipment sold.)
2. Sanchez Company uses the indirect method for the Operating Activities section of the cash flow statement. What amount related to the sale would be added or subtracted in the computation of Net Cash Flows from Operating Activities?
3. What amount related to the sale would be added or subtracted in the computation of Net Cash Flows from Investing Activities?

Analyzing Cash Flows from Operating Activities; Interpreting the Quality of Income Ratio

E12-15
LO12-2, 12-3
PepsiCo

A recent annual report for **PepsiCo** contained the following information for the period (dollars in millions):

Net income	$6,462
Depreciation and amortization	2,737
Increase in accounts receivable	666
Increase in inventory	331
Increase in prepaid expense	27
Increase in accounts payable	520
Decrease in taxes payable	340
Increase in other current liabilities	589
Cash dividends paid	3,157
Share repurchases	2,489

Source: PepsiCo

Required:

1. Compute cash flows from operating activities for PepsiCo using the indirect method.
2. Compute the quality of income ratio.
3. What were the major reasons that PepsiCo's quality of income ratio did not equal 1.0?

Reporting Cash Flows from Investing and Financing Activities

E12-16
LO12-4, 12-6

Oering's Furniture Corporation is a Virginia-based manufacturer of furniture. In a recent year, it reported the following activities:

Net income	$ 5,135
Purchase of property, plant, and equipment	2,071
Borrowings under line of credit (bank)	1,117
Proceeds from issuance of stock	11
Cash received from customers	37,164
Payments to reduce long-term debt	46
Sale of marketable securities	219
Proceeds from sale of property and equipment	6,894
Dividends paid	277
Interest paid	90
Purchase of treasury stock (stock repurchase)	2,583

Required:

Based on this information, present the investing and financing activities sections of the cash flow statement.

Preparing a Statement of Cash Flows (Indirect Method)

E12-17
LO12-2, 12-4, 12-6

Shallow Waters Company was started several years ago by two diving instructors. The company's comparative balance sheets and income statement are presented below, along with additional information.

	Current Year	Prior Year
Balance Sheet at December 31		
Cash	$ 4,000	$4,500
Accounts receivable	1,300	800
Prepaid expenses	100	250
Equipment	700	0
	$ 6,100	$5,550
Wages payable	$ 650	$1,100
Common stock and additional paid-in capital	1,700	1,400
Retained earnings	3,750	3,050
	$ 6,100	$5,550
Income Statement for Current Year		
Lessons revenue	$34,550	
Wages expense	(30,200)	
Other expenses	(3,650)	
Net income	$ 700	

Additional Data:

a. Prepaid expenses relate to rent paid in advance.
b. Other expenses were paid in cash.
c. Purchased equipment for $700 cash at the end of the current year to be used starting in the following year.
d. An owner contributed capital by paying $300 cash in exchange for the company's stock.

Required:
Prepare the statement of cash flows for the year ended December 31, current year, using the indirect method.

E12-18 Preparing a Statement of Cash Flows (Indirect Method)

LO12-2, 12-4, 12-6

Computer Service and Repair was started five years ago by two college roommates. The company's comparative balance sheets and income statement are presented below, along with additional information.

	Current Year	Prior Year
Balance Sheet at December 31		
Cash	$ 3,300	$4,000
Accounts receivable	700	500
Prepaid expenses	100	50
Equipment	350	0
Accumulated depreciation	(50)	0
	$ 4,400	$4,550
Wages payable	$ 350	$1,100
Short-term note payable	300	0
Common stock	1,000	1,000
Retained earnings	2,750	2,450
	$ 4,400	$4,550
Income Statement for Current Year		
Service revenue	$ 34,000	
Depreciation expense	(50)	
Salaries expense	(30,000)	
Other expenses	(3,650)	
Net income	$ 300	

Additional Data:

a. Prepaid expenses relate to rent paid in advance.
b. Other expenses were paid in cash.
c. Purchased equipment for $350 cash at the beginning of the current year and recorded $50 of depreciation expense at the end of the current year.
d. At the end of the current year, the company signed a short-term note payable to the bank for $300.

Required:
Prepare the statement of cash flows for the year ended December 31, current year, using the indirect method.

Reporting and Interpreting Cash Flows from Investing and Financing Activities with Discussion of Management Strategy

E12-19
LO12-4, 12-5, 12-6
Gibraltar Industries

Gibraltar Industries is a Buffalo, New York–based manufacturer and distributor of building products for residential, industrial, infrastructure, renewable energy, and conservation markets. In a recent year, it reported the following activities:

Acquisitions (investments in other companies)	$(313,686)
Increase in inventories	(5,719)
Depreciation and amortization	20,915
Long-term debt reduction	(6,656)
Net cash provided by operating activities	89,104
Net income	64,566
Net proceeds from issuance of common stock	1,119
Net proceeds from sale of property and equipment	77
Proceeds from long-term debt	85,000
Proceeds from sale of other equity investments	2,000
Purchases of property, plant, and equipment	(13,068)

Source: Gibraltar Industries

Required:

1. Based on this information, present the investing and financing activities sections of the cash flow statement.
2. Compute the capital acquisitions ratio. What does the ratio tell you about Gibraltar's ability to finance purchases of property, plant, and equipment with cash provided by operating activities?
3. What main purpose do you think Gibraltar's management had in mind for the cash generated by issuing long-term debt?

Reporting Noncash Transactions on the Statement of Cash Flows; Interpreting the Effect on the Capital Acquisitions Ratio

E12-20
LO12-5, 12-7

An analysis of Courtney Corporation's operational asset accounts provided the following information:

a. Acquired a large machine that cost $36,000. Courtney paid for it by giving a $15,000, 12 percent interest-bearing note due at the end of two years and 500 shares of its common stock, with a par value of $10 per share and a market value of $42 per share.
b. Acquired a small machine that cost $12,700. Full payment was made by transferring a tract of land that had a book value of $12,700.

Required:

1. Show how this information should be reported on the statement of cash flows.
2. What would be the effect of these transactions on the capital acquisitions ratio? How might these transactions distort one's interpretation of the ratio?

(Chapter Supplement A) Reporting Cash Flows from Operating Activities from an Analyst's Perspective (Direct Method)

E12-21

Refer to the information for Peak Heights Company in Exercise 12-7.

Required:
Present the operating activities section of the statement of cash flows for Peak Heights Company using the direct method.

E12-22 (Chapter Supplement A) Reporting and Interpreting Cash Flows from Operating Activities from an Analyst's Perspective (Direct Method)

Refer to the information for Rodriguez Company in Exercise 12-8.

Required:
1. Present the operating activities section of the statement of cash flows for Rodriguez Company using the direct method. Assume that other accrued liabilities relate to other expenses on the income statement.
2. What were the major reasons that Rodriguez was able to report a net loss but positive cash flow from operations? Why are the reasons for the difference between cash flow from operations and net income important to financial analysts?

E12-23 (Chapter Supplement A) Reporting and Interpreting Cash Flows from Operating Activities from an Analyst's Perspective (Direct Method)

Refer to the following summarized income statement and additional selected information for Trumansburg, Inc.

Income Statement	
Revenues	$150,800
Cost of sales	55,500
Gross margin	95,300
Salary expense	55,400
Depreciation and amortization	33,305
Other expense	9,600
Net loss before tax	(3,005)
Income tax expense	1,500
Net loss	$ (4,505)
Other information:	
Decrease in receivables	$ 800
Decrease in inventories	230
Increase in prepaid expenses	1,500
Increase in accounts payable	1,750
Decrease in accrued liabilities	602
Increase in income taxes payable	1,280

Required:
1. Based on this information, compute cash flow from operating activities using the direct method. Assume that prepaid expenses and accrued liabilities relate to other expense.
2. What were the major reasons that Trumansburg was able to report a net loss but positive cash flow from operations? Why are the reasons for the difference between cash flows from operations and net income important to financial analysts?

E12-24 (Chapter Supplement C) Preparing a Statement of Cash Flows, Indirect Method: T-Account Method

GolfGear & More, Inc., is a regional and online golf equipment retailer. The company reported the following for the current year:

Purchased a long-term investment for cash, $15,000.

Paid cash dividend, $12,000.

Sold equipment for $6,000 cash (cost, $21,000; accumulated depreciation, $15,000).

Issued shares of no-par stock, 500 shares at $12 per share cash.

Net income was $20,200.

Depreciation expense was $3,000.

Its comparative balance sheet is presented below.

	Balances 12/31/Current Year	Balances 12/31/Prior Year
Cash	$ 19,200	$ 20,500
Accounts receivable	22,000	22,000
Merchandise inventory	75,000	68,000
Investments	15,000	0
Equipment	93,500	114,500
Accumulated depreciation	(20,000)	(32,000)
Total	$204,700	$193,000
Accounts payable	$ 14,000	$ 17,000
Wages payable	1,500	2,500
Income taxes payable	4,500	3,000
Notes payable	54,000	54,000
Common stock and additional paid-in capital	106,000	100,000
Retained earnings	24,700	16,500
Total	$204,700	$193,000

Required:

1. Following Chapter Supplement C, complete a T-account worksheet to be used to prepare the statement of cash flows for the current year.
2. Based on the T-account worksheet, prepare the statement of cash flows for the current year in proper format.

PROBLEMS

Preparing a Statement of Cash Flows (Indirect Method) (AP12-1)

P12-1
LO12-1, 12-2, 12-4, 12-6

Sharp Screen Films, Inc., is developing its annual financial statements at December 31, current year. The statements are complete except for the statement of cash flows. The completed comparative balance sheets and income statement are summarized as follows:

	Current Year	Prior Year
Balance sheet at December 31		
Cash	$ 73,250	$ 63,500
Accounts receivable	15,250	21,350
Merchandise inventory	23,450	18,000
Property and equipment	209,250	160,350
Less: Accumulated depreciation	(57,450)	(45,750)
	$263,750	$217,450
Accounts payable	$ 16,500	$ 19,000
Wages payable	2,000	2,700
Note payable, long-term	56,300	71,000
Common stock and additional paid-in capital	103,950	65,900
Retained earnings	85,000	58,850
	$263,750	$217,450
Income statement for current year		
Sales	$205,000	
Cost of goods sold	(123,500)	
Depreciation expense	(11,700)	
Other expenses	(43,000)	
Net income	$ 26,800	

Additional Data:

a. Bought equipment for cash, $48,900.
b. Paid $14,700 on the long-term note payable.
c. Issued new shares of stock for $38,050 cash.
d. Dividends of $650 were declared and paid.
e. Other expenses all relate to wages.
f. Accounts payable includes only inventory purchases made on credit.

Required:

1. Prepare the statement of cash flows using the indirect method for the year ended December 31, current year.
2. Based on the cash flow statement, write a short paragraph explaining the major sources and uses of cash by Sharp Screen Films during the current year.

P12-2 LO12-1, 12-2, 12-4, 12-6

Preparing a Statement of Cash Flows (Indirect Method) (AP12-2)

BGP Electrical Supply is developing its annual financial statements at December 31, current year. The statements are complete except for the statement of cash flows. The completed comparative balance sheets and income statement are summarized:

	Current Year	Prior Year
Balance sheet at December 31		
Cash	$ 37,000	$ 29,000
Accounts receivable	32,000	28,000
Merchandise inventory	41,000	38,000
Property and equipment	132,000	111,000
Less: Accumulated depreciation	(41,000)	(36,000)
	$201,000	$170,000
Accounts payable	$ 36,000	$ 27,000
Accrued wages expense	1,200	1,400
Note payable, long-term	38,000	44,000
Common stock and additional paid-in capital	88,600	72,600
Retained earnings	37,200	25,000
	$201,000	$170,000
Income statement for current year		
Sales	$120,000	
Cost of goods sold	(70,000)	
Other expenses	(37,800)	
Net income	$ 12,200	

Additional Data:

a. Bought equipment for cash, $21,000.
b. Paid $6,000 on the long-term note payable.
c. Issued new shares of stock for $16,000 cash.
d. No dividends were declared or paid.
e. Other expenses included depreciation, $5,000; wages, $20,000; taxes, $6,000; other, $6,800.
f. Accounts payable includes only inventory purchases made on credit. Because there are no liability accounts relating to taxes or other expenses, assume that these expenses were fully paid in cash.

Required:

1. Prepare the statement of cash flows for the year ended December 31, current year, using the indirect method.
2. Based on the cash flow statement, write a short paragraph explaining the major sources and uses of cash during the current year.

(Chapter Supplement A) Preparing a Statement of Cash Flows (Direct Method) (AP12-3)

P12-3

Use the information concerning Sharp Screen Films, Inc., provided in Problem 12-1 to fulfill the following requirements.

Required:

1. Prepare the statement of cash flows using the direct method for the year ended December 31, current year.
2. Based on the cash flow statement, write a short paragraph explaining the major sources and uses of cash by Sharp Screen Films during the current year.

(Chapter Supplement A) Comparing Cash Flows from Operating Activities (Direct and Indirect Methods) (AP12-4)

P12-4

Omega Company's accountants have just completed the income statement and balance sheet for the year and have provided the following information (dollars in thousands):

INCOME STATEMENT		
Sales revenue		$ 22,600
Expenses		
Cost of goods sold	$10,500	
Depreciation expense	2,000	
Salaries expense	4,070	
Rent expense	3,200	
Insurance expense	1,100	
Utilities expense	850	
Interest expense on bonds	450	
Loss on sale of investments	650	22,820
Net loss		$ (220)

SELECTED BALANCE SHEET ACCOUNTS	Current Year	Prior Year
Merchandise inventory	$150	$ 65
Accounts receivable	440	620
Accounts payable	285	212
Salaries payable	38	23
Rent payable	4	10
Prepaid rent	6	7
Prepaid insurance	17	4

Other Data:
The company issued $30,000, 8 percent bonds payable at par during the year.

Required:

1. Prepare the cash flows from operating activities section of the statement of cash flows using the direct method.
2. Prepare the cash flows from operating activities section of the statement of cash flows using the indirect method.

(Chapter Supplement B) Preparing a Statement of Cash Flows with Gain on Sale of Equipment (Indirect Method) (AP12-5)

P12-5
LO12-2, 12-4, 12-6

XS Supply Company is developing its annual financial statements at December 31, current year. The statements are complete except for the statement of cash flows. The completed comparative balance sheets and income statement are summarized below:

	Current Year	Prior Year
Balance sheet at December 31		
Cash	$ 34,000	$ 29,000
Accounts receivable	35,000	28,000
Merchandise inventory	41,000	38,000
Property and equipment	121,000	100,000
Less: Accumulated depreciation	(30,000)	(25,000)
	$201,000	$170,000
Accounts payable	$ 36,000	$ 27,000
Wages payable	1,200	1,400
Note payable, long-term	38,000	44,000
Common stock and additional paid-in capital	88,600	72,600
Retained earnings	37,200	25,000
	$201,000	$170,000
Income statement for current year		
Sales	$120,000	
Gain on sale of equipment	1,000	
Cost of goods sold	(70,000)	
Other expenses	(38,800)	
Net income	$ 12,200	

Additional Data:

a. Bought equipment for cash, $31,000. Sold equipment with original cost of $10,000, accumulated depreciation of $7,000, for $4,000 cash.
b. Paid $6,000 on the long-term note payable.
c. Issued new shares of stock for $16,000 cash.
d. No dividends were declared or paid.
e. Other expenses included depreciation, $12,000; wages, $13,000; taxes, $6,000; and other, $7,800.
f. Accounts payable includes only inventory purchases made on credit. Because there are no liability accounts relating to taxes or other expenses, assume that these expenses were fully paid in cash.

Required:

1. Prepare the statement of cash flows for the year ended December 31, current year, using the indirect method.
2. Evaluate the statement of cash flows.

P12-6 (Chapter Supplement C) Preparing a Statement of Cash Flows, Indirect Method, Using the T-Account Approach (AP12-6)

Hanks Company is developing its annual financial statements at December 31, current year. The statements are complete except for the statement of cash flows. The completed comparative balance sheets and income statement are summarized as follows:

	Current Year	Prior Year
Balance sheet at December 31		
Cash	$ 33,000	$ 18,000
Accounts receivable	26,000	28,000
Merchandise inventory	39,000	36,000
Fixed assets (net)	80,000	72,000
	$178,000	$154,000

(Continued)

	Current Year	Prior Year
Accounts payable	$ 27,000	$ 21,000
Wages payable	1,500	1,000
Note payable, long-term	42,000	48,000
Common stock, no par	78,500	60,000
Retained earnings	29,000	24,000
	$178,000	$154,000
Income statement for current year		
Sales	$ 80,000	
Cost of goods sold	(43,000)	
Expenses	(30,000)	
Net income	$ 7,000	

Additional Data:

a. Bought fixed assets for cash, $12,000.
b. Paid $6,000 on the long-term note payable.
c. Sold unissued common stock for $18,500 cash.
d. Declared and paid a $2,000 cash dividend.
e. Incurred the following expenses: depreciation, $4,000; wages, $12,000; taxes, $2,000; and other, $12,000.

Required:

1. Prepare the statement of cash flows T-accounts using the indirect method to report cash flows from operating activities.
2. Prepare the statement of cash flows.
3. Prepare a schedule of noncash investing and financing activities if necessary.

ALTERNATE PROBLEMS

Preparing a Statement of Cash Flows (Indirect Method) (P12-1)

AP12-1
LO12-1, 12-2, 12-4, 12-6

Ingersol Construction Supply Company is developing its annual financial statements at December 31, current year. The statements are complete except for the statement of cash flows. The completed comparative balance sheets and income statement are summarized as follows:

	Current Year	Prior Year
Balance sheet at December 31		
Cash	$ 34,000	$ 29,000
Accounts receivable	45,000	28,000
Merchandise inventory	32,000	38,000
Property and equipment	121,000	100,000
Less: Accumulated depreciation	(30,000)	(25,000)
	$202,000	$170,000
Accounts payable	$ 36,000	$ 27,000
Wages payable	2,200	1,400
Note payable, long-term	40,000	46,000
Common stock and additional paid-in capital	86,600	70,600
Retained earnings	37,200	25,000
	$202,000	$170,000
Income statement for current year		
Sales	$135,000	
Cost of goods sold	(70,000)	
Other expenses	(37,800)	
Net income	$ 27,200	

Additional Data:

a. Bought equipment for cash, $21,000.
b. Paid $6,000 on the long-term note payable.
c. Issued new shares of stock for $16,000 cash.
d. Dividends of $15,000 were declared and paid in cash.
e. Other expenses included depreciation, $5,000; wages, $20,000; taxes, $6,000; and other, $6,800.
f. Accounts payable includes only inventory purchases made on credit. Because there are no liability accounts relating to taxes or other expenses, assume that these expenses were fully paid in cash.

Required:

1. Prepare the statement of cash flows using the indirect method for the year ended December 31, current year.
2. Evaluate the statement of cash flows.

AP12-2 Preparing a Statement of Cash Flows (Indirect Method) (P12-2)

LO12-1, 12-2, 12-4, 12-6

Audio House, Inc., is developing its annual financial statements at December 31, current year. The statements are complete except for the statement of cash flows. The completed comparative balance sheets and income statement are summarized as follows:

	Current Year	Prior Year
Balance sheet at December 31		
Cash	$ 64,000	$ 65,000
Accounts receivable	15,000	20,000
Inventory	22,000	20,000
Property and equipment	210,000	150,000
Less: Accumulated depreciation	(60,000)	(45,000)
	$251,000	$210,000
Accounts payable	$ 8,000	$ 19,000
Taxes payable	2,000	1,000
Note payable, long-term	86,000	75,000
Common stock and additional paid-in capital	75,000	70,000
Retained earnings	80,000	45,000
	$251,000	$210,000
Income statement for Current Year		
Sales	$190,000	
Cost of goods sold	(90,000)	
Other expenses	(60,000)	
Net income	$ 40,000	

Additional Data:

a. Bought equipment for cash, $60,000.
b. Borrowed an additional $11,000 and signed an additional long-term note payable.
c. Issued new shares of stock for $5,000 cash.
d. Dividends of $5,000 were declared and paid in cash.
e. Other expenses included depreciation, $15,000; wages, $20,000; and taxes, $25,000.
f. Accounts payable includes only inventory purchases made on credit.

Required:

1. Prepare the statement of cash flows for the year ended December 31, current year, using the indirect method.
2. Based on the cash flow statement, write a short paragraph explaining the major sources and uses of cash during the current year.

(Chapter Supplement A) Preparing a Statement of Cash Flows (Direct Method) (P12-3)

AP12-3

Use the information concerning Ingersol Construction Supply Company provided in Alternate Problem 12-1 to fulfill the following requirements.

Required:

1. Prepare the statement of cash flows using the direct method for the year ended December 31, current year.
2. Evaluate the statement of cash flows.

(Chapter Supplement A) Comparing Cash Flows from Operating Activities (Direct and Indirect Methods) (P12-4)

AP12-4

Athena Company's accountants have just completed the income statement and balance sheet for the year and have provided the following information (dollars in thousands):

INCOME STATEMENT		
Sales revenue		$64,900
Expenses		
Cost of goods sold	$32,300	
Depreciation expense	7,500	
Salaries expense	12,100	
Rent expense	9,000	
Insurance expense	3,600	
Utilities expense	2,400	
Interest expense on bonds	2,250	
Loss on sale of investments	1,050	
Total expenses		70,200
Net loss		$(5,300)

SELECTED BALANCE SHEET ACCOUNTS	Current Year	Prior Year
Merchandise inventory	$350	$480
Accounts receivable	520	370
Accounts payable	310	290
Salaries payable	130	170
Rent payable	90	80
Prepaid rent	160	110
Prepaid insurance	70	100

Other Data:

The company issued $50,000, 9 percent bonds payable at par during the year.

Required:

1. Prepare the cash flows from operating activities section of the statement of cash flows using the direct method.
2. Prepare the cash flows from operating activities section of the statement of cash flows using the indirect method.

(Chapter Supplement B) Preparing a Statement of Cash Flows with Gain on Sale of Equipment (Indirect Method) (P12-5)

AP12-5
LO12-2, 12-4, 12-6

Golden Deer Company is developing its annual financial statements at December 31, current year. The statements are complete except for the statement of cash flows. The completed comparative balance sheets and income statement are summarized below:

(Continued)

	Current Year	Prior Year
Balance sheet at December 31		
Cash	$ 57,000	$ 61,000
Accounts receivable	37,000	41,000
Merchandise inventory	63,000	57,000
Property and equipment	65,000	39,000
Less: Accumulated depreciation	(38,000)	(26,000)
	$184,000	$172,000
Accounts payable	$ 42,000	$ 38,000
Wages payable	3,000	12,000
Note payable, long-term	22,000	30,000
Common stock and additional paid-in capital	67,000	58,000
Retained earnings	50,000	34,000
	$184,000	$172,000
Income statement for current year		
Sales	$165,000	
Gain on sale of equipment	2,000	
Cost of goods sold	(102,000)	
Other expenses	(49,000)	
Net income	$ 16,000	

Additional Data:

a. Bought equipment for cash, $40,000. Sold equipment with original cost of $14,000, accumulated depreciation of $10,000, for $6,000 cash.
b. Paid $8,000 on the long-term note payable.
c. Issued new shares of stock for $9,000 cash.
d. No dividends were declared or paid.
e. Other expenses included depreciation, $22,000; wages, $16,300; taxes, $5,000; and other, $5,700.
f. Accounts payable includes only inventory purchases made on credit. Because there are no liability accounts relating to taxes or other expenses, assume that these expenses were fully paid in cash.

Required:

1. Prepare the statement of cash flows for the year ended December 31, current year, using the indirect method.
2. Evaluate the statement of cash flows.

AP12-6 (Chapter Supplement C) Preparing a Statement of Cash Flows, Indirect Method, Using the T-Account Approach (P12-6)

Murray Company is developing its annual financial statements at December 31, current year. The statements are complete except for the statement of cash flows. The completed comparative balance sheets and income statement are summarized as follows:

	Current Year	Prior Year
Balance sheet at December 31		
Cash	$ 40,000	$ 36,000
Accounts receivable	34,000	29,000
Inventory	55,000	44,000
Property, plant, and equipment	85,000	68,000
Less: Accumulated depreciation	(45,000)	(38,000)
	$169,000	$139,000

(Continued)

Accounts payable	$ 19,000	$ 12,000
Wages payable	5,000	4,000
Long-term debt	35,000	45,000
Common stock and additional paid-in capital	78,000	58,000
Retained earnings	32,000	20,000
	$169,000	$139,000
Income statement for current year		
Sales	$ 98,000	
Cost of goods sold	(41,000)	
Other expenses	(40,000)	
Net income	$ 17,000	

Additional Data:

a. Bought fixed assets for cash, $17,000.
b. Paid $10,000 of principal on the long-term note payable.
c. Sold unissued common stock for $20,000 cash.
d. Declared and paid a $5,000 cash dividend.
e. Incurred the following expenses: depreciation, $7,000; wages, $18,000; taxes, $4,000; and other, $11,000.

Required:

1. Prepare the statement of cash flows T-accounts using the indirect method to report cash flows from operating activities.
2. Prepare the statement of cash flows.
3. Prepare a schedule of noncash investing and financing activities if necessary.

CONTINUING PROBLEM

Preparing the Statement of Cash Flows (Indirect Method)

CON12-1
LO12-1, 12-2, 12-4, 12-6, 12-7
Pool Corporation

Presented in alphabetical order below are the line items including the subtotals and totals (with some simplifications) from **Pool Corporation**'s recent statement of cash flows prepared using the indirect method. Using these line items, prepare Pool Corporation's statement of cash flows in good form for the year ended December 31 following the format presented in Exhibit 12.1 (all dollar amounts in thousands).

Accounts payable	$ 6,402
Accrued expenses and other current liabilities	20,682
Acquisition of businesses	(5,934)
Amortization	1,559
Cash and cash equivalents at beginning of year	9,721
Cash and cash equivalents at end of year	17,487
Change in cash and cash equivalents	7,766
Depreciation	9,746
Loss on sale of property and equipment	263
Net cash provided by operating activities	75,103
Net cash used in financing activities	(41,759)
Net cash used in investing activities	(25,578)
Net income	71,993
Other financing activities	944
Other operating assets	8,635
Payments of cash dividends	(26,470)
Payments on long-term debt and other long-term liabilities	(149)

(Continued)

Payments on revolving line of bank credit	(700,749)
Prepaid expenses	(2,951)
Proceeds from revolving line of bank credit	749,349
Proceeds from stock issued under share-based compensation plans	13,085
Product inventories	(35,339)
Purchases of property and equipment	(19,844)
Purchases of treasury stock	(77,769)
Receivables	(5,887)
Sale of property and equipment	200

Source: Pool Corporation

CASES AND PROJECTS

Annual Report Cases

CP12-1
LO12-2, 12-4, 12-6, 12-7
Target Corporation

Finding Financial Information

Refer to the financial statements of **Target** given in Appendix B at the end of this book.

Required:

1. Does Target, use the direct or indirect method to report cash flows from operating activities? How did you know?
   a. Direct because it lists the individual sources and uses of cash resulting from operations.
   b. Direct because it reconciles or explains the differences between net earnings and cash provided by operations.
   c. Indirect because it reconciles or explains the differences between net earnings and cash provided by operations.
   d. Indirect because is separates cash flows into operating, investing, and financing activities.
   e. None of the above.
2. What was the largest "Changes in operating accounts" in the operating section of the most recent cash flow statement? Explain the direction of its effect in the reconciliation.
   a. Depreciation and amortization which is added because it is a non-cash expense.
   b. Accounts payable which increased. The increase in borrowing caused an increase in cash, all other things being equal.
   c. Inventory which increased. The increase in inventory purchases caused a decrease in cash, all other things being equal.
   d. Other assets which increased. The small change means that the resulting change in cash is very large, all other things being equal.
   e. None of the above.
3. Explain why the "Share-based compensation" and "Depreciation and amortization" items were added in the reconciliation of net income to net cash provided by operating activities.
   a. They are expenses that do not affect cash or other operating assets or liabilities.
   b. They are financing and investing cash flows, respectively.
   c. They are "Changes in operating accounts."
   d. All of the above.
   e. None of the above.
4. What was free cash flow (in millions of dollars) for the year ended January 30, 2021 (denoted as fiscal 2020 in Target's statements)? ______________

CP12-2
LO12-2, 12-4, 12-6, 12-7
Walmart Inc.

Finding Financial Information

Refer to the financial statements of **Walmart** given in Appendix C at the end of this book.

Required:

1. On the statement of cash flows, what was the largest item (in absolute value) listed under "Adjustments to reconcile consolidated net income to net cash provided by operating activities" during the most recent reporting year? Explain the direction of its effect in the reconciliation.
   a. "Depreciation and amortization" which is added because it is an expense that does not affect cash or other operating assets or liabilities.
   b. "Accounts payable" which increased. The increase in borrowing caused an increase in cash, all other things being equal.
   c. "Losses on disposal of business operations" which is an investing cash outflow.
   d. "Dividends paid" which decreases net income and Net cash provided by operating activities.
   e. None of the above.
2. What amount of tax payments did the company make during the most recent reporting year? Where did you find the information?
   a. $6,858 from the "Provision for income taxes" on the Consolidated Statements of Income.
   b. $1,911 under "Deferred income taxes" in the operating activities section of the Consolidated Statements of Cash Flows.
   c. $5,271 in the "Supplemental disclosure of cash flow information" located near the bottom of the Consolidated Statements of Cash Flows.
   d. It is not disclosed in Walmart's annual report.
   e. None of the above.
3. Has the company paid cash dividends during the last three years? If so, how much have they paid in total (in millions of dollars)? (Ignore dividends paid to noncontrolling interest.)
   ☐ Yes ____________
   ☐ No
4. Examine Walmart's *investing and financing* activities. List the company's three largest *uses of cash* during the most recent year.
   a. "Payments for property and equipment," "Proceeds from disposal of property and equipment," and "Other investing activities."
   b. "Repayments of long-term debt," "Proceeds from disposal of property and equipment," and "Payments for business acquisitions."
   c. "Repayments of long-term debt," "Dividends paid," and "Purchase of company stock."
   d. "Payments for property and equipment," "Repayments of long-term debt," and "Dividends paid."
   e. None of the above.

Comparing Companies within an Industry

CP12-3
LO12-3, 12-5
Target Corporation
Walmart Inc.

Refer to the financial statements of **Target** (Appendix B) and **Walmart** (Appendix C), and the Industry Ratio Report (Appendix D) at the end of this book.

Required:

1. Compute the quality of income ratio for both companies for the most recent reporting year. Which company has a better quality of income ratio?

   Target = ____________ **Walmart** = ____________

2. Compare the quality of income ratio for both companies to the industry average. Are these companies producing more or less cash from operating activities relative to net income than the average company in the industry?
   a. Target and Walmart are generating less cash from operating activities per dollar of net income than the industry average.
   b. Target and Walmart are generating more cash from operating activities per dollar of net income than the industry average.
   c. Target is generating less and Walmart is generating more cash from operating activities per dollar of net income than the industry average.
   d. Target is generating more and Walmart is generating less cash from operating activities per dollar of net income than the industry average.
3. Compute the capital acquisitions ratio for both companies for the most recent reporting year.

   Target = ____________ **Walmart** = ____________

Compare their abilities to finance purchases of property, plant, and equipment with cash provided by operating activities (select one).

☐ Target has a greater ability to finance purchases of property, plant, and equipment with cash provided by operating activities.

☐ Walmart has a greater ability to finance purchases of property, plant, and equipment with cash provided by operating activities.

4. Compare the capital acquisitions ratio for both companies to the industry average. How does each company's ability to finance the purchase of property, plant, and equipment with cash provided by operating activities compare with that of other companies in the industry?
   a. Target and Walmart are less able to finance purchases of property, plant, and equipment with cash provided by operating activities than the industry average.
   b. Target and Walmart are more able to finance purchases of property, plant, and equipment with cash provided by operating activities than the industry average.
   c. Target is less able and Walmart is more able to finance purchases of property, plant, and equipment with cash provided by operating activities than the industry average.
   d. Target is more able and Walmart is less able to finance purchases of property, plant, and equipment with cash provided by operating activities than the industry average.

Financial Reporting and Analysis Cases

CP12-4
LO12-1, 12-2, 12-4, 12-6
Rocky Mountain Chocolate Factory

Preparing a Complex Statement of Cash Flows (Indirect Method)

Rocky Mountain Chocolate Factory manufactures an extensive line of premium chocolate candies for sale at its franchised and company-owned stores in malls throughout the United States. Its balance sheet as of May 31, the end of the first quarter of a recent year, is presented along with an analysis of selected accounts and transactions:

ROCKY MOUNTAIN CHOCOLATE FACTORY, INC.
Balance Sheets

Assets	May 31 (Unaudited)	February 29
Current assets		
Cash and cash equivalents	$ 921,505	$ 528,787
Accounts and notes receivable–trade, less allowance for doubtful accounts of $43,196 at May 31 and $28,196 at February 29	1,602,582	1,463,901
Inventories	2,748,788	2,504,908
Deferred tax asset	59,219	59,219
Other	581,508	224,001
Total current assets	5,913,602	4,780,816
Property and equipment–at cost	14,010,796	12,929,675
Less accumulated depreciation and amortization	(2,744,388)	(2,468,084)
	11,266,408	10,461,591
Other assets		
Notes and accounts receivable due after one year	100,206	111,588
Goodwill and other intangibles, net of accumulated amortization of $259,641 at May 31 and $253,740 at February 29	330,359	336,260
Other	574,130	624,185
	1,004,695	1,072,033
	$18,184,705	$16,314,440

(Continued)

Liabilities and Equity	May 31 (Unaudited)	February 29
Current liabilities		
Short-term debt	$ 0	$ 1,000,000
Current maturities of long-term debt	429,562	134,538
Accounts payable–trade	1,279,455	998,520
Accrued liabilities	714,473	550,386
Income taxes payable	11,198	54,229
Total current liabilities	2,434,688	2,737,673
Long-term debt, less current maturities	4,193,290	2,183,877
Deferred income taxes	275,508	275,508
Stockholders' Equity		
Common stock–authorized 7,250,000 shares, $0.03 par value; issued 3,034,302 shares at May 31 and at February 29	91,029	91,029
Additional paid-in capital	9,703,985	9,703,985
Retained earnings	2,502,104	2,338,267
	12,297,118	12,133,281
Less common stock held in treasury, at cost–129,153 shares at May 31 and at February 29	1,015,899	1,015,899
	11,281,219	11,117,382
	$18,184,705	$16,314,440

The accompanying notes are an integral part of these statements.

Source: Rocky Mountain Chocolate Factory, Inc.

Analysis of Selected Accounts and Transactions:

a. Net income was $163,837. Notes and accounts receivable due after one year relate to operations.
b. Depreciation and amortization totaled $282,205.
c. No "other" noncurrent assets (which relate to investing activities) were purchased this period.
d. No property, plant, and equipment were sold during the period. No goodwill was acquired or sold.
e. Proceeds from issuance of long-term debt were $4,659,466, and principal payments were $2,355,029. (Combine the current maturities with the long-term debt in your analysis.)
f. No dividends were declared or paid.
g. Ignore the "deferred tax asset" and "deferred income taxes" accounts.

Required:
Prepare a statement of cash flows for the quarter ended May 31, using the indirect method.

Making a Decision as a Financial Analyst: Analyzing Cash Flow for a New Company

CP12-5
LO12-2

Carlyle Golf, Inc., was formed in September of last year. The company designs, contracts for the manufacture of, and markets a line of men's golf apparel. A portion of the statement of cash flows for Carlyle follows:

CURRENT YEAR	
Cash flows from operating activities	
Net income	$(460,089)
Depreciation	3,554
Noncash compensation (stock)	254,464
Deposits with suppliers	(404,934)
Increase in prepaid assets	(42,260)
Increase in accounts payable	81,765
Increase in accrued liabilities	24,495
Net cash flows from operating activities	$(543,005)

Management expects a solid increase in sales in the near future. To support the increase in sales, it plans to add $2.2 million to inventory. The company did not disclose a sales forecast. At the end of the current year, Carlyle had less than $1,000 in cash. It is not unusual for a new company to experience a loss and negative cash flows during its start-up phase.

Required:
As a financial analyst recently hired by a major investment bank, you have been asked to write a short memo to your supervisor evaluating the problems facing Carlyle. Emphasize typical sources of financing that may or may not be available to support the expansion.

Critical Thinking Case

CP12-6
LO12-1, 12-2, 12-6
Enron

Ethical Decision Making: A Real-Life Example

In February 19, 2004, press release, the Securities and Exchange Commission described a number of fraudulent transactions that **Enron** executives concocted in an effort to meet the company's financial targets. One particularly well-known scheme is called the "Nigerian barge" transaction, which took place in the fourth quarter of 1999. According to court documents, Enron arranged to sell three electricity-generating power barges moored off the coast of Nigeria. The "buyer" was the investment banking firm of **Merrill Lynch**. Although Enron reported this transaction as a sale in its income statement, it turns out this was no ordinary sale. Merrill Lynch didn't really want the barges and had only agreed to buy them because Enron guaranteed, in a secret side deal, that it would arrange for the barges to be bought back from Merrill Lynch within six months of the initial transaction. In addition, Enron promised to pay Merrill Lynch a hefty fee for doing the deal. In an interview on National Public Radio on August 17, 2002, Michigan Senator Carl Levin declared, "(T)he case of the Nigerian barge transaction was, by any definition, a loan."

Required:

1. Discuss whether the Nigerian barge transaction should have been considered a loan rather than a sale. As part of your discussion, consider the following questions. Doesn't the Merrill Lynch payment to Enron at the time of the initial transaction automatically make it a sale, not a loan? What aspects of the transaction are similar to a loan? Which aspects suggest that the four criteria for revenue recognition (summarized near the end of Chapter 3) were not fulfilled?
2. The income statement effect of recording the transaction as a sale rather than a loan is fairly clear: Enron was able to boost its revenues and net income. What is somewhat less obvious, but nearly as important, are the effects on the statement of cash flows. Describe how recording the transaction as a sale rather than as a loan would change the statement of cash flows.
3. How would the two different statements of cash flows (described in your response to requirement 2) affect financial statement users?

You as Analyst: Online Company Research

CP12-7
LO12-1, 12-2, 12-3, 12-4, 12-5, 12-6

Team Project: Analyzing Cash Flows

In your web browser, search for the investor relations page of a public company you are interested in (e.g., Papa John's investor relations). Select SEC Filings or Annual Report or Financials to obtain the 10-K for the most recent year available.*

Required:
Answer the following questions based on the annual report (10-K) that you have downloaded:

1. Which of the two basic reporting approaches for cash flows from operating activities did the company adopt?
2. What is the quality of income ratio for the most current year? What were the major causes of differences between net income and cash flow from operations?

3. What is the capital acquisitions ratio for the three-year period presented in total? How is the company financing its capital acquisitions?
4. What portion of the cash from operations in the current year is being paid to stockholders in the form of dividends?

*Alternatively, you can go to sec.gov, click on Company Filings (under the search box), type in the name of the public company you want to find. Once at the list of filings, type 10-K in the Filing Type box. The most recent 10-K annual report will be at the top of the list. Click on Interactive Data for a list of the parts or the entire report to examine.

BUSINESS ANALYTICS AND DATA VISUALIZATION WITH EXCEL AND TABLEAU

Connect offers a variety of exercises to assess Excel skills, data visualization, interpretation, and analysis, including auto-graded Tableau Dashboard Activities, Applying Excel problems, and Integrated Excel problems.

Images used throughout chapter: Question of ethics: mushmello/Shutterstock; Pause for feedback: McGraw Hill; Guided help: McGraw Hill; Financial analysis: McGraw Hill; Focus on cash flows: Hilch/Shutterstock; Key ratio analysis: guillermain/123RF; Data analytics: Hilch/Shutterstock; Tip: McGraw Hill; ESG reporting: McGraw Hill; International perspective: Hilch/Shutterstock

13 chapter

Analyzing Financial Statements

The history of **The Home Depot** is an unusual success story. Founded in 1978 in Atlanta, The Home Depot has grown to be America's largest home improvement retailer, with over 2,200 stores in the United States, Canada, and Mexico. Financial statements for The Home Depot are presented in Exhibit 13.1. As you can see, The Home Depot has grown both sales and net income over the last three years. As you analyze Exhibit 13.1 and read other disclosures in this chapter, it is helpful to keep in mind that The Home Depot's fiscal year ends on the Sunday nearest to January 31. This means that "fiscal 2020" ended on January 31, 2021; "fiscal 2019" ended on February 2, 2020; and "fiscal 2018" ended on February 3, 2019.

With the recent improvement in the company's financial results, would you want to invest in The Home Depot? A number of professional analysts think you should, including those who work for Guggenheim Securities, a full-service, integrated investment banking and brokerage company. In a January 2021 research report on The Home Depot, Guggenheim analysts wrote: "We believe shares are poised to outperform. . .As a result, we are upgrading the shares to BUY from NEUTRAL. . ."

Professional analysts consider a large number of factors in developing the type of recommendation contained in the Guggenheim research report, including information reported in a company's financial statements. In this chapter, we use accounting information and a variety of analytical tools to study The Home Depot and its major competitor, **Lowe's**.

LEARNING OBJECTIVES

After studying this chapter, you should be able to:

Melissa Golden/Redux

FOCUS COMPANY

The Home Depot

FINANCIAL ANALYSIS: BRINGING IT ALL TOGETHER

homedepot.com

UNDERSTANDING THE BUSINESS

Companies spend billions of dollars each year preparing financial reports as well as other information that is important to investors like corporate sustainability reports. These statements are then made available to current and prospective investors. Most companies no longer mail this information to investors, but rather make it available online. **The Home Depot**'s financial information, as well as its sustainability report, are available from its Investor Relations website at ir.homedepot.com.

The reason that The Home Depot and other companies spend so much money to provide information to investors is simple: Financial statements and related information help people make better economic decisions. In fact, the information is designed primarily to meet the needs of external decision makers, including present and potential owners, investment analysts, and creditors.

EXHIBIT 13.1

The Home Depot Select Financial Statements

THE HOME DEPOT
REAL WORLD EXCERPT:
Annual Report

THE HOME DEPOT, INC.
CONSOLIDATED STATEMENTS OF EARNINGS

in millions, except per share data	**Fiscal 2020**	**Fiscal 2019**	**Fiscal 2018**
Net sales	$132,110	$110,225	$108,203
Cost of sales	87,257	72,653	71,043
Gross profit	44,853	37,572	37,160
Operating Expenses:			
Selling, general and administrative	24,447	19,740	19,513
Depreciation and amortization	2,128	1,989	1,870
Impairment loss	–	–	247
Total operating expenses	26,575	21,729	21,630
Operating income	18,278	15,843	15,530
Interest and other (income) expense:			
Interest and investment income	(47)	(73)	(93)
Interest expense	1,347	1,201	1,051
Other	–	–	16
Interest and other, net	1,300	1,128	974
Earnings before provision for income taxes	16,978	14,715	14,556
Provision for income taxes	4,112	3,473	3,435
Net Earnings	$ 12,866	$ 11,242	$ 11,121
Basic weighted average common shares	1,074	1,093	1,137
Basic earnings per share	$ 11.98	$ 10.29	$ 9.78
Diluted weighted average common shares	1,078	1,097	1,143
Diluted earnings per share	$ 11.94	$ 10.25	$ 9.73

THE HOME DEPOT, INC.
CONSOLIDATED BALANCE SHEETS

in millions, except per share data	**End of Fiscal 2020**	**End of Fiscal 2019**
Assets		
Current assets:		
Cash and cash equivalents	$ 7,895	$ 2,133
Receivables, net	2,992	2,106
Merchandise inventories	16,627	14,531
Other current assets	963	1,040
Total current assets	28,477	19,810
Net property and equipment	24,705	22,770
Operating lease right-of-use assets	5,962	5,595
Goodwill	7,126	2,254
Other assets	4,311	807
Total assets	$70,581	$51,236
Liabilities and Stockholders' Equity		
Current liabilities:		
Short-term debt	$ –	$ 974
Accounts payable	11,606	7,787
Accrued salaries and related expenses	2,463	1,494
Sales taxes payable	774	605
Deferred revenue	2,823	2,116
Income taxes payable	193	55
Current installments of long-term debt	1,416	1,839

(Continued)

EXHIBIT 13.1

Continued

in millions, except per share data	End of Fiscal 2020	End of Fiscal 2019
Current operating lease liabilities	828	828
Other accrued expenses	3,063	2,677
Total current liabilities	23,166	18,375
Long-term debt, excluding current installments	35,822	28,670
Long-term operating lease liabilities	5,356	5,066
Deferred income taxes	1,131	706
Other long-term liabilities	1,807	1,535
Total liabilities	67,282	54,352
Common stock, par value $0.05; authorized: 10,000 shares; issued: 1,789 shares at end of Fiscal 2020, and 1,786 shares at end of Fiscal 2019; outstanding: 1,077 shares at end of Fiscal 2020 and end of Fiscal 2019	89	89
Paid-in capital	11,540	11,001
Retained earnings	58,134	51,729
Accumulated other comprehensive loss	(671)	(739)
Treasury stock, at cost, 712 shares at end of Fiscal 2020, and 709 shares at end of Fiscal 2019	(65,793)	(65,196)
Total stockholders' equity (deficit)	3,299	(3,116)
Total liabilities and stockholders' equity	$70,581	$51,236

THE HOME DEPOT, INC.

CONSOLIDATED STATEMENTS OF CASH FLOWS

in millions	Fiscal 2020	Fiscal 2019	Fiscal 2018
Cash Flows from Operating Activities:			
Net earnings	$12,866	$11,242	$11,121
Reconciliation of net earnings to net cash provided by operating activities:			
Depreciation and amortization	2,519	2,296	2,152
Stock-based compensation expense	310	251	282
Impairment loss	–	–	247
Changes in receivables, net	(465)	(170)	33
Changes in merchandise inventories	(1,657)	(593)	(1,244)
Changes in other current assets	43	(135)	(257)
Changes in accounts payable and accrued expenses	5,118	32	870
Changes in deferred revenue	702	334	80
Changes in income taxes payable	(149)	44	(42)
Changes in deferred income taxes	(569)	202	26
Other operating activities	121	184	(103)
Net cash provided by operating activities	18,839	13,687	13,165
Cash Flows from Investing Activities:			
Capital expenditures	(2,463)	(2,678)	(2,442)
Payments for businesses acquired, net	(7,780)	–	(21)
Other investing activities	73	25	47
Net cash used in investing activities	(10,170)	(2,653)	(2,416)
Cash Flows from Financing Activities:			
Repayments of short-term debt, net	(974)	(365)	(220)
Proceeds from long-term debt, net of discount and premiums	7,933	3,420	3,466
Repayments of long-term debt	(2,872)	(1,070)	(1,209)

(Continued)

EXHIBIT 13.1

Concluded

in millions	Fiscal 2020	Fiscal 2019	Fiscal 2018
Repurchases of common stock	(791)	(6,965)	(9,963)
Proceeds from sales of common stock	326	280	236
Cash dividends	(6,451)	(5,958)	(4,704)
Other financing activities	(154)	(140)	(153)
Net cash used in financing activities	(2,983)	(10,798)	(12,547)
Change in cash and cash equivalents	5,686	236	(1,798)
Effect of exchange rate changes on cash and cash equivalents	76	119	(19)
Cash and cash equivalents at beginning of year	2,133	1,778	3,595
Cash and cash equivalents at end of year	$ 7,895	$ 2,133	$ 1,778
Supplemental Disclosures:			
Cash paid for income taxes	$ 4,654	$ 3,220	$ 3,774
Cash paid for interest, net of interest capitalized	1,241	1,112	1,035
Non-cash capital expenditures	274	136	248

Source: The Home Depot, Inc.

ORGANIZATION OF THE CHAPTER

The Investment Decision

Understanding a Company's Strategy

Financial Statement Analysis

- Time Series Analysis
- Cross Sectional Analysis

Component Percentages and Ratio Analysis

- Component Percentages
- Ratio Analysis
- Profitability Ratios
  1. Return on Equity Ratio (ROE)
  2. Return on Assets Ratio (ROA)
  3. Gross Profit Margin Ratio
  4. Net Profit Margin Ratio
  5. Earnings per Share Ratio (EPS)
  6. Quality of Income Ratio
- Asset Turnover Ratios
  7. Total Asset Turnover Ratio
  8. Fixed Asset Turnover Ratio
  9. Receivables Turnover Ratio
  10. Inventory Turnover Ratio
- Liquidity Ratios
  11. Current Ratio
  12. Quick Ratio
  13. Cash Ratio
- Solvency Ratios
  14. Times Interest Earned Ratio
  15. Cash Coverage Ratio
  16. Debt-to-Equity Ratio
- Market Ratios
  17. Price/Earnings (P/E) Ratio
  18. Dividend Yield Ratio

Interpreting Ratios and Other Analytical Considerations

- Other Financial Information

THE INVESTMENT DECISION

Of the people who use financial statements, investors are perhaps the single largest group. They often rely on the advice of professional analysts, who develop recommendations on widely held stocks such as **The Home Depot**. Investors who use analysts' reports pay close attention to their recommendations. As this book was being written, 14 professional analysts issued the following investment recommendations for The Home Depot:

Source: NASDAQ.com.

Perhaps the most important thing to notice about this summary of investment recommendations is that not all analysts agree on whether investors should purchase The Home Depot's stock. This level of disagreement shows that financial analysis is part art and part science.

In considering an investment in stock, investors should evaluate the company's future income and growth potential on the basis of three factors:

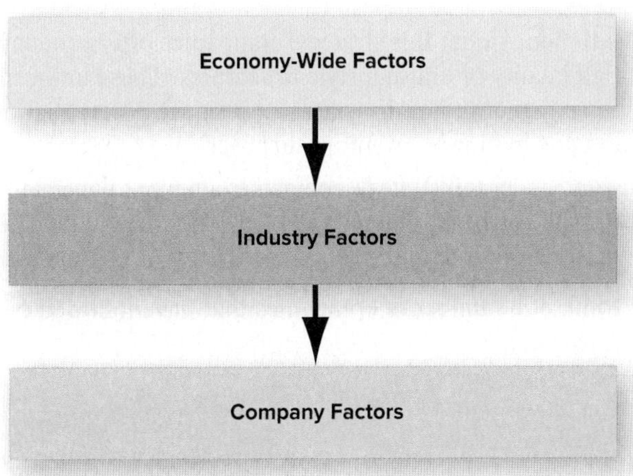

1. **Economy-wide factors.** Often the overall health of the economy has a direct impact on the performance of an individual company. Investors should consider data such as the unemployment rate, general inflation rate, and changes in interest rates. For example, **J.P. Morgan**'s research report discusses both "disposable income" and "consumer savings" as factors to consider when analyzing The Home Depot (*J.P. Morgan North America Equity Research, January 7, 2021*).
2. **Industry factors.** Certain events can impact a specific industry differently than other industries or the economy as a whole. For example, a research report from **Oppenheimer** Equity Research emphasizes that even during a general economic downturn due to the COVID-19 pandemic, data ". . .highlights clearly continued, persistent outsized demand growth within the home improvement category, as consumers spend more time at home. . ." (*Oppenheimer Equity Research, January 29, 2021*).
3. **Individual company factors.** To properly analyze a company, good analysts do not rely solely on the information reported in a company's financial statements and other reports. They visit the company, buy its products, and read about it in the business press. If you are considering an investment in The Home Depot, you should visit its stores and assess its product offerings and the service it provides to customers in addition to analyzing its financial statements and other reports. An example of company-specific information is contained in the J.P. Morgan report, which states that The Home Deport ". . .believes its supply chain capabilities and overall proposition (price and assortment) are differentiating factors for the Pro customer vs. its competitors. . ." (*J.P. Morgan North America Equity Research, January 7, 2021*). Analysts who, over time, have repeatedly visited The Home Depot stores are in a good position to assess whether the company's statements about price and assortment are true.

Besides considering these factors, investors should understand a company's business strategy when evaluating its financial statements. A company's business strategy directly affects the accounts you will see on its financial statements.

LEARNING OBJECTIVE 13-1

Explain how a company's business strategy affects financial statement analysis.

UNDERSTANDING A COMPANY'S STRATEGY

Financial statement analysis involves more than just "crunching numbers." Before you start looking at numbers, you should know what you are looking for. While financial statements reflect transactions, each of those transactions is the result of a company's operating decisions as it implements its business strategy.

Businesses can earn a high rate of return by following different strategies. There are two fundamental strategies:

1. **Product differentiation.** Under this strategy, companies offer products with unique benefits, such as high quality or unusual style or features. These unique benefits allow a company to charge higher prices. In general, a product differentiation strategy results in higher profit margins but lower inventory turnover.
2. **Cost differentiation.** Under this strategy, companies attempt to operate more efficiently than their competitors, which permits them to offer lower prices to attract customers. In general, a cost differentiation strategy results in lower profit margins but higher inventory turnover.

You can probably think of a number of companies that have followed one of these two basic strategies. Here are some examples:

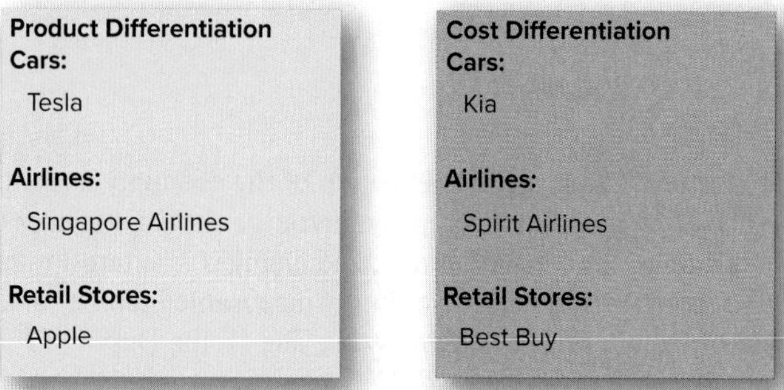

The best place to start financial analysis is with a solid understanding of a company's business strategy. To evaluate how well a company is doing, you must know what managers are trying to do. You can learn a great deal about a company's business strategy by reading its annual report or 10-K, especially the letter from the president and management's discussion and analysis (MD&A). It also is useful to read other reports (e.g., sustainability or ESG reports) and articles about the company in the business press.

The Home Depot's business strategy is described in its 10-K report as follows:

THE HOME DEPOT
REAL WORLD EXCERPT:
10-K Report

> Our ability to operate successfully and meet the needs of our customers in the pandemic environment successfully was due in significant part to the transformational journey we began in 2017 to create the One Home Depot experience, our vision of an interconnected, frictionless shopping experience that enables our customers to seamlessly blend the digital and physical worlds. Our multi-year accelerated investment program to create this experience is now largely complete. Our investments have been guided by the following strategies:
>
> - Invest using a "customer-back" approach
> - Reinforce our position as the product authority in home improvement

- Deliver a best-in-class, interconnected shopping experience
- Extend our low-cost provider position

These strategic investments are designed to extend our current competitive advantages. We believe our primary competitive advantages are: (1) our culture and associates, (2) our premium real estate, (3) our world-class merchandising organization, (4) our flexible supply chain, and (5) our digital experience. Taken together, our One Home Depot vision and execution of the related strategies are helping us to meet our two principal business objectives: continue to grow our share of the highly competitive market in which we operate and deliver shareholder value. We believe that our efforts to build the One Home Depot experience, and the groundwork we laid in these areas over the past decade, position us well to meet our objectives in any environment and have been particularly important in navigating the challenges created by the pandemic. We achieved record sales in fiscal 2020, while remaining focused on two key priorities: the safety and well-being of our associates and customers and providing our customers and communities with the products and services they need.

Source: The Home Depot, Inc.

This description of The Home Depot's strategy serves as a guide for our financial analysis.

FINANCIAL STATEMENT ANALYSIS

LEARNING OBJECTIVE 13-2

Discuss ways to analyze financial statements.

Analyzing financial data without a basis for comparison is not informative. For example, would you be impressed with a company that earned $1 million last year? You are probably thinking, "It depends." A $1 million profit might be very good for a company that lost money the year before but not good for a company that made $500 million the preceding year. It might be good for a small company but not for a very large company. And it might be considered good if all the other companies in the industry lost money the same year but not good if they all earned much larger profits.

As you can see from this simple example, financial results cannot be evaluated in isolation. To properly analyze the information reported in financial statements, you must develop appropriate comparisons. The task of finding appropriate comparisons requires judgment and is not always easy. Financial analysis is a sophisticated skill, not a mechanical process.

There are two general methods for making financial comparisons. The first compares a company to itself in prior years. The second compares a company to other companies at a point in time or across time.

1. **Comparing across time.** In this type of analysis, which often is referred to as "time-series analysis," information is compared over time. For example, a key measure of performance for most retail companies is the change in sales at existing stores, which often is referred to as "comparable store sales." The time-series chart below shows that **The Home Depot**'s comparable store sales growth over the last five years. This chart clearly shows the uptick in home improvement projects in 2020.

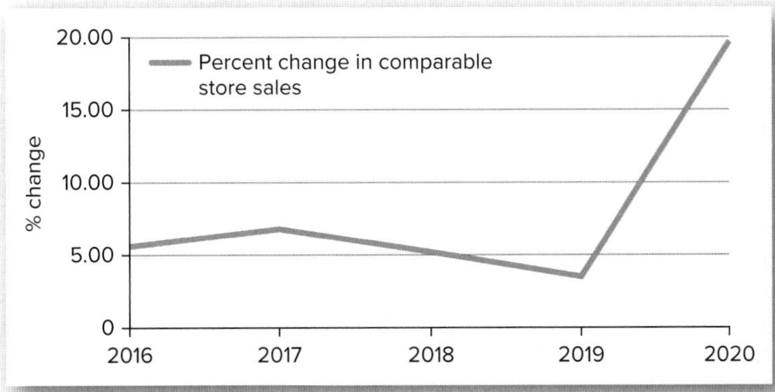

Source: The Home Depot, Inc.

The notes to the financial statements help explain why:

THE HOME DEPOT
REAL WORLD EXCERPT:
10-K Report

> Comparable sales is a measure that highlights the performance of our existing locations and websites by measuring the change in net sales for a period over the comparable prior-period of equivalent length. Comparable sales includes sales at all locations, physical and online, open greater than 52 weeks (including remodels and relocations) and excludes closed stores. Retail stores become comparable on the Monday following their 52nd week of operation.
> Total comparable sales increased 19.7 percent in fiscal 2020, reflecting a 10.5 percent increase in comparable average ticket and an 8.6 percent increase in comparable customer transactions.

Source: The Home Depot, Inc.

2. **Comparing across companies.** In this type of analysis, which often is referred to as "cross-sectional analysis," information for multiple companies is compared at a point in time or across time. We have seen that financial results are often affected by industry and economy-wide factors. By comparing a company with other companies in the same line of business, an analyst can gain better insight into the company's performance.

Finding comparable companies is often difficult. Few companies do the exact same thing as their competitors. For example, **Gap**, **Nordstrom**, **Target**, **Walmart**, and **Urban Outfitters** are all apparel retailers, but not all could be considered comparable companies for purposes of financial analysis. These retailers offer different levels of quality and appeal to different types of customers.

Tip Remember the phrase "garbage in, garbage out" when considering industry information found on the Internet. Make sure you know what formulas are being used to calculate a ratio and where the ratio inputs are coming from before relying on the ratio's output for financial analysis.

The federal government has developed the North American Industry Classification System (NAICS) for use in reporting economic data. The system assigns a specific industry code to each corporation based on its business operations. Analysts often use these six-digit codes to identify companies that have similar business operations. In addition, you can find multiple online resources, such as Yahoo! Finance or Google Finance, that provide industry information. Because of the diversity of companies included in any given industry classification, and the potential difference in how ratios are calculated, these data should be used with great care. For this reason, some analysts prefer to compare two companies that are very similar instead of using industry-wide comparisons.

A QUESTION OF ETHICS

Insider Information

A company's accountants often are aware of important financial information before it is made available to the public. This is called *insider information.* Some people might be tempted to buy or sell stock based on insider information, but to do so is a serious criminal offense. The Securities and Exchange Commission has brought a number of cases against individuals who traded on insider information. Their convictions resulted in large fines and time served in jail.

In some cases, determining whether something is insider information is difficult. For example, an individual could overhear a comment made in the company elevator by two executives. Is this insider information? A well-respected Wall Street investment banker offers good advice on dealing with such situations: "If you are not sure if something is right or wrong, apply the newspaper headline test. Ask yourself how you would feel to have your family and friends read about what you had done in the newspaper." Interestingly, many people who have spent time in jail and lost small fortunes in fines because of insider trading say that the most difficult part of the process was telling their families.

To uphold the highest ethical standard, many public accounting firms have adopted rules that prevent their staff from investing in companies that they audit. Such rules are designed to ensure that a company's auditors will not be tempted to engage in insider trading.

COMPONENT PERCENTAGES AND RATIO ANALYSIS

LEARNING OBJECTIVE 13-3

Compute and interpret component percentages.

Component Percentages

All analysts use various tools to analyze a company's financial statements. Two popular tools are **component percentages** and **ratio analysis**. Component percentages express each item on a financial statement as a percentage of a single base amount. The base amount on the income statement is net sales. To compute component percentages on the income statement, each amount reported is divided by net sales. The base amount on the balance sheet is total assets. To compute component percentages on the balance sheet, each amount is divided by total assets.

Exhibit 13.2 shows a component percentage analysis for **The Home Depot**'s income statement. The percentages reported in Exhibit 13.2 were calculated by taking the dollar amounts reported on The Home Depot's income statement shown in Exhibit 13.1 and dividing them by net sales. If you simply reviewed the dollar amounts on the income statement, you might miss important insights. For example, cost of sales expense increased by $14,604 million in fiscal 2020. This increase might seem to reflect a decline in operating efficiency until it is compared with sales productivity. A component percentage analysis provides an important insight: This expense category essentially stayed constant at approximately 66 percent from 2018 to 2020, reflecting that The Home Depot was able to increase sales without having to pay more on average for the items sold to generate those sales.

The component analysis (in Exhibit 13.2) also reflects that net income (which The Home Depot refers to as "net earnings") has remained relatively constant at just below or just above 10 percent over the three-year period. This suggests that The Home Depot is finding ways to maintain its operating efficiency across time.

EXHIBIT 13.2 Component Percentages for The Home Depot

	Fiscal 2020		Fiscal 2019		Fiscal 2018	
dollars in millions	$	% of Net Sales	$	% of Net Sales	$	% of Net Sales
Net sales	$132,110		$110,225		$108,203	
Cost of sales		66.0%		65.9%		65.7%
Gross profit	44,853	34.0	37,572	34.1	37,160	34.3
Operating expenses:						
Selling, general and administrative	24,447	18.5	19,740	17.9	19,513	18.0
Depreciation and amortization	2,128	1.6	1,989	1.8	1,870	1.7
Impairment loss	–	–	–	–	247	0.2
Total operating expenses	26,575	20.1	21,729	19.7	21,630	20.0
Operating income	18,278	13.8	15,843	14.4	15,530	14.4
Interest and other (income) expense:						
Interest and investment income	(47)	–	(73)	(0.1)	(93)	(0.1)
Interest expense	1,347	1.0	1,201	1.1	1,051	1.0
Other	–	–	–	–	16	–
Interest and other, net	1,300	1.0	1,128	1.0	974	0.9
Earnings before provision for income taxes	16,978	12.9	14,715	13.3	14,556	13.5
Provision for income taxes	4,112	3.1	3,473	3.2	3,435	3.2
Net earnings	$ 12,866	9.7%	$ 11,242	10.2%	$ 11,121	10.3

Source: The Home Depot, Inc.

BUSINESS ANALYTICS

Using Data Visualization Tools to Assess a Company's Performance

Many analysts use data visualization tools (e.g., Tableau or Microsoft BI) to help them analyze a company's financial data. This type of data analytics is especially useful when communicating findings during meetings or in printed form. The nearby bar chart visually displays key income percentages for **The Home Depot** from Exhibit 13.2, along with comparable data from its competitor, **Lowe's**. The chart allows you to easily see that The Home Depot and Lowe's have comparable gross profit margins, but that The Home Depot has higher operating, pre-tax, and net income margins.

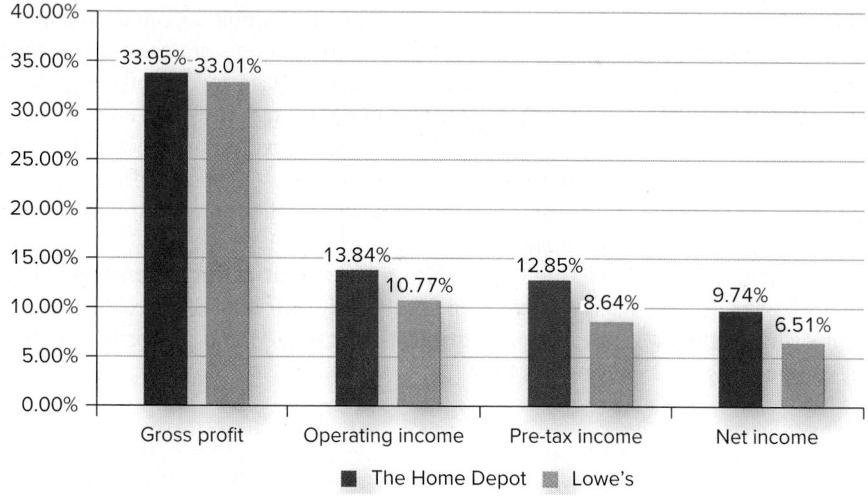

Source: Data from The Home Depot, Inc., and Lowe's

Ratio Analysis

Component percentages are a type of ratio. Ratios simply express one number relative to another number. With component percentages, both the numerator and the denominator of the ratio come from the same financial statement, either the income statement or the balance sheet. This does not have to be the case. As an example, assume you want to know how effective a company is in using its assets to generate net income. Answering this question is difficult if you only know that the company earned net income of \$500,000. Comparing income to total assets provides additional insights. If total assets are \$5 million, for example, then the relationship of earnings to assets is \$500,000 ÷ \$5,000,000 = 10%. This measure indicates a different level of performance than would be the case if total assets were \$250 million. Ratio analysis helps decision makers identify significant relationships and make meaningful comparisons.

Of the many ratios that can be computed using a company's financial statements, analysts focus on those that are most useful in a given situation. Comparing cost of goods sold to long-term debt is not meaningful because these items have no natural relationship. Instead, an analyst often will compute certain widely used ratios and then decide which additional ratios could be relevant to a particular decision. Research and development costs as a percentage of sales is not a meaningful ratio for some companies, for example, but it is useful when analyzing companies that depend on new products, such as a pharmaceutical company.

When you compute ratios, remember a basic fact about financial statements: Balance sheet amounts are as of a specific point in time while income statement amounts relate to a period of time. To adjust for this difference, most analysts use the average balance sheet amount when comparing a balance sheet number to an income statement number. The average is computed by adding the beginning and ending amounts of a balance sheet account and dividing the total by two. Making this adjustment allows you to compare the average balance sheet amount that corresponds to the period for which the income statement number was generated. In specific cases, analysts will use the ending balance sheet amount. Doing so is appropriate only if there is not a significant difference between the beginning and ending balances. For consistency, we use average balance sheet amounts unless there is a specific reason to use the ending balance. When that is the case, we will provide the logic behind our choice.

Financial statement analysis involves a lot of judgment. The more clearly you define the questions you want answered, the easier it is to select the most appropriate ratios to compute. We will discuss several ratios that are appropriate to most situations. They can be grouped into the categories shown in Exhibit 13.3.[1]

Tip Remember that when a ratio compares an income statement amount to a balance sheet amount, the average balance sheet amount is typically used. You can calculate the average by adding the beginning and ending amounts of the balance sheet account and dividing the total by two.

Profitability Ratios

LEARNING OBJECTIVE 13-4

Compute and interpret profitability ratios.

Profitability is a primary measure of the overall success of a company. **Profitability ratios** focus on net income and how it compares to other amounts reported on the financial statements. Return on equity is a widely used measure of profitability.

1. Return on Equity Ratio (ROE)

Return on equity relates income earned to the investment made by a company's owners. This ratio reflects the simple fact that investors expect to earn a return on the money they invest in a company. The return on equity ratio is computed as follows:

$$\text{Return on Equity Ratio (ROE)} = \frac{\text{Net Income}}{\text{Average Total Stockholders'' Equity}}$$

$$\text{The Home Depot 2020} = \frac{\$12{,}866}{\$3{,}299^*} = 390.00\%$$

*We normally use average stockholders' equity for the denominator; however, because The Home Depot reported negative stockholders' equity in fiscal 2019, we are using the ending balance for fiscal year 2020. For comparability reasons, we are also using the ending balance for Lowe's.

The Home Depot earned 390.00 percent on the owners' investment. Another way to interpret this number is to say that, on average, for every $1.00 equity investors contributed to The Home Depot, the company earned $3.90 in fiscal 2020. Was this return good or bad? To answer this question, we need to compare 390.00 percent to what The Home Depot's ROE was in prior years, or to its competitors' ROE in 2020. ROE for **Lowe's** was 406.05 percent, indicating that Lowe's produced a better return on its owners' investment than did The Home Depot in fiscal 2020. We must interpret this ratio with caution, however, given The Home Depot has recently repurchased a considerable amount of treasury stock from the market, which has caused its stockholders' equity to be negative in fiscal 2019 and fiscal 2018.

2. Return on Assets Ratio (ROA)

Another test of profitability compares income to the total assets used to generate the income. Return on assets is computed as follows:

$$\text{Return on Assets Ratio (ROA)} = \frac{\text{Net Income}}{\text{Average Total Assets}}$$

$$\text{The Home Depot 2020} = \frac{\$12{,}866}{\$60{,}909^*} = 21.12\%$$

$$\frac{^*(\$51{,}236 + \$70{,}581)}{2} = \$60{,}909$$

This implies that, on average, for every $1.00 of assets reported on The Home Depot's balance sheet, the company earned just over 21 cents in fiscal 2020. The ROA for Lowe's was

[1]The numbers for The Home Depot used throughout the following examples are taken from the financial statements in Exhibit 13.1.

EXHIBIT 13.3

Widely Used Accounting Ratios

RATIO	BASIC COMPUTATION*
Profitability Ratios	
1. Return on equity ratio (ROE)	$\frac{\text{Net Income}}{\text{Average Total Stockholders' Equity}}$
2. Return on assets ratio (ROA)	$\frac{\text{Net Income}}{\text{Average Total Assets}}$
3. Gross profit margin ratio	$\frac{\text{Gross Profit}}{\text{Net Sales Revenue}}$
4. Net profit margin ratio	$\frac{\text{Net Income}}{\text{Net Sales Revenue}}$
5. Earnings per share ratio (EPS)	$\frac{\text{Net Income}}{\text{Weighted Average Number of Common Shares Outstanding}}$
6. Quality of income ratio	$\frac{\text{Cash Flows from Operating Activities}}{\text{Net Income}}$
Asset Turnover Ratios	
7. Total asset turnover ratio	$\frac{\text{Net Sales Revenue}}{\text{Average Total Assets}}$
8. Fixed asset turnover ratio	$\frac{\text{Net Sales Revenue}}{\text{Average Net Fixed Assets}}$
9. Receivables turnover ratio	$\frac{\text{Net Credit Sales}}{\text{Average Net Receivables}}$
10. Inventory turnover ratio	$\frac{\text{Cost of Goods Sold}}{\text{Average Inventory}}$
Liquidity Ratios	
11. Current ratio	$\frac{\text{Current Assets}}{\text{Current Liabilities}}$
12. Quick ratio	$\frac{\text{Cash \& Cash Equivalents + Net Accounts Receivable + Marketable Securities}}{\text{Current Liabilities}}$
13. Cash ratio	$\frac{\text{Cash \& Cash Equivalents}}{\text{Current Liabilities}}$
Solvency Ratios	
14. Times interest earned ratio	$\frac{\text{Net Income + Interest Expense + Income Tax Expense}}{\text{Interest Expense}}$
15. Cash coverage ratio	$\frac{\text{Cash Flows from Operating Activities}}{\text{Interest Paid}}$
16. Debt-to-equity ratio	$\frac{\text{Total Liabilities}}{\text{Total Stockholders' Equity}}$
Market Ratios	
17. Price/Earnings (P/E) ratio	$\frac{\text{Market Price per Share}}{\text{Earnings per Share}}$
18. Dividend yield ratio	$\frac{\text{Dividends per Share}}{\text{Market Price per Share}}$

*We list the basic computation for each ratio. Analysts sometimes adjust these basic computations depending on the analysis they are conducting.

13.54 percent, considerably lower than the ROA for **The Home Depot**. This comparison indicates that The Home Depot is utilizing its assets to generate income more effectively than Lowe's.

Some analysts modify the basic ROA computation listed above by adding interest expense (net of tax) to the numerator of the ratio. The logic for making this adjustment is that the denominator of the ratio includes resources (assets) provided by both owners and creditors, so the numerator should include the return that was available to both groups. Interest expense is therefore added back because it was previously deducted in the computation of net income. Note, too, that when making this adjustment, interest expense often is measured net of income tax. The net of tax amount is used when interest is deductible for tax purposes, which it is up to a cap.

3. Gross Profit Margin Ratio

The gross profit margin ratio (also referred to as the gross profit percentage) reflects gross profit as a percent of sales. If not shown separately on a company's income statement, gross profit is computed by subtracting cost of sales from net sales. The gross profit margin ratio is computed as follows:

$$\text{Gross Profit Margin Ratio} = \frac{\text{Gross Profit}}{\text{Net Sales Revenue}}$$

$$\text{The Home Depot 2020} = \frac{\$44{,}853}{\$132{,}110} = 33.95\%$$

Lowe's had a similar gross profit margin ratio: 33.01 percent. This implies that, after subtracting the direct costs associated with selling products, both The Home Depot and Lowe's had between 33 and 34 cents of each dollar of sales remaining to cover other expenses. The fact that The Home Depot and Lowe's have almost identical gross profit margin ratios indicates that the two companies likely follow similar business strategies and sell similar products, perhaps even sourced from the same suppliers.

4. Net Profit Margin Ratio

The net profit margin ratio reflects net income as a percent of sales. It is computed as follows:

$$\text{Net Profit Margin Ratio} = \frac{\text{Net Income}}{\text{Net Sales Revenue}}$$

$$\text{The Home Depot 2020} = \frac{\$12{,}866}{\$132{,}110} = 9.74\%$$

For fiscal 2020, each dollar of The Home Depot's sales generated over 9 cents of profit. In comparison, Lowe's earned 6.51 percent, or approximately 6.5 cents for each dollar of sales. These numbers reflect that for each dollar of sales, The Home Depot is subtracting just under 91 cents in expenses while Lowe's is subtracting approximately 94 cents.

While both the gross profit margin ratio and the net profit margin ratio are good measures of operating efficiency, you should be careful not to analyze them in isolation because they do not consider the resources needed to earn income. It is very difficult to compare profit margins for companies in different industries. For example, profit margins are low in the food industry while profit margins in the jewelry industry are high. Both types of businesses can be quite profitable, however, because a high sales volume can compensate for a low profit margin. Grocery stores have low profit margins, but they generate a high sales volume from a broad customer base that tends to purchase items on a daily or weekly basis. Although jewelry stores earn comparatively more profit from each sales dollar, fewer people purchase jewelry and typically do so only occasionally. Thus, jewelry stores tend to have fewer sales transactions than grocery stores.

The trade-off between profit margin and sales volume can be stated in simple terms: Would you prefer to have 5 percent of $1,000,000 or 10 percent of $100,000? As you can see, a larger profit margin percentage is not always better in terms of total dollars earned.

5. Earnings per Share Ratio (EPS)

The earnings per share ratio is a measure of return on investment that is based on the number of common shares outstanding. EPS is computed as follows:

$$\text{Earnings per Share Ratio (EPS)} = \frac{\text{Net Income}}{\text{Weighted Average Number of Shares Outstanding}}$$

$$\text{The Home Depot 2020} = \frac{\$12{,}866}{1{,}074} = \$11.98 \text{ per share}$$

You often can obtain the weighted average number of shares outstanding, as well as EPS, from the bottom of a company's income statement (see Exhibit 13.1). Earnings per share is probably the single most widely reported ratio, and it is the only ratio required by GAAP. Analysts develop their own estimates of future EPS and the stock price of a company may change significantly if the actual EPS differs from their estimate. Lowe's EPS in fiscal 2020 was \$7.77 per share, so less than **The Home Depot**'s EPS. When analyzing EPS numbers for a company, keep in mind that managers can significantly alter EPS by selling shares of common stock or repurchasing shares of common stock. For example, when managers choose to repurchase shares of common stock, it reduces the denominator of the EPS ratio but does not affect the numerator. The overall effect is an increase in EPS.

6. Quality of Income Ratio

Most financial analysts are concerned about the quality of a company's income because some accounting procedures can be used to report higher income. For example, a company that uses a short estimated life for a depreciable asset will report lower income in the asset's early years relative to an identical company that uses a longer estimated life. One method of evaluating the quality of a company's income is to compare its reported income to its cash flows from operating activities, as follows:

$$\text{Quality of Income Ratio} = \frac{\text{Cash Flows from Operating Activities}}{\text{Net Income}}$$

$$\text{The Home Depot 2020} = \frac{\$18{,}839}{\$12{,}866} = 1.46$$

A general rule of thumb is that a quality of income ratio that is higher than 1.00 indicates high-quality income because each dollar of income is supported by one or more dollars of cash flows. A ratio that is below 1.00 represents lower-quality income. Lowe's quality of income ratio is 1.89, so both Lowe's and The Home Depot have quality of income ratios above 1.00.

PAUSE FOR FEEDBACK

We have discussed several profitability ratios. Profitability ratios focus on income and how it compares to other amounts reported on the financial statements. Next we will discuss asset turnover ratios. Before you move on, complete the following to test your understanding of the concepts we have covered so far.

SELF-STUDY QUIZ

Show how to compute the following ratios:

1. Return on equity ratio =
2. Return on assets ratio =
3. Net profit margin ratio =

Answers are on the next page.

GUIDED HELP 13-1 

For additional step-by-step video instruction on calculating ratios, go to mhhe.com/libby_gh13-1.

Recommended Homework: M13-3, M13-4, E13-5, P13-3

Asset Turnover Ratios

LEARNING OBJECTIVE 13-5

Compute and interpret asset turnover ratios.

Asset turnover ratios focus on capturing how efficiently a company uses its assets. For example, acquiring and selling inventory is a key activity for many companies. The inventory turnover ratio helps analysts evaluate a company's ability to sell its inventory. Another example is the receivables turnover ratio, which helps analysts evaluate a company's ability to collect its receivables. These and other asset turnover ratios are discussed below.

7. Total Asset Turnover Ratio

The total asset turnover ratio captures how well a company uses its assets to generate revenue. The ratio is computed as follows:

$$\text{Total Asset Turnover Ratio} = \frac{\text{Net Sales Revenue}}{\text{Average Total Assets}}$$

$$\text{The Home Depot 2020} = \frac{\$132{,}110}{\$60{,}909^*} = 2.17$$

$$\frac{^*(\$51{,}236 + \$70{,}581)}{2} = \$60{,}909$$

A total asset turnover ratio of 2.17 implies that, on average, each dollar of assets on **The Home Depot**'s balance sheet generates $2.17 of revenue. **Lowe's** total asset turnover ratio is 2.08. Comparing the two indicates that The Home Depot is slightly more effective than Lowe's at using its assets to generate revenue. As the table below indicates, The Home Depot's total asset turnover has declined over the last three years. This decline is likely something analysts will keep a close eye on in the future.

	2020	**2019**	**2018**
Total Asset Turnover	2.17	2.31	2.44

Solutions to SELF-STUDY QUIZ

1. $\text{Return on Equity Ratio} = \frac{\text{Net income}}{\text{Average Total Stockholders' Equity}}$

2. $\text{Return on Assets Ratio} = \frac{\text{Net Income}}{\text{Average Total Assets}}$

3. $\text{Net Profit Margin Ratio} = \frac{\text{Net Income}}{\text{Net Sales Revenue}}$

8. Fixed Asset Turnover Ratio

Whereas the total asset turnover ratio captures how well a firm uses *all* of its assets to generate revenues, the fixed asset turnover ratio focuses more narrowly on how well a company uses its *fixed assets* to generate revenues. The term *fixed assets* is synonymous with property, plant, and equipment. The ratio is computed as follows:

$$\text{Fixed Asset Turnover Ratio} = \frac{\text{Net Sales Revenue}}{\text{Average Net Fixed Assets}}$$

$$\text{The Home Depot 2020} = \frac{\$132{,}110}{\$23{,}738^*} = 5.57$$

$$\frac{^*(\$22{,}770 + \$24{,}705)}{2} = \$23{,}738$$

Lowe's fiscal 2020 fixed asset turnover ratio is 4.73. The Home Depot's ratio is higher, indicating it is more effective at using its fixed assets to generate revenues. For each dollar The Home Depot invested in property, plant, and equipment, the company was able to generate $5.57 in sales revenue, while Lowe's could generate only $4.73.

9. Receivables Turnover Ratio

Being able to efficiently collect accounts receivable is critical to a company. Analysts know this and therefore keep close watch on a company's receivables turnover ratio. The receivables turnover ratio is computed as follows:

$$\text{Receivables Turnover Ratio} = \frac{\text{Net Credit Sales}^*}{\text{Average Net Receivables}}$$

$$\text{The Home Depot 2020} = \frac{\$132{,}110}{\$2{,}549^\dagger} = 51.83 \text{ Times}$$

$$\frac{^\dagger(\$2{,}106 + \$2{,}992)}{2} = \$2{,}549$$

*If credit sales are not reported separately (which is typically the case), use total net sales as an approximation.

A high receivables turnover ratio suggests that a company collects its accounts receivable many times during a year. The Home Depot, on average, collects its accounts receivable over 51 times a year. Granting credit to customers with poor credit and ineffective collection efforts will produce a low receivables turnover ratio. While a very low ratio is obviously a problem, a very high ratio also can be troublesome because it suggests an overly stringent credit policy that could cause lost sales and profits.

Steve Hix/Corbis/Getty Images

The receivables turnover ratio often is converted to reflect the number of days, on average, it takes a company to collect its receivables. The computation is as follows:

$$\text{Average Days to Collect Receivables} = \frac{\text{Days in a Year}}{\text{Receivables Turnover Ratio}}$$

$$\text{The Home Depot 2020} = \frac{365}{51.83} = 7.04 \text{ Days}$$

The Home Depot's average days to collect receivables ratio implies that it takes the company an average of just over seven days to collect its accounts receivable. Although the receivables turnover ratio normally provides useful insights, the one for The Home Depot is not meaningful. It is highly unlikely that The Home Depot collects cash from its credit customers in just seven days. Because we did not know the amount of The Home Depot's credit sales, we used total sales as an approximation. In this case, the approximation is not reasonable. Most customers use a bank credit card such as MasterCard or Visa. From The Home Depot's perspective, a sales transaction involving a bank credit card is recorded as a cash sale because the credit card company quickly transfers cash to The Home Depot and then takes on the responsibility of collecting from the customer. As a result, many of The Home Depot's sales are actually cash sales, invalidating the assumption that total sales are a reasonable proxy for credit sales. This situation illustrates that ratio analysis involves more than the mere computation of numbers. Analysts must evaluate the results based on their understanding of a company's business strategy.

10. Inventory Turnover Ratio

Like the receivables turnover ratio, the inventory turnover ratio is a measure of operating efficiency. It is computed as follows:

$$\text{Inventory Turnover Ratio} = \frac{\text{Cost of Goods Sold}}{\text{Average Inventory}}$$

$$\text{The Home Depot 2020} = \frac{\$87{,}257}{\$15{,}579^*} = 5.60 \text{ Times}$$

$$\frac{^*(\$14{,}531 + \$16{,}627)}{2} = \$15{,}579$$

Because a company normally realizes profit each time inventory is sold, an increase in this ratio is usually favorable. If the ratio is too high, however, it may be an indication that sales were lost because desired items were not in stock. A company must balance the cost of holding inventory with the potential cost of losing a sale.

On average, The Home Depot's inventory was acquired and sold to customers over 5 times during the year. The inventory turnover ratio is critical for The Home Depot because of its business strategy. It wants to be able to offer customers the right product when they need it at a price that beats the competition. Inventory turnover for Lowe's was 4.09. Historically, The Home Depot has enjoyed an advantage over Lowe's in terms of inventory management. The Home Depot's effectiveness in inventory management means that the company is able to tie up less money in carrying inventory compared to Lowe's.

Turnover ratios vary significantly from one industry to the next. Companies in the food industry (grocery stores and restaurants) have high inventory turnover ratios because their inventory is subject to rapid deterioration. Companies that sell expensive merchandise (automobiles and high-fashion clothes) have much lower ratios because sales tend to be less frequent, but customers want to have a selection to choose from so companies in these industries must still carry significant inventory.

Like the receivables turnover ratio, the inventory turnover ratio often is converted to reflect the number of days, on average, it takes a company to sell its inventory. The computation is

$$\text{Average Days to Sell Inventory} = \frac{\text{Days in a Year}}{\text{Inventory Turnover Ratio}}$$

$$\text{The Home Depot 2020} = \frac{365}{5.60} = 65.18 \text{ Days}$$

Using Ratios to Analyze the Operating Cycle In Chapter 3, we introduced the concept of a company's operating cycle, which is the time it takes for a company to pay cash to its suppliers, sell goods to its customers, and collect cash from its customers. Analysts are interested in the operating cycle because it helps them evaluate a company's cash needs and is a good indicator of operating efficiency.

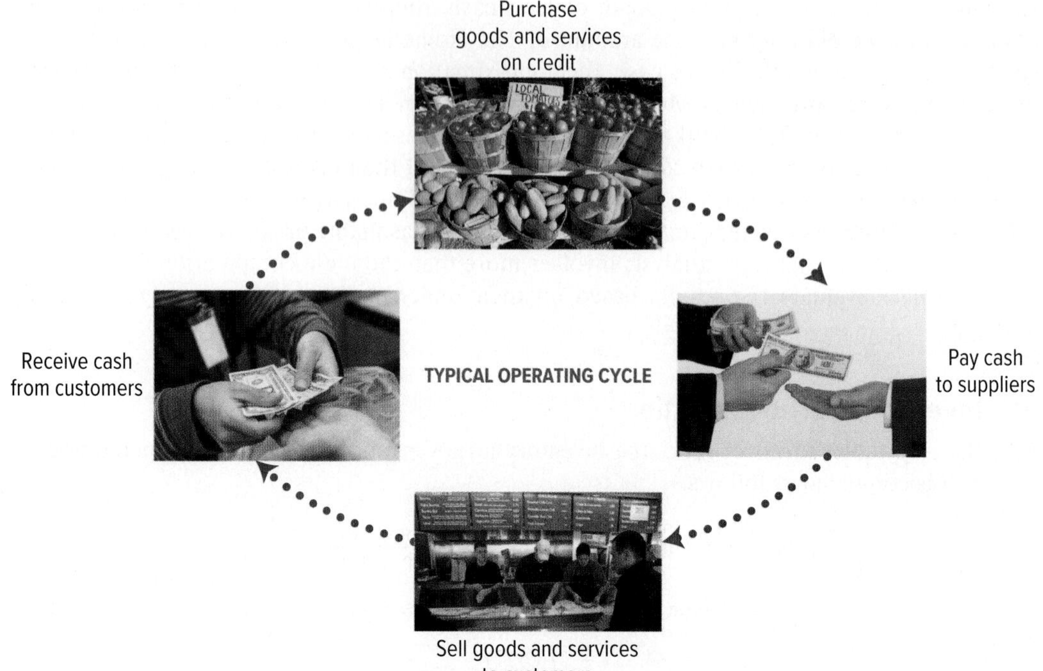

Top: Digital Vision/Getty Images; Left: Juanmonino/Getty Images; Right: Tetra Images/Getty Images; Bottom: Jeff Kowalsky/Bloomberg/Getty Images

The operating cycle for most companies involves three distinct phases: the acquisition of inventory, the sale of the inventory, and the collection of cash from the customer. We have discussed several ratios that are helpful when evaluating a company's operating cycle:

Ratio*	Operating Activity
Accounts payable turnover ratio	Purchase of inventory
Inventory turnover ratio	Sale of inventory
Receivables turnover ratio	Collection of cash from customers

*We discussed the accounts payable turnover ratio in Chapter 9. The inventory turnover ratio and the receivables turnover ratio are discussed in this chapter.

Each of the ratios measures the number of days it takes, on average, to complete an operating activity. We already have computed two of the needed ratios for The Home Depot, so if we compute the accounts payable turnover ratio, we can analyze the company's operating cycle:

$$\text{Accounts Payable Turnover Ratio} = \frac{\text{Cost of Goods Sold}}{\text{Average Accounts Payable}}$$

$$\text{The Home Depot 2020} = \frac{\$87{,}257}{\$9{,}697^*} = 9.00 \text{ Times}$$

$$\frac{^*(\$7{,}787 + \$11{,}606)}{2} = \$9{,}697$$

$$\text{Average Days to Pay Payables} = \frac{\text{Days in Year}}{\text{Accounts Payable Turnover Ratio}}$$

$$\text{The Home Depot 2017} = \frac{365}{9.00} = 40.56 \text{ Days}$$

The numbers of days it takes The Home Depot to complete each phase of its operating cycle are

Ratio	Time
Average days to pay payables	40.56 days
Average days to sell inventory	65.17 days
Average days to collect receivables	7.04 days

Examining each phase of the operating cycle helps us understand the cash needs of the company. **The Home Depot**, on average, pays for its inventory 40 days after it receives it. It takes, on average, just over 72 days (65.17 + 7.04) for it to sell its inventory and collect cash from its customers. Therefore, The Home Depot must invest cash in its operating activities 32 days (72 days − 40 days) between the time it pays its vendors and the time it collects from its customers. Companies prefer to minimize the time between paying vendors and collecting cash from customers because it frees up cash for other productive purposes. The Home Depot could reduce this time by slowing payments to creditors or by increasing how quickly it turns over its inventory.

FINANCIAL ANALYSIS

ROA Profit Driver Analysis and the DuPont Model

As introduced in Chapter 5, one of the most general frameworks for evaluating a company's profit drivers is to examine its Return on Assets (ROA). ROA can be broken down into two components:

ROA = **Net Profit Margin** × **Total Asset Turnover**

$$\frac{\textbf{Net Income}}{\textbf{Average Total Assets}} = \frac{\textbf{Net Income}}{\textbf{Net Sales Revenue}} \times \frac{\textbf{Net Sales Revenue}}{\textbf{Average Total Assets}}$$

In mathematical terms, canceling out like items on the right side of the above equation shows that the left and right sides are equivalent. Examining the additional information on the right side allows an analyst to tell a much richer story about a company's performance than can be told by examining just ROA. For example, a company can increase its ROA by increasing its net profit margin or by increasing the revenue it generates from its asset base (its total asset turnover).

Breaking down ROA into its two components allows you to more fully understand what underlies a company's performance. With this knowledge, you can better assess whether a company is effectively implementing its business strategy, especially when you examine how the ratios change across time. For example, The Home Depot's ROA in 2019 was 23.61 percent. ROA decreased to 21.12 percent in 2020. What drove the decrease? Examining the components of ROA reflects that The Home Depot's ROA decreased as a result of both its profit margin decreasing (from 10.20 percent in 2019 to 9.74 percent in 2020) and its asset turnover ratio decreasing (from 2.31 in 2019 to 2.17 in 2020). This implies that The Home Depot was less effective at using its assets to generate revenues and less effective at earning a profit on the revenues it did earn.

Some analysts include a third component in their analysis: financial leverage $\left(\frac{\text{average total assets}}{\text{average total stockholders' equity}}\right)$. When financial leverage is added to the model, it is commonly referred to as the **DuPont model.**

ROE = **Net Profit Margin** × **Total Asset Turnover** × **Financial Leverage**

$$\frac{\textbf{Net Income}}{\textbf{Average Total Stockholders' Equity}} = \frac{\textbf{Net Income}}{\textbf{Net Sales Revenue}} \times \frac{\textbf{Net Sales Revenue}}{\textbf{Average Total Assets}} \times \frac{\textbf{Average Total Assets}}{\textbf{Average Total Stockholders' Equity}}$$

Financial leverage is the difference between Return on Equity (ROE) and Return on Assets (ROA) and reflects the extent to which a company uses its liabilities to leverage up its return to stockholders. Financial leverage and the full DuPont model are discussed in more detail in Financial Statement Analysis classes.

LEARNING OBJECTIVE 13-6

Compute and interpret liquidity ratios.

Liquidity Ratios

Liquidity refers to a company's ability to meet its short-term obligations. Because most short-term obligations will be paid with current assets, **liquidity ratios** focus on the relationship between current assets and current liabilities. The ability to pay current liabilities is an important factor in evaluating a company's short-term financial strength. In this section, we discuss three ratios that are used to measure liquidity: the current ratio, the quick ratio, and the cash ratio.

11. Current Ratio

The current ratio measures to what extent a company's total current assets cover its total current liabilities on a specific date. It is computed as follows:

$$\text{Current Ratio} = \frac{\text{Current Assets}}{\text{Current Liabilities}}$$

$$\text{The Home Depot 2020} = \frac{\$28{,}477}{\$23{,}166} = 1.23$$

A ratio greater than 1 implies that a company's current assets are sufficient to cover its current liabilities. If a company's current ratio is less than 1, analysts will want to understand how the company intends to meet its short-term obligations. At the end of fiscal 2020, **The Home Depot** had $1.23 in current assets for each $1.00 in current liabilities. **Lowe's** had $1.19 in current assets for each $1.00 in current liabilities.

To properly use the current ratio, analysts must understand the nature of a company's business. Many manufacturing companies have developed sophisticated systems to minimize the amount of inventory they must hold. These systems, called *just-in-time inventory,* are designed to have an inventory item arrive just when it is needed. While these systems can work well for manufacturing companies, they typically do not work well for retail companies. Customers expect to find merchandise in the store when they want it, and it has proven difficult to precisely forecast consumer behavior. As a result, most retailers have comparatively high current ratios because they must carry large inventories. The Home Depot, for example, maintains an inventory of 35,000 different products in a typical store, and 1 million different products online.

The optimal level of the current ratio depends on the business environment in which a company operates. If cash flows are predictable and stable, the current ratio can be low, even less than 1. For example, **Procter & Gamble**, a strong and fiscally conservative company, often has a current ratio less than one; its current ratio for fiscal 2020 was 0.85. When cash flows are highly variable, a higher current ratio is desirable.

Analysts become concerned if a company's current ratio is high compared to that of other companies in its industry. A firm is operating inefficiently when it ties up too much money in inventory or accounts receivable. It is also important to keep in mind that current assets other than cash need to be converted to cash before they can be used to satisfy current obligations.

Erik S. Lesser/Bloomberg/Getty Images

12. Quick Ratio

The quick ratio, sometimes referred to as the **acid test**, is a more stringent test of short-term liquidity than is the current ratio. The quick ratio compares quick assets, defined as *cash and near-cash assets,* to current liabilities. Quick assets include cash, net accounts receivable, and marketable securities. Inventory is omitted from quick assets because of the uncertainty of the timing of cash flows from its sale. Prepaid expenses also are excluded from quick assets. The quick ratio is computed as follows:

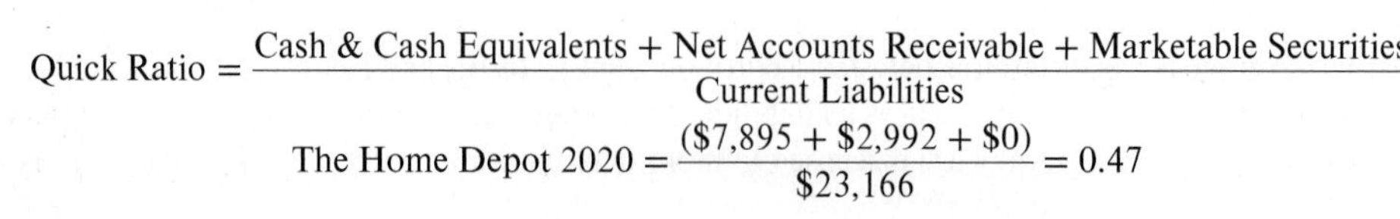

$$\text{Quick Ratio} = \frac{\text{Cash \& Cash Equivalents} + \text{Net Accounts Receivable} + \text{Marketable Securities}}{\text{Current Liabilities}}$$

$$\text{The Home Depot 2020} = \frac{(\$7{,}895 + \$2{,}992 + \$0)}{\$23{,}166} = 0.47$$

The quick ratio is a measure of whether the highly liquid assets of a company, those that can be converted to cash quickly, are sufficient to cover current liabilities. **The Home Depot** has 47 cents in cash and near-cash assets for every $1.00 in current liabilities. This margin of safety is typical of the retail industry and would be considered a sufficient margin in light of the large amount of cash The Home Depot generates from its operating activities ($18.8 billion in fiscal 2020). In comparison, the quick ratio for **Lowe's** is significantly lower (0.28).

13. Cash Ratio

Cash is the lifeblood of a business. Without cash, a company cannot pay its employees or meet its obligations to creditors. Even a profitable business will fail without sufficient cash. One measure of the adequacy of available cash, called the *cash ratio,* is computed as follows:

$$\text{Cash Ratio} = \frac{\text{Cash \& Cash Equivalents}}{\text{Current Liabilities}}$$

$$\text{The Home Depot 2020} = \frac{\$7{,}895}{\$23{,}166} = 0.34$$

In fiscal 2020, The Home Depot's cash ratio was 0.34. The Home Depot's cash ratio indicates that the company has on hand 34 cents of cash for each $1.00 of current liabilities. Would analysts be concerned about this number? Not likely. It is important to keep in mind that not all of The Home Depot's current liabilities need to be paid immediately. It therefore does not need to keep enough cash on hand at any point in time to cover all of its short-term obligations. As mentioned previously, The Home Depot's statement of cash flows shows that the company generated $18.8 billion in cash from its operating activities in fiscal 2020. As a result, it is highly likely that The Home Depot will have sufficient cash on hand when the time comes to meet any given current liability. Many analysts believe the cash ratio should not be too high because holding excessive amounts of cash implies that the company is not investing the cash in more productive assets to grow the business.

PAUSE FOR FEEDBACK

We have discussed several asset turnover ratios and liquidity ratios. Asset turnover ratios capture how efficiently a company uses its assets. Liquidity ratios focus on a company's ability to meet its short-term obligations. Next we will discuss solvency ratios. Before you move on, complete the following to test your understanding of the concepts we have covered so far.

SELF-STUDY QUIZ

Show how to compute the following ratios:

1. Current ratio =
2. Quick ratio =
3. Cash ratio =

After you have completed your answers, check them below.

GUIDED HELP 13-2 

For additional step-by-step video instruction on calculating ratios, go to mhhe.com/libby_gh13-2.

Recommended Homework: M13-5, M13-6, E13-8, E13-9, E13-10, E13-12, P13-3

Solutions to SELF-STUDY QUIZ

1. Current Ratio = Current Assets ÷ Current Liabilities
2. Quick Ratio = (Cash & Cash Equivalents + Net Accounts Receivable + Marketable Securities) ÷ Current Liabilities
3. Cash Ratio = Cash & Cash Equivalents ÷ Current Liabilities

LEARNING OBJECTIVE 13-7

Compute and interpret solvency ratios.

Solvency Ratios

Solvency refers to a company's ability to meet its long-term obligations. **Solvency ratios** measure this ability and include the times interest earned, cash coverage, and debt-to-equity ratios.

14. Times Interest Earned Ratio

Interest payments are a fixed obligation. If a company fails to make required interest payments, creditors may force it into bankruptcy. Because of the importance of meeting interest payments, analysts often compute a ratio called *times interest earned:*

$$\text{Times Interest Earned} = \frac{\text{Net Income} + \text{Interest Expense} + \text{Income Tax Expense}}{\text{Interest Expense}}$$

$$\text{The Home Depot 2020} = \frac{(\$12{,}866 + \$1{,}347 + \$4{,}112)}{\$1{,}347} = 13.60 \text{ Times}$$

The times interest earned ratio compares the income available to pay interest in a period to a company's interest obligation for the same period. Interest expense and income tax expense are included in the numerator because these amounts are available to pay interest. The times interest earned ratio represents a margin of protection for creditors. In fiscal 2020, **The Home Depot** generated $13.60 in income for each $1.00 of interest expense, a high ratio that indicates a secure position for creditors.

Some analysts believe that the times interest earned ratio is flawed because interest expense is paid in cash, not with net income. These analysts prefer to use the cash coverage ratio.

15. Cash Coverage Ratio

Given the importance of having enough cash on hand to make required interest payments, it is easy to understand why many analysts use the cash coverage ratio. It is computed as follows:

$$\text{Cash Coverage Ratio} = \frac{\text{Cash Flows from Operating Activities}}{\text{Interest Paid}}$$

$$\text{The Home Depot 2020} = \frac{\$18{,}839}{\$1{,}241} = 15.18 \text{ Times}$$

The Home Depot's cash coverage ratio shows that the company generated $15.18 in cash for every $1.00 of interest paid, which is strong coverage. Some analysts modify the basic cash coverage ratio by adding back to the numerator interest paid and income taxes paid. These amounts are typically disclosed separately at the bottom of a company's statement of cash flows, as they are for The Home Depot in Exhibit 13.1.

16. Debt-to-Equity Ratio

The debt-to-equity ratio expresses a company's debt as a proportion of its stockholders' equity. It is computed as follows:

$$\text{Debt-to-Equity Ratio} = \frac{\text{Total Liabilities}}{\text{Total Stockholders' Equity}}$$

$$\text{The Home Depot 2020} = \frac{\$67{,}282}{\$3{,}299} = 20.39$$

In fiscal 2020, for each $1.00 of stockholders' equity, The Home Depot had $20.39 of liabilities. By comparison, **Lowe's** debt-to-equity ratio was higher at $31.52.

Debt is risky for a company because specific interest payments must be made even if the company has not earned sufficient income to pay them. In contrast, dividends are always at the company's discretion and are not legally enforceable until they are declared by the board of directors. Thus, equity capital is associated with fewer contractual payments than is debt.

Despite the risk associated with debt, however, most companies obtain significant amounts of resources from creditors because of the advantages of borrowing money. For example, interest expense is a deductible expense, up to a cap, on a company's income tax return. Weighing these benefits against the contractual obligations that accompany debt results in companies using a mix of debt and equity financing. Analysts evaluate this mix by computing the debt-to-equity ratio.

Market Ratios

Some ratios, often called **market ratios**, relate the current price per share of a company's stock to the return that accrues to stockholders. Analysts find these ratios helpful because they are based on the current value of an owner's investment in a company.

LEARNING OBJECTIVE 13-8

Compute and interpret market ratios.

17. Price/Earnings (P/E) Ratio

The price/earnings (P/E) ratio measures the relationship between the current market price of a company's stock and its earnings per share. At the end of fiscal 2020, **The Home Depot**'s stock was trading at $269.13 per share. EPS for fiscal 2020 was $11.98. With this information, we can compute The Home Depot's P/E ratio as follows:

$$\text{Price/Earnings Ratio} = \frac{\text{Market Price per Share}}{\text{Earnings per Share}}$$

$$\text{The Home Depot 2020} = \frac{\$269.13}{\$11.98} = 22.47$$

This P/E ratio indicates that The Home Depot's stock was selling at a price that was just over 20 times its earnings per share. The P/E ratio reflects the stock market's assessment of a company's future performance. A high ratio indicates that earnings are expected to grow rapidly. **Lowe's** P/E ratio is 21.33. The P/E ratios for The Home Depot and Lowe's indicate that the market expects them to perform well in the future.

In economic terms, the value of a stock is determined by calculating the present value of the company's future earnings. Thus, a company that expects to increase its earnings in the future is worth more than one that cannot grow its earnings (assuming other factors are the same). However, while a high P/E ratio and good growth prospects are considered favorable, there are risks. When a company with a high P/E ratio does not meet the level of earnings expected by the market, the negative impact on its stock can be dramatic.

18. Dividend Yield Ratio

When investors buy stock, they can earn a return on their investment through dividends or price appreciation. The dividend yield ratio reflects the return on investment absent any capital appreciation, or, said differently, the return attributed solely to the dividends a company pays. Not all companies report the cash dividend they paid per share on their statement of cash flows or statement of stockholders' equity, so you may need to search their 10-K to find the information. **The Home Depot** paid dividends of $6.00 per share in fiscal 2020. At the end of fiscal 2020, its stock price was $269.13 per share. Its dividend yield ratio is computed as follows:

$$\text{Dividend Yield Ratio} = \frac{\text{Dividends per Share}}{\text{Market Price per Share}}$$

$$\text{The Home Depot 2020} = \frac{\$6.00}{\$269.13} = 2.23\%$$

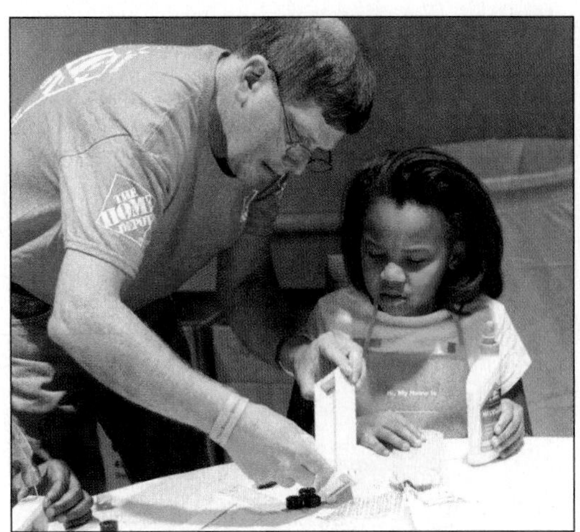

AB Forces News Collection/
Alamy Stock Photo

In recent years, the dividend yield for The Home Depot has been between 2.23 and 2.46 percent, so relatively stable. The dividend yield for most stocks is not high compared to alternative investments. Investors are willing to accept low dividend yields if they expect that the price of a stock will increase while they own it. Investors who bought The Home Depot stock did so knowing they would receive a dividend, but they also were expecting its stock price to increase. In contrast, stocks with low growth potential tend to offer much higher dividend yields than do stocks with high growth potential. Stocks with high dividend yields often appeal to retired investors who need current income rather than future growth potential.

The dividend yield for Lowe's is slightly less than that for The Home Depot, 1.38 percent in fiscal 2020. The nearby chart shows average dividend yields for several different industries.

PAUSE FOR FEEDBACK

We have discussed several solvency and market ratios. Solvency ratios focus on a company's ability to meet its long-term obligations. Market ratios relate the current price per share of a company's stock to the return that accrues to stockholders. Next we will discuss important analytical considerations. Before you move on, complete the following to test your understanding of the concepts we have covered so far.

SELF-STUDY QUIZ

Show how to compute the following ratios:

1. Cash coverage ratio =
2. Debt-to-equity ratio =
3. Price/earnings ratio =

After you have completed your answers, check them below.

GUIDED HELP 13-3

For additional step-by-step video instruction on calculating ratios, go to mhhe.com/libby_gh13-3.

Recommended Homework: M13-8, M13-9, E13-12, E13-13, P13-3, P13-10

Solutions to SELF-STUDY QUIZ

1. Cash Coverage Ratio = Cash Flows from Operating Activities ÷ Interest Paid
2. Debt-to-Equity Ratio = Total Liabilities ÷ Total Stockholders' Equity
3. Price/Earnings Ratio = Market Price per Share ÷ Earnings per Share

INTERPRETING RATIOS AND OTHER ANALYTICAL CONSIDERATIONS

Except for earnings per share, the computation of financial ratios has not been standardized by the accounting profession. Thus, analysts must decide which ratios to use and how to compute them based on their decision objective. When using ratios computed by others, analysts are careful to note how each ratio is computed.

As we have seen, ratios can be interpreted only by comparing them to other ratios or a benchmark value. Some ratios, by their very nature, are unfavorable at either very high or very low values. For example, a very low current ratio may indicate an inability to meet short-term obligations, while a very high current ratio may indicate excessive current assets. Furthermore, an optimal ratio for one company may not be optimal for another. Comparing ratios for two firms is appropriate only if the companies are comparable in terms of their industry, operations, and accounting policies.

> **Tip** Remember that only earnings per share (EPS) is defined by GAAP. It is therefore critical that you understand the formula being used, and the source of the inputs, before relying on the output of any ratio computation. Just remember, "garbage in, garbage out."

Because ratios are based on the aggregation of information, they may obscure underlying factors that are of interest to the analyst. For example, a current ratio that is considered optimal can obscure a short-term liquidity problem in a company with a large amount of inventory but a minimal amount of cash with which to meet short-term obligations. Examining multiple ratios, like the quick ratio and cash ratio in conjunction with the current ratio, can uncover this type of problem.

In other cases, analysis cannot uncover obscured problems. For example, consolidated statements include financial information about a parent company and its subsidiaries. The parent company could have a low current ratio and the subsidiary a high one, but when their statements are consolidated, their current ratios are in effect averaged and can fall within an acceptable range. The fact that the parent company could have a serious liquidity problem is obscured.

A company's accounting policy choices will influence its ratios. This is important because different companies rarely use exactly the same accounting policies. For example, two companies that purchase the exact same asset will report different net income amounts if one uses accelerated depreciation while the other uses straight-line depreciation. These different amounts will influence any ratios that include net income. Analysts who do not understand how a company's accounting choices influence its ratios could draw inappropriate conclusions. It is therefore critical that analysts understand a company's accounting policies before interpreting its ratios. A company's accounting policies are described in the footnotes to its financial statements.

Other Relevant Information

Understanding the broader economic environment in which a company operates and other relevant information is important when interpreting its ratios and analyzing a company. Some things that analysts commonly consider are:

1. **Rapid growth.** Growth in total sales does not always indicate that a company is successful. Total sales can increase as a result of a company selling more at its existing stores, it can increase as a result of a company opening new stores, or it can increase as a result of a company purchasing another company. Growth driven by purchasing another company or new-store sales might obscure the fact that existing stores are not meeting customer needs and are experiencing declining sales. To help analysts sort out what is driving sales growth, companies often report a figure we discussed at the beginning of this chapter called "comparable store sales." This figure captures the growth in sales for stores that have been in existence for some period of time, typically 13 months or more. **The Home Depot** discusses comparable store sales growth in its 2020 10-K:

THE HOME DEPOT
REAL WORLD EXCERPT:
10-K Report

Total comparable sales increased 19.7 percent in fiscal 2020, reflecting a 10.5 percent increase in comparable average ticket and an 8.6 percent increase in comparable customer transactions. The increase in comparable sales reflected a number of factors, including increased consumer demand across our core categories and the execution of our strategic efforts to drive an enhanced interconnected experience in both the physical and digital worlds. The increase in comparable average ticket and comparable customer transactions was primarily driven by an increase in the number of products sold per transaction and stronger in-store and online customer engagement, as well as commodity price inflation primarily from lumber.

Source: The Home Depot, Inc.

2. **Uneconomical expansion.** In the pursuit of growth, some companies will open stores in less desirable locations. These poor locations can cause a company's average productivity to decline. One measure of productivity in the retail industry is sales volume per square foot of selling space. The Home Depot reports sales volume per square foot in its 2020 10-K report:

Year	Sales per Square Foot
2020	$543.74
2019	454.82
2018	446.86
2017	417.02
2016	390.78

   As the table shows, sales per square foot has grown from $390.78 in 2016 to $543.74 in 2020, a good sign that The Home Depot is not opening stores in undesirable locations.

3. **Non-financial information.** Remember that analyzing a company involves much more than simply analyzing its financial statements and ratios. For example, to get a sense for how a company is implementing its strategy, analysts will often visit individual stores and perhaps talk to customers and suppliers. Information obtained during these visits helps analysts better understand how a company's strategy is actually being implemented in its stores. Another example pertains to researching and understanding how a company is addressing risks associated with the environmental, social and governance issues it faces. With an understanding of these broad non-financial factors, analysts are better able to interpret a company's current financial information as well as make more informed predictions about future performance.

ENVIRONMENTAL, SOCIAL, & GOVERNANCE (ESG) REPORTING

As you learned in Chapter 5, most large public companies have started to publish a report on the sustainability of their operations. These reports go by various names. Two of the most common names are corporate social responsibility (CSR) report and environmental, social and governance (ESG) report. The Home Depot uses the term "responsibility report," which can be accessed from its investor relations website (ir.homedepot.com). In its 10-K, The Home Depot also extensively discusses its goals related to diversity, sustainability, and environmental impact. Below is an excerpt from this section of its 10-K.

Our Environmental Goals. We currently have several major commitments to help combat climate change and reduce our environmental footprint:

Year Announced	Goal	Progress
2015	**Store Energy Usage:** Reduce our U.S. stores' kilowatt-hour energy use by 20% over 2010 levels by 2020	**Completed**
2015	**Renewable/Alternative Energy Sources:** Produce and procure, on an annual basis, 135 megawatts of energy through renewable or alternative energy sources, such as wind, solar and fuel cell technology, by 2020	**Completed**
2017	**Customer Greenhouse Gas Emissions:** Help reduce North American customers' greenhouse gas emissions by 20 million metric tons by 2020	**Completed**
2017	**Customer Energy and Water Savings:** Help customers save $2.5 billion in electricity costs and reduce water use by 250 billion gallons by 2020	**Completed**
2017	**Paint Chemical Reduction:** Reduce suspect chemicals in paints by 2020	**Completed**
2018	**Cleaning Products Chemical Reduction:** Reduce suspect chemicals in cleaning products by 2022	**In Process**
2018	**Science-Based Carbon Emissions Targets:** Commit to 2.1% annual reduction in carbon emissions, with the goal to achieve a 40% reduction by 2030 and 50% reduction by 2035	**In Process**
2019	**Recyclable Packaging:** Exclude expanded polystyrene foam (EPS) and polyvinyl chloride (PVC) film from the packaging of private-brand products we sell, replacing them with easier-to-recycle materials by 2023	**In Process**
2020	**NEW GOAL for Renewable/Alternative Energy Sources:** Produce or procure, on an annual basis, 335 megawatts of renewable or alternative energy by 2025	**In Process**

Home Depot

CHAPTER TAKE-AWAYS

13-1. Explain how a company's business strategy affects financial statement analysis. **p. 692**

Financial statements reflect transactions. Transactions are the result of a company carrying out its operating decisions as it implements its business strategy. Thus, an understanding of a company's business strategy provides the context for conducting financial statement analysis.

13-2. Discuss ways to analyze financial statements. **p. 693**

Analysts use financial statements to understand a company's current and past performance, as well as to make predictions about future performance. The data reported in a company's financial statements can be used for either time-series analysis (comparing a company or companies over time) or cross-sectional analysis (comparing similar companies at a point in time).

13-3. Compute and interpret component percentages. **p. 695**

Component percentages express each item on a financial statement as a percentage of a single base amount. The base amount on the income statement is net sales. To compute component percentages on the income statement, each amount reported is divided by net sales. The base amount on the balance sheet is total assets. To compute component percentages on the balance sheet, each amount is divided by total assets. Component percentages are evaluated by comparing them over time or by comparing them with percentages for similar companies.

13-4. Compute and interpret profitability ratios. p. 697

Profitability ratios focus on income and how it compares to other amounts reported on the financial statements. Exhibit 13.3 lists these ratios and shows how to compute them. Profitability ratios are evaluated by comparing them over time or by comparing them with ratios for similar companies.

13-5. Compute and interpret asset turnover ratios. p. 701

Asset turnover ratios focus on capturing how effectively a company uses its assets. Exhibit 13.3 lists these ratios and shows how to compute them. Asset turnover ratios are evaluated by comparing them over time or by comparing them with ratios for similar companies.

13-6. Compute and interpret liquidity ratios. p. 706

Liquidity ratios focus on evaluating a company's ability to meet its short-term obligations. Exhibit 13.3 lists these ratios and shows how to compute them. Liquidity ratios are evaluated by comparing them over time or by comparing them with ratios for similar companies.

13-7. Compute and interpret solvency ratios. p. 708

Solvency ratios focus on evaluating a company's ability to meet its long-term obligations. Exhibit 13.3 lists these ratios and shows how to compute them. Solvency ratios are evaluated by comparing them over time or by comparing them with ratios for similar companies.

13-8. Compute and interpret market ratios. p. 709

Market ratios relate the current price per share of a company's stock to the return that accrues to stockholders. Exhibit 13.3 lists these ratios and shows how to compute them. Market ratios are evaluated by comparing them over time or by comparing them with ratios for similar companies.

FINDING FINANCIAL INFORMATION

Balance Sheet

Ratios are not reported on the balance sheet. Analysts do, however, use balance sheet information to compute various ratios. Most analysts use an average of the beginning and ending amounts for balance sheet accounts when comparing balance sheet numbers to income statement numbers.

Income Statement

Earnings per share is the only ratio that is required to be reported on the financial statements. It is reported at the bottom of the income statement.

Statement of Cash Flows

Ratios are not reported on the statement of cash flows. Analysts, however, do use cash flow information to compute various ratios.

Statement of Stockholders' Equity

Ratios are not reported on the statement of stockholders' equity. Analysts, however, do use amounts from this statement to compute various ratios.

Notes

Under Summary of Significant Accounting Policies

This note describes a company's accounting policies. Understanding a company's accounting policies is critical to interpreting its ratios, especially when comparing ratios across companies.

Under Separate Notes

There is a vast amount of information reported in a company's footnotes. At times, you will need to retrieve information from a footnote in order to calculate a specific ratio.

KEY TERMS

Asset Turnover Ratios Ratios that capture how efficiently a company uses its assets. **p. 701**

Component Percentages Express each item on a particular financial statement as a percentage of a single base amount. **p. 695**

Liquidity Ratios Ratios that measure a company's ability to meet its currently maturing obligations. **p. 706**

Market Ratios Ratios that relate the current price per share of a company's stock to the return that accrues to stockholders. **p. 709**

Profitability Ratios Ratios that compare income with one or more primary activities. **p. 697**

Ratio Analysis An analytical tool that measures the proportional relationship between two financial statement amounts. **p. 695**

Solvency Ratios Ratios that measure a company's ability to meet its long-term obligations. **p. 708**

QUESTIONS

1. Who are the primary users of a company's financial statements?
2. When considering an investment in stock, investors should evaluate the company's future income and growth potential on the basis of what three factors?
3. How does product differentiation differ from cost differentiation?
4. What are the two general methods for making financial comparisons?
5. What are component percentages? Why are they useful?
6. What is ratio analysis? Why is it useful?
7. What do profitability ratios focus on? What is an example of a profitability ratio and how is it computed?
8. What do turnover ratios focus on? What is an example of a turnover ratio and how is it computed?
9. What do liquidity ratios focus on? What is an example of a liquidity ratio and how is it computed?
10. What do solvency ratios focus on? What is an example of a solvency ratio and how is it computed?
11. What do market ratios focus on? What is an example of a market ratio and how is it computed?
12. Explain how a company's accounting policy choices can affect its ratios.
13. Explain why rapid growth in total sales might not necessarily be a good thing for a company.

MULTIPLE-CHOICE QUESTIONS

1. A company has total assets of $500,000 and noncurrent assets of $400,000. Current liabilities are $40,000. What is the current ratio?
   a. 12.5
   b. 10.0
   c. 2.5
   d. Cannot be determined without additional information.
2. Which of the following would **not** change the receivables turnover ratio for a retail company?
   a. Increases in the retail prices of inventory.
   b. A change in credit policy.
   c. Increases in the cost incurred to purchase inventory.
   d. None of the above.
3. Which of the following ratios is used to analyze liquidity?
   a. Earnings per share ratio.
   b. Debt-to-equity ratio.
   c. Current ratio.
   d. Both (a) and (c).
4. The two components of the return on asset ratio are
   a. Gross profit margin ratio and return on equity ratio.
   b. Net profit margin ratio and earnings per share ratio.
   c. Net profit margin ratio and total asset turnover ratio.
   d. Return on equity ratio and earnings per share ratio.

5. Which of the following ratios is required by GAAP?
   a. Earnings per share ratio.
   b. Price/earnings ratio.
   c. Dividend yield ratio.
   d. All of the above are required by GAAP.
6. A company has quick assets of $300,000 and current liabilities of $150,000. The company purchased $50,000 in inventory on credit. After the purchase, the quick ratio would be
   a. 2.0
   b. 2.3
   c. 1.5
   d. 1.75
7. The inventory turnover ratio for Natural Foods Stores is 14.6. The company reported cost of goods sold in the amount of $1,500,000 and total sales of $2,500,000. What is the average amount of inventory for Natural Foods?
   a. $102,740
   b. $171,233
   c. $100,000
   d. $60,000
8. Given the following ratios for four companies, which company is **least** likely to experience problems paying its current liabilities promptly?

	Quick Ratio	Receivables Turnover Ratio
a.	1.2	58
b.	1.2	25
c.	1.0	55
d.	0.5	60

9. A decrease in selling and administrative expenses would impact what ratio?
   a. Fixed asset turnover ratio.
   b. Times interest earned ratio.
   c. Quick ratio.
   d. Current ratio.
10. A creditor is **least** likely to use what ratio when analyzing a company that has borrowed funds on a long-term basis?
    a. Cash coverage ratio.
    b. Debt-to-equity ratio.
    c. Times interest earned ratio.
    d. Dividend yield ratio.

MINI-EXERCISES

M13-1 Inferring Financial Information Using Component Percentages
LO13-3

A large retailer reported revenue of $1,665,000. The company's gross profit percentage was 44 percent. What amount of cost of goods sold did the company report?

M13-2 Inferring Financial Information Using Component Percentages
LO13-3

A consumer products company reported a 5.4 percent increase in sales from Year 1 to Year 2. Sales in Year 1 were $29,600. In Year 2, the company reported cost of goods sold in the amount of $9,107. What was the gross profit percentage in Year 2?

M13-3 Computing the Return on Equity Ratio
LO13-4

Compute the return on equity ratio for Year 2 given the following data:

	Year 2	Year 1
Net income	$ 183,000	$ 159,000
Stockholders' equity	1,100,000	1,250,000
Total assets	2,460,000	2,630,000
Interest expense	42,000	32,000

Computing the Return on Asset Ratio

M13-4
LO13-4

Compute the return on asset ratio for Year 2 given the following data:

	Year 2	Year 1
Total asset turnover ratio	2.10	1.90
Net profit margin ratio	12.00%	10.00%

Analyzing the Inventory Turnover Ratio

M13-5
LO13-5

A manufacturer reported an inventory turnover ratio of 8.6 last year. This year, management introduced a new inventory control system that was expected to reduce average inventory levels by 25 percent. Cost of goods sold is expected to increase due to the price of raw materials increasing. Given this information, would you expect the inventory turnover ratio to increase or decrease this year relative to last year? Explain.

Using the Current Ratio to Infer Financial Information

M13-6
LO13-6

Kamrath Company reported total assets of $1,400,000 and noncurrent assets of $480,000. The company also reported a current ratio of 3.5. What amount of current liabilities did the company report?

Analyzing Financial Relationships

M13-7
LO13-6

Ramesh Company has prepared preliminary financial results that are now being reviewed by the accountants. You notice that the current ratio is 2.4 and the quick ratio is 3.7. You recognize that this is unusual. Does it imply that a mistake has been made? Explain.

Calculating the Times Interest Earned Ratio

M13-8
LO13-7

In the current year, Salmon Company reported sales of $1,420,000, interest expense of $12,000, income tax expense of $13,000, and net income of $52,000. What is Salmon's times interest earned ratio?

Inferring Financial Information Using a Ratio

M13-9
LO13-8

Zion Company earned $6.50 per share and paid dividends of $3.50 per share. The company reported a dividend yield of 5 percent. What was the price of the stock?

Analyzing the Impact of Accounting Alternatives

M13-10
LO13-4, 13-5, 13-6

Seattle Corporation is considering changing its inventory method from FIFO to LIFO. Assume that inventory prices have been increasing. All else equal, what impact would you expect the change to have on the following ratios: net profit margin, fixed asset turnover ratio, current ratio, and quick ratio?

EXERCISES

Using Financial Information to Identify Companies

E13-1
LO13-1, 13-2, 13-3, 13-5, 13-6

The following selected financial data pertain to four unidentified companies:

	COMPANIES			
	1	2	3	4
Balance Sheet Data (component %)				
Cash	3.5%	4.7%	8.2%	11.7%
Accounts receivable	16.9	28.9	16.8	51.9
Inventory	46.8	35.6	57.3	0.0
Property and equipment	18.3	21.7	7.6	18.7
Income Statement Data (component %)				
Cost of goods sold	78.0%	77.5%	55.8%	0.0%
Profit before taxes	2.1	0.7	1.2	3.2
Selected Ratios				
Current ratio	1.3	1.5	1.6	1.2
Inventory turnover ratio	3.6	9.8	1.5	N/A*

*N/A = Not applicable

In no particular order, the four unidentified companies are:

a. High-end clothing store
b. Advertising agency
c. Wholesale candy company
d. Car manufacturer

Required:
Match each company with its financial information.

E13-2 Using Financial Information to Identify Companies

LO13-1, 13-2, 13-3, 13-5, 13-6

The following selected financial data pertain to four unidentified companies:

	COMPANIES			
	1	2	3	4
Balance Sheet Data (component %)				
Cash	7.3%	21.6%	6.1%	11.3%
Accounts receivable	28.2	39.7	3.2	22.9
Inventory	21.6	0.6	1.8	27.5
Property and equipment	32.1	18.0	74.6	25.1
Income Statement Data (component %)				
Cost of goods sold	84.7%	0.0%	0.0%	56.6%
Profit before taxes	1.7	3.2	2.4	6.9
Selected Ratios				
Current ratio	1.5	1.2	0.6	1.9
Inventory turnover ratio	27.4	N/A*	N/A*	3.3

*N/A = Not applicable

In no particular order, the four unidentified companies are:

a. Travel agency
b. Hotel
c. Meat processing company
d. Drug company

Required:
Match each company with its financial information.

E13-3 Using Financial Information to Identify Companies

LO13-1, 13-2, 13-3, 13-5, 13-6

The following selected financial data pertain to four unidentified companies:

	COMPANIES			
	1	2	3	4
Balance Sheet Data (component %)				
Cash	5.1%	8.8%	6.3%	10.4%
Accounts receivable	13.1	41.5	13.8	4.9
Inventory	4.6	3.6	65.1	35.8
Property and equipment	53.1	23.0	8.8	35.7
Income Statement Data (component %)				
Cost of goods sold	0.0%	0.0%	54.8%	77.5%
Profit before taxes	0.3	16.0	3.9	1.5
Selected Ratios				
Current ratio	0.7	2.2	1.9	1.4
Inventory turnover ratio	N/A*	N/A*	1.4	15.5

*N/A = Not applicable

In no particular order, the four unidentified companies are:

a. Cable TV company
b. Grocery store
c. Accounting firm
d. High-end jewelry store

Required:
Match each company with its financial information.

Using Financial Information to Identify Companies

E13-4
LO13-1, 13-2, 13-3, 13-5, 13-6

The following selected financial data pertain to four unidentified companies:

	COMPANIES			
	1	2	3	4
Balance Sheet Data (component %)				
Cash	11.6%	6.6%	5.4%	7.1%
Accounts receivable	4.6	18.9	8.8	35.6
Inventory	7.0	45.8	65.7	26.0
Property and equipment	56.0	20.3	10.1	21.9
Income Statement Data (component %)				
Cost of goods sold	43.3%	63.6%	85.9%	84.2%
Profit before taxes	2.7	1.4	1.1	0.9
Selected Ratios				
Current ratio	0.7	2.1	1.2	1.3
Inventory turnover ratio	30.0	3.5	5.6	16.7

In no particular order, the four unidentified companies are:

a. Full-line department store
b. Wholesale fish company
c. Automobile dealer (low-priced used cars)
d. Restaurant

Required:
Match each company with its financial information.

Calculating Component Percentages

E13-5
LO13-3

Compute the component percentages for Trixy Magic's income statement below. Discuss any trends you observe.

TRIXY MAGIC, INC.
Consolidated Statements of Earnings
(in millions)

	Fiscal 2021	% Sales	Fiscal 2020	% Sales	Fiscal 2019	% Sales
Net sales	**$56,223**	**100.00%**	**$53,417**	**100.00%**	**$50,521**	**100.00%**
Cost of sales	36,665		34,941		33,194	
Gross margin	**19,558**		**18,476**		**17,327**	
Expenses:						
Selling, general, and administrative	13,281		12,865		12,244	
Depreciation	1,485		1,462		1,523	
Interest–net	516		476		423	
Total expenses	**15,282**		**14,803**		**14,190**	
Pre-tax earnings	4,276		3,673		3,137	
Income tax provision	1,578		1,387		1,178	
Net earnings	**$ 2,698**		**$ 2,286**		**$ 1,959**	

E13-6 Matching Each Ratio with Its Formula

LO13-4, 13-5, 13-6, 13-7, 13-8

Match each ratio or percentage with its formula.

Ratio or Percentage	Formulas
1. Net profit margin ratio	A. Net Income ÷ Net Sales Revenue
2. Inventory turnover ratio	B. Days in Year ÷ Receivables Turnover Ratio
3. Average days to collect receivables	C. Net Income ÷ Average Total Stockholders' Equity
4. Dividend yield ratio	D. Net Income ÷ Weighted Average Number of Common Shares Outstanding
5. Return on equity ratio	E. (Cash & Cash Equivalents + Net Accounts Receivable + Marketable Securities) ÷ Current Liabilities
6. Current ratio	F. Current Assets ÷ Current Liabilities
7. Debt-to-equity ratio	G. Cost of Goods Sold ÷ Average Inventory
8. Price/earnings ratio	H. Net Credit Sales ÷ Average Net Receivables
9. Receivables turnover ratio	I. Days in Year ÷ Inventory Turnover Ratio
10. Average days to sell inventory	J. Total Liabilities ÷ Total Stockholders' Equity
11. Earnings per share ratio	K. Dividends per Share ÷ Market Price per Share
12. Return on assets ratio	L. Market Price per Share ÷ Earnings per Share
13. Quick ratio	M. Net Income ÷ Average Total Assets
14. Times interest earned ratio	N. Cash Flows from Operating Activities ÷ Interest Paid
15. Cash coverage ratio	O. Net Sales Revenue ÷ Average Net Fixed Assets
16. Fixed asset turnover ratio	P. (Net Income + Interest Expense + Income Tax Expense) ÷ Interest Expense

E13-7 Computing Turnover Ratios

LO13-3, 13-5

Procter & Gamble

Procter & Gamble is a multinational corporation that manufactures and markets many household products. In a recent year, sales for the company were $83,062 (all amounts in millions). The annual report did not disclose the amount of credit sales, so we will assume that 90 percent of sales were on credit. The average gross profit on sales was 49 percent. Additional account balances were

	Ending	Beginning
Accounts receivable (net)	$6,386	$6,508
Inventory	6,759	6,909

Required:

Compute Procter & Gamble's receivables turnover ratio and its inventory turnover ratio. On average, how many days does it take for the company to collect its accounts receivable and sell its inventory?

E13-8 Computing Turnover Ratios

LO13-3, 13-5

Sales for the year for Fuji Company were $1,000,000, 70 percent of which were on credit. The average gross profit on sales was 40 percent. Additional account balances were

	Ending	Beginning
Accounts receivable (net)	$60,000	$45,000
Inventory	25,000	70,000

Required:

Compute the turnover for the accounts receivable and inventory, the average days to collect receivables, and the average days to sell inventory.

E13-9 Analyzing the Impact of Selected Transactions on the Current Ratio

LO13-6

Assume current assets totaled $120,000 and the current ratio was 1.5 before the following independent transactions:

(1) Purchased merchandise for $40,000 on short-term credit.

(2) Purchased a delivery truck for $25,000. Paid $3,000 cash and signed a two-year interest-bearing note for the balance.

Required:

Compute the current ratio after each independent transaction.

Analyzing the Impact of Selected Transactions on the Current Ratio

E13-10
LO13-6
The Bombay Company, Inc.

The Bombay Company, Inc., sold a line of home furnishings that included furniture, wall decor, and decorative accessories. Bombay operated through a network of retail locations throughout the United States and Canada, as well as through its direct-to-customer operations and international licensing arrangements. The company was forced to file for bankruptcy. In its last financial statement prior to bankruptcy, Bombay reported current assets of $161,604,000 and current liabilities of $113,909,000.

Required:
Determine the impact of the following independent transactions on the current ratio for Bombay:

1. Sold long-term assets for cash.
2. Accrued severance pay and benefits for employees who were terminated.
3. Wrote down the carrying value of certain inventory items that were deemed to be obsolete.
4. Acquired new inventory; supplier was not willing to provide normal credit terms, so an 18-month interest-bearing note was signed.

Inferring Financial Information from Ratios

E13-11
LO13-3, 13-5
Dollar General Corporation

Dollar General Corporation operates general merchandise stores that feature quality merchandise at low prices. All stores are located in the United States, predominantly in small towns in midwestern and southeastern states. In a recent year, the company reported average inventories of $1,668 million and an inventory turnover ratio of 8.0. Average total fixed assets were $2,098 million, and the fixed asset turnover ratio was 9.0. What amount did Dollar General report as gross profit in the current year?

Computing Asset Turnover, Liquidity, and Solvency Ratios

E13-12
LO13-5, 13-6, 13-7
Cintas

Cintas designs and manufactures uniforms for corporations throughout the United States and Canada. The company's stock is traded on the NASDAQ. Selected information from the company's financial statements follows.

CINTAS (in millions)		
	Current Year	**Prior Year**
Select Income Statement Information		
Net revenue	$4,552	$4,316
Cost of goods sold	2,637	2,529
Selling, general, and administrative expenses	1,303	1,222
Interest expense	72	70
Income tax expense	233	184
Net income	374	315
Select Statement of Cash Flows Information		
Cash paid for interest	65	69
Cash flows from operating activities	608	553
Select Balance Sheet Information		
Cash and equivalents	513	352
Marketable securities	—	6
Accounts receivable	508	505
Inventories	251	240
Prepaid expense and other current assets	26	25
Accounts payable	150	121
Current accrued expenses	377	342
Current portion of long-term debt	1	8
Other current liabilities	102	85
Long-term debt	1,300	1,301

Required:
Compute the following ratios for the current year:

- Receivables turnover ratio (assume that all sales were credit sales)
- Inventory turnover ratio
- Current ratio
- Cash ratio
- Times interest earned ratio
- Cash coverage ratio

E13-13 LO13-8 **Inferring Financial Information Using Market Ratios**

Wakon Company earned $3.25 per share and paid dividends of $0.75 per share. The company reported a dividend yield of 3 percent. What was the price of Wakon's stock?

PROBLEMS

P13-1 LO13-1, 13-2, 13-3, 13-4, 13-6, 13-7, 13-8 **Analyzing Ratios (AP13-1)**

Company X and Company Y are two giants of the retail industry. Both offer full lines of moderately priced merchandise. In the last fiscal year, annual sales for Company X totaled $53 billion and annual sales for Company Y totaled $20 billion. Compare the two companies as a potential investment based on the following ratios:

Ratios for Current Year	Company X	Company Y
P/E	11.0	12.9
Gross profit margin ratio	28.6	39.3
Net profit margin ratio	2.8	5.7
Current ratio	2.0	1.4
Cash coverage ratio	0.7	2.2
Debt-to-equity ratio	1.4	2.0
Return on equity ratio	12.0	27.8
Return on assets ratio	5.2	9.3
Dividend yield ratio	Not applicable	1.4
Earnings per share ratio	$5.17	$5.20

P13-2 LO13-2, 13-5, 13-6, 13-7, 13-8 **Analyzing an Investment by Comparing Selected Ratios (AP13-2)**

You have the opportunity to invest $10,000 in one of two companies from a single industry. The only information you have is below. Which company would you select? Justify your choice.

Ratios for Current Year	Company A	Company B	Industry Average
Current ratio	1.30	1.00	1.20
Quick ratio	0.80	0.75	0.80
Debt-to-equity ratio	0.90	3.45	1.10
Inventory turnover ratio	18.20	12.00	12.20
Price/earnings ratio	22.01	19.20	21.25
Dividend yield ratio	1.84	1.02	1.04

Calculating Profitability, Turnover, Liquidity, and Solvency Ratios (AP13-3)

P13-3
LO13-4, 13-5, 13-6, 13-7

Using the financial information presented in Exhibit 13.1, calculate the following ratios for fiscal 2020 for The Home Depot:

- Return on equity ratio
- Return on assets ratio
- Total asset turnover ratio
- Inventory turnover ratio
- Current ratio
- Quick ratio
- Cash coverage ratio
- Debt-to-equity ratio

Computing Ratios and Comparing Alternative Investment Opportunities (AP13-4)

P13-4
LO13-3, 13-4, 13-5, 13-6, 13-7, 13-8

The current year financial statements for Blue Water Company and Prime Fish Company are presented below.

	Blue Water	Prime Fish
Balance Sheet		
Cash	$ 41,000	$ 21,000
Accounts receivable (net)	38,000	31,000
Inventory	99,000	40,000
Property & equipment (net)	140,000	401,000
Other assets	84,000	305,000
Total assets	$ 402,000	$ 798,000
Current liabilities	$ 99,000	$ 49,000
Long-term debt (interest rate: 10%)	65,000	60,000
Capital stock ($10 par value)	148,000	512,000
Additional paid-in capital	29,000	106,000
Retained earnings	61,000	71,000
Total liabilities and stockholders' equity	$ 402,000	$ 798,000
Income Statement		
Sales revenue (1/3 on credit)	$ 447,000	$ 802,000
Cost of goods sold	(241,000)	(400,000)
Operating expenses	(161,000)	(311,000)
Net income	$ 45,000	$ 91,000
Other data		
Per share stock price at end of current year	$ 22	$ 15
Average income tax rate	30%	30%
Dividends declared and paid in current year	$ 33,000	$ 148,000

Both companies are in the fish catching and manufacturing business. Both have been in business approximately 10 years, and each has had steady growth. The management of each has a different viewpoint in many respects. Blue Water is more conservative, and as its president has said, "We avoid what we consider to be undue risk." Neither company is publicly held.

Required:

1. Using year-end balances for all ratios, compute the following ratios:

   PROFITABILITY RATIOS:

   1. Return on equity
   2. Return on assets
   3. Gross profit margin

4. Net profit margin
5. Earnings per share

ASSET TURNOVER RATIOS

6. Total asset turnover
7. Fixed asset turnover
8. Receivables turnover
9. Inventory turnover

LIQUIDITY RATIOS

10. Current ratio
11. Quick ratio
12. Cash ratio

SOLVENCY RATIO

13. Debt to equity ratio

MARKET RATIOS:

14. Price/earnings ratio
15. Dividend yield ratio

2. Based on the ratios you computed, which company is more efficient at collecting its accounts receivable and turning over its inventory?

P13-5 Computing Differences and Comparing Financial Statements Using Percentages (AP13-5)

LO13-3, 13-6

The comparative financial statements for Chinook Company are below:

	Year 2	Year 1
Income Statement		
Sales revenue	$190,000	$167,000
Cost of goods sold	112,000	100,000
Gross profit	78,000	67,000
Operating expenses and interest expense	56,000	53,000
Pretax income	22,000	14,000
Income tax	8,000	4,000
Net income	$ 14,000	$ 10,000
Balance Sheet		
Cash	$ 4,000	$ 7,000
Accounts receivable (net)	14,000	18,000
Inventory	40,000	34,000
Property and equipment (net)	45,000	38,000
Total assets	$103,000	$ 97,000
Current liabilities (no interest)	$ 16,000	$ 17,000
Long-term liabilities (interest rate: 10%)	45,000	45,000
Common stock ($5 par value, 6,000 shares outstanding)	30,000	30,000
Retained earnings	12,000	5,000
Total liabilities and stockholders' equity	$103,000	$ 97,000

Required:

1. Complete the following columns for each line item in the preceding comparative financial statements:

INCREASE (DECREASE) from Year 1 to Year 2		
Line Item Name	**Amount**	**Percent**

2. By what amount did the current ratio change from Year 1 to Year 2?

Computing Comparative Financial Statements and ROA Profit Driver Ratios (AP13-6)

P13-6
LO13-3, 13-4, 13-5

Use the data given in P13-5 for Chinook Company.

Required:
1. Compute component percentages for Year 2.
2. Compute return on assets, total asset turnover, and the net profit margin for Year 2.

Analyzing Financial Statements Using Ratios (AP13-7)

P13-7
LO13-4, 13-6, 13-8

Use the data in P13-5 for Chinook Company. Assume that the stock price per share is $28 and that dividends in the amount of $3.50 per share were paid during Year 2. Compute the following ratios:

- Earnings per share ratio
- Current ratio
- Quick ratio
- Cash ratio
- Price/earnings ratio
- Dividend yield ratio

Analyzing the Impact of Alternative Inventory Methods on Selected Ratios (AP13-8)

P13-8
LO13-4, 13-5, 13-6, 13-7

Company A uses the FIFO method to account for inventory and Company B uses the LIFO method. The two companies are exactly alike except for the difference in inventory cost flow assumptions. Costs of inventory items for both companies have been rising steadily in recent years, and each company has increased its inventory each year. Ignore tax effects.

Required:
Identify which company will report the higher amount for each of the following ratios.
1. Net profit margin ratio
2. Earnings per share ratio
3. Inventory turnover ratio
4. Current ratio
5. Debt-to-equity ratio

Computing and Analyzing Ratios (AP13-9)

P13-9
LO13-4, 13-5, 13-6, 13-7, 13-8

The financial statements for Lainey's Famous Pizza are below. Lainey's operates more than 250 locations in 30 states and 11 countries.

Required:
1. Compute the following ratios for Year 3 using information from the company's financial statements.
   a. Return on equity ratio
   b. Net profit margin ratio
   c. Inventory turnover ratio
   d. Current ratio
   e. Quick ratio
   f. Debt-to-equity ratio
   g. Price/earnings ratio (assume a market price per share of $1.12)
2. Does Lainey's Famous Pizza's inventory turnover ratio seem reasonable to you?

LAINEY'S FAMOUS PIZZA, INC., AND SUBSIDIARIES
Consolidated Statements of Operations
(amounts in thousands, except for per share data)

	Year 3	Year 2	Year 1
Revenues:			
Restaurant sales	$659,606	$652,185	$665,616
Royalties from licensing agreement	6,122	7,739	6,580
Domestic franchise revenues	3,100	2,684	2,757
International franchise revenues	2,403	2,078	2,121
Total revenues	671,231	664,686	677,074

(Continued)

	Year 3	Year 2	Year 1
Costs and expenses:			
Food, beverage, and paper supplies	158,732	154,181	165,526
Labor	247,133	247,350	247,276
Direct operating and occupancy	142,420	141,973	140,367
Cost of sales	548,285	543,504	553,169
General and administrative	50,731	50,791	51,642
Depreciation and amortization	37,006	40,181	40,299
Pre-opening costs	3,269	1,843	4,478
Loss on impairment of property and equipment	18,702	22,941	13,336
Store closure costs	1,708	539	1,033
Litigation, settlement, and other costs	8,759	1,609	736
Total costs and expenses	668,460	661,408	664,693
Operating income	2,771	3,278	12,381
Interest expense, net	(16)	(788)	(1,324)
Income before income tax (benefit)/provision	2,755	2,490	11,057
Income tax (benefit)/provision	(5,839)	(2,091)	2,395
Net income	$ 8,594	$ 4,581	$ 8,662
Net income per common share:			
Basic	$ 0.35	$ 0.19	$ 0.34
Diluted	$ 0.35	$ 0.19	$ 0.34
Weighted average shares used in calculating net income per common share:			
Basic	24,488	24,064	25,193
Diluted	24,488	24,143	25,211

LAINEY'S FAMOUS PIZZA, INC., AND SUBSIDIARIES
Consolidated Balance Sheets
(in thousands, except for share data)

	Year 3	Year 2
Assets		
Current assets:		
Cash and cash equivalents	$ 21,230	$ 21,424
Receivables	11,594	12,541
Inventories	5,827	5,557
Current deferred tax asset, net	8,225	7,076
Prepaid rent	231	4,957
Other prepaid expenses	2,518	2,031
Total current assets	49,625	53,586
Property and equipment, net	250,446	255,416
Noncurrent deferred tax asset, net	22,101	25,011
Goodwill	4,622	4,622
Other intangibles, net	4,837	4,714
Other assets	8,313	6,909
Total assets	$339,944	$350,258
Liabilities and Stockholders' Equity		
Current liabilities:		
Accounts payable	$ 17,075	$ 11,263
Accrued compensation and benefits	23,273	23,201

	Year 3	Year 2
Accrued rent	20,424	19,287
Deferred rent credits	4,058	3,745
Other accrued liabilities	13,690	10,915
Gift card liability	14,577	20,640
Store closure reserve	54	326
Total current liabilities	93,151	89,377
Long-term debt	—	22,300
Other liabilities	9,886	7,728
Deferred rent credits, net of current portion	33,177	32,478
Income taxes payable, net of current portion	319	9,125
Commitments and contingencies		
Stockholders' equity:		
Common stock–$0.01 par value, 80,000,000 shares authorized, 24,579,797 and 24,195,800 shares issued and outstanding at the end of Year 3 and Year 2, respectively	246	242
Additional paid-in capital	179,563	174,000
Retained earnings	23,602	15,008
Total stockholders' equity	203,411	189,250
Total liabilities and stockholders' equity	$339,944	$350,258

Identifying Companies Based on the Price/Earnings Ratio (AP13-10)

P13-10
LO13-8
Apple
Peabody Energy Corporation
Tesla

The price/earnings ratio provides important information concerning the stock market's assessment of the growth potential of a business. The following are price/earnings ratios for selected companies. Match the company with its ratio and explain how you made your selections. If you are not familiar with a company, you should visit its website.

Company	Price/Earnings Ratio
1. **Apple**	A. 2
2. **Peabody Energy Corporation (coal)**	B. 1,053
3. **Tesla**	C. 35

Mc Graw Hill connect

ALTERNATE PROBLEMS

Analyzing Ratios (P13-1)

AP13-1
LO13-1, 13-2, 13-3, 13-4, 13-6, 13-7, 13-8
Coca-Cola
PepsiCo

Coca-Cola and **PepsiCo** are well-known international beverage and snack companies. Compare the two companies as a potential investment based on the following ratios:

Ratio	Coca-Cola	PepsiCo
P/E	65.0	26.5
Gross profit margin ratio	69.3	58.4
Net profit margin ratio	12.2	8.8
Quick ratio	0.4	0.7
Current ratio	0.6	1.1
Debt-to-equity ratio	0.7	0.4
Return on equity ratio	27.4	29.1
Return on assets ratio	28.0	16.6
Dividend yield ratio	1.0	1.6

AP13-2 Analyzing an Investment by Comparing Selected Ratios (P13-2)

LO13-2, 13-5, 13-6, 13-7, 13-8

You have the opportunity to invest $10,000 in one of two companies from a single industry. The only information you have is below. Which company would you select? Justify your choice.

Ratios for Current Year	Company A	Company B	Industry Average
Current ratio	1.00	1.02	1.20
Quick ratio	0.80	0.79	0.95
Debt-to-equity ratio	1.25	1.34	0.70
Inventory turnover ratio	8.20	14.00	18.20
Price/earnings ratio	4.01	9.20	21.25
Dividend yield ratio	1.74	2.24	6.04

AP13-3 Calculating Profitability, Turnover, Liquidity, Solvency, and Market Ratios (P13-3)

LO13-4, 13-5, 13-6, 13-7, 13-8

Using the financial information presented in Exhibit 13.1, calculate the following ratios for fiscal 2020 for The Home Depot:

- Net profit margin ratio
- Quality of income ratio
- Receivables turnover ratio
- Cash ratio
- Times interest earned ratio
- Price/earnings ratio (assume a market price per share of $250)

AP13-4 Computing and Interpreting Ratios (P13-4)

LO13-5, 13-6, 13-7

Tabor Company has just prepared the following comparative annual financial statements for the current year:

TABOR COMPANY
Comparative Income Statement
For the Years Ended December 31

	Current Year	Prior Year
Sales revenue (one-half on credit)	$110,000	$99,000
Cost of goods sold	52,000	48,000
Gross profit	58,000	51,000
Expenses (including $4,000 interest expense each year)	40,000	37,000
Pretax income	18,000	14,000
Income tax expense (30%)	5,400	4,200
Net income	$ 12,600	$ 9,800

TABOR COMPANY
Comparative Balance Sheet
At December 31

	Current Year	Prior Year
Assets		
Cash	$ 49,500	$ 18,000
Accounts receivable	37,000	32,000
Inventory	25,000	38,000
Property & equipment (net)	95,000	105,000
Total assets	$206,500	$193,000
Liabilities		
Accounts payable	$ 42,000	$ 35,000
Income taxes payable	1,000	500
Note payable, long-term	40,000	40,000

(Continued)

	Current Year	Prior Year
Stockholders' equity		
Capital stock ($5 par value)	90,000	90,000
Retained earnings	33,500	27,500
Total liabilities and stockholders' equity	$206,500	$193,000

Required:

1. Using average balances for balance sheet accounts and year-end balances for all income statement accounts, compute the following ratios for the current year:

   ASSET TURNOVER RATIOS

   1. Total asset turnover
   2. Fixed asset turnover
   3. Receivables turnover
   4. Inventory turnover

   LIQUIDITY RATIOS

   5. Current ratio
   6. Quick ratio
   7. Cash ratio

   SOLVENCY RATIO

   8. Times interest earned
   9. Cash coverage ratio
   10. Debt to equity ratio

   Assume cash flows from operating activities were $14,600 and cash paid for interest was $3,800.
2. Comment on the receivables turnover and inventory turnover ratios. Any concerns?

AP13-5 LO13-3, 13-6

Computing Differences and Comparing Financial Statements Using Percentages (P13-5)

The comparative financial statements for Summer Corporation are below:

	Year 2	Year 1
Income Statement		
Sales revenue	$453,000	$447,000
Cost of goods sold	250,000	241,000
Gross profit	203,000	206,000
Operating expenses (including interest on bonds)	167,000	168,000
Pretax income	36,000	38,000
Income tax	10,800	11,400
Net income	$ 25,200	$ 26,600
Balance Sheet		
Cash	$ 6,800	$ 3,900
Accounts receivable (net)	42,000	29,000
Merchandise inventory	25,000	18,000
Prepaid expenses	200	100
Property and equipment (net)	130,000	120,000
Total assets	$204,000	$171,000
Accounts payable	$ 17,000	$ 18,000
Income taxes payable	1,000	1,000
Bonds payable (interest rate: 10%)	70,000	50,000
Common stock ($10 par value, 10,000 shares outstanding)	100,000	100,000
Retained earnings	16,000	2,000
Total liabilities and stockholders' equity	$204,000	$171,000

Required:

1. Complete the following columns for each line item in the preceding comparative financial statements:

INCREASE (DECREASE) from Year 1 To Year 2		
Line Item Name	**Amount**	**Percent**

2. By what amount did the current ratio change from Year 1 to Year 2?

AP13-6 Computing Comparative Financial Statements and ROA Profit Driver Ratios (P13-6)

LO13-3, 13-4, 13-5

Use the data given in AP13-5 for Summer Corporation.

Required:

1. Compute component percentages for Year 2.
2. Compute return on assets, total asset turnover, and the net profit margin for Year 2.

AP13-7 Analyzing Financial Statements Using Ratios (P13-7)

LO13-4, 13-6, 13-8

Use the data in AP13-5 for Summer Corporation. Assume that the stock price per share is $22 and that dividends in the amount of $5.00 per share were paid during Year 2. Compute the following ratios:

- Earnings per share ratio
- Current ratio
- Quick ratio
- Cash ratio
- Price/earnings ratio
- Dividend yield ratio

AP13-8 Analyzing the Impact of Alternative Inventory Methods on Selected Ratios (P13-8)

LO13-4, 13-5, 13-6, 13-7

Wolf Company uses the LIFO method to account for inventory and Tiger Company uses the FIFO method. The two companies are exactly alike except for the difference in inventory cost flow assumptions. Costs of inventory items for both companies have been rising steadily in recent years, and each company has increased its inventory each year. Ignore tax effects.

Required:

Identify which company will report the higher amount for each of the following ratios.

1. Net profit margin ratio
2. Earnings per share ratio
3. Inventory turnover ratio
4. Current ratio
5. Debt-to-equity ratio

AP13-9 Computing and Analyzing Ratios (P13-9)

LO13-4, 13-5, 13-6, 13-7

The financial statements for Lainey's Famous Pizza are below. Lainey's operates more than 250 locations in 30 states and 11 countries.

Required

1. Compute the following ratios for Year 3 using information from the company's financial statements.
   a. Return on assets ratio
   b. Gross profit margin ratio
   c. Fixed asset turnover ratio
   d. Receivables turnover ratio (use total revenues as a proxy for net credit sales)
   e. Cash ratio
   f. Debt-to-equity ratio
2. Does Lainey's Famous Pizza's receivables turnover ratio concern you at all? Assume that receivables turned over 65 times in Year 2.

LAINEY'S FAMOUS PIZZA, INC., AND SUBSIDIARIES
Consolidated Statements of Operations
(amounts in thousands, except for per share data)

	Year 3	Year 2	Year 1
Revenues:			
Restaurant sales	$659,606	$652,185	$665,616
Royalties from licensing agreement	6,122	7,739	6,580
Domestic franchise revenues	3,100	2,684	2,757
International franchise revenues	2,403	2,078	2,121
Total revenues	671,231	664,686	677,074
Costs and expenses:			
Food, beverage, and paper supplies	158,732	154,181	165,526
Labor	247,133	247,350	247,276
Direct operating and occupancy	142,420	141,973	140,367
Cost of sales	548,285	543,504	553,169
General and administrative	50,731	50,791	51,642
Depreciation and amortization	37,006	40,181	40,299
Pre-opening costs	3,269	1,843	4,478
Loss on impairment of property and equipment	18,702	22,941	13,336
Store closure costs	1,708	539	1,033
Litigation, settlement, and other costs	8,759	1,609	736
Total costs and expenses	668,460	661,408	664,693
Operating income	2,771	3,278	12,381
Interest expense, net	(16)	(788)	(1,324)
Income before income tax (benefit)/provision	2,755	2,490	11,057
Income tax (benefit)/provision	(5,839)	(2,091)	2,395
Net income	$ 8,594	$ 4,581	$ 8,662
Net income per common share:			
Basic	$ 0.35	$ 0.19	$ 0.34
Diluted	$ 0.35	$ 0.19	$ 0.34
Weighted average shares used in calculating net income per common share:			
Basic	24,488	24,064	25,193
Diluted	24,488	24,143	25,211

LAINEY'S FAMOUS PIZZA, INC., AND SUBSIDIARIES
Consolidated Balance Sheets
(in thousands, except for share data)

	Year 3	Year 2
Assets		
Current assets:		
Cash and cash equivalents	$ 21,230	$ 21,424
Receivables	11,594	12,541
Inventories	5,827	5,557
Current deferred tax asset, net	8,225	7,076
Prepaid rent	231	4,957
Other prepaid expenses	2,518	2,031
Total current assets	49,625	53,586
Property and equipment, net	250,446	255,416
Noncurrent deferred tax asset, net	22,101	25,011

(Continued)

	Year 3	Year 2
Goodwill	4,622	4,622
Other intangibles, net	4,837	4,714
Other assets	8,313	6,909
Total assets	$339,944	$350,258
Liabilities and Stockholders' Equity		
Current liabilities:		
Accounts payable	$ 17,075	$ 11,263
Accrued compensation and benefits	23,273	23,201
Accrued rent	20,424	19,287
Deferred rent credits	4,058	3,745
Other accrued liabilities	13,690	10,915
Gift card liability	14,577	20,640
Store closure reserve	54	326
Total current liabilities	93,151	89,377
Long-term debt	—	22,300
Other liabilities	9,886	7,728
Deferred rent credits, net of current portion	33,177	32,478
Income taxes payable, net of current portion	319	9,125
Commitments and contingencies		
Stockholders' equity:		
Common stock–$0.01 par value, 80,000,000 shares authorized, 24,579,797 and 24,195,800 shares issued and outstanding at the end of Year 3 and Year 2, respectively	246	242
Additional paid-in capital	179,563	174,000
Retained earnings	23,602	15,008
Total stockholders' equity	203,411	189,250
Total liabilities and stockholders' equity	$339,944	$350,258

AP13-10
LO13-8
Boeing
Zoom Video Communications
A-Mark Precious Metals

Identifying Companies Based on the Price/Earnings Ratio (P13-10)

The price/earnings ratio provides important information concerning the stock market's assessment of the growth potential of a business. The following are price/earnings ratios for selected companies. Match the company with its ratio and explain how you made your selections. If you are not familiar with a company, you should visit its website.

Company	Price/Earnings Ratio
1. **Boeing**	A. 46
2. **Zoom Video Communications**	B. 5
3. **A-Mark Precious Metals**	C. 147

CONTINUING PROBLEM

CON13-1
LO13-4, LO13-5, LO13-6, LO13-7, LO13-8
Pool Corporation, Inc.

Computing Ratios

Pool Corporation, Inc., sells swimming pool supplies and equipment. It is a publicly traded corporation that trades on the NASDAQ exchange. The majority of Pool's customers are small, family-owned businesses.

Required:

1. Using the SEC EDGAR service at sec.gov or the company's investor relations website, download the current annual report for Pool Corporation.

2. Compute the following ratios:
   a. Return on assets ratio
   b. Net profit margin ratio
   c. Inventory turnover ratio
   d. Current ratio
   e. Cash coverage ratio
   f. Debt-to-equity ratio
   g. Price/earnings ratio (**Hint:** You will need to go to another source, such as Google Finance, to get the market price per share at the end of the fiscal year.)

CASES AND PROJECTS

Annual Report Cases

CP13-1
LO13-4, 13-5, 13-6,
Target

Finding Financial Information

Refer to the financial statements and footnotes of **Target** given in Appendix B at the end of this book. All dollar amounts are in millions. Round your answers to two decimal places.

Required:

1. For the most recent fiscal year, compute the return on equity ratio for Target.
   a. 36.91 percent
   b. 30.25 percent
   c. 24.98 percent
   d. 33.25 percent
   e. None of the above
2. For the most recent fiscal year, compute the return on assets ratio for Target.
   a. 9.29 percent
   b. 10.21 percent
   c. 8.52 percent
   d. 13.91 percent
   e. None of the above
3. For the most recent fiscal year, compute the net profit margin for Target.
   a. 6.99 percent
   b. 4.67 percent
   c. 8.52 percent
   d. 4.73 percent
   e. None of the above
4. For the most recent fiscal year, compute the inventory turnover ratio for Target.
   a. 6.22
   b. 7.36
   c. 5.15
   d. 6.74
   e. None of the above
5. For the most recent fiscal year, compute the current ratio for Target.
   a. 0.89
   b. 1.03
   c. 0.97
   d. 1.24
   e. None of the above

CP13-2
LO13-4, 13-5, 13-6,
Walmart

Finding Financial Information

Refer to the financial statements and footnotes of **Walmart** given in Appendix C at the end of this book. All dollar amounts are in millions. Round your answers to two decimal places. For calculations that require net income, use the "Consolidated net income" amount reported by Walmart.

Required:

1. For the most recent fiscal year, compute the return on equity ratio for Walmart. ______________
2. For the most recent fiscal year, compute the return on assets ratio for Walmart. ______________
3. For the most recent fiscal year, compute the net profit margin for Walmart. ______________
4. For the most recent fiscal year, compute the inventory turnover ratio for Walmart. ______________
5. For the most recent fiscal year, compute the current ratio for Walmart. ______________

CP13-3
LO13-2, 13-4, 13-5, 13-6, 13-7, 13-8

Comparing Companies within an Industry

Refer to the financial statements of Target (Appendix B) and Walmart (Appendix C) and the Industry Ratio Report (Appendix D) at the end of this book.

Required:

1. Compute the total asset turnover ratio for both companies for the most recent fiscal year. Round your answer to two decimal places.

   Target = ______ **Walmart** = ______

2. Compare the total asset turnover ratios for Target and Walmart to the average total asset turnover ratio for the retail industry. Are Target and Walmart more or less effective at using their assets to generate revenue compared to the industry average?
   a. Both Target and Walmart are more effective at using their assets to generate revenue than the industry average.
   b. Walmart is more effective at using their assets to generate revenue compared to the industry average, but Target is less effective.
   c. Target is more effective at using their assets to generate revenue compared to the industry average, but Walmart is less effective.
   d. Both Target and Walmart are less effective at using their assets to generate revenue than the industry average.
3. Compute the cash coverage ratio for both companies for the most recent fiscal year. Round your answer to two decimal places.

   Target = ______ **Walmart** = ______

4. Which company generated a greater amount of cash from operating activities relative to interest paid during the most recent fiscal year?
   ☐ Target
   ☐ Walmart
5. Compute the price/earnings ratio for both companies for the most recent fiscal year. Round your answer to two decimal places. (*Note:* Target and Walmart's stock price at the end of the most recent fiscal year was $181.17 and $139.27, respectively.)

   Target = ______ **Walmart** = ______

6. According to their price/earnings ratio, which company does the market expect will increase their earnings more rapidly in the future?
   ☐ Target
   ☐ Walmart

Financial Reporting and Analysis Case

CP13-4
LO13-1, 13-4 13-5

Interpreting Financial Results Based on Corporate Strategy

In this chapter, we discussed the importance of analyzing financial results based on an understanding of the company's business strategy. Using the two components of the ROA ratio (net profit margin and total asset turnover), we illustrated how different strategies could earn high returns for investors. Assume that two companies in the same industry adopt fundamentally different strategies. One manufactures high-end consumer electronics. Its products employ state-of-the-art technology, and the company offers a high level of customer service both before and after the sale. The other company emphasizes low cost with good performance. Its products utilize well-established technology but are never innovative. Customers buy these products at large, self-service warehouses and are expected to install the products using information contained in printed brochures. Which of the two components of the ROA ratio would you expect to differ for these companies as a result of their different business strategies?

Inferring Information from the Two Components of the ROA Ratio

CP13-5
13-4, 13-5

In this chapter, we discussed the two components of the ROA ratio (net profit margin and total asset turnover). Using your knowledge of the two components, find the missing amount in each of the following cases:

Case 1: ROA is 10 percent; net income is $20,000; the total asset turnover ratio is 5; and net sales are $1,000,000. What is the amount of average total assets?

Case 2: Net income is $1,500,000; net sales are $8,000,000; and the total asset turnover ratio is 8. What is the amount of average total assets?

Case 3: ROA is 50 percent; the net profit margin is 10 percent; average total assets are $1,000,000; and the total asset turnover ratio is 5. What are net sales?

Case 4: Net income is $50,000; the total asset turnover ratio is 5; and net sales are $1,000,000. What is ROA?

Critical Thinking Case

Evaluating an Ethical Dilemma

CP13-6
LO13-6

Barton Company requested a large loan from First Federal Bank to acquire a tract of land for future expansion. Barton reported current assets of $1,900,000 ($430,000 in cash) and current liabilities of $1,075,000. First Federal denied the loan request for a number of reasons, including the fact that the current ratio was below 2:1. When Barton was informed of the loan denial, the controller of the company immediately paid $420,000 that was owed to several trade creditors. The controller then asked First Federal to recompute the current ratio and reconsider the loan application. Based on these abbreviated facts, would you recommend that First Federal approve the loan request? Why? Are the controller's actions ethical?

You as Analyst: Online Company Research

Examining an Annual Report

CP13-7
LO13-3, 13-4, 13-5, 13-6, 13-7, 13-8

In your web browser, search for the investor relations page of a public company you are interested in (e.g., Zoom investor relations). Select SEC Filings or Annual Report or Financials to obtain the 10-K for the most recent year available.

Required:
For the company you selected, compute and interpret each of the ratios in Exhibit 13.3. Most of the information you need will be in the financial statements, though some may come from the footnotes or management's discussion and analysis section.

Images used throughout chapter: Question of ethics: mushmello/Shutterstock; Pause for feedback: McGraw Hill; Guided help: McGraw Hill; Financial analysis: McGraw Hill; Focus on cash flows: Hilch/Shutterstock; Key ratio analysis: guillermain/123RF; Data analytics: Hilch/Shutterstock; Tip: McGraw Hill; ESG reporting: McGraw Hill; International perspective: Hilch/Shutterstock

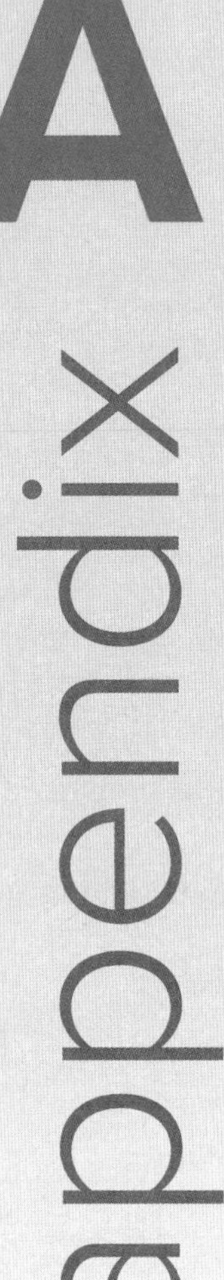

Reporting and Interpreting Investments in Other Corporations

One of the world's most recognizable and powerful brands is Disney, with Mickey Mouse® at its center. The Disney company started in 1923 as a cartoon studio in Hollywood, California. Once Mickey Mouse became a "star" in 1928, the creative entrepreneurs Walt and Roy Disney soon developed a vision of branding, merchandising the characters in the cartoons, and creating comic strips for newspapers. Then they produced the first Disney movie—*Snow White and the Seven Dwarfs.* In 1954, Walt Disney ventured into television with its *Wonderful World of Disney* series that lasted 29 years (under various titles). The brand expanded in 1955 when Disneyland opened.

Disney's original corporate strategy had film production as its core business, with other operations interconnected as the brands developed. Today, this vision remains true with the addition of technology into each of the segments. **The Walt Disney Company** is now a diversified, worldwide entertainment company, with five business segments:

(1) Theme parks and resorts across the globe, including the newest Shanghai Disney Resort;

(2) Media networks, including ESPN, ABC Television Network, and, in late 2018, 21st Century Fox;

(3) Studio entertainment, including *Toy Story* and *Star Wars* movies, and theatrical shows such as *The Lion King;*

(4) Consumer products and interactive media; and

(5) Direct-to-Consumer & International, a subscription-based video streaming service Disney+.

LEARNING OBJECTIVES

After studying this material, you should be able to:

A-1 Analyze and report investments in debt securities using the amortized cost and fair value methods. p. A-5

A-2 Analyze and report passive investments in equity securities using the fair value method. p. A-12

A-3 Analyze and report investments involving significant influence using the equity method. p. A-15

A-4 Analyze and report investments in controlling interests. p. A-24

parrysuwanitch/123RF

FOCUS COMPANY

The Walt Disney Company

INVESTMENT STRATEGIES IN A DIVERSIFIED COMPANY

thewaltdisneycompany.com

From its website, The Walt Disney Company's mission is

> . . . to entertain, inform and inspire people around the globe through the power of unparalleled storytelling, reflecting the iconic brands, creative minds and innovative technologies that make ours the world's premier entertainment company.

To accomplish this mission, The Walt Disney Company invests in a wide variety of other companies. In 1995, Disney acquired **ABC** for $19 billion and has since purchased many other companies, including **Pixar Animation Studios** for $7.4 billion, **Marvel Entertainment** for $4 billion, **Lucasfilm** for $4.05 billion, and **21st Century Fox** for $69.5 billion. Other recent investments allow Disney to expand its brands using new technologies, such as **Hulu** (digital subscription service) and **BAMTech** (direct-to-consumer business that distributes sports programming including Major League Baseball's streaming technology and content delivery).

UNDERSTANDING THE BUSINESS

Many strategic factors motivate managers to invest in securities. A company that has extra cash and simply wants to earn a return on the idle funds can invest those funds in the stocks and bonds of other companies, either long or short term. We say these investments are *passive* because the managers of the investing company are not interested in influencing or controlling the other companies.

EXHIBIT A.1

The Walt Disney Company Consolidated Balance Sheets (Condensed)

THE WALT DISNEY COMPANY
Consolidated Balance Sheets
(in millions)

	October 3, 2020	September 28, 2019
ASSETS		
Current assets *(summarized)*	$ 35,251	$ 28,124
Film and television costs	25,022	22,810
Investments	3,903	3,224
Parks, resorts, and other property	32,078	31,603
Goodwill	77,689	80,293
Other assets	27,606	27,930
Total assets	$201,549	$193,984
LIABILITIES AND EQUITY		
Current liabilities *(summarized)*	$ 26,628	$ 31,341
Long-term liabilities *(summarized)*	86,658	68,754
Equity:		
Common stock	54,497	53,907
Retained earnings	38,315	42,494
Accumulated other comprehensive loss	(8,322)	(6,617)
Treasury stock	(907)	(907)
Noncontrolling interests	4,680	5,012
Total equity	88,263	93,889
Total liabilities and equity	$201,549	$193,984

Source: The Walt Disney Company

Sometimes a company decides to invest more heavily in another company with the purpose of influencing that company's policies and activities. As shown in Exhibit A.1, **The Walt Disney Company**'s balance sheets ending on October 3, 2020, and September 28, 2019, report the asset "Investments," which includes both passive investments and investments aimed at influencing affiliated companies.

Finally, managers may determine that controlling another company, by either purchasing it directly or becoming the majority shareholder, is desirable. If the acquired company goes out of existence, its assets and liabilities are added at fair value to the assets and liabilities of the buyer. If the acquired company continues as a separate legal entity, then the two companies' financial reports are combined into consolidated financial statements, as Disney has done (see the word **consolidated** in its statement title, Consolidated Balance Sheets in Exhibit A.1).

In this appendix, we discuss the accounting for four types of investments. First, we discuss investments in debt securities to be held to maturity using the amortized cost method, followed by the fair value method for those not held to maturity. Then, we examine the fair value method of accounting for passive investments in equity securities. For stock investments involving significant influence over another company, we then present the equity method. The appendix closes with a discussion of accounting for mergers and consolidated statements.

ORGANIZATION OF THE APPENDIX

Types of Investments and Accounting Methods	Passive Investment in Debt Securities	Passive Investment in Equity Securities	Investments for Significant Influence: Equity Method	Controlling Interests: Mergers and Acquisitions
• Passive Investments in Debt and Equity Securities • Investments in Stock for Significant Influence • Investments in Stock for Control	• Purchasing Debt Securities • Earning Interest Revenue • If Held to Maturity • If Actively Traded • If Not Held to Maturity or Actively Traded • Comparison of Financial Statement Effects of Using Fair Value	• Purchasing Equity Securities • Earning Dividend Revenue • Applying the Fair Value Method • Financial Statement Effects of Using Fair Value	• Recording Investments under the Equity Method • Reporting Investments under the Equity Method	• Recording a Merger • Reporting for the Combined Companies

TYPES OF INVESTMENTS AND ACCOUNTING METHODS

The accounting methods used to record investments are directly related to the type of investment (debt or equity security), how much is owned of the equity security, and how long management intends to hold the investments. The investment categories and the appropriate measuring and reporting methods are summarized as follows.

Passive Investments in Debt and Equity Securities

Passive investments are made to earn a return on funds that may be needed for future short-term or long-term purposes. This category includes both investments in debt (bonds and notes) and equity (stock) securities.

Debt securities. Because there is no ownership stake, debt securities are always considered passive investments. There are three types:

- **Held-to-maturity investments**–When the company intends and demonstrates the ability to hold the debt securities until they reach maturity, they are:
  - Measured at **amortized cost.**
  - Classified as noncurrent held-to-maturity investments, unless they mature within the next 12 months (then they are reported as current assets).
- **Trading securities**–When the investments are to be sold before maturity and are actively traded, they are:
  - Measured using the **fair value method.**
  - Classified as current assets.

Tip **Under the Fair Value Method:** Investments in securities that do not have readily determinable fair value are reported at cost and assessed each period for impairment.

- **Available-for-sale securities**—By default, when the debt securities are not intended to be held to maturity or actively traded, they are:
  - Measured using the **fair value method.**
  - Classified as current or noncurrent, depending on management's intent.

Equity securities. When the investing company **owns less than 20 percent** of the outstanding voting shares of another company and has no significant influence over the investee, the equity securities are considered passive:

- **Investments in equity securities**—They are:
  - Measured using the **fair value method.**
  - Classified as current or noncurrent equity investments, depending on management's intent.

Investments in Stock for Significant Influence

Significant influence is the ability to have an important impact on the operating, investing, and financing policies of another company. Significant influence is presumed if the investing company **owns from 20 to 50 percent** of the outstanding voting shares of the other company. However, other factors also may indicate that significant influence exists, such as membership on the board of directors of the other company, participation in the policy-making processes, evidence of material transactions between the two companies, an interchange of management personnel, or technological dependency. The **equity method** is used to measure and report this category of investments.

Investments in Stock for Control

Control is the ability to determine the operating and financing policies of another company through ownership of voting stock. Control is presumed when the investing company **owns more than 50 percent** of the outstanding voting stock of the other company. The **acquisition method** of accounting and consolidation are applied to combine the companies.

Exhibit A.2 summarizes the measuring and reporting methods and balance sheet classifications.

EXHIBIT A.2 Summary of Measuring and Reporting Methods for Investments

	Investment in Debt Securities of Another Entity			Investment in the Voting Common Stock of Another Entity		
Investment Category	**Passive**			**Passive**	**Significant Influence**	**Control**
Level of Ownership	**HELD-TO-MATURITY**	**TRADING**	**AVAILABLE FOR SALE**	**<20%** of outstanding voting shares†	**20–50%** of outstanding voting shares‡	**>50%** of outstanding voting shares
Measuring and Reporting Method	**Amortized cost**	**Fair value** (through Net Income)	**Fair value** (through Other Comprehensive Income)	**Fair value** (through Net Income)	**Equity method**	**Acquisition accounting and consolidation**
Balance Sheet Classification	Noncurrent; amount maturing next year would be classified as current	Current	Current or noncurrent	Current or noncurrent	Noncurrent	N/A; financial statements are consolidated

†<20% of company's voting common stock; investor is presumed not to have significant influence. Includes investments in preferred stock and other equity securities that are nonvoting.

‡20–50% of a company's voting common stock is presumed to represent significant influence; however, there are exceptions, including (1) if below 20% ownership with evidence of interlocking directorates, use equity method and (2) if 20–50% ownership but unable to obtain financial information from affiliate, use fair value method.

PASSIVE INVESTMENT IN DEBT SECURITIES

LEARNING OBJECTIVE A-1

Analyze and report investments in debt securities using the amortized cost and fair value methods.

Purchasing Debt Securities

On the date of purchase, a debt security (typically, a bond or note) may be acquired at the maturity amount (at **par**), for less than the maturity amount (at a **discount**), or for more than the maturity amount (at a **premium**).[1] The total cost of the investment, including all incidental acquisition costs such as transfer fees and broker commissions, is debited to the Investments account.

EXAMPLE:

To illustrate accounting for investments in debt securities of another company, assume that on October 1, 2023, **The Walt Disney Company** paid the *par value* of $150,000 for 6 percent bonds that mature on September 30, 2028.[2] Interest at 6 percent per year is paid on March 31 and September 30.

The journal entry to record the purchase of the bonds and its effect on the accounting equation follow:

	Debit	Credit
Investments (+A)	150,000	
Cash (−A)		150,000

Assets		=	Liabilities	+	Stockholders' Equity
Investments	+150,000				
Cash	−150,000				

Earning Interest Revenue

The Walt Disney Company's fiscal year ends on the Saturday closest to September 30. The bonds in this illustration were purchased at par or face value on October 1, 2023, and pay interest March 31 and September 30. Because no premium or discount needs to be amortized (because the bonds were purchased at par), interest revenue of $4,500 ($150,000 × 0.06 × ½ year) is earned and received in cash on March 31, 2024, and again on September 30, 2024. The following journal entry records the receipt of interest:

	Debit	Credit
Cash (+A)	4,500	
Interest revenue (+R, +SE)		4,500

Assets		=	Liabilities	+	Stockholders' Equity	
Cash	+4,500				Interest revenue (+R)	+4,500

This entry will be made every March 31 and September 30 during the period that Disney holds the bonds.

However, at the end of each fiscal year, measuring and reporting investments in debt securities depend on management's purpose. Will the debt instruments be

- Held to their maturity dates (classified as either current or noncurrent investments depending on the maturity date),

[1]The determination of the price of the bond is based on the present value techniques discussed in Chapter 9 and illustrated in Chapter 10. Many analysts refer to a bond price as a percentage of par. For example, *The Wall Street Journal* might report that an ExxonMobil bond with a par value of $1,000 is selling at 82.97. This means it would cost $829.70 (82.97 percent of $1,000) to buy the bond.

[2]When bond investors accept a rate of interest on a bond investment that is the same as the stated rate of interest on the bonds, the bonds will sell at par (i.e., at 100 or 100 percent of face value). For illustration of the journal entries of a bond purchased at other than par value, see Appendix Supplement at the end of this appendix.

- Traded actively over a short period of time (classified as current assets), or
- Neither held to maturity nor actively traded (classified as current or noncurrent investments based on management's intent)?

If Held To Maturity

When management has the intent and ability to hold debt securities (bonds or notes) until their maturity date (when the principal is due), they are considered appropriately as **held-to-maturity investments**. These investments in debt instruments are reported at cost adjusted for the amortization of any discount or premium (**amortized cost method**), not at their fair value. That means that **no fair value adjusting entry** is necessary at the end of the fiscal period because the debt securities already are measured at amortized cost.

When the bonds in the illustration mature on September 30, 2028, the journal entry to record receipt of the principal payment would be:

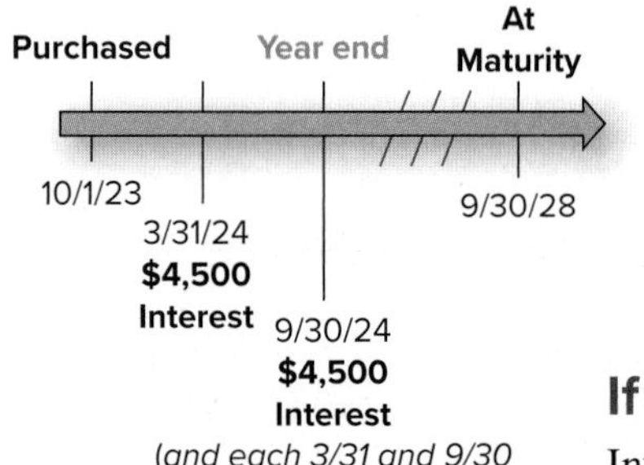

	Debit	Credit
Cash (+A)	150,000	
Investments (−A)		150,000

Assets		=	Liabilities	+	Stockholders' Equity
Cash	+150,000				
Investments	−150,000				

If Actively Traded

Investments in debt securities that are actively traded over short periods of time are accounted for as **trading securities**. The objective is to generate profits on short-term changes in the price of the securities. This approach is similar to the one taken by many financial institutions. The portfolio manager actively seeks opportunities to buy and sell securities. Trading securities with readily determinable market values are recorded by applying the **fair value method** and are reported as current assets on the balance sheet. To apply the **fair value method**, at the end of each fiscal year, the trading securities portfolio is adjusted **up or down** to the portfolio's fair value. Fair value is a security's current market value (the amount that would be received in an orderly sale). The adjusting journal entry will cause total assets to increase or decrease. The offsetting effect is reported **on the income statement as an unrealized gain or loss** (that is, the amount associated with the price change from holding the investment–no actual exchange transaction has been made). The unrealized gain or loss is subsequently closed to Retained Earnings to keep the balance sheet in balance.

Let's illustrate the year-end valuation of trading securities by assuming **The Walt Disney Company** decides to actively trade its $150,000 investment in debt securities provided in the prior example. Assume that:

- Disney has no prior trading securities,
- the investment in debt securities has a fair value at the end of the fiscal year on September 30, 2024, of $140,000, and
- the investment is sold on September 30, 2025 (end of the next fiscal year), for $165,000.

At the end of fiscal year 2024 First, compute the adjustment that is needed, as demonstrated in Exhibit A.3. The book value of the trading securities portfolio is the $150,000 balance in

EXHIBIT A.3

Fair Value Adjustment Illustration—Trading Securities

Fiscal Year Ending in	Fair Value	−	Book Value	=	Adjustment
2024	$140,000	−	$150,000	=	$(10,000)
2025	165,000	−	140,000	=	25,000

the account before the adjustment. The $140,000 is the fair value of the trading securities. **The difference is the unrealized loss of $10,000 that is reported on the Income Statement.** The adjusting entry to record the trading securities at fair value is

	Debit	Credit
Unrealized loss (+E, −SE)	10,000	
Investments (−A)		10,000

Assets		=	Liabilities	+	Stockholders' Equity	
Investments	−10,000				Unrealized loss (+E)	−10,000

Tip **Reminder:** Losses and gains, including Unrealized Loss or Gain on trading securities, are components of net income and are closed to Retained Earnings at the end of the accounting year.

Investments (Trading Securities)			
10/1/23 Purchase	150,000		
		10,000	9/30/24 AJE
9/30/24 Balance	140,000		

Trading securities sold in 2025 When the securities are traded (sold) on September 30, 2025, there are **two** journal entries: (1) the trading securities first are adjusted to fair value of $165,000 on September 30, 2025 (an increase of $25,000 since September 30, 2024 as shown in Exhibit A.3), with the unrealized gain reported on the Income Statement, and (2) then the sale is recorded.

Trading Securities:
Purchased — Year end — Sold
10/1/23
3/31/24 $4,500 Interest
AJE
9/30/24 $4,500 Interest
3/31/25 $4,500 Interest
9/30/25 $4,500 Interest
1. Adjust to fair value
2. Record sale

(1) Adjustment to fair value:

	Debit	Credit
Investments (+A)	25,000	
Unrealized gain (+R, +SE)		25,000

Assets		=	Liabilities	+	Stockholders' Equity	
Investments	+25,000				Unrealized gain (+R)	+25,000

(2) Sale of trading securities:

	Debit	Credit
Cash (+A)	165,000	
Investments (−A)		165,000

Assets		=	Liabilities	+	Stockholders' Equity
Cash	+165,000				
Investments	−165,000				

Investments (Trading Securities)			
10/1/23 Purchase	150,000		
		10,000	9/30/24 AJE
9/30/24 Balance	140,000		
9/30/25 AJE	**25,000**	**165,000**	9/30/25 Sale
9/30/25 Balance	0		

Note that, over the two years, the total net unrealized gain of $15,000 ($10,000 unrealized loss in 2024 plus $25,000 unrealized gain in 2025) is equal to the difference between the sales price of $165,000 and the original cost of $150,000.

If Not Held to Maturity or Actively Traded

If investments in debt securities are not held to maturity or traded actively, then, by default, the investments are considered **available-for-sale securities**. This is a common category of investments for most companies interested in earning a return on funds needed for future purposes. Available-for-sale securities with readily determinable market values are reported at **fair value** (those typically available on securities exchanges) and may be classified as current or noncurrent assets depending on whether management intends to sell the securities during the upcoming year.

Tip **Key difference:** Any unrealized gain or loss is treated differently between:

- **Trading securities→ to Net Income** (which is closed to Retained Earnings)
- **Available-for-sale securities→ to Other Comprehensive Income** (which is a component of stockholders' equity)

For reporting the investments, the available-for-sale securities portfolio is adjusted **up or down** to the portfolio's **fair value**.[3] The adjusting journal entry for the unrealized holding gain or loss will cause total assets to increase or decrease. The offsetting effect is **not reported on the income statement, unlike the treatment for trading securities**. Instead, any **unrealized gain or loss** is recorded **as a component of Other Comprehensive Income on the Statement of Comprehensive Income**. When a sale takes place, the investment portfolio is first adjusted to fair value on the sale date. Then, the accumulated net unrealized gain or loss for those investments that are sold is reclassified out of Other Comprehensive Income and reported on the current period's income statement as **a realized gain or loss.**

To illustrate the year-end valuation and then subsequent sale of available-for-sale debt securities, assume that **The Walt Disney Company** purchases the $150,000 in bonds at par and intends to hold the securities for a couple of years. The purchase and interest revenue earned journal entries are the same as for the held-to-maturity bond investment (illustrated previously). What is different is how to report and record fair value adjustments and subsequent sales of securities. Let's assume that:

- Disney has no additional investments in available-for-sale securities,
- the investment in debt securities has a fair value at the end of the fiscal year on September 30, 2024, of $140,000, and
- the entire investment is sold on September 30, 2025 (in the next fiscal year), for $165,000 in cash.

At the end of fiscal year 2024 First, compute the adjustment that is needed as demonstrated in Exhibit A.4. The book value of the available-for-sale securities portfolio is the $150,000 balance in the account before the adjustment. The $140,000 after the adjustment is the fair value of the investment. **The difference is the $10,000 unrealized loss that is reported on the Statement of Comprehensive Income** as a component of Other Comprehensive Income (OCI for short). The September 2024 adjusting entry to record the available-for-sale securities at fair value is:

	Debit	Credit
Unrealized loss (−OCI, −SE)	10,000	
Investments (−A)		10,000

Assets		=	Liabilities	+	Stockholders' Equity	
Investments	−10,000				Unrealized loss (−OCI)	−10,000

Investments (Available-for-Sale Securities)			
10/1/23 Purchase	150,000		
		10,000	9/30/24 AJE
9/30/24 Balance	140,000		

EXHIBIT A.4

Fair Value Adjustment Illustration—Available-for-Sale Debt Securities

Fiscal Year Ending in	Fair Value	−	Book Value	=	Adjustment
2024	$140,000	−	$150,000	=	$ (10,000)
2025	165,000	−	140,000	=	25,000
Balance in Other Comprehensive Income for these securities					$ 15,000 (Balance before reclassification)

[3]Companies often keep the asset value at cost and record the change in fair value in a related valuation allowance that is added to or subtracted from the asset. This does not change the financial statement presentation.

Available-for-sale securities sold in 2025 There are **three** entries that need to be recorded for the sale of available-for-sale debt securities:

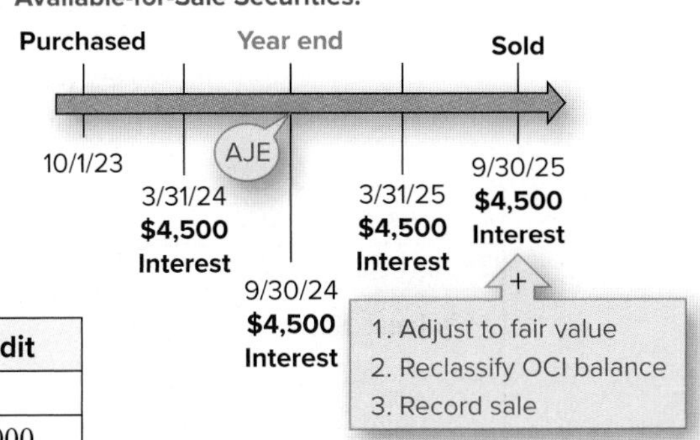

(1) *Adjust to fair value:* The investment account is again adjusted to its fair value on the date of sale of September 30, 2025. In our illustration, the current fair value is $165,000 and the book value is $140,000. The adjustment is an increase to the investment account of $25,000 with the unrealized gain increasing Other Comprehensive Income (OCI).

	Debit	Credit
Investments (+A)	25,000	
Unrealized gain (+OCI, +SE)		25,000

Assets		=	Liabilities	+	Stockholders' Equity	
Investments	+25,000				Unrealized gain (+OCI)	+25,000

(2) *Reclassify the Other Comprehensive Income balance:* Then, the total net unrealized gain or loss accumulated in Other Comprehensive Income for the securities that are sold is reclassified as a **realized** gain or loss to be reported on the income statement. In our illustration, the realized gain is $15,000, equal to the difference between the original cost of $150,000 and the current fair value of $165,000. It also is equal to the net adjustments over the holding period in Other Comprehensive Income ($(10,000) + $25,000).

	Debit	Credit
Unrealized gain (−OCI, −SE)	15,000	
Gain on sale of investments (+R, +SE)		15,000

Assets	=	Liabilities	+	Stockholders' Equity	
				Unrealized gain (−OCI)	−15,000
				Gain on sale of investments (+R)	+15,000

(3) *Record the sale of the available-for-sale securities:* Finally, the sale is recorded with the investments account decreased by its book value (equal to fair value after the adjustment in (1) above) and cash received of $165,000.

	Debit	Credit
Cash (+A)	165,000	
Investments (−A)		165,000

Assets		=	Liabilities	+	Stockholders' Equity
Cash	+165,000				
Investments	−165,000				

Investments (Available-for-Sale Securities)			
10/1/23 Purchase	150,000		
		10,000	9/30/24 AJE
9/30/24 Balance	140,000		
9/30/25 AJE	**25,000**	**165,000**	9/30/25 Sale
9/30/25 Balance	0		

Comparison of Financial Statement Effects of Using Fair Value

Based on the illustrations above for investments in debt securities reported at fair value, the following comparison summarizes the effects on financial statements across years for trading securities and available-for-sale securities. **Note that the difference between the two portfolios is how unrealized gains and losses are reported.** For trading securities, the $10,000 unrealized loss is reported on the 2024 income statement and the $25,000 unrealized gain is reported on the 2025 income statement. However, for available-for-sale securities, the $15,000 net unrealized gain is accumulated in Other Comprehensive Income and then reclassified as a $15,000 realized gain on the 2025 income statement. The overall effect after two years is that net income is increased by $33,000 under both types of investments–$15,000 related to the positive change in the investment value and $18,000 due to interest revenue earned on the investments.

Ignoring income taxes		2024	2025	
Trading Securities				
Balance Sheet	*Investments*	$140,000	$0	
			(Sold for $165,000)	
	Retained earnings (effect, not balance)	(1,000)	34,000	
Income Statement	*Interest revenue ($4,500 two times per year)*	9,000	9,000	
	Unrealized gains (losses)	(10,000)	25,000	
Available-for-Sale Securities				
Balance Sheet	*Investments*	$140,000	$0	
			(Sold for $165,000)	
	Retained earnings (effect, not balance)	9,000	24,000	
	Accumulated other comprehensive income	(10,000)	0	Balance after reclassification
Income Statement	*Interest revenue ($4,500 two times per year)*	9,000	9,000	
	Gain on sale of investments	–	15,000	Net unrealized gain reclassified out of OCI and into income
Statement of Comprehensive Income	*Unrealized gains (losses)*	(10,000)	25,000	
	Reclassification adjustment		(15,000)	

Includes net income plus/minus other effects not on income statement

PAUSE FOR FEEDBACK

Other than debt investments held to maturity that are reported at amortized cost, **passive investments in debt securities** are recorded at cost and adjusted to fair value at year-end. The resulting unrealized gain or loss is recorded.

- For trading securities, the net unrealized gains and losses are reported in net income (which is closed to retained earnings).
- For available-for-sale securities, the net unrealized gains and losses are included in Other Comprehensive Income (which is reported as part of stockholders' equity as Accumulated Other Comprehensive Income [Loss]).

Any interest earned is reported as revenue. To see if you understand passive debt investments accounting and reporting, complete the following quiz.

SELF-STUDY QUIZ

On January 1, 2023, Rosa Food Corporation invested in bonds of **Amazon.com**. Rosa's reporting period ends December 31.

a. Record the purchase of $500,000, 4 percent bonds at par.
b. The bond investment pays interest annually on December 31. Record the interest earned and received in cash on December 31, 2023.
c. Record the fair value adjustment on December 31, 2023, assuming the fair value is $508,000.
d. Record the interest earned and received in cash on December 31, 2024.

e. Record all of the entries related to the sale of the securities on December 31, 2024, for $505,000 cash.
f. What are the accounts and amounts reported on the 2024 income statement?
g. What are the line items and amounts reported on the 2024 statement of comprehensive income, excluding net income?

Required:

1. Prepare the journal entries for transactions (*a*) through (*e*) using the side-by-side table below, first assuming the investments are treated as trading securities and then as available-for-sale securities.
2. Then, answer questions (*f*) and (*g*) in the same side-by-side table.

	Trading Securities			Available-for-Sale Securities		
		Debit	**Credit**		**Debit**	**Credit**
a.						
b.						

After you have completed your answers, check them below.

GUIDED HELP A-1

For additional step-be-step video instruction on recording transactions related to trading securities and available-for-sale securities, go to mhhe.com/libby_gha-1.

Related Homework: MA-3, MA-4, EA-2, EA-3, PA-2, PA-3

Solutions to SELF-STUDY QUIZ

	Trading Securities			Available-for-Sale Securities		
		Debit	**Credit**		**Debit**	**Credit**
a.	Investments (+A)	500,000		Investments (+A)	500,000	
	Cash (−A)		500,000	Cash (−A)		500,000
b.	Cash (+A)	20,000		Cash (+A)	20,000	
	Interest revenue (+R, +SE)		20,000	Interest revenue (+R, +SE)		20,000
	$500,000 × 0.04 × 12/12					
c.	Investments (+A)	8,000		Investments (+A)	8,000	
	Unrealized gain (+R, +SE)		8,000	Unrealized gain (+OCI, +SE)		8,000
	FV $508,000 – BV $500,000					
d.	Cash (+A)	20,000		Cash (+A)	20,000	
	Interest revenue (+R, +SE)		20,000	Interest revenue (+R, +SE)		20,000
e.	(1) Unrealized loss (+E, −SE)	3,000		(1) Unrealized loss (−OCL, −SE)	3,000	
	Investments (−A)		3,000	Investments (−A)		3,000
	FV $505,000 – BV $508,000					
				(2) Unrealized gain (−OCI, −SE)	5,000	
				Gain on sale of investments (+R, +SE)		5,000
				2023 OCI gain $8,000 – 2024 OCI loss $3,000		
	(2) Cash (+A)	505,000		(3) Cash (+A)	505,000	
	Investments (−A)		505,000	Investments (−A)		505,000
f.	Interest revenue	$20,000		Interest revenue	$20,000	
	Unrealized loss	(3,000)		Gain on sale of investments	5,000	
g.	Unrealized gains and losses are not reported on the statement of comprehensive income.			Unrealized loss	(3,000)	
				Reclassification of net unrealized gain	5,000	

LEARNING OBJECTIVE A-2

Analyze and report passive investments in equity securities using the fair value method.

PASSIVE INVESTMENT IN EQUITY SECURITIES

When a company purchases and owns less than 20 percent of the outstanding voting stock of another company, the investment in these equity securities is usually considered passive. Passive investments in equity securities, whether current or noncurrent, are reported **at fair value** with any year-end adjustments for **unrealized gains or losses reported in net income** (similar to the accounting for debt securities actively traded).

EXAMPLE:

To illustrate accounting for investment in equity securities, assume that on October 1, 2023, **The Walt Disney Company** purchased 10 percent of the voting common stock of Green Light Pictures[4] for $15 per share. Green Light, an independent film studio, has 100,000 shares of stock outstanding. In addition, the studio pays a dividend of $0.50 per share each year at the end of September, its fiscal year end.

Purchasing Equity Securities

In the example, Disney purchased 10,000 shares (10 percent of Green Light's 100,000 shares outstanding) for $150,000 (10,000 shares × $15 per share). The journal entry to record the purchase of the stock and its effect on the accounting equation follow:

	Debit	Credit
Investments (+A)	150,000	
Cash (−A)		150,000

Assets		=	Liabilities	+	Stockholders' Equity
Investments	+150,000				
Cash	−150,000				

Earning Dividend Revenue

Green Light declares and pays dividends at the end of September each year. The following journal entry records the receipt of dividends of $5,000 (10,000 shares × $0.50 per share):

	Debit	Credit
Cash (+A)	5,000	
Dividend revenue (+R, +SE)		5,000

Assets		=	Liabilities	+	Stockholders' Equity	
Cash	+5,000				Dividend revenue (+R)	+5,000

These will be the same accounts used in the entry each year that dividends are declared by Green Light.

Applying the Fair Value Method

Because Disney owns less than 20 percent of the outstanding voting common stock of Green Light Pictures, Disney accounts for its investment in equity securities by applying the **fair value method.** Regardless of how actively the equity investments are traded, they are classified as current or noncurrent assets on the balance sheet, depending on management's intent.

Adjustments to fair value at year-end are treated similarly to what is done for trading securities discussed earlier. As such, the equity investments portfolio is **increased or decreased each period** with the offsetting effect reported on the income statement as an **unrealized gain or loss** (from holding the investment).

[4]Green Light Pictures is a fictitious company.

Let's illustrate the year-end valuation and subsequent sale of investments in equity securities by assuming that:

- Disney has no other investments in equity securities,
- the fair value of Green Light's common stock was $12 per share at September 30, 2024 ($120,000), and $16.50 per share at September 30, 2025 ($165,000), and
- Disney sold the stock portfolio on March 31, 2026, for $19 per share ($190,000) (before Green Light declared any dividends).

At the end of fiscal year 2024 First, compute the adjustment that is needed, as demonstrated in Exhibit A.5. Fair value of $120,000 is below book value of $150,000, the balance in the investments account before the adjustment. The adjusting entry to record the investments in equity securities at fair value is

	Debit	Credit
Unrealized loss (+E, −SE)	30,000	
Investments (−A)		30,000

Assets		=	Liabilities	+	Stockholders' Equity	
Investments	−30,000				Unrealized loss (+E)	−30,000

Investments (Equity Securities)

10/1/23 Purchase	150,000		
		30,000	9/30/24 AJE
9/30/24 Balance	120,000		

At the end of fiscal year 2025 At the end of 2025, the portfolio is adjusted again to fair value. As shown in Exhibit A.5, the adjustment is the amount needed to bring the investments from the account's $120,000 book value to the $165,000 current year-end fair value–an increase of $45,000.

	Debit	Credit
Investments (+A)	45,000	
Unrealized gain (+R, +SE)		45,000

Assets		=	Liabilities	+	Stockholders' Equity	
Investments	+45,000				Unrealized gain (+R)	+45,000

Investments (Equity Securities)

10/1/23 Purchase	150,000		
		30,000	9/30/24 AJE
9/30/24 Balance	120,000		
9/30/25 AJE	**45,000**		
9/30/25 Balance	165,000		

Fiscal Year Ending in	Fair Value	−	Book Value	=	Adjustment
2024	$120,000	−	$150,000	=	$(30,000)
2025	165,000	−	120,000	=	45,000
2026	190,000	−	165,000	=	25,000

EXHIBIT A.5

Fair Value Method—Passive Investment in Equity Securities Illustration

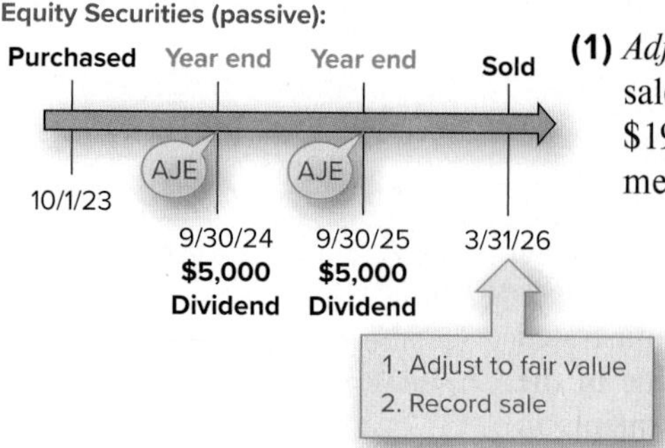

Investments in equity securities sold in 2026 There are **two** entries that need to be recorded for the sale of investments in equity securities:

(1) *Adjust to fair value:* The investment account is again adjusted to its fair value on the sale date of March 31, 2026. In our illustration in Exhibit A.5, the current fair value is $190,000 and the book value is $165,000. The adjustment is an increase to the investment account of $25,000.

	Debit	Credit
Investments (+A)	25,000	
Unrealized gain (+R, +SE)		25,000

Assets		=	Liabilities	+	Stockholders' Equity	
Investments	+25,000				Unrealized gain (+R)	+25,000

(2) *Record the sale of the equity securities:* The sale is recorded with the investments account decreased by its book value (equal to fair value after the adjustment in (1) above) and cash received of $190,000.

	Debit	Credit
Cash (+A)	190,000	
Investments (−A)		190,000

Assets		=	Liabilities	+	Stockholders' Equity
Cash	+190,000				
Investments	−190,000				

Investments (Equity Securities)			
10/1/23 Purchase	150,000		
		30,000	9/30/24 AJE
9/30/24 Balance	120,000		
9/30/25 AJE	45,000		
9/30/25 Balance	165,000		
3/31/26 AJE	**25,000**	**190,000**	3/31/26 Sale
9/30/26 Balance	0		

Financial Statement Effects of Using Fair Value

Based on the illustrations above for investments in equity securities reported at fair value, the following summarizes the effects on financial statements across years for equity securities investments.

		2024	2025	2026
Equity Securities				
Balance Sheet	*Investments*	$120,000	$165,000	$0 (Sold for $190,000)
	Retained earnings (effect, not balance)	(25,000)	50,000	25,000
Income Statement	*Dividend revenue*	5,000	5,000	0
	Unrealized gains (losses)	(30,000)	45,000	25,000

PAUSE FOR FEEDBACK

Ownership of less than 20 percent of the outstanding voting stock of another company is presumed to be a passive investment. The investment is reported at fair value with year-end adjustments for unrealized gains or losses reported on the income statement. Complete the following quiz to ensure that you understand accounting and reporting for passive equity investments and that you can apply the fair value method.

SELF-STUDY QUIZ

On August 1, Year 1, Noelle Corp. purchased 60,000 shares of BeckyCo. common stock (400,000 shares outstanding) for $31 per share as a long-term investment. Noelle's year ends on December 31. The following information pertains to the price per share of BeckyCo. stock:

Stock Price	
12/31/Year 1	$33
12/31/Year 2	30

BeckyCo. reported $6,000,000 in net income and declared dividends of $0.75 per share each year (paid on January 10 of the following year). Noelle sold all of the BeckyCo. stock on February 12, Year 3, at a price of $34 per share.

Required:
Prepare any journal entries that are required by the facts presented.

Related Homework: MA-7, EA-4, EA-7, PA-3, PA-4, PA-5, CONA-1

Solutions to SELF-STUDY QUIZ

		Debit	Credit	
8/1/Year 1	Investments (+A)	1,860,000		← *60,000 shares × $31 per share*
Purchase	Cash (−A)		1,860,000	
12/31/Year 1	Dividends receivable (+A)	45,000		← *60,000 shares × $0.75 per share*
Dividends	Dividend revenue (+R, +SE)		45,000	
Adjustment	Investments (+A)	120,000		
	Unrealized gain (+R, +SE)*		120,000	
1/10/Year 2	Cash (+A)	45,000		
	Dividends receivable (−A)		45,000	
12/31/Year 2	Dividends receivable (+A)	45,000		← *60,000 shares × $0.75 per share*
Dividends	Dividend revenue (+R, +SE)		45,000	
Adjustment	Unrealized loss (+E, −SE)*	180,000		
	Investments (−A)		180,000	
1/10/Year 3	Cash (+A)	45,000		
	Dividends receivable (−A)		45,000	
2/12/Year 3	Investments (+A)	240,000		
Adjustment	Unrealized gain (+R, +SE)*		240,000	
Sale	Cash (+A)	2,040,000		
	Investments (+A)		2,040,000	

* Adjustment computations:

DATE	FAIR VALUE	−	BOOK VALUE BEFORE ADJUSTMENT	=	ADJUSTMENT
12/31/Year 1	60,000 shares × $33 = $1,980,000		$1,860,000		$120,000
12/31/Year 2	60,000 shares × $30 = 1,800,000		1,980,000		(180,000)
12/31/Year 3	60,000 shares × $34 = 2,040,000		1,800,000		240,000

LEARNING OBJECTIVE A-3

Analyze and report investments involving significant influence using the equity method.

INVESTMENTS FOR SIGNIFICANT INFLUENCE: EQUITY METHOD

On its balance sheet in Exhibit A.1, **The Walt Disney Company**'s investment account includes both debt and equity securities as passive investments *and* investments in the stock of other companies in which Disney takes a more active role as an investor (i.e., it exerts significant influence over the affiliated companies).

For a variety of reasons, an investor may want to exert influence (presumed by owning 20 to 50 percent of the outstanding voting stock) without becoming the controlling shareholder (presumed when owning more than 50 percent of the voting stock). Examples follow:

- A retailer may want to influence a manufacturer to be sure that it can obtain certain products designed to its specifications.
- A manufacturer may want to influence a computer consulting firm to ensure that it can incorporate the consulting firm's cutting-edge technology in its manufacturing processes.
- A manufacturer may recognize that a parts supplier lacks experienced management and could prosper with additional managerial support.

The **equity method** must be used when an investor can exert **significant influence over an affiliate.** As of October 3, 2020, Disney appropriately applied the equity method to its 20 to 50 percent owned investments in other companies, including **A+E Television Networks** (50 percent owned), **CTV Specialty Television** (a variety of Canadian networks, 30 percent owned), **Seven TV** (a 20 percent-owned Disney channel in Russia), and **Tata Sky Limited** (a direct-to-home distribution platform in India, 30 percent owned). On the balance sheet, these investments are classified as noncurrent assets.

Recording Investments under the Equity Method

Under the equity method, the investor's 20 to 50 percent ownership of a company presumes significant influence over the affiliate's process of earning income. As a consequence, the investor reports its portion of the affiliate's net income (or net loss) as its income (or loss) and increases (or decreases if a net loss) the investment account by the same amount.[5] Similarly, the receipt of dividends by the investor is treated as a reduction of the investment account, not revenue. A summary follows:

+ Investments (in Affiliates) (A) –	
Beginning balance • Purchases of investments	• Sales of investments
• Company's % share of affiliate's net income *(credit Equity in investee earnings)* **↑ income**	• Company's % share of affiliates' net losses *(debit Equity in investee losses)* **↓ income**
	• Company's share of affiliate's dividends declared for the period (*debit Dividends Receivable*) **No effect on income**
Ending balance	

Purchase of Stock

For simplification, let's assume the following:

- On September 30, 2023 (end of its fiscal year), The Walt Disney Company had no long-term investment in companies over which it exerted significant influence,

[5]Likewise, the investor also reports its portion of the affiliate's other comprehensive income (e.g., from unrealized gains and losses in its investment in available-for-sale debt securities) in a similar manner, with the offsetting account Equity in Other Comprehensive Income of Investees.

- At the beginning of its next fiscal year, Disney purchased a 40 percent interest in Green Light Pictures for $400,000 cash (40,000 shares of Green Light's 100,000 outstanding voting common stock shares), and
- Green Light earns differing amounts of net income each year and declares and pays dividends annually. Green Light's fiscal year ends on September 30, the same as Disney.

Disney was presumed to have significant influence over the affiliate. Therefore, Disney must use the equity method to account for this investment. The purchase of the asset would be recorded at cost.

	Debit	Credit
Investments (+A)	400,000	
Cash (−A)		400,000

Assets		=	Liabilities	+	Stockholders' Equity
Investments	+400,000				
Cash	−400,000				

Earnings of Affiliates

Because the investor can influence the process of earning income for the affiliates, the investor company bases its investment income on the affiliates' earnings rather than the dividends affiliates declare. During the fiscal year ending in 2024, Green Light Pictures reported a net income of $500,000 for the year. The Walt Disney Company's percentage share of Green Light's income is $200,000 (40% × $500,000) and is recorded as follows:

	Debit	Credit
Investments (+A)	200,000	
Equity in investee earnings (+R, +SE)		200,000

Assets		=	Liabilities	+	Stockholders' Equity	
Investments	+200,000				Equity in investee earnings (+R)	+200,000

If the affiliates report a net loss for the period, the investor records its percentage share of the loss by decreasing the investment account and recording Equity in Investee Losses. The Equity in Investee Earnings (or Losses) is reported in the Other Items section of the income statement, with interest revenue, dividend revenue, and interest expense.[6]

Dividends Declared

Because Disney can influence the dividend policies of its equity-method investments, any dividends declared by the affiliate should **not** be recorded as investment income. Instead, dividends declared by the affiliate reduce Disney's investment account. During the fiscal year ending in 2024, Green Light declared a cash dividend of $0.50 per share to stockholders. Disney will receive $20,000 ($0.50 × 40,000 shares) from Green Light in the future.

	Debit	Credit
Dividends receivable (+A)	20,000	
Investments (−A)		20,000

Assets		=	Liabilities	+	Stockholders' Equity
Dividends receivable	+20,000				
Investments	−20,000				

[6]In this illustration, if Green Light Pictures also reported other comprehensive income of $100,000 for the year, an additional $40,000 ($100,000 × 0.40) would be recorded by Walt Disney as Equity in Other Comprehensive Income of Investees.

In summary, the effects for the fiscal year ending September 30, 2024, are reflected in the following T-accounts:

Investments (in Affiliates) (A)			
9/30/23 Balance	0		
2024 Purchase	400,000		
2024 Share of affiliate's earnings	200,000	20,000	2024 Share of affiliate's dividends
9/30/24 Balance	580,000		

Equity in Investee Earnings (R)			
		0	10/1/23 Balance
		200,000	2024 Share of affiliate's earnings
		200,000	9/30/24 Balance

Reporting Investments under the Equity Method

The Investments account is reported on the balance sheet as a long-term asset. However, subsequent to the investment purchase, the investment account **does not reflect either cost or fair value.** Instead, the following occurs:

- The investment account is increased by the cost of shares that were purchased and the proportional share of the affiliates' net income.
- The account is reduced by the proportional amount of dividends declared from affiliate companies, the proportional share of affiliates' net losses, and the cost of any shares that were sold.

At the end of the accounting period, accountants **do not adjust the investment account to reflect changes in the fair value** of the securities that are held.[7] When the securities are sold, the difference between the cash received and the book value of the investment is recorded as a gain or loss on the sale of the investment and is reported on the income statement in the Other Items section.

PAUSE FOR FEEDBACK

If between 20 and 50 percent of the outstanding voting shares are owned, significant influence over the affiliate firm's operating and financing policies is presumed, and the equity method is applied. Under the **equity method,** the investor records the investment at cost on the acquisition date. Each period thereafter, the investment account is increased (or decreased) by the proportionate interest in the income (or loss) reported by the affiliate corporation and decreased by the proportionate share of the dividends declared by the affiliate corporation.

SELF-STUDY QUIZ

To test your understanding of these concepts, answer the following.

At the beginning of 2024, Weld Company purchased 30 percent (20,000 shares) of the outstanding voting stock of another company for $600,000 cash. During 2024, the affiliate declared $50,000 in cash dividends. For 2024, the affiliate reported net income of $150,000 and no other

[7]FAS 159 (ASC 825-10) does allow companies to elect fair value treatment for equity method investments, but few companies are expected to make the election.

comprehensive income. The stock had a fair value of $34 per share on December 31, 2024, Weld's fiscal year end.

Required:

1. For 2024, record the following:
   a. Record the purchase by Weld.
   b. Record Weld's entry for the affiliate's declaration of dividends.
   c. Record Weld's equity in the affiliate's earnings.
   d. Record any year-end adjustment to Weld's investments account.
2. What would be reported on Weld's balance sheet for the investment in the affiliate at the end of 2024? (*Hint:* Construct a T-account.)
3. What would be reported on Weld's 2024 income statement for the investment in the affiliate?

After you have completed your answers, check them below.

Related Homework: M-8, EA-5, EA-6, EA-7, PA-4, PA-5, PA-6

FINANCIAL ANALYSIS

Transaction Structuring: Selecting Accounting Methods for Minority Investments

Managers can choose freely between LIFO and FIFO or accelerated depreciation and straight-line depreciation. In the case of minority (≤50 percent owned) investments, investments of less than 20 percent of a company's outstanding stock are usually accounted for under the fair value method and investments of 20 to 50 percent are accounted for under the equity method.

However, managers may be able to structure the acquisition of stock in a manner that permits them to use the accounting method that they prefer. For example, a company that wants to use the fair value method could purchase only 19.9 percent of the outstanding stock of another company and achieve the same investment goals as it would with a 20 percent investment. Why might managers want to avoid

Solutions to SELF-STUDY QUIZ

1. Journal entries:

		Debit	Credit	
a.	Investments (+A)	600,000		← *30 percent interest*
	Cash (−A)		600,000	
b.	Dividends receivable (+A)	15,000		← *$50,000 × 0.30*
	Investments (−A)		15,000	
c.	Investments (+A)	45,000		← *$150,0000 × 0.30*
	Equity in investee earnings (+R, +SE)		45,000	

   d. Under the equity method, no adjustment to fair value is recorded or reported.
2. Balance in Investments at December 31, 2024 = $630,000 [$600,000 − $15,000 + $45,000]
3. Equity in investee earnings = $45,000

Investments (in Affiliates) (A)

1/1/24 Balance	0		
2024 Purchase	600,000		
2024 Share of affiliate's earnings	45,000	15,000	2024 Share of affiliate's dividends
12/31/24 Balance	630,000		

using the equity method? Most managers prefer to minimize variations in reported earnings. If a company were planning to buy stock in a firm that reported large earnings in some years and large losses in others, it might want to use the fair value method to avoid reporting its share of the affiliate's earnings and losses.

Auditors will review management's application of the fair value and equity methods for investments near the 20 percent ownership level to determine if the proper method was used because significant influence still may be present. For example, the company has the ability to influence the timing or amount of dividends and/or production decisions, and has the ability to have individuals elected to the affiliate's board of directors.

Analysts who compare several companies must understand management's reporting choices and the way in which differences between the fair value and equity methods can affect earnings.

FOCUS ON CASH FLOWS

Investments

Many of the effects of applying the fair value method to passive investments and the equity method to investments held for significant influence affect net income but not cash flow. These items require adjustments under the indirect method when converting net income to cash flows from operating activities.

In General Investments have a number of effects on the statement of cash flows:

1. The cash resulting from the sale or purchase is reflected in the Investing Activities section.
2. In the Operating Activities section, there are a number of adjustments to net income:
   a. Any gain (loss) on the sale is subtracted from (added to) net income.
   b. Any unrealized holding gain (loss) on trading securities (debt) and equity securities (from applying the fair value method) is subtracted from (added to) net income.
   c. Equity in income (losses) of investees (from applying the equity method) is subtracted from (added to) net income because no cash was involved in the recording of the revenue under the equity method.
   d. Any dividends received from an affiliate are added to net income because, when cash was received, no revenue was recorded under the equity method.

Effect on the Statement of Cash Flows	
	Effect on Cash Flows
Operating Activities	
Net income	$xxx
Adjusted for	
Gains/losses on sale of investments	-/+
Net unrealized holding gains/losses on trading and passive equity securities	-/+
Equity in investee earnings/losses	-/+
Dividends received from affiliated companies	+
Investing Activities	
Purchase of investments	-
Sale of investments	+

CONTROLLING INTERESTS: MERGERS AND ACQUISITIONS

LEARNING OBJECTIVE A-4

Analyze and report investments in controlling interests.

Before we discuss financial reporting issues for situations in which a company owns more than 50 percent of the outstanding common stock of another corporation, we should consider management's reasons for acquiring this level of ownership:

1. **Vertical integration.** In this type of acquisition, a company acquires another at a different level in the channels of distribution. For example, oil companies such as **ExxonMobil** are active at vertical integration, from locating oil deposits, drilling and extracting the crude, and transporting it, to refining it into various petroleum products and distributing the fuel to company-owned retail stations.
2. **Horizontal growth.** These acquisitions involve companies at the same level in the channels of distribution. For example, in early 2015, **Heinz** merged with **Kraft Foods** in a $45 billion deal that created the world's fifth-largest food and beverage company.
3. **Synergy.** The operations of two companies together may be more profitable than the combined profitability of the companies as separate entities. The Heinz-Kraft merger was expected to provide for $1.5 billion in annual cost savings. In addition, Heinz earns 60 percent of its sales from regions beyond North America, whereas Kraft's sales are mostly in North America. The merger provides opportunities to sell Kraft brands globally, realizing higher profits.

Scott Olson/Getty Images

Understanding why one company has acquired control over other companies is a key factor in understanding the company's overall business strategy.

Recording a Merger

The easiest way to understand the statements that result from the purchase of another company is to consider the case of a simple merger, where one company purchases all of the assets and liabilities of another and the acquired company goes out of existence as a separate corporation. We will consider the case in which **The Walt Disney Company** acquires all of the assets and liabilities of Green Light Pictures for $1,000,000 cash.

The acquisition method is the only method allowed by U.S. GAAP and IFRS for recording a merger or acquisition. It requires that the assets and liabilities of Green Light be recorded by Disney at their **fair value** on the date of the merger. So the acquiring company, in this case Disney, must go through a two-step process, often called the **purchase price allocation,** to determine how to record the acquisition:

Step 1: **Estimate the fair value of the acquired company's tangible assets, identifiable intangible assets, and liabilities.** This includes all assets and liabilities, regardless of whether and at what amount they were recorded on the books of the acquired company.

Step 2: **Compute goodwill, the excess of the total purchase price over the fair value of the acquired assets minus any assumed liabilities listed in Step 1.**

Tip **Reminder → Goodwill** was already defined and discussed in Chapter 8; it is an intangible asset and is computed as follows:

Purchase price	
−Fair value of acquired assets minus liabilities assumed	
Goodwill	

For our example, assume that Green Light owned two assets (equipment and a patent) and had one liability (a note payable). Disney followed the two steps and produced the following:

Step 1: Estimate the fair value of the acquired company's tangible assets, identifiable intangible assets, and liabilities.

Fair value of Green Light's −	Equipment	$350,000	$950,000 total assets
	Patents	600,000	
	Note Payable	100,000	

Step 2: Compute goodwill as follows:

Purchase price for Green Light	$1,000,000
Less: Fair value of assets ($950,000) minus liabilities ($100,000)	850,000
Premium paid above fair value (recorded as goodwill)	$ 150,000

Disney would then account for the merger by recording the assets and liabilities listed above and reducing cash for the amount paid as follows:

	Debit	Credit
Equipment (+A)	350,000	
Patents (+A)	600,000	
Goodwill (+A)	150,000	
Notes payable (+L)		100,000
Cash (−A)		1,000,000

Assets		=	Liabilities		+	Stockholders' Equity
Equipment	+350,000		Notes payable	+100,000		
Patents	+600,000					
Goodwill	+150,000					
Cash	−1,000,000					

FINANCIAL ANALYSIS

Disney Buys Fox

In March 2019, **The Walt Disney Company** (the world's largest media conglomerate) completed a major acquisition of **21st Century Fox** (the world's third-largest media conglomerate, now renamed **TFCF Corporation**). Disney purchased most of Fox's assets, with a fair value of $74.2 billion, and assumed $53.8 billion in liabilities for $69.5 billion in stock and cash. The purchase price exceeded the fair value of the net assets acquired by $49.1 billion–all allocated to goodwill.

The deal gave Disney more content, including 20th Century Fox movies (e.g., *X-Men, War for the Planet of the Apes, Bohemian Rhapsody,* and *Hidden Figures*), Fox television shows (e.g., *The Simpsons, Family Guy, The Masked Singer,* and *Prodigal Son*), and Fox Sports Networks. In announcing the acquisition, the deal was expected to provide cost-saving synergies of at least $2 billion.

In summary, when performing a purchase price allocation, it is important to remember two points:

- The book values on the acquired company's balance sheet are irrelevant unless they represent fair value.
- Goodwill is reported only if it is acquired in a merger or acquisition transaction.

In its 2020 annual report, The Walt Disney Company describes its policy for accounting for and reporting mergers and acquisitions in the following note:

THE WALT DISNEY COMPANY

REAL WORLD EXCERPT:

Fiscal Year 2020 Annual Report

2 Summary of Significant Accounting Policies

Principles of Consolidation

The consolidated financial statements of the Company include the accounts of The Walt Disney Company and its majority-owned and controlled subsidiaries. Intercompany accounts and transactions have been eliminated in consolidation.

Source: The Walt Disney Company

Reporting for the Combined Companies

After the merger in the Disney-Green Light illustration above, **The Walt Disney Company** will treat the acquired assets and liabilities in the same manner as if they were acquired individually. For example, the company will depreciate the $350,000 added to equipment over its remaining useful life and amortize the $600,000 for patents over their remaining useful life. As we noted in Chapter 8, goodwill is considered to have an indefinite life. As a consequence, it is not amortized, but, like all long-lived assets, goodwill is reviewed for possible impairment of value. Recording an impairment loss would increase expenses for the period and reduce the amount of goodwill on the balance sheet.[8]

The COVID-19 pandemic had a severe impact on Disney, beginning in 2020. This included significantly reduced capacity at theme parks, suspension of cruise ship sailings, and closing retail stores for most of the year; delays or cancellations of studio, film, television, theatrical, and stage play productions and releases; reduced advertising sales on media networks and direct-to-consumer productions; and the shifting of key live sports programming until later in the year. As a result, Disney determined that goodwill and intangible assets were impaired and were written down, as reported in its 2020 annual report:

NOTES TO THE FINANCIAL STATEMENTS

NOTE 1. Description of the Business and Segment Information

Impact of COVID-19

. . .

In fiscal 2020, the Company recorded goodwill and intangible asset impairments totaling $5.0 billion, in part due to the negative impact COVID-19 has had on the International Channels business.

THE WALT DISNEY COMPANY

REAL WORLD EXCERPT:

2020 Annual Report

When a company acquires another, and both companies continue their separate legal existence, **consolidated financial statements** must be presented. The parent company is the company that gains control over the other company. The subsidiary company is the company that the parent acquires. When the parent buys 100 percent of the subsidiary, the resulting consolidated financial statements look the same as they would if the companies were combined into one in a simple merger as discussed above. The procedures involved in preparation of consolidated statements are discussed in advanced accounting courses.

PAUSE FOR FEEDBACK

Mergers and ownership of a controlling interest in another corporation (more than 50 percent of the outstanding voting shares) must be accounted for using the acquisition method. The acquired company's assets and liabilities are measured at their fair value. Any amount paid above the fair value of the net assets is reported as goodwill by the buyer. To make sure you understand how to apply these concepts, answer the following questions.

[8]In Chapter 8, accounting for impairments of tangible and intangible assets is discussed. Assessing goodwill impairment is a different, more complex process that is beyond the scope of this text.

SELF-STUDY QUIZ

PT Don Corporation purchased 100 percent of Keryn Company for $10 and merged Keryn into PT Don. On the date of the merger, the fair value of Keryn's assets was $11 and the fair value of Keryn's liabilities was $4. What amounts would be added to PT Don's balance sheet as a result of the merger for

1. Goodwill?
2. Other Assets (excluding Goodwill)?

After you have completed your answers, check them below.

Related Homework: EA-8, PA-8

DEMONSTRATION CASE A

PASSIVE INVESTMENTS USING THE FAIR VALUE METHOD

(Try to resolve the requirements before proceeding to the suggested solution that follows.) Howell Equipment Corporation sells and services a major line of farm equipment. Both sales and service operations have been profitable. On January 1, 2023, Howell purchased at par $250,000 in 5 percent bonds as an investment to be traded actively. The bonds pay interest every June 30 and December 31. The bonds were sold on December 31, 2023, when the bonds had a fair value of $252,000. Howell's year ends on December 31.

Required:

1. Prepare the journal entries for each of Howell Equipment's transactions in 2023.
2. What account(s) and amount(s) will be reported on the Corporation's balance sheet at the end of 2023?
3. What account(s) and amount(s) will be reported on its 2023 income statement?
4. Assuming the bond investment is not to be held to maturity or actively traded, prepare the journal entries for each of Howell Equipment's transactions in 2023.
5. What account(s) and amount(s) will be reported on the Corporation's 2023 income statement for the investment in (4).
6. Assume instead that Howell Equipment purchased 3,000 of the 60,000 outstanding voting shares of common stock of Red Jaguar Company for $15 per share on March 1, 2023. Red Jaguar does not pay dividends. At December 31, 2023, Red Jaguar's stock price was $21 per share. Howell Equipment sold the shares on September 15, 2024, for $23 per share. Prepare Howell Equipment's journal entries for the sale in 2024.

SUGGESTED SOLUTION FOR CASE A

1. Because management intends to trade the bonds actively, the bonds are accounted for using the fair value method with any unrealized gains and losses reported on the income statement. The investments would be classified as current assets on the balance sheet.

Solutions to SELF-STUDY QUIZ

1 Purchase price $10 – Fair value of net assets $7 ($11 assets – $4 liabilities) = Goodwill $3
2. Keryn Company's other assets (at fair value) = $11

		Debit	Credit
January 1, 2023:	Investments (+A)	250,000	
	Cash (−A)		250,000
June 30, 2023:	Cash (+A) [$250,000 × 0.05 × ½]	6,250	
	Interest revenue (+R, +SE)		6,250
December 31, 2023:	Cash (+A) [$250,000 × 0.05 × ½]	6,250	
	Interest revenue (+R, +SE)		6,250
Fair value AJE	Investments (+A) [$252,000 – $250,000]	2,000	
	Unrealized gain (+R, +SE)		2,000
Sale	Cash (+A)	252,000	
	Investments (−A)		252,000

2. On the December 31 balance sheet, there would be no investment account for the bonds because they were sold on December 31, 2023.

3. On the 2023 income statement under Other Items:

Interest revenue	$12,500
Unrealized gain	2,000

4. Under this assumption, the bonds would be considered available-for-sale, accounted for using the fair value method with any unrealized gains or losses reported on the Statement of Comprehensive Income. The investments would be classified as either current or noncurrent assets on the balance sheet, depending on management's intention, until sold. When sold, the net amount of the accumulated unrealized gains and losses are reclassified from the Statement of Comprehensive Income to the income statement as a gain or loss on sale of the investments.

		Debit	Credit
January 1, 2023:	Investments (+A)	250,000	
	Cash (−A)		250,000
June 30, 2023:	Cash (+A) [$250,000 × 0.05 × ½]	6,250	
	Interest revenue (+R, +SE)		6,250
December 31, 2023:	Cash (+A) [$250,000 × 0.05 × ½]	6,250	
	Interest revenue (+R, +SE)		6,250
Fair value AJE	Investments (+A) [$252,000 – $250,000]	2,000	
	Unrealized gain (+OCI, +SE)		2,000
Reclassification	Unrealized gain (−OCI, −SE)	2,000	
	Gain on sale of investments (+R, +SE)		2,000
Sale	Cash (+A)	252,000	
	Investments (−A)		252,000

5. On the 2023 income statement under Other Items: Interest revenue, $12,500, and Gain on sale of investments, $2,000.

6. Investments in equity securities that represent less than 20 percent of the outstanding voting shares of the investee company are presumed to be passive investments and are accounted for using the fair value method with any unrealized gains and losses reported on the income statement (similar to bond investments categorized as trading securities). Howell Equipment acquired 5 percent of the outstanding voting common stock (3,000 shares ÷ 60,000 shares outstanding) as a passive investment. First, determine the amount of the adjustment to fair value in each year:

Date	Fair Value	–	Book Value	=	Adjustment
12/31/2023	$63,000 (3,000 shares × $21)	–	$45,000 (3,000 shares × $15)	=	$18,000
9/15/2024	69,000 (3,000 shares × $23)	–	63,000	=	6,000

When sold on September 15, 2024:

September 15, 2024:		Debit	Credit
Fair value AJE	Investments (+A)	6,000	
	Unrealized gain (+R, +SE)		6,000
Sale	Cash (+A)	69,000	
	Investments (−A)		69,000

DEMONSTRATION CASE B

INVESTMENTS WITH SIGNIFICANT INFLUENCE USING EQUITY METHOD

On January 1, 2024, Connaught Company purchased 40 percent of the outstanding voting shares of London Company on the open market for $85,000 cash. London declared and paid $10,000 in cash dividends on December 1 and reported net income of $60,000 for the year. Both companies have a December 31 year-end.

Required:

1. Prepare the journal entries for Connaught Company for 2024.
2. What account(s) and amount(s) were reported on Connaught's balance sheet at the end of 2024?
3. What account(s) and amount(s) were reported on Connaught's 2024 income statement?

SUGGESTED SOLUTION FOR CASE B

1. Because Connaught acquired between 20 and 50 percent of the outstanding voting shares of its investee, the investment is accounted for using the equity method. The investment account increases (decreases) by Connaught's percentage share of the investee's income (loss) each year with the amount reported on the income statement as equity in investee earnings (losses). The investment account also is decreased by Connaught's percentage share of any dividends declared by the investee, and the dividends are not considered income due to the influence Connaught is presumed to have over the investee's financing and operating activities. The investment is not reported at fair value.

		Debit	Credit
January 1, 2024:	Investments (+A)	85,000	
	Cash (−A)		85,000
December 1, 2024:	Cash (+A) [$10,000 × 0.40]	4,000	
	Investments (−A)		4,000
December 31, 2024:	Investments (+A) [$60,000 × 0.40]	24,000	
	Equity in investee earnings (+R, +SE)		24,000

2. On the balance sheet at December 31, 2024, under noncurrent assets: Investments, $105,000 [$85,000 – $4,000 + $24,000].
3. On the 2024 income statement under Other Items: Equity in investee earnings, $24,000.

DEMONSTRATION CASE C

MERGER USING ACQUISITION METHOD

On January 1, 2023, Ohio Company purchased 100 percent of the outstanding voting shares of Allegheny Company in the open market for $85,000 cash, and Allegheny was merged into Ohio Company. On the date of acquisition, the fair value of Allegheny Company's plant and equipment was $89,000 and the fair value of a note payable was $10,000. Allegheny had no other assets or liabilities.

Required:

1. Analyze the merger to determine the amount of goodwill purchased.
2. Give the journal entry that Ohio Company should make on the date of the acquisition. If none is required, explain why.
3. Should Allegheny Company's assets be included on Ohio's balance sheet at book value or fair value? Explain.

SUGGESTED SOLUTION FOR CASE C

1.

Purchase price for Allegheny Company	$85,000	
Less: Fair value of net assets purchased	79,000	[$89,000 assets – $10,000 liabilities]
Goodwill	$ 6,000	

2.

		Debit	Credit
January 1, 2023:	Plant and equipment (+A)	89,000	
	Goodwill (+A)	6,000	
	Notes payable (+L)		10,000
	Cash (−A)		85,000

3. Allegheny Company's assets should be included on the post-merger balance sheet at their fair values as of the date of acquisition. The cost principle applies as it does with all asset acquisitions.

Appendix Supplement

Held-to-Maturity Bonds Purchased at Other Than Par Value: Amortized Cost Method

Bond Purchases

On the date of purchase, a bond may be acquired at the maturity amount (at par), for less than the maturity amount (at a discount), or for more than the maturity amount (at a premium). The total cost of the bond, including all incidental acquisition costs such as transfer fees and broker commissions, is debited to the Held-to-Maturity Investments account.

To illustrate accounting for bond investments acquired **at other than par,** assume that on October 1, 2023, **The Walt Disney Company** paid $92,278 cash for an 8 percent, 5-year $100,000 bond that paid interest semiannually (on March 31 and September 30). Each semiannual payment is $4,000 ($100,000 × 0.08 × ½ year). The bond's yield was 10 percent. The $92,278 represents the present value of the bond on the purchase date, computed as follows:

Present value of the bond investment = Present value of the face + Present value of the interest annuity
$92,278 = ($100,000 × 0.61391) + ($4,000 × 7.72173)
[n = 10 periods; interest rate per period = 5%]

Using Excel:	rate (i) = 5, nper (n) = 10, pmt = −4,000, FV = −100,000
Using Calculator:	rate (i) = 5, periods (n) = 10, pmt = −4,000, FV = −100,000

Management intends to hold the bonds until maturity. The journal entry to record the purchase of the bonds follows:

	Debit	Credit
Investments (+A)	92,278	
Cash (−A)		92,278

Assets		=	Liabilities	+	Stockholders' Equity
Investments	+92,278				
Cash	−92,278				

Interest Earned

The bonds in this illustration were purchased at a discount that will need to be amortized over the life of the investment. Using the effective interest amortization method (discussed in Chapter 10), the cash received is $4,000, the face amount of the bond ($100,000) multiplied by the stated rate of interest for half a year (4 percent). Revenue earned is $4,614, computed by multiplying the current book value of the bond ($92,278) times the market rate for half of a year (5 percent). The following journal entry records the receipt of interest on March 31, 2024 (the first interest payment date after the purchase of the bond investment):

	Debit	Credit
Cash (+A)	4,000	
Investments (+A)	614	
Interest revenue (+R, +SE)		4,614

Assets		=	Liabilities	+	Stockholders' Equity	
Investments	+4,000				Interest revenue (+R)	+4,614
Cash	+614					

The balance of the Investments account after this first receipt of interest on March 31, 2024, is $92,892 ($92,278 + $614), which will be the book value of the bond used in determining interest revenue on the next payment date of September 30, 2024. If the bond investment must be sold before maturity, any difference between market value on the date of sale and net book value would be reported as a gain or loss on sale.

APPENDIX TAKE-AWAYS

A-1. Analyze and report investments in debt securities using the amortized cost and fair value methods. **p. A-5**

When management intends to hold an investment in a debt security (such as a bond or note) until it matures, the held-to-maturity security is recorded at cost when acquired and reported at **amortized cost** on the balance sheet. Any interest earned during the period is reported on the income statement.

If the investments are intended to be held actively, the trading securities are reported at **fair value,** with unrealized gains and losses reported on the income statement.

If the investments in debt securities are not to be held to maturity or actively traded, the available-for-sale securities are reported at **fair value,** with unrealized gains and losses reported on the statement of comprehensive income. When sold, the net unrealized gains/losses for the securities are reclassified from the statement of comprehensive income to realized gains/losses on the income statement.

A-2. Analyze and report passive investments in equity securities using the fair value method. **p. A-12**

Acquiring less than 20 percent of the outstanding voting shares of another company's common stock is presumed to be a passive investment. These investments are recorded at cost and adjusted to **fair value** at year-end. The resulting unrealized gain or loss is reported on the income statement, the same treatment as trading securities (debt).

Any dividends earned are reported as revenue.

A-3. **Analyze and report investments involving significant influence using the equity method.** **p. A-16**

If between 20 and 50 percent of the outstanding voting shares are owned, significant influence over the affiliate firm's operating and financing policies is presumed, and the equity method is applied. Under the **equity method,** the investor records the investment at cost on the acquisition date. Each period thereafter, the investment account is increased (or decreased) by the proportionate interest in the income (or loss) reported by the affiliate corporation and decreased by the proportionate share of the dividends declared by the affiliate corporation.

A-4. **Analyze and report investments in controlling interests.** **p. A-25**

Mergers occur when one company purchases all of the net assets of another and the target company ceases to exist as a separate legal entity. Mergers and ownership of a controlling interest of another corporation (more than 50 percent of the outstanding voting shares) must be accounted for using the **acquisition method.** The acquired company's assets and liabilities are measured at their fair values on the date of the transaction. Any amount paid above the fair value of the assets less liabilities is reported as goodwill by the buyer.

FINDING FINANCIAL INFORMATION

Balance Sheet

Current Assets:
- Investments (trading securities (debt) and equity securities if intended to be current)

Noncurrent Assets:
- Investments (available-for-sale debt securities, equity securities if intended to be noncurrent, and those held for significant influence)

Stockholders' Equity:
- Other comprehensive income (for unrealized gains/losses in available-for-sale debt securities)

Statement of Comprehensive Income

Net income

Other comprehensive income:
- Unrealized gains/losses (from available-for-sale debt securities)
- Reclassification of unrealized gains/losses (due to sale)

Notes

In Various Notes
- Accounting policies for investments
- Details about trading and available-for-sale debt securities, passive equity securities, and equity method investments

Income Statement

Under "Other Items":
- Dividend and interest revenue
- Gains or losses on sale of investments
- Net unrealized gains/losses (on trading securities or passive equity investments)
- Equity in investee earnings/losses (equity method)

Statement of Cash Flows

Operating Activities:

Net income adjusted for:
- Gains/losses on sale of investments
- Net unrealized gains/losses (from trading securities and passive equity securities)
- Dividends received from equity method investees
- Equity in investee earnings/losses (equity method)

Investing Activities:

Purchase/sale of investments

KEY TERMS

Acquisition Method Records assets and liabilities acquired in a merger or acquisition at their fair value on the transaction date **p. A-21**

Amortized Cost Method Reports investments in debt securities held to maturity at cost minus any premium amortization or plus any discount amortization **p. A-6**

Available-for-Sale Securities All debt investments other than trading securities and debt investments held to maturity (classified as either current or noncurrent) **p. A-7**

Equity Method Used when an investor can exert significant influence over an affiliate; the method permits recording the investor's share of the affiliate's income as part of the investor's earnings **p. A-16**

Fair Value Method Reports securities at their current market value (the amount that would be received in an orderly sale) **p. A-6**

Held-to-Maturity Investments Investments in debt securities that management has the ability and intent to hold until maturity **p. A-6**

Merger Occurs when one company purchases all of the net assets of another and the acquired company goes out of existence **p. A-21**

Trading Securities All investments in debt instruments that are held primarily for the purpose of active trading (buying and selling) in the near future (classified as short term) **p. A-6**

Unrealized Gain or Loss Amounts associated with price changes of securities that are held—no actual exchange transaction (e.g., sale) has yet taken place **p. A-6**

QUESTIONS

1. Explain the difference between a short-term investment and a long-term investment.
2. Explain the difference in accounting methods used for passive investments, investments in which the investor can exert significant influence, and investments in which the investor has control over another entity.
3. Explain how bonds held to maturity are reported on the balance sheet.
4. Under the fair value method, when and how does the investor company measure revenue?
5. Under the equity method, why does the investor company measure revenue on a proportionate basis when income is reported by the affiliate company rather than when dividends are declared?
6. Under the equity method, dividends declared by the affiliate company are not recorded as revenue. To record dividends as revenue involves double counting. Explain.
7. When one company acquires control of another, how are the acquired company's assets and liabilities recorded?
8. What is goodwill?

MULTIPLE-CHOICE QUESTIONS

1. Company X owns 40 percent of Company Y and exercises significant influence over the management of Company Y. Therefore, Company X uses what method of accounting for reporting its ownership of stock in Company Y?
   a. The amortized cost method.
   b. The equity method.
   c. The fair value method.
   d. Consolidation of the financial statements of companies X and Y.
2. Company W purchases at par $250,000 in 10 percent bonds of Company Z and intends to hold the bonds for at least five years. At the end of the current year, how would Company W's investment in Company Z bonds be reported on Company W's December 31 (year-end) balance sheet?
   a. At the December 31 fair value in the long-term assets section.
   b. At original cost in the current assets section.
   c. At the December 31 fair value in the current assets section.
   d. At original cost in the long-term assets section.
3. Dividends received from a passive stock investment that is reported in the long-term assets section of the balance sheet are reported as which of the following?
   a. An increase to cash and a decrease to the investment in stock account.
   b. An increase to cash and an increase to revenue.
   c. An increase to cash and an unrealized gain on the income statement.
   d. An increase to cash and an unrealized gain on the balance sheet.
4. Realized gains and losses are recorded on the income statement for which of the following transactions in trading securities and available-for-sale securities?
   a. When adjusting a trading security to its fair value.
   b. Only when recording the sale of a trading security.
   c. When adjusting an available-for-sale security to its fair value.
   d. When recording the sale of an available-for-sale security.
5. When recording dividends declared by a stock investment accounted for using the equity method, which of the following statements is true?
   a. Total assets are increased and net income is increased.
   b. Total assets are increased and total stockholders' equity is increased.

c. Total assets and total stockholders' equity do not change.
d. Total assets are decreased and total stockholders' equity is decreased.

6. When using the equity method of accounting, when is revenue recorded on the books of the investor company?
   a. When a dividend is declared by the affiliate.
   b. When the fair value of the affiliate stock increases.
   c. When the affiliate company reports net income.
   d. Both (a) and (c).
7. Bott Company acquired 500 shares of Barus Company at $53 per share as a long-term investment. This represents 10 percent of the outstanding voting shares of Barus. During the year, Barus paid stockholders $3 per share in dividends. At year-end, Barus reported net income of $60,000. Barus's stock price at the end of the year was $55 per share. For Bott Company, the amount of investments reported on the balance sheet at year-end and the amount reported on the income statement for the year are

	Balance Sheet	Income Statement
a.	$31,000	$6,000
b.	$27,500	$2,500
c.	$27,500	$6,000
d.	$31,000	$1,500

8. Bott Company acquired 500 shares of Barus Company at $53 per share as a long-term investment. This represents 40 percent of the outstanding voting shares of Barus. During the year, Barus paid stockholders $3 per share in dividends. At year-end, Barus reported net income of $60,000. Barus's stock price at the end of the year was $55 per share. For Bott Company, the amount of investments reported on the balance sheet at year-end and the amount reported on the income statement for the year are

	Balance Sheet	Income Statement
a.	$31,000	$ 6,000
b.	$27,500	$ 2,500
c.	$49,000	$24,000
d.	$27,500	$ 1,500

9. Jordan Company purchased 100 percent of the outstanding voting shares of Phil Corporation in the open market for $230,000 cash, and Phil was merged into Jordan Company. On the date of acquisition, the fair value of Phil Corporation's property and equipment was $300,000 and the fair value of its long-term debt was $130,000. Phil has no other assets or liabilities. What amount of goodwill would Jordan Company record related to the purchase of Phil Corporation?
   a. No goodwill should be recorded by Jordan.
   b. $170,000
   c. $60,000
   d. $40,000

MINI-EXERCISES

Matching Measurement and Reporting Methods

MA-1
LOA-1, A-2, A-3, A-4

Match the following. Answers may be used more than once:

Measurement Method	Reporting Method
A. Amortized cost	____ 1. Less than 20 percent voting stock ownership.
B. Equity method	____ 2. Current fair value.
C. Acquisition method and consolidation	____ 3. More than 50 percent voting stock ownership.
D. Fair value method	____ 4. At least 20 percent but not more than 50 percent voting stock ownership.
	____ 5. Bonds held to maturity.
	____ 6. Original cost less any amortization of premium or discount with the purchase.
	____ 7. Original cost plus proportionate part of the income of the affiliate less proportionate part of the dividends declared by the affiliate.

MA-2 LOA-1

Recording a Bond Investment Purchase

James Company purchased $800,000, 8 percent bonds issued by Heidi Company on January 1 of the current year. The purchase price of the bonds was $900,000. Interest is payable semiannually each June 30 and December 31. Record the purchase of the bonds on January 1 of the current year.

MA-3 LOA-1

Recording a Bond Investment Held as Available-for-Sale

On January 1, 2024, Brian Company purchased at par $800,000, 6 percent bonds issued by Laura Company to be held as available-for-sale securities. At December 31, 2024, the bonds had a fair value of $775,000. The bond investment was sold on July 1, 2025, for $802,000. Brian Company's fiscal year ends on December 31. Record (1) the adjustment of the bond investment on December 31, 2024, and (2) the sale of the bonds on July 1, 2025. Ignore interest.

MA-4 LOA-1

Recording a Bond Investment Held as Trading Securities

Using the data in MA-3, assume that Brian Company purchased the bond investment to be actively traded instead of the available-for-sale portfolio. Record (1) the adjustment of the bond investment on December 31, 2024, and (2) the sale of the bonds on July 1, 2025. Ignore interest.

MA-5 LOA-1

Determining Financial Statement Effects of Available-for-Sale Securities Transactions

Using the following categories, indicate the effects of the transactions listed in MA-3, assuming the securities are available-for-sale. Use + for increase and – for decrease and indicate the amounts.

	Balance Sheet			Income Statement		
Transaction Date	Assets	Liabilities	Stockholders' Equity	Revenues/ Gains	Expenses/ Losses	Net Income

MA-6 LOA-1

Determining Financial Statement Effects of Trading Securities Transactions

Using the following categories, indicate the effects of the transactions listed in MA-4, assuming the securities are traded actively. Use + for increase and – for decrease and indicate the amounts.

	Balance Sheet			Income Statement		
Transaction Date	Assets	Liabilities	Stockholders' Equity	Revenues/ Gains	Expenses/ Losses	Net Income

MA-7 LOA-2

Recording Passive Investment in Equity Securities

During December of the current year, James Company acquired some of the 50,000 outstanding shares of the common stock, par $12, of Andrew Corporation as a long-term passive investment. The accounting period for both companies ends December 31. Give the journal entries for James Company for each of the following transactions that occurred during the current year:

Dec. 2 Purchased 6,250 shares of Andrew common stock at $15 per share.
Dec. 15 Andrew Corporation declared a cash dividend of $2 per share.
Dec. 31 Determined the current market price of Andrew stock to be $12 per share.

MA-8 LOA-3

Recording Equity Method Securities Transactions

On January 1 of the current year, PurchaseAgent.com acquired 35 percent (800,000 shares) of the common stock of E-Transaction Corporation. The accounting period for both companies ends December 31. Give the journal entries for each of the following transactions that occurred during the current year for PurchaseAgent.com:

July 2 E-Transaction declared a cash dividend of $0.25 per share.
July 16 E-Transaction paid the cash dividend declared on July 2.
Dec. 31 E-Transaction reported net income of $400,000.

Determining Financial Statement Effects of Equity Method Securities

MA-9
LOA-3

Using the following categories, indicate the effects of the transactions listed in MA-8. Use + for increase and – for decrease and indicate the amounts.

	Balance Sheet			Income Statement		
Transaction Date	Assets	Liabilities	Stockholders' Equity	Revenues/ Gains	Expenses/ Losses	Net Income

Interpreting Goodwill Disclosures

MA-10
LOA-4
Cisco Systems, Inc.

Cisco Systems, Inc., is a global conglomerate that develops, manufactures, and sells networking hardware (e.g., switches, routers, and cybersecurity), software, telecommunications equipment, and other high-technology services and products. Its balance sheet recently reported goodwill in the amount of $33.8 billion, which is over 35 percent of the company's total assets. This percentage is very large compared to that of most companies. Explain why you think Cisco has such a large amount of goodwill reported on its balance sheet.

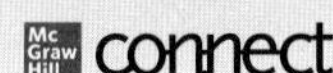

EXERCISES

Recording Bonds Held to Maturity

EA-1
LOA-1
Electronic Arts Inc.

Electronic Arts Inc. "is a global leader in digital interactive entertainment. We develop, market, publish and deliver games, content and services that can be played and watched on game consoles, PCs, mobile phones and tablets." Popular brands include *Battlefield, The Sims, Madden NFL,* and *Star Wars.* The company reported over $5.5 billion in revenue in a recent year.

Assume that as part of its cash management strategy, Electronic Arts purchased $12 million in bonds at par for cash on July 1 of the current year. The bonds pay 8 percent interest annually, with payments on June 30 and December 31, and mature in 10 years. The company plans to hold the bonds until maturity.

Required:

1. Record the purchase of the bonds on July 1 of the current year.
2. Record the receipt of interest on December 31 of the current year.

Recording Transactions in the Available-for-Sale Securities Portfolio

EA-2
LOA-1

On July 1, 2024, Slick Rocks, Inc., purchased at par $350,000, 6 percent bonds of Sandstone Company as an investment that the management intends to hold for a few years but not to maturity. The bonds pay interest each June 30 and December 31. Slick Rocks' fiscal year ends on December 31. The following information pertains to the price of the Sandstone bonds:

	Bond Price
12/31/2024	$356,000
12/31/2025	352,000

Slick Rocks sold the Sandstone bonds on June 30, 2026, at a price of $353,000. Prepare any journal entries that are required by the facts presented in the case.

Recording Transactions in the Trading Securities Portfolio

EA-3
LOA-1

Using the data in EA-2, assume that Slick Rocks' management purchased the Sandstone bonds for the trading securities portfolio instead of the available-for-sale securities portfolio. Prepare any journal entries that are required by the facts presented in the case.

Recording Transactions in the Equity Securities Portfolio

EA-4
LOA-2

On March 10, 2023, Dearden, Inc., purchased 15,000 shares (2 percent) of Jaffa stock for $35 per share. Management intends to hold the securities long term. Dearden's year ends on December 31. The following information pertains to the price per share of Jaffa stock:

	Stock Price
12/31/2023	$33
12/31/2024	36
12/31/2025	32

Dearden sold all of the Jaffa stock on September 12, 2026, at a price of $30 per share. Prepare any journal entries that are required by the facts presented in this case.

EA-5 Recording and Reporting an Equity Method Investment

LOA-3

Gioia Company acquired some of the 65,000 shares of outstanding common stock (no par) of Tristezza Corporation during the current year as a long-term investment. The annual accounting period for both companies ends December 31. The following transactions occurred during the current year:

Jan. 10 Purchased 17,875 shares of Tristezza common stock at $11 per share.

Dec. 31
a. Received the current year financial statements of Tristezza Corporation that reported net income of $80,000.
b. Tristezza Corporation declared a cash dividend of $0.60 per share.
c. Tristezza Corporation paid the cash dividend declared in *(b).*
d. Determined the market price of Tristezza stock to be $10 per share.

Required:

1. What accounting method should the company use? Why?
2. Give the journal entries for each of these transactions. If no entry is required, explain why.
3. Show how the long-term investment and the related revenue should be reported on the current year's financial statements (balance sheet and income statement) of Gioia Company.

EA-6 Interpreting the Effects of Equity Method Investments on Cash Flow from Operations

LOA-3

Using the data in EA-5, answer the following questions:

Required:

1. On the current year cash flow statement, how would the investing section of the statement be affected by the preceding transactions?
2. On the current year cash flow statement (indirect method), how would the equity in the earnings of the affiliated company and the dividends from the affiliated company affect the operating section? Explain the reasons for the effects.

EA-7 Comparing Fair Value and Equity Methods

LOA-2, A-3

Company A purchased a certain number of Company B's outstanding voting shares at $20 per share as a long-term investment. Company B had outstanding 20,000 shares of $10 par value stock. Complete the following table relating to the measurement and reporting by Company A after acquisition of the shares of Company B stock.

	Fair Value Method	Equity Method
Assume number of Company B shares acquired →	**2,500**	**7,000**
a. What level of ownership by Company A of Company B is required to apply the method?	______	______
b. What events should cause Company A to recognize revenue related to the investment in Company B?	______	______
c. After the acquisition date, how should Company A change the balance of the investment account with respect to the stock owned in Company B (other than for the disposal of the investments)?	______	______

Additional information:	
Net income reported by Company B in the first year	$59,000
Dividends declared by Company B in the first year	$12,000
Market price of Company B stock at the end of the first year	$17 per share

d. At acquisition, the investment account on the books of Company A should be debited for what amount?	$______	$______
e. What is the balance in the investment account on the balance sheet of Company A at the end of the first year?	$______	$______
f. What amount of revenue from the investment in Company B should Company A report at the end of the first year?	$______	$______
g. What amount of unrealized loss should Company A report at the end of the first year?	$______	$______

Determining the Appropriate Accounting Treatment for an Acquisition

EA-8
LOA-4
Colgate-Palmolive Company

The notes to recent financial statements of the **Colgate-Palmolive Company** contained the following information (dollar amounts in millions):

3. Acquisitions and Divestitures

On June 20, 2011, the Company . . . finalized the Company's acquisition from Unilever of the Sanex personal care business . . . for an aggregate purchase price of $966. . . . This strategic acquisition is expected to strengthen Colgate's personal care business in Europe, primarily in the liquid body cleansing and deodorants business. Total purchase price consideration of $966 has been allocated to the net assets acquired based on their respective fair values at June 20, 2011. . . .

Source: Colgate-Palmolive

Colgate-Palmolive acquired 100 percent of the fair value of the net assets of **Sanex** for $966 million in cash. Assume that Sanex's assets *(not detailed)* at the time of the acquisition had a book value of $480 million and a fair value of $625 million. Colgate-Palmolive also assumed Sanex's liabilities of $70 million (book value and fair value of the liabilities are the same, *not detailed*). Prepare the entry on the date of acquisition as a merger.

(Appendix Supplement) Recording Bonds Held to Maturity (Purchased at a Premium)

EA-9
Electronic Arts Inc.

Electronic Arts Inc. "is a global leader in digital interactive entertainment. We develop, market, publish and deliver games, content and services that can be played and watched on game consoles, PCs, mobile phones and tablets." Popular brands include Battlefield, *The Sims, Madden NFL,* and *Star Wars.* The company reported over $5.5 billion in revenue in a recent year.

Assume that, as part of its cash management strategy, Electronic Arts purchased as a long-term investment $12 million in 10-year bonds for $13,785,346 cash on July 1 of the current year. The bonds pay 8 percent interest semiannually on June 30 and December 31. The market rate on the bonds on the date of purchase was 6 percent.

Required:

1. Record the purchase of the bonds on July 1 of the current year.
2. Record the receipt of interest on December 31 of the current year (apply the effective interest amortization method).

PROBLEMS

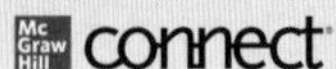

PA-1
LOA-1
Starbucks

Determining Financial Statement Effects for Bonds Held to Maturity (APA-1)

Starbucks is a global company that provides high-quality coffee products. Assume that as part of its expansion strategy, Starbucks plans to open numerous new stores in Mexico in a few years. The company has $7 million to support the expansion and has decided to invest the funds in corporate bonds until the bonds reach maturity in three years. Assume that Starbucks purchased bonds with $7 million face value at par for cash on July 1 of the current year. The bonds pay 7 percent interest each June 30 and December 31.

Required:

1. What accounts are affected when the bonds are purchased on July 1 of the current year?
2. What accounts are affected when interest is received on December 31 of the current year?
3. Should Starbucks prepare a journal entry if the fair value of the bonds decreased to $6,000,000 on December 31 of the current year? Explain.

PA-2
LOA-1

Recording Passive Investments (APA-2)

On January 1, 2024, Rain Technology purchased at par $80,000, 5 percent, bonds of Lightyear Services Company. The bonds pay interest quarterly on March 31, June 30, September 30, and December 31. Rain Technology's year ends on December 31. The following information applies to the fair value of Lightyear Services' bonds:

	Bond Price
12/31/2024	$78,000
12/31/2025	87,000
12/31/2026	81,000

Rain Technology sold the bonds on July 14, 2027, for $83,000.

Required:

1. Prepare Rain Technology's entry to record interest received on March 31, 2024.
2. Assuming that Rain purchased the bonds as trading securities, prepare journal entries at the end of each year and on the date of sale. Ignore interest.
3. Assuming that Rain purchased the bonds as available-for-sale securities, prepare journal entries at the end of each year and on the date of sale. Ignore interest.

PA-3
LOA-1, A-2

Recording and Reporting Passive Investments (APA-3)

During January 2023, Optimum Glass Company purchased the following securities for its long-term investment portfolio:

- D-Light Corporation common stock: 14,250 shares (95,000 outstanding) at $11 per share
- Fluorescent Company bonds: $400,000 (20-year, 7 percent) purchased at par (not to be held to maturity or actively traded)

All companies have a December 31 year-end. Subsequent to acquisition, the following data were available:

	2023	2024
Net income reported at December 31:		
D-Light Corporation	$ 31,000	$ 41,000
Fluorescent Company	360,000	550,000
Dividends and interest paid during the year:		
D-Light Corporation (cash dividends per share)	$ 0.50	$ 0.70
Fluorescent Company (annual interest)	28,000	28,000
Fair value at December 31:		
D-Light Corporation (per share)	$ 10.00	$ 11.50
Fluorescent Company	375,000	385,000

Required:

1. What accounting method should be used for the investment in D-Light common stock? Fluorescent bonds? Why?
2. Give the journal entries for the Optimum Glass Company for each year in parallel columns (if none, explain why) for each of the following:
   a. Purchase of the investments.
   b. Income reported by D-Light Corporation and Fluorescent Company.
   c. Dividends and interest received from D-Light Corporation and Fluorescent Company.
   d. Fair value effects at year-end.
3. For each year, show how the following amounts should be reported on the financial statements:
   a. Long-term investments.
   b. Other comprehensive income for unrealized gains/losses.
   c. Revenues and gains/losses.

Recording Passive Investments and Investments for Significant Influence (APA-4)

PA-4
LOA-2, A-3

On August 4, 2024, Bennett Corporation purchased 2,000 shares of Plummer Company for $180,000. The following information applies to the stock price of Plummer Company:

	Price
12/31/2024	$85
12/31/2025	91
12/31/2026	94

Plummer Company declares cash dividends of $3.50 per share on June 1 of each year and pays the dividends on July 1 of each year.

Required:

1. Prepare journal entries to record the facts in the case, assuming that Bennett purchased the shares as a passive investment.
2. Prepare journal entries to record the facts in the case, assuming that Bennett used the equity method to account for the investment. Bennett owns 30 percent of Plummer and Plummer reported $30,000 in income each year.

Comparing Methods to Account for Various Levels of Ownership of Voting Stock (APA-5)

PA-5
LOA-2, A-3

Company T had 25,000 outstanding shares of common stock, par value $10 per share. On January 1 of the current year, Company P purchased some of Company T's shares as a long-term investment at $25 per share. At the end of the current year, Company T reported the following: income, $45,000, and cash dividends declared during the year, $16,500. The fair value of Company T stock at the end of the current year was $22 per share.

Required:

1. For both of the following cases (Case A and Case B, shown in the tabulation), identify the method of accounting that Company P should use. Explain why.
2. Give the journal entries for Company P at the dates indicated for each of the two independent cases (Case A and Case B), assuming that the investments will be held long term. Use the following format:

	Case A: 3,000 Shares Purchased	Case B: 8,750 Shares Purchased
a. To record the acquisition on January 1.		
b. To recognize the income reported by Company T for the current year.		
c. To recognize the dividends declared and then paid by Company T (two entries).		
d. To recognize the fair value effect at the end of the current year.		

3. Complete the following schedule to show the separate amounts that should be reported on the current year's financial statements of Company P:

	Dollar Amounts	
	Case A	Case B
Balance sheet		
Investments		
Income Statement		
Dividend revenue		
Unrealized gain/(loss)		
Equity in investee earnings		

4. Explain why assets and revenues for the two cases are different.

PA-6 LOA-3 Recording Investments for Significant Influence (APA-6)

Below are selected T-accounts related to equity investments for William Company.

Investments			
1/1 Balance	56,432		
Purchase	15,685		
Share of affiliates' earnings	?	8,564	Share of affiliates' dividends
12/31 Balance	67,450		

Equity in Investee Earnings			
		0	1/1 Balance
		?	Share of affiliates' earnings
		3,897	12/31 Balance

Required:

a. Prepare the journal entry for the purchase of additional investments in affiliated companies for cash.
b. Prepare the journal entry for the declaration of cash dividends on the investments.
c. At year-end, the investments account had a fair value of $62,000; the affiliates also reported $8,120 in net income for the year. Prepare the year-end journal entry.
d. What would be reported on the balance sheet related to the investments in affiliates on December 31?
e. What would be reported on the income statement for the year?

PA-7 LOA-3 Determining Cash Flow Statement Effects of Investments for Significant Influence (APA-7)

During the current year, Bradford Company purchased some of the 90,000 shares of common stock, par $6, of Hall, Inc., as a long-term investment. The annual accounting period for each company ends December 31. The following transactions occurred during the current year:

Jan. 7	Purchased 40,500 shares of Hall stock at $30 per share.
Dec. 31	*a.* Received the current year financial statements of Hall, which reported net income of $215,000.
	b. Hall declared and paid a cash dividend of $1.50 per share.
	c. Determined that the current market price of Hall stock was $41 per share.

Required:
Indicate how the Operating Activities and Investing Activities sections of the cash flow statement (indirect method) will be affected by each transaction.

PA-8 LOA-4 Analyzing Goodwill and Reporting a Merger (APA-8)

On January 4, David Company acquired all of the net assets (assets and liabilities) of William Company for $145,000 cash. The two companies merged, with David Company surviving. On the date of acquisition, William's balance sheet included the following.

Balance Sheet at January 4	William Company
Cash	$23,000
Property and equipment (net)	70,000
Total assets	$93,000
Liabilities	$16,000
Common stock (par $5)	41,000
Retained earnings	36,000
Total liabilities and stockholders' equity	$93,000

The property and equipment had a fair value of $85,000. William also owned an internally developed patent with a fair value of $3,000 (thus, not recorded as an asset on William's balance sheet). The book values of the cash and liabilities were equal to their fair values.

Required:

1. How much goodwill was involved in this merger? Show computations.
2. Give the journal entry that David would make to record the merger on January 4.

ALTERNATE PROBLEMS

Determining Financial Statement Effects for Bonds Held to Maturity (PA-1)

APA-1
LOA-1
Sonic Corp.

Sonic Corp. operates and franchises a chain of quick-service drive-in restaurants in the United States. Customers order at a drive thru, dine on the patio, or drive up to a canopied parking space. A carhop then delivers the food to the customer. Assume that Sonic has $15 million in cash to support future expansion and has decided to invest the funds in corporate bonds until the money is needed. Sonic purchases bonds with $15 million face value at par for cash on January 1 of the current year. The bonds mature in four years and pay 9 percent interest annually, with payments on each June 30 and December 31. Sonic plans to hold the bonds until maturity.

Required:

1. What accounts were affected when the bonds were purchased on January 1 of the current year?
2. What accounts were affected when interest was received on June 30 of the current year?
3. Should Sonic prepare a journal entry if the fair value of the bonds increased to $16,300,000 on December 31 of the current year? Explain.

Recording Passive Investments (PA-2)

APA-2
LOA-1

On October 1, 20x1, Hill-Nielsen purchased at par $170,000, 4 percent, bonds of Community Communications Company. The bonds pay interest quarterly on March 31, June 30, September 30, and December 31. Hill-Nielson Corporation's year ends on December 31. The following information applies to the fair value of Community Communications' bonds:

	Bond Price
12/31/20x1	$173,000
12/31/20x2	168,000
12/31/20x3	165,000

Hill-Nielson sold the bonds on March 17, 20x4, for $164,000.

Required:

1. Prepare the entry to record interest received on December 31, 20x1.
2. Assuming that Hill-Nielson purchased the bonds as trading securities, prepare journal entries at the end of each year and on the date of sale. Ignore interest.
3. Assuming that Hill-Nielson purchased the bonds as available-for-sale securities, prepare journal entries at the end of each year and on the date of sale. Ignore interest.

APA-3 Recording and Reporting Passive Investments (PA-3)

LOA-1, A-2

During January 2023, Pentagon Company purchased the following securities for its long-term investment portfolio:

- Square Company common stock: 12,000 shares (200,000 outstanding) at $25 per share
- Rectangle Corporation bonds: $200,000 (10-year, 5 percent) purchased at par (not to be held to maturity or actively traded)

All companies have a December 31 year-end. Subsequent to acquisition, the following data were available:

	2023	2024
Net income reported at December 31:		
Square Company	$ 941,000	$ 986,000
Rectangle Corporation	1,250,000	1,320,000
Dividends and interest paid during the year:		
Square Company (cash dividends per share)	$ 0.75	$ 1.00
Rectangle Corporation (annual interest)	10,000	10,000
Fair value at December 31:		
Square Company (per share)	$ 29.00	$ 24.50
Rectangle Corporation	210,000	225,000

Required:

1. What accounting method should be used for the investment in Square common stock? Rectangle bonds? Why?
2. Give the journal entries for Pentagon Company for each year in parallel columns for each of the following (if no entry is necessary, explain why):
   a. Purchase of the investments.
   b. Income reported by Square Company and Rectangle Corporation.
   c. Dividends and interest received from Square Company and Rectangle Corporation.
   d. Fair value effects at year-end.
3. For each year, show how the following amounts should be reported on the financial statements:
   a. Long-term investments.
   b. Other comprehensive income for unrealized gains/losses.
   c. Revenues and gains/losses.

APA-4 Recording Passive Investments and Investments for Significant Influence (PA-4)

LOA-2, A-3

On March 31, 20x1, Robert Electronics Company purchased 4,000 shares of Pat Company for $250,000. The following information applies to the stock of Pat Company:

	Bond Price
12/31/20x1	$65
12/31/20x2	63
12/31/20x3	64

Pat Company declares cash dividends of $2 per share on November 1 of each year and pays dividends on December 1 of each year.

Required:

1. Prepare journal entries to record the facts in the case, assuming that Robert purchased the shares as a passive investment.
2. Prepare journal entries to record the facts in the case, assuming that Robert used the equity method to account for the investment. Robert owns 40 percent of Pat Company and Pat Company reported $120,000 in income each year.

Recording and Reporting Passive Investments (PA-5)

APA-5
LOA-2, A-3

Arbor Company had 200,000 outstanding shares of common stock, par value $1 per share. On January 10 of the current year, Cardinal Corporation purchased some of Arbor's shares as a long-term investment at $12 per share. At the end of the current year, Arbor reported the following: income, $90,000, and cash dividends declared and paid during the year, $15,000. The fair value of Arbor Company stock at the end of the current year was $14 per share.

Required:

1. For both of the following cases (Case A and Case B, shown in the tabulation), identify the method of accounting that Cardinal Corporation should use. Explain why.
2. Give the journal entries for Cardinal Corporation at the dates indicated for each of the two independent cases (Case A and Case B), assuming that the investments will be held long term. Use the following format:

	Case A: 10,000 Shares Purchased	Case B: 84,000 Shares Purchased
a. To record the acquisition on January 10.		
b. To recognize the income reported by Arbor Company for the current year.		
c. To recognize the dividends declared and then paid by Arbor Company (two entries).		
d. To recognize the fair value effect at the end of the current year.		

3. Complete the following schedule to show the separate amounts that should be reported on the current year's financial statements of Cardinal Corporation:

	Dollar Amounts	
	Case A	Case B
Balance sheet		
Investments		
Income Statement		
Dividend revenue		
Unrealized gain/(loss)		
Equity in investee earnings		

4. Explain why assets and revenues for the two cases are different.

Recording Investments for Significant Influence (PA-6)

APA-6
LOA-3

Below are selected T-accounts related to equity investments for Lois Corporation.

Investments

	Debit	Credit	
1/1 Balance	321,652		
Purchase	34,990		
Share of affiliates' earnings	?	6,210	Share of affiliates' dividends
12/31 Balance	472,025		

Equity in Investee Earnings

Debit	Credit	
	0	1/1 Balance
	?	Share of affiliates' earnings
	121,593	12/31 Balance

Required:

a. Prepare the journal entry for the purchase of additional investments in affiliated companies for cash.
b. Prepare the journal entry for the declaration of cash dividends on the investments.

c. At year-end, the investments account had a fair value of $350,000; the affiliates also reported $386,676 in net income for the year. Prepare the year-end journal entry.
d. What would be reported on the balance sheet related to the investments in affiliates on December 31?
e. What would be reported on the income statement for the year?

APA-7
LOA-3

Determining Cash Flow Statement Effects of Passive Investments and Investments for Significant Influence (PA-7)

For each of the transactions in APA-5, indicate how the operating activities and investing activities sections of the cash flow statement (indirect method) will be affected.

APA-8
LOA-4

Analyzing Goodwill and Reporting a Merger (PA-8)

On June 1, Gamma Company acquired all of the net assets of Pi Company for $140,000 cash. The two companies merged, with Gamma Company surviving. On the date of acquisition, Pi Company's balance sheet included the following:

Balance Sheet at June 1	Pi Company
Inventory	$ 13,000
Property and equipment (net)	165,000
Total assets	$178,000
Liabilities	$ 82,000
Common stock (par $1)	65,000
Retained earnings	31,000
Total liabilities and stockholders' equity	$178,000

On the date of acquisition, the inventory had a fair value of $12,000 and the property and equipment had a fair value of $180,000. The fair value of the liabilities equaled their book value.

Required:

1. How much goodwill was involved in this merger? Show computations.
2. Give the journal entry that Gamma Company would make to record the merger on June 1.

CONTINUING PROBLEM

CONA-1
LOA-1, A-2, A-3
Pool Corporation, Inc.

Accounting for Passive Investments

Pool Corporation, Inc., is the world's largest wholesale distributor of swimming pool supplies and equipment.

Required:

1. Assume that Pool Corporation purchased for cash 40,000 of the 4,600,000,000 voting shares of common stock outstanding of **The Walt Disney Company** on November 21, 2023, at $103 per share as an investment. The following information applies to the stock price of Disney:

	Price
12/31/2023	$100
12/31/2024	105
12/31/2025	104

On September 15, 2026, Pool Corporation sold all of the Disney securities at $106 per share.

Prepare journal entries to record the purchase, each year-end adjustment, and the sale of the Disney stock as an investment. Ignore dividends.

2. Assume that Pool Corporation purchases The Walt Disney Company bonds at par for $4,120,000 cash on November 21, 2023, as an investment to be held long-term, not held to maturity. The following information applies to the price of Disney bonds:

	Price
12/31/2023	$4,121,000
12/31/2024	4,115,000
12/31/2025	4,124,000

On September 15, 2026, Pool Corporation sold all of the Disney securities for $4,130,000 cash.

Prepare journal entries to record the purchase, each year-end adjustment, and the sale of the Disney bonds. Ignore interest.

3. Prepare journal entries to record the facts in (2) above, assuming that Pool Corporation purchased the bonds to be traded actively.

McGraw Hill connect

CASES AND PROJECTS

Annual Report Cases

Finding Financial Information

CPA-1
LOA-2, A-4
Target Corporation

Refer to the financial statements of **Target Corporation** in Appendix B at the end of this book. All dollar amounts are in millions.

1. Target does not report separate lines for short- or long-term investments on its balance sheets. However, the notes to the statements provide information. What does Target report as the amount of short-term investments for the most recent year and where is this reported on the balance sheet?
   a. $8,511 in cash and cash equivalents
   b. $2,577 in other current assets
   c. $7,644 in cash and cash equivalents
   d. $1,810 in other current assets
2. What type of short-term investments are reported by Target as cash equivalents for the most recent year? Check all that apply.
   a. Debt instruments
   b. Highly liquid investments
   c. Securities having an original maturity of three months or less from the time of purchase
   d. Equity securities
   e. Securities classified as available-for-sale
3. In 2017, Target invested $75 million in the stock of **Casper Sleep Inc.** for a 7.3 percent ownership stake. What method should Target have used to account for the investment and why?
   a. Held-to-maturity method because Casper was not a public company.
   b. Equity method because it was an investment in common stock.
   c. Available-for-sale method because Target did not intend to trade the securities.
   d. Fair value method because it was a passive investment in common stock.
4. How much goodwill did Target report in the most recent year?
   a. $633
   b. $668
   c. $631
   d. $686
   e. Goodwill is not reported by Target.

Finding Financial Information

CPA-2
LOA-1, A-2, A-4
Walmart Inc.

Refer to the financial statements of **Walmart Inc.** in Appendix C at the end of this book. All dollar amounts are in millions, except where noted.

1. What amount does the company report for goodwill for the most recent year (in millions)?
2. In what account on the balance sheet are investments reported?
3. How are the investments in debt securities classified?
4. Which of the following measurement methods are Investments in equity securities with readily determinable market values reported?
   a. At cost
   b. At net realizable value
   c. At fair value
   d. At present value
5. In 2018, Walmart acquired 77 percent of **Flipkart**, India's leading e-commerce marketplace, for $16 billion in cash. In the deal, Walmart acquired current assets of $1.2 billion (not detailed), tradenames of $4.7 billion, and technology of $0.3 billion, and assumed $3.7 billion in liabilities (not detailed).
   a. What method did Walmart use for the purchase?
   b. Record the journal entry for the acquisition (in billions).

Financial Reporting and Analysis Cases

CPA-3 LOA-2, A-3 Using Financial Reports: Analyzing the Financial Effects of the Fair Value and Equity Methods

On January 1 of the current year, Sheena Company purchased 30 percent of the outstanding common stock of Maryn Corporation at a total cost of $485,000. Management intends to hold the stock for the long term. On the current year's December 31 balance sheet, the investment in Maryn Corporation was $556,000, but no additional Maryn stock was purchased. The company received $90,000 in cash dividends from Maryn. The dividends were declared and paid during the current year. The company used the equity method to account for its investment in Maryn. The market price of Sheena Company's share of Maryn stock increased during the current year to a total value of $550,000.

Required:

1. Explain why the investment account balance increased from $485,000 to $556,000 during the current year.
2. What amount of revenue from the investment was reported during the current year?
3. If Sheena did not have significant influence over Maryn and used the fair value method, what amount of revenue from the investment should have been reported in the current year?
4. If Sheena did not have significant influence over Maryn and used the fair value method, what amount should be reported as the investment in Maryn Corporation on the current year's December 31 balance sheet?

CPA-4 LOA-1 Inferring Passive Investments Transactions

Below are selected T-accounts for the RunnerTech Company, which reported its investments as noncurrent assets.

Investments (available-for-sale securities)

	Debit	Credit	
1/1	10,000		
Purchase	50,000		
Sale AJE	1,500	31,500	Sale
Year-end AJE	?		
12/31	31,200		

Unrealized Gains (in OCI)

	Debit	Credit	
		300	1/1
Reclassification	1,600	1,500	Sale AJE
		?	Year-end AJE
		1,400	12/31

Interest Revenue

	Debit	Credit	
		0	1/1
		?	Earned
		3,000	12/31

Gain on Sale of Investments

	Debit	Credit	
		0	1/1
		?	Reclassification
		?	12/31

Required:
For the current year:

a. Prepare the entry for the purchase of the available-for-sale bond securities for cash.
b. Prepare the entry for the receipt of interest on the bond investments.
c. Prepare the entry for the sale of half of the portfolio when the fair value was $31,500.
d. Prepare the entry at year-end when the remaining securities in the portfolio had a fair value of $31,200.
e. What would be reported on the balance sheet related to the available-for-sale bond investments on December 31?
f. What would be reported on the income statement for the year?
g. How would year-end reporting change if the investments were categorized as trading securities instead of available-for-sale securities?

Critical Thinking Cases

Evaluating an Ethical Dilemma: Using Inside Information

CPA-5
LOA-4

Assume that you are on the board of directors of a company that has decided to buy 80 percent of the outstanding stock of another company within the next three or four months. The discussions have convinced you that this company is an excellent investment opportunity, so you decide to buy $10,000 worth of the company's stock for your personal portfolio. Is there an ethical problem with your decision? Would your answer be different if you planned to invest $500,000? Are there different ethical considerations if you don't buy the stock but recommend that your brother does so?

Evaluating an Acquisition from the Standpoint of a Financial Analyst

CPA-6
LOA-4

Assume that you are a financial analyst for a large investment banking firm. You are responsible for analyzing companies in the retail sales industry. You have just learned that a large West Coast retailer has acquired a large East Coast retail chain for a price more than the net book value of the acquired company. You have reviewed the separate financial statements for the two companies before the announcement of the acquisition. At the request of your boss, write a brief report explaining what will happen when the financial results of the companies are consolidated under the acquisition method.

You as Analyst: Online Company Research

Analysis of Investments of a Public Company (an Individual or Team Project)

CPA-7
LOA-1, A-2, A-3, A-4

In your web browser, search for the investor relations page of a public company you are interested in (e.g., Papa Johns investor relations). Select SEC Filings or Annual Report or Financials to obtain the 10-K for the most recent year available.*

Required:
1. Go to the Balance Sheets and/or the Notes for the most recent year:
   a. Does the company have greater than 50 percent ownership in other companies?
      i. If so, what method did it use to account for its investment in the other companies?
      ii. Where did you find this information?
      iii. List any other companies that were acquired during the year and what was the percentage of ownership of each?
   b. Does the company use the equity method for any investments?
      i. If so, what disclosure does the company include about the equity method investments?
   c. Does the company have any held-to-maturity investments?

2. Go to the Income Statement and/or Notes for the most recent year:
   a. What did the company report as unrealized gains or losses in net income?
   b. What did the company report as gains or losses from disposal of investments?
3. Go to the Statement of Comprehensive Income for the most recent year:
   a. What does the company report for unrealized gains or losses?
   b. What does the company report for reclassifications of net unrealized gains or losses?
4. Go to the Statement of Cash Flows for the most recent year:
   a. In the operating activities section, what adjustments to net income does the company indicate related to its investments?
   b. In the investing activities section:
      i. What was the cash flow effect of any acquisitions of other companies?
      ii. What was the cash flow effect of any disposals of investments?

*Alternatively, you can go to sec.gov, click on Company Filings (under the search box), type in the name of the public company you want to find. Once at the list of filings, type 10-K in the Filing Type box. The most recent 10-K annual report will be at the top of the list. Click on Interactive Data for a list of the parts or the entire report to examine.

Images used throughout chapter: Question of ethics: mushmello/Shutterstock; Pause for feedback: McGraw Hill; Guided help: McGraw Hill; Financial analysis: McGraw Hill; Focus on cash flows: Hilch/Shutterstock; Key ratio analysis: guillermain/123RF; Data analytics: Hilch/Shutterstock; Tip: McGraw Hill; ESG reporting: McGraw Hill; International perspective: Hilch/Shutterstock

Partial 10-K report for teaching purposes.
For the complete 10-K, go to sec.gov or investors.target.com/sec-filings.

UNITED STATES
SECURITIES AND EXCHANGE COMMISSION

Washington, D.C. 20549

FORM 10-K

(Mark One)

☒ ☒ **ANNUAL REPORT PURSUANT TO SECTION 13 OR 15(d) OF THE SECURITIES EXCHANGE ACT OF 1934**

For the fiscal year ended January 30, 2021

OR

☐ ☐ **TRANSITION REPORT PURSUANT TO SECTION 13 OR 15(d) OF THE SECURITIES EXCHANGE ACT OF 1934**

For the transition period from ____ to ____

Commission File Number 1-6049

TARGET CORPORATION

(Exact name of registrant as specified in its charter)

Minnesota
(State or other jurisdiction of incorporation or organization)
1000 Nicollet Mall, Minneapolis, Minnesota
(Address of principal executive offices)

41-0215170
(I.R.S. Employer Identification No.)
55403
(Zip Code)

Registrant's telephone number, including area code: 612/304-6073
Former name, former address and former fiscal year, if changed since last report: N/A

Securities registered pursuant to Section 12(b) of the Securities Exchange Act of 1934:

Title of each class	Trading Symbol(s)	Name of each exchange on which registered
Common stock, par value $0.0833 per share	**TGT**	**New York Stock Exchange**

Securities registered pursuant to Section 12(g) of the Act: **None**

Indicate by check mark if the registrant is a well-known seasoned issuer, as defined in Rule 405 of the Securities Act. Yes ☒ No ☐ Indicate by check mark if the registrant is not required to file reports pursuant to Section 13 or Section 15(d) of the Act. Yes o No ☒

Note – Checking the box above will not relieve any registrant required to file reports pursuant to Section 13 or 15(d) of the Exchange Act from their obligations under those Sections.

Indicate by check mark whether the registrant (1) has filed all reports required to be filed by Section 13 or 15(d) of the Securities Exchange Act of 1934 during the preceding 12 months (or for such shorter period that the registrant was required to file such reports), and (2) has been subject to such filing requirements for the past 90 days. Yes ☒ No ☐

Indicate by check mark whether the registrant has submitted electronically every Interactive Data File required to be submitted pursuant to Rule 405 of Regulation S-T (§232.405 of this chapter) during the preceding 12 months (or for such shorter period that the registrant was required to submit such files). Yes X No ☐

Indicate by check mark if disclosure of delinquent filers pursuant to Item 405 of Regulation S-K (§229.405 of this chapter) is not contained herein, and will not be contained, to the best of registrant's knowledge, in definitive proxy or information statements incorporated by reference in Part III of this Form 10-K or any amendment to this Form 10-K. ☒

Indicate by check mark whether the registrant is a large accelerated filer, an accelerated filer, a non-accelerated filer, smaller reporting company, or an emerging growth company (as defined in Rule 12b-2 of the Exchange Act).

Large accelerated filer x	Accelerated filer o	Non-accelerated filer o
Smaller reporting company ☐		Emerging growth company ☐

If an emerging growth company, indicate by check mark if the registrant has elected not to use the extended transition period for complying with any new or revised financial accounting standards provided pursuant to Section 13(a) of the Exchange Act. ☐

Indicate by check mark whether the registrant has filed a report on and attestation to its management's assessment of the effectiveness of its internal control over financial reporting under Section 404(b) of the Sarbanes-Oxley Act (15 U.S.C. 7262(b)) by the registered public accounting firm that prepared or issued its audit report. ☒

Indicate by check mark whether the registrant is a shell company (as defined in Rule 12b-2 of the Act). Yes ☐ No ☒

The aggregate market value of the voting stock held by non-affiliates of the registrant as of July 31, 2020, was $62,803,635,300 based on the closing price of $125.88 per share of Common Stock as reported on the New York Stock Exchange Composite Index.

Indicate the number of shares outstanding of each of registrant's classes of Common Stock, as of the latest practicable date. Total shares of Common Stock, par value $0.0833, outstanding as of March 4, 2021, were 498,616,180.

DOCUMENTS INCORPORATED BY REFERENCE

Portions of Target's Proxy Statement for the Annual Meeting of Shareholders to be held on June 9, 2021, are incorporated into Part III.

PART I

Item 1. Business

General

Target Corporation (Target, the Corporation or the Company) was incorporated in Minnesota in 1902. We offer to our customers, referred to as "guests," everyday essentials and fashionable, differentiated merchandise at discounted prices. Our ability to deliver a preferred shopping experience to our guests is supported by our supply chain and technology, our devotion to innovation, our loyalty offerings and suite of fulfillment options, and our disciplined approach to managing our business and investing in future growth. We operate as a single segment designed to enable guests to purchase products seamlessly in stores or through our digital channels. Since 1946, we have given 5 percent of our profit to communities.

Seasonality

A larger share of annual revenues and earnings traditionally occurs in the fourth quarter because it includes the November and December holiday sales period.

Merchandise

We sell a wide assortment of general merchandise and food. The majority of our general merchandise stores offer an edited food assortment, including perishables, dry grocery, dairy, and frozen items. Nearly all of our stores larger than 170,000 square feet offer a full line of food items comparable to traditional supermarkets. Our small format stores, generally smaller than 50,000 square feet, offer curated general merchandise and food assortments. Our digital channels include a wide merchandise assortment, including many items found in our stores, along with a complementary assortment.

A significant portion of our sales is from national brand merchandise. Approximately one-third of 2020 sales was related to our owned and exclusive brands, including but not limited to the following:

Owned Brands

A New Day™
All in Motion™
Archer Farms™
Art Class™
Auden™
Ava & Viv™
Boots & Barkley™
Bullseye's Playground™
Casaluna™
Cat & Jack™
Cloud Island™
Colsie™
Embark™
Everspring™
Good & Gather™
Goodfellow & Co™
Hearth & Hand™ with Magnolia
heyday™
Hyde & EEK! Boutique™
JoyLab™
Knox Rose™
Kona Sol™
Made By Design™
Market Pantry™
More Than Magic™
Opalhouse™
Open Story™
Original Use™
Pillowfort™
Project 62™
Prologue™
Room Essentials™
Shade & Shore™
Simply Balanced™
Smartly™
Smith & Hawken™
Sonia Kashuk™
Spritz™
Stars Above™
Sun Squad™
Threshold™
Universal Thread™
up & up™
Wild Fable™
Wondershop™
Xhilaration™

Exclusive Adult Beverage Brands

California Roots™
Mystic Reef™
Rosé Bae™
The Collection™
Wine Cube™

We also sell merchandise through periodic exclusive design and creative partnerships and generate revenue from in-store amenities such as Target Café and leased or licensed departments such as Target Optical, Starbucks, and other food service offerings. CVS Pharmacy, Inc. (CVS) operates pharmacies and clinics in our stores under a perpetual operating agreement from which we generate annual occupancy income. In 2020, we announced a partnership with Ulta Beauty under which we will operate *Ulta Beauty at Target*, a shop-in-shop experience debuting on Target.com and in more than 100 Target locations beginning in 2021, with plans to scale to hundreds more over time.

Customer Loyalty Programs

Our guests receive a 5 percent discount on nearly all purchases and receive free shipping at Target.com when they use their Target Debit Card, Target Credit Card, or Target™ MasterCard® (collectively, RedCards™). We also seek to drive customer loyalty and trip frequency through our Target Circle program, where members earn 1 percent rewards on nearly all non-RedCard purchases, among other benefits.

Distribution

The vast majority of merchandise is distributed to our stores through our network of distribution centers. Common carriers ship merchandise to and from our distribution centers. Vendors or third-party distributors ship certain food items and other merchandise directly to our stores. Merchandise sold through our digital channels is distributed to our guests via common carriers (from stores, distribution centers, vendors, and third-party distributors), delivery via our wholly owned subsidiary, Shipt, Inc. (Shipt), and through guest pick-up at our stores. Our stores fulfill the majority of the digitally originated sales, which allows improved product availability, faster fulfillment times, reduced shipping costs, and allows us to offer guests a suite of same-day fulfillment options such as Order Pickup, Drive Up, and Shipt.

Human Capital Management

At Target, our purpose is to help all families discover the joy of everyday life. In support of this purpose we invest in our team, our most important asset, by giving them opportunities to grow professionally, take care of themselves, each other and their families, and to make a difference for our guests and our communities. We are among the largest private employers in the U.S., and our workforce has varying goals and expectations of their employment relationship, from team members looking to build a career to students, retirees and others who are seeking to supplement their income in an enjoyable atmosphere. We seek to be an employer of choice to attract and retain top talent no matter their objectives in seeking employment. To that end, we strive to foster an engaged, diverse, inclusive, safe, purpose-driven culture where employees, referred to as "team members," have equitable opportunities for success.

As of January 30, 2021, we employed approximately 409,000 full-time, part-time, and seasonal team members. Because of the seasonal nature of the retail business, employment levels peak in the holiday season. We also engage independent contractors, most notably in our Shipt subsidiary.

Talent Development and Engagement

We offer a compelling work environment with meaningful experiences and abundant growth and career-development opportunities. This starts with the opportunity to do challenging work and learn on the job and is supplemented by programs and continuous learning that help our team build skills at all levels, including programs focused on specialized skill development, leadership opportunities, coaching, and mentoring. Our talent and succession planning process supports the development of a diverse talent pipeline for leadership and other critical roles. We monitor our team members' perceptions of these commitments through a number of surveys and take steps to address areas needing improvement.

Diversity and Inclusion

We champion workplace diversity and inclusion and focus on developing, advancing, and recruiting diverse talent. We monitor the representation of women and racially or ethnically diverse team members at different levels throughout the company and disclose the composition of our team in our annual Workforce Diversity Report (which, beginning with our 2019 report, includes demographic information using the categories disclosed in our EEO-1 report). Developing teams where team members feel heard, respected, and included is a core Target value and is also fundamental to creating an inclusive guest experience.

Compensation and Benefits

Our compensation and benefits are designed to support the financial, mental, and physical well-being of our team members and their families. We believe in paying team members equitably, regardless of gender, race or ethnicity, and we regularly review the pay data of U.S. team members to confirm that we are doing so. Our compensation packages include a $15 per-hour minimum starting wage for US hourly team members (who comprise the vast majority of our team), a 401(k) plan with matching contributions up to five percent of eligible earnings, paid vacation and holidays, family leave, merchandise and other discounts, disability insurance, life insurance, healthcare and dependent care flexible spending accounts, tuition reimbursement, various team member assistance programs, an annual short-term incentive program, long-term equity awards, and health insurance benefits. Eligibility for, and the level of, benefits vary depending on team members' full-time or part-time status, work location, compensation level, and tenure.

Workplace Health and Safety

We strive to maintain a safe and secure work environment and have specific safety programs. This includes administering a comprehensive occupational injury- and illness-prevention program and training for team members.

COVID-19

In 2020 we invested more than $ 1 billion in the well-being, health, and safety of our team members and guests. We extended certain benefits to our team members in light of the COVID-19 pandemic, including bonuses, fully-paid leaves for up to 30 days, free back-up dependent care, and a variety of mental, emotional, and physical wellness resources. We also enacted dozens of safety, social distancing, and cleaning measures designed to protect our team and guests during the COVID-19 pandemic.

Working Capital

Effective inventory management is key to our ongoing success, and we use various techniques including demand forecasting and planning and various forms of replenishment management. We achieve effective inventory management by staying in-stock in core product offerings, maintaining positive vendor relationships, and carefully planning inventory levels for seasonal and apparel items to minimize markdowns.

Competition

We compete with traditional and internet retailers, including department stores, off-price general merchandise retailers, wholesale clubs, category-specific retailers, drug stores, supermarkets, and other forms of retail commerce. Our ability to positively differentiate ourselves from other retailers and provide compelling value to our guests largely determines our competitive position within the retail industry.

Intellectual Property

Our brand image is a critical element of our business strategy. Our principal trademarks, including Target, our "Expect More. Pay Less." brand promise, and our "Bullseye Design," have been registered with the United States (U.S.) Patent and Trademark Office. We also seek to obtain and preserve intellectual property protection for our brands.

Geographic Information

Nearly all of our revenues are generated within the U.S. The vast majority of our property and equipment is located within the U.S.

Available Information

Our Annual Report on Form 10-K, quarterly reports on Form 10-Q, current reports on Form 8-K, proxy statements, and amendments to those reports filed or furnished pursuant to Section 13(a) or 15(d) of the Exchange Act are available free of charge at investors.target.com as soon as reasonably practicable after we file such material with, or furnish it to, the U.S. Securities and Exchange Commission (SEC). In addition, the SEC maintains a website (http://www.sec.gov) that contains information we electronically file with, or furnish to, the SEC. Our Corporate Governance Guidelines, Code of Ethics, Corporate Responsibility Report, and the charters for the committees of our Board of Directors are also available free of charge in print upon request or at investors.target.com. Information on our website is not part of this or any other report we file with, or furnish to, the SEC.

Item 8. Financial Statements and Supplementary Data

Report of Management on the Consolidated Financial Statements

Management is responsible for the consistency, integrity, and presentation of the information in the Annual Report. The consolidated financial statements and other information presented in this Annual Report have been prepared in accordance with accounting principles generally accepted in the United States and include necessary judgments and estimates by management.

To fulfill our responsibility, we maintain comprehensive systems of internal control designed to provide reasonable assurance that assets are safeguarded and transactions are executed in accordance with established procedures. The concept of reasonable assurance is based upon recognition that the cost of the controls should not exceed the benefit derived. We believe our systems of internal control provide this reasonable assurance.

The Board of Directors exercised its oversight role with respect to the Corporation's systems of internal control primarily through its Audit Committee, which is comprised of independent directors. The Committee oversees the Corporation's systems of internal control, accounting practices, financial reporting and audits to assess whether their quality, integrity, and objectivity are sufficient to protect shareholders' investments.

In addition, our consolidated financial statements have been audited by Ernst & Young LLP, independent registered public accounting firm, whose report also appears on this page.

/s/ Brian C. Cornell

Brian C. Cornell
Chairman and Chief Executive Officer

/s/ Michael J. Fiddelke

Michael J. Fiddelke
Executive Vice President and
Chief Financial Officer

March 10, 2021

Report of Independent Registered Public Accounting Firm

To the Shareholders and the Board of Directors of Target Corporation

Opinion on the Financial Statements

We have audited the accompanying consolidated statements of financial position of Target Corporation (the Corporation) as of January 30, 2021 and February 1, 2020, the related consolidated statements of operations, comprehensive income, cash flows and shareholders' investment for each of the three years in the period ended January 30, 2021, and the related notes (collectively referred to as the "consolidated financial statements"). In our opinion, the consolidated financial statements present fairly, in all material respects, the financial position of the Corporation at January 30, 2021 and February 1, 2020, and the results of its operations and its cash flows for each of the three years in the period ended January 30, 2021, in conformity with U.S. generally accepted accounting principles.

We also have audited, in accordance with the standards of the Public Company Accounting Oversight Board (United States) (PCAOB), the Corporation's internal control over financial reporting as of January 30, 2021, based on criteria established in Internal Control-Integrated Framework issued by the Committee of Sponsoring Organizations of the Treadway Commission (2013 framework) and our report dated March 10, 2021 expressed an unqualified opinion thereon.

Basis for Opinion

These financial statements are the responsibility of the Corporation's management. Our responsibility is to express an opinion on the Corporation's financial statements based on our audits. We are a public accounting firm registered with the PCAOB and are required to be independent with respect to the Corporation in accordance with the U.S. federal securities laws and the applicable rules and regulations of the Securities and Exchange Commission and the PCAOB.

We conducted our audits in accordance with the standards of the PCAOB. Those standards require that we plan and perform the audit to obtain reasonable assurance about whether the financial statements are free of material misstatement, whether due to error or fraud. Our audits included performing procedures to assess the risks of material misstatement of the financial statements, whether due to error or fraud, and performing procedures that respond to those risks. Such procedures included examining, on a test basis, evidence regarding the amounts and disclosures in the financial statements. Our audits also included evaluating the accounting principles used and significant estimates made by management, as well as evaluating the overall presentation of the financial statements. We believe that our audits provide a reasonable basis for our opinion.

Critical Audit Matters

The critical audit matters communicated below are matters arising from the current period audit of the financial statements that were communicated or required to be communicated to the audit committee and that: (1) relate to accounts or disclosures that are material to the financial statements and (2) involved our especially challenging, subjective or complex judgments. The communication of critical audit matters does not alter in any way our opinion on the consolidated financial statements, taken as a whole, and we are not, by communicating the critical audit matters below, providing separate opinions on the critical audit matters or on the accounts or disclosures to which they relate.

Valuation of Inventory and related Cost of Sales

Description of the Matter

At January 30, 2021, the Corporation's inventory was $10,653 million. As described in Note 9 to the consolidated financial statements, the Corporation accounts for the vast majority of its inventory under the retail inventory accounting method (RIM) using the last-in, first-out (LIFO) method. RIM is an averaging method that has been widely used in the retail industry due to its practicality. Under RIM, inventory cost and the resulting gross margins are calculated by applying a cost-to-retail ratio to the inventory retail value.

Auditing inventory requires extensive audit effort including significant involvement of more experienced audit team members, including the involvement of our information technology (IT) professionals, given the relatively higher level of automation impacting the inventory process including the involvement of multiple information systems used to capture the high volume of transactions processed by the Corporation. Further, the inventory process is supported by a number of automated and IT dependent controls that elevate the importance of the IT general controls that support the underlying information systems utilized to process transactions. In addition, in March 2020, as a result of COVID-19, the Company temporarily suspended physical inventory counts at its stores. The Company resumed physical inventory counts in June 2020 using a statistical sampling method. Historically, the Company counted nearly all of its stores annually.

How We Addressed the Matter in Our Audit

We obtained an understanding, evaluated the design and tested the operating effectiveness of controls over the Corporation's inventory process, including the underlying IT general controls. For example, we tested automated controls performed by the Corporation's information systems and controls over the completeness of data transfers between information systems used in performing the Corporation's RIM calculation. Our audit procedures included, among others, testing the processing scenarios of the automated controls by evaluating configuration settings and performing a transaction walkthrough for each scenario. In addition, we evaluated the design and tested the effectiveness of controls over the Company's modified store inventory count process, including the determination of the number of stores counted and evaluation of the results from the sample it counted.

Our audit procedures also included, among others, testing the key inputs into the RIM calculation, including purchases, sales, shortage, and price changes (markdowns) by comparing the key inputs back to source information such as third-party vendor invoices, third-party inventory count information and cash receipts. We performed extensive analytical procedures. For example, we performed store square footage analytics to predict ending inventory values at each store location, as well as predictive markdown analytics based on inquiries held with members of the merchant organization to assess the level of price changes within a category. In addition, we tested the existence of inventories by observing physical inventory counts for a sample of stores and distribution centers.

Valuation of Vendor Income Receivables

Description of the Matter	At January 30, 2021, the Corporation's vendor income receivables totaled $504 million. As discussed in Note 5 of the consolidated financial statements, the Corporation receives consideration for a variety of vendor-sponsored programs, which are primarily recorded as a reduction of cost of sales when earned. The Corporation records a receivable for amounts earned but not yet received. Auditing the Corporation's vendor income receivables was complex due to the estimation required in measuring the receivables. The estimate was sensitive to significant assumptions, such as forecasted vendor income collections, and estimating the time period over which the collections have been earned, which is primarily based on historical trending and data.
How We Addressed the Matter in Our Audit	We obtained an understanding, evaluated the design and tested the operating effectiveness of controls over the Corporation's vendor income receivable process, including controls over management's review of the significant assumptions described above. To test the estimated vendor income receivables, we performed audit procedures that included, among others, assessing the estimation methodology used by management and evaluating the forecasted vendor income collections and the time period over which collections have been earned as used in the receivable estimation model. For a sample of the vendor rebates and concessions, we evaluated the nature and source of the inputs used and the terms of the contractual agreements. We recalculated the amount of the vendor income earned based on the inputs and the terms of the agreements. In addition, we recalculated the time period over which the vendor income collection had been earned to assess the accuracy of management's estimates. We also performed sensitivity analyses of significant assumptions to evaluate the significance of changes in the receivables that would result from changes in assumptions.

/s/ Ernst & Young LLP

We have served as the Corporation's auditor since 1931.
Minneapolis, Minnesota
March 10, 2021

Report of Management on Internal Control over Financial Reporting

Our management is responsible for establishing and maintaining adequate internal control over financial reporting, as such term is defined in Exchange Act Rules 13a-15(f). Under the supervision and with the participation of our management, including our chief executive officer and chief financial officer, we assessed the effectiveness of our internal control over financial reporting as of January 30, 2021, based on the framework in *Internal Control—Integrated Framework (2013)*, issued by the Committee of Sponsoring Organizations of the Treadway Commission (2013 framework). Based on our assessment, we conclude that the Corporation's internal control over financial reporting is effective based on those criteria.

Our internal control over financial reporting as of January 30, 2021, has been audited by Ernst & Young LLP, the independent registered public accounting firm who has also audited our consolidated financial statements, as stated in their report which appears on this page.

/s/ Brian C. Cornell	/s/ Michael J. Fiddelke
Brian C. Cornell Chairman and Chief Executive Officer	Michael J. Fiddelke Executive Vice President and Chief Financial Officer

March 10, 2021

Report of Independent Registered Public Accounting Firm

To the Shareholders and the Board of Directors of Target Corporation

Opinion on Internal Control over Financial Reporting

We have audited Target Corporation's internal control over financial reporting as of January 30, 2021, based on criteria established in Internal Control—Integrated Framework issued by the Committee of Sponsoring Organizations of the Treadway Commission (2013 framework) (the COSO criteria). In our opinion, Target Corporation (the Corporation) maintained, in all material respects, effective internal control over financial reporting as of January 30, 2021, based on the COSO criteria.

We also have audited, in accordance with the standards of the Public Company Accounting Oversight Board (United States) (PCAOB), the consolidated statements of financial position of the Corporation as of January 30, 2021 and February 1, 2020, the related consolidated statements of operations, comprehensive income, cash flows and shareholders' investment for each of the three years in the period ended January 30, 2021, and the related notes and our report dated March 10, 2021 expressed an unqualified opinion thereon.

Basis for Opinion

The Corporation's management is responsible for maintaining effective internal control over financial reporting and for its assessment of the effectiveness of internal control over financial reporting included in the accompanying Report of Management on Internal Control over Financial Reporting. Our responsibility is to express an opinion on the Corporation's internal control over financial reporting based on our audit. We are a public accounting firm registered with the PCAOB and are required to be independent with respect to the Corporation in accordance with the U.S. federal securities laws and the applicable rules and regulations of the Securities and Exchange Commission and the PCAOB.

We conducted our audit in accordance with the standards of the PCAOB. Those standards require that we plan and perform the audit to obtain reasonable assurance about whether effective internal control over financial reporting was maintained in all material respects.

Our audit included obtaining an understanding of internal control over financial reporting, assessing the risk that a material weakness exists, testing and evaluating the design and operating effectiveness of internal control based on the assessed risk, and performing such other procedures as we considered necessary in the circumstances. We believe that our audit provides a reasonable basis for our opinion.

Definition and Limitations of Internal Control Over Financial Reporting

A company's internal control over financial reporting is a process designed to provide reasonable assurance regarding the reliability of financial reporting and the preparation of financial statements for external purposes in accordance with generally accepted accounting principles. A company's internal control over financial reporting includes those policies and procedures that (1) pertain to the maintenance of records that, in reasonable detail, accurately and fairly reflect the transactions and dispositions of the assets of the company; (2) provide reasonable assurance that transactions are recorded as necessary to permit preparation of financial statements in accordance with generally accepted accounting principles, and that receipts and expenditures of the company are being made only in accordance with authorizations of management and directors of the company; and (3) provide reasonable assurance regarding prevention or timely detection of unauthorized acquisition, use, or disposition of the company's assets that could have a material effect on the financial statements.

Because of its inherent limitations, internal control over financial reporting may not prevent or detect misstatements. Also, projections of any evaluation of effectiveness to future periods are subject to the risk that controls may become inadequate because of changes in conditions, or that the degree of compliance with the policies or procedures may deteriorate.

/s/ Ernst & Young LLP

Minneapolis, Minnesota
March 10, 2021

Consolidated Statements of Operations

(millions, except per share data)	2020	2019	2018
Sales	$92,400	$77,130	$74,433
Other revenue	1,161	982	923
Total revenue	93,561	78,112	75,356
Cost of sales	66,177	54,864	53,299
Selling, general and administrative expenses	18,615	16,233	15,723
Depreciation and amortization (exclusive of depreciation included in cost of sales)	2,230	2,357	2,224
Operating income	6,539	4,658	4,110
Net interest expense	977	477	461
Net other (income) / expense	16	(9)	(27)
Earnings from continuing operations before income taxes	5,546	4,190	3,676
Provision for income taxes	1,178	921	746
Net earnings from continuing operations	4,368	3,269	2,930
Discontinued operations, net of tax	—	12	7
Net earnings	$ 4,368	$ 3,281	$ 2,937
Basic earnings per share			
Continuing operations	$ 8.72	$ 6.39	$ 5.54
Discontinued operations	—	0.02	0.01
Net earnings per share	$ 8.72	$ 6.42	$ 5.55
Diluted earnings per share			
Continuing operations	$ 8.64	$ 6.34	$ 5.50
Discontinued operations	—	0.02	0.01
Net earnings per share	$ 8.64	$ 6.36	$ 5.51
Weighted average common shares outstanding			
Basic	500.6	510.9	528.6
Diluted	505.4	515.6	533.2
Antidilutive shares	—	—	—

Note: Per share amounts may not foot due to rounding.

See accompanying Notes to Consolidated Financial Statements.

Consolidated Statements of Comprehensive Income

(millions)	2020	2019	2018
Net earnings	$ 4,368	$ 3,281	$ 2,937
Other comprehensive income / (loss), net of tax			
Pension benefit liabilities	102	(65)	(52)
Currency translation adjustment and cash flow hedges	10	2	(6)
Other comprehensive income / (loss)	112	(63)	(58)
Comprehensive income	$ 4,480	$ 3,218	$ 2,879

See accompanying Notes to Consolidated Financial Statements.

Consolidated Statements of Financial Position

(millions, except footnotes)	January 30, 2021	February 1, 2020
Assets		
Cash and cash equivalents	$ 8,511	$ 2,577
Inventory	10,653	8,992
Other current assets	1,592	1,333
Total current assets	20,756	12,902
Property and equipment		
Land	6,141	6,036
Buildings and improvements	31,557	30,603
Fixtures and equipment	5,914	6,083
Computer hardware and software	2,765	2,692
Construction-in-progress	780	533
Accumulated depreciation	(20,278)	(19,664)
Property and equipment, net	26,879	26,283
Operating lease assets	2,227	2,236
Other noncurrent assets	1,386	1,358
Total assets	$ 51,248	$ 42,779
Liabilities and shareholders' investment		
Accounts payable	$ 12,859	$ 9,920
Accrued and other current liabilities	6,122	4,406
Current portion of long-term debt and other borrowings	1,144	161
Total current liabilities	20,125	14,487
Long-term debt and other borrowings	11,536	11,338
Noncurrent operating lease liabilities	2,218	2,275
Deferred income taxes	990	1,122
Other noncurrent liabilities	1,939	1,724
Total noncurrent liabilities	16,683	16,459
Shareholders' investment		
Common stock	42	42
Additional paid-in capital	6,329	6,226
Retained earnings	8,825	6,433
Accumulated other comprehensive loss	(756)	(868)
Total shareholders' investment	14,440	11,833
Total liabilities and shareholders' investment	$ 51,248	$ 42,779

Common Stock Authorized 6,000,000,000 shares, $0.0833 par value; 500,877,129 shares issued and outstanding as of January 30, 2021; 504,198,962 shares issued and outstanding as of February 1, 2020.

Preferred Stock Authorized 5,000,000 shares, $0.01 par value; no shares were issued or outstanding during any period presented.

See accompanying Notes to Consolidated Financial Statements.

Consolidated Statements of Cash Flows

(millions)	2020	2019	2018
Operating activities			
Net earnings	$ 4,368	$ 3,281	$ 2,937
Earnings from discontinued operations, net of tax	—	12	7
Net earnings from continuing operations	4,368	3,269	2,930
Adjustments to reconcile net earnings to cash provided by operations:			
Depreciation and amortization	2,485	2,604	2,474
Share-based compensation expense	200	147	132
Deferred income taxes	(184)	178	322
Loss on debt extinguishment	512	10	—
Noncash losses / (gains) and other, net	86	29	95
Changes in operating accounts:			
Inventory	(1,661)	505	(900)
Other assets	(137)	18	(299)
Accounts payable	2,925	140	1,127
Accrued and other liabilities	1,931	199	89
Cash provided by operating activities—continuing operations	10,525	7,099	5,970
Cash provided by operating activities—discontinued operations	—	18	3
Cash provided by operations	10,525	7,117	5,973
Investing activities			
Expenditures for property and equipment	(2,649)	(3,027)	(3,516)
Proceeds from disposal of property and equipment	42	63	85
Other investments	16	20	15
Cash required for investing activities	(2,591)	(2,944)	(3,416)
Financing activities			
Additions to long-term debt	2,480	1,739	—
Reductions of long-term debt	(2,415)	(2,069)	(281)
Dividends paid	(1,343)	(1,330)	(1,335)
Repurchase of stock	(745)	(1,565)	(2,124)
Stock option exercises	23	73	96
Cash required for financing activities	(2,000)	(3,152)	(3,644)
Net increase / (decrease) in cash and cash equivalents	5,934	1,021	(1,087)
Cash and cash equivalents at beginning of period	2,577	1,556	2,643
Cash and cash equivalents at end of period	$ 8,511	$ 2,577	$ 1,556
Supplemental information			
Interest paid, net of capitalized interest	$ 939	$ 492	$ 476
Income taxes paid	1,031	696	373
Leased assets obtained in exchange for new finance lease liabilities	428	379	130
Leased assets obtained in exchange for new operating lease liabilities	262	464	246

See accompanying Notes to Consolidated Financial Statements.

Consolidated Statements of Shareholders' Investment

(millions)	Common Stock Shares	Stock Par Value	Additional Paid-in Capital	Retained Earnings	Accumulated Other Comprehensive (Loss) / Income	Total
February 3, 2018	541.7	$ 45	$ 5,858	$ 6,495	$ (747)	$ 11,651
Net earnings	—	—	—	2,937	—	2,937
Other comprehensive loss	—	—	—	—	(58)	(58)
Dividends declared	—	—	—	(1,347)	—	(1,347)
Repurchase of stock	(27.2)	(2)	—	(2,068)	—	(2,070)
Stock options and awards	3.3	—	184	—	—	184
February 2, 2019	517.8	$ 43	$ 6,042	$ 6,017	$ (805)	$ 11,297
Net earnings	—	—	—	3,281	—	3,281
Other comprehensive loss	—	—	—	—	(63)	(63)
Dividends declared	—	—	—	(1,345)	—	(1,345)
Repurchase of stock	(16.0)	(1)	—	(1,520)	—	(1,521)
Stock options and awards	2.4	—	184	—	—	184
February 1, 2020	504.2	$ 42	$ 6,226	$ 6,433	$ (868)	$ 11,833
Net earnings	—	—	—	4,368	—	4,368
Other comprehensive income	—	—	—	—	112	112
Dividends declared	—	—	—	(1,367)	—	(1,367)
Repurchase of stock	(5.7)	—	—	(609)	—	(609)
Stock options and awards	2.4	—	103	—	—	103
January 30, 2021	500.9	$ 42	$ 6,329	$ 8,825	$ (756)	$ 14,440

We declared $2.70, $2.62, and $2.54 dividends per share for the twelve months ended January 30, 2021, February 1, 2020, and February 2, 2019, respectively.

See accompanying Notes to Consolidated Financial Statements.

Notes to Consolidated Financial Statements

1. Summary of Accounting Policies

Organization We are a general merchandise retailer selling products to our guests through our stores and digital channels.

We operate as a single segment that includes all of our continuing operations, which are designed to enable guests to purchase products seamlessly in stores or through our digital channels. Nearly all of our revenues are generated in the United States (U.S.). The vast majority of our long-lived assets are located within the U.S.

Consolidation The consolidated financial statements include the balances of Target and its subsidiaries after elimination of intercompany balances and transactions. All material subsidiaries are wholly owned. We consolidate variable interest entities where it has been determined that Target is the primary beneficiary of those entities' operations.

Use of estimates The preparation of our consolidated financial statements in conformity with U.S. generally accepted accounting principles (GAAP) requires management to make estimates and assumptions affecting reported amounts in the consolidated financial statements and accompanying notes. Actual results may differ significantly from those estimates.

Fiscal year Our fiscal year ends on the Saturday nearest January 31. Unless otherwise stated, references to years in this report relate to fiscal years, rather than to calendar years. Fiscal 2020, 2019 and 2018 ended January 30, 2021, February 1, 2020, and February 2, 2019, respectively, and consisted of 52 weeks. Fiscal 2021 will end January 29, 2022, and will consist of 52 weeks.

Accounting policies Our accounting policies are disclosed in the applicable Notes to the Consolidated Financial Statements. Certain prior-year amounts have been reclassified to conform to the current-year presentation.

3. Revenues

General merchandise sales represent the vast majority of our revenues. We also earn revenues from a variety of other sources, most notably credit card profit-sharing income from our arrangement with TD Bank Group (TD).

Revenues (millions)	2020	2019	2018
Apparel and accessories *(a)*	$ 14,772	$ 14,304	$ 13,434
Beauty and household essentials *(b)*	24,461	20,616	19,296
Food and beverage *(c)*	18,135	15,039	14,585
Hardlines *(d)*	16,626	12,595	12,709
Home furnishings and décor *(e)*	18,231	14,430	14,298
Other	175	146	111
Sales	92,400	77,130	74,433
Credit card profit sharing	666	680	673
Other	495	302	250
Other revenue	1,161	982	923
Total revenue	$ 93,561	$ 78,112	$ 75,356

(a) Includes apparel for women, men, boys, girls, toddlers, infants and newborns, as well as jewelry, accessories, and shoes.
(b) Includes beauty and personal care, baby gear, cleaning, paper products, and pet supplies.
(c) Includes dry grocery, dairy, frozen food, beverages, candy, snacks, deli, bakery, meat, produce, and food service in our stores.
(d) Includes electronics (including video game hardware and software), toys, entertainment, sporting goods, and luggage.
(e) Includes furniture, lighting, storage, kitchenware, small appliances, home décor, bed and bath, home improvement, school/office supplies, greeting cards and party supplies, and other seasonal merchandise.

Merchandise sales – We record almost all retail store revenues at the point of sale. Digitally originated sales may include shipping revenue and are recorded upon delivery to the guest or upon guest pickup at the store. Total revenues do not include sales tax because we are a pass-through conduit for collecting and remitting sales taxes. Generally, guests may return national brand merchandise within 90 days of purchase and owned and exclusive brands within one year of purchase. Sales are recognized net of expected returns, which we estimate using historical return patterns and our expectation of future returns. As of January 30, 2021, February 1, 2020, and February 2, 2019, the liability for estimated returns was $139 million, $117 million, and $116 million, respectively.

We routinely enter into arrangements with vendors whereby we do not purchase or pay for merchandise until the merchandise is ultimately sold to a guest. Under the vast majority of these arrangements, which represent less than 5 percent of consolidated sales, we record revenue and related costs gross. We concluded that we are the principal in these transactions for a number of reasons, most notably because we 1) control the overall economics of the transactions, including setting the sales price and realizing the majority of cash flows from the sale, 2) control the relationship with the customer, and 3) are responsible for fulfilling the promise to provide goods to the customer. Merchandise received under these arrangements is not included in Inventory because the purchase and sale of this inventory are virtually simultaneous.

Revenue from Target gift card sales is recognized upon gift card redemption, which is typically within one year of issuance. Our gift cards do not expire. Based on historical redemption rates, a small and relatively stable percentage of gift cards will never be redeemed, referred to as "breakage." Estimated breakage revenue is recognized over time in proportion to actual gift card redemptions.

Gift Card Liability Activity

(millions)	February 1, 2020	Gift Cards Issued During Current Period But Not Redeemed [b]	Revenue Recognized From Beginning Liability	January 30, 2021
Gift card liability [a]	$ 935	$ 739	$ (639)	$ 1,035

[a] Included in Accrued and Other Current Liabilities.
[b] Net of estimated breakage.

Guests receive a 5 percent discount on nearly all purchases and receive free shipping at Target.com when they use their Target Debit Card, Target Credit Card, or Target MasterCard (RedCards). The discount is included as a sales reduction and was $1.1 billion, $962 million, and $953 million in 2020, 2019, and 2018, respectively.

Target Circle program members earn 1 percent rewards on nearly all non-RedCard purchases. As of January 30, 2021, deferred revenue of $72 million related to this loyalty program was included in Accrued and Other Current Liabilities. Amounts related to this program were insignificant at February 1, 2020.

Credit card profit sharing – We receive payments under a credit card program agreement with TD. Under the agreement, we receive a percentage of the profits generated by the Target Credit Card and Target MasterCard receivables in exchange for performing account servicing and primary marketing functions. TD underwrites, funds, and owns Target Credit Card and Target MasterCard receivables, controls risk management policies, and oversees regulatory compliance.

Other – Includes advertising, Shipt membership and service revenues, rental income, and other miscellaneous revenues, none of which are individually significant.

4. Cost of Sales and Selling, General and Administrative Expenses

The following table illustrates the primary items classified in each major expense category:

Cost of Sales	Selling, General and Administrative Expenses
Total cost of products sold including • Freight expenses associated with moving merchandise from our vendors to and between our distribution centers and our retail stores • Vendor income that is not reimbursement of specific, incremental, and identifiable costs	Compensation and benefit costs for stores and headquarters, except ship from store costs classified as cost of sales Occupancy and operating costs of retail and headquarters facilities
Inventory shrink	Advertising, offset by vendor income that is a reimbursement of specific, incremental, and identifiable costs
Markdowns	Pre-opening and exit costs of stores and other facilities
Outbound shipping and handling expenses associated with sales to our guests	Credit cards servicing expenses
Payment term cash discounts	Costs associated with accepting third-party bank issued payment cards
Distribution center costs, including compensation and benefits costs and depreciation	Litigation and defense costs and related insurance recoveries
Compensation and benefit costs associated with shipment of merchandise from stores	Other administrative costs
Import costs	

Note: The classification of these expenses varies across the retail industry.

7. Fair Value Measurements

Fair value measurements are reported in one of three levels based on the lowest level of significant input used: Level 1 (unadjusted quoted prices in active markets); Level 2 (observable market inputs, other than quoted prices included in Level 1); and Level 3 (unobservable inputs that cannot be corroborated by observable market data).

Fair Value Measurements - Recurring Basis			Fair Value as of	
(millions)	Classification	Pricing Category	January 30, 2021	February 1, 2020
Assets				
Short-term investments [(a)]	Cash and Cash Equivalents	Level 1	$ 7,644	$ 1,810
Prepaid forward contracts [(b)]	Other Current Assets	Level 1	38	23
Equity securities [(c)]	Other Current Assets	Level 1	—	39
Interest rate swaps [(d)]	Other Noncurrent Assets	Level 2	188	137

(a) Carrying value approximates fair value because maturities are less than three months.
(b) Initially valued at transaction price. Subsequently valued by reference to the market price of Target common stock.
(c) Represents our investment in Casper common stock.
(d) Valuations are based on observable inputs to the valuation model (e.g., interest rates and credit spreads).

In 2020 and 2019, we recorded pretax losses of $19 million and $41 million, respectively, related to our investment in Casper within Net Other (Income) / Expense. We sold our investment during 2020.

8. Cash and Cash Equivalents

Cash equivalents include highly liquid investments with an original maturity of three months or less from the time of purchase. Cash equivalents also include amounts due from third-party financial institutions for credit and debit card transactions. These receivables typically settle in five days or less.

Cash and Cash Equivalents (millions)	January 30, 2021	February 1, 2020
Cash	$ 307	$ 326
Short-term investments	7,644	1,810
Receivables from third-party financial institutions for credit and debit card transactions	560	441
Cash and cash equivalents [(a)]	$ 8,511	$ 2,577

(a) We have access to these funds without any significant restrictions, taxes or penalties.

As of January 30, 2021, and February 1, 2020, we reclassified book overdrafts of $240 million and $209 million, respectively, to Accounts Payable and $24 million and $23 million, respectively, to Accrued and Other Current Liabilities.

9. Inventory

The vast majority of our inventory is accounted for under the retail inventory accounting method (RIM) using the last-in, first-out (LIFO) method. Inventory is stated at the lower of LIFO cost or market. Inventory cost includes the amount we pay to our suppliers to acquire inventory, freight costs incurred to deliver product to our distribution centers and stores, and import costs, reduced by vendor income and cash discounts. Distribution center operating costs, including compensation and benefits, are expensed in the period incurred. Inventory is also reduced for estimated losses related to shrink and markdowns. The LIFO provision is calculated based on inventory levels, markup rates, and internally measured retail price indices.

Under RIM, inventory cost and the resulting gross margins are calculated by applying a cost-to-retail ratio to the inventory retail value. RIM is an averaging method that has been widely used in the retail industry due to its practicality. The use of RIM will result in inventory being valued at the lower of cost or market because permanent markdowns are taken as a reduction of the retail value of inventory.

10. Other Current Assets

Other Current Assets (millions)	January 30, 2021	February 1, 2020
Accounts and other receivables	$ 631 $	$ 498
Vendor income receivable	504	464
Prepaid expenses	171	154
Other	286	217
Total	$ 1,592 $	$ 1,333

11. Property and Equipment

Property and equipment, including assets acquired under finance leases, is depreciated using the straight-line method over estimated useful lives or lease terms if shorter. We amortize leasehold improvements purchased after the beginning of the initial lease term over the shorter of the assets' useful lives or a term that includes the original lease term, plus any renewals that are reasonably certain at the date the leasehold improvements are acquired. Depreciation expense for 2020, 2019, and 2018 was $2.5 billion, $2.6 billion, and $2.5 billion, respectively, including depreciation expense included in Cost of Sales. For income tax purposes, accelerated depreciation methods are generally used. Repair and maintenance costs are expensed as incurred. Facility pre-opening costs, including supplies and payroll, are expensed as incurred.

Estimated Useful Lives	Life (Years)
Buildings and improvements	8-39
Fixtures and equipment	2-15
Computer hardware and software	2-7

We review long-lived assets for impairment when store performance expectations, events, or changes in circumstances—such as a decision to relocate or close a store or distribution center, discontinue a project, or make significant software changes—indicate that the asset's carrying value may not be recoverable. We recognized impairment losses of $62 million, $23 million, and $92 million during 2020, 2019, and 2018, respectively. For asset groups classified as held for sale, measurement of an impairment loss is based on the excess of the carrying amount of the asset group over its fair value. We estimate fair value by obtaining market appraisals, obtaining valuations from third-party brokers, or using other valuation techniques. Impairments are recorded in SG&A Expenses.

12. Other Noncurrent Assets

Other Noncurrent Assets (millions)	January 30, 2021	February 1, 2020
Goodwill and intangible assets	$ 668	$ 686
Company-owned life insurance investments, net of loans	450	418
Other	268	254
Total	$ 1,386	$ 1,358

13. Goodwill and Intangible Assets

Goodwill totaled $631 million and $633 million as of January 30, 2021, and February 1, 2020, respectively. No impairments were recorded in 2020, 2019, or 2018 as a result of the annual goodwill impairment tests performed.

Intangible assets, net of accumulated amortization, totaled $ 37 million and $53 million as of January 30, 2021, and February 1, 2020, respectively, and primarily related to trademarks and customer relationships. We use both accelerated and straight-line methods to amortize definite-lived intangible assets over 4 to 15 years. The weighted average life of intangible assets was 8 years as of January 30, 2021. Amortization expense was $ 15 million, $13 million, and $14 million in 2020, 2019, and 2018, respectively, and is estimated to be less than $15 million annually through 2025.

14. Accrued and Other Current Liabilities

Accrued and Other Current Liabilities (millions)	January 30, 2021	February 1, 2020
Wages and benefits	$ 1,677	$ 1,158
Real estate, sales, and other taxes payable	1,103	601
Gift card liability, net of estimated breakage	1,035	935
Income tax payable	473	129
Dividends payable	341	333
Current portion of operating lease liabilities	211	200
Workers' compensation and general liability [(a)]	169	155
Interest payable	79	69
Other	1,034	826
Total	$ 6,122	$ 4,406

[(a)] We retain a substantial portion of the risk related to general liability and workers' compensation claims. We estimate our ultimate cost based on analysis of historical data and actuarial estimates. General liability and workers' compensation liabilities are recorded at our estimate of their net present value.

16. Commercial Paper and Long-Term Debt

As of January 30, 2021, the carrying value and maturities of our debt portfolio were as follows:

Debt Maturities	January 30, 2021	
(dollars in millions)	Rate [(a)]	Balance
Due 2021-2025	3.0 %	$ 3,607
Due 2026-2030	3.0	3,392
Due 2031-2035	6.6	507
Due 2036-2040	6.8	936
Due 2041-2045	4.0	1,084
Due 2046-2050	3.8	1,117
Total notes and debentures	3.7	10,643
Swap valuation adjustments		183
Finance lease liabilities		1,854
Less: Amounts due within one year		(1,144)
Long-term debt and other borrowings		$ 11,536

[(a)] Reflects the dollar weighted average stated interest rate as of year-end.

Required Principal Payments (millions)	2021	2022	2023	2024	2025
Total required principal payments	$1,056	$ 63	—	$ 1,000	$ 1,500

In October 2020, we repurchased $1.77 billion of debt before its maturity at a market value of $2.25 billion. We recognized a loss on early retirement of $512 million, which was recorded in Net Interest Expense.

In March 2020, we issued unsecured fixed rate debt of $1.5 billion at 2.250 percent that matures in April 2025 and $1.0 billion at 2.650 percent that matures in September 2030.

In January 2020, we issued $750 million of 10-year unsecured fixed rate debt at 2.350 percent, and separately, we redeemed $1.0 billion of 3.875 percent unsecured fixed rate debt before its maturity. We recognized a loss on early retirement of approximately $10 million, which was recorded in Net Interest Expense.

In March 2019, we issued $1.0 billion of 10-year unsecured fixed rate debt at 3.375 percent, and in June 2019, we repaid $1.0 billion of 2.3 percent unsecured fixed rate debt at maturity.

We obtain short-term financing from time to time under our commercial paper program.

Commercial Paper (dollars in millions)	2020	2019	2018
Maximum daily amount outstanding during the year	$ —	$ 744	$ 658
Average amount outstanding during the year	—	41	63
Amount outstanding at year-end	—	—	—
Weighted average interest rate	— %	2.36 %	2.00 %

We have a committed $2.5 billion unsecured revolving credit facility that expires in October 2023. No balances were outstanding at any time during 2020, 2019, or 2018.

Substantially all of our outstanding borrowings are senior, unsecured obligations. Most of our long-term debt obligations contain covenants related to secured debt levels. In addition to a secured debt level covenant, our credit facility also contains a debt leverage covenant. We are, and expect to remain, in compliance with these covenants, which have no practical effect on our ability to pay dividends.

Partial 10-K report for teaching purposes.
For the complete 10-K, go to sec.gov or stock.walmart.com/investors/financial-information/sec-filings/.

UNITED STATES
SECURITIES AND EXCHANGE COMMISSION
Washington, D.C. 20549

FORM 10-K

☒ Annual report pursuant to section 13 or 15(d) of the Securities Exchange Act of 1934

For the fiscal year ended January 31, 2021, or

☐ Transition report pursuant to section 13 or 15(d) of the Securities Exchange Act of 1934

Commission file number 001-06991.

WALMART INC.
(Exact name of registrant as specified in its charter)

DE	71-0415188
(State or other jurisdiction of incorporation or organization)	(IRS Employer Identification No.)
702 S.W. 8th Street Bentonville, AR	72716
(Address of principal executive offices)	(Zip Code)

Registrant's telephone number, including area code: (479) 273-4000

Securities registered pursuant to Section 12(b) of the Act:

Title of each class	Trading Symbol(s)	Name of each exchange on which registered
Common Stock, par value $0.10 per share	WMT	NYSE
1.900% Notes Due 2022	WMT22	NYSE
2.550% Notes Due 2026	WMT26	NYSE

Securities registered pursuant to Section 12(g) of the Act: None

Indicate by check mark if the registrant is a well-known seasoned issuer, as defined in Rule 405 of the Securities Act.
Yes ý No ¨

Indicate by check mark if the registrant is not required to file reports pursuant to Section 13 or Section 15(d) of the Exchange Act.
Yes ¨ No ý

ITEM 8. FINANCIAL STATEMENTS AND SUPPLEMENTARY DATA

Report of Independent Registered Public Accounting Firm

To the Shareholders and the Board of Directors of Walmart Inc.

Opinion on the Financial Statements

We have audited the accompanying consolidated balance sheets of Walmart Inc. (the Company) as of January 31, 2021 and 2020, the related consolidated statements of income, comprehensive income, shareholders' equity and cash flows for each of the three years in the period ended January 31, 2021, and the related notes (collectively referred to as the "Consolidated Financial Statements"). In our opinion, the Consolidated Financial Statements present fairly, in all material respects, the financial position of the Company at January 31, 2021 and 2020, and the results of its operations and its cash flows for each of the three years in the period ended January 31, 2021, in conformity with U.S. generally accepted accounting principles.

We also have audited, in accordance with the standards of the Public Company Accounting Oversight Board (United States) (PCAOB), the Company's internal control over financial reporting as of January 31, 2021, based on criteria established in Internal Control-Integrated Framework issued by the Committee of Sponsoring Organizations of the Treadway Commission (2013 framework) and our report dated March 19, 2021 expressed an unqualified opinion thereon.

Basis for Opinion

These financial statements are the responsibility of the Company's management. Our responsibility is to express an opinion on the Company's financial statements based on our audits. We are a public accounting firm registered with the PCAOB and are required to be independent with respect to the Company in accordance with the U.S. federal securities laws and the applicable rules and regulations of the Securities and Exchange Commission and the PCAOB.

We conducted our audits in accordance with the standards of the PCAOB. Those standards require that we plan and perform the audit to obtain reasonable assurance about whether the financial statements are free of material misstatement, whether due to error or fraud. Our audits included performing procedures to assess the risks of material misstatement of the financial statements, whether due to error or fraud, and performing procedures that respond to those risks. Such procedures included examining, on a test basis, evidence regarding the amounts and disclosures in the financial statements. Our audits also included evaluating the accounting principles used and significant estimates made by management, as well as evaluating the overall presentation of the financial statements. We believe that our audits provide a reasonable basis for our opinion.

Critical Audit Matters

The critical audit matters communicated below are matters arising from the current period audit of the financial statements that were communicated or required to be communicated to the audit committee and that: (1) relate to accounts or disclosures that are material to the financial statements and (2) involved our especially challenging, subjective or complex judgments. The communication of critical audit matters does not alter in any way our opinion on the Consolidated Financial Statements, taken as a whole, and we are not, by communicating the critical audit matters below, providing separate opinions on the critical audit matters or on the accounts or disclosures to which they relate.

Contingencies

Description of the Matter

As described respect in Note 10 to the Consolidated Financial Statements, at January 31, 2021, the Company is involved in a number of legal proceedings and has made accruals with to these matters, where appropriate. For some matters, a liability is not probable, or the amount cannot be reasonably estimated and therefore an accrual has not been made. Where a liability is reasonably possible and may be material, such matters have been disclosed. Management assessed the probability of occurrence and the estimation of any potential loss based on the ability to predict the number of claims that may be filed or whether any loss or range of loss can be reasonably estimated. For example, in assessing the probability of occurrence in a particular legal proceeding, management exercises judgment to determine if it can predict the number of claims that may be filed and whether it can reasonably estimate any loss or range of loss that may arise from that proceeding. In connection with the sale of Asda, the Company is no longer liable for the Asda Equal Value Claims; however, the Company has agreed to provide indemnification for any potential Asda liability related to these claims up to a contractually determined amount.

Auditing management's accounting for, and disclosure of, loss contingencies and the estimated fair value of related indemnifications was complex and highly judgmental as it involved our assessment of the significant judgments made by management when assessing the probability of occurrence for contingencies or related indemnifications or when determining whether an estimate of the loss or range of loss could be made.

How We Addressed the Matter in Our Audit

We obtained an understanding, evaluated the design and tested the operating effectiveness of controls over the identification and evaluation of contingencies and related indemnities. For example, we tested controls over the Company's assessment of the likelihood of loss and the Company's determinations regarding the measurement of loss.

To test the Company's assessment of the probability of occurrence or determination of an estimate of loss, or range of loss, among other procedures, we read the minutes of the meetings of the Board of Directors and committees of the Board of Directors, reviewed opinions provided to the Company by certain outside legal counsel, read letters received directly by us from internal and external counsel, and evaluated the current status of contingencies based on discussions with internal legal counsel. We also evaluated the appropriateness of the related disclosures. To test the estimated fair value of indemnities, we involved a valuation specialist to evaluate the valuation methodologies and significant assumptions including, among others, the discount rate.

Valuation of Indefinite-Lived Intangible Assets

Description of the Matter

At January 31, 2021, the Company has $4.9 billion of indefinite-lived intangible assets which primarily consist of acquired tradenames. As disclosed in Notes 1, 8 and 12 to the Consolidated Financial Statements, these assets are evaluated for impairment at least annually using valuation techniques to estimate fair value. These fair value estimates are sensitive to certain significant assumptions including revenue growth rates, discount rates, and royalty rates.

Auditing management's annual indefinite-lived intangible assets impairment tests was complex and highly judgmental due to the significant measurement uncertainty in determining the fair values of the indefinite-lived intangibles. For example, the fair value estimates are sensitive to significant assumptions identified above that are affected by future market or economic conditions.

How We Addressed the Matter in Our Audit

We obtained an understanding, evaluated, the design and tested the operating effectiveness of controls over the Company's indefinite-lived intangible asset impairment review process. Our procedures included, among others, testing controls over management's review of the significant assumptions described above used to estimate the fair values of the indefinite-lived intangible assets.

To test the estimated fair values of the indefinite-lived intangible assets, we performed audit procedures that included, among others, assessing methodologies used to determine the fair value, testing the significant assumptions discussed above and testing the completeness and accuracy of the underlying data used by the Company. For example, we evaluated management's forecasted revenue growth rates used in the fair value estimates by comparing those assumptions to the historical results of the Company and current industry, market and economic forecasts. We involved a valuation specialist to assist in evaluating the valuation methodologies and the significant assumptions such as discount rates and royalty rates. Additionally, we performed sensitivity analyses of significant assumptions to evaluate the effect on the fair value estimates of the indefinite-lived assets.

Ernst & Young LLP

We have served as the Company's auditor since 1969.

Rogers, Arkansas
March 19, 2021

Walmart Inc.
Consolidated Statements of Income

(Amounts in millions, except per share data)	Fiscal Years Ended January 31, 2021	2020	2019
Revenues:			
Net sales	$ 555,233	$ 519,926	$ 510,329
Membership and other income	3,918	4,038	4,076
Total revenues	559,151	523,964	514,405
Costs and expenses:			
Cost of sales	420,315	394,605	385,301
Operating, selling, general and administrative expenses	116,288	108,791	107,147
Operating income	22,548	20,568	21,957
Interest:			
Debt	1,976	2,262	1,975
Finance, capital lease and financing obligations	339	337	371
Interest income	(121)	(189)	(217)
Interest, net	2,194	2,410	2,129
Other (gains) and losses	(210)	(1,958)	8,368
Income before income taxes	20,564	20,116	11,460
Provision for income taxes	6,858	4,915	4,281
Consolidated net income	13,706	15,201	7,179
Consolidated net income attributable to noncontrolling interest	(196)	(320)	(509)
Consolidated net income attributable to Walmart	$ 13,510	$ 14,881	$ 6,670
Net income per common share:			
Basic net income per common share attributable to Walmart	$ 4.77	$ 5.22	$ 2.28
Diluted net income per common share attributable to Walmart	4.75	5.19	2.26
Weighted-average common shares outstanding:			
Basic	2,831	2,850	2,929
Diluted	2,847	2,868	2,945
Dividends declared per common share	$ 2.16	$ 2.12	$ $2.08

See accompanying notes.

Walmart Inc.
Consolidated Statements of Comprehensive Income

(Amounts in millions)	Fiscal Years Ended January 31, 2021	2020	2019
Consolidated net income	$ 13,706	$ 15,201	$ 7,179
Consolidated net income attributable to noncontrolling interest	(196)	(320)	(509)
Consolidated net income attributable to Walmart	13,510	14,881	6,670
Other comprehensive income (loss), net of income taxes			
Currency translation and other	842	286	(226)
Net investment hedges	(221)	122	272
Cash flow hedges	235	(399)	(290)
Minimum pension liability	(30)	(1,244)	131
Other comprehensive income (loss), net of income taxes	826	(1,235)	(113)
Other comprehensive (income) loss attributable to noncontrolling interest	213	(28)	188
Other comprehensive income (loss) attributable to Walmart	1,039	(1,263)	75
Comprehensive income, net of income taxes	14,532	13,966	7,066
Comprehensive (income) loss attributable to noncontrolling interest	17	(348)	(321)
Comprehensive income attributable to Walmart	$ 14,549	$ 13,618	$ 6,745

See accompanying notes.

Walmart Inc.
Consolidated Balance Sheets

(Amounts in millions)	As of January 31, 2021	2020
ASSETS		
Current assets:		
Cash and cash equivalents	$ 17,741	$ 9,465
Receivables, net	6,516	6,284
Inventories	44,949	44,435
Prepaid expenses and other	20,861	1,622
Total current assets	90,067	61,806
Property and equipment, net	92,201	105,208
Operating lease right-of-use assets	13,642	17,424
Finance lease right-of-use assets, net	4,005	4,417
Goodwill	28,983	31,073
Other long-term assets	23,598	16,567
Total assets	$ 252,496	$ 236,495
LIABILITIES AND EQUITY		
Current liabilities:		
Short-term borrowings	$ 224	$ 575
Accounts payable	49,141	46,973
Accrued liabilities	37,966	22,296
Accrued income taxes	242	280
Long-term debt due within one year	3,115	5,362
Operating lease obligations due within one year	1,466	1,793
Finance lease obligations due within one year	491	511
Total current liabilities	92,645	77,790
Long-term debt	41,194	43,714
Long-term operating lease obligations	12,909	16,171
Long-term finance lease obligations	3,847	4,307
Deferred income taxes and other	14,370	12,961
Commitments and contingencies		
Equity:		
Common stock	282	284
Capital in excess of par value	3,646	3,247
Retained earnings	88,763	83,943
Accumulated other comprehensive loss	(11,766)	(12,805)
Total Walmart shareholders' equity	80,925	74,669
Noncontrolling interest	6,606	6,883
Total equity	87,531	81,552
Total liabilities and equity	$ 252,496	$ 236,495

See accompanying notes.

Walmart Inc.
Consolidated Statements of Shareholders' Equity

(Amounts in millions)	Common Stock		Capital in Excess of Par Value	Retained Earnings	Accumulated Other Comprehensive Income (Loss)	Total Walmart Shareholders' Equity	Noncontrolling Interest	Total Equity
	Shares	Amount						
Balances as of February 1, 2018	2,952	$ 295	$ 2,648	$85,107	$ (10,181)	$ 77,869	$ 2,953	$80,822
Adoption of new accounting standards, net of income taxes	—	—	—	2,361	(1,436)	925	(1)	924
Consolidated net income	—	—	—	6,670	—	6,670	509	7,179
Other comprehensive income (loss), net of income taxes	—	—	—	—	75	75	(188)	(113)
Cash dividends declared ($2.08 per share)	—	—	—	(6,102)	—	(6,102)	—	(6,102)
Purchase of Company stock	(80)	(8)	(245)	(7,234)	—	(7,487)	—	(7,487)
Cash dividend declared to noncontrolling interest	—	—	—	—	—	—	(488)	(488)
Noncontrolling interest of acquired entity	—	—	—	—	—	—	4,345	4,345
Other	6	1	562	(17)	—	546	8	554
Balances as of January 31, 2019	2,878	288	2,965	80,785	(11,542)	72,496	7,138	79,634
Adoption of new accounting standards on February 1, 2019, net of income taxes	—	—	—	(266)	—	(266)	(34)	(300)
Consolidated net income	—	—	—	14,881	—	14,881	320	15,201
Other comprehensive income (loss), net of income taxes	—	—	—	—	(1,263)	(1,263)	28	(1,235)
Cash dividends declared ($2.12 per share)	—	—	—	(6,048)	—	(6,048)	—	(6,048)
Purchase of Company stock	(53)	(5)	(199)	(5,435)	—	(5,639)	—	(5,639)
Cash dividend declared to noncontrolling interest	—	—	—	—	—	—	(475)	(475)
Other	7	1	481	26	—	508	(94)	414
Balances as of January 31, 2020	2,832	284	3,247	83,943	(12,805)	74,669	6,883	81,552
Consolidated net income	—	—	—	13,510	—	13,510	196	13,706
Other comprehensive income (loss), net of income taxes	—	—	—	—	1,039	1,039	(213)	826
Cash dividends declared ($2.16 per share)	—	—	—	(6,116)	—	(6,116)	—	(6,116)
Purchase of Company stock	(20)	(2)	(97)	(2,559)	—	(2,658)	—	(2,658)
Cash dividends declared to noncontrolling interest	—	—	—	—	—	—	(365)	(365)
Other	9	—	496	(15)	—	481	105	586
Balances as of January 31, 2021	2,821	$ 282	$ 3,646	$88,763	$ (11,766)	$ 80,925	$ 6,606	$87,531

See accompanying notes.

Walmart Inc.
Consolidated Statements of Cash Flows

(Amounts in millions)	Fiscal Years Ended January 31, 2021	2020	2019
Cash flows from operating activities:			
Consolidated net income	$ 13,706	$ 15,201	$ 7,179
Adjustments to reconcile consolidated net income to net cash provided by operating activities:			
Depreciation and amortization	11,152	10,987	10,678
Net unrealized and realized (gains) and losses	(8,589)	(1,886)	3,516
Losses on disposal of business operations	8,401	15	4,850
Asda pension contribution	—	(1,036)	—
Deferred income taxes	1,911	320	(499)
Other operating activities	1,521	1,981	1,734
Changes in certain assets and liabilities, net of effects of acquisitions and dispositions:			
Receivables, net	(1,086)	154	(368)
Inventories	(2,395)	(300)	(1,311)
Accounts payable	6,966	(274)	1,831
Accrued liabilities	4,623	186	183
Accrued income taxes	(136)	(93)	(40)
Net cash provided by operating activities	36,074	25,255	27,753
Cash flows from investing activities:			
Payments for property and equipment	(10,264)	(10,705)	(10,344)
Proceeds from the disposal of property and equipment	215	321	519
Proceeds from the disposal of certain operations	56	833	876
Payments for business acquisitions, net of cash acquired	(180)	(56)	(14,656)
Other investing activities	102	479	(431)
Net cash used in investing activities	(10,071)	(9,128)	(24,036)
Cash flows from financing activities:			
Net change in short-term borrowings	(324)	(4,656)	(53)
Proceeds from issuance of long-term debt	—	5,492	15,872
Repayments of long-term debt	(5,382)	(1,907)	(3,784)
Dividends paid	(6,116)	(6,048)	(6,102)
Purchase of Company stock	(2,625)	(5,717)	(7,410)
Dividends paid to noncontrolling interest	(434)	(555)	(431)
Other financing activities	(1,236)	(908)	(629)
Net cash used in financing activities	(16,117)	(14,299)	(2,537)
Effect of exchange rates on cash, cash equivalents and restricted cash	235	(69)	(438)
Net increase in cash, cash equivalents and restricted cash	10,121	1,759	742
Cash and cash equivalents reclassified as assets held for sale	(1,848)	—	—
Cash, cash equivalents and restricted cash at beginning of year	9,515	7,756	7,014
Cash, cash equivalents and restricted cash at end of year	$ 17,788	$ 9,515	$ 7,756
Supplemental disclosure of cash flow information:			
Income taxes paid	$ 5,271	$ 3,616	$ 3,982
Interest paid	2,216	2,464	2,348

See accompanying notes.

Walmart Inc.
Notes to Consolidated Financial Statements

Note 1. Summary of Significant Accounting Policies

General

Walmart Inc. ("Walmart" or the "Company") helps people around the world save money and live better – anytime and anywhere – by providing the opportunity to shop in retail stores and through eCommerce. Through innovation, the Company is striving to continuously improve a customer-centric experience that seamlessly integrates eCommerce and retail stores in an omni-channel offering that saves time for its customers.

The Company's operations comprise three reportable segments: Walmart U.S., Walmart International and Sam's Club.

Principles of Consolidation

The Consolidated Financial Statements include the accounts of Walmart and its subsidiaries as of and for the fiscal years ended January 31, 2021 ("fiscal 2021"), January 31, 2020 ("fiscal 2020") and January 31, 2019 ("fiscal 2019"). Intercompany accounts and transactions have been eliminated in consolidation. The Company consolidates variable interest entities where it has been determined that the Company is the primary beneficiary of those entities' operations. Investments for which the Company exercises significant influence but does not have control are accounted for under the equity method. These variable interest entities and equity method investments are immaterial to the Company's Consolidated Financial Statements.

The Company's Consolidated Financial Statements are based on a fiscal year ending on January 31 for the United States ("U.S.") and Canadian operations. The Company consolidates all other operations generally using a one-month lag and based on a calendar year. There were no significant intervening events during the month of January 2021 related to the operations consolidated using a lag that materially affected the Consolidated Financial Statements.

Use of Estimates

The Consolidated Financial Statements have been prepared in conformity with U.S. generally accepted accounting principles. Those principles require management to make estimates and assumptions, including potential impacts arising from the COVID-19 pandemic and related government actions, that affect the reported amounts of assets and liabilities. Management's estimates and assumptions also affect the disclosure of contingent assets and liabilities at the date of the financial statements and the reported amounts of revenues and expenses during the reporting period. Actual results may differ from those estimates.

Cash and Cash Equivalents

The Company considers investments with a maturity when purchased of three months or less to be cash equivalents. All credit card, debit card and electronic transfer transactions that process in less than seven days are classified as cash and cash equivalents. The amounts due from banks for these transactions classified as cash and cash equivalents totaled $4.1 billion and $1.7 billion as of January 31, 2021 and 2020, respectively.

The Company's cash balances are held in various locations around the world. Of the Company's $17.7 billion and $9.5 billion in cash and cash equivalents as of January 31, 2021 and January 31, 2020, approximately 40% and 80% were held outside of the U.S., respectively. Cash and cash equivalents held outside of the U.S. are generally utilized to support liquidity needs in the Company's non-U.S. operations.

The Company uses intercompany financing arrangements in an effort to ensure cash can be made available in the country in which it is needed with the minimum cost possible.

As of January 31, 2021 and 2020, cash and cash equivalents of approximately $2.8 billion and $2.3 billion, respectively, may not be freely transferable to the U.S. due to local laws or other restrictions. Of the $2.8 billion as of January 31, 2021, approximately $1.0 billion can only be accessed through dividends or intercompany financing arrangements subject to approval of Flipkart Private Limited ("Flipkart") minority shareholders; however, this cash is expected to be utilized to fund the operations of Flipkart.

Receivables

Receivables are stated at their carrying values, net of a reserve for doubtful accounts, and are primarily due from the following: customers, which also includes insurance companies resulting from pharmacy sales, banks for customer credit, debit cards and electronic transfer transactions that take in excess of seven days to process; suppliers for marketing or incentive programs; governments for income taxes; and real estate transactions. As of January 31, 2021 and January 31, 2020, receivables from transactions with customers, net were $2.7 billion and $2.9 billion, respectively.

Inventories

The Company values inventories at the lower of cost or market as determined primarily by the retail inventory method of accounting, using the last-in, first-out ("LIFO") method for the Walmart U.S. segment's inventories. The inventory for the Walmart International segment is valued primarily by the retail inventory method of accounting, using the first-in, first-out ("FIFO") method. The retail inventory method of accounting results in inventory being valued at the lower of cost or market, since permanent markdowns are immediately recorded as a reduction of the retail value of inventory. The inventory at the Sam's Club segment is valued using the weighted-average cost LIFO method. As of January 31, 2021 and January 31, 2020, the Company's inventories valued at LIFO approximated those inventories as if they were valued at FIFO.

Property and Equipment

Property and equipment are initially recorded at cost. Gains or losses on disposition are recognized as earned or incurred. Costs of major improvements are capitalized, while costs of normal repairs and maintenance are expensed as incurred. The following table summarizes the Company's property and equipment balances, and includes the estimated useful lives that are generally used to depreciate the assets on a straight-line basis:

		As of January 31,	
(Amounts in millions)	Estimated Useful Lives	2021	2020
Land	N/A	$ 19,308	$ 24,619
Buildings and improvements	3 - 40 years	97,582	105,674
Fixtures and equipment	1 - 30 years	56,639	58,607
Transportation equipment	3 - 15 years	2,301	2,377
Construction in progress	N/A	4,741	3,751
Property and equipment		180,571	195,028
Accumulated depreciation		(88,370)	(89,820)
Property and equipment, net		$ 92,201	$ 105,208

Leasehold improvements are depreciated or amortized over the shorter of the estimated useful life of the asset or the remaining expected lease term. Total depreciation and amortization expense for property and equipment, property under finance leases and financing obligations, property under capital leases and intangible assets for fiscal 2021, 2020 and 2019 was $11.2 billion, $11.0 billion and $10.7 billion, respectively.

Leases

For any new or modified lease, the Company, at the inception of the contract, determines whether a contract is or contains a lease. The Company records right-of-use ("ROU") assets and lease obligations for its finance and operating leases, which are initially recognized based on the discounted future lease payments over the term of the lease. As the rate implicit in the Company's leases is not easily determinable, the Company's applicable incremental borrowing rate is used in calculating the present value of the sum of the lease payments.

Impairment of Long-Lived Assets

Management reviews long-lived assets for indicators of impairment whenever events or changes in circumstances indicate that the carrying amount may not be recoverable. The evaluation is performed at the lowest level of identifiable cash flows, which is at the individual store or club level. Undiscounted cash flows expected to be generated by the related assets are estimated over the assets' useful lives based on updated projections. If the evaluation indicates that the carrying amount of the assets may not be recoverable, any potential impairment is measured based upon the fair value of the related asset or asset group as determined by an appropriate market appraisal or other valuation technique.

Goodwill and Other Acquired Intangible Assets

Goodwill represents the excess of the purchase price over the fair value of net assets acquired in business combinations and is allocated to the appropriate reporting unit when acquired. Other acquired intangible assets are stated at the fair value acquired as determined by a valuation technique commensurate with the intended use of the related asset. Goodwill and indefinite-lived intangible assets are not amortized; rather, they are evaluated for impairment annually and whenever events or changes in circumstances indicate that the value of the asset may be impaired. Definite-lived intangible assets are considered long-lived assets and are amortized on a straight-line basis over the periods that expected economic benefits will be provided.

Goodwill is assigned to the reporting unit which consolidates the acquisition. Components within the same reportable segment are aggregated and deemed a single reporting unit if the components have similar economic characteristics. As of January 31, 2021, the Company's reporting units consisted of Walmart U.S., Walmart International and Sam's Club. Goodwill is evaluated for impairment using either a qualitative or quantitative approach for each of the Company's reporting units. Generally, a qualitative assessment is first performed to determine whether a quantitative goodwill impairment test is necessary. If management determines, after performing an assessment based on the qualitative factors, that the fair value of the reporting unit is more likely than not less than the carrying amount, or that a fair value of the reporting unit substantially in excess of the carrying amount cannot be assured, then a quantitative goodwill impairment test would be required. The quantitative test for goodwill impairment is performed by determining the fair value of the related reporting units. Fair value is measured based on the discounted cash flow method and relative market-based approaches. After evaluation, management determined the fair value of each reporting unit is significantly greater than the carrying amount and, accordingly, the Company has not recorded any impairment charges related to goodwill.

The following table reflects goodwill activity, by reportable segment, for fiscal 2021 and 2020:

(Amounts in millions)	**Walmart U.S.**	**Walmart International**	**Sam's Club**	**Total**
Balances as of February 1, 2019	$ 2,552	$ 28,316	$ 313	$ 31,181
Changes in currency translation and other	—	(149)	—	(149)
Acquisitions	41	—	—	41
Balances as of January 31, 2020	2,593	28,167	313	31,073
Changes in currency translation and other	—	10	—	10
Acquisitions	103	—	8	111
Amounts reclassified related to operations held for sale(1)	—	(2,211)	—	(2,211)
Balances as of January 31, 2021	$ 2,696	$ 25,966	$ 321	$ 28,983

(1) Represents goodwill associated with operations in the U.K. and Japan which are classified as held for sale as of January 31, 2021.

Intangible assets are included in other long-term assets in the Company's Consolidated Balance Sheets. As of January 31, 2021 and 2020, the Company had $4.9 billion and $5.2 billion, respectively, in indefinite-lived intangible assets which primarily consists of acquired trade names. There were no significant impairment charges related to intangible assets for fiscal 2021. During fiscal 2020, the Company incurred approximately $0.7 billion in impairment charges related to its intangible assets.

Investments

Investments in equity securities with readily determinable fair values are recorded at fair value in other long-term assets in the Consolidated Balance Sheets with changes in fair value recognized in other gains and losses in the Consolidated Statements of Income. Equity investments without readily determinable fair values are carried at cost in other long-term assets in the Consolidated Balance Sheets, and adjusted for any observable price changes or impairments recorded in other gains and losses in the Consolidated Statements of Income.

Investments in debt securities classified as held-to-maturity are reported at amortized cost in other long-term assets in the Consolidated Balance Sheets with interest or dividend income recorded in interest income in the Consolidated Statements of Income.

Revenue Recognition

Net Sales

The Company recognizes sales revenue, net of sales taxes and estimated sales returns, at the time it sells merchandise or services to the customer. eCommerce sales include shipping revenue and are recorded upon delivery to the customer. Estimated sales returns are calculated based on expected returns.

Membership Fee Revenue

The Company recognizes membership fee revenue both in the U.S. and internationally over the term of the membership, which is typically 12 months. Membership fee revenue was $1.7 billion for fiscal 2021, $1.5 billion for fiscal 2020 and $1.4 billion for fiscal 2019, respectively. Membership fee revenue is included in membership and other income in the Company's Consolidated Statements of Income. Deferred membership fee revenue is included in accrued liabilities in the Company's Consolidated Balance Sheets.

Gift Cards

Customer purchases of gift cards are not recognized as sales until the card is redeemed and the customer purchases merchandise using the gift card. Gift cards in the U.S. and some countries do not carry an expiration date; therefore, customers and members can redeem their gift cards for merchandise and services indefinitely. Gift cards in some countries where the Company does business have expiration dates. While gift cards are generally redeemed within 12 months, a certain number of gift cards, both with and without expiration dates, will not be fully redeemed. Management estimates unredeemed balances and recognizes revenue for these amounts in membership and other income in the Company's Consolidated Statements of Income over the expected redemption period.

Financial and Other Services

The Company recognizes revenue from service transactions at the time the service is performed. Generally, revenue from services is classified as a component of net sales in the Company's Consolidated Statements of Income.

Cost of Sales

Cost of sales includes actual product cost, the cost of transportation to the Company's distribution facilities, stores and clubs from suppliers, the cost of transportation from the Company's distribution facilities to the stores, clubs and customers and the cost of warehousing for the Sam's Club segment and import distribution centers. Cost of sales is reduced by supplier payments that are not a reimbursement of specific, incremental and identifiable costs.

Payments from Suppliers

The Company receives consideration from suppliers for various programs, primarily volume incentives, warehouse allowances and reimbursements for specific programs such as markdowns, margin protection, advertising and supplier-specific fixtures. Payments from suppliers are accounted for as a reduction of cost of sales, except in certain limited situations when the payment is a reimbursement of specific, incremental and identifiable costs, and are recognized in the Company's Consolidated Statements of Income when the related inventory is sold.

Operating, Selling, General and Administrative Expenses

Operating, selling, general and administrative expenses include all operating costs of the Company, except cost of sales, as described above. As a result, the majority of the cost of warehousing and occupancy for the Walmart U.S. and Walmart International segments' distribution facilities is included in operating, selling, general and administrative expenses. Because the Company only includes a portion of the cost of its Walmart U.S. and Walmart International segments' distribution facilities in cost of sales, its gross profit and gross profit as a percentage of net sales may not be comparable to those of other retailers that may include all costs related to their distribution facilities in cost of sales and in the calculation of gross profit.

Advertising Costs

Advertising costs are expensed as incurred, consist primarily of print, television and digital advertisements and are recorded in operating, selling, general and administrative expenses in the Company's Consolidated Statements of Income. In certain limited situations, reimbursements from suppliers that are for specific, incremental and identifiable advertising costs are recognized as a reduction of advertising costs in operating, selling, general and administrative expenses. Advertising costs were $3.2 billion, $3.7 billion and $3.5 billion for fiscal 2021, 2020 and 2019, respectively.

Note 3. Shareholders' Equity

The total authorized shares of $0.10 par value common stock is 11.0 billion, of which 2.8 billion were issued and outstanding as of January 31, 2021 and 2020.

Share Repurchase Program

From time to time, the Company repurchases shares of its common stock under share repurchase programs authorized by the Company's Board of Directors. All repurchases made during fiscal 2021 were made under the $20.0 billion share repurchase program approved in October 2017, of which authorization for $3.0 billion of share repurchases remained as of January 31, 2021. On February 18, 2021, the Board of Directors approved a new $20.0 billion share repurchase program which, beginning February 22, 2021, replaced the previous share repurchase program. Any repurchased shares are constructively retired and returned to an unissued status.

The Company regularly reviews share repurchase activity and considers several factors in determining when to execute share repurchases, including, among other things, current cash needs, capacity for leverage, cost of borrowings, results of operations and the market price of the Company's common stock. The following table provides, on a settlement date basis, the number of shares repurchased, average price paid per share and total amount paid for share repurchases for fiscal 2021, 2020 and 2019:

	Fiscal Years Ended January 31,		
(Amounts in millions, except per share data)	2021	2020	2019
Total number of shares repurchased	19.4	53.9	79.5
Average price paid per share	$ 135.20	$ 105.98	$ 93.18
Total cash paid for share repurchases	$ 2,625	$ 5,717	$ 7,410

Note 5. Accrued Liabilities

The Company's accrued liabilities consist of the following as of January 31, 2021 and 2020:

	January 31,	
(Amounts in millions)	2021	2020
Liabilities held for sale(1)	$ 12,734	$ —
Accrued wages and benefits(2)	7,654	6,093
Self-insurance(3)	4,698	4,469
Accrued non-income taxes(4)	3,328	3,039
Deferred gift card revenue	2,310	1,990
Other(5)	7,242	6,705
Total accrued liabilities	$ 37,966	$ 22,296

(1)Liabilities held for sale relate to the Company's operations in Japan and the U.K. classified as held for sale as of January 31, 2021.

(2)Accrued wages and benefits include accrued wages, salaries, vacation, bonuses and other incentive plans.

(3)Self-insurance consists of insurance-related liabilities, such as workers' compensation, general liability, auto liability, product liability and certain employee-related healthcare benefits.

(4)Accrued non-income taxes include accrued payroll, property, value-added, sales and miscellaneous other taxes.

(5)Other accrued liabilities consist of various items such as interest, maintenance, utilities, legal contingencies, and advertising.

Note 6. Short-term Borrowings and Long-term Debt

Short-term borrowings consist of commercial paper and lines of credit. Short-term borrowings as of January 31, 2021 and 2020 were $0.2 billion and $0.6 billion, respectively, with weighted-average interest rates of 1.9% and 5.0%, respectively. Short-term borrowings as of January 31, 2020 were primarily outside of the U.S.

The Company has various committed lines of credit in the U.S. to support its commercial paper program and are summarized in the following table:

	January 31, 2021			January 31, 2020		
(Amounts in millions)	**Available**	**Drawn**	**Undrawn**	**Available**	**Drawn**	**Undrawn**
Five-year credit facility	$ 5,000	$ —	$ 5,000	$ 5,000	$ —	$ 5,000
364-day revolving credit facility(1)	10,000	—	10,000	10,000	—	10,000
Total	$ 15,000	$ —	$ 15,000	$ 15,000	$ —	$ 15,000

(1) In April 2020, the Company renewed and extended its existing 364-day revolving credit facility.

The committed lines of credit in the table above mature at various times between April 2021 and May 2024, carry interest rates generally ranging between LIBOR plus 10 basis points and LIBOR plus 75 basis points, and incur commitment fees ranging between 1.5 and 4.0 basis points. In conjunction with the committed lines of credit listed in the table above, the Company has agreed to observe certain covenants, the most restrictive of which relates to the maximum amount of secured debt. Additionally, the Company has syndicated and fronted letters of credit available which totaled $1.8 billion as of January 31, 2021 and 2020, of which $1.8 billion and $1.6 billion was drawn as of January 31, 2021 and 2020, respectively.

The Company's long-term debt, which includes the fair value instruments, consists of the following as of January 31, 2021 and 2020:

	January 31, 2021			January 31, 2020	
(Amounts in millions)	**Maturity Dates By Fiscal Year**	**Amount**	**Average Rate(1)**	**Amount**	**Average Rate(1)**
Unsecured debt					
Fixed	2022 - 2050	$ 35,216	3.9%	$ 39,752	3.8%
Variable	2022	750	0.5%	1,500	2.1%
Total U.S. dollar denominated		35,966		41,252	
Fixed	2023 - 2030	3,034	3.3%	2,758	3.3%
Variable		—		—	
Total Euro denominated		3,034		2,758	
Fixed	2031 - 2039	3,682	5.4%	3,518	5.4%
Variable		—		—	
Total Sterling denominated		3,682		3,518	
Fixed	2023-2028	1,624	0.3%	1,652	0.4%
Variable		—		—	
Total Yen denominated		1,624		1,652	
Total unsecured debt		44,306		49,180	
Total other(2)		3		(104)	
Total debt		44,309		49,076	
Less amounts due within one year		(3,115)		(5,362)	
Long-term debt		$ 41,194		$ 43,714	

(1)The average rate represents the weighted-average stated rate for each corresponding debt category, based on year-end balances and year-end interest rates.

(2)Includes deferred loan costs, discounts, fair value hedges, foreign-held debt and secured debt.

Annual maturities of long-term debt during the next five years and thereafter are as follows:

(Amounts in millions) **Fiscal Year**	**Annual Maturities**
2022	$ 3,115
2023	3,014
2024	4,721
2025	4,360
2026	1,480
Thereafter	27,619
Total	$ 44,309

Debt Issuances

There were no long-term debt issuances in fiscal 2021. Information on long-term debt issued during fiscal 2020, for general corporate purposes, is as follows:

(Amounts in millions)

Issue Date	**Principal Amount**	**Maturity Date**	**Fixed vs. Floating**	**Interest Rate**	**Net Proceeds**
April 23, 2019	$1,500	July 8, 2024	Fixed	2.850%	$ 1,493
April 23, 2019	$1,250	July 8, 2026	Fixed	3.050%	1,242
April 23, 2019	$1,250	July 8, 2029	Fixed	3.250%	1,243
September 24, 2019	$500	September 24, 2029	Fixed	2.375%	497
September 24, 2019	$1,000	September 24, 2049	Fixed	2.950%	975
Various	$42	Various	Various	Various	42
Total					$ 5,492

The fiscal 2020 issuances are senior, unsecured notes which rank equally with all other senior, unsecured debt obligations of the Company, and are not convertible or exchangeable. These issuances do not contain any financial covenants which restrict the Company's ability to pay dividends or repurchase company stock.

APPENDIX D

INDUSTRY RATIO REPORT

Retail Industry

Liquidity	
Current Ratio	1.10
Quick Ratio	0.45

Activity	
Inventory Turnover	8.63
Fixed Asset Turnover	9.29
Total Asset Turnover	2.20
Accounts Payable Turnover	8.21

Profitability	
Earnings Per Share	10.66
Gross Profit Percentage	27.12%
Net Profit Margin	4.53%
Return on Equity	24.51%
Return on Assets	9.27%
Quality of Income Ratio	3.34

Leverage	
Cash Coverage	35.01
Debt-to-Equity	8.23
Times Interest Earned	17.20

Dividends	
Dividend Yield	1.71%

Other	
Capital Acquisitions Ratio	4.31
Price/Earnings	33.09

COMPANIES USED IN INDUSTRY ANALYSIS

Company Name	Ticker Symbol
Amazon.com, Inc.	AMZN
Best Buy Co., Inc.	BBY
Costco Wholesale Corp.	COST
Dollar General Corp.	DG
Home Depot Inc.	HD
The Kroger Co.	KR
Lowe's Inc.	LOW
Target Corp.	TGT
Walgreens Boots Alliance Inc.	WBA
Walmart Inc.	WMT

TABLE E.1

Present Value of $1

Periods	1.0%	2.0%	3.0%	3.75%	4.0%	4.25%	5.0%	6.0%	7.0%
1	0.99010	0.98039	0.97087	0.96386	0.96154	0.95923	0.95238	0.94340	0.93458
2	0.98030	0.96117	0.94260	0.92902	0.92456	0.92013	0.90703	0.89000	0.87344
3	0.97059	0.94232	0.91514	0.89544	0.88900	0.88262	0.86384	0.83962	0.81630
4	0.96098	0.92385	0.88849	0.86307	0.85480	0.84663	0.82270	0.79209	0.76290
5	0.95147	0.90573	0.86261	0.83188	0.82193	0.81212	0.78353	0.74726	0.71299
6	0.94205	0.88797	0.83748	0.80181	0.79031	0.77901	0.74622	0.70496	0.66634
7	0.93272	0.87056	0.81309	0.77283	0.75992	0.74725	0.71068	0.66506	0.62275
8	0.92348	0.85349	0.78941	0.74490	0.73069	0.71679	0.67684	0.62741	0.58201
9	0.91434	0.83676	0.76642	0.71797	0.70259	0.68757	0.64461	0.59190	0.54393
10	0.90529	0.82035	0.74409	0.69202	0.67556	0.65954	0.61391	0.55839	0.50835

Present Value of $1

Periods	1.0%	2.0%	3.0%	3.75%	4.0%	4.25%	5.0%	6.0%	7.0%
11	0.89632	0.80426	0.72242	0.66701	0.64958	0.63265	0.58468	0.52679	0.47509
12	0.88745	0.78849	0.70138	0.64290	0.62460	0.60686	0.55684	0.49697	0.44401
13	0.87866	0.77303	0.68095	0.61966	0.60057	0.58212	0.53032	0.46884	0.41496
14	0.86996	0.75788	0.66112	0.59726	0.57748	0.55839	0.50507	0.44230	0.38782
15	0.86135	0.74301	0.64186	0.57568	0.55526	0.53562	0.48102	0.41727	0.36245
16	0.85282	0.72845	0.62317	0.55487	0.53391	0.51379	0.45811	0.39365	0.33873
17	0.84438	0.71416	0.60502	0.53481	0.51337	0.49284	0.43630	0.37136	0.31657
18	0.83602	0.70016	0.58739	0.51548	0.49363	0.47275	0.41552	0.35034	0.29586
19	0.82774	0.68643	0.57029	0.49685	0.47464	0.45348	0.39573	0.33051	0.27651
20	0.81954	0.67297	0.55368	0.47889	0.45639	0.43499	0.37689	0.31180	0.25842
25	0.77977	0.60953	0.47761	0.39838	0.37512	0.35326	0.29530	0.23300	0.18425
30	0.74192	0.55207	0.41199	0.33140	0.30832	0.28689	0.23138	0.17411	0.13137

Present Value of $1

Periods	8.0%	9.0%	10.0%	11.0%	12.0%	13.0%	14.0%	15.0%	20.0%	25.0%
1	0.92593	0.91743	0.90909	0.90090	0.89286	0.88496	0.87719	0.86957	0.83333	0.80000
2	0.85734	0.84168	0.82645	0.81162	0.79719	0.78315	0.76947	0.75614	0.69444	0.64000
3	0.79383	0.77218	0.75131	0.73119	0.71178	0.69305	0.67497	0.65752	0.57870	0.51200
4	0.73503	0.70843	0.68301	0.65873	0.63552	0.61332	0.59208	0.57175	0.48225	0.40960
5	0.68058	0.64993	0.62092	0.59345	0.56743	0.54276	0.51937	0.49718	0.40188	0.32768
6	0.63017	0.59627	0.56447	0.53464	0.50663	0.48032	0.45559	0.43233	0.33490	0.26214
7	0.58349	0.54703	0.51316	0.48166	0.45235	0.42506	0.39964	0.37594	0.27908	0.20972
8	0.54027	0.50187	0.46651	0.43393	0.40388	0.37616	0.35056	0.32690	0.23257	0.16777
9	0.50025	0.46043	0.42410	0.39092	0.36061	0.33288	0.30751	0.28426	0.19381	0.13422
10	0.46319	0.42241	0.38554	0.35218	0.32197	0.29459	0.26974	0.24718	0.16151	0.10737

Present Value of $1

Periods	8.0%	9.0%	10.0%	11.0%	12.0%	13.0%	14.0%	15.0%	20.0%	25.0%
11	0.42888	0.38753	0.35049	0.31728	0.28748	0.26070	0.23662	0.21494	0.13459	0.08590
12	0.39711	0.35553	0.31863	0.28584	0.25668	0.23071	0.20756	0.18691	0.11216	0.06872
13	0.36770	0.32618	0.28966	0.25751	0.22917	0.20416	0.18207	0.16253	0.09346	0.05498
14	0.34046	0.29925	0.26333	0.23199	0.20462	0.18068	0.15971	0.14133	0.07789	0.04398
15	0.31524	0.27454	0.23939	0.20900	0.18270	0.15989	0.14010	0.12289	0.06491	0.03518
16	0.29189	0.25187	0.21763	0.18829	0.16312	0.14150	0.12289	0.10686	0.05409	0.02815
17	0.27027	0.23107	0.19784	0.16963	0.14564	0.12522	0.10780	0.09293	0.04507	0.02252
18	0.25025	0.21199	0.17986	0.15282	0.13004	0.11081	0.09456	0.08081	0.03756	0.01801
19	0.23171	0.19449	0.16351	0.13768	0.11611	0.09806	0.08295	0.07027	0.03130	0.01441
20	0.21455	0.17843	0.14864	0.12403	0.10367	0.08678	0.07276	0.06110	0.02608	0.01153
25	0.14602	0.11597	0.09230	0.07361	0.05882	0.04710	0.03779	0.03038	0.01048	0.00378
30	0.09938	0.07537	0.05731	0.04368	0.03338	0.02557	0.01963	0.01510	0.00421	0.00124

TABLE E.2

Present Value of Annuity of $1

Periods	1.0%	2.0%	3.0%	3.75%	4.0%	4.25%	5.0%	6.0%	7.0%
1	0.99010	0.98039	0.97087	0.96386	0.96154	0.95923	0.95238	0.94340	0.93458
2	1.97040	1.94156	1.91347	1.89287	1.88609	1.87936	1.85941	1.83339	1.80802
3	2.94099	2.88388	2.82861	2.78831	2.77509	2.76198	2.72325	2.67301	2.62432
4	3.90197	3.80773	3.71710	3.65138	3.62990	3.60861	3.54595	3.46511	3.38721
5	4.85343	4.71346	4.57971	4.48326	4.45182	4.42073	4.32948	4.21236	4.10020
6	5.79548	5.60143	5.41719	5.28507	5.24214	5.19974	5.07569	4.91732	4.76654
7	6.72819	6.47199	6.23028	6.05790	6.00205	5.94699	5.78637	5.58238	5.38929
8	7.65168	7.32548	7.01969	6.80280	6.73274	6.66378	6.46321	6.20979	5.97130
9	8.56602	8.16224	7.78611	7.52077	7.43533	7.35135	7.10782	6.80169	6.51523
10	9.47130	8.98259	8.53020	8.21279	8.11090	8.01089	7.72173	7.36009	7.02358

Present Value of Annuity of $1

Periods	1.0%	2.0%	3.0%	3.75%	4.0%	4.25%	5.0%	6.0%	7.0%
11	10.36763	9.78685	9.25262	8.87979	8.76048	8.64354	8.30641	7.88687	7.49867
12	11.25508	10.57534	9.95400	9.52269	9.38507	9.25039	8.86325	8.38384	7.94269
13	12.13374	11.34837	10.63496	10.14236	9.98565	9.83251	9.39357	8.85268	8.35765
14	13.00370	12.10625	11.29607	10.73962	10.56312	10.39090	9.89864	9.29498	8.74547
15	13.86505	12.84926	11.93794	11.31530	11.11839	10.92652	10.37966	9.71225	9.10791
16	14.71787	13.57771	12.56110	11.87017	11.65230	11.44031	10.83777	10.10590	9.44665
17	15.56225	14.29187	13.16612	12.40498	12.16567	11.93315	11.27407	10.47726	9.76322
18	16.39827	14.99203	13.75351	12.92046	12.65930	12.40590	11.68959	10.82760	10.05909
19	17.22601	15.67846	14.32380	13.41731	13.13394	12.85938	12.08532	11.15812	10.33560
20	18.04555	16.35143	14.87747	13.89620	13.59033	13.29437	12.46221	11.46992	10.59401
25	22.02316	19.52346	17.41315	16.04320	15.62208	15.21734	14.09394	12.78336	11.65358
30	25.80771	22.39646	19.60044	17.82925	17.29203	16.77902	15.37245	13.76483	12.40904

Present Value of Annuity of $1

Periods	8.0%	9.0%	10.0%	11.0%	12.0%	13.0%	14.0%	15.0%	20.0%	25.0%
1	0.92593	0.91743	0.90909	0.90090	0.89286	0.88496	0.87719	0.86957	0.83333	0.80000
2	1.78326	1.75911	1.73554	1.71252	1.69005	1.66810	1.64666	1.62571	1.52778	1.44000
3	2.57710	2.53129	2.48685	2.44371	2.40183	2.36115	2.32163	2.28323	2.10648	1.95200
4	3.31213	3.23972	3.16987	3.10245	3.03735	2.97447	2.91371	2.85498	2.58873	2.36160
5	3.99271	3.88965	3.79079	3.69590	3.60478	3.51723	3.43308	3.35216	2.99061	2.68928
6	4.62288	4.48592	4.35526	4.23054	4.11141	3.99755	3.88867	3.78448	3.32551	2.95142
7	5.20637	5.03295	4.86842	4.71220	4.56376	4.42261	4.28830	4.16042	3.60459	3.16114
8	5.74664	5.53482	5.33493	5.14612	4.96764	4.79877	4.63886	4.48732	3.83716	3.32891
9	6.24689	5.99525	5.75902	5.53705	5.32825	5.13166	4.94637	4.77158	4.03097	3.46313
10	6.71008	6.41766	6.14457	5.88923	5.65022	5.42624	5.21612	5.01877	4.19247	3.57050

Present Value of Annuity of $1

Periods	8.0%	9.0%	10.0%	11.0%	12.0%	13.0%	14.0%	15.0%	20.0%	25.0%
11	7.13896	6.80519	6.49506	6.20652	5.93770	5.68694	5.45273	5.23371	4.32706	3.65640
12	7.53608	7.16073	6.81369	6.49236	6.19437	5.91765	5.66029	5.42062	4.43922	3.72512
13	7.90378	7.48690	7.10336	6.74987	6.42355	6.12181	5.84236	5.58315	4.53268	3.78010
14	8.24424	7.78615	7.36669	6.98187	6.62817	6.30249	6.00207	5.72448	4.61057	3.82408
15	8.55948	8.06069	7.60608	7.19087	6.81086	6.46238	6.14217	5.84737	4.67547	3.85926
16	8.85137	8.31256	7.82371	7.37916	6.97399	6.60388	6.26506	5.95423	4.72956	3.88741
17	9.12164	8.54363	8.02155	7.54879	7.11963	6.72909	6.37286	6.04716	4.77463	3.90993
18	9.37189	8.75563	8.20141	7.70162	7.24967	6.83991	6.46742	6.12797	4.81219	3.92794
19	9.60360	8.95011	8.36492	7.83929	7.36578	6.93797	6.55037	6.19823	4.84350	3.94235
20	9.81815	9.12855	8.51356	7.96333	7.46944	7.02475	6.62313	6.25933	4.86958	3.95388
25	10.67478	9.82258	9.07704	8.42174	7.84314	7.32998	6.87293	6.46415	4.94759	3.98489
30	11.25778	10.27365	9.42691	8.69379	8.05518	7.49565	7.00266	6.56598	4.97894	3.99505

TABLE E.3

Future Value of $1

Periods	1.0%	2.0%	3.0%	3.75%	4.0%	4.25%	5.0%	6.0%	7.0%
1	1.01000	1.02000	1.03000	1.03750	1.04000	1.04250	1.05000	1.06000	1.07000
2	1.02010	1.04040	1.06090	1.07641	1.08160	1.08681	1.10250	1.12360	1.14490
3	1.03030	1.06121	1.09273	1.11677	1.12486	1.13300	1.15763	1.19102	1.22504
4	1.04060	1.08243	1.12551	1.15865	1.16986	1.18115	1.21551	1.26248	1.31080
5	1.05101	1.10408	1.15927	1.20210	1.21665	1.23135	1.27628	1.33823	1.40255
6	1.06152	1.12616	1.19405	1.24718	1.26532	1.28368	1.34010	1.41852	1.50073
7	1.07214	1.14869	1.22987	1.29395	1.31593	1.33824	1.40710	1.50363	1.60578
8	1.08286	1.17166	1.26677	1.34247	1.36857	1.39511	1.47746	1.59385	1.71819
9	1.09369	1.19509	1.30477	1.39281	1.42331	1.45440	1.55133	1.68948	1.83846
10	1.10462	1.21899	1.34392	1.44504	1.48024	1.51621	1.62889	1.79085	1.96715

Future Value of $1

Periods	1.0%	2.0%	3.0%	3.75%	4.0%	4.25%	5.0%	6.0%	7.0%
11	1.11567	1.24337	1.38423	1.49923	1.53945	1.58065	1.71034	1.89830	2.10485
12	1.12683	1.26824	1.42576	1.55545	1.60103	1.64783	1.79586	2.01220	2.25219
13	1.13809	1.29361	1.46853	1.61378	1.66507	1.71786	1.88565	2.13293	2.40985
14	1.14947	1.31948	1.51259	1.67430	1.73168	1.79087	1.97993	2.26090	2.57853
15	1.16097	1.34587	1.55797	1.73709	1.80094	1.86699	2.07893	2.39656	2.75903
16	1.17258	1.37279	1.60471	1.80223	1.87298	1.94633	2.18287	2.54035	2.95216
17	1.18430	1.40024	1.65285	1.86981	1.94790	2.02905	2.29202	2.69277	3.15882
18	1.19615	1.42825	1.70243	1.93993	2.02582	2.11529	2.40662	2.85434	3.37993
19	1.20811	1.45681	1.75351	2.01268	2.10685	2.20519	2.52695	3.02560	3.61653
20	1.22019	1.48595	1.80611	2.08815	2.19112	2.29891	2.65330	3.20714	3.86968
25	1.28243	1.64061	2.09378	2.51017	2.66584	2.83075	3.38635	4.29187	5.42743
30	1.34785	1.81136	2.42726	3.01747	3.24340	3.48564	4.32194	5.74349	7.61226

Future Value of $1

Periods	8.0%	9.0%	10.0%	11.0%	12.0%	13.0%	14.0%	15.0%	20.0%	25.0%
1	1.08000	1.09000	1.10000	1.11000	1.12000	1.13000	1.14000	1.15000	1.20000	1.25000
2	1.16640	1.18810	1.21000	1.23210	1.25440	1.27690	1.29960	1.32250	1.44000	1.56250
3	1.25971	1.29503	1.33100	1.36763	1.40493	1.44290	1.48154	1.52088	1.72800	1.95313
4	1.36049	1.41158	1.46410	1.51807	1.57352	1.63047	1.68896	1.74901	2.07360	2.44141
5	1.46933	1.53862	1.61051	1.68506	1.76234	1.84244	1.92541	2.01136	2.48832	3.05176
6	1.58687	1.67710	1.77156	1.87041	1.97382	2.08195	2.19497	2.31306	2.98598	3.81470
7	1.71382	1.82804	1.94872	2.07616	2.21068	2.35261	2.50227	2.66002	3.58318	4.76837
8	1.85093	1.99256	2.14359	2.30454	2.47596	2.65844	2.85259	3.05902	4.29982	5.96046
9	1.99900	2.17189	2.35795	2.55804	2.77308	3.00404	3.25195	3.51788	5.15978	7.45058
10	2.15892	2.36736	2.59374	2.83942	3.10585	3.39457	3.70722	4.04556	6.19174	9.31323

Future Value of $1

Periods	8.0%	9.0%	10.0%	11.0%	12.0%	13.0%	14.0%	15.0%	20.0%	25.0%
11	2.33164	2.58043	2.85312	3.15176	3.47855	3.83586	4.22623	4.65239	7.43008	11.64153
12	2.51817	2.81266	3.13843	3.49845	3.89598	4.33452	4.81790	5.35025	8.91610	14.55192
13	2.71962	3.06580	3.45227	3.88328	4.36349	4.89801	5.49241	6.15279	10.69932	18.18989
14	2.93719	3.34173	3.79750	4.31044	4.88711	5.53475	6.26135	7.07571	12.83918	22.73737
15	3.17217	3.64248	4.17725	4.78459	5.47357	6.25427	7.13794	8.13706	15.40702	28.42171
16	3.42594	3.97031	4.59497	5.31089	6.13039	7.06733	8.13725	9.35762	18.48843	35.52714
17	3.70002	4.32763	5.05447	5.89509	6.86604	7.98608	9.27646	10.76126	22.18611	44.40892
18	3.99602	4.71712	5.55992	6.54355	7.68997	9.02427	10.57517	12.37545	26.62333	55.51115
19	4.31570	5.14166	6.11591	7.26334	8.61276	10.19742	12.05569	14.23177	31.94800	69.38894
20	4.66096	5.60441	6.72750	8.06231	9.64629	11.52309	13.74349	16.36654	38.33760	86.73617
25	6.84848	8.62308	10.83471	13.58546	17.00006	21.23054	26.46192	32.91895	95.39622	264.69780
30	10.06266	13.26768	17.44940	22.89230	29.95992	39.11590	50.95016	66.21177	237.37631	807.79357

TABLE E.4

Future Value of Annuity of $1

Periods	1.0%	2.0%	3.0%	3.75%	4.0%	4.25%	5.0%	6.0%	7.0%
1	1.00000	1.00000	1.00000	1.00000	1.00000	1.00000	1.00000	1.00000	1.00000
2	2.01000	2.02000	2.03000	2.03750	2.04000	2.04250	2.05000	2.06000	2.07000
3	3.03010	3.06040	3.09090	3.11391	3.12160	3.12931	3.15250	3.18360	3.21490
4	4.06040	4.12161	4.18363	4.23068	4.24646	4.26230	4.31013	4.37462	4.43994
5	5.10101	5.20404	5.30914	5.38933	5.41632	5.44345	5.52563	5.63709	5.75074
6	6.15202	6.30812	6.46841	6.59143	6.63298	6.67480	6.80191	6.97532	7.15329
7	7.21354	7.43428	7.66246	7.83861	7.89829	7.95848	8.14201	8.39384	8.65402
8	8.28567	8.58297	8.89234	9.13255	9.21423	9.29671	9.54911	9.89747	10.25980
9	9.36853	9.75463	10.15911	10.47503	10.58280	10.69182	11.02656	11.49132	11.97799
10	10.46221	10.94972	11.46388	11.86784	12.00611	12.14622	12.57789	13.18079	13.81645

Future Value of Annuity of $1

Periods	1.0%	2.0%	3.0%	3.75%	4.0%	4.25%	5.0%	6.0%	7.0%
11	11.56683	12.16872	12.80780	13.31288	13.48635	13.66244	14.20679	14.97164	15.78360
12	12.68250	13.41209	14.19203	14.81212	15.02581	15.24309	15.91713	16.86994	17.88845
13	13.80933	14.68033	15.61779	16.36757	16.62684	16.89092	17.71298	18.88214	20.14064
14	14.94742	15.97394	17.08632	17.98135	18.29191	18.60879	19.59863	21.01507	22.55049
15	16.09690	17.29342	18.59891	19.65565	20.02359	20.39966	21.57856	23.27597	25.12902
16	17.25786	18.63929	20.15688	21.39274	21.82453	22.26665	23.65749	25.67253	27.88805
17	18.43044	20.01207	21.76159	23.19497	23.69751	24.21298	25.84037	28.21288	30.84022
18	19.61475	21.41231	23.41444	25.06478	25.64541	26.24203	28.13238	30.90565	33.99903
19	20.81090	22.84056	25.11687	27.00471	27.67123	28.35732	30.53900	33.75999	37.37896
20	22.01900	24.29737	26.87037	29.01739	29.77808	30.56250	33.06595	36.78559	40.99549
25	28.24320	32.03030	36.45926	40.27112	41.64591	43.07648	47.72710	54.86451	63.24904
30	34.78489	40.56808	47.57542	53.79924	56.08494	58.48553	66.43885	79.05819	94.46079

Future Value of Annuity of $1

Periods	8.0%	9.0%	10.0%	11.0%	12.0%	13.0%	14.0%	15.0%	20.0%	25.0%
1	1.00000	1.00000	1.00000	1.00000	1.00000	1.00000	1.00000	1.00000	1.00000	1.00000
2	2.08000	2.09000	2.10000	2.11000	2.12000	2.13000	2.14000	2.15000	2.20000	2.25000
3	3.24640	3.27810	3.31000	3.34210	3.37440	3.40690	3.43960	3.47250	3.64000	3.81250
4	4.50611	4.57313	4.64100	4.70973	4.77933	4.84980	4.92114	4.99337	5.36800	5.76563
5	5.86660	5.98471	6.10510	6.22780	6.35285	6.48027	6.61010	6.74238	7.44160	8.20703
6	7.33593	7.52333	7.71561	7.91286	8.11519	8.32271	8.53552	8.75374	9.92992	11.25879
7	8.92280	9.20043	9.48717	9.78327	10.08901	10.40466	10.73049	1 1.06680	12.91590	15.07349
8	10.63663	11.02847	11.43589	11.85943	12.29969	12.75726	13.23276	13.72682	16.49908	19.84186
9	12.48756	13.02104	13.57948	14.16397	14.77566	15.41571	16.08535	16.78584	20.79890	25.80232
10	14.48656	15.19293	15.93742	16.72201	17.54874	18.41975	19.33730	20.30372	25.95868	33.25290

Future Value of Annuity of $1

Periods	8.0%	9.0%	10.0%	11.0%	12.0%	13.0%	14.0%	15.0%	20.0%	25.0%
11	16.64549	17.56029	18.53117	19.56143	20.65458	21.81432	23.04452	24.34928	32.15042	42.56613
12	18.97713	20.14072	21.38428	22.71319	24.13313	25.65018	27.27075	29.00167	39.58050	54.20766
13	21.49530	22.95338	24.52271	26.21164	28.02911	29.98470	32.08865	34.35192	48.49660	68.75958
14	24.21492	26.01919	27.97498	30.09492	32.39260	34.88271	37.58107	40.50471	59.19592	86.94947
15	27.15211	29.36092	31.77248	34.40536	37.27971	40.41746	43.84241	47.58041	72.03511	109.68684
16	30.32428	33.00340	35.94973	39.18995	42.75328	46.67173	50.98035	55.71747	87.44213	138.10855
17	33.75023	36.97370	40.54470	44.50084	48.88367	53.73906	59.11760	65.07509	105.93056	173.63568
18	37.45024	41.30134	45.59917	50.39594	55.74971	61.72514	68.39407	75.83636	128.11667	218.04460
19	41.44626	46.01846	51.15909	56.93949	63.43968	70.74941	78.96923	88.21181	154.74000	273.55576
20	45.76196	51.16012	57.27500	64.20283	72.05244	80.94683	91.02493	102.44358	186.68800	342.94470
25	73.10594	84.70090	98.34706	114.41331	133.33387	155.61956	181.87083	212.79302	471.98108	1054,79118
30	113.28321	136.30754	164.49402	199.02088	241.33268	293.19922	356.78685	434.74515	1181,88157	3227,17427

GLOSSARY

A

Account A standardized format that organizations use to accumulate the dollar effect of transactions on each financial statement item.

Accounting A system that collects and processes (analyzes, measures, and records) financial information about an organization and reports that information to decision makers.

Accounting Cycle The process used by entities to analyze and record transactions, adjust the records at the end of the period, prepare financial statements, and prepare the records for the next cycle.

Accounting Entity The organization for which financial data are to be collected.

Accounting Period The time period covered by the financial statements.

Accounts Receivable (Trade Receivables, Receivables) Open accounts owed to the business by trade customers.

Accrual Basis Accounting Revenues are recognized when goods and services are provided to customers, and expenses are recognized in the same period as the revenues to which they relate, regardless of when cash is received or paid.

Accrued Expenses Liabilities (payables) created when expenses are incurred, but cash will be paid in the future; created at end of period during the adjustment process to reflect the amount of expense incurred that the company will pay in the future.

Accrued Liabilities Expenses that have been incurred but have not been paid at the end of the accounting period.

Accrued Revenues Assets (receivables) created when revenues are earned, but cash will be collected from customers in the future; created at end of period during the adjustment process to reflect the amount of revenue earned by providing goods or services over time to customers who will pay in the future.

Acquisition Cost The net cash equivalent amount paid or to be paid for an asset.

Acquisition Method Records assets and liabilities acquired in a merger or acquisition at their fair value on the transaction date.

Additional Paid-in Capital (Paid-in Capital, Contributed Capital in Excess of Par) The amount of contributed capital less the par value of the stock.

Adjusting Entries Entries necessary at the end of the accounting period to measure all revenues and expenses of that period and update assets and liabilities.

Aging of Accounts Receivable Method Estimates uncollectible accounts based on the age of each account receivable.

Allowance for Doubtful Accounts (Allowance for Bad Debts, Allowance for Uncollectible Accounts) Contra-asset account containing the estimated uncollectible accounts receivable.

Allowance Method Bases bad debt expense on an estimate of uncollectible accounts.

Amortization Systematic and rational allocation of the acquisition cost of an intangible asset over its useful life.

Amortized Cost Method Reports investments in debt securities held to maturity at cost minus any premium amortization or plus any discount amortization.

Annuity A series of periodic cash receipts or payments that are equal in amount each interest period.

Assets Economic resources owned or controlled by a company that have a measurable value and benefit the company by producing cash inflows or reducing cash outflows in the future.

Asset Turnover Ratios Ratios that capture how efficiently a company uses its assets.

Audit An examination of the financial reports to ensure that they represent what they claim and conform with generally accepted accounting principles.

Authorized Shares The maximum number of shares of stock a corporation can issue as specified in its charter.

Available-for-Sale Securities All debt investments other than trading securities and debt investments held to maturity (classified as either short term or long term).

Average Cost Method Uses the weighted average unit cost of the goods available for sale for both cost of goods sold and ending inventory.

B

Bad Debt Expense (Doubtful Accounts Expense, Uncollectible Accounts Expense, Provision for Uncollectible Accounts) Expense associated with estimated uncollectible accounts receivable.

Balance Sheet (Statement of Financial Position) Reports the amount of assets, liabilities, and stockholders' equity of an accounting entity at a point in time.

Bank Reconciliation Process of verifying the accuracy of both the bank statement and the cash accounts of a business.

Bank Statement A monthly report from a bank that shows deposits recorded, checks cleared, other debits and credits, and a running bank balance. This same information is available on a daily basis from the bank's online banking site.

Basic Accounting Equation (Balance Sheet Equation) Assets = Liabilities + Stockholders' Equity.

Board of Directors Elected by the shareholders to represent their interests; its audit committee is responsible for maintaining the integrity of the company's financial reports.

Bond Certificate The document investors receive when they purchase bond securities.

Bond Discount The difference between the selling price of a bond and the bond's face value when the bond is sold for less than par.

Bond Premium The difference between the selling price of a bond and the bond's face value when the bond is sold for more than par.

Bond Principal (Face Value, Par Value, Maturity Value) The amount a company pays bondholders on the maturity date and the amount used to compute the bond's periodic cash interest payments.

C

Callable Bonds Bonds containing a call feature that allows the bond issuer the option of retiring the bonds early.

Capitalized Interest Interest expenditures included in the cost of a self-constructed asset.

Cash Money or any instrument that banks will accept for deposit and immediate credit to a company's account, such as a check, money order, or bank draft.

Cash Basis Accounting Records revenues when cash is received and expenses when cash is paid.

Cash Equivalents Short-term investments with original maturities of three months or less that are readily convertible to cash and whose value is unlikely to change.

Cash Flows from Financing Activities Cash inflows and outflows related to external sources of financing (owners and creditors) for the enterprise.

Cash Flows from Investing Activities Cash inflows and outflows related to the acquisition or sale of productive facilities and investments in the securities of other companies.

Cash Flows from Operating Activities (Cash Flows from Operations) Cash inflows and outflows directly related to earnings from normal operations.

Closing Entries Made at the end of the accounting period to transfer balances in temporary accounts to Retained Earnings and to establish a zero balance in each of the temporary accounts for beginning the next accounting period.

Common Stock The basic voting stock issued by a corporation.

Component Percentages Express each item on a particular financial statement as a percentage of a single base amount.

Contingent Liability A potential liability that has arisen as the result of a past event; it is not a definitive liability until some future event occurs.

Contra-Account An account that is an offset to, or reduction of, the primary account or financial statement section.

Convertible Bonds Unsecured bonds that may be converted to common stock at some point in the future.

Copyright Exclusive right to publish, use, and sell a literary, musical, or artistic work.

Corporate Governance The procedures designed to ensure that the company is managed in the interests of the shareholders.

Cost (Historical Cost) The cash-equivalent value of an asset on the date of the transaction.

Cost of Goods Sold Equation BI + P − EI = CGS.

Coupon Rate (Stated Rate, Contract Rate, Nominal Rate) The interest rate specified on a bond, and the rate used to compute the bond's periodic cash interest payment.

Covenants Legally binding agreements between a bond issuer and a bondholder.

Credit The right side of an account.

Credit Card Discount Fee charged by the credit card company for its services.

Cumulative Dividend Preference Requires any unpaid dividends on preferred stock to accumulate. These cumulative preferred dividends must be paid before any common dividends can be paid.

Current Assets Assets that will be used or turned into cash within one year. Inventory is always considered a current asset regardless of the time needed to produce and sell it.

Current Dividend Preference Requires that dividends be paid to preferred stockholders before any dividends are paid to common stockholders.

Current Liabilities Short-term obligations that will be paid or settled within the coming year in cash, goods, other current assets, or services.

D

Debenture An unsecured bond; no assets are specifically pledged to guarantee repayment.

Debit The left side of an account.

Declaration Date The date on which the board of directors officially approves a dividend.

Declining-Balance Depreciation Method that allocates the net book value (cost minus accumulated depreciation) of an asset over its useful life based on a multiple of the straight-line rate, thus assigning more depreciation to early years and less depreciation to later years of an asset's life.

Deferred (Unearned) Revenues Liabilities created from collecting cash from customers before providing goods or services to customers; need to be adjusted at the end of the period to reflect the amount of revenue earned by providing goods or services over time to customers.

Deferred Expenses Assets created when purchased in the past before being used to generate revenues; need to be adjusted at the end of the accounting period to reflect the amount of expense incurred by using the asset to generate revenue over time.

Deferred Tax Liability Created when differences in financial reporting and tax reporting cause accounting income to be higher than tax income in a given period.

Depletion Systematic and rational allocation of the cost of a natural resource over the period of its exploitation.

Depreciable Cost Cost minus residual value; the amount to be allocated over an asset's useful life.

Depreciation The process of allocating the cost of buildings and equipment (but not land) over their productive lives using a systematic and rational method.

Direct Labor The earnings of employees who work directly on the products being manufactured.

Direct Method A method of presenting the operating activities section of the statement of cash flows that reports components of cash flows from operating activities as gross receipts and gross payments.

Dividends in Arrears Dividends on cumulative preferred stock that have not been paid in prior years.

E

Earnings Forecasts Predictions of earnings for future accounting periods, prepared by financial analysts.

Effective-Interest Amortization A method of amortizing a bond discount or bond premium that reflects the effective interest rate a company pays bondholders over the life of a bond.

Equity Method A method used when an investor can exert significant influence over an affiliate; the method permits recording the investor's share of the affiliate's income as part of the investor's earnings.

Estimated Residual (or Salvage) Value The estimated amount to be recovered by the company, less disposal costs, at the end of an asset's estimated useful life.

Estimated Useful Life The expected service life of an asset to the present owner.

Expenses The costs of operating the business that are incurred to generate revenues during the period.

Expense Recognition Principle (or Matching Principle) Expenses are recorded in the same time period when incured to generate revenue.

F

Factory Overhead Manufacturing costs that are not raw material or direct labor costs.

Fair Value Method A method for reporting securities at their current market value (the amount that would be received in an orderly sale).

Faithful Representation Requires that the information be complete, neutral, and free from error.

Finance Lease Longer-term leases in which the effective control of the leased asset is transferred to the lessee.

Financial Accounting Standards Board (FASB) The private sector body given the primary responsibility to work out the detailed rules that become generally accepted accounting principles.

Finished Goods Inventory Manufactured goods that are complete and ready for sale.

First-In, First-Out (FIFO) Method An inventory costing method that assumes that the first goods purchased (the first in) are the first goods sold.

Form 8-K The report used by publicly traded companies to disclose any material event not previously reported that is important to investors.

Form 10-K The annual report that publicly traded companies must file with the SEC.

Form 10-Q The quarterly report that publicly traded companies must file with the SEC.

Franchise A contractual right to sell certain products or services, use certain trademarks, or perform activities in a geographical region.

Free Cash Flow Cash Flows from Operating Activities less Dividends less Capital Expenditures.

Future Value The sum to which an amount will increase as the result of compound interest.

G

Gains Result primarily from the disposal of assets for more than their cost minus the amount of cost depreciated in the past.

Generally Accepted Accounting Principles The measurement and disclosure rules used to develop the information in financial statements.

Going Concern Assumption States that businesses are assumed to continue to operate into the foreseeable future (also called the continuity assumption).

Goods Available for Sale The sum of beginning inventory and purchases (or transfers to finished goods) for the period.

Goodwill (Cost in Excess of Net Assets Acquired) For accounting purposes, the excess of the purchase price of a acquired business over the fair value of the acquired business's assets and liabilities.

Gross Profit (Gross Margin) Net sales less cost of goods sold.

H

Held-to-Maturity Investments Investments in debt securities that management has the ability and intent to hold until maturity.

I

Improvements Expenditures that increase the productive life, operating efficiency, or capacity of an asset and are recorded as increases in asset accounts, not as expenses.

Income before Income Taxes (Pretax Earnings) Revenues minus all expenses except income tax expense.

Income Statement (Statement of Income, Statement of Earnings, Statement of Operations, Statement of Comprehensive Income) Reports the revenues less the expenses of the accounting period.

Indenture A legal document that describes all the details of a debt security to potential buyers.

Indirect Method A method of presenting the operating activities section of the statement of cash flows that adjusts net income to compute cash flows from operating activities.

Institutional Investors Managers of pension, mutual, endowment, and other funds that invest on the behalf of others.

Intangible Assets Assets that have special rights but not physical substance.

Internal Controls Processes by which a company provides reasonable assurance regarding the reliability of the company's financial reporting, the effectiveness and efficiency of its operations, and its compliance with applicable laws and regulations.

Inventory Tangible property held for sale in the normal course of business or used in producing goods or services for sale.

Issued Shares The total number of shares of stock that have been sold.

J

Journal Entry An accounting method for expressing the effects of a transaction on accounts in a debits-equal-credits format.

L

Last-In, First-Out (LIFO) Method An inventory costing method that assumes that the most recently purchased units (the last in) are sold first.

Leasehold Improvements Modifications that a lessee makes to a leased property.

Legal Capital The permanent amount of capital defined by state law that must remain invested in the business; serves as a cushion for creditors.

Lenders (Creditors) Suppliers and financial institutions that lend money to companies.

Lessee The party that pays for the right to use the leased asset.

Lessor The party that owns a leased asset.

Liabilities Measurable obligations resulting from a past transaction; they are expected to be settled in the future by transferring assets or providing services.

Licenses and Operating Rights Obtained through agreements with governmental units or agencies; permit owners to use public property in performing their services.

LIFO Reserve A contra-asset for the excess of FIFO over LIFO inventory.

Liquidity The ability to pay current obligations.

Liquidity Ratios Ratios that measure a company's ability to meet its currently maturing obligations.

Long-Term Liabilities All of the entity's obligations that are not classified as current liabilities.

Losses Result primarily from the disposal of assets for less than their cost minus the amount of cost depreciated in the past.

Lower of Cost or Net Realizable Value Valuation method departing from the cost principle; it serves to recognize a loss when net realizable value drops below cost.

M

Market Interest Rate (Yield, Effective Interest Rate) The rate of return investors demand for a company's bonds on the date the bonds are issued, and the rate used to compute the bond's interest expense each period.

Market Ratios Ratios that relate the current price per share of a company's stock to the return that accrues to stockholders.

Material Amounts Amounts that are large enough to influence a user's decision.

Merchandise Inventory Goods held for resale in the ordinary course of business.

Merger Occurs when one company purchases all of the net assets of another and the acquired company goes out of existence.

Monetary Unit Assumption States that accounting information should be measured and reported in the national monetary unit without any adjustment for changes in purchasing power.

N

Natural Resources Assets occurring in nature, such as mineral deposits, timber tracts, oil, and gas.

Net Book Value (Carrying Value or Book Value) The acquisition cost of an asset less its accumulated depreciation, depletion (of natural resources), or amortization (of intangible assets).

Net Realizable Value (NRV) The expected sales price less selling costs (e.g., repair and disposal costs).

Net Sales The top line reported on the income statement. Net Sales = Sales Revenue − (Credit card discounts + Sales discounts + Sales returns and allowances).

No-Par Value Stock Capital stock that has no-par value as specified in the corporate charter.

Noncash Investing and Financing Activities Transactions that do not have direct cash flow effects; reported as a supplement to the statement of cash flows in narrative or schedule form.

Notes (Footnotes) Provide supplemental information about the financial condition of a company, without which the financial statements cannot be fully understood.

Notes Receivable Written promises that require another party to pay the business under specified conditions (amount, time, interest).

O

Operating (Cash-to-Cash) Cycle The time it takes for a company to pay cash to suppliers, sell goods and services to customers, and collect cash from customers.

Operating Income (Income from Operations) Net sales (operating revenues) less operating expenses (including cost of goods sold).

Operating Lease Longer-term leases in which the effective control of the leased asset remains with the lessor.

Ordinary Repairs and Maintenance Expenditures that maintain the productive capacity of an asset during the current accounting period only and are recorded as expenses.

Outstanding Shares The total number of shares of stock that are owned by stockholders on any particular date.

Overfunded When the plan's assets are greater than its liability.

P

Par Value The nominal value per share of stock as specified in the corporate charter.

Patent Granted by the federal government for an invention; gives the owner the exclusive right to use, manufacture, and sell the subject of the patent.

Payment Date The date on which a cash dividend is paid to the stockholders of record.

Pension An amount of money paid to a retired employee.

Percentage of Credit Sales Method Bases bad debt expense on the historical percentage of credit sales that result in bad debts.

Periodic Inventory System An inventory system in which ending inventory and cost of goods sold are determined at the end of the accounting period based on a physical inventory count.

Permanent Accounts The balance sheet accounts that carry their ending balances into the next accounting period.

Perpetual Inventory System An inventory system in which a detailed inventory record is maintained, recording each purchase and sale during the accounting period.

Post-Closing Trial Balance Prepared as an additional step in the accounting cycle to check that debits equal credits and all temporary accounts have been closed (have zero balances).

Preferred Stock Stock that has specified rights over common stock.

Present Value The current value of an amount to be received in the future; a future amount discounted for compound interest.

Press Release A written public news announcement normally distributed to major news services.

Primary Objective of Financial Reporting to External Users To provide financial information about the reporting entity that is useful to existing and potential investors, lenders, and other creditors in making decisions about providing resources to the entity.

Private Investors Individuals who purchase shares in companies.

Profitability Ratios Ratios that compare income with one or more primary activities.

Prospectus A regulatory filing that describes all the details of a debt or equity security to potential buyers.

Public Company Accounting Oversight Board (PCAOB) The private sector body given the primary responsibility to work out detailed auditing standards.

Purchase Discount Cash discount received for prompt payment of an account.

Purchase Returns and Allowances A reduction in the cost of purchases associated with unsatisfactory goods.

R

Ratio Analysis An analytical tool that measures the proportional relationship between two financial statement amounts.

Raw Materials Inventory Items acquired for the purpose of processing into finished goods.

Record Date The date on which the corporation prepares the list of current stockholders who will receive the dividend when paid.

Relevant Information Information that can influence a decision; it has predictive and/or feedback value.

Retained Earnings Cumulative earnings of a company that are not distributed to the owners and are reinvested in the business.

Revenues The amounts earned and recorded from a company's day-to-day business activities, mostly when a company sells products or provides services to customers or clients.

Revenue Recognition Principle Revenues are recognized (1) when the company transfers promised goods or services to customers; (2) in the amount it expects to be entitled to receive.

S

Sales (or Cash) Discount Cash discount offered to encourage prompt payment of an account receivable.

Sales Returns and Allowances A reduction of sales revenues for return of or allowances for unsatisfactory goods.

Secured Bond Specific assets are pledged as a guarantee of repayment at maturity.

Securities and Exchange Commission (SEC) The U.S. government agency that determines the financial statements that public companies must provide to stockholders and the measurement rules that they must use in producing those statements.

Separate Entity Assumption States that business transactions are separate from the transactions of the owners.

Short-Term Lease A lease for 12 months or less (including expected renewals and extensions) that does not contain a purchase option that the lessee is expected to exercise.

Solvency Ratios Ratios that measure a company's ability to meet its long-term obligations.

Specific Identification Method An inventory costing method that identifies the cost of the specific item that was sold.

Statement of Cash Flows (Cash Flow Statement) Reports inflows and outflows of cash during the accounting period in the categories of operating, investing, and financing.

Statement of Stockholders' Equity The statement reports the changes in each of the company's stockholders' equity accounts during the period.

Stock Dividend A distribution of additional shares of a corporation's own stock on a pro rata basis at no cost to existing stockholders.

Stock Split Gives stockholders a specified number of additional shares for each share that they currently hold.

Stockholders' Equity (Shareholders' or Owners' Equity) The financing provided by the owners and the operations of the business.

Straight-Line Amortization An alternative method of amortizing bond discounts and premiums that allocates an equal dollar amount to each interest period. It is only permitted by GAAP under specific circumstances.

Straight-Line Depreciation Method that allocates the depreciable cost of an asset in equal periodic amounts over its useful life.

T

T-account A tool for summarizing transaction effects for each account, determining balances, and drawing inferences about a company's activities.

Tangible Assets Assets that have physical substance.

Technology Includes costs capitalized for computer software and website development.

Temporary Accounts Income statement (and sometimes dividends declared) accounts that are closed to Retained Earnings at the end of the accounting period.

Temporary Tax Differences Result from companies reporting revenues and expenses on their income statements in a different time period than they report them on their tax returns.

Time Period Assumption The long life of a company can be reported in shorter time periods, such as months, quarters, and years.

Time Value of Money Principle that a given amount of money deposited in an interest-bearing account increases over time.

Trademark An exclusive legal right to use a special name, image, or slogan.

Trading Securities All investments in debt instruments that are held primarily for the purpose of active trading (buying and selling) in the near future (classified as short term).

Transaction (1) An exchange between a business and one or more external parties to a business or (2) a measurable internal event such as the use of assets in operations.

Transaction Analysis The process of studying a transaction to determine its economic effect on the business in terms of the accounting equation.

Treasury Stock A corporation's own stock that has been repurchased. Shares held as treasury stock are considered issued shares but not outstanding shares.

Trial Balance A list of all accounts with their balances to provide a check on the equality of the debits and credits.

Trustee An independent party appointed to represent the bondholders.

U

Units-of-Production Depreciation Method that allocates the depreciable cost of an asset over its useful life based on the relationship of its periodic output or activity level to its total estimated output or activity level.

Unqualified (Clean) Audit Opinion Auditor's statement that the financial statements are fair presentations in all material respects in conformity with GAAP.

Unrealized Gain or Loss Amounts associated with price changes of securities that are held—no actual exchange transaction (e.g., sale) has yet taken place.

W

Work in Process Inventory Goods in the process of being manufactured.

Working Capital The dollar difference between total current assets and total current liabilities.

COMPANY INDEX

A

B

C

I

J

K

L

A

B

C

E

G

H

I

J

K

L

O

P

Q

R

S

V

W

X

Y

Z